Jaegwon Kim is William Perry Faunce Professor of Philosophy at Brown University. His publications include a number of influential papers on metaphysics and philosophy of mind. He is the author of *Supervenience and Mind* (1993), *Mind in a Physical World* (1998), *Physicalism, or Something Near Enough* (2005), and *Essays in the Metaphysics of Mind* (2010) and the co-editor of Blackwell's *Epistemology: An Anthology,* second edition (2008).

Daniel Z. Korman is Assistant Professor of Philosophy at the University of Illinois, Urbana-Champaign. He specializes in metaphysics and has published articles in *Oxford Studies in Metaphysics, Noûs,* and the *Journal of Philosophy*.

Ernest Sosa taught from 1964 to 2007 at Brown University, and is currently Board of Governors Professor of Philosophy at Rutgers University. Among his books are *Knowledge in Perspective* (1991), *Epistemic Justification* (with Laurence BonJour; Blackwell, 2003), *A Virtue Epistemology* (2007), *Reflective Knowledge* (2009), and *Knowing Full Well* (2010). He is also co-editor of Blackwell's *Epistemology: An Anthology,* second edition (2008).

BLACKWELL PHILOSOPHY ANTHOLOGIES

Each volume in this outstanding series provides an authoritative and comprehensive collection of the essential primary readings from philosophy's main fields of study. Designed to complement the *Blackwell Companions to Philosophy* series, each volume represents an unparalleled resource in its own right, and will provide the ideal platform for course use.

1 Cottingham: *Western Philosophy: An Anthology* (second edition)
2 Cahoone: *From Modernism to Postmodernism: An Anthology* (expanded second edition)
3 LaFollette: *Ethics in Practice: An Anthology* (third edition)
4 Goodin and Pettit: *Contemporary Political Philosophy: An Anthology* (second edition)
5 Eze: *African Philosophy: An Anthology*
6 McNeill and Feldman: *Continental Philosophy: An Anthology*
7 Kim, Sosa, and Korman: *Metaphysics: An Anthology* (second edition)
8 Lycan and Prinz: *Mind and Cognition: An Anthology* (third edition)
9 Kuhse and Singer: *Bioethics: An Anthology* (second edition)
10 Cummins and Cummins: *Minds, Brains, and Computers – The Foundations of Cognitive Science: An Anthology*
11 Sosa, Kim, Fantl, and McGrath: *Epistemology: An Anthology* (second edition)
12 Kearney and Rasmussen: *Continental Aesthetics – Romanticism to Postmodernism: An Anthology*
13 Martinich and Sosa: *Analytic Philosophy: An Anthology* (second edition)
14 Jacquette: *Philosophy of Logic: An Anthology*
15 Jacquette: *Philosophy of Mathematics: An Anthology*
16 Harris, Pratt, and Waters: *American Philosophies: An Anthology*
17 Emmanuel and Goold: *Modern Philosophy – From Descartes to Nietzsche: An Anthology*
18 Scharff and Dusek: *Philosophy of Technology – The Technological Condition: An Anthology*
19 Light and Rolston: *Environmental Ethics: An Anthology*
20 Taliaferro and Griffiths: *Philosophy of Religion: An Anthology*
21 Lamarque and Olsen: *Aesthetics and the Philosophy of Art – The Analytic Tradition: An Anthology*
22 John and Lopes: *Philosophy of Literature – Contemporary and Classic Readings: An Anthology*
23 Cudd and Andreasen: *Feminist Theory: A Philosophical Anthology*
24 Carroll and Choi: *Philosophy of Film and Motion Pictures: An Anthology*
25 Lange: *Philosophy of Science: An Anthology*
26 Shafer-Landau and Cuneo: *Foundations of Ethics: An Anthology*
27 Curren: *Philosophy of Education: An Anthology*
28 Shafer-Landau: *Ethical Theory: An Anthology*
29 Cahn and Meskin: *Aesthetics: A Comprehensive Anthology*
30 McGrew, Alspector-Kelly and Allhoff: *The Philosophy of Science: An Historical Anthology*
31 May: *Philosophy of Law: Classic and Contemporary Readings*
32 Rosenberg and Arp: *Philosophy of Biology: An Anthology*

METAPHYSICS
AN ANTHOLOGY

Second Edition

Edited by

Jaegwon Kim, Daniel Z. Korman

and

Ernest Sosa

WILEY-BLACKWELL

A John Wiley & Sons, Ltd., Publication

This edition first published 2012
Editorial material and organization © 2012 by Blackwell Publishing Ltd

Blackwell Publishing was acquired by John Wiley & Sons in February 2007. Blackwell's publishing program has been merged with Wiley's global Scientific, Technical, and Medical business to form Wiley-Blackwell.

Registered Office
John Wiley & Sons Ltd, The Atrium, Southern Gate, Chichester, West Sussex, PO19 8SQ, United Kingdom

Editorial Offices
350 Main Street, Malden, MA 02148-5020, USA
9600 Garsington Road, Oxford, OX4 2DQ, UK
The Atrium, Southern Gate, Chichester, West Sussex, PO19 8SQ, UK

For details of our global editorial offices, for customer services, and for information about how to apply for permission to reuse the copyright material in this book please see our website at www.wiley.com/wiley-blackwell.

Library of Congress Cataloging-in-Publication Data

Metaphysics : an anthology / edited by Jaegwon Kim, Daniel Z. Korman, Ernest Sosa. – 2nd ed.
     p.   cm. – (Blackwell philosophy anthologies)
   Includes bibliographical references and index.
   ISBN 978-1-4443-3101-1 (hardback) – ISBN 978-1-4443-3102-8 (paperback)
 1. Metaphysics.   I. Kim, Jaegwon.   II. Korman, Daniel Z.   III. Sosa, Ernest.
   BD111.M55 2012
   110–dc23

                              2011023056

A catalogue record for this book is available from the British Library.

Set in 9.5/11.5pt Minion by SPi Publisher Services, Pondicherry, India
Printed in Singapore by Ho Printing Singapore Pte Ltd

1   2012

Contents

Source Acknowledgments

The editors and publisher gratefully acknowledge the permission granted to reproduce the copyright material in this book:

1   W. V. Quine, "On What There Is," *Review of Metaphysics*, 2 (1948): 21–38. Copyright © 1948 by The Review of Metaphysics. Reprinted by permission.

2   Rudolf Carnap, "Empiricism, Semantics, and Ontology," in *Meaning and Necessity* (Chicago: University of Chicago Press, 1956), pp. 205–21. Reproduced by permission.

3   David Lewis and Stephanie Lewis, "Holes," *Australasian Journal of Philosophy*, 48/(1970): 206–12. Routledge Publishing. Reproduced by permission.

4   Roderick Chisholm, "Beyond Being and Nonbeing," *Philosophical Studies*, 24/4 (1973): 245–57. Reproduced by kind permission of Springer Science + Business Media B.V.

5   Stephen Yablo, "Does Ontology Rest on a Mistake?," *Proceedings of the Aristotelian Society*, NS, supp. vol. 72 (1998): 229–61. Reprinted by permission of John Wiley & Sons, Inc.

6   Amie L. Thomasson, "If We Postulated Fictional Objects, What Would They Be?", in *Fiction and Metaphysics*, Cambridge Studies in Philosophy (Cambridge: Cambridge University Press, 1999), ch. 1. Reproduced by permission.

7   Jonathan Schaffer, "On What Grounds What," in David Chalmers, David Manley, and Ryan Wasserman (eds.), *Metametaphysics* (Oxford: Oxford University Press, 2009), pp. 347–83. Reproduced by permission.

8   Max Black, "The Identity of Indiscernibles," *Mind*, 51 (1952), reprinted in Max Black, *Problems of Analysis* (1954), pp. 204–16. Reproduced by permission.

9   Robert M. Adams, "Primitive Thisness and Primitive Identity," *Journal of Philosophy*, 76/1 (Jan. 1979): pp. 5–26. Reproduced by permission.

10 Saul Kripke, "Identity and Necessity," in *Identity and Individuation* (New York: New York University Press, 1971), pp. 135–64. Copyright New York University. Reproduced by permission.

11 Allan Gibbard, "Contingent Identity," *Journal of Philosophical Logic*, 4 (1975): 187–221. Reproduced by kind permission of Springer Science + Business Media B.V.

12 Gareth Evans, "Can There Be Vague Objects?", *Analysis*, 38/4 (Oct. 1978): 208. Published by Oxford University Press on behalf of the Analysis Committee. Reproduced by permission.

13 Robert C. Stalnaker, "Vague Identity," in David F. Austin (ed.), *Philosophical Analysis: A Defense by Example,* (Dordrecht: Kluwer, 1988), 349–60. Reproduced by kind permission of Springer Science + Business Media B.V.

14 Alvin Plantinga, "Modalities: Basic Concepts and Distinctions," from chapters 1 and 2 of

Plantinga, *Nature of Necessity* (Oxford: Oxford University Press, 1974). Reproduced by permission.

15 Robert M. Adams, "Actualism and Thisness," *Synthese*, 49/1, Demonstrative and Indexical Reference, Part I (Oct. 1981): 3–41. Used with kind permission of Springer Science + Business Media B.V.

16 David Lewis, "A Philosopher's Paradise: The Plurality of Worlds," from chapter 1 of Lewis, *On the Plurality of Worlds* (Oxford: Blackwell, 1986). Reprinted by permission of John Wiley & Sons, Inc.

17 Robert C. Stalnaker, "Possible Worlds," *Noûs*, 10 (1976): 65–75.

18 Gideon Rosen, "Modal Fictionalism," *Mind*, NS 99/395 (July 1990): 327–54. Published by Oxford University Press on behalf of the Mind Association. Reproduced by permission.

19 Kit Fine, "Essence and Modality," in *Philosophical Perspectives*, vol. 8: *Logic and Language* (1994), pp. 1–16. Reproduced by permission of John Wiley & Sons, Inc.

20 W. V. Quine, "Natural Kinds," in *Essays in Honor of Carl G. Hempel* (1969). Copyright W. V. Quine. Reproduced by kind permission of Springer Science + Business Media B.V.

21 Sydney Shoemaker, "Causality and Properties," in Peter van Inwagen (ed.), *Time and Cause* (Dordrecht: Reidel, 1980). Reproduced by kind permission of Springer Science + Business Media B.V.

22 Keith Campbell, "The Metaphysic of Abstract Particulars," *Midwest Studies in Philosophy*, 6 (1981): 477–88.

23 David Lewis, "New Work for a Theory of Universals," *Australasian Journal of Philosophy*, 61 (Dec. 1983): 343–77. Reproduced by permission.

24 D. M. Armstrong, "Universals as Attributes," originally published in D. M. Armstrong, *Universals: An Opinionated Introduction* (1989), ch. 5. Copyright by Westview Press. Reprinted by permission of the publisher.

25 Bertrand Russell, "On the Notion of Cause," *Proceedings of the Aristotelian Society*, NS 13 (1912–13): 1–26. Reprinted by permission of John Wiley & Sons, Inc.

26 J. L. Mackie, "Causes and Conditions," *American Philosophical Quarterly*, 2 (1965): 245–64. Reproduced by permission.

27 Donald Davidson, "Causal Relations," *Journal of Philosophy*, 64/21 (Nov. 1967): 692–703. Copyright by Donald Davidson. Reprinted by permission of the author's estate and Columbia University.

28 G. E. M. Anscombe, "Causality and Determination: An Inaugural Lecture," © Cambridge University Press 1971. Reproduced with permission.

29 David Lewis, "Causation," *Journal of Philosophy*, 70/17 (10 Oct. 1973): 556–67. Reproduced by permission.

30 Wesley C. Salmon, "Causal Connections," in *Scientific Explanation and the Causal Structure of the World* (Princeton, NJ: Princeton University Press, 1984). © 1984 Princeton University Press. Reprinted by permission of Princeton University Press.

31 Michael Tooley, "Causation: Reductionism versus Realism," *Philosophy and Phenomenological Research*, 50, supplement (Autumn 1990): 215–36. Reproduced by permission of John Wiley & Sons, Inc.

32 Ned Hall, "Two Concepts of Causation," in John Collins, Ned Hall, and L. A. Paul (eds.), *Causation and Counterfactuals* (Cambridge, MA: MIT Press, 2004), pp. 225–276, © 2004 Massachusetts Institute of Technology, by permission of the MIT Press.

33 Roderick M. Chisholm, "Identity Through Time," in R. M. Chisholm, *Person and Object* (Chicago: Open Court, 1976). Reprinted by permission of Open Court Publishing Company, a division of Carus Publishing Company, Chicago, IL. Copyright © 1976 by Open Court.

34 W. V. O. Quine, "Identity, Ostension, and Hypostasis," *Journal of Philosophy*, 47/22 (26 Oct. 1950): 621–33. Reprinted by permission of the Journal of Philosophy and Dr. Douglas B. Quine, literary executor.

35 Judith Jarvis Thomson, "Parthood and Identity Across Time," *Journal of Philosophy*, 80 (1983): 201–20. Reproduced by permission.

36 Mark Heller, "Temporal Parts of Four-Dimensional Objects," in *The Ontology of Physical Objects* (Cambridge: Cambridge University Press, 1990), ch. 1 (pp. 1–29). © Cambridge University Press 1990. Reproduced by permission.

37   David Lewis, from chapter 4 of *On the Plurality of Worlds* (Oxford: Blackwell, 1986). Reprinted by permission of John Wiley & Sons, Inc.

38   Sally Haslanger, "Endurance and Temporary Intrinsics," *Analysis*, 49/3 (June 1989): 119–25. Reproduced by permission.

39   Theodore Sider, "All the World's a Stage," *Australasian Journal of Philosophy*, 74/3 (Sept. 1996): 433–53. Reproduced by permission.

40   Sydney Shoemaker, "Persons and their Pasts," *American Philosophical Quarterly*, 7 (1970). Reproduced by permission.

41   Bernard Williams, "The Self and the Future." In the public domain. Currently published by Duke University Press.

42   Derek Parfit, "Personal Identity." In the public domain. Currently published by Duke University Press.

43   David K. Lewis, "Survival and Identity," from David Lewis, *Philosophical Papers*, vol. 1 (Oxford: Oxford University Press), pp. 55–77.

44   Jaegwon Kim, "Lonely Souls: Causality and Substance Dualism," in Kevin Corcoran (ed.), *Soul, Body, and Survival: The Metaphysics of the Human Person* (Ithaca, NY: Cornell University Press, 2001). Copyright © 2001 by Cornell University. Reproduced by permission of the publisher.

45   Lynne Rudder Baker, "The Ontological Status of Persons," *Philosophy and Phenomenological Research*, 65/2 (Sept. 2002): 370–88. Reproduced by permission.

46   Eric T. Olson, "An Argument for Animalism," in R. Martin and J. Barresi (eds.), *Personal Identity* (Oxford: Blackwell 2003), pp. 318–24. Reprinted by permission of John Wiley & Sons, Inc.

47   Peter van Inwagen, "When are Objects Parts?", in James E. Tomberlin (ed.), *Philosophical Perspectives*, 1: *Metaphysics* (1987). Copyright by Ridgeview Publishing Co., Atascadero, CA. Reprinted by permission of Ridgeview Publishing Company.

48   David Lewis, "Many, But Almost One," in John Bacon, Keith Campbell, and Lloyd Reinhardt (eds.), *Ontology, Causality, and Mind* (Cambridge: Cambridge University Press, 1993), pp. 23–39. © 1993 Cambridge University Press. Reproduced by permission.

49   Ernest Sosa, "Existential Relativity," *Midwest Studies in Philosophy*, 23 (1999): 132–43. Reprinted by permission of John Wiley & Sons, Inc.

50   Theodore Sider, "The Argument from Vagueness," in *Four Dimensionalism: An Ontology of Persistence and Time* (Oxford: Oxford University Press, 2001), ch. 4, sect. 9 (pp. 120–39).

51   Trenton Merricks, "Epiphenomenalism and Eliminativism," in *Objects and Persons* (Oxford: Oxford University Press, 2001), ch. 3. Reproduced by permission.

52   Eli Hirsch, "Against Revisionary Ontology," *Philosophical Topics*, 30/1 (Spring 2002): 102–27. Reproduced by permission of the author and the University of Arkansas Press, www.uapress.com.

53   Daniel Z. Korman, "Strange Kinds, Familiar Kinds, and the Charge of Arbitrariness," *Oxford Studies in Metaphysics*, 5 (2010). Reproduced by permission.

Every effort has been made to trace copyright holders and to obtain their permission for the use of copyright material. The publisher apologizes for any errors or omissions in the above list and would be grateful if notified of any corrections that should be incorporated in future reprints or editions of this book.

Preface

Metaphysics is a philosophical inquiry into the most basic and general features of reality and our place in it. Because of its very subject matter, metaphysics is often philosophy at its most theoretical and abstract. But, as the works in this book show, simple, intuitive reflections on our familiar experiences of everyday life and the concepts that we use to describe them can lead us directly to some of the most profound and intractable problems of metaphysics.

This anthology, intended as a companion to Blackwell's *A Companion to Metaphysics*, is a collection of writings chosen to represent the state of discussion on the central problems of contemporary metaphysics. Many of the selections are "contemporary classics," and many of the rest will likely join their ranks in due course. Throughout the selection process we tried to be responsive to the needs of students who are relatively new to metaphysics. Given the overall aim of the volume and the nature of the field, it is unavoidable that some of the writings should contain somewhat technical parts that demand close study; however, we believe that most of the essential selections are accessible to the attentive reader without an extensive background in metaphysics or technical philosophy.

The selections are grouped into eight parts. Each part is preceded by a brief editorial introduction, including a list of works for further reading. These introductions are not intended as comprehensive surveys of the problems, positions, and arguments on the topic of each part; for such guidance the reader is encouraged to consult *A Companion to Metaphysics*. Rather, their aim is to give the reader some orientation, by indicating the scope of the problems dealt with in the works included in that section and what their authors attempt to accomplish.

Part I focuses on questions of ontology: questions about what sorts of things there are (properties? meanings? fictional characters?), about the nature of existence claims, and about the correct methodology for settling ontological disputes. Part II concerns questions about identity: whether there can be distinct but indiscernible objects, whether the identity relation can hold contingently, whether it can be vague, and so on. Part III includes various discussions of modal notions: necessity and possibility, essence and essential properties, and "possible worlds." Part IV is devoted to age-old issues concerning the nature and existence of properties, for instance, whether properties can exist without having instances, what individuates properties, and which properties there are (if any). Part V is devoted to the nature of causation, the relation that David Hume famously called "the cement of the universe." The central question of Part VI is what it takes for an object to persist through time and change, that is, what it is for a thing at one time and a thing at a later time to be the same thing. Part VII addresses questions about the nature of persons and about what it is in virtue of which persons persist through time and change. There is a clear difference between someone living through the night and someone being replaced overnight by an exact "molecule-for-molecule" duplicate; but in what does this difference consist? Part VIII includes various selections that bear upon the question of which material objects there are: is common sense right about which kinds of macroscopic objects there are, or are there – right before our eyes – far more or far fewer than we ordinarily take there to be?

It was difficult in many cases to neatly segregate the works into separate parts; the reader should be aware that many of the selections are of relevance to problems dealt with in more than one part. For instance, Quine's "On What There Is" (chapter 1) is directly relevant to the issues under discussion in Part IV (Properties); many of the entries in Part IV, in turn, have direct bearing on the issues in Part V (Causation); and questions about material constitution (the relationship between objects and what they are made of) are represented in Parts II (Identity), VI (Persistence), VII (Persons), and VIII (Objects).

The topics represented in this book by no means exhaust the field of metaphysics. For reasons of space we have had to leave out many important topics, among them the following: facts, events, and propositions; primary and secondary qualities; space and time; the existence and nature of mathematical objects; the objective and the subjective; and determinism. Even on the topics included here, many important and worthy works have had to be left out, either on account of limited space or because of the difficulty of extracting from them something of reasonable length that would be self-contained. In choosing the works to be included, our primary focus has been on seminal primary literature that represents major contemporary positions and arguments in metaphysics. In consequence, we have had to forgo many valuable follow-up discussions and elaborations, objections, and expository surveys. We hope that the interested reader will pursue the threads of discussion inspired by the materials included here.

During much of the middle half of the last century, metaphysics was in the doldrums, at least within the analytic tradition. This was largely due to the anti-metaphysical influence of the two then dominant philosophical trends. Logical positivism and its formalistic, hyper-empiricist legacies lingered through the 1950s and 1960s in the United States, nourishing an atmosphere that did not encourage serious metaphysics, while in Britain the anti-metaphysical animus derived from "ordinary language" philosophy and the later works of Wittgenstein. However, metaphysics began a surprisingly swift, robust comeback in the 1960s, and has attracted many talented philosophers over the last few decades. It is now flourishing as never before, showing perhaps that our need for metaphysics is as basic as our need for philosophy itself. We believe that this collection gives a broad glimpse of metaphysics during the twentieth century and the beginnings of the twenty-first.

We would like to thank Alex Baia, Sara Bernstein, Matti Eklund, Rob Koons, Trenton Merricks, Dave Robb, Alex Skiles, and especially Chad Carmichael for valuable advice on the second edition. We are also deeply grateful to Janet Moth, Wiley-Blackwell's answer to Winston Wolfe.

Jaegwon Kim
Daniel Z. Korman
Ernest Sosa

April 2011

PART I
Ontology

Introduction

Ontology is an inquiry into what there is, and your ontology is a list, or structured taxonomy, of the sorts of things that you believe there to be. For instance, most all of us accept an ontology that includes material objects (baseballs, mountains, molecules) and physical events (earthquakes, parties, home runs). Whenever possible, one would like to avoid "overpopulating" one's ontology with exotic or seemingly superfluous entities. But this is sometimes difficult to avoid. For instance, red houses and red roses have something in common. So there is something that they have in common: namely, their color. So there are colors. There is therefore pressure to include not only colored things, but also colors themselves as entities in their own right, in a complete inventory of everything that there is. Another example: In order for a sentence like 'Pegasus flies' to be meaningful, there must be something that the sentence is about. So there must be some object that 'Pegasus' picks out, namely, Pegasus. So it seems that fictional characters must be included in our ontology as well.

In "On What There Is" (chapter 1), W. V. Quine attempts to resist these and other arguments for allowing such entities as properties, fictional characters, and meanings into our ontology. Quine shows how claims that make apparent reference to such entities can often be paraphrased as claims that refer only to more "respectable" entities, and he insists that it is the paraphrases that reveal one's true ontological commitments. Quine also proposes an influential methodology for adjudicating ontological disputes, that is, for determining what our ontological commitments *should* be. For Quine, we ought to admit only those entities that would need to be quantified over in our best scientific theories.

In "Empiricism, Semantics, and Ontology" (chapter 2), Rudolf Carnap argues that one who accepts a way of talking that involves reference to abstract objects (like properties and numbers) is not thereby committed, in any robust sense, to there being such entities. So, contra Quine, one cannot read a philosopher's ontological commitments off of the "linguistic frameworks" within which she presents and develops her theories. A framework itself might have certain commitments, which is just to say that the linguistic rules that govern that framework permit making certain existence claims within that framework. For instance, the rules governing mathematical discourse entail the truth of 'There are prime numbers greater than three', and the truth of 'There are numbers' follows directly from this.

Metaphysics: An Anthology, Second Edition. Edited by Jaegwon Kim, Daniel Z. Korman and Ernest Sosa.

Apart from ("internal") questions about whether such existence claims are true within a framework, the only other meaningful question that one can ask about such claims, according to Carnap, is whether it is theoretically useful to employ a given framework, which is a question to be settled on pragmatic (not philosophical) grounds. Carnap observes that philosophers are trying to ask an altogether different ("external") question, a question about whether there really is a realm of entities corresponding to certain linguistic frameworks. But, insofar as these questions are meant to be answerable independently of any linguistic framework, Carnap dismisses them as meaningless "pseudo-questions," on the grounds that there can be no way of verifying or disconfirming claims about the reality of these objects independently of a given linguistic framework.

David and Stephanie Lewis's "Holes" (chapter 3) nicely illustrates the sorts of maneuvers that philosophers make in debates over the reality of various suspect entities, such as numbers, properties, fictional characters, and (in this case) holes. Their imaginary dialogue – between "Argle" and "Bargle" – centers around the worry that the existence of holes is in tension with the attractive view that everything that exists is material. Argle at first denies that there are holes and (in true Quinean fashion) attempts to paraphrase away talk of holes. Argle ultimately opts for a different strategy: admitting that there are holes, but identifying them with material objects, specifically, "hole-linings" (i.e., the physical boundaries surrounding the empty space). Bargle shows that this sort of maneuver, like related maneuvers in other discussions of ontology, forces one to say various things that are at odds with common sense, and the dialogue ends with some methodological reflections on the significance of embracing the counterintuitive implications of theoretically motivated views.

In "Beyond Being and Nonbeing" (chapter 4), Roderick M. Chisholm clarifies and defends the Meinongian view (due to Alexius Meinong) that a complete ontology must include objects that do not exist. One sort of argument for Meinongianism was mentioned above: there must be something for the sentence 'Pegasus does not exist' to be about, in which case it must be about some nonexistent object. Chisholm examines strategies for paraphrasing away apparent reference to nonexistent objects, and he attempts to show that they are not equipped to handle such statements as 'John fears a ghost' or 'The mountain I am thinking of is golden'. In order to account for the truth of such statements, Chisholm argues, we may have to postulate nonexistent items after all.

In "Does Ontology Rest on a Mistake?" (chapter 5), Stephen Yablo raises an important challenge to the Quinean approach to ontology. He observes that a great deal of our discourse – even in science – is to some extent figurative and that metaphors and certain kinds of make-believe have a valuable, and perhaps indispensable, role to play in communication and reasoning. So one might expect figurative talk to show up even in our best theories. If so, then, unless we can reliably distinguish between the figurative and literal aspects of our discourse (and Yablo offers reason to believe that we can't), we can't be sure that inspection of our best theories will reveal our true ontological commitments. Yablo's fictionalist approach to ontological claims also promises to vindicate the dismissive Carnapian attitude that many have toward serious ontological investigation. If our talk of numbers and the like is largely a matter of pretense or make-believe, this would explain why asking whether there are *really* such things as numbers – independently of the frameworks that license talk of numbers – strikes us as so odd.

It is often taken for granted that fictional characters do not exist, and this supposition plays a key role both in Quine's discussion of ontological commitment and in many discussions of Meinongian objects. In "Fictional Objects" (chapter 6) – the first chapter of her book *Fiction and Metaphysics* – Amie L. Thomasson defends a view of fictional characters on which they do in fact exist. Fictional characters, on her account, are abstract artifacts: *abstract* in that they do not have spatial locations, and *artifacts* in that they are brought into existence as the result of our creative acts. Thomasson sketches an account of their existence conditions – that is, what it takes for them to come into existence and to remain in existence – and she argues that an account of fictional characters as abstract artifacts is superior to accounts on which they are held to be Meinongian objects or merely possible objects.

In "On What Grounds What" (chapter 7), Jonathan Schaffer presents an alternative to the Quinean conception of the task and methodology of metaphysics. According to Schaffer, the questions of ontology are not concerned primarily with which entities there are but rather which entities are *fundamental.* Schaffer maintains that questions of what there is are, for the most part, entirely trivial – of course there are numbers, properties, and fictional characters! – and he shows that the perennial questions in metaphysics are typically questions about relations of dependency, or grounding, among various kinds of entities, not about whether there are such entities. Schaffer also argues that the Quinean project of reading our commitments off of our best theories is viable only to the extent that it presupposes a structured ontology of fundamental and nonfundamental (derivative) entities. In the final section, Schaffer endorses the monist view that, fundamentally, there is only one material object: the cosmos.

Further Reading

Azzouni, J. (2004). *Deflating Existential Consequence.* Oxford: Oxford University Press.

Chalmers, D. J., Manley, D., and Wasserman, R. (2009). *Metametaphysics: New Essays on the Foundations of Ontology.* Oxford: Oxford University Press.

Hirsch, E. (2002). "Quantifier Variance and Realism," *Philosophical Issues, Realism and Relativism* 12: 51–73.

Hofweber, T. (2005). "A Puzzle About Ontology," *Noûs* 39: 256–83.

Kalderon, M. (2005). *Fictionalism in Metaphysics.* Oxford: Oxford University Press.

Merricks, T. (2007). *Truth and Ontology.* Oxford: Oxford University Press.

Parsons, T. (1980). *Nonexistent Objects.* New Haven: Yale University Press.

Putnam, H. (1987). "Truth and Convention: On Davidson's Refutation of Conceptual Relativism," *Dialectica* 41: 69–77.

Rosen, G. (1993). "A Refutation of Nominalism(?)" *Philosophical Topics* 21: 149–86.

Stanley, J. (2001). "Hermeneutic Fictionalism," *Midwest Studies in Philosophy* 25: 36–71.

Thomasson, A. (1999). *Fiction and Metaphysics,* Cambridge: Cambridge University Press.

1

On What There Is

W. V. Quine

A curious thing about the ontological problem is its simplicity. It can be put in three Anglo-Saxon monosyllables: 'What is there?' It can be answered, moreover, in a word – 'Everything' – and everyone will accept this answer as true. However, this is merely to say that there is what there is. There remains room for disagreement over cases; and so the issue has stayed alive down the centuries.

Suppose now that two philosophers, McX and I, differ over ontology. Suppose McX maintains there is something which I maintain there is not. McX can, quite consistently with his own point of view, describe our difference of opinion by saying that I refuse to recognize certain entities. I should protest, of course, that he is wrong in his formulation of our disagreement, for I maintain that there are no entities, of the kind which he alleges, for me to recognize; but my finding him wrong in his formulation of our disagreement is unimportant, for I am committed to considering him wrong in his ontology anyway.

When *I* try to formulate our difference of opinion, on the other hand, I seem to be in a predicament. I cannot admit that there are some things which McX countenances and I do not, for in admitting that there are such things I should be contradicting my own rejection of them.

It would appear, if this reasoning were sound, that in any ontological dispute the proponent of the negative side suffers the disadvantage of not being able to admit that his opponent disagrees with him.

This is the old Platonic riddle of nonbeing. Non-being must in some sense be, otherwise what is it that there is not? This tangled doctrine might be nicknamed *Plato's beard*; historically it has proved tough, frequently dulling the edge of Occam's razor.

It is some such line of thought that leads philosophers like McX to impute being where they might otherwise be quite content to recognize that there is nothing. Thus, take Pegasus. If Pegasus *were* not, McX argues, we should not be talking about anything when we use the word; therefore it would be nonsense to say even that Pegasus is not. Thinking to show thus that the denial of Pegasus cannot be coherently maintained, he concludes that Pegasus is.

McX cannot, indeed, quite persuade himself that any region of space-time, near or remote, contains a flying horse of flesh and blood. Pressed for further details on Pegasus, then, he says that Pegasus is an idea in men's minds. Here, however, a confusion begins to be apparent. We may for the

W. V. Quine, "On What There Is," *Review of Metaphysics*, 2 (1948): 21–38. Copyright © 1948 by The Review of Metaphysics. Reprinted by permission.

Metaphysics: An Anthology, Second Edition. Edited by Jaegwon Kim, Daniel Z. Korman and Ernest Sosa.
Editorial material and organization © 2012 Blackwell Publishing Ltd. Published 2012 by Blackwell Publishing Ltd.

sake of argument concede that there is an entity, and even a unique entity (though this is rather implausible), which is the mental Pegasus-idea; but this mental entity is not what people are talking about when they deny Pegasus.

McX never confuses the Parthenon with the Parthenon-idea. The Parthenon is physical; the Parthenon-idea is mental (according anyway to McX's version of ideas, and I have no better to offer). The Parthenon is visible; the Parthenon-idea is invisible. We cannot easily imagine two things more unlike, and less liable to confusion, than the Parthenon and the Parthenon-idea. But when we shift from the Parthenon to Pegasus, the confusion sets in – for no other reason than that McX would sooner be deceived by the crudest and most flagrant counterfeit than grant the nonbeing of Pegasus.

The notion that Pegasus must be, because it would otherwise be nonsense to say even that Pegasus is not, has been seen to lead McX into an elementary confusion. Subtler minds, taking the same precept as their starting point, come out with theories of Pegasus which are less patently misguided than McX's, and correspondingly more difficult to eradicate. One of these subtler minds is named, let us say, Wyman. Pegasus, Wyman maintains, has his being as an unactualized possible. When we say of Pegasus that there is no such thing, we are saying, more precisely, that Pegasus does not have the special attribute of actuality. Saying that Pegasus is not actual is on a par, logically, with saying that the Parthenon is not red; in either case we are saying something about an entity whose being is unquestioned.

Wyman, by the way, is one of those philosophers who have united in ruining the good old word 'exist'. Despite his espousal of unactualized possibles, he limits the word 'existence' to actuality – thus preserving an illusion of ontological agreement between himself and us who repudiate the rest of his bloated universe. We have all been prone to say, in our common-sense usage of 'exist', that Pegasus does not exist, meaning simply that there is no such entity at all. If Pegasus existed he would indeed be in space and time, but only because the word 'Pegasus' has spatio-temporal connotations, and not because 'exists' has spatio-temporal connotations. If spatio-temporal reference is lacking when we affirm the existence of the cube root of 27, this is simply because a cube root is not a spa-

tio-temporal kind of thing, and not because we are being ambiguous in our use of 'exist'.[1] However, Wyman, in an ill-conceived effort to appear agreeable, genially grants us the nonexistence of Pegasus and then, contrary to what *we* meant by nonexistence of Pegasus, insists that Pegasus *is*. Existence is one thing, he says, and subsistence is another. The only way I know of coping with this obfuscation of issues is to *give* Wyman the word 'exist'. I'll try not to use it again; I still have 'is'. So much for lexicography; let's get back to Wyman's ontology.

Wyman's overpopulated universe is in many ways unlovely. It offends the aesthetic sense of us who have a taste for desert landscapes, but this is not the worst of it. Wyman's slum of possibles is a breeding ground for disorderly elements. Take, for instance, the possible fat man in that doorway; and, again, the possible bald man in that doorway. Are they the same possible man, or two possible men? How do we decide? How many possible men are there in that doorway? Are there more possible thin ones than fat ones? How many of them are alike? Or would their being alike make them one? Are no *two* possible things alike? Is this the same as saying that it is impossible for two things to be alike? Or, finally, is the concept of identity simply inapplicable to unactualized possibles? But what sense can be found in talking of entities which cannot meaningfully he said to be identical with themselves and distinct from one another? These elements are well-nigh incorrigible. By a Fregean therapy of individual concepts, some effort might be made at rehabilitation; but I feel we'd do better simply to clear Wyman's slum and be done with it.

Possibility, along with the other modalities of necessity and impossibility and contingency, raises problems upon which I do not mean to imply that we should turn our backs. But we can at least limit modalities to whole statements. We may impose the adverb 'possibly' upon a statement as a whole, and we may well worry about the semantical analysis of such usage; but little real advance in such analysis is to be hoped for in expanding our universe to include so-called *possible entities*. I suspect that the main motive for this expansion is simply the old notion that Pegasus, for example, must be because otherwise it would be nonsense to say even that he is not.

Still, all the rank luxuriance of Wyman's universe of possibles would seem to come to naught when we make a slight change in the example and speak not of Pegasus but of the round square cupola on Berkeley College. If, unless Pegasus were, it would be nonsense to say that he is not, then by the same token, unless the round square cupola on Berkeley College were, it would be nonsense to say that it is not. But, unlike Pegasus, the round square cupola on Berkeley College cannot be admitted even as an unactualized possible. Can we drive Wyman now to admitting also a realm of unactualizable impossibles? If so, a good many embarrassing questions could be asked about them. We might hope even to trap Wyman in contradictions, by getting him to admit that certain of these entities are at once round and square. But the wily Wyman chooses the other horn of the dilemma and concedes that it is nonsense to say that the round square cupola on Berkeley College is not. He says that the phrase 'round square cupola' is meaningless.

Wyman was not the first to embrace this alternative. The doctrine of the meaninglessness of contradictions runs a way back. The tradition survives, moreover, in writers who seem to share none of Wyman's motivations. Still, I wonder whether the first temptation to such a doctrine may not have been substantially the motivation which we have observed in Wyman. Certainly the doctrine has no intrinsic appeal; and it has led its devotees to such quixotic extremes as that of challenging the method of proof by *reductio ad absurdum* – a challenge in which I sense a *reductio ad absurdum* of the doctrine itself.

Moreover, the doctrine of meaninglessness of contradictions has the severe methodological drawback that it makes it impossible, in principle, ever to devise an effective test of what is meaningful and what is not. It would be forever impossible for us to devise systematic ways of deciding whether a string of signs made sense – even to us individually, let alone other people – or not. For it follows from a discovery in mathematical logic, due to Church,[2] that there can be no generally applicable test of contradictoriness.

I have spoken disparagingly of Plato's beard, and hinted that it is tangled. I have dwelt at length on the inconveniences of putting up with it. It is time to think about taking steps.

Russell, in his theory of so-called singular descriptions, showed clearly how we might meaningfully use seeming names without sup-

posing that there be the entities allegedly named. The names to which Russell's theory directly applies are complex descriptive names such as 'the author of *Waverley*', 'the present King of France', 'the round square cupola on Berkeley College'. Russell analyzes such phrases systematically as fragments of the whole sentences in which they occur. The sentence 'The author of *Waverley* was a poet', for example, is explained as a whole as meaning 'Someone (better: something) wrote *Waverley* and was a poet, and nothing else wrote *Waverley*'. (The point of this added clause is to affirm the uniqueness which is implicit in the word 'the', in '*the* author of *Waverley*'.) The sentence 'The round square cupola on Berkeley College is pink' is explained as 'Something is round and square and is a cupola on Berkeley College and is pink, and nothing else is round and square and a cupola on Berkeley College'.

The virtue of this analysis is that the seeming name, a descriptive phrase, is paraphrased *in context* as a so-called incomplete symbol. No unified expression is offered as an analysis of the descriptive phrase, but the statement as a whole which was the context of that phrase still gets its full quota of meaning – whether true or false.

The unanalyzed statement 'The author of *Waverley* was a poet' contains a part, 'the author of *Waverley*', which is wrongly supposed by McX and Wyman to demand objective reference in order to be meaningful at all. But in Russell's translation, 'Something wrote *Waverley* and was a poet and nothing else wrote *Waverley*', the burden of objective reference which had been put upon the descriptive phrase is now taken over by words of the kind that logicians call bound variables, variables of quantification: namely, words like 'something', 'nothing', 'everything'. These words, far from purporting to be names specifically of the author of *Waverley*, do not purport to be names at all; they refer to entities generally, with a kind of studied ambiguity peculiar to themselves. These quantificational words or bound variables are, of course a basic part of language, and their meaningfulness, at least in context, is not to be challenged. But their meaningfulness in no way presupposes there being either the author of *Waverley* or the round square cupola on Berkeley College or any other specifically preassigned objects.

Where descriptions are concerned, there is no longer any difficulty in affirming or denying being. 'There *is* the author of *Waverley*' is explained by Russell as meaning 'Someone (or, more strictly, something) wrote *Waverley* and nothing else wrote *Waverley*. 'The author of *Waverley* is not' is explained, correspondingly, as the alternation 'Either each thing failed to write *Waverley* or two or more things wrote *Waverley*'. This alternation is false, but meaningful; and it contains no expression purporting to name the author of *Waverley*. The statement 'The round square cupola on Berkeley College is not' is analyzed in similar fashion. So the old notion that statements of nonbeing defeat themselves goes by the board. When a statement of being or nonbeing is analyzed by Russell's theory of descriptions, it ceases to contain any expression which even purports to name the alleged entity whose being is in question, so that the meaningfulness of the statement no longer can be thought to presuppose that there be such an entity.

Now what of 'Pegasus'? This being a word rather than a descriptive phrase, Russell's argument does not immediately apply to it. However, it can easily be made to apply. We have only to rephrase 'Pegasus' as a description, in any way that seems adequately to single out our idea; say, 'the winged horse that was captured by Bellerophon'. Substituting such a phrase for 'Pegasus', we can then proceed to analyze the statement 'Pegasus is', or 'Pegasus is not', precisely on the analogy of Russell's analysis of 'The author of *Waverley* is' and 'The author of *Waverley* is not'.

In order thus to subsume a one-word name or alleged name such as 'Pegasus' under Russell's theory of description, we must, of course, be able first to translate the word into a description. But this is no real restriction. If the notion of Pegasus had been so obscure or so basic a one that no pat translation into a descriptive phrase had offered itself along familiar lines, we could still have availed ourselves of the following artificial and trivial-seeming device: we could have appealed to the *ex hypothesi* unanalyzable, irreducible attribute of *being Pegasus*, adopting, for its expression, the verb 'is-Pegasus', or 'pegasizes'. The noun 'Pegasus' itself could then be treated as derivative, and identified after all with a description: 'the thing that is-Pegasus', 'the thing that pegasizes'.

If the importing of such a predicate as 'pegasizes' seems to commit us to recognizing that there is a corresponding attribute, pegasizing, in Plato's heaven or in the minds of men, well and good. Neither we nor Wyman nor McX have been contending, thus far, about the being or nonbeing of universals, but rather about that of Pegasus. If in terms of pegasizing we can interpret the noun 'Pegasus' as a description subject to Russell's theory of descriptions, then we have disposed of the old notion that Pegasus cannot be said not to be without presupposing that in some sense Pegasus is.

Our argument is now quite general. McX and Wyman supposed that we could not meaningfully affirm a statement of the form 'So-and-so is not', with a simple or descriptive singular noun in place of 'so-and-so', unless so-and-so is. This supposition is now seen to be quite generally groundless, since the singular noun in question can always be expanded into a singular description, trivially or otherwise, and then analyzed out *à la* Russell.

We commit ourselves to an ontology containing numbers when we say there are prime numbers larger than a million; we commit ourselves to an ontology containing centaurs when we say there are centaurs; and we commit ourselves to an ontology containing Pegasus when we say Pegasus is. But we do not commit ourselves to an ontology containing Pegasus or the author of *Waverley* or the round square cupola on Berkeley College when we say that Pegasus or the author of *Waverley* or the cupola in question is *not*. We need no longer labor under the delusion that the meaningfulness of a statement containing a singular term presupposes an entity named by the term. A singular term need not name to be significant.

An inkling of this might have dawned on Wyman and McX even without benefit of Russell if they had only noticed – as so few of us do – that there is a gulf between *meaning* and *naming* even in the case of a singular term which is genuinely a name of an object. The following example from Frege will serve.[3] The phrase 'Evening Star' names a certain large physical object of spherical form, which is hurtling through space some scores of millions of miles from here. The phrase 'Morning Star' names the same thing, as was probably first established by some observant Babylonian. But the two phrases cannot be regarded as having the same meaning; otherwise that Babylonian could have dispensed with his observations and contented himself with reflecting on the meanings of his words. The meanings, then, being different from one another, must be other than the named object, which is one and the same in both cases.

Confusion of meaning with naming not only made McX think he could not meaningfully repudiate Pegasus; a continuing confusion of meaning with naming no doubt helped engender his absurd notion that Pegasus is an idea, a mental entity. The structure of his confusion is as follows. He confused the alleged *named object* Pegasus with the *meaning* of the word 'Pegasus', therefore concluding that Pegasus must be in order that the word have meaning. But what sorts of things are meanings? This is a moot point; however, one might quite plausibly explain meanings as ideas in the mind, supposing we can make clear sense in turn of the idea of ideas in the mind. Therefore Pegasus, initially confused with a meaning, ends up as an idea in the mind. It is the more remarkable that Wyman, subject to the same initial motivation as McX, should have avoided this particular blunder and wound up with unactualized possibles instead.

Now let us turn to the ontological problem of universals: the question whether there are such entities as attributes, relations, classes, numbers, functions. McX, characteristically enough, thinks there are. Speaking of attributes, he says: 'There are red houses, red roses, red sunsets; this much is prephilosophical common sense in which we must all agree. These houses, roses, and sunsets, then, have something in common; and this which they have in common is all I mean by the attribute of redness.' For McX, thus, there being attributes is even more obvious and trivial than the obvious and trivial fact of there being red houses, roses, and sunsets. This, I think, is characteristic of metaphysics, or at least of that part of metaphysics called ontology: one who regards a statement on this subject as true at all must regard it as trivially true. One's ontology is basic to the conceptual scheme by which he interprets all experiences, even the most commonplace ones. Judged within some particular conceptual scheme – and how else is judgment possible? – an ontological statement goes without saying, standing in need of no separate justification at all. Ontological statements follow immediately from all manner of casual statements of commonplace fact, just as – from the point of view, anyway, of McX's conceptual scheme – 'There is an attribute' follows from 'There are red houses, red roses, red sunsets'.

Judged in another conceptual scheme, an ontological statement which is axiomatic to McX's mind may, with equal immediacy and triviality, be adjudged false. One may admit that there are red houses, roses, and sunsets, but deny, except as a popular and misleading manner of speaking, that they have anything in common. The words 'houses', 'roses', and 'sunsets' are true of sundry individual entities which are houses and roses and sunsets, and the word 'red' or 'red object' is true of each of sundry individual entities which are red houses, red roses, red sunsets; but there is not, in addition, any entity whatever, individual or otherwise, which is named by the word 'redness', nor, for that matter, by the word 'househood', 'rosehood', 'sunsethood'. That the houses and roses and sunsets are all of them red may be taken as ultimate and irreducible, and it may be held that McX is no better off, in point of real explanatory power, for all the occult entities which he posits under such names as 'redness'.

One means by which McX might naturally have tried to impose his ontology of universals on us was already removed before we turned to the problem of universals. McX cannot argue that predicates such as 'red' or 'is-red', which we all concur in using, must be regarded as names each of a single universal entity in order that they be meaningful at all. For we have seen that being a name of something is a much more special feature than being meaningful. He cannot even charge us – at least not by *that* argument – with having posited an attribute of pegasizing by our adoption of the predicate 'pegasizes'.

However, McX hits upon a different strategem. 'Let us grant,' he says, 'this distinction between meaning and naming of which you make so much. Let us even grant that "is red", "pegasizes", etc., are not names of attributes. Still, you admit they have meanings. But these *meanings*, whether they are *named* or not, are still universals; and I venture to say that some of them might even be the very things that I call attributes, or something to much the same purpose in the end.'

For McX, this is an unusually penetrating speech; and the only way I know to counter it is by refusing to admit meanings. However, I feel no reluctance toward refusing to admit meanings, for I do not thereby deny that words and statements are meaningful. McX and I may agree to the letter in our classification of linguistic forms into the meaningful and the meaningless, even though McX construes meaningfulness as the *having* (in some sense of 'having') of some abstract entity which he calls a meaning, whereas I do not. I remain free to maintain that the fact that a given linguistic utterance is meaningful (or *significant*, as I prefer to say so as not to invite hypostasis of meanings as entities) is an ultimate and irreducible matter of fact; or, I may undertake to analyze it in terms directly of what people do in the presence of the linguistic utterance in question and other utterance similar to it.

The useful ways in which people ordinarily talk or seem to talk about meanings boil down to two: the *having* of meanings, which is significance, and *sameness* of meaning, or synonymy. What is called *giving* the meaning of an utterance is simply the uttering of a synonym, couched, ordinarily, in clearer language than the original. If we are allergic to meanings as such, we can speak directly of utterances as significant or insignificant, and as synonymous or heteronymous one with another. The problem of explaining these adjectives 'significant' and 'synonymous' with some degree of clarity and rigor – preferably, as I see it, in terms of behavior – is as difficult as it is important.[4] But the explanatory value of special and irreducible intermediary entities called meanings is surely illusory.

Up to now I have argued that we can use singular terms significantly in sentences without presupposing that there are the entities which those terms purport to name. I have argued further that we can use general terms, for example, predicates, without conceding them to be names of abstract entities. I have argued further that we can view utterances as significant, and as synonymous or heteronymous with one another, without countenancing a realm of entities called meanings. At this point McX begins to wonder whether there is any limit at all to our ontological immunity. Does *nothing* we may say commit us to the assumption of universals or other entities which we may find unwelcome?

I have already suggested a negative answer to this question, in speaking of bound variables, or variables of quantification, in connection with Russell's theory of descriptions. We can very easily involve ourselves in ontological commitments by saying, for example, that *there is something* (bound variable) which red houses and sunsets have in common; or that *there is something* which is a prime number larger than a million. But this is, essentially, the *only* way we can involve ourselves in ontological commitments: by our use of bound variables. The use of alleged names is no criterion, for we can repudiate their namehood at the drop of a hat unless the assumption of a corresponding entity can be spotted in the things we affirm in terms of bound variables. Names are, in fact, altogether immaterial to the ontological issue, for I have shown, in connection with 'Pegasus' and 'pegasize', that names can be converted to descriptions, and Russell has shown that descriptions can be eliminated. Whatever we say with the help of names can be said in a language which shuns names altogether. To be assumed as an entity is, purely and simply, to be reckoned as the value of a variable. In terms of the categories of traditional grammar, this amounts roughly to saying that to be is to be in the range of reference of a pronoun. Pronouns are the basic media of reference; nouns might better have been named propronouns. The variables of quantification, 'something', 'nothing', 'everything', range over our whole ontology, whatever it may be; and we are convicted of a particular ontological presupposition if, and only if, the alleged presupposition has to be reckoned among the entities over which our variables range in order to render one of our affirmations true.

We may say, for example, that some dogs are white and not thereby commit ourselves to recognizing either doghood or whiteness as entities. 'Some dogs are white' says that some things that are dogs are white; and, in order that this statement be true, the things over which the bound variable 'something' ranges must include some white dogs, but need not include doghood or whiteness. On the other hand, when we say that some zoological species are cross-fertile, we are committing ourselves to recognizing as entities the several species themselves, abstract though they are. We remain so committed at least until we devise some way of so paraphrasing the statement as to show that the seeming reference to species on the part of our bound variable was an avoidable manner of speaking.[5]

Classical mathematics, as the example of primes larger than a million clearly illustrates, is up to its neck in commitments to an ontology of abstract entities. Thus it is that the great medieval controversy over universals has flared up anew in the modern philosophy of mathematics. The issue is clearer now than of old, because we now have a more explicit standard whereby to decide what ontology a given theory or form of discourse is committed to: a theory is committed to those and only those entities to which the bound variables of the theory must be capable of referring in order that the affirmations made in the theory be true.

Because this standard of ontological presupposition did not emerge clearly in the philosophical tradition, the modern philosophical mathematicians have not on the whole recognized that they were debating the same old problem of universals in a newly clarified form. But the fundamental cleavages among modern points of view on foundations of mathematics do come down pretty explicitly to disagreements as to the range of entities to which the bound variables should be permitted to refer.

The three main medieval points of view regarding universals are designated by historians as *realism*, *conceptualism*, and *nominalism*. Essentially these same three doctrines reappear in twentieth-century surveys of the philosophy of mathematics under the new names *logicism*, *intuitionism*, and *formalism*.

Realism, as the word is used in connection with the medieval controversy over universals, is the Platonic doctrine that universals or abstract entities have being independently of the mind; the mind may discover them but cannot create them. *Logicism*, represented by Frege, Russell, Whitehead, Church, and Carnap, condones the use of bound variables to refer to abstract entities known and unknown, specifiable and unspecifiable, indiscriminately.

Conceptualism holds that there are universals but they are mind-made. *Intuitionism*, espoused in modern times in one form or another by Poincaré, Brouwer, Weyl, and others, countenances the use of bound variables to refer to abstract entities only when those entities are capable of being cooked up individually from ingredients specified in advance. As Fraenkel has put it, logicism holds that classes are discovered while intuitionism holds that they are invented – a fair statement indeed of the old opposition between realism and conceptualism. This opposition is no mere quibble; it makes an essential difference in the amount of classical mathematics to which one is willing to subscribe.

Logicists, or realists, are able on their assumptions to get Cantor's ascending orders of infinity; intuitionists are compelled to stop with the lowest order of infinity, and, as an indirect consequence, to abandon even some of the classical laws of real numbers. The modern controversy between logicism and intuitionism arose, in fact, from disagreements over infinity.

Formalism, associated with the name of Hilbert, echoes intuitionism in deploring the logicist's unbridled recourse to universals. But formalism also finds intuitionism unsatisfactory. This could happen for either of two opposite reasons. The formalist might, like the logicist, object to the crippling of classical mathematics; or he might, like the *nominalists* of old, object to admitting abstract entities at all, even in the restrained sense of mind-made entities. The upshot is the same: the formalist keeps classical mathematics as a play of insignificant notations. This play of notations can still be of utility – whatever utility it has already shown itself to have as a crutch for physicists and technologists. But utility need not imply significance, in any literal linguistic sense. Nor need the marked success of mathematicians in spinning out theorems, and in finding objective bases for agreement with one another's results, imply significance. For an adequate basis for agreement among mathematicians can be found simply in the rules which govern the manipulation of the notations – these syntactical rules being, unlike the notations themselves, quite significant and intelligible.[6]

I have argued that the sort of ontology we adopt can be consequential – notably in connection with mathematics, although this is only an example. Now how are we to adjudicate among rival ontologies? Certainly the answer is not provided by the semantical formula 'To be is to be the value of a variable'; this formula serves rather, conversely, in testing the conformity of a given remark or doctrine to a prior ontological standard. We look to bound variables in connection with ontology not in order to know what there is, but in order to know what a given remark or doctrine, ours or someone else's, *says* there is; and this much is quite properly a problem involving language. But what there is is another question.

In debating over what there is, there are still reasons for operating on a semantical plane. One reason is to escape from the predicament noted at the beginning of this essay: the predicament of my not being able to admit that there are things which McX countenances and I do not. So long as I adhere to my ontology, as opposed to McX's, I cannot allow my bound variables to refer to entities which belong to McX's ontology and not to mine. I can, however, consistently describe our disagreement by characterizing the statements which McX affirms. Provided merely that my ontology countenances linguistic forms, or at least concrete inscriptions and utterances, I can talk about McX's sentences.

Another reason for withdrawing to a semantical plane is to find common ground on which to argue. Disagreement in ontology involves basic disagreement in conceptual schemes; yet McX and I, despite these basic disagreements, find that our conceptual schemes converge sufficiently in their intermediate and upper ramifications to enable us to communicate successfully on such topics as politics, weather, and, in particular, language. Insofar as our basic controversy over ontology can be translated upward into a semantical controversy about words and what to do with them, the collapse of the controversy into question-begging may be delayed.

It is no wonder, then, that ontological controversy should tend into controversy over language. But we must not jump to the conclusion that what there is depends on words. Translatability of a question into semantical terms is no indication that the question is linguistic. To see Naples is to bear a name which, when prefixed to the words 'sees Naples', yields a true sentence; still there is nothing linguistic about seeing Naples.

Our acceptance of an ontology is, I think, similar in principle to our acceptance of a scientific theory, say a system of physics: we adopt, at least insofar as we are reasonable, the simplest conceptual scheme into which the disordered fragments of raw experience can be fitted and arranged. Our ontology is determined once we have fixed upon the over-all conceptual scheme which is to accommodate science in the broadest sense; and the considerations which determine a reasonable construction of any part of that conceptual scheme, for example, the biological or the physical part, are not different in kind from the considerations which determine a reasonable construction of the whole. To whatever extent the adoption of any system of scientific theory may be said to be a matter of language, the same – but no more – may be said of the adoption of an ontology.

But simplicity, as a guiding principle in constructing conceptual schemes, is not a clear and unambiguous idea; and it is quite capable of presenting a double or multiple standard. Imagine, for example, that we have devised the most economical set of concepts adequate to the play-by-play reporting of immediate experience. The entities under this scheme – the values of bound variables – are, let us suppose, individual subjective events of sensation or reflection. We should still find, no doubt, that a physicalistic conceptual scheme, purporting to talk about external objects, offers great advantages in simplifying our over-all reports. By bringing together scattered sense events and treating them as perceptions of one object, we reduce the complexity of our stream of experience to a manageable conceptual simplicity. The rule of simplicity is indeed our guiding maxim in assigning sense-data to objects: we associate an earlier and a later round sensum with the same so-called penny, or with two different so-called pennies, in obedience to the demands of maximum simplicity in our total world-picture.

Here we have two competing conceptual schemes, a phenomenalistic one and a physicalistic one. Which should prevail? Each has its advantages; each has its special simplicity in its own way. Each, I suggest, deserves to be developed. Each may be said, indeed, to be the more fundamental, though in different senses: the one is epistemologically, the other physically, fundamental.

The physical conceptual scheme simplifies our account of experience because of the way myriad scattered sense events come to be associated with single so-called objects; still there is no likelihood that each sentence about physical objects can actually be translated, however deviously and complexly, into the phenomenalistic language. Physical objects are postulated entities which round out and simplify our account of the flux of experience, just as the introduction of irrational numbers simplifies laws of arithmetic. From the point of view of the conceptual scheme of the elementary arithmetic of rational numbers alone, the broader arithmetic of rational and irrational numbers would have the status of a convenient myth, simpler than the literal truth (namely, the arithmetic of rationals) and yet containing that literal truth as a scattered part. Similarly, from a phenomenalistic point of view, the conceptual scheme of physical objects is a convenient myth, simpler than the literal truth and yet containing that literal truth as a scattered part.[7]

Now what of classes or attributes of physical objects, in turn? A platonistic ontology of this sort is, from the point of view of a strictly physicalistic conceptual scheme, as much a myth as that physicalistic conceptual scheme itself is for phenomenalism. This higher myth is a good and useful one, in turn, insofar as it simplifies our account of physics. Since mathematics is an integral part of this higher myth, the utility of this myth for physical science is evident enough. In speaking of it nevertheless as a myth, I echo that philosophy of mathematics to which I alluded earlier under the name of formalism. But an attitude of formalism may with equal justice be adopted toward the physical conceptual scheme, in turn, by the pure aesthete or phenomenalist.

The analogy between the myth of mathematics and the myth of physics is, in some additional and perhaps fortuitous ways, strikingly close. Consider, for example, the crisis which was precipitated in the foundations of mathematics, at the turn of the century, by the discovery of Russell's paradox and other antinomies of set theory. These contradictions had to be obviated by unintuitive, *ad hoc* devices; our mathematical myth-making became deliberate and evident to all. But what of physics? An antinomy arose between the undular and the corpuscular accounts of light; and if this was not as out-and-out a contradiction as Russell's paradox, I suspect that the reason is that physics is not as out-and-out as mathematics. Again, the second great modern crisis in the foundations of mathematics — precipitated in 1931 by Gödel's proof that there are bound to be undecidable statements in arithmetic[8] — has its companion piece in physics in Heisenberg's indeterminacy principle.

In earlier pages I undertook to show that some common arguments in favor of certain ontologies are fallacious. Further, I advanced an explicit standard whereby to decide what the ontological commitments of a theory are. But the question what ontology actually to adopt still stands open, and the obvious counsel is tolerance and an experimental spirit. Let us by all means see how much of the physicalistic conceptual scheme can be reduced to a phenomenalistic one; still, physics also naturally demands pursuing, irreducible *in toto* though it be. Let us see how, or to what

degree, natural science may be rendered independent of platonistic mathematics; but let us also pursue mathematics and delve into its platonistic foundations.

From among the various conceptual schemes best suited to these various pursuits, one — the phenomenalistic — claims epistemological priority. Viewed from within the phenomenalistic conceptual scheme, the ontologies of physical objects and mathematical objects are myths. The quality of myth, however, is relative; relative, in this case, to the epistemological point of view. This point of view is one among various, corresponding to one among our various interests and purposes.

Notes

1 The impulse to distinguish terminologically between existence as applied to objects actualized somewhere in space-time and existence (or subsistence or being) as applied to other entities arises in part, perhaps, from an idea that the observation of nature is relevant only to questions of existence of the first kind. But this idea is readily refuted by counter-instances such as 'the ratio of the number of centaurs to the number of unicorns'. If there were such a ratio, it would be an abstract entity, viz., a number. Yet it is only by studying nature that we conclude that the number of centaurs and the number of unicorns are both 0 and hence that there is no such ratio.

2 Alonzo Church, 'A note on the *Entscheidungsproblem*', *Journal of Symbolic Logic* I (1936), pp. 40–1, 101–2.

3 Gottlob Frege, 'On sense and nominatum', in Herbert Feigl and Wilfrid Sellars (eds), *Readings in Philosophical Analysis* (New York: Appleton-Century-Crofts, 1949), pp. 85–102.

4 See 'Two dogmas of empiricism' and 'The problem of meaning in linguistics', in W. V. Quine, *From a Logical Point of View* (Cambridge, Mass.: Harvard University Press, 1953).

5 W. V. Quine, 'Logic and the reification of universals', in *From a Logical Point of View*.

6 See Nelson Goodman and W. V. Quine, 'Steps toward a constructive nominalism', *Journal of Symbolic Logic* 12 (1947), pp. 105–22.

7 The arithmetical analogy is due to Philip Frank, *Modern Science and its Philosophy* (Cambridge, Mass.: Harvard University Press, 1949), pp. 108f.

8 Kurt Gödel, 'Über formal unertscheidbare Sätze der Principia Mathematica and verwander Systeme', *Monatshefle fur Mathematik and Physik* 38 (1931), pp. 173–98.

2

Empiricism, Semantics, and Ontology

Rudolf Carnap

1   The Problem of Abstract Entities

Empiricists are in general rather suspicious with respect to any kind of abstract entities like properties, classes, relations, numbers, propositions, etc. They usually feel much more in sympathy with nominalists than with realists (in the medieval sense). As far as possible they try to avoid any reference to abstract entities and to restrict themselves to what is sometimes called a nominalistic language, i.e., one not containing such references. However, within certain scientific contexts it seems hardly possible to avoid them. In the case of mathematics, some empiricists try to find a way out by treating the whole of mathematics as a mere calculus, a formal system for which no interpretation is given or can be given. Accordingly, the mathematician is said to speak not about numbers, functions, and infinite classes, but merely about meaningless symbols and formulas manipulated according to given formal rules. In physics it is more difficult to shun the suspected entities, because the language of physics serves for the communication of reports and predictions and hence cannot be taken as a mere calculus. A physicist who is suspicious of abstract entities may perhaps try to declare a certain part of the language of physics as uninterpreted and uninterpretable, that part which refers to real numbers as space-time coordinates or as values of physical magnitudes, to functions, limits, etc. More probably he will just speak about all these things like anybody else but with an uneasy conscience, like a man who in his everyday life does with qualms many things which are not in accord with the high moral principles he professes on Sundays. Recently the problem of abstract entities has arisen again in connection with semantics, the theory of meaning and truth. Some semanticists say that certain expressions designate certain entities, and among these designated entities they include not only concrete material things but also abstract entities, e.g., properties as designated by predicates and propositions as designated by sentences.[1] Others object strongly to this procedure as violating the basic principles of empiricism and leading back to a metaphysical ontology of the Platonic kind.

It is the purpose of this article to clarify this controversial issue. The nature and implications of the acceptance of a language referring to abstract entities will first be discussed in general; it will be shown that using such a language does not imply embracing a Platonic ontology but is

Rudolf Carnap, "Empiricism, Semantics, and Ontology," in *Meaning and Necessity* (Chicago: University of Chicago Press, 1956), pp. 205–21. Reproduced by permission.

Scientists work within the framework
Philosophers work on the framework

perfectly compatible with empiricism and strictly scientific thinking. Then the special question of the role of abstract entities in semantics will be discussed. It is hoped that the clarification of the issue will be useful to those who would like to accept abstract entities in their work in mathematics, physics, semantics, or any other field; it may help them to overcome nominalistic scruples.

2 Linguistic Frameworks

Are there properties, classes, numbers, propositions? In order to understand more clearly the nature of these and related problems, it is above all necessary to recognize a fundamental distinction between two kinds of questions concerning the existence or reality of entities. If someone wishes to speak in his language about a new kind of entities, he has to introduce a system of new ways of speaking, subject to new rules; we shall call this procedure the construction of a linguistic *framework* for the new entities in question. And now we must distinguish two kinds of questions of existence: first, questions of the existence of certain entities of the new kind *within the framework*; we call them *internal questions*; and second, questions concerning the existence or reality *of the system of entities as a whole*, called *external questions*. Internal questions and possible answers to them are formulated with the help of the new forms of expressions. The answers may be found either by purely logical methods or by empirical methods, depending upon whether the framework is a logical or a factual one. An external question is of a problematic character which is in need of closer examination.

The world of things. Let us consider as an example the simplest kind of entities dealt with in the everyday language: the spatio-temporally ordered system of observable things and events. Once we have accepted the thing language with its framework for things, we can raise and answer internal questions, e.g., "Is there a white piece of paper on my desk?," "Did King Arthur actually live?," "Are unicorns and centaurs real or merely imaginary?," and the like. These questions are to be answered by empirical investigations. Results of observations are evaluated according to certain rules as

confirming or disconfirming evidence for possible answers. (This evaluation is usually carried out, of course, as a matter of habit rather than a deliberate, rational procedure. But it is possible, in a rational reconstruction, to lay down explicit rules for the evaluation. This is one of the main tasks of a pure, as distinguished from a psychological, epistemology.) The concept of reality occurring in these internal questions is an empirical, scientific, nonmetaphysical concept. To recognize something as a real thing or event means to succeed in incorporating it into the system of things at a particular space-time position so that it fits together with the other things recognized as real, according to the rules of the framework.

From these questions we must distinguish the external question of the reality of the thing world itself. In contrast to the former questions, this question is raised neither by the man in the street nor by scientists, but only by philosophers. Realists give an affirmative answer, subjective idealists a negative one, and the controversy goes on for centuries without ever being solved. And it cannot be solved because it is framed in a wrong way. To be real in the scientific sense means to be an element of the system; hence this concept cannot be meaningfully applied to the system itself. Those who raise the question of the reality of the thing world itself have perhaps in mind not a theoretical question, as their formulation seems to suggest, but rather a practical question, a matter of a practical decision concerning the structure of our language. We have to make the choice whether or not to accept and use the forms of expression in the framework in question.

In the case of this particular example, there is usually no deliberate choice because we all have accepted the thing language early in our lives as a matter of course. Nevertheless, we may regard it as a matter of decision in this sense: we are free to choose to continue using the thing language or not; in the latter case we could restrict ourselves to a language of sense-data and other 'phenomenal' entities, or construct an alternative to the customary thing language with another structure, or, finally, we could refrain from speaking. If someone decides to accept the thing language, there is no objection against saying that he has accepted the world of things. But this must not be interpreted as if it meant his acceptance of a *belief* in the reality of the thing world; there is no such belief or assertion or assumption, because it is not a theoretical question. To accept the thing world means nothing more than to accept a certain form of language, in other words, to accept rules for forming statements and for testing, accepting, or rejecting them. The acceptance of the thing language leads, on the basis of observations made, also to the acceptance, belief, and assertion of certain statements. But the thesis of the reality of the thing world cannot be among these statements, because it cannot be formulated in the thing language or, it seems, in any other theoretical language.

The decision of accepting the thing language, although itself not of a cognitive nature, will nevertheless usually be influenced by theoretical knowledge, just like any other deliberate decision concerning the acceptance of linguistic or other rules. The purposes for which the language is intended to be used, for instance, the purpose of communicating factual knowledge, will determine which factors are relevant for the decision. The efficiency, fruitfulness, and simplicity of the use of the thing language may be among the decisive factors. And the questions concerning these qualities are indeed of a theoretical nature. But these questions cannot be identified with the question of realism. They are not yes–no questions but questions of degree. The thing language in the customary form works indeed with a high degree of efficiency for most purposes of everyday life. This is a matter of fact, based upon the content of our experiences. However, it would be wrong to describe this situation by saying: "The fact of the efficiency of the thing language is confirming evidence for the reality of the thing world"; we should rather say instead: "This fact makes it advisable to accept the thing language."

The system of numbers. As an example of a system which is of a logical rather than a factual nature let us take the system of natural numbers. The framework for this system is constructed by introducing into the language new expressions with suitable rules: (1) numerals like "five" and sentence forms like "there are five books on the table"; (2) the general term "number" for the new entities, and sentence forms like "five is a number"; (3) expressions for properties of numbers (e.g., "odd," "prime"), relations (e.g., "greater than"), and functions (e.g.,

"plus"), and sentence forms like "two plus three is five"; (4) numerical variables ("m," "n," etc.) and quantifiers for universal sentences ("for every n, …") and existential sentences ("there is an n such that …") with the customary deductive rules.

Here again there are internal questions, e.g., "Is there a prime number greater than a hundred?" Here, however, the answers are found, not by empirical investigation based on observations, but by logical analysis based on the rules for the new expressions. Therefore the answers are here analytic, i.e., logically true.

What is now the nature of the philosophical question concerning the existence or reality of numbers? To begin with, there is the internal question which, together with the affirmative answer, can be formulated in the new terms, say, by "There are numbers" or, more explicitly, "There is an n such that n is a number." This statement follows from the analytic statement "five is a number" and is therefore itself analytic. Moreover, it is rather trivial (in contradistinction to a statement like "There is a prime number greater than a million," which is likewise analytic but far from trivial), because it does not say more than that the new system is not empty; but this is immediately seen from the rule which states that words like "five" are substitutable for the new variables. Therefore nobody who meant the question "Are there numbers?" in the internal sense would either assert or even seriously consider a negative answer. This makes it plausible to assume that those philosophers who treat the question of the existence of numbers as a serious philosophical problem and offer lengthy arguments on either side, do not have in mind the internal question. And, indeed, if we were to ask them: "Do you mean the question as to whether the framework of numbers, *if* we were to accept it, would be found to be empty or not?," they would probably reply: "Not at all; we mean a question *prior* to the acceptance of the new framework." They might try to explain what they mean by saying that it is a question of the ontological status of numbers; the question whether or not numbers have a certain metaphysical characteristic called reality (but a kind of ideal reality, different from the material reality of the thing world) or subsistence or status of "independent entities." Unfortunately, these philosophers have so far not given a formulation of their question in terms of the common scientific language. Therefore our judgment must be that they have not succeeded in giving to the external question and to the possible answers any cognitive content. Unless and until they supply a clear cognitive interpretation, we are justified in our suspicion that their question is a pseudo-question, that is, one disguised in the form of a theoretical question while in fact it is non-theoretical; in the present case it is the practical problem whether or not to incorporate into the language the new linguistic forms which constitute the framework of numbers.

The system of propositions. New variables, "p," "q," etc., are introduced with a rule to the effect that any (declarative) sentence may be substituted for a variable of this kind; this includes, in addition to the sentences of the original thing language, also all general sentences with variables of any kind which may have been introduced into the language. Further, the general term "proposition" is introduced. "p is a proposition" may be defined by "p or not p" (or by any other sentence form yielding only analytic sentences). Therefore, every sentence of the form "…is a proposition" (where any sentence may stand in the place of the dots) is analytic. This holds, for example, for the sentence:

(a) "Chicago is large is a proposition."

(We disregard here the fact that the rules of English grammar require not a sentence but a that-clause as the subject of another sentence; accordingly, instead of (a) we should have to say "That Chicago is large is a proposition".) Predicates may be admitted whose argument expressions are sentences; these predicates may be either extensional (e.g., the customary truth-functional connectives) or not (e.g., modal predicates like "possible," "necessary," etc.). With the help of the new variables, general sentences may be formed, e.g.,

(b) "For every p, either p or not-p."
(c) "There is a p such that p is not necessary and not-p is not necessary."
(d) "There is a p such that p is a proposition."

(c) and (d) are internal assertions of existence. The statement "There are propositions" may be meant in the sense of (d); in this case it is analytic (since it follows from (a)) and even trivial. If, however, the statement is meant in an external sense, then it is noncognitive.

It is important to notice that the system of rules for the linguistic expressions of the propositional framework (of which only a few rules have here been briefly indicated) is sufficient for the introduction of the framework. Any further explanations as to the nature of the propositions (i.e., the elements of the system indicated, the values of the variables "p," "q," etc.) are theoretically unnecessary because, if correct, they follow from the rules. For example, are propositions mental events (as in Russell's theory)? A look at the rules shows us that they are not, because otherwise existential statements would be of the form: "If the mental state of the person in question fulfils such and such conditions, then there is a p such that…." The fact that no references to mental conditions occur in existential statements (like (c), (d), etc.) shows that propositions are not mental entities. Further, a statement of the existence of linguistic entities (e.g., expressions, classes of expressions, etc.) must contain a reference to a language. The fact that no such reference occurs in the existential statements here shows that propositions are not linguistic entities. The fact that in these statements no reference to a subject (an observer or knower) occurs (nothing like: "There is a p which is necessary for Mr X") shows that the propositions (and their properties, like necessity, etc.) are not subjective. Although characterizations of these or similar kinds are, strictly speaking, unnecessary, they may nevertheless be practically useful. If they are given, they should be understood, not as ingredient parts of the system, but merely as marginal notes with the purpose of supplying to the reader helpful hints or convenient pictorial associations which may make his learning of the use of the expressions easier than the bare system of the rules would do. Such a characterization is analogous to an extra-systematic explanation which a physicist sometimes gives to the beginner. He might, for example, tell him to imagine the atoms of a gas as small balls rushing around with great speed, or the electromagnetic field and its oscillations as quasi-elastic tensions and vibrations in an ether. In fact, however, all that can accurately be said about atoms or the field is implicitly contained in the physical laws of the theories in question.[2]

The system of thing properties. The thing language contains words like "red," "hard," "stone," "house," etc., which are used for describing what things are like. Now we may introduce new variables, say "*f*," "*g*," etc., for which those words are substitutable and furthermore the general term "property." New rules are laid down which admit sentences like "Red is a property," "Red is a color," "These two pieces of paper have at least one color in common" (i.e., "There is an *f* such that *f* is a color, and …"). The last sentence is an internal assertion. It is of an empirical, factual nature. However, the external statement, the philosophical statement of the reality of properties – a special case of the thesis of the reality of universals – is devoid of cognitive content.

The systems of integers and rational numbers. Into a language containing the framework of natural numbers we may introduce first the (positive and negative) integers as relations among natural numbers and then the rational numbers as relations among integers. This involves introducing new types of variables, expressions substitutable for them, and the general terms "integer" and "rational number."

The system of real numbers. On the basis of the rational numbers, the real numbers may be introduced as classes of a special kind (segments) of rational numbers (according to the method developed by Dedekind and Frege). Here again a new type of variables is introduced, expressions substitutable for them (e.g., "$\sqrt{2}$"), and the general term "real number."

The spatio-temporal coordinate system for physics. The new entities are the space-time points. Each is an ordered quadruple of four real numbers, called its coordinates, consisting of three spatial and one temporal coordinates. The physical state of a spatio-temporal point or region is described either with the help of qualitative predicates (e.g., "hot") or by ascribing numbers as values of a physical magnitude (e.g., mass, temperature, and the like). The step from the system of things (which does not contain space-time points but only extended objects with spatial and temporal relations between them) to the physical coordinate system is again a matter of decision. Our choice of certain features, although itself not theoretical, is suggested by theoretical knowledge, either logical or factual. For example, the choice of real numbers rather than rational numbers or integers as coordinates is not much influenced by the facts of experience but mainly due to considerations of mathematical simplicity. The restriction to rational coordinates would not be in conflict with any experimental knowledge we have, because the result of any measurement is a rational number. However, it would prevent the use of ordinary geometry (which says, e.g., that the diagonal of a square with the side 1 has the irrational value $\sqrt{2}$) and thus lead to great complications. On the other hand, the decision to use three rather than two or four spatial coordinates is strongly suggested, but still not forced upon us, by the result of common observations. If certain events allegedly observed in spiritualistic séances, e.g., a ball moving out of a sealed box, were confirmed beyond any reasonable doubt, it might seem advisable to use four spatial coordinates. Internal questions are here, in general, empirical questions to be answered by empirical investigations. On the other hand, the external questions of the reality of physical space and physical time are pseudo-questions. A question like "Are there (really) space-time points?" is ambiguous. It may be meant as an internal question; then the affirmative answer is, of course, analytic and trivial. Or it may be meant in the external sense: "Shall we introduce such and such forms into our language?"; in this case it is not a theoretical but a practical question, a matter of decision rather than assertion, and hence the proposed formulation would be misleading. Or finally, it may be meant in the following sense: "Are our experiences such that the use of the linguistic forms in question will be expedient and fruitful?" This is a theoretical question of a factual, empirical nature. But it concerns a matter of degree; therefore a formulation in the form "real or not?" would be inadequate.

3　What Does Acceptance of a Kind of Entities Mean?

Let us now summarize the essential characteristics of situations involving the introduction of a new kind of entities, characteristics which are common to the various examples outlined above.

The acceptance of a new kind of entities is represented in the language by the introduction of a framework of new forms of expressions to be used according to a new set of rules. There may be new names for particular entities of the kind in question; but some such names may already occur in the language before the introduction of the new framework. (Thus, for example, the thing language contains certainly words of the type of "blue" and "house" before the framework of properties is introduced; and it may contain words like "ten" in sentences of the form "I have ten fingers" before the framework of numbers is introduced.) The latter fact shows that the occurrence of constants of the type in question – regarded as names of entities of the new kind after the new framework is introduced – is not a sure sign of the acceptance of the new kind of entities. Therefore the introduction of such constants is not to be regarded as an essential step in the introduction of the framework. The two essential steps are rather the following. First, the introduction of a general term, a predicate of higher level, for the new kind of entities, permitting us to say of any particular entity that it belongs to this kind (e.g., "Red is a *property*," "Five is a *number*"). Second, the introduction of variables of the new type. The new entities are values of these variables; the constants (and the closed compound expressions, if any) are substitutable for the variables.[3] With the help of the variables, general sentences concerning the new entities can be formulated.

After the new forms are introduced into the language, it is possible to formulate with their help internal questions and possible answers to them. A question of this kind may be either empirical or logical; accordingly a true answer is either factually true or analytic.

From the internal questions we must clearly distinguish external questions, i.e., philosophical questions concerning the existence or reality of the total system of the new entities. Many philosophers regard a question of this kind as an ontological question which must be raised and answered *before* the introduction of the new language forms. The latter introduction, they believe, is legitimate only if it can be justified by an ontological insight supplying an affirmative answer to the question of reality. In contrast to this view, we take the position that the introduction of the new ways of speaking does not

need any theoretical justification because it does not imply any assertion of reality. We may still speak (and have done so) of "the acceptance of the new entities," since this form of speech is customary; but one must keep in mind that this phrase does not mean for us anything more than acceptance of the new framework, i.e., of the new linguistic forms. Above all, it must not be interpreted as referring to an assumption, belief, or assertion of "the reality of the entities." There is no such assertion. An alleged statement of the reality of the system of entities is a pseudo-statement without cognitive content. To be sure, we have to face at this point an important question; but it is a practical, not a theoretical question; it is the question of whether or not to accept the new linguistic forms. The acceptance cannot be judged as being either true or false because it is not an assertion. It can only be judged as being more or less expedient, fruitful, conducive to the aim for which the language is intended. Judgments of this kind supply the motivation for the decision of accepting or rejecting the kind of entities.[4]

Thus it is clear that the acceptance of a linguistic framework must not be regarded as implying a metaphysical doctrine concerning the reality of the entities in question. It seems to me due to a neglect of this important distinction that some contemporary nominalists label the admission of variables of abstract types as "Platonism."[5] This is, to say the least, an extremely misleading terminology. It leads to the absurd consequence that the position of everybody who accepts the language of physics with its real number variables (as a language of communication, not merely as a calculus) would be called Platonistic, even if he is a strict empiricist who rejects Platonic metaphysics.

A brief historical remark may here be inserted. The noncognitive character of the questions which we have called here external questions was recognized and emphasized already by the Vienna Circle under the leadership of Moritz Schlick, the group from which the movement of logical empiricism originated. Influenced by ideas of Ludwig Wittgenstein, the Circle rejected both the thesis of the reality of the external world and the thesis of its irreality as pseudo-statements;[6] the same was the case for both the thesis of the reality of universals (abstract entities, in our present terminology) and the nominalistic thesis that they are not real and that their alleged names are not

There being such things as designata

names of anything but merely *flatus vocis*. (It is obvious that the apparent negation of a pseudo-statement must also be a pseudo-statement). It is therefore not correct to classify the members of the Vienna Circle as nominalists, as is sometimes done. However, if we look at the basic anti-metaphysical and pro-scientific attitude of most nominalists (and the same holds for many materialists and realists in the modern sense), disregarding their occasional pseudo-theoretical formulations, then it is, of course, true to say that the Vienna Circle was much closer to those philosophers than to their opponents.

4 Abstract Entities in Semantics

The problem of the legitimacy and the status of abstract entities has recently again led to controversial discussions in connection with semantics. In a semantical meaning analysis certain expressions in a language are often said to designate (or name or denote or signify or refer to) certain extra-linguistic entities.[7] As long as physical things or events (e.g., Chicago or Caesar's death) are taken as designata (entities designated), no serious doubts arise. But strong objections have been raised, especially by some empiricists, against abstract entities as designata, e.g., against semantical statements of the following kind:

1. "The word 'red' designates a property of things."
2. "The word 'color' designates a property of properties of things."
3. "The word 'five' designates a number."
4. "The word 'odd' designates a property of numbers."
5. "The sentence 'Chicago is large' designates a proposition."

Those who criticize these statements do not, of course, reject the use of the expressions in question, like "red" or "five"; nor would they deny that these expressions are meaningful. But to be meaningful, they would say, is not the same as having a meaning in the sense of an entity designated. They reject the belief, which they regard as implicitly presupposed by those semantical statements, that to each expression of the types in question (adjectives like "red," numerals like "five," etc.) there is a

particular real entity to which the expression stands in the relation of designation. This belief is rejected as incompatible with the basic principles of empiricism or of scientific thinking. Derogatory labels like "Platonic realism," "hypostatization," or "'Fido'–Fido principle" are attached to it. The latter is the name given by Gilbert Ryle to the criticized belief, which, in his view, arises by a naïve inference of analogy: just as there is an entity well known to me, viz., my dog Fido, which is designated by the name "Fido," thus there must be for every meaningful expression a particular entity to which it stands in the relation of designation or naming i.e., the relation exemplified by "Fido"–Fido.[8] The belief criticized is thus a case of hypostatization, i.e., of treating as names expressions which are not names. While "Fido" is a name, expressions like "red," "five," etc. are said not to be names, not to designate anything.

Our previous discussion concerning the acceptance of frameworks enables us now to clarify the situation with respect to abstract entities as designata. Let us take as an example the statement:

(a) "'Five' designates a number."

The formulation of this statement presupposes that our language L contains the forms of expressions which we have called the framework of numbers, in particular, numerical variables and the general term "number." If L contains these forms, the following is an analytic statement in L:

(b) "Five is a number."

Further, to make the statement (a) possible, L must contain an expression like "designates" or "is a name of" for the semantical relation of designation. If suitable rules for this term are laid down, the following is likewise analytic:

(c) "'Five' designates five."

(Generally speaking, any expression of the form "'…' designates…" is an analytic statement provided the term "…" is a constant in an accepted framework. If the latter condition is not fulfilled, the expression is not a statement.) Since (a) follows from (c) and (b), (a) is likewise analytic.

Thus it is clear that *if* someone accepts the framework of numbers, then he must acknowledge (c) and (b) and hence (a) as true statements. Generally speaking, if someone accepts a framework for a certain kind of entities, then he is bound to admit the entities as possible designata. Thus the question of the admissibility of entities of a certain type or of abstract entities in general as designata is reduced to the question of the acceptability of the linguistic framework for those entities. Both the nominalistic critics, who refuse the status of designators or names to expressions like "red," "five," etc., because they deny the existence of abstract entities, and the skeptics, who express doubts concerning the existence and demand evidence for it, treat the question of existence as a theoretical question. They do, of course, not mean the internal question; the affirmative answer to *this* question is analytic and trivial and too obvious for doubt or denial, as we have seen. Their doubts refer rather to the system of entities itself; hence they mean the external question. They believe that only after making sure that there really is a system of entities of the kind in question are we justified in accepting the framework by incorporating the linguistic forms into our language. However, we have seen that the external question is not a theoretical question but rather the practical question whether or not to accept those linguistic forms. This acceptance is not in need of a theoretical justification (except with respect to expediency and fruitfulness), because it does not imply a belief or assertion. Ryle says that the "Fido"–Fido principle is "a grotesque theory." Grotesque or not, Ryle is wrong in calling it a theory. It is rather the practical decision to accept certain frameworks. Maybe Ryle is historically right with respect to those whom he mentions as previous representatives of the principle, viz., John Stuart Mill, Frege, and Russell. If these philosophers regarded the acceptance of a system of entities as a theory, an assertion, they were victims of the same old, metaphysical confusion. But it is certainly wrong to regard *my* semantical method as involving a belief in the reality of abstract entities, since I reject a thesis of this kind as a metaphysical pseudo-statement.

The critics of the use of abstract entities in semantics overlook the fundamental difference between the acceptance of a system of entities and an internal assertion, e.g., an assertion that there are elephants or electrons or prime numbers greater than a million. Whoever makes an internal assertion is certainly obliged to justify it by providing evidence, empirical evidence in the case of electrons, logical proof in the case of the prime numbers. The demand for a theoretical justification, correct in the case of internal assertions, is sometimes wrongly applied to the acceptance of a system of entities. Thus, for example, Ernest Nagel asks for "evidence relevant for affirming with warrant that there are such entities as infinitesimals or propositions."[9] He characterizes the evidence required in these cases – in distinction to the empirical evidence in the case of electrons – as "in the broad sense logical and dialectical." Beyond this no hint is given as to what might be regarded as relevant evidence. Some nominalists regard the acceptance of abstract entities as a kind of superstition or myth, populating the world with fictitious or at least dubious entities, analogous to the belief in centaurs or demons. This shows again the confusion mentioned, because a superstition or myth is a false (or dubious) internal statement.

Let us take as example the natural numbers as cardinal numbers, i.e., in contexts like "Here are three books." The linguistic forms of the framework of numbers, including variables and the general term "number," are generally used in our common language of communication; and it is easy to formulate explicit rules for their use. Thus the logical characteristics of this framework are sufficiently clear (while many internal questions, i.e., arithmetical questions, are, of course, still open). In spite of this, the controversy concerning the external question of the ontological reality of the system of numbers continues. Suppose that one philosopher says: "I believe that there are numbers as real entities. This gives me the right to use the linguistic forms of the numerical framework and to make semantical statements about numbers as designata of numerals." His nominalistic opponent replies: "You are wrong; there are no numbers. The numerals may still be used as meaningful expressions. But they are not names, there are no entities designated by them. Therefore the word 'number' and numerical variables must not be used (unless a way were found to introduce them as merely abbreviating devices, a way of translating them into the nominalistic thing language)." I cannot think of any possible evidence that would be regarded as relevant by both philosophers, and therefore, if actually found, would decide the controversy or at least make one of the opposite theses more probable than the other. (To construe the numbers as classes or properties of the second level, according to the Frege–Russell method, does, of course, not solve the controversy, because the first philosopher would affirm and the second deny the existence of the system of classes or properties of the second level.) Therefore I feel compelled to regard the external question as a pseudo-question, until both parties to the controversy offer a common interpretation of the question as a cognitive question; this would involve an indication of possible evidence regarded as relevant by both sides.

There is a particular kind of misinterpretation of the acceptance of abstract entities in various fields of science and in semantics that needs to be cleared up. Certain early British empiricists (e.g., Berkeley and Hume) denied the existence of abstract entities on the ground that immediate experience presents us only with particulars, not with universals, e.g., with this red patch, but not with Redness or Color-in-General; with this scalene triangle, but not with Scalene Triangularity or Triangularity-in-General. Only entities belonging to a type of which examples were to be found within immediate experience could be accepted as ultimate constituents of reality. Thus, according to this way of thinking, the existence of abstract entities could be asserted only if one could show either that some abstract entities fall within the given, or that abstract entities can be defined in terms of the types of entity which are given. Since these empiricists found no abstract entities within the realm of sense-data, they either denied their existence, or else made a futile attempt to define universals in terms of particulars. Some contemporary philosophers, especially English philosophers following Bertrand Russell, think in basically similar terms. They emphasize a distinction between the data (that which is immediately given in consciousness, e.g., sense-data, immediately past experiences, etc.) and the constructs based on the data. Existence or

reality is ascribed only to the data; the constructs are not real entities; the corresponding linguistic expressions are merely ways of speech not actually designating anything (reminiscent of the nominalists' *flatus vocis*). We shall not criticize here this general conception. (As far as it is a principle of accepting certain entities and not accepting others, leaving aside any ontological, phenomenalistic, and nominalistic pseudo-statements, there cannot be any theoretical objection to it.) But if this conception leads to the view that other philosophers or scientists who accept abstract entities thereby assert or imply their occurrence as immediate data, then such a view must be rejected as a misinterpretation. References to space-time points, the electromagnetic field, or electrons in physics, to real or complex numbers and their functions in mathematics, to the excitatory potential or unconscious complexes in psychology, to an inflationary trend in economics, and the like, do not imply the assertion that entities of these kinds occur as immediate data. And the same holds for references to abstract entities as designata in semantics. Some of the criticisms by English philosophers against such references give the impression that, probably due to the misinterpretaion just indicated, they accuse the semanticist not so much of bad metaphysics (as some nominalists would do) but of bad psychology. The fact that they regard a semantical method involving abstract entities not merely as doubtful and perhaps wrong, but as manifestly absurd, preposterous and grotesque, and that they show a deep horror and indignation against this method, is perhaps to be explained by a misinterpretation of the kind described. In fact, of course, the semanticist does not in the least assert or imply that the abstract entities to which he refers can be experienced as immediately given either by sensation or by a kind of rational intuition. An assertion of this kind would indeed be very dubious psychology. The psychological question as to which kinds of entities do and which do not occur as immediate data is entirely irrelevant for semantics, just as it is for physics, mathematics, economics, etc., with respect to the examples mentioned above.[10]

5 Conclusion

For those who want to develop or use semantical methods, the decisive question is not the alleged ontological question of the existence of abstract entities but rather the question whether the use of abstract linguistic forms or, in technical terms, the use of variables beyond those for things (or phenomenal data) is expedient and fruitful for the purposes for which semantical analyses are made, viz., the analysis, interpretation, clarification, or construction of languages of communication, especially languages of science. This question is here neither decided nor even discussed. It is not a question simply of yes or no, but a matter of degree. Among those philosophers who have carried out semantical analyses and thought about suitable tools for this work, beginning with Plato and Aristotle and, in a more technical way on the basis of modern logic, with C. S. Peirce and Frege, a great majority accepted abstract entities. This does, of course, not prove the case. After all, semantics in the technical sense is still in the initial phases of its development, and we must be prepared for possible fundamental changes in methods. Let us therefore admit that the nominalistic critics may possibly be right. But if so, they will have to offer better arguments than they have so far. Appeal to ontological insight will not carry much weight. The critics will have to show that it is possible to construct a semantical method which avoids all references to abstract entities and achieves by simpler means essentially the same results as the other methods.

The acceptance or rejection of abstract linguistic forms, just as the acceptance or rejection of any other linguistic forms in any branch of science, will finally be decided by their efficiency as instruments, the ratio of the results achieved to the amount and complexity of the efforts required. To decree dogmatic prohibitions of certain linguistic forms instead of testing them by their success or failure in practical use, is worse than futile; it is positively harmful because it may obstruct scientific progress. The history of science shows examples of such prohibitions based on prejudices deriving from religious, mythological, metaphysical, or other irrational sources, which slowed up the developments for shorter or longer periods of time. Let us learn from lessons of history. Let us grant to those work in any special field of investigation the freedom to use any form of expression which seems useful to them; the work in the field will sooner or later lead to the elimination of those forms which have no useful function. *Let us be cautious in making assertions and critical in examining them, but tolerant in permitting linguistic forms.*

Notes

1 The terms "sentence" and "statement" are here used synonymously for declarative (indicative, propositional) sentences.

2 In my book *Meaning and Necessity* (Chicago: University of Chicago Press, 1947) I have developed a semantical method which takes propositions as entities designated by sentences (more specifically, as intensions of sentences). In order to facilitate the understanding of the systematic development, I added some informal, extra-systematic explanations concerning the nature of propositions. I said that the term "proposition" "is used neither for a linguistic expression nor for a subjective, mental occurrence, but rather for something objective that may or may not be exemplified in nature.... We apply the term 'proposition' to any entities of a certain logical type, namely, those that may be expressed by (declarative) sentences in a language" (p. 27). After some more detailed discussions concerning the relation between propositions and facts, and the nature of false propositions, I added: "It has been the purpose of the preceding remarks to facilitate the understanding of our conception of propositions. If, however, a reader should find these explanations more puzzling than clarifying, or even unacceptable, he may disregard them" (p. 31) (that is, disregard these extra-systematic explanations, not the whole theory of the propositions as intensions of sentences, as one reviewer understood). In spite of this warning, it seems that some of those readers who were puzzled by the explanations, did not disregard them but thought that by raising objections against them they could refute the theory. This is analogous to the procedure of some laymen who by (correctly) criticizing the other picture or other visualizations of physical theories, thought they had refuted those theories. Perhaps the discussions in the present paper will help in clarifying the role of the system of linguistic rules for the introduction of a framework for entities on the one

hand, and that of extra-systematic explanations concerning the nature of the entities on the other.

3 W. V. Quine was the first to recognize the importance of the introduction of variables as indicating the acceptance of entities. "The ontology to which one's use of language commits him comprises simply the objects that he treats as falling…within the range of values of his variables" (W. V. Quine, "Notes on existence and necessity," *Journal of Philosophy* 40 (1943), pp. 113–27, at p. 118; compare also his "Designation and existence" *Journal of Philosophy* 36 (1939), pp. 702–9, and "On universals," *Journal of Symbolic Logic* 12 (1947), pp. 74–84.

4 For a closely related point of view on these questions see the detailed discussions in Herbert Feigl, "Existential hypotheses," *Philosophy of Science* 17 (1950), pp. 35–62.

5 Paul Bernays, "Sur le platonisme dans les mathématiques," *L'Enseignement math.* 34 (1935), pp. 52–69. W. V. Quine, see previous note and a recent paper "On what there is," this volume, ch. 1. Quine does not acknowledge the distinction which I emphasize above, because according to his general conception there are no sharp boundary lines between logical and factual truth, between questions of meaning and questions of fact, between the acceptance of a language structure and the acceptance of an assertion formulated in the language. This conception, which seems to deviate considerably from customary ways of thinking, will be explained in his article "Semantics and abstract objects," *Proceedings of the American Academy of Arts and Sciences* 80 (1951), pp. 90–6. When Quine in the above article classifies my logicistic conception of mathematics (derived from Frege and Russell) as "platonic realism" (p. 9), this is meant (according to a personal communication from him) not as ascribing to me agreement with Plato's metaphysical doctrine of universals, but merely as referring to the fact that I accept a language of mathematics containing variables of higher levels. With respect to the basic attitude to take in choosing a language form (an "ontology" in Quine's terminology, which seems to me misleading), there appears now to be agreement between us: "the obvious counsel is tolerance and an experimental spirit" (ibid., p. 12).

6 See Rudolf Carnap, *Scheinprobleme in der Philosophie; das Fremdpsychische und der Realismusstreit* (Berlin, 1928); Moritz Schlick, *Positivismus und Realismus*, repr. in *Gesammelte Aufsätze* (Vienna: 1938).

7 See Rudolf Carnap, *Introduction to Semantics* (Cambridge, Mass.: Harvard University Press, 1942); *idem, Meaning and Necessity*. The distinction I have drawn in the latter book between the method of the name-relation and the method of intension and extension is not essential for our present discussion. The term "designation" is used in the present article in a neutral way; it may be understood as referring to the name-relation or to the intension-relation or to the extension-relation or to any similar relations used in other semantical methods.

8 Gilbert Ryle, "Meaning and necessity," *Philosophy* 24 (1949), pp. 69–76.

9 Ernest Nagel, review of Rudolf Carnap, *Meaning and Necessity*, 1st edn, *Journal of Philosophy* 45 (1948), pp. 467–72.

10 Wilfrid Sellars, "Acquaintance and description again," *Journal of Philosophy* 46 (1949), pp. 496–504, at pp. 502 f. analyzes clearly the roots of the mistake "of taking the designation relation of semantic theory to be a reconstruction of *being present to an experience*."

3

Holes

David and Stephanie Lewis

Argle. I believe in nothing but concrete material objects.

Bargle. There are many of your opinions I applaud; but one of your less pleasing characteristics is your fondness for the doctrines of nominalism and materialism. Every time you get started on any such topic, I know we are in for a long argument. Where shall we start this time: numbers, colors, lengths, sets, force-fields, sensations, or what?

Argle. Fictions all! I've thought hard about every one of them.

Bargle. A long evening's work. Before we start, let me find you a snack. Will you have some crackers and cheese?

Argle. Thank you. What spendid Gruyère!

Bargle. You know, there are remarkably many holes in this piece.

Argle. There are.

Bargle. Got you!

* * *

Bargle. You admit there are many holes in that piece of cheese. Therefore, there are some holes in it. Therefore, there are some holes. In other words, holes exist. But holes are not made of matter; to the contrary, they result from the absence of matter.

Argle. I did say that there are holes in the cheese; but that is not to imply that there are holes.

Bargle. However not? If you say that there are A's that are B's, you are committed logically to the conclusion that there are A's.

Argle. When *I* say that there are holes in something, I mean nothing more nor less than that it is perforated. The synonymous shape-predicates '...is perforated' and 'there are holes in...' – just like any other shape-predicate, say '...is a dodecahedron' – may truly be predicated of pieces of cheese, without any implication that perforation is due to the presence of occult, immaterial entities. I am sorry my innocent predicate confuses you by sounding like an idiom of existential quantification, so that you think that inferences involving it are valid when they are not. But I have my reasons. You, given a perforated piece of cheese and believing as you do that it is perforated because it contains immaterial entities called holes, employ an idiom of existential quantification to say falsely 'There are holes in it'. Agreeable fellow that I am, I wish to have a sentence that sounds like yours and that is true exactly when you falsely suppose your existential quantification over immaterial things to be true. That way we could talk about the

David Lewis and Stephanie Lewis, "Holes," *Australasian Journal of Philosophy*, 48 (1970): 206–12. Routledge Publishing. Reproduced by permission.

Metaphysics: An Anthology, Second Edition. Edited by Jaegwon Kim, Daniel Z. Korman and Ernest Sosa.

cheese without philosophizing, if only you'd let me. You and I would understand our sentences differently, but the difference wouldn't interfere with our conversation until you start drawing conclusions which follow from your false sentence but not from my homonymous true sentence.[1]

Bargle. Oh, very well. But behold: there are as many holes in my piece of cheese as in yours. Do you agree?

Argle. I'll take your word for it without even counting: there are as many holes in mine as in yours. But what I mean by that is that either both pieces are singly-perforated, or both are doubly-perforated, or both are triply-perforated, and so on.

Bargle. What a lot of different shape-predicates you know! How ever did you find time to learn them all? And what does 'and so on' mean?[2]

Argle. Let me just say that the two pieces are equally-perforated. Now I have used only one two-place predicate.

Bargle. Unless I singly-perforate each of these crackers, how will you say that there are as many holes in my cheese as crackers on my plate? Be so kind as not to invent another predicate on the spot. I am quite prepared to go on until you have told me about all the predicates you have up your sleeve. I have a good imagination, and plenty of time.

Argle. Oh, dear ... (ponders)

* * *

Argle. I was wrong. There *are* holes.

Bargle. You recant?

Argle. No. Holes are material objects.

Bargle. I expected that sooner. You are thinking, doubtless, that every hole is filled with matter: silver amalgam, air, interstellar gas, luminiferous ether or whatever it may be.

Argle. No. Perhaps there are no truly empty holes; but I cannot deny that there might be.

Bargle. How can something utterly devoid of matter be made of matter?

Argle. You're looking for the matter in the wrong place. (I mean to say, that's what you would be doing if there were any such things as places, which there aren't.) The matter isn't inside the hole. It would be absurd to say it was: nobody wants to say that holes are inside themselves. The matter surrounds the hole. The lining of a hole, you agree, is a material object. For every hole there is a hole-lining; for every hole-lining there is a hole. I say the hole-lining *is* the hole.

* * *

Bargle. Didn't you say that the hole-lining surrounds the hole? Things don't surround themselves.

Argle. Holes do. In my language, 'surrounds' said of a hole (described as such) means 'is identical with'. 'Surrounds' said of other things means just what you think it means.

Bargle. Doesn't it bother you that your dictionary must have two entries under 'surrounds' where mine has only one?

Argle. A little, but not much. I'm used to putting up with such things.

Bargle. Such *whats*?

Argle. Such dictionary entries. They're made of dried ink, you recall.

Bargle. Oh. I suppose you'll also say that '... is in ...' or '... is through ...' said of a hole means '... is part of ...'.

Argle. Exactly so, Bargle.

Bargle. Then do you still say that 'There are holes in the cheese' contains an unanalyzed shape-predicate synonymous with '... is perforated'?

Argle. No; it is an existential quantification, as you think it is. It means that there exist material objects such that they are holes and they are parts of the piece of cheese.

* * *

Bargle. But we wouldn't say, would we, that a hole is made out of cheese?

Argle. No; but the fact that we wouldn't say it doesn't mean it isn't true. We wouldn't have occasion to say, unless philosophizing, that these walls are perpendicular to the floor; but they are. Anyhow we *do* say that caves are holes in the ground and that some of them are made out of limestone.

* * *

Bargle. Take this paper-towel roller. Spin it on a lathe. The hole-lining spins. Surely you'd never say the hole spins?

Argle. Why not?

Bargle. Even though the hole might continue to be entirely filled with a dowel that didn't spin or move at all?

Argle. What difference does that make?

Bargle. None, really. But now I have you: take a toilet-paper roller, put it inside the paper-towel roller, and spin it the other way. The big hole spins clockwise. The little hole spins counter-clockwise. But the little hole is part of the big hole, so it spins clockwise along with the rest of the big hole. So if holes can spin, as you think, the little hole turns out to be spinning in both directions at once, which is absurd.

Argle. I see why you might think that the little hole is part of the big hole, but you can't expect me to agree. The little hole is inside the big hole, but that's all. Hence I have no reason to say that the little hole is spinning clockwise.

* * *

Bargle. Consider a thin-walled hole with a gallon of water inside. The volume of the hole is at least a gallon, whereas the volume of the hole-lining is much less. If the hole is the hole-lining, then whatever was true of one would have to be true of the other. They could not differ in volume.

Argle. For 'hole' read 'bottle'; for 'hole-lining' also read 'bottle'. You have the same paradox. Holes, like bottles, have volume – or, as I'd rather say, are voluminous or equi-voluminous with other things – in two different senses. There's the volume of the hole or bottle itself, and there's the volume of the largest chunk of fluid which could be put inside the hole or bottle without compression. For holes, as for bottles, contextual clues permit us to keep track of which we mean.

* * *

Bargle. What is the volume of the hole itself? How much of the cheese do you include as part of one of these holes? And how do you decide? Arbitrarily, that's how. Don't try saying you include as little of the cheese as possible, for however much you include, you could have included less.

Argle. What we call a single hole is really many hole-linings. Some include more of the cheese, some include less. Therefore I need not decide, arbitrarily or otherwise, how much cheese is part of the hole. Many different decisions are equally correct.

Bargle. How can a single hole be identical with many hole-linings that are not identical with one another?

Argle. Really there are many different holes, and each is identical with a different hole-lining. But all these different holes are the same hole.

Bargle. You contradict yourself. Don't you mean to say that they all *surround* the same hole – where by 'surround' I mean 'surround', not 'be identical with'?

Argle. Not at all. I would contradict myself if I said that two different holes were identical. But

I didn't; what I said was that they were the same hole. Two holes are the same hole when they have a common part that is itself a hole.

Bargle. You agreed before that there were as many holes in my cheese as crackers on my plate. Are there still?

Argle. Yes; there are two of each left.

Bargle. Two crackers, to be sure, but how can you say there are two holes?

Argle. Thus: there is a hole, and there is another hole that is not the same hole, and every hole in the cheese is the same hole as one or the other.

Bargle. Be so kind as to say 'co-perforated', not 'same', and stop pretending to talk about identity when you are not. I understand you now: co-perforation is supposed to be an equivalence relation among hole-linings, and when you say there are two holes you are trying to say that there are two non-identical co-perforation-classes of hole-linings. Really you identify holes not with hole-linings but with *classes* of hole-linings.

Argle. I would if I could, but I can't. No; holes are hole-linings; but when I speak of them as holes, I find it convenient to use 'same' meaning 'co-perforated' wherever a man of your persuasion would use 'same' meaning 'identical'. You know my reason for this trickery: my sentences about sameness of holes will be true just when you wrongly suppose your like-sounding sentences to be. The same goes for sentences about number of holes, since we both analyse these in terms of sameness.[3]

* * *

Bargle. You still haven't told me how you say there are as many holes in my cheese as crackers on my plate, without also saying how many there are.

Argle. Here goes. There exist three things X, Y, and Z, X is part of the sum of the crackers, Y is part of the cheese, and Z is part of Y. Every maximal connected part of Y is a hole, and every hole in the cheese is the same hole as some maximal connected part of Y. X overlaps each of the crackers and Z overlaps each maximal connected part of Y. Everything which is either the intersection of X and a cracker or the intersection of Z and some maximal connected part of Y is the same size as any other such thing. X is the same size as Z.[4]

* * *

Bargle. Your devices won't work because co-perforation is not an equivalence relation. *Any*

two overlapping parts of my cheese have a common part that is a hole-lining, though in most cases the hole-lining is entirely filled with cheese. To be co-perforated is therefore nothing more than to overlap, and overlapping is no equivalence relation. The result is that although, as you say, you can find two hole-linings in this cheese that are not co-perforated, you can find another one that is co-perforated with both of them.

Argle. If you were right that a hole made of cheese could be entirely filled with the same kind of cheese, you could find far more than two non-co-perforated hole-linings; and there would be no such thing as cheese without holes in it. But you are wrong. A hole is a hole not just by virtue of its own shape but also by virtue of the way it contrasts with the matter inside it and around it. The same is true of other shape-predicates; I wouldn't say that any part of the cheese is a dodecahedron, though I admit that there are parts – parts that do not contrast with their surroundings – that are *shaped like* dodecahedra.

Bargle. Consider the paper-towel roller. How many holes?

Argle. One. You know what I mean: many, but they're all the same.

Bargle. I think you must say there are at least two. The left half and the right half are not the same hole. They have no common part, so no common part that is a hole.

Argle. They're not holes, they're two parts of a hole.

Bargle. Why aren't they holes themselves? They are singly-perforated and they are made of matter unlike the matter inside them. If I cut them apart you'd have to say they were holes?

Argle. Yes.

Bargle. You admit that a hole can be a proper part of a bigger – say, thicker-skinned – hole?

Argle. Yes.

Bargle. You admit that they are shaped like holes?

Argle. Yes, but they aren't holes. I can't say why they aren't. I know which things are holes, but I can't give you a definition. But why should I? You already know what hole-linings are. I say the two halves of the roller are only parts of a hole because I – like you – would say they are only parts of a hole-lining. What isn't a hole-lining isn't a hole.

Bargle. In that case, I admit that co-perforation may be an equivalence relation at least among singly-perforated hole-linings.

Argle. All holes are singly-perforated. A doubly-perforated thing has two holes in it that are not the same hole.

Bargle. Are you sure? Take the paper-towel roller and punch a little hole in its side. Now you have a hole in a hole-lining. You'd have to say you have a hole in a hole. You have a little hole which is part of a big hole; the big hole is not singly-perforated; and the little hole and the big hole are the same hole, since the little hole is a common part of each.

Argle. I think not. You speak of *the* big hole; but what we have are two big holes, not the same, laid end to end. There is also the little hole, not the same as either big hole, which overlaps them both. Of course we sometimes call something a hole, in a derivative sense, if it is a connected sum of holes. Any decent cave consists of many holes that are not the same hole, so I must have been speaking in this derivative sense when I said that caves are holes.

Bargle. What peculiar things you are driven to say when philosophy corrupts your mind! Tell me the truth; would you have dreamt for a moment of saying there were two big holes rather than one if you were not suffering under the influence of a philosophical theory?

Argle. No; I fear I would have remained ignorant.

Bargle. I see that I can never hope to refute you, since I no sooner reduce your position to absurdity than you embrace the absurdity.

Argle. Not absurdity; disagreement with common opinion.

Bargle. Very well. But I, for one, have more trust in common opinions than I do in any philosophical reasoning whatever. In so far as you disagree with them, you must pay a great price in the plausibility of your theories.

Argle. Agreed. We have been measuring that price. I have shown that it is not so great as you thought; I am prepared to pay it. My theories can earn credence by their clarity and economy; and if they disagree a little with common opinion, then common opinion may be corrected even by a philosopher.

Bargle. The price is still too high.

Argle. We agree in principle; we're only haggling.

Bargle. We do. And the same is true of our other debates over ontic parsimony. Indeed, this argument has served us as an illustration – novel, simple, and self-contained – of the nature of our customary disputes.

Argle. And yet the illustration has interest in its own right. Your holes, had I been less successful, would have punctured my nominalistic materialism with the greatest of case.

Bargle. Rehearsed and refreshed, let us return to – say – the question of classes.[5]

Notes

1 *Cf.* W. V. Quine, 'On What There Is', *From a Logical Point of View*, 2nd edition (Cambridge, Mass.: Harvard University Press, 1961): 13.

2 *Cf.* Donald Davidson, 'Theories of Meaning and Learnable Languages', in Y. Bar-Hillel, *Logic, Methodology and Philosophy of Science, Proceedings of the 1964 International Congress* (Amsterdam, 1965): 383–94.

3 *Cf.* Quine's maxim of identification of indiscernibles in 'Identity, Ostension, and Hypostasis', *From a Logical Point of View*, 71; P. T. Geach, 'Identity', *Review of Metaphysics* 21 (1967): 3–12.

4 This translation adapts a device from Nelson Goodman and W. V. Quine, 'Steps toward a Constructive Nominalism', *Journal of Symbolic Logic* 12 (1947): 109–110.

5 There would be little truth to the guess that Argle is one of the authors and Bargle is the other. We thank Charles Chastain, who also is neither Argle nor Bargle, for many helpful comments.

4

Beyond Being and Nonbeing

Roderick M. Chisholm

Meinong wrote: "There are objects of which it is true that there are no such objects."[1] But he was well aware that this statement of his doctrine of *Aussersein* was needlessly paradoxical. Other statements were: "The non-real" is not "a mere nothing" and "The object as such…stands 'beyond being and non-being'."[2] Perhaps the clearest statement was provided by Meinong's follower, Ernst Mally: "*Sosein* is independent of *Sein*."[3] We could paraphrase Mally's statement by saying: "An object may have a set of characteristics whether or not it exists and whether or not it has any other kind of being."

It is commonly supposed that this doctrine of *Aussersein* is absurd and that whatever grounds Meinong may have had for affirming it were demolished by Russell's theory of descriptions. I believe, however, that this supposition is false. I shall attempt here to set forth the doctrine in its most extreme form and I shall then consider what may be said in its favor.

I

The fundamental theses of Meinong's theory of objects are (1) that there are objects which do not exist and (2) that objects which are such that there

are *no* such objects are nonetheless constituted in some way or other and thus may be made the subject of true predication. The second of these two theses is the doctrine of *Aussersein*. The first thesis, as Meinong says, is familiar to traditional metaphysics. But traditional metaphysics, he adds, has had "a prejudice in favor of the actual."[4] Though it has had a proper concern for "ideal objects", those things that merely subsist [*bestehen*] and do not exist, it has neglected those things that have no being at all. Hence the need for a more encompassing theory of objects.

Among the characteristic tenets of the theory of objects are the following.

Of objects, some exist and others do not exist. Thus horses are included among objects that exist, and unicorns and golden mountains are included among objects that do not exist.

Of objects that do not exist, some may yet be said to be, or to subsist, and others may not be said to be at all.

Thus if existence is thought of as implying a spatio-temporal locus, then there are certain ideal objects that do not exist. Among these are properties or attributes and the objects of mathematics, as well as states of affairs (what Meinong calls '*Objektive*'). Since there are horses, for example,

Roderick Chisholm, "Beyond Being and Nonbeing," *Philosophical Studies*, 24/4 (1973): 245–57. Reproduced by kind permission of Springer Science + Business Media B.V.

Metaphysics: An Anthology, Second Edition. Edited by Jaegwon Kim, Daniel Z. Korman and Ernest Sosa.
Editorial material and organization © 2012 Blackwell Publishing Ltd. Published 2012 by Blackwell Publishing Ltd.

there is also the being of horses, the being of the being of horses, the nonbeing of the nonbeing of horses, and the being of the nonbeing of the nonbeing of horses. And since there are no unicorns, there is also the nonbeing of unicorns, the being of the nonbeing of unicorns, the nonbeing of the being of unicorns, and the nonbeing of the nonbeing of unicorns.[5]

But, though every object may correctly be said to be something or other, it is not the case that every object may correctly be said to be.[6] Unicorns, golden mountains, and round squares may not be said to be at all. Everything, however, *is* an object, whether or not it exists or has any other kind of being, and indeed whether or not it is even thinkable. (Whatever is unthinkable, after all, at least has the property of *being* unthinkable.) And every object, clearly, has the characteristics it does have whether or not it has any kind of being. This last is the proposition Mally expressed by saying that the *Sosein* of an object is independent of its *Sein*.

The theory of *Aussersein*, therefore, should be distinguished both from Platonism, as this term is currently interpreted, and from the reism, or concretism, of Brentano and Kotarbinski. Thus the Platonist might be said to reason as follows: "(*P*) Certain objects that do not exist have certain properties; but (*Q*) an object has properties if and only if it is real; hence (*R*) there are real objects that do not exist." The reist, on the other hand, reasons from not-*R* and *Q* to not-*P*; that is to say, he takes as his premises Plato's second premise and the contradictory of Plato's conclusion and then derives the contradictory of Plato's first premise. But Meinong, like Plato and unlike the reist, accepts *P* as well as *R*; unlike both Plato and the reist, he rejects *Q*; and then *he* derives a conclusion that is unacceptable both to the Platonist and to the reist – namely, "(*S*) The totality of objects extends far beyond the confines of what is merely real."[7]

Once this conclusion is accepted, a number of interesting distinctions may be made. These would seem to be peculiar to Meinong's theory of objects.

Thus objects may be subdivided into those which are possible and those which are impossible. (We should note, incidentally, that to say of an object that it is only a possible object is *not* to say of it that it is only possibly an object. For possible objects, as well as impossible objects, *are* objects.) Possible objects, unlike impossible objects, have non-contradictory *Soseins*. Golden mountains, for example, although they have no kind of being, may be possible objects; for the *Sosein* of a golden mountain need not preclude its *Sein*. But some golden mountains are impossible objects – for example, those that are both golden and nongolden, and those that are both round and square. An impossible object is thus an object with a contradictory *Sosein* – a *Sosein* that precludes its object's *Sein*.[8]

Soseins, too, are objects and therefore every *Sosein* has itself a *Sosein*. An object which is not itself a *Sosein* is an impossible object if it *has* a contradictory *Sosein*. May a *Sosein*, too, be an impossible object? Mally answers this question in a remarkable paragraph which may be paraphrased as follows:

"Like any other object a *Sosein* is an impossible object if *it* has a *Sosein* which precludes its *Sein*; that is to say, a *Sosein* is an impossible object if its own *Sosein* is contradictory. A *Sosein* would have a contradictory *Sosein* if it had the property of being the *Sosein* of an object which does *not* have that *Sosein*. The circularity of a possible square is thus an impossible *Sosein*. For the circularity of a possible square has itself a contradictory *Sosein*: that of being the circularity of something that isn't circular. But an impossible *Sosein* is not the same as a contradictory *Sosein*. The circularity of a possible square must be distinguished from the circularity (and squareness) of a *round* square; the former is an impossible *Sosein*, but the latter is not. The circularity of a round square is a contradictory *Sosein* but *not* an impossible *Sosein*. What is impossible is that there be an object that is both round and square. But it is *not* impossible that a round square be both round and square. Indeed, it is *necessary* that a round square be both round and square."[9]

Objects may also be classified as being either complete or incomplete. Where an impossible object is an object having a *Sosein* that violates the law of contradiction, an *incomplete object* is one having a *Sosein* that violates the law of excluded middle. Of the round squares that were being contemplated just now, it may be neither true nor false to say of the one that was contemplated by you that it is larger than the one that was contemplated by me.[10]

Of all objects, the most poorly endowed would seem to be what Meinong calls *defective objects*. Indeed, they are so poorly endowed that Meinong seems to be uncertain as to whether they are objects at all. If I wish that your wish will come true, then the object of my wish is whatever it is that you happen to wish. And if, unknown to me, *your* wish is that my wish will come true, then the object of your wish is what it is that I happen to wish. But this object, in the circumstances imagined, would seem to have very little *Sosein* beyond that of being our mutual object. Meinong felt, incidentally, that this concept of a defective object might be used to throw light upon the logical paradoxes.[11]

It is a mistake, then, to express the doctrine of *Aussersein* by saying that according to Meinong, such objects as golden mountains and round squares have a kind of being other than existence or subsistence. Meinong's point is that they have no kind of being at all. They are "homeless objects", not even to be found in Plato's heaven.[12]

Why assume, then, that an object may have a *Sosein* and yet no *Sein* – that an object may have a set of characteristics and yet no kind of being at all?

II

The prima facie case for this doctrine of *Aussersein* lies in the fact that there are many truths which *seem*, at least, to pertain to objects which are such that there are no such objects. It is reasonable to assume that this prima facie case would be weakened if we could show, with respect to these truths, that they need not be construed as pertaining to these homeless objects. It is also reasonable to assume, I think, that Meinong's case will be strengthened to the extent that we find ourselves *unable* to show, with respect to any one of these truths, that it need not be construed as pertaining to such objects.

There are at least five groups of such truths that have been singled out in recent literature. (The groups are not mutually exclusive and they may not be exhaustive.) For there would seem to be at least five different sorts of things that we may say of an object that does not exist or have any other kind of being: (1) we may say that the object does not exist; (2) we may say what the

object is without implying either that it exists or that it does not exist; (3) we may note what expressions in our language are used to refer to that object; (4) we may say that the object is involved in myth or fiction and that, as so involved, it is richly endowed with attributes; or (5) we may say that someone's intentional attitude is directed upon that object.

Meinong's best case, I think, lies with the final group – with those truths that seem to pertain to the nonexistent objects of our intentional attitudes. But let us consider them all in as favorable a light as we can.

(1) Examples of the first group are "Things that are both round and square do not exist" and "Unicorns do not exist". Can we paraphrase these in such a way that they may be seen to involve no reference to nonexistent objects? The first example presents fewer problems than the second, but it is doubtful that we can paraphrase it in a way that would satisfy Meinong.

The obvious paraphrase of "Things that are both round and square do not exist" would be "Everything that does exist is such that it is not both round and square". But, Meinong would say, where the subject-term of the paraphrase may be taken to refer to any piece of reality one chooses, the subject-term of the original is intended to refer to "what does not exist and is therefore not a piece of reality at all."[13]

The obvious paraphrase of "Unicorns do not exist" would be "Everything that does exist is such that it is not unicorn". But this, Meinong could say, leaves us with a reference to nonexistent objects. To say of a thing that it is not a unicorn is to say of it that it is not identical with any unicorn; and to say of a thing that it is not identical with any unicorn is to relate it to objects that do not exist.

Hence we may wish to replace 'a unicorn', in "Everything that does exist is such that it is not a unicorn", by certain predicates. But what predicates, and how do we decide? Let us suppose (to oversimplify somewhat) that we are satisfied with 'single-horned' and 'equine'. Then paraphrase "Unicorns do not exist" as "Everything that does exist is such that it is not both single-horned and equine". Meinong may now repeat the objection he had made to our attempted paraphrase of the first example above. And he may add still another.

How did we happen to choose the particular predicates "single-horned" and "equine"? We chose them, Meinong would say, because we know, *a priori*, that all and only unicorns are both single-horned and equine. And this *a priori* statement – "All and only unicorns are both equine and single-horned" – is one in which, once again, we have a subject-term that refers, or purports to refer, to nonexistent objects. This statement, however, belongs to the second group and not to the first.

(2) Meinong writes: "If one judges that a perpetual motion machine does not exist, then it is clear that the object whose existence he is denying must have certain properties and indeed certain characteristic properties. Otherwise the judgment that the object does not exist would have neither sense nor justification."[14] Applying a similar observation to our previous example, we may say, of the judgment that unicorns do not exist, that it presupposes that unicorns are both single-horned and equine. "Unicorns are both single-horned and equine" may also be expressed as "Every existing thing is such that if it were a unicorn then it would be both equine and single-horned." But the presence of 'a unicorn' in the latter sentence, as we have noted, ennables Meinong to say that the sentence does tell us something about unicorns – namely, that if any existing thing were identical with any one of them, then that thing would be both equine and single-horned.[15]

These truths about nonexistent objects which are presupposed, whenever we say of anything that it does not exist, are *a priori*, according to Meinong. Much of what we know about objects, he says, is thus '*daseinsfrei*'.[16]

There are some *a priori* statements, according to Meinong, in which nonexistent objects are singled out by means of definite descriptions. "Not only is the much heralded gold mountain made of gold, but the round square is as surely round as it is square."[17] What are we to say of "The golden mountain is golden"? According to Russell's theory of descriptions, some sentences of the form "The thing which is *F* is *G*" may be paraphrased into sentences of the following form: "There exists an *x* such that *x* is *F* and *x* is *G*, and for every (existing) *y*, if *y* is *F* then *y* is identical with *x*". Hence if we paraphrase "The golden mountain is golden" in this way, we will have: "There exists an *x* such that *x* is both golden and a mountain, and *x* is golden, and, for every (existing) *y*, if *y* is both golden and a mountain, then *y* is identical with *y*." The resulting sentence

would seem to refer only to objects that do exist. But is it an adequate paraphrase?

"The golden mountain is golden", according to Meinong, is *true*. But Russell's paraphrase implies "There exists an *x* such that *x* is both golden and a mountain" and is therefore *false*. How can a false statement be an adequate paraphrase of a true one?

Russell, of course, would say that Meinong is mistaken in insisting that "The golden mountain is golden" is true. But how are we to decide who is right, without begging the basic question that is involved?

(3) Semantical statements may seem to provide another type of reference to objects that do not exist or to objects such that there are no such objects. For example, "The word '*Einhorn*' in German designates unicorns"; or "The word '*Einhorn*' in German purports to designate unicorns"; or "The word '*Einhorn*' is used in German ostensibly to designate unicorns". And analogously for the word "unicorn" and its use in English. But Meinong would say – quite correctly, it seems to me – that semantical statements are really a subclass of intentional statements, statements about psychological attitudes and their objects, and hence that they belong to fifth group below. To say that "*Einhorn*" is used to designate unicorns, according to Meinong, is to say that "*Einhorn*" is used to express those thoughts and other intentional attitudes that take unicorns as their object.[18]

(4) Statements about objects of fiction and mythology are sometimes taken as paradigm cases of statements about nonexistent objects. Examples are "Sam Weller was Mr. Pickwick's servant" and "Sam Weller was a fictitious character who didn't really exist". But if I am not mistaken, these belong with our intentional statements, below. Thus the first example, as it would ordinarily be intended, pertains to one of the objects of a certain story (if we take 'story' in the widest sense of the word). But to say of a thing that it is an object of a certain story is to say, in essence, either that someone has told a story about that thing or that someone has thought of a story about that thing. And to say that someone has told a story, or that someone has thought of a story, is to make an intentional statement. When we say "Sam Weller was a fictitious character who didn't really exist", we are not only making an

intentional statement, about an object of someone's story, but we are also making a statement that belongs to our first group above – a statement saying that the object does not exist. Statements about the objects of mythology are analogous, except that it may be necessary to add, again intentionally, that the story in question is one that someone believes.

(5) Meinong's best case, then, would seem to lie with those true *intentional* statements that seem to pertain to objects that do not exist. I shall distinguish four types of such statement.

The first type is exemplified by

(a)　John fears a ghost.

Here we seem to have a straightforward affirmation of a relation between John and a nonexistent object. It is of the essence of an intentional attitude, according to Meinong, that it may thus 'have' an object "even though the object does not exist."[19] Can we paraphrase our statement (a) in such a way that the result can be seen to involve no such apparent reference to a nonexistent object? So far as I have been able to see, we cannot. (It is true, of course, that philosophers often invent new terms and then profess to be able to express what is intended by such statements as "John fears a ghost" in their own technical vocabularies. But when they try to convey to us what their technical terms are supposed to mean, then they, too, refer to nonexistent objects such as unicorns.)

It is sometimes said that Meinong did not properly understand the use of words in intentional contexts – or, in the terms of our example, that he did not properly understand the use of the expression "a ghost" in such a sentence as "John fears a ghost". He mistakenly supposed, it is suggested, that the word 'ghost' has a *referential* use in "John fears a ghost". But just what was the mistake that Meinong made? He did not make the mistake of supposing that the word 'ghost' in "John fears a ghost" is used to refer to something that exists or to something that is real. Is it that the word has a certain nonreferential use in such sentences and that Meinong was not aware of this use? But what *is* that nonreferential use – other than that of being used to tell us that John fears a ghost? I know of four positive suggestions, but they all seem to leave Meinong untouched. Thus

it has been said (i) that the word 'ghost', in "John fears a ghost", is used, not to describe the object of John's fears, but only to contribute to the description of John himself. This was essentially Brentano's suggestion.[20] But just *how* does 'ghost' here contribute to the description of John? It isn't being used to tell us that *John* is a ghost, or that John's *thought* is a ghost, for these things are false, but "John fears a ghost", we may suppose, is true. Surely the only way in which the word 'ghost' here contributes to the description of John is by telling us *what* the object is that he fears. It has also been suggested (ii) that the word 'ghost', in "John fears a ghost", functions only as part of the longer expression "fears a ghost" and that its use in such contexts has no connection at all with the use it has in such sentences as "There is a ghost." (Compare the use of 'unicorn' in "The Emperor decorated his tunic ornately.") That this suggestion is false, however, may be seen by noting that "John fears a ghost" and "John's fears are directed only upon things that really exist" together imply "There is a ghost." It has also been suggested (iii) that the word 'ghost', in "John fears a ghost", is used to refer to what in other uses would constitute the sense or connotation of 'ghost.'[21] In this case, "John fears a ghost" would be construed as telling us that there is a certain relation holding between John and a certain set of attributes or properties. But what attributes or properties, and what relation? John himself may remind us at this point that what he fears is a certain *concretum* and not a set of attributes or properties. It has even been suggested (iv) that the word 'ghost', in "John fears a ghost", is being used, in "the material mode", to refer to itself.[22] But John, of course, may not fear the *word* 'ghost.' What, then, would "John fears a ghost" be used to tell us about John and the word 'ghost'?

The second type of intentional statement is exemplified by

(b)　The mountain I am thinking of is golden.

To supply a context for such a statement, we imagine a game in which the participants are told to contemplate a mountain, such as might be found in Atlantis, and are then asked to describe the mountain they have contemplated. Meinong's "The golden mountain is golden", of our second group above, may well leave us speechless, but surely "The mountain I am thinking of is golden" may express a proposition that is true.

Russell's theory of desciptions does not provide us with a way of paraphrasing the statement, for, once again, Russell's procedure would provide us with a statement that is *false* ("There exists an x such that x is a mountain I am thinking of and x is golden, and, for every y, if y is a mountain I am thinking of, then y is identical with x").[23]

The participants in the game we have imagined may well compare mountains: "The mountain you are thinking of differs in interesting respects from the mountain I am thinking of." May we also say that the nonexistent object of one man's intentional attitude is *identical with* the nonexistent object of another man's intentional attitude? I think that we may often assume that this is the case. Such an identity statement provides us with our third example of a Meinongian intentional statement. Thus we may be agnostic and yet affirm:

(c) All Mohammedans worship the same God.

But this example, I think, is more problematic than the others. If the statement in question were true, we could say, of any two Mohammedans, that the God that is worshipped by the one is identical with the God that is worshipped by the other. But can we really say this if, as we are also inclined to say, "the God that is worshipped by Mohammedans does not exist". Shouldn't we say, at most, that for any two Mohammedans, x and y, the God that x worships is *very much like* the God that y worships?[24] (And instead of saying "The God that is worshipped by Mohammedans does not exist", we might express ourselves more accurately by saying "Every Mohammedan is such that the God that he worships does not exist.") But for Meinong's purpose, of course, it is enough to say that one nonexistent object is very much like another.

If we can never be sure that the nonexistent object upon which one man's intentional attitude is directed is identical with the nonexistent object upon which another man's intentional attitude is directed, we can be sure, on occasion, that the nonexistent object upon which one of a certain man's intentional attitudes is directed is identical with a nonexistent object upon which another one of that same man's intentional attitudes is directed. Thus we may say of an obsessed believer:

(d) The thing he fears the most is the same as the thing he loves the most.

Any adequate theory of the emotions would seem to imply that a man may have at any particular time a great variety of attitudes and feelings all directed upon a single object – even though that object does not exist.[25]

The latter example reminds us of what Meinong pointed out in a somewhat different connection – "we can also count what does not exist."[26] For a man may be able to say truly "I fear exactly three people" where all three people are objects that do not exist.

Such intentional statements, then, are what provide the best possible case for Meinong's doctrine of *Aussersein*. I think it must be conceded to Meinong that there is no way of paraphrasing any of them which is such that we know both (i) that it is adequate to the sentence it is intended to paraphrase and (ii) that it contains no terms ostensibly referring to objects that do not exist. Doubtless many philosophers are prejudiced against Meinong's doctrine because of the fact that Russell's theory of descriptions, as well as the theory of quantification in the way in which it is interpreted in *Principia Mathematica*, is not adequate to the statements with which Meinong is concerned. But this fact, Meinong could say, does not mean that the statements in question are suspect. It means only that such logic, as it is generally interpreted, is not adequate to intentional phenomena.

Notes

1   A. Meinong, 'Über Gegenstandstheorie', *Gesammelte Abhandlungen* (Leipzig, Johann Ambrosius Barth, 1929), II, p. 490. This work first appeared in 1904, in the collection *Untersuchungen zur Gegenstandstheorie und Psychologie* (Leipzig, Johann Ambrosius Barth), edited by Meinong. It is translated as 'The Theory of Objects', in *Realism and the Background of Phenomenology* (Glencoe, III., The Free Press, 1960), ed. by Roderick M. Chisholm; the quotation above appears on page 83.

2   *Gesammelte Abhandlungen* II, pp. 486, 489; English translation in *Realism and the Background of Phenomenology*, pp. 79, 86.

3   'Untersuchungen zur Gegenstandstheorie des Messens', in *Untersuchungen zur Gegenstandstheorie und Psychologie*, pp. 51–120; the quotation may be found on page 127.

4   *Gesammelte Abhandlungen* II, p. 485; English translation, p. 78.

5   See *Gesammelte Abhandlungen* II, pp. 486–8; English translation, pp. 79–80. The most complete statement of Meinong's theory of states of affairs, or *Objektive*, may be found in Chapter III ('Das Objektiv') of *Über Annahmen*, second edition (Leipzig, Johann Ambrosius Barth, 1910).

6   "Jeder Gegenstand ist *etwas*, aber nicht jedes Etwas *ist*." Mally, op. cit., p. 126.

7   The quotation is from Meinong's posthumous *Zur Grundlegung der allgemeinen Werttheorie* (Graz, Leuschner und Lubensky, 1923), ed. by Ernst Mally, p. 158.

8   Once we grasp the nature of an impossible object, according to Meinong, we become aware of "the necessity of its nonbeing". Meinong does not use the expression "necessary object", but he says, with respect to abstract objects, that once we grasp *their* nature, we become aware of "the necessity of their being". See *Über die Stellung der Gegenstandstheorie im System der Wissenschaften (Leipzig, R. Voitländer Verlag, 1907)*, p. 76.

9   Paraphrased from Ernst Mally, op. cit., pp. 128–9. I have translated '*Viereck*' as 'square', have added italics, and have written 'possible square' in two places where Mally wrote only '*Viereck*'.

10 On incomplete objects, see Meinong's *Über Möglichkeit und Wahrscheinlichkeit* (Leipzig, Johann Ambrosius Barth, 1915), pp. 179–80; also *Über die Stellung der Gegenstandstheorie im System der Wissenschaften*, pp. 118–23.

11 Meinong discusses defective objects in *Über emotionale Präsentation* (Vienna, Alfred Hölder, 1917), pp. 10–26.

12 See *Über die Stellung der Gegenstandstheorie im System der Wissenschaften*, Section One ('Heimatlose Gegenstände'), p. 8ff. In the *Introduction to Mathematical Philosophy* (London: George Allen and Unwin, Ltd., 1919) Russell said that, according to Meinong, such objects as the golden mountain and the round square "must have some kind of logical being" (p. 169). But in 'On Denoting' and in his earlier writings on Meinong, he does not make this mistake.

13 *Über die Stelling der Gegenstandstheorie im System der Wissenschaften*, p. 38. Meinong's remarks were directed toward the distinction between "Ghosts do not exist [*Gespenster existieren nicht*]" and "No real thing is ghostly [*Kein Wirkliches ist Gespenst*]". Compare Richard L. Cartwright, "Negative Existentials," *Journal of Philosophy*, LVII (1960), 629–39.

14 *Über Annahmen*, p. 79.

15 By confusing use and mention, one may try to render "Unicorns are both single-horned and equine" into a statement which mentions only words. (Such a statement as "The word 'unicorn' refers to things that are both single-horned and equine" belongs to our third group, below.)

16 A considerable part of Meinong's *Über die Stellung der Gegenstandstheorie im System der Wissenschaften* is devoted to '*Daseinsfreiheit*' and '*Apriorität*'.

17 English translation of 'The Theory of Objects', p. 82; *Gesammelte Abhandlungen* II, p. 490. Russell said that if "The round square is round" is true, then "The existent round square is existent" is also true; and the latter statement, he pointed out, implies that there is a round square; see his review of *Untersuchungen zur Gegenstandstheorie und Psychologie*, *Mind* XIV (1905), 530–8, esp. p. 533. Meinong replied that 'existent' is not a predicate, not a *Soseinsbestimmung*, and hence he should have said that "The existent round square is existent" is false. Unfortunately, however, he attempted to draw a distinction between "is existent" and "exists" and then said that although the existent round square is existent it does not exist. See *Über die Stellung der Gegenstandstheorie im System der Wissenschaften*, pp. 16–19. Reviewing the latter work, Russell replied: "I must confess that I see no difference between existing and being existent; and beyond this I have no more to say", *Mind* XVI (1907), 436–9, esp. p. 439. Meinong also had difficulties with "The possible round square is possible"; see *Über Möglichkeit und Wahrscheinlichkeit*, pp. 277–89. What he should have said, I think, is that "possible" is not a predicate, not a "*Soseinsbestimmung*," and hence that "The possible round square is possible" is false.

18 See *Über Annahmen*, second edition, p. 26.

19 See *Gesammelte Abhandlungen*, Vol. II, p. 383.

20 See Franz Brentano, *The True and the Evident* (London, Routledge and Kegan Paul, 1966), English edition edited by Roderick M. Chisholm, pp. 68–9.

21 This interpretation may be suggested by Frege's "Über Sinn und Bedeutung," *Zeitschrift für Philosophische Kritik*, vol. C (1892), pp. 25–50; translated as "On Sense and Nominatum," in *Readings in Philosophical Analysis* (New York, Appleton-Century-Crofts, Inc., 1949), edited by Herbert Feigl and Wilfrid Sellars, pp. 85–102.

22 Carnap once suggested that "Charles thinks (asserts, believes, wonders about) *A*", where "*A*" is thought of as being the abbreviation of some sentence, may be translated as "Charles thinks '*A*'"; *The Logical Syntax of Language* (New York, Harcourt, Brace and Company, 1937), p. 248.

23 In "On Denoting" Russell said that "the chief objection" to Meinong's nonexistent objects "is that such objects, admittedly, are apt to infringe the law of contradiction"; see Bertrand Russell, *Logic and Knowledge* (London, George Allen and Unwin, 1956), p. 45. Thus the round square that I am thinking of may be an object that is both round and nonround. Meinong's reply was that the law of contradiction (in the form, "For any attribute *F*, there is nothing that exemplifies *F* and also does not exemplify *F*") applies only to what is real or possible; one could hardly expect it to apply to impossible objects such as the round square. See *Über die Stellung der Gegenstandstheorie im System der Wissenschaften*, p. 16. One may also argue that certain possible objects would seem to infringe upon other logical laws. Suppose Jones, who mistakenly believes that F.D.R. was assassinated, tells us that the man he is now thinking about is the assassin of F.D.R. From Jones' true statement it follows that the man he is thinking about murdered F.D.R.; but for any *x* and *y*, if *x* murdered *y*, then *y* was murdered by *x*; hence F.D.R. *was* murdered – and by a nonexistent object! See James Mish'alani, "Thought and Object," *The Philosophical Review* LXXI (1962), pp. 185–201. Meinong's reply could be: The statement "For any *x* and *y*, if *x* murdered *y*, then *y* was murdered by *x*" is true only if our variables range over objects that exist; and, more generally, from the fact that it is a part of the *Sosein* of a nonexistent object *x* that *x* stands in a certain relation *R* to an existent object *y*, it does not follow that it is a part of the *Sosein* of *y* either that *y* is related by the converse of *R* to *x* or that *x* is related by *R* to *y*.

24 P. T. Geach cites this example: "Hob thinks a witch has blighted Bob's mare, and Nob wonders whether she (the same witch) killed Cob's sow"; in "Intentional Identity", *Journal of Philosophy*, LXVI (1967), pp. 627–32. There is a certain ambiguity in the example, for it may be taken to imply either that the object of Hob's thought *is* identical with the object of Nob's wondering or only that Nob *thinks* that it is. Taking it in its first sense, how could we ever find out that it is true? Hob may assure us that he thinks there is one and only one witch who blighted Bob's mare and that he also thinks that that witch is *F*, *G*, *H*, and … (where '*F*', '*G*', and '*H*' may be thought of as abbreviating certain predicates); and Nob may assure us that he, too, thinks there is one and only witch who blighted Bob's mare, that that witch is *F*, *G*, *H*, and … , and also, perhaps, that he, Nob, thinks that that witch is the same as the one that Hob believes to have blighted Bob's mare. But our statement of these facts does not entail that the object of Hob's thought is identical with the object of Nob's wondering. And, given that there are no witches, it is difficult to think of anything we could learn from Hob and Nob that would entail it.

25 Thus Meinong's theory of value is based upon this assumption; see *Zur Grundlegung der allgemeinen Werttheorie*, Part II ("*Die Werterlebnisse*").

26 "The Theory of Objects," English translation, p. 79; *Gesammelte Abhandlungen*, Vol. II, p. 487.

5

Does Ontology Rest on a Mistake?

Stephen Yablo

Not that I would undertake to limit my use of the words 'attribute' and 'relation' to contexts that are excused by the possibility of such paraphrase… consider how I have persisted in my vernacular use of 'meaning', 'idea', and the like, long after casting doubt on their supposed objects. True, the use of a term can sometimes be reconciled with rejection of its objects; but I go on using the terms without even sketching any such reconciliation.[1]

Quine, *Word and Object*

I

Introduction. Ontology the progressive research program (not to be confused with ontology the swapping of hunches about what exists) is usually traced back to Quine's 1948 paper 'On What There Is'. According to Quine in that paper, the ontological problem can be stated in three words – 'what is there?' – and answered in one: 'everything'. Not only that, Quine says, but 'everyone will accept this answer as true'.

If Quine is right that the ontological problem has an agreed-on answer, then what excuse is there for a subject called ontology?

Quine's own view on this comes in the very next sentence: 'there remains room for disagreement over cases'. Of course, we know or can guess the kind of disagreement Quine is talking about.[2] Are there or are there not such entities as the number nineteen, the property of roundness, the chance that it will rain, the month of April, the city of Chicago, and the language Spanish? Do 'they' really exist or do we have here just grammar-induced illusions?

And yet, there is a certain cast of mind that has trouble taking questions like these seriously. Some would call it the *natural* cast of mind: it takes a good deal of training before one can bring oneself to believe in an undiscovered fact of the matter as to the existence of nineteen, never mind Chicago and Spanish. And even after the training, one feels just a teensy bit ridiculous pondering the ontological status of these things.

Stephen Yablo, "Does Ontology Rest on a Mistake?," *Proceedings of the Aristotelian Society*, NS, supp. vol. 72 (1998): 229–61. Reprinted by permission of John Wiley & Sons, Inc.

Metaphysics: An Anthology, Second Edition. Edited by Jaegwon Kim, Daniel Z. Korman and Ernest Sosa.

Quine of course takes existence questions dead seriously.[3] He even outlines a program for their resolution: Look for the best overall theory – best by ordinary scientific standards or principled extensions thereof – and then consider what has to exist for the theory to be true.

Not everyone likes this program of Quine's. Such opposition as there has been, though, has centred less on its goals than on technical problems with the proposed method. Suppose a best theory were found; why shouldn't there be various ontologies all equally capable of conferring truth on it? Isn't a good theory in part an ontologically plausible one, making the approach circular?[4]

But again, there is a certain cast of mind that balks rather at the program's goals. A line of research aimed at determining whether Chicago, April, Spanish, etc. really exist strikes this cast of mind as naive to the point of comicality. It's as though one were to call for research into whether April is really the cruellest month, or Chicago the city with the big shoulders, or Spanish the loving tongue. (The analogy is not entirely frivolous as we will see.)

II

Curious/Quizzical. Here then are two possible attitudes about philosophical existence-questions: the *curious*, the one that wants to find the answers, and the *quizzical*, the one that doubts there is anything to find and is inclined to shrug the question off.

Among analytic philosophers the dominant attitude is one of curiosity.[5] Not only do writers on numbers, worlds, and so on give the impression of trying to work out whether these entities are in fact there, they almost always adopt Quine's methodology as well. An example is the debate about sets. One side maintains with Putnam and Quine that the indispensability of sets in science argues for their reality; the other side holds with Field and perhaps Lewis that sets are not indispensable and (so) can safely be denied. Either way, the point is to satisfy curiosity about what there is.

How many philosophers lean the other way is not easy to say, because the quizzical camp has been keeping a low profile of late. I can think of

two reasons for this, one principled and the other historical.

The principled reason is that no matter how oddly particular existence-claims, like 'Chicago exists', may fall on the ear, existence as such seems the very paradigm of an issue that has to admit of a determinate resolution. Compare in this respect questions about *whether* things are with questions about *how* they are.

How a thing is, what characteristics it has, can be moot due to features of the descriptive apparatus we bring to bear on it. If someone wants to know whether France is hexagonal, smoking is a dirty habit, or the Liar sentence is untrue, the answer is that no simple answer is possible. This causes little concern because there's a story to be told about why not; the predicates involved have vague, shifty, impredicative, or otherwise unstraightforward conditions of application.

But what could prevent there from being a fact of the matter as to *whether* a thing is? The idea of looking for trouble in the application conditions of 'exists' makes no sense, because these conditions are automatically satisfied by whatever they are tested against.

Don't get me wrong; the feeling of mootness and pointlessness that some existence-questions arouse in us is a real phenomenological datum that it would be wrong to ignore. But a feeling is, well, only a feeling. It counts for little without a *vindicating explanation* that exhibits the feeling as worthy of philosophical respect. And it is unclear how the explanation would go, or how it could possibly win out over the non-vindicating explanation that says that philosophical existence-questions are just very hard.

This connects up with the second reason why the quizzical camp has not been much heard from lately. The closest thing the quizzicals have had to a champion lately is Rudolf Carnap in 'Empiricism, Semantics, and Ontology'. This is because Carnap *had* a vindicating explanation to offer of the pointless feeling: The reason it feels pointless to ponder whether, say, numbers exist is that 'numbers exist', as intended by the philosopher, has no meaning.[6] Determined to pronounce from a position external to the number-framework, all the philosopher achieves is to cut himself off from the rules governing the use of 'number', which then drains his pronouncements of all significance.

Quine's famous reply (see below) is that the internal/external distinction is in deep cahoots with the analytic/synthetic distinction and just as misconceived. That Carnap is widely seen to have *lost* the ensuing debate is a fact from which the quizzical camp has never quite recovered. Carnap's defeat was indeed a double blow. Apart from embarrassing the quizzicals' champion, it destroyed the only available model of how quizzicalism might be philosophically justified.

III

Preview. I don't especially want to argue with the assessment of Carnap as loser of his debate with Quine. Internal/external[7] as Carnap explains it *does* depend on analytic/synthetic. But I think that it can be freed of this dependence, and that once freed it becomes something independently interesting: the distinction between statements made within make-believe games and those made without them – or, rather, a special case of it with some claim to be called the metaphorical/literal distinction.

This make-believish twist turns the tables somewhat. Not even Quine considers it ontologically committing to say in a *figurative* vein that there are Xs. His program for ontology thus presupposes a distinction in the same ballpark as the one he rejects in Carnap. And he needs the distinction to be tolerably clear and sharp; otherwise there will be no way of implementing the exemption from commitment that he grants to the non-literal.

Now, say what you like about analytic/synthetic, compared to the literal/metaphorical distinction it is a marvel of philosophical clarity and precision. Even those with use for the notion admit that the boundaries of the literal are about as blurry as they could be, the clear cases on either side enclosing a vast interior region of indeterminacy.

An argument can thus be made that it is Quine's side of the debate, not Carnap's, that is invested in an overblown distinction. It goes like this: To determine our commitments, we need to be able to ferret out all traces of non-literality in our assertions. If there is no feasible project of doing *that*, then there is no feasible project of Quinean ontology. There may be quicker ways of developing this objection, but the approach

through 'Empiricism, Semantics, and Ontology' is rich enough in historical ironies to be worth the trip.

IV

Carnap's proposal. Existence-claims are not singled out for special treatment by Carnap; he asks only that they meet a standard to which all meaningful talk is subject, an appropriate sort of discipline or rule-governedness. Run through his formal theory of language, this comes to the requirement that meaningful discussion of Xs – material objects, numbers, properties, spacetime points, or whatever – has got to proceed under the auspices of a *linguistic framework*, which lays down the 'rules for forming statements [about Xs] and for testing, accepting, or rejecting them'.[8] An ontologist who respects this requirement by querying 'the existence of [Xs] *within the framework*' is said by Carnap to be raising an *internal* existence-question.[9]

A good although not foolproof way to recognize internal existence-questions is that they tend to concern, not the Xs as a class, but the Xs meeting some further condition: 'is there a piece of paper on my desk?' rather than 'are there material objects?' I say 'not foolproof' because one *could* ask in an internal vein about the Xs generally; are there these entities or not? The question is an unlikely one because for any framework of interest, the answer is certain to be yes'. (What use would the X-framework be if having adopted it, you found yourself with no Xs to talk about?) But both forms of internal question are possible.

The point about internal existence-questions of either sort is that they raise no difficulties of principle. It is just a matter of whether applicable rules authorize you to say that there are Xs, or Xs of some particular kind. If they do, the answer is *yes*; otherwise *no*; end of story.[10] This alone shows that the internal existence-question is not the one the philosopher meant to be asking: it is not the 'question of realism'. A system of rules making 'there are material objects' or 'there are numbers' *unproblematically* assertible is a system of rules in need of external validation, or the opposite. Are the rules right to counsel acceptance of 'there are Xs'? It is no good consulting the framework for the answer; we know what *it* says. No, the existence of Xs will have to queried from a position outside the X-framework. The philosopher's question is an *external* question.

Now, Carnap respects the ambition to cast judgment on the framework from without. He just thinks philosophers have a wrong idea of what is coherently possible here. How can an external deployment of 'there are Xs' mean anything, when by definition it floats free of the rules whence alone meaning comes?

There are of course meaningful questions in the vicinity. But these are questions that mention 'X' rather than using it: e.g., the practical question 'should we adopt a framework requiring us to use 'X' like so?'[11] If the philosopher protests that she meant to be asking a question about Xs, not the term 'X', Carnap has a ready reply: 'You also thought to be asking a meaningful question, and one external to the X-framework. And it turns out that these conditions cannot be reconciled. The best I can do by way of indulging your desire to query the framework itself is to hear you as asking a question of advisability'.

So that is what he does; the 'external question' becomes the practical question, and the 'question of realism' which the philosopher thought to be asking is renounced as impossible. There is something that the 'question of realism' was *supposed* to be; there is a concept of the question, if you like. But the concept has no instances.[12]

V

Internal/external and the dogma of reductionism. Quine has a triple-barrelled response, set out in the next three sections.[13] The key to Carnap's position (as he sees it) is that 'the statements commonly thought of as ontological are proper matters of contention only in the form of linguistic proposals'.[14] But now, similar claims have been made about the statements commonly thought of as *analytic*; theoretical-sounding disputes about whether, say, the square root of −1 is a number are best understood as practical disputes about how to use 'number'. So, *idea*: the external existence-claims can be (re)conceived as the analytic ones. The objection thus looks to be one of guilt-by-association-with-the-first-dogma: 'if there is no proper distinction between analytic and synthetic, then no basis at all remains for the contrast which

Carnap urges between ontological statements and empirical statements of existence'.[15]

Trouble is, the association thus elaborated doesn't look all that close. For one thing, existence-claims of the kind Carnap would call analytic show no particular tendency to be external. Quine appreciates this but pronounces himself unbothered: 'there is in these terms no contrast between analytic statements of an ontological kind and other analytic statements of existence such as "There are prime numbers above a hundred"; but I don't see why he should care about this'.[16] Quine's proposal also deviates from Carnap in the opposite way; existence-claims can fail to be analytic without (on that account) failing to be external. An example that Carnap himself might give is 'there are material objects'. Quine apparently considers it a foregone conclusion that experience should take a course given which 'there are material objects' is assertible in the thing framework.[17] How could it be? It is not analytic that experience even occurs.[18]

All of that having been said, Carnap agrees that the distinctions are linked: 'Quine does not acknowledge [my internal/external] distinction' because according to him 'there are no sharp boundary lines between logical and factual truth, questions of meaning and questions of fact, between acceptance of a language structure and the acceptance of an assertion formulated in the language'.[19] The parallel here between 'logical truth', 'questions of meaning', and 'acceptance of a language structure' suggests that analytic/synthetic may define internal/external (not directly, by providing an outright equivalent, but) *indirectly* through its role in the notion of a framework. The assertion rules that make up frameworks are not statements, and so there is no question of calling them analytically *true*. But they are the nearest thing to, namely, analytically *valid* or *correct*. The rules are what give X-sentences their meanings, hence they 'cannot be wrong' as long as those meanings hold fixed.

Pulling these threads together, internal/external presupposes analytic/synthetic by presupposing frameworkhood; for frameworks are made up inter alia of analytic assertion rules. Some might ask, 'why should analytic rules be as objectionable as analytic truths?' But that is essentially to ask why Quine's second dogma – the reductionism that finds every statement to be linkable by fixed correspondence rules to a determinate range of confirming observations – should be as objectionable to him as the first. The objection is the same in both cases. Any observation can work for or against any statement in the right doctrinal/methodological context. Hence no assertion *or rule of assertion* can lay claim to being indefeasibly correct, as it would have to be were it correct as a matter of meaning. Quine may be right that the two dogmas are at bottom one; still, our finding *narrowly* drawn is one of guilt-by-association-with-the-second-dogma.

VI

Internal/external & double effect. Quine's attack on internal/external begins with his anti-reductionism, but it doesn't end there. Because up to a point, Carnap *agrees*: any link between theory and observation can be broken, and any can in the right context be forged.[20] It is just that he puts a different spin on these scenarios. There is indeed (thinks Carnap) a possibility that can never be foreclosed. But it is not the possibility of our correcting the rules to accommodate some new finding about the conditions under which X-statements are 'really true';[21] it is that we should decide for *practical* reasons to trade the going framework for another, thereby imbuing 'X' with a new and different meaning.[22]

That Carnap to this extent *shares* Quine's anti-reductionism forces Quine to press his objection from the other side. Having previously argued that the 'internal' life, in which we decide between particular statements, is a looser and more pragmatic affair than Carnap paints it, he needs now to argue that the 'external' life, in which we decide between frameworks, is more evidence-driven and theoretical.

Imagine that the choice before me is whether to adopt a rule making 'there are Xs' assertible under such and such observational conditions. And assume, as may well be the case, that these conditions are known to obtain; they might obtain trivially, as when 'X' = 'number'. Then my decision is (in part) a decision about whether to say 'there are Xs'. Since Carnap gives no hint that these words are to be uttered with anything less than complete sincerity, what I am really deciding

is whether to regard 'there are Xs' as *true* and to *believe* in Xs.[23] How then does adopting the rule fall short of being the acceptance of new doctrine?

Carnap could play it straight here and insist that adopting the rule involves only a *conditional* undertaking to assent to 'there are Xs' under specified observational conditions, while adopting the doctrine is categorically aligning myself with the view that there are Xs. But this is the kind of manoeuvre that gives the doctrine of double effect a bad name. Surely the decision to ϕ cannot disclaim all responsibility for ϕ's easily foreseeable (perhaps analytically foreseeable) consequences? To portray adopting the rule as taking a stand on what I am going to *mean* by 'X', as opposed to a stand on the facts, is just another version of the same manoeuvre; it is not going to make much of an impression on the man who called it 'nonsense, and the root of much nonsense, to speak of a linguistic component and a factual component in the truth of any individual statement'.[24]

VII

Internal/external & pragmatism. Carnap has his work cut out for him. Can he *without* appeal to analytic/synthetic, and *without* assuming the separability of meaning and 'how things are' as factors in truth, explain why the adoption of new assertion rules is not a shift in doctrine?

He might try the following. *If* the decision to make 'there are Xs' assertible were based in some independent insight into the ontological facts, or even in evidence relevant to those facts, then yes, it would probably deserve to be called a change of doctrine. If anything has been learned, though, from the long centuries of wheel-spinning debate, it is that independent insight and evidence are lacking. The decision to count 'there are Xs' assertible has got to be made on the basis of *practical* considerations: efficiency, simplicity, applicability, fruitfulness, and the like. And what practical considerations rationalize is not change in doctrine, but change in action or policy.

This is where push famously comes to shove. Efficiency and the rest are *not* for Quine 'practical considerations', not if that is meant to imply a lack of evidential relevance. They are exactly the sorts of factors that scientists point to as favouring one theory over another, hence as supporting this or that view of the world. As he puts it in the last sentence of 'Carnap's Views on Ontology', 'ontological questions [for Carnap] are questions not of fact but of choosing a convenient conceptual scheme or framework for science;... with this I agree only if the same be conceded for every scientific hypothesis'.[25]

A three-part objection, then: anti-reductionism, double effect, and finally pragmatism. The objection ends as it began, by disparaging not the idea of a Carnapian linguistic framework so much as its bearing on actual practice.[26] The special framework-directed attitudes Carnap points to are, to the extent that we have them at all, attitudes we also take towards our theories. Between acceptance of a *theory* and acceptance of particular theoretical claims, there is indeed not much of a gap. But it is all the gap that is left between external and internal if Quine is right.

VIII

Superficiality of the Quinean critique. Here is Quine's critique in a nutshell. The factors governing assertion are an inextricable mix of the semantic and the cognitive; any serious question about the assertive use of 'X' has to do both with the word's meaning *and* the X-ish facts. Accordingly Carnap's external stance, in which we confront a purely practical decision about which linguistic rules to employ, and his internal stance, in which we robotically apply these rules to determine existence, are both of them philosophical fantasies.

I want to say that even if all of this is correct, Quine wins on a technicality. His objection doesn't embarrass internal/external as such, only Carnap's way of developing the distinction. To see why, look again at the objection's three stages. The 'anti-reductionist' stage takes issue with Carnap's construal of the framework rules as something like analytic. But analyticity is a red herring. The key point about frameworks for Carnap's purposes is that

(*) they provide a context in which we are to say $--X--$ under these conditions, $==X==$ under those conditions, and so on, entirely without regard to whether these statements are in a framework-independent sense true.

This is all it takes for there to be an internal/external distinction. And it seems just irrelevant to (*) whether the rules telling us what to say when are conceived as analytically fixed.

Someone might object that analytical fixity was forced on us by semantic autonomy (by the fact that X has no other meaning than what it gets from the rules), and that semantic autonomy is non-negotiable since it is what licenses (*)'s insouciance about external truth. Numerical calculation does not answer to external facts about numbers for the same reason that players of tag don't see themselves as answerable to game-independent facts about who is really 'IT', just as apart from the game there's no such thing as being 'IT'; apart from the framework there's no such thing as being 'the sum of seven and five'.

But now wait. If the object is to prevent external claims from 'setting a standard' that internal claims would then be expected to live up to, depriving them of all meaning seems like overkill. A more targeted approach would be to *allow* X-talk its external meaning – allow it to that extent to 'set a standard' – but make clear that internal X-talk is not *bound* by that standard. How to make it clear is the question, and this is where the second or 'double effect' stage comes in.

Must internal utterances have the status of assertions? Carnap's stated goal, remember, is to calm the fears of researchers tempted by Platonic languages; he wants to show that 'using such a language does not imply embracing a Platonic ontology but is perfectly compatible with empiricism and strictly scientific thinking'.[27] If the issue is really one of use and access, then it would seem immaterial whether Carnap's researchers are asserting the sentences they utter or putting them forward in some other and less committal spirit.[28] This takes us to the third or 'pragmatic' stage of Quine's critique.

That frameworks are chosen on practical grounds proves nothing, Quine says, since practical reasons can also be evidential. Of course he's right. But why can't Carnap retort that it was the *other* (the non-evidential) sort of practical reason he had in mind – the other sort of practical reason he took to be at work in these cases? The claim Quine needs is that when it comes to indicative-mood speech behaviour, *no other sort of practical reason is possible.* There is no such thing, in other words, as just putting on a way of talking for the practical advantages it brings, without regard to whether the statements it recommends are in a larger sense true. (If there were, Carnap could take *that* as his model for adopting a framework.)

Does Quine allow for the possibility of ways of talking that are useful without being true, or regarded as true? A few tantalizing passages aside,[29] it seems clear that he not only allows for it, he revels in it. The overall trend of *Word & Object* is that a *great deal* of our day to day talk, and a great deal of the talk even of working scientists, is not to be taken ultimately seriously. This is Quine's famous doctrine of the 'double standard'. Intentional attributions, subjunctive conditionals, and so on are said to have 'no place in an austere canonical notation for science',[30] suitable for 'limning the true and ultimate structure of reality'.[31] Quine does not for a moment suggest these idioms are not useful. He goes out of his way to hail them as indispensable, both to the person in the street and the working scientist.[32] When the physicist (who yields to no one in her determination to limn ultimate structure) espouses a doctrine of 'ideal objects' (e.g., point masses and frictionless planes), this is welcomed by Quine as

> a deliberate myth, useful for the vividness, beauty, and substantial correctness with which it portrays certain aspects of nature even while, on a literal reading, it falsifies nature in other respects.[33]

Other examples could be mentioned;[34] their collective upshot is that Quine does not really doubt that practical reasons can be given for asserting what are on balance untruths. There is no in-principle mystery (even for him) about the kind of thing Carnap is talking about: a well-disciplined, practically advantageous way of talking that makes no pretence of being 'really true'.

IX

What is a framework and what should it be? About one thing Quine is right. Frameworks cannot remain what they were; they will have to evolve or die. Quine's own view is that he has pushed frameworks in the direction of theories.

But his objection really argues, I think, for a different sort of evolution.

Look again at the three stages. The first tells us that frameworks are not to be seen as sole determinants of meaning. All right, let '*X*''s meaning depend on factors that the framework has no idea of; let '*X*' have its meaning quite *independently* of the framework. The second tells us that the rules about what to say when had better not be rules about what to believingly assert. All right, let them be rules about what to *put forward*, where this is a conversational move falling short of assertion. The third tells us that if frameworks are non-doctrinal, this is not because they are adopted for reasons like simplicity, fruitfulness, and familiarity. All right, let the conclusion be reached by another and more direct route; let us identify frameworks outright with practices of such and such a type, where it is independently obvious that to engage in these practices is not thereby to accept any particular doctrine.

Now, what is our usual word for an enterprise where sentences are put at the service of something other than their usual truth-conditions, by people who may or may not believe them, in a disciplined but defeasible way? It seems to me that our usual word is 'make-believe game' or 'pretend game'. Make-believe games are the paradigm activities in which we 'assent' to sentences with little or no regard for their actual truth-values.

Indications are that Carnap would have resisted any likening of the internal to the make-believe. He take pains to distance himself from those who 'regard the acceptance of abstract entities as a kind of superstition or myth, populating the world with fictitious…entities'.[35] Why, when the make-believe model appears to achieve the freedom from external critique that Carnap says he wants?[36]

First there is a difference of terminology to deal with. A 'myth' for Carnap is 'a false (or dubious) internal statement' – something along the lines of 'there are ghosts' conceived as uttered in the thing framework.[37] A 'myth' or fiction for me is a *true* internal statement (that is, a statement endorsed by the rules) whose external truth value is as may be, the point being that that truth value is from an internal standpoint quite irrelevant. So while a Carnapian myth *cannot* easily be true, a myth in my sense *must* be internally true and may be externally true as well. (Studied indecision about which of them *are* externally true will be playing an increasing role as we proceed.)

Now, clearly, that 'internal truths' are not myths$_1$ = *statements that pertinent rules of evidence tell us to believe-false* doesn't show they aren't myths$_2$ = *statements that pertinent rules of make-believe tell us to imagine-true*. That said, I suspect that Carnap would not want internal truths to be myths$_2$ either. This is because freedom from external critique is only part of what Carnap is after, and the negative part at that. There is also the freedom *to* carry on in the familiar sort of unphilosophical way. The internal life Carnap is struggling to defend is the *ordinary* life of the ontologically unconcerned inquirer. And that inquirer does not see herself as playing games, she sees herself as describing reality.

X

The effect on Quine's program. Playing games vs. describing reality – more on that dilemma in due course.[38] Our immediate concern is not the bearing of make-believe games on Carnap's program, it's the bearing on Quine's. Quine has not much to say on the topic but it is satisfyingly direct:

> One way in which a man may fail to share the ontological commitments of his discourse is… by taking an attitude of frivolity. The parent who tells the Cinderella story is no more committed to admitting a fairy godmother and a pumpkin coach into his own ontology than to admitting the story as true.[39]

Note that the imputation of frivolity is not limited just to explicit self-identified pieces of play-acting. Who among us has not slipped occasionally into 'the essentially dramatic idiom of propositional attitudes',[40] or the subjunctive conditional with its dependence on 'a dramatic projection',[41] or the 'deliberate myths'[42] of the infinitesimal and the frictionless plane? Quine's view about all these cases is that we can protect ourselves from ontological scrutiny by keeping the element of drama well in mind, and holding our tongues in moments of high scientific seriousness.

Now, the way Quine is usually read, we are to investigate what exists by reworking our overall theory of the world with whatever tools science and philosophy have to offer, asking all the while what has to exist for the theory to be true. The advice at any particular stage is to

> (Q) count a thing as existing iff it is a commitment of your best theory, i.e., the theory's truth requires it.

What though if my best theory contains elements *S* that are there not because they are such very good things to believe but for some other reason, like the advantages that accrue if I *pretend* that *S*? Am I still to make *S*'s commitments my own? One certainly hopes not; I can hardly be expected to take ontological guidance from a statement I don't accept, and may well regard as false!

It begins to look as though (Q) overshoots the mark. At least, I see only two ways of avoiding this result. One is to say that the make-believe elements are never going to make it into our theories in the first place. As theorists we are in the business of describing the world; and to the extent that a statement is something to be pretended true, that statement is not descriptive. A second and likelier thought is that any make-believe elements that do make their way in will eventually drop out. As theory evolves it bids stronger and stronger to be accepted as the honest to God truth. These options are considered in the next few sections; after that we ask what sense can still be made of the Quinean project.

XI

Can make-believe be descriptive?[43] The thread that links all make-believe games together is that they call upon their participants to pretend or imagine that certain things are the case. These to-be-imagined items make up the game's *content*, and to elaborate and adapt oneself to this content is typically the game's very point.[44]

An alternative point suggests itself, though, when we reflect that all but the most boring games are played with *props*, whose game-independent properties help to determine what it is that players are supposed to imagine. That Sam's pie is too big for the oven doesn't follow from the rules of mud pies alone; you have to throw in the fact that Sam's clump of mud fails to fit into the hollow stump. If readers of 'The Final Problem' are to think of

Holmes as living nearer to Hyde Park than Central Park, the facts of nineteenth century geography deserve a large part of the credit.

Now, a game whose content reflects the game-independent properties of worldly props can be seen in two different lights. What ordinarily happens is that we take an interest in the props because and to the extent that they influence the content; one tramps around London in search of 221B Baker street for the light it may shed on what is true according to the Holmes stories.

But in principle it could be the other way around: we could be interested in a game's content because and to the extent that it yielded information about the props. This would not stop us from playing the game, necessarily, but it would tend to confer a different significance on our moves. Pretending within the game to assert that BLAH would be a way of giving voice to a fact holding *outside* the game: the fact that the props are in such and such a condition, viz., the condition that makes BLAH a proper thing to pretend to assert.

Using games to talk about game-independent reality makes a certain in principle sense, then. Is such a thing ever actually done? A case can be made that it is done all the time – not indeed with explicit self-identified games like 'mud pies' but impromptu everyday games hardly rising to the level of consciousness. Some examples of Kendall Walton's suggest how this could be so:

Where in Italy is the town of Crotone? I ask. You explain that it is on the arch of the Italian boot. 'See that thundercloud over there – the big, angry face near the horizon', you say; 'it is headed this way'.... We speak of the saddle of a mountain and the shoulder of a highway.... All of these cases are linked to make-believe. We think of Italy and the thundercloud as something like pictures. Italy (or a map of Italy) depicts a boot. The cloud is a prop which makes it fictional that there is an angry face... The saddle of a mountain is, fictionally, a horse's saddle. But our interest, in these instances, is not in the make-believe itself, and it is not for the sake of games of make-believe that we regard these things as props... [The make-believe] is useful for articulating, remembering, and communicating facts about the props – about the geography of Italy, or the identity of the storm cloud...or mountain topography. It is by thinking of Italy or the thundercloud...as potential if not actual props that I understand where Crotone is, which cloud is the one being talked about.[45]

A certain kind of make-believe game, Walton says, can be 'useful for articulating, remembering, and communicating facts' about aspects of the game-independent world. He might have added that make-believe games can make it easier to reason about such facts, to systematize them, to visualize them, to spot connections with other facts, and to evaluate potential lines of research. That similar virtues have been claimed for metaphors is no accident, if metaphors are themselves moves in world-oriented pretend games:

The metaphorical statement (in its context) implies or suggests or introduces or calls to mind a (possible) game of make-believe... In saying what she does, the speaker describes things that are or would be props in the implied game. [To the extent that paraphrase is possible] the paraphrase will specify features of the props by virtue of which it would be fictional in the implied game that the speaker speaks truly, if her utterance is an act of verbal participation in it.[46]

A metaphor on this view is an utterance that represents its objects as being *like so*: the way that they *need* to be to make the utterance pretence-worthy in a game that it itself suggests. The game is played not for its own sake but to make clear which game-independent properties are being attributed. They are the ones that do or would confer legitimacy upon the utterance construed as a move in the game.

Assuming the make-believe theory is on the right track, it will not really do to say that sentences meant only to be pretended-true are nondescriptive and hence unsuited to scientific theorizing. True, to pretend is not itself to describe. But on the one hand, the pretence may only be alluded to, not actually undertaken. And on the other, the reason for the pretence may be to portray the world as holding up its end of the bargain, by being in a condition to make a pretence like that appropriate. All of this may proceed with little conscious attention. Often in fact the metaphorical content is the one that 'sticks to the mind' and the literal content takes

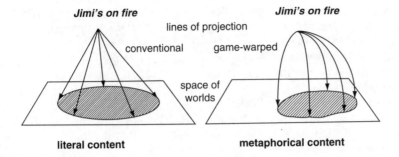

Figure 5.1

effort to recover. (Figurative speech is like that; compare the effort of remembering that 'that wasn't such a great idea', taken literally, leaves open that it was a very *good* idea.)

XII

Flight from figuration. What about the second strategy for salvaging (Q)? Our theories may start out partly make-believe (read now metaphorical), but as inquiry progresses the make-believe parts gradually drop out. Any metaphor that is not simply junked – the fate Quine sometimes envisages for intentional psychology – will give way to a paraphrase serving the same useful purposes without the figurative distractions.[47] An example is Weierstrass with his epsilon–delta definition of limit showing how to do away with talk of infinitesimals.

This appears to be the strategy Quine would favour. Not only does he look to science to beat the metaphors back, he thinks it may be the only human enterprise up to the task. He appreciates, of course, that we are accustomed to thinking of 'linguistic usage as literalistic in its main body and metaphorical in its trimming'. The familiar thought is however

> a mistake.... Cognitive discourse at its most dryly literal is largely a refinement rather, characteristic of the neatly worked inner stretches of science. It is an open space in the tropical jungle, created by cleaning tropes away.[48]

The question is really just whether Quine is *right* about this – not about the prevalence of metaphor outside of science, but about its eventual dispensability within.[49] And here we have to ask

what might have drawn us to metaphorical ways of talking in the first place.

A metaphor has in addition to its *literal* content – given by the conditions under which it is true and to that extent belief-worthy – a *metaphorical* content given by the conditions under which it is 'fictional' or pretence-worthy in the relevant game. If we help ourselves to the (itself perhaps metaphorical[50]) device of possible worlds, we can put it like so:

$$S\text{'s} \begin{Bmatrix} \text{literal} \\ \text{metaphorical} \end{Bmatrix} \text{content} =$$

the set of worlds that,
considered as actual, make $S \begin{Bmatrix} \text{true} \\ \text{fictional} \end{Bmatrix}$.

The role of pretend games on this approach is to warp the usual lines of semantic projection, so as to reshape the region a sentence defines in logical space.[51] In Figure 5.1, the straight lines on the left are projected by the ordinary, conventional meaning of 'Jimi's on fire'; they pick out the worlds which make 'Jimi's on fire' true. The bent lines on the right show what happens when worlds are selected according to whether they make the very same sentence, meaning the very same thing, fictional or pretence-worthy.

If it is granted that there are these metaphorical contents – these ensembles of worlds picked out by their shared property of legitimating a certain pretence – then here is what we want explained: what are the reasons for accessing them *metaphorically*? I can think of at least three sorts of reason, corresponding to three progressively more interesting sorts of metaphor.

Representationally essential metaphors. The most obvious reason is lack of a literal alternative; the language might have no more to offer in the way of a unifying principle for the worlds in a given content than that *they* are the ones making the relevant sentence fictional. It seems at least an open question, for example, whether the clouds we call *angry* are the ones that are literally *F*, for any *F* other than 'such that it would be natural and proper to regard them as angry if one were going to attribute emotions to clouds'. Nor does a literal criterion immediately suggest itself for the pieces of computer code called *viruses*, the markings on a page called *tangled* or *loopy*, the glances called *piercing*, or the topographical features called *basins*, *funnels*, and *brows*.

The topic being ontology, though, let's try to illustrate with an *existential* metaphor: a metaphor making play with a special sort of object to which the speaker is not committed (not by the metaphorical utterance, anyway) and to which she adverts only for the light it sheds on other matters. An example much beloved of philosophers is *the average so-and-so*.[52] When someone says that

(S) The average star has 2.4 planets,

she is not quite serious; she is pretending to describe an (extraordinary) entity called 'the average star' as a way of really talking about what the (ordinary) stars are like on average. Of course, this *particular* metaphor can be paraphrased away, as follows:

(T) The number of planets divided by the number of stars is 2.4,

But the numbers in *T* are from an intuitive perspective just as remote from the cosmologist's intended subject matter as the average star in *S*. And this ought to make us, or the more nominalistic among us, suspicious. Wasn't it Quine who stressed the possibility of unacknowledged myth-making in even the most familiar constructions? The nominalist therefore proposes that *T* is metaphorical too; it provides us with access to a content more literally expressed by

(U) There are 12 planets and 5 stars or 24 planets and 10 stars or...[53]

And now here is the rub. The rules of English do not allow infinitely long sentences; so the most literal route of access *in English* to the desired content is *T*, and *T* according to the nominalist is a metaphor. It is only by making *as if* to countenance numbers that one can give expression in English to a fact having nothing to do with numbers, a fact about stars and planets and how they are numerically proportioned.[54]

Presentationally essential metaphors. Whether you buy the example or not, it gives a good indication of what it would be like for a metaphor to be 'representationally essential', that is, unparaphrasable at the level of content; we begin to see how the description a speaker wants to offer of his *intended* objects might be inexpressible until *unintended* objects are dragged in as representational aids.

Hooking us up to the right propositional contents, however, is only one of the services that metaphor has to offer. There is also the fact that a metaphor (with any degree of life at all) 'makes us see one thing as another';[55] It 'organizes our view'[56] of its subject matter; it lends a special 'perspective' and makes for 'framing-effects'.[57] Dick Moran has a nice example:

> To call someone a tail-wagging lapdog of privilege is not simply to make an assertion of his enthusiastic submissiveness. Even a pat metaphor deserves better than this, and [the] analysis is not essentially improved by tacking on a... list of further dog-predicates that may possibly be part of the metaphor's meaning...the comprehension of the metaphor involves *seeing* this person as a lapdog, and ...experiencing his dogginess.[58]

The point is not essentially about seeing-as, though, and it is not only conventionally 'picturesque' metaphors that pack a cognitive punch no literal paraphrase can match. This is clear already from scientific metaphors like *feedback loop*, *underground economy*, and *unit of selection*, but let me illustrate with a continuation of the example started above.

Suppose that I am wrong and 'the average star has 2.4 planets' is representationally accidental; the infinite disjunction 'there are five stars and twelve planets etc.' turns out to be perfect English. The formulation in terms of the average star is still on the whole hugely to be preferred – for its easier visualizability, yes, but also its greater suggestiveness ('that makes me wonder how many moons the average planet has'), the way it lends itself to comparison with other data ('the average planet has nine times as many moons as the average star has planets'), and so on.[59]

Along with its representational content, then, we need to consider a metaphor's *presentational force*. Just as it can make all the difference in the world whether I grasp a proposition under the heading '*my* pants are on fire', grasping it as the retroimage of 'Crotone is in the arch of the boot' or 'the average star has 2.4 planets' can be psychologically important too. To think of Crotone's location as the place it would *need* to be to put it in the arch of Italy imagined as a boot, or of the stars and planets as proportioned the way they would need to be for the average star to come out with 2.4 planets, is to be affected in ways going well beyond the proposition expressed. That some of these ways are cognitively advantageous gives us a second reason for accessing contents metaphorically.

Procedurally essential metaphors. A metaphor with only its propositional content to recommend it probably deserves to be considered *dead*; thus 'my watch has a broken hand' and 'planning ahead saves time' and perhaps even 'the number of Democrats is decreasing'. A metaphor (like the Crotone example) valued in addition for its presentational force is *alive*, in one sense of the term, but it is not yet, I think, all that a metaphor can be. This is because we are still thinking of the speaker as someone with a definite *message* to get across. And the insistence on a message settled in advance is apt to seem heavy-handed. 'The central error about metaphor', says Davidson, is to suppose that

associated with [each] metaphor is a cognitive content that its author wishes to convey and that the interpreter must grasp if he is to get the message. This theory is false… It should make us suspect the theory that it is so hard to decide, even in the case of the simplest metaphors, exactly what the content is supposed to be.[60]

Whether or not all metaphors are like this, one can certainly agree that a lot are: perhaps because, as Davidson says, their 'interpretation reflects as much on the interpreter as on the originator';[61] perhaps because their interpretation reflects ongoing real-world developments that neither party feels in a position to prejudge. A slight elaboration of the make-believe story brings this third grade of metaphorical involvement under the same conceptual umbrella as the other two:

> Someone who utters S in a metaphorical vein is recommending the project of (i) looking for games in which S is a promising move, and (ii) accepting the propositions that are S's inverse images in those games under the modes of presentation that they provide.

The overriding principle here is *make the most of it*;[62] construe a metaphorical utterance in terms of the game or games that retromap it onto the most plausible and instructive contents in the most satisfying ways.

Now, should it happen that the speaker has definite ideas about the best game to be playing with S, I myself see no objection to saying that she intended to convey a certain metaphorical message – the first grade of metaphorical involvement – perhaps under a certain metaphorical mode of presentation – the second grade.[63] The reason for the third grade of metaphorical involvement is that one can imagine various *other* cases, in which the speaker's sense of the potential metaphorical *truthfulness* of a form of words outruns her sense of the particular truth(s) being expressed. These include the case of the *pregnant* metaphor, which yields up indefinite numbers of contents on continued interrogation;[64] the *prophetic* metaphor, which expresses a single content whose identity, however, takes time to emerge;[65] and, importantly for us, the *patient* metaphor, which hovers unperturbed above competing interpretations, as though waiting to be told where its advantage really lies.[66]

Three grades of metaphorical involvement, then, each with its own distinctive rationale.[67] The

Quinean is in effect betting that these rationales are short-term only – that in time we are going to outgrow the theoretical needs to which they speak. I suppose this means that every theoretically important content will find literal expression; every cognitively advantageous mode of presentation will confer its advantages and then slink off; every metaphorical 'pointer' will be replaced by a literal statement of what it was pointing at. If he has an argument for this, though, Quine doesn't tell us what it is. I therefore want to explore the consequences of allowing that like the poor, metaphor will be with us always.

XIII

Can the program be rijiggered? An obvious and immediate consequence is that the traditional ontological program of believing in the entities to which our best theory is committed stands in need of revision. The reason, again, is that our best theory may well include metaphorical sentences (whose literal contents are) not meant to be believed. Why should we be moved by the fact that *S* as literally understood cannot be true without *X*s, if the truth of *S* so understood is not something we have an opinion about?

I take it that any workable response to this difficulty is going to need a way of *sequestering* the metaphors as a preparation for some sort of special treatment. Of course, we have no idea as yet what the special treatment would be; some metaphors are representationally essential and so not paraphrasable away. But never mind that for now. Our problem is much more basic.

If metaphors are to be given special treatment, there had better be a way of telling *which statements the metaphors are*. What is it? Quine doesn't tell us, and it may be doubted whether a criterion is possible. For his program to stand a chance, something must be done to fend off the widespread impression that the boundaries of the literal are so unclear that there is no telling, in cases of interest, whether our assertions are to be taken ontologically seriously.

This is not really the place (and I am not the person) to try to bolster the sceptical impression. But if we did want to bolster it, we could do worse than to take our cue from Quine's attack on the analytic/synthetic distinction in 'Two Dogmas'.

One of his criticisms is phenomenological. Quine says he cannot tell whether 'Everything green is extended' is analytic, and he feels this reflects not an incomplete grasp of 'green' or 'extended' but the obscurity of 'analytic'. Suppose we were to ask ourselves in a similar vein whether 'extended' is metaphorical in 'after an extended delay, the game resumed'. Is 'calm' literal in connection with people and metaphorical as applied to bodies of water, or the other way around – or literal in connection with these and metaphorical when applied to historical eras? What about the 'backs' and 'fronts' of animals, houses, pieces of paper, and parades? Questions like these seem unanswerable, and not because one doesn't understand 'calm' and 'front'.

A second criticism Quine makes is that analyticity has never been explained in a way that enables us to decide difficult cases; we lack even a rough criterion of analyticity. All that has been written on the demarcation problem for metaphor notwithstanding, the situation there is no better and almost certainly worse.

A lot of the criteria in circulation are either extensionally incorrect or circular: often both at the same time, like the idea that metaphors (taken at face value) are outrageously false.[68] The criteria that remain tend to reinforce the impression of large-scale indeterminacy. Consider the 'silly question' test; because they share with other forms of make believe the feature of settling only so much, metaphors invite outrageously inappropriate questions along the lines of 'where exactly is the hatchet buried?' and 'do you plan to *drop*-forge the uncreated conscience of your race in the smithy of your soul, or use some alternative method?' But is it silly, or just mind-bogglingly *naive*, to wonder where *the number of planets* might be found, or how much *the way we do things around here* weighs or how it is coloured? It seems to me that it is silly if these phrases are metaphorical, naive if they are literal; and so we are no further ahead.

The heart of Quine's critique is his vision of what it is to put a sentence forward as (literally) true. As against the reductionist's claim that the content of a statement is renderable directly in terms of experience, Quine holds that connections with experience are mediated by surrounding theory. This liberalized vision is supposed to cure us of the *expectation* of a sharp divide between the analytic statements, which no experience can threaten, and the synthetic ones, which are empirically refutable as a matter of meaning.

As it happens, though, we have advanced a similarly liberalized vision of what it is to put a sentence forward as metaphorically true. By the time the third level of metaphorical involvement is reached, the speaker may or may not be saying anything cashable at the level of worlds. This is because a statement's truth-conditions have come to depend on posterity's judgment as to what game(s) it is best seen as a move in.[69] And it cannot be assumed that this judgment will be absolute and unequivocal: or even that the judgment will be made, or that anyone expects it to be made, or cares about the fact that matters are left forever hanging.

Strange as it may seem, it is this third grade of metaphorical involvement, supposedly at the furthest remove from the literal, that most fundamentally prevents a sharp delineation of the literal.[70] The reason is that *one* of the contents that my utterance may be up for, when I launch S into the world in the make-the-most-of-it spirit described above, is its *literal* content. I want to be understood as meaning what I literally *say* if my statement is literally true – count me a player of the 'null game', if you like – and meaning whatever my statement projects onto via the right sort of 'non-null' game if my statement is literally false. It is thus indeterminate from my point of view whether I am advancing S's literal content or not.[71]

Isn't this in fact our common condition? When speakers declare that there are three ways something can be done, that the number of As = the number of Bs, that they have tingles in their legs, that the Earth is widest at the equator, or that Nixon had a stunted superego, they are more sure that S is getting at *something* right than that the thing it is getting at is the proposition that S, as some literalist might construe it. If numbers exist, then yes, we are content to regard ourselves as having spoken literally. If not, then the claim was that the As and Bs are equinumerous.[72]

Still, why should it be a bar to ontology that it is indeterminate from my point of view whether I am advancing S's literal content? One can imagine Quine saying: I always told you that ontology was a long-run affair. See how it turns out; if and

when the literal interpretation prevails, that will be the moment to count yourself committed to the objects your sentence quantifies over.

Now though we have come full circle – because how the literality issue turns out depends on how the ontological issue turns out. Remember, we are content to regard our numerical quantifiers as literal precisely if, so understood, our numerical statements are true; that is, precisely if there *really are* numbers. Our problem was how to take the latter issue seriously, and it now appears that Quine is giving us no help with this at all. His advice is to countenance numbers iff the *literal* part of our theory quantifies over them; and to count the part of our theory that quantifies over numbers literal iff there turn out to really be numbers.[73]

XIV

The trouble with 'really'. The goal of philosophical ontology is to determine what really exists. Leave out the 'really' and there's no philosophy; the ordinary judgment that there exists a city called Chicago stands unopposed. But 'really' is a device for shrugging off pretences, and assessing the remainder of the sentence from a perspective uncontaminated by art. ('That guy's not *really* Nixon, just in the opera'.) And what am I supposed to do with the request to shrug off an attitude that, as far as I can tell, I never held in the first place?

One problem is that I'm not sure what it would *be* to take 'there is a city of Chicago' more literally than I already do.[74] But suppose that this is somehow overcome; I teach myself to focus with laserlike intensity on the truth value of 'there is a city of Chicago, *literally speaking*'. Now my complaint is different: Where are the methods of inquiry supposed to be found that test for the truth of existence-claims thus elaborated? All of our ordinary methods were designed with the unelaborated originals in mind. They can be expected to receive the 'literally speaking' not as a welcome clarification but an obscure and unnecessary twist.

Quine's idea was that our ordinary methods could be 'jumped up' into a test of literal truth by applying them in a sufficiently principled and long-term way. I take it as a given that this is the one idea with any hope of attaching believable truth values to philosophical existence-claims. Sad to say, the more controversial of these claims are equipoised between literal and metaphorical in a way that Quine's method is powerless to address.[75] It is not out of any dislike for the method – on the contrary, it is because I revere it as ontology's last, best hope – that I conclude that the existence-questions of most interest to philosophers are moot. If they had answers, (Q) would turn them up; it doesn't, so they don't.[76]

Notes

1 Quine 1960, 210.
2 Quine 1960 lists 'disagreement on whether there are wombats, unicorns, angels, neutrinos, classes, points, miles, propositions' (233).
3 I am talking about the 'popular', pre-late-1960s, Quine: the one who wrote 'A logistical approach to the ontological problem', 'On what there is' (ignoring the ontological relativism), 'Two dogmas of empiricism', 'On Carnap's views on ontology', and *Word & Object* (ignoring the ontological relativity). Quine's later writings are not discussed here at all.
4 Doubts have been expressed too about the extensionality of Quinean commitment. Particularly helpful on these topics are Chomsky & Scheffler 1958–9, Stevenson 1976, and Jackson 1980.
5 It might be safer to say that curiosity is the analytic movement's 'official' attitude, the one that most published research unapologetically presupposes. (This after a period of ordinary-language-inspired quizzicality, as in Ryle 1954, 'The World of Science and the Everyday World'.)
6 So says my Carnap, anyway; for a sense of the interpretive options see Haack, Stroud, Hookway, and Bird.
7 'Internal/external' is short for 'the internal/external distinction'; likewise 'analytic/synthetic'.
8 Carnap 1956, 208.
9 Carnap 1956, 206.
10 I am slurring over the possibility that the rules yield no verdict; cf. the treatment of solubility judgments in Carnap 1936/7.
11 Also mentioned is the theoretical question, 'how well would adopting this framework serve our interests as inquirers?'.
12 Is the concept incoherent? On my interpretation, yes. Yet as Bird remarks, Carnap says only that the question of realism has not been made out. I read the relevant passages as leaving the door open, not to the question of realism as he defines it (*his* definition can't be satisfied), but to an alternative definition.
13 Quine devotes most of his 1951b to another, seemingly much sillier, objection. See Bird for criticism.
14 Quine 1951b, 71.
15 Quine 1951b, 71.
16 What is so hard to see? Internal/external was supposed to shed light on the felt difference between substantive, 'real world', existence-questions and those of the sort that only a philosopher could take seriously. 'Are there primes over a hundred?' as normally understood falls on one side of this line; 'are there numbers?' as normally understood falls on the other. Carnap should thus care very much if Quine's version of his distinction groups these questions together. The problem is by no means an isolated one. According to Carnap in the Schilpp volume, existence-claims about abstract objects are '*usually* analytic and trivial' (Schilpp 1963, 871, emphasis added).
17 He includes it on a list of sentences said to be 'analytic or contradictory given the language' (Quine 1951b, 71). Why a true-in-virtue-of-meaning sentence would be well suited for the role of a sentence that is untrue-in-virtue-of-being-cognitively-meaningless is not altogether clear.
18 On the other hand: 'Accepting a new kind of entity' involves, for Carnap, adopting a new style of variable with corresponding general term. 'There are material objects' thus translates as $(\exists m)$ MATOBJ (m); which, given how the variable and term are coordinated, is equivalent to $(\exists m)m=m$; which, to come at last to the point, is logically valid in standard quantificational logic. On the third hand, Carnap *objected* to this feature of standard quantificational logic: 'If logic is to be independent of empirical knowledge, then it must assume nothing concerning the *existence of objects*' (Carnap 1937, 140). In his 'physical language', he notes, 'whether anything at all exists – that is to say, whether there is ... a non-trivially occupied position – can only be expressed by means of a synthetic sentence' (ibid., 141).
19 Carnap 1956, 215.
20 It is too often forgotten where Quine *gets* his anti-reductionism: 'The dogma of reductionism survives in the supposition that each statement, taken in isolation from its fellows, can admit of confirmation or infirmation at all. My countersuggestion, issuing essentially from Carnap's doctrine of the physical world in the *Aufbau*, is that our statements about the external world face the tribunal of sense experience not individually but only as a corporate body' (Quine 1951a, 41).

21 There is no scope for such a finding, since there is no external vantage point from which X-statements can be evaluated.

22 This was Carnap's view already in the 1930s: 'all rules are laid down with the reservation that they may be altered as soon as it seems expedient to do so' (Carnap 1937, 318).

23 'The acceptance of the thing language leads, on the basis of observations made, also to the acceptance, belief and assertion of certain statements' (Carnap 1956, 208).

24 Quine 1951a, 42. The situation here is more complicated than it may look. Until the framework is adopted, 'there are Xs' has no meaning for me. I am thus faced with a package deal: do I want to mean a certain thing by 'there are Xs', and accept 'there are Xs' with that meaning? Since the meaning is not, pre-adoption, mine, it is questionable whether I can be described, pre-adoption, as considering whether there are Xs, or even considering whether to believe that there are Xs.

25 Quine 1951b, 72.

26 Quine on the back of his copy of Carnap 1956: 'When are rules really adopted? Ever? Then what application of your theory to what I am concerned with (language now)?' (Creath 1990, 417).

27 Carnap 1956, 206.

28 Compare van Fraassen on 'the realist and antirealist pictures of scientific activity. When a scientist advances a new theory, the realist sees him as asserting the (truth of the) postulates. But the antirealist sees him as displaying this theory, holding it up to view, as it were, and claiming certain virtues for it' (van Fraassen 1980, 57). A fuller treatment would explore analogies with constructive empiricism; see note 75 for a point of disanalogy.

29 See especially 'Posits & Reality', originally intended as the opening chapter of Quine 1960. 'Might the molecular doctrine be ever so useful in organizing and extending our knowledge of the behavior of observable things, and yet be factually false? One may question, on closer consideration, whether this is really an intelligible possibility' (Quine 1976, 248). 'Having noted that man has no evidence of the existence of bodies beyond the fact that their assumption helps him organize experience, we should have done well...to conclude: such then, at bottom, is what evidence is...' (ibid., 251).

30 Quine 1960, 225.

31 Quine 1960, 221.

32 'Not that I would forswear daily use of intentional idioms, or maintain that they are practically dispensable. But they call, I think, for bifurcation in canonical notation' (Quine 1960, 221). 'Not that the idioms thus renounced are supposed to be unneeded in the market place or the laboratory....

The doctrine is that all traits of reality worthy of the name can be set down in an idiom of this austere form if in any idiom' (ibid., 228).

33 Quine 1960, 250.

34 Just as the immaterialist 'stoop[s] to our [materialist] idiom...when the theoretical question is not at issue', and the nominalist 'agree[s] that there are primes between 10 and 20', condoning 'that usage as a mere manner of speaking', many of our own 'casual remarks in the "there are" form would want dusting up when our thoughts turn seriously ontological'. This causes no confusion provided that 'the theoretical use is...respected as literal and basic' (Quine 1966a, 99ff).

35 Carnap 1956, 218.

36 The make-believe interpretation also offers certain advantages. Carnap says that practical decisions as between frameworks are informed by theoretical discussions about ease of use, communicability, and so on. But theoretical statements are always internal, and we are now by hypothesis occupying an external vantage point. Carnap might reply that internal/external is a relative distinction, and that we occupy framework A when considering whether to adopt framework B. But since the one framework may be just as much in need of evaluation as the other, this makes for a feeling of intellectual vertigo. A cleaner solution is to say that we occupy the external perspective when we in a non-make-believe spirit consider the practicality of engaging in make-believe. See also note 47.

37 Carnap 1956, 218.

38 I have hopes of enticing the Carnapians back on board by representing it as a false dilemma.

39 Quine 1961, 103.

40 Quine 1960, 219.

41 Dramatic in that 'we feign belief in the antecedent and see how convincing we then find the consequent' (Quine 1960, 222). This hints (quite by accident) at an analogy between the make-believe theory and 'if-thenism' that I hope to pursue elsewhere.

42 Quine, 248ff.

43 This section borrows from Yablo 1997.

44 Better, such and such is part of the game's content if 'it is to be imagined.... should the question arise, it being understood that often the question shouldn't arise' (Walton 1990, 40). Subject to the usual qualifications, the ideas about make-believe and metaphor in the next few paragraphs are all due to Walton (1990, 1993).

45 Walton 1993, 40–1.

46 Ibid., 46. I should say that Walton does not take himself to be offering a general theory of metaphor.

47 The notion of paraphrase has always been caught between an aspiration to symmetry – paraphrases

are supposed to *match* their originals along some semantic dimension – and an aspiration to the opposite – paraphrases are supposed to *improve* on their originals by shedding unwanted ontological commitments. (See Alston 1957.) Quine avoids the paradox by sacrificing matching to improvement; he expects nothing like synonymy but just a sentence that 'serves any purposes of [the original] that seem worth serving' (Quine 1960, 214). But while this is technically unanswerable, there is still the feeling in many cases that the paraphrase 'says the same' as what it paraphrases, or the same as what we were trying to say by its means. A reversion to the poetry-class reading of 'paraphrase' – a paraphrase of S expresses in literal terms what S says metapharically – solves the paradox rather neatly.

48 Quine 1981, 188–9.

49 Quine speaks of the 'inner stretches' of science; is that to concede that 'total science' has no hope of achieving a purely literal state?

50 Yablo 1997. Derrida was right; one uses metaphor to explain metaphor.

51 A lot of metaphors are literally impossible: 'I am a rock'. Assuming we want a non-degenerate region on the left, the space of worlds should embrace all 'ways for things to be', not just the 'ways things could have been'. The distinction is from Salmon 1989.

52 I am indebted to Melia 1995. Following the example of Quine, I will be using 'metaphor' in a very broad sense; the term will cover anything exploiting the same basic semantic mechanisms as standard 'Juliet is the sun'-type metaphors, no matter how banal and unpoetic.

53 Why not a primitive '2.4-times-as-many' predicate? Because 2.4 is not the only ratio in which quantities can stand; 'we will never find the time to learn all the infinitely many [q-times-as-many] predicates', with q a schematic letter taking rational substituends, much less the r-times-as-long predicates, with r ranging schematically over the reals (Melia 1995, 228). A fundamental attraction of existential metaphor is its promise of ontology-free semantic productivity. How real the promise is – how much metaphor can do to get us off the ontology/ideology treadmill – strikes me as wide open and very much in need of discussion.

54 Compare Quine on states of affairs: 'the particular range of possible physiological states, each of which would count as a case of [the cat] wanting to get on that particular roof, is a gerry-mandered range of states that could surely not be encapsulated in any manageable anatomical description even if we knew all about cats…. Relations to states of affairs,… such as wanting and fearing,

afford some very special and seemingly indispensable ways of grouping events in the natural world' (Quine 1966b, 147). Quine sees here an argument for counting states of affairs (construed as sets of worlds!) into his ontology. But the passage reads better as an argument that the *metaphor* of states of affairs allows us access to theoretically important contents unapproachable in any other way.

55 Davidson 1978.

56 Max Black in Ortony 1993.

57 Moran 1989, 108.

58 Moran 1989, 90.

59 Similarly with Quine's cat example: the gerrymandered anatomical description *even if available* could never do the cognitive work of 'What Tabby wants is that she gets onto the roof'.

60 Sacks 1978, 44.

61 Sacks 1978, 29. I hasten to add that Davidson would have no use for even the unsettled sort of metaphorical content about to be proposed.

62 David Hills's phrase, and idea.

63 This of course marks a difference with Davidson.

64 Thus, each in its own way, 'Juliet is the sun', 'Eternity is a spider in a Russian hathhouse', and 'The state is an organism'.

65 Examples: An apparition assures Macbeth that 'none of woman born' shall harm him; the phrase's meaning hangs in the air until Macduff, explaining that he was 'from his mother's womb untimely ripped', plunges in the knife. Martin Luther King Jr. told his followers that 'The arc of the moral universe is long, but it bends toward justice'; recent work by Josh Cohen shows that a satisfyingly specific content can be attached to these words. A growing technical literature on verisimilitude testifies to the belief that 'close to the truth' admits of a best interpretation.

66 'Patience is the key to content' (Mohammed).

67 I don't say this list is exhaustive; consider a fourth grade of metaphorical involvement. Sometimes the point is not to advance a game-induced content but to map out the contours of the inducing game, e.g., to launch a game, or consolidate it, or make explicit some consequence of its rules, or extend the game by adjoining new rules. Thus the italicized portions of the following: 'you said he was a Martian, right? well, *Mars is the angry planet*'; '*the average star has a particular size* – it is so many miles in diameter – *but it is not in any particular place*'; 'that's close to right, but *close only counts in horseshoes*'; '*life is a bowl of cherries*; sweet at first but then the pits'. A fair portion of pure mathematics, it seems to me, consists of just such gameskeeping.

68 'Taken at face value' means 'taken literally'; and plenty of metaphors are literally true, e.g, 'no man

is an island'. A general discussion of 'tests for figuration' can be found in Sadock's 'Figurative Speech and Linguistics' (Ortony 1993).

69 There are limits, of course; I should say, posterity's *defensible* judgment.

70 It prevents a sharp delineation, not of the literal *utterances*, but of the utterances in which speakers are committing themselves to the literal *contents* of the sentences coming out of their mouths. This indeterminacy would remain if, as seems unlikely, a sharp distinction between literal and metaphorical utterances could be drawn.

71 Indeterminacy is also possible about whether I am advancing a content at all, as opposed to (see note 67 on the fourth grade of metaphorical involvement) articulating the rules of some game relative to which contents are figured, i.e., doing some gameskeeping. An example suggested by David Hills is 'there are continuum many spatiotemporal positions', uttered by one undecided as between the substantival and relational theories of spacetime. One might speak here of a fifth grade of metaphorical involvement, which – much as the third grade leaves it open *what* content is being expressed – takes no definite stand on whether the utterance *has* a content.

72 'When it was reported that Hemingway's plane had been sighted, wrecked, in Africa, the New York *Mirror* ran a headline saying, "Hemingway Lost in Africa", the word 'lost' being used to suggest he was dead. When it turned out he was alive, the *Mirror* left the headline to be taken literally' (Davidson 1978, 40). I suspect that something like this happens more often than we suppose, with the difference that there is no conscious equivocation and that it is the metaphorical content that we fall back on.

73 If literal/metaphorical is as murky as all that, how can it serve Carnapian goals to equate external with literal and internal with metaphorical? Two goals need to be distinguished: Carnap's 'official' goal of making quantification over abstract entities nominalistically acceptable in principle; and his more quizzicalistic goal of construing *actual* such quantification in such a way that nominalistic doubts come to appear ingenuous if not downright silly. The one is served by arranging for the quantification to be clearly, convincingly, and invincibly metaphorical; I have said nothing to suggest that a determined metaphor-maker is dragged against her will into the region of indeterminacy. The other is served by construing our actual quantificational practice as metaphorical-iff-necessary, that is, literal-iff-literally-true.

74 Or to commit myself to taking it more literally than I already may. I have a slightly better idea of what it would be to commit myself to the literal content of 'the number of As = the number of Bs'. This is why I lay more weight on a second problem; see immediately below.

75 Which existence-claims am I talking about here? One finds more of an equipoise in some cases than others. These are the cases where the automatic presumption in favour of a literal interpretation is offset by one or more of the following hints of possible metaphoricality. *Insubstantiality*: The objects in question have no more to their natures than is entailed by our conception of them, e.g., there is not much more to the numbers than what follows from the 2nd-order Peano Axioms. *Indeterminacy*: It is indeterminate which of them are identical to which, e.g., which sets the real numbers are. *Silliness*: They give rise to 'silly questions' probing areas the make-believe does not address. *Unaboutness*: They turn up in the truth-conditions of sentences that do not intuitively concern them, e.g., 'this argument is valid' is not intuitively about models. *Paraphrasability*: They are oftentimes paraphrasable away with no felt loss of subject matter; 'there are more Fs than Gs' captures all we meant by 'the number of Fs exceeds the number of Gs'. *Expressiveness*: They boost the language's power to express facts about less controversial entities, as in the average star example. *Irrelevance*: They are called on to 'explain' phenomena that would not on reflection suffer by their absence; if all the one–one functions were killed off today, there would still be as many left shoes in my closet as right. *Disconnectedness*: Their lack of naturalistic connections threatens to prevent reference relations and epistemic access. I take it that mathematical objects exhibit these features to a higher degree than, say, God, or theoretical entities in physics.

76 I owe thanks to David Velleman, Ken Walton, Jamie Tappenden, Marc Kelly, Eunice Lee, Jacob Howard, George Wilson, Susan Wolf, Bas van Fraassen, Laura Bugge Schroeter, and especially David Hills.

References

Alston, W. 1958. 'Ontological commitment', *Philosophical Studies*, Vol. 9, No. 1, pp. 8–17.

Bird, G. 1995. 'Carnap and Quine: Internal and External Questions', *Erkenntnis*, Vol. 42, pp. 41–6.

Carnap, R. 1936/7. 'Testability and Meaning', *Philosophy of Science*, Vol. 3, 419–471, and Vol. 4, 1–40.

Carnap, R. 1937. *The Logical Syntax of Language* (London: Routledge & Kegan Paul).

Carnap, R. 1956. 'Empiricism, Semantics, & Ontology', in his *Meaning & Necessity*, 2nd edition (Chicago: University of Chicago Press).

Carnap, R. 1969. *The Logical Structure of the World & Pseudoproblems in Philosophy* (Berkeley: University of California Press).

Chomsky, N. & I. Scheffler, 1958–9. 'What is said to be', *Proceedings of the Aristotelian Society*, Vol. LIX, pp. 71–82.

Creath, R. ed. 1990. *Dear Carnap, Dear Van* (Los Angeles: UCLA Press).

Davidson, D. 1978. 'What metaphors mean', in Sacks 1979.

Haack, S. 1976. 'Some preliminaries to ontology', *Journal of Philosophical Logic*, Vol. 5, pp. 457–74.

Hills, D. 1998. 'Aptness and Truth in Metaphorical Utterance', *Philosophical Topics* Vol. 25, pp. 117–53.

Hookway, C. 1988. *Quine* (Stanford: Stanford University Press).

Jackson, F. 1980. 'Ontological commitment and paraphrase', *Philosophy*, Vol. 55, pp. 303–15.

Melia, J. 1995. 'On what there's not', *Analysis*, Vol. 55, No. 4, pp. 223–9.

Moran, R. 1989. 'Seeing and Believing: Metaphor, Image, and Force', *Critical Inquiry*, Vol. 16, pp. 87–112.

Ortony, A. 1993. *Metaphor and Thought*, second edition (Cambridge: Cambridge University Press).

Quine, W. V. 1939. 'A logistical approach to the ontological problem', preprint from (the 'destined never to appear') *Journal of Unified Science*; reprinted in Quine 1961.

Quine, W. V. 1948. 'On what there is', *Review of Metaphysics*, Vol. II, No. 5, reprinted in Quine 1961.

Quine, W. V. 1951a. 'Two dogmas of empiricism', *Philosophical Review*, Vol. 60, pp. 20–43, reprinted in Quine 1961.

Quine, W. V. 1951b. 'On Carnap's views on ontology', *Philosophical Studies*, Vol. II, No. 5, pp. 65–72, reprinted in Quine 1976.

Quine, W. V. 1960. *Word & Object* (Cambridge: MIT Press).

Quine, W. V. 1961. *From a Logical Point of View*, 2nd edition (New York, Harper & Row).

Quine, W. V. 1964. 'Ontological reduction and the world of numbers', *Journal of Philosophy*, Vol. 61, reprinted with changes in Quine 1976.

Quine, W. V. 1966a and b. 'Existence and Quantification' and 'Propositional Objects', in *Ontological Relativity and Other Essays* (New York: Columbia University Press).

Quine, W. V. 1976. *The Ways of Paradox & Other Essays*, revised edition (New York: Columbia University Press).

Quine, W. V. 1979. 'A Postscript on Metaphor', in Sacks 1978, reprinted in Quine 1981.

Quine, W. V. 1981. *Theories and Things* (Cambridge: Harvard University Press).

Ryle, G. 1954. *Dilemmas* (London: Cambridge University Press).

Sacks, S. ed., 1978. *On Metaphor* (Chicago: University of Chicago Press).

Salmon, N. 1989. 'The Logic of What Might Have Been', *Philosophical Review*, Vol. 98, pp. 3–34.

Schilpp, P. A. 1963. *The Philosophy of Rudolf Carnap* (La Salle, Illinois: Open Court).

Stevenson, L. 1976. 'On what sorts of thing there are', *Mind*, Vol. 85, pp. 503–21.

Stroud, B. 1984. *The Significance of Philosophical Skepticism* (Oxford: Oxford University Press).

van Fraassen, B. 1980. *The Scientific Image* (Oxford: Clarendon Press).

Walton, K. 1990. *Mimesis & Make-Believe* (Cambridge, Mass.: Harvard University Press).

Walton, K. 1993. 'Metaphor and Prop Oriented Make-Believe', *European Journal of Philosophy*, Vol. 1, No. 1. pp. 39–57.

Yablo, S. 1997. 'How in the World?', *Philosophical Topics*, Vol. 24, No. 1.

6

If We Postulated Fictional Objects, What Would They Be?

Amie L. Thomasson

If we are to postulate fictional characters at all, it seems advisable to postulate them as entities that can satisfy or at least make sense of our most important beliefs and practices concerning them. Often theories of fiction are driven not by an independent sense of what is needed to understand talk and practices regarding fiction, but rather by a desire to show how fictional characters may find their place in a preconceived ontology of possible, nonexistent, or abstract objects – to demonstrate one more useful application of the ontology under discussion, or to provide catchy and familiar examples. Instead of starting from a ready-made ontology and seeing how we can fit fictional characters into it, I suggest that we begin by paying careful attention to our literary practices so that we can see what sorts of things would most closely correspond to them. I thus begin by discussing what sorts of entities our practices in reading and discussing works of fiction seem to commit us to, and I draw out the *artifactual theory* of fiction as a way of characterizing the sort of entity that seems best suited to do the job of fictional characters.

1 What Fictional Characters Seem To Be

Fictional objects as I discuss them here include such characters as Emma Woodhouse, Sherlock Holmes, Hamlet, and Tom Sawyer – characters who appear in works of literature and whose fortunes we follow in reading those works. In our everyday discussions of literature we treat fictional characters as created entities brought into existence at a certain time through the acts of an author. If someone contended that George Washington was a great fan of Sherlock Holmes, we might object that in Washington's time there was no Sherlock Holmes – the Holmes character was not created until 1887. The term "fiction" derives from the Latin *fingere* meaning "to form," and this linguistic root is still evident in our practices in treating fictional characters as entities formed by the work of an author or authors in composing a work of fiction.[2] We do not describe authors of fictional works as discovering their characters or selecting them from an ever-present set of abstract, nonexistent, or possible objects. Instead, we describe authors as inventing their characters, making them up, or

Amie L. Thomasson, "If We Postulated Fictional Objects, What Would They Be?", in *Fiction and Metaphysics*, Cambridge Studies in Philosophy (Cambridge: Cambridge University Press, 1999), ch. 1. Reproduced by permission.

Metaphysics: An Anthology, Second Edition. Edited by Jaegwon Kim, Daniel Z. Korman and Ernest Sosa.
Editorial material and organization © 2012 Blackwell Publishing Ltd. Published 2012 by Blackwell Publishing Ltd.

AMIE L. THOMASSON

creating them, so that before being written about by an author, there is no fictional object. Taking authors to be genuinely creative as they make up fictional characters is central to our ordinary understanding of fiction. One of the things we admire about certain authors is their ability to make up sympathetic, multidimensional characters rather than cardboard cut-outs, and at times we count our good luck that certain characters like Sherlock Holmes were created when, given a busier medical practice, Arthur Conan Doyle might never have created him.

Thus, if we are to postulate fictional characters that satisfy our apparent practices regarding them, it seems that we should consider them to be entities that can come into existence only through the mental and physical acts of an author – as essentially created entities. Once we begin to treat fictional characters as created entities, a further issue arises. Do they simply need to be created at some time, by someone, or is the identity of a fictional character somehow tied to its particular origin in the work of a particular author or authors taking part in a particular literary tradition? Unexamined intuitions may provide no clear answer to this question, but our goal is to draw out a view of fictional characters that corresponds as closely as possible to our practices in studying fictional characters. Such critical practices provide grounds for taking the latter view, that a particular fictional character not only has to be created but is necessarily tied to its particular origin.

Suppose that a student happens on two literary figures remarkably similar to each other; both, for example, are said to be maids, warding off attempts at seduction, and so on. Under what conditions would we say that these are works about one and the same fictional character? It seems that we would say that the two works are about the same character only if we have reason to believe that the works derived from a common origin – if, for example, one work is the sequel to the other, or if both are developments of the same original myth. Literary scholars mark this difference by distinguishing "sources" drawn on by an author in composing a work from coincidentally similar characters or works, mere "analogs." If one can show that the author of the latter work had close acquaintance with the earlier work, it seems we have good support for the claim that

the works are about the same character (as for example in the Pamela Andrews of Richardson's and Fielding's tales). But if someone can prove that the authors of the two works bore no relation to each other or to a common source but were working from distinct traditions and sources, it seems that the student has at best uncovered a coincidence – that different individuals and cultures generated remarkably similar analogous characters.

So it seems that if we wish to postulate fictional objects that correspond to our ordinary practices about identifying them, fictional characters should be considered entities that depend on the particular acts of their author or authors to bring them into existence. Naturally the process of creating a particular character may be diffuse: It may be created by more than one author, over a lengthy period of time, involving many participants in a story-telling tradition, and so on. But the fact that the process of creating a fictional character may be diffuse does not disrupt the general point that, whatever the process of creation for a given character may be, for coming into existence it depends on those particular creative acts. Such a requirement not only is consistent with critical practices in identifying characters but also is crucial to treating characters as identical across different sequels, parodies, and other literary developments.

Once created, clearly a fictional character can go on existing without its author or his or her creative acts, for it is preserved in literary works that may long outlive their author. If we treat fictional characters as creations invented by authors in creating works of literature, and existing because of their appearance in such works, then it seems that for a fictional character to be preserved, some literary work about it must remain in existence. And so we have uncovered a second dependency: Characters depend on the creative acts of their authors in order to come into existence and depend on literary works in order to remain in existence.[3] Here again the question arises: Does a fictional character depend on one particular literary work for its preservation, or does a fictional character need only to appear in some literary work or other to remain in existence? It certainly seems that a character may survive as long as some work in which it appears remains. If we could not allow that the same

What if even no literary work remains, but the fictional character is remembered by some such entity that read the work prior?

FICTIONAL OBJECTS 61

character may appear in more than one literary work, or even slightly different editions of a work, then we would be unable to account for literary critical discourse about the development of a character across different works, and we would even be unable to admit that readers of different editions of *The Great Gatsby* are discussing one and the same Jay Gatsby. In short, we would be left postulating many characters in cases in which there seems to be but one. So it seems we should allow that one character may appear in more than one work, and if it can appear in more than one work, it must remain in existence as long as one literary work about it does. Thus even if "A Scandal in Bohemia" should exist no longer, the character Sherlock Holmes can go on existing provided that one or more of the other works in which he appears remains in existence. So, although a fictional character depends on a literary work for its continued existence, it depends only on the maintenance of some work in which it appears.[4]

The dependence of a character on a literary work forces us to address a second question: If a character depends on a work of literature, what does a work of literature depend on? When can we say that a literary work exists? Because characters depend on literary works, anything on which literary works depend is also, ultimately, something on which characters depend. As ordinarily treated in critical discourse, a literary work is not an abstract sequence of words or concepts waiting to be discovered but instead is the creation of a particular individual or group at a particular time in particular social and historical circumstances. Thus, as with characters, it seems that literary works must be created by an author or authors at a certain time in order to come into existence.

Like a character, it also seems that a work of literature depends rigidly on the acts of its particular author to exist, so that, even if two authors coincidentally composed the same words in the same order, they would not thereby have composed the same work of literature. One way to see the essentiality of a work's origin to its identity is by observing that literary works take on different properties based on the time and circumstances of their creation and creator. By virtue of originating in a different place in literary, social, and political history, at the hands of a different

author, or in a different place in an author's *oeuvre*, one and the same sequence of words can provide the basis for two very different works of literature with different aesthetic and artistic properties.[5] The same sequence of words appearing in *Animal Farm* could have been written in 1905, but that literary work could not have had the property of being a satire of the Stalinist state, a central property of Orwell's tale. If the same words of *Portrait of the Artist as a Young Man* were written by James Joyce not in 1916, but instead after *Ulysses* came out in 1922, that work would lack the property of exhibiting a highly original use of language, which *Portrait of the Artist* has. Two mysteries based on the same sequence of words written in 1816 and today, both ending with "the butler did it," might have the property of having a surprise ending in the former but not the latter case. A screenplay with the same sequence of words as Oliver Stone's *Nixon*, if written in 1913, could have the properties neither of being about (the real) Richard Nixon, nor of being a sympathetic portrayal of the main character, nor of being revisionary and speculative. Similar cases could be brought to bear to show that a wide variety of aesthetic and artistic properties central to discussions of works of literature – being a work of high modernism, a parody, horrifying, reactionary, exquisitely detailed, an updated retelling of an old story – depend on the context and circumstances of creation, so that literary works may be based on the same series of words but have different aesthetic and artistic properties. In at least some cases, these properties seem essential to the literary work, e.g., being a satire seems essential to *Animal Farm* considered as a work of literature. For that reason, it seems that a literary work is best conceived not as an abstract sequence of words but as an artifact that had to be created in those original circumstances in which it was created.

Like fictional characters, literary works, once created, can clearly survive the death of their author; indeed the great majority of literary works we have today persist despite the deaths of their authors. But does a literary work, once created, always exist, or can a work once again cease to exist even after it is created? If we take seriously the view that literary works are artifacts created at a certain time, it seems natural to allow that, like other artifacts from umbrellas to unions to universities, they can also be destroyed. It would surely seem bizarre to claim that all of the lost stories of past cultures still exist as much as ever. On the contrary, one of the things that is often lamented about the destruction of cultures, be they ancient Greek or Native American, is the loss of the stories and fictional worlds they created. We treat literary tales as entities that can cease to exist, that at times take special efforts and government projects to preserve (e.g., by recording the oral folktales of Appalachia), or that may be destroyed by a temperamental author burning unpublished manuscripts. Treating works of literature as entities that may be destroyed – at least if all copies and memories of them are destroyed – seems a natural consequence of considering them to be cultural artifacts rather than Platonistic abstracta.

Yet certainly there are many who do not share the intuition that literary works may cease to exist after being created. The idea that literary works, if they exist, must exist eternally (once created) seems to me to be a hangover of a Platonism that assimilates all abstract entities to the realm of the changeless and timeless, and in particular a consequence of viewing literary works roughly as series of words or concepts that can survive the destruction of any collection of copies of them. To the extent that it is a hangover of Platonism, this position should lose its appeal if one accepts the earlier arguments that literary works are, instead, artifacts individuated in part by the particular circumstances of their creation.

Apart from a lingering Platonism, one feature of our language might incline some to the view that literary works cannot cease to exist: We often speak not of *destroyed* or *past* works, but rather of *lost* works, as if all that were missing was our ability to find these (still existing) works of ancient, careless, or temperamental authors. This language practice, however, is easily explained without adopting the odd view that works of literature, once created, exist eternally despite even the destruction of the whole real world. The explanation is simply that, because a literary work does not require any *particular* copy to remain in existence, it is hard to be certain that there is not some copy of the work, somewhere, that has survived, and with it the work of literature. Who knows what may be lurking in the basement corridors of the Bodleian Library? A formerly lost sonnet of Shakespeare's was discovered there

not so long ago. Unlike in the case of a unique painting, of which we can find the ashes, we can always hold out hope in the case of a literary work that a copy of it remains in some library, attic room, or perfect memory, so that the literary work might be "found" again. (This is reinforced by noting that, although we ordinarily speak of old or ancient works as lost, in the case of a modern manuscript burned by its author, we are more prone to count the work "destroyed" than merely lost.) But none of this speaks against the idea that, provided all copies and memories of a literary work are destroyed, never to be recovered, the literary work is gone as well – or, to put it another way, the literary work is then lost not in the sense in which sets of keys are lost, but in the sense in which an exploded battleship is lost, or a doctor can lose a patient.

If we consider characters to be creations owing their continued existence to the literary works in which they appear, then if all of the works regarding a character can fall out of existence, so can that character. Thus it is a consequence of this view that if all copies of all of the works regarding some ancient Greek heroine have been destroyed, never to be recovered or recalled, then she has fallen out of existence with those works and become a "past" fictional object in much the same way as a person can become a dead, past, concrete object. If we take seriously the idea of fictional characters as artifacts, it seems equally natural to treat them as able to be destroyed just as other artifacts are.[6] Thus fictional characters as well as the literary works in which they appear may fall out of existence with the literature of a culture.

One objection that might be raised to the idea that both fictional characters and literary works may fall out of existence is that it seems we can still think of them, refer to them, and so on, even after their founding texts have all been destroyed. But this is no different than in the case of other perishable objects and artifacts: We may still think of and refer to people after they have died, buildings long since destroyed, civilizations long gone by. If fictional characters and literary works cease to exist, I am not suggesting that they then enter a peculiar realm of Meinongian nonexistence or that it is as if such objects never were, but rather that they become past objects just like the other contingent objects around us. The problem of how we can think of and refer to past objects is no small one but is not unique to fiction.

Ordinarily, a literary work is maintained in existence by the presence of some copy or other of the relevant text (whether on paper, film, tape, or CD-ROM). It is in this way that the literature of past ages has been handed down to our present day. But even if printed words on a page survive, that is not enough to guarantee the ongoing existence of the work. A literary work is not a mere bunch of marks on a page but instead is an intersubjectively accessible recounting of a story by means of a public language. Just as a language dies out without the continued acceptance and understanding of a group of individuals, so do linguistically based literary works. A literary work as such can exist only as long as there are some individuals who have the language capacities and background assumptions they need to read and understand it. If all conscious agents are destroyed, then nothing is left of fictional works or the characters represented in them but some ink on paper. Similarly, if all speakers of a language die out, with the language never to be rediscovered, then the literary works peculiar to that tongue die out as well.[7] Thus preserving some printed or recorded document is not enough to preserve a literary work – some competent readers are also required. If competent readers and a printed text survive, however, that is enough to preserve a literary work.

In other cases, however, we speak of a work of literature as being preserved even if there are no printed copies of the text. In oral traditions, for example, the work is preserved in memory even if it is not being spoken or heard, and (as in *Fahrenheit 451*) it seems that a work could be preserved in memories during times of censorship, even if all printed copies of it were destroyed. So even if a literary work is typically maintained by a printed, comprehensible text, it seems that such is not necessary. A latent memory of the work (disposed to produce an oral or written copy of the work, given the appropriate circumstances) may be enough to maintain it in existence.[8] Thus we can say that, for its maintenance, a character depends generically on the existence of some literary work about it; a literary work, in turn, may be maintained either in a copy of the text and a readership capable of understanding it or in memory.[9]

exacting, memorized

In sum, it looks as if, if we are to postulate entities that would correspond to our ordinary beliefs and practices about fictional characters, these should be entities that depend on the creative acts of authors to bring them into existence and on some concrete individuals such as copies of texts and a capable audience in order to remain in existence. Thus fictional objects, in this conception, are not the inhabitants of a disjoint ontological realm but instead are closely connected to ordinary entities by their dependencies on both concrete, spatiotemporal objects and intentionality. Moreover, they are not a strange and unique type of entity: Similar dependencies are shared with objects from tables and chairs to social institutions and works of art.

Artifacts of all kinds, from tables and chairs to tools and machines, share with fictional characters the feature of requiring creation by intelligent beings. But it might be thought that the way in which fictional characters are created does make them strange, for although one cannot simply create a table, toaster, or automobile by describing such an object, fictional characters are created merely with words that posit them as being a certain way. For example, because characters are created by being written about by their authors, Jane Austen creates the fictional character Emma Woodhouse and brings her into existence (assuming she did not exist before) in writing the sentence:

> Emma Woodhouse, handsome, clever, and rich, with a comfortable home and happy disposition, seemed to unite some of the best blessings of existence, and had lived nearly twenty-one years in the world with very little to distress or vex her.

But the fact that a character can be created merely through such linguistic acts should cause no peculiar difficulties for a theory of fiction. It has long been noticed that a common feature of so-called conventional or effective illocutionary acts such as appointing, resigning, adjourning, and marrying is that they bring into existence the state of affairs under discussion. Thus, for example, the celebrant of a marriage pronounces a couple husband and wife, a pronouncement that itself creates the couple's new status as husband and wife.[10] More recently, it has been noticed that it is a common feature of many cultural and institutional entities that they can be brought into existence merely by being represented as existing. Searle discusses this general feature using money as the example. A dollar bill may read:

> "This note is legal tender for all debts public and private." But that representation is now, at least in part, a declaration: It creates the institutional status by representing it as existing. It does not represent some prelinguistic natural phenomenon.[11]

A contract, similarly, may be created simply by the utterance of words such as "I hereby promise to." Searle even cites as a general feature of institutional reality that institutional facts can be brought into existence by being represented as existing and can exist only if they are represented as existing (62–3).[12]

What I am suggesting is a parallel with fictional characters: Just as marriages, contracts, and promises may be created through the performance of linguistic acts that represent them as existing, a fictional character is created by being represented in a work of literature. If there is no preexistent object to whom Austen was referring in writing the words above, writing those words brings into existence the object therein described: The fictional character Emma Woodhouse.[13] Thus even the feature that fictional characters may be created not through hard labor on physical materials but through the utterance of words, rather than placing them in a peculiarly awkward situation, points again to their being at home among other cultural entities. Human consciousness is creative. It is that creativity that enables us to increase our chances of survival by formulating plans and examining scenarios not physically before us. It is also that creativity that enables the human world of governments, social institutions, works of art, and even fictional characters to be constructed on top of the independent physical world by means of our intentional representations.[14]

Nor are fictional characters alone in requiring certain forms of human understanding and practice for their ongoing preservation as well as creation. It has often been argued that works of art in general are not mere physical objects but instead depend both on some instantiation in physical form (in a performance, on canvas, in a printed

copy), and – for their intentional properties such as expressiveness and meaning – on the intentional acts of humans.[15] Similarly, cultural and institutional facts regarding money, contracts, and property are plausibly characterized as depending not only on certain physical objects like pieces of paper with a certain history, but also on maintaining forms of human agreement.[16] For something to be money, it is not enough that it be a piece of paper with a certain history, it must also, both initially and continually, be accepted as what people collectively agree to count as money in a particular society.

In short, on this view fictional characters are a particular kind of cultural artifact. Like other cultural objects, fictional characters depend on human intentionality for their existence. Like other artifacts, they must be created in order to exist, and they can cease to exist, becoming past objects. It is primarily in its treatment of fictional characters as ordinary cultural artifacts rather than as the odd inhabitants of a different realm that the artifactual theory differs most markedly from other ways of characterizing fictional objects. It is also their place as cultural artifacts that makes fictional objects of broader philosophical interest, for the ontology of fiction can thus serve as a model for the ontology of other social and cultural objects in the everyday world.

It may help to locate the artifactual theory in conceptual space by briefly contrasting it with other views of what fictional objects are. Some of its advantage vis-à-vis these other theories only show up when we attempt to overcome the problems of developing identity conditions for fictional objects and handling reference to and discourse about them.[17] Nonetheless, a brief comparison should help elucidate the differences between this theory and other treatments of fiction.

2   Meinongian Theories of Fiction

The most popular and well-developed theories of fiction that have been available are those broadly construable as Meinongian theories, including those that take fictional characters to be either nonexistent or abstract entities, such as those developed by Parsons, Zalta, and Rapaport. Neither Meinong's theory nor contemporary Meinongian theories are devised specifically as theories of fiction; they concern the wider realm of nonexistent objects generally.[18] Nonetheless, much of the motivation for and many of the applications of Meinongian theories of nonexistent objects concern fictional objects. Many different theories have been devised that may roughly be labeled Meinongian; despite their differences, they typically share certain fundamental characteristics captured by the following principles:

$\exists x \exists P\ P x$

1 There is at least one object correlated with every combination of properties.[19]
2 Some of these objects (among them fictional objects) have no existence whatsoever.[20]
3 Although they do not exist, they (in some sense) have the properties with which they are correlated.[21]

The first principle is sometimes known as a "comprehension principle," ensuring a multitude of nonexistent objects. Meinongian theories differ with respect to which properties count in principle one. Parsons's theory, for example, limits properties to simple, nuclear properties such as "is blue" or "is tall"; Zalta's theory permits so-called extranuclear properties (such as "is possible" and "is thought about") and complex properties. Meinongians also vary with respect to how nonexistent objects "have" their properties according to the third principle; for views like Parsons's, there are two kinds of property (nuclear and extranuclear), but only one kind of predication, enabling "have" to be read straightforwardly, as (in this theory) nonexistents have their properties in the same way as real objects do. For views like Zalta's or Rapaport's, there are two modes of predication; nonexistent objects have properties in a different way than their real counterparts. Although ordinary objects exemplify their properties, nonexistent objects "encode" the properties with which they are correlated (Zalta) or have them as "constituents" (Rapaport).[22]

Meinongian theories of fiction resemble the artifactual theory in that both allow that there are fictional objects, that we can refer to them, that they play an important role in experience, and so on. Moreover, Meinongians are largely to be credited with showing that consistent theories of fiction can be developed and with undermining the paradigm according to which there are only

real entities (a paradigm Parsons refers to as the "Russellian rut").

But there are also important differences between the artifactual theory and any such Meinongian theory of fiction. First, the theories differ with respect to where they apply the word "exists"; I am willing to claim that fictional characters exist; the Meinongian (by principle two) grants them no existence whatsoever. But because the Meinongian famously maintains that there are such objects, that we can think of them, refer to them, and so on, this difference is largely linguistic.[23] *exists in linguistic frame*

A deeper difference between the theories regards how many objects they say there are. Unlike the Meinongian, I do not employ any kind of comprehension principle and so do not claim that there is an infinite, ever-present range of nonexistent (or abstract) objects. In the artifactual theory, the only fictional objects there are are those that are created. This points to a further difference between this view and that of the Meinongian: In the artifactual view, fictional objects are created at a certain point in time, not merely discovered or picked out. According to the Meinongian, fictional characters are merely some of the infinite range of ever-present nonexistent or abstract objects – namely, those that are described in some story.

Accordingly, if an author writes of a character, she or he is merely picking out or referring to an object that was already available for reference. Authors can then be said to discover their characters or pick them out from the broad range of objects available, but not to bring these objects into existence. They *can* be said to make these objects *fictional*, for an abstract or nonexistent object does not become fictional until it is written about. Nonetheless, the object remains the same; it simply bears a new relation to contingent acts of authoring.[24] As Parsons writes:

I have said that, in a popular sense, an author *creates* characters, but this too is hard to analyze. It does not mean, for example, that the author brings those characters into existence, for they do not exist. Nor does he or she make them objects, for they were objects before they appeared in stories. We might say, I suppose, that the author makes them *fictional* objects, and that they were not fictional objects before the creative act.[25]

Meinongian: objects are transformed from abstract into fictional when written

In short, the only kind of creation permitted in Meinongian accounts is the author's taking an available object and making it fictional (by writing about it in a story). This, it seems to me, is not robust enough to satisfy the ordinary view that authors are genuinely creative in the sense of creating new objects, not merely picking out old objects and thereby making them fictional. By contrast, in the artifactual theory, authors genuinely bring new characters into being that were not around before – they invent their characters rather than discovering them. In short, the Meinongian might be said to offer a top-down approach to fiction that begins by positing an infinite range of nonexistent or abstract objects and then carves out a portion of those (those described in works of literature) to serve as the fictional characters. In contrast, the artifactual theory attempts to take a bottom-up approach to fictional characters by treating them as constructed entities created by authors and depending on ordinary objects such as stories and a competent audience.

... [T]here are also many differences between Meinongian theories and the artifactual theory regarding identity conditions for fictional objects and how reference to and discourse about fictional objects are handled. Some shortcomings of the Meinongian view include an inability to genuinely treat fictional characters as created entities and consequent difficulties in offering adequate identity conditions for fictional characters (especially identity conditions across texts).[26] Other problems arise for Meinongian treatments of fictional discourse, notably in handling fictional discourse about real individuals. Thus, despite the merits of Meinongian theories in offering a consistent and well-developed view of fictional characters, I argue that the artifactual theory provides a better conception of them overall. The main difference underlying the two theories and responsible for the advantages I claim for the artifactual theory lies in a fundamental difference in approach, as the Meinongian sees fictional characters as part of a separate realm of abstract or nonexistent objects, disjoint from and dissimilar to that of ordinary objects, and in the artifactual theory their similarities and connections to entities in the ordinary world are taken as fundamental.

3 Possibilist Theories of Fiction

Whether in an attempt to provide a complete account of fiction or as motivation for an ontology of possibilia, an attempt is often made to locate fictional characters among unactualized possibilia. Fictional characters have long provided some of the most appealing examples of merely possible entities and have often been used in arguments in favor of postulating unactualized possibilia. Kripke, for example, uses Sherlock Holmes as an example (which he later retracts) of an entity that "does not exist, but in other states of affairs he would have existed," and Plantinga treats the view that "Hamlet and Lear do not in fact exist; but clearly they could have" as one of the most persistent arguments in favor of unactualized possibilia.[27] And at first glance it seems plausible that, even if there is no actual person who has all of the properties ascribed to Hamlet in the play, surely there is some possible person exhibiting all of those properties, making Hamlet a member of another possible world.

This is a fundamentally different approach to fiction from that of the artifactual theory, because in the artifactual theory fictional objects are not possible people but actual characters. Although it is a tempting way to accommodate fictional characters, and fictional characters may provide fun (purported) examples of mere possibilia, major problems arise if we try to identify a fictional character with that merely possible individual exhibiting all and only those properties ascribed to the character in the story. First, as has been frequently acknowledged, there seem to be simply too many possible individuals that fit the bill, and no means to choose among them.[28] For the descriptions provided in literary works fail to completely specify what the characters described in them are like, leaving indeterminate a wide range of properties such as, typically, a character's blood type, weight, diet, and mundane daily activities. Thus we run into trouble immediately if we try to identify characters with possible people, for the features of a character left open by the story could be filled out in an infinite variety of ways by different possible people. Selecting any one as identical with a particular character seems hopelessly arbitrary. On the other hand, if the character is described as bearing incompatible

such as a round square copula

properties, making it an impossible object, we have not too many possibilia to do the job, but too few.

A further problem arises in that possibilist views, like Meinongian views, give us no way of accounting for the created status of fictional characters. Even if we could find a single candidate possible detective to identify with Sherlock Holmes, this would be a possible man with the property of being born in the nineteenth century, not of being created by Arthur Conan Doyle. Finally, possibilist theories, Meinongian theories, or any theories that base the identity of a character on the properties ascribed to it eliminate the possibility that there can be more than one story about a single character. For if the character is ascribed even a single different property, it is a different character. Thus these views provide no means to admit that the same character may appear in different stories, sequels, or even slightly altered new editions or translations of an old story. Perhaps it is because of such problems that this view has been far less popular among those working seriously with fiction. Indeed Kripke and Plantinga both, after considering it, reject this view. In light of these problems it seems that possible objects are not candidates well suited to do the job of fictional characters. Because this view of fiction seems hardly able to get off the ground, I do not spend much time discussing it.[29]

4   Fictional Characters as Objects of Reference

Other views of fiction consider fictional objects mere objects of reference that we must postulate to make sense of a certain kind of literary discourse. Such views are developed by Crittenden, who treats fictional objects as "grammatical objects," and by van Inwagen, who considers fictional objects to be the "theoretical entities" referred to in works of literary criticism. These views parallel the artifactual view in many important respects, and the differences between such theories and the artifactual theory lie less in direct conflicts than simply in the artifactual theory's filling in areas left blank by the other theories. Nonetheless, there are also important differences of approach between these theories and the artifactual theory.

Working within a broadly Wittgensteinian view of language, Crittenden postulates fictional objects as (mere) objects of reference, or grammatical objects. Although he takes fictional names as referring to certain objects, he repeatedly emphasizes that the status of these objects is merely that of objects of reference, available to be referred to by readers, critics, and other practitioners of the relevant language games of fiction, although they do not exist and are "not to be understood as having any sort of reality whatever."[30]

Although Crittenden denies that fictional characters exist, many of the features he assigns to fictional characters (based on the commitments of language practices) conform to those assigned by the artifactual theory. He too takes fictional objects to be entities created by authors through writing stories, and entities that are dependent on certain kinds of intentionality and practices involving language. But he seems to take dependence as marking a sort of honorary nonexistence and is keenest to point out that fictional objects have no *independent* existence when he is trying to emphasize that they have no "sort of reality whatever." [...] *like also have no 'independent' existence*

I am sympathetic to taking our language practices regarding fiction seriously. I also agree that our literary practices in general may serve as a valuable guide in developing a theory of fiction because ideally, we want to postulate fictional characters as entities that can make sense of as large a portion of common practice as possible. But Crittenden's Wittgensteinian antimetaphysical stance leads him to rely on practice too heavily and eschew talk of the ontology of fiction by replacing ontological issues with a mere discussion of practice. As he writes:

> Fictional discourse has no grounding in any further metaphysical reality; this linguistic practice itself and not some independent ontological realm is the fundamental fact in any account of the status of fictional characters (69).

Thus, instead of using practice as a guide to understanding what sorts of things fictional characters would be, Crittenden allows it to constitute what is true and false of fictional characters. Even in particular cases in which substantive issues arise regarding what is true or false of a fictional character, he simply reduces the issue to one of inquiring after our current practices. Thus he reduces the truth-values of claims about fictional characters to the accepted practices regarding their truth or falsehood, for example writing:

> Such [fictional] objects ... have properties just in that property-attributing expressions are appropriately applied to them in types of discourse such as fiction and myth. Whether these expressions are truly or falsely applied depends on purely linguistic or conceptual considerations and not on external, independent reality (97).

But in talking about fiction we should recognize that here, as elsewhere, we could – even as a group – be wrong. We could be wrong, for example, regarding whether characters treated as identical really are, and we could be wrong regarding the attributes we commonly ascribe to a character. Our practices themselves appeal to features beyond practice to decide issues of substance regarding the identity and properties of a fictional character – features like the character's origin. Crittenden himself occasionally acknowledges the important role played in character identity by external criteria such as the history behind the writing of the stories (43–44). Using these criteria to determine the identity conditions for fictional characters requires a willingness to reach beyond practice to discuss what the objects that would justify our practices and revisions of our practices would be like. It also requires that we treat fictional characters as more than mere objects of reference – as objects (albeit dependent ones) able to make true or false, reasonable or unreasonable, our claims and practices regarding them. The move to a detailed ontological discussion of fictional objects, not just practices regarding them, is still required.

Among current analytic treatments of fiction, that closest to the artifactual theory is perhaps that which van Inwagen develops, according to which fictional characters are "theoretical entities of literacy criticism."[31] In treating fictional characters as the entities described in literary criticism, van Inwagen rightly emphasizes the importance of postulating fictional characters to make sense of critical discourse about them. The two positions coincide at many points, first and foremost in the claim that fictional characters exist.[32]

The most important difference between the artifactual theory and van Inwagen's, like that between it and Crittenden's, lies in the fact that van Inwagen does little to describe the ontological status of the creatures of fiction he postulates. He describes fictional characters as "theoretical entities"; theoretical entities in general he describes only as those referred to by the special vocabularies of theoretical disciplines, and which make some of those sentences true. So, in the case of creatures of fiction:

> [S]ometimes, if what is said in a piece of literary criticism is to be true, then there must be entities of a certain type, entities that are never the subjects of non-literary discourse, and which make up the extensions of the theoretical general terms of literary criticism. It is these that I call "theoretical entities of literary criticism."[33]

This, however, does not tell us what fictional characters are like, but only that they are the things that make at least some (which?) of the sentences of literary criticism true. He does not discuss, for example, whether or not they are created, whether they can appear in more than one text, or how they relate to readers, and so we have no way of offering identity conditions for them or of evaluating the truth-value of critical sentences apparently about them. We also have little way of knowing how these creatures of fiction compare with other sorts of entities. Van Inwagen places them in the same category as other entities discussed in literary criticism such as plots, novels, rhyme schemes, and imagery, but it is not clear how they compare with other types of entities such as works of music, copies of texts, and universals. Thus we are left with no means of fitting fictional characters into a general ontological picture or of determining the relative parsimony of theories that do and do not postulate them.

I suspect that the omission of such aspects of a genuine metaphysical theory of fiction is no accident, for both theories attempt to hold a largely deflationary account of fictional characters as entities we must postulate merely to make sense

Artifactual theory combines an ontological assertion of fictional objects and an analysis of our practices regarding them

FICTIONAL OBJECTS   69

of certain odd types of (theoretical or fictional) discourse; Crittenden at least would see asking such metaphysical questions as going astray in taking these mere objects of reference too ontologically seriously. Both such accounts thus still treat fiction (and for van Inwagen, theoretic discourse generally) as presenting a special case in which we must posit theoretic objects or mere objects of reference to make sense of our discourse. In this respect both theories differ importantly from the artifactual theory because, in this view, fictional characters are not to be considered theoretic entities or mere objects of reference any more than tables and chairs, committee meetings, and works of art are. Instead they are a certain type of object referred to, and indeed not a peculiar type of object but a type of object relevantly similar to stories, governments, and other everyday objects.

5   Fictional Characters as Imaginary Objects

One view that has a certain similarity in spirit to the artifactual theory, although the two differ in substance, is the view that treats fictional characters as imaginary objects – entities created and sustained by imaginative acts. It is a view developed, for example, by Sartre in his work on the imagination, which he takes to apply not only to imagined objects but also to objects represented in works of art, and even to works of art themselves. An imagined object, in this view, is an entity created in an imaginative act of consciousness and that exists only as long as it is being imagined. As Sartre writes:

> We have seen that the act of imagination is a magical one. It is an incantation destined to produce the object of one's thought, the thing one desires. … The faint breath of life we breathe into [imaginary objects] comes from us, from our spontaneity. If we turn away from them they are destroyed.[34]

Such a view is similar in spirit to the artifactual theory in that both insist that fictional characters are created objects, indeed objects created by the intentional acts of their authors. They are likewise similar in that both take fictional characters to remain dependent even after they are created.

But Sartre's view, and similar views of imaginary objects, treat them as existing only as long as someone is thinking of them. As a result two large problems confront this view *qua* theory of fiction. First, the idea that these objects exist only as long as they are being thought of runs counter to our usual practices in treating Holmes, Hamlet, and the rest as enduring through those periods of time in which no one is imagining them. It seems to have the odd consequence that such characters "flit in and out of existence."[35] Second, if, as Sartre has it, a fictional character is not only created by the author's imaginative acts but (re)created afresh by the imaginative acts of each reader, it is difficult to see how we can legitimately say that two or more readers are each reading about or experiencing one and the same fictional character.

It was Ingarden who first suggested how to avoid these problems and still conceive of fictional characters as, in some sense, dependent on intentionality. In Ingarden's view, a fictional character is a "purely intentional object," an object created by consciousness and having "the source of its existence and total essence" in intentionality.[36] More precisely, a fictional character is created by an author who constructs sentences about it, but it is maintained in its existence thereafter not by the imagination of individuals, but by the words and sentences themselves. Words and sentences have what Ingarden calls "borrowed intentionality," a representational ability derived from intentional acts that confer meaning on phonetic (and typographic) formations. Thus, although fictional characters remain mediately dependent on intentionality, the immediate dependence of fictional characters on words and sentences gives them a relative independence from any particular act of consciousness:

> Both isolated words and entire sentences possess a borrowed intentionality, one that is conferred on them by acts of consciousness. It allows the purely intentional objects to free themselves, so to speak, from immediate contact with the acts of consciousness in the process of execution and thus to acquire a relative independence from the latter (125–6).

Because these pieces of language are public and enduring, different people may all think of one and the same fictional character, and the character may survive even if no one is thinking of it provided its representation in such pieces of language remains. In sum, Ingarden showed the way to acknowledge the consciousness-dependence of fictional characters without losing their status as lasting, publicly accessible entities; his work provides the true historical predecessor of the theory here defended.

The artifactual theory similarly avoids the problems of Sartre's view by nothing that, although the intentional acts of an author are required to bring a fictional character into existence, it is not the case that it exists only for as long as someone imagines it. On the contrary, fictional characters are ordinarily maintained in existence by the existence of some copy or copies of the literary work concerning them. Although that literary work requires the ongoing existence of a community capable of reading and understanding the text, it does not require that someone constantly be reading it or thinking of it in order to remain in existence, just as the ongoing existence of money requires a community willing to accept it as money although it does not constantly require that someone be explicitly thinking "this is money." Thus literary characters on this model do not flit in and out of existence depending on whether people are thinking of them; they exist as long as literary works regarding them remain. Moreover, fictional characters on this view are not created afresh with each person's thinking of them; on the contrary, by reading the same work many different readers may all access one and the same fictional object.[37]

Thomasson, starting from Ingarden's view, externalizes fictional objects from formerly being thought of as merely imaginary

Notes

1   As I use the term, I do not mean to limit fictional characters to the people said to take part in the story; fictional animals, inanimate objects, events, and processes share the same status and the same analysis. Focusing on the case of literary fictions enables the discussion to be more precise and detailed. But I do not mean to rule out the possibility that there may be something like a fictional character appearing in a painting, in imagination, or even in a hallucination, and the theory developed here should suggest how to handle those cases as well. I simply do not presuppose that the issues in these cases are exactly the same, or that the theory

developed automatically applies to these so-called fictional or imaginary entities as well.

2   It is also telling that Roget's *Thesaurus* lists "product" as its first meaning under the heading "fiction," again pointing to the idea that fictional characters are things produced.

3   Here again I am speaking specifically of the characters *qua* literary fictions and do not mean to rule out that characters can also appear in movies, paintings, or acts of imagination. The conditions under which the same character can appear represented via other media would need to be drawn out separately but should proceed along the same lines as those for transtextual character identity, which are drawn out in Chapter 5. [Chapter references in the notes are to Thomasson's *Fiction and Metaphysics*, from which this selection is taken].

4   More precise conditions regarding whether we can say that one and the same character appears in two or more stories are developed in Chapter 5.

5   Levinson (*Music, Art, and Metaphysics*, 68–73) offers parallel arguments that a musical work is not identical with a pure sound structure.

6   Any discomfort with the idea that fictional characters can cease to exist probably stems from discomfort with admitting that they ever existed at all. In Chapter 7 I discuss how to interpret claims that fictional characters do not exist.

7   The possibility always remains, however, that these stories, and the characters represented in them, may be brought back on the basis of these texts if the language is once again discovered and understood. That one and the same character or story may exist, cease to exist, and exist once more is not so strange. Given that fictional characters and stories are not spatiotemporally located entities, there seems no reason to require spatiotemporal continuity as an identity condition.

8   Naturally that memory must be by a comprehending individual. If someone merely memorizes the right sounds in the right order without understanding their meaning, a comprehending audience is required in addition to the memory of sounds.

9   Precise identity conditions for stories are laid out in Chapter 5.

10 Bach and Harnish (*Linguistic Communication*, 113–15) discuss such "effective" linguistic acts and the institutional states of affairs they produce.

11 Searle, *Construction of Social Reality*, 74.

12 My own view is that it overstates the case to claim that all institutional facts can exist only if they are represented as existing. Institutional facts, I would say, depend on intentionality but not always on our representing those facts as being the way that they

are. A recession, for example, depends on economic systems that depend on human intentionality, but we can be in a recession even if no one represents us as being in a recession. In any case, however, Searle is certainly right that many institutional facts may be brought into existence by being represented as existing and require representations for their existence. It is that common feature that it is important to draw out here.

13 In Chapter 6 I develop and defend the *intentional object theory of intentionality*, according to which every intentional act has a content and an object. It is this creative capacity of intentionality, to make an object if there is none referred to, that guarantees the availability of an object for all kinds of intentional acts.

14 Further discussion of the human world as one dependent on intentionality may be found in my work (Thomasson, "Ontology").

15 See, e.g., Margolis "Ontological Peculiarity," 257–259. Other arguments that at least some works of art are not physical entities may be found in Wollheim, *Art and Its Objects*, sections 4–10; Ingarden, *Literary Work of Art*, sections 2–5; and Wolterstorff, *Worlds of Art*, 42.

16 For discussion of such institutional facts and argument that they depend on human agreement, see Searle, *The Construction of Social Reality*.

17 See Chapter 5, 4, and 7 (respectively) for discussion of how the artifactual theory handles these issues and why its solution presents advantages over Meinongian theories.

18 My criticisms of such theories do not concern their suitability for handling other abstract objects or so-called nonexistents, and in fact theories such as Parsons's and Zalta's have a variety of interesting and fruitful applications. I only claim that these abstract or nonexistent entities are not suited to do the job of handling fictional characters.

19 For Parsons there is exactly one object correlated with each combination of nuclear properties; some of these are real and some nonexistent. For Zalta there is exactly one *abstract* object that *encodes* each combination of properties. In addition, for some combinations of properties there is also an ordinary object *exemplifying* exactly those properties. The original such principle may be found in Meinong's *Über Möglichkeit und Wahrscheinlichkeit*, 282; for Parsons see *Nonexistent Objects*, 19; for Zalta see *Abstract Objects*, 12.

20 Zalta's formalized theory of abstract objects admits of two possible interpretations. According to the first, Meinongian, interpretation the quantifier ranging over abstract objects asserts only that "there is" such

an object, leaving abstract objects as Meinongian nonexistents. According to the second, Platonist, interpretation, the quantifier may be read as "there exists" even if ranging over abstract entities. Thus it is only under the first interpretation that Zalta's theory shares this common characteristic of Meinongian theories. See Zalta, *Abstract Objects*, 50–2; *Intensional Logic*, 102–4.

21 This is the so-called principle of independence formulated by Meinong's student Ernst Mally. For discussion see Lambert's *Principle of Independence*.

22 For a more detailed discussion of the differences between two-types-of-property views and two-types-of-predication views and how each handles the problems of fictional predication, see Chapter 7.

23 In the Platonist interpretation, Zalta's theory does not share this characteristic, as it asserts the existence of abstract objects. The availability of two different interpretations of Zalta's theory, one of which claims existence for abstract objects and the other of which does not, is a further sign that – provided one admits that there are such objects – the issue of whether or not one is willing to say that they *exist* is primarily one of labeling.

24 This follows from Zalta's (*Abstract Objects*, 91–2) definitions of stories and fictional characters.

25 Parsons, *Nonexistent Objects*, 188.

26 See Chapters 3, 5, and 7.

27 Kripke, "Semantical Considerations," 65 (see also his retraction, 172). Plantinga considers and argues against this case for the existence of unactualized possibilia (*Nature of Necessity*, 153 ff).

28 Versions of this problem are discussed by Kripke (*Naming and Necessity*, 157–8) and by Plantinga (*Nature of Necessity*, 154–5).

29 It does, however, provide a useful contrast case in discussing the place of fictional characters in modal metaphysics, so I return to it briefly in Chapter 3.

30 Crittenden, *Unreality*, 69.

31 van Inwagen, "Creatures of Fiction."

32 The two views also handle predications of fictional objects similarly, although the accounts of the reference of fictional names differ. See Chapters 7 and 4, respectively.

33 van Inwagen, "Creatures of Fiction," 303.

34 Sartre, *Psychology of Imagination*, 177–8.

35 This phrase is borrowed from Wolterstorff, who advances similar criticisms against R. G. Collingwood's treatment of works of art as imaginary entities (Wolterstorff, *Works and Worlds*, 43).

36 Ingarden, *Literary Work of Art*, 117.

37 In Chapter 6 I have more to say about how we can legitimately claim that different readers have experiences of the same fictional character.

References

Bach, Kent, and Robert M. Harnish. *Linguistic Communication and Speech Acts.* Cambridge, Mass.: MIT Press, 1979.

Collingwood, R. G. *The Principles of Art.* New York: Oxford University Press, 1958.

Crittenden, Charles. *Unreality: The Metaphysics of Fictional Objects.* Ithaca, New York: Cornell University Press, 1991.

Ingarden, Roman. *The Literary Work of Art,* trans. George G. Grabowicz. Evanston, Ill.: Northwestern University Press, 1973.

Kripke, Saul. *Naming and Necessity.* Cambridge, Mass.: Harvard University Press, 1972.

Kripke, Saul. "Semantical Considerations on Modal Logic." In Leonard Linsky (ed.), *Reference and Modality.* Oxford: Oxford University Press, 1971.

Lambert, Karel. *Meinong and the Principle of Independence.* Cambridge: Cambridge University Press, 1983.

Levinson, Jerrold. *Music, Art and Metaphysics.* Ithaca, NY: Cornell University Press, 1990.

Margolis, Joseph. "The Ontological Peculiarity of Works of Art." In *Philosophy Looks at the Arts,* 3rd edn. Philadelphia: Temple University Press, 1987.

Meining, Alexius. *Über Möglichkeit und Wahrscheinlichkeit.* In *Alexius Meinong Gesamtausgabe,* vol. VI, ed. Roderick Chisholm. Graz, Austria: Akademische Druck u. Verlagsanstalt, 1972.

Parsons, Terence. *Nonexistent Objects.* New Haven: Yale University Press, 1980.

Plantinga, Alvin. *The Nature of Necessity.* Oxford: Clarendon Press, 1974.

Rapaport, William J. "Meinongian Theories and a Russellian Paradox." *Noûs* 12 (1978): 153–80.

Sartre, Jean-Paul. *The Psychology of Imagination.* New York: Carol Publishing Group, 1991.

Searle, John. *The Construction of Social Reality.* New York: The Free Press, 1995.

Thomasson, Amie L. "The Ontology of the Social World in Searle, Husserl and Beyond." *Phenomenological Inquiry* 21 (October 1997): 109–136.

van Inwagen, Peter. "Creatures of Fiction." *American Philosophical Quarterly* 14, no. 4 (1977): 299–308.

van Inwagen, Peter. "Fiction and Metaphysics." *Philosophy and Literature* 7 (1983): 67–77.

Wollheim, Richard. *Art and its Objects.* New York: Harper & Row, 1968.

Wolterstorff, Nicholas. *Works and Worlds of Art.* Oxford: Clarendon Press, 1980.

Zalta, Edward. *Abstract Objects.* The Netherlands: Reidel, 1983.

Zalta, Edward. *Intensional Logic and the Metaphysics of Intentionality.* Cambridge, Mass.: MIT Press, 1988.

Zalta, Edward. "Referring to Fictional Characters." Unpublished manuscript. A version translated into German appears in *Zeitschrift fiir Semiotik* 9 nos. 1–2 (1987): 85–95.

7

On What Grounds What

Jonathan Schaffer

Substance is the subject of our inquiry; for the principles and the causes we are seeking are those of substances. For if the universe is of the nature of a whole, substance is its first part; …

Aristotle (1984: 1688; *Meta.* 1069a18–20)

On the now dominant Quinean view, metaphysics is about what there is. Metaphysics so conceived is concerned with such questions as whether properties exist, whether meanings exist, and whether numbers exist. I will argue for the revival of a more traditional Aristotelian view, on which metaphysics is about what grounds what. Metaphysics so revived does not bother asking whether properties, meanings, and numbers exist. Of course they do! The question is whether or not they are *fundamental*.

In §1 I will distinguish three conceptions of metaphysical structure. In §2 I will defend the Aristotelian view, coupled with a permissive line on existence. In §3 I will further develop a neo-Aristotelian framework, built around primitive grounding relations.

1 Three Conceptions of Metaphysical Structure

Contemporary textbooks usually introduce metaphysics through the Quine-Carnap debate, with Quine awarded the victory. The main resistance comes from neo-Carnapians who challenge Quine's laurels. But why start with the Quine-Carnap debate? Why think that the best understanding of metaphysics is to be found in a debate between a positivist teacher and his post-positivist student, both of whom share explicitly anti-metaphysical sympathies?

Among the many assumptions Quine and Carnap share is that metaphysical questions are *existence questions*, such as whether numbers exist. They only disagree on the further issue of

Jonathan Schaffer, "On What Grounds What," in David Chalmers, David Manley, and Ryan Wasserman (eds.), *Metametaphysics* (Oxford: Oxford University Press, 2009), pp. 347–83. Reproduced by permission.

whether such questions are meaningful (at least as the metaphysician might pose them). But why think that metaphysical questions are existence questions of this sort?

Return to Aristotle's *Metaphysics*. There are virtually no existence questions posed. The whole discussion is about *substances* (fundamental units of being). At one point Aristotle does pause to ask if numbers exist, and his answer is a brief and dismissive *yes*: "it is true also to say, without qualification, that the objects of mathematics exist, and with the character ascribed to them by mathematicians" (1984: 1704; *Meta*.1077b32–3). For Aristotle, the serious question about numbers is whether they are transcendent substances, or grounded in concreta. The question is not *whether* numbers exist, but *how*.

1.1   The Quinean view: on what there is

According to Quine, metaphysics addresses the question of "What is there?" (1963a: 1) He notes that the question has a trivial answer ("everything"), but adds "there remains room for disagreement over cases" (1963a: 1). Among the cases he mentions are properties, meanings, and numbers. Thus Quine sees metaphysics as addressing the question of what exists, by addressing questions such as whether properties, meanings, and numbers exist. This should be familiar.

To be more precise about the Quinean view, it will prove useful to begin by distinguishing between the *task* and *method* of metaphysics. Thus:

Quinean task: The task of metaphysics is to say what exists.

What exists forms the domain of quantification. The domain is a set (or class, or plurality) – it has no internal structure. In other words, the Quinean task is to *list the beings*.

The Quinean task of saying what exists is to be achieved by the following method:

Quinean method: The method of metaphysics is to extract existence commitments from our best theory.

In slightly more detail, the Quinean method is to begin with our best theory and canonical logic, translate the former into the latter, and see what

the bound variables must range over for the result to be true (see §2.3 for further details). That is, the method is to solve for the domain of quantification required for the truth of an apt regimentation of our best theory. The elements of the domain are the posits of the best theory, and insofar as we accept the theory, these are the entities we get committed to (1963a: 12–3). That is the ontology. The rest is ideology.

The Quinean view deserves praise for providing an integrated conception of the discipline. Part of what makes the Quinean task worth assigning is that there seems to be viable method for accomplishing it, and part of what makes the Quinean method worth pursuing is that there seems to be a valuable task it accomplishes.

The Quinean view deserves further praise for promising progress. Indeed, Quine himself felt compelled to move from eliminativism about numbers to realism (1960a, 1966b), on grounds that quantification over numbers seems indispensable to formally regimented physics. Thus the Quinean view promises what Yablo calls "Ontology the progressive research program (not to be confused with ontology the swapping of hunches about what exists)" (1998: 229).

The Quinean view deserves even more praise for its historical role in helping revive metaphysics from its positivistic stupor. Quine was primarily arguing against Carnap, who rejected metaphysical existence claims as *meaningless*.[1] Carnap's views develop the anti-metaphysical positivism of his day, as expressed by Schlick: "The empiricist does not say to the metaphysician 'what you say is false,' but, 'what you say asserts nothing at all!' He does not contradict him, but says 'I don't understand you'" (1959: 107). To consider Quine the victor of the Quine-Carnap debate is to consider this extreme anti-metaphysical position defeated.

Yet victory for the Quinean view should not be considered victory for traditional metaphysics. For the Quinean view is *revisionary by design*. Thus when Carnap criticizes Quine for "giving meaning to a word which belongs to traditional metaphysics and should therefore be meaningless" (Quine 1966a: 203), Quine rejoins: "meaningless words are precisely the words which I feel freest to specify meanings for" (1966a: 203). Indeed, though the textbooks cast Quine and Carnap as opponents, Quine is better understood as an anti-metaphysical ally of his mentor (c.f. Price

1997). *The Quine-Carnap debate is an internecine debate between anti-metaphysical pragmatists* (concerning the analytic-synthetic distinction, with implication for whether the locus of pragmatic evaluation is molecular or holistic). As Quine himself says:

> Carnap maintains that ontological questions, … are questions not of fact but of choosing a convenient conceptual scheme or framework for science; and with this I agree only if the same be conceded for every scientific hypothesis. (1966a: 211)[2]

The Quinean view of the task and method of metaphysics remains dominant. Indeed, the contemporary landscape in meta-metaphysics may be described as featuring a central Quinean majority, amid a scattering of Carnapian dissidents. Few other positions are even on the map.[3]

1.2   The Aristotelian view: on what grounds what

There are views of metaphysics other than Quine's or Carnap's. The traditional view – what Carnap would dismiss and Quine revise – is of course rooted in Aristotle. For Aristotle, metaphysics is about what grounds what. Thus Aristotle leads into the *Metaphysics* with: "we must inquire of what kind are the causes and the principles, the knowledge of which is wisdom" (1984: 1553: *Meta*.982a4–5). He concludes:

> [I]t is the work of one science to examine being *qua* being, and the attributes which belong to it *qua* being, and the same science will examine not only substances but also their attributes, both those above named and what is prior and posterior, genus and species, whole and part, and the others of this sort. (1984: 1587; *Meta*.1005a14–17)

Aristotle then characterizes metaphysical inquiry as centered on substance: "Substance is the subject of our inquiry; for the principles and the causes we are seeking are those of substances. For if the universe is of the nature of a whole, substance is its first part; …" (1984: 1688: *Meta*.1069a18–20).

Aristotle's notion of substance, developed in the *Categories*, is multifaceted. But perhaps the core notion is that of a *basic, ultimate, fundamental*

unit of being. This emerges in the passage that Wedin refers to as "the grand finale of the *Categories*" (2000: 81), namely: "So if the primary substances did not exist it would be impossible for any of the other things to exist" (1984: 5; *Cat*.2b6–7; c.f. 1984: 1609; *Meta*.1019a2–4). As Gill aptly summarizes:

> In the *Categories* the main criterion [for selecting the primary substances] is ontological priority. An entity is ontologically primary if other things depend for its existence on it, while it does not depend in a comparable way on them. The primary substances of the *Categories*, such as particular men and horses, are subjects that ground the existence of other things; some of the nonprimary things, such as qualities and quantities, exist because they modify the primary substances, and others, such as substantial species and genera, exist because they classify the primary entities … Therefore the existence of other things depends upon the existence of these basic entities; … (1989: 3)

Thus, on Aristotle's view, metaphysics is the discipline that studies substances and their modes and kinds, by studying the fundamental entities and what depends on them.[4]

Putting this together, the neo-Aristotelian will conceive of the task of metaphysics as:

Aristotelian task: The task of metaphysics is to say what grounds what.

That is, the neo-Aristotelian will begin from a *hierarchical view of reality* ordered by *priority in nature*. The primary entities form the sparse structure of being, while the grounding relations generate an abundant superstructure of posterior entities. The primary is (as it were) all God would need to create. The posterior is grounded in, dependent on, and derivative from it. The task of metaphysics is to limn this structure.

What of the method? A very general answer may be given as:

Aristotelian method: The method of metaphysics is to deploy diagnostics for what is fundamental, together with diagnostics for grounding.

Different versions of the neo-Aristotelian view may deploy different diagnostics for what is fundamental as well as for grounding. I will offer specific diagnostics in §3.3. But for present purposes this general conception of the Aristotelian method will suffice.

For present purposes I am interested in how the Quinean and Aristotelian views differ. While Quine is interested in existence questions (such as whether there are numbers), Aristotle seems to take a permissive disinterest in such questions. Thus consider how he launches the *Categories*, with a catalogue of types of entity: "Of things said without any combination, each signifies either substance or quantity or qualification or a relative or where or when or being-in-a-position or having or doing or being-affected" (1984: 4; *Cat.*1b25–7). He simply assumes that all such types of entity exist, without need for further discussion (cf. Frede 1987).

Indeed, in one of the few places in the *Metaphysics* where Aristotle even considers an existence question – concerning numbers – he answers with an immediate affirmative:

> Thus since it is true to say without qualification that not only things which are separable but also things which are inseparable exist – for instance, that moving things exist – it is true also to say, without qualification, that the objects of mathematics exist, and with the character ascribed to them by mathematicians. (1984: 1704; *Meta.*1077b31–3)

As Corkum explains, "the philosophical question is not *whether* such things exist but *how* they do" (2008: 76). Aristotle elsewhere considers existence questions with respect to time, place, the void, and the infinite (*inter alia*). But throughout he is primarily concerned with *how* something exists. Thus he comes to say of the infinite:

> The infinite, then, exists in no other way, but in this way it does exist, potentially and by reduction. It exists in fulfillment in the sense in which we say "it is day" or "it is the games"; and potentially as matter exists, not independently as what is finite does. (1984: 352; *Phys.*206b13–16)

As Owen summarizes Aristotle's approach, using the example of time, "The philosophical query "Does time exist?" is answered by saying 'Time is such and such' and showing the answer innocent of logical absurdities" (1986b: 275).

What emerges is that the neo-Aristotelian and Quinean views will differ on at least two points. First, while the Quinean will show great concern with questions such as whether numbers exist, the neo-Aristotelian will answer such questions with a dismissive *yes, of course*. Second, while the neo-Aristotelian will show great concern with questions such as whether numbers are fundamental or derivative, the Quinean will have no concern with this further question. (Or the Quinean concern will be expressed in terms she mistakenly thinks are analyzable via supervenience; or in terms she admittedly considers dark: or in terms that belie an implicitly Aristotelian hierarchical view: §2.2.)

Existence questions do play a role for my sort of neo-Aristotelian. What exists are the grounds, grounding relations, and the grounded entities. Hence, existence claims constrain the grounds and groundings, to be basis enough for the grounded. So for instance, given that numbers exist, they must either be counted as substances (grounds), or else explanation is required for how they are grounded in the real substances.

But the existence questions are doubly transformed. First, they no longer represent the end of metaphysical inquiry. For one must still determine whether an existent is a ground, grounding relation, or a grounded entity (and if so, how). Second, there is no longer anything directly at stake. For there is no longer any harm in positing an abundant roster of existents, *provided it is grounded on a sparse basis*. (This is why the neo-Aristotelian can be so permissive about what exists. She need only be stingy when it comes to what is fundamental: §2.1.)

While the Quine-Carnap debate remains the official starting point of contemporary discussions, vestiges of the Aristotelian view linger. For example, Armstrong makes crucial use of the notion of "the ontological free lunch":

> [W]hatever supervenes or, as we can also say, is entailed or necessitated, … is not something ontologically additional to the subvenient, or necessitating, entity or entities. What supervenes is no addition to being. (1997: 12)

But what could this mean? In Quinean terms, whatever supervenes is an addition to being in the only available sense – it is an additional entry on the list of beings. But in Aristotelian terms, there is a straightforward way to understand Armstrong: *whatever is dependent is not fundamental*, and thus *no addition to the sparse basis*. Thus, Armstrong's notion of an ontological free lunch seems best understood against an Aristotelian background.

To take another example, Lewis invokes a naturalness ordering on properties: "Some few properties are *perfectly* natural. Others, even though they may be somewhat disjunctive or extrinsic, are at least somewhat natural in a derivative way." (1986: 61). In Aristotelian terms, Lewis is suggesting a hierarchical grounding structure, albeit one restricted to properties.[5]

Perhaps the best example of a neo-Aristotelian view is to be found in Fine's *constructional ontology*, which has "a tripartite structure; there are domains for the elements, for the givens, and for the constructors" (1991: 266). The elements are the existents, the givens are the grounds, and the constructors are the grounding relations. Fine also speaks of "a primitive metaphysical concept of reality" (2001: 1), where what counts as really the case is "settled by considerations of ground" (2001: 1). To revive the Aristotelian view is thus to further unearth what is already resurfacing (to varying degrees) in Armstrong, Lewis, Fine, and all those who would revive traditional metaphysics.

There is a tension in contemporary metaphysics. On the one hand the Quinean view of the discipline remains dominant (§1.1). On the other hand there has been a revival of interest in questions of what is fundamental, and a revival of interest in traditional metaphysics. The tension is that the post-positivist Quinean view is (by design) unsuited for the traditional questions. The revival of traditional metaphysics demands a revival of the traditional Aristotelian view, which involves concepts one will not find in Quine or Carnap.

1.3 Metaphysical structures: flat, sorted, and ordered

What emerges is that Quine and Aristotle offer different views of metaphysical structure. That is, the Quinean and Aristotelian tasks involve structurally distinct conceptions of the target of metaphysical inquiry. For the Quinean, the target is *flat*. The task is to solve for E = the set (or class, or plurality) of entities. There is no structure to E. For

any alleged entity, the flat conception offers two classificatory options: either the entity is in E, or not.

For the neo-Aristotelian, the target is *ordered*. The task is to solve for the pair $\langle F, G \rangle$ of fundamental entities and grounding relations, which generate the hierarchy of being. For any alleged entity, the ordered conception offers not two but four major classificatory options: either the entity is in F, in G, in neither but generated from F through G, or else in the rubbish bin of the non-existent. (If the entity is in the third class, then there will be further sub-options as to how the entity is grounded.)[6]

Maybe also worth mentioning is a third view of metaphysical structure (perhaps inspired by Aristotle's *Categories*), on which the target is *sorted*. The task is to solve for the number of categories n, and solve for the sets $E_1 - E_n$ of entities in each category. For any alleged entity, the sorted conception offers $n + 1$ classificatory options for n many categories: either the entity is in E_1 or E_2 or ... or E_n, or else binned as non-existent.

Putting all of this together, and moving the sorted view second:

Flat structure: The target of metaphysical inquiry is an unstructured list of existents E.

Sorted structure: The target of metaphysical inquiry is (i) the number of categories n, and (ii) lists $E_1 - E_n$ of entities in each category.

Ordered structure: The target of metaphysical inquiry is an ordered hierarchy generated from (i) a list of the substances F, plus (ii) a list of the grounding relations G.

In lieu of three thousand further words, see the figure below.

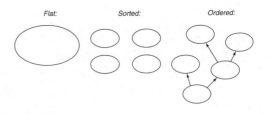

Flat: Sorted: Ordered:

Here are three structurally distinct conceptions of metaphysics. Never mind the historical views of Quine or Aristotle. Just ask: *which is the best conception of the target of metaphysical inquiry?*

Flat structure is strictly weaker than sorted structure, which in turn is strictly weaker than ordered structure. First, a flat ontology does not subsume a sorted or an ordered ontology. Given a list of entities, there is no guarantee that one can sort or order them. E determines neither $E_1 - E_n$ nor $<F, G>$. Next, a sorted ontology subsumes a flat ontology ($U(E_1 - E_n)$ determines E) but does not subsume an ordered ontology. E_f does not determine what is basic among entities of that sort, nor does anything determine priority between entities of sorts E_j and E_k. Finally, an ordered ontology subsumes a flat ontology ($x \in E$ iff x is in the closure of F under the Gs), and might well subsume a sorted ontology, if the categories are determined by the different grounding relations (if not one should also consider a sorted-and-ordered ontology).

I will not be paying further attention to the prospects for the sorted (or sorted-and-ordered) conception, because I think the categories are indeed determined by the grounding relations. That is, categories just are *ways things depend on substances*. This view is plausibly attributed to Aristotle, for whom categorical distinctions arise from the many senses of "being." These many senses are in turn held to derive from a single *focal sense*, that of "being" as attributed to a substance:

> [T]here are many senses in which a thing is said to be, but all refer to one starting-point; some things are said to be because they are substances, others because they are affections of substances, others because they are a process towards substance, or destructions or privations or qualities of substance, or productive or generative of substance, or of things which are relative to substance, or negations of some of these things or of substance itself. (1984: 1584; *Meta.* 1003b5–10)

Thus the categories themselves, the different ways of being, are best understood as different ways of depending on the primary beings. As Cohen explains:

> Substances are unique in being independent things; the items in other categories all depend somehow on substances. That is, qualities are the qualities of substances; quantities are the amounts and sizes that substances come in; relations are the way substances stand to one another. These

various non-substances all owe their existence to substances … (2003: 3)

Thus, a sorting presupposes a prior dependence ordering over the entities. *Categories are places in the dependence ordering.* Substance, for instance, serves as both root node and focal category.

I have not said what substances or grounding relations there are (though see §3.3 for some speculations), and so have not offered any schedule of categories. All I have suggested is that the sorting must derive from the ordering. If so then the sorted ontology (and the sorted-and-ordered ontology) can be ignored in favor of the ordered ontology it must derive from. To conclude this section: the question of *the task of metaphysics* is the question of *the target of metaphysical inquiry*, and, this question may be made more precise as the question of *whether the appropriate target of metaphysical inquiry is flat or ordered.*

2 Three Arguments for Ordered Structure Plus Permissivism

So is the appropriate target of metaphysical inquiry flat or ordered? I will argue that an ordered conception – packaged with a permissive stance on existence – proves best. I will begin by arguing that the Quinean existence questions are trivial (§2.1), while the Aristotelian fundamentality questions are interesting (§2.2). This will vindicate the neo-Aristotelian conception of the task of metaphysics. I will then turn to matters of method, and argue that the Quinean method is inextricably interwoven with questions of grounding (§2.3). Grounding questions will emerge as both deep and unavoidable.

2.1 Permissivism: the triviality of existence questions

Contemporary metaphysics, under the Quinean regime, has focused on existence questions such as whether properties, meanings, and numbers exist, as well as whether possible worlds exists, whether and when mereological composites exist, etc. I will glance at the debates over (i) whether numbers exist, (ii) whether properties exist, (iii) whether mereological composites exist, and (iv) whether fictional characters exist, and will use these examples to suggest that the contemporary existence debates are *trivial*, in that *the entities in question obviously do exist*. (What is not trivial is whether they are fundamental.)

Start with the debate over numbers. Here, without further ado, is a proof of the existence of numbers:

1. There are prime numbers.
2. Therefore there are numbers.

1 is a mathematical truism. It commands *Moorean certainty*, as being more credible than any philosopher's argument to the contrary. Any metaphysician who would deny it has *ipso facto* produced a *reductio* for her premises. And 2 follows immediately, by a standard adjective-drop inference.[7] Thus numbers exist. End of story. (Perhaps there are no completely knock-down arguments in metaphysics, but this one seems to me to be as forceful as they come: cf. Fine 2001: 2.)

I anticipate three replies. First, one might reply by paraphrasing 1. For instance, one might hold that it is only *according to the fiction of numbers* that there are prime numbers. I reply that this does not touch the argument. 1 does not make any claims about fictions (nor is there any covert fictive operator lurking in the syntax). So presumably this is a way of saying that 1 is false, and only some suitable paraphrase is true. But 1 is obviously true, as stated. Whatever philosophical concerns might motivate this paraphrasing fictionalist have met their *reductio*.[8]

Second, one might reply that the sense of "are" has shifted from 1 to 2, perhaps (as Carnap would have it) from some sort of number-framework-internal meaning, to some sort of distinct framework-external meaning. I answer that there is no shift in meaning. There is no linguistic evidence of any ambiguity in our idioms of existential quantification.[9] Indeed, if there were such meaning shifts then no adjective-drop inference would be valid. One could not automatically infer "there are roses" from "there are red roses" for fear of meaning shift. But one can. Likewise one can automatically infer "there are numbers" from "there are prime numbers."

Third, one might reply that all quantification is ontologically neutral, and thus accept 2 while denying that numbers exist (Azzouni 2007). To my mind (and here I follow Quine), 2 just says

that numbers exist. There is no gap. Indeed, the neutralist seems committed to the following unfathomable conjunction: "Numbers do not exist, and there are numbers."

Obviously the committed rejecter of numbers can continue the debate on all these fronts. I lack the space for further discussion. I am *not* suggesting that impermissivism is completely indefensible. What I *am* trying to suggest is that permissivism is very plausible, and (as I will argue below) quite unobjectionable.

Turn to the debate over properties. Here is a proof of the existence of properties:

3. There are properties that you and I share.
4. Therefore there are properties.

3 is an everyday truism. And 4, like 2, follows from its preceding premise. Thus properties exist.

Just as with the question of numbers, one might reply by offering a paraphrase of 3. But likewise the paraphrase is irrelevant. 3 itself remains (obviously) true, as stated.[10] Similarly one might reply by claiming a meaning shift with respect to the quantification in 3 and 4. But likewise there is no meaning shift. There is just plain old existential quantification all the way through, and it is existentially committal.

Shift to the debate over mereology. Here is an anti-nihilist proof of the existence of mereological composites (things with proper parts):

5. My body has proper parts (e.g., my hands).
6. Therefore there are things with proper parts.

5 is a biological banality, and 6 follows. Thus mereological nihilism is false.[11]

As to the debate over fictional characters, here is a proof of the existence of a particular fictional character:

7. Arthur Conan Doyle created Sherlock Holmes.
8. Therefore Sherlock Holmes exists.

7 is a literary fact, and 8 follows, given that to create something is to make it exist.[12]

So I would suggest that the contemporary existence debates are trivial. While I obviously cannot speak to every contemporary existence debate here, perhaps it will suffice to speak to one other debate that may stand in as a best case for a metaphysical existence question, namely the question of whether God exists. I think even this is a trivial *yes* (and I am an atheist). *The atheistic view is that God is a fictional character.* The atheist need not be committed to the claim that there are no fictional characters! (To put this point another way, if the theism debate *were* about the existence of God, then the following would count as a *defense* of theism: (i) God is a fictional character, and (ii) fictional characters exist, hence (iii) God exists. But obviously that is no defense of theism! Hence the theism debate is *not* about existence.[13])

So I recommend a broad permissivism about existence. Note that I have not attempted to state the limits of permissivism. I certainly do not mean to suggest that every candidate entity should count as an existent (the neo-Aristotelian does retain a rubbish bin for the non-existent: §1.3). For instance, if a candidate entity is described in such a way as to entail grounding information (e.g., "a Platonic number," understood as a transcendent substance), or so as to engender contradictions (e.g., "a non-self-identical creature"), one need not remain permissive. My point is only that one should be permissive about those very entities Quineans typically consider most controversial.

Note also that the permissivism suggested is *not* Meinongian. I draw no distinctions between what exists, what subsists, and what there is (as per Meinong 1960). I am not introducing new quantifiers (as per the Routley view discussed in Lewis 1999c). Rather, I am invoking *the one and only sense of existence*, and merely holding that very much exists.

Note finally that this permissivism is *not* "lightweight" (in the sense of Chalmers 2009), at least in the sense in which the lightweight realist treats existence claims as *analytic*, grounded in allegedly analytic ampliative conditionals such as "if there are particles arranged tablewise, then there is a table." I take no such deflationist stance on existence, offer no analytic claims, and say nothing of particles. Rather, I take entities like tables to be full-blown "heavyweight" entries on the roster of entities, and merely add that their existence is *obvious*.

I anticipate three objections. First, one might object that there are perfectly good proposals, such as that of Field 1980, that allow us to eliminate such "spooky creatures" as numbers.

I answer that one should distinguish such proposals from any Quinean gloss that might accompany them. If Field's construction works, for instance, I say it shows how numbers do exist in a world of concrete substances, as grounded in certain features of such substances (e.g., betweenness and congruence relations between substantival spacetime points). This is a better interpretation of the Field construction than Field's own Quinean eliminativist interpretation, because it reconciles Field's view with the obvious fact that there are prime numbers.[14]

Second, one might object that there are countervailing intuitions of unreality. Indeed, with fictional characters like Santa Claus, it is often natural to say that Santa is not real (e.g., this is a natural way to correct the child who believes in a flesh and blood Santa). But "real" is used flexibly in ordinary English to mark a multitude of distinctions. For instance, it can be used to mark the existent/non-existent distinction, the objective/subjective distinction, and the basic/derivative distinction, *inter alia*.[15] Further, even intuitions directly targeted to non-existence can be explained away via *quantifier domain restriction*. When the nominalist denies that numbers exist, and when the atheist denies that God exists, what both are denying is that the entities in question are among the *mind-independent* entities.[16] When the mereological nihilist denies that fusions exist, what she is denying is that such entities *ultimately* exist – she is denying that such entities are fundamental.[17]

Third, one might object that permissivism violates some crucial methodological, epistemological, or metaphysical dictum. For instance, permissivism might be said to fall afoul of Occam's Razor in multiplying entities; or violate empiricist scruples in admitting things beyond what our senses reveal; or conflict with nominalistic demands by countenancing spooky abstracta. I answer that there need be no conflict with any reasonable dictum. Occam's Razor should only be understood to concern substances: *do not multiply basic entities without necessity.* There is no problem with the multiplication of derivative entities – they are an "ontological free lunch" (§1.2). Indeed a better methodology would be the "bang for the buck" principle. What one ought to have is the strongest theory (generating the most derivative entities) on the simplest basis (from the fewest substances). Empiricist scruples and nominalistic demands may be met if the entities in question are grounded. For instance, if numbers are indeed grounded in the concrete realm, then (i) they may be known via their concrete grounds, and (ii) they would be brought down to earth.

So do not be alarmed. Permissivism only concerns the shallow question of what exists. One can and should still be restrictive about the deep question of what is *fundamental*, and one still owes an account of *how* these very many things exist in virtue of what little is fundamental. (For instance, on my preferred view [§3.3] there is only one fundamental entity – *the whole concrete cosmos* – from which all else exists by *abstraction*.)

I conclude that contemporary metaphysics, insofar as it has been inspired by the Quinean task, has confused itself with trivialities. Hofweber 2005 speaks of "a puzzle about ontology," namely how it could be that (i) metaphysics seems to ask deep and difficult questions, when (ii) the existence questions seem shallow and trivial. *This is only a puzzle on the Quinean assumption that metaphysics is asking existence questions.* The deep questions about numbers, properties, and parts (*inter alia*) are not *whether* there are such things, but *how*.

2.2 Ordering: the importance of dependence structure

The philosopher raised on the Quine-Carnap debate who turns to the central metaphysical questions will leave confused. She will find debates such as: (i) metaphysical realism versus idealism, (ii) realism about numbers versus constructivism, (iii) realism about universals versus nominalism, (iv) substratum versus bundle theories of objects, (v) dualistic versus materialistic theories of mind, (vi) substantival versus relational theories of space, and (vii) monistic versus pluralistic theories of the cosmos. She will find little disagreement about what exists, but profound dispute over what is fundamental.

Starting with (i), the debate over metaphysical realism, both the realist and idealist accept the existence of rocks.[18] There is no dispute about what exists. Rather, the dispute is over *mind-dependence*: are entities like rocks grounded in ideas, or independent of them? The debate between the realist and constructivist about numbers in (ii)

likewise concerns mind-dependence. The questions is whether numbers are independent of the mind, or based on our concepts.[19]

Turning to (iii), the debate over universals, both the realist and nominalist accept the existence of general properties. The dispute is over whether properties are fundamental, or whether they are derivative. For the predicate nominalist who treats properties as 'shadows cast by predicates,' the issue is once again not one of existence but one of mind-dependence.

Moving to the debate over substrata as per (iv), both the substratum and bundle theorists accept the existence of objects and properties. The dispute is over *priority*. For the substratum theorist, objects are prior, and properties are dependent modes. Thus, Descartes says:

> We should notice something very well known by the natural light: nothingness possesses no attributes or qualities. It follows that, whenever we find some attributes or qualities, there is necessarily some thing or substance to be found for them to belong to; ... (1985: 196; cf. Armstrong 1997: 99)

For the bundle theorist, properties (be they universals or tropes) are prior, being what Campbell calls "the independent, primitive elements which in combination constitute the variegated and somewhat intelligible world in which we find ourselves" (1997: 127). Objects are then bundled out of compresent property complexes.

Likewise, debate (v) over the mind is not a dispute over whether mind or matter exists, but rather over whether mind is based in matter. The debate (vi) over substantival space is not a dispute over whether there is space, but rather over whether space is grounded in its occupants. And, finally, debate (vii) over monism is not a dispute over whether wholes or parts exist, but rather over which is prior. The core monistic thesis is that the whole is prior to its parts (Schaffer 2010a).

I thus submit that a meta-metaphysics that would make sense of these central questions must make sense of claims of grounding. These central metaphysical questions are not questions about *whether* entities exist, but only about *how* they do.

I anticipate three replies. First, one might reply that there are *other* central metaphysical questions which are existence questions.[20] I answer that the neo-Aristotelian need not contest this, since she has room for both grounding and existence questions. Recall that the Aristotelian view subsumes the Quinean view (§1.3). There is no problem making room for existence questions on the Aristotelian view – rather, the problem is finding any room for grounding questions on the Quinean view.

That said, I also doubt that there are many important metaphysical existence questions. Or at least I would maintain that the usual candidates (e.g., the question of whether numbers exist) fail, and would ask the provider of this first reply for better examples.

The second reply I anticipate is that grounding questions can be analyzed into existence questions, via supervenience claims. For instance, take the debate over the mind. The Quinean might maintain that she can understand this as a dispute over whether mental states *supervene* on physical states, where supervenience is analyzed in terms of patterns of existences (albeit across possible worlds). Supervenience is invoked to fake ordering structure within a flat ontology. Many contemporary Quineans do in fact claim to be interested in limning the ultimate structure of reality. But when pressed on what they mean by this, they retreat to supervenience.[21]

My answer to this second reply is that the supervenience analyses of grounding all fail (cf. McLaughlin and Bennett 2005: §3.5). There are two evident and systematic problems with using supervenience to simulate grounding. The first is that supervenience has the wrong formal features: supervenience is reflexive, and non-asymmetric, while grounding is irreflexive and asymmetric. The second problem is that supervenience is an intensional relational while grounding is hyperintensional. For instance, there are substantive grounding questions for necessary entities (like numbers), but supervenience claims go vacuous for necessary entities.[22]

Supervenience is mere modal correlation. As Kim suggests, it is the supervenience correlation that should be explained via grounding:

> Supervenience itself is not an explanatory relation. It is not a "deep" metaphysical relation; rather, it is a "surface" relation that reports a pattern of property covariation, suggesting the presence of an interesting dependency relation that might explain it. (1993: 167)

There is an interesting question about the modal consequences of grounding. This opens up the prospect of using supervenience for *something* – the right sort of supervenience failure can show grounding failure. Modal correlation is at best a symptom.

There have been other attempts to analyze grounding, including those centered around existential dependence counterfactuals (the simplest version: *x* depends on *y* iff: if *y* did not exist then *x* would not exist, but if *x* did not exist then *y* might still exist).[23] But such counterfactuals are problematically contextually variable, and the analysis goes vacuous on necessary entities. Obviously, I cannot address all further analyses here, but suffice it to say that I know of none that succeed.

Grounding should rather be taken as *primitive*, as per the neo-Aristotelian approach (cf. Fine 2001: 1). Grounding is an unanalyzable but needed notion – it is *the primitive structuring conception of metaphysics*. It is the notion the physicalist needs to explicate such plausible claims as "the fundamental properties and facts are physical and everything else obtains *in virtue of* them" (Loewer 2001: 39). It is the notion the truthmaker theorist needs to explicate such plausible claims as: "Must there not be something about the world that makes it to be the case, that serves as an ontological ground, for this truth?" (Armstrong 1997: 115; cf. Schaffer 2010b). (Of course one might ask for further clarification of a proposed primitive, including paradigm cases and inferential patterns: §3.2.)

The third reply I anticipate is that grounding questions can be rephrased as existence questions, by packing grounding information into the description of a candidate entity. For instance, take the debate over whether numbers are abstract substances (Plato), grounded in concrete instances (Aristotle), or grounded in the mind (Kant). Now define a "transcendent number" as a number that is an abstract substance, define an "immanent number" as a number that is independent of the mind but grounded in the concrete realm, and define a "conceptual number" as a number that is grounded in the mind. Then the classical debate about numbers can be rephrased in terms of whether there exist transcendent numbers (Plato), immanent numbers (Aristotle), or only conceptual numbers (Kant). Likewise the debate between the metaphysical realist and idealist can be rephrased in terms of whether there exist mind-independent rocks.

My answer to this third reply is that, first, the existence questions this reply invokes are not the ones the Quinean considers. There is still no question of whether such things as properties, meanings, and numbers exist. There is only a question of whether such beasts as "substantial universals," "fundamental meanings," and "transcendent numbers" exist.

Second, metaphysics is still not about existence questions *per se*. The most this third reply can show is that metaphysics can be framed as concerning *existence questions of a specific sort*, namely *those that pack grounding information into the description of the entity in question*. To answer such questions one still needs to determine what grounds what.

Really virtually any question can be rephrased as an existence question. Suppose I wonder whether the whole cosmos is a single integrated substance, or a mere aggregate of particles. Then my question can be rephrased as the question of whether there is an entity such that it is the cosmos and it is fundamental. Likewise suppose I wonder whether this rose is red. Then my question can be rephrased as the question of whether there is an entity such that it is this rose and it is red. With sufficient perversity, every branch of human inquiry can be characterized as inquiry into what exists. Just don't be misled. What is characteristic of the most central metaphysical questions, however perversely they may be phrased, is that they concern grounding.

2.3 Substantial presuppositions: the Quinean method presupposes Aristotelian structure

Having argued that the Quinean task is philosophically trivial (§2.1) and misses the most central metaphysical questions (§2.2), it remains to reconsider the Quinean method. It will prove useful to divide this method into five stages. First one must identify the best theory and canonical logic:

Quinean method, stage 1: Identify the best theory (physics, for Quine).

Quinean method, stage 2: Identify the canonical logic (first-order logic, for Quine).

Then one must translate the theory into the logic, determine what domain is needed for the result to be true, and read the entity commitments off this domain:

Quinean method, stage 3: Translate the best theory into the canonical logic (some paraphrasing allowed, for Quine).

Quinean method, stage 4: Determine the domain of quantification required to render this translation true (all equinumerous domains are equally good, for Quine).

Quinean method, stage 5: Read the entity commitments off the elements of the required domain (with radically eliminativist consequences, for Quine).

I will be arguing that the Quinean method requires presuppositions about ordering structure *at every single stage*. (This is not to claim that the grounding questions must be answered *before* the existence questions, but only that the questions are inseparable – recall that ordered structure addresses both together: §1.3.)

Starting with the first stage, I ask: *what makes a theory best?* One's conception of what is fundamental impacts this question. To illustrate, suppose one is choosing from among the following three candidates: (i) Bohmian mechanics, (ii) the many-minds interpretation of quantum mechanics,[24] and (iii) Bohmian mechanics plus geology. Presumably one will want to eliminate (iii) at the start, and then select between (i) and (ii). But note that both (i) and (ii) are incomplete, in the sense that they won't say a word about geology, simply because they haven't got the terms. Note also that (i) and (ii) are empirically equivalent (Albert 1992: 176).

I suggest that a good reason for eliminating (iii) would be that *geology is not fundamental*. Geological features are grounded in physical features. I further suggest that one good way to select between (i) and (ii) would be to consider whether *mind is fundamental*. If one has reason to be a materialist about minds (§2.1), then one has reason to prefer Bohmian mechanics to the many-minds view. Or if one has reason to be a dualist, then one has reason to prefer the many-minds view to Bohmian mechanics. So it seems that the question of what makes a theory best is interwoven with the question of what is basic, in the following way:

Aristotelian presuppositions at stage 1: The best theory is a theory of the fundamental.

It may be worth noting that Quine himself took physics to provide the best theory, for reasons that seem to concern what is basic. Thus Quine speaks of physics as investigating "the essential nature of the world" (1981: 93), defends behaviorism by speaking of "limning the true and ultimate structure of reality" (1960a: 221), and defends physicalism by invoking the dependence of all else on the physical:

> Why, Goodman asks, this special deference to physical theory? This is a good question, and part of its merit is that it admits of a good answer. The answer is not that everything worth saying can be translated into the technical vocabulary of physics; not even that all good science can be translated into that vocabulary. The answer is rather this: nothing happens in the world, not the flutter of an eyelid, not the flicker of a thought, without some redistribution of microphysical states. (1981: 98)

Aristotelian metaphysics is thus built into the Quinean method from the first stage. Part of what makes a theory best (even by Quine's own lights) is that it is a theory of what is fundamental (the "ultimate structure of reality").

Turning to the second stage of the Quinean method, I ask: *what makes a logic canonical?* One's conception of what is fundamental impacts this question. To illustrate, suppose one is choosing from among the following three candidates: (i) first-order classical logic, (ii) first-order intuitionist logic, and (iii) first-order dialetheist logic. This can affect what one quantifies over. For instance, first-order dialetheist logic allows for the existence of contradictory states of affairs.

Consider the dispute over intuitionism. Perhaps the key motivation for intuitionism is the Kantian view of numbers as mind-dependent. In this vein Dummett considers "the celebrated thesis that mathematical statements do not relate to an objective mathematical reality existing independently of us" (1978: 227–8). He continues:

> [W]e have first to resolve the metaphysical question whether mathematical objects – natural numbers, for example – are, as on the constructivist view, creations of the human mind, or, as on the platonist view, independently existing abstract objects. (1978: 229)[25]

Or consider the debate over dialetheism. One motivation for dialetheism is the view that there are impossible worlds.[26] And one of the issues

that then arises is whether worlds are basic entities (as per Lewis 1986), or some sort of set-theoretic constructions. In this vein, Nolan argues that the set-theoretic account can reconcile impossibilia with classical logic:

> Possible worlds for Lewis, notoriously, are just large objects much like our own cosmos – so the worlds where there are blue swans are just cosmoi with blue swans (among other things) in them. Extending this approach to impossible objects produces literal impossibilities … Abstract impossibilia … would not pose the same risk of incoherence as impossibilia which literally had the features associated with them … Someone who took possible worlds to be sets of propositions, or sets of sentence-like representations, is probably already committed to sets of sentences which are not maximal … or consistent … (1997: 541–2)

Thus questions about the substantiality of entities such as numbers and worlds (e.g., whether numbers are basic or mind-dependent creations, whether worlds are basic or set-theoretic constructions) are intertwined with the foundations of logic:

Aristotelian presuppositions at stage 2: The canonical logic turns (in part) on what is fundamental.

And so fundamentality questions remain unavoidable, even when deciding on a logic.[27]

Moving to the third stage of the Quinean method, I ask: *which are the apt translations?* One's conception of the substances impacts this question. To illustrate, suppose our best theory says that the Big Bang exists. Plausibly an apt translation should involve existential quantification over the Big Bang. But consider the following three rivals: (i) the functorese translation, which packs all seeming reference to individuals into adverbial modifications of the copula ("it is Big Bang-ish there-ly"); (ii) the fictionalist translation, which prefixes an "according to the fiction" operator ("according to the fiction of cosmology, the Big Bang exists"); and (iii) the inverted translation, which runs any Quinean paraphrases in the unintended direction.

The functorese translation replaces individual variables with predicate functors. Functorese may be developed with individual terms only for places (Strawson 1959: 217–21), so that "the Big

Bang exists" would be translated as "there exists a place that is Big-Bang-ish." Or functorese may deploy only a single individual term for the world (Prior 1969): "there exists a world that is Big-Bang-ish." Or functorese may even go without individual terms altogether (Hawthorne and Cortens 1995), producing: "it is Big-Bang-ish here-ish," where the "it" is a semantically empty syntactic reflex (expletive "it").[28] Quine himself develops functorese in his 1960b and 1963b, noting that his "criterion of ontological commitment is of course inapplicable to discourse constructed by means of [functors]" (1963b: 104). His conclusion on this matter was a further "defusal" of metaphysics:

> To entertain the notion of an ontology at all … for the speakers of [functorese] would be an unwarranted projection on our part of a parochial category appropriate only to our linguistic circle. Thus I do recognize that the question of ontological commitment is parochial, though within a much broader parish than that of the speakers and writers of symbolic logic. (1992: 28)

The fictionalist translation prefixes fictive operators. Thus "the Big Bang exists" might be translated as "According to the fiction of cosmology, the Big Bang exists." The prefixed operator blocks any direct ontological commitment. So Yablo maintains: "Someone whose sentences are commited to so-and-sos need not share in the commitment if the sentences are advanced in a fictional or make-believe spirit" (2001: 74).[29] Yablo thus concludes:

> The more controversial of these [philosophical existence claims] are equipoised between literal and metaphorical in a way that Quine's method is powerless to address. It is not out of any dislike for the method – on the contrary, it is because I revere it as ontology's last, best hope – that I conclude that the existence-questions of most interest to philosophers are moot. If they had answers, [the Quinean method] would turn them up; it doesn't, so they don't. (1998: 259–60)

So unless constraints are placed on translations involving predicate functors and fictive operators, there is *no constraint whatsoever* on which references will survive translation.

Inverted translations pose a different threat, that of reversing paraphrases. To illustrate with an example from Alston, suppose the following are equivalent: (i) "There is a possibility that James will come," and (ii) "The statement that James will come is not certainly false." Paraphrasing (i) into (ii) might seem to remove commitment to possibilities, but as Alston notes:

> [I]t is puzzling to me that anyone should claim that these translations 'show that we need not assert the existence of' possibilities, … For if the translation of' [(i)] into [(ii)], for example, is adequate, then they are normally used to make the same assertion … Hence the point of the translation cannot be put in terms of some assertion or commitment from which it saves us. (1998: 47)

Some basis for the *direction* of analysis is needed. If paraphrase is licensed by a symmetric notion like synonymy, or even by some non-asymmetric relation, then there will be at least some opportunities for inversions.

I suggest that a good way to constrain the application of predicate functors and fictive operators, and to impose direction on paraphrasing, is via the asymmetry of grounding. One should translate groundwards:

Aristotelian presuppositions at stage 3: The apt translations are into talk of the fundamental.

Thus consider functorese, and suppose for the sake of argument that what is fundamental are point particles, and a few physical magnitudes. Then there will be symmetry between the particle-positing translation of the best theory that assigns the physical magnitudes to the point particles, and the functorese translation that locates being-particle-like-in-such-and-such-ways at various places. The fundamental structure of the world breaks the linguistic symmetry, and blocks the functorese translation. Thus the question of what counts as an apt translation is interwoven with the question of what counts as fundamental.[30]

Continuing on to the fourth stage of the Quinean method, I ask: *which are the required domains?* The required domain is the domain of the fundamental. Formally speaking, all equinumerous domains can render the same formulae true. Indeed, by the Löwenheim-Skolem theorem, any formulae that have a true interpretation in a nonempty universe have a true interpretation in the universe of positive integers. Some constraints on proper domains are needed.

Recall Quine's own conclusion that ontology is doubly relative, both to a manual of translation and a background theory (§1.1). The manual of translation tells us whether, for instance, "gavagai" is to be rendered "as 'rabbit' or as 'undetached rabbit part' or as 'rabbit stage'" (1969: 30; see also 1960a: §12). The background theory tells us whether one of these options, say "rabbit," is to be interpreted as designating Peter Cottontail, the whole cosmos minus Peter, or Peter's singleton, since: "Reinterpreting the rest of our terms for bodies in the corresponding fashion, we come out with an ontology interchangeable with our familiar one" (1992: 33). The different background theories are isomorphic and thus contribute the same "neutral nodes to the structure of the theory."

I am suggesting that substantiality considerations play a role in determining the right domain. *Some domains are metaphysically privileged.* Here I am following Lewis, who suggests:

> Among all the things and classes that there are, most are miscellaneous, gerrymandered, ill-demarcated. Only an elite minority are carved at the joints, … Only these elite things and classes are eligible to serve as referents. The world – any world – has the makings of many interpretations that satisfy many theories; but most of these interpretations are disqualified because they employ ineligible referents. (1999b: 65)

So for instance, if (*per impossibile*) singletons were perfectly natural, then the referent of "gavagai" would gravitate to Peter's singleton. The Lewisian notion of naturalness is already a notion of an ordering (§1.2). Lewis himself vacillates on whether the ordering extends (i) only over the properties, (ii) over both objects and properties (as the above passage suggests), or (iii) more widely still. But there is no reason whatsoever to restrict priority relations in any way. By extending priority generally, one gets a better account of reference magnetism that covers all sorts of reference, and one can formulate interesting theses about priority between various entities (e.g., the nominalist proposal that objects are prior to properties).[31]

Thus, the Quinean method needs guidance in choosing a domain, on pain of the twofold relativity Quine embraced. I suggest turning to the priority ordering for such guidance, as follows:

Aristotelian presuppositions at stage 4: The right domain is the domain of the fundamental.

Substantial metaphysics is thus entangled with issues of domain choice.

As to the fifth and final stage of the Quinean method, I ask: *where are the tables and chairs?* The Quinean method is eliminativist by design. After all, if one regiments physics into first-order classical logic (with no functorialist or fictionalist tricks), all one will have to quantify over will be whatever particles or fields or whatnot the physics invokes. One will certainly not have any people and horses, tables and chairs, or apples and pebbles. When Moore intones "Here is one hand … and here is another" (1959: 146), such a Quinean must demur. This is madness. There may be a method to such madness, but madness it remains.

The thing to say about people, tables, pebbles, and their ilk is that these are *derivative*. Suppose for the sake of argument that what is basic is the spatiotemporal manifold and a handful of fundamental fields that fill it. Nevertheless, the way the fields fill spacetime grounds the existence of various pieces of furniture, *inter alia*. Were all the previous objections somehow surmounted, the best the Quinean method could claim to produce would be *the basic entities*. Grounding would still be required to preserve the method from the madness of eliminativism.

What I am suggesting is that the commitments of the regimented translation of the best theory are to *the fundamental entities*. The existence commitments are not just to these ultimate grounds, but also to grounding relations and what is grounded:

Aristotelian presuppositions at stage 5: The ontic commitments are to the fundamental grounds *plus* grounding relations and what is grounded.

Putting this together, I have suggested that the Quinean method will only deliver decent results if one brings to it Aristotelian presuppositions concerning what is fundamental. If one supposes that being forms a hierarchy with foundations, then one will be in a better position to determine the best theory, the canonical logic, the apt translations, the required domains, and the existence commitments of what results.

I am *not* suggesting that the Aristotelian account is enough to save the Quinean method, but only that it helps. The question of what is the canonical logic, for instance, remains underdetermined even by the invocation of ordering structure. *Nor* am I suggesting that the Aristotelian questions of grounding are prior to the Quinean existence questions. I am merely suggesting that they are interwoven. What I *am* trying to suggest is that traditional metaphysics is so tightly interwoven into the fabric of philosophy that it cannot be torn out without the whole tapestry unraveling. Substantial metaphysics is unavoidable. One might at least try to do it well.

3 Towards a neo-Aristotelian Framework

I have argued for a revival of a neo-Aristotelian meta-metaphysics, targeting a structured hierarchy rather than a flat list. So far the focus has been on distinguishing the Quinean and neo-Aristotelian views (§1), and arguing for the latter (§2). I will conclude by further developing the neo-Aristotelian framework, in three interrelated ways. I will begin by using grounding as a primitive to analyze a family of useful structural concepts (§3.1). I will then turn to clarifying this primitive via intuitive exemplars and formal constraints (§3.2). Finally I will illustrate one particular neo-Aristotelian approach (§3.3).

3.1 The grounding family

Part of what makes grounding a useful notion is that it can be used to define a cluster of useful metaphysical notions. In this respect grounding is like proper parthood, which can be used to define a cluster of useful mereological notions.

To begin, the key notions of *a fundamental entity* (a prior, primary, independent, ground entity) and *derivative entity* (a posterior, secondary, dependent, grounded entity) can both be defined in terms of *grounding* (ontological dependence, priority in nature), as follows:

Fundamental: x is fundamental $=_{df}$ nothing grounds x.

Further:

Derivative: x is derivative $=_{df}$ something grounds x.[32]

Given these definitions, the categories of *being fundamental* and *being derivative* come out exhaustive and exclusive. So one gets the following material equivalence:

Existent: x is an existent iff x is fundamental or x is derivative.

Note that this is not intended as a definition of "existence" – I take that term to be too fundamental to be definable, and in any case have already appealed to it by using existential quantifiers to define the previous notions. This is merely an informative equivalence.

The notion of grounding may be put to further use to capture a crucial mereological distinction (missing from classical mereology) between *an integrated whole* which exhibits a genuine unity, and *a mere aggregate* which is a random assemblage of parts. Thus, Aristotle speaks of "that which is compounded out of something so that the whole is one – not like a heap, however, but like a syllable, ..." (1984: 1644: *Meta*.1041b11–2). This intuitive distinction may be defined via:

Integrated whole: x is an integrated whole $=_{df}$ x grounds each of its proper parts.

Mere aggregate: x is a mere aggregate $=_{df}$ each of x's proper parts ground x.

Obviously mixed cases are possible as well. What it is for two entities to be *interdependent* may now be defined:

Interdependence: x and y are interdependent $=_{df}$ there is an integrated whole of which x and y are both proper parts.

This has the correct result that *if* the universe is an integrated whole, then all its proper parts would turn out interdependent.

I leave off further exploration of the grounding family at this point. But I would note that at least one other alternative primitive would equally serve my definitional purposes, that of *improper grounding*. Improper grounding may be defined via grounding as:

Improper grounding: x improperly grounds $y =_{df} x$ grounds y, or $x = y$.

But the definition may equally be run in the other direction, since:

Grounding: x grounds y iff x improperly grounds y, and $x \neq y$.

In this sense the grounding family is even further akin to the mereological family (which may be defined starting from proper parthood or improper parthood, *inter alia*). Further parallels will emerge below.

3.2 Grounding Itself

So far I have attempted to show that a family of notions may be constructed around the relation of grounding. To the extent these notions were antecedently comprehensible, the notion of grounding may be comprehended by its definitive role. But I think that there is more to be said about the notion of grounding itself. Grounding is a natural and intuitive notion, for which there exist clear examples, and clear formal constraints.

To show how natural and intuitive the notion of grounding is, it may be most useful to work historically. Plato brings the notion of natural priority to prominence in the *Euthyphro* dilemma, asking: "Is what is holy holy because the gods approve it, or do they approve it because it is holy?" (1961: 178; 10a). Many of us teach this dilemma to our first year students. They get it. Priority then resurfaces in the metaphor of the cave in *Republic*, where the form of the good is compared to the sun, and declared ultimately prior: "the objects of knowledge not only receive from the presence of the good their being known, but their very existence and essence is derived to them from it, ..." (1961: 744; 509b). Aristotle then codifies the notion of priority in nature, characterizes substances as ultimately prior, and conceives of metaphysics as the study of such substances. These notions reverberate through the history of metaphysics (e.g., Descartes 1985: 210; Spinoza 1960: 179).

For some clear examples of grounding, consider the relations between: (i) the entity and its singleton, (ii) the Swiss cheese and its holes,

(iii) natural features and moral features, (iv) sparse properties and abundant properties, and (v) truthmakers and truths. Thus with respect to set theory it is natural to think that $\emptyset$ is basic, and that the other pure sets are founded on it (Fine 1994). For holes, a plausible position is that the material host is prior, with the holes formed from it (Casati and Varzi 1994). And for truth, the intuition that truth is grounded in being comes to us from Aristotle himself:

> [I]f there is a man, the statement whereby we say that there is a man is true, and reciprocally – since if the statement whereby we say that there is a man is true, there is a man. And whereas the true statement is in no way the cause of the actual thing's existence, the actual thing does seem in some way the cause of the statement's being true: it is because the actual thing exists or does not exist that the statement is called true or false. (1984: 22: *Cat*.14a14–22)

As to the logical features of grounding, it is best modeled as a two-place predicate, which I will write as "\". Thus "$x \backslash y$" means that x grounds y. As with the identity sign, terms for entities of arbitrary ontological category may flank the grounding sign.[33] This notion of grounding is that of *partial* and *relative* grounding. It is partial in that $x \backslash y$ is compatible with $z \backslash y$ (where $x \neq z$) – entities may have a plurality of grounds, "$x \backslash y$" just means that x is one among y's grounds.[34] It is relative in that $x \backslash y$ is compatible with $y \backslash z$ – entities may be grounded in entities that have still deeper grounds.

Grounding is then irreflexive, asymmetric, and transitive. It thus induces a partial ordering over the entities (*the great chain of being*), with foundations (the substances, the foundation post for the great chain of being).[35] Formally this may be modeled by a directed acyclic graph, for which every path has a starting point.

In its formal structure, grounding is similar to causation and proper parthood, in that both are irreflexive, asymmetric, and transitive (thus inducing partial orderings). It differs from both in requiring minimal elements. Grounding is, however, exactly like the classical mereological relation of *having as a proper part*, which is irreflexive, asymmetric, and transitive, and whose ordering provably is well-founded (in fact it provably has a unique foundation, *the whole universe*).

So I say that grounding passes every test for being a metaphysical primitive worth positing. It is unanalyzable. It is useful. And it is clear what we mean. (Of course the notion of grounding may be *unfamiliar* to some metaphysicians raised only on Quine and Carnap. The best advice I can give is *work with the notion*, and see if you then come to grasp it.)

I digress to consider a possible objection, according to which there are many distinct notions of grounding, united only in name. Whereas Aristotle claimed that there were many notions of priority, singling out priority in nature as foremost among them (cf. Owen 1986a: 186), this objector goes further, holding that priority in nature is *itself* "said in many ways." By way of reply, I see no more reason to consider this a case of mere homonymy, than to consider various cases of identity as merely homonymous. In both cases, there is a common term, and the same formal structure. This is some evidence of real unity. At the very least, I would think it incumbent on the objector to provide further reason for thinking that the general term 'grounding' denotes no unified notion.

Perhaps the 'mere homonymy' objection will be more pressing for some implementations of the Aristotelian view than others, depending on how diverse a roster of grounding relations they adduce. For what it is worth, on my preferred view (§3.3) all the grounding relations are relations of *abstraction*. The concrete whole is always prior in nature to its abstracted aspects. Perhaps this evinces a still deeper unity to the notion of grounding.

3.3   Illustration: a neo-Aristotelian metaphysic

I conclude with an illustration of a neo-Aristotelian metaphysic. This is intended to further explicate the general neo-Aristotelian framework, to be suggestive of the tremendous diversity of specific views compatible with such a framework, and perhaps even to hold independent interest.[36]

Recall (§1.2) that the Aristotelian method involves diagnostics for what is fundamental as well as for the grounding relations. Here are three diagnostics I would provide for the fundamental substances:

Minimal Completeness: The substances are minimally complete.

A set *S* of entities at *w* is *complete* for *w* iff *S* serves to characterize *w*, by providing a supervenience base for *w*. *S is minimally* complete for *w* iff (i) *S* is complete for *w*, and (ii) no proper subset of *S* is complete for *w*.

Metaphysical Generality: The substances have a form that fits all metaphysical possibilities.

The form of a collection is its most general features, and a form fits all metaphysical possibilities iff these features exist at all metaphysically possible worlds. The ways the substances could be just are the ways the world could be.

Empirical Specifiability: the substances have a content informed by fundamental physics.

The content of an inventory is its most specific features, and the content is empirically specifiable iff these features fit those found in fundamental physics.

Here are two diagnostics for the grounding relations:

Permissiveness: The grounding relations generate very many entities.

In other words, the grounding relations should provide a lot of bang for very little substantial buck. This is intended to mesh with the permissivism about existence espoused in §2.2.

Abstraction: The grounding relations are relations of abstraction.

The derivative entities, in order to be an "ontological free lunch" and count as no further addition, ought to be already latent within the substances. In other words, the grounding relations should just be ways of separating out aspects that are implicitly present from the start.[37]

Here is the sort of picture of substances that these diagnostics converge upon:

Priority Monism: There is exactly one substance, the whole concrete cosmos.

Insofar as there can be no difference in the world without a difference somewhere in the cosmos, priority monism delivers a complete roster of substances.[38] This roster is trivially minimal, since the only proper subset of {the cosmos} is Ø, which obviously is not complete. Moreover, this roster is clearly metaphysically general – the ways the cosmos could be just are the ways the world could be.[39] And this roster is empirically specifiable since advanced physics is field theoretic physics, and field theory has a natural monistic interpretation in terms of a spacetime bearing properties.[40]

These diagnostics also converge on:

Thick Particularism: Substances are thick particulars (concrete things).

That is, substances have both a *that*-aspect – the thin particular, the substrat-um – and a *what*-aspect – the thickening features, the modes (cf. Armstrong 1997: 123–6). Plugging in priority monism, the *that*-aspect of the cosmos is spacetime, and the *what*-aspect of it is its fields.

So among the derivative categories are those of substratum and mode:

Substratum and Mode as Derivative: substratum and mode are abstractions from thick particulars.

Another derivative category will be the *partialia*, abstracted via:

Universal Decomposition: The cosmos may be arbitrarily decomposed into parts.

From priority monism plus universal decomposition, the entirety of the actual concrete mereological hierarchy of thick particulars is generated (whether or not the world is gunky). Wholes are complete and concrete unities, and *partialia* their incomplete aspects, arising from a process of "one-sided abstraction" (Bradley 1978: 124).

With the *partialia* thus grounded, it remains to ground *abstracta* (such as *numbers* and *possibilia*) in the actual concrete realm. Here matters are too complicated to discuss further within the scope of this paper. But perhaps I have said enough to illustrate how at least one of the many possible neo-Aristotelian programs might look.

To conclude: metaphysics as I understand it is about what grounds what. It is about the structure of the world. It is about what is fundamental, and what derives from it.

Notes

Thanks especially to Ted Sider for detailed and helpful comments or multiple drafts. Many thanks also to Dave Chalmers, Phil Corkum, Janelle Derstine, Matti Eklund, Dan Giberman, Katherine Hawley, Thomas Hofweber, Kathrin Koslicki, David Manley, Kris McDaniel, Casey Perin, Ryan Wasserman, Dean Zimmerman, and audiences at Western Washington University. Australian National University, the Southeast Graduate Philosophy Conference, the Inland Northwest Philosophy Conference, and the St. Andrews Metaphysics Reading Group.

1 Slightly more precisely, Carnap holds that existence claims are either framework-external and thus meaningless, or framework-internal and thus either analytic or empirical. At best he would acknowledge that there is a *pragmatic* question of which frameworks to accept: "[T]he decisive question is not the alleged ontological question of the existence of abstract entities but rather the question of whether the use of abstract linguistic forms … is expedient and fruitful…" (1956: 221).

2 Quine's own conclusions about metaphysics are then utterly deflationary. For Quine also held the thesis of *ontological relativity* (1969: 54–5; see §2.3 for further discussion), which led him to conclude: "What is empirically significant in an ontology is just its contribution of neutral nodes to the structure of the theory" (1992: 33: from a section entitled "*Ontology Defused*"). So for Quine, not only is the only task of metaphysics to provide *a list*, but the only salient feature of the list is its *cardinality*. For as long as two lists have the same cardinality, there will be a reductive one-one mapping between them (1969: 57). Thus, for Quine, there is no real difference between positing chairs or dragons or numbers. In this vein, Quine considers whether the Löwenheim-Skolem theorem should lead him to approve of an ontology of *just the positive integers*. He has no complaint whatsoever against such Pythagoreanism, save that:

[W]e could not have arrived at our science in the first place under that interpretation, since the numbers do not correspond one by one to the reifications that were our stepping stones. Practically, heuristically, we must presumably pursue science in the old way … (1992: 33)

Thus, for Quine, the only metaphysical question is *how many entities are there*. By Löwenheim-Skolem the cardinality of the positive integers is provably sufficient. So metaphysics is already done. To every great question of metaphysics, a permissible final answer: what exists is {1, 2, 3, …}.

Such a view invites the reply: if that was the answer, what was supposed to be the question? In Douglas Adams's *The Hitchhiker's Guide to the Galaxy*, the computer *Deep Thought* (second only to *Earth* as the greatest computer ever) is designed to answer the great question of Life, the Universe and Everything. *Deep Thought* spits, churns, and gurgles for 7.5 million years, before finally answering: "42." The story continues: "Forty-two!" yelled Loonquawl. "Is that all you've got to show for seven and a half million years' work?" "I checked it very thoroughly," said the computer, "and that quite definitely is the answer. I think the problem to be quite honest with you, is that you've never actually known what the question *is*" (p. 182).

3   Here the exceptions prove the rule, in that those few who challenge Quine usually then champion Carnap. For instance, Price 1997, Azzouni 1998, Yablo 1998, Hofweber 2005, and Chalmers 2009 all oppose the Quinean regime (albeit in different ways), under a Carnapian banner.

4   There are of course great controversies concerning Aristotle's *Metaphysics*, such as whether he continues to treat individuals as substances (as per the *Categories*) or has shifted to substantial forms, and whether he conceives of substantial forms as universals or as particulars (tropes). But the claims made in the main text should be fairly uncontroversial (cf. Loux 1991: 2).

5   Though Lewis elsewhere (1999b: 65) does speak of naturalness for objects, and Sider 2001: (xxi–xxiv) has argued for an extension of Lewisian naturalness beyond properties. To reach the sort of neo-Aristotelian position I am recommending one must (i) extend the priority-in-nature ordering to all entities, and (ii) be permissive about the abundant realm of derivative entities.

6   My sort of neo-Aristotelian will also be *permissive* about existence, in that she will not toss many candidate entities into the rubbish bin. Or at least, with respect to such entities as properties, meanings, and numbers, these will all go into either the first or third classes (fundamental or derivative entities). Such permissivism, though, is strictly additional to the postulation of an ordered target.

7   This is the same inference pattern as seen in "there are red roses, therefore there are roses." Strictly speaking, adjective-drop inferences are valid only for intersective adjectives. There is a special class of non-intersective adjectives like "fake" for which they fail ("this is a fake diamond, therefore this is a

diamond" is a poor inference). But "prime" is evidently intersective, as is "composite" and "even" and "rational" and other adjectives that could be used in its place in the argument.

8   Here I follow Lewis: "I'm moved to laughter at the thought of how *presumptuous* it would be to reject mathematics for philosophical reasons" (1991: 59). The sort of concerns one finds typically involve substantive causal and/or epistemic theses, aimed to show that entities like numbers would have to be causally inert or epistemically inaccessible. These concerns are interesting. Indeed they might help us learn about the nature of causality, or the limits of knowledge, or the need for concrete grounds for numbers. The point is just that mathematical truisms such as 1 deserve far greater credence than any causal and/or epistemic philosophical dictums they may conflict with.

9   Indeed, there is plenty of evidence against ambiguity. For instance, (i) other languages do not use distinct terms for these allegedly distinct existence claims, and (ii) our language has systematically related expressions ("there are numbers" "numbers exist," etc.) for the same claims.

10   Quine himself denounces claims like 3 as "popular and misleading" (1963a: 10). A strange conjunction! Somehow Quine has managed to insult a claim for being intuitive.

11   This is merely an argument for the existence of *some* mereologically composite entities. It is not an argument for *universal composition* or any further thesis about exactly when composition occurs. I am happy to accept universal composition, on the grounds that (i) there are heaps (and piles and stacks and other individuals with no integral unity), and (ii) arbitrary composites are no less unified than heaps – indeed any arbitrary composite can be considered to be a heap. That said, I do consider this argument for universal composition to be less obvious than the anti-nihilist argument of the main text. Not every contemporary existence question is *equally* obvious!

12   Thus, consider the following passage, cited by van Inwagen: "To hear some people talk, you would think that all of Dickens's working-class characters were comic grotesques; although such characters certainly exist, there are fewer of them than is commonly supposed" (2000: 245).

13   In this light, consider Feuerbach's classic statement of atheism, that "Man … creates God in his own image, …" (1989: 118). Likewise, consider how Nietzsche puts the question: "Is man merely a mistake of God's? Or God merely a mistake of man's?" (1987: 467) Theists have also traditionally framed the issue in terms of dependence on the human mind. Thus, Anselm argues that God "cannot exist

in the mind alone," since God "can be thought to exist in reality also, which is greater" (1965: 217).

14 Field himself swallows the claim that "there are prime numbers" is false. But if one reinterprets Field's construction as vindicating the Aristotelian picture that abstracta like numbers have concrete grounds, then (i) "there are prime numbers" can be recognized as true, and (ii) Platonism is still avoided. The question for those who would want to retain the eliminativist construal of such constructions is *why*? This takes us forward to the question of whether there are any *other* problems with permissivism.

15 "Real" can also be used to mark distinctions such as that between paradigm and deviant cases. For instance, someone can fail to count as "a real man," not for failing to exist, or merely appearing male, but only for failing to satisfy some cultural norm of masculinity.

16 Azzouni 1998, for instance, in the course of defending the claim that numbers are not real, explicitly equates being real with being mind-independent. But if an entity is mind-dependent, and minds exist, doesn't the entity exist thereby? For instance, if a rock is mind-dependent as per Berkeley (for the rock to be is for it to be perceived), and it is in fact perceived, then does is not thereby have being? I conjecture that Azzouni's intuitions of "non-existence" are the product of (i) his intuition that numbers are mind-dependent entities, and (ii) his implicit restriction of the domain to the mind-independent.

17 Thus, Dorr, defending mereological nihilism, says: "What we debate in the ontology room is the question what there *is strictly speaking* – what there *really, ultimately is* – what there is *in the most fundamental sense*" (2005: 24). I conjecture that the italics are driving Dorr's intuitions.

18 As Berkeley introduces his idealism: "a certain color, taste, smell, figure and consistence, having been observed to go together, are accounted one distinct thing, signified by the name 'apple.' Other collections of ideas constitute a stone, a tree, a book, and the like sensible things;..." (1974: 151) This is why kicking a rock is no refutation – the idealist believes in rocks. For she believes in ideas, and holds rocks to be ideal.

19 Thus, Kant claims that number is "the unity of the synthesis of the manifold of a homogeneous intuition in general" (1965: 184). Kant is not denying the existence of number, but merely explaining how number might be grounded in our concepts (specifically, in the pure concepts of the understanding).

20 One might even reserve "ontology" for these metaphysical questions. Such is a revisionary usage – historically the term "ontology" comes from Aristotle's definition of first philosophy as the study of being *qua* being, and is properly used for an account of the nature of *being*, not for a list of beings (cf. Taylor 1961: 42–3). But never mind that.

21 In this vein, Lewis advertises supervenience as "a stripped-down form of reductionism, unencumbered by dubious denials of existence, claims of ontological priority, or claims of translatability" (1999a: 29).

22 For instance, it seems very plausible- especially given the iterative conception of sets (Boolos 1971) – that {Ø} is founded upon Ø (and not *vice versa*), but in this case the supervenience relations run in both directions (Fine 1994).

23 See Lowe 2005 for a sophisticated survey of accounts in this vein.

24 The many-minds interpretation associates each observer with continuum-many indeterministically evolving minds (Albert and Loewer 1988).

25 *Point of clarification*: Dummett is ultimately skeptical of the appeal to metaphysics here, since: "the puzzle is to know on what basis we could possibly resolve the metaphysical question" (1978: 229). Dummett's own suggestion is to appeal to the theory of meaning (somehow questions in this realm are supposed to be more tractable). The point in the main text is simply to illustrate how metaphysical questions about grounding can bear on the debate over the canonical logic.

26 Thus consider Priest's story of Sylvan's Box, which "was absolutely empty, but also had something in it" (1997: 575). Among the conclusions Priest draws is: "There are, in some undeniable sense, logically impossible situations or worlds. The story describes (or at least, partially describes) one such" (1997: 580).

27 There are many other places where metaphysics and logic intertwine, such as (i) issues of the existence of relations and sets arising with respect to *second-order logic*, and (ii) the issue of whether it is possible for there to be nothing as with *free logic*. The discussion in the main text is only meant to be illustrative.

28 See Burgess and Rosen (1997: 185–8) for a concise summary of the formal techniques involved. Borges (in "Tlön, Uqbat, Orbis Tertius", 73) offers the following lovely fiction of what such a language would be like:
There are no nouns in Tlön's conjectural *Ursprache*, from which the "present" languages and dialects are derived: there are impersonal verbs, modified by monosyllabic suffixes (or prefixes) with adverbial value. For example: there is no word corre-

sponding to the word "moon," but there is a verb which in English would be "to moon" or "to moonate." "The moon rose above the river" is *hlör u fang axaxaxas mlö*, or literally: "upward behind the on-streaming it moon[at]ed."

29 *Point of clarification*: Yablo 2001 distinguishes several fictionalisms, of which a prefixed fictive operator is one ("meta-fictionalism"). Yablo's own preferred version is "figuralism," which does without the fictive operator, in favor of direct but metaphorical assertion of the content (assertion with a wink, as it were).

30 This idea harkens back to the logical atomists's notion of analysis as "picturing the structure of reality." Thus, Wisdom says that the point of analysis is "clearer insight into the ultimate structure of F; i.e. clearer insight into the Structure of the situation which 'F' finally locates" (1933: 195), and Urmson explains the direction of analysis as being "towards a structure ... more nearly similar to the structure of the fact," adding that this metaphysical picture is needed as a "rationale of the practice of analysis" (1956: 24–5).

31 Here I am following Sider 2001 (xxi–xxiv) in extending the Lewisian idea of *eligibility* for reference.

32 *Complication*: what about the grounding relations themselves? Surely they exist, so are they fundamental or derivative? I am undecided. If fundamental then they are conflated with substances. But if derivative there is a worrisome regress, because then the grounding relations themselves would need grounding. A third option would be to redefine fundamentality to leave room for a third option, such as via:
*Fundamentality**: x is fundamental* $=_{df}$ nothing grounds x, and x grounds something.
Now the grounding relations can be understood via the following material equivalence:
*Grounding**: x is a grounding* relation iff (i) nothing grounds x, and (ii) x grounds nothing.
On this picture, grounding stands outside the priority ordering altogether, imposing structure upon it.

33 If grounding were notated as a relation "Gxy" it would be restricted to individuals, and if it were notated as an operator G<A, B> it would be restricted to propositions. Yet we might want to speak of the dependence of individuals or propositions on entities in other categories, and of various cross-categorical dependencies (e.g., that of modes on the substances they modify).

34 A notion of total grounding requires plural terms. We might notate this with "\\," and write "$x\backslash\backslash Ys$" to mean that x is totally grounded in the Ys, where y is among the Ys iff $x\backslash y$. I have started with singular grounding as basic and used it to define plural grounding but this could be reversed. I would have no objection to taking "\\" as primitive and defining "\" therefrom, as follows: $x\backslash y$ iff for some Xs, x is one of the Xs, and $Xs\backslash\backslash y$.

35 The intuition that being requires a ground is defended by Aristotle (1984: 1570: *Meta*.994a1–19), and endorsed by Leibniz (1989: 85), *inter alia*. It is the analogue of the set-theoretic axiom of *Foundedness*, and resurfaces in Fine's principle of *Foundation*: "Necessarily, any element of the ontology can be constructed from the basic elements of the ontology by means of constructors in the ontology" (1991: 267).

36 This discussion is connected to my discussion of priority monism in Schaffer 2010a.

37 Scaltsas imputes a similar view to Aristotle: "for Aristotle a substance is complex, not because it is a conglomeration of distinct abstract components like matter, form, or properties; a substance is complex because such items can be separated out by abstraction, which is a kind of division of the unified substance" (1994: 109)

38 To see the bite of completeness, note that a pluralistic roster comprising point particles in spatiotemporal relations would fail completeness if the whole had *emergent* features, as are arguably present in entangled quantum systems (Schaffer 2010a §2.2).

39 In contrast, a pluralistic roster of mereological simples fails generality, since the world could be *gunky*. That would be a way the world that could be that is not a way that any roster of simples could be (Schaffer 2010a: §2.4).

40 For instance, general relativistic models are <M, g, T> triples, where M is a four-dimensional continuously differentiable point manifold, g is a metric-field tensor, and t is a stress-energy tensor (with both g and t defined at every point of M). The obvious ontology here is that of a spacetime manifold bearing fields. Thus Norton notes: "a spacetime is a manifold of events with certain fields defined on the manifold. The literal reading is that this manifold is an independently existing structure that bears properties" (2004). Quantum field theory invites a similar monistic reading. As d'Espagnat explains: "Within [quantum field theory] particles are admittedly given the status of mere properties, ... But they are properties of something. This something is nothing other than space or space-time, ..." (1983: 84). See Schaffer (2009) for some further defense of the spacetime-bearing-fields view of what is fundamental.

References

Adams, Douglas 1980. *The Hitchhiker's Guide to the Galaxy*. Ballantine Books.

Albert, David 1992. *Quantum Mechanics and Experience*. Harvard University Press.

Albert, David and Barry Loewer 1988. "Interpreting the Many-Worlds Interpretation", *Synthése* 77: 195–213.

Alston, William 1998. "Ontological Commitments", in *Contemporary Readings in the Foundations of Metaphysics*, eds Stephen Laurence and Cynthia MacDonald: 46–54. Basil Blackwell.

Anselm 1965. *St. Anselm's Proslogion*, ed. and trans. M. H. Charlesworth. Oxford University Press.

Aristotle 1984. *The Complete Works of Aristotle: The Revised Oxford Translation*, vols 1 and 2, ed. Jonathan Barnes. Princeton University Press.

Armstrong, D. M. 1997. *A World of States-of-Affairs*. Cambridge University Press.

Azzouni, Jody 1998. "On 'On What There Is'", *Pacific Philosophical Quarterly* 79: 1–18.

Azzouni, Jody 2007. "Ontological Commitment in the Vernacular", *Noûs* 41: 204–26.

Berkeley, George 1974. "A Treatise Concerning the Principles of Human Knowledge", in *The Empiricists*: 135–215. Anchor Press.

Boolos, George 1971. "The Iterative Conception of Set", *Journal of Philosophy* 68: 215–31.

Borges, Jorge Luis 1999. "Tlön, Uqbar, Orbis Tertius", in *Collected Fictions*, trans. Andrew Hurley: 68–81. Penguin Books.

Bradley, F. H. 1978. *Appearance and Reality*. Oxford University Press.

Burgess, John and Gideon Rosen 1997. *A Subject with no Object*. Oxford University Press.

Campbell, Keith 1997. "The Metaphysic of Abstract Particulars", in *Properties*, ed. D. H. Mellor and Alex Oliver: 125–39. Oxford University Press.

Carnap, Rudolph 1956. "Empiricism, Semantics, and Ontology", in *Meaning and Necessity*: 205–21. University of Chicago Press.

Casati, Roberto and Achille Varzi 1994. *Holes and Other Superficialities*. MIT Press.

Chalmers, David 2009. "Ontological Anti-Realism", in David Chalmers, David Manley, and Ryan Wasserman (eds.), *Metametaphysics*. 77–129. Oxford University Press.

Cohen, S. Marc 2003. "Aristotle's Metaphysics", *Stanford Encyclopedia of Philosophy*.

Corkum, Phil 2008. "Aristotle on Ontological Dependence", *Phronesis* 53: 65–92.

Descartes, René 1985. *The Philosophical Writings of Descartes*, trans. and ed. John Cottingham, Robert Stoothoff, and Dugald Murdoch. Cambridge University Press.

d'Espagnat, Bernard 1983. *In Search of Reality*. Springer-Verlag.

Dorr, Cian 2005. "What We Disagree About When We Disagree About Ontology", in *Fictionalism in Metaphysics*, ed. Mark Kalderon. Oxford University Press.

Dummett, Michael 1978. "The Philosophical Basis of Intuitionistic Logic", in *Truth and Other Enigmas*: 215–47. Harvard University Press.

Feuerbach, Ludwig 1989. *The Essence of Christianity*, trans. George Eliot. Prometheus Books.

Field, Hartry 1980. *Science without Numbers*. Princeton University Press.

Fine, Kit 1991. "The Study of Ontology", *Noûs* 25: 263–94.

Fine, Kit 1994. "Ontological Dependence", *Proceedings of the Aristotelian Society* 95: 269–90.

Fine, Kit 2001. "The Question of Realism", *Philosophers' Imprint* 1: 1–30.

Frede, Michael 1987. "Substance in Aristotle's Metaphysics", in *Essays in Ancient Philosophy*. University of Minnesota Press.

Gill, Mary Louise 1989. *Aristotle on Substance: The Paradox of Unity*. Princeton University Press.

Hawthorne, John and Andrew Cortens 1995. "Towards Ontological Nihilism", *Philosophical Studies* 79: 143–65.

Hofweber, Thomas 2005. "A Puzzle about Ontology", *Noûs* 39: 256–83.

Kant, Immanuel 1965. *Critique of Pure Reason*, trans. Norman Kemp Smith. St. Martin's Press.

Kim, Jaegwon: 1993. "Postscripts on Supervenience", in *Supervenience and Mind: Selected Philosophical Essays*: 161–74. Cambridge University Press.

Leibniz, G. W. F. 1989. *Philosophical Essays*, trans. and ed. Roger Ariew and Daniel Garber. Hackett.

Lewis, David 1986. *On the Plurality of Worlds*. Basil Blackwell.

Lewis, David 1991. *Parts of Classes*. Basil Blackwell.

Lewis, David 1999a. "New work for a theory of universals", in *Papers in Metaphysics and Epistemology*: 8–55. Cambridge University Press.

Lewis, David 1999b. "Putnam's paradox", in *Papers in Metaphysics and Epistemology*: 56–77. Cambridge University Press.

Lewis, David 1999c. "Noneism or allism?" in *Papers in Metaphysics and Epistemology*: 152–63. Cambridge University Press.

Loewer, Barry 2001. "From Physics to Physicalism", in *Physicalism and its Discontents*, ed. Carl Gillet and Barry Loewer: 37–56. Cambridge University Press.

Loux, Michael 1991. *Primary Ousia: An Essay on Aristotle's Metaphysics Z and H*. Cornell University Press.

Lowe, E. J. 2005. "Ontological Dependence", *Stanford Encyclopedia of Philosophy*.

McLaughlin, Brian and Karen Bennett 2005. "Supervenience", *Stanford Encyclopedia of Philosophy*.

Meinong, Alexius 1960. "The Theory of Objects", in *Realism and the Background of Phenomenology*, ed. Roderick M. Chisholm, trans. Isaac Levi, B. D. Terrell, and Roderick M. Chisholm: 76–117. Ridgeview Publishing.

Moore, G. E. 1959. "Proof of an External World", in *Philosophical Papers by George Edward Moore*: 127–50. George Allen & Unwin.

Nietzsche, Friedrich 1987. "The Twilight of the Idols", in *The Portable Nietzsche*, ed. and trans. Walter Kaufmann: 463–564. Penguin Books.

Nolan, Daniel 1997. "Impossible Worlds: A Modest Approach", in *Note Dame Journal of Formal Logic* 38: 535–72.

Norton, John 2004. "The Hole Argument", *Stanford Encyclopedia of Philosophy*.

Owen, G. E. L. 1986a. "Logic and Metaphysics in Some Earlier Works of Aristotle", in *Logic, Science, and Dialectic: Collected Papers in Greek Philosophy*, ed. Martha Nussbaum: 180–99. Cornell University Press.

Owen, G. E. L. 1986b. "Aristotle on the Snares of Ontology", in *Logic, Science, and Dialectic: Collected Paper in Greek Philosophy*: 259–78.

Plato 1961. *Collected Dialogues*, ed. Edith Hamilton and Huntington Cairus. Princeton University Press.

Price. Huw 1997. "Carnap, Quine and the fate of metaphysics", *Electronic Journal of Analytic Philosophy* 5: <http://ejap.louisiana.edu/EJAP/1997.spring/price 976.html>

Priest, Graham 1997. "Sylvan's Box", *Notre Dame Journal of Formal Logic* 38: 573–82.

Prior, Arthur 1969. *Past, Present, and Future*. Oxford University Press.

Quine, W. V. O. 1960a. *Word and Object*. M. I. T. Press.

Quine, W. V. O. 1960b. "Variables Explained Away", *Proceedings of the American Philosophical Society* 104: 343–7.

Quine, W. V. O. 1963a. "On What There Is", in *From a Logical Point of View*: 1–19. Harper & Row.

Quine, W. V. O. 1963b. "Logic and the Reification of Universals", in *From a Logical Point of View*: 102–29.

Quine, W. V. O. 1966a. "On Carnap's Views on Ontology", in *The Ways of Paradox and Other Essays*: 203–11. Harvard University Press.

Quine, W. V. O. 1966b. "Ontological Reduction and the World of Numbers", in *The Ways of Paradox and Other Essays*: 212–20.

Quine, W. V. O. 1969. "Ontological Relativity", in *Ontological Relativity and Other Essays*: 26–68.

Quine, W. V. O. 1981. "Things and their Place in Theories", in *Theories and Things*: 1–23. Harvard University Press.

Quine, W. V. O. 1992. *Pursuit of Truth*. Harvard University Press.

Scaltsas, Theodore 1994. "Substantial Holism", in *Unity, Identity, and Explanation in Aristotle's Metaphysics*, eds Theodore Scaltsas, David Charles, and Mary Louise Gill: 107–28. Clarendon Press.

Schaffer, Jonathan 2010a. "Monism: The Priority of the Whole", *Philosophical Review* 119: 31–76.

Schaffer, Jonathan 2010b. "The Least Discerning and Most Promiscuous Truthmaker", *Philosophical Quarterly* 60 (239): 307–24.

Schaffer, Jonathan 2009. "Spacetime the One Substance". *Philosophical Studies* 145: 131–48.

Schlick, Moritz 1959. "Positivism and Realism", in *Logical Positivism*, ed. A. J. Ayer: 82–107. Macmillan Publishing.

Sider, Theodore 2001. *Four-Dimensionalism: An Ontology of Persistence and Time*. Oxford University Press.

Spinoza, Benedict 1960. "The Ethics", in *The Rationalists*: 179–406. Anchor Press.

Strawson, P. F. 1959. *Individuals: An Essay in Descriptive Metaphysics*. Routledge.

Taylor, A. E. 1961. *Elements of Metaphysics*. Barnes & Noble.

Urmson, J. O. 1956. *Philosophical Analysis: Its Development Between the Two World Wars*. Oxford University Press.

Van Inwagen, Peter 2000. "Quantification and Fictional Discourse", in *Empty Names, Fiction, and the Puzzles of Non-Existence*, eds Anthony Everett and Thomas Hofweber: 235–47. CSLI Publications.

Wedin, Michael 2000. *Aristotle's Theory of Substance: The Categories and Metaphysics Z*. Oxford University Press.

Wisdom, John 1933. "Logical Constructions (V)", *Mind* 42: 186–202.

Yablo, Stephen 1998. "Does Ontology Rest on a Mistake?" *Proceedings of the Aristotelian Society*, 72 (Supp.): 229–61.

Yablo, Stephen 2001. "Go Figure: A Path through Fictionalism", *Midwest Studies in Philosophy* 25: 72–102.

PART II
Identity

Introduction

On the face of it, identity seems like the simplest of relations: everything is identical with itself and with nothing else. Much of the philosophical interest in identity revolves around the proposal that there is a certain tight connection between identity and shared properties: for any objects x and y, x is identical to y if and only if x has every property that y has and vice versa. This biconditional claim is the conjunction of two conditional claims. First, the Indiscernibility of Identicals: if x and y are identical, then they share all of their properties. Second, the Identity of Indiscernibles: if x and y share all of their properties, then they are identical. (The label "Leibniz's Law" is often used in connection with these claims, sometimes to refer to the biconditional and sometimes for one or the other of the conditional claims.)

The Indiscernibility of Identicals is irresistible. For suppose that o_1 and o_2 are identical but that o_1 has different properties from o_2. Since, by hypothesis, o_2 *just is* o_1, to say that o_2 has different properties from o_1 would be to say that o_1 has different properties from o_1. But it's simply incoherent to say that something has different properties from itself. So identical items can't differ with respect to their properties. The Identity of Indiscernibles may seem less obvious. Why couldn't there be two different objects that have all the same properties? To see why one would be inclined to accept it, it helps to consider the full range of properties that an object can be said to have. o_1 has the property of being identical to o_1. This is o_1's "identity property." On the supposition that o_1 and o_2 have *all* the same properties, o_2 must have o_1's identity property as well. So o_2 has the property of being identical to o_1. It therefore seems to follow trivially from some things' sharing all of their properties that they are identical.

Max Black's "The Identity of Indiscernibles" (chapter 8) is a dialogue – between the characters A and B – about the truth of the Identity of Indiscernibles. A begins by presenting arguments for this principle which (like the one sketched above) turn on the fact that distinct objects will always differ with respect to their identity properties. B balks at these supposed properties, and insists that – if this is going to be an interesting principle – 'properties' must be construed more narrowly, to exclude identity properties. B then presents a now-famous counterexample to the Identity of Indiscernibles: it is possible for there to be a world containing nothing but two iron spheres that are indistinguishable in all respects but nevertheless distinct. A attempts to resist the counterexample by finding properties that they would not

Metaphysics: An Anthology, Second Edition. Edited by Jaegwon Kim, Daniel Z. Korman and Ernest Sosa.
Editorial material and organization © 2012 Blackwell Publishing Ltd. Published 2012 by Blackwell Publishing Ltd.

share in common – for instance, relational properties that they bear to one another or to the places that they occupy – as well as by trying to show that there is something incoherent about the envisaged scenario.

In "Primitive Thisness and Primitive Identity" (chapter 9), Robert M. Adams defends a view about the nature of identity properties, or, as he calls them, "thisnesses." Adams argues that thisnesses are nonqualitative, that is, they cannot be reduced to any general, qualitative features of the individuals whose thisnesses they are. Some of Adams's arguments turn on Black-style counterexamples, but he also supplies a novel style of argument which turns on the less controversial claim that there can be objects that merely are *nearly* indiscernible. Adams goes on to defend the view that transworld identity is primitive – that is, facts about which individuals in a world are identical to which individuals in other worlds are not entirely determined by facts about the distribution of qualities in those worlds. He does so by arguing that it is possible for there to be entire worlds that are qualitatively identical and yet nevertheless contain different individuals.

In "Identity and Necessity" (chapter 10), Saul Kripke presents a number of insights which, in the words of Richard Rorty, "stood analytic philosophy on its ear," changing the face of metaphysics as well as the philosophy of language and the philosophy of mind. Kripke's aim was to challenge (what was at the time) the received view that empirical identity claims – for instance, that Hesperus is Phosphorus and that heat is molecular motion – are all contingent. Along the way, he introduces his distinction between rigid and non-rigid designators, challenges "telescope views" of knowledge about possible scenarios, presents his famous "Humphrey objection" to David Lewis's counterpart theory, shows that some necessary truths cannot be known a priori, and argues for the necessity of scientific identities. He also overturns the very attractive and (at the time) widely held contingent identity thesis in the philosophy of mind, that is, that mental properties are in fact identical to their neural correlates, but could have failed to be identical to them.

In "Contingent Identity" (chapter 11), Allan Gibbard argues that there are at least *some* cases of objects that are only contingently identical. He focuses on a case in which a statue, "Goliath," and the lump of clay of which it is constituted, "Lumpl," are created simultaneously and later destroyed simultaneously. It is extremely tempting to suppose that Lumpl and Goliath are identical: after all they occupy exactly the same location and share all the same parts for the entirety of their existence. But it is possible for them to have been distinct. For instance, if Lumpl had been squashed into a ball, it would have existed in the absence of Goliath and therefore would not have been identical to Goliath. This proposal, although highly attractive, seems to run afoul of the Indiscernibility of Identicals principle mentioned above. Lumpl, but not Goliath, has the property of being able to survive squashing. Goliath, but not Lumpl, has the property of necessarily being identical to Goliath. Gibbard defends his proposal against this sort of objection by invoking a Quinean treatment of modal predicates. (See chapters 35, 36, and 39 for discussion of alternative treatments of this problem of material constitution, and see chapter 14 for further discussion of this Quinean treatment.)

The final two papers are on the topic of vague identity. Can it sometimes be vague whether something at one time is identical to something at an earlier or later time? On the face of it, it seems intuitively obvious that there can be vague identities. For instance, suppose that the Los Angeles Lakers get a new general manager, who promptly renames the team, trades over half of the players, hires a new head coach, and moves the resultant team to a new city. Is this team the very team that was once called "the Lakers"? Or is it a new team, which first came into existence sometime after these changes began? There may seem to be no determinate fact of the matter whether this team is the Lakers (under a new name) or a brand new team. Intuitively, it can be vague whether a thing at one time and a thing at a different time are the same thing, just as it can be vague whether a certain shade of turquoise counts as blue or whether a certain person counts as bald.

In "Can There Be Vague Objects?" (chapter 12), Gareth Evans argues that vague identity is impossible. His argument runs roughly as follows: If it were indeterminate whether A is identical to B, then A and B would have different properties. After all, A would have the property of being determinately identical to A, and B would lack this property. But if they have different properties then, by the Indiscernibility of Identicals (or, more cautiously, the Nonidentity of Discernibles), A and B must not be identical. So the assumption that we had a case of vague identity turns out to be unstable, since that assumption leads to the conclusion that this is a case of nonidentity.

So what should we say about the intuitive cases of vague identities, in light of Evans's argument? In "Vague Identity" (chapter 13), Robert C. Stalnaker maintains that the conclusion of the argument is compatible with our intuitions about these cases. (Stalnaker attributes the argument to Nathan Salmon, who discovered the argument independently from Evans.) Stalnaker observes that the argument against vague identity shows only that 'is identical to' cannot itself be vague. But identity statements as a whole may nevertheless be vague if 'is identical to' is flanked by vague expressions. For instance, 'Sue is Harry's best friend' might be vague because 'Harry's best friend' is vague. Stalnaker argues that paradigm cases of vague identity over time can be accommodated in the same way, that is, by maintaining that it is indeterminate which of various objects are referred to by the names flanking the identity predicate. He shows that this response is available on both of the leading theories of persistence (see Part VI on three-dimensionalism and four-dimensionalism).

Further Reading

Baker, L. R. (1997). "Why Constitution is not Identity," *The Journal of Philosophy*, 94: 599–621.

Chisholm, R. M. (1967). "Identity through Possible Worlds: Some Questions," *Noûs* 1: 1–8.

Geach, P. T. (1972). "Identity" and "Identity – A Reply," in *Logic Matters*. Oxford: Basil Blackwell.

Hawthorne, J. (1995). "The Bundle Theory of Substance and the Identity of Indiscernibles," *Analysis* 55: 191–6.

Hawthorne, J. (2003). "Identity," in M. J. Loux and D. W. Zimmerman (eds.), *The Oxford Handbook of Metaphysics*. Oxford: Oxford University Press, pp. 99–130.

Johnston, M. (1992). "Constitution Is Not Identity," *Mind* 101: 89–106.

Lowe, E. J. (1989). "What is a Criterion of Identity?," *Philosophical Quarterly* 39: 1–21.

Parsons, T. (1987). "Entities Without Identity," *Philosophical Perspectives* 1: 1–19.

Perry, J. (1970). "The Same F," *Philosophical Review* 79: 181–200.

Wiggins, D. (2001). *Sameness and Substance Renewed*. New York: Cambridge University Press.

8

The Identity of Indiscernibles

Max Black

A: The principle of the Identity of Indiscernibles seems to me obviously true. And I don't see how we are going to define identity or establish the connection between mathematics and logic without using it.

B: It seems to me obviously false. And your troubles as a mathematical logician are beside the point. If the principle is false, you have no right to use it.

A: You simply *say* it's false – and even if you said so three times, that wouldn't make it so.

B: Well, you haven't done anything more yourself than assert the principle to be true. As Bradley once said, 'assertion can demand no more than counter-assertion; and what is affirmed on the one side, we on the other can simply deny.'

A: How will this do for an argument? If two things, *a* and *b*, are given, the first has the property of being identical with *a*. Now *b* cannot have this property, for else *b* would be *a*, and we should have only one thing, not two as assumed. Hence *a* has at least one property, which *b* does not have, that is to say the property of being identical with *a*.

B: This is a roundabout way of saying nothing, for '*a* has the property of being identical with *a*' means no more than '*a* is *a*'. When you begin to say '*a* is …' I am supposed to know what thing you are referring to as '*a*' and I expect to be told something about that thing. But when you end the sentence with the words '… is *a*', I am left still waiting. The sentence '*a* is *a*' is a useless tautology.

A: Are you as scornful about difference as about identity? For *a* also has, and *b* does not have, the property of being different from *b*. This is a second property that the one thing has but not the other.

B: All you are saying is that *b* is different from *a*. I think the form of words '*a* is different from *b*' does have the advantage over '*a* is *a*' that it might be used to give information. I might learn from hearing it used that '*a*' and '*b*' were applied to different things. But this is not what you want to say, since you are trying to use the names, not mention them. When I already know what '*a*' and '*b*' stand for, '*a* is different from *b*' tells me nothing. It, too, is a useless tautology.

A: I wouldn't have expected you to treat 'tautology' as a term of abuse. Tautology or not, the sentence has a philosophical use. It expresses the necessary truth that different things have at least one property not in common. Thus different things must be discernible; and hence, by contraposition, indiscernible things must be identical. Q.E.D.

B: Why obscure matters by this old-fashioned language? By 'indiscernible' I suppose you mean the same as 'having all properties in common'. Do

Max Black, "The Identity of Indiscernibles," *Mind*, 51 (1952), reprinted in Max Black, *Problems of Analysis* (1954), pp. 204–16. Reproduced by permission.

Metaphysics: An Anthology, Second Edition. Edited by Jaegwon Kim, Daniel Z. Korman and Ernest Sosa.

you claim to have proved that two things having all their properties in common are identical?

A: Exactly.

B: Then this is a poor way of stating your conclusion. If a and b are identical, there is just one thing having the two names 'a' and 'b'; and in that case it is absurd to say that a and b are two. Conversely, once you have supposed there are two things having all their properties in common, you can't without contradicting yourself say that they are 'identical'.

A: I can't believe you were really misled. I simply meant to say it is logically impossible for two things to have all their properties in common. I showed that a must have at least two properties – the property of being identical with a and the property of being different from b – neither of which can be a property of b. Doesn't this prove the principle of Identity of Indiscernibles?

B: Perhaps you have proved something. If so, the nature of your proof should show us exactly what you have proved. If you want to call 'being identical with a' a 'property' I suppose I can't prevent you. But you must then accept the consequences of this way of talking. All you mean when you say 'a has the property of being identical with a' is that a is a. And all you mean when you say 'b does not have the property of being identical with a' is that b is not a. So what you have 'proved' is that a is a and b is not a; that is to say, b and a are different. Similarly, when you said that a, but not b, had the property of being different from b, you were simply saying that a and b were different. In fact you are merely redescribing the hypothesis that a and b are different by calling it a case of 'difference of properties'. Drop the misleading description and your famous principle reduces to the truism that different things are different. How true! And how uninteresting!

A: Well, the properties of identity and difference may be uninteresting, but they are properties. If I had shown that grass was green, I suppose you would say I hadn't shown that grass was coloured.

B: You certainly would not have shown that grass had any colour other than green.

A: What it comes to is that you object to the conclusion of my argument following from the premise that a and b are different.

B: No, I object to the triviality of the conclusion. If you want to have an interesting principle to

defend, you must interpret 'property' more narrowly – enough so, at any rate, for 'identity' and 'difference' not to count as properties.

A: Your notion of an interesting principle seems to be one which I shall have difficulty in establishing. Will you at least allow me to include among 'properties' what are sometimes called 'relational characteristics' – like being married to Caesar or being at a distance from London?

B: Why not? If you are going to defend the principle, it is for you to decide what version you wish to defend.

A: In that case, I don't need to count identity and difference as properties. Here is a different argument that seems to me quite conclusive. The only way we can discover that two different things exist is by finding out that one has a quality not possessed by the other or else that one has a relational characteristic that the other hasn't.

If both are blue and hard and sweet and so on, and have the same shape and dimensions and are in the same relations to everything in the universe, it is logically impossible to tell them apart. The supposition that in such a case there might really be two things would be unverifiable in principle. Hence it would be meaningless.

B: You are going too fast for me.

A: Think of it this way. If the principle were false, the fact that I can see only two of your hands would be no proof that you had just two. And even if every conceivable test agreed with the supposition that you had two hands, you might all the time have three, four, or any number. You might have nine hands, different from one another and all indistinguishable from your left hand, and nine more all different from each other but indistinguishable from your right hand. And even if you really did have just two hands, and no more, neither you nor I nor anybody else could ever know that fact. This is too much for me to swallow. This is the kind of absurdity you get into, as soon as you abandon verifiability as a test of meaning.

B: Far be it from me to abandon your sacred cow. Before I give you a direct answer, let me try to describe a counter-example.

Isn't it logically possible that the universe should have contained nothing but two exactly similar spheres? We might suppose that each was made of chemically pure iron, had a diameter of one mile, that they had the same temperature, colour, and so on, and that nothing else existed. Then every quality and relational characteristic of the one would also be a property of the other. Now if what I am describing is logically possible, it is not impossible for two things to have all their properties in common. This seems to me to *refute* the Principle.

A: Your supposition, I repeat, isn't verifiable and therefore can't be regarded as meaningful. But supposing you *have* described a possible world, I still don't see that you have refuted the principle. Consider one of the spheres, *a*,...

B: How can I, since there is no way of telling them apart? *Which* one do you want me to consider?

A: This is very foolish. I mean either of the two spheres, leaving you to decide which one you wished to consider. If I were to say to you 'Take any book off the shelf', it would be foolish on your part to reply 'Which?'

B: It's a poor analogy. I know how to take a book off a shelf, but I don't know how to identify one of two spheres supposed to be alone in space and so symmetrically placed with respect to each other that neither has any quality or character the other does not also have.

A: All of which goes to show as I said before, the unverifiability of your supposition. Can't you imagine that one sphere has been designated as '*a*'?

B: I can imagine only what is logically possible. Now it is logically possible that somebody should enter the universe I have described, see one of the spheres on his left hand and proceed to call it '*a*'. I can imagine that all right, if that's enough to satisfy you.

A: Very well, now let me try to finish what I began to say about *a* ...

B: I still can't let you, because you, in your present situation, have no right to talk about *a*. All I have conceded is that if something were to happen to introduce a change into my universe, so that an observer entered and could see the two spheres, one of them could then have a name. But this would be a different supposition from the one I wanted to consider. My spheres don't yet have names. If an observer were to enter the scene, he could perhaps put a red mark on one of the spheres. You might just as well say 'By "*a*" I mean the sphere which would be the first to be

marked by a red mark if anyone were to arrive and were to proceed to make a red mark!' You might just as well ask me to consider the first daisy in my lawn that would be picked by a child, if a child were to come along and do the picking. This doesn't now distinguish any daisy from the others. You are just pretending to use a name.

A: And I think you are just pretending not to understand me. All I am asking you to do is to think of one of your spheres, no matter which, so that I may go on to say something about it when you give me a chance.

B: You talk as if naming an object and then thinking about it were the easiest thing in the world. But it isn't so easy. Suppose I tell you to name any spider in my garden: if you can catch one first or describe one uniquely, you can name it easily enough. But you can't pick one out, let alone 'name' it, by just thinking. You remind me of the mathematicians who thought that talking about an Axiom of Choice would really allow them to choose a single member of a collection when they had no criterion of choice.

A: At this rate you will never give me a chance to say anything. Let me try to make my point without using names. Each of the spheres will surely differ from the other in being at some distance from that other one, but at no distance from itself – that is to say, it will bear at least one relation to itself – *being at no distance from*, or *being in the same place as* – that it does not bear to the other. And this will serve to distinguish it from the other.

B: Not at all. *Each* will have the relational characteristic *being at a distance of two miles*, say, *from the centre of a sphere one mile in diameter*, etc. And each will have the relational characteristic (if you want to call it that) of *being in the same place as itself*. The two are alike in this respect as in all others.

A: But look here. Each sphere occupies a different place; and this at least will distinguish them from one another.

B: This sounds as if you thought the places had some independent existence, though I don't suppose you really think so. To say the spheres are in 'different places' is just to say that there is a distance between the two spheres; and we have already seen that that will not serve to distinguish them. Each is at a distance – indeed the same distance – from the other.

A: When I said they were at different places, I didn't mean simply that they were at a distance from one another. That one sphere is in a certain place does not entail the existence of any *other* sphere. So to say that one sphere is in its place, and the other in its place, and then to add that these places are different seems to me different from saying the spheres are at a distance from one another.

B: What does it mean to say 'a sphere is in its place'? Nothing at all, so far as I can see. Where else could it be? *All* you are saying is that the spheres are in different places.

A: Then my retort is, What does it mean to say 'Two spheres are in different places'? Or, as you so neatly put it, 'Where else could they be?'

B: You have a point. What I should have said was that your assertion that the spheres occupied different places said nothing at all, unless you were drawing attention to the necessary truth that different physical objects must be in different places. Now if two spheres must be in different places, as indeed they must, to say that the spheres occupy different places is to say no more than they are two spheres.

A: This is like a point you made before. You won't allow me to deduce anything from the supposition that there are two spheres.

B: Let me put it another way. In the two-sphere universe, the only reason for saying that the places occupied were different would be that different things occupied them. So in order to show the places were different, you would first have to show, in some other way, that the spheres were different. You will never be able to distinguish the spheres by means of the places they occupy.

A: A minute ago, you were willing to allow that somebody might give your spheres different names. Will you let me suppose that some traveller has visited your monotonous 'universe' and has named one sphere 'Castor' and the other 'Pollux'?

B: All right – provided you don't try to use those names yourself.

A: Wouldn't the traveller, at least, have to recognize that *being at a distance of two miles from Castor* was not the same property as being at a distance of two miles *from Pollux*?

B: I don't see why. If he were to see that Castor and Pollux had exactly the same properties, he would see that 'being at a distance of two miles from Castor' meant exactly the same as 'being at a distance of two miles from Pollux'.

A: They couldn't mean the same. If they did, '*being at a distance of two miles from Castor and at the same time not being at a distance of two miles from Pollux*' would be a self-contradictory description. But plenty of bodies could answer to this description. Again, if the two expressions meant the same, anything which was two miles from Castor would have to be two miles from Pollux – which is clearly false. So the two expressions don't mean the same, and the two spheres have at least two properties not in common.

B: Which?

A: *Being at a distance of two miles from Castor* and *being at a distance of two miles from Pollux*.

B: But now you are *using* the words 'Castor' and 'Pollux' as if they really stood for something. They are just our old friends '*a*' and '*b*' in disguise.

A: You surely don't want to say that the arrival of the name-giving traveller creates spatial properties? Perhaps we can't name your spheres and therefore can't name the corresponding properties; but the properties must be there.

B: What can this mean? The traveller has not visited the spheres, and the spheres have no names – neither 'Castor', nor 'Pollux', nor '*a*', nor '*b*', nor any others. Yet you still want to say they have certain properties which cannot be referred to without using names for the spheres. You want to say 'the property of being at a distance from Castor', though it is logically impossible for you to talk in this way. You can't speak, but you won't be silent.

A: How eloquent, and how unconvincing! But since you seem to have convinced yourself, at least, perhaps you can explain another thing that bothers me: I don't see that you have a right to talk as you do about places or spatial relations in connection with your so-called universe. So long as we are talking about our own universe – *the* universe – I know what you mean by 'distance', 'diameter', 'place' and so on. But in what you want to call a universe, even though it contains only two objects, I don't see what such words could mean. So far as I can see, you are applying these spatial terms in their present usage to a hypothetical situation which contradicts the presuppositions of that usage.

B: What do you mean by 'presupposition'?

A: Well, you spoke of measured distances, for one thing. Now this presupposes some means of measurement. Hence your 'universe' must contain at least a third thing – a ruler or some other measuring device.

B: Are you claiming that a universe must have at least three things in it? What is the least number of things required to make a world?

A: No, all I am saying is that you cannot describe a configuration as *spatial* unless it includes at least three objects. This is part of the meaning of 'spatial' – and it is no more mysterious than saying you can't have a game of chess without there existing at least thirty-five things (thirty-two pieces, a chessboard, and two players).

B: If this is all that bothers you, I can easily provide for three or any number of things without changing the force of my counter-example. The important thing, for my purpose, was that the configuration of two spheres was symmetrical. So long as we preserve this feature of the imaginary universe, we can now allow any number of objects to be found in it.

A: You mean any *even* number of objects.

B: Quite right. Why not imagine a plane running clear through space, with everything that happens on one side of it always exactly duplicated at an equal distance in the other side.

A: A kind of cosmic mirror producing real images.

B: Yes, except that there wouldn't be any mirror! The point is that in *this* world we can imagine any degree of complexity and change to occur. No reason to exclude rulers, compasses and weighing machines. No reason, for that matter, why the Battle of Waterloo shouldn't happen.

A: Twice over, you mean – with Napoleon surrendering later in two different places simultaneously!

B: Provided you wanted to call both of them 'Napoleon'.

A: So your point is that everything could be duplicated on the other side of the non-existent Looking Glass. I suppose whenever a man got married, his identical twin would be marrying the identical twin of the first man's fiancée?

B: Exactly.

A: Except that 'identical twins' wouldn't be *numerically* identical?

B: You seem to be agreeing with me.

A: Far from it. This is just a piece of gratuitous metaphysics. If the inhabitants of your world had enough sense to know what was sense and what wasn't, they would never suppose all the events in their world were duplicated. It would be much more sensible for them to regard the 'second' Napoleon as a mere mirror image – and similarly for all the other supposed 'duplicates'.

B: But they could walk through the 'mirror' and find water just as wet, sugar just as sweet, and grass just as green on the other side.

A: You don't understand me. They would not postulate 'another side'. A man looking at the 'mirror' would be seeing *himself*, not a duplicate. If he walked in a straight line toward the 'mirror', he would eventually find himself back at his starting point, not at a duplicate of his starting point. This would involve their having a different geometry from ours – but that would be preferable to the logician's nightmare of the reduplicated universe.

B: They might think so – until the twins really began to behave differently for the first time!

A: Now it's you who are tinkering with your supposition. You can't have your universe and change it too.

B: All right, I retract.

A: The more I think about your 'universe', the queerer it seems. What would happen when a man crossed your invisible 'mirror'? While he was actually crossing, his body would have to change shape, in order to preserve the symmetry. Would it gradually shrink to nothing and then expand again?

B: I confess I hadn't thought of that.

A: And here is something that explodes the whole notion. Would you say that one of the two Napoleons in your universe had his heart in the right place – literally, I mean?

B: Why, of course.

A: In that case his 'mirror-image' twin would have the heart on the opposite side of the body. One Napoleon would have his heart on the left of his body, and the other would have it on the right of his body.

B: It's a good point, though it would still make objects like spheres indistinguishable. But let me try again. Let me abandon the original idea of a *plane* of symmetry and suppose instead that we have only a *centre* of symmetry. I mean that everything that happened at any place would be exactly duplicated at a place an equal distance on the opposite side of the centre of symmetry. In short, the universe would be what the mathematicians call 'radially symmetrical'. And to avoid complications, we could suppose that the centre of symmetry itself was physically inaccessible, so that it would be impossible for any material body to pass through it. Now in *this* universe, identical twins would have to be either both right-handed or both left-handed.

A: Your universes are beginning to be as plentiful as blackberries. You are too ingenious to see the force of my argument about verifiability. Can't you see that your supposed description of a universe in which everything has its 'identical twin' doesn't describe anything verifiably different from a corresponding universe without such duplication? This must be so, no matter what kind of symmetry your universe manifested.

B: You are assuming that in order to verify that there are two things of a certain kind, it must be possible to show that one has a property not possessed by the other. But this is not so. A pair of very close but similar magnetic poles produce a characteristic field of force which assures me that there are two poles, even if I have no way of examining them separately. The presence of two exactly similar stars at a great distance might be detected by some resultant gravitational effect or by optical interference – or in some such similar way – even though we had no way of inspecting one in isolation from the other. Don't physicists say something like this about the electrons inside an atom? We can verify *that* there are two, that is to say a certain property of the whole configuration, even though there is no way of detecting any character that uniquely characterises any element of the configuration.

A: But if you were to approach your two stars one would have to be on your left and one on the right. And this would distinguish them.

B: I agree. Why shouldn't we say that the two stars are distinguishable – meaning that it would be possible for an observer to see one on his left and the other on his right, or more generally, that it would be *possible* for one star to come to have a relation to a third object that the second star would not have to that third object.

A: So you agree with me after all.

B: Not if you mean that the two stars do not have all their properties in common. All I said was that it was logically possible for them to enter into different relationships with a third object. But this would be a change in the universe.

A: If you are right, nothing unobserved would be observable. For the presence of an observer would always change it, and the observation would always be an observation of something else.

B: I don't say that every observation changes what is observed. My point is that there isn't any *being to the right or being to the left* in the two-sphere universe until an observer is introduced, that is to say until a real change is made.

A: But the spheres themselves wouldn't have changed.

B: Indeed they would: they would have acquired new relational characteristics. In the absence of any asymmetric observer, I repeat, the spheres would have all their properties in common (including, if you like, the power to enter into different relations with other objects). Hence the principle of Identity of Indiscernibles is false.

A: So perhaps you really do have twenty hands after all?

B: Not a bit of it. Nothing that I have said prevents me from holding that we can verify *that* there are exactly two. But we could know *that* two things existed without there being any way to distinguish one from the other. The Principle is false.

A: I am not surprised that you ended in this way, since you assumed it in the description of your fantastic 'universe'. Of course, if you began by assuming that the spheres were numerically different though qualitatively alike, you could end by 'proving' what you first assumed.

B: But I wasn't 'proving' anything. I tried to support my contention that it is logically possible for two things to have all their properties in common by giving an illustrative description. (Similarly, if I had to show it is logically possible for nothing at all to be seen, I would ask you to imagine a universe in which everybody was blind.) It was for you to show that my description concealed some hidden contradiction. And you haven't done so.

A: All the same I am not convinced.

B: Well, then, you ought to be.

9

Primitive Thisness and Primitive Identity

Robert M. Adams

Is the world – and are all possible worlds – constituted by purely qualitative facts, or does thisness hold a place beside suchness as a fundamental feature of reality? Some famous philosophers – Leibniz, Russell, and Ayer, for example – have believed in a purely qualitative constitution of things; others, such as Scotus, Kant, and Peirce, have held to primitive thisness. Recent discussions of direct, nondescriptive reference to individuals have brought renewed interest in the idea of primitive, nonqualitative thisness.

I am inclined to accept primitive thisness, but for reasons that do not depend very heavily on recent semantics. In the present essay I will try to justify my position – but even more to sort out some issues that are easily and often confused. I will begin (in section 1) by trying to elucidate some terms that will be important in the discussion. Leibniz will be discussed in section 2 as the archetypal believer in a purely qualitative universe. I will argue that his position is not inconsistent with the semantics of direct reference, and that proponents of primitive thisness must attack rather a certain doctrine of the Identity of Indiscernibles. Two types of argument against that doctrine will be analyzed and defended in sections 3 and 4.

Primitive thisness has been associated or even identified, in recent discussion, with primitive identity and non-identity of individuals in different possible worlds.[1] The association is appropriate, but the main issue about primitive transworld identity is quite different from that about primitive thisness, as will be argued in section 5, where I will also defend the primitive-ness of transworld identity. The sixth and final section of the paper will be devoted to some problems about necessary connections between qualitative properties and primitive thisnesses.

1 Thisness and Suchness

Three notions that we will use call for some elucidation at the outset. They are the notions of an *individual*, of a *thisness*, and of a purely qualitative property or (as I shall call it) a *suchness*.

By "individual" here I mean particulars such as persons, physical objects, and events. It is assumed that numbers and universals are not individuals in this sense, and that particular places and times are individuals if they have an absolute being and identity independent of their relation to particular physical objects and events.

Robert M. Adams, "Primitive Thisness and Primitive Identity," *Journal of Philosophy*, 76/1 (Jan. 1979): pp. 5–26. Reproduced by permission.

Metaphysics: An Anthology, Second Edition. Edited by Jaegwon Kim, Daniel Z. Korman and Ernest Sosa.

A thisness[2] is the property of being identical with a certain particular individual – not the property that we all share, of being identical with some individual or other, but my property of being identical with me, your property of being identical with you, etc. These properties have recently been called "essences,"[3] but that is historically unfortunate; for essences have normally been understood to be constituted by qualitative properties, and we are entertaining the possibility of nonqualitative thisnesses. In defining "thisness" as I have, I do not mean to deny that universals have analogous properties – for example, the property of being identical with the quality red. But since we are concerned here principally with the question whether the identity and distinctness of individuals is purely qualitative or not, it is useful to reserve the term "thisness" for the identities of individuals.

It may be controversial to speak of a "property" of being identical with me. I want the word "property" to carry as light a metaphysical load here as possible. "Thisness" is intended to be a synonym or translation of the traditional term "haecceity" (in Latin, *haecceitas*), which so far as I know was invented by Duns Scotus. Like many medieval philosophers, Scotus regarded properties as components of the things that have them. He introduced haecceities (thisnesses), accordingly, as a special sort of metaphysical component of individuals.[4] I am not proposing to revive this aspect of his conception of a haecceity, because I am not committed to regarding properties as components of individuals. To deny that thisnesses are purely qualitative is not necessarily to postulate "bare particulars," substrata without qualities of their own, which would be what was left of the individual when all its qualitative properties were subtracted. Conversely, to hold that thisnesses are purely qualitative is not to imply that individuals are nothing but bundles of qualities, for qualities may not be components of individuals at all.

We could probably conduct our investigation, in somewhat different terms, without referring to thisnesses as properties; but the concept of a *suchness* is not so dispensable. Without the distinction between the qualitative and the nonqualitative, the subject of this paper does not exist. I believe the concept, and the distinction, can be made clear enough to work with, though not, I fear, clear enough to place them above suspicion.

We might try to capture the idea by saying that a property is purely qualitative – a suchness – if and only if it could be expressed, in a language sufficiently rich, without the aid of such referential devices as proper names, proper adjectives and verbs (such as "Leibnizian" and "pegasizes"), indexical expressions, and referential uses of definite descriptions. That seems substantially right, but may be suspected of circularity, on the ground that the distinction between qualitative and nonqualitative might be prior to the notions of some of those referential devices. I doubt that it really is circular, in view of the separation between semantic and metaphysical issues for which I shall argue in section 2; but it would take us too far afield to pursue the issue of circularity here.

There is another and possibly more illuminating approach to the definition of "suchness". All the properties that are, in certain senses, general (capable of being possessed by different individuals) and nonrelational are suchnesses. More precisely, let us say that a *basic suchness* is a property that satisfies the following three conditions. (1) It is not a thisness and is not equivalent to one. (2) It is not a property of being related in one way or another to one or more particular individuals (or to their thisnesses). This is not to deny that some basic suchnesses are in a sense relational (and thus do not fall in the Aristotelian category of Quality, though they count as "purely qualitative" for present purposes). An example may help to clarify this. The property of owning the house at 1011 Rose Avenue, Ann Arbor, Michigan, is not a basic suchness, although several different individuals have had it, because it involves the thisness of that particular house. But the property of being a home-owner is a basic suchness, although relational, because having it does not depend on which particular home one owns. (3) A basic suchness is not a property of being identical with or related in one way or another to an extensionally defined set that has an individual among its members, or among its members' members, or among its members' members' members, etc. Thus, if being an American is to be analyzed as a relation to a set of actual people and places, it is not a basic suchness.

These three conditions may be taken as jointly sufficient for being a suchness, but it is not clear that they are also necessary for being a suchness.

For it seems intuitively that any property that is constructed by certain operations out of purely qualitative properties must itself be purely qualitative. The operations I have in mind for the construction are of two sorts. (1) They may be logical, such as those expressed by "not", "or", and $\ulcorner(\exists x)\phi(\ ,x)\urcorner$, where the property ascribed to x by $\ulcorner(\exists y)\phi(y,x)\urcorner$ is a basic suchness or constructed by allowed operations out of basic suchnesses. Or (2) they may be epistemic, such as those expressed by $\ulcorner$believes that $p\urcorner$ and $\ulcorner$wishes that $p\urcorner$, where p is a proposition constructed, by allowed operations, solely out of basic suchnesses. So if your thisness, or a property equivalent to the property of being (identical with) you, could be constructed in these ways as a complex of basic suchnesses, it would seem intuitively to be a suchness, although (by definition) it is not a *basic* suchness. Indeed, as we shall see, this is precisely the way in which Leibniz attempts to account for individuality in a purely qualitative universe.

So as not to beg the question against him, let us define a *suchness* as a property that is either a basic suchness or constructed out of basic suchnesses in such a way as I have indicated. This recursive definition of "suchness" seems to me to capture the notion I want to discuss; but it depends on notions of property construction and of being a relation to a particular individual which may themselves be somewhat unclear or otherwise debatable. In any event, I am prepared to accept the notion of a suchness, and related notions of qualitativeness of facts, similarities, differences, etc., as primitive if they cannot be satisfactorily defined. Some philosophers may entirely reject this distinction between the qualitative and the nonqualitative, or may doubt that there are any properties that really ought to count as suchnesses under it. We shall not be concerned here with these doubts, but rather with what can be said, within the framework of the distinction, against those philosophers who think that all properties are suchnesses and all facts purely qualitative.

2   The Leibnizian Position

Leibniz held, as I have suggested, that the thisness of each particular individual *is* a suchness. "Singulars," he said, "are in fact *infimae species*," the lowest or final species, the most specific members of the system of kinds. In this, as he sometimes remarked, he was extending to all individuals the doctrine of Thomas Aquinas about angels, that each one constitutes a separate species.[5]

The idea behind this claim is fairly simple, though the structure it postulates for thisnesses is infinitely complex. According to Leibniz, the terms of all propositions, at least as they are apprehended by the omniscience of God, are analyzable into simple, purely qualitative concepts. The construction of complex concepts out of simple ones is by logical operations; Leibniz thinks principally of conjunction and negation. The concept of an individual, which as we may put it expresses the property of being that individual, differs from more general concepts in being *complete*.[6] What makes a thing an individual, in other words, is that, in the logical construction of its concept, differentia is added to differentia until a concept is reached so specific that no new content can consistently be added to it.

Leibniz expresses this notion of completeness by saying that the concept of an individual implies every predicate of the individual. He inferred, notoriously, that alternative careers cannot be possible for the same individual. If a man never marries, for example, the concept of him must contain the predicate of never marrying, and so it would have been contradictory for *him* to have married.[7] I see no need to incorporate this implausible thesis in the theory of purely qualitative thisnesses. For if God can form complete concepts in the way that Leibniz supposes, he can also form the concept of a being that satisfies *either* one *or* another *or* another … of them.[8] If individuals are defined by disjunctive concepts of the latter sort, there are alternative careers, in different possible worlds, that they could have had. And if Leibnizian complete concepts are purely qualitative, so are disjunctions of them. The completeness of individual concepts, at least in the form actually maintained by Leibniz, is therefore not to be regarded as an integral part of the "Leibnizian position" under discussion here.

If we want an up-to-date argument for primitive, *non*qualitative thisnesses, we may be tempted to seek it in the semantics of direct reference. Several philosophers have made a persuasive case for the view that we often succeed in referring to a particular individual without knowing any clearly qualitative property, or even any disjunction of such properties, that a thing must possess in order to be that individual. Such direct reference is commonly effected by the use of proper names and indexical expressions, and sometimes by what has been called the "referential" use of descriptions.[9] If these claims are correct (as I believe they are), doesn't it follow that thisnesses are primitive and nonqualitative?

Yes and no. It follows that thisnesses are *semantically* primitive – that is, that we can express them (and know that we express them) without understanding each thisness (the property of being this or that individual) in terms of some other property or properties, better known to us, into which it can be analyzed or with which it is equivalent. But it does not follow that thisnesses *are* not analyzable into, equivalent with, or even identical with, purely qualitative properties or suchnesses, as claimed by Leibniz. Thus it does not follow that we are entitled to say that thisnesses are *metaphysically* primitive in the sense that interests us here, or (more precisely) that they are nonqualitative.

For Leibniz could certainly accept direct reference without giving up his conception of thisnesses as qualitative properties. All he must say is that we can refer to individuals, and thus express their thisnesses, without understanding the analyses that show the thisnesses to be qualitative. And that he believed in any case. On his view the complete, definitive concept of an individual is infinitely complex and, therefore, cannot be distinctly apprehended by any finite mind, but only by God. Hence *we* must refer to the concept of the individual by reference to the individual (as "the individual notion or haecceity of Alexander,"[10] for example), rather than referring to the individual as the one who satisfies the concept.

We may rely intuitively on direct reference in arguing for nonqualitative thisnesses, but the issue of direct reference is not the center of our metaphysical inquiry. The purely qualitative conception of individuality stands or falls, rather, with a certain doctrine of the Identity of Indiscernibles.

The Identity of Indiscernibles might be defined, in versions of increasing strength, as the doctrine that no two distinct individuals can share (1) all their properties, or (2) all their suchnesses, or (3) all their nonrelational suchnesses. Leibniz takes no pains to distinguish these three doctrines, because he holds all of them; but it is only the second that concerns us here. The first is utterly trivial. If thisnesses are properties, of course two distinct individuals, Castor and Pollux, cannot have all their properties in common. For Castor must have the properties of being identical with Castor and not being identical with Pollux, which Pollux cannot share.[11] The third doctrine, rejecting the possibility of individuals differing in relational suchnesses alone, is a most interesting thesis, but much more than needs to be claimed in holding that reality must be purely qualitative. Let us therefore here reserve the title "Identity of Indiscernibles" for the doctrine that any two distinct individuals must differ in some suchness, *either* relational *or* nonrelational.

I say, the doctrine that they *must* so differ. Leibniz commonly states this principle, and the stronger principle about relations, in the language of necessity. And well he might; for he derives them from his theory of the nature of an individual substance, and ultimately from his conception of the nature of truth, which he surely regarded as absolutely necessary.[12] He was not perfectly consistent about this. He seemed to admit to Clarke that there could have been two perfectly indiscernible things. But, as Clarke remarked, some of Leibniz's arguments require the claim of necessity.[13] And it is only if necessity is claimed, that philosophically interesting objections can be raised to the Identity of Indiscernibles. For surely we have no reason to believe that there actually are distinct individuals that share all their qualitative properties, relational as well as nonrelational.

Here we are concerned with the necessary connection between the Identity of Indiscernibles, in the sense I have picked out, and Leibniz's conception of thisnesses as suchnesses. If individuals are *infimae species*, then "the principle of individuation is always some specific difference";[14] individuals must be distinguished by their suchnesses. Conversely, the clearest way of proving the distinctness of two properties is usually to find a possible case in which one would be exemplified without the other. In order to establish the distinctness of thisnesses from all suchnesses, therefore, one might try to exhibit possible cases in which two things would possess all the same suchnesses, but with different thisnesses. That is, one might seek counter-examples to refute the Identity of Indiscernibles.

Indeed a refutation of that doctrine is precisely what is required for the defense of nonqualitative thisnesses. For suppose the Identity of Indiscernibles is true. And suppose further, as Leibniz did and as believers in the doctrine may be expected to suppose, that it is true of possible worlds as well as of individuals, so that no two possible worlds are exactly alike in all qualitative respects. Then for each possible individual there will be a suchness of the disjunctive form:

having suchnesses S_{t1} in a world that has suchnesses $S_{\omega1}$, or

having suchnesses S_{t2} in a world that has suchnesses $S_{\omega2}$, or ...

which that individual will possess in every world in which it occurs, and which no other individual will possess in any possible world.[15] This suchness will, therefore, be necessarily equivalent to the property of being that individual, and, since there will be such a suchness for every individual, it follows that every individual's thisness will be equivalent to a suchness.

Perhaps it does not follow immediately that every possible individual's thisness will *be* a suchness. If being an even prime and being the successor of 1 may be distinct though necessarily equivalent properties, some thisness and some suchness might also be distinct though necessarily equivalent. But if *every* thisness must be necessarily equivalent to a suchness, it will be hard to show that thisnesses distinct from suchnesses cannot be dispensed with, or that possible worlds cannot all be constituted purely qualitatively.

On the other hand, if it is possible for there to be distinct but qualitatively indiscernible individuals, it is possible for there to be individuals whose thisnesses are both distinct from all suchnesses and necessarily equivalent to no suchness. And in that case there is some point to distinguishing the thisnesses of individuals systematically from their suchnesses. For it is plausible to suppose that the structure of individuality is sufficiently similar in all cases that, if in some possible cases thisnesses would be distinct from all suchnesses, then thisnesses are universally distinct from suchnesses – even if some thisnesses (including, for all we know, those of all actual individuals) are necessarily equivalent to some suchnesses.

3 The Dispersal Arguments against the Identity of Indiscernibles

The standard argument against the Identity of Indiscernibles, going back at least to Kant,[16] is from spatial dispersal. Max Black's version[17] is fairly well known. We are to imagine a universe consisting solely of two large, solid globes of iron. They always have been, are, and always will be exactly similar in shape (perfectly spherical), size, chemical composition, color – in short, in every qualitative respect. They even share all their relational suchnesses; for example, each of them has the property of being two diameters from another iron globe similar to itself. Such a universe seems to be logically possible; hence it is concluded that there could be two qualitatively indiscernible things and that the Identity of Indiscernibles is false.

Similar arguments may be devised using much more complicated imaginary universes, which may have language-users in them. Such universes may be perfectly symmetrical about a central point, line, or plane, throughout their history. Or they may always repeat themselves to infinity in every direction, like a monstrous three-dimensional wallpaper pattern.

The reason that is assumed to show that the indiscernibles in these imaginary universes are not identical is not that they have different properties, but that they are spatially dispersed, spatially distant from one another. The axiom about identity that is used here is not that the same thing cannot both have and lack the same property, but that the same thing cannot be in two places at once – that is, cannot be spatially distant from itself.[18]

An argument for the possibility of non-identical indiscernibles, very similar to the argument from spatial dispersal, and as good, can also be given from *temporal* dispersal. For it seems that there could be a perfectly cyclical universe in which each event was preceded and followed by infinitely many other events qualitatively indiscernible from itself. Thus there would be distinct but indiscernible *events*, separated by temporal rather than spatial distances. And depending on our criteria of transtemporal identity, it might also be argued that there would be indiscernible persons and physical objects, similarly separated by temporal distances.

In a recent interesting article Ian Hacking argues that "it is vain to contemplate possible spatiotemporal worlds to refute or establish the identity of indiscernibles."[19] He holds that

> Whatever God might create, we are clever enough to describe it in such a way that the identity of indiscernibles is preserved. This is a fact not about God but about description, space, time, and the laws that we ascribe to nature.[20]

The dichotomy between what God might create and our descriptions is important here. Hacking allows that there are consistent descriptions of non-identical indiscernibles and that there are possible states of affairs in which those descriptions would not exactly be false. On the other hand, he thinks that those same possible states of affairs could just as truly (not more truly, but just as truly) be described as containing only one thing in place of each of the sets of indiscernibles. The two descriptions are very different, but there is no difference at all in the possible reality that they represent. Thus Hacking is not exactly asserting the Identity of Indiscernibles. But his rejection of primitive, nonqualitative thisness runs at least as deep as Leibniz's. He thinks that there cannot be any objective fact of the matter about how many individuals are present in the cases that seem to be counterexamples to the Identity of Indiscernibles. And on his view the constitution of reality, of what "God might create," as distinct from our descriptions of it, is purely qualitative.

Hacking's criticisms are directed against both the spatial- and the temporal-dispersal arguments for the possibility of non-identical indiscernibles. The most telling point he makes against them is that they overlook the possibility of alternative geometries and chronometries. If we have a space or time that is curved, then an individual can be spatially or temporally distant from itself, and distance does not prove distinctness. Hacking makes this point most explicitly about time,[21] but he could also use it to criticize the spatial argument, as follows: "The most that God could create of the world imagined by Black is a globe of iron, having internal qualities Q, which can be reached by traveling two diameters in a straight line from a globe of iron having qualities Q. This possible reality can be described as two globes in Euclidean space, or as a single globe in a non-Euclidean space so tightly curved that the globe can be reached by traveling two diameters in a straight line from itself. But the difference between these descriptions represents no difference in the way things could really be."

There are at least two possible replies to Hacking. (1) He acknowledges that if "absolute space-time" is accepted, the spatial and temporal dispersal arguments are quite successful in refuting the Identity of Indiscernibles. But to hold, as he seems to,[22] that no weaker assumption would vindicate the arguments is to demand more than is needed. The dispersal arguments hold up very well even if places and times are defined in terms of relations of objects, provided that certain spatiotemporal relational properties of objects are accepted as primitive. For example, if it is a primitive feature of a possible reality that an iron globe such as Black describes can be reached by traveling some distance in one direction on a *Euclidean* straight line from an exactly similar globe, then non-identical indiscernibles are possible in reality and not just in description.

In order to reply to Hacking in this way, one must assume that a difference in geometries makes, in its own right, a difference in possible worlds, so the same paths in the same universe could not be described, without error, both as Euclidean straight paths and as non-Euclidean straight paths. One must assume that facts about what geometry the universe has are not reducible to facts about what laws of nature best explain other, more primitive facts about objects in space; in particular, one must assume that what geometry the universe has does not depend on a determination of the number of objects in space. Some philosophers may accept these assumptions, and I do not have any better than intuitive grounds for rejecting them. Like Hacking, nonetheless, I am inclined to reject them.

(2) The most obvious and fundamental difference between Black's imaginary Euclidean (or gently Riemannian) two-globe universe and its tightly curved one-globe counterpart seems to be that in one of them there are two iron globes, and in the other only one. Why can't that be a difference between possible realities in its own right? Indeed, I think it is extremely plausible to regard it so.[23]

To give this answer, of course, is to hold that the thisnesses of the two globes are metaphysically primitive. The function of the imaginary spatiotemporal world here is not to show how individual distinctness can be explained by spatiotemporal relations; no such explanation is needed if thisnesses are metaphysically primitive. The imaginary world simply provides an example in which it seems intuitively that two individuals would be distinct although it is clear that they would have all the same suchnesses.

The intuition involved here is akin to those which support belief in direct reference. This will be clearer if we imagine that we are on one of the two globes, with indiscernible twins on the other, so that the use of demonstratives will be possible. Then we can appeal to the intuition that it means something, which we understand quite well and which if true expresses a metaphysical reality, to say that this globe is not identical with that one, even in a situation in which we are not able to distinguish them qualitatively. But the argument goes beyond direct reference in one important respect: it incorporates a judgment that the assertion of individual distinctness is not only intelligible independently of qualitative difference, but also consistent with the assumption that there is no qualitative difference.

4 Arguments from the Possibility of Almost Indiscernible Twins

We may just have an intuition that there could be distinct, though indiscernible, globes in these circumstances. But there may also be an argument for this view – which will depend in turn on other intuitions, like all arguments in these matters. The argument might rest on an intuition that the possibility of there being two objects in a given spatiotemporal relation to each other is not affected by any slight changes in such features as the color or chemical composition of one or both objects.[24] If we accept that intuition, we can infer the possibility of indiscernible twins from the uncontroversial possibility of *almost* indiscernible twins. No one doubts that there could be a universe like the universe of our example in other respects, if one of the two globes had a small chemical impurity that the other lacked. Surely, we may think, the absence of the impurity would not make such a universe impossible.

Spatiotemporal dispersal still plays a part in this argument. But one can argue against the Identity of Indiscernibles from the possibility of almost indiscernible twins in quite a different way, using an example that has to do primarily with minds rather than with bodies. Suppose I have an almost indiscernible twin. The only qualitative difference between him and me, and hence between his part of the universe and mine, is that on one night of our lives (when we are 27 years old) the fire-breathing dragon that pursues me in my nightmare has ten horns, whereas the monster in his dream has only seven. I assume that the number of horns is little noted nor long remembered, and that any other, causally associated differences between his and my lives and parts of the world are slight and quite local. No doubt there is a possible world (call it w) in which there are almost indiscernible twins of this sort; it is only an expository convenience to assume that I am one of them and that w is actual. But if such a world is even possible, it seems to follow that a world with perfectly indiscernible twins is also possible. For surely I could have existed, and so could my twin, if my monster had had only seven horns, like his. And that could have been even if there were no other difference from the lives we live in w, except in the details causally connected with the number of horns in my dream. In that case we would have been distinct but qualitatively indiscernible – a relation which seems therefore to be logically possible.

Several points in this argument call for further mention or explanation. (1) The non-identity obtaining between me and my twin in w is proved by a qualitative difference between us there. (2) The argument depends on an intuition of transworld identity – that in a possible world (call it w'), otherwise like w, but in which my dragon has only seven horns, there could exist an individual identical with me and an individual identical with my twin, even though we would not be qualitatively different in that case. (3) The transitivity of identity is relied on in arguing that since my twin and I are not identical in w (as shown by the difference in our suchnesses there), it follows that we are not identical in any possible world, and therefore are distinct in w', if we both exist in it.

(4) Because differences in modal properties can be purely qualitative, the conclusion that my twin and I would be qualitatively indiscernible in w' depends, additionally, on the assumption that in w' he as well as I would be a person who could

have dreamed of a ten-horned monster in the circumstances in which I did in *w*. In other words, it is assumed that if *w* and *w'* are possible, so is a world *w''* just like *w* except that in *w''* it is my twin's beast that has ten horns and mine that has seven. (More precisely, it is assumed that *w* and *w''* would be equally possible if *w'* were actual.) The implications of the supposition that there are possible worlds that differ, as *w* and *w''* do, only by a transposition of individuals will be studied further in section 5 below.

(5) But we may notice here a consideration about time that seems to me to support assumptions (2) and (4). The mutual distinctness of two individual persons already existing cannot depend on something that has not yet happened. The identity and non-identity of most individuals, and surely of persons, are conceived of as determined, at any time of their existence, by their past and present. This is doubtless connected with the importance that origins seem to have in questions of transworld identity. Consider the state of *w* when my twin and I are 22, five years before the distinctive dreams. We are already distinct from each other, though nothing has yet happened to distinguish us qualitatively. I think it follows that our mutual distinctness is independent of the qualitative difference arising from our later dreams. We would be distinct, therefore, even if our dreams did not differ at age 27 – that is, even if we were perfectly indiscernible qualitatively, as we would be in *w'*. Moreover, since my twin and I have our identities already established by age 22, which of us is which cannot depend on which has which dream five years later; it is possible that the seven-horned monster trouble my sleep, and the ten-horned his, when we are 27, as in *w''*. This argument depends, of course, on the assumption that in *w* my twin and I have histories that differ qualitatively during a certain period after we are 22, but not before then. It follows that *w* is not completely deterministic, but that does not keep *w* from being at least logically possible.[25]

5　Primitive Transworld Identity

Issues of modality *de re* turn on identity questions. To say that a certain individual is only contingently a parent, but necessarily an animal, for example, is to say that there could have been a nonparent, but not a non-animal, that would have been the same individual as that one. It has become customary, and has been at least heuristically helpful, to represent such identities as identities of individuals in different possible worlds – "transworld identities" for short – although (as we have just seen) modal claims *de re* can be understood as identity claims even without the imagery of possible worlds. Whether modality *de re* really adds anything important to the stock of modal facts depends, I think, on whether there are transworld identities or non-identities, and if so, whether they are primitive or are rather to be analyzed in terms of some more fundamental relation(s) among possible worlds. I will try to show here that, if we are prepared to accept nonqualitative thisnesses, we have a very plausible argument for primitive transworld identities and non-identities.

It might be thought, indeed, that we would have a more than plausible argument – that if, by refuting the Identity of Indiscernibles, we can show that thisnesses are metaphysically primitive, it will follow trivially that transworld identity of individuals is also primitive. For the property of being identical with (for example) Aristotle is the same property in every possible world in which it occurs. Hence it cannot be distinct from all suchnesses when possessed by a famous philosopher in the actual world if it is identical with a suchness when possessed by one of Alexander the Great's tax collectors in some other possible world.

This argument is correct insofar as it makes the point that the thisness or identity of a particular individual is nonqualitative either at all places, times, and possible worlds at which it occurs, or at none of them. By the same token, however, there is nothing special about transworld identity in this connection. But the issue on which I wish to focus here is specifically about the primitiveness of *transworld* identities. It therefore cannot be the issue of whether they are purely qualitative.

When we ask about the primitiveness of a kind of identity, we typically want to know, about a certain range of cases, whether the belonging of two properties to a single subject can be explained as consisting in other, more basic relations obtaining between distinct subjects of the same or related properties.[26] Thus Aristotle is the subject of the diverse properties expressed by "is a philosopher" and "could have been a tax collector". In asking whether the identity of the actual philosopher with the possible tax collector is primitive, we want to know whether it consists in some more fundamental relation between Aristotle's actual career and a career in which he would have been a tax collector. This issue is quite distinct from that of the qualitative or nonqualitative character of Aristotle's identity, in the same or in different worlds, as may be seen by reflecting on some other sorts of identity.

The claim that there are nonqualitative thisnesses does not clearly entail that *transtemporal* identity, for example, is primitive. For suppose there are two persisting individuals, Indi and Scerni, acknowledged to be qualitatively indiscernible, and therefore to possess non-qualitative thisnesses. It is not obvious that the identity of Indi at time t_1 with Indi at time t_2 (or the belonging of Indi's t_1 states and t_2 states to a single individual) cannot be explained as consisting in other, more basic relations among successive events or states or stages of Indi, without presupposing the transtemporal identity of any individual. Perhaps this can be done in terms of spatiotemporal continuity or memory links or causal connections or some other relation. The property of being Indi at any given time would still not be equivalent to any suchness. It could be analyzed in terms of the more basic relations among Indi's temporal stages. But the distinctness of those stages from the corresponding stages of Scerni would still be irreducibly nonqualitative, and this nonqualitative character would be passed on to the property of being Indi (at any time). The transtemporal aspect of Indi's identity, however, would not be indispensably primitive. In the present state of philosophical research it is probably unclear whether any transtemporal identity is indeed primitive; my point here is just that the thesis of the nonqualitativeness of thisnesses can be separated from that of the primitiveness of transtemporal identity.

If, to complete the separation of issues, we seek an example of a philosopher who is committed, with apparent consistency, both to the purely qualitative character of all thisnesses and to the primitiveness of some sort of individual identity, we can find it in Leibniz. He regards thisnesses as conjunctions of simpler, logically independent suchnesses. That the combination of properties is

effected by the logical operation of conjunction is an essential part of his conceptual atomism. He assumes that there are some cases in which the instantiation of a conjunction of properties cannot be analyzed as consisting in any more fundamental fact. But if it is a primitive fact that the property *F and G* is instantiated, the identity of some possessor of *F* with a possessor of *G* must also be primitive, rather than analyzable as consisting in some more basic relation obtaining between distinct possessors of *F* and of *G* or related properties. The primitiveness of identity in such cases is in no way inconsistent with Leibniz's opinion that thisnesses are suchnesses; it is indeed required by the way in which he thinks thisnesses are constructed out of simpler suchnesses.

The primitive identities for Leibniz would probably not be transtemporal, and would certainly not be transworld. But no distance in space, time, or "logical space" is needed for questions of identity. Suppose one of Aristotle's momentary perceptual states includes both tasting an olive and hearing a bird sing. In this supposition it is implied, and not yet explained by any more basic relation, that some individual that is tasting an olive is *identical* with one that is hearing a bird sing. And it seems that this sort of identity (identity of the individual subject of simultaneous qualities) could be primitive in a purely qualitative construction of reality.

So questions of the primitiveness of identity relations are in general distinct from the question of the qualitativeness or nonqualitativeness of thisnesses. But, in the case of transworld identity in particular, I think that primitive identities are much more plausible if nonqualitative thisnesses are accepted than if they are rejected. Suppose, on the one hand, that all thisnesses are purely qualitative. Then the thisness of any individual can be constructed as a disjunction of suchnesses, each suchness representing one possible career of the individual (as explained in section 2 above). It seems quite possible that in every case the grouping of disjuncts as alternative careers of a single individual could be explained by general principles about transworld identity of one or another kind of individuals, and the transworld identity of the particular individual could be analyzed as consisting in the satisfaction of the general principles by the relevant disjuncts. And if there should be borderline cases, in which the issue of transworld identity is not settled by general principles, one might well conclude that transworld identity or non-identity is undefined, rather than primitive, in those cases.

If, on the other hand, we reject the Identity of Indiscernibles in favor of nonqualitative thisnesses, it will not be hard to find examples that will provide support of great intuitive plausibility for primitive transworld identities and non-identities. Consider, again, a possible world w_1 in which there are two qualitatively indiscernible globes; call them Castor and Pollux.[27] Being indiscernible, they have of course the same duration; in w_1 both of them have always existed and always will exist. But it seems perfectly possible, logically and metaphysically, that either or both of them cease to exist. Let w_2 then, be a possible world just like w_1 up to a certain time t at which in w_2 Castor ceases to exist while Pollux goes on forever; and let w_3 be a possible world just like w_2 except that in w_3 it is Pollux that ceases to exist at t while Castor goes on forever. That the difference between w_2 and w_3 is real, and could be important, becomes vividly clear if we consider that, from the point of view of a person living on Castor before t in w_1 and having (of course) an indiscernible twin on Pollux, it can be seen as the difference between being annihilated and somebody else being annihilated instead. But there is no qualitative difference between w_2 and w_3. And there are no qualitative necessary and sufficient conditions for the transworld identity or non-identity of Castor and Pollux; for every qualitative condition satisfied by Castor in w_2 is satisfied by Pollux in w_1 and vice versa.[28]

A similar example can be constructed for transworld identity of *events*. Suppose all that happens in w_1 is that Castor and Pollux approach and recede from each other in an infinite series of indiscernible pulsations of the universe. In w_1 their pulsations go on forever, but they might not have. For every pair of them there is surely a possible world in which one member of the pair is the last pulsation, and a different possible world in which the other is the last pulsation. But there is no qualitative difference between these possible worlds; each contains the same number ($\aleph_0$ the first infinite number) of exactly similar pulsations. There are therefore no qualitative necessary and sufficient conditions for the transworld identities and non-identities of the events in these possible worlds.

Any case of this sort, in which two possible worlds differ in the transworld identities of their individuals but not in their suchnesses, provides us at once with a clearer proof of a primitive transworld identity than has yet been found for a primitive transtemporal identity.[29] For the geometrical, topological, psychological, and causal relations out of which philosophers have hoped to construct transtemporal identity do not obtain among the alternative possible careers of an individual. 'Logical space' is not a space to which the concepts of physical space apply literally. There is no causal interaction between different possible worlds. One cannot remember events in another possible world in the same sense in which one's memory of events in the actual past might be important to personal identity. The most important transworld relations of individuals, which seem to be the foundation of all their other transworld relations, are qualitative similarity – which cannot explain different transworld identities in worlds that are qualitatively indiscernible – and identity itself. One might try to analyze the transworld identity of an individual in terms of qualitative similarities plus having the same parts, or the same parents; but then the transworld identity of some individuals (the parts or the parents) is presupposed. If the Identity of Indiscernibles is rejected, there seems to be no plausible way of analyzing transworld identity and non-identity in general in terms of other, more basic relations.

6   Thisness and Necessity

I have argued that there are possible cases in which no purely qualitative conditions would be both necessary and sufficient for possessing a given thisness. It may be thought that this is too cautious a conclusion – that if thisnesses are nonqualitative, there cannot be any qualitative necessary conditions at all for possessing them. The following argument could be given for this view.

Let T be a thisness, and let S be a suchness. Many philosophers have believed that all necessary truths are *analytic*, in the sense that they are either truths of formal logic or derivable by valid logical rules from correct analyses of concepts or properties. This may be regarded as a broadly Leibnizian conception of necessity.

Suppose it is right; and suppose that thisnesses are irreducibly nonqualitative. We may well wonder, then, how it could be a necessary truth that whatever has T has S. For it is surely not a truth of formal logic. And suchnesses are not analyzable in terms of thisnesses; so if thisnesses are not analyzable in terms of suchnesses, how can any connection between T and S fail to be synthetic?

The conclusion, that there cannot be any purely qualitative necessary condition for the possession of any given thisness, is absurd, however. It implies that you and I, for example, could have been individuals of any sort whatever – plutonium atoms, noises, football games, places, or times, if those are all individuals.[30] If we cannot trust our intuition that we could not have been any of those things, then it is probably a waste of time to study *de re* modalities at all. If there are any transworld identities and non-identities, there are necessary connections between thisnesses and some suchnesses.

But it is difficult to understand what makes these connections necessary; and that difficulty has doubtless motivated some philosophical doubts about *de re* modality.[31] Those who accept nonqualitative thisnesses but cling to the dogma that all necessary truths are analytic in the sense explained above may suppose that every nonqualitative thisness that is necessarily connected with suchnesses is analyzable as a conjunction of some or all of the suchnesses it implies, plus a relation to one or more particular individuals of some more fundamental sort. Either the latter individuals (or others still more basic to which one would come by recursive applications of the view) would have no qualitative necessary conditions of their identity at all, or there would be an infinite regress (perhaps virtuous) of thisnesses analyzable in terms of more fundamental thisnesses. Neither alternative seems particularly plausible.

It is better to abandon the identification of necessity with analyticity and suppose that necessities *de re* are commonly synthetic. Perhaps the best answer that can be given to the question, What makes it necessary that Jimmy Carter (for example) is not a musical performance? is this: It is a fact, which we understand very well to be true, though not analytic, that Jimmy Carter is a person. And there are necessary conditions of intra- and transworld identity which follow (analytically, indeed) from the concept or property of being a person and which entail that no individual that is in fact a person could under any circumstances be a musical performance.

There are many notoriously perplexing questions about what suchnesses belong necessarily to which individuals. "Could Cleopatra have been male?" "Could I (who am blue-eyed) have been brown-eyed?" And so forth. It may be that some of these questions call for conceptual legislation rather than metaphysical discovery, for some of our concepts of kinds of individual may be somewhat vague with respect to necessary conditions of transworld identity. The acceptance of nonqualitative thisnesses does not oblige us to settle doubtful cases in favor of contingency. Indeed, I am inclined to decide a very large proportion of them in favor of necessity (or impossibility, as the case may be).

If a name is desired for the position I have defended here, according to which thisnesses and transworld identities are primitive but logically connected with suchnesses, we may call it *Moderate Haecceitism*.

Notes

Versions of this paper were read to colloquia at UCLA, UC Irvine, and Stanford. I am indebted to many, and particularly to Marilyn Adams, Kit Fine, Dagfinn Føllesdal, Ian Hacking, Robert Hambourger, David Kaplan, Kenneth Olson, John Perry, and Peter Woodruff, for discussion that helped in writing and rewriting the paper. My interest in the project grew out of discussions with Kaplan.

1 See David Kaplan, "How to Russell a Frege-Church," *Journal of Philosophy* 72 (1975, Nov. 6), pp. 716–29, at pp. 722–7.

2 "Thisness" is the inevitable and historic word here. But we must not suppose that everything important that is expressed by a demonstrative is caught up in the relevant thisness. You might know many facts involving the thisness (in my sense) of Gerald Ford, for example, and yet be ignorant that *that* man (disappearing over the hill in a golf cart) is Ford. I believe this is a translation into my terminology of a point John Perry has made; see his "Frege on demonstratives," *Philosophical Review* 86/4 (Oct. 1977), pp. 474–97, and "Indexicality and belief," unpublished.

3 E.g., by Alvin Plantinga, *The Nature of Necessity* (Oxford: Clarendon Press, 1974), pp. 71f.

4   Johannes Duns Scotus, *Quaestiones in libros metaphysicorum*, VII. xii. schol. 3; cf. *Ordinatio*, II.3.1.2, 57. I am indebted to Marilyn McCord Adams for acquainting me with these texts and views of Scotus, and for much discussion of the topics of this paragraph.

5   Gottfried Wilhelm Leibniz, *Fragments zur Logik*, ed. Franz Schmidt (Berlin: Akademic-Verlag, 1960), p. 476; cf. Leibniz, *Discourse on Metaphysics*, trans. P. G. Lucas and L. Griut (Manchester: Manchester University Press, 1953), sect. 9. This is not the place to debate points of interpretation, and I will sometimes speak of "properties" where Leibniz usually restricts himself to "concept" and "predicate"; but I think I do not substantially misrepresent him on the points that concern us.

6   *Discourse on Metaphysics*, sect. 8.

7   See Leibniz's letter of 4/14 July, 1686 to Antoine Arnauld, in *The Leibniz–Arnaud Correspondence*, trans. H. T. Mason, (Manchester: Manchester University Press, 1967), pp. 53–66.

8   This point could also be put in terms of constructing complete concepts from predicates that are indexed to possible worlds. This possible amendment of Leibniz's position, and its analogy with Leibniz's commitment to the indexing of predicates to times, were noted by Benson Mates, "Individuals and modality in the philosophy of Leibniz," *Studia Leibnitiana* 4 (1972), p. 109.

9   Cf. Keith S. Donnellan, "Reference and definite descriptions," *Philosophical Review*, 75/3 (July 1966), pp. 281–304, and *idem*, "Proper names and identifying descriptions," in D. Davidson and G. Harman (eds), *The Semantics of Natural Languages*, 2nd edn. (Boston: Reidel, 1972), pp. 356–79; Saul Kripke, "Naming and necessity," in Davidson and Harman (eds), pp. 253–355.

10 Leibniz, *Discourse on Metaphysics*, sect. 8.

11 This way of establishing a trivial version of the Identity of Indiscernibles was noticed by Whitehead and Russell, *Principia Mathematica*, vol. 1, 2nd edn. (Cambridge: Cambridge University Press, 1957), p. 57. It is the initial topic in Max Black's "The identity of indiscernibles," this volume, ch. 8, and I think that Black does not quite distinguish it from any interesting version of the doctrine, because he does not explicitly distinguish relational properties that are suchnesses from those which are not.

12 See esp. his famous paper "First truths," and his *Discourse on Metaphysics*, sects. 8, 9.

13 *The Leibniz–Clarke Correspondence*, ed. H. G. Alexander (Manchester: Manchester University Press, 1956), Leibniz's fifth letter, sects. 25, 26, and Clarke's fifth reply, sects. 21–5 and 26–32. Clarke could not have seen the papers in which Leibniz most clearly implied the claim of necessity.

14 Leibniz, *Fragmente zur Logik*, p. 476.

15 Of course the suchness will be constituted by a single disjunct if, as Leibniz held, each individual exists in only one possible world.

16 Immanuel Kant, *Critique of Pure Reason*, A263 f. = B319 f.

17 This volume, ch. 8.

18 This axiom might be doubted, but I simply assume it here. Occam denied that it is a necessary truth (*Reportario*, IV, q. 4N and q. 5J, in *Opera Plurima* (Lyon, 1494–6); I am indebted to Marilyn Adams for this information).

19 Ian Hacking, "The identity of indiscernibles," *Journal of Philosophy* 72, 9 (8 May 1975), pp. 249–56, at p. 249.

20 Ibid., pp. 255–6.

21 Ibid., p. 255. The point was also suggested, about space, by Black, this volume, ch. 8.

22 Hacking, "The identity of indiscernibles," pp. 251f, 254f.

23 Strictly speaking, I think it is highly plausible to regard it so *if* physical objects are accepted as primitive features of reality. Like Leibniz, I am inclined to take a phenomenalistic view of physical objects, and hence doubt the primitiveness of *their* thisnesses. Unlike Leibniz, I think there could be distinct but indiscernible sentient beings and mental events; cases that help to show the plausibility of this view may be provided by temporal dispersal arguments, or by another type of argument to be discussed in section 4 below.

24 If we assume that differences in color or chemical composition necessarily involve microscopic differences in spatiotemporal configuration, the intuition would have to be that slight differences of that sort do not affect the logical or metaphysical possibility of a given macroscopic configuration of objects.

25 I do not claim that Leibniz would accept this judgment of possibility.

26 Cf. John Perry, "Can the self divide?," *Journal of Philosophy* 59/6 (7 Sept. 1972), pp. 463–88, at pp. 466–8.

27 The question may be raised whether giving names to the globes is consistent with their qualitative indiscernibility (cf. Black, this volume, ch. 8). Two answers may be given. The imaginative answer is that we may suppose that the globes have (indiscernible) societies of language-users on them and we are speaking the language of the Castor-dwellers; in the language of the Pollux-dwellers, of course, "Castor" names Pollux and "Pollux" Castor, but that does not keep Castor from *being* Castor and Pollux Pollux. The sober answer is that "Castor" and "Pollux" are informal equivalents of variables bound by the existential quantifiers that would be used to introduce the example in a formal way.

28 We rely here on an intuition that the Castor-dweller can refer directly to the same individual (namely herself) in different possible worlds, despite the absence of qualitative necessary and sufficient conditions for the identity. This is related, in ways that should by now be familiar to us, to intuitions that have been used to support the semantics of direct reference – as, for example, that when we say, "Nixon might have lost the 1968 election," we refer to the actual individual, Nixon, in a non-actual situation even if we do not know any clearly qualitative property that the possible loser must have in order to be identical with the actual President. (The example is Kripke's; see his "Naming and necessity," pp. 264ff.)

29 It is not essential to the argument to start from a world in which (as in w_1) there are non-identical indiscernibles. An essentially similar argument can be based on the case presented in section 4 above, in which I have an *almost* indiscernible twin. But, since the crux of the argument will be that every qualitative condition satisfied by me in w is satisfied by him in w'', and vice versa, we must still be prepared to accept nonqualitative thisnesses. And, as we saw in section 4, the case can also be used to argue for the possibility of a world containing perfectly indiscernible twins.

30 In his *Examination of McTaggart's Philosophy*, vol. 1 (Cambridge: Cambridge University Press, 1933), p. 177, C. D. Broad pointed out that rejection of the Identity of Indiscernibles does not imply "that it is logically possible that [a particular] P, which *in fact has* the nature N, should *instead* have had some other nature N'; e.g., that I might have been born in Rome in 55 BC, or that the Albert Memorial might have been a volcano in South America."

31 Cf. W. V. Quine, *From a Logical Point of View*, 2nd edn (New York: Harper Torchbooks, 1963), p. 155.

10

Identity and Necessity

Saul Kripke

A problem which has arisen frequently in contemporary philosophy is: "How are *contingent* identity statements possible?" This question is phrased by analogy with the way Kant phrased his question "How are synthetic a priori judgments possible?" In both cases, it has usually been taken for granted in the one case by Kant that synthetic a priori judgments were possible, and in the other case in contemporary philosophical literature that contingent statements of identity are possible. I do not intend to deal with the Kantian question except to mention this analogy: After a rather thick book was written trying to answer the question how synthetic a priori judgments were possible, others came along later who claimed that the solution to the problem was that synthetic a priori judgments were, of course, impossible and that a book trying to show otherwise was written in vain. I will not discuss who was right on the possibility of synthetic a priori judgments. But in the case of contingent statements of identity, most philosophers have felt that the notion of a contingent identity statement ran into something like the following paradox. An argument like the following can be given against the possibility of contingent identity statements:[1]

First, the law of the substitutivity of identity says that, for any objects x and y, if x is identical to y, then if x has a certain property F, so does y:

$$(1) \quad (x)(y)[(x = y) \supset (Fx \supset Fy)]$$

On the other hand, every object surely is necessarily self-identical:

$$(2) \quad (x)\Box(x = x)$$

But

$$(3) \quad (x)(y)(x = y) \supset [\Box(x = x) \supset \Box(x = y)]$$

is a substitution instance of (1), the substitutivity law. From (2) and (3), we can conclude that, for every x and y, if x equals y, then, it is necessary that x equals y:

$$(4) \quad (x)(y)((x = y) \supset \Box \, (x = y))$$

This is because the clause $\Box(x = x)$ of the conditional drops out because it is known to be true.

This is an argument which has been stated many times in recent philosophy. Its conclusion,

Saul Kripke, "Identity and Necessity," in *Identity and Individuation* (New York: New York University Press, 1971), pp. 135–64. Copyright New York University. Reproduced by permission.

Metaphysics: An Anthology, Second Edition. Edited by Jaegwon Kim, Daniel Z. Korman and Ernest Sosa.
Editorial material and organization © 2012 Blackwell Publishing Ltd. Published 2012 by Blackwell Publishing Ltd.

however, has often been regarded as highly paradoxical. For example, David Wiggins, in his paper, "Identity-Statements," says.

> Now there undoubtedly exist contingent identity-statements. Let $a = b$ be one of them. From its simple truth and (5) [=(4) above] we can derive "$\Box(a = b)$". But how then can there be any contingent identity-statements?[2]

He then says that five various reactions to this argument are possible, and rejects all of these reactions, and reacts himself. I do not want to discuss all the possible reactions to this statement, except to mention the second of those Wiggins rejects. This says:

> We might accept the result and plead that provided 'a' and 'b' are proper names nothing is amiss. The consequence of this is that no contingent identity-statements can be made by means of proper names.

And then he says that he is discontented with this solution, and many other philosophers have been discontented with this solution, too, while still others have advocated it.

What makes the statement (4) seem surprising? It says, for any objects x and y, if x is y, then it is necessary that x is y. I have already mentioned that someone might object to this argument on the grounds that premise (2) is already false, that it is not the case that everything is necessarily self-identical. Well, for example, am I myself necessarily self-identical? Someone might argue that in some situations which we can imagine I would not even have existed, and therefore the statement "Saul Kripke is Saul Kripke" would have been false, or it would not be the case that I was self-identical. Perhaps, it would have been neither true nor false, in such a world, to say that Saul Kripke is self-identical. Well, that may be so, but really it depends on one's philosophical view of a topic that I will not discuss: that is, what is to be said about truth-values of statements mentioning objects that do not exist in the actual world or any given possible world or counterfactual situation. Let us interpret necessity here weakly. We can count statements as necessary if, whenever the objects mentioned therein exist, the statement would be true. If we wished to be very careful

about this, we would have to go into the question of existence as a predicate and ask if the statement can be reformulated in the form: For every x it is necessary that, if x exists, then x is self-identical. I will not go into this particular form of subtlety here because it is not going to be relevant to my main theme. Nor am I really going to consider formula (4). Anyone who believes formula (2) is, in my opinion, committed to formula (4). If x and y are the same things and we can talk about modal properties of an object at all, that is, in the usual parlance, we can speak of modality *de re* and an object *necessarily* having certain properties as such, then formula (1), I think, has to hold. Where x is any property at all, including a property involving modal operators, and if x and y are the same object and x has a certain property F, then y has to have the same property F. And this is so even if the property F is itself of the form of necessarily having some other property G, in particular that of necessarily being identical to a certain object. Well, I will not discuss the formula (4) itself because by itself it does not assert, of any particular true statement of identity, that it is necessary. It does not say anything about *statements* at all. It says for every *object x* and *object y*, if x and y are the same object, then it is necessary that x and y are the same object. And this, I think, if we think about it (anyway, if someone does not think so, I will not argue for it here), really amounts to something very little different from the statement (2). Since x, by definition of identity, is the only object identical with x, "$(y)(y = x \supset Fy)$" seems to me to be little more than a garrulous way of saying "Fx," and thus $(x)(y)(y = x \supset Fx)$ says the same as $(x)Fx$ no matter what "F" is – in particular, even if "F" stands for the property of necessary identity with x. So if x has this property (of necessary identity with x), trivially everything identical with x has it, as (4) asserts. But, from statement (4) one may apparently be able to deduce that various particular statements of identity must be necessary, and this is then supposed to be a very paradoxical consequence.

Wiggins says, "Now there undoubtedly exist contingent identity-statements." One example of a contingent identity statement is the statement that the first Postmaster General of the United States is identical with the inventor of bifocals, or that both of these are identical with the man claimed by the *Saturday Evening Post* as its founder (*falsely* claimed, I gather, by the way). Now some such statements are plainly contingent. It plainly is a contingent fact that one and the same man both invented bifocals and took on the job of Postmaster General of the United States. How can we reconcile this with the truth of statement (4)? Well, that, too, is an issue I do not want to go into in detail except to be very dogmatic about it. It was, I think, settled quite well by Bertrand Russell in his notion of the scope of a description. According to Russell, one can, for example, say with propriety that the author of *Hamlet* might not have written *Hamlet*, or even that the author of *Hamlet* might not have been the author of *Hamlet*. Now here, of course, we do not deny the necessity of the identity of an object with itself; but we say it is true concerning a certain man that he in fact was the unique person to have written *Hamlet* and secondly that the man, who in fact was the man who wrote *Hamlet*, might not have written *Hamlet*. In other words, if Shakespeare had decided not to write tragedies, he might not have written *Hamlet*. Under these circumstances, the man who in fact wrote *Hamlet* would not have written *Hamlet*. Russell brings this out by saying that in such a statement the first occurrence of the description "the author of *Hamlet*" has large scope.[3] That is, we say, "The author of *Hamlet* has the following property: that he might not have written *Hamlet*." We *do not* assert that the following statement might have been the case, namely that the author of *Hamlet* did not write *Hamlet*, for that is not true. That would be to say that it might have been the case that someone wrote *Hamlet* and yet did not write *Hamlet*, which would be a contradiction. Now, aside from the details of Russell's particular formulation of it, which depends on his theory of descriptions, this seems to be the distinction that any theory of descriptions has to make. For example, if someone were to meet the President of Harvard and take him to be a Teaching Fellow, he might say: "I took the President of Harvard for a Teaching Fellow." By this he does not mean that he took the proposition "The President of Harvard is a Teaching Fellow" to be true. He could have meant this, for example, had he believed that some sort of democratic system had gone so far at Harvard that the President of it decided to take on the task of being a Teaching Fellow. But that probably is not what he means.

What he means instead, as Russell points out, is "Someone is President of Harvard and I took him to be a Teaching Fellow." In one of Russell's examples someone says, "I thought your yacht is much larger than it is." And the other man replies, "No, my yacht is not much larger than it is."

Provided that the notion of modality *de re*, and thus of quantifying into modal contexts, makes any sense at all, we have quite an adequate solution to the problem of avoiding paradoxes if we substitute descriptions for the universal quantifiers in (4) because the only consequence we will draw,[4] for example, in the bifocals case, is that there is a man who both happened to have invented bifocals and happened to have been the first Postmaster General of the United States, and is necessarily self-identical. There is an object x such that x invented bifocals, and as a matter of contingent fact an object y, such that y is the first Postmaster General of the United States, and finally, it is necessary, that x is y. What are x and y here? Here, x and y are both Benjamin Franklin, and it can certainly be necessary that Benjamin Franklin is identical with himself. So, there is no problem in the case of descriptions if we accept Russell's notion of scope.[5] And I just dogmatically want to drop that question here and go on to the question about names which Wiggins raises. And Wiggins says he might accept the result and plead that, provided *a* and *b* are proper names, nothing is amiss. And then he rejects this.

Now what is the special problem about proper names? At least if one is not familiar with the philosophical literature about this matter, one naïvely feels something like the following about proper names. First, if someone says "Cicero was an orator," then he uses the name "Cicero" in that statement simply to pick out a certain object and then to ascribe a certain property to the object, namely, in this case, he ascribes to a certain man the property of having been an orator. If someone else uses another name, such as, say, "Tully," he is still speaking about the same man. One ascribes the same property, if one says "Tully is an orator," to the same man. So to speak, the fact, or state of affairs, represented by the statement is the same whether one says "Cicero is an orator" or one says "Tully is an orator." It would, therefore, seem that the function of names is *simply* to refer, and not to describe the objects so named by such properties as "being the inventor of bifocals" or "being the first Postmaster General." It would seem that Leibniz's law and the law (1) should not only hold in the universally quantified form, but also in the form "if $a = b$ and Fa, then Fb," wherever "a" and "b" stand in place of names and "F" stands in place of a predicate expressing a genuine property of the object:

$$(a = b \cdot Fa) \supset Fb$$

We can run the same argument through again to obtain the conclusion where "a" and "b" replace any names, "If $a = b$, then necessarily $a = b$." And so, we could venture this conclusion: that whenever "a" and "b" are proper names, if a is b, that it is necessary that a is b. Identity statements between proper names have to be necessary if they are going to be true at all. This view in fact has been advocated, for example, by Ruth Barcan Marcus in a paper of hers on the philosophical interpretation of modal logic.[6] According to this view, whenever, for example, someone makes a correct statement of identity between two names, such as, for example, that Cicero is Tully, his statement has to be necessary if it is true. But such a conclusion *seems* plainly to be false. (I, like other philosophers, have a habit of understatement in which "it seems plainly false" means "it is plainly false." Actually, I think the view is true, though not quite in the form defended by Marcus.) At any rate, it seems plainly false. One example was given by Professor Quine in his reply to Professor Marcus at the symposium: "I think I see trouble anyway in the contrast between proper names and descriptions as Professor Marcus draws it. The paradigm of the assigning of proper names is tagging. We may tag the planet Venus some fine evening with the proper name 'Hesperus'. We may tag the same planet again someday before sunrise with the proper name 'Phosphorus'." (Quine thinks that something like that actually was done once.) "When, at last, we discover that we have tagged the same planet twice, our discovery is empirical, and not because the proper names were descriptions." According to what we are told, the planet Venus seen in the morning was originally thought to be a star and was called "the Morning Star," or (to get rid of any question of using a description) was called "Phosphorus." One and the same planet, when seen in the evening, was thought to be another star, the Evening Star, and was called "Hesperus." Later on, astronomers discovered that Phosphorus and Hesperus were one and the same. Surely no amount of a priori ratiocination on their part could conceivably have made it possible for them to deduce that Phosphorus is Hesperus. In fact, given the information they had, it might have turned out the other way. Therefore, it is argued, the statement "Hesperus is Phosphorus" has to be an ordinary contingent, empirical truth, one which might have come out otherwise, and so the view that true identity statements between names are necessary has to be false. Another example which Quine gives in *Word and Object* is taken from Professor Schrödinger, the famous pioneer of quantum mechanics: A certain mountain can be seen from both Tibet and Nepal. When seen from one direction, it was called "Gaurisanker"; when seen from another direction, it was called "Everest"; and then, later on, the empirical discovery was made that Gaurisanker *is* Everest. (Quine further says that he gathers the example is actually geographically incorrect. I guess one should not rely on physicists for geographical information.)

Of course, one possible reaction to this argument is to deny that names like "Cicero," "Tully," "Gaurisanker," and "Everest" really are proper names. Look, someone might say (someone has said it: his name was "Bertrand Russell"), just because statements like "Hesperus is Phosphorus" and "Gaurisanker is Everest" are contingent, we can see that the names in question are not really purely referential. You are not, in Marcus's phrase, just "tagging" an object; you are actually describing it. What does the contingent fact that Hesperus is Phosphorus amount to? Well, it amounts to the fact that *the* star in a certain portion of the sky in the evening is *the* star in a certain portion of the sky in the morning. Similarly, the contingent fact that Gaurisanker is Everest amounts to the fact that the mountain viewed from such and such an angle in Nepal is the mountain viewed from such and such another angle in Tibet. Therefore, such names as "Hesperus" and "Phosphorus" can only be abbreviations for descriptions. The term "Phosphorus" *has* to mean "the star seen ...," or (let us be cautious because it actually turned out not to be a star), "the *heavenly body* seen from such and such a position at such and such a time in the morning," and the name "Hesperus" has to mean "the heavenly body seen in such and such a position at such and such a time in the evening." So, Russell concludes, if we want to reserve the term "name" for things which really just name an object without describing it, the only real proper names we can have are names of our own immediate sense-data, objects of our own "immediate acquaintance." The only such names which occur in language are demonstratives like "this" and "that." And it is easy to see that this requirement of necessity of identity, understood as exempting identities between names from all imaginable doubt, can indeed be guaranteed only for demonstrative names of immediate sense-data; for only in such cases can an identity statement between two different names have a general immunity from Cartesian doubt. There are some other things Russell has sometimes allowed as objects of acquaintance, such as one's self; we need not go into details here. Other philosophers (for example, Marcus in her reply, at least in the verbal discussion as I remember it – I do not know if this got into print, so perhaps this should not be "tagged" on her[7]) have said, "If names are really just tags, genuine tags, then a good dictionary should be able to tell us that they are names of the same object." You have an object *a* and an object *b* with names "John" and "Joe." Then, according to Marcus, a dictionary should be able to tell you whether or not "John" and "Joe" are names of the same object. Of course, I do not know what ideal dictionaries should do, but ordinary proper names do not seem to satisfy this requirement. You certainly *can*, in the case of ordinary proper names, make quite empirical discoveries that, let's say, Hesperus is Phosphorus, though we thought otherwise. We can be in doubt as to whether Gaurisanker is Everest or Cicero is in fact Tully. Even now, we could conceivably discover that we were wrong in supposing that Hesperus was Phosphorus. Maybe the astronomers made an error. So it seems that this view is wrong and that if by a name we do not mean some artificial notion of names such as Russell's, but a proper name in the ordinary sense, then there can be contingent identity statements using proper names, and the view to the contrary seems plainly wrong.

In recent philosophy a large number of other identity statements have been emphasized as examples of contingent identity statements, different, perhaps, from either of the types I have mentioned before. One of them is, for example, the statement "Heat is the motion of molecules." First, science is supposed to have discovered this. Empirical scientists in their investigations have been supposed to discover (and, I suppose, they did) that the external phenomenon which we call "heat" is, in fact, molecular agitation. Another example of such a discovery is that water is H_2O, and yet other examples are that gold is the element with such and such an atomic number, that light is a stream of photons, and so on. These are all in some sense of "identity statement" identity statements. Second, it is thought, they are plainly contingent identity statements, just because they were scientific discoveries. After all, heat might have turned out not to have been the motion of molecules. There were other alternative theories of heat proposed, for example, the caloric theory of heat. If these theories of heat had been correct, then heat would not have been the motion of molecules, but instead, some substance suffusing the hot object, called "caloric." And it was a matter of course of science and not of any logical necessity that the one theory turned out to be correct and the other theory turned out to be incorrect.

So, here again, we have, apparently, another plain example of a contingent identity statement. This has been supposed to be a very important example because of its connection with the mind-body problem. There have been many philosophers who have wanted to be materialists, and to be materialists in a particular form, which is known today as "the identity theory." According to this theory, a certain mental state, such as a person's being in pain, is identical with a certain state of his brain (or, perhaps, of his entire body, according to some theorists), at any rate, a certain material or neural state of his brain or body. And so, according to this theory, my being in pain at this instant, if I were, would be identical with my body's being or my brain's being in a certain state. Others have objected that this cannot be because, after all, we can imagine my pain existing even if the state of the body did not. We can perhaps imagine my not being embodied at all and still being in pain, or, conversely, we could imagine my body existing and being in the very same state even if there were no pain. In fact, conceivably, it could be in this state even though there were no mind "back of it," so to speak, at all. The usual reply has been to concede that all of these things might have been the case, but to argue that these are irrelevant to the question of the identity of the mental state and the physical state. This identity, it is said, is just another contingent scientific identification, similar to the identification of heat with molecular motion, or water with H_2O. Just as we can imagine heat without any molecular motion, so we can imagine a mental state without any corresponding brain state. But, just as the first fact is not damaging to the identification of heat and the motion of molecules, so the second fact is not at all damaging to the identification of a mental state with the corresponding brain state. And so, many recent philosophers have held it to be very important for our theoretical understanding of the mind-body problem that there can be contingent identity statements of this form.

To state finally what *I* think, as opposed to what seems to be the case, or what others think, I think that in both cases, the case of names and the case of the theoretical identifications, the identity statements are necessary and not contingent. That is to say, they are necessary if *true*; of course, false identity statements are not necessary. How can one possibly defend such a view? Perhaps I lack a complete answer to this question, even though I am convinced that the view is true. But to begin an answer, let me make some distinctions that I want to use. The first is between a *rigid* and a *nonrigid designator*. What do these terms mean? As an example of a nonrigid designator, I can give an expression such as "the inventor of bifocals." Let us suppose it was Benjamin Franklin who invented bifocals, and so the expression, "the inventor of bifocals," designates or refers to a certain man, namely, Benjamin Franklin. However, we can easily imagine that the world could have been different, that under different circumstances someone else would have come upon this invention before Benjamin Franklin did, and in that case, *he* would have been the inventor of bifocals. So, in this sense, the expression "the inventor of bifocals' is non-rigid: Under certain circumstances one man would have been the inventor of bifocals; under other

circumstances, another man would have. In contrast, consider the expression "the square root of 25." Independently of the empirical facts, we can give an arithmetical proof that the square root of 25 is in fact the number 5, and because we have proved this mathematically, what we have proved is necessary. If we think of numbers as entities at all, and let us suppose, at least for the purpose of this lecture, that we do, then the expression "the square root of 25" necessarily designates a certain number, namely 5. Such an expression I call "a *rigid* designator." Some philosophers think that anyone who even uses the notions of rigid or nonrigid designator has already shown that he has fallen into a certain confusion or has not paid attention to certain facts. What do I mean by "rigid designator"? I mean a term that designates the same object in all possible worlds. To get rid of one confusion, which certainly is not mine, I do not use "might have designated a different object" to refer to the fact that language might have been used differently. For example, the expression "the inventor of bifocals" might have been used by inhabitants of this planet always to refer to the man who corrupted Hadleyburg. This would have been the case, if, first, the people on this planet had not spoken English, but some other language, which phonetically overlapped with English; and if, second, in that language the expression "the inventor of bifocals" meant the "man who corrupted Hadleyburg." Then it would refer, of course, in their language, to whoever in fact corrupted Hadleyburg in this counterfactual situation. That is not what I mean. What I mean by saying that a description might have referred to something different, I mean that in *our* language as *we* use it in describing a counterfactual situation, there might have been a different object satisfying the descriptive conditions *we* give for reference. So, for example, we use the phrase "the inventor of bifocals," when we are talking about another possible world or a counterfactual situation, to refer to whoever in that counterfactual situation would have invented bifocals, not to the person whom people *in* that counterfactual situation would have called "the inventor of bifocals." *They* might have spoken a different language which phonetically overlapped with English in which "the inventor of bifocals" is used in some other way. I am *not* concerned with that question here. For that matter, they might have been deaf and dumb, or there might have been no people at all. (There still could have been an inventor of bifocals even if there were no people – God, or Satan, will do.)

Second, in talking about the notion of a rigid designator, I do not mean to imply that the object referred to has to exist in all possible worlds, that is, that it has to necessarily exist. Some things, perhaps mathematical entities such as the positive integers, if they exist at all, necessarily exist. Some people have held that God both exists and necessarily exists; others, that he contingently exists; others, that he contingently fails to exist; and others, that he necessarily fails to exist:[8] all four options have been tried. But at any rate, when I use the notion of rigid designator, I do not imply that the object referred to necessarily exists. All I mean is that in any possible world where the object in question *does* exist, in any situation where the object *would* exist, we use the designator in question to designate that object. In a situation where the object does not exist, then we should say that the designator has no referent and that the object in question so designated does not exist.

As I said, many philosophers would find the very notion of rigid designator objectionable *per se*. And the objection that people make may be stated as follows: Look, you're talking about situations which are counterfactual, that is to say, you're talking about other possible worlds. Now these worlds are completely disjoint, after all, from the actual world which is not just another possible world; it is the actual world. So, before you talk about, let us say, such an object as Richard Nixon in another possible world at all, you have to say which object in this other possible world would *be* Richard Nixon. Let us talk about a situation in which, as *you* would say, Richard Nixon would have been a member of SDS. Certainly the member of SDS you are talking about is someone very different in many of his properties from Nixon. Before we even can say whether this man would have been Richard Nixon or not, we have to set up criteria of identity across possible worlds. Here are these other possible worlds. There are all kinds of objects in them with different properties from those of any actual object. Some of them resemble Nixon in some ways, some of them resemble Nixon in other ways. Well, which of these objects is

Nixon? One has to given a criterion of identity. And this shows how the very notion of rigid designator runs in a circle. Suppose we designate a certain number as the number of planets. Then, if that is our favorite way, so to speak, of designating this number, then in any other possible worlds we will have to identify whatever number is the number of planets with the number 9, which in the actual world is the number of planets. So, it is argued by various philosophers, for example, implicitly by Quine, and explicitly by many others in his wake, we cannot really ask whether a designator is rigid or nonrigid because we first need a criterion of identity across possible worlds. An extreme view has even been held that, since possible worlds are so disjoint from our own, we cannot really say that any object in them is the *same* as an object existing now but only that there are some objects which resemble things in the actual world, more or less. We, therefore, should not really speak of what would have been true of Nixon in another possible world but, only of what "counterparts" (the term which David Lewis uses[9]) of Nixon there would have been. Some people in other possible worlds have dogs whom they call "Checkers." Others favor the ABM but do not have any dog called Checkers. There are various people who resemble Nixon more or less, but none of them can really be said to be Nixon; they are only *counterparts* of Nixon, and you choose which one is the best counterpart by noting which resembles Nixon the most closely, according to your favorite criteria. Such views are widespread, both among the defenders of quantified modal logic and among its detractors.

All of this talk seems to me to have taken the metaphor of possible worlds much too seriously in some way. It is as if a "possible world" were like a foreign country, or distant planet way out there. It is as if we see dimly through a telescope various actors on this distant planet. Actually David Lewis's view seems the most reasonable if one takes this picture literally. No one far away on another planet can be strictly identical with someone here. But, even if we have some marvelous methods of transportation to take one and the same person from planet to planet, we really need some epistemological criteria of identity to be able to say whether someone on this distant planet is the same person as someone here.

All of this seems to me to be a totally misguided way of looking at things. What it amounts to is the view that counterfactual situations have to be described purely qualitatively. So, we cannot say, for example, "If Nixon had only given a sufficient bribe to Senator X, he would have gotten Carswell through," because that refers to certain people, Nixon and Carswell, and talks about what things would be true of them in a counterfactual situation. We must say instead "If a man who has a hairline like such and such, and holds such and such political opinions had given a bribe to a man who was a senator and had such and such other qualities, then a man who was a judge in the South and had many other qualities resembling Carswell would have been confirmed." In other words, we must describe counterfactual situations purely qualitatively and then ask the question, "Given that the situation contains people or things with such and such qualities, which of these people is (or is a counterpart of) Nixon, which is Carswell, and so on?" This seems to me to be wrong. Who is to prevent us from saying "Nixon might have gotten Carswell through had he done certain things"? We are speaking of *Nixon* and asking what, in certain counterfactual situations, would have been true of *him*. We can say that if Nixon had done such and such, he would have lost the election to Humphrey. Those I am opposing would argue, "Yes, but how do you find out if the man you are talking about is in fact Nixon?" It would indeed be very hard to find out, if you were looking at the whole situation through a telescope, but that is not what we are doing here. Possible worlds are not something to which an epistemological question like this applies. And if the phrase "possible worlds" is what makes anyone think some such question applies, he should just *drop* this phrase and use some other expression, say "counterfactual situation," which might be less misleading. If we say "If Nixon had bribed such and such a senator, Nixon would have gotten Carswell through," what is *given* in the very description of that situation is that it is a situation in which we are speaking of Nixon, and of Carswell, and of such and such a senator. And there seems to be no less objection to *stipulating* that we are speaking of certain *people* than there can be objection to stipulating that we are speaking of certain *qualities*. Advocates of the other view take speaking of certain qualities as

unobjectionable. They do not say, "How do we know that this quality (in another possible world) is that of redness?" But they do find speaking of certain *people* objectionable. But I see no more reason to object in the one case than in the other. I think it really comes from the idea of possible worlds as existing out there, but very far off, viewable only through a special telescope. Even more objectionable is the view of David Lewis. According to Lewis, when we say "Under certain circumstances Nixon would have gotten Carswell through," we really mean "Some man, other than Nixon but closely resembling him, would have gotten some judge, other than Carswell but closely resembling him, through." Maybe that is so, that some man closely resembling Nixon could have gotten some man closely resembling Carswell through. But *that* would not comfort either Nixon or Carswell, nor would it make Nixon kick himself and say "*I* should have done such and such to get Carswell through." The question is whether under certain circumstances Nixon *himself* could have gotten *Carswell* through. And I think the objection is simply based on a misguided picture.

Instead, we can perfectly well talk about rigid and nonrigid designators. Moreover, we have a simple, intuitive test for them. We can say, for example, that the number of planets might have been a different number from the number it in fact is. For example, there might have been only seven planets. We can say that the inventor of bifocals might have been someone other than the man who *in fact* invented bifocals.[10] We cannot say, though, that the square root of 81 might have been a different number from the number it in fact is, for that number just has to be 9. If we apply this intuitive test to proper names, such as for example "Richard Nixon," they would seem intuitively to come out to be rigid designators. First, when we talk even about the counterfactual situation in which we suppose Nixon to have done different things, we assume we are still talking about Nixon himself. We say, "If Nixon had bribed a certain senator, he would have gotten Carswell through," and we assume that by "Nixon" and "Carswell" we are still referring to the very same people as in the actual world. And it seems that we cannot say "Nixon might have been a different man from the man he in fact was," unless, of course, we mean it metaphorically: He might have been a different *sort* of person (if you believe in free will and that people are not inherently corrupt). You might think the statement true in that sense, but Nixon could not have been in the other literal sense a different person from the person he, in fact, is, even though the thirty-seventh President of the United States might have been Humphrey. So the phrase "the thirty-seventh President" is nonrigid, but "Nixon," it would seem, is rigid.

Let me make another distinction before I go back to the question of identity statements. This distinction is very fundamental and also hard to see through. In recent discussion, many philosophers who have debated the meaningfulness of various categories of truths, have regarded them as identical. Some of those who identify them are vociferous defenders of them, and others, such as Quine, say they are all identically meaningless. But usually they're not distinguished. These are categories such as "analytic," "necessary," "a priori," and sometimes even "certain." I will not talk about all of these but only about the notions of aprioricity and necessity. Very often these are held to be synonyms. (Many philosophers probably should not be described as holding them to be synonyms; they simply *use* them interchangeably.) I wish to distinguish them. What do we mean by calling a statement *necessary*? We simply mean that the statement in question, first, is true, and, second, that it could not have been otherwise. When we say that something is *contingently* true, we mean that, though it is in fact the case, it could have been the case that things would have been otherwise. If we wish to assign this distinction to a branch of philosophy, we should assign it to metaphysics. To the contrary, there is the notion of an *a priori truth*. An a priori truth is supposed to be one which can be *known* to be true independently of all experience. Notice that this does not in and of itself say anything about all possible worlds, unless this is put into the definition. All that it says is that it can be known to be true of the actual world, independently of all experience. It may, by some philosophical argument, follow from our knowing, independently of experience, that something is true of the actual world, that it has to be known to be true also of all possible worlds. But if this is to be established, it requires some philosophical argument to establish it. Now, *this* notion, if we

were to assign it to a branch of philosophy, belongs, not to metaphysics, but to epistemology. It has to do with the way we can know certain things to be in fact true. Now, it may be the case, of course, that anything which is necessary is something which *can* be known a priori. (Notice, by the way, the notion a priori truth as thus defined has in it *another* modality: it *can* be known independently of all experience. It is a little complicated because there is a double modality here.) I will not have time to explore these notions in full detail here, but one thing we can see from the outset is that these two notions are by no means trivially the same. If they are coextensive, it takes some philosophical argument to establish it. As stated, they belong to different domains of philosophy. One of them has something to do with *knowledge*, of what can be known in certain ways about the *actual* world. The other one has to do with *metaphysics*, how the world *could* have been; given that it is the way it is, could it have been otherwise, in certain ways? Now I hold, as a matter of fact, that neither class of statements is contained in the other. But all we need to talk about here is this: Is everything that is necessary knowable a priori or known a priori? Consider the following example: the Goldbach conjecture. This says that every even number is the sum of two primes. It is a mathematical statement, and if it is true at all, it has to be necessary. Certainly, one could not say that though in fact every even number is the sum of two primes, there could have been some extra number which was even and not the sum of two primes. What would that mean? On the other hand, the answer to the question whether every even number *is* in fact the sum of two primes is unknown, and we have no method at present for deciding. So we certainly do not know, a priori or even a posteriori, that every even number is the sum of two primes. (Well, perhaps we have some evidence in that no counterexample has been found.) But we certainly do not know a priori anyway, that every even number is, in fact, the sum of two primes. But, of course, the definition just says "*can* be known independently of experience," and someone might say that if it is true, we *could* know it independently of experience. It is hard to see exactly what this claim means. It might be so. One thing it might mean is that if it were true we could *prove* it. This claim is certainly wrong if it is generally applied to mathematical statements and we have to work within some fixed system. This is what Gödel proved. And even if we mean an "intuitive proof in general," it might just be the case (at least, this view is as clear and as probable as the contrary) that though the statement is true, there is just no way the human mind could ever prove it. Of course, one way an *infinite* mind might be able to prove it is by looking through each natural number one by one and checking. In this sense, of course, it can, perhaps, be known a priori, but only by an infinite mind, and then this gets into other complicated questions. I do not want to discuss questions about the conceivability of performing an infinite number of acts like looking through each number one by one. A vast philosophical literature has been written on this: Some have declared it is logically impossible; others that it is logically possible; and some do not know. The main point is that it is not trivial that just because such a statement is necessary it can be known a priori. Some considerable clarification is required before we decide that it can be so known. And so this shows that even if everything necessary is a priori in some sense, it should not be taken as a trivial matter of definition. It is a substantive philosophical thesis which requires some work.

Another example that one might give relates to the problem of essentialism. Here is a lectern. A question which has often been raised in philosophy is: What are its essential properties? What properties, aside from trivial ones like self-identity, are such that this object has to have them if it exists at all,[11] are such that if an object did not have it, it would not be this object?[12] For example, being made of wood, and not of ice, might be an essential property of this lectern. Let us just take the weaker statement that it is not made of ice. That will establish it as strongly as we need it, perhaps as dramatically. Supposing this lectern is in fact made of wood, could this very lectern have been made from the very beginning of its existence from ice, say frozen from water in the Thames? One has a considerable feeling that it could *not*, though in fact one certainly could have made a lectern of water from the Thames, frozen it into ice by some process, and put it right there in place of this thing. If one had done so, one would have made, of course, a *different* object. It

would not have been *this very lectern*, and so one would not have a case in which this very lectern here was made of ice, or was made from water from the Thames. The question of whether it could afterward, say in a minute from now, turn into ice is something else. So, it would seem, if an example like this is correct – and this is what advocates of essentialism have held – that this lectern could not have been made of ice, that is, in any counterfactual situation of which we would say that this lectern existed at all, we would have to say also that it was not made from water from the Thames frozen into ice. Some have rejected, of course, any such notion of essential property as meaningless. Usually, it is because (and I think this is what Quine, for example, would say) they have held that it depends on the notion of identity across possible worlds, and that this is itself meaningless. Since I have rejected this view already, I will not deal with it again. We can talk about *this very object*, and whether it could have had certain properties which it does not in fact have. For example, it could have been in another room from the room it in fact is in, even at this very time, but it could not have been made from the very beginning from water frozen into ice.

If the essentialist view is correct, it can only be correct if we sharply distinguish between the notions of a posteriori and a priori truth on the one hand, and contingent and necessary truth on the other hand, for although the statement that this table, if it exists at all, was not made of ice, is necessary, it certainly is not something that we know a priori. What we know is that first, lecterns usually are not made of ice, they are usually made of wood. This looks like wood. It does not feel cold, and it probably would if it were made of ice. Therefore, I conclude, probably this is not made of ice. Here my entire judgment is a posteriori. I could find out that an ingenious trick has been played upon me and that, in fact, this lectern is made of ice; but what I am saying is, given that it is in fact not made of ice, in fact is made of wood, one cannot imagine that under certain circumstances it could have been made of ice. So we have to say that though we cannot know a priori whether this table was made of ice or not, given that it is not made of ice, it is *necessarily* not made of ice. In other words, if *P* is the statement that the lectern is not made of ice, one knows by a priori philosophical analysis, some conditional of the form "if P, then necessarily P." If the table is not made of ice, it is necessarily not made of ice. On the other hand, then, we know by empirical investigation that P, the antecedent of the conditional, is true – that this table is not made of ice. We can conclude by *modus ponens*:

$$P \supset \Box P$$
$$\underline{P \qquad\qquad}$$
$$\Box P$$

The conclusion – "$\Box P$" – is that it is necessary that the table not be made of ice, and this conclusion is known a posteriori, since one of the premises on which it is based is a posteriori. So, the notion of essential properties can be maintained only by distinguishing between the notions of a priori and necessary truth, and I do maintain it.

Let us return to the question of identities. Concerning the statement "Hesperus is Phosphorus" or the statement "Cicero is Tully," one can find all of these out by empirical investigation, and we might turn out to be wrong in our empirical beliefs. So, it is usually argued, such statements must therefore be contingent. Some have embraced the other side of the coin and have held "Because of this argument about necessity, identity statements between names have to be knowable a priori, so, only a very special category of names, possibly, really works as names; the other things are bogus names, disguised descriptions, or something of the sort. However, a certain very narrow class of statements of identity are known a priori, and these are the ones which contain the genuine names." If one accepts the distinctions that I have made, one need not jump to either conclusion. One can hold that certain statements of identity between names, though often known a posteriori, and maybe not knowable a priori, are in fact necessary, if true. So, we have some room to hold this. But, of course, to have some room to hold it does not mean that we should hold it. So let us see what the evidence is. First, recall the remark that I made that proper names seem to be rigid designators, as when we use the name "Nixon" to talk about a certain man, even in counterfactual situations. If we say, "If Nixon had not written the letter to Saxbe, maybe he would have gotten Carswell through," we are in this statement talking about Nixon, Saxbe, and Carswell, the very same men as

in the actual world, and what would have happened to them under certain counterfactual circumstances. If names are rigid designators, then there can be no question about identities being necessary, because "a" and "b" will be rigid designators of a certain man or thing x. Then even in every possible world, a and b will both refer to this same object x, and to no other, and so there will be no situation in which a might not have been b. That would have to be a situation in which the object which we are also now calling "x" would not have been identical with itself. Then one could not possibly have a situation in which Cicero would not have been Tully or Hesperus would not have been Phosphorus.[13]

Aside from the identification of necessity with a priority, what has made people feel the other way? There are two things which have made people feel the other way.[14] Some people tend to regard identity statements as metalinguistic statements, to identify the statement "Hesperus is Phosphorus" with the metalinguistic statement "'Hesperus' and 'Phosphorus' are names of the same heavenly body." And that, of course, might have been false. We might have used the terms "Hesperus" and "Phosphorus" as names of *two* different heavenly bodies. But, of course, this has nothing to do with the necessity of identity. In the same sense "$2 + 2 = 4$" might have been false. The phrases "$2 + 2$" and "4" might have been used to refer to two different numbers. One can imagine a language, for example, in which "$+$," "2," and "$=$" were used in the standard way, but "4" was used as the name of, say, the square root of minus 1, as we should call it, "i." Then "$2 + 2 = 4$" would be false, for 2 plus 2 is not equal to the square root of minus 1. But this is not what we want. We do not want just to say that a certain statement which we in fact use to express something true could have expressed something false. We want to use the statement in *our* way and see if it could have been false. Let us do this. What is the idea people have? They say, 'Look, Hesperus might not have been Phosphorus. Here a certain planet was seen in the morning, and it was seen in the evening; and it just turned out later on as a matter of empirical fact that they were one and the same planet. If things had turned out otherwise, they would have been two different planets, or two different heavenly bodies, so how can you say that such a statement is necessary?'

Now there are two things that such people can mean. First, they can mean that we do not know a priori whether Hesperus is Phosphorus. This I have already conceded. Second, they may mean that they can actually imagine circumstances that they would call circumstances in which Hesperus would not have been Phosphorus. Let us think what would be such a circumstance, using these terms here as *names* of a planet. For example, it could have been the case that Venus did indeed rise in the morning in exactly the position in which we saw it, but that on the other hand, in the position which is in fact occupied by Venus in the evening, Venus was not there, and Mars took its place. This is all counterfactual because in fact Venus is there. Now one can also imagine that in this counterfactual other possible world, the Earth would have been inhabited by people and that they should have used the names "Phosphorus" for Venus in the morning and "Hesperus" for Mars in the evening. Now, this is all very good, but would it be a situation in which Hesperus was not Phosphorus? Of course, it is a situation in which people would have been able to *say*, truly, "Hesperus is not Phosphorus"; but we are supposed to describe things in our language, not in theirs. So let us describe it in our language. Well, how could it actually happen that Venus would not be in that position in the evening? For example, let us say that there is some comet that comes around every evening and yanks things over a little bit. (That would be a very simple scientific way of imagining it: not really too simple – that is very hard to imagine actually.) It just happens to come around every evening, and things get yanked over a bit. Mars gets yanked over to the very position where Venus is, then the comet yanks things back to their normal position in the morning. Thinking of this planet which we now call "Phosphorus," what should we say? Well, we can say that the comet passes it and yanks Phosphurus over so that it is not in the position normally occupied by Phosphorus in the evening. If we do say this, and really use "Phosphorus" as the name of a planet, then we have to say that, under such circumstances, Phosphorus in the evening would not be in the position in which we, in fact, saw it; or alternatively, Hesperus in the evening would not be in the position in which we, in fact, saw it. We might say that under such circumstances, we would not have called Hesperus

"Hesperus" because Hesperus would have been in a different position. But that still would not make Phosphorus different from Hesperus; what would then be the case instead is that Hesperus would have been in a different position from the position it in fact is and, perhaps, not in such a position that people would have called it "Hesperus." But that would not be a situation in which Phosphorus would not have been Hesperus.

Let us take another example which may be clearer. Suppose someone uses "Tully" to refer to the Roman orator who denounced Cataline and uses the name "Cicero" to refer to the man whose works he had to study in third-year Latin in high school. Of course, he may not know in advance that the very same man who denounced Cataline wrote these works, and that is a contingent statement. But the fact that this statement is contingent should not make us think that the statement that Cicero is Tully, if it is true, and it is in fact true, is contingent. Suppose, for example, that Cicero actually did denounce Cataline, but thought that this political achievement was so great that he should not bother writing any literary works. Would we say that these would be circumstances under which he would not have been Cicero? It seems to me that the answer is no, that instead we would say that, under such circumstances, Cicero would not have written any literary works. It is not a necessary property of Cicero – the way the shadow follows the man – that he should have written certain works; we can easily imagine a situation in which Shakespeare would not have written the works of Shakespeare, or one in which Cicero would not have written the works of Cicero. What may be the case is that we *fix the reference* of the term "Cicero" by use of some descriptive phrase, such as "the author of these works." But once we have this reference fixed, we then use the name "Cicero" *rigidly* to designate the man who in fact we have identified by his authorship of these works. We do not use it to designate whoever would have written these works in place of Cicero, if someone else wrote them. It might have been the case that the man who wrote these works was not the man who denounced Cataline. Cassius might have written these works. But we would not then say that Cicero would have been Cassius, unless we were speaking in a very loose and metaphorical way. We would say that Cicero, whom we may have identified and come to know by his works, would not have written them, and that someone else, say Cassius, would have written them in his place.

Such examples are not grounds for thinking that identity statements are contingent. To take them as such grounds is to misconstrue the relation between a *name* and a *description used to fix its reference*, to take them to be *synonyms*. Even if we fix the reference of such a name as "Cicero" as the man who wrote such and such works, in speaking of counterfactual situations, when we speak of Cicero, we do not then speak of whoever in such counterfactual situations *would* have written such and such works, but rather of Cicero, whom we have identified by the contingent property that he is the man who in fact, that is, in the actual world, wrote certain works.[15]

I hope this is reasonably clear in a brief compass. Now, actually I have been presupposing something I do not really believe to be, in general, true. Let us suppose that we do fix the reference of a name by a description. Even if we do so, we do not then make the name *synonymous* with the description, but instead we use the name *rigidly* to refer to the object so named, even in talking about counterfactual situations where the thing named would not satisfy the description in question. Now, this is what I think in fact is true for those cases of naming where the reference is fixed by description. But, in fact, I also think, contrary to most recent theorists, that the reference of names is rarely or almost never fixed by means of description. And by this I do not just mean what Searle says: "It's not a single description, but rather a cluster, a family of properties which fixes the reference." I mean that properties in this sense are not used *at all*. But I do not have the time to go into this here. So, let us suppose that at least one half of prevailing views about naming is true, that the reference is fixed by descriptions. Even were that true, the name would not be synonymous with the description, but would be used to *name* an object which we pick out by the contingent fact that it satisfies a certain description. And so, even though we can imagine a case where the man who wrote these works would not have been the man who denounced Cataline, we should not say that that would be a case in which Cicero would not have been Tully. We should say that it is a case in which Cicero did not write these works, but rather that Cassius did. And the identity of Cicero and Tully still holds.

Let me turn to the case of heat and the motion of molecules. Here, surely, is a case that is contingent identity! Recent philosophy has emphasized this again and again. So, if it is a case of contingent identity, then let us imagine under what circumstances it would be false. Now, concerning this statement I hold that the circumstances philosophers apparently have in mind as circumstances under which it would have been false are not in fact such circumstances. First, of course, it is argued that "Heat is the motion of molecules" is an a posteriori judgment; scientific investigation might have turned out otherwise. As I said before, this shows nothing against the view that it is necessary – at least if I am right. But here, surely, people had very specific circumstances in mind under which, so they thought, the judgment that heat is the motion of molecules would have been false. What were these circumstances? One can distill them out of the fact that we found out empirically that heat is the motion of molecules. How was this? What did we find out first when we found out that heat is the motion of molecules? There is a certain external phenomenon which we can sense by the sense of touch, and it produces a sensation which we call "the sensation of heat." We then discover that the external phenomenon which produces this sensation, which we sense, by means of our sense of touch, is in fact that of molecular agitation in the thing that we touch, a very high degree of molecular agitation. So, it might be thought, to imagine a situation in which heat would not have been the motion of molecules, we need only imagine a situation in which we would have had the very same sensation and it would have been produced by something other than the motion of molecules. Similarly, if we wanted to imagine a situation in which light was not a stream of photons, we could imagine a situation in which we were sensitive to something else in exactly the same way, producing what we call visual experiences, though not through a stream of photons. To make the case stronger, or to look at another side of the coin, we could also consider a situation in which we *are* concerned with the motion of molecules but in which such motion does not give us the sensation of heat. And it might also have happened that we, or, at least, the creatures inhabiting this planet, might have been so constituted that, let us say, an increase in the motion of molecules did not give us this sensation but that, on the contrary, a slowing down of the molecules did give us the very same sensation. This would be a situation, so it might be thought, in which heat would not be the motion of molecules, or, more precisely, in which temperature would not be mean molecular kinetic energy.

But I think it would not be so. Let us think about the situation again. First, let us think about it in the actual world. Imagine right now the world invaded by a number of Martians, who do indeed get the very sensation that we call "the sensation of heat" when they feel some ice which has slow molecular motion, and who do not get a sensation of heat – in fact, maybe just the reverse – when they put their hand near a fire which causes a lot of molecular agitation. Would we say, "Ah, this casts some doubt on heat being the motion of molecules, because there are these other people who don't get the same sensation"? Obviously not, and no one would think so. We would say instead that the Martians somehow feel the very sensation we get when we feel heat when they feel cold, and that they do not get a sensation of heat when they feel heat. But now let us think of a counterfactual situation.[16] Suppose the earth had from the very beginning been inhabited by such creatures. First, imagine it inhabited by no creatures at all: then there is no one to feel any sensations of heat. But we would not say that under such circumstances it would necessarily be the case that heat did not exist; we would say that heat might have existed, for example, if there were fires that heated up the air.

Let us suppose the laws of physics were not very different: Fires do heat up the air. Then there would have been heat even though there were no creatures around to feel it. Now let us suppose evolution takes place, and life is created, and there are some creatures around. But they are not like us, they are more like the Martians. Now would we say that heat has suddenly turned to cold, because of the way the creatures of this planet sense it? No, I think we should describe this situation as a situation in which, though the creatures on this planet got our sensation of heat, they did not get it when they were exposed to heat. They got it when they were exposed to cold. And that is something we can surely well imagine. We can imagine it just as we can imagine our planet being invaded by creatures of this sort. Think of it in two steps. First there is a stage where there are no creatures at all, and one can certainly

imagine the planet still having both heat and cold, though no one is around to sense it. Then the planet comes through an evolutionary process to be peopled with beings of different neural structure from ourselves. Then these creatures could be such that they were insensitive to heat; they did not feel it in the way we do; but on the other hand, they felt cold in much the same way that we feel heat. But still, heat would be heat, and cold would be cold. And particularly, then, this goes in no way against saying that in this counterfactual situation heat would still *be* the molecular motion, *be* that which is produced by fires, and so on, just as it would have been if there had been no creatures on the planet at all. Similarly, we could imagine that the planet was inhabited by creatures who got visual sensations when there were sound waves in the air. We should not therefore say, "Under such circumstances, sound would have been light." Instead we should say, "The planet was inhabited by creatures who were in some sense visually sensitive to sound, and may be even visually sensitive to light." If this is correct, it can still be and will still be a necessary truth that heat is the motion of molecules and that light is a stream of photons.

To state the view succinctly: we use both the terms "heat" and "the motion of molecules" as rigid designators for a certain external phenomenon. Since heat is in fact the motion of molecules, and the designators are rigid, by the argument I have given here, it is going to be *necessary* that heat is the motion of molecules. What gives us the illusion of contingency is the fact we have identified the heat by the contingent fact that there happen to be creatures on this planet – (namely, ourselves) who are sensitive to it in a certain way, that is, who are sensitive to the motion of molecules or to heat – these are one and the same thing. And this is contingent. So we use the description, 'that which causes such and such sensations, or that which we sense in such and such a way,' to identify heat. But in using this fact we use a contingent property of heat, just as we use the contingent property of Cicero as having written such and such works to identify him. We then use the terms "heat" in the one case and "Cicero" in the other *rigidly* to designate the objects for which they stand. And of course the term "the motion of molecules" is rigid; it always stands for the motion of molecules, never for any other phenomenon. So, as Bishop Butler said, "everything is what it is and not another thing." Therefore, "Heat is the motion of molecules" will be necessary, not contingent, and one only has the *illusion* of contingency in the way one could have the illusion of contingency in thinking that this table might have been made of ice. We might think one could imagine it, but if we try, we can see on reflection that what we are really imagining is just there being another lectern in this very position here which was in fact made of ice. The fact that we may identify this lectern by being the object we see and touch in such and such a position is something else.

Now how does this relate to the problem of mind and body? It is usually held that this is a contingent identity statement just like "Heat is the motion of molecules." That cannot be. It cannot be a contingent identity statement just like "Heat is the motion of molecules" because, if I am right, "Heat is the motion of molecules" is not a contingent identity statement. Let us look at this statement. For example, "My being in pain at such and such a time is my being in such and such a brain state at such and such a time," or "Pain in general is such and such a neural (brain) state."

This is held to be contingent on the following grounds. First, we can imagine the brain state existing though there is no pain at all. It is only a scientific fact that whenever we are in a certain brain state we have a pain. Second, one might imagine a creature being in pain, but not being in any specified brain state at all, maybe not having a brain at all. People even think, at least prima facie, though they may be wrong, that they can imagine totally disembodied creatures, at any rate certainly not creatures with bodies anything like our own. So it seems that we can imagine definite circumstances under which this relationship would have been false. Now, if these circumstances are circumstances, notice that we cannot deal with them simply by saying that this is just an illusion, something we can apparently imagine, but in fact cannot in the way we thought erroneously that we could imagine a situation in which heat was not the motion of molecules. Because although we can say that we pick out heat contingently by the contingent property that it affects us in such and such a way, we cannot similarly say that we pick out pain contingently by the fact that it affects us in such and such a way. On such a picture there

would be the brain state, and we pick it out by the contingent fact that it affects us as pain. Now that might be true of the brain state, but it cannot be true of the pain. The experience itself has to be *this experience*, and I cannot say that it is a contingent property of the pain I now have that it is a pain.[17] In fact, it would seem that the terms "my pain" and "my being in such and such a brain state" are, first of all, both rigid designators. That is, whenever anything is such and such a pain, it is essentially that very object, namely, such and such a pain, and wherever anything is such and such a brain state, it is essentially that very object, namely, such and such a brain state. So both of these are rigid designators. One cannot say this pain might have been something else, some other state. These are both rigid designators.

Second, the way we would think of picking them out – namely, the pain by its being an experience of a certain sort, and the brain state by its being the state of a certain material object, being of such and such molecular configuration – both of these pick out their objects essentially and not accidentally, that is, they pick them out by essential properties. Whenever the molecules *are* in this configuration, we *do* have such and such a brain state. Whenever you feel *this*, you do have a pain. So it seems that the identity theorist is in some trouble, for, since we have two rigid designators, the identity statement in question is necessary. Because they pick out their objects essentially, we cannot say the case where you seem to imagine the identity statement false is really an illusion like the illusion one gets in the case of heat and molecular motion, because that illusion depended on the fact that we pick out heat by a certain contingent property. So there is very little room to maneuver, perhaps none.[18] The identity theorist, who holds that pain is the brain state, also has to hold that it necessarily is the brain state. He therefore cannot concede, but has to deny, that there would have been situations under which one would have had pain but not the corresponding brain state. Now usually in arguments on the identity theory, this is very far from being denied. In fact, it is conceded from the outset by the materialist as well as by his opponent. He says, "Of course, it *could* have been the case that we had pains without the brain states. It is a contingent identity." But that cannot be. He has to hold that we are under some illusion in thinking that we can imagine that there could have been pains without brain states. And the only model I can think of for what the illusion might be, or at least the model given by the analogy the materialists themselves suggest, namely, heat and molecular motion, simply does not work in this case. So the materialist is up against a very stiff challenge. He has to show that these things we think we can see to be possible are in fact not possible. He has to show that these things which we can imagine are not in fact things we can imagine. And that requires some very different philosophical argument from the sort which has been given in the case of heat and molecular motion. And it would have to be a deeper and subtler argument than I can fathom and subtler than has ever appeared in any materialist literature that I have read. So the conclusion of this investigation would be that the analytical tools we are using go against the identity thesis and so go against the general thesis that mental states are just physical states.[19]

The next topic would be my own solution to the mind-body problem, but that I do not have.

Notes

1   This paper was presented orally, without a written text, to the New York University lecture series on identity which makes up the volume *Identity and Individuation*. The lecture was taped, and the present paper represents a transcription of these tapes, edited only slightly with no attempt to change the style of the original. If the reader imagines the sentences of this paper as being delivered, extemporaneously, with proper pauses and emphases, this may facilitate his comprehension. Nevertheless, there may still be passages which are hard to follow, and the time allotted necessitated a condensed presentation of the argument. (A longer version of some of these views, still rather compressed and still representing a transcript of oral remarks, has appeared in Donald Davidson and Gilbert Harman (eds), *Semantics of Natural Language* (Dordrecht: Reidel, 1972).) Occasionally, reservations, amplifications and gratifications of my remarks had to be repressed, especially in the discussion of theoretical identification and the mind-body problem. The notes, which were added to the original, would have become even more unwieldly if this had not been done.

2   R.J. Butler (ed.), *Analytical Philosophy, Second Series* (Oxford: Blackwell, 1965), p. 41.

3   The second occurrence of the description has small scope.

4   In Russell's theory, $F(\imath xGx)$ follows from $(x)Fx$ and $(\exists!x)\,Gx$, provided that the description in $F(\imath xGx)$ has the entire context for its scope (in Russell's 1905 terminology, has a "primary occurrence"). Only then is $F(\imath xGx)$ "about" the denotation of "$\imath xGx$." Applying this rule to (4), we get the results indicated in the text. Notice that, in the ambiguous form $\square(\imath xGx = \imath xHx)$, if one or both of the descriptions have "primary occurrences," the formula does not assert the necessity of $\imath xGx = \imath xHx$; if both have secondary occurrences, it does. Thus in a language without explicit scope indicators, descriptions must be construed with the smallest possible scope – only then will $\sim A$ be the negation of A, $\square A$ the necessitation of A, and the like.

5   An earlier distinction with the same purpose was, of course, the medieval one of *de dicto-de re*. That Russell's distinction of scope eliminates modal paradoxes has been pointed out by many logicians, especially Smullyan.

So as to avoid misunderstanding, let me emphasize that I am of course not asserting that Russell's notion of scope solves Quine's problem of "essentialism", what it does show, especially in conjunction with modern model-theoretic approaches to modal logic, is that quantified modal logic need not deny the truth of all instances of $(x)(y)(x = y \cdot \supset \cdot Fx \supset Fy)$, nor of all instances of "$(x)(Gx \supset Ga)$" (where "a" is to be replaced by a nonvacuous definite description whose scope is all of "Ga"), in order to avoid making it a necessary truth that one and the same man invented bifocals and headed the original Postal Department. Russell's contextual definition of description need not be adopted in order to ensure these results; but other logical theories, Fregean or other, which take descriptions as primitive must somehow express the same logical facts. Frege showed that a simple, non-iterated context containing a definite description with small scope, which cannot be interpreted as being "about" the denotation of the description, can be interpreted as about its "sense." Some logicians have been interested in the question of the conditions under which, in an intensional context, a description with small scope is equivalent to the same one with large scope. One of the virtues of a Russellian treatment of descriptions in modal logic is that the answer (roughly that the description be a "rigid designator" in the sense of this lecture) then often follows from the other postulates for quantified modal logic: no special postulates are needed, as in Hintikka's treatment. Even if descriptions are taken as primitive, special postulation of when scope is irrelevant can often be deduced from more basic axioms.

6   R. B. Marcus, "Modalities and intensional languages," in *Boston Studies in the Philosophy of Science*, vol. 1 (New York: Humanities Press, 1963), pp. 71ff. See also the "Comments" by Quine and the ensuing discussion.

7   It should. See her remark in *Boston Studies in the Philosophy of Science*, vol. 1, p. 115, in the discussion following the papers.

8   If there is no deity, and especially if the nonexistence of a deity is *necessary*, it is dubious that we can use "he" to refer to a deity. The use in the text must be taken to be nonliteral.

9   David K. Lewis, "Counterpart theory and quantified modal logic," *Journal of Philosophy* 65 (1968), pp. 113ff.

10 Some philosophers think that definite descriptions, in English, are ambiguous, that sometimes "the inventor of bifocals" rigidly designates the man who in fact invented bifocals. I am tentatively inclined to reject this view, construed as a thesis about English (as opposed to a possible hypothetical language), but I will not argue the question here.

What I do wish to note is that, contrary to some opinions, this alleged ambiguity cannot replace the Russellian notion of the scope of a description. Consider the sentence "The number of planets might have been necessarily even." This sentence plainly can be read so as to express a truth; had there been eight planets, the number of planets would have been necessarily even. Yet without scope distionctions, both a "referential" (rigid) and a nonrigid reading of the description will make the statement false. (Since the number of planets in the rigid reading amounts to the falsity that 9 might have been necessarily even.)

The "rigid" reading is equivalent to the Russellian primary occurrence; the nonrigid, to innermost scope – some, following Donnellan, perhaps loosely, have called this reading the "attributive" use. The possibility of intermediate scopes is then ignored. In the present instance, the intended reading of $\Diamond\Box$ (the number of planets is even) makes the scope of the description $\Box$(the number of planets is even), neither the largest nor the smallest possible.

11 This definition is the usual formulation of the notion of essential property, but an exception must be made for existence itself: on the definition given, existence would be trivially essential. We should regard existence as essential to an object only if the object necessarily exists. Perhaps there are other recherché properties, involving existence, for which the definition is similarly objectionable. (I thank Michael Slote for this observation.)

12 The two clauses of the sentence noted give equivalent definitions of the notion of essential property, since $\Box((\exists x)(x = a) \supset Fa)$ is equivalent to $\Box(x)$ $(\sim Fx \supset x = a)$. The second formulation, however, has served as a powerful seducer in favor of theories of "identification across possible worlds." For it suggests that we consider 'an object *b* in another possible world' and test whether it is identifiable with *a* by asking whether it lacks any of the essential properties of *a*. Let me therefore emphasize that, although an essential property is (trivially) a property without which an object cannot be *a*, it by no means follows that the essential, purely qualitative properties of *a* jointly form a sufficient condition for being *a*, nor that *any* purely qualitative conditions are sufficient for an object to be *a*. Further, even if necessary and sufficient qualitative conditions for an object to be Nixon may exist, there would still be little justification for the demand for a purely qualitative description of all counterfactual situations. We can ask whether Nixon might have been a Democrat without engaging in these subtleties.

13 I thus agree with Quine, that "Hesperus is Phosphorus" is (or can be) an empirical discovery; with Marcus, that it is necessary. Both Quine and Marcus, according to the present standpoint, err in identifying the epistemological and the metaphysical issues.

14 The two confusions alleged, especially the second, are both related to the confusion of the metaphysical question of the necessity of "Hesperus is Phosphorus" with the epistemological question of its aprioricity. For if Hesperus is identified by its position in the sky in the evening, and Phosphorus by its position in the morning, an investigator may well know, in advance of empirical research, that Hesperus is Phosphorus if and only if one and the same body occupies position *x* in the evening and position *y* in the morning. The a priori material equivalence of the two statements, however, does not imply their strict (necessary) equivalence. (The same remarks apply to the case of heat and molecular motion.) Similar remarks apply to some extent to the relationship between "Hesperus is Phosphorus" and "'Hesperus' and 'Phosphorus' name the same thing." A confusion that also operates is, of course, the confusion between what *we* say of a counterfactual situation and how people *in* that situation would have described it; this confusion, too, is probably related to the confusion between aprioricity and necessity.

15   If someone protests, regarding the lectern, that it *could* after all have *turned out* to have been made of ice, and therefore could have been made of ice, I would reply that what he really means is that *a lectern* could have looked just like this one, and have been placed in the same position as this one, and yet have been made of ice. In short, I could have been in the *same epistemological situation* in relation to *a lectern made of ice* as I actually am in relation to *this* lectern. In the main text, I have argued that the same reply should be given to protests that Hesperus could have turned out to be other than Phosphorus, or Cicero other than Tully. Here, then, the notion of "counterpart" comes into its own. For it is not this table, but an epistemic "counterpart," which was hewn from ice; not Hesperus–Phosphorus–Venus, but two distinct counterparts thereof, in two of the roles Venus actually plays (that of Evening Star and Morning Star), which are different. Precisely because of this fact, it is not *this table* which could have been made of ice. Statements about the modal properties of *this table* never refer to counterparts. However, if someone confuses the epistemological and the metaphysical problems, he will be well on the way to the counterpart theory Lewis and others have advocated.

16   Isn't the situation I just described also counterfactual? At least it may well be, if such Martians never in fact invade. Strictly speaking, the distinction I wish to draw compares how we *would* speak *in* a (possibly counterfactual) situation, *if* it obtained, and how we *do* speak *of* a counterfactual situation, knowing that it does not obtain – i.e., the distinction between the language we would have used in a situation and the language we *do* use to describe it. (Consider the description: "Suppose we all spoke German." This description is in English.) The former case can be made vivid by imagining the counterfactual situation to be actual.

17   The most popular identity theories advocated today explicitly fail to satisfy this simple requirement. For these theories usually hold that a mental state is a brain state, and that what makes the brain state into a mental state is its "causal role," the fact that it tends to produce certain behavior (as intentions produce actions, or pain, pain behavior) and to be produced by certain stimuli (e.g., pain, by pinpricks). If the relations between the brain state and its causes and effects are regarded as contingent, then *being such-and-such-a-mental-state* is a contingent property of the brain state. Let X be a pain. The causal-role identity theorist holds (1) that X is a brain state, (2) that the fact that X is a pain is to be analyzed (roughly) as the fact that X is produced by certain stimuli and produces certain

behavior. The fact mentioned in (2) is, of course, regarded as contingent; the brain state X might well exist and not tend to produce the appropriate behavior in the absence of other conditions. Thus (1) and (2) assert that a certain pain X might have existed, yet not have been a pain. This seems to me self-evidently absurd. Imagine any pain: is it possible that *it itself* could have existed, yet not have been a pain?

If $X = Y$, then X and Y share all properties, including modal properties. If X is a pain and Y the corresponding brain state, then *being a pain* is an essential property of X, and *being a brain state* is an essential property of Y. If the correspondence relation is, in fact, identity, then it must be *necessary* of Y that it corresponds to a pain, and *necessary* of X that it correspond to a brain state, indeed to this particular brain state, Y. Both assertions seem false; it *seems* clearly possible that X should have existed without the corresponding brain state; or that the brain state should have existed without being felt as pain. Identity theorists cannot, contrary to their almost universal present practice, accept these intuitions; they must deny them, and explain them away. This is none too easy a thing to do.

18   A brief restatement of the argument may be helpful here. If "pain" and "C-fiber stimulation" are rigid designators of phenomena, one who identifies them must regard the identity as necessary. How can this necessity be reconciled with the apparent fact that C-fiber stimulation might have turned out not to be correlated with pain at all? We might try to reply by analogy to the case of heat and molecular motion; the latter identity, too, is necessary, yet someone may believe that, before scientific investigation showed otherwise, molecular motion might have turned out not to be heat. The reply is, of course, that what really is possible is that people (or some rational or sentient beings) could have been in the *same epistemic situation* as we actually are, and identify *a phenomenon* in the same way we identify heat, namely, by feeling it by the sensation we call "the sensation of heat," without the phenomenon being molecular motion. Further, the beings might not have been sensitive to molecular motion (i.e., to heat) by any neural mechanism whatsoever. It is impossible to explain the apparent possibility of C-fiber stimulations not having been pain in the same way. Here, too, we would have to suppose that we could have been in the same epistemological situation, and identify something in the same way we identify pain, without its corresponding to C-fiber stimulation. But the way we identify pain is by feeling it, and if a C-fiber stimulation could have occurred without

our feeling any pain, then the C-fiber stimulation could have occurred without there *being* any pain, contrary to the necessity of the identity. The trouble is that although "heat" is a rigid designator, heat is picked out by the contingent property of its being felt in a certain way; pain, on the other hand, is picked out by an essential (indeed necessary and sufficient) property. For a sensation to be *felt* as pain is for it to *be* pain.

19 All arguments against the identity theory which rely on the necessity of identity, or on the notion of essential property, are, of course, inspired by Descartes's argument for his dualism. The earlier arguments which superficially were rebutted by the analogies of heat and molecular motion, and the bifocals inventor who was also Postmaster General, had such an inspiration; and so does my argument here. R. Albritton and M. Slote have informed me that they independently have attempted to give essentialist arguments against the identity theory, and probably others have done so as well.

The simplest Cartesian argument can perhaps be restated as follows: Let "*A*" be a *name* (rigid designator) of Descartes's body. Then Descartes argues that since he could exist even if *A* did not, $\lozenge$(Descartes $\neq A$), hence Descartes $\neq A$. Those who have accused him of a modal fallacy have forgotten that "*A*" is rigid. His argument is valid, and his conclusion is correct, provided its (perhaps dubitable) premise is accepted. On the other hand, provided that Descartes is regarded as having ceased to exist upon his death, "Descartes $\neq A$" can be established without the use of a modal argument; for if so, no doubt *A* survived Descartes when *A* was a corpse. Thus *A* had a property (existing at a certain time) which Descartes did not. The same argument can establish that a statue is not the hunk of stone, or the congery of molecules, of which it is composed. Mere non-identity, then, may be a weak conclusion. (See D. Wiggins, *Philosophical Review* 77 (1968), pp. 90ff.) The Cartesian modal argument, however, surely can be deployed to maintain relevant stronger conclusions as well.

11

Contingent Identity

Allan Gibbard

This brief for contingent identity begins with an example. Under certain conditions, I shall argue, a clay statue is identical with the piece of clay of which it is made – or at least it is plausible to claim so. If indeed the statue and the piece of clay are identical, I shall show, then the identity is contingent: that is to say, where s is the statue and c the piece of clay.

(1) $s = c$ & $\lozenge(s$ exists & c exists & $s \neq c)$

This claim of contingent identity, if true, has important ramifications. Later I shall develop theories of concrete things and proper names which are needed to fit the claim. These theories together form a coherent alternative to theories which hold that all true identities formed with proper names are necessary – a plausible alternative, I shall argue, with many advantages.

Most purported examples of such contingent identity fail: that much, I think, has been shown by Saul Kripke's recent work.[1] Kripke's work has transformed the subjects of necessity and reference, and the usual examples of contingent identity depend on accounts of those subjects which Kripke's attacks undermine. Take, for instance,

one of Frege's examples of *a posteriori* identity, somewhat reworded:[2]

(2) If Hesperus exists, then Hesperus = Phosphorus.

On the account of necessity which prevailed before Kripke, a truth is necessary only if it can be known a priori. Now as Frege pointed out, (2) is clearly a posteriori, since it reports a discovery which could only have been made by observation. On the old account, then, (2), although true, is not a necessary truth. Kripke's attacks undermine this account of necessary truth as a priori truth. Whether something is a necessary truth, he argues, is not a matter of how we can know it, but of whether it might have been false if the world had been different: a proposition is a necessary truth if it would have been true in any possible situation. The necessary–contingent distinction and the a priori–a posteriori distinction, then, are not drawn in the same way, and to prove a truth contingent, it is not enough simply to show that it is a posteriori.[3]

Kripke's attacks also undermine accounts of reference which would make (2) a contingent truth. On both Russell's theory of descriptions[4]

Allan Gibbard, "Contingent Identity," *Journal of Philosophical Logic*, 4 (1975): 187–221.
Reproduced by kind permission of Springer Science + Business Media B.V.

and the later "cluster" theory, a name gets its reference in some way from the beliefs of the person who uses it. On Russell's view, the heavenly body Hesperus of which the ancients spoke would be the thing which fitted certain beliefs they had about Hesperus; on the cluster theory, it would be the thing which fitted a preponderance of their beliefs about it. Now the ancients' beliefs about Hesperus and their beliefs about Phosphorus were such that, in some possible worlds, one thing would fit the former and another the latter. On such an account of proper names, then, (2) would be false in some possible worlds, and is therefore contingent.

I shall not repeat Kripke's attacks on the description and cluster theories of proper names.[5] My purpose here is to argue that even if these attacks are successful, there may well remain some contingent identities consisting of proper names. The identity of Hesperus and Phosphorus is not contingent, on the theories I shall develop, but I shall give an example which is. Kripke's attacks, if I am right, transform the subject of contingent identity, but they do not eliminate it.

I

In what sort of case might a statue s be identical with the piece of clay, c, of which it is made? Identity here is to be taken in a strict, timeless sense, not as mere identity during some period of time. For two things to be strictly identical, they must have all properties in common. That means, among other things, that they must start to exist at the same time and cease to exist at the same time. If we are to construct a case in which a statue is identical with a piece of clay, then, we shall need persistence criteria for statues and pieces of clay – criteria for when they start to exist and when they cease to exist.

Take first the piece of clay. Here I do not mean the portion of clay of which the piece consists, which may go on existing after the piece has been broken up or merged with other pieces. I shall call this clay of which the piece consists a *portion* of clay; a portion of clay, as I am using the term, can be scattered widely and continue to exist. Here I am asking about a *piece* or *lump* of clay.

A lump sticks together: its parts stick to each other, directly or through other parts, and no part

of the lump sticks to any portion of clay which is not part of the lump. The exact nature of this sticking relation will not matter here; it is a familiar relation which holds between parts of a solid object, but not between parts of a liquid, powder, or heap of solid objects. We know, then, what it is for two portions of clay to be parts of the same lump of clay at a time t, and if they are, I shall say that they are *stuck to* each other *at t*.

For how long, then, does a piece of clay persist? As a first approximation, the criteria might be put as follows. A piece of clay consists of a portion P of clay. It comes into existence when all the parts of P come to be stuck to each other, and cease to be stuck to any clay which is not part of P. It ceases to exist when the parts of P cease to be stuck to each other or come to be stuck to clay which is not in P. Thus a piece of clay can be formed either by sticking smaller pieces of clay together or by breaking it off a larger piece of clay, and it can be destroyed either by breaking it apart or by sticking it to other pieces of clay.

This standard is probably too strict; we ought to allow for such things as wear and the adherence of clay dust to a wet piece of clay. Nothing will change, though, for my purposes, if we allow the portion of clay which composes a piece of clay to change slowly over time. In the actual world, then, a piece of clay might be characterized by a function P from instants to portions of clay. In order for it to characterize a piece of clay, the function P would have to satisfy the following conditions.

(a)   The domain of P is an interval of time T.

(b)   For any instant t in T, $P(t)$ is a portion of clay the parts of which, at t, are both stuck to each other and not stuck to any clay particles which are not part of $P(t)$.

(c)   The portions of clay $P(t)$ change with t only slowly, if at all. (I shall give no exact standard of slowness here, but one might be stipulated if anything hinged on it.)

(d)   No function P^* which satisfies (a), (b), and (c) *extends* P^*, in the sense that the domain of P^* properly includes the domain of P and the function P is P^* with its domain restricted.

Both on this standard, then, and on the earlier, stricter one, a piece of clay comes into existence when parts in it are stuck to each other and unstuck from all other clay, and goes out of existence when its parts cease to be stuck to each other or become stuck to other clay. That is what I shall need for what follows.

What, now, are the persistence criteria for clay statues? By a statue here, I do not mean a shape of which there could be more than one token, but a concrete particular thing: distinct clay statues, as I am using the term, may come out of the same mold. A clay statue consists of a piece of clay in a specific shape. It lasts, then, as long as the piece of clay lasts and keeps that shape. It comes into being when the piece of clay first exists and has that shape, and it goes out of existence as soon as the piece of clay ceases to exist or to have that shape.

These criteria too may be overly strict: again we may want to allow for slow changes of shape from wear, accretion, and slight bending. So let us say, a clay statue persists as long as the piece of clay it is made of persists and changes shape only slowly.

I do not claim that the criteria I have given are precisely set forth that way in our conceptual scheme. I do think that the criteria I have given fit at least roughly what we say about statues and pieces of clay. My argument will depend on no such claim, though, and for all I shall have to say, the criteria I have given might have been purely stipulative. I do need to make one claim for those criteria: I claim that as I have defined them, pieces of clay and clay statues are objects. That is to say, they can be designated with proper names, and the logic we ordinarily use will still apply. That is all, strictly speaking, that I need to claim for the criteria I have given.

Now we are in a better position to ask, are a clay statue and the piece of clay of which it is made identical? The persistence criteria I have given make it clear that often the two are distinct. In a typical case, a piece of clay is brought into existence by breaking it off from a bigger piece of clay. It then gets shaped, say, into the form of an elephant. With the finishing touches, a statue of an elephant comes into being. The statue and the piece of clay therefore have different properties: the times they start to exist are different, and whereas the statue has the property of being elephant-shaped as long as it exists, the piece of clay does not. Since one has properties the other lacks, the two are not identical.[6]

Suppose, though, a clay statue starts to exist at the same time as the piece of clay of which it is made, and ceases to exist at the same time as the piece of clay ceases to exist. Will the statue then be identical with the piece of clay? It is indeed possible for a statue to endure for precisely the same period of time as its piece of clay, as the persistence criteria I have given make clear. Consider the following story.

I make a clay statue of the infant Goliath in two pieces, one the part above the waist and the other the part below the waist. Once I finish the two halves, I stick them together, thereby bringing into existence simultaneously a new piece of clay and a new statue. A day later I smash the statue, thereby bringing to an end both statue and piece of clay. The statue and the piece of clay persisted during exactly the same period of time.

Here, I am tempted to say, the statue and the piece of clay are identical. They began at the same time, and on any usual account, they had the same shape, location color, and so forth at each instant in their history, everything that happened to one happened to the other, and the act that destroyed the one destroyed the other. If the statue is an entity over and above the piece of clay in that shape, then statues seem to take on a ghostly air. No doubt other explanations of what the statue is can be offered, but the hypothesis that the statue and piece of clay are identical seems well worth exploring.

If indeed the statue and piece of clay are the same thing, then their identity is contingent. It is contingent, that is to say in the sense of (1) at the beginning of this paper. (1) uses proper names, and so let me name the statue and the lump: the statue I shall call "*Goliath*"; the piece of clay, "Lumpl." Naming the piece of clay, to be sure, seems strange, but that, presumably, is because it is unusual to name pieces of clay, not because pieces of clay are unnamable. With these names, (1) becomes

(3) *Goliath* = Lumpl & ◊ (*Goliath* exists & Lumpl exists & *Goliath* ≠ Lumpl).

It is in this sense that I want to claim that *Goliath* = Lumpl contingently.

Suppose, then, that *Goliath* = Lumpl. Then their identity is contingent in the sense of (3). For suppose I had brought Lumpl into existence as

Goliath, just as I actually did, but before the clay had a chance to dry, I squeezed it into a ball. At that point, according to the persistence criteria I have given, the statue *Goliath* would have ceased to exist, but the piece of clay Lumpl would still exist in a new shape. Hence Lumpl would not be *Goliath*, even though both existed. We would have

Lumpl exists & *Goliath* exists & *Goliath* ≠ Lumpl

If in fact, then, *Goliath* = Lumpl, then here is a case of contingent identity. In fact *Goliath* = Lumpl, but had I destroyed the statue *Goliath* by squeezing it, then it would have been the case that, although both existed, *Goliath* ≠ Lumpl. The identity is contingent, then, in the sense given in (3).

II

The claim that *Goliath* = Lumpl, then, has important consequences for the logic of identity. How can the claim be evaluated?

Initially, at least, the claim seems plausible. *Goliath* and Lumpl exist during precisely the same period of time, and at each instant during that period, they have, it would seem, the same shape, color, weight, location, and so forth: they share all their obvious properties.

The claim that *Goliath* = Lumpl, moreover, fits a systematic account of statues and piece of clay. A clay statue ordinarily begins to exist only after its piece of clay does. In such cases, it seems reasonable to say, the statue is a temporal segment of the piece of clay – a segment which extends for the period of time during which the piece of clay keeps a particular, statuesque shape. Here, then, is a systematic account of the relation between a statue and its piece of clay. By that account, however, there will be cases in which a clay statue is identical with its piece of clay. For in some cases the very temporal segment of the piece of clay which constitutes the statue extends for the entire life of the piece of clay. In such a case, the segment is the piece of clay in its entire extent: the statue and the piece of clay are identical.[7]

That leads to my main reason for wanting to say that *Goliath* = Lumpl. Concrete things, like statues and pieces of clay, are a part of the physical world, and we ought, it seems to me, to have a

systematic physical account of them. Concrete things, I want to maintain, are made up in some simple, canonical way from fundamental physical entities. Now what I have said of the relation between a statue and its piece of clay fits such a general view of concrete things. Suppose, for example, we take point-instants to be our fundamental physical entities, and let a concrete thing be a set of point-instants. In that case, *Goliath* = Lumpl simply because they are the same set of point-instants. Suppose instead we take particles to be our fundamental physical entities, and let a concrete thing be a changing set of particles – which might mean a function from instants in time to sets of particles. Then again, *Goliath* = Lumpl, because at each instant they consist of the same set of particles. Now particles and point-instants are the sorts of things we might expect to appear in a well-confirmed fundamental physics – in that part of an eventual physics which gives the fundamental laws of the universe. A system according to which *Goliath* = Lumpl, then, may well allow concrete things to be made up in a simple way from entities that appear in well-confirmed fundamental physics. Concrete things, then, can be given a place in a comprehensive view of the world.

In the rest of this paper, then, I shall work out a theory according to which *Goliath* = Lumpl. Concrete things, for all I shall say, may be either sets of point-instants or changing sets of particles. The sections which follow develop a theory of proper names and a theory of modal and dispositional properties for concrete things.

III

If, as I want to claim, *Goliath* = Lumpl, then how do proper names like "*Goliath*" and "Lumpl" work? Kripke gives an account of proper names from which it follows that *Goliath* cannot be identical with Lumpl; thus if Kripke's were the only plausible account of proper names, then the claim that *Goliath* = Lumpl would have to be abandoned. In fact, though, accepting that *Goliath* = Lumpl leads to an alternative account of proper names, which, I shall argue, is fully coherent and at least at plausible as Kripke's.

Kripke's account of proper names is roughly this. We in the actual world use proper names both to talk about the actual world and to talk about ways the world might have been. According to Kripke, if a proper name denotes a thing in the actual world, then in talk of non-actual situations, the name, if it denotes at all, simply denotes that same thing. A proper name is a *rigid designator*: it refers to the same thing in talk of any possible world in which that thing exists, and in talk of any other possible world, it refers to nothing in that world.[8]

Now if all proper names are rigid designators, then *Goliath* cannot be identical with Lumpl as I have claimed. For suppose they are identical. Call the actual world W_0 and the world as it would be if I had squeezed the clay into a ball W'; then

(i)   In W_0, *Goliath* = Lumpl,

but as I have shown,

(ii)   In W', *Goliath* ≠ Lumpl.

Now if the names "*Goliath*" and "Lumpl" are both rigid designators, then (i) and (ii) cannot both hold. For suppose (i) is true. Then the names "*Goliath*" and "Lumpl" both denote the same thing in W_0. Hence if they are both rigid designators, they both denote that thing in every possible world in which it exists, and denote nothing otherwise. Since they each denote something in W', they must therefore both denote the same thing in W', and thus (ii) must be false.

The claim that *Goliath* = Lumpl, then, is incompatible with Kripke's account of proper names. Suppose, then, that *Goliath* is indeed identical with Lumpl; what view of proper names emerges? How, on that supposition, could we decide whether the name "*Goliath*" is a rigid designator? Consider the situation. In the actual world, "*Goliath*" refers to a thing which I made and then broke, which is both a statue and a piece of clay. Hence the name "*Goliath*" is a rigid designator if it refers to that same thing in any possible situation in which the thing exists, and refers to nothing otherwise.

What, though, would constitute "that same thing" if the statue and the piece of clay were different? Take the situation in W': suppose instead of breaking the statue, as I actually did, I had squeezed the clay into a ball. Would that

single thing which in fact I made and then broke – which in fact was both a piece of clay and a statue – then be the statue *Goliath* which I squeezed out of existence, or the piece of clay Lumpl which went on existing after I squeezed it?

I can find no sense in the question. To ask meaningfully what that thing would be, we must designate it either as a statue or as a piece of clay. It makes sense to ask what the statue *Goliath* would be in that situation: it would be a statue; likewise, it makes sense to ask what the piece of clay Lumpl would be in that situation: it would be a piece of clay. What that thing would be, though, apart from the way it is designated, is a question without meaning.

A rough theory begins to emerge from all this. If *Goliath* and Lumpl are the same thing, asking what that thing would be in W' apart from the way the thing is designated, makes no sense. Meaningful cross-world identities of such things as statues, it begins to seem, must be identities *qua* something: *qua* statue or *qua* lump,[9] *qua* *Goliath* or *qua* Lumpl. It makes sense to talk of the "same statue" in different possible worlds, but no sense to talk of the "same thing."

Put more fully, what seems to be happening is this. Proper names like "*Goliath*" or "Lumpl" refer to a thing as a thing of a certain kind: "*Goliath*" refers to something as a statue; "Lumpl," as a lump. For each such kind of thing, there is a set of persistence criteria, like the ones I gave for statues and for lumps.[10] In rare cases, at least, one thing will be of two different kinds, with different persistence criteria, and whereas one proper name refers to it as a thing of one kind, another proper name will refer to it as a thing of another kind. In such cases, the identity formed with those names is contingently true. It is true because the two names designate the same thing, which ceases to exist at the same time on both sets of criteria. It is contingent because if the world had gone differently after the thing came into existence, the thing might have ceased to exist at different times on the two sets of criteria: it would have been one thing on one set of persistence criteria, and another thing – perhaps a temporal segment of the first – on the second set of criteria.

If all that is so, it makes no sense to call a designator rigid or nonrigid by itself. A designator may be rigid with respect to a sortal: it may be statue-rigid, as "*Goliath*" is, or it may be lump-rigid, as "Lumpl" is. A designator, for instance, is *statue-rigid* if it designates the same statue in every possible world in which that statue exists and designates nothing in any other possible world. What is special about proper names like "*Goliath*" and "*Lumpl*" is not that they are rigid designators. It is rather that each is rigid with respect to the sortal it invokes. "*Goliath*" refers to its bearer as a statue and is statue-rigid; "*Lumpl*" refers to its bearer as a lump and is lump-rigid.

In short, then, if we accept that *Goliath* = *Lumpl* and examine the situation, a rough theory of proper names emerges. A proper name like "*Goliath*" denotes a thing in the actual world, and invokes a sortal with certain persistence criteria. It then denotes the same thing-of-that-sort in every possible world in which it denotes at all. The name "*Goliath*" itself, for instance, denotes a lump of clay and invokes the sortal *statue*; hence it denotes the same statue in every possible world in which that statue exists.

That leaves two questions unanswered. First, how does a name like "*Goliath*" get its reference in the actual world? Second, what makes a thing in another possible world "the same statue" as the one which in fact I made and then broke? I shall tackle this second question first.

Once I made my statue, that statue existed, and nothing that happened from then on could change the fact that it had existed or the way it had come to exist. It would be that same statue whether I subsequently broke it, squeezed it, or sold it. Its origin, then, makes a statue the statue that it is, and if statues in different possible worlds have the same beginning, then they are the same statue.

The name "*Goliath*" picks out in W' the one statue which begins in W' like *Goliath* in W_0. Consider the case more fully. The world W' bears an important relation to W_0 and the statue *Goliath* in W_0: W' *branches* from W_0 after *Goliath* begins to exist; that is, until some time after *Goliath* begins to exist in W_0, the histories of W_0 and W' are exactly the same. In the branching world W', then, *Goliath* is the statue which has exactly the same history before the branching as *Goliath* in W_0. The name "*Lumpl*" too picks out a thing in W' which begins exactly like the statue *Goliath* in W_0. "*Lumpl*," though, picks out, not the unique statue in W' which begins that way, but the unique piece of clay in W' which begins that way. Since that piece of clay in W' is distinct from

that statue in W', the two names pick out different things in W' – different things which both start out in the same way.

Here, then, is a theory of reference for the special case of branching possible worlds. Let proper name α denote a thing X in the actual world W_0; the theory will apply to any possible world W which branches from W_0 after X begins to exist in W_0. According to the theory, α not only denotes X in W_0, but also invokes a set C of persistence criteria which X satisfies in W_0. The reference of α in W, then, is the thing in W which has the same history before the branching as X has in W_0 and which satisfies the persistence criteria in set C.

According to the theory, then, the reference of a name in branching world W depends on two things: its reference in the actual world, and the persistence criteria it invokes. The reference of the name in the actual world determines how the thing it denotes in W begins; the persistence criteria it invokes determine which of the various things that begin that way in W the name denotes.

That leaves the problem of possible worlds which do not branch from the actual world, or which branch too early. How to handle reference to things in such obdurate worlds I do not know. Perhaps the best course is to deny that any such reference is possible. The clearest cases of reference by a speaker in one possible world to a thing in another are ones like the clay statue case, where a world branches from the actual one after the thing to which reference is made starts to exist. I am inclined, then, for the sake of clarity, to rule out any other sort of reference to concrete entities in other possible worlds. If, though, a clear criterion which allowed such reference were devised, that criterion could probably be adopted without much changing the system I am proposing.

There remains the question of how a name gets its reference in the actual world. Its reference in branching worlds, I have said, depends partly on its reference in the actual world. Until we say how a name gets its reference in the actual world, then, even the theory of reference for branching worlds is incomplete. Nothing I have said about the names "*Goliath*" and "*Lumpl*" has any direct bearing on the question of reference in the actual world. The account Kripke gives[11] seems plausible to me, and everything I have said in this paper is compatible with it.

On that account, a name gets its reference from a causal chain that connects the person who uses the name with the thing denoted. In my mouth and in the mouth of anyone else who uses the names "Goliath" and "Lumpl," those names denote the actual thing they do because I applied those names to it directly and others got the names from me. Other people, then, are connected to that clay statue by a tradition through which the name was handed down; I am connected more directly, by having perceived the thing and named it.

Persistence criteria play a role in starting the tradition. I named the thing I did by pointing to it and invoking persistence criteria: "I name this statue 'Goliath,'" I said, "and this piece of clay 'Lumpl.'" The name "Goliath," then, denoted the unique thing at which I was pointing which satisfied the persistence criteria for statues – that is, the unique statue at which I was pointing. Since the same thing satisfied both the criteria for statues and the criteria for pieces of clay, both names denoted the same thing, but if I had invoked different persistence criteria, I might have named a different thing. When I pointed at the statue, I pointed at a number of things of various durations. I pointed, for instance, at the portion of clay which made up the statue. I might have said, "I name the portion of clay which makes up this statue 'Portia.'" If I had done so, I would have named a portion of clay which survived the breaking of the statue. Thus when the tradition is started which gives a name a concrete reference in the actual world, the persistence criteria invoked help determine what entity bears that name.

I have given a theory of proper names, and on that theory, it is clear why the identity "Goliath = Lumpl" is contingent. It is equally clear, on that theory, why the identity "Hesperus = Phosphorus" is necessary, in the sense that it holds in any possible world in which Hesperus exists. At least, it is clear if identity of concrete things across possible worlds is confined to branching cases in the way I have described. Both names, "Hesperus" and "Phosphorus," invoke the persistence criteria for heavenly bodies. Both refer to Venus. Hence in any possible world W which branches from the actual world after Venus begins to exist, they both refer to the heavenly body in W which starts out in W like Venus in W_0. Both, then, refer to the same thing in W. On the theory here, then, as on Kripke's theory, the identity "Hesperus =

Phosphorus," even though a posteriori, is a necessary truth: it would hold in any situation in which Hesperus or Phosphorus existed.

In short, then, if we accept that Goliath = Lumpl, the following theory of proper names for concrete objects emerges. The reference of a name in the actual world is fixed partly by invoking a set of persistence criteria which determine what thing it names. The name may then be passed on through a tradition, and the reference is fixed by the origin of that tradition. The name can also be used to refer to a thing in a possible world which branches from the actual world after the thing named in the actual world begins to exist. In that case the name refers to the unique thing in that possible world which both satisfies the persistence criteria the name invokes and starts out exactly like the bearer of the name in the actual world.

IV

Kripke's theory of proper names is incompatible with the theory I have developed, and Kripke gives a number of forceful arguments for his theory. Do any of those arguments tell against the theory here? Let me try to pick out arguments Kripke gives which are germane.

According to the theory here, it makes no sense to call a designator rigid and leave it at that, because it makes no strict sense to call things in different possible worlds identical and leave it at that: identity across possible worlds makes sense only with respect to a sortal. According to Kripke, qualms about identity across possible worlds are unfounded, and plain talk of rigid designators makes perfectly good sense. What Kripke says most directly on this point, however, shows no more than what I have already accepted: that it makes sense to call a designator rigid with respect to a sortal, like statue, number or man. "... we can perfectly well talk about rigid and nonrigid designators. Moreover, we have a simple, intuitive test for them. We can say, for example, that the number of planets might have been a different number from the number it in fact is." The designator "the number of planets," then, is nonrigid. "If we apply this intuitive test to proper names, such as for example 'Richard Nixon,' they would seem intuitively to come out as rigid designators.... It seems that we cannot say 'Nixon might have been a different man from the man he in fact was,' unless, of course, we mean it metaphorically."[12]

Does it make sense, then, to call a designator "rigid" independently of a sortal it invokes? Kripke's examples here prove no such thing. Nixon indeed could not have been a different *man* from the man he in fact is. That, however, shows only that the designator "Nixon" is rigid with respect to the sortal *man*, not that it is rigid independently of any sortal. To show it rigid independently of any sortal, one would have to go beyond what Kripke says in the passage I have quoted, and show that Nixon could not have been a different *entity* from the one he in fact is.

For that purpose, the "simple, intuitive test" Kripke offers will not help. We speak and think of "the same person" but not of "the same entity." The point at issue is how everyday talk of "the same person" best fits into systematic talk of "entities." To this issue, everyday intuitions about entities, if we had them, would be irrelevant: the matter has to be settled by working out rival systems and comparing their implications.

Kripke attacks qualms about cross-world identity in another way: those qualms, he says, may just grow out of a confusion about what possible worlds are. Talk of "possible worlds" suggests that they are like distant planets to be explored. If that were what they were like, I might explore a possible world and discover someone who looked like Benjamin Franklin; I would then have to determine whether it actually was Franklin I had discovered, or just someone who looked like him.[13]

Instead, according to Kripke, possible worlds are situations which we stipulate – "counterfactual situations" may be the best term. What thing is what in a counterfactual situation is not something I find out; it is part of what I stipulate: it is "given in the very description" of the stipulated situation. "And there seems to be no less objection to *stipulating* that we are speaking of certain *people* than there can be to stipulating that we are speaking of certain *qualities*."[14]

Is that so? The statue example seems to provide an objection – an objection, at least, to stipulating that we are speaking of certain *entities*. In that example, a possible situation was stipulated, just as Kripke demands. "For suppose I had brought Lumpl into existence as *Goliath*, just as I actually did, but before the clay had a chance to dry, I squeezed it into a ball." In this stipulated situation, I showed, there are two distinct things, a statue and a piece of clay. It might be tempting to ask which of the two is the one thing which, in the actual world, I made and then broke. To that question, though, there is no plain answer – or so I argued. Now the problem is not one of under-stipulation. It is not as if the thing I actually made could appear in two different possible situations in which I squeezed it: in one as a statue that ceased to exist when squeezed, and in another as a piece of clay which persisted after it was squeezed. After I made that thing, I held it in my hands and I could have squeezed it; if I suppose that I did squeeze it, I have stipulated as much about the identities of the things in that supposed situation as can be stipulated. A situation, then, can be fully stipulated even though questions of identity across possible worlds remain unsettled.

Kripke agrees to something like this. "Given certain counterfactual vicissitudes in the history of the molecules of a table, T, one may ask whether T would exist, in that situation, or whether a certain bunch of molecules, which in that situation would constitute a table, constitute the very same table T." Such a conception of "transworld identification," he says, "differs considerably from the usual one"; for one thing, "the attempted notion deals with criteria of identity of particulars in terms of other particulars, not qualities" – in terms of particular molecules, that is to say.[15] This qualification, though, has no bearing on the point in question here. Take a possible world in which I squeeze Lumpl into a ball, and suppose all the molecules involved are clearly identified. There are still two distinct things in that world, the statue *Goliath* which I destroy by squeezing, and the piece of clay Lumpl which survives the squeezing. The question remains, then, which of those two distinct things in that possible world is the single thing which in fact I made and then broke. There is, in short, a genuine problem with cross-world identification – Kripke's arguments notwithstanding.

V

The most prominent objection to contingent identity remains to be tackled: the objection that it violates Leibniz' Law. If *Goliath* is contingently identical with Lumpl, then although

(4)   □(Lumpl exists → Lumpl = Lumpl)

is true,

(5)   □(Lumpl exists → *Goliath* = Lumpl)

is false. Yet (5) is derived from (4) and

(6)   *Goliath* = Lumpl

by substitutivity of identicals. Thus, the objection goes, *Goliath* cannot be contingently identical with Lumpl.

The usual answer will serve my purpose here. Leibniz' Law settles very little by itself: put as a general law of substitutivity of identicals, it is just false; in its correct version, it is a law about properties and relations: *If x = y, then for any property, if x has it, then y has it, and for any relation and any given things, if x stands in that relation to those things, then y stands in that relation to those things.* The law so stated yields substitutivity of identicals only for contexts that attribute properties and relations. (5) follows from (4) and (6) by Leibniz' Law, then, only if the context

(7)   □(Lumpl exists → — = Lumpl)

attributes a property. We can block the inference to (5), then, simply by denying that the context (7) attributes a property.

It may seem arbitrary to deny that (7) attributes a property, but whether it does is the very point in question here. A property, if it is to be a property, must apply or not apply to a thing independently of the way the thing is designated. (7) gives a property, then, only if it gives something that is true of Lumpl or false of Lumpl independently of the way Lumpl is designated, and whether it does is the point in question.

The proponent of contingent identity, then, has a reasonable, consistent position open to him – a position that is familiar in the literature on the subject.[16] Expressions constructed with modal operators, he can say, simply do not give properties of *concrete things*, such as statues and pieces of clay. Modal expressions do not apply to concrete things independently of the way they are designated. Lumpl, for instance, is the same thing

as *Goliath*: it is a clay statue of the infant *Goliath* which I put together and then broke. Necessary identity to Lumpl, though, is not a property which that thing has or lacks, for it makes no sense to ask whether that thing, as such, is necessarily identical with Lumpl. Modal contexts, then, do not attribute properties or relations to concrete things – so the proponent of contingent identity can respond to Leibniz' Law.

Now this response comes at a stiff price. Quantificational contexts must attribute properties or relations; they must be true or false of things independently of the way those things are designated. If modal contexts do not attribute properties or relations to concrete things, it follows that such contexts are not open to quantification with variables whose values are concrete things. A large number of formulas, then, must be ruled out as ill formed.

Although, for instance, the sentence

◊ (Lumpl exists & *Goliath* ≠ Lumpl)

is well formed, the expression

(8)   ◊ (Lumpl exists & x ≠ Lumpl)

turns out to be ill formed – at least, that is, if the variable x can take *Goliath* as a value. Now on the basis of what I have said, that seems reasonable. Take the expression (8), and consider the thing I made and then broke, which is both a statue and a lump. There is no apparent way of saying that (8) is true or false of that thing; it is true of it *qua* statue but not *qua* piece of clay. By that test, the free variable x does not belong in its context in (8) if it takes concrete things like statues and lumps among its values.

Here, then, may be a telling objection to contingent identity: if in order to maintain contingent identity we must restrict quantification so drastically, the objector can argue, we shall be unable to say many of the things we need to say, both in scientific talk and in daily life. Concrete things will have no modal properties: there will, that is, be no such thing as *de re* modality for concrete things. Indeed on some accounts, there will also be problems with dispositions – as I shall later show. Perhaps we can maintain contingent identity only at the cost of tying our tongues, and that, if it is true, might be a strong reason for rejecting contingent identity.

The remainder of my argument for the plausibility of the system I am advocating will concern this issue. I shall give devices which I think will enable us to say anything that we ought seriously to regard as meaningful, and say it in the system I am advocating. What I have to say will center around the system Carnap proposed in *Meaning and Necessity* for quantifying into modal contexts.[17] Carnap's system, I think, is the best one for handling quantified modal talk of concrete things. In what follows, I shall draw loosely both on Carnap's system and on Aldo Bressan's extension of it[18] to give ways of saying what we need to say.

Carnap's system has many advantages. It fits my claim that *Goliath* = Lumpl, and it allows variables in any context in which a proper name can appear. Indeed on Carnap's account, variables in modal contexts act almost exactly as proper names do on the account in section III of this paper. Carnap, in short, gives a clear, consistent theory which fits what I have been saying.

There is, to be sure, a price for all this: Carnap gives a nonstandard account of the way predicates and variables behave in modal contexts. The account he gives, though, makes sense, and it departs from the standard account of quantifiers in much the same way as I departed in section III from the standard account of proper names. It is nonstandard, then, in ways that fit nicely the theory in this paper.

Carnap's treatment of variables is suggested by part of Frege's treatment of proper names. According to Frege,[19] a proper name in a modal context refers *obliquely*: its reference there is its usual sense. Hence in

(9) $\Diamond$ (Lumpl exists & Goliath $\neq$ Lumpl),

the name "*Goliath*" refers, not to a statue, but to a statue-concept which is the normal sense of the name. Any other name with that same normal sense could be substituted for "*Goliath*" in (9) without changing its truth-value. This part of Frege's account fits what I have said of proper names, as I shall later illustrate.

Now just as, on Frege's account, proper names shift their reference in modal contexts, on Carnap's account, variables in modal contexts

shift their range of values: they range over senses. In the formula

$\Diamond$ (Lumpl exists & $x \neq$ Lumpl),

then, x ranges not over concrete things, like statues and pieces of clay, but over what Carnap calls "individual concepts" – including statue-concepts and lump-concepts. Call things of the kind the variables take as values in nonmodal contexts *individuals*: an *individual concept* is a function whose domain is a set of possible worlds, and which assigns to each world W in its domain an individual that exists in W.

I spell out what is roughly Carnap's proposal in the appendix;[20] here I give it by example. Let the individuals in the system be concrete things, like statues and lumps. Let "*E*" in nonmodal contexts be the predicate *exists*, and let "*H*" in such contexts be the predicate *is humanoid*, by which I shall mean *is human-shaped throughout its early history*. Then in the formula

(10) $\Box(Ex \to Hx)$,

on Carnap's proposal, both the variable and the predicates make a shift. The variable x in (10) now ranges over individual concepts, and the predicates in (10) make compensating shifts as follows: "*E*" now means not *exists*, but rather *is a concept of an individual that exists*. "*H*" now means not *is humanoid*, but rather *is a concept of an individual that is humanoid*. For any possible world W and individual concept f, that is to say, "*H*" in modal contexts is true of f in W if and only if the individual f assigns to W is humanoid in W.[21]

That gives (10) a clear interpretation: the open sentence (10) is true of any individual concept f such that for every world W, if f assigns an individual to W, then f assigns to W an individual that is humanoid in W. In particular, then, (10) is true of the *Goliath*-concept – the individual concept that assigns the statue *Goliath* to each possible world in which that statue exists, and assigns nothing to any other possible world. For *Goliath* in any possible world, according to the theory I have given, is humanoid: in any world in which it exists, it starts out in the shape of the actual *Goliath*, and changes shape only slowly. (10) is false of the Lumpl-concept correspondingly defined, since in possible worlds in which I squeeze Lumpl into a ball, Lumpl loses its human shape during its early history, and thus is not humanoid in the stipulated sense. To such a possible world, then, the Lumpl-concept does not assign an individual which is humanoid.

Variables on this proposal work very much like proper names on my account of them in section III. Just as on that earlier account,

(11) $\Box(E\ Goliath \rightarrow H\ Goliath)$

is true and

(12) $\Box(E\ Lumpl \rightarrow H\ Lumpl)$

is false, so on the Carnapian account I am now giving, the open sentence $\Box(Ex \rightarrow Hx)$ is true of the *Goliath*-concept and false of the *Lumpl*-concept.

Indeed, just as, on Carnap's account, variables in modal contexts range over individual concepts, so on the account in section III, proper names in modal contexts can be construed as denoting individual concepts. Proper names work, in other words, roughly as Frege claims. Let the name "*Goliath*" in (11), for instance, denote the *Goliath*-concept, and suppose predicates shift in modal contexts as Carnap suggests. Then (11) attributes to the *Goliath*-concept the property

$\Box(E\_\_ \rightarrow H\_\_)$,

that in every possible world W, if it assigns to W an existing individual, then it assigns to W an individual that is humanoid. The *Goliath*-concept has that property, and so (11) on this construal is true. The Lumpl-concept does not have that property, and so (12) on this construal is false. That is as it should be on the account in section III. Modal properties can be construed as attributing properties and relations to individual concepts, much as Frege claims.

VI

What happens to identity on this account? Identity of individual concepts x and y is not now expressed as "$x = y$"; that, in modal contexts,

means just that x and y are concepts of the same individual. The way to say that x and y are the same individual concept is

$$\Box[(Ex \lor Ey) \rightarrow x = y].$$

I shall abbreviate this "$x \equiv y$".

It could now be objected that the thesis of contingent identity has collapsed. Identity in the system here, it seems, is given not by "$=$," but by "$\equiv$" and the relation "$\equiv$" is never contingent; if it holds between two individual concepts, then it holds between them in every possible world. No genuine relation of identity, then, is contingent; the illusion that there are contingent identities came from using the identity sign "$=$" to mean something other than true identity.

To this objection the following answer can be given. "$=$" indeed is the identity sign for individuals in the system, and if I am right that a piece of clay is an individual in the Carnapian sense, then "$=$" is the identity sign for pieces of clay. For consider: in non-modal contexts, I stipulated, the variables range over individuals. Now "$=$" in such contexts holds only for identical individuals; it is the relation a piece of clay, for instance, bears to itself and only to itself. Moreover, applied to individuals, "$=$" satisfies Leibniz' Law: individuals related by it have the same properties in the strict sense, and stand in the same relations in the strict sense. The contexts where "$=$" is not an identity sign are modal contexts, but there the variables range not over individuals, but over individual concepts. "$=$" in the system, then, is the identity sign for individuals, and according to the system, "$=$" can hold contingently for individuals: A sentence of the form "$a = b$," then, asserts the identity of two individuals, and it may be contingent.

Quine would object to this answer. It depends on a "curious double interpretation of variables": outside modal contexts they are interpreted as ranging over individuals; inside modal contexts, over individual concepts. "This complicating device," Quine says, "has no essential bearing, and is better put aside."[22] "Since the duality in question is a peculiarity of a special metalinguistic idiom and not of the object-language itself, there is nothing to prevent our examining the object-language from the old point of view and asking what the values of its variables are in the old-fashioned non-dual sense of the term."[23] The values in the old-fashioned sense,

Quine says, are individual concepts, for "$(\forall x)x \equiv x$" is a logical truth, and on "the old point of view," that means that entities between which the relation $\equiv$ fails are distinct entities. In all contexts, then, the values of the variables are individual concepts, and identity is given by "$\equiv$."

All this can be accepted, however, and the point I have made stands: "=" in the system expresses identity of individuals. "$a = b$," on Quine's interpretation, says that a and b are concepts of the same individual. That amounts to saying that the individual of which a is the concept is identical with the individual of which b is the concept. Even on Quine's interpretation, then, "$a = b$" in effect asserts the identity of individuals, and does so in the most direct way the system allows.

On either Quine's interpretation or Carnap's, then, to assert

(13) *Goliath* = Lumpl

is in effect to assert the identity of an individual. For all Carnap's system says, (13) may be true, though *Goliath* might not have been identical with Lumpl. If (13) is true but contingent, then it seems reasonable to call it a contingent identity. The claim that there are contingent identities in a natural sense, then, is consistent with Carnap's modal system on either Carnap's or Quine's interpretation of values of variables.

VII

One further Quinean objection needs to be answered. I am embracing "essentialism" for individual concepts. Essentialism, if I understand Quine, is the view that necessity properly applies "to the fulfillment of conditions by objects ... apart from special ways of specifying them."[24] Now what I have said, as I shall explain, requires me to reject essentialism for concrete things but accept it for individual concepts. That discriminatory treatment needs to be justified.

First, a more precise definition of essentialism: *Essentialism for* a class of entities U, I shall say, is the claim that for any entity e in U and any condition ϕ which e fulfills, the question of whether e necessarily fulfills ϕ has a definite answer apart from the way e is specified.[25]

Now according to what I have said, essentialism for the class of concrete things is false. In the clay statue example, I said, the same concrete thing fulfills the condition

$$E \_\_ \to H \_\_$$

necessarily under the specification "*Goliath*" and only contingently under the specification "Lumpl"; whether that thing, apart from any special designation, necessarily fulfills that condition is a meaningless question.

Essentialism for the class of individual concepts, on the other hand, must be true if Carnap's system is to work. That is so because Carnap's system allows quantification into modal contexts without restriction. For let ϕ be a condition and e an individual concept which fulfills ϕ. Then $\Box\phi x$ is well formed and the variable "x" ranges over individual concepts, so that e is in the range of "x." Thus e either definitely satisfies the formula $\Box\phi x$ or definitely fails to satisfy it. The question of whether e necessarily fulfills ϕ must have a definite answer even apart from the way e is specified. Thus essentialism holds for individual concepts.

Why this discriminatory treatment? Why accept essentialism for individual concepts and reject it for individuals? The point of doing so is this: my arguments against essentialism for concrete things rested not on general logical considerations, but on considerations that apply specifically to concrete things. I argued that it makes no sense to talk of a concrete thing as fulfilling a condition ϕ in every possible world – as fulfilling ϕ necessarily, in other words – apart from its designation. Essentialism, then, is false for concrete things because apart from a special designation, it is meaningless to talk of the same concrete thing in different possible worlds.

For this last, I had two arguments, both of which apply specifically to concrete things. First I considered the clay statue example, gave reasons for saying that *Goliath* is identical to Lumpl, and showed that the same statue in a different situation would not be the same piece of clay. Second, in section III, I gave a theory of identity of concrete things across certain possible worlds, according to which such identity made sense only with respect to a kind. These arguments applied only to concrete things.[26]

It makes good sense, on the other hand, to speak of the same individual concept in different possible worlds. An individual concept is just a function which assigns to each possible world in a set an individual in that world. There is no problem of what that function would be in a possible world different from the actual one. Whereas, then, there is no good reason for rejecting essentialism indiscriminately, there are strong grounds for rejecting essentialism for concrete things.

VIII

An objection broached in section V remains to be tackled. There is, according to the system here, no such thing as *de re* modality for concrete things: in a formula of the form $\Box Fx$, the variable ranges over individual concepts rather than concrete things. Now without *de re* modality for concrete things, the objection goes, our tongues will be tied: we will be left unable to say things that need to be said, both for scientific and for daily purposes.

In fact, though, the system here ties our tongues very little. It allows concrete things to have modal properties of a kind, and those permissible modal properties will do any job that *de re* modalities could reasonably be asked to do. To see how such legitimate modal properties can be constructed, return to the statue example.

According to the theory given here, the concrete thing *Goliath* or Lumpl has neither the property of being essentially humanoid nor the property of being possibly nonhumanoid. There is a modal property, though, which it does have: it is essentially humanoid *qua* statue. That can be expressed in the Carnapian system I have given. Let δ be the predicate "is a statue-rigid individual concept." δ is intensional, then, in the sense that it applies to individual concepts, so that variables in its scope take individual concepts as values, just as they do in the scope of a modal operator. The sentence

x is essentially humanoid *qua* statue,

then, means this:

(14) $(\exists y)[y = x \ \& \ \delta y \ \& \ \Box(Ey \rightarrow Hy)]$.[27]

Here the variable y is free within the scope of a modal operator, and hence ranges over individual concepts; but x occurs only outside the scope of modal operators, and hence ranges over individuals. In "$y = x$," then, the predicate "=" makes a compensating shift of the kind shown in section V, but only in its left argument. Thus "$y = x$" here means that y is a concept of an individual identical to x – in other words, y is a concept of x. (14), then, says the following: "There is an individual concept y which is a statue-concept, and is a concept of something humanoid in any possible world in which it is a concept of anything." That gives a property which applies to concrete things: only the variable x is free in (14), and since it occurs only outside the scope of modal operators, it ranges over individuals. (14), then, gives a property of the concrete thing Lumpl, a property which we might call "being essentially humanoid *qua* statue."

Concrete things, then, in the system given here, have no *de re* modal properties – no properties of the form $\Box F$. They do, however, have modal properties of a more devious kind: modal properties *qua* a sortal. Such properties should serve any purpose for which concrete things really need modal properties.

IX

Dispositional properties raise problems of much the same kind as do modal properties. At least one promising account of dispositions is incompatible with the system given here.

Here is the account. A disposition like solubility is a property which applies to concrete things, and it can be expressed as a counterfactual conditional: "x is soluble" means "If x were placed in water, then x would dissolve." This counterfactual conditional in turn means something like this: "In the possible world which is, of all those worlds in which x is in water, most like the actual world, x dissolves."[28]

Now this account is incompatible with the system I have given, because it requires identity of concrete things across possible worlds. For without such cross-world identity, it makes no sense to talk of "the possible world which is, of all those worlds in which x is in water, most like the actual world." For such talk makes sense only if there is a definite set of worlds in which x is in water, and there is such a definite set only if for each possible world, either x is some definite entity in that world – so that it makes definite sense to say that x is in water in that world – or x definitely does not exist in that world. The account of dispositions I have sketched, then, requires identity of concrete things across possible worlds, which on the theory in this paper is meaningless.

The point is perhaps most clear in the statue example. It makes no sense to say of the concrete thing *Goliath*, or Lumpl, that if I squeezed it, it would cease to exist. If I squeezed the statue *Goliath*, *Goliath* would cease to exist, but if I squeezed the piece of clay Lumpl, Lumpl would go on existing in a different shape. Take, then, the property "If I squeezed x, then x would cease to exist," which I shall write

(15)   I squeeze $x \,\square\!\!\rightarrow\, x$ ceases to exist.

That is not a property which the single concrete thing, *Goliath* or Lumpl, either has or straightforwardly lacks.

Counterfactual properties, then, have much the same status as modal properties. A concrete thing – a piece of salt, for instance – cannot have the counterfactual property

x is in water $\square\!\!\rightarrow\, x$ dissolves,

or as I shall write it,

(16) $Wx \,\square\!\!\rightarrow\, Dx$.

Put more precisely, the point is this: a concrete thing can have no such property if, first, the account of counterfactuals which I have given is correct and, second, identity of concrete things across possible worlds makes no sense. Call a property of the form given in (15) and (16) a *straightforward counterfactual property*; then on the theories I have given, concrete things can have no straightforward counterfactual properties.

Individual concepts, in contrast, can perfectly well have straightforward counterfactual properties, since they raise no problems of identity across possible worlds. Indeed we can treat the

connective "$\square\!\!\rightarrow$" as inducing the same shifts as do modal operators: making the variables in its scope range over individual concepts, and shifting the predicates appropriately. On that interpretation, (15) is true of the *Goliath*-concept but false of the Lumpl-concept; (15) says, "In the possible world which, of all those worlds in which I squeeze the thing picked out by concept x, is most like the actual world, the thing picked out by x ceases to exist." That holds of the *Goliath*-concept but not of the Lumpl-concept. Likewise on this interpretation, (16) is true not of a piece of salt, but of a piece-of-salt individual concept. (16) now says the following: "In the possible world which is, of all those worlds in which the thing picked out by x is in water, most like the actual world, the thing picked out by x dissolves."

So far the situation is grave. The moral seems to be this: concrete things have no dispositional properties, but individual concepts do. Water-solubility, or something like it, may be a property of a piece-of-salt individual concept, but it cannot be a property of the concrete thing, that piece of salt. That is a sad way to leave the matter. On close examination, many seeming properties look covertly dispositional – mass and electric charge are prime examples. Strip concrete things of their dispositional properties, and they may have few properties left.

Fortunately, though, individuals do turn out to have dispositional properties of a kind. The device used for modal properties in the last section works here too. A concrete thing like a piece of salt cannot, it is true, have the straightforward counterfactual property $Wx \,\square\!\!\rightarrow\, Dx$. Only an individual concept could have that property. A piece of salt does, though, have the more devious counterfactual property given by "*Qua* piece of salt, if x were in water then x would dissolve," which I shall write

(17) $(x \ qua \ \text{piece})[Wx \,\square\!\!\rightarrow\, Dx]$.

This expands as follows: let $\mathscr{S}$ mean "is a piece-rigid individual concept"; then (17) means

(18) $(\exists y)[y = x \ \& \ \mathscr{S}y(Wy \,\square\!\!\rightarrow\, Dy)]$

As in the corresponding formula (14) for modal properties, "x" here is free of modal entanglements, and so it ranges over concrete things. (18) seems a good way to interpret water solubility as a property of pieces of salt.

Concrete things, then, can have dispositional properties. The dispositional property *is water-soluble* is not the straightforward counterfactual property given by (16), but the more devious counterfactual property given by (18). A system with contingent identity can still allow dispositions to be genuine properties of concrete things.

X

From the claim that *Goliath* = Lumpl, I think I have shown, there emerges a coherent system which stands up to objections. Why accept this system? In section II, I gave one main reason: the system lets concrete things be made up in a simple way from entities that appear in fundamental physics. It thus gives us machinery for putting into one coherent system both our beliefs about the fundamental constitution of the world and our everyday picture of concrete things.

Another important reason for accepting the system is one of economy. I think I have shown how to get along without *de re* modality for concrete things and still say what needs to be said about them. That may be especially helpful when we deal with causal necessity; indeed, the advantages of doing without *de re* causal necessity go far beyond mere economy. What I have said in this paper about plain necessity applies equally well to causal necessity, and the notion of causal necessity seems especially unobjectionable – even Quine thinks it may be legitimate.[29] Causally necessary truths are what scientists are looking for when they look for fundamental scientific laws, and it surely makes sense to look for fundamental scientific laws. Now we might expect fundamental scientific laws to take the form $\square_c \phi$, "It is causally necessary that ϕ," where ϕ is extensional – contains no modal operators. If so, then scientific laws contain *de dicto* causal necessity, but no *de re* necessity. To get significant *de re* causal necessities, we would need to make metaphysical assumptions with no grounding in scientific law. If we can get along without *de re* physical necessity, that will keep puzzling metaphysical questions about essential properties out of physics. The system here shows how to do that.

None of the reasons I have given in favor of the system here are conclusive. The system has to be judged as a whole: it is coherent and withstands objections; the remaining question is whether it is superior to its rivals. What, then, are the alternatives?

Kripke gives an alternative formal semantics,[30] but no systematic directions for applying it. To use Kripke's semantics, one needs extensive intuitions that certain properties are essential and others accidental. Kripke makes no attempt to say how concrete things might appear in a theory of fundamental physics; whether such an account can be given in Kripke's system remains to be seen.

One other alternative to the theory in this paper is systematic: statues and pieces of clay can be taken, not to be "individuals" in the Carnapian sense of the term which I have been using, but to be Carnapian "individual concepts." They may be regarded, that is, as functions from possible worlds, whose values are Carnapian individuals.[31] On such a view, a Carnapian individual would be regarded as a sort of "proto-individual" from which concrete things are constructed.

Such a view has its advantages: it allows standard quantification theory, with no Carnapian shift of the range of variables in modal contexts. Indeed, as Quine points out, a Carnapian semantics can be interpreted so that variables always range over individual concepts.[32]

One reason for preferring the Carnapian system is this. I expect that the variables used in expressing fundamental laws can most simply be interpreted as ranging over Carnapian individuals. If so, then I would be reluctant to regard those Carnapian individuals as mere proto-individuals, with genuine individuals as functions which take these proto-individuals as values at possible worlds. Fundamental physics, I would like to say, deals with genuine individuals.

If the system I have given is accepted, the ramifications are wide. Take just one example: the question of whether a person is identical with his body. If there is no consciousness after death, then, it would seem, a person ceases to exist when he dies. A person's body normally goes on existing after he dies. Ordinarily, then, a person is not identical with his body. In some cases, however, a person's body is destroyed when he dies. In such cases, according to the system in this paper, there is no purely logical reason against saying the following: the person in this case is identical with his body, but had he died a normal death, he would have been distinct from his body. If there are reasons against such a view, they must be nonlogical reasons.

Whether or not the system I have advocated is the best one, I have at least done the following. First, I have shown that there is a problem with identity across possible worlds, even in the simple case of possible worlds which branch after the entity in question begins to exist. In such cases, I have shown, certain assumptions, not easily refuted, lead to contingent identity. Second, I have given a theory of proper names which fits much of what Kripke says about proper names when he considers examples, and which, in rare cases, allows contingent identity. Finally, I have shown how, while accepting contingent identity and rejecting *de re* modality for concrete things, we can still allow concrete things to have modal and dispositional properties.

The system I advocate is worked out in more detail in the appendix.[33] In that system, I think, concrete things and possible worlds lose some of their mystery: they arise naturally from a systematic picture of the physical world.

Notes

I am grateful for the comments and criticisms of many people. I was helped in the early stages of revision by discussion at the University of Pittsburgh philosophy colloquium, by the written comments of Richard Gale and Paul Teller, and by discussion with Allen Hazen, Robert Kraut, and Storrs McCall. I am especially grateful to Anil Gupta for his extensive help, both in the early and the late stages of revision.

1   Saul Kripke, "Identity and necessity," this volume, ch. 10; *idem*, "Naming and necessity," in D. Davidson and G. Harman (eds), *Semantics of Natural Language* (Dordrecht: Reidel, 1972).

2   Gottlob Frege, "On sense and reference," trans. M. Black, in P. Geach and M. Black, *Translations from the Philosophical Writings of Gottlob Frege* (Oxford: Blackwell, 1966), pp. 55–78, at p. 57; orig. German pub. 1892.

3   This volume, pp. 130–2; Kripke, "Naming and necessity," pp. 260–4.

4   Bertrand Russell, "On denoting," in Robert Marsh (ed.), *Logic and Knowledge* (New York: Macmillan, 1956), pp. 41–56; orig. pub. 1905.

5   Kripke, "Naming and necessity," pp. 254–60, 284–308.

6   W. V. O. Quine, "Identity, ostension, and hypostasis," this volume, ch. 34, sect. 1.

7   This fits the view put forth ibid.

8   Kripke, "Naming and necessity," pp. 269–70.

9   David Lewis, "Counterparts of persons and their bodies," *Journal of Philosophy* 68 (1971), pp. 203–11, gives a theory very much like this. There are, according to Lewis, a diversity of counterpart relations which hold between entities in different possible worlds – the "personal" counterpart relation and the "bodily" counterpart relation are two (p. 208). The counterpart relation appropriate to a given modal context may be selected by a term, such as "I" or "my body," or it may be selected by a phrase, "regarded as a –," which works like one of my "qua" phrases. In these respects, then, my theory fits Lewis's. In other respects, it differs. My relation of being an *F*-counterpart is an equivalence relation, and it holds between any two entities in different worlds which are both *F*'s and which share a common past. Lewis's counterpart relations "are a matter of overall resemblance in a variety of respects" (p. 208), and are not equivalence relations (p. 209).

10 Peter Geach *Reference and Generality* (Ithaca, NY: Cornell University Press, 1962), sect. 34, contends that a proper name conveys a "nominal essence" – "requirements as to identity" that can be expressed by a common noun. The name "Thames," for instance, conveys the nominal essence expressed by the common noun "river." In this respect, my theory follows Geach's. Geach, however, (sect. 31), thinks that even in the actual world, identity makes no sense except with respect to a general term. According to the theory in this paper, non-relative identity makes sense in talk of any one possible world; it is only cross-world identity that must be made relative to a sortal.

11 Kripke, "Naming and necessity," pp. 298–9.

12 This volume, p. 129.

13 Kripke, "Naming and necessity," p. 268.

14 This volume, p. 129.

15 Kripke, "Naming and necessity," pp. 271–2.

16 Cf. W. V. O. Quine, "Reference and modality," in *From a Logical Point of View*, 2nd edn (New York: Harper & Row, 1961), pp. 139–59, sect. 2.

17 See esp. Rudolf Carnap, *Meaning and Necessity* (Chicago: University of Chicago Press, 1947), sect. 41. I shall not follow Carnap in detail, nor, for the most part, shall I try to say in what precise ways I follow him and in what ways I deviate from what he says.

18 Aldo Bressan, *A General Interpreted Modal Calculus* (New Haven, Conn.: Yale University Press, 1972).

19 Frege, "On sense and reference," p. 59.

20 The original paper included an appendix, omitted here.

21 The talk of "shifts" is not Carnap's; it is part of my own informal reading of Carnap's semantics. Carnap does think "that individual variables in modal sentences … must be interpreted as referring, not to individuals, but to individual concepts" (*Meaning and Necessity*, p. 180). He does not, however, allow variables to shift their ranges of values within a single language. Rather, he constructs two languages, a non-modal language S_1 in which variables range over individuals and a modal language S_2 in which variables range over individual concepts. Any sentence of S_1 is a sentence of S_2 and is its own translation into S_2 (see ibid., pp. 200–2). The semantics I give in the appendix (not included in this volume) is roughly that of Carnap's S_2 (see ibid., pp. 183–4). In informal discussion in the body of this paper, though, I take a variable to range over individuals whenever such an interpretation is possible.

Carnap does not talk of predicates shifting in the way I describe, but once variables are taken to range over individual concepts, such a reinterpretation of predicates allows a straightforward reading of Carnap's semantics. Quine discussed this point in his letter to Carnap (*Meaning and Necessity*, p. 197).

22 Quine, "Reference and modality," p. 153.

23 Letter in Carnap, *Meaning and Necessity*, p. 196.

24 Quine, "Reference and modality," p. 151.

25 For other characterizations of essentialism, see Terence Parsons, "Essentialism and quantified modal logic," *Philosophical Review* 78 (1969), pp. 35–52, sect. 2.

26 Quine objects to essentialism even for abstract entities. "Essentialism," he writes, "is abruptly at variance with the idea, favored by Carnap, Lewis, and others, of explaining necessity by analyticity" ("Reference and modality," p. 155). That, however, cannot be true: Carnap does explain his system in terms of analyticity, and his system involves essentialism, as I have explained. Carnap's system is thus a counterexample to Quine's claim; it shows that one can consistently both accept essentialism for individual concepts and explain necessity by analyticity.

27 Anil Gupta has shown me a formula similar to this one, which he attributes to Nuel Belnap.

28 See Robert Stalnaker, "A theory of conditionals," in *Studies in Logical Theory*, American Philosophical Quarterly Monograph Series, no. 2 (1968), and Stalnaker and Richmond Thomason, "A semantic analysis of conditional logic," *Theoria* 36 (1970), pp. 23–42. For a somewhat different theory which raises similar problems, see David K. Lewis, *Counterfactuals* (Oxford: Blackwell, 1973).

29 See Quine, "Reference and modality," pp. 158–9.

30 Saul Kripke, "Semantical considerations on modal logic," *Acta Philosophica Fennica* 16 (1963), pp. 83–94.

31 See Richmond Thomason and Robert Stalnaker, "Modality and reference," *Noûs* 2 (1968), pp. 359–72.

32 Letter in Carnap, *Meaning and Necessity*, p. 196.

33 See n. 20 above.

12

Can There Be Vague Objects?

Gareth Evans

It is sometimes said that the world might itself *be* vague. Rather than vagueness being a deficiency in our mode of describing the world, it would then be a necessary feature of any true description of it. It is also said that amongst the statements which may not have a determinate truth value as a result of their vagueness are identity statements. Combining these two views we would arrive at the idea that the world might contain certain objects about which it is a *fact* that they have fuzzy boundaries. But is this idea coherent?

Let '*a*' and '*b*' be singular terms such that the sentence '*a* = *b*' is of indeterminate truth value, and let us allow for the expression of the idea of indeterminacy by the sentential operator '∇'. Then we have:

(1) $\nabla(a = b)$.

(1) reports a fact about *b* which we may express by ascribing to it the property '$\hat{x}[\nabla(x = a)]$':

(2) $\hat{x}\,[\nabla(x = a)]b$.

But we have:

(3) $\sim \nabla(a = a)$

and hence:

(4) $\sim \hat{x}[\nabla(x = a)]a$.

But by Leibniz's Law, we may derive from (2) and (4):

(5) $\sim (a = b)$

contradicting the assumption, with which we began, that the identity statement '*a* = *b*' is of indeterminate truth value.

If 'Indefinitely' and its dual, 'Definitely' ('Δ') generate a modal logic as strong as S5, (1)–(4) and, presumably, Leibniz's Law, may each be strengthened with a 'Definitely' prefix, enabling us to derive

(5′) $\Delta \sim (a = b)$

which is straightforwardly inconsistent with (1).

Gareth Evans, "Can There Be Vague Objects?", *Analysis*, 38/4 (Oct. 1978): 208. Published by Oxford University Press on behalf of the Analysis Committee. Reproduced by permission.

Metaphysics: An Anthology, Second Edition. Edited by Jaegwon Kim, Daniel Z. Korman and Ernest Sosa.

13

Vague Identity

Robert C. Stalnaker

Can the identity relation be vague, or semantically indeterminate? The following argument, offered by Nathan Salmon, suggests that it cannot be:

> Suppose there is a pair of entities x and y ... such that it is vague ... whether they are one and the very same thing. Then the pair $\langle x, y \rangle$ is quite definitely not the same pair as $\langle x, x \rangle$, since it is determinately true that x is one and the very same thing as itself. It follows that x and y must be distinct. But then it is not vague whether they are identical or distinct.[1]

This is, I think, a sound argument for something, but one may be misled about what it shows, particularly about identity across time and across possible worlds. In this paper, I will try to get clearer about just what the conclusion of the argument is: about what kinds of semantic indeterminacy it excludes, and what kinds it permits.

The first point to make is that the argument does not show, and does not pretend to show, that identity *statements* cannot be vague. It is clear that if there is any semantic indeterminacy in the language at all, then it will be possible to construct vague identity statements. There are at least two different kinds of cases. First, consider the statement "Harry's best friend is Sue." Suppose that the relation 'is best friend of' is a vague relation, and that it is semantically indeterminate whether it is Sue or George who stands in this relation to Harry. Then the definite description, 'Harry's best friend' will be a semantically indeterminate singular term. Harry's best friend is either Sue or George, but there is no fact of the matter about which of the two it is.[2]

One might be tempted to think that Salmon's argument showed that this kind of indeterminacy is impossible. Following the strategy of the argument, one might reason as follows: It is determinately true that Sue is Sue, and so if it is not determinately true that Sue is Harry's best friend, then the pair <Sue, Sue> is definitely not the same as the pair, <Sue, Harry's best friend>. But if these pairs are definitely distinct, then Sue is definitely not Harry's best friend. The fallacy in this argument is in the move from the premise that a certain relational statement is indeterminate to the conclusion that there is a determinate pair of persons such that it is indeterminate whether *they* stand in the relation. But of course if it is indeterminate whether Sue is Harry's best friend, then it is indeterminate which pair of

Robert C. Stalnaker, "Vague Identity," in David F. Austin (ed.), *Philosophical Analysis: A Defense by Example,* (Dordrecht: Kluwer, 1988), 349–60. Reproduced by kind permission of Springer Science + Business Media B.V.

Metaphysics: An Anthology, Second Edition. Edited by Jaegwon Kim, Daniel Z. Korman and Ernest Sosa.
Editorial material and organization © 2012 Blackwell Publishing Ltd. Published 2012 by Blackwell Publishing Ltd.

persons is denoted by the expression, '<Sue, Harry's best friend>'.

Here is a different kind of example of an indeterminate identity statement, used in several places by Sydney Shoemaker.[3] Two multistory structures are connected by a covered passage. Is this one building with two wings, or two connected buildings? Suppose neither the concept of building nor the linguistic practices of the users of this/these building(s) determine an answer. Jones is in room 201 on one side, while Smith is in room 395 on the other side. There is no fact of the matter about whether the building Jones is in is the same as the building Smith is in. Here the indeterminacy does not necessarily derive from a vague definite description. One might use demonstratives to pick out the building(s) without resolving the ambiguity. (Smith may wonder, "is *this* building the same as *that* one?") But in this example, as in the first one, the source of the semantic indeterminacy in the identity statement is indeterminacy about what things are being said to be identical.[4]

Some relational statements may lack a truth value even when it is clear what things the statement relates. For example, even where it is clear who we are referring to with the name 'Sam', and determinate who Sam's father is, there may be no fact of the matter about whether Sam is more successful than his father. What Salmon's argument shows is that this cannot happen with identity. Once it is clear that this is all the argument purports to prove, there should be no controversy about it. Identity is a very simple relation. Its extension (relative to a domain of individuals D) is the set of pairs $<d,d>$ such that d is a member of D. If there is any question about whether a given pair of individuals is in this set, it obviously must be a question about what pair we are talking about.

Salmon gives his argument in the context of a discussion of identity across possible worlds. Suppose we describe, uniquely, a possible table, that exists in some nonactual possible world, and ask whether that table is or is not identical with some particular actual table. Does Salmon's argument show that if there is only one possible table that fits our description, then there must be a fact of the matter about whether or not it is one and the same table as some actual table? Or consider the related issue concerning identity across time:

does the argument show that there must be a fact of the matter about which ship (if either) is the original Ship of Theseus? These are the kinds of examples that have led philosophers to suggest that identity is in some cases vague, and it is this response to the examples that Salmon's argument aims to refute. I will consider some examples that make a *prima facie* case for vague identity over time, and across possible worlds, asking what Salmon's argument shows about how we must describe such examples.

I will begin with a temporal example. In Philadelphia there are two prominent seafood restaurants named 'Bookbinder's' that carry on a rather unseemly rivalry. One calls itself 'Bookbinder's Seafood House.' ("The Bookbinder's Family serves classic seafood only in Center City"); I will call it 'B_1'. The other describes itself as 'The old original Bookbinder's' ("There is only one!" "Imitated … never duplicated"); I will call this one B_2. Each lays claim to a tradition going back to 1865 when a single restaurant named 'Bookbinder's' was founded. I will call this original restaurant 'B_0'. Now I don't know the historical facts; perhaps one of the two restaurants is really the original, while the other is a new restaurant started later by the descendants of the original family. But it could be that the history is somewhat tangled, with several changes in ownership and location, branches opened, buildings sold, partners or heirs dividing the property. Perhaps – and this is what I will assume – each of the two current restaurants has some legitimate claim to *be* that restaurant that was founded in 1865. Does Salmon's argument show that there must be facts about the histories of these two restaurants that determine which of the two is the original, or that determine that neither of the two presently existing restaurants is the original? It is clearly false that $B_1 = B_2$, and so, because of the transitivity of identity, it cannot be that both $B_0 = B_1$ and $B_0 = B_2$, but there is some temptation to say, given the historical assumptions I am making, that these latter two identity claims are semantically indeterminate. Can we reconcile this temptation with Salmon's argument? I want to suggest that we can.

In defining my notation for describing the example, I said that B_0 is the original restaurant. There are at least two ways to take this stipulation. On the most natural way to take it, a description is used to pick out a restaurant in 1865. 'B_0'

reaches back to that time, referring directly to a certain restaurant existing then. But we might instead understand the stipulation as saying that 'B_0' is to be the name of a certain presently existing restaurant, the one that has a certain historical property. B_0 is the one of the two presently existing restaurants called 'Bookbinder's' that has the property, *was founded in 1865*. On the second way of understanding the stipulation, the example resembles the vague definite description case. 'B_0' is an ambiguous name, since its reference was fixed by an ambiguous definite description. It is indeterminate which restaurant, B_1 or B_2, has the historical property *was founded in 1865*, and so it is indeterminate whether the name 'B_0' refers to B_1 or to B_2. But on the first way of understanding the stipulation, 'B_0' seems to have a determinate referent since (it seems) in 1865 there was only one restaurant named 'Bookbinder's.' If a Philadelphian had said, in 1865, "Let's have dinner at Bookbinder's," he would, it seems, have referred unambiguously; 'B_0' names the restaurant that he would have named. It seems also clear that 'B_1' and 'B_2' are unambiguous. So, given Salmon's argument, how can it be indeterminate whether $B_0 = B_2$?

The answer to this question will depend on how we understand enduring things: persons, physical objects, and institutions such as restaurants that exist through time. One kind of account is this: enduring things are four dimensional objects – things with temporal as well as spatial parts, things that are extended in time in the same way that they are extended in space. A thing, on this way of understanding things, is the same as its history; a person is the same as his or her life. If we understand continuant things in this way, then the restaurant example will be just like the building example. When I say "*this* building," it is indeterminate whether I refer to a larger or a smaller structure, and the indeterminacy is explained in terms of an indeterminacy in the general concept of a building. It is indeterminate whether the larger structure is one building or two, and whether the smaller structure is a whole building or merely a part of one. In the same way, there are two temporally extended restaurant-like objects, each containing a common temporal part – the part that existed in 1865 and for some time after. But it is indeterminate which of these things is a *restaurant*, and which is a composite of two temporal parts of different restaurants. For this reason, it is indeterminate which of these entities 'B_0' refers to.

It might appear that we have succeeded in referring to a determinate thing with 'B_0' since it is determinately true (true on both ways of understanding of the concept of restaurant) that there was, in 1865, exactly one restaurant in Philadelphia named 'Bookbinder's.' Similarly, it might appear that I have referred to a determinate thing when I said "*this* building," since on either of the two construals of the concept of building I was in exactly one building (I was not straddling two buildings). But it is clear (assuming this conception of a continuant thing) that this appearance of determinacy is an illusion.

I think this is a satisfactory explanation of the indeterminacy of reference in the restaurant example, assuming that it is right to identify persons, physical objects and restaurants with their lives or histories. But some will protest that this is just not what such things are. They will insist that continuant things, unlike events or lives, don't have temporal parts. They exist through time, but are wholly present at each time. It is not entirely clear what this protest amounts to – some philosophers would complain that it makes no sense, since to endure through time just *is* to have temporal parts.[5] But even if this is a dark doctrine, difficult to make sense of, there is some intuitive inclination to assent to it. I don't want either to defend or to criticize this doctrine, nor will I try to explain what it means. But I will consider whether, if we assumes that sense can be made of it, and that it is correct, we will have a harder time explaining *prima facie* cases of vague identity as cases of indeterminacy of reference.

The proponent of this conception of enduring objects might argue as follows:

First, consider the domain of restaurants that existed in Philadelphia in 1865. There is only one named 'Bookbinder's.' It is the one we are calling 'B_0.' Not only are there no other *restaurants* that are candidates to be the referent of this name, there are (on this way of understanding enduring objects) no other restaurant-like entities – entities that would be correctly called 'restaurants' on some different way of disambiguating the term 'restaurant' – that are candidates to be referents of the name 'B_0.' For even if our 'criteria of identity' for restaurants are indeterminate, this can't affect the domain of things that are restaurants at a given time, since the restaurants that exist at that time are wholly present then. So it seems that we have achieved determinate reference to a particular enduring thing. Now consider the domain of restaurants that exist in Philadelphia today. There is just one that we are calling 'B_1,' and it is clear which one it is. Again, we seem to have determinate reference. So if we accept the validity of Salmon's argument, it seems that there must be a fact of the matter whether the determinate thing B_0 is or is not identical with the determinate thing B_1.

Against this argument, I will contend that the indeterminacy may be more subtle on the assumptions we are making, but it is still there. To help bring it out, let me first consider an argument about a related question concerning identity over time. Consider the proverbial statue and lump of clay out of which it is made. Yesterday, the statue did not exist, although the lump of clay did, so the statue cannot *be* the lump of clay, even today. The two things have (today) different historical properties: one has the property of having existed yesterday, while the other does not. Notice that this familiar argument does not require that we think of the statue and the lump as four dimensional things, only parts of which exist today. Even if we insist that (in some sense to be explained) both the statue and the lump are wholly present now, the argument still shows that they must be (now) distinct. The argument does not depend on claiming that the two things have different *parts*; it requires only that they have different historical properties. Now consider again the restaurants. Suppose that the concept of restaurant is indeterminate in that it is indeterminate what counts as the same restaurant at different times (as a concept would be indeterminate if it were indeterminate whether it picked out statues or lumps of clay). On some ways of arbitrarily refining our concept, B_0 will become B_1, and on others B_0 will become B_2. So on some disambiguations, B_0 had (in 1865) temporal properties (for example, being such that it will be located in Center City in 121 years) that B_0 lacked on other disambiguations. The referent of 'B_0' will thus depend on how we disambiguate, and so will be indeterminate.

I recognize that in giving this argument I am supposing things that Salmon regards as incoherent, but I don't think I am begging any questions. What is at issue is whether Salmon's argument shows that what I am supposing is incoherent. My argument is that what I am supposing commits me to indeterminacy of reference, and not to indeterminacy of identity between determinate objects. But Salmon's argument refutes only the latter commitment.

Salmon's argument shows us that if we succeed in picking out entities, of any kind, a and b, there must be a fact of the matter whether a and b are one thing or two. Or to put it contrapositively, the argument shows that if it is indeterminate whether $a = b$, then it is indeterminate what 'a' refers to, or what 'b' refers to. This simple abstract argument cannot, by itself, give us reason to think that the facts, together with our conceptual resources *must* decide the question whether a given identity statement is true. All it tells us is that if the facts and our concepts do not decide the question, then it is undetermined what the terms in the identity statement are referring to.

Imagine someone who responded to the building example this way: "I am perfectly clear what buildings I am referring to: I am referring to *this* one, and to *that* one (pointing to the other structure). So, because of Salmon's argument, I conclude that our concept of a building *must* determine an answer to the question whether this building is that one." This is obviously not a reasonable response. The building case is a *prima facie* case of indeterminate identity, and what Salmon's argument shows is that a *prima facie* case of indeterminate identity just is a *prima facie* case of indeterminacy of reference. Our problem is to explain the source of the indeterminacy.

The cases of identity over time show that the indeterminacy of reference can be of a subtle kind. Just as we can distinguish intimately related things such as an artifact and what it is made of, a person and his or her body, by distinguishing their temporal properties, so we can distinguish subtly different potential referents of indeterminate terms by distinguishing their temporal properties. But while Salmon's argument can force us to recognize such subtle indeterminacies, it cannot make a plausible case that our conceptual resources must be doing more work than they seem to be doing.

I want to conclude by commenting, more briefly, about what Salmon's argument has to say about *prima facie* cases of indeterminate identity across possible worlds. There are strategies here that parallel those available to reconcile the phenomena about identity through time with the argument, but there are also some significant differences. Strategies that are plausible in one context may be implausible in the other. I will begin by sketching an example – the example from Saul Kripke's *Naming and Necessity* that provided the context for Salmon's argument – and then discuss four contrasts between the case of identity through time and the case of identity across possible worlds.

Suppose we consider a particular counterfactual variation on the history of the molecules that constitute some actual table – call it T.

> One may ask whether T would exist, in that situation, or whether a certain bunch of molecules, which in that situation would constitute a table, constitute the very same table T ... [I]n some cases the answer may be indeterminate.[6]

The molecules that constitute the table, at least at its beginning, must be substantially the same as those that constitute the actual table if the counterfactual table is to *be* the actual table, but presumably they need not be exactly the same molecules. If this is right, there will surely be borderline cases. That is, surely there will be a possible world at which there exists a table whose origin and constitution in that world make it indeterminate whether or not it is numerically the same table as the actual table T. How is this to be reconciled with the argument? Our thesis is that where there is indeterminacy of identity there is indeterminacy of reference, but in this kind of case, where is the indeterminacy of reference? In answering this question, we cannot follow the temporal analogy too closely; there are a number of contrasts.

First, while there is some plausibility to the conception of continuant objects as four dimensional things, with temporal parts, there is no plausibility to the corresponding conception of objects and persons as spread out across possible worlds, existing only partly in each one. On such a conception, we would have to say that only a small part of our table is actual; most of it is merely possible. If we are to distinguish potential referents of the terms we use to talk about tables, we will have to do it in terms of their contrasting modal properties, and not in terms of their contrasting parts.

Second, while it is not entirely unnatural to distinguish things (such as statues and hunks of clay) solely by their historical properties, and so to distinguish potential referents of terms in this way, it is much more artificial, at least in some cases, to distinguish things solely by their modal properties.[7] Consider, not Bookbinder's, but Turback's, a restaurant in Ithaca with a shorter and less checkered history: continuous management and the same location since its beginning. But of course Turback's *might* have had a history similar to Bookbinder's. Does this counterfactual possibility, in which there would exist restaurants that are neither determinately identical to Turback's nor determinately distinct from it, force us to say that our actual references to Turback's in ordinary statements about it, are indeterminate? We should hope that it does not.

Third, there is an option open to us in the cross-world case that does not parallel any available in the temporal cases. We can attribute the indeterminacy to the fact that we have not picked out a single possible world, but only a set of them. One might say that if specifying the identity and arrangement of the molecules in a given possible world does not determine whether the table that those molecules constitute is *this* very table, then it is open to us to decide whether it is or not. In so deciding, we are making a further stipulation about which possible world we choose to describe. But there are at least two problems with this strategy. First, as Salmon brings out in his discussion, we can make this move only if we reject a very plausible supervenience assumption: the assumption that the totality of facts about the molecular constituents of the world determines all the facts about physical objects. If we use this strategy to eliminate the cross-world indeterminacy, we have to distinguish not just possible worlds that are qualitatively indiscernible, but worlds that are constituted by numerically identical components arranged in exactly the same ways throughout their histories. Two such indiscernible worlds might differ only in this way: in one of them, a certain table is *this* table, while in the other the corresponding table (made in the same way of the same molecules) is not *this* table.

Second, even if we were willing to reject the supervenience assumption, there is an additional problem with this response. Presumably, the reason we are inclined to say that it is indeterminate whether the possible world we describe is one in which table T exists is that we are inclined to say that it is indeterminate whether it is possible for this table to have that origin and constitution. But if we solve the problem of indeterminacy by proliferating possibilities, we will have to conclude that it is determinately possible for the table to have that origin and constitution.[8]

Finally, if we are actualists, we must keep in mind the following contrast between the temporal and the worldly cases, a contrast that may underlie all the others. Past times are parts of reality on a par with our own time, but other possible 'worlds' are just alternative ways that the one world there is might have been. We can refer directly across time to a past thing by interacting with the thing as it was then, since causal relations are relations that hold across time. But reference to 'things' in other possible worlds is really just a way of talking about the potentialities of things in the actual world. The only *things* there are, of any kind, are the actual things. What it is for some actual thing to exist in the domain of some alternative possible world is for that possible world to represent that actual thing as existing, and being some particular way. Questions about whether some thing in the domain of a counterfactual world is identical to some particular actual thing are questions about whether a certain representation is a representation of that actual thing. This relation – the relation between a representation and what it represents – is not the identity relation, and it, unlike identity, may be vague even if it is clear what the relata are.

Exactly how does this actualist interpretation of the possible worlds rhetoric help us to reconcile Salmon's argument with Kripke's example? Suppose that T is a determinate table, and that we have got hold of a particular possible world – call it w – that contains a single table – call it T' – with the sort of origin and composition to make it indeterminate whether it is the same table as T. So, it would seem, '$T = T'$' is indeterminate, yet it also seems that both 'T' and 'T'' have determinate reference.

But first, we must keep in mind that the question whether '$T = T'$' is true, false or indeterminate is the question whether it is true, false or indeterminate *in the actual world*, since for the actualist, truth and falsity are the same as actual truth and falsity. So our two names, if they succeed in picking out tables, will do so in quite different ways. 'T' names a table unproblematically, but if 'T'' names a table (an actual table) and not just a table-representation, it will have to do so in virtue of some relation between a table-representation expressed by 'T'' and a table. The question is, does T have, in the actual world, the modal property 'would be T' if w were actual'? This question depends on whether the table-representation, T', which is a feature or component of the possible state of the world w, stands in a certain relation – a relation that is obviously not identity – to the table T. If it does, then 'T'' denotes, in the actual world, T, and so the identity statement is true. But if it is indeterminate whether T has this modal property, then the name 'T'' is indeterminate, in the actual world, and so the identity statement can be indeterminate without conflicting with Salmon's argument. T' may appear to be determinate because it picks out a determinate table in w. But this is only to say that if w were actual, the table-representation T' would represent a unique table.[9]

Identity is often confused with other relations – composition, genidentity, unity, counterparthood – and when it is discussions of identity may be discussions of interesting metaphysical questions. But identity itself is a very simple and a very abstract relation. There are no limits on its domain of application: restaurants and rivers, nations and numbers, persons, pigs, pictures, powers, possibilities and propositions are all things that, if they exist at all, are identical to themselves, and to nothing else. If we are not clear what we are talking about, it may be unclear whether a statement that ascribes this relation is true, but the relation itself is unproblematic and uninteresting. That some entity stands in this relation with itself says nothing about the nature of the entity, and so one should be suspicious of any argument that purports to get substantive metaphysical conclusions out of the logic of identity – conclusions about what kinds of things there can be in the world, or about what the things that are there must be like.[10]

Notes

1 Salmon (1981), 243. There is a similar argument in Evans (1978), 208. Evans described his argument as an argument against the coherence of the idea of vague objects in the world, but the argument itself is against semantically indeterminate identity statements. Thomason (1982), uses a supervaluation semantics to argue that Evans's argument is fallacious.

2 One could adopt a semantic account of definite descriptions according to which statements containing vague descriptions were false, rather than neither true nor false. But it would be a mistake to think that Salmon's argument shows that one must adopt such a semantic account.

3 See, for example, note 5 in Shoemaker's reply to Swinburne in Shoemaker and Swinburne (1984), 145.

4 In the building example, the kind of semantic indeterminacy seems to be ambiguity rather than vagueness since there is a small number of alternative interpretations. But there are also cases with a continuous range of alternative interpretations that look more like cases of vagueness. Consider, for example, the concept of a mountain (cf. Quine (1960), 125ff. and also Hughes (1985)). Obviously one could not say, nonarbitrarily, exactly which square inches of territory are parts of a given mountain, and which were parts of the plain or foothills surrounding it. Should we say that it is semantically indeterminate just which precise parcel of land the name 'Mt. Rainier' refers to, or should we say that this name refers determinately to a vague individual? Some say that the latter description is confused, since vagueness is in the language, not in the world. But it is not clear to me that one description is better than the other, or what hangs on the difference. Intuitively, it does not seem unnatural to say that there are objects with vague boundaries. But if we insist that, say, Mt. Rainier is a vague individual, and that the name 'Mt. Rainier' refers determinately to this individual, we do not thereby commit ourselves to vague identities. Suppose I define a precise piece of territory whose boundaries are within the range of vagueness of the boundary of Mt. Rainier. Call this piece of land 'M.' Is it false that Mt. Rainier = M, or is it indeterminate? If Mt. Rainier is a vague individual, then it seems we ought to say 'false,' since M is not a vague individual, and so cannot be the same thing. On the other hand, if we say that this identity statement is indeterminate, then it seems reasonable to say that it is not determinate whether or not 'Mt. Rainier' refers to M. We might ask a parallel question about vagueness in the expression of properties. Are there vague properties, or just vague predicates – predicates that indeterminately express one of a range of precise properties? For example, does the predicate 'is short' determinately express a vague property, *being short*, or is it indeterminate which of a range of precise properties, such as *being less than 161.3 centimeters tall*, it expresses? If we say the latter, then we should say that the statement, 'the property of being short just is the property of being less than 161.3 centimeters tall' is semantically indeterminate, rather than false.

5 David Lewis, for example, argues that the only way to make sense of the dark saying (continuant things don't have temporal parts – they persist through time, but are wholly present at each time) is to assume that its defender is using the concepts *part* and *whole* in a restricted way, to exclude temporal parts. See Lewis (1986), 203. But this cannot be quite right, since the defender of this conception of continuant things will grant that some kinds of things – football games, wars, eras and centuries – can have temporal parts.

6 Kripke (1981), 50–1.

7 Allan Gibbard, discussing a cross-world version of the statue-lump of clay example, allows that one may distinguish things from what they are made of by their different temporal properties, but argues that if the statue and the lump of clay coincide throughout their history, they will be contingently identical. Apparently he finds it less plausible to distinguish things by their modal properties. See Gibbard (1975) (chapter 11 of this volume).

8 Salmon's solution to the problem is to allow that the world at which the table with the problematic origin and constitution is *this* table may be an impossible world – a world that is inaccessible to the actual world. Or, perhaps the accessibility relation is vague, in which case it is indeterminate whether this world is possible or impossible (relative to the actual world). Salmon also seems to think that his solution is compatible with the supervenience assumption, since there cannot be two distinct *possible* worlds (relative to any world) that are indiscernible on the molecular level. See Salmon (1981), Appendix I.

9 In a footnote commenting on this example, and the general problem of the vagueness of cross-world identity, Kripke suggested that "some sort of 'counterpart' notion (though not with Lewis's philosophical underpinnings of resemblance, foreign country worlds, etc.), may have some utility here." Kripke (1981), p. 51, n18. I think this is right, and I have tried to motivate such an application of counterpart theory in Stalnaker (1987). The focus there is on contingent identity statements rather than vague identity statements. It is important to keep in mind that the relevant counterpart relation is not a weaker relation between things that some take to be

identical (like, say, the relation of composition between a substance and what it is made of). The counterpart relation holds between representations rather than between the things represented. Very roughly, the idea is this: if representation *a* is a counterpart of representation *b*, then the thing represented by *a* is identical with the thing represented by *b*. The counterpart relation can be vague, and intransitive, even though the identity relation can be neither. See also Forbes (1984) for a defense of the application of counterpart theory to these problems.

10   In thinking about these issues, I have benefited from correspondence and conversation with a number of people, including Hugh Chandler, Graeme Forbes, Christopher Hughes, Nathan Salmon, Sydney Shoemaker and Peter van Inwagen.

References

Evans, Gareth (1978), 'Can There Be Vague Objects?', *Analysis* 38: 208.

Forbes, Graeme (1984), 'Two Solutions to Chisholm's Paradox,' *Philosophical Studies*, 46: 171–87.

Gibbard, Allan (1975), 'Contingent Identity,' *Journal of Philosophical Logic*, 4 187–222.

Hughes, Christopher (1985), 'Is a Thing Just the Sum of Its Parts?' *Proceedings of the Aristotelian Society*, new series 86.

Kripke, Saul (1981), *Naming and Necessity* (Cambridge: Harvard University Press).

Lewis, David (1986), *On the Plurality of Worlds*. (Oxford: Basil Blackwell).

Quine, Willard Van Orman (1960), *Word and Object* (New York and London: John Wiley & Sons).

Salmon, Nathan U. (1981), *Reference and Essence* (Princeton, NJ: Princeton University Press).

Shoemaker, Sydney & Richard Swinburne (1984), *Personal Identity* (Oxford: Basil Blackwell).

Stalnaker, Robert (1987), 'Counterparts and Identity,' *Midwest Studies in Philosophy* 11: 121–40.

Thomason, Richmond (1982), 'Identity and Vagueness,' *Philosophical Studies* 42: 329–32.

PART III
Modality

Introduction

Some propositions are necessarily true, for instance, the proposition that eight is greater than five and the proposition that horses are animals. Other propositions are only contingently true, for instance, that Socrates was wise (he could have been foolish) or that there are horses (evolution could have taken a different course and they would never have come into existence). Others are false but possibly true, for instance, that Socrates was eight feet tall or that some horses are bright blue. Modality is the study of necessity, possibility, and other such "modes" of truth. Necessity and possibility are of central interest in philosophy in part because philosophical claims tend to take the form of claims, not just about how things happen to be, but about how things *must* be. And to assess claims about how things must be, one must often look beyond what happens to be true and consider what could possibly be true. For instance, the claim that, necessarily, a person exists only if her body exists would be undermined if it were so much as possible for people to survive the annihilation of their bodies. Or, as some philosophers would put it, we need only consider whether there is a "possible world" in which people outlive their bodies. (More on issues of personal identity in Part VII.)

The modalities mentioned above are known as *de dicto* modalities, that is, attributions of necessity or contingency to propositions, statements, or sentences. But modal notions can also be used to characterize the way in which an *object* possesses a property. We can say of Socrates that he was only contingently wise, and we can say of the number eight that it is necessarily greater than five. These are known as *de re* modal attributions. Some (most prominently, W. V. Quine) have cast doubt on the notion of *de re* modality. One reason for skepticism is that whether we are willing to say that a given item has a certain property necessarily or only contingently seems suspiciously dependent on how we choose to describe the item. We are tempted to say that the number between seven and nine is necessarily greater than five, while the number of planets in the solar system is only contingently greater than five. But 'the number between seven and nine' and 'the number of planets in the solar system' pick out exactly the same number (now that Pluto has been "demoted"), and a single item cannot both be contingently and necessarily greater than five. This description-dependence suggests that *de re* modal properties are something that we project onto objects, not genuine, objective features

Metaphysics: An Anthology, Second Edition. Edited by Jaegwon Kim, Daniel Z. Korman and Ernest Sosa.
Editorial material and organization © 2012 Blackwell Publishing Ltd. Published 2012 by Blackwell Publishing Ltd.

of those objects. In "Modalities: Basic Concepts and Distinctions" (chapter 14), Alvin Plantinga defends *essentialism* – the view that objects do have some of their properties as a matter of *de re* necessity – against a variety of such skeptical challenges. Plantinga begins the selection by helpfully distinguishing the notion of a necessary truth from a number of associated notions: logical truth, a priori truth, self evidence, and immunity from rational rejection.

In "Actualism and Thisness" (chapter 15), Robert M. Adams defends the actualist thesis that everything that exists is actual. Although philosophers are prone to talking about merely possible individuals, most believe that (strictly speaking) there are no such things. On the view that Adams had defended in "Primitive Thisness and Primitive Identity" (chapter 9), every object has an individual essence, or "thisness" – a property that is instantiated (and can be instantiated) by it and only it. A question that divides actualists is whether there exist any individual essences for nonexistent objects (for instance, for each of the infinitely many possible siblings that you did not have but could have had). Adams argues that there are no uninstantiated individual essences, on the grounds that the only viable account of the nature of these essences requires their bearers to exist in order for the thisnesses themselves to exist. Adams also addresses the following prima facie problem for his view: If there is a world in which neither you nor your identity properties exist, then it would seem that there could be no propositions about you in that world. (What would such propositions be "built up out of" in such a world?) But then the proposition that you do not exist cannot exist in such a world, let alone be true. So there can be no world in which it is true that you do not exist. So it seems to follow that you exist necessarily, which is absurd. Adams responds by drawing a (now well-known) distinction between being true *in* a world and being true *at* a world.

Adams appeals at numerous points to what happens in certain "possible worlds," as does virtually every other author in this anthology. There is a possible world in which there are blue swans. There is no possible world in which $2 + 1 = 4$. Some treat talk of possible worlds merely as shorthand for talking about what could and could not have been the case. But others invoke them to do genuine explanatory work, and they owe us some account of what these worlds are. In chapter 16 – the heavily abridged first chapter of his book *On the Plurality of Worlds* – David Lewis presents and defends his possibilist (i.e., anti-actualist) thesis of modal realism. According to modal realism, possible worlds, like the actual world, are real, existent universes. The view has the seemingly outlandish implication that blue swans really do exist, as do talking donkeys and all other sorts of entities that we regard as merely possible. They do not *actually* exist (i.e., they do not exist in the actual world) but they do exist. Lewis defends this radical account of possible worlds by showing that it has numerous theoretical benefits and applications (in regard to modality, counterfactuals, content, and properties) that might outweigh its more unpalatable aspects.

In "Possible Worlds" (chapter 17), Robert C. Stalnaker defends an alternative theory of possible worlds, one which does not involve commitment to a plurality of concrete universes. Stalnaker begins by showing that one can accept certain plausible aspects of Lewis's conception of worlds – specifically, his understanding of worlds as ways things might have been and his indexical treatment of 'actual' – without taking possible worlds to be the same *sorts* of things as the actual world. (This is sometimes known as an *ersatz* conception of possible worlds.) Stalnaker goes on to suggest that we ought to treat worlds as irreducible, on the grounds that such a view has more explanatory power than one that reduces worlds to sets of propositions.

In "Modal Fictionalism" (chapter 18), Gideon Rosen examines a way of avoiding commitment to possible worlds altogether. According to Rosen, what is going on when we talk about possible worlds is similar to what is going on when we tell stories. We do not actually mean to commit ourselves to the existence of Sherlock Holmes when we say 'There is a brilliant detective at 221 B Baker Street'. We only mean to say that *according to the Holmes stories* there is a brilliant detective there. Rosen examines the prospects of a fictionalist account of our talk about possible worlds on which ordinary modal claims are true just in case associated nonmodal claims are true according to a Lewis-style story of possible worlds. Rosen argues that modal fictionalism is, in virtually all respects, on a par with Lewis's modal realism with regard to its explanatory power, but without the intolerable commitment to a plurality of concrete worlds!

In "Essence and Modality" (chapter 19), Kit Fine examines the relationship between necessary properties and essential properties. He challenges the widespread view that the notion of an essential property can be understood in purely modal terms, for instance, that an object has a property essentially just in case it is necessary that it has that property. By that criterion, not only is it essential to {Socrates} (that is, the set whose only member is Socrates) that it has Socrates as a member, but it is also essential to Socrates that he is a member of the set {Socrates}. Surely, however, this is not part of Socrates' nature – being a member of that set is no part of what it is for Socrates to be the object that he is – and therefore, Fine contends, it is not essential to Socrates that he be a member of {Socrates}. Intuitively, what accounts for its being necessary that Socrates is a member of {Socrates} is the nature of {Socrates}, not the nature of Socrates. Fine defends a definitional conception of essence which can account for this asymmetry in a way that the modal conception evidently cannot.

Further Reading

Adams, R. M. (1974). "Theories of Actuality," *Noûs* 8: 211–31.

Armstrong, D. M. (1986). "The Nature of Possibility," *The Canadian Journal of Philosophy* 16: 575–94.

Bennett, K. (2005). "Two Axes of Actualism," *The Philosophical Review* 114: 297–326.

Divers, J. (2002). *Possible Worlds*. New York: Routledge.

Fine, K. (2003). "The Problem of Possibilia," in M. J. Loux and D. W. Zimmerman (eds.), *The Oxford Handbook of Metaphysics*. Oxford: Oxford University Press, pp. 161–79.

Kripke, S. (1980). *Naming and Necessity*. Cambridge, MA: Harvard University Press.

Lewis, D. (1986). *On the Plurality of Worlds*. Oxford: Blackwell.

Loux, M. J. (1979). *The Possible and the Actual*. Ithaca, NY: Cornell University Press.

Marcus, R. B. (1993). *Modalities*. Oxford: Oxford University Press.

Merricks, T. (2003). "The End of Counterpart Theory," *The Journal of Philosophy* 100: 521–49.

Plantinga, A. (1974). *The Nature of Necessity*. Oxford: Oxford University Press.

Quine, W. V. (1953). "Reference and Modality," in Quine, *From a Logical Point of View*. Cambridge, MA: Harvard University Press, pp. 139–59.

14

Modalities: Basic Concepts and Distinctions

Alvin Plantinga

1 Preliminary Distinctions and Remarks

A. *Necessity circumscribed*

The distinction between necessary and contingent truth is as easy to recognize as it is difficult to explain to the sceptic's satisfaction. Among true propositions[1] we find some, like

(1) The average annual rainfall in Los Angeles is about 12 inches

that are contingent, while others, like

(2) $7 + 5 = 12$

or

(3) If all men are mortal and Socrates is a man, then Socrates in mortal

that are necessary.

But what exactly do these words – 'necessary' and 'contingent' – mean? What distinction do they mark? Just what is supposed to be the difference between necessary and contingent truths? We can hardly explain that p is necessary if and only if its denial is impossible; this is true but insufficiently enlightening. It would be a peculiar philosopher who had the relevant concept of impossibility well in hand but lacked that of necessity. Instead, we must give examples and hope for the best. In the first place, truths of logic – truths of propositional logic and first-order quantification theory, let us say – are necessary in the sense in question. Such truths are logically necessary in the narrow sense; (3) above would be an example. But the sense of necessity in question – call it 'broadly logical necessity' – is wider than this. Truths of set theory, arithmetic and mathematics generally are necessary in this sense, as are a host of homelier items such as

No one is taller than himself
Red is a colour
If a thing is red, then it is coloured
No numbers are human beings

and

No prime minister is a prime number.

And of course there are many propositions debate about whose status has played an important role in philosophical discussion – for example,

Every person is conscious at some time or other

Alvin Plantinga, "Modalities: Basic Concepts and Distinctions," from chapters 1 and 2 of Plantinga, *Nature of Necessity* (Oxford: Oxford University Press, 1974). Reproduced by permission.

Metaphysics: An Anthology, Second Edition. Edited by Jaegwon Kim, Daniel Z. Korman and Ernest Sosa.
Editorial material and organization © 2012 Blackwell Publishing Ltd. Published 2012 by Blackwell Publishing Ltd.

Every human person has a body
No one has a private language
There never was a time when there was space but
　　no material objects

and

There exists a being than which it is not possible
　　that there be a greater.

So the sense of necessity in question is wider than
that captured in first-order logic. On the other
hand, it is narrower than that of *causal* or *natural*
necessity.

　　　　Voltaire once swam the Atlantic

for example is surely implausible. Indeed, there is
a clear sense in which it is impossible. Eighteenth-
century intellectuals (as distinguished from
dolphins) simply lacked the physical equipment
for this kind of feat. Unlike Superman,
furthermore, the rest of us are incapable of leaping
tall buildings at a single bound, or (without
auxiliary power of some kind) travelling faster
than a speeding bullet. These things are impossible
for us; but not in the broadly logical sense. Again,
it may be necessary – causally necessary – that any
two material objects attract each other with a
force proportional to their mass and inversely
proportional to the square of the distance between
them; it is not necessary in the sense in question.

　　Another notion that must carefully be
distinguished from necessity is what (for want of a
better name) we might call 'unrevisability' or
perhaps 'ungiveupability'. Some philosophers
hold that *no* proposition – not even the austerest
law of logic – is in principle immune from
revision. The future development of science
(though presumably not that of theology) could
lead us rationally to abandon any belief we now
hold, including the law of non-contradiction and
modus ponens itself. So Quine:

> … it becomes folly to seek a boundary between
> synthetic statements which hold contingently on
> experience, and analytic statements, which hold
> come what may. Any statement can be held come
> what may, if we make drastic enough adjustments
> elsewhere in the system. Even a statement very
> close to the periphery can be held true in the face of
> recalcitrant experience by pleading hallucination

or by amending certain statements of the kind
called logical laws. Conversely, by the same token,
no statement is immune to revision. Revision even
of the logical law of excluded middle has been proposed as a means of simplifying quantum mechanics; and what difference is there in principle
between such a shift and the shift whereby Kepler
superseded Ptolemy, or Einstein Newton, or
Darwin Aristotle?[2]

Giving up a truth of logic – *modus ponens*, let us
say – in order to simplify physical theory may
strike us as like giving up a truth of arithmetic in
order to simplify the Doctrine of the Trinity. In
any event, Quine's point is that no statement is
immune from revision; for each there are
circumstances under which (perhaps with a
reluctant wave) we should give it up, and do so
quite properly.

　　Here Quine may or may not be right. But
suppose we temporarily and ironically concede
that every statement, *modus ponens* included, is
subject to revision. Are we then obliged to follow
those who conclude that there are no genuinely
necessary propositions? No; for their conclusion
displays confusion. To say of *modus ponens* that it
(or its corresponding conditional) is a necessary
truth is not, of course, to say that people will
never give it up, as if necessity were a trait
conferred by long-term popular favour. I may be
unprepared to give up the belief that I am a fine
fellow in the face of even the most recalcitrant
experience; it does not follow either that this
belief is necessarily true or that I take it to be so.
Nor would the unlikely event of everyone's
sharing my truculence on this point make any
difference. Just as obviously, a proposition might
be necessarily true even if most people thought it
false or held no opinion whatever on the matter.

　　So necessity has little or nothing to do with
what people would *in fact* give up under various
happy or unhappy circumstances. But it must also
be distinguished from what cannot be *rationally*
rejected. For clearly a proposition might be both
necessary and such that on a given occasion the
rational thing to do is to give up or deny it. Suppose
I am a mathematical neophyte and have heard and
accepted rumours to the effect that the continuum
hypothesis has been shown to be independent of
Zermelo–Fraenkel set theory. I relate this rumour
to a habitually authoritative mathematician, who

smiles indulgently and produces a subtly fallacious argument for the opposite conclusion – an argument which I still find compelling after careful study. I need not be irrational in believing him and accepting his argument, despite the fact that in this instance his usual accuracy has deserted him and he has told me what is necessarily false. To take a more homely example: I have computed the sum $97 + 342 + 781$ four times running, and each time got the answer 1120; so I believe, naturally enough, that $97 + 342 + 781 = 1120$. The fact, however, is that I made the same mistake each time – carried a '1' instead of a '2' in the third column. But my belief may none the less be rational. I do not know whether circumstances could arise in which the reasonable thing to do would be to give up *modus ponens*; but if such circumstances could and did arise, it would not follow that *modus ponens* is not a necessary truth. Broadly logical necessity, therefore, must be distinguished from unrevisability as well as from causal necessity and logical necessity strictly so called.

It must also be distinguished from the *self-evident* and the a priori. The latter two are epistemological categories, and fairly vaporous ones at that. But consider the first. What does self-evidence come to? The answer is by no means easy. In so far as we can make rough and intuitive sense of this notion, however, to say that a proposition p is self-evident is to answer the question 'how do you know that p?' It is to claim that p is utterly obvious – obvious to anyone or nearly anyone who understands it. If p is self-evident, then on understanding it we simply see that it is true; our knowledge of *modus ponens* may be cited as of this sort. Now obviously many questions arise about this notion; but in so far as we do apprehend it, we see that many necessary propositions are not thus transparent. $97 + 342 + 781 = 1220$ is indeed necessary, but certainly not self-evident – not to most of us, at any rate.

Still, perhaps we could say that this truth is self-evident in an extended sense: it is a consequence of self-evident truths by argument forms whose corresponding conditionals are themselves self-evident. Could we add that all necessary truths are self-evident in this extended sense? Not with any show of plausibility. The axiom of choice and the continuum hypothesis are either necessarily true or necessarily false; there is little reason to think that either of these, or either of their denials, are

deducible from self-evident propositions by self-evident steps. You may think it inappropriate to speak of truth in connection with such an item as, say, the continuum hypothesis. If so, I disagree; I think this proposition just as true or just as false as the commonest truths and falsities of arithmetic. But no matter; there are simpler and more obvious examples. Each of Goldbach's conjecture and Fermat's last theorem, for example, is either necessarily true or necessarily false; but each may turn out to be such that neither it nor its denial is self-evident in the extended sense. That is to say, for all I know, and, so far as I know, for all *anyone* knows, this may be so. I do not mean to assert that this is *possibly* so, in the broadly logical sense; for (as could plausibly be argued) where S is the set of self-evident propositions and R that of self-evident argument forms, a proposition p *possibly* follows from S by R only if p *actually*, and, indeed, *necessarily* thus follows. And since I do not know whether Goldbach's conjecture or Fermat's theorem *do* follow from S by R, I am not prepared to say that it is *possible* that they do so. My point is only that the question whether, for example, Goldbach's conjecture is self-evident in the extended sense is distinct from the question whether it is a necessary truth.

So not all necessary propositions are self-evident. What about the converse? Are some contingent propositions self-evident? The question is vexed, and the answer not obvious. Is the proposition I express by saying '$2 + 2 = 4$ is self-evident for me now' self-evident for me now? Perhaps so, perhaps not. Perhaps the idea of self-evidence is not sharp enough to permit an answer. What is once more important is that a negative answer is not immediate and obvious; self-evidence must be distinguished, initially, at least, from necessity.

Not strictly to the point but worth mentioning is the fact that some propositions *seem* or *appear* to be self-evident although they are not necessarily true or, for that matter, true at all. Some of the best examples are furnished by the Russellian paradoxes. It seems self-evident that for every condition or property P there is the set of just those things displaying P; it seems equally self-evident that there is such a condition or property as that of *being non-self-membered*. But of course these (together with some other apparently self-evident propositions) self-evidently yield the conclusion that there is a set that is and is not a member of itself; and this is self-evidently false. Some may see in this the bankruptcy of self-evidence. It is not my purpose, in these introductory pages, to defend self-evidence or answer the question how we know the truth of such propositions as *modus ponens*. Still, the conclusion is hasty. Our embarrassment in the face of such paradoxes shows that a proposition may seem to be self-evident when in fact it is false. How does it follow that *modus ponens*, for example, is not self-evident, or that there is some other or better answer to the question of how we know that it is true? The senses sometimes deceive us; square towers sometimes appear round. It does not follow either that we do not know the truth of such propositions as *The Empire State Building is rectangular* or that we have some non-empirical method of determining its truth.

Finally, the distinction between the necessary and the contingent must not be confused with the alleged cleavage between the a priori and the a posteriori. The latter distinction, indeed, is shrouded in obscurity. But given the rough and intuitive understanding we have of the terms involved, it is clear that the distinction they mark, like that between what is self-evident and what is not (and unlike that between the necessary and contingent), is *epistemological*. Furthermore, the relation between what is known a priori and what is necessarily true is by no means simple and straightforward. It is immediately obvious that not all necessary truths are known a priori; for there are necessary truths – Fermat's last theorem or its denial, for example – that are not known at all, and *a fortiori* are not known a priori. Is it rather that every necessary truth that is known, is known a priori? This question divides itself: (*a*) is every necessary truth that is known, known a priori to everyone who knows it? and (*b*) is every necessary truth that is known to someone or other, known a priori to someone or other? The answer to (*a*) is clear. Having taken the trouble to understand the proof, you may know a priori that the Schroeder–Bernstein theorem is a consequence of some standard formulation of set theory. If I know that you are properly reliable in these matters and take your word for it, then I may know that truth a posteriori – as I may if I've forgotten the proof but remember having verified that indeed there is one. To learn the value of the sine of 54 degrees, I consult a handy table of trigonometric functions: my

knowledge of this item is then a posteriori. In the same way, even such simple truths of arithmetic as that $75 + 36 = 111$ can be known a posteriori. So the answer to (*a*) is obvious. The answer to question (*b*) is perhaps not quite so clear; but elsewhere I give some examples of truths that are necessary but probably not known *a priori* to any of us.[3]

So necessity cannot be identified with what is known a priori. Should we say instead that a proposition is necessary if and only if it is know*able* a priori? But by whom? We differ widely in our ability to apprehend necessary truths; and no doubt some are beyond the grasp of even the best of us. Is the idea, then, that a proposition is necessarily true, if and only if it is *possible*, in the broadly logical sense, that some person, human or divine, knows it a priori? Perhaps this is true. Indeed, perhaps every truth whatever is possibly known a priori to some person – to God if not to man. But suppose we avoid the turbid waters of speculative theology and restrict our question to *human* knowledge: must a contingent proposition, if known, be known a posteriori? The question is as vexed as the notion of a priori knowledge is obscure. What is known a priori is known independently, somehow or other, of experience. My knowledge of *modus ponens* or that $7 + 5 = 12$ would be cited by way of example. But how about my knowledge that I do know that $7 + 5 = 12$? Is that independent of experience in the requisite fashion? Suppose

(4)   I know that $7 + 5 = 12$;

cannot I know a priori that (4) is true? And this despite the contingency of (4)? Perhaps you will say that I know (4) only if I know

(4′)   I believe that $7 + 5 = 12$

and perhaps you will add that knowledge of this last item must be a posteriori. But is this really true? On a strict construction of 'independent of experience' it may seem so; for surely I must have had *some* experience to know that I thus believe – if only that needed to acquire the relevant concepts. But on such a strict construction it may seem equally apparent that I know no truths at all a priori; even to know that $7 + 5 = 12$, I must have had some experience. There is no specific *sort* of experience I need, to know that $7 + 5 = 12$; and this (subject, of course, to all the difficulty of saying what counts as a *sort* here) is perhaps what distinguishes my knowledge of this truth as a priori. But the same thing holds for my knowledge of (4′). Belief is not (*pace* Hume) a special brilliance or vividness of idea or image; there is no specific sort of experience I must have to know that I believe that 7 + 5 = 12. So perhaps I know a priori that I believe that 7 + 5 = 12. If so, then I have a priori knowledge of a contingent truth. Similarly, perhaps my knowledge that I *exist* is a priori. For perhaps I know a priori that I believe that I exist; I also know a priori that if I believe that I exist, then indeed I do exist. But then nothing but exceptional obtuseness could prevent my knowing a priori that I exist, despite the contingency of that proposition.

It is fair to say, therefore, that I probably know some contingent truths a priori. At any rate it seems clearly *possible* that I do so. So necessity cannot be identified with what is knowable a priori.[4] Unrevisability, self-evidence, and a priori knowledge are difficult notions; but conceding that we do have a grasp – one that is perhaps halting and infirm – of these notions, we must also concede that the notion of necessary truth coincides with none of them.

B. Modality de dicto and modality de re

I have spoken of necessity as a property or trait of *propositions* and tried to distinguish it from others sometimes confused with it. This is the idea of modality *de dicto*. An assertion of modality *de dicto*, for example

(5)   necessarily nine is composite

predicates a modal property – in this instance *necessary truth* – of another *dictum* or proposition:

(6)   nine is composite.

Much traditional philosophy, however, bids us distinguish this notion from another. We may attribute necessary truth to a proposition; but we may also ascribe to some object – the number 9, let us say – the *necessary* or *essential possession* of such a property as that of *being composite*. The distinction between modality *de dicto* and modality *de re* is apparently embraced by Aristotle, who observes (*Prior Analytics*, i. 9) that 'It happens sometimes

that the conclusion is necessary when only one premiss is necessary; not, however, either premiss taken at random, but the major premiss'.[5] Here Aristotle means to sanction such inferences as

(7)   Every human being is necessarily rational
(8)   Every animal in this room is a human being

so

(9)   Every animal in this room is necessarily rational;

he means to reject such inferences as

(10)   Every rational creature is in Australia
(11)   Every human being is necessarily a rational creature

so

(12)   Every human being is necessarily in Australia.

Now presumably Aristorle would accept as sound the inference of (9) from (7) and (8) (granted the truth of (8)). If he is right, therefore, then (9) is not to be read as

(9′)   It is neccessarily true that every animal in this room in rational;

for (9′) is clearly false. Instead, (9) must be construed (if Aristotle is correct) as the claim that each animal in this room has a certain property – the property of being rational – *necessarily* or *essentially*. That is to say, (9) must be taken as an expression of modality *de re* rather than modality *de dicto*. And what this means is that (9) is not the assertion that a certain *dictum* or proposition – *every animal in this room is rational* – is necessarily true, but is instead the assertion that each *res* of a certain kind has a certain property essentially or necessarily – or, what comes to the same, the assertion that each such thing has the modal property of being essentially rational.

In *Summa Contra Gentiles*, St Thomas considers the question whether God's foreknowledge of human action – a foreknowledge that consists, according to St Thomas, in God's simply *seeing* the relevant action's taking place – is consistent with human freedom. In this connection he inquires into the truth of

> (13)   What is seen to be sitting in necessarily sitting.

For suppose at t_1 God sees that Theaetetus is sitting at t_2. If (13) is true, then presumably Theaetetus is *necessarily* sitting at t_2, in which case he was not free, at that time, to do anything *but* sit.

St Thomas concludes that (13) is true taken *de dicto* but false taken *de re*; that is

> (13′)   It is necessarily true that whatever is seen to be sitting is sitting

is true but

> (13″)   Whatever is seen to be sitting has the property of sitting necessarily or essentially

is false. The deterministic argument, however, requires the truth of (13″); and hence that argument fails. Like Aristotle, then, Aquinas appears to believe that modal statements are of two kinds. Some predicate a modality of another statement (modality *de dicto*); but others predicate of an object the necessary or essential possession of a property; and these latter express modality *de re*.

But what is it, according to Aristotle and Aquinas, to say that a certain object has a certain property essentially or necessarily? That, presumably, the object in question could not conceivably have lacked the property in question; that under no possible circumstances could that object have failed to possess that property. Here, as in the case of modality *de dicto*, no mere definition is likely to be of much use; what we need instead is example and articulation. I am thinking of the number 5; what I am thinking of then, is prime. *Being prime*, furthermore, is a property that it could not conceivably have lacked. Of course, the proposition

> (14)   What I am thinking of is prime

is not necessarily true. This has no bearing on the question whether what I am thinking of could have failed to be prime; and indeed it could not. No doubt the number 5 could have lacked many

properties that in fact it has: the property of numbering the fingers on a human hand would be an example. But that it should have lacked the property of being prime is quite impossible. And a statement of modality *de re* asserts of some object that it has some property essentially in this sense.

Aquinas points out that a given statement of modality *de dicto* – (13′) for example – may be true when the corresponding statement of modality *de re* – (13″) in this instance – is false. We might add that in other such pairs the *de dicto* statement is false but the *de re* statement true; if I am thinking of the number 17, then

> (15)   What I am thinking of is essentially prime

is true, but

> (15′)   Necessarily, what I am thinking of is prime

is false.

The distinction between modality *de re* and modality *de dicto* is not confined to ancient and medieval philosophy. G. E. Moore discusses the idealistic doctrine of internal relations;[6] he concludes that it is false or confused or perhaps both. What is presently interesting is that he takes this doctrine to be the claim that all relational properties are *internal* – which claim, he thinks, is just the proposition that every object has each of its relational properties essentially in the above sense. The doctrine of internal relations, he says, 'implies, in fact, quite generally, that any term which does in fact have a particular relational property, could not have existed without having that property. And in saying this it obviously flies in the face of common sense. It seems quite obvious that in the case of many relational properties which things have, the fact that they have them is a mere matter of fact; that the things in question might have existed without having them.'[7] Now Moore is prepared to concede that objects do have some of their relational properties essentially. Like Aristotle and Aquinas, therefore, Moore holds that some objects have some of their properties essentially and others non-essentially or accidentally.

One final example: Norman Malcolm believes that the Analogical Argument for other minds requires the assumption that one must learn what, for example, *pain* is 'from his own case'. But, he says, 'if I were to learn what pain is from perceiving my own pain then I should, necessarily, have learned that pain is something that exists only when I feel pain. For the pain that serves as my paradigm of pain (i.e. my own) has the property of existing only when I feel it. That property is essential, not accidental; it is nonsense to suppose that the pain I feel could exist when I did not feel it.'[8] This argument appears to require something like the following premiss:

(16) If I acquire my concept of *C* by experiencing objects and all the objects that serve as my paradigms have a property *P* essentially, then my concept of *C* is such that the proposition *Whatever is an instance of C has P* is necessarily true.

Is (16) true? I shall not enter that question here. But initially, at least, it looks as if Malcolm means to join Aristotle, Aquinas and Moore in support of the thesis that objects typically have both essential and accidental properties; apparently he means to embrace the conception of modality *de re*.

There is a prima facie distinction, then, between modality *de dicto* and modality *de re*. This distinction, furthermore, has a long and distinguished history. Many contemporary philosophers who find the idea of modality *de dicto* tolerably clear, however, look utterly askance at that of modality *de re*, suspecting it a source of boundless confusion. Indeed, there is abroad the subtle suggestion that the idea of modality *de re* is not so much confused as vaguely immoral or frivolous – as if to accept or employ it is to be guilty of neglecting serious work in favour of sporting with Amaryllis in the shade. In the next section, therefore, we shall examine objections to modality *de re*.

2   Modality *De Re*: Objections

A.   The problem

One who accepts the idea of modality *de re* typically holds that some objects – 9, for example – have some of their properties – being composite, for example – *essentially* or *necessarily*.[9] That is to say, 9 has this property and could not conceivably have lacked it. And here the force of 'could have' is

that broadly logical notion of possibility outlined in section 1. This is a notion of possibility broader than that of *causal* or *natural* possibility: it is causally impossible that David should have the attribute of travelling from Boston to Los Angeles at a velocity greater than the speed of light, but not impossible in the sense in question. On the other hand, this sense is narrower than that of logical possibility strictly so called. That someone should have the attribute of knowing that $7 + 5 = 13$ is impossible, and impossible in the sense in question; the resources of logic alone, however, do not suffice to demonstrate this impossibility. The claim that objects have some of their properties essentially or necessarily is part of what we may call *essentialism*. To this contention the essentialist, as I shall understand him, adds the claim that objects have accidental as well as essential properties. Socrates, for example, has self-identity essentially, but is accidentally snub-nosed; while he could not have been self-diverse, he could have been non-snub-nosed. Still further, essentialism (as here understood) includes the idea that some properties are essential to some but not all objects; thus 9 but not 5 is essentially composite. So the essentialist holds that objects have both essential and accidental properties; and that some properties are had essentially by some but not all objects.

According to Quine, essentialism 'is the doctrine that some of the attributes of a thing (quite independently of the language in which the thing is referred to, if at all) may be essential to the thing and others accidental'.[10] I take the point to be this. When the essentialist says of something *x* that it has a certain property *P* essentially, he means to be predicating a property of *x* – a property distinct from *P*.[11] For every property *P* there is the property of having *P* essentially; and if *x* has *P* essentially, then *x* has the property *having P essentially*. This has two important consequences. In the first place, a proposition of the form *x has P essentially* entails that *something* has *P* essentially and is therefore properly subject to existential generalization. To say that 9 is essentially composite is to predicate a property – that of being essentially composite – of 9; hence

(1)   9 is essentially composite

entails

(2)   There is at least one thing that is essentially composite.

A second consequence: if *x* has *P* essentially, then the same claim must be made for anything identical with *x*. If 9 is essentially composite, so is Paul's favourite number, that number being 9. This follows from the principle sometimes called 'Leibniz's Law' or 'The Indiscernibility of Identicals':

(3)   For any property *P* and any objects *x* and *y*, if *x* is identical with *y*, then *x* has *P* if and only if *y* has *P*.

Like Caesar's wife Calpurnia, this principle is entirely above reproach.[12] But then, if an object *x* has a property *P* essentially, it has the property of having *P* essentially; by (3), therefore, anything identical with *x* shares that distinction with it. Accordingly, if an object has a property essentially, so does anything identical with it. *Having P essentially* is a property of an object *x*; it is not, for example, a three-termed relation involving *x, P*, and (say) some description of *x*.

The essentialist, therefore, holds that some objects have both accidental and essential properties – properties not everything has essentially. He adds that where *P* is a property, so is *having P essentially*. And many philosophers view these claims with suspicion, if not outright disdain. What are the objections to it?

B.   Essentialism and set-theoretical reduction

Some who accept essentialism point, by way of illustration, to the fact that the number 9 has the property *being composite* essentially or necessarily. Gilbert Harman is unsympathetic to this notion.[13] Arguing that 'the claim that numbers have such essential properties is incompatible with the familiar idea that number theory can be reduced to set theory in various ways',[14] he taxes those who accept *de re* modality with putting forward this idea 'less as an empirical hypothesis than as a metaphysical or religious doctrine'[15] and he rhetorically asks 'Why should we take them seriously?'

While I have no ready answer to this last question, I do feel that the theory of *de re* modality, taken as a religious doctrine, is a bit thin. It will never replace the Heidelberg Catechism, or even Supralapsarianism. What is presently interesting, however, is Harman's argument for the thesis that 9's being essentially composite *is* incompatible with this familiar idea. How does it go? According to the familiar idea, says Harman,

> the natural numbers can be identified with any of various sequences of sets. Zero might be identified with the null set, and each succeeding natural number with the set whose only member is the set identified with the previous number. Or a natural number might be identified with the set of all natural numbers less than it. And there are an infinity of other possible identifications all of which allow the full development of number theory.[16]

So far, so good. That the natural numbers can be identified, in this fashion, with various distinct set-theoretical structures is indeed a familiar idea. But of course there is no reason to stick thus unimaginatively to sets; we may, if we wish, identify President Nixon with zero and the remaining numbers with propositions about him: *Nixon is less than one foot tall, Nixon is less than two feet tall,* … All we need for such 'identification' is a countably infinite set of objects together with a relation[17] under which they form an infinite sequence or progression. Since practically any object you please is the tenth element in some progression, any object you please can be 'identified', in this fashion, with 9.

'But', continues Harman, 'being a composite number is not an essential property of any set. Therefore', he says, 'if numbers can be identified with sets and *de re* necessity is in question, no number is necessarily a composite number. Being a composite number is not an essential property of any number.'[18]

Here there may be less than meets the eye. How, exactly, are we to construe this argument? Taken at face value, it appears to involve an application of Leibniz's Law; perhaps we can outline it as follows:

(4)   No set is essentially a composite number,

that is,

(5)   No set has the property of being essentially composite.

But

(6)   Numbers can be identified with sets.

Therefore (given Leibniz's Law),

(7)   No number has the property of being essentially composite.

Put thus baldly, this argument, obviously, is about as imperforate as an afghan knit by an elephant. We might as well argue that 9 does not have the property of being divisible by 3, since Nixon does not, and it can be identified with him.

The point is this. That number theory can be reduced to set theory in various ways is indeed, in Harman's words, a familiar idea. It is widely recognized and accepted as accurate and as part of the current lore about numbers and sets. And according to this familiar idea, a given number can be 'identified' with any of many distinct sets. But what this comes to (in so far as the idea in question *is* widely accepted) is only this: there are many denumerable families of sets that form a progression under some (recursive) relation. Accordingly, for any number *n*, there are many distinct sets each of which is the *n*+1st element in some progression and can therefore play the role of *n* in some set-theoretical development of number theory. But of course the fact that numbers can be identified in *this* sense with Nixon or with various distinct set-theoretical objects does not suggest that any number is in fact *identical with* Nixon or some set; it is this latter, however, that is required for an application of Leibniz's Law.

C.   *Essentialism and the number of apostles*

According to the essentialist, for each property *P* there is the property of having *P* essentially – a property an object has (if at all) in itself, regardless of how it may be described or referred to. If 9 is essentially composite, so is Paul's favourite number, that number being 9. The essentialist therefore rejects the idea that 9 *qua*, as they say, Paul's favourite number has the property of being his favourite number essentially, but *qua* the successor of 8 has that property accidentally; this would be to say that *being essentially Paul's favourite number* is not a property at all but perhaps a relation involving 9, the property of being Paul's

favourite number, and a designation of 9. He holds instead that such an item as *being essentially composite* is a property – in this case, one enjoyed by 9; hence it is a property of Paul's favourite number, if indeed Paul's favourite number is 9.

It is here that he makes his mistake, according to William Kneale.[19] For, says Kneale, an object does not have a property *P* essentially *just as an object* (to speak oracularly); instead it has *P* essentially (if at all) *relative to* certain ways of specifying or selecting it for attention – and perhaps accidentally, relative to other ways. When we say that *x* has *P* essentially or necessarily, this must be construed as 'an elliptical statement of relative necessity';[20] that is, as short for something like '*x* has *P* necessarily relative to *D*' where *D* is some description. Of course if *P* is a *truistic* property – one which, like *is red or is not red*, is had necessarily by every object relative to every way of describing it – then this reference to ways of selecting *x* may perhaps be suppressed without undue impropriety, so that we may say *simpliciter* that *P* is essential to *x*. In these cases, then, the reference to a description is otiose; but where *P* is not truistic, such a reference is crucial, even if implicit. Fundamentally, therefore, Kneale holds that there is no such thing, for a property *P*, as the property of having *P* essentially; these are only three-termed relations involving *P*, an object *x*, and the various ways of selecting *x* for attention.

But why so? The opposite view, he says, is based on the mistaken assumption that

properties may be said to belong to individuals necessarily or contingently, as the case may be, without regard to the ways in which the individuals are selected for attention. It is no doubt true to say that the number 12 is necessarily composite, but it is certainly not correct to say that the number of apostles is necessarily composite, unless the remark is to be understood as an elliptical statement of relative necessity. And again, it is no doubt correct to say that this at which I am pointing is contingently white, but it is certainly not correct to say that the white paper at which I am looking is contingently white, unless again, the remark is to be understood as elliptical.[21]

Kneale's argument does not wear its structure upon its sleeve. How, exactly, does it go? What are the premises? The *conclusion*, pretty clearly, is that an object does not have a property necessarily *in itself* or just as an object; it has it necessarily or contingently, as the case may be, *relative to* certain descriptions of the object. There is no such thing as the property of being necessarily composite; and a proposition like

(8)   The number 12 is necessarily composite

does not predicate a property of 12; instead it predicates a relation of 12, the property of being composite, and a 'way of selecting 12 for attention'. But why should we think so? How are we to construe the argument? Perhaps it has something like the following premises:

(9)   12 = the number of apostles
(8)   The number 12 is necessarily composite
(10)   If (8), then if there is such a property as *being necessarily composite*, 12 has it
(11)   The number of apostles is not necessarily composite
(12)   If (11), then if there is such a property as *being necessarily composite*, the number of the apostles lacks it.

It therefore follows that there is no such property as *being necessarily composite*; hence, it is false that for any property *P*, there is the property of having *P* essentially or necessarily; and hence the essentialist thesis is mistaken.

Now clearly Kneale's argument requires Leibniz's Law as an additional premiss – a principle the essentialist will be happy to concede. And if we add this premiss, then the argument is apparently valid. But why should we accept (11)? Consider an analogous argument for the unwelcome conclusion that *necessary truth* or *being necessarily true* is not a property that a proposition has in itself or just as a proposition, but only relative to certain descriptions of it:

(13)   The proposition that $7 + 5 = 12$ is necessarily true
(14)   The proposition I am thinking of is not necessarily true
(15)   The proposition that $7 + 5 = 12$ is identical with the proposition I am thinking of.

Therefore

(16)   *Being necessarily* true is not a property.

This argument is feeble and unconvincing; if (15) is true, then (14) must be false. But is not the very same comment appropriate to (11) and (9)? If (9) is true, then presumably (11) is false. And so the question becomes acute: why *does* Kneale take (11) to be true? The answer, I suspect, is that he reads (11) as

(11′)   The proposition *the number of apostles is composite* is not necessarily true.

More generally, Kneale seems to think of sentences of the form '— has … essentially' (where the first blank is filled by a singular term and the second by an expression denoting a property) as short for or a stylistic variant of the corresponding sentences of the form 'the proposition — has … is necessarily true'; where α ranges over singular terms and '*B*' over expressions denoting properties, Kneale apparently means to ascribe something like the following definitional schema to the essentialist:

D₁ ⌜α has *B* essentially⌝ = def. ⌜The proposition α *has B* is necessarily true⌝.

But this ascription is at best uncharitable as an account of what the essentialist means by his characteristic assertions. As noted above, the latter holds that a proposition like

(17)   12 is essentially composite

predicates a property of 12, and hence entails (by way of existential generalization)

(18)   There is at least one object *x* such that *x* is essentially composite.

Applying D₁ (and making appropriate grammatical adjustments) we have

(19)   There is at least one object *x* such that the proposition *x* is composite is necessarily true.

But of course (19) as it stands is grotesque; there is no such thing as the proposition *x is composite*; the words '*x* is composite' do not express a proposition. The essentialist may be benighted, but he does not confound (18), which he accepts, with such a darkling hodge-podge as (19).

Fundamentally, however, to saddle the essentialist with D_1 is to ignore his claim that an item like (17) is a *de re* assertion that predicates a *property* of the number 12. If he accepts (17), then he will also hold that the number of apostles is essentially composite; and he will be utterly unshaken by the *de dicto* truth that

> (11′)   *the number of apostles is composite* is not necessarily true.

A central feature of his programme, after all, is to distinguish such *de re* propositions as (17) from such *de dicto* items as (11′); and to ascribe D_1 to him is to ignore, not discredit, his claim that there is such a distinction to be drawn.

But perhaps we were being hasty. Suppose we look again at Kneale's argument. Perhaps he does not mean to ascribe D_1 to the essentialist: perhaps we are to understand his argument as follows. We have been told that '*x* has *P* essentially' means that it is impossible or inconceivable that *x* should have lacked *P*; that there is no conceivable set of circumstances such that, should they have obtained, *x* would not have had *P*. Well, consider the number 12 and the number of apostles. Perhaps it *is* impossible that *the number 12* should have lacked the property of being composite; but it is certainly possible that *the number of apostles* should have lacked it; for clearly the number of apostles could have been 11, in which case it would not have been composite. Hence *being essentially composite* is not a property, and the essentialist thesis fails.

How could the defender of essentialism respond? The relevant portion of the argument may perhaps be stated as follows:

> (20)   The number of apostles could have been 11
>
> (21)   If the number of apostles had been 11, then the number of apostles would have been prime

Hence

> (22)   It is possible that the number of apostles should have been prime

and therefore

> (23)   The number of apostles is not essentially composite.

But the essentialist has an easy retort. The argument is successful only if (23) is construed as the assertion *de re* that a certain number – 12 as it happens – does not have the property of being essentially composite. Now (22) can be read *de dicto* as

> (22a)   The proposition *the number of apostles is prime* is possible;

it may also be read *de re*, that is, as

> (22b)   The number that numbers the apostles (that is, the number that *as things in fact stand* numbers the apostles) could have been prime.

The latter entails (23); the former, of course, does not. Hence to preserve the argument we must take (22) as (22b). Now consider (20). The same *de re/de dicto* ambiguity is once again present. Read *de dicto* it makes the true (if unexciting) assertion that

> (20a)   The proposition *there are just 11 apostles* is possible.

Read *de re*, however – that is, as

> (20b)   The number that (as things in fact stand) numbers the apostles could have been 11

– it will be indignantly repudiated by the essentialist; for the number that numbers the apostles is 12, and accordingly could not have been 11. We must therefore take (20) as (20a).

This brings us to (21). If (20a) and (21) are to entail (22b), then (21) must be construed as

> (21a)   If the proposition *the number of apostles is 11* had been true, then the number that (as things in fact stand) numbers the apostles would not have been composite.

But surely this is false. For what it says is that if there had been 11 apostles, then the number that in fact does number the apostles – the number 12 – would not have been composite; and at best this is outrageous. No doubt any inclination to accept (21a) may be traced to an unremarked penchant for confusing it with

> (24) If the proposition *the number of apostles is 11* had been true, then the number that *would have* numbered the apostles would have been prime.

(24), of course, though true, is of no use to Kneale's argument. Accordingly, Kneale's objection to essentialism is at best inconclusive.

D. Essentialism and the mathematical cyclist

Let us therefore turn to a different but related complaint. Quine argues that talk of a difference between necessary and contingent attributes of an object is baffling:

> Perhaps I can evoke the appropriate sense of bewilderment as follows. Mathematicians may conceivably be said to be necessarily rational and not necessarily two-legged; and cyclists necessarily two-legged and not necessarily rational. But what of an individual who counts among his eccentricities both mathematics and cycling? Is this concrete individual necessarily rational and contingently two-legged or vice versa? Just insofar as we are talking referentially of the object, with no special bias towards a background grouping of mathematicians as against cyclists or vice versa, there is no semblance of sense in rating some of his attributes as necessary and others as contingent. Some of his attributes count as important and others as unimportant, yes, some as enduring and others as fleeting; but none as necessary or contingent.[22]

Noting the existence of a philosophical tradition in which this distinction *is* made, Quine adds that one attributes it to Aristotle 'subject to contradiction by scholars, such being the penalty for attributions to Aristotle'. None the less, he says, the distinction is 'surely indefensible'.

Now this passage reveals that Quine has little enthusiasm for the distinction between essential and accidental attributes; but how exactly are we to understand him? Perhaps as follows. The essentialist, Quine thinks, will presumably accept

> (25) Mathematicians are necessarily rational but not necessarily bipedal

and

> (26) Cyclists are necessarily bipedal but not necessarily rational.

But now suppose that

> (27) Paul K. Zwier is both a cyclist and a mathematician.

From these we may infer both that

> (28) Zwier is necessarily rational but not necessarily bipedal

and

> (29) Zwier is necessarily bipedal but not necessarily rational

which appear to contradict each other twice over: (28) credits Zwier with the property of being necessarily rational, while (29) denies him that property; (29) alleges that he has the property of being essentially bipedal, an allegation disputed by (28).

This argument is unsuccessful as a refutation of the essentialist, whatever its merits as an evocation of a sense of bewilderment. For consider the inference of (29) from (26) and (27). (29) is a conjunction, as are (26) and (27). And presumably its first conjunct

> (30) Zwier is necessarily bipedal

is supposed to follow from the first conjuncts of (26) and (27), viz.

> (31) Cyclists are necessarily bipedal

and

> (32) Zwier is a cyclist.

But sensitive, as by now we are, to *de re/de dicto* ambiguity, we see that (31) can be read *de dicto* as

(31a)   Necessarily, all cyclists are bipedal

or *de re* as

(31b)   Every cyclist has the property of being necessarily bipedal.

And if (30) is to follow from (32) and (31), the latter must be seen as predicating of every cyclist the property (30) ascribes to Zwier; (31), that is, must be read as (31b). So taken, there is less than a ghost of a chance the essentialist will accept it. No doubt he will concede the necessary truth of

(33)   All (well-formed) cyclists are bipedal

and thus the truth of (31a); he will accept no obligation to infer that such well-formed cyclists as Zwier are essentially bipedal. And the same comments apply, *mutatis mutandis*, to the inference of the second conjunct of (29) from those of (26) and (27). Accordingly, (26) is true but of no use to the argument if we read it *de dicto*; read *de re*, it will be repudiated by the essentialist.

Taken as a refutation of the essentialist, therefore, this passage misses the mark; but perhaps we should emphasize its second half and take it instead as an expression of a sense of bewildered puzzlement as to what *de re* modality might conceivably be. Similar protestations may be found elsewhere in Quine's works:

> An object, of itself and by whatever name or none, must be seen as having some of its traits necessarily and others contingently, despite the fact that the latter traits follow just as analytically from some ways of specifying the object as the former do from other ways of specifying it.

And

> This means adapting an invidious attitude towards certain ways of specifying *x* ... and favouring other ways ... as somehow better revealing the 'essence' of the object.

But 'such a philosophy', he says, 'is as unreasonable by my lights as it is by Carnap's or Lewis's'.[23]

Here Quine's central complaint is this: a given object, according to the essentialist, has *some* of its properties essentially and others accidentally, despite the fact that the latter follow from certain ways of specifying the object just as the former do from others. So far, fair enough. Snub-nosedness (we may suppose) is not one of Socrates' essential attributes; none the less it follows (in the sense in question) from the description 'the snub-nosed teacher of Plato'. As we construe him, furthermore, the essentialist holds that among the essential attributes of an object are certain non-truistic properties – properties which, unlike the property of being red or not red, do not follow from every description; so it will indeed be true, as Quine suggests, that ways of uniquely specifying an object are not all on the same footing. Those from which each of its essential properties follows must be awarded the accolade as best revealing the essence of the object.

But what, exactly, is 'unreasonable' about this? And how, precisely, is it baffling? The real depth of Quine's objection, as I understand it, is this: he holds that 'A's are necessarily B's' must, if it means anything at all, mean something like 'necessarily, A's are B's'; for 'necessity resides in the way we talk about things, not in the things we talk about'.[24] And hence the bafflement in asking, of some specific individual who is both cyclist and mathematician, whether he is essentially rational and contingently two-legged, or vice versa. Perhaps the claim is, finally, that while we can make a certain rough sense of modality *de dicto*, we can understand modality *de re* only if we can explain it in terms of the former. I turn to such explanation in Chapter III [not included in this selection].

Notes

1   Necessity, truth and allied properties are at bottom (as I see it) properties of propositions, not sentences. A sentence is true, on a given occasion of its use, if on that occasion it expresses a true proposition. My conception of proposition as non-linguistic entity expressed by but distinct from sentences parallels Moore's idea of proposition, Frege's of *Gedanke*, and Bolzano's of *Satz*. Some find propositions objectionable – on the grounds, apparently, that they lack 'a clear criterion of identity'. In so far as the alleged debility can be made tolerably clear, it is one that propositions share with electrons, mountains, wars – and sentences.

2   W. V. O. Quine, 'Two dogmas of empiricism', in *From a Logical Point of View*, 2nd edn (Cambridge, Mass.: Harvard University Press, 1961), p. 43.

3   See A. Plantinga, *The Nature of Necessity* (Oxford: Clarendon Press, 1974), ch. 5, sect. 2. See also *idem*, 'World and essence', *Philosophical Review* 79 (1970), p. 481.

4   In 'Naming and necessity', in D. Davidson and G. Harman (eds), *Semantics of Natural Language* (Dordrecht: Reidel, 1972, p. 253), Saul Kripke suggests that another kind of proposition is contingent but knowable a priori. Suppose, he says, that I fix the reference of the term 'one metre' as the length of a certain stick (call it S) at a time t. Then 'one metre' is not synonymous with the phrase 'the length of S at t' but is instead a proper name or 'rigid designator' of the length S actually has at t. And under these conditions, he adds, my knowledge of the proposition *S is one metre long at t* is a priori despite the contingency of that proposition. 'If he used stick S to fix the reference of the term "one metre", then as a result of this kind of "definition" (which is not an abbreviative or synonymous definition) he knows automatically without further investigation, that S is one metre long' (p. 275). Here we may have doubts. Suppose I have never seen S and hold no views as to its length. I propose none the less to use 'one metre' as a rigid designator of the length, whatever it is, that S actually displays at t. After thus determining the reference of 'one metre', I know that the *sentence* 'S is one metre long at t' expresses a truth in my language; the truth it does express, however, is one I neither know nor believe. So my thus determining the reference of 'one metre' is not sufficient for my knowing a priori that S is one metre long.

What I do know a priori (or so it seems to me) is that if I use 'one metre' as a rigid designator of the length of S (and given the appropriate function of the phrase 'S is ... long at t'), then the sentence 'S is one metre long at t' expresses a truth in my language. This conditional, however, is necessary rather than contingent.

The issues here are complex, and much more must be said; unfortunately 'Naming and necessity' came into my hands too late for the detailed consideration I should like to have given this and other issues it raises.

5   Quoted by William Kneale in 'Modality *de dicto* and *de re*', in E. Nagel, P. Suppes, and A. Tarski (eds), *Logic, Methodology, and Philosophy of Science*

(Stanford, Calif.: Stanford University Press, 1962), p. 623.

6   G. E. Moore, *Philosophical Studies* (London: Routledge & Kegan Paul, 1951), p. 276.

7   Ibid., p. 289.

8   Norman Malcolm, 'Wittgenstein's *Philosophical Investigations*', *Philosophical Review* 63 (1954); repr. in *idem, Knowledge and Certainty* (Englewood Cliffs, NJ: Prentice-Hall Inc., 1963). The quoted passage is on p. 105 of the latter volume.

9   In speaking of the view in question, I use the words 'necessarily' and 'essentially' as synonyms. Of course I neither assume nor suggest that these words are in fact synonyms as ordinarily employed. See R. Marcus, 'Essential attribution', *Journal of Philosophy* 68 (Apr. 1971), p. 193.

10 W. V. O. Quine, 'Three grades of modal involvement', in *The Ways of Paradox* (New York: Random House, 1966), p. 173.

11 Alternatively, we might take it that what he asserts is a proposition predicating of *x* and *P* a special relation of *property-inherence*: that in which an object and a property stand if the former has the latter essentially. Such a proposition, presumably, will be equivalent to one predicating of *x* the property of having *P* essentially.

12 Apparently Leibniz himself did not clearly distinguish (3) from:

(3′) Singular terms denoting the same object can replace each other in any context *salva veritate*

a 'principle' that does not hold for such excellent examples of language as English.

13 Gilbert Harman, 'A nonessential property', *Journal of Philosophy* 67 (Apr. 1970), p. 183.

14 Ibid., p. 184.

15 Ibid., p. 185.

16 Ibid., p. 184.

17 Perhaps recursive; see Paul Benacerraf, 'What numbers could not be', *Philosophical Review* 74 (1965), p. 51.

18 Harman, 'Nonessential property', p. 184.

19 Kneale, 'Modality *de dicto* and *de re*', p. 622.

20 Ibid., p. 629.

21 Ibid.

22 W. V. Quine, *Word and Object* (Cambridge, Mass.: MIT Press, 1960), p. 199.

23 *From a Logical Point of View*, 2nd edn (New York: Harper & Row, 1963), pp. 155–6.

24 Quine, *Ways of Paradox*, p. 174.

15

Actualism and Thisness

Robert M. Adams

1 The Thesis

My thesis is that all possibilities are purely qualitative except insofar as they involve individuals that actually exist. I have argued elsewhere (Adams, 1979b) that thisness holds a place beside suchness as a fundamental feature of reality – and not only of reality but also of some possibilities. There are facts, and also possibilities, that are not purely qualitative. The thesis of the present essay is that all the non-qualitative possibilities are possibilities for actual individuals. I will begin by trying to explain the meaning of this claim (Section 1); then I will defend it (Section 2), and develop some of its implications for modality, of which the chief is that what modal facts *de re* there are depends on what individuals actually exist (Sections 3 and 4).

1.1 Essences

We may be aided in understanding my thesis by contrasting it with an opposing position. Alvin Plantinga has proposed (very elegantly) to assure that there are all the possibilities *de re* there could have been, by holding that while there are not all the individuals there could possibly have been,

there are essences of all the individuals there could possibly have been (Plantinga, 1976). An *essence* of an individual *a*, in Plantinga's sense, is a property that *a* would possess in every possible world in which *a* would exist, and that no other individual would possess in any possible world.[1] It is a property that is essential to *a* and that no other individual could possess.

A possibility is presumably a proposition that could have been true or a state of affairs that could have obtained. Plantinga and I cannot consistently say that a possibility for an individual that does not actually exist is a proposition or state of affairs that has that individual as a constituent, for we think that there *are* no such individuals (though there *could* have been individuals other than those that there actually are). But maybe a possibility for a non-actual individual could be a proposition or state of affairs that has an essence of that individual, rather than the individual itself, as a constituent. From this point of view, whether there are non-qualitative possibilities for non-actual individuals depends on whether there are non-qualitative essences of non-actual individuals; I think that with some possible qualifications, there are not. Plantinga has not committed himself as to whether

Robert M. Adams, "Actualism and Thisness," *Synthese*, 49/1, Demonstrative and Indexical Reference, Part I (Oct. 1981): 3–41. Used with kind permission of Springer Science + Business Media B.V.

there are non-qualitative facts at all; but he is committed to the view that there actually exist all the essences there could have been, including non-qualitative essences if there could be any of them.

The chief reason he gives for affirming this is that "Properties, like propositions and possible worlds, are necessary beings" (Plantinga, 1976; in Loux, 1979, p. 268). I agree that it is plausible to think of properties (and also propositions and perhaps possible worlds) as existing necessarily, *if* we think of them as constituted purely qualitatively. I shall argue, however, that there is good reason to deny that *non*-qualitative properties are necessary beings (cf. Fine, 1977, p. 129f.).

Three types of essences there might be will concern us. (i) The most important are *thisnesses*. A thisness, in the sense intended here,[2] is the property of being a particular individual, or of being identical with that individual. It is not the property we all share, of being identical with some particular individual or other. But my thisness is the property of being me; that is, of being identical with me. Your thisness is the property of being you. Jimmy Carter's thisness is the property of being identical with Jimmy Carter (*not*: of being called "Jimmy Carter"); and so forth. All thisnesses are essences in Plantinga's sense, and every essence of an individual is necessarily coextensive with the thisness of that individual. Plantinga seems to imply that there are thisnesses, as well as other essences, of all the individuals there could possibly have been, including many individuals that do not actually exist (Plantinga, 1976; in Loux, 1979, pp. 268f., cf. 262f.). I have argued in an earlier paper (Adams, 1979b) that there could be thisnesses that would not be equivalent to any purely qualitative property, and that thisnesses are therefore primitive in the sense of being in principle distinct from all purely qualitative properties. Here I will argue that there are no thisnesses of individuals that never actually exist – although of course there could have been other individuals than those that there are, and if they had existed they would have had thisnesses. I think this is a necessary truth; in no possible world would there be thisnesses of individuals that do not exist in that world.

(ii) A *qualitative essence* would be a purely qualitative property that is an essence. Suppose, for example, there is some conjunction C (perhaps infinite) of purely qualitative properties that are jointly possessed, in actual fact, by me

alone, and that could not possibly be jointly possessed by any other individual. In that case the property of *possibly possessing C* (that is, of being something that possesses or could have possessed C) could plausibly be regarded as a qualitative essence of me. Part of what I have argued in Adams, 1979b is that there could be individuals that would not have qualitative essences. Indeed we do not know that *we* have them.

(iii) Even if we do not have qualitative essences, perhaps we have α-*relational essences* in addition to our thisnesses. 'α' is employed here, following Plantinga's useful convention, as a proper name of the actual world (α would still be α even if it were not actual, though of course it would not be the actual world if it were not actual). By 'α-relational essence' I mean an essence that has the form, *bearing R to* $a_1, a_2, a_3, \ldots$, where $a_1, a_2, a_3, \ldots$ are certain individuals that exist in α, and R is a relation such that *bearing R to some* (unspecified) $x_1, x_2, x_3, \ldots$ *or other* is a purely qualitative property. For example, let the sperm and egg cells from which I sprang be named "Dick" and "Jane" respectively. I think some philosophers would say that the property of being the sole person that sprang from the union of Dick and Jane is an essence of me. This would be an α-relational essence. It would also be a non-qualitative essence, because it involves the thisnesses of Dick and Jane. And though if it really is an essence it is necessarily coextensive with my thisness, I think it is distinct from my thisness. It is the property of bearing a certain relation to Dick and Jane, whereas my thisness is the property of bearing a certain relation (identity) to me.

If there are qualitative or α-relational essences at all, perhaps there are such essences of non-actual individuals. That is, perhaps there are properties, not actually possessed by any individual, which would be such essences of any individual that had them. I am not denying that. And if I have a qualitative or α-relational essence, it might have existed without me. The property of being the sole person that sprang from the union of Dick and Jane, for instance, is a property that could have existed, unexemplified, if Dick and Jane had existed but never come together and I had never existed. And any qualitative essence could have existed, as an unexemplified abstract object, without the individual to which it belongs. There is nothing in this that is inconsistent with the thesis that all possibilities are purely qualitative except insofar as they involve individuals that actually exist.

We will not need a special classification for another possible type of essence that plays a part in Plantinga's argument. If P is a property and w is a possible world, then the *world-indexed* property P_w is the property of having P in w. Thus P_α (the "α-transform" of P) is the property of having P in α (the actual world). Plato, for example, has the property of being-a-great-philosopher-in-α. Plantinga holds that α-transforms, and world-indexed properties in general, are essential to whatever individuals have them; and further, that if P belongs to exactly one individual in w, P_w is an essence of that individual.

We need not pay separate attention here to world-indexed essences for the following reason. A world-indexed essence, P_w, could form the basis of a *non-qualitative* possibility *not founded on actual individuals* only if one or both of two conditions obtained – namely if (i) P were neither purely qualitative nor an α-relational property, or if (ii) w were a possible world not constituted by purely qualitative propositions alone, nor by purely qualitative propositions plus propositions about individuals that exist in α. But I deny that there are any properties or possible worlds of these sorts. Of course it is open to anyone to argue against me on this point by trying to show how there could be non-qualitative propositions not founded on actual individuals. But until that is done it would be begging the question against me to appeal to world-indexed essences *in order to* explain how there could be non-qualitative possibilities not founded on actual individuals.

1.2 Singular propositions

Another notion that will play an important part in our discussion is that of a singular proposition. A singular proposition is, roughly, a proposition that involves or refers to an individual directly, and not by way of its qualitative properties or its relations to another individual. A proposition that has an individual x itself, or a thisness of x, as a constituent would be a singular proposition about x. A proposition that has a qualitative or α-relational essence of x as a constituent, however, would not as such be a singular proposition about x. If there were singular propositions about

non-actual individuals, possibilities for non-actual individuals could be founded on them. But the reasons I will give for thinking there are no thisnesses of non-actual individuals will also be reasons for thinking there are no singular propositions about non-actual individuals.

1.3 Actualism

My thesis is an *actualist* thesis. Actualism is the doctrine that there *are* no things that do not exist in the actual world. The actualist agrees, of course, that there could have been things that do not actually exist; in particular, there could have been individuals other than those that there are. But he disagrees with those (whom we may call "possibilists") who think this point can be put, in sober metaphysical truth, by saying that there *are* infinitely many possible individuals that do not exist in the actual world but that do exist in other possible worlds. Possibilists affirm, and actualists deny, that possible but non-actual entities can enter into relations and have properties, and can therefore be values of variables in the logic of predicates.

If possibilism is true, my thesis is false. If there is a non-actual individual, there is also its thisness, the property of being identical with that individual, and there are presumably all the singular propositions, and all the non-qualitative possibilities, about that individual that there would be if the individual actually existed. I believe, however, that possibilism is false and actualism is true (cf. Adams, 1974). I will not argue for that here, but will argue that *if* actualism is true, then there are no thisnesses of non-actual individuals, no singular propositions about them, and no possibilities that are non-qualitative except insofar as actual individuals are involved. It is indeed one of the substantive differences between actualism and possibilism, in my opinion, that actualism restricts the entry of thisness into mere possibility in a way that possibilism does not.

1.4 Construction

What I have said in Section 1.3 is subject to one important qualification. The entities, relations, and predications affirmed by possibilists and denied by actualists are to be understood as *primitive* features of a metaphysical scheme. For suppose definitions could be devised by which a "non-actual individual" with many properties could be logically constructed out of things that actually exist. A "hard" actualist (cf. Adams, 1974, p. 224) might insist on rejecting such definitions. But that would be sticking at a verbal point. The actualism that I espouse might be more accurately characterized, therefore, as the doctrine that there *is* (tenselessly) nothing but what (tenselessly) exists, and whatever is logically constructed out of things that actually exist.

The most important metaphysical issues in this area will have to do with the primitive entities and primitive facts. If we want to know whether all possibilities are purely qualitative except insofar as they involve actual individuals, we want to know whether the possibilities are purely qualitative at the primitive level, and whether they involve actual individuals at the primitive level. For if the primitive data for the construction are purely qualitative or α-relational, a constructed possibility will not be non-qualitative, at bottom, except insofar as it involves actual individuals.

1.5   Illustrations

We may be able to understand the meaning of my thesis better and more concretely with the aid of two examples of its consequences. (A) The thesis makes a particularly large and clear metaphysical difference in a case of the following sort. I have argued (in Adams, 1979b) that there could be a pair of individuals that would be qualitatively indiscernible from each other (having all their purely qualitative properties in common), and that such individuals would have, in effect, no qualitative essence. Any purely qualitative property that one of them could have had, the other could have had. Let us suppose[3] that there could have been a pair of individuals, qualitatively indiscernible from each other, which do not exist in α, and neither of which could have borne any relation to any individual that does exist in α that the other could not have borne to that same individual. It will be convenient to introduce an abbreviation and say that any pair of individuals meeting those conditions would be an "I-pair." Since the members of an I-pair would differ from each other neither in the qualitative nor in the α-relational properties they could have

had, they would have neither qualitative nor α-relational essences. (Here we must remember that 'α' is a proper name of a possible world that is only contingently actual. To say that there could have been individuals that would not have had α-relational essences is not necessarily to deny that if a world *w*, in which such individuals exist, had been actual, they would have had *w*-relational essences.) By considering the possibility of individuals that would not differ α-relationally in what could be true of them, we exclude the involvement of actual individuals. By supposing also that they would not differ qualitatively in what could be true of them, we set up a case in which the difference between qualitative and non-qualitative possibilities can be clearly manifested. These two features together make a case for which particularly interesting consequences follow from the thesis that all possibilities are purely qualitative except insofar as they involve actual individuals.

If an I-pair *existed*, there *would* be a difference between possibilities regarding the one member and possibilities regarding the other – for example, between the possibility of this one ceasing to exist and the possibility of that one ceasing to exist. And the difference between these possibilities could not be stated in purely qualitative terms. (That is also part of what I tried to show in Adams, 1979b.) Given that the members of an I-pair do not actually exist, however, it follows from the thesis of the present paper that there *is* not, in fact, any difference between possibilities regarding the one and possibilities regarding the other. There is not actually any such thing as a difference between the possibility of this one ceasing to exist and the possibility of that one ceasing to exist. For no such difference could be understood either qualitatively or in terms of the involvement of actual individuals, since there is neither a qualitative nor an α-relational difference between the members of an I-pair.

(B) I find it natural, and others may at least find it vivid, to think of my thesis in a theological context. I suppose that God, in deciding whether and how to create a world, knew all the *kinds* of things that could have existed or happened. That is, He had before His mind a complete array of all the suchnesses or purely qualitative properties that could possibly have been exemplified. But did He also have before His mind an infinite array of merely possible individuals, or thisnesses of them, or singular propositions about them, or possibilities regarding them, in such a way that He could have chosen from a number of individuals, possibly indiscernible in every purely qualitative respect, one to be created rather than another?[4] I think not. God can create a woman of such and such a qualitative character. And when He has done so, she is an individual and has a thisness, which is the property of being her; and there may be non-qualitative possibilities regarding her. But that property and those possibilities are parasitic on her actual existence. They did not pre-exist her in a storehouse of properties and possibilities eternally and necessarily at God's disposal. There are no non-qualitative possibilities except insofar as they involve individuals about whom it is a fact, and not an uncertainty still up for decision, that they are actual individuals.[5]

2   The Argument

My thesis rests on the view that there is, so to speak, no ontological foundation for non-qualitative possibilities except in actual individuals. What this means can perhaps best be seen in the example of I-pairs. I claim that there is no way in which there can be possibilities for one member of an I-pair that are distinct from similar possibilities for the other member. For if there are such possibilities, how do they differ from similar possibilities for the other member? Not qualitatively, nor in their relation to actual individuals, for it is part of the definition of an I-pair that there is neither a qualitative nor an α-relational difference between what could be true of one member and what could be true of the other. An actualist cannot be satisfied with the answer that the possibilities differ simply in that this possibility is related to *this* member of the pair in the way that that possibility is related to *that* member of the pair, and that this difference is primitive and not further analyzable. For the members of an I-pair do not actually exist, and therefore they cannot enter into any primitive relation, according to actualism.

It remains to consider the suggestions that the possibilities in question could differ in their relation to singular propositions about the members of the I-pair, or in their relation to the thisnesses of the members of the I-pair, or in their relation to some other sort of non-qualitative essences of the members of the I-pair. I shall argue that none of these foundations for distinct non-qualitative possibilities is available – first by trying to show that there are no thisnesses of any individuals that do not actually exist, and that there are no singular propositions about non-actual individuals; then by arguing that it is not plausible to suppose that there is another sort of non-qualitative, non-α-relational essence that could belong to non-existent individuals. In effect I shall be arguing both that there are no essences at all that could be essences of members of an I-pair, and more generally, that there is no way in which there can be non-qualitative possibilities except by relation to actual individuals.

It is hard to see how an actualist could consistently maintain that there is a thisness of a non-actual individual. For if there were one, it would be the property of being identical with that individual. To be the property of being identical with a particular individual is to stand, primitively, in a unique relation with that individual. This relation between an individual and its thisness is the crux of the argument. It would be absurd to suppose that being the property of being identical with me could be a purely internal feature of my thisness, not implying any relation to *me*. The relation between an individual and its thisness is essential to both of them. My thisness is a property that I would have in every possible world in which I would exist – but equally, my thisness could not exist without being *mine*. It could not exist without being the thisness *of* Robert Merrihew Adams. So if there were a thisness of a non-actual individual, it would stand, primitively, in a relation to that individual. But according to actualism non-actual individuals cannot enter primitively into any relation. It seems to follow that according to actualism there cannot be a thisness of a non-actual individual.

It would not be plausible to suppose that the relation between an individual and the property of being identical with that individual need not be primitive, but could be analyzed in terms of that property's relations to other individuals or to purely qualitative properties. Moreover this supposition would not provide thisnesses for members of I-pairs. For by the definition of an I-pair there are not actually any individuals, nor any purely qualitative properties, that are related differently to the two members of an I-pair. Hence a thisness cannot be related to one member of an I-pair rather than the other by virtue of any relation to actual individuals or purely qualitative properties. And in general it seems evident that a relation constructed from other relations to individuals (which must be actual individuals, according to actualism), and to purely qualitative properties, cannot provide a foundation for non-qualitative possibilities that are not founded in actual individuals.

A similar argument shows that an actualist must deny that there are singular propositions about non-actual individuals. A singular proposition about an individual x is a proposition that involves or refers to x directly, and not by way of x's qualitative properties or relations to another individual. This relation is surely part of what makes the proposition what it is; it is essential to the proposition, and the proposition could not exist without being directly related to x. But according to actualism a proposition cannot bear such a relation to any non-actual individual.

I believe these arguments are conclusive so long as the thisness of an individual x is conceived, as I conceive it, as the property of being identical with x, and so long as a corresponding conception of singular propositions is maintained. But some may object that these conceptions are too narrow, and that thisnesses have sometimes been conceived, historically, as non-qualitative essences, or perhaps more broadly as non-qualitative entities, of a different sort, which could exist without the individuals whose thisnesses they are. According to such an alternative conception I depend on my thisness in a way that it does not depend on me; for certainly I could not have existed without it. And it might be held that singular propositions should be conceived as having thisnesses in this alternative sense as constituents.

The crucial question here, metaphysically, is whether there are any non-qualitative essences or other non-qualitative entities that could play this role. We are particularly concerned to know whether there are any that could do it for non-actual individuals that would have no qualitative or α-relational essence, such as members of an I-pair. I shall argue that there are not. In doing so, to avoid confusion, I shall reserve the term ⌜thisness of x⌝ for the property of being identical with x, and use ⌜haecceity of x⌝ for the

supposed non-qualitative entities that could largely play the part of a thisness of x even if x never existed.

It is not easy to say what haecceities would be. That is indeed the chief objection to them. Suppose H* is my haecceity. What would H* have been if I had never existed? It would be misleading at best for an actualist to claim that H* would have been *my haecceity* in that case, for he thinks there would have been no me for it to be related to. But one might hold that H* would have been something that *could* have been a haecceity of an individual, and that could not have been a haecceity of different individuals in different possible worlds. That would fit it to represent me in worlds in which I myself would not exist. Likewise it might be claimed that there are infinitely many such entities in the actual world, deputizing here for individuals that would exist in other possible worlds. But what would these entities be?

If H* existed and I never did, I do not see how H* or anything else could be the property of *being identical with me*; for a primitive relation to me is surely essential to that property. But maybe there could be the unactualized property of *having H* as a haecceity*. Perhaps H* itself would (self-referentially) be this property; or perhaps H* would not be a property at all. Even if *having H* as a haecceity* were necessarily coextensive with *being identical with me*, I think they would be distinct.

Here we can see clearly the nature of the difference between a theory of thisnesses, in my sense, and a theory of haecceities that could exist without their individuals. On my view the individuals themselves provide the basis for non-qualitative facts, by their identity and distinctness. In the theory of haecceities this basis is provided instead by the haecceities, and they are necessarily existent entities (perhaps abstract entities) which are not qualitative properties. Specifically, the basis for non-qualitative facts is provided by the incommunicability of the haecceities – that is, by their inability to bear a certain relation to more than one individual in the same or in different possible worlds. Hence on my view the fundamental non-qualitative properties are of the form, *being identical with x*; but on the other view they are of something like the form, *having h as a haecceity*.

The nature of the supposed haecceities is still very obscure, however. To see this, we may begin by thinking again of an I-pair. Make their description as detailed as you like, provided only they remain indiscernible with respect to their qualitative properties and their relations (if any) to actual individuals. Now ask yourself, which member of the I-pair would you rather have exist, if only one of them were to exist. The question is absurd, not merely because you have no reason to prefer one to the other, but because you have no way of picking out or referring to one of them rather than the other, éven in your own mind. You can of course say, "Let us call one of them 'Castor' and the other 'Pollux,'" but that does not enable you to refer to one of them rather than the other, any more than the variables in

$$(\exists x)(\exists y)(x \text{ is a horse } \& \ y \text{ is a horse } \& \ x \neq y)$$

refer to one horse rather than another. You cannot pick out one member of an I-pair, rather than the other, because you have no acquaintance with any haecceity (or indeed any essence at all) of either of them.

"Of course not; but is that just an unfortunate limitation of our cognitive powers?" you may ask. I think it is more than that; at any rate I cannot see how even a superhuman mind could pick out one of such a pair of indiscernible non-actual objects, or be acquainted with haecceities of them. Of course that does not prove that there are no haecceities of such non-actual objects, but such obscurity surely makes belief in them less attractive.

It may be objected that we do seem to apprehend some singular propositions about non-actual individuals – namely, about fictitious individuals; and that we must therefore be acquainted with haecceities of fictitious individuals. Must we not, for example, be acquainted with a haecceity of Sherlock Holmes in order to understand the proposition that Sherlock Holmes was a detective? This is not the place to try to give a positive account of the role of proper names in fiction, but I think there is good reason to deny that there are primitive haecceities of fictitious individuals. For consider the following sequence of events, which surely could have happened, though probably it did not.

In 1870, before Sir Arthur Conan Doyle had written any of his famous stories, a retired schoolteacher in Liverpool wrote a story called "The Hound of the Joneses" about an amateur detective named "Sherlock Holmes." And the name was not the only coincidence. "The Hound of the Joneses" was not a very good story, but the characteristics of the detective in it were so similar to those that Sherlock Holmes has in Conan Doyle's stories that if Doyle had written and published "The Hound of the Joneses" in 1920, it would certainly have been accepted (if not applauded) as a story about Sherlock Holmes. As it was, however, it was destined for oblivion. It was never read by anyone but its author, who died in 1872. The only manuscript was burned by the author's niece when she cleaned the house in 1873, and it never had the slightest influence on Conan Doyle. Now the question I want to raise is whether "The Hound of the Joneses" was a story about Sherlock Holmes, or in other words whether the detective in "The Hound of the Joneses" was Sherlock Holmes – that is, whether he was identical with that prince of fictitious detectives known to us from Conan Doyle's stories.

Three answers seem possible. (i) The detective in "The Hound of the Joneses" certainly was Sherlock Holmes, because of the qualitative similarity he bears to the hero of Conan Doyle's stories. (ii) The protagonist of "The Hound of the Joneses" may or may not have been Sherlock Holmes, depending on whether its author and Doyle happen to have attached the same haecceity (or equivalent haecceities) to their heroes. (How likely it is that they hit on the same haecceity will presumably depend on the mechanism by which we are acquainted with haecceities.) (iii) Sherlock Holmes (the famous Sherlock Holmes, that is) certainly does not appear in "The Hound of the Joneses," because it is a necessary condition of a story's being about Sherlock Holmes that it be appropriately connected by historical influences to Conan Doyle's stories.

Of these answers the second seems to be the one that ought to be given by those who believe there are primitive haecceities of fictitious individuals. But I think it is absurd, and the third answer is pretty clearly the right one. This suggests that such individuality as fictitious individuals have is parasitic on the individuality of their (actual) authors.

Even the *incommunicability* of haecceities, which is supposed to provide a basis for non-qualitative facts, is mysterious. If relation to a particular individual is not essential to haecceities, what keeps God from using the same haecceity twice, to create two different individuals with the same haecceity, even in the same world? Why couldn't Woodrow Wilson and Harry Truman, for example, have had the same haecceity? Was Wilson's haecceity "used up," perhaps, in making Wilson? Someone who holds a theory of haecceities may reply that these questions are silly, because the central point of his theory is the postulation of haecceities as entities that are incommunicable in the relevant respects. And no doubt it is an analytic truth that nothing is a haecceity unless it is incommunicable in the indicated sense. But that does not answer the question about the entities that are supposed to be haecceities, what it is about them that makes them incommunicable and thus enables them to count as haecceities.

Haecceities (as distinct from thisnesses) are postulated as "something, we know not what" to fill some metaphysical role. Sometimes they have been postulated to play a part in a theory according to which properties – indeed universals – are constituents of which individuals are (at least partly) composed. Such a theory naturally gives rise to a problem of individuation: what keeps an individual from being a (complicated) universal? What must be added to the universals that are constituents of the individual, to particularize or individuate it? The haecceity is postulated as a *constituent* of the individual, to perform this individuating function.[6] (On this theory the fundamental non-qualitative properties would be of the form, *having h as a constituent*, where h is a haecceity.)

The idea of the haecceity as a constituent of the individual may help to explain why the haecceity could exist without the individual but the individual could not exist without the haecceity; for such a relationship often obtains between an individual and one of its constituents. But the nature of this constituent is still a mystery. Indeed another problem may be mentioned here that seems quite acute on this theory. Presumably every haecceity is compatible with some but not all consistent qualitative properties. For example, I am a person but could not possibly have been a musical performance. My haecceity constituent must therefore be, necessarily, capable of being combined with personhood but incapable of being combined with the property of being a musical performance. But what is the ground of

this necessary capacity and incapacity? We cannot *explain* them by pointing out that I can be a person but could not have been a musical performance; for my modal properties are supposed to be explained by those of my haecceity, since the latter would exist and have its modal properties even if I never existed and had no properties. It may be pointed out that there is a great categorial difference between persons, as substances, and musical performances, as events. But this only pushes the problem to a deeper level, since there is (as I argued in Adams, 1979b, pp. 14, 23) as much reason to postulate non-qualitative essences of events as of substances. If my haecceity is an entity independent of me, and distinct from all qualitative properties (including the property of substantiality), what is it about this entity by virtue of which it could join with substantiality, but could not join with eventhood, to form an individual? I do not see an answer to this question.

Moreover I do not believe that properties are constituents of which individuals are wholly or partly composed. If we do not think of individuals as composed in that way, we will not need to postulate a special constituent to "individuate" them or keep them from being universals. Neither do we need a special constituent to make them identical with themselves or distinct from each other. Those can be seen as primitive relations of the individuals to themselves and to each other. Of course this presupposes that the individuals themselves actually are given; for an actualist it presupposes that they actually exist.

The idea of non-qualitative facts has suffered from its historic association with the idea of a mysterious individuating constituent of individuals. Perhaps in order to avoid such obscurity some have been inclined to see the world as constituted by purely qualitative facts. But we can have a primitive thisness, with much less mystery, as the property of being identical with a certain individual, if we do not suppose that the thisness could exist independently of the individual. The property of being identical with me can be thought of as formed by a partial abstraction (innocent, so far as I can see) from the proposition that Robert Merrihew Adams is identical with me. Or perhaps my thisness could be conceived as the ordered pair whose first member is the relation of identity and whose second member is me. In that case I would be a constituent of my thisness, rather than my thisness of me, and it would be particularly obvious that my thisness could not have existed if I had never existed.

The arguments for non-qualitative facts are directly arguments for the non-qualitative character of properties or facts of identity and non-identity with given individuals (Adams, 1979b), and thus give rise naturally to the conception of thisnesses in my sense. That conception also provides answers to questions corresponding to important perplexities that we found in thinking about haecceities. If my thisness is the property of being identical with me, the incommunicability of thisnesses is easily understood, because it follows from the logical character of identity that a property of the form, *being identical with x*, cannot be possessed by more than one individual in the same or in different possible worlds. If we understand thisnesses as identities of actually existing individuals, moreover, we can give a fairly plausible account of why my thisness could not have been combined with the property of being a musical performance. The explanation is that I am (in fact) a person, and there are necessary conditions of trans-temporal and trans-world identity which follow (perhaps analytically) from the concept of a person and which entail that no musical performance could have been the same individual as one that is in fact a person – from which it follows that no musical performance could have had the property of being identical with me, which is my thisness (Adams, 1979b, p. 24f.).

3 Our Possible Non-Existence and its Logic

3.1 An objection

I hold that there are no things that never exist. No such things have properties or enter into relations. I hold further that there are no thisnesses of non-actual individuals, and no singular propositions about them. And I hold that these are necessary truths. But now consider a singular negative existential proposition – for example, the proposition that I never exist. That proposition expresses a logical and metaphysical possibility, for I am not a necessary being. Doesn't it follow, then, that there is a possible world in which the proposition is true? But a proposition must *be* in order to be true. So it seems there is a possible

world in which there *is* a singular proposition (indeed a true one) about an individual (me) that never exists in that world – contrary to what I have claimed (cf. Plantinga, 1974, pp. 144–8). Moreover it seems that in that world this individual that never exists enters into a relation (non-identity) with all the things that do exist in that world – again contrary to what I have claimed.

At this point we face a temptation. If we believe that I have a qualitative or an α-relational essence, we could agree that if I never existed there would be no singular propositions about me, in the strict sense of 'singular proposition' that I have adopted, but we could maintain that if I never existed there would still have been propositions involving my qualitative or α-relational essence. Among such propositions, at least one would presumably be equivalent to the proposition that I do not exist, and the possibility of my non-existence could be explained in terms of the possible truth of that proposition. Similarly, my non-identity with the individuals that would exist in a world in which I would not exist could be explained in terms of their relation to my qualitative or α-relational essence. This solution to the problem would yield a neater and easier basis for modal logic, in some ways, than we shall get by rejecting the temptation.

Nevertheless I think it is wise to reject it. As to qualitative essences, we do not know that we have them. As to α-relational essences, it is at least philosophically controversial whether we have them; and if we do have them, they probably involve individuals that would not exist in some of the possible worlds in which we would not exist. In those worlds our α-relational essences would no more exist than our thisnesses, and they could therefore not be used to explain the possibility of our not existing in those worlds. Thus it seems that we cannot *count* on qualitative or α-relational essences in solving this problem. So I will set the temptation aside, and assume henceforth that our possible non-existence is to be accounted for in terms of thisnesses and singular propositions that would not exist if we did not exist.

In reply to this objection I deny, then, that ⌜It is possible that *p*⌝ always implies that the proposition that-*p* could have been true. Philosophers have often found it natural to characterize possibilities and necessities in terms of what propositions would have been true in some or all possible situations (or possible worlds, as we like to say). This seems harmless enough so long as it is assumed that all propositions are necessary beings. But it is misleading if (as I hold) some propositions exist only contingently. From an actualist point of view, modalities (especially non-qualitative modalities) are not to be understood in terms of a non-modal property (truth) that propositions could have had, but in terms of modal properties that actually existing entities do have. To say that I might never have existed is not to say that the proposition that I never exist could have been true. There is such a proposition; but if I ever exist it is false, and if I never existed it would not be true because it would not exist. To say that I might never have existed is to say something about the modal properties that I actually have – and by implication about the modal properties that my thisness, and the proposition that I exist, actually have. It is equivalent to saying that I am a contingent being, that my thisness is not necessarily exemplified, and that the proposition that I exist is not a necessary truth. It seems to me evident that these entities all exist and actually have these modal properties; but I have argued that if actualism is correct, none of them would have existed or had any properties if I had never existed. I conclude that an actualist should hold that whether there are possibilities about an individual depends on whether there *actually* are propositions about the individual, rather than on whether there would have been such propositions if the possibilities in question had been realized.

Similarly, it is true that if I never existed the things that did exist would not be identical with me, but that is not to say that I would enter into a relation of non-identity with them. It is rather to say that the proposition that I would in that case be identical with them is false; and that proposition is one that actually exists but would not exist if I never existed. The foundation of the fact that things that might have existed if I never did would not be identical with me is not in a relation that they *would* bear to me, but rather in the logic of identity together with my *actual* possession of the property of being something that might never have existed even if some things did exist.

3.2   Truth at a world

Contemporary treatments of modality make so much use of the notions of possible worlds, and of propositions true and false in (or at) such worlds, that we can hardly rest content with the solution proposed in Section 3.1 until we see more clearly what it implies about a possible worlds semantics for the modal notions with which we are concerned. In beginning to develop such implications, however, I wish to state plainly that I do not pretend to be giving a complete formulation of a modal logic, or of a semantics for a modal logic – much less to be proving the completeness of anything. My aim is rather to clarify and justify the metaphysical constraints I think a modal logic must satisfy if it is to be suitable for the understanding of possibility and necessity that interests us here.

If there are any possible worlds, actualism implies that they, like anything else, must be, or be constructed from, things that exist in the actual world. More than one actualistic treatment of possible worlds is available, no doubt; but as a working hypothesis let us assume that possible worlds are, or are constructed from, maximal consistent sets of actually existing propositions. Such sets may be called "world-stories." They are consistent in the sense, not merely that there is no provable contradiction in them, but that all the propositions in each world-story could possibly be true together; 'possibly' is accepted as a primitive here. The intuitive idea behind calling the world-stories "maximal" is that for every proposition *p*, each world-story contains either *p* or the negation of *p*. This idea needs to be modified in some ways; two limitations on the completeness of world-stories will concern us here.

(i) In a typical non-actual world there would exist some individuals that never exist in the actual world (cf. Section 4.1 below). If such a world were actual, there would be singular propositions about those individuals, and some of them would be true. But no such propositions are included in the world-stories of such worlds, since no such propositions actually exist. The world-stories therefore do not include all the propositions that would exist and be true if the corresponding worlds were actual. Some world-stories may not even contain enough to determine a world completely. I think there could be a pair of possible worlds that differed from each other only by the interchange of two individuals (or sets of individuals) that do not exist in the actual world (Adams, 1979b, p. 22f.; cf. Section 4.4 below). The only propositions that would be true in one of those worlds and false in the other are singular propositions that do not exist in the actual world. Therefore both these worlds are represented by a single world-story that does not discriminate between them. I said there "could be" such a pair of worlds rather than there "is" one, because I believe there is no more of non-actual possible worlds than is given by their world-stories. In this sort of case the world-story gives us a *type* of world rather than a completely determinate world. Out of public and private habit I shall continue to speak of "possible worlds." but when I do, it should be understood that some of the "worlds" are types that could be further differentiated by the addition of singular propositions about individuals that do not exist in the actual world. This may be less than we wanted in the way of possible worlds, but actualist intuitions make extremely plausible the claim that it's all there is. Of course nothing that has been said here keeps the possible worlds or world-types from being completely determinate in every *purely qualitative* respect.

(ii) Intuitively, a world-story should be complete with respect to singular propositions about those actual individuals that would still be actual if all the propositions in the story were true, and should contain no singular propositions at all about those actual individuals that would not exist in that case. For the propositions would not exist and therefore could not be true, if the individuals did not exist. Let us say, therefore that if *w* is a set of propositions, and *s* is the set of all the actual individuals that *w* contains any singular propositions about, and *p* is a singular proposition that is exclusively about one or more members of *s*, then *w* is not a world-story unless *w* includes either *p* or its negation. Furthermore, if a world-story contains any singular proposition at all about an individual *i*, it must contain the proposition that *i* exists. But a consistent set of propositions, otherwise maximal, still counts as a world-story if it contains no singular propositions at all about one or more actual individuals, provided that the existence of those individuals is

not entailed by any propositions that are included in the world-story. The singular proposition that I exist, for example, may entail the singular proposition about my mother, that she exists. If so, every world-story that includes the former proposition must also include the latter.

A world-story that includes no singular proposition about me constitutes and describes a possible world in which I would not exist. It represents my possible non-existence, not by including the proposition that I do not exist but simply by omitting me. That I would not exist if all the propositions it includes, and no other actual propositions, were true is not a fact internal to the world that it describes, but an observation that we make from our vantage point in the actual world, about the relation of that world-story to an individual of the actual world.

Let us mark this difference in point of view by saying that the proposition that I never exist is (in the actual world) true *at* many possible worlds, but *in* none. Only propositions that are included in a world-story are true *in* the world it describes. Among actual propositions they are the ones that would be true if that world were actual. Thus it is true *at* possible worlds in which Napoleon would exist and I would not, that I am not identical with Napoleon; but that proposition is not true *in* those worlds, because it would not exist in them (and I would not enter into any relation of non-identity if one of them were actual).

In Section 3.1 I argued that whether there are possibilities about an individual depends on whether there actually are propositions about the individual, rather than on whether there would have been such propositions if the possibilities in question had been realized. This conclusion can be incorporated in a possible worlds semantics by stating the conditions for the truth of modal propositions in terms of truth *at* a possible world instead of truth *in* a possible world. '◊ ~ (I exist)' ['It is possible that it be not the case that I exist'] should turn out to be true in our modal logic. Therefore, since '~ (I exist)' is not true *in* any possible world, we should not conceive of ⌈◊p⌉ as true if and only if ⌈p⌉ is true *in* some possible world. Rather, we shall say that ⌈◊p⌉ is true if and only if ⌈p⌉ is true *at* some possible world; and similarly ⌈□p⌉ is true if and only if ⌈p⌉ is true *at* all possible worlds.

If the notion of truth *at* a possible world is going to play such a central role in our modal logic, we shall have to give a more precise account of it. Our first inclination may be to say that what is true about me at a world in which I do not exist is only that I do not exist. I think we cannot quite get away with that; I shall argue that '~ (I have blue eyes),' for example is true at any world at which '~ (I exist)' is true. What we can insist is that what is true about me *at* a world in which I do not exist must be determined, in accordance with some logical criterion, by the proposition that I do not exist, together with other propositions, true at that world, which are *not about me*.[7] For in a world in which I do not exist I have no properties; so what else about me could determine anything there? The criterion I propose will be developed in stages. In the simplest cases truth-functional form, the logical form pertaining to the non-modal logic of propositions, is the only logical form that we need to consider.

Let *w* be a possible world, and *a* an actual individual that would not exist in *w*; then:

(C1)　All propositions that are included in the world-story of *w* are true at *w* as well as in *w*.

(C2)　If ⌜*p*⌝ is an atomic singular proposition about *a*, then ⌜~*p*⌝ is true at *w*.

(C3)　All propositions that follow truth-functionally from propositions true at *w* are true at *w*.

Among the singular propositions about me that are true at worlds in which I would not exist, by this criterion, are those expressed by '~ (I exist),' '~(I have blue eyes),' '~(I am a person),' '~(I am a fish),' '~(Robert Merrihew Adams = Robert Merrihew Adams),' and '(I exist) ⊃ (I am a fish).' On the other hand, 'I am a non-fish' is atomic and therefore false at worlds in which I would not exist.

This is as it should be, intuitively. If I did not exist, would I be a fish? No, I would be nothing at all. Is it true then that in that case I would not be a fish? Yes. We capture these intuitions by saying that 'I am a fish' is false, and '~(I am a fish)' true, *at* all possible worlds in which I would not exist. But 'I am a non-fish' means that I am something that is not a fish; it ascribes to me the *property* of being a non-fish. If I did not exist, might I have that property? Might I be something that is not a fish?

No, I would be nothing at all, and would have no properties. Hence 'I am a non-fish' is appropriately counted false in worlds in which I do not exist.

In effect I am treating every atomic singular proposition about *a* as ascribing a property to *a*,[8] and therefore as saying that *a* is *something* that has the property. The denial of such a proposition correctly characterizes not only states of affairs in which *a* would be something that lacked the property, but also states of affairs in which *a* would not be anything of any sort at all. I would not claim that we always use logically atomic and non-atomic expressions in accordance with this principle; but it imposes, at worst, a minor regimentation on our ordinary linguistic habits.

3.3　Quantification and truth at a world

By (C2), 'I am shorter than the Empire State Building' is false, and its negation is true, at worlds in which I do not exist, even if they do contain the Empire State Building. But what about '(∃x)(I am shorter than x)'? It ought to be false too, and its negation ought to be true, at worlds in which I do not exist; for I cannot enter into any relation where I do not exist. My criterion must be extended to provide for this.

Let *w* be a possible world, and *a* an actual individual that would not exist in *w*; then:

(C4)　If ⌜$\phi(a, x_1,...,x_n)$⌝ is an atomic propositional function from $x_1,...,x_n$ to singular propositions about *a*, then ⌜~(∃x_1)... (∃x_n)($\phi(a, x_1,...,x_n)$)⌝ is true at *w*.

Other questions about quantification remain to be answered. I might never have existed even if Napoleon had been a general. So there should be possible worlds in which

(1)　~ (I exist) & Napoleon is a general

is true. It is plausible to think that

(2)　(∃x)(~ (I exist) & x is a general)

is also true at those worlds. But this is not provided for by (C4), because '~ (I exist) & x is a general' is not an *atomic* propositional function. (2) does follow from (1) by Existential Generalization

(EG); and that might suggest we ought to say that any proposition is true at a possible world w if it follows by standard predicate logic (including EG) from propositions that are true at w.

This suggestion has unacceptable consequences, however. For '~ (I exist)' is true at many possible worlds, but '$(\exists x) \sim (x$ exists),' which follows from it by EG, is false at all possible worlds, according to actualism. There is a similar problem about the rule of Universal Instantiation (UI). '$(\forall x)$ (x exists)' is true at all possible worlds, but 'I exist,' which follows from it by UI, is false at many possible worlds.

Several logicians have developed what is known as a "free logic," which may be characterized, for our present purpose, as a logic of quantifiers and predicates in which the rules of EG and UI are restricted to permit the inference of $\ulcorner(\exists x)(\phi(x))\urcorner$ from $\ulcorner\phi(a)$ & a exists,$\urcorner$ but not from $\ulcorner\phi(a)\urcorner$ alone,[9] and of $\ulcorner\phi(a)\urcorner$ from $\ulcorner a$ exists & $(\forall x)(\phi(x)),\urcorner$ but not from $\ulcorner(\forall x)(\phi(x))\urcorner$ alone. This conception can be used in our criterion.

Let w be a possible world, and a an actual individual that would not exist in w; then:

(C5) All propositions that follow by a "free" quantification logic from propositions true at w are true at w.

It would not do to replace (C3) and (C5) by the simpler statement that all propositions that "follow" from propositions true at w are true at w. For there is a variety of cases in which the *truth* of a proposition q follows from the *truth* of another proposition p although there are possible worlds at which p is true and q is false. There are several important logical relations that obtain among all true propositions, and indeed among all the propositions that are true *in* any one possible world, but not among all the propositions that are true *at* any one possible world. The standard, unrestricted rule of EG is our first example of this.

If a singular proposition $\ulcorner\phi(a)\urcorner$ is true *in* any possible world, a must exist, and satisfy $\ulcorner\phi(\ )\urcorner$ in that world. Therefore something that exists in that world satisfies $\ulcorner\phi(\ )\urcorner$ there; so $\ulcorner(\exists x)(\phi(x))\urcorner$ is true *in* that world. Thus unrestricted EG preserves truth *in* any possible world; applying EG to a proposition true *in* the world will lead us only to a proposition that is also true in the world. Since truth is coextensive with truth *in* the actual world, the same reasoning shows that unrestricted EG preserves *truth*.[10]

We have seen, however, that unrestricted EG does not preserve truth *at* every possible world. Applying it to a proposition that is true *at* some possible world (such as '~ (I exist)') sometimes takes us to a proposition that is false at that world, and indeed at all possible worlds (such as '$(\exists x) \sim$ (x exists)'). But there is no counterexample here to the thesis that unrestricted EG preserves *truth*, and truth *in* any one possible world; for '~ (I exist)' is neither *true*, nor true *in* any possible world, because it exists only in worlds at which it is false.

For these reasons the *truth* of

(3) $(\exists x)(x$ exists $\supset x$ is a son of Arthur and Margaret Adams)

follows from the *truth* of

(4) I exist $\supset$ I am a son of Arthur and Margaret Adams,

even though (4) is true *at*, and (3) is false *at*, possible worlds in which neither I nor any other son of my parents would exist.

Unrestricted EG gives rise to propositional forms that have a sort of *validity*, in that they have no instances that are *false*, or false *in* any possible world, but that lack *necessity* because they have instances that are false *at* some possible world. In particular,

(5) $\phi(y) \supset (\exists x)(\phi(x))$

is a singular propositional form all of whose instances are *true*; and all of its instances that exist in any possible world are true *in* that world. But it has instances that are false *at* worlds in which they, and the individual they are about, do not exist. And therefore its necessitation,

(6) $\Box[\phi(y) \supset (\exists x)(\phi(x))]$,

has instances that are simply *false*.

This suggests that the problems here arise, not from EG alone, but from EG in combination with the *rule of Necessitation*, which provides that if $\ulcorner p\urcorner$

is a theorem, so is ⌈□p⌉. Perhaps we can safely rely on standard quantification logic (including unrestricted EG and UI) for inferring *truths* from *truths*, if we restrict the rule of Necessitation to provide only that if ⌈p⌉ is a theorem of a "free" fragment of our system (a fragment in which EG and UI are restricted) then ⌈□p⌉ is a theorem of our system. This will enable us to have (5) as a theorem (which we want, since all its instances are true) without having (6) as a theorem (which we don't want, since it has false instances). We might want to say that (5) is a "contingent theorem."

The rule of Necessitation, as an expression of the idea that logical principles are necessary truths, must be treated in general with great caution, if what possibilities there are varies from one possible world to another. A famous thesis about truth provides another case, having nothing to do with quantification, in which an important logical principle is acceptable but its necessitation is not.

(7)　The proposition that-*p* is true if, and only if, *p*

has instances that are false *at* some possible worlds, but no false instances and no instances that are false *in* any possible world. For example, 'I never exist' expresses a proposition (call it P*) that is true *at* some possible worlds. But 'The proposition that I never exist is true' is false *at* those worlds, because it expresses an atomic singular proposition about P*, and P* does not exist in those worlds. *In* any possible world, however, a proposition can be true only if it exists, and then the proposition that it is true will also be true in that world. Hence if a proposition is (actually) *true*, so is the proposition that it is true. (7) may be admitted as a "contingent theorem" in a formal system, but its necessitation,

(8)　□(The proposition that-*p* is true if, and only if, *p*)

must not be accepted as a theorem if singular propositions are allowed as substitution instances.[11] Another restriction on the rule of Necessitation is required here, if (7) is to be a theorem.

These logical relations (and others I shall suggest) that obtain among all true propositions but not among all propositions that are true *at* any one possible world may make the notion of truth *at* a possible world seem rather anomalous. Perhaps indeed there is something odd about it; we are using it to do something that is inherently awkward, although I think we have plenty of reason to do it anyway. A possible world involves two diverse groups of propositions: one group that could all be true together, and a second group that expresses certain relations of the first group to actual individuals. Intuitively we think of the two groups as jointly defining a single way things could have been; and that is right. But they do not form a seamless whole. They could not all be true together, for the second group would not have existed, and therefore would not have been true, if the possible world the two groups jointly define had been actual. The first group define a possible world from within, so to speak, while the second group characterize it only from our point of view in the actual world.

The awkwardness is not due to the notion of possible worlds, however. That (6) and (8) have false instances though (5) and (7) do not, follows, I think, from any satisfactory actualistic treatment of the possibility of our non-existence, with or without possible worlds semantics. It is as if we were trying to paint a picture of my non-existence. We could do a portrait of my family, leaving me out of it and perhaps including a figure that is not a likeness of anyone in particular instead of me; but that does not seem to capture unambiguously all that we meant to express. The classic and obvious solution is to frame the picture and put a plaque on the frame saying, "The Non-existence of Robert M. Adams"; and that is probably the thing to do. But we must not expect the message of the plaque to be related to the figures in the picture in the same way that they are related to each other.

3.4　Which modal propositions are true at which worlds?

The most difficult problem, in developing a criterion for truth *at* a world, is to determine which singular *modal* propositions, if any, should be counted as true at worlds in which individuals they are about would not exist. I believe that such propositions as '◊(Jimmy Carter exists)' and '□ ~ (I am a musical performance)' should be regarded as ascribing properties to the individuals they are about, and should be treated here in the same way as atomic propositions (and that propositions such as '$(\exists x)\Diamond(x$ is stronger than Muhammed Ali)' should receive a corresponding treatment).

Let w be a possible world, and a an actual individual that would not exist in w; then:

(C6) If $\ulcorner\Diamond p\urcorner$ and $\ulcorner\Box p\urcorner$ are singular propositions about a, then $\ulcorner\sim\Diamond p\urcorner$ and $\ulcorner\sim\Box p\urcorner$ are true at w.

(C7) If $\ulcorner\sim(\exists x_1)\ldots(\exists x_n)\Diamond(\phi(a, x_1,\ldots, x_n))\urcorner$ and $\ulcorner\sim(\exists x_1)\ldots(\exists x_n)\Box(\phi(a, x_1,\ldots, x_n))\urcorner$ are singular propositions about a, then they are true at w.

This treatment of singular modal propositions is metaphysically satisfying, though formally inconvenient.

It is metaphysically satisfying, from an actualist point of view, because there *are* no possibilities or necessities *de re* about non-actual individuals. So if I were not an actual individual there would be none about me. The singular propositions that I exist and that I do not exist would not exist to have the logical properties, or enter into the relations with some or all world-stories, by virtue of which my existence or non-existence would be possible or necessary. I therefore say that '$\Diamond$(I exist),' '$\Diamond\sim$(I exist),' '$\Box$(I exist),' and '$\Box\sim$(I exist)' are all false, and their negations true, at worlds in which I do not exist. Neither my existence nor my non-existence would be possible or necessary if I did not exist.

In accepting (C6) and (C7) one opts for a modal logic that reflects the idea that what modal facts there are (or would be) depends on what individuals there are (or would be). Inasmuch as there would be different individuals in different possible worlds, the modal facts *de re* differ from world to world. This should not be surprising. I have already argued that what possible worlds there are will differ from world to world. It is characteristic of actualism that modal facts, like all other facts, have their whole ontological basis in the actual world. This makes it possible to understand how the modal facts might be different if another world were actual.

The most disturbing consequence of my treatment of singular modal propositions is that the familiar modal axiom '$p \supset \Diamond p$' will have instances that are not necessarily true. For '$\sim$(I exist) $\supset \Diamond \sim$ (I exist)' is an instance of '$p \supset \Diamond p$' that is false at worlds in which I do not exist. I was initially inclined to resist this conclusion, but on reflection it seems to me metaphysically plausible. When we say that what is actual must be possible, we are leaving out of account the possibility that there might be no entity there to bear the relevant modal property; but what I have been arguing is that if I had never existed neither I nor the proposition that I do not exist would have been there to have any property of possibility.

Nonetheless there is a sense in which I agree that what is actual must be possible. The axiom '$p \supset \Diamond p$' is another logical principle that has no instances that are *false*, or false *in* any possible world, even though it has instances that are false *at* some possible worlds. For all its instances will be true in any world in which they exist. It could therefore be admitted as a contingent theorem; but its necessitation, '$\Box(p\supset\Diamond p)$,' has false instances and would have to be excluded by a suitable restriction on the rule of Necessitation.[12]

To say that my non-existence would not be possible if I did not exist is not to say that it would be impossible. '$p \supset \sim \Box \sim p$' has no instances that are false at any possible world, and may be regarded as a "weak" version of '$p \supset \Diamond p$.' Indeed '$\sim\Box\sim$' may function as a "weak possibility operator," and '$\sim\Diamond\sim$' as a "weak necessity operator";[13] for clearly on the view that I am advancing they are not necessarily equivalent to '$\Diamond$' and '$\Box$' respectively, as they are in most familiar modal logics.

The axioms characteristic of the systems S4 and S5 of modal logic can be divided into "weak" versions, which hold for all instances at all possible worlds, and "strong" versions, which do not (if singular propositions are admitted as instances). The following are only some examples:

strong	*Weak*
$\Box p \supset\Box\Box p$	$\Box p \supset\Box\sim\Diamond\sim p$
$\Diamond p \supset\Box\Diamond p$	$\Diamond p \supset\Box\sim\Box\sim p$
$\sim\Box\sim p \supset\Box\sim\Box\sim p$	$\sim\Box\sim p \supset\sim\Diamond\Box\sim p$

The modal logic generated by (C6) and (C7) will thus be weaker and more complicated than we may have wanted.

I believe (C6) and (C7) are justified anyway, on metaphysical grounds; but I grant that their correctness is far more doubtful than that of the first five clauses of my criterion. So let us look at three alternatives to my treatment of singular modal propositions. (i) It could be held that unlike other singular propositions, singular modal propositions, negative as well as affirmative, are true *at* a possible world if and only if they are true *in* it. This would have the consequence that neither '◊(I exist)' nor '~◊ (I exist)' would be true at worlds in which I do not exist. It seems unfortunate to admit such a truth-value gap into our modal logic at this point, when there are (as I have argued) strong reasons for responding with a clear 'No' to the question whether, if I never existed, it would be the case that ◊(I exist). Moreover this approach still leaves us with the consequence that '◊~(I exist)' is not true at worlds in which I do not exist, and therefore that '$p \supset ◊p$' has instances that are not true at all possible worlds.

(ii) It may occur to us to try to deal with the problem in terms of a relation of accessibility, or relative possibility, between worlds. We could say that a possible world w_2 is possible in (or accessible from) a possible world w_1 if and only if every individual that exists in w_2 and also exists in the actual world exists in w_1. The reason for saying this is that the complete world-story of w_2 will exist in w_1 only if this condition is satisfied. We could then say that ⌜□p⌝ and ⌜◊q⌝ are true *at* a possible world w if and only if ⌜p⌝ is true at all, and ⌜q⌝ is true at least at one, of the worlds that are possible in w. Since the accessibility relation defined here is easily seen to be reflexive and transitive but not symmetrical, S4 would be the right modal logic for it. That is a formally convenient result.[14]

I have passed over certain refinements in this theory, because they do not affect the strongest objection to it, which is that it implies that '□ ~ (I exist)' is true at w if I do not exist in w. For all the worlds possible in such a world must be worlds in which I do not exist. In other words, the theory has the consequence that if I had not existed, my non-existence would have been necessary. This is intuitively unacceptable. If I had not existed, I think my existence would not have been possible; but it seems even clearer that my non-existence would not have been necessary.

(iii) The most tempting alternative to my treatment of singular modal propositions, I think, would begin by rejecting the whole idea of relativizing their truth and falsity to different possible worlds. Modal propositions, it might be claimed, are not to be included in world-stories. They arise only when the finished system of world-stories (as it *actually* exists, of course) is surveyed. There is on this view no non-arbitrary sense in which modal propositions are true *in* or *at* possible worlds. But we could stipulate arbitrarily that

(C6′) No matter what the form of ⌜p⌝, a proposition of the form ⌜◊p,⌝ ⌜□p,⌝ ⌜~◊p,⌝ or ⌜~□p⌝ is true at all possible worlds if and only if it is *true* (actually true).

Then we could help ourselves to the powerful and convenient modal logic of S5.

This stipulation would violate the requirement (laid down in §3.2 above) that what is true about an individual a at a world in which a does not exist must be determined by a's non-existence there, together with propositions, true at that world, that are *not about a*. Suppose a is the actual world premiere of Beethoven's ninth symphony, and w is a possible world in which neither a nor I would exist. Then I think (C6′) implies that at w it would still be true that a could have been a musical performance and I could not. This difference between a and me at w could hardly have been determined by our (common) non-existence there plus some propositions that are not about us. To suppose such a difference at w between two individuals that would not exist in w seems at least uncomfortably close to ascribing properties at w to individuals that would not exist in w.

Of course if we are firmly agreed that the truth of modal propositions at a possible world is a matter of arbitrary stipulation, it is hard to raise a metaphysical objection. But are we really reduced to arbitrary stipulation here? If there cannot be singular propositions about individuals that never exist, then there is a non-arbitrary difference in the relations of singular modal propositions to different possible worlds. I think it would be good for this difference to be reflected in our modal logic, as it is not in S5.

(C6′) is an alternative to (C6); we cannot get an alternative to (C7) in the same way. For (C7)

determines (in the negative) questions about whether, in a possible world in which an individual *a* would not exist, there would be individuals of one sort or another that would be *possibly related to a* in one way or another. We cannot just say that the answer is affirmative if it is actually true that the individual in question could be so related to *a*, and negative if it is actually false that the individual in question could be so related to *a*. For the "other individual" we are asking about might well be one that does not exist in α (the actual world); and in that case there are not actually any singular propositions about that individual, and it is neither actually true nor actually false that that individual could be related to *a* in the relevant way. An alternative to (C7), therefore, would require some approach and rationale other than those on which (C6′) is based.

4 Some Problems of Construction

Among the various things that most of us sometimes say about what might have been the case with reference to various actual individuals, or to non-actual individuals of various sorts, there are some about which we may well wonder what sense can be made of them on the views I have advocated here. Some consideration of the extent to which a few of these supposed possibilities can be constructed in accordance with my principles may be helpful both in understanding and in assessing those principles.[15]

4.1 Non-actual individuals

It may be asked how I can assert 'There could have been an individual that would not have been identical with any of the individuals that actually exist' without admitting primitive relations (of non-identity) between individuals that may exist only in different possible worlds. I take the assertion to be equivalent to

> $(\exists w)(\exists \phi)(w$ is a world-story & w includes the proposition that $(\exists x)(\phi(x))$ & $\sim (\exists x)$ (w includes the proposition that $\phi(x)))$

– where ϕ ranges over infinitely as well as finitely complex properties or propositional functions.

4.2. Trans-world relationships

My parents could have had, instead of me, a different son whose eyes would have been just a little bluer than mine are. But how can that be possible? It seems that we want to assert the possibility of a world in which I would not exist but there would be a man who does not exist in α (the actual world) and who would have the property of having eyes just a little bluer than mine are in α. That property appears to be a relation between him and me, however; and my metaphysical views imply that there could not be a relation between him and me in a world in which I would never exist (nor in α, since he does not exist here). (Let us ignore for the time being any additional problems there may be about things being related to α in worlds in which one or more of the individuals of α would not exist.)

One approach to this problem is to construct in terms of world-stories a relation between the actual color of my eyes and colors that other people's might be if I did not exist. We could say,

> $(\exists c)(\exists x)(\exists y)(\exists w)(c$ is the color of my eyes & x and y are my parents & w is a world-story & w contains no singluar propositions about me & $\sim (\exists z)(w$ contains the proposition that z is a son of x and y) & w does contain the proposition that $(\exists z)(z$ is a son of x and y & z has eyes just a little bluer than $c))$.

In addition to being rather laborious, this approach has what some may regard as a metaphysical disadvantage in that it involves quantifying over qualities (in this case, shades of color). But I doubt that we can find a significantly better construction in terms of possible worlds.

A less artificial approach is available so long as we do not try to dress all our modal judgments in the panoply of possible worlds. Comparisons with actual samples are probably our most natural and primitive way of indicating shades of color. "What shade of blue do you mean?" "Just a little bluer than this." It is natural to ascribe shades of color in this way when describing non-actual as well as actual situations. "What color are you thinking his eyes might have been?" "Just a little bluer than mine are." The actual color of my eyes is used to say how blue his might have been.

Here we are describing a possible but non-actual situation from our perspective in the actual world, as we do when we say that I might not have existed. If we were describing "from inside" a world in which I would not exist, we could not use my eyes as a color sample.

This "external" characterization of the possible in terms of the actual may be regarded as primitive. It does not have to be constructed in terms of possible worlds. Metaphysically, however, it may be doubted whether this approach would really free us from an ontological commitment to colors.

4.3   Similar worlds with disjoint domains

It is a controversial question whether there is a possible world just like the actual world qualitatively but with none of the same individuals as the actual world. Nothing maintained in the present essay settles this question. It is not difficult to construct such a world on my principles: there is one if there is a world-story containing no singular propositions and no propositions that are not true. The question remains whether there is such a world-story – or in other words, whether what would be constructed in that way is possible.

My metaphysical views begin to be more constraining, however, when the question is raised whether there could be *two* possible worlds just like the actual world qualitatively but sharing no individual with the actual world or with each other. We can take a first step toward the construction of such worlds. If there is a world-story containing no singular propositions and no propositions that are not true, by virtue of its completeness as a world-story it must contain all true non-singular propositions. Hence it itself contains the proposition,

(9)   There is a world-story containing no singular propositions and no propositions that are not true.

For (9) is a non-singular proposition, and true in this case. So if there were a world w just like the actual world qualitatively, but with entirely different individuals, it would be true in w that there is a possible world w' just like w qualitatively but with entirely different individuals.

The next stage of the construction collapses into the abyss of non-being, however. For the question whether w' is distinct from α (the world that in fact is actual) has no answer. It is not a fact that the individuals of w' are the same as those of α, nor that all or some of them are distinct from the individuals of α. There are no relations at all between w' and α; indeed it is somewhat misleading to speak of them in the same sentence. For in α there is no distinction between w and w', since there is in α only *one* world-story containing no singular propositions and no propositions that are not true. And in w, for the same reason, there would be no distinction between w' and α.

From the standpoint of a first world (α), figuratively speaking, there may be a second possible world just like the first but with entirely different individuals. In the first world, however, there is no distinction between the individuals of a second such world and those of a third, since the individuals of the second world do not exist and there are no singular propositions about them. *In* a second such world its individuals would indeed be distinguishable from those of other similar worlds, but there the identity of the individuals of the first world would be lost. Thus there is no standpoint from which *three* perfectly similar worlds can be distinguished. I think this should be accepted as a consequence of the dependence of non-qualitative possibilities on actual individuals.

Of course we have not considered here every possible approach to the construction of three perfectly similar possible worlds, but I doubt that any approach will succeed, except perhaps for very special sorts of world. (For example, could there be three perfectly similar possible worlds entirely populated by disjoint sets of individuals that exist in α?)

4.4   Interchange of non-actual individuals

The problems explored in Section 4.3 may leave the reader wondering how I can say (as I did in Section 3.2) that there could be a pair of possible worlds that differed from each other only by the interchange of two individuals that do not exist in the actual world. One answer to this question is that there could be such a pair of possible worlds if the following is true:

$(\exists w)(\exists\phi)(\exists\psi)(\exists\phi')(\exists\psi')(w$ is a world-story & $\sim(\exists x)(w$ contains the proposition that $\phi(x))$ & $\sim(\exists y)(w$ contains the proposition that $\psi(y))$ & w does contain the proposition that $(\exists x)(\exists y)(\exists w')(\exists w'')(\phi(x)$ & $\psi(y)$ & w' is a world-story & w'' is a world-story & w' is just like w'' except that the propositions that $\phi'(x)$ and that $\psi'(y)$ are contained in w' and not in w'', and the propositions that $\phi'(y)$ and that $\psi'(x)$ are contained in w'' and not in $w'))$[16]

– where ϕ, ψ, ϕ', and ψ' range over infinitely as well as finitely complex propositional functions. In other words, the possibility of worlds that would differ only by the interchange of two individuals can be expressed in terms of a perfectly general characterization of a possible world in which both of the individuals would exist; we do not need singular propositions about the individuals for this construction.

4.5   I-pairs

An important part of the argument of Section 2 was stated in terms of I-pairs. An I-pair was defined as a pair of individuals, qualitatively indiscernible from each other, which do not exist in α (the actual world), and neither of which could have borne any relation to any individual that does exist in α that the other could not have borne to that same individual. It may be suspected that this definition violates constraints imposed by my own position. The notion of an I-pair is related to the problem discussed in Section 4.4; for if an I-pair existed, there would presumably be possible worlds differing only by interchange of the members of the I-pair (or of sets each including one member of the I-pair). But there is also a more difficult problem about I-pairs. What do I mean by saying that neither member of the I-pair *could* have had relations that the other could not have had to any individual of α? Very likely the members of the I-pair would exist only in possible worlds from which some individual (some event, at least) that exists in α would be absent. Perhaps there is no possible world in which there would be both singular modal propositions about one or both members of the I-pair, and universal generalizations about all the individuals of α and what relations they could have had.

For this reason there may indeed be no acceptable construction of I-pairs in terms of what would be true *in* one or more possible worlds. But from my point of view there is an acceptable construction in terms of what would be true *at* some possible world. An I-pair would exist in any possible world w that satisfies, from the standpoint of α, the following three conditions with respect to some property or propositional function ϕ:

(10) $\sim(\exists x)(\text{at } w \text{ it is true that } \phi(x))$

(11)   At w it is true that $(\exists x)(\exists y)(\phi(x)$ & $\phi(y)$ & x is qualitatively indiscernible from $y)$

(12) $\sim(\exists z)(\text{at } w \text{ it is true that } (\exists\psi)[(\exists x)(\phi(x)$ & $\Diamond\psi(x, z))$ & $(\exists y)(\phi(y)$ & $\sim\Diamond\psi(y, z))])$

These conditions will be satisfied by any possible world represented or constituted, in α, by a world-story that contains no singular propositions but contains the proposition that $(\exists x)(\exists y)(x$ is qualitatively indiscernible from $y)$. That any such world satisfies (10) and (11), with respect to some property or propositional function ϕ (existence, for example) is obvious. It also satisfies (12) with respect to any ϕ at all. For a world-story, in α, that contains no singular propositions represents or constitutes a possible world in which no individual of α would exist. And at any such world, for any individual z that exists in α, it is false that $(\exists\psi)(\exists x)\Diamond(\psi(x,z))$, by a natural extension of (C7) to deal with quantification over variables in predicate position.

The satisfaction of (12) is trivial in this case (and perhaps in all cases in which all three conditions are satisfied). This triviality may give rise to a suspicion that (10), (11), and (12) are not jointly equivalent to any set of conditions that one would regard as jointly sufficient for the possibility of an I-pair if one held metaphysical views that differed from mine on some of the issues discussed in the present paper.

Even if this construction should fail to capture the original notion of an I-pair, however, that notion is a ladder by which we have climbed up but which we could afford to kick away now. I assumed that *if* my thesis, that all possibilities are purely qualitative except insofar as they involve actual individuals, is false, *then* there should be *both* possibilities of I-pairs *and* possibilities for one member of an I-pair that are distinct from similar possibilities for the other. Then I argued that there are no distinct possibilities of the latter sort. The force of my argument would not be impaired if I were obliged to conclude that there are no possibilities of I-pairs at all. It is those who reject my thesis who have reason to insist (and no reason to deny) that there could be I-pairs.

Notes

In writing and revising this paper I have been helped by current and past discussions with many people, including Marilyn McCord Adams, Keith Donnellan, Daniel Hunter, David Kaplan, Saul Kripke, Alvin Plantinga, and Nathan Salmon. I am particularly indebted to Tyler Burge, Kit Fine, and David Lewis, for reading versions of the paper and giving me helpful comments. Thanks are due to all the participants in discussions at the New Jersey Regional Philosophical Association (December 1979), the Rice University Spring Philosophy Conference (March 1980), and the Catholic University of America (April 1980), where versions or parts of the paper were read. It was written during a sabbatical leave granted by UCLA and spent as a visiting fellow at Princeton University and Princeton Theological Seminary; I am happy to express my appreciation to all three institutions.

1   I used to object to this broad use of 'essence,' on the ground that historically 'essence' has referred only to purely qualitative properties (Adams, 1977, p. 187; 1979b, p. 6). I have changed my mind, chiefly because we need a term with the sense that Plantinga assigns to 'essence,' and 'essence' is the term currently in use for that purpose. My historical scruples are slightly undercut also by the observation that while Scotus does insist that haecceities are "distinct from every quidditative entity," he also seems to regard the haecceity as the bottom term ("*infimum*") in the ordering of predicates "*sub ratione essentiae*," where essence is being contrasted with existence (Duns Scotus, 1973, pp. 480 and 419f. – i.e., Dist. 3, Part 1, Questions 5–6 and 3). Nonetheless we must be very clear that the properties most often spoken of historically as "essences" are purely qualitative.

2   See Adams, 1979b, pp. 6–9, for more on this and on the meaning of 'purely qualitative.'

3   Plausibly enough; but cf. Section 4.5 below.

4   For interesting discussions of this question see Edwards, 1957, p. 391, and Prior, 1978, p. 142. The

position I am defending in this essay is reminiscent of views of Prior's, though with some differences; see especially Prior, 1960.

5   This bears on a question discussed (too briefly) in Adams, 1979a, p. 55f. Could God have created *you* without all the evils that preceded your coming to be? It might be suggested that He could have done so by simply deciding to create something having your thisness in a world without those evils. But I am claiming here that thisnesses of possible individuals are not available to God for that kind of decision. This thesis may be of some use for theodicy, but some theologians may be offended by the implication that God does not know as possible all the singular propositions that would actually be true if He created certain sorts of world (cf. Duns Scotus, 1894, p. 35, col. 2, top – i.e., Book 2, Dist. 12, qu. 7). And we may speculate that Leibniz (i) believed that primitive thisnesses would depend on the actual existence of the thisses, (ii) saw that primitive thisnesses would therefore be a feature of the world that God could not have known as possible independently of which world He actualized, and (iii) regarded this consequence as theologically objectionable. I think this may have been one of Leibniz's motives for rejecting primitive thisnesses and affirming the necessity of the identity of indiscernibles.

6   Duns Scotus, to whom we owe the term 'haecceity,' seems to have held a theory of this sort. See especially Duns Scotus, 1973, pp. 416–421 and 474–484 – i.e., Dist. 3, Part 1, Questions 2, 3 and 5–6. I am indebted to Marilyn McCord Adams for acquainting me with relevant Scotistic texts and views, and for much discussion about them. See also Brown, 1979.

7   Something similar, called "the Indifference Principle," is advocated in Fine, 1977, p. 132. Fine there provisionally adopts a "Falsehood Convention" that is (at least roughly) equivalent to (C2) and (C4) in the criterion I shall develop below; but I do not regard (C2) and (C4) as merely conventional.

8   Thus I am essentially in agreement with the treatment of this problem in terms of a distinction between "predicative" and "impredicative" singular propositions in Plantinga, 1974, pp. 149–51. The distinction seems both more intelligible and more attractive to me now than it did in Adams, 1977, p. 185f.

9   The inference from $\ulcorner\phi(a)\urcorner$ alone can be allowed if $\ulcorner\phi(a)\urcorner$ is atomic. This refinement does not matter in (C5) because atomic $\ulcorner\phi(a)\urcorner$ will not be true at any possible world unless $\ulcorner\phi(a)$ & a exists$\urcorner$ is true at that world too.

10 It is crucial to this argument that it is about *propositions*, and I hold that there are no singular

propositions about non-actual individuals. I do not mean to be making any pronouncement, one way or the other, about the validity of EG, in the actual world, as applied to *linguistic utterances* containing proper names or other individual constants.

11   That (8) will not hold "once the contingent existence of propositions is allowed," is pointed out by Fine, 1977, p. 136.

12   There are related problems about the notion of a qualitative essence of an individual. Such an essence would be equivalent, in a way, to the individual's thisness. Under my preferred treatment of singular modal propositions, however, interchange of the qualitative essence and the thisness in a proposition will not always preserve truth *at* a possible world, and therefore will not always preserve *truth* in a modal proposition. If $\ulcorner\phi(\ )\urcorner$ expresses a qualitative essence of a contingent being *a*, then $\ulcorner\Diamond(\exists x)(\phi(x))\urcorner$ as a purely qualitative modal proposition, will be true, and $\ulcorner\Diamond(\exists x)(x = a)\urcorner$ as a singular modal proposition about *a*, will be false, *at* possible worlds in which *a* does not exist, although the two propositions will have the same truth value in every possible world in which they both exist. And $\ulcorner\Box\Diamond(\exists x)(x = a)\urcorner$ will be simply *false* although $\ulcorner\Box\Diamond(\exists x)(\phi(x))\urcorner$ will be true. This pattern should be familiar to us by now. And we can say in general, if $\ulcorner\phi(\ )\urcorner$ expresses a qualitative essence of *a*,

(13) $\Box(\forall x)(\phi(x) \equiv x = a)$

is true: at every possible world, nothing but *a* is ϕ and *a* is ϕ if *a* exists. But by clause (C6) of my criterion for truth at a possible world, (13) is false *at* possible worlds in which *a* does not exist. Therefore

(14) $\Box\Box(\forall x)(\phi(x) \equiv x = a)$,

the necessitation of (13), is simply false.

13   An analogous distinction between strong and weak modal operators was proposed in Prior, 1957, ch. 5, for dealing with the problem under discussion here. In Prior's system Q, however, singular propositions are neither true nor false at worlds in which individuals they are about do not exist.

14   It is noted by Fine, 1977, p. 139.

15   After considerable thought and discussion I am uncertain to what extent the proposals for actualistic construction of possibilist quantifiers and of various entities from the universe of possibilism in Fine, 1977, can be reconciled with my principles. This is left as a problem to the reader. (Hint: Is the motivation of some of Fine's definitions in conflict with (C6) and (C7)?)

16   This is a construction for a pair of worlds in which both of the interchanged individuals would exist in both worlds. It is easy to modify it to construct a pair of worlds in which each of the interchanged individuals would exist in only one world of the pair (though both would exist in a common world that provides a starting point).

References

Adams, Robert Merrihew: 1974, 'Theories of Actuality,' *Noûs* 8, 211–31; reprinted in Loux, 1979.

Adams, Robert Merrihew: 1977, 'Critical Study: The *Nature of Necessity* (A. Plantinga),' *Noûs* 11, 175–91.

Adams, Robert Merrihew: 1979a, 'Existence, Self-Interest, and the Problem of Evil,' *Noûs* 13, 53–65.

Adams, Robert Merrithew: 1979b, 'Primitive Thisness and Primitive Identity,' *The Journal of Philosophy* 76, 5–26.

Brown, O. J.: 1979, 'Individuation and Actual Existence in Scotistic Metaphysics: A Thomistic Assessment,' *New Scholasticism* 53, 347–61.

Duns Scotus, Joannes: 1894, *Opera Omnia* (Wadding edition, revised), vol. 23 (*Reportata Parisiensia*), Vivès, Paris.

Duns Scotus, Joannes: 1973, *Opera Omnia* (Vatican edition), vol. 7 (*Ordinatio*, Book 2, Dist. 1–3), Vatican Press, Vatican City.

Edwards, Jonathan: 1957, *Freedom of the Will*, ed. by Paul Ramsey, Yale University Press, New Haven and London.

Fine, Kit: 1977, 'Postscript' in A. N. Prior and Kit Fine, *Worlds, Times and Selves*. University of Massachusetts Press, Amherst.

Loux, Michael J. (editor): 1979, *The Possible and the Actual: Readings in the Metaphysics of Modality*, Cornell University Press, Ithaca.

Plantinga, Alvin: 1974, *The Nature of Necessity*, Clarendon Press, Oxford.

Plantinga, Alvin: 1976, 'Actualism and Possible Worlds,' *Theoria* 42, 139–60; reprinted in Loux, 1979.

Prior, A. N.: 1957, *Time and Modality*, Clarendon Press, Oxford.

Prior, A. N.: 1960, 'Identifiable Individuals,' *Review of Metaphysics* 13, 684–96.

Prior, A. N.: 1978, *Past, Present and Future*, Clarendon Press, Oxford.

16

A Philosopher's Paradise

David Lewis

1.1 The Thesis of Plurality of Worlds

The world we live in is a very inclusive thing. Every stick and every stone you have ever seen is part of it. And so are you and I. And so are the planet Earth, the solar system, the entire Milky Way, the remote galaxies we see through telescopes, and (if there are such things) all the bits of empty space between the stars and galaxies. There is nothing so far away from us as not to be part of our world. Anything at any distance at all is to be included. Likewise the world is inclusive in time. No long-gone ancient Romans, no long-gone pterodactyls, no long-gone primordial clouds of plasma are too far in the past, nor are the dead dark stars too far in the future, to be part of this same world. Maybe, as I myself think, the world is a big physical object; or maybe some parts of it are entelechies or spirits or auras or deities or other things unknown to physics. But nothing is so alien in kind as not to be part of our world, provided only that it does exist at some distance and direction from here, or at some time before or after or simultaneous with now.

The way things are, at its most inclusive, means the way this entire world is. But things might have been different, in ever so many ways. This book of mine might have been finished on schedule. Or, had I not been such a commonsensical chap, I might be defending not only a plurality of possible worlds, but also a plurality of impossible worlds, whereof you speak truly by contradicting yourself. Or I might not have existed at all – neither I myself, nor any counterpart of me. Or there might never have been any people. Or the physical constants might have had somewhat different values, incompatible with the emergence of life. Or there might have been altogether different laws of nature; and instead of electrons and quarks, there might have been alien particles, without charge or mass or spin but with alien physical properties that nothing in this world shares. There are ever so many ways that a world might be; and one of these many ways is the way that this world is.

Are there other worlds that are other ways? I say there are, I advocate a thesis of plurality of worlds, or *modal realism*,[1] which holds that our world is but one world among many. There are countless other worlds, other very inclusive things. Our world consists of us and all our surroundings, however remote in time and space; just as it is one big thing having lesser things as

David Lewis, "A Philosopher's Paradise: The Plurality of Worlds," from chapter 1 of Lewis, *On the Plurality of Worlds* (Oxford: Blackwell, 1968). Reprinted by permission of John Wiley & Sons, Inc.

Metaphysics: An Anthology, Second Edition. Edited by Jaegwon Kim, Daniel Z. Korman and Ernest Sosa.
Editorial material and organization © 2012 Blackwell Publishing Ltd. Published 2012 by Blackwell Publishing Ltd.

parts, so likewise do other worlds have lesser otherworldly things as parts. The worlds are something like remote planets; except that most of them are much bigger than mere planets, and they are not remote. Neither are they nearby. They are not at any spatial distance whatever from here. They are not far in the past or future, nor for that matter near; they are not at any temporal distance whatever from now. They are isolated: there are no spatiotemporal relations at all between things that belong to different worlds. Nor does anything that happens at one world cause anything to happen at another. Nor do they overlap; they have no parts in common, with the exception, perhaps, of immanent universals exercising their characteristic privilege of repeated occurrence.

The worlds are many and varied. There are enough of them to afford worlds where (roughly speaking) I finish on schedule, or I write on behalf of *impossibilia*, or I do not exist, or there are no people at all, or the physical constants do not permit life, or totally different laws govern the doings of alien particles with alien properties. There are so many other worlds, in fact, that absolutely *every* way that a world could possibly be is a way that some world *is*. And as with worlds, so it is with parts of worlds. There are ever so many ways that a part of a world could be; and so many and so varied are the other worlds that absolutely every way that a part of a world could possibly be is a way that some part of some world is.

The other worlds are of a kind with this world of ours. To be sure, there are differences of kind between things that are parts of different worlds – one world has electrons and another has none, one has spirits and another has none – but these differences of kind are no more than sometimes arise between things that are parts of one single world, for instance in a world where electrons coexist with spirits. The difference between this and the other worlds is not a categorial difference.

Nor does this world differ from the others in its manner of existing. I do not have the slightest idea what a difference in manner of existing is supposed to be. Some things exist here on earth, other things exist extraterrestrially, perhaps some exist no place in particular; but that is no difference in manner of existing, merely a difference in location or lack of it between things that exist. Likewise some things exist here at our world, others exist at other worlds; again, I take this to be a difference between

things that exist, not a difference in their existing. You might say that strictly speaking, only this-worldly things *really* exist; and I am ready enough to agree; but on my view this 'strict' speaking is *restricted* speaking, on a par with saying that all the beer is in the fridge and ignoring most of all the beer there is. When we quantify over less than all there is, we leave out things that (unrestrictedly speaking) exist *simpliciter*. If I am right, other-worldly things exist *simpliciter*, though often it is very sensible to ignore them and quantify restrictedly over our worldmates. And if I am wrong, other-worldly things fail *simpliciter* to exist. They exist, as the Russell set does, only according to a false theory. That is not to exist in some inferior manner – what exists only according to some false theory just does not exist at all.

The worlds are not of our own making. It may happen that one part of a world makes other parts, as we do; and as other-worldly gods and demiurges do on a grander scale. But if worlds are causally isolated, nothing outside a world ever makes a world; and nothing inside makes the whole of a world, for that would be an impossible kind of self-causation. We make languages and concepts and descriptions and imaginary representations that apply to worlds. We make stipulations that select some worlds rather than others for our attention. Some of us even make assertions to the effect that other worlds exist. But none of these things we make are the worlds themselves.

Why believe in a plurality of worlds? – Because the hypothesis is serviceable, and that is a reason to think that it is true. The familiar analysis of necessity as truth at all possible worlds was only the beginning. In the last two decades, philosophers have offered a great many more analyses that make reference to possible worlds, or to possible individuals that inhabit possible worlds. I find that record most impressive. I think it is clear that talk of *possibilia* has clarified questions in many parts of the philosophy of logic, of mind, of language, and of science – not to mention metaphysics itself. Even those who officially scoff often cannot resist the temptation to help themselves abashedly to this useful way of speaking.

Hilbert called the set-theoretical universe a paradise for mathematicians. And he was right (though perhaps it was not he who should have said it). We have only to believe in the vast hierarchy of sets, and there we find entities suited to meet the needs of all the branches of mathematics;[2] and we find that the very meagre primitive vocabulary of set theory, definitionally extended, suffices to meet our needs for mathematical predicates; and we find that the meagre axioms of set theory are first principles enough to yield the theorems that are the content of the subject. Set theory offers the mathematician great economy of primitives and premises, in return for accepting rather a lot of entities unknown to *Homo javanensis*. It offers an improvement in what Quine calls ideology, paid for in the coin of ontology. It's an offer you can't refuse. The price is right; the benefits in theoretical unity and economy are well worth the entities. Philosophers might like to see the subject reconstructed or reconstrued; but working mathematicians insist on pursuing their subject in paradise, and will not be driven out. Their thesis of plurality of sets is fruitful; that gives them good reason to believe that it is true.

Good reason; I do not say it is conclusive. Maybe the price is higher than it seems because set theory has unacceptable hidden implications – maybe the next round of set-theoretical paradoxes will soon be upon us. Maybe the very idea of accepting controversial ontology for the sake of theoretical benefits is misguided – so a sceptical epistemologist might say, to which I reply that mathematics is better known than any premise of sceptical epistemology. Or perhaps some better paradise might be found. Some say that mathematics might be pursued in a paradise of *possibilia*, full of unactualised idealisations of things around us, or of things we do – if so, the parallel with mathematics serves my purpose better than ever! Conceivably we might find some way to accept set theory, just as is and just as nice a home for mathematics, without any ontological commitment to sets. But even if such hopes come true, my point remains. It has been the judgement of mathematicians, which modest philosophers ought to respect, that *if* that is indeed the choice before us, then it is worth believing in vast realms of controversial entities for the sake of enough benefit in unity and economy of theory.

As the realm of sets is for mathematicians, so logical space is a paradise for philosophers. We have only to believe in the vast realm of *possibilia*, and there we find what we need to advance our endeavours. We find the wherewithal to reduce the diversity of notions we must accept as primitive, and thereby to improve the unity and economy of the theory that is our professional concern – total theory, the whole of what we take to be true. What price paradise? If we want the theoretical benefits that talk of *possibilia* brings, the most straightforward way to gain honest title to them is to accept such talk as the literal truth. It is my view that the price is right, if less spectacularly so than in the mathematical parallel. The benefits are worth their ontological cost. Modal realism is fruitful; that gives us good reason to believe that it is true.

Good reason; I do not say it is conclusive. Maybe the theoretical benefits to be gained are illusory, because the analyses that use *possibilia* do not succeed on their own terms. Maybe the price is higher than it seems, because modal realism has unacceptable hidden implications. Maybe the price is *not* right; even if I am right about what theoretical benefits can be had for what ontological cost, maybe those benefits just are not worth those costs. Maybe the very idea of accepting controversial ontology for the sake of theoretical benefits is misguided. Maybe – and this is the doubt that most interests me – the benefits are not worth the cost, because they can be had more cheaply elsewhere. Some of these doubts are too complicated to address here, or too simple to address at all; others will come in for discussion in the course of this book.

1.2 Modal Realism at Work: Modality

In the next four sections, I consider what possible worlds and individuals are good for. Even a long discussion might be too short to convince all readers that the applications I have in mind are workable at all, still less that approaches employing *possibilia* are superior to all conceivable rivals. (Still less that *possibilia* are absolutely indispensable, something I don't believe myself.) Each application could have a book of its own. Here I shall settle for less.

The best known application is to modality. Presumably, whatever it may mean to call a world actual (see section 1.9), it had better turn out that the world we are part of is the actual world. What actually is the case, as we say, is what goes on here. That is one possible way for a world to be. Other worlds are other, that is *un*actualised, possibilities. If there are many worlds, and every way that a world could possibly be is a way that some world is, then whenever such-and-such might be the case, there is some world where such-and-such is the case. Conversely, since it is safe to say that no world is any way that a world could not possibly be, whenever there is some world at which such-and-such is the case, then it might be that such-and-such is the case. So modality turns into quantification: possibly there are blue swans iff, for some world W, at W there are blue swans.

But not just quantification: there is also the phrase 'at W' which appears within the scope of the quantifier, and which needs explaining. It works mainly by restricting the domains of quantifiers in its scope, in much the same way that the restricting modifier 'in Australia' does. In Australia, all swans are black – all swans are indeed black, if we ignore everything not in Australia; quantifying only over things in Australia, all swans are black. At some strange world W, all swans are blue – all swans are indeed blue, if we ignore everything not part of the world W; quantifying only over things that are part of W, all swans are blue.

[...]

As possibility amounts to existential quantification over the worlds, with restricting modifiers inside the quantifiers, so necessity amounts to universal quantification. Necessarily all swans are birds iff, for any world W, quantifying only over parts of W, all swans are birds. More simply: iff all swans, no matter what world they are part of, are birds. The other modalities follow suit. What is impossible is the case at no worlds; what is contingent is the case at some but not at others.

More often than not, modality is *restricted* quantification; and restricted from the standpoint of a given world, perhaps ours, by means of so-called 'accessibility' relations. Thus it is nomologically necessary, though not unrestrictedly necessary, that friction produces heat: at every world that obeys the laws of our world, friction produces heat. It is contingent which world is ours; hence what are the laws of our world; hence which worlds are nomologically 'accessible' from ours; hence what is true throughout these worlds, i.e. what is nomologically necessary.

Likewise it is historically necessary, now as I write these words, that my book is at least partly

written: at every world that perfectly matches ours up to now, and diverges only later if ever, the book is at least partly written.

Putting together nomological and historical accessibility restrictions, we get the proper treatment of predetermination – a definition free of red herrings about what can in principle be known and computed, or about the analysis of causation. It was predetermined at his creation that Adam would sin iff he does so at every world that both obeys the laws of our world and perfectly matches the history of our world up through the moment of Adam's creation.

As other worlds are alternative possibilities for an entire world, so the parts of other worlds are alternative possibilities for lesser individuals. Modality *de re*, the potentiality and essence of things, is quantification over possible individuals. As quantification over possible worlds is commonly restricted by accessibility relations, so quantification over possible individuals is commonly restricted by counterpart relations. In both cases, the restrictive relations usually involve similarity. A nomologically or historically accessible world is similar to our world in the laws it obeys, or in its history up to some time. Likewise a counterpart of Oxford is similar to Oxford in its origins, or in its location *vis-à-vis* (counterparts of) other places, or in the arrangement and nature of its parts, or in the role it plays in the life of a nation or a discipline. Thus Oxford might be noted more for the manufacture of locomotives than of motor cars, or might have been a famous centre for the study of paraconsistent hermeneutics, iff some other-worldly counterpart of our Oxford, under some suitable counterpart relation, enjoys these distinctions.

Sometimes one hears a short list of the restricted modalities: nomological, historical, epistemic, deontic, maybe one or two more. And sometimes one is expected to take a position, once and for all, about what is or isn't possible *de re* for an individual. I would suggest instead that the restricting of modalities by accessibility or counterpart relations, like the restricting of quantifiers generally, is a very fluid sort of affair: inconstant, somewhat indeterminate, and subject to instant change in response to contextual pressures. Not anything goes, but a great deal does. And to a substantial extent, saying so makes it so: if you say what would only be true under

adhering to identical natural laws / logic

certain restrictions, and your conversational partners acquiesce, straightway those restrictions come into force.[3]

The standard language of modal logic provides just two modal expressions: the diamond, read as 'possibly', and the box, read as 'necessarily'. Both are sentential operators: they attach to sentences to make sentences, or to open formulas to make open formulas. So a modal logician will write

◊ for some x, x is a swan and x is blue

to mean that possibly some swan is blue, i.e. that there might be a blue swan; or

□ for all x, if x is a swan then x is a bird

to mean that necessarily all swans are birds. Likewise

◊ x is blue

is a formula satisfied by anything that could possibly be blue, and

□ x is a bird

is a formula satisfied by anything that must necessarily be a bird. When they attach to sentences we can take the diamond and the box as quantifiers, often restricted, over possible worlds. How to take them when they attach to open formulas – sentential expressions with unbound variables – is more questionable.

A simple account would be that in that case also they are just quantifiers over worlds. But that raises a question. Start with something that is part of this world: Hubert Humphrey, say. He might have won the presidency but didn't, so he satisfies the modal formula 'possibly x wins' but not the formula 'x wins'. Taking the diamond 'possibly' as a quantifier over worlds, (perhaps restricted, but let me ignore that), that means that there is some world W such that, at W, he satisfies 'x wins'. But how does he do that if he isn't even part of W?

You might reply that he *is* part of W as well as part of this world. If this means that the whole of him is part of W, I reject that for reasons to be

given in section 4.2 [chapter 4 is not included in this selection]; if it means that part of him is part of W, I reject that for reasons to be given in section 4.3. Then to save the simple account, we have to say that Humphrey needn't be part of a world to satisfy formulas there; there is a world where somehow he satisfies 'x wins' *in absentia*.

We might prefer a more complex account of how modal operators work.[4] We might say that when 'possibly' is attached to open formulas, it is a quantifier not just over worlds but also over other-worldly counterparts of this-worldly individuals; so that Humphrey satisfies 'possibly x wins' iff, for some world W, for some counterpart of Humphrey in W, that counterpart satisfies 'x wins' at W. The satisfaction of 'x wins' by the counterpart is unproblematic. Now we need no satisfaction *in absentia*.

The simple and complex accounts are not in competition. Both do equally well, because there is a counterpart-theoretic account of satisfaction *in absentia* that makes them come out equivalent. Satisfaction *in absentia* is vicarious satisfaction: Humphrey satisfies 'x wins' vicariously at any world where he has a winning counterpart. Then according to both accounts alike, he satisfies 'possibly x wins' iff at some world he has a counterpart who wins.

The box and diamond are interdefinable: 'necessarily' means 'not possibly not'. So what I have said for one carries over to the other. According to the simple account, Humphrey satisfies the modal formula 'necessarily x is human' iff it is not the case that there is some world W such that, at W, he satisfies 'x is not human'; that is, iff at no world does he satisfy – *in absentia* or otherwise – x is not human'. According to the complex account, Humphrey satisfies 'necessarily x is human' iff it is not the case that for some world W, for some counterpart of Humphrey in W, that counterpart satisfies 'x is not human' at W; that is, iff there is no counterpart in any world of Humphrey who satisfies 'x is not human'. Taking satisfaction *in absentia* to be vicarious satisfaction through a counterpart, the simple and complex accounts again agree: Humphrey satisfies 'necessarily x is human' iff he has no non-human counterpart at any world.

(It is plausible enough that Humphrey has no non-human counterpart. Or, if I am right to say that counterpart relations are an inconstant and indeterminate affair, at any rate it is plausible enough that there is *some* reasonable counterpart relation under which Humphrey has no non-human counterpart – so let's fix on such a counterpart relation for the sake of the example.)

The alert or informed reader will know that if what I've said about how Humphrey satisfies modal formulas sounds right, that is only because I took care to pick the right examples. A famous problem arises if instead we consider whether Humphrey satisfies modal formulas having to do with the contingency of his existence. According to what I've said, be it in the simple or the complex formulation, Humphrey satisfies 'necessarily x exists' and fails to satisfy 'possibly x does not exist' iff he has no counterpart at any world W who does not exist at W. But what can it mean to say that the counterpart is 'at W' if not that, at W, the counterpart exists?[5] So it seems that Humphrey *does* satisfy 'necessarily x exists' and *doesn't* satisfy 'possibly x does not exist'. That is wrong. For all his virtues, still it really will not do to elevate Humphrey to the ranks of the Necessary Beings.

What I want to say, of course, is that Humphrey exists necessarily iff at every world he has some counterpart, which he doesn't; he has the possibility of not existing iff at some world he lacks a counterpart, which he does. It's all very well to say this; but the problem is to square it with my general account of the satisfaction of modal formulas.

So shall we give a revised account of the satisfaction of modal formulas? Should we say that Humphrey satisfies 'necessarily ϕx' iff at every world he has some counterpart who satisfies 'ϕx'? Then, by the interdefinability of box and diamond, Humphrey satisfies 'possibly x is a cat' iff it is not the case that at every world he has some counterpart who satisfies 'not x is a cat': and indeed that is not the case, since at some worlds he has no counterparts at all; so it seems that he *does* satisfy 'possibly x is a cat' even if he has not a single cat among his counterparts! This is no improvement. What next?

Shall we dump the method of counterparts? – That wouldn't help, because we can recreate the problem in a far more neutral framework. Let us suppose only this much. (1) We want to treat the modal operators simply as quantifiers over worlds. (2) We want to grant that Humphrey somehow satisfies various formulas at various other worlds, never mind how he does it. (3) We want it to come out that he satisfies the modal formula 'necessarily x is human', since that seems to be the way to say something true, namely that he is essentially human. (4) We want it to come out that he satisfies the modal formula 'possibly x does not exist', since that seems to be the way to say something else true, namely that he might not have existed. (5) We want it to come out that he does *not* satisfy the model formula 'possibly x is human and x does not exist' since that seems to be the way to say something false, namely that he might have been human without even existing. So he satisfies 'x is human' at all worlds and 'x does not exist' at some worlds; so he satisfies both of them at some worlds; yet though he satisfies both conjuncts he doesn't satisfy their conjunction! How can that be?

There might be a fallacy of equivocation. Maybe what it means for Humphrey to satisfy a formula *in absentia* is different in the case of different kinds of formulas, or in the case of different kinds of worlds. Maybe, for instance, he can satisfy 'x does not exist' at a world by not having a counterpart there; but to satisfy 'x is human' at a world he has to have a counterpart there who is human, and to satisfy 'x is human and x does not exist' he would have to have one who was human and yet did not exist. Or maybe the language is uniformly ambiguous, and different cases invite different disambiguations. Either way, that would disappoint anyone who hopes that the language of quantified modal logic will be a well-behaved formal language, free of ambiguity and free of devious semantic rules that work different ways in different cases.

Or maybe the satisfying of modal formulas does not always mean what we would intuitively take it to mean after we learn how to pronounce the box and diamond. Maybe, for instance, saying that Humphrey satisfies 'necessarily x is human' is *not* the right way to say that he is essentially human. That would disappoint anyone who hopes that the language of boxes and diamonds affords a good regimentation of our ordinary modal thought.

Whichever it is, the friend of boxes and diamonds is in for a disappointment. He can pick his disappointment to suit himself. He can lay down uniform and unambiguous semantic rules for a regimented formal language – and re-educate his intuitions about how to translate between that language and ordinary modal talk. He can

[margin, handwritten] Perhaps just speak of Humphrey's counterpart x to ϕx → still bearing a relation to humphrey, but not 'as humphrey'.

discipline himself, for instance, never to say 'necessarily human' when he means 'essentially human'; but instead, always to say 'necessarily such that it is human if it exists'. Alternatively, he can build his language more on the pattern of what we ordinarily say – and equip it either with outright ambiguities, or else with devious rules that look at what a formula says before they know what it means to satisfy it.[6]

What is the correct counterpart-theoretic interpretation of the modal formulas of the standard language of quantified modal logic? – Who cares? We can make them mean whatever we like. We are their master. We needn't be faithful to the meanings we learned at mother's knee – because we didn't. If this language of boxes and diamonds proves to be a clumsy instrument for talking about matters of essence and potentiality, let it go hang. Use the resources of modal realism *directly* to say what it would mean for Humphrey to be essentially human, or to exist contingently.

[…]

Another modal notion which is badly served by diamonds and boxes is supervenience. The idea is simple and easy: we have supervenience when there could be no difference of one sort without differences of another sort. At least, this *seems* simple and easy enough; and yet in recent discussions[7] we get an unlovely proliferation of non-equivalent definitions. Some stick close to the original idea but seem too weak; others seem strong enough but out of touch with the original idea. A useful notion threatens to fade away into confusion. I offer this diagnosis of the trouble. There really *is* just one simple, easy, useful idea. However, it is unavailable to those who assume that all modality must come packaged in boxes and diamonds. Therefore we get a plethora of unsatisfactory approximations and substitutes.

To see why there is a problem about formulating supervenience theses, we need a few examples. First, a fairly uncontroversial one. A dot-matrix picture has global properties – it is symmetrical, it is cluttered, and whatnot – and yet all there is to the picture is dots and non-dots at each point of the matrix. The global properties are nothing but patterns in the dots. They supervene: no two pictures could differ in their global properties without differing, somewhere, in whether there is or isn't a dot.

A second example is more controversial and interesting. The world has its laws of nature, its chances and causal relationships; and yet – perhaps! – all there is to the world is its point-by-point distribution of local qualitative character. We have a spatiotemporal arrangement of points. At each point various local intrinsic properties may be present, instantiated perhaps by the point itself or perhaps by point-sized bits of matter or of fields that are located there. There may be properties of mass, charge, quark colour and flavour, field strength, and the like; and maybe others besides, if physics as we know it is inadequate to its descriptive task. Is that all? Are the laws, chances, and causal relationships nothing but patterns which supervene on this point-by-point distribution of properties? Could two worlds differ in their laws without differing, somehow, somewhere, in local qualitative character? (I discuss this question of 'Humean supervenience', inconclusively, in the Introduction to my *Philosophical Papers*, volume II.)

A third example. A person has a mental life of attitudes and experiences and yet – perhaps! – all there is to him is an arrangement of physical particles, interacting in accordance with physical laws. Does the mental supervene on the physical? We can distinguish two questions. (1) *Narrow* psychophysical supervenience: could two people differ mentally without also themselves differing physically? (2) *Broad* psychophysical supervenience: could two people differ mentally without there being a physical difference somewhere, whether in the people themselves or somewhere in their surroundings? We can also distinguish questions in another way, cross-cutting the distinction of narrow and broad, depending on how restricted a range of possibilities we consider. If we restrict ourselves to worlds that obey the actual laws of nature, then even a dualist might accept some kind of psychophysical supervenience, if he believes in strict laws of psychophysical correlation. If we impose no restriction at all, then even a staunch materialist might reject all kinds of psychophysical supervenience, if he takes materialism to be a contingent truth. If we want to define materialism in terms of psychophysical supervenience, we will have to steer between these extremes.[8]

Supervenience means that there *could* be no difference of the one sort without difference of the other sort. Clearly, this 'could' indicates modality. Without the modality we have nothing of interest. No two dot-for-dot duplicate pictures differ in symmetry; they could not, and that is why symmetry is nothing but a pattern in the arrangement of dots. Maybe also it happens that no two dot-for-dot duplicate pictures differ in their origins. But if so, that just means that a certain sort of coincidence happens not to have occurred; it doesn't mean that the origin of a picture is nothing but a pattern in the arrangement of dots. Dot-for-dot duplicates perfectly well could come from different origins, whether or not they ever actually do.

So we might read the 'could' as a diamond – a modal operator 'possibly' which modifies sentences. 'There could be no difference of the one sort without difference of the other sort' – read this to mean that it is not the case that, possibly, there are two things which have a difference of the one sort without any difference of the other sort. That is: it is not the case that there is some world W such that, at W, two things have a difference of the one sort but not the other. That is, taking 'at W' as usual as a restricting modifier: there is no world wherein two things have a difference of the one sort but not the other. Is this an adequate way to formulate supervenience?

Sometimes it is. It will do well enough to state our supervenience theses about dot-matrix pictures. Symmetry (or whatnot) supervenes on the arrangement of the dots iff there is no world wherein two pictures differ in symmetry without differing in their arrangement of dots. It will do also to state narrow psychophysical supervenience: that thesis says that there is no world (or, none within a certain restriction) wherein two people differ mentally without themselves differing physically. So far, so good.

But sometimes the formulation with a diamond is not adequate. We start to hit trouble with the thesis of broad psychophysical supervenience. The idea is that the mental supervenes on the physical; however, the physical pattern that is relevant to a given person's mental life might extend indefinitely far outside that person and into his surroundings. Then the thesis we want says that there could be no mental difference between two people without there being some physical difference, whether intrinsic or extrinsic, between them. Reading the 'could' as a diamond, the thesis becomes this:

there is no world (or, none within a certain restriction) wherein two people differ mentally without there being some physical difference, intrinsic or extrinsic, between them. That is not quite right. We have gratuitously limited our attention to physical differences between two people in the same world, and that means ignoring those extrinsic physical differences that only ever arise between people in different worlds. For instance, we ignore the difference there is between two people if one inhabits a Riemannian and the other a Lobachevskian spacetime. So what we have said is not quite what we meant to say, but rather this: there could be no mental differences without some physical difference *of the sort that could arise between people in the same world.* The italicised part is a gratuitous addition. Perhaps it scarcely matters here. For it doesn't seem that the sort of very extrinsic physical difference that could never arise between people in the same world would make much difference to mental life. Nevertheless, insistence on reading the 'could' as a diamond has distorted the intended meaning.

For a case where the distortion is much more serious, take my second example: the supervenience of laws. We wanted to ask whether two worlds could differ in their laws without differing in their distribution of local qualitative character. But if we read the 'could' as a diamond, the thesis in question turns into this: it is not the case that, possibly, two worlds differ in their laws without differing in their distribution of local qualitative character. In other words: there is no world wherein two worlds differ in their laws without differing in their distribution of local qualitative character. That's trivial – there is no world wherein two worlds do anything. At any one world W, there is only the one single world W. The sentential modal operator disastrously restricts the quantification over worlds that lies within its scope. Better to leave it off. But we need *something* modal – the thesis is not just that the one actual world, with its one distribution of local qualitative character, has its one system of laws![9]

What we want is modality, but not the sentential modal operator. The original simple statement of supervenience is the right one, in all cases: there *could* be no difference of the one sort without difference of the other sort. What got us into trouble was to insist on reading 'could' as a diamond. Just as in the case of modalised comparatives, the real effect of the 'could' seems to be to *un*restrict quantifiers which would normally range over this-worldly things. Among all the worlds, or among all the things in all the worlds (or less than all, in case there is some restriction), there is no difference of the one sort without difference of the other sort. Whether the things that differ are part of the same world is neither here nor there. Again the moral is that we'd better have other-worldly things to quantify over – not just a primitive modal modifier of sentences.

[…]

1.3   Modal Realism at Work: Counterfactuals

A counterfactual (or 'subjunctive') conditional is an invitation to consider what goes on in a selected 'counterfactual situation'; which is to say, at some other possible world. Partly, the world in question is specified explicitly by the antecedent of the conditional: 'If kangaroos had no tails....' Partly, it is specified by a permanent understanding that there is to be no gratuitous departure from the background of fact: ignore worlds where the kangaroos float around like balloons, since the kangaroos of our world are much too heavy for that. Partly, it is specified by temporary contextual influences that indicate what sorts of departures would be especially gratuitious; for instance, facts just mentioned may have a special claim to be held fixed.

Partly, it is not specified at all: no telling whether the kangaroos have stumps where the tails should be. So it is an idealisation to think that we have to do with a single world, rather than an ill-defined class. Under that idealisation, we can say that a counterfactual conditional 'If it were that A, then it would be that C' is true iff C is true at the selected A-world. More generally, the conditional is true at a world W iff C is true at the A-world selected from the standpoint of W.[10]

[…]

If counterfactuals were no good for anything but idle fantasies about unfortunate kangaroos, then it might be faint praise to say that possible worlds can help us with counterfactuals. But, in fact, counterfactuals are by no means peripheral or dispensable to our serious thought. They are as central as causation itself. As I touch these keys,

luminous green letters appear before my eyes, and afterward black printed letters will appear before yours; and if I had touched different keys – a counterfactual supposition – then correspondingly different letters would have appeared. That is how the letters depend causally upon the keystrokes, and that is how the keystrokes cause letters to appear.

Suppose that two wholly distinct events occur, C and E; and if C had not occurred, E would not have occurred either. I say that if one event depends counterfactually on another in this way (and if it's the right sort of counterfactual, governed by the right sort of closeness of worlds) then E depends causally on C, and C is a cause of E. To be sure, this is only the beginning of a counterfactual analysis of causation. Not all counterfactuals are of the right sort, and it is a good question how to distinguish the ones that are from the ones that aren't. We need an account of eventhood, and of distinctness of events. And not all effects depend counterfactually on their causes; for instance, we may have causation by a chain of stepwise dependence, in which E depends on D which depends on C, and thereby C causes E, yet E does not depend directly on C because of some alternate cause waiting in reserve.[11] You may or may not share my optimism about an analysis of causation in terms of counterfactual dependence of events. But even if you give up hope for an analysis, still you can scarcely deny that counterfactuals and causation are well and truly entangled.

Causal theories of this, that, and the other have been deservedly popular in recent years. These theories are motivated by imagining cases where normal patterns of counterfactual dependence fail. Normally, my perceptual experience depends on what is going on around me, in such a way as to make its content largely correct. Normally, my movements depend on my beliefs and desires, in such a way that they tend to serve my beliefs according to my desires. Normally, the way I am depends on the way I was just before, in such a way as to keep change gradual. What if these normal dependences were absent? If my perceptual experience would be the same no matter what was going on around me, I would not be perceiving the world. If the movements of my body would be the same no matter what I believed and desired, those movements would not be my actions. If the man who will wake up in my bed tomorrow would be exactly the same regardless of what befell me today, he would be an impostor.

If possible worlds help with counterfactuals, then, they help with many parts of our thought that we could scarcely imagine being without.

[…]

1.4 Modal Realism at Work: Content

An inventory of the varieties of modality may include *epistemic* and *doxastic* necessity and possibility. Like other modalities, these may be explained as restricted quantification over possible worlds. To do so, we may use possible worlds to characterise the content of thought. The content of someone's knowledge of the world is given by his class of *epistemically accessible* worlds. These are the worlds that might, for all he knows, be his world; world W is one of them iff he knows nothing, either explicitly or implicitly, to rule out the hypothesis that W is the world where he lives. Likewise the content of someone's system of belief about the world (encompassing both belief that qualifies as knowledge and belief that fails to qualify) is given by his class of *doxastically accessible* worlds. World W is one of those iff he believes nothing, either explicitly or implicitly, to rule out the hypothesis that W is the world where he lives.

Whatever is true at some epistemically or doxastically accessible world is epistemically or doxastically possible for him. It might be true, for all he knows or for all he believes. He does not know or believe it to be false. Whatever is true throughout the epistemically or doxastically accessible worlds is epistemically or doxastically necessary; which is to say that he knows or believes it, perhaps explicitly or perhaps only implicitly.

Since only truths can be known, the knower's own world always must be among his epistemically accessible worlds. Not so for doxastic accessibility. If he is mistaken about anything, that is enough to prevent his own world from conforming perfectly to his system of belief.[12]

No matter how we might originally characterise the content of knowledge or belief, it ought to be possible afterward to introduce the distinction between worlds that do and worlds that do not conform to that content. That done, we could go on to introduce the epistemic and doxastic modalities. For instance if we began with a notion of belief as some sort of acceptance of interpreted sentences – perhaps of our language, perhaps of some public language the believer speaks, or perhaps of the believer's hypothetical 'language of thought' – then we could say that a doxastically accessible world is one where all the accepted sentences are true. I am quite sceptical about this order of proceeding, for reasons that need not be reviewed here.[13] A more promising plan, I think, is to characterise the content of knowledge or belief from the outset in terms of something rather like the epistemically or doxastically accessible worlds. (Let me concentrate simply on belief, passing over the added complications that arise when we distinguish someone's knowledge from the rest of his system of belief.) The class of doxastically accessible worlds is roughly what we want, but it isn't exactly right; some changes must be made.

For one thing, I said that the doxastically accessible worlds give the content of one's system of belief *about the world*; but not all belief is about the world. Some of it is egocentric belief; or, as I have called it elsewhere, 'irreducibly *de se*'.[14] Imagine someone who is completely opinionated, down to the last detail, about what sort of world he lives in and what goes on there. He lacks no belief about the world. For him, only one world is doxastically accessible. (Or, at most, one class of indiscernible worlds – let me ignore this complication.) And yet there may be questions on which he has no opinion. For instance he may think he lives in a world of one-way eternal recurrence, with a beginning but no end, with a certain course of history repeated exactly in every epoch; and he may have no idea which epoch he himself lives in. Every epoch of the world he takes to be his contains someone who might, for all he believes, be himself. He has no idea which one of them he is. If he did, for instance if he somehow became persuaded that he lived in the seventeenth epoch, he would believe more than he does. But he would not believe more about the world. The added belief would be not about the world, but about his own place therein. → still a belief about something in the world

So if we want to capture the entire content of someone's system of belief, we must include the egocentric part. We should characterise the content not by a class of possible worlds, but by a class of possible individuals – call them the believer's

the domain of these worlds will vary subject to subject → the more knowledge one has, the smaller the domain of epistemically accessible worlds *doxastic alternatives* – who might, for all he believes, be himself. Individual X is one of them iff nothing that the believer believes, either explicitly or implicitly, rules out the hypothesis that he himself is X. These individuals are the believer's doxastic possibilities. But they are not different possible ways for the world to be; rather, they are different possible ways for an individual to be, and many of them may coexist within a single world. [...] Suppose that all of someone's doxastic alternatives have a certain property; then he believes, explicitly or implicitly, that he himself has that property. [...]

1.5   Modal Realism at Work: Properties

We have frequent need, in one connection or other, to quantify over properties. If we believe in possible worlds and individuals, and if we believe in set-theoretic constructions out of things we believe in, then we have entities suited to play the role of properties.

The simplest plan is to take a property just as the set of all its instances – *all* of them, this- and other-worldly alike. Thus the property of being a donkey comes out as the set of all donkeys, the donkeys of other worlds along with the donkeys of ours.[15]

The usual objection to taking properties as sets is that different properties may happen to be coextensive. All and only the creatures with hearts are creatures with kidneys; all and only the talking donkeys are flying pigs, since there are none of either. But the property of having a heart is different from the property of having a kidney, since there could have been an animal with a heart but no kidneys. Likewise the property of being a talking donkey is different from the property of being a flying pig. If we take properties as sets, so it is said, there is no distinguishing different but accidentally coextensive properties.

But according to modal realism, these 'accidentally coextensive' properties are not coextensive at all. They only appear so when we ignore their other-worldly instances. If we consider all the instances, then it never can happen that two properties are coextensive but might not have been. It is contingent whether two properties have the same this-worldly instances. But it is not contingent whether they have the same instances *simpliciter*.

It is a mistake to say that if a property were a set, then it would have its instances – its members –

essentially, and therefore it never could be contingent whether something has or lacks it. Consider the property of being a talking donkey, which I say is the set of all talking donkeys throughout the worlds. The full membership of this set does not vary from world to world. What does vary from world to world is the subset we get by restricting ourselves to the world in question. That is how the number of instances is contingent; for instance, it is contingently true that the property has no instances. Further, it is a contingent matter whether any particular individual has the property. Take Brownie, an other-worldly talking donkey. Brownie himself is, once and for all, a member of the set; hence, once and for all, an instance of the property. But it is contingent whether Brownie talks; Brownie has counterparts who do and counterparts who don't. In just the same way, it is contingent whether Brownie belongs to the set: Brownie has counterparts who do and counterparts who don't. That is how it is contingent whether Brownie has the property.

As it is for properties, so it is for relations. An instance of a dyadic relation is an ordered pair of related things; then we may take the relation again to be the set of its instances – all of them, this- and other-worldly alike. Again, it is no problem that different relations may happen to be coextensive; for this is only to say that the this-worldly parts of the sets are the same, and there is more to a set than its this-worldly part. Again, a pair may stand in a relation contingently, if it has counterpart pairs that do and counterpart pairs that don't.[16] In the same way, a triadic relation can be taken as a set of ordered triples, and so on. Also we can include relations of variable degree, since there is no reason why pairs and triples, for instance, cannot both belong to a single set.[17]

[...]

I identify propositions with certain properties – namely, with those that are instantiated only by entire possible worlds. Then if properties generally are the sets of their instances, a proposition is a set of possible worlds. A proposition is said to *hold* at a world, or to be *true at* a world. The proposition is the same thing as the property of being a world where that proposition holds; and that is the same thing as the set of worlds where that propositions holds. A proposition holds at just those worlds that are members of it.[18]

Just as it is sometimes said that properties are had relative to this or that, so it is sometimes said that propositions hold relative to this or that. No harm in their holding at worlds, of course; but other relative holding requires a switch in what we mean by 'propositions'. For instance a *tensed* proposition, which is said to hold at some times but not others, can be taken as a set of world-time pairs; in other words a relation of worlds and times. If as I think (see section 1.6) no time is identically a common part of two different worlds, then this can be simplified: we can say that the tensed proposition is simply a property, that is a set, of times.

Likewise an *egocentric* proposition, which holds for some people but not others, could be taken as a property, that is a set, of people. And if we generalise, and countenance also egocentric propositions which hold for things other than people – such as the proposition that one is a poached egg – then we should say that the egocentric proposition is a property, that is a set, of possible individuals. But if we can already call it a 'property', what's the sense of also calling the same thing an 'egocentric proposition'?

There might be a good reason. The conception we associate with the word 'proposition' may be something of a jumble of conflicting *desiderata*. Part of the idea is that propositions are supposed to be true or-false *simpliciter*. Or at any rate, their truth or falsity is not supposed to be relative to anything except the world – unlike a sentence, a proposition is not supposed to be true on one interpretation but false on another, true on one resolution of vagueness but false on another, true in Melbourne but false in Adelaide, true yesterday but false today, true for me but false for you. But another part of the idea is that propositions are supposed to be the objects of thought. They are supposed to be capable of giving the content of what we know, believe, and desire. But it is clear that some thought is egocentric, irreducibly *de se*, and then its content cannot be given by the propositions whose truth is relative to nothing but worlds; for those propositions do not discriminate between inhabitants of the same world. If you insist that propositions, rightly so called, must be true or false relative to worlds and nothing else, then you had better say that the objects of at least some thought turn out not to be propositions. Whereas if you insist that propositions, rightly so

called, are the things that serve as objects of all thought, then you had better admit that some propositions are egocentric. The point is the same whichever way you say it: the objects of thought in general are not sets of possible worlds; they sometimes must be, and always can be, taken instead as sets of possible individuals.

Everyone agrees that it won't do to take a property as the sets of its this-worldly instances, because then two properties will be taken to be identical if they happen to be coextensive. Some will say that it is just as bad to take a property as the set of all its instances throughout the worlds, because then two properties will be taken to be identical if they are necessarily coextensive. The stock example concerns the properties of triangularity and of trilaterality. Necessarily, a planar figure bounded by line segments has the same number of angles as sides. So, throughout the worlds, all and only triangles are trilaterals. Yet don't we want to say that these are two different properties?

Sometimes we do, sometimes we don't. I don't see it as a matter for dispute. Here there is a rift in our talk of properties, and we simply have two different conceptions. It's not as if we have fixed once and for all, in some perfectly definite and unequivocal way, on the things we call 'the properties', so that now we are ready to enter into debate about such questions as, for instance, whether two of them ever are necessarily coextensive. Rather, we have the word 'property', introduced by way of a varied repertory of ordinary and philosophical uses. The word has thereby become associated with a role in our commonsensical thought and in a variety of philosophical theories. To deserve the name of 'property' is to be suited to play the right theoretical role; or better, to be one of a class of entities which together are suited to play the right role collectively. But it is wrong to speak of *the* role associated with the word 'property', as if it were fully and uncontroversially settled. The conception is in considerable disarray. It comes in many versions, differing in a number of ways. The question worth asking is: which entities, if any, among those we should believe in, can occupy which versions of the property role? My answer is, in part, that sets of *possibilia* are entities we should believe in which are just right for *one* version of the property role.

There's no point in insisting that this one is the only rightful conception of the properties.

Another version of the property role ties the properties more closely to the meanings of their standard names, and to the meanings of the predicates whereby they may be ascribed to things. 'Triangular' means having three angles, 'trilateral' means having three sides. These meanings differ. (Or do they? The conception of 'meaning' also is in disarray!) So on this conception of properties, we want to distinguish triangularity from trilaterality, though we never can distinguish their instances. We can put the distinction to use, for instance, in saying that one of the two properties is trivially coextensive with triangularity, whereas the other is non-trivially coextensive with triangularity.

This conception demands that properties should be *structured*. If we want to match up properties with the meanings of linguistic expressions that have syntactic structure, then we want to give the properties themselves some kind of quasi-syntactic structure. We can construct structured properties on the model of the structured 'meanings' considered in the previous section. We needn't build them from scratch; we can begin with the unstructured properties and relations we have already, the sets of this- and other-worldly instances. So these structured properties will require *possibilia* just as much as the unstructured ones did. We will need not only properties and relations of individuals; also we will make use of a higher-order unstructured relation that holds between properties and relations of individuals. It is a relation all the same – a set of pairs – and it is constructed out of *possibilia* just as much as first-order properties and relations of individuals are.

Let A be the relation of being an angle of; let S be the relation of being a side of. Suppose for simplicity that these can be left as unstructured relations; we could go to a deeper level of analysis if we like, but that would complicate the construction without showing anything new. Let T be the higher-order unstructured relation which holds between an unstructured property F of individuals and an unstructured relation G of individuals iff F is the property of being something which exactly three things bear relation G to. A certain unstructured property is the unique thing which bears T to A, and therefore it is the (unstructured) property of triangularity; it also is the unique thing which bears T to S, and therefore it is the (unstructured) property of

trilaterality. Therefore let us take the structured property of triangularity as the pair $\langle T, A \rangle$, and the structured property of trilaterality as the pair $\langle T, S \rangle$. Since S and A differ, we have the desired difference between the two pairs that we took to be our two structured properties. [...]

1.6   Isolation

I hope that by saying what theoretical purposes it is meant to serve, I have helped to make clear what my thesis of plurality of worlds is. Now I shall address some further questions of formulation and state some further tenets of my position.

A possible world has parts, namely possible individuals. If two things are parts of the same world, I call them *worldmates*.[19] A world is the mereological sum[20] of all the possible individuals that are parts of it, and so are worldmates of one another. It is a maximal sum: anything that is a worldmate of any part of it is itself a part. (This is just a consequence of my denial that worlds overlap.) But not just any sum of parts of worlds is itself a world. It might, of course, be only part of a world. Or it might consist of parts of two or more different worlds; thus it might be spread over logical space, not wholly within any one world, and its parts might not all be worldmates of one another.

What, then, is the difference between a sum of possible individuals that is a possible world, and one that is not? What makes two things worldmates? How are the worlds demarcated one from another? Why don't all the *possibilia* comprise one big world? Or, at the other extreme, why isn't each possible neutrino a little world of its own? In Perry's terminology: what is the unity relation for possible worlds?[21]

I gave part of the answer in my opening section, when I said that nothing is so far away from us in space, or so far in the past or the future, as not to be part of the same world as ourselves. The point seems uncontroversial, and it seems open to generalisation: whenever two possible individuals are spatiotemporally related, they are worldmates. If there is any distance between them – be it great or small, spatial or temporal – they are parts of one single world.

(Better: for any two possible individuals, if every particular part of one is spatiotemporally related to every particular part of the other that is wholly distinct from it, then the two are worldmates. This formulation avoids difficults that might be raised concerning partial spatiotemporal relatedness of trans-world mereological sums; difficulties about multiply located universals; and difficulties about whether we ought to say that overlapping things are spatiotemporally related.)

[...]

So we have a sufficient condition: if two things are spatiotemporally related, then they are world-mates. The converse is much more problematic. Yet that is more or less the doctrine that I propose. Putting the two halves together: things are worldmates iff they are spatiotemporally related. A world is underlined, then, by the spatiotemporal interrelation of its parts. There are no spatiotemporal relations across the boundary between one world and another; but no matter how we draw a boundary within a world, there will be spatiotemporal relations across it.

A first, and simplest, objection is that a world might possibly consist of two or more completely disconnected spacetimes. (Maybe *our* world does, if indeed such disconnection is possible.) But whatever way a world might be is a way that some world is; and one world with two disconnected spacetimes is a counterexample against my proposal. Against this objection, I must simply deny the premise. I would rather not; I admit some inclination to agree with it. But it seems to me that it is no central part of our modal thinking, and not a consequence of any interesting general principle about what is possible. So it is negotiable. Given a choice between rejecting the alleged possibility of disconnected spacetimes within a single world and (what I take to be the alternative) resorting to a primitive worldmate relation, I take the former to be more credible.

I cannot give you disconnected spacetimes within a single world; but I can give you some passable substitutes. One big world, spatiotemporally interrelated, might have many different world-like parts. *Ex hypothesi* these are not complete worlds, but they could seem to be. They might be four-dimensional; they might have no boundaries; there might be little or no causal interaction between them. Indeed, each of these world-like parts of one big world might be a duplicate of some genuinely complete world.

[...]

There is a second way in which the worlds are isolated: there is no causation from one to another. If need be, I would put this causal isolation alongside spatiotemporal isolation as a principle of demarcation for worlds. But there is no need. Under a counterfactual analysis of causation, the causal isolation of worlds follows automatically. Therefore it contributes nothing to the demarcation of one world from another. No matter how we solve the demarcation problem, trans-world causation comes out as nonsense.

When we have causation within a world, what happens is roughly as follows. (For simplicity I ignore complications having to do with causal pre-emption and overdetermination, and with the idealisation of supposing that we always have closest antecedent-worlds. Taking these matters into account would do nothing in favour of trans-world causation.) We have a world W where event C causes event E. Both these events occur at W, and they are distinct events, and it is the case at W that if C had not occurred, E would not have occurred either. The counterfactual means that at the closest worlds to W at which C does not occur, E does not occur either.

Try to adapt this to a case of trans-world causation, in which the events of one world supposedly influence those of another. Event C occurs at world W_C, event E occurs at world W_E, they are distinct events, and if C had not occurred, E would not have occurred either. This counterfactual is supposed to hold – where? It means that at the closest worlds to – where? – at which C does not occur, E does not occur – where? – either.

[...]

1.7 Concreteness

Because I said that other worlds are of a kind with this world of ours, doubtless you will expect me to say that possible worlds and individuals are concrete, not abstract. But I am reluctant to say that outright. Not because I hold the opposite view; but because it is not at all clear to me what philosophers mean when they speak of 'concrete' and 'abstract' in this connection. Perhaps I would agree with it, whatever it means, but still I do not find it a useful way of explaining myself.

I can say this much, even without knowing what 'concrete' is supposed to mean. I take it, at least, that donkeys and protons and puddles and stars are supposed to be paradigmatically concrete. I take it also that the division between abstract and concrete is meant to divide entities into fundamentally different kinds. If so, then it is out of the question that an abstract entity and a concrete entity should be exactly alike, perfect duplicates. According to my modal realism, the donkeys and protons and puddles and stars that are parts of this world have perfect duplicates that are parts of other worlds. This suffices to settle, whatever exactly it may mean, that at least some possible individuals are 'concrete'. And if so, then at least some possible worlds are at least partly 'concrete'.

[...]

1.8 Plenitude

At the outset, I mentioned several ways that a world might be; and then I made it part of my modal realism that

(1)   absolutely every way that a world could possibly be is a way that some world is, and
(2)   absolutely every way that a part of a world could possibly be is a way that some part of some world is.

But what does that mean? It *seems* to mean that the worlds are abundant, and logical space is somehow complete. There are no gaps in logical space; no vacancies where a world might have been, but isn't. It seems to be a principle of plenitude. But is it really?

Given modal realism, it becomes advantageous to identify 'ways a world could possibly be' with worlds themselves. Why distinguish two closely corresponding entities: a world, and also the maximally specific way that world is? Economy dictates identifying the 'ways' with the worlds.

But as Peter van Inwagen pointed out to me, that makes (1) contentless. It says only that every world is identical to some world. That would be true even if there were only seventeen worlds, or one, or none. It says nothing at all about abundance or completeness. Likewise for (2).

Suppose we thought a maximally specific 'way' should be the same kind of things as a less specific 'way': namely a property, taken as a set. Then a maximally specific 'way' would be a unit set. Now

indeed the 'ways' are distinct from the worlds. Further, they are abstract in whatever sense sets are. But this does nothing to restore content to (1). A 'possible way' is a *non-empty* set, and (1) now says trivially that each of the unit sets has a member.[22]

Or perhaps a 'way' should be not a unit set, but an equivalence class under indiscernibility. I am agnostic about whether there are indiscernible worlds. If there are, I myself would wish to say that there are indiscernible ways a world could be, just as I would say that a world of two-way eternal recurrence affords countless indiscernible ways – one per epoch – for a person to be. But others might not like the idea of indiscernible 'ways'. They might therefore welcome a guarantee that, whether or not worlds ever are indiscernible, 'ways' never will be. Now (1) says trivially that each of the equivalence classes has a member.

Or suppose we thought a 'way' should be the intrinsic nature of a world, a highly complex structural universal (as in Forrest, 'Ways Worlds Could Be'.) Given that thesis, a 'possible way' is an *instantiated* universal. Now (1) says trivially that each of these has a world to instantiate it.

We might read (1) as saying that every way we *think* a world could possibly be is a way that some world is; that is, every seemingly possible description or conception of a world does fit some world. Now we have made (1) into a genuine principle of plenitude. But an unacceptable one. So understood, (1) indiscriminately endorses offhand opinion about what is possible.

I conclude that (1), and likewise (2), cannot be salvaged as principles of plenitude. Let them go trivial. Then we need a new way to say what (1) and (2) seemed to say: that there are possibilities enough, and no gaps in logical space.

To which end, I suggest that we look to the Humean denial of necessary connections between distinct existences. To express the plenitude of possible worlds, I require a *principle of recombination* according to which patching together parts of different possible worlds yields another possible world. Roughly speaking, the principle is that anything can coexist with anything else, at least provided they occupy distinct spatiotemporal positions. Likewise, anything can fail to coexist with anything else. Thus if there could be a dragon, and there could be a unicorn, but there couldn't be a dragon and a unicorn side by side, that would be an unacceptable gap in logical space, a failure of plenitude. And if there could be a talking head contiguous to the rest of a living human body, but there couldn't be a talking head separate from the rest of a human body, that too would be a failure of plenitude.

[...]

I cannot altogether accept the formulation: anything can coexist with anything. For I think the worlds do not overlap, hence each thing is part of only one of them. A dragon from one world and a unicorn from a second world do not themselves coexist either in the dragon's world, or in the unicorn's world, or in a third world. An attached head does not reappear as a separated head in some other world, because it does not reappear at all in any other world.

Ordinarily I would replace trans-world identity by counterpart relations, but not here. I cannot accept the principle: a counterpart of anything can coexist with a counterpart of anything else. Counterparts are united by similarity, but often the relevant similarity is mostly extrinsic. In particular, match of origins often has decisive weight. Had my early years gone differently, I might be different now in ever so many important ways – here I envisage an other-worldly person who is my counterpart mainly by match of origins, and very little by intrinsic similarity in later life. It might happen (at least under some resolutions of the vagueness of counterpart relations) that nothing could be a counterpart of the dragon unless a large part of its surrounding world fairly well matched the dragon's world; and likewise that nothing could be a counterpart of the unicorn unless a large part of its surrounding world fairly well matched the unicorn's world; and that no one world matches both the dragon's world and the unicorn's world well enough; and therefore that there is no world where a counterpart of the dragon coexists with a counterpart of the unicorn. Considered by themselves, the dragon and the unicorn are compossible. But if we use the method of counterparts, we do not consider them by themselves; to the extent that the counterpart relation heeds extrinsic similarities, we take them together with their surroundings.

It is right to formulate our principle of recombination in terms of similarity. It should say,

for instance, that there is a world where something like the dragon coexists with something like the unicorn. But extrinsic similarity is irrelevant here, so I should not speak of coexisting *counterparts*. Instead, I should say that a *duplicate* of the dragon and a *duplicate* of the unicorn coexist at some world, and that the attached talking head has at some world a separated duplicate.

[...]

Among all the possible individuals there are, some are parts of this world; some are not, but are duplicates of parts of this world; some, taken whole, are not duplicates of any part of this world, but are divisible into parts each of which is a duplicate of some part of this world. Still other possible individuals are not thus divisible: they have parts, no part of which is a duplicate of any part of this world. These I call *alien* individuals. (That is, they are alien *to* this world; similarly, individuals could be alien to another world. For instance, many individuals in this world are alien to more impoverished worlds.) A world that contains alien individuals – equivalently, that is itself an alien individual – I call an alien world.

In 'New Work for a Theory of Universals', I defined an alien natural property as one that is not instantiated by any part of this world, and that is not definable as a conjunctive or structural property build up from constituents that are all instantiated by parts of this world.[23] Anything that instantiates an alien property is an alien individual; any world within which an alien property is instantiated is an alien world.

But not conversely: we could have an alien individual that did not instantiate any alien properties, but instead combined non-alien properties in an alien way. Suppose that positive and negative charge are not, strictly speaking, incompatible; but suppose it happens by accident or by contingent law that no this-worldly particle has both these properties. Then an other-worldly particle that does have both is an alien individual but needn't have any alien properties.

A world to which no individuals, worlds, or properties are alien would be an especially rich world. There is no reason to think we are privileged to inhabit such a world. Therefore any acceptable account of possibility must make provision for alien possibilities.

So it won't do to say that all worlds are generated by recombination from parts of this world, individuals which are possible because they are actual. We can't get the alien possibilities just by rearranging non-alien ones. Thus our principle of recombination falls short of capturing all the plenitude of possibilities.

A principle which allowed not only recombination of spatiotemporal parts of the world but also recombination of non-spatiotemporal parts – universals or tropes – would do a bit more. It would generate those alien individuals that do not instantiate alien properties. But I say (1) that such a principle, unlike mine, would sacrifice neutrality about whether there exist universals or tropes, and (2) that it still wouldn't go far enough, since we also need the possibility of alien properties.

Although recombination will not generate alien worlds out of the parts of this world, it nevertheless applies to alien worlds. It rules out that there should be only a few alien worlds. If there are some, there are many more. Anything alien can coexist, or fail to coexist, with anything else alien, or with anything else not alien, in any arrangement permitted by shape and size.

1.9 Actuality

I say that ours is one of many worlds. Ours is the actual world; the rest are not actual. Why so? – I take it to be a trivial matter of meaning. I use the word 'actual' to mean the same as 'this-worldly'. When I use it, it applies to my world and my worldmates; to this world we are part of, and to all parts of this world. And if someone else uses it, whether he be a worldmate of ours or whether he be unactualised, then (provided he means by it what we do) it applies likewise to his world and his worldmates. Elsewhere I have called this the 'indexical analysis' of actuality and stated it as follows.

> I suggest that 'actual' and its cognates should be analyzed as *indexical* terms: terms whose reference varies, depending on relevant features of the context of utterance. The relevant feature of context, for the term 'actual', is the world at which a given utterance occurs. According to the indexical analysis I propose, 'actual' (in its primary sense) refers at any world w to the world w. 'Actual' is analogous to 'present', an indexical term whose reference varies depending on a

different feature of context: 'present' refers at any time t to the time t. 'Actual' is analogous also to 'here', 'I', 'you', and 'aforementioned' – indexical terms depending for their reference respectively on the place, the speaker, the intended audience, the speaker's acts of pointing, and the foregoing discourse. ('Anselm and Actuality', pp. 184–5)

This makes actuality a relative matter: every world is *actual at* itself, and thereby all worlds are on a par. This is *not* to say that all worlds are actual – there's no world at which that is true, any more than there's ever a time when all times are present. The 'actual at' relation between worlds is simply identity.

Given my acceptance of the plurality of worlds, the relativity is unavoidable. I have no tenable alternative. For suppose instead that one world alone is *absolutely* actual. There is some special distinction which that one world alone posseses, not relative to its inhabitants or to anything else but *simpliciter*. I have no idea how this supposed absolute distinction might be understood, but let us go on as if we did understand it. I raise two objections.

The first objection concerns our knowledge that we are actual. Note that the supposed absolute distinction, even if it exists, doesn't make the relative distinction go away. It is still true that one world alone is ours, is this one, is the one we are part of. What a remarkable bit of luck for us if the very world we are part of is the one that is absolutely actual! Out of all the people there are in all the worlds, the great majority are doomed to live in worlds that lack absolute actuality, but we are the select few. What reason could we ever have to think it was so? How could we ever know? Unactualised dollars buy no less unactualised bread, and so forth. And yet we *do* know for certain that the world we are part of is the actual world – just as certainly as we know that the world we are part of is the very world we are part of. How could this be knowledge that we are the select few?

D. C. Williams asks the same question. Not about 'actuality' but about 'existence'; but it comes to the same thing, since he is discussing various doctrines on which so-called 'existence' turns out to be a special status that distinguishes some of the things there are from others. He complains that Leibniz 'never intimates, for example, how he can tell that *he* is a member of the existent world and not a mere possible monad on the shelf of essence' ('Dispensing with Existence', p. 752).

Robert M. Adams, in 'Theories of Actuality', dismisses this objection. He says that a simple-property theory of absolute actuality can account for the certainty of our knowledge of our own actuality by maintaining that we are as immediately acquainted with our own absolute actuality as we are with our thoughts, feelings, and sensations. But I reply that if Adams and I and all the other actual people really have this immediate acquaintance with absolute actuality, wouldn't my elder sister have had it too, if only I'd had an elder sister? So there she is, unactualised, off in some other world getting fooled by the very same evidence that is supposed to be giving me my knowledge.

This second objection concerns contingency. (It is due to Adams, and this time he and I agree.) Surely it is a contingent matter which world is actual. A contingent matter is one that varies from world to world. At one world, the contingent matter goes one way; at another, another. So at one world, one world is actual; and at another, another. How can this be *absolute* actuality? – The relativity is manifest!

The indexical analysis raises a question. If 'actual' is an indexical, is it or is it not a rigidified indexical? In a context where other worlds are under consideration, does it still refer to the world of utterance, or does it shift its reference? Compare 'now', which is normally rigidified, with 'present', which may or may not be. So you say 'Yesterday it was colder than it is now', and even in the scope of the time-shifting adverb, 'now' still refers to the time of utterance. Likewise you say 'Yesterday it was colder than it is at present', and the reference of 'present' is unshifted. But if you say 'Every past event was once present', then the time-shifting tensed verb shifts the reference of 'present'. I suggest that 'actual' and its cognates are like 'present': sometimes rigidified, sometimes not. What if I'd had an elder sister? Then there would have been someone who doesn't actually exist. (Rigidified.) Then she would have been actual, though in fact she is not. (Unrigidified.) Then someone would have been actual who actually isn't actual. (Both together.) In the passage just quoted I called the unrigidified sense 'primary'; but not for any good reason.[24]

I said that when I use it, 'actual' applies to my world and my worldmates; that is, to the world I am part of and to other parts of that world. Likewise, *mutatis mutandis*, when some other-worldly being uses the word with the same meaning. But that left out the sets. I would not wish to say that any sets are *parts of* this or other worlds,[25] but nevertheless I would like to say that sets of actual things are actual. Sometimes we hear it said that sets are one and all unlocated; but I don't know any reason to believe this, and a more plausible view is that a set is where its members are. It is scattered to the extent that its members are scattered; it is unlocated if, but only if, its members are unlocated. That applies as much to location among the worlds as it does to location within a single world. Just as a set of stay-at-home Australians is in Australia, so likewise a set of this-wordly things is this-worldly, in other words actual. In the same way, a set of sets that are all in Australia is itself in Australia, and likewise a set of actual sets is itself actual; and so on up the iterative hierarchy.

I might sometimes prefer to use the word 'actual' a bit more broadly still. There is no need to decide, once and for all and inflexibly, what is to be called actual. After all, that is not the grand question: what is there? It is only the question which of all the things there are stand in some special relation to us, but there are special relations and there are special relations. Suppose there are things that are not our world, and not parts of our world, and not sets built up entirely from things that are parts of our world – but that I might nevertheless wish to quantify over even when my quantification is otherwise restricted to this-worldly things. If so, no harm done if I sometimes call them 'actual' by courtesy. No harm done, in fact, if I decline to adopt any official position on the question whether they are actual or whether they are not! It is no genuine issue.

The numbers, for instance, might well be candidates to be called 'actual' by courtesy. But it depends on what the numbers are. If they are universals, and some or all of them are non-spatiotemporal parts of their this-worldly instances which in turn are parts of this world, then those numbers, at least, are actual not by courtesy but because they are parts of this world. Likewise for other mathematical entities.

Properties, taken as sets of all their this- and other-worldly instances, are another candidate.

By what I said above about actuality of sets, only those properties are actual whose instances are confined to the actual world. But most of the properties we take an interest in have instances both in and out of this world. Those ones might be called 'partly actual'; or they might as well just be called 'actual', since very often we will want to include them in our otherwise this-worldly quantifications.

Events fall in with the properties; for I see no reason to distinguish between an event and the property of being a spatiotemporal region, of this or another world, wherein that event occurs. (See my 'Events'.) An event that actually occurs, then, is a set that includes exactly one this-worldly region. That makes it partly actual, and we may as well just call it 'actual'.

Propositions, being sets of worlds, also fall in with the properties taken as sets. A proposition is partly actual at just those worlds where it is true, for it has just those worlds as its members. So we might call at least the true propositions 'actual'; or we might just call all propositions 'actual', distinguishing however between those that are and are not actually true.

Not only sets but individuals may be partly actual – big individuals, composed of parts from more worlds than one, and so partly in each of several worlds. If there are any such trans-world individuals that are partly in this world, hence partly actual, should we call them 'actual' *simpliciter*? – That depends. We needn't, if we think of them just as oddities that we can mostly ignore. I think they are exactly that. But if we were reluctant to ignore them in our quantifying, perhaps because we thought that we ourselves were among them, then we might appropriately call them 'actual'.[26]

Notes

1 Or 'extreme' modal realism, as Stalnaker calls it – but in what dimension does its extremity lie?
2 With the alleged exception of category theory – but here I wonder if the unmet needs have more to do with the motivational talk than with the real mathematics.
3 Kratzer, 'What "Must" and "Can" Must and Can Mean'; and my 'Scorekeeping in a Language Game'.
4 This is essentially the account I gave in 'Counterpart Theory and Quantified Modal Logic'.

5 We might just *say* it, and not mean anything by it. That is Forbes's solution to our present difficulty, in his so-called 'canonical counterpart theory' – my own version is hereby named 'official standard counterpart theory' – in which, if Humphrey has no ordinary counterpart among the things which exist at W, he does nevertheless have a counterpart at W. This extraordinary counterpart is none other than Humphrey himself – he then gets in as a sort of associate member of W's population, belonging to its 'outer domain' but not to the 'inner domain' of things that exist there fair and square. This isn't explained, but really it needn't be. It amounts to a stipulation that there are two different ways that Humphrey – he himself, safe at home in this world – can satisfy formulas *in absentia*. Where he has proper counterparts, he does it one way, namely the ordinary vicarious way. Where he doesn't, he does it another way – just by not being there he satisfies 'x does not exist'.
6 If he likes, he can give himself more than one of these disappointments. As I noted, Forbes's talk of non-existent counterparts in outer domains amounts to a stipulation that satisfaction *in absentia* works different ways in different cases; so I find it strange that he offers it in rejoinder to a proposal of Hunter and Seager that modal formulas of parallel form needn't always be given parallel counterpart-theoretic translations. But this divided treatment does not pay off by making the modal formulas mean what we would offhand expect them to – it is exactly the non-existent counterparts in the outer domains that keep Humphrey from satisfying 'necessarily x is human' even if he is essentially human.
7 Surveyed in Teller, 'A Poor Man's Guide to Supervenience and Determination'.
8 See Kim, 'Psychophysical Supervenience', and my 'New Work for a Theory of Universals'.
9 One more example of the same sort of distortion. Let *naturalism* be the thesis that whether one's conduct is right supervenes on natural facts, so that one person could do right and another do wrong only if there were some difference in natural facts between the two – as it might be, a difference in their behaviour or their circumstances. Consider the theory that, necessarily, right conduct is conduct that conforms to divinely willed universal maxims. Suppose it is contingent what, if anything, is divinely willed. And suppose that facts about what is divinely willed are supernatural, not natural, facts. You might well expect that this divine-will theory of rightness would contradict naturalism; for if two people are alike so far as natural facts are concerned, but one of them lives in a world where

prayer is divinely willed and the other lives in a world where blasphemy is divinely willed, then what is right for the first is not right for the second. But if we read the 'could' as a diamond, we get an unexpected answer. A difference in what universal maxims are divinely willed never could be a difference between two people in the same world. Within a single world, the only differences relevant to rightness are natural differences, such as the difference between one who prays and one who blasphemes. So indeed there is no world wherein one person does right and another does wrong without any difference in natural facts between the two. So either this divine-will theory of rightness is naturalistic after all; or else – more likely – something has gone amiss with our understanding of supervenience.

10 See my *Counterfactuals* and Stalnaker, 'A Theory of Conditionals'.

11 I discuss these issues in my *Philosophical Papers*, vol. II, part 6.

12 See Hintikka, *Knowledge and Belief*, and his subsequent discussions of knowledge and belief in *Models for Modalities* and *The Intentions of Intentionality*.

13 See Stalnaker, *Inquiry*, chapters 1 and 2.

14 See my 'Attitudes *De Dicto* and *De Se*' and 'Individuation by Acquaintance and by Stipulation'; and see Chisholm, *The First Person*, for a parallel theory in a somewhat different framework.

15 I say 'set' not 'class'. The reason is that I do not want to restrict myself to properties of individuals alone; properties themselves have properties. Properties must therefore be sets so that they may be members of other sets.

When I use the term 'set' and 'class' in this book, the reader would not go far wrong to suppose that I am following the standard usage: 'class' is the more general term, and covers not only sets but also 'proper classes'. Those are supposed to be set-like things which, by reason of the boundless rank of their members, are somehow disqualified from membership in any class or set. But in fact I use the terms to mark a somewhat different distinction, as follows. It is sometimes suggested that there is an irreducibly plural way of referring to things, or quantifying over them. I say 'There are some critics such that they admire only one another' or 'There are all the non-self-members, and they do not comprise any sort of set or class', and I am not quantifying in the ordinary way over any set or class of critics or of non-self-members; rather I am quantifying over nothing but critics or non-self-members themselves, however I am quantifying

over them in an irreducibly plural w[...] Stenius; Armstrong, *Universals [...] Realism*, vol. I, pp. 32–4; and espec[...] find it very plausible that there is i[...] thing as ontologically innocent plural quantification, and that it can indeed replace quantification over sets – sometimes. It would be delightful (except when I want to cite belief in sets as a precedent for my modal realism) if plural quantification could be iterated up the hierarchy, so that some fancy kind of plurally plural quantification over individuals could replace *all* quantification over sets or classes. But I think this project has very little hope of success. So I consider some apparent quantification over sets or classes of whatnots to carry genuine ontological commitment not only to the whatnots, but also to sets or classes of them; and then I use the word 'set'. But sometimes I think my quantification could be read as, or replaced by, innocent plural quantification that carries no commitment except to the whatnots themselves; and then I use the word 'class'.

An exception: since the phrase 'equivalence class' is standard, I use it whether or not I take there to be genuine ontological commitment.

16 Not just any pair of counterparts should count as a counterpart pair; it may be that pair $\langle X, Y \rangle$ counts as a counterpart of pair $\langle V, W \rangle$ partly because the relations between X and Y resemble those between V and W. See Hazen, 'Counterpart-Theoretic Semantics for Modal Logic'; my *Philosophical Papers*, vol. I, pp. 44–5; and the discussion of joint possibilities in section 4.4.

17 There is a choice between various set-theoretic constructions of ordered pairs, triples, etc. I shall leave the choice unmade, since making it would serve no useful purpose. [...] So all that I say of pairs, triples, ..., and relations is systematically ambiguous. No harm, unless I said something that would have different truth values on different disambiguations; which I have no intention of doing.

18 Distinguish my proposal from a different way of unifying propositions, properties, and relations. The idea is that relations properly speaking are two-place, three-place, and on up; properties are one-place relations; and propositions are zero-place relations. See, for instance, Montague, *Formal Philosophy*, pp. 122–3. This strikes me as misguided elegance. How can we make sense of it? – Only by giving *everything* one more place than meets the eye. The so-called n-place relations are instantiated not *simpliciter* but relative to a world. (Or for Montague, relative to an index that might or might not be a world.) I say that means they all have an

extra, hidden place to them. Thus a proposition is supposed to be a zero-place relation, but it turns out to be a one-place relation – that is, a set of one-tuples of worlds. A so-called property is supposed to be a one-place relation, but it turns out to be a two-place relation of things to worlds; what is supposed to be a two-place relation turns out to be three-place; and so on up. The treatment of propositions is the only satisfactory part. If we identified a one-tuple of a world with the world itself, as we might but needn't, it is exactly my own treatment; if not, still sets of worlds and sets of their one-tuples would correspond so closely that we needn't care which ones get called the propositions. The rest of the unified treatment is not satisfactory because it relies on the obfuscatory notion of relative instantiation. Therefore the whole idea is best abandoned.

19 Worldmates are compossible in the strongest sense of the word. Two things are compossible in another sense if they are vicariously worldmates, in virtue of their counterparts; that is, iff some one world contains counterparts of both of them. Two things are compossible in yet another sense iff some one world contains intrinsic duplicates of both. In this third sense, any two possible individuals are compossible (except, perhaps, when one is too big to leave room for the other); see section 1.8.

20 The *mereological sum*, or *fusion*, of several things is the least inclusive thing that includes all of them as parts. It is composed of them and of nothing more; any part of it overlaps one or more of them; it is a proper part of anything else that has all of them as parts. Equivalently: the mereological sum of several things is that thing such that, for any X, X overlaps it iff X overlaps one of them. For background on the mereology that I shall be using, see Leonard and Goodman; or Goodman, *Structure of Appearance*, section II.4.

21 The question is raised by Richards. I am grateful to him, and to David Johnson, for helpful discussion of it.

22 Some critics have thought it very important that the 'ways' should be 'abstract' entities and distinct from the worlds. For instance, see Stalnaker, 'Possible Worlds'; and van Inwagen, who writes 'the cosmos, being concrete, is not a way things could have been. ... And surely the cosmos cannot itself be identical with any way the cosmos could have been: to say this would be like saying that Socrates is identical with the way Socrates is, which is plain bad grammar.' ('Indexicality and Actuality', p. 406.) But to me, the choice whether to take a 'way' as a unit set or as its sole member seems to be of the utmost unimportance, on a par with the arbitrary choice between speaking of a set or of its characteristic function.

23 Perhaps, as Armstrong has suggested in discussion, I should have added a third clause: '... and that is not obtainable by interpolation or extrapolation from a spectrum of properties that are instantiated by parts of this world'.

24 For various examples that require or forbid rigidification if they are to make sense, see my *Philosophical Papers*, vol. 1, p. 22; for further discussion, see Hazen, 'One of the Truths about Actuality' and van Inwagen, 'Indexicality and Actuality'.

25 But not because I take it that the part-whole relation applies only to individuals and not sets, as I said in *Philosophical Papers*, vol. I, p. 40; rather, because I now take it that a set is never part of an individual.

26 In *Philosophical Papers*, vol. 1, pp. 39–40, I distinguished three ways of 'being in a world': (1) being *wholly* in it, that is, being part of it; (2) being *partly* in it, that is, having a part that is wholly in it; and (3) existing *from the standpoint of* it, that is, 'belonging to the least restricted domain that is normally – modal metaphysics being deemed abnormal – appropriate in evaluating the truth at that world of quantifications'. If the world in question is actual, that is almost my present distinction between being actual, being partly actual, and being actual by courtesy; the only difference in the terminologies being that I would not now throw all sets into the lower grade. I distinguish all of the above from (4) existing *according to* a world: I claim that something exists according to a world – for instance, Humphrey both exists and wins the presidency according to certain worlds other than ours – by having a counterpart that is part of that world. [...]

References

Adams, Robert M. 'Theories of Actuality', *Noûs*, 8 (1974), pp. 211–31.

Armstrong, D. M. *Universals and Scientific Realism*, 2 vols. Cambridge: Cambridge University Press, 1978.

Black, Max. 'The Elusiveness of Sets', *Review of Metaphysics*, 24 (1971), pp. 614–36.

Boolos, George. 'To Be is To Be a Value of a Variable (or To Be Some Values of Some Variables)', *Journal of Philosophy*, 82 (1984), pp. 430–49.

Forbes, Graeme. 'Canonical Counterpart Theory', *Analysis*, 42 (1982), pp. 33–7.

Goodman, Nelson. *The Structure of Appearance.* Cambridge, MA: Harvard University Press, 1951.

Hazen, Allen. 'Counterpart-Theoretic Semantics for Modal Logic', *Journal of Philosophy*, 76 (1979), pp. 319–38.

Hazen, Allen. 'One of the Truths about Actuality', *Analysis*, 39 (1977), pp. 1–3.

Hintikka, Jaakko. *The Intentions of Intentionality and Other New Models for Modalities.* Dordrecht: Reidel, 1975.

Hintikka, Jaakko. *Knowledge and Belief.* Ithaca, NY: Cornell University Press, 1962.

Hintikka, Jaakko. *Models for Modalities: Selected Essays.* Reidel, 1969.

Kim, Jaegwon, 'Psychophysical Supervenience', *Philosophical Studies*, 41 (1982), pp. 51–70.

Kratzer, Angelika. 'What "Must" and "Can" Must and Can Mean', *Linguistics and Philosophy*, 1 (1977), pp. 337–55.

Leonard, Henry S., and Goodman, Nelson. 'The Calculus of Individuals and its Uses', *Journal of Symbolic Logic*, 5 (1940), pp. 45–55.

Lewis, David. 'Attitudes *De Dicto* and *De Se*', *Philosophical Review*, 88 (1979), pp. 513–43.

Lewis, David. *Counterfactuals.* Oxford: Basil Blackwell, 1973.

Lewis, David. 'Counterpart Theory and Quantified Modal Logic', *Journal of Philosophy*, 65 (1968), pp. 113–26.

Lewis, David. 'Events', in *Philosophical Papers*, vol. II.

Lewis, David. 'Individuation by Acquaintance and by Stipulation', *Philosophical Review*, 92 (1983), pp. 3–32.

Lewis, David. *Philosophical Papers*, 2 vols. New York: Oxford University Press, 1983, 1986.

Lewis, David. 'Scorekeeping in a Language Game', *Journal of Philosophical Logic*, 8 (1979): 339–59.

Montague, Richard. *Formal Philosophy: Selected Papers of Richard Montague.* New Haven: Yale University Press, 1974.

Perry, John, 'Can the Self Divide?', *Journal of Philosophy*, 69 (1972), pp. 463–88.

Richards, Tom. 'The Worlds of David Lewis', *Australasian Journal of Philosophy*, 53 (1975), pp. 105–18.

Stalnaker, R. *Inquiry.* Cambridge, MA: MIT Press, 1984.

Stalnaker, R. 'Possible Worlds', *Noûs*, 10 (1976), pp. 65–75.

Stalnaker, R. 'A Theory of Conditionals', in Nicholas Rescher (ed.), *Studies in Logical Theory.* Oxford: Blackwell, 1968.

Stenius, Eric. 'Sets', *Synthese*, 27 (1974), pp. 161–88.

Teller, Paul. 'A Poor Man's Guide to Supervenience and Determination', *Southern Journal of Philosophy*, supp. to vol. 22 (1984), pp. 137–62.

van Inwagen, Peter. 'Indexicality and Actuality', *Philosophical Review*, 89 (1980), pp. 403–26.

Williams, Donald C. 'Dispensing with Existence', *Journal of Philosophy*, 59 (1962), pp. 748–63.

17

Possible Worlds

Robert C. Stalnaker

According to Leibniz, the universe – the actual world – is one of an infinite number of possible worlds existing in the mind of God. God created the universe by actualizing one of these possible worlds – the best one. It is a striking image, this picture of an infinite swarm of total universes, each by its natural inclination for existence striving for a position that can be occupied by only one, with God, in his infinite wisdom and benevolence, settling the competition by selecting the most worthy candidate. But in these enlightened times, we find it difficult to take this metaphysical myth any more seriously than the other less abstract creation stories told by our primitive ancestors. Even the more recent expurgated versions of the story, leaving out God and the notoriously chauvinistic thesis that our world is better than all the rest, are generally regarded, at best, as fanciful metaphors for a more sober reality. J. L. Mackie, for example, writes "... talk of possible worlds ... cries out for further analysis. There *are* no possible worlds except the actual one; so what are we up to when we talk about them?" (Mackie: 90). Lawrence Powers puts the point more bluntly: "The whole idea of possible worlds (perhaps laid out in space like raisins in a pudding) seems ludicrous" (Powers).

These expressions of skepticism and calls for further analysis are of course not directed at Leibniz but at recent uses of parts of his metaphysical myth to motivate and give content to formal semantics for modal logics. In both formal and philosophical discussions of modality, the concept of a possible world has shown itself to have considerable heuristic power. But, critics have argued, a heuristic device should not be confused with an explanation. If analyses of modal concepts (or of the concept of a proposition) in terms of possible worlds are to be more than heuristic aids in mapping the relationships among the formulae of a modal logic, the concept of a possible world itself must be explained and justified.

Although it is commonly taken to be an obvious truth that there really are no such things as possible worlds – that the myth, whether illuminating or misleading, explanatory or obfuscating, is nevertheless a myth – this common opinion can be challenged. That is, one might respond to the possible worlds skeptic not by explaining the metaphor but by taking the story to be the literal truth. David Lewis responds in this way, and he cites common opinion and ordinary language on his side:

Robert C. Stalnaker, "Possible Worlds," *Noûs*, 10 (1976): 65–75.

Metaphysics: An Anthology, Second Edition. Edited by Jaegwon Kim, Daniel Z. Korman and Ernest Sosa.

I believe there are possible worlds other than the one we happen to inhabit. If an argument is wanted, it is this: It is uncontroversially true that things might have been otherwise than they are. I believe, and so do you, that things could have been different in countless ways. But what does this mean? Ordinary language permits the paraphrase: there are many ways things could have been besides the way that they actually are. On the face of it, this sentence is an existential quantification. It says that there exist many entities of a certain description, to wit, 'ways things could have been'. I believe things could have been different in countless ways. I believe permissible paraphrases of what I believe; taking the paraphrase at its face value, I therefore believe in the existence of entities which might be called 'ways things could have been'. I prefer to call them 'possible worlds'. (Lewis: 84.)

Lewis does not intend this as a knockdown argument. It is only a presumption that the sentences of ordinary language be taken at face value, and the presumption can be defeated if the naive reading of the sentences leads to problems which can be avoided by an alternative analysis. The aim of the argument is to shift the burden to the skeptic who, if he is to defeat the argument, must point to the problems which commitment to possible worlds creates, and the alternative analysis which avoids those problems. Lewis does not think the skeptic can do either.

The rhetorical force of Lewis's argument is in the suggestion that possible worlds are really not such alien entities as the metaphysical flavor of this name seems to imply. The argument suggests not that ordinary language and our common beliefs commit us to a weighty metaphysical theory, but rather that what appears to be a weighty metaphysical theory is really just some ordinary beliefs by another name. Believing in possible worlds is like speaking prose. We have been doing it all our lives.

But for this to be convincing, the shift from "ways things might have been" to "possible worlds" must be an innocent terminological substitution, and I do not believe that, as Lewis develops the concept of a possible world, it is. To argue this point I will state four theses about possible worlds, all defended by Lewis. Together they constitute a doctrine which I will call extreme realism about possible worlds. It is this doctrine against which the

skeptic is reacting, and against which, I shall argue, he is justified in reacting. I believe the doctrine is false, but I also believe that one need not accept or reject the theses as a package. The main burden of my argument will be to show the independence of the more plausible parts of the package, and so to defend the coherence of a more moderate form of realism about possible worlds – one that might be justified by our common modal opinions and defended as a foundation for a theory about the activities of rational agents.

Here are Lewis's four theses:

1. *Possible worlds exist*. Other possible worlds are just as real as the actual world. They may not *actually* exist, since to actually exist is to exist in the actual world, but they do, nevertheless, exist.

2. *Other possible worlds are things of the same sort as the actual world* – "I and all my surroundings" (Lewis: 86). They differ "not in kind, but only in what goes on at them. Our actual world is only one world among others. We call it alone actual not because it differs in kind from all the rest, but because it is the world we inhabit" (Lewis: 85).

3. *The indexical analysis of the adjective 'actual' is the correct analysis*. "The inhabitants of other worlds may truly call their own world actual if they mean by 'actual' what we do; for the meaning we give to 'actual' is such that it refers at any world i to that world i itself. 'Actual' is indexical, like 'I' or 'here' or 'now': it depends for its reference on the circumstances of utterance, to wit, the world where the utterance is located" (Lewis: 85–6).

4. *Possible worlds cannot be reduced to something more basic*. "Possible worlds are what they are and not another thing." It would be a mistake to identify them with some allegedly more respectable entity, for example a set of sentences of some language. Possible worlds are "respectable entities in their own right" (Lewis: 85).

The first thesis, by itself, is compatible with Lewis's soothing claim that believing in possible worlds is doing no more than believing that things might have been different in various ways. What is claimed to exist are things which ordinary language calls "ways things might have been", things that truth is defined relative to, things that our modal idioms may be understood as quantifiers over. But the first thesis says nothing about the nature of the entities that play these roles. It is the second thesis which gives realism about possible worlds its metaphysical bite, since it implies that possible worlds are not shadowy ways things could be, but concrete particulars, or at least entities which are made up of concrete particulars and events. The actual world is "I and my surroundings". Other possible worlds are more things like that. Even a philosopher who had no qualms about abstract objects like numbers, properties, states and kinds might balk at this proliferation of fullblooded universes which seem less real to us than our own only because we have never been there.

The argument Lewis gives for thesis one, identifying possible worlds with ways things might have been, seems even to be incompatible with his explanation of possible worlds as more things of the same kind as I and all my surroundings. If possible worlds are ways things might have been, then the actual world ought to be *the way things are* rather than *I and all my surroundings. The way things are* is a property or a state of the world, not the world itself. The statement that the world is the way it is is true in a sense, but not when read as an identity statement (Compare: "the way the world is is the world"). This is important, since if properties can exist uninstantiated, then *the way the world is* could exist even if a world that is that way did not. One could accept thesis one – that there really are many ways that things could have been – while denying that there exists anything else that is like the actual world.

Does the force of thesis two rest, then, on a simple equivocation between "the actual world", in the sense that is roughly captured in the paraphrase "I and all my surroundings", and the sense in which it is equivalent to "the way things are"? In part, I think, but it also has a deeper motivation. One might argue from thesis three – the indexical analysis of actuality – to the conclusion that the essential difference between our world and the others is that we are here, and not there.

Thesis three seems to imply that the actuality of the actual world – the attribute in virtue of which it is actual – is a world-relative attribute. It is an attribute which our world has relative to itself, but which all the other worlds have relative to themselves too; so the *concept* of actuality does not distinguish, from an absolute standpoint, the actual world from the others. But if there is no absolute property of actuality, does this not mean that, looking at things from an objective point of view, merely possible people and their surroundings are just as real as we and ours?

The mistake in this reasoning, I think, is in the assumption that the absolute standpoint is a neutral one, distinct from the view from within any possible world. The problem is avoided when one recognizes that the standpoint of the actual world *is* the absolute standpoint, and that it is part of the concept of actuality that this should be so. We can grant that fictional characters are as right, from their point of view, to affirm their fullblooded reality as we are to affirm ours. But their point of view is fictional, and so what is right from it makes no difference as far as reality is concerned.

My point is that the *semantical* thesis that the indexical analysis of "actual" is correct can be separated from the metaphysical thesis that the actuality of the actual world is nothing more than a relation between it and things existing in it. Just as one could accept the indexical analysis of personal pronouns and be a solipsist, and accept the indexical analysis of tenses and believe that the past exists only as memory and the future only as anticipation, one can accept the indexical analysis of actuality while excluding from one's ontology any universes that *are* the way things might have been.

In fact, I want to argue, one must exclude those analogues of our universe from one's ontology. The thesis that the actual world alone is real is superficially analogous to solipsism – the thesis that I alone am real, but solipsism has content, and can be coherently denied, because it says something substantive about what alone is real. In effect, solipsism says that the actual world is a person, or a mind. But the thesis that the actual world alone is real has content only if "the actual world" means something other than the totality of everything there is, and I do not believe that it does. The thesis that there is no room in reality for other things than the actual world is not, like solipsism, based on a restrictive theory of what there is room for in reality, but rather on the metaphysically neutral belief that "the actual world" is just another name for reality.

So the moderate realism whose coherence I am trying to defend accepts theses one and three, and rejects thesis two. What about thesis four? If we identify possible worlds with ways things might have been, can we still hold that they are "respectable entities in their own right", irreducible to anything more fundamental? Robert Adams has argued that to avoid extreme realism we must find an eliminative reduction of possible worlds. "If there are any true statements in which there are said to be non-actual possible worlds," he argues, "they must be reducible to statements in which the only things there are said to be are things which are in the actual world, and which are not identical with non-actual possibles" (Adams: 224). Unless the reminder that by "possible world" we mean nothing more than "way things might have been" counts as such a reduction, I do not see why this should be necessary. Why cannot *ways things might have been* be elements of the actual world, as they are?

Two problems need to be separated: the first is the general worry that the notion of a possible world is a very obscure notion. How can explanations in terms of possible worlds help us to understand anything unless we are told what possible worlds are, and told in terms which are independent of the notions which possible worlds are intended to explain? The second problem is the specific problem that believing in possible worlds and in the indexical analysis of actuality seems to commit one to extreme realism, which (many believe) is obviously false. Now to point to the difference between a way our world might have been and a world which *is* the way our world might have been, and to make clear that the possible worlds whose existence the theory is committed to are the former kind of thing and not the latter, is to do nothing to solve the first problem; in fact it makes it more acute since it uses a modal operator to say what a possible world is. But this simple distinction does, I think, dissolve the second problem which was the motivation for Adams's demand for an analysis.

Not only is an eliminative reduction of possible worlds not necessary to solve the second problem, it also may not be sufficient to solve the first. I shall argue that the particular reduction that Adams proposes – a reduction of possible worlds to propositions – by itself says nothing that answers the critic who finds the concept of a possible world obscure. His reduction says no more, and in fact says less, about propositions and possible worlds than the reverse analysis that I would defend – the analysis of propositions in terms of possible worlds.

Adams's analysis is this: "Let us say that a *world-story* is a maximal consistent set of propositions. That is, it is a set which has as its members one member of every pair of mutually contradictory propositions, and which is such that it is possible for all of its members to be true together. The notion of a possible world can be given a contextual analysis in terms of world-stories" (Adams: 225). For a proposition to be true in some or all possible worlds is for it to be a member of some or all world-stories. Other statements that seem to be about possible worlds are to be replaced in a similar way by statements about world-stories.

There are three undefined notions used in Adams's reduction of possible worlds: *proposition, possibility*, and *contradictory*. What are propositions? Adams leaves this question open for further discussion; he suggests that it might be answered in various ways. Little is said about them except that they are to be thought of as language independent abstract objects, presumably the potential objects of speech acts and propositional attitudes.

What is possibility? The notion used in the definition of world-story is a property of *sets* of propositions. Intuitively, a set of propositions is possible if all its members can be true together. This notion cannot, of course, be defined in terms of possible worlds, or world-stories, without circularity, but it should be a consequence of the theory that a set of propositions is possible if and only if its members are simultaneously true in some possible world (are all members of some world-story). Presumably, an explicit formulation of the world-story theory would contain postulates sufficient to ensure this.

What is a contradictory? This relation between propositions might be defined in terms of possibility as follows: A and B are contradictories if and only if $\{A, B\}$ is not possible, and for every possible set of propositions Γ either $\Gamma \cup \{A\}$ or $\Gamma \cup \{B\}$ is possible. The theory tacitly assumes that every proposition has a contradictory; in an explicit formulation, this would be an additional postulate.

These definitions and postulates yield a minimal world-story theory. It is minimal in that it imposes no structure on the basic elements of the theory except what is required to justify what Adams calls the "intuitively very plausible thesis that possibility is holistic rather than atomistic, in the sense that what is possible is possible only as part of a possible completely determinate world" (Adams: 225). But the theory justifies this thesis only by postulating it.

It will be useful to compare this reduction of possible worlds to propositions with the competing reduction of propositions to possible worlds. What is at stake in choosing which of these two notions to define in terms of the other? Adams refers to the "not unfamiliar trade-off between non-actual possibles and intensions (such as propositions); given either, we may be able to construct the other, or do the work that was supposed to be done by talking about the other" (Adams: 228). But the two proposals are not equivalent. Part of what distinguishes them is an elusive question of conceptual priority, but there are also more substantive differences, both in the structure imposed on propositions and possible worlds and in the questions left to be answered by further developments of the respective theories.

If we set aside questions of conceptual priority – of which concepts and principles should be primitive and which defined or derived – what is the difference between the two analyses? The world-story theory is weaker, leaving open questions which are settled by the possible worlds analysis of propositions. The following two theses are consequences of the possible worlds analysis, but not of the world-story theory; the first concerns identity conditions; the second is a closure condition:

(I) Necessarily equivalent propositions are identical.

(C) For every set of propositions, there is a proposition which, necessarily, is true if and only if every member of the set is true.

Are these consequences of the possible worlds analysis welcome or not? I believe that thesis (I) can be defended independently of the possible worlds analysis of propositions, but that is a long story for another occasion. The thesis does have some notoriously problematic consequences, but I believe, first, that it is implied by a widely held and plausible assumption about the nature of

propositional attitudes – the assumption that attitudes like belief and desire are dispositions of agents displayed in their rational behavior – and second, that the apparently paradoxical consequences of the thesis can be explained away. But for now let me just point out that the possible worlds analysis has this substantive consequence, and leave the part of my argument which depends on it conditional on the assumption that this consequence is welcome. The thesis is not implied by the minimal world-story theory, but it is compatible with it, so the world-story theorist who agrees with me about thesis (I) can add it to his theory as an additional postulate.

Thesis (C) seems reasonable on almost any theory of propositions and propositional attitudes. Whatever propositions are, if there are propositions at all then there are sets of them, and for any set of propositions, it is something determinately true or false that all the members of the set are true. If one is willing to talk of propositions at all, one will surely conclude that that something is a proposition. It may not be possible to express all such propositions since it may not be possible, in any actual language, to refer to all such sets; it may not be humanly possible to believe or disbelieve some such propositions, since it may not be humanly possible to grasp them. But if this is so, it is surely a contingent human limitation which should not restrict the range of potential objects of propositional attitudes. So I will assume that the world-story theorist will want to add thesis (C) to his theory.

If (I) and (C) are added as postulates to the minimal world-story theory, then it becomes equivalent to the possible worlds analysis with respect to the structure it imposes on the set of propositions, and on the relation between propositions and possible worlds. The sole difference that remains between the two theories is that one takes as primitive what the other defines. And even this difference will be eliminated if we make one more change in response to a question about the further development of the world-story theory.

The next question for the world-story theorist is this: can he say more about his fundamental concept, the concept of a proposition? In particular, are there some *basic* propositions out of which all the rest can be constructed? The usual way to answer this question is to model basic propositions on the atomic sentences of a first order language; propositions are constructed out of individuals and primitive properties and relations in the same way that sentences are constructed out of names and predicates. But this strategy requires building further structure into the theory. There is another way to answer the question which needs no further assumption. We can deduce from what has already been built into the world-story theory that there is a set of propositions of which all propositions are truth-functions: this is the set of strongest contingent propositions – those propositions which are members of just one world-story. It is thus a harmless change, a matter of giving the theory a more economical formulation, to take these to be the basic propositions. (This change does not foreclose a further reduction of what are here called basic propositions. Any alternative reduction could be expressed as a further reduction; this is why the move is harmless.) We can then define propositions generally as sets of basic propositions (or, for a neater formulation, call the basic elements *propositional elements* and let their unit sets be the basic propositions.) A non-basic proposition will be true just in case one of its members is true. This reduction has the added advantage that it allows us to define the previously primitive property of possibility, and to derive all of the postulates. With these primitive notions and assumptions eliminated, the world-story theory looks as good as the theory that takes possible worlds as primitive and defines propositions. This is, of course, because it is exactly the same theory.

I have gone through this exercise of changing the world-story theory into the possible worlds analysis of propositions in order to make the following point: first, the minimal world-story theory with which I began is indeed a minimal theory of propositions, a theory that assumes nothing about them except that they have truth values and are related to each other by the standard propositional relations (entailment, compatibility, and so forth). But second, every step in the metamorphosis of this minimal theory into the possible worlds analysis is motivated by independently plausible assumptions about propositions or by theory-neutral considerations of economy of formulation. If this is right, then the possible worlds analysis is not just one theory which makes the assumptions about propositions that I have made. More than this, it is the whole content of that analysis to impose the minimal structure on propositions which is appropriate to a theory which understands propositions in this way. Anyone who believes that there are objects of propositional attitudes, and who accepts the assumptions about the formal properties of the set of these objects, must accept that there are things which have all the properties that the possible worlds theory attributes to possible worlds, and that propositions can be reduced to these things.

Is the form of realism about possible worlds that I want to defend really realism? It is in the sense that it claims that the concept of a possible world is a basic concept in a true account of the way we represent the world in our propositional acts and attitudes. A full defense of this kind of realism would require a development and defense of such an account. All I have tried to do here is show that there is a coherent thesis about possible worlds which rejects extreme realism, but which takes possible worlds seriously as irreducible entities, a thesis that treats possible worlds as more than a convenient myth or a notational shortcut, but less than universes that resemble our own.[1]

Note

1 I am indebted to the John Simon Guggenheim Memorial Foundation for support during the time when this paper was written.

References

Robert Merrihew Adams, "Theories of Actuality" *Noûs* 8(1974): 211–31.

David Lewis, *Counterfactuals* (Cambridge, Mass.: Harvard University Press, 1973).

J. L. Mackie, *Truth, Probability and Paradox* (Oxford: Clarendon Press, 1973).

Lawrence Powers, Comments on R. Stalnaker, "Propositions" in Alfred F. MacKay and Daniel D. Merrill (eds.), *Issues in the Philosophy of Language* (New Haven: Yale University Press, 1976).

18

Modal Fictionalism

Gideon Rosen

1   The Problem

Like most people, Ed does not believe in blue swans. However, he does believe that such creatures *might* have existed. That is, he believes such things are possible.

Now according to the standard possible worlds account of modality,

(1)   There might have been blue swans iff there is a world W such that, at W, there are blue swans.

So given what Ed already believes, if he embraces this analysis his beliefs will deductively entail that

(2)   There is a (non-actual) possible world at which there are blue swans.

Thus for someone like Ed – someone with ordinary modal opinions – to accept the possible worlds analysis is to take on a *commitment* to believing in other possible worlds. Or at least, this is what our trivial deduction seems to show.

Unfortunately, again like many people, Ed just cannot bring himself to endorse this commitment. He cannot believe that other possible worlds exist. Thus it appears that Ed has no choice: on pain of inconsistency, he must reject the possible worlds approach to modality.

Now this may not seem like much of a tragedy. But we have left out one detail. What lends the situation its peculiar poignancy is that Ed is a philosopher; and as a philosopher he knows that in discussions of modal subtleties – discussions which can hardly be avoided nowadays – the language of possible worlds has become a nearly indispensible tool. For it permits the articulation of modal views with a clarity and vividness that cannot be achieved by other means – so much so that even philosophers who officially renounce the idiom often find themselves talking about possible worlds anyway when it becomes important to make a modal claim precise or a modal argument rigorous. There is a great risk of doublethink in such circumstances: asserting the existence of worlds at one moment while denying it at another. Ed suffers a debilitating anxiety at the prospect of ontological hypocrisy. Something must be done. But what?

If we suppose that the employment of the possible worlds framework inevitably involves asserting, for instance, that there is a world with blue swans, then it would appear that Ed has only

Gideon Rosen, "Modal Fictionalism," *Mind*, NS 99/395 (July 1990): 327–54. Published by Oxford University Press on behalf of the Mind Association. Reproduced by permission.

Metaphysics: An Anthology, Second Edition. Edited by Jaegwon Kim, Daniel Z. Korman and Ernest Sosa.

two choices short of abstinence: he can submit to whatever cognitive psychotherapy he might need to overcome his aversion to possible worlds; or he can look for a way to interpret his apparent quantification over worlds in such claims as a misleading *façon de parler*, lacking the usual implications of existential quantification.

If Ed chooses the psychotherapeutic route, he will find no shortage of willing therapists, and an abundance of useful self-help literature. These are the writings of those who openly advocate an ontology of things called 'possible worlds'; and here we should distinguish two fundamentally different approaches.

The first is what Lewis has called *ersatz modal realism*.[1] This is really a family of views, unified by the idea that talk of 'possible worlds' is not to be taken literally. There are indeed a vast number of 'worlds'; but they are not really *worlds* on a par with the spatially extended universe we inhabit. Rather they are *abstract representations* of various ways our world might have been. Thus one typical ersatzist proposal identifies worlds with sets of sentences which represent possible states of the World by describing them.[2] Other forms of ersatzism identify worlds with other, possibly less familiar abstract objects.[3] In each case, however, the response to the charge of ontological impropriety is much the same: people like Ed who are put off by the possible worlds approach have been misled by the colourful terminology into thinking that worlds must be bizarre things, more fit for science fiction than serious philosophy. But this is a mistake. So-called 'possible worlds' are really nothing but *actually existing abstract objects*, the likes of which most philosophers already believe in. To call them 'non-actual' is not to say that they inhabit some shadowy purgatory between being and non-being, but only that they fail to represent things as they are. From an ontological point of view, at any rate, nothing could be more straightforward.

The other approach is Lewis's own *modal realism*. For reasons I will not pursue, Lewis doubts that the ersatz modal realist can produce an account of worlds adequate to every task for which worlds might be wanted. (*Pl.*, ch. 3). He maintains instead that the full benefits of the framework can only be had if we suppose that the non-actual 'worlds' are literally *worlds* –

distinct universes as real and robust as ̸ yet wholly isolated from one another an̸

Obviously the modal realist's res̸ sceptics like Ed cannot be as quick as the ersatzer's, since the realist actually believes what the sceptic finds incredible; namely, that besides our universe there are countless others, populated with blue swans, talking donkeys, and every other beast, conceivable or not. The realist must allay such worries while he answers head on every weighty metaphysical argument which purports to show that our world is the only world there is. And this is only the beginning. Critics have claimed to see in modal realism the seeds of every pernicious intellectual trend from inductive scepticism to moral nihilism. Lewis's recent book is devoted largely to the heroic task of answering these charges, as well as to positive argument for his position. The aim, ultimately, is to persuade people like Ed that despite our initial shock and horror, we all have good reason to revise our naive ontological view by taking on a commitment to robust possible worlds.

I will not stop to weigh the relative merits of realism and ersatzism here. In fact I am going to assume that this dispute has been settled in the realist's favour. That is, I will assume that Lewis is right to say that *if* there are entities fit to play the role of possible worlds in a general account of modality, they must be the robust, largely concrete objects the realist believes in. I will also suppose that Lewis has successfully blunted the more *philosophical* objections to modal realism, like the charge that it renders modal knowledge impossible or that it leads to paradoxes of various sorts.

The only objection I will not suppose answered is perhaps the most famous: the incredulous stare.[4] As Lewis says, 'modal realism *does* disagree, to an extreme extent, with firm common sense opinion about what there is' (*Pl.*, p. 133). To embrace it is to undertake a massive revision in the world-view we bring with us to philosophy. And it may be that in spite of everything Lewis says, in spite of the many ways in which he shows his hypothesis to be fruitful in systematic metaphysics, one still finds oneself unable to assent to it. This is the significance of the incredulous stare; and Lewis is right to say that he cannot refute it, because it is not an argument. It is rather an expression of the degree to which, given our starting point, modal realism, with its commitment to countless non-actual talking donkeys and the like, must strike us as utterly incredible.

When I said that Ed was unwilling to take on a commitment to possible worlds, this was the character I had in mind – a theorist who rejects ersatzism, perhaps for Lewis's reasons, but at the same time finds the realist's metaphysical picture impossible to accept. Such a theorist has good reason to look into Ed's remaining option – to interpret his apparent quantification over possible worlds as an innocent *façon de parler*, involving no commitment to worlds of any sort.

I will call any interpretation with this feature a *deflationist* interpretation of the possible worlds framework.[5] According to deflationism, you can have all the benefits of talking about possible worlds without the ontological costs. You can legitimately say in one breath (perhaps in the course of explaining what you mean by some modal claim) 'there is a world where blue swans exist' and in the next breath; 'but really, I don't believe in possible worlds'. The trick is to explain why this is not a plain contradiction.

A complete survey of the deflationist's options would, I suppose, have to recognize as a potential starting point each of the myriad dodges philosophers have devised to explain away their apparent quantification over entities they profess not to believe in. Thus the deflationist might try to maintain that his quantifier over worlds is not the familiar existential quantifier but some more exotic bird. Perhaps it is a substitutional quantifier; or possibly Routley's Meinongian 'particular' quantifier which ranges indiscriminately over what there is and what there is not.[6] Alternatively, the deflationist might try to argue that the surface form of his assertion is more radically misleading, perhaps by claiming that his utterances of 'there are blue swan worlds' when properly understood contain no quantifier over worlds of any kind, much as claims about *the average family* are shown upon analysis to contain no term purporting to refer to such a creature.

I want to discuss the prospects for deflationism. But I will not survey the landscape here. Instead my procedure will be to describe at the outset a new deflationist strategy which strikes me as especially promising. The aim is to see what sort of balm it might offer for someone in Ed's sad condition.

2   Fictionalism

The deflationist strategy I want to discuss might fittingly be called 'fictionalism' about possible worlds.[7] The central idea is that sentences about, for example, blue swan worlds – sentences which look like straightforward existential generalizations – should be understood by analogy with (3):

(3)   There is a brilliant detective at 221b Baker street.

Taken as a straightforward existential claim, this is false, and anyone who asserts it with the intention that it be so understood speaks falsely. Yet we know that there are conversational contexts in which utterances of (3) may be perfectly *correct* – even true; namely, conversations about what happens in Sherlock Holmes stories. In these contexts, utterances of (3) are not intended straightforwardly. Rather, when the participants are mutually aware that the topic is a certain body of fiction, and not, for example, the history of British criminology, utterances of (3) will be read as elliptical renderings of (4):

(4)   In the Holmes stories, there is a brilliant detective at 221b Baker Street.

Now this claim is perfectly true; and so, therefore, are utterances of (3) where the context can be counted upon to supply the silent prefix 'In the Holmes stories ...'[8]

For us, however, the important thing about (4) and its ellipsis (3) is not that they are true, but rather that someone may unflinchingly believe or assert what they say without committing himself to believing that a detective lives in Baker Street. The Holmes stories are *fictions*. And one characteristic feature of fictions is that we may legitimately have opinions about their contents without believing that what they say is true, or that the objects they purport to describe exist.

Call any sentential operator of the form 'In the fiction F, ...' or 'According to such and such a story ...' a *story prefix*. The moral of the last paragraph, then, is that as we ordinarily understand these expressions, quantification within the scope of a story prefix is not existentially committing. You can believe 'According to the fiction F, $\exists x P x$' without believing '$\exists x P x$'; for as a rule, the former does not entail the latter.

We may generalize further by noting that the story mentioned in a story prefix need not be a literary fiction, nor for that matter, any sort of fiction in the usual sense. Russell thought that *according to Leibniz's monadology*, the table is really a colony of souls. But we do not conclude on this basis that Russell was himself committed to the animist metaphysic. In general, the fiction mentioned in a story prefix can be *any representation whatsoever*: a story, a scientific theory, or a metaphysical speculation. The basic point is unaffected: so long as you are not independently committed to regarding this representation as true, when you assent to 'In F, P' you incur no obligation to assent to 'P' by itself.

The fictionalist about possible worlds hopes to take advantage of this fact by interpreting his own apparent quantification over worlds as quantification within the scope of a story prefix. As with (3), the prefix will sometimes be *silent*; so the fictionalist will often sound just like the modal realist. Yet the fictionalist's claims about possible worlds will always be elliptical for claims about the content of a story; and the ellipsis can always be expanded. In this way, the fictionalist hopes to earn honest title to the language of possible worlds – that is, title to talk as if there were such things – while retaining a sensible one-World ontology.

The first and most obvious problem in developing this strategy is to specify the story the fictionalist plans to exploit. The chief constraint, of course, is that it be one according to which the usual claims about possible worlds – for example, the claim that there are blue swan worlds – are true. There may be more than one story or theory of possible worlds which meets this constraint. But one is particularly salient, especially in the present dialectical context. I have in mind Lewis's own modal realism, a theory explicitly designed to meet this constraint. This suggests a starting point: the fictionalist will explain that his own talk about possible worlds is to be understood, not as talk about what exists in fact, but rather as talk about what exists according to the realist's hypothesis of an immense plurality of robust universes.[9]

In other words, what the realist regards as true metaphysics, the fictionalist regards as a (probably) false story, to be mentioned *but not asserted* in his account of modality. For example, although the fictionalist does not for a moment believe that there are worlds with blue swans, he does believe (as anyone should) that

(5)   According to the hypothesis of a plurality of worlds, there is at world W such that at W there are blue swans.

The fictionalist maintains that when he utters, as he might, 'there is a blue swan world' what he really means to assert is (5). This uncontroversial metafictional thesis is the fictionalist's paraphrase of the equally uncontroversial modal claim that there might have been blue swans.

More generally, let P be an arbitrary modal proposition. The modal realist will have ready a non-modal paraphrase of P in the language of possible worlds; call it P^*. The realist's assertions about possible worlds are guided by explicit adherence to the schema P *iff* P^*. The fictionalist's parasitic proposal is therefore to assert every instance of the schema: P *iff according to the hypothesis of the plurality of worlds*, P^*. Like modal realism, the theory would seem to provide truth conditions for modal claims in a systematic way. Indeed, if the prefix is allowed to go silent, the two theories will be verbally indiscernible. The difference is that the fictionalist's account does not presuppose an ontology of possible worlds.

3   The Fictionalist's Fiction

Before we can begin to evaluate this proposal, we need to be a bit more explicit about this fiction I have called 'the hypothesis of the plurality of worlds'. We begin with a set of informal postulates.

(6a)   Reality consists in a plurality of *universes* or "worlds".

(6b)   One of these is what we ordinarily call *the* universe: the largest connected spatiotemporal system of which we are parts.

(6c)   The others are things of roughly the same kind: systems of objects, many of them concrete, connected by a network of external relations like the spatiotemporal distances that connect objects in our universe. (*Pl.*, pp. 2, 74–6)

(6d)   Each universe is isolated from the others; that is, particulars in distinct universes are not spatiotemporally related. (It follows that universes do not overlap; no particular inhabits two universes.) (*Pl.*, p. 78)

(6e)   The totality of universes is closed under a principle of recombination. Roughly: for any collection of objects from any number of universes, there is a single universe containing any number of duplicates of each, provided there is a spacetime large enough to hold them. (*Pl.*, pp. 87–90)[10]

(6f)   There are no arbitrary limits on the plenitude of universes. (*Pl.*, p. 103)[11]

(6g)   Our universe is not special. That is, there is nothing remarkable about it from the point of view of the system of universes.[12]

These postulates – whose significance will become clearer as we go on – are meant to capture in a preliminary way the ontological core of Lewis's modal realism. They describe the objects a modal realist *qua* modal realist must believe in.

In one important sense, however, the postulates fail to capture the full force of modal realism. To see why, it is enough to note that (6) is formulated without modal vocabulary. The postulates are all theses about what there *is*, not what there *must* or *might be*.[13] And this has the odd consequence that the theory they determine is (in some sense) compatible with the view that everything is actual. That is, we can imagine an extravagant actualist embracing (6) while adding that only actual things exist. There is no contradiction here. It is simply the eccentric view that actuality is much bigger than we ordinarily think – a vast sea of 'island universes' – a cosmology that might appeal to an actualist metaphysician driven by the converse of Quine's taste for clear skies and desert landscapes.[14]

I take it, however, that modal realism is incompatible with actualism by definition. To be a modal realist is to believe that some things are real but not actual. In order to capture this aspect, then, more needs to be said. For example, we might supplement the postulates with some remark such as (7):

(7)   The universes are *possible worlds*; our universe and its parts are actual individuals; the others are *merely possible*.

(6) and (7) together clearly entail that some things are real but non-actual. The theory they determine deserves the name 'modal realism' (MR), and anyone who believes it is a modal realist.

I labour this point mainly to point out that the fictionalist's fiction is not exactly MR. With the addition of (7), MR contains overt (albeit defined) modal vocabulary in its formulation. For reasons of clarity, however, the fictionalist does well to keep his fiction non-modal. Still, he wants to retain the realist's idea that our universe is one of many. He therefore takes as his starting point the original postulates (6); the supplementary modal bridge laws in (7) will play no role in his account.

But these original postulates are not quite enough for the fictionalist's purposes. They tell us a great deal about the realist's general conception of the totality of universes. Yet they say rather little about what sorts of objects the various universes contain. Thus nothing in (6) guarantees that some of the universes contain people or clouds or stars, much less blue swans and tailless kangaroos. As we will shortly see, however, it is crucial that the fictionalist's fiction provide a rich and detailed picture of what goes on in the various universes. Towards this end, the fictionalist proposes that the original postulates be supplemented with an *encyclopaedia*: a list of the non-modal truths about the intrinsic character of this universe.[15] The encyclopaedia specifies, for example, that our universe contains objects which are rather like ordinary kangaroos but for the lack of a tail (at least in the form of undetached kangaroo-parts). So, by recombination (6e), other universes contain free-standing tailless kangaroos, duplicates of these residents of our world. This new theory – (6) together with the complete catalogue of non-modal intrinsic truths about our world – is the fictionalist's fiction. Call it *PW*.

4 The Fictionalist Theory of Possibility

We can now state the fictionalist's proposal in a more precise way. Let P be an arbitrary modal claim, and P^* the modal realist's non-modal paraphrase of P in the language of possible worlds. (If the realist's claim to provide a reductive analysis is sound, P^* must always exist.) The modal realist asserts the biconditional P iff P^*, which, as we have seen, leads directly to a commitment to possible worlds when conjoined with common-sense modal opinion. The fictionalist's ploy is to borrow P^*, the fruit of the realist's labour, without asserting it, and to assert instead instances of the schema:

P iff according to PW, P^*.

As Russell might have said, the method has (at least) the advantages of theft over honest toil. What remains to be seen is whether it has any others.

To illustrate, consider Ed's conviction that

(8)   There might have been blue swan.

For the modal realist, this is equivalent to an existential generalization about possible worlds:

(8r)   There is a universe containing blue swans.

The fictionalist therefore offers the following paraphrase:

(8f)   According to PW, there is a universe containing blue swans.

The example brings out the central contrast between fictionalism and modal realism. If, like Ed, you are at all sceptical about the real existence of blue swans, you should not believe (8r). But no one should doubt that (8f) is true. It should be utterly uncontroversial that *according to the realist's conception of the plurality of universes*, there is a universe with a blue swan in it. And this is as it should be, because it is equally uncontroversial that there might have been blue swans. And for the fictionalist these come to the same thing.

To get some sense of the intended range of the fictionalist analysis, consider a counterfactual.

(9)   If swans were blue, ducks would be pink.

Glossing over certain subtleties, we may suppose that the realist construes this as a restricted universal generalization:

(9r)   In each universe that differs from ours as little as the blueness of swans permits, duck are pink.

So the fictionalist offers the obvious parasitic analysis:

(9f)   According to PW, every universe that differs as little from ours as the blueness of swans permits is a universe where ducks are pink.

Here the sceptic about other universes can plausibly endorse the realist's paraphrase. If ours is the only universe, (9r) is vacuously true. In contrast, (9f), like the counterfactual itself, is obviously false. On the realist's view there are universes very much like ours with blue swans and ordinary ducks; and these are more like our world in the relevant respects than is any universe featuring both non-standard ducks and swans.

These examples are elementary, of course. They contain none of the iterated modalities or other syntactic complexities which the cognoscenti will recognize as potential sources of difficulty. Still, they bring out the central contrast: by and large, the fictionalist will paraphrase uncontroversially true (false) modal statements with similarly uncontroversial statements about the content of the theory PW. And other things being equal, this is an advantage, since the realist paraphrase of even the most trivial modal thesis is generally a highly contentious metaphysical speculation, sharply at odds with what most of us (including Ed) ordinarily believe.

I will come back to the relative merits of the two positions in a moment. But first I would like to stress one important respect in which the views are on a par. The examples suggest (without of course proving it) that in central cases, *the realist and the fictionalist will concur in their theoretically informed modal judgements.* That is, whenever the realist believes that his paraphrase of a modal claim is true, the fictionalist should have the same view of *his* paraphrase. This is a straightforward consequence of the fictionalist's shameless parasitism. When the realist believes his account P^* of the modal claim P, this can only be because he judges P^* true on the basis of a theory he accepts. But this is precisely what the fictionalist is interested in: the truth value of the realist's paraphrase according to the realist's theory. The realist and the fictionalist therefore generate theoretically informed modal judgements by considering precisely the same range of facts. And this guarantees that the two will generally agree about the modal truths. (But see section 7 below.)

Now one plausible desideratum for a philosophical account of modal discourse is that it should *ratify* a substantial body of prior modal opinion. The theorist should do his best, in other words, to paraphrase modal claims we all believe with propositions that he is entitled to believe in light of his theory. The upshot of the last paragraph is therefore the following conditional correctness claim: if the modal realist is in a position to regard his analysis as adequate in this minimal sense, the fictionalist is as well.[16]

Of course, such fidelity to common-sense modal opinion is not the only constraint on an adequate account of modality. More generally, we should hope that our approach will be largely compatible with the rest of what we believe about the world and our place in it. For example, I take it as given that we possess a great deal of modal knowledge. Hence it is a grave fault in any philosophical account of the modal facts if it makes it mysterious that we can know them, given what we firmly believe about the limits of our faculties. We also bring a relatively firm ontological view to the analysis of modality; and any theory that requires us to abandon important parts of it is faulty for a similar reason. How then does fictionalism fare with respect to these further constraints on our project?

5 Ontology

As I have said, perhaps the most powerful objection to Lewis's view is that, seen in light of things we firmly believe, modal realism is simply incredible. Normally we do not think that there are countless universes besides our own, much less that they are populated by an infinity of blue swans, talking donkeys, and the rest. Yet modal realism tells us that these things exist. To embrace

it is therefore to undertake a substantial revision in the world-view we bring with us to this metaphysical problem.

Now strangeness can never be a decisive objection. But I believe it must count for something. We have little use in the end for a philosophy we cannot seriously believe. Hence when we are exhorted to change our view over to one which by our present lights seems fantastically unlikely, we are entitled to ask for correspondingly strong reasons. Lewis's main strategy is to motivate modal realism by showing how *useful* it is in systematic philosophy to suppose that there are many worlds. One may doubt that modal realism really is as useful as Lewis says; but even granting this, one may still wonder whether such considerations of utility could ever be enough to motivate so radical a revision in our conception of what there is.[17]

The first and most obvious advantage of fictionalism, then, is that it appears to have no revisionary ontological consequences whatsoever. At the very least, you can believe everything the fictionalist says about the truth conditions for modal statements without having to believe in possibilia. For as we have seen, the fictionalist's claims are claims about the content of a story. And because they do not presuppose the truth of that story, you can believe them without inheriting a commitment to the items the story purports to describe.

This is not to say that fictionalism is altogether silent on ontological matters. It may well be that in talking about stories, theories, and other representations as he does, the fictionalist takes on a commitment to these entities. And since it is conventional to regard these representations as *abstract* entities, fictionalism may not appeal to certain nominalists.[18] Now this conventional view is hardly sacrosanct. It may be possible, for all I know, to give a nominalistically acceptable treatment of the fictionalist's ontology. But even if this is not possible, it must be admitted that, given our starting point, a commitment to abstract objects is not nearly so weighty as the realist's commitment to possible worlds. Nominalism was no part of the sensible, naive ontology that Ed, for one, was so concerned to preserve. Most of us already believe in stories, theories, and the rest, even if we lack a neat theory of them. In any case, the point is not that fictionalism says nothing about what exists, but rather that, unlike modal realism, it requires no large scale change in view; and other things being equal, this must seem a distinct virtue of the fictionalist approach.

6 Epistemology

If fictionalism aspires (as modal realism surely does) to provide an account of the nature of modal truth, then the fictionalist must show his account to be compatible with the manifest fact of our modal knowledge. He must convince us that the modal facts as he conceives them are the sort of fact that creatures like us can know. In this section I will only take up part of this problem. I would like to ask whether fictionalism is compatible with the view that our usual methods for forming modal beliefs are generally a good guide to the modal truth. This is a central question for any account. A theory that cannot ground our confidence in the reliability of our best methods would seem to lead rather quickly to modal scepticism, the view that we have no modal knowledge; a claim which, like most strong sceptical theses, is very hard to believe.

Modal realism, of course, is often said to violate this condition. The worry is that if modal statements are understood as claims about a domain of physical objects from which we are causally isolated, it may seem hard to see why we should credit our world-bound faculties with the capacity to deliver the modal truth. I will not review Lewis's response to this challenge: I find it (sometimes) compelling (cf. *Pl.*, pp. 108–15). Instead I would like to focus on certain important remarks he makes along the way. Responding to the demand for a naturalistic account of the sources of modal belief, Lewis writes:

In the mathematical case, the answer is that we come by our opinions largely by reasoning from general principles that we already accept … I suppose the answer in the modal case is similar. I think our everyday modal opinions are, in large measure, consequences of a principle of recombination … One could imagine reasoning rigorously from a precise formulation of it, but in fact our reasoning is more likely to take the form of imaginative experiments. We try to think how duplicates of things already accepted as

possible … might be rearranged to fit the description of an alleged possibility. Having imagined various arrangements – not in complete detail, of course – we consider how they might be aptly described. (*Pl.*, pp. 113–14)

This passage sketches a plausible account of the role of imagination in modal reasoning. Imagination does not put us in 'contact' with a special realm of being. Rather, when we imagine we consider the consequences of certain principles which guide our thought – in the modal case, principles which seem well captured by the postulates of *PW*. We construct representations of situations in accordance with our empirical knowledge, the principles of recombination, non-arbitrariness, and so on.[19] And if one of the situations we imagine by this route is aptly described by the statement *P*, we conclude that 'Possibly *P*' is true.

Now if something along these lines is right, any account of modality must somehow explain why we should regard this imaginative method as a reliable way of finding out the modal truth. Discovering the consequences of principles that guide the imagination is, after all, a broadly psychological enquiry. Why should that be a good way of discovering what might have been?

The realist's answer is deceptively simple. (i) the modal truths are truths about a domain of universes; (ii) the principles which guide our imagination are true of that domain; so (iii) by and large, when we imagine in accordance with these principles the states of affairs we imagine are realized somewhere among the universes.

Straightforward, perhaps; but this line of response ought to seem profoundly puzzling. Letting the first premiss pass, (ii) remains a striking conjecture. We may ask: is it just a coincidence that the principles which guide our imaginations truly describe a domain of objects with which human beings had absolutely no contact when those principles were being shaped, presumably by a perfectly natural evolutionary process? After all, there might have been creatures whose imaginative principles were quite out of step with the distribution of worlds in modal space. How is it that we are so lucky as to have been given the *right* imaginative dispositions? Surely the realist owes us an explanation.

I will not presume to answer for the realist, who will no doubt begin by pointing to other cognitive domains (e.g., inductive reasoning) where the reliability of our faculties must be allowed to be an historically contingent matter. The only point I want to stress is that no analogous problem arises for the fictionalist. If the realist is right in suggesting that we are guided in the imaginative construction of possibilities by principles like the postulates of *PW*, then when we engage in imaginative experiments, *the least we discover is what is true according to PW*. But for the fictionalist, that is enough. The modal facts just are facts of this kind. Thus for the fictionalist there is no special mystery as to why we should trust our imaginations as a guide to the modal truth. And once again, this seems to me an important point in fictionalism's favour.[20]

7   The Incompleteness Problem

I hope fictionalism is beginning to look like a potentially attractive solution to Ed's dilemma: a way to exploit the possible worlds framework for various purposes without believing in worlds besides our own. Unfortunately, as the reader will no doubt have guessed, the picture is not so unreservedly rosy. In the sequel I shall discuss three problems for fictionalism. None is decisive against the view, but they give a fair picture of the complexities it may involve. For someone in Ed's position, they may be just the thing to tip the scales against the strategy we have been discussing.

Earlier I made the modest claim that fictionalism and modal realism agree with one another (and with everyday opinion) about a large body of modal doctrine – the modal statements that strike us either as obviously true or obviously false. A more general equivalence claim fails, however, and this may mean trouble for the fictionalist. It turns out that in some rather marginal cases, the fictionalist and the realist must disagree about what the modal truths are; and for a theorist whose intuitions clearly favour the latter, this may count against the fictionalist proposal.

To see the difficulty, we need as an example a modal claim which, from the realist's point of view, has a determinate truth value of which we are ignorant. Moreover, we require that this ignorance not be due to ignorance about the empirical facts of our universe. It must be a robust modal ignorance – an ignorance that would survive an arbitrary extension of our scientific and historical knowledge. Now it may not be obvious that such statements exist. But on Lewis's view, certain claims about how 'large' the universe might have been fit into this category. For example, let κ be a cardinal number larger than the number of space-time regions in our universe, and consider the claim that

(10)   There might have been κ non-overlapping physical objects.

For the realist, of course, this amounts to a claim about the size of the largest universes:

(10r)   There is a universe containing κ non-overlapping physical objects.

But this claim differs importantly from the others we have considered. As mentioned earlier, Lewis holds that there must be an upper bound κ^* to the number of non-overlapping objects that inhabit the most populous words (see n. 10). Yet we do not know what this upper bound is; and for all we know, even if we were fully informed about the empirical character of our universe we might still have no insight into this global aspect of the totality of universes. Thus for the realist, the modal claim (10) has a definite truth value; but we cannot say what it is, because we do not know – and may never know – whether $\kappa < \kappa^*$.

Now consider the fictionalist's attitude towards (10). For him, (10) is equivalent to

(10f)   According to *PW*, there is a universe containing κ non-overlapping physical objects.

What is the truth value of this sentence? Well, this much seems clear: the upshot of the last paragraph is that even if we had a full specification of *PW* – a list of the postulates, together with a complete account of the non-modal intrinsic nature of our world – we might still be in no position to affirm that according to *PW*, there are universes containing *k* objects. *The story is simply silent on this point.* But (10f) implies that it gives a definite positive answer. So (10f) is not true.

The fictionalist therefore has two options: (10*f*) is false or it is truth-valueless. In either case, because (10*f*) is not true, the fictionalist must say that the modal claim (10) with which he takes it to be equivalent is not true. And this is already a departure from realism. The fictionalist who takes *PW* as his governing fiction can rule out in advance the possibility that there might have been *κ* objects; the realist cannot. So if for some reason you have a positive intuition that this ought to remain an open question, you may find this form of fictionalism counter-intuitive. But we can go even further. For it seems that whichever course the fictionalist takes he must say something implausible.

The more natural option is surely to call (10*f*) false. After all, (10*f*) says that the realist's theory settles whether there are worlds of a certain size; but the theory does not settle that question. So (10*f*) attributes to *PW* a property it does not have. To see why this natural verdict leads to trouble for the fictionalist, consider (11):

(11)   It is not the case that there might have been *κ* non-overlapping physical objects.

On the face of it, this is the negation of our original modal claim (10). And it is an important feature of our understanding of modal discourse that here, as everywhere, a statement and its negation are contradictories. That is, they must have different truth values if they have truth values at all. The fictionalist has to respect this appearance, I think. Hence if he declares (10) *false*, he must declare (11) *true*.

Unfortunately, this assignment of truth values is ruled out by symmetry considerations. The fictionalist's analysis of (11),

(11*f*)   According to *PW*, no universe con-tatins *κ* physical objects.

has exactly the same form as (10*f*): the story *PW* is silent about the truth value of the embedded sentence. But since this was our reason for calling (10*f*) false, symmetry requires that we declare (11*f*) – and hence (11) – false as well. The intuitive claim that (10*f*) is false therefore seems to force the fictionalist to concede that (10) and (11) – a modal claim and its negation – have the same truth value, in violation of what I take to be a

fairly firm commitment of ordinary usage to the effect that such claims are always contradictory.[21]

The fictionalist can avoid this result by declaring that in general when the paraphrase *P** of a modal claim *P* is not determinately settled as true or false by the theory *PW*, the modal claim *P* is to lack a truth value. (10) and (11) would then both be truth valueless, which is compatible with their being contradictories.

I am going to suppose that the fictionalist makes this stipulation. Unfortunately, besides being less natural than the first, it has one or two worrying consequences. The first is that with this stipulation, the ordinary logical connectives when applied to modal statements are no longer truth-functional. (10) and (11) are truth valueless. But their disjunction is a logical truth, as is its paraphrase into the language of *PW*. And I assume that all such logical truths are true according to *PW*. So the fictionalist must allow that in the modal case we may have a true disjunction with neither disjunct true. A similar situation arises in other areas, of course, most notably in certain philosophical treatments of vagueness and the truth-predicate which employ a supervaluational approach to the semantics of truth value gaps.[22] Still it may seem troubling to see the phenomenon repeated here, in a domain where our ordinary ways of thinking give us no reason to expect a complicated propositional logic, and where the only reason for proposing one is, to say the least, generated by concerns rather distant from the linguistic practice in question.

A second problem is more troubling. Recall that in the intuitive explanation of the fiction-alist's strategy I relied on an understanding of how story prefixes generally work. We understand what sort of expression the fictionalist's operator 'According to *PW*' is supposed to be only because we are told that it is a member of the familiar class of expressions that includes, for example, 'In the Holmes stories …'. Unfortunately, it seems fairly clear that the familiar story prefixes do not give rise to truth value gaps like those we have just proposed on the fictionalist's behalf. The Holmes stories are silent about Moriarty's blood type just as *PW* is silent about the size of the largest worlds. Yet if someone were to assert 'In the Holmes stories, Moriarty has blood type A +' we would naturally suppose that he had said something *false*, not something lacking in truth value. Again: quantum mechanics is silent on the panpsychism question. But when avatars of the new age say that according to quantum mechanics, the universe is conscious, they speak *falsely*. Quantum mechanics says no such thing. The solution to the problem of modal contradictories has the consequence that the fictionalist's operator departs from the paradigm by giving rise to gaps rather than falsehoods in analogous circumstances. And this should leave us wondering how well we really understand it. If it differs in this way from other story prefixes, how else does it differ and why? Unless he can answer, the fictionalist's view is infected by unclarity at its core.

8 Primitive Modality

So far we have treated the fictionalist's operator as an intuitively understood but undefined primitive expression. Yet these last remarks suggest that it is in fact a potentially puzzling creature; and one may legitimately suspect that a serious effort to explain its semantic behaviour will reveal hidden complexity in the fictionalist's view.

Further reason to worry emerges when we consider what we might say by way of explication to someone who did not already understand the expression 'According to *PW*, *P*'. We might begin by offering any of the following glosses: *If PW were true then P would be true; If we suppose PW, P follows; It would be impossible for PW to be true without P being true as well*. These are not perfect paraphrases. None the less, each seems to give a fair preliminary indication of what we mean when we use the fictionalist's prefix. And the trouble is that in every case the key phrase is an overtly modal locution. This suggests that the fictionalist's device should itself be classed as a modal operator.

Two kinds of objection spring to mind at this suggestion. The weaker claims that, at the very least, the fictionalist cannot boast the comprehensiveness of the modal realist; for the realist claims to be able to analyse *all* modal locutions in non-modal terms – a full reduction of the modal to the non-modal – whereas the fictionalist's analyses invariably contain an unreduced modal component. The stronger maintains that the fictionalist's theory is not just less comprehensive

than we might have hoped: it is altogether unhelpful. For the fictionalist's modal primitive is an especially obscure one – far more obscure, in fact, than the modal notions he would explain by means of it.

In response, the fictionalist should first allow that *if* the prefix is to be called a modal operator, then he has not furnished the materials for an eliminative reduction. What he has done (if his account succeeds in other respects) is to suggest a way of reducing a wide variety of modal notions to this one. Now this may not seem as impressive as a thoroughgoing eliminative reduction. But it remains a non-trivial analytic advance. No similar claim can be made, for example, by those who would take the logician's standard modal operators as primitive. For as several writers have pointed out, many recognizably modal judgements cannot be expressed in a language whose modal vocabulary is restricted to boxes and diamonds.[23]

Second, the fictionalist should point out that if his prefix is a modal operator, then it is by no means obvious that the realist has given a fully reductive treatment of modality; for it remains unclear how the realist proposes to eliminate occurrences of this very locution. True, the realist does have a powerful strategy for eliminating a large class of story prefixes as part of his account of truth in fiction. This theory identifies the content of a story S with a set of possible worlds, C_S, determined by several factors, including the explicit text of the fiction, the intentions of the story teller, the circumstances of its telling, and so on. A sentence P is said to be true *according to S* iff P is true at every world in C_S. To take a simple example: the content of 'A Study in Scarlet' might be given by the set of all worlds least different from the actual world in which the text of that story is inscribed as a record of known fact. What is true in the story is what is true in all these worlds.[24]

This style of analysis admits of variations. The important point, however, is that even if one of them is ultimately successful as an account of truth in simple narrative fiction, the account does not generalize to metaphysical 'stories' like the realist's hypothesis. The fictions for which the possible worlds analysis is suited are in an intuitive sense stories about how things might *actually* have transpired. That is why they are naturally represented as sets of possible worlds. *PW*, however, is not a story in this mould. It is a representation of all of modal reality, not just our small corner of it. And this is an important difference.

To see this more clearly, consider a recent, justifiably ignored novel called *This Lonely World*. The author is a committed modal realist, and his book is a dystopia modelled loosely on certain anti-totalitarian fables of the thirties: in this case, a nightmare vision of the actualist's conception of reality. The reader is invited to imagine or pretend that there is only one world – ours – and then to contemplate the grim implications. In the story, whatever happens happens necessarily. Nothing is possible but what is actual. Thus, as the author makes quite clear, regret is misplaced; deliberation is pointless; and most tragic of all, the most elegant and fruitful of metaphysical theories is false.

Never mind whether these are the right implications. This is fiction after all. Our question is whether the modal realist armed with his reductive account of truth in fiction can represent the content of this story (which is, after all, not so different in its ontological aspect from what many of us actually think). That is, how does the realist propose to analyse statements of the form 'In *This Lonely World*, P' so as to eliminate occurrence of the story prefix?

If the analysis is to follow the paradigm, the content of the tale should be a set of worlds. But which set? Not the set containing the actual world alone: this represents a complete account of what is actually the case, and that is not what the book contains. Perhaps the set of lonely worlds – worlds according to which there are no other worlds? If there were such worlds it might make sense to say that everything that happens in them happens necessarily. The trouble is that the modal realist has no reason to believe in lonely worlds, if indeed he can make any sense of the idea.[25]

Clearly, the problem is that for the realist, a representation of the totality of worlds is either necessarily true or necessarily false. The content, if it is to be a set of worlds, must therefore be either the set of all worlds or the null set. And neither will do to capture the very determinate content of stories like *This Lonely World*, or for that matter, *PW* itself. Thus from the realist's own point of view, story-telling about the actual world is a very different activity from story-telling about all the worlds. The realist has an elegant reductive treatment for story prefixes of the first kind; but

he lacks a parallel account for the second, a class that includes the prefix 'according to *PW*'.

Notice now that the fictionalist is in precisely the same position. Suppose, as we have, that he regards his operator as primitive. This done, he can parrot in his usual way the realist's account of truth in well-behaved fiction, for example, by saying that when *F* is an ordinary narrative fiction, '*In F, P*' is true iff according to *PW, the closest universes in which F is told as known fact are universes in which P*. This is borrowed, of course, but there is no circularity, since the fictionalist does not intend 'According to *PW*' to fall within the scope of the analysis.

If you are keeping score, the fictionalist can so far match the realist analysis for analysis, and both are without an account of the operator 'According to *PW* …'. The standoff might not last, of course. The realist might some day be able to give an account of the fictionalist's prefix. And if that account crucially involves the apparatus of possible worlds, the fictionalist will not be able to borrow it without circularity. I stress, it is not at all obvious how this account might go; yet even if we suppose it given, it may still seem at this stage that the fictionalist has done remarkably well. He has offered a powerful reduction of a wide variety of modal notions to one – a streamlining of ideology – with no cost in ontology. His account is adequate to common sense modal opinion; it makes good sense of the sources of modal knowledge … . Is not one modal primitive a fair price to pay for all that?

Some will no doubt be put off by the conception of philosophical method presupposed by the question. But let it stand. Even so, it may still be objected that our accounting is far too charitable. The difference between the two views is not just that the fictionalist must take as primitive a modal notion the realist defines, much as some treatments of propositional logic take negation and disjunction as primitive while others define both in terms of the Sheffer stroke. The trouble is that there is something deeply *unsatisfying* about the fictionalist's choice of primitive. First, as our discussion of the incompleteness problem shows, it is not nearly as clear as one might like a primitive to be. Insofar as the fictionalist tells us anything about how it works, he says that it works like the story prefixes we already understand. But the fact is that it differs importantly in two respects: in giving rise to truth value gaps and in resisting the standard possible worlds analysis. Second, and perhaps more importantly, this primitive just does not *feel* primitive. Truth relative to a story sounds like the sort of thing one ought to be able to explain, in stark contrast to more plausible primitives like negation. Lastly, it seems clear that a theory whose bedrock includes a notion as obscure as 'true according to *PW*' does little to address one traditional anxiety about the legitimacy of modal language. I have in mind the spectre of the Humeo-Quinean sceptic, who objects to the use of modal language in philosophy on the grounds that it is simply too poorly understood to serve a solid intellectual purpose. I have not stressed the project of answering this last, confessedly protean, sort of worry here. But pressure from this direction has persistently fuelled the search for a reductive account of modality in the empiricist tradition; and it would be a disappointment for many, I think, if the fictionalist were utterly powerless against it.

Considerations like these may lead the reduction-bent fictonalist to look for some more substantive account of his central notion – a procedure for analysing it away in terms of more basic non-modal notions. Unfortunately, I suspect the prospects are dim. As with all fictions, more is true according to *PW* than is given explicitly in the text – in this case, the postulates plus the encyclopaedia. And the problem is to specify the *consequence relation* which determines this larger class in a non-modal way. I will simply report, however, that I do not know how to do this. We may count on firm intuitions about whether a sentence *P* is true according to the realist's hypothesis. But I know of no illuminating non-modal characterization of the relation between the hypothesis and *P* which these intuitions are meant to capture.

This may reflect nothing more than a lack of ingenuity on my part.[26] Still, we must face the fact that primitive modality may well be an ineliminable feature of the fictionalist's view. Whether one regards this as a serious flaw will depend very much on how one conceives the project we have been engaged in – that is, the project of producing an 'account' or 'analysis' of modal language that involves no commitment to possible worlds. If one seriously believes that, in the absence of a reductive account, the modal notions are somehow philosophically suspect, then fictionalism as I have presented it is not much of an advance. Alternatively, one might think (with Lewis) that although a reductive analysis of modality is a nice thing to have, it is best thought of as a virtue to be entered into the balance along with the others we have discussed. From this point of view, fictionalism's failure to provide for reduction may be outweighed by the utter plausibility of its ontology, by its compatibility with a broadly naturalistic epistemology, and so on. Finally, one may be simply uninterested in the reductive project. For many writers, a world-view purged of modality is no part of the interest of the possible worlds approach; and in this case the fictionalist's failure to ground a reduction may not matter at all.[27]

This is worth stressing. Various interests might be served by the sort of deflationism we have been discussing, and we have not kept them altogether separate. We began with the modest project of earning the right, as it were, to move back and forth between the modal idiom and the idiom of possible worlds without incurring egregious metaphysical commitments. This aim is separable from the realist's ambition to provide a reduction of the modal to the non-modal; and for all we have said, Ed's concerns would be perfectly well served by a deflationism that failed to provide such reduction. True, to the extent that the fictionalist's primitive operator is unclear, this is grounds for worry. Clarity is presumably a desideratum no matter what the project. But for Ed this may not seem at all conclusive. After all, the fact that we can engage in conversation about what's true according to the realist's hypothesis in order to test his theory against intuition is testimony to our understanding. We know how to use the prefix 'According to *PW*' tolerably well, and insofar as we do, we understand it. Whether this sort of understanding is enough to keep fictionalism in the running as a live option for someone like Ed is now a matter of somewhat delicate judgement.

9   The Argument from Concern[28]

I would like to close with a rather different challenge, one which invites further clarification of our project. The problem may be developed by analogy with Kripke's well-known objection to Lewis's counterpart theory. Kripke writes:

> The counterpart of something in another possible world is *never* identical with the thing itself. Thus if we say 'Humphrey might have won the election …' we are not talking about something that might have happened to *Humphrey* but to someone *else*, a 'counterpart'. Probably, however, Humphrey could not care less whether someone else, no matter how much resembling him, would have been victorious in another possible world. Thus Lewis's view seems to me even more bizarre than the usual notions of transworld identification it replaces.[29]

Of course, there is a minor infelicity here. Lewis does not identify what might have happened to Humphrey with what *might* have happened to someone else. Rather, the truth conditions for claims about what might have happened to Humphrey refer to what *does* happen to others, namely, Humphrey's counterparts in other worlds. But this hardly affects the main point. Humphrey, we may suppose, cares a great deal that he might have defeated Nixon, but could not care less that someone rather like him – but still a complete stranger – did defeat someone rather like Nixon. One fact is a matter of immediate concern; the other, an occasion for indifference. Hence there is something paradoxical – or, as Kripke says, 'bizarre' – in the identification of the two.

Let us be clear about the nature of the objection. Humphrey apparently takes different attitudes towards the modal fact about himself and the non-modal fact about his counterpart; but this by itself is not a logical objection to the claim that the facts are identical. It is perfectly possible to have different attitudes towards a single thing under distinct descriptions. Lois loves Superman; she is merely fond of Clark. This is possible because, even though Superman *is* Clark Kent, Lois has not figured this out. Similarly, it would seem possible for someone to care that *P* without caring that *P**, even when *P* and *P** pick out the same state of affairs, provided he does not believe that they do.

The objection is, I believe, more 'pragmatic' than logical. An 'account' of modality must answer to a range of phenomena. So far we have emphasized fidelity to our prior beliefs – fidelity to our beliefs about what might have been, to our views on the sources of modal knowledge, to our general conception of what there is, and so on. What Kripke has done is to point to a rather different but equally important phenomenon – our palpable *concern* for the modal facts – and to urge fidelity here as well. An adequate account will preserve the intelligibility of our caring about the modal truth as we do; of our responding emotionally, morally, and practically to our modal thoughts. The objection is that counterpart theory fails this constraint. We simply do not care about the fortunes of perfect strangers in the immediate way in which we care about our own modal properties. Hence it is implausible to identify the two sorts of fact.

In general, fidelity constraints may be seen as expressions of the methodological conservatism that guides our search for 'accounts' or 'analyses'. The requirement of fidelity to prior modal opinion, for example, may be seen as the requirement that anyone who takes the proposed analysis to heart should not thereby be forced to modify his corpus of modal belief in a radical way. Similarly, the constraint behind Kripke's objection may be viewed as the requirement that an adequate account must be acceptable without forcing a radical revision in our patterns of concern for the modal facts. To accept Lewis's counterpart theory, Kripke seems to be saying, would practically force the view that the modal facts do not much matter. Ordinarily, we have a vital moral and emotional concern for what might have happened to us. Yet to accept counterpart theory is to view these modal facts as no more vital than the day-to-day lives of strangers on another planet, that is, as matters of practical indifference. And this is a substantial revision.

Once the objection is put this way, there is an obvious – if not obviously correct – response. In taking counterpart theory to heart one might aim to revise, not one's interest in modality, but rather one's concern for certain distant strangers. Humphrey thinks he has no special reason to care about his counterparts. But when he accepts Lewis's analysis he will believe that the modal facts about him *just are* facts about his counterparts; and since he cares about the former, he will come to care about the latter.[30]

This is Lewis's preferred answer, I believe. And it would take us afield to evaluate it on its own terms. What needs stressing is that this is still a revisionary stance. To respond in this way is to grant that to accept modal realism is to revise, not just one's ontology, but one's patterns of interest and concern. Now the requirement of fidelity to these practices is, like all such requirements, a defeasible one. A well-motivated analysis may actually give us grounds for changing our view of what is worth caring about. The question for modal realism – a question we need not answer – is whether we have been given adequate grounds for the revision the theory seems to force.

It should be easy to see how all this bears on the adequacy of fictionalism. Just as modal realism strains credulity by identifying facts of vital concern with apparently indifferent facts about distant simulacra, so fictionalism may be thought to strain credulity by identifying these same facts with facts about the content of an arcane story. Humphrey cares that he might have won. Perhaps he regrets some decision because he thinks that had he acted differently, he might have won. Now imagine that Humphrey comes to embrace the fictionalist's view of the content of his modal thoughts. He comes to believe that the fact that he might have won *just is* the fact that, according to the story *PW*, there is a world in which someone rather like him – his counterpart – does win. Could his pattern of concern conceivably survive this identification? Could he coherently feel *regret* – and this can be a powerful, crippling sentiment – at the thought that in some philosopher's story, someone resembling Humphrey won an election like the election Humphrey lost? Do not imagine that the story is taken as *evidence* for the distinct modal fact that Humphrey might have won. For the fictionalist, the fact about the story just is the modal fact; and a lucid fictionalist must have the same attitude towards both.

We begin, I suppose, thinking that what happens in fiction is not centrally important to us. Someone who does not care about what happens to Isabelle Archer may be a Philistine; but he need not be a moral or psychological monster. Indifference to the modal facts, however, is quite another thing. Consider the sentiment of regret, to take only a simple case. Regret is, in part, an emotional response to a modal thought. To regret having acted in a certain way, one must think that had one acted differently, things might have been better; and further, that one could have acted differently.[31] A sentiment is not regret

unless such modal thoughts lie behind it. And if this is right, to be indifferent to the modal is to be incapable of regret.[32]

But regret is not a trivial thing. The character who feels no regret is a moral monster *par excellence*. That we think so is shown by the lengths we go to to inculcate a capacity for regret in children. Moreover, it seems to me that we do this, not simply for the cynical reason that someone with this capacity is easier to socialize, but because we also think that to feel regret when regret is called for is a sign of good character, worth having for its own sake.

If this is right – and I grant that it is only the barest sketch of an undoubtedly complex phenomenon – then a view which leads to indifference to the modal truth entails a revision in patterns of concern that is simply out of the question. Just as it is not a serious option for Ed to believe in a countless infinity of talking donkeys, it is not a serious option for any of us to abandon concern for the modal facts. If fictionalism really does require this, then taking fictionalism seriously is, if nothing else, a practical impossibility.

But does fictionalism require this? A response parallel to Lewis's is of course available. That is, the fictionalist may say that, although a revision is required, it is not the pernicious one just described. Rather, the lucid fictionalist may come to think that truth in the fiction *PW* is important to him in a way he had not previously imagined. The fact that things would have gone better if he had only acted differently *just is* the fact that according to *PW*, worlds most like the actual world in which his counterparts act differently are worlds where things go better. But this only means that he must care – perhaps desperately – about what happens to these characters in this fiction. True, he did not always care about such things. But now he does; and moreover, the transition was not that hard – not nearly as hard as the alternative, which is to become indifferent to the modal facts.

Now whether this transition is really possible for us is, I suppose, a psychological question; and I do not know the answer. But the objection may still be pressed. The fictionalist is now passionately concerned with the content of a certain fiction about alternative universes, namely, *PW*. Yet presumably he does not care about other similar fictions in the same way. Consider, for example, the story that says there are just two universes: ours and one populated only by blue swans. Just as modal truth is defined in terms of the fiction *PW*, we can define an analogous body of truth – the schmodal truth (?) – in terms of the new fiction. Thus we might say that *P* is *s-possible* iff, according to the two-world story, there is world at which *P*; and similarly for *s*-necessity, the *s*-counterfactual, and so on. Now schmodality is not modality. Yet for the lucid fictionalist, the modal facts and the schmodal facts are facts of the same kind: namely, facts about the content of a story about alternative universes. We may then ask the fictionalist: why do you care so much about the one and not at all about the other?

The question is designed to exploit what is plausibly a norm governing patterns of concern or interest. If you care especially for some members of a class but not for others, you should be able to point to some feature which distinguishes the items you care about – a feature which *grounds* your difference in attitude. The worry is that the fictionalist cannot adhere to this norm in his concern for the modal and indifference to the schmodal. They are both facts about the content of certain false stories. And unless one of these stories has some *authority* which the other lacks, the fictionalist's concern may seem purely arbitrary – a *fetish* ungrounded in distinctive valuable features of its object.[33]

I know of no simple answer to this challenge. One response, I suppose, is to argue that the norm is too stringent – that by this criterion, all our concerns are fetishistic. It is chimerical to require that whenever we care about some things more than others we should be able to point to a feature that grounds this concern, since the question will always return: why do you care about things with that feature more than things which lack it? But if some of our legitimate concerns are in this sense ungrounded, it is no decisive objection that the lucid fictionalist's concern for the modal must fit this pattern. Obviously this line of response requires careful handling. I will not pursue it here except to say that if there is to be a practice of criticizing passions as arbitrary or vain, then it cannot depend crucially on this problematic model. So it remains possible that once we understand this critical practice better, the fictionalist's special concern for the fiction *PW* will still appear objectionably fetishistic.

Another response is to accept the norm and to look for some feature to distinguish the fiction *PW* from other fictions about possible worlds. This may seem hopeless. After all, what could possibly distinguish one bizarre science fiction scenario from another sufficiently to make one deserve the non-derivative concern we accord modality? Yet there may be an answer. Recall that in discussing the epistemology of modality I suggested in passing that the principles which guide the imagination when we construct possible states of affairs are in some sense well captured by the postulates of *PW*. I did not defend this claim – and it would be a subtle problem. But if there is something to it, then the fictionalist might try to argue that *PW* derives its 'authority' from being an explicit formulation of our own imaginative habits. So construed, fictionalism's affinities for 'conceptualist' theories of possibility is obvious. These theories aim to locate the source of modal distinctions in us, in our capacity to imagine or conceive alternatives to the actual state of things. Some of the problems of such approaches are well-known – and more would have to be said to show that fictionalism skirts them. For now I will only say that this strikes me as a potentially fruitful approach for the fictionalist bent on answering the challenge at hand.

One last response deserves mention.[34] Throughout I have supposed that fictionalism, like modal realism, aims to be a *theory of possibility*, that is, an account of the truth conditions for modal statements, and hence of the facts that make modal statements true. But note that this assumption is not strictly necessary given the modest problem we began with. All Ed ever wanted was license to move back and forth between modal claims and claims about worlds. Such transitions are guided by biconditionals: for the realist, *P* iff *P**; for the fictionalist, *P* iff according to *PW*, *P**. But it is one thing to embrace these biconditionals – even to embrace them as a body of necessary truths – and another to regard them as providing analyses. The fictionalist who aims only to solve Ed's problem may therefore conceivably reject the stronger reading. He may claim to offer not a theory of possibility, but merely a theory linking the modal facts with facts about the story *PW*. The theory licenses transitions from one idiom to the other, without purporting to shed light on the nature of modal truth. This timid fictionalism of course raises as many questions as it answers. Still it must be granted that many of the objections we have mentioned, including the argument from concern, simply do not arise for this view. If the modal facts are distinct from facts about the fictionalist's fiction, there is nothing wrong with displaying divergent attitudes towards them.

10   Conclusion

Whether fictionalism is a viable deflationist alternative to modal realism depends very much on what one wants the theory for. Given the realist's interest in an account of the nature of modality, fictionalism has the advantage of being relatively modest in its ontology and sensible in its epistemology. It has the defect, however, of a primitive modal component (at least until a more ingenious exponent comes along) and perhaps of inviting what seems like an extraordinary revision in our patterns of concerns. The more modest one's aims, the more congenial fictionalism may seem. As a solution to Ed's dilemma, the timid fictionalism mentioned in the last section may in fact be wholly satisfactory. It is now up to theorists of modality who talk about possible worlds without believing in them to ask themselves whether, given their purposes, some form of fictionalism may not constitute an attractive option.

Notes

Versions of this paper were presented at Princeton, Cornell, and the Universities of Pittsburgh, Pennsylvania and Michigan; and I thank everyone who participated. Some of the individuals whose comments have been especially helpful are mentioned in the footnotes. I owe a debt of a rather different order to David Lewis, both for extensive comments on earlier drafts, and for much needed encouragement throughout.

1   D. Lewis, *On the Plurality of Worlds*, Oxford, Basil Blackwell, 1986; hereafter *Pl.*

2   E.g., the state descriptions of R. Carnap, *Meaning and Necessity*, Chicago, University of Chicago Press, 1947, p. 9.

3   Cf. A. Plantinga, *The Nature of Necessity*, Oxford, Oxford University Press, 1974; R. Stalnaker, *Inquiry*, Cambridge, MA, MIT Press, 1984; P. van Inwagen,

'Two Concepts of Possible Worlds', *Midwest Studies in Philosophy*, 1986, pp. 185–213.

4   Cf. D. Lewis, *Counterfactuals*, Oxford, Basil Blackwell, 1973, p. 86; also *Pl.*, ch. 2, sec. 8.

5   Cf. G. Forbes, *The Metaphysics of Modality*, Oxford, Oxford University Press, 1985, where such approaches are called 'anti-realist'.

6   R. Routley, *Exploring Meinong's Jungle and Beyond*, Canberra: Philosophy Department, Research School of Social Sciences, Australian National University, Monograph #3, 1980, p. 176.

7   As the name suggests, the view has affinities for certain so-called 'fictionalist' positions in the philosophy of mathematics. Cf. C. Chihara, *Ontology and the Vicious Circle Principle*, Ithaca, Cornell, 1973, ch. 2; H. Hodes, 'Logicism and the Ontological Commitments of Arithmetic', *Journal of Philosophy*, 1984, pp. 123–49.

8   This approach to fictional truth is articulated in D. Lewis, 'Truth in Fiction', *American Philosophical Quarterly*, 1978, pp. 37–46; cf. N. Wolterstorff, *Works and Worlds of Art*, Oxford, Oxford University Press, 1980. For another, rather different approach which may also lend itself to a fictionalist construal of possible worlds, Cf., K. Walton, 'Fearing Fictions', *Journal of Philosophy*, 1978, pp. 5–27.

9   For a theory of possible worlds that might serve as the basis for an alternative fictionalism, cf. D. M. Armstrong, 'The Nature of Possibility', *Canadian Journal of Philosophy*, 1986.

10 The final proviso is required to forestall the paradox presented in P. Forrest and D. M. Armstrong, 'An Argument Against David Lewis's Theory of Possible Worlds', *Australasian Journal of Philosophy*, 1984, pp. 164–8. As Lewis understands this condition it has the effect that there is an (unknown) upper bound to the dimensionality of the largest spacetimes represented among the universes, and so an upper bound to the number of non-overlapping objects that inhabit the most populous worlds. This will be important below, sect. 7.

11 As with recombination, adequate formulation of this principle is tricky. It is meant to guarantee, e.g., that the upper bounds mentioned in the previous note are *natural* ones. Thus it may be that the largest worlds possess a countable infinity of spatial dimensions. But it is ruled out that they have, say, $10^{17} + 1$ dimensions. To suppose so would be to imagine that the plenitude of worlds was in this sense arbitrarily restricted.

12 Lewis does not distinguish this requirement from non-arbitrariness. But they strike me as importantly different. The present principle is concerned with the status of our universe with respect to the others. Thus (6g), but not (6f) entails that there must be properties or universals that are not

instantiated in our universe, but are instantiated in others. If our universe contained an instance of every possible natural property, it would be a remarkably rich world, in violation of (6g).

13 That such a specification is possible is of course crucial for the modal realist, who hopes to exploit his theory of possible worlds in a fully reductive analysis of the modal notions.

14 For a striking anticipation, cf. Poe's *Eureka*:

> I myself feel impelled to the *fancy* – without of course calling it more – that there does exist a limitless succession of Universes, more or less similar to that of which we have cognizance – to that of which alone we shall ever have cognizance …. *If* such clusters exist, however – *and they do* – it is abundantly clear that, having had no part in our origin, they have no portion in our laws. They neither attract us nor we them. Their material – their spirit is not ours – is not that which obtains in any part of our universe. They could not impress our senses or our souls. And between them and us … there are no influences in common. Each exists apart and independently, in the bosom of its proper and particular god!

In *The Complete Works of Edgar Allen Poe*, New York, AMS Press, 1965, 16: 256. Cf. P. Unger, 'Minimizing Arbitrariness: Toward a Metaphysics of Infinitely Many Isolated Concrete Worlds', *Midwest Studies*, 1984.

15 For our purposes, S is non-modal intrinsic truth about our universe if it contains no modal vocabulary and entails neither the existence nor the non-existence of things outside our universe. It suffices for the latter that all quantifiers and names in S be restricted to the inhabitants of this universe.

16 Of course I do not claim to have shown that the realist's analysis is adequate in this sense. This is the burden of much of Lewis's book.

17 Indeed, one may wonder why such arguments from utility should be even prima facie compelling for Lewis given his other views. For Lewis, our aim in metaphysics as in physics is to believe the truth. And because he is a realist (in every sense) about truth, Lewis grants that there is no necessary connection between a theory's being useful, elegant, etc., and it's being true. Of course we may *hope* that the truth may be captured by a beautiful, fruitful theory, and our theory construction may be guided by this hope; but we have no independent reason to believe it must be so. Now the arguments for modal realism may establish that it is useful, elegant, and so on. So I can see how they might give someone reason to hope that it is true. As Lewis says, if modal realism is right we inhabit a paradise for philosophers, and we are all supposed to hope to dwell in paradise. The trouble is that reason to hope is not in general reason to believe. To suppose otherwise is to countenance wishful thinking as a sound policy for fixing belief in metaphysics.

18 Chihara (op. cit.) maintains that fictionalism in the mathematical case is nominalistically acceptable because prefixes of the form 'In F,…' may be thought of as simple symbols, not open to quantification in the 'F' place. I have my doubts, if only because the fictionalist's explanatory remarks seem inevitably to involve quantification over representations. Of course even if this is right it should not bother a liberal nominalist like Chihara: anyone who admits an ontology of linguistic entities that outstrips the totality of concrete inscriptions can easily construe the fictionalist's fictions as entities of this type.

19 Lewis's remarks may suggest, by analogy with the mathematical case, that we accept or believe the principles which tacitly guide the imagination. But this seems wrong. The principles in question are principles about possible worlds. So if we believe them we are committed to modal realism from the cradle, simply because we reason about what might have been. It seems clear, however, that with one or two exceptions, modal realists are made, not born.

20 This is not to say that there is not a deep epistemological question as to how we discover through imaginative reasoning the consequences of these imaginative principles. The point is only that the realist and the fictionalist both agree that such discovery is possible. So any problem this view presents is a problem for both of them.

21 It may be objected that we have a precedent for making just this claim in a domain quite close to our subject. According to many accounts of truth in fiction, the sentences 'Moriarty had blood type A +' and 'It is not the case that Moriarty had blood type A +' are not genuine contradictories; for as they are standardly intended they are elliptical for prefixed sentences where the prefix 'In the Holmes stories …' takes wide scope. 'In F, not-P' is not the negation of 'In F, P'. Hence both may be false. The fictonalist, however, cannot appeal to this precedent to explain how the modal theses (10) and (11) can both be false. For it is no part of his view that modal statements (in contrast with statements about possible worlds) are ever supplied with a tacit prefix.

22 Cf. B. van Fraassen, 'Singular Terms, Truth-Value Gaps, and Free Logic', *Journal of Philosophy*, 1966, pp. 481–95; D. Lewis, 'General Semantics', reprinted in his *Philosophical Papers*, v.1, New York,

Oxford, 1983; S. Kripke, 'Outline of a Theory of Truth', *Journal of Philosophy*, 1975, pp. 690–715.

23 Cf. *Pl.*, p. 13; A. Hazen, 'Expressive Completeness in Modal Languages', *Journal of Philosophical Logic*, 1976, pp. 25–46. In the system of Forbes (op. cit.), the language of modal logic is extended with a countable infinity of modal operators to render it comparable in expressive power to the language of modal realism.

24 Lewis, 'Truth in Fiction'; Wolterstorff, op. cit.

25 I suppose a lonely world would have to be a world relative to which no others are possible. Presumably, however, any notion of relative possibility that might be introduced into a realist treatment would rely heavily on facts about similarity of worlds. The lonely worlds would then be worlds not relevantly similar to any others. Recombination guarantees, however, that for any world there are worlds very much like it in any respect that could possibly matter.

26 For reason to think the problem intractable in principle, cf. *Pl.*, pp. 150 ff. The most obvious approach is to construe the relation as a logical one: i.e., to view the postulates and encyclopaedia (*PW*) as axioms and to define 'In *PW*, *P*' as *PW* ⇒ *P*. Now given minimal abstract apparatus, various purely formal relations of logical consequence can of course be defined non-modally. But there is reason to think that ⇒ cannot be such a relation. First, the language of the theory is an unregimented fragment of English, for which no purely formal notion of consequence is available. But more importantly, even if we imagine the language regimented as, say, a first order language, a purely formal relation of consequence will not do justice to our intuitions, for the familiar reason that it will flout certain intuitively necessary but non-logical connections between terms in the language. Thus: necessarily, gold is a metal. And intuitively, according to *PW*, in all universes, gold is a metal. Yet the embedded sentence here is not one of the postulates, nor is it included in the encyclopaedia, since it involves quantification over other worlds. And what is highly implausible is that it should be a *purely formal* consequence of any regimentation of these.

27 Cf. Stalnaker, op. cit.; and Kripke's remarks on possible worlds in *Naming and Necessity*, Cambridge MA, Harvard, 1980, esp. p. 19, n. 18.

28 Some comments from Simon Blackburn suggested what follows. Cf. his *Spreading the Word*, Oxford, Oxford University Press, 1984, pp. 212–16.

29 *Naming and Necessity*, p. 45.

30 Or, perhaps, to insist that he has cared about the latter all along without knowing it.

31 Note: this 'could' denotes, not metaphysical possibility, but rather the agent's freedom – still a modal notion, but one whose connection with the main topic of this paper is far from straight-forward.

32 Regret is a telling test case because here our concern for the modal is arguably non-derivative, in contrast, e.g., to our interest in counterfactuals like 'If I had slipped I would have broken my neck', which may well derive from an interest in what the counterfactual implies about the non-modal features of the actual world.

33 Here the objection parallels Blackburn's discussion of counterpart theory; Blackburn, op. cit.

34 I owe the suggestion to Wm. Taschek.

19

Essence and Modality

Kit Fine

The concept of essence has played an important role in the history and development of philosophy; and in no branch of the discipline is its importance more manifest than in metaphysics.

Its significance for metaphysics is perhaps attributable to two main sources. In the first place, the concept may be used to characterize what the subject, or at least part of it, is about. For one of the central concerns of metaphysics is with the identity of things, with what they are. But the metaphysician is not interested in every property of the objects under consideration. In asking 'What is a person?', for example, he does not want to be told that every person has a deep desire to be loved, even if this is in fact the case.

What then distinguishes the properties of interest to him? What is it about a property which makes it bear, in the metaphysically significant sense of the phrase, on what an object is? It is in answer to this question that appeal is naturally made to the concept of essence. For what appears to distinguish the intended properties is that they are essential to their bearers.

But the concept of essence is not merely of help in picking out the properties and concepts of interest to the metaphysician; it is itself one of those concepts. It plays not only an external role, in helping to characterize the subject, but also an internal role, in helping to constitute it. In one respect, this internal role is simply a consequence of the external one. For if a given property is essential, then so is the property of essentially having that property; and hence an interest in the given "lower level" property will transfer to an interest in the derived "higher level" property.

However, in addition to these derivative uses of the concept, there are other more significant uses. For the metaphysician may want to say that a person is essentially a person or that having a body is not essential to a person or that a person's essence is exhausted by his being a thing that thinks. And there is no natural way of seeing any of these claims as arising from some general essentialist function of a corresponding non-essentialist claim.

Furthermore, the concept is not only of use in the formulation of metaphysical claims; it is also of use in the definition of metaphysical concepts. An obvious example is the concept of an essential being; for an essential being is one whose essence includes its own existence. But there are other, less obvious, cases. Two, of great significance for

Kit Fine, "Essence and Modality," in *Philosophical Perspectives*, vol. 8: *Logic and Language* (1994), pp. 1–16. Reproduced by permission of John Wiley & Sons, Inc.

Metaphysics: An Anthology, Second Edition. Edited by Jaegwon Kim, Daniel Z. Korman and Ernest Sosa.
Editorial material and organization © 2012 Blackwell Publishing Ltd. Published 2012 by Blackwell Publishing Ltd.

the subject, are the concepts of substance and ontological dependence. For a substance (at least in one sense of the term) is something whose essence does not preclude it from existing on its own; and one object depends upon another (again in one sense of the term) if its essence prevents it from existing without the other object.

Given the importance of the concept of essence, it is not surprising that philosophers have attempted to get clearer on what it is; and as we survey their endeavours, we find that two main lines of thought have been pursued. On the one hand, essence has been conceived on the model of definition. It has been supposed that the notion of definition has application to both words and objects – that just as we may define a word, or say what it means, so we may define an object, or say what it is. The concept of essence has then been taken to reside in the "real" or objectual cases of definition, as opposed to the "nominal" or verbal cases.

On the other hand, the concept has been elucidated in modal terms. It has been supposed that the notion of necessity may relate either to propositions or to objects – that not only may a proposition be said to be necessary, but also an object may be said to be necessarily a certain way. The concept of essence has then been located in the "de re", as opposed to the "de dicto", cases of modal attribution.

Both lines of thought go at least as far back as Aristotle. The definitional approach is trumpeted throughout his metaphysical writings; in the *Metaphysics* 1031a12, for example, he writes "clearly, then, definition is the formula of the essence". He does not, as far as I know, give a modal account of essence. But he does provide a modal account of two cognate notions. For his preferred definition of 'accident' is as 'something which may either belong or not belong to some self-same thing' (*Topics*, 102b6–7); and he follows Plato in taking things to be "prior and posterior ... in respect of nature and substance" when the priors "can be without the other things, while the others cannot be without them" (*Metaphysics*, 1019a1–4).

Similar accounts, though sometimes with an admixture of both elements, recur throughout the history of philosophy. To take but two examples, Locke follows the definitional tradition in taking an essence of a thing to be "the being of any thing, whereby it is what it is" (*Essay*, Bk. 3,

Ch. 3, §15), while Mill is closer to modal tradition in treating the essence of a thing as "that without which the thing could neither be, nor be conceived to be" (*System of Logic*, Bk. 1, chapter vi, §2).

When we come to the contemporary period in analytic philosophy, we find that, as a result of a sustained empiricist critique, the idea of real definition has been more or less given up (unless it is taken to be vestigially present in the notion of a sortal). But the idea of understanding essence in terms of de re modality has lived on. The first philosopher from this period to provide a rigorous account of the connection between essence and modality appears to be G. E. Moore. In his famous paper *External and Internal Relations*, he defines what it is for a property to be internal (which I take to be the same as the property's being essential): P is *internal* to A just in case "(x=A) entails xP" (p. 293) or, equivalently, just in case the material implication $(x=A) \rightarrow xP$ is a necessary truth (p. 302). Moore is also remarkably sympathetic to discussions of internality and provides various interesting examples of internal and external properties throughout his writings.

However, it is only in the last twenty years or so that the modal approach to essentialist metaphysics has really come into its own. For with the advent of quantified modal logic, philosophers have been in a better position to formulate essentialist claims; and with clarification of the underlying modal notions, they have been better able to ascertain their truth. These developments have also had a significant impact on our understanding of metaphysics. For there would appear to be nothing special about the modal character of essentialist claims beyond their being de re. It therefore appears reasonable to treat the metaphysics of identity as merely part of a broader study of modality de re. The subject becomes, in effect, a part of applied modal logic.

It is my aim in this paper to show that the contemporary assimilation of essence to modality is fundamentally misguided and that, as a consequence, the corresponding conception of metaphysics should be given up. It is not my view that the modal account fails to capture anything which might reasonably be called a concept of essence. My point, rather, is that the notion of essence which is of central importance to the metaphysics of identity is not to be understood in modal terms or even to be regarded as extensionally equivalent to a modal notion. The one notion is, if I am right, a highly refined version of the other; it is like a sieve which performs a similar function but with a much finer mesh.

I shall also argue that the traditional assimilation of essence to definition is better suited to the task of explaining what essence is. It may not provide us with an analysis of the concept, but it does provide us with a good model of how the concept works. Thus my overall position is the reverse of the usual one. It sees real definition rather than de re modality as central to our understanding of the concept.

Let us turn first to the modal account. There are somewhat different ways the account can go. At its very simplest, it takes an object to have a property essentially just in case it is necessary that the object has the property. But there are two variants on the basic account, which make the necessary possession of the property conditional on something else. One variant makes the necessary possession conditional on existence: an object is taken to have a property essentially just in case it is necessary that the object has the property if it exists. The other variant makes the necessary possession conditional upon identity: an object is taken to have a property essentially just in case it is necessary that the object has the property if it is identical to that very object.

The last formulation is, in effect, the account proposed by Moore. However, it might be argued that, properly viewed, it should be identified with one of the two other formulations. For either the identity of an object with itself has existential import, in which case there is a collapse to the second, or it is without existential import, in which case there is a collapse to the first.

Even before we embark on a detailed criticism of these accounts, we should note that there is something suspicious about them. For we have an informal way of saying that an object essentially has a certain property. We say 'the object must have that property if it is to be the object that it is'. Somehow this form of words manages to convey what we wish to convey. But how? And how, in particular, are we to understand the role of the qualifying phrase 'if it is to be the object that it is'?

We can think of the various modal accounts as providing us with an answer to this question. On the categorical account, the qualification is taken to be redundant. But then why is it made? Under

one version of the conditional account, the phrase is taken to convey existence. But then why is the existence of the object expressed so perversely in terms of identity? Under the other version of the conditional account, the phrase conveys a vacuous condition. But then, again, why is the qualification made and whence our feeling that it points to something significant?

We do not have here an argument against the modal accounts. But it is hard, all the same, to avoid the suspicion that they are somehow based upon a misreading of the standard informal way of expressing essentialist claims.

Let us now turn to the detailed considerations. My objection to the modal accounts will be to the sufficiency of the proposed criterion, not to its necessity. I accept that if an object essentially has a certain property then it is necessary that it has the property (or has the property if it exist); but I reject the converse. For the time being, we shall confine our attention to the existentially conditioned form of the criterion. Once the objection is developed for this form, it will be clear how it is to be extended to the categorical form.

Consider, then, Socrates and the set whose sole member is Socrates. It is then necessary, according to standard views within modal set theory, that Socrates belongs to singleton Socrates if he exists; for, necessarily, the singleton exists if Socrates exists and, necessarily, Socrates belongs to singleton Socrates if both Socrates and the singleton exist. It therefore follows according to the modal criterion that Socrates essentially belongs to singleton Socrates.

But, intuitively, this is not so. It is no part of the essence of Socrates to belong to the singleton. Strange as the literature on personal identity may be, it has never been suggested that in order to understand the nature of a person one must know to which sets he belongs. There is nothing in the nature of a person, if I may put it this way, which demands that he belongs to this or that set or which demands, given that the person exists, that there even be any sets.

It is not critical to the example that appeal be made to an abstract entity. Consider two objects whose natures are unconnected, say Socrates and the Eiffel Tower. Then it is necessary that Socrates and the Tower be distinct. But it is not essential to Socrates that he be distinct from the Tower, for there is nothing in his nature which connects him in any special way to it.

Nor is it critical to the example that the reader actually endorse the particular modal and essentialist claims to which I have made appeal. All that is necessary is that he should recognize the intelligibility of a position which makes such claims. For any reasonable account of essence should not be biased towards one metaphysical view rather than the other. It should not settle, as a matter of definition, any issue which we are inclined to regard as a matter of substance.

I am aware, though, that there may be readers who are so in the grip of the modal account of essence that they are incapable of understanding the concept in any other way. One cannot, of course, argue a conceptually blind person into recognizing a conceptual distinction, any more than one can argue a colour blind person into recognizing a colour distinction. But it may help such a reader to reflect on the difference between saying that singleton Socrates essentially contains Socrates and saying that Socrates essentially belongs to singleton Socrates. For can we not recognize a sense of nature, or of "what an object is", according to which it lies in the nature of the singleton to have Socrates as a member even though it does not lie in the nature of Socrates to belong to the singleton?

Once we recognize the asymmetry between these two cases, we have the means to present the objection. For no corresponding modal asymmetry can be made out. If the singleton essentially contains Socrates, then it is necessary that Socrates belongs to the singleton if the singleton exists. Granted that it is necessary that the singleton exists if Socrates does, it follows that it is necessary that Socrates belongs to the singleton if Socrates exists. But then Socrates essentially belongs to the singleton, which is the conclusion we wished to avoid.

The modal account is subject to further difficulties. For consider any necessary truth; it could be a particular mathematical truth, for example, or even the conjunction of all necessary truths. Then it is necessarily the case that this truth should hold if Socrates exists. But it is no part of Socrates' essence that there be infinitely many prime numbers or that the abstract world of numbers, sets, or what have you, be just as it is.

Among the necessary truths, if our modal theorist is to be believed, are statements of essence. For a statement of essence is a statement of necessity and so it will, like any statement of necessity, be necessarily true if it is true at all. It follows that it will part of the essence of any object that every other object has the essential properties that it has: it will be part of the essence of the Eiffel Tower for Socrates to be essentially a person with certain parents, let us say, or part of the essence of Socrates for the Eiffel Tower to be essentially spatio-temporally continuous. O happy metaphysician! For in discovering the nature of one thing, he thereby discovers the nature of all things.

The second of our two objections applies directly to the categorical account. The first also applies under either of two modifications. One possibility is to use necessary existents in place of contingent existents. Thus we may talk of 2 and singleton 2 rather than of Socrates and singleton Socrates. The other possibility is to make the attributed property conditional upon existence. Thus instead of asking whether Socrates is essentially a member of singleton Socrates, we ask whether he is essentially a member of the singleton *if he exists*. Under each of these two proposals, the difference between the conditional and categorical accounts disappears while the discrepancy with the essentialist claims remains.

In addition to the difficulties which are common to the two forms of the modal account, there is a difficulty which is peculiar to the conditional form. Consider Socrates again: it is necessarily the case that he exists if he exists. But we do not want to say that he essentially exists.

This difficulty has been recognized before, but I do not think that its significance has been properly appreciated. For existence is not an isolated example; there are many other cases of this sort. If, for instance, there is nothing in the nature of Socrates which demands that he exists, then presumably there is nothing in the nature of Socrates which demands that his parents exist. However, it is necessary (we may suppose) that his parents exist if Socrates does.

One can understand what motivates the conditional form of the account. For the categorical form provides us, in effect, with a vacuous interpretation of the qualifying phrase "if the object is to be the object that it is". This is clearly too weak. The conditional account can therefore be seen as an attempt to provide us with a more substantive interpretation of the phrase.

Unfortunately, the resulting interpretation is too strong. This is most simply seen, as we did above, by asking whether existence is an essential property of any object; for whatever property we take the phrase to attribute to the object must be an essential property of that object. But, of course, once one non-essential property is countenanced many others will follow as necessary consequences of it.

There is no obvious way around any of the above difficulties. To get round the first difficulty, one might try to add a condition of relevance to the modal criterion. One would demand, if a property is to be essential to an object, that it somehow be relevant to the object. However, the case of Socrates and his singleton makes it hard to see how the required notion of relevance could be understood without already presupposing the concept of essence in question. For we want to say that it is essential to the singleton to have Socrates as a member, but that it is not essential to Socrates to be a member of the singleton. But there is nothing in the "logic" of the situation to justify an asymmetric judgement of relevance; the difference lies entirely in the nature of the objects in question.

To get round the second difficulty, one might make the additional demand on an essential property that it not be an essential property, in the original sense, of every object whatever. The counterexamples which were constructed from necessary truths would then be overturned. But these examples could be readily reinstated by conjoining the given degenerate essential property with one which was not degenerate.

Nor does it help here to impose a condition of relevance, as in the first case. For I assume that we do not want to impose a general ban on "improper" properties being essential; we might be happy to say, for example, that it is essential to the null set that there be sets. And it would be possible, in any case, to construct related counter-examples using "proper" properties.

It is important to appreciate that the problem cases here do not simply arise from the requirement that the essential properties of an object be closed under logical consequence. For even with this requirement is in force, we would not want to say that it is essential to Socrates that

the various necessary truths (as opposed to logical truths) be the case. Thus the problem is not an instance of the familiar problem of "logical omniscience".

To get round the third difficulty, one might suppose that the term 'essentially' is being used ambiguously, having a categorical meaning in application to properties like existence and having a conditional meaning in the other cases. There are, however, no independent reasons for believing in such an ambiguity. We have no "feeling" when we say that Socrates is essentially a man but not essentially existent that there has been a shift in the use of the term. If the term had these two senses, then there should be a sense in which Socrates was not essentially a man (in addition to the sense in which he is essentially a man). But there appears to be no such sense.

A sophisticated variant of this defence would make 'essentiality' disjunctive rather than ambiguous. Thus it would be supposed that in saying that an object essentially had a certain property we were claiming that either the property is existence-like and the object has the property essentially in the categorical sense or the property is not existence-like and the object has the property essentially in the conditional sense. But such a view is ad hoc. Why should the essentiality of existence consist in anything different from the essentiality of other properties?

The double standard also leads, as one might have expected, to incoherence. For what drives us to submit the property of being a man to the conditional criterion is the belief that it is impossible for something to be a man without existing. It would then seem to follow that the property of being an existent man should also submit to the conditional criterion; for this latter property merely makes explicit the existential commitment which is implicit in the former property. Granted that Socrates is essentially a man, we should therefore accept that Socrates is essentially an existent man. But how can Socrates be essentially an existent man without also being essentially existent?

Nor is it clear how the double standard is to be generalized so as to exclude the other troublesome cases, such as the one concerning the existence of Socrates' parents.

Thus the difficulties are not to be avoided. But might there not be some other, perhaps quite different, version of the modal criterion which is not subject to these difficulties? Although it is hard to be definitive on such a matter, I think it can plausibly be made out that no such alternative account is to found. For it seems to be possible to agree on all of the modal facts and yet disagree on the essentialist facts. But if any modal criterion of essence were correct, such a situation would be impossible.

Consider, for example, the mind-body problem. What is the relationship between a person, his body and his mind? We can imagine two philosophers agreeing on the modal facts; they accept that a person, his body and his mind are all distinct, that it is necessary that a person have just one body and one mind and that a mind or body belong to just one person, that a person necessarily has the mind and body that he has (if he exists) and that a mind or body necessarily belong to the person that they belong to (if they exist), and so on. But all the same, they may disagree on the essential properties of persons, bodies and minds. For the one philosopher may think of the body and the mind as some kind of abstraction from a person. For him therefore it is of the essence of a body or of a mind to belong to the person that they belong to, though not of the essence of a person to have the body or mind that he has. The other philosopher, though, may think of a person and his mind as some kind of abstraction from the body. For him therefore it will be of the essence of a person and mind to belong to the body that they belong to, though not of the essence of a body to belong to the person or the mind.

If no modal account of essence is possible, then this is important for our understanding of the metaphysics of identity. For it shows that even when all questions of necessity have been resolved, questions of their source will remain. The example shows further that these questions will not always be unproblematic; they may raise real issues. Thus the subject should not be taken to be constituted, either in principle or practice, by its claims of necessity.

Why has the modal criterion let us down so badly? What is it about the concept of necessity which makes it so inappropriate for understanding the concept of essence?

Certainly, there is a connection between the two concepts. For any essentialist attribution will give rise to a necessary truth; if certain objects are essentially related then it is necessarily true that the objects are so related (or necessarily true given that the objects exist). However, the resulting necessary truth is not necessary simpliciter. For it is true in virtue of the identity of the objects in question; the necessity has its source in those objects which are the subject of the underlying essentialist claim.

Thus different essentially induced truths may have their source in the identities of different objects – Socrates being a man having its source in the identity of Socrates, 2 being a number having its source in the identity of 2. In particular, an induced truth which concerns various objects may have its source in the nature of some of these objects but not of others. This is how it is with our standard example of Socrates being a member of singleton Socrates; for this is true in virtue of the identity of singleton Socrates, but not of the identity of Socrates.

The concept of metaphysical necessity, on the other hand, is insensitive to source: all objects are treated equally as possible grounds of necessary truth; they are all grist to the necessitarian mill. What makes it so easy to overlook this point is the confusion of subject with source. One naturally supposes, given that a subject-predicate proposition is necessary, that the subject of the proposition is the source of the necessity. One naturally supposes, for example, that what makes it necessary that singleton 2 contains (or has the property of containing) the number 2 is something about the singleton. However, the concept of necessity is indifferent to which of the many objects in a proposition is taken to be its subject. The proposition that singleton 2 contains 2 is necessary whether or not the number or the set is taken to be the subject of the proposition.

Given the insensitivity of the concept of necessity to variations in source, it is hardly surprising that it is incapable of capturing a concept which is sensitive to such variation. Each object, or selection of objects, makes its own contribution to the totality of necessary truths; and one can hardly expect to determine from the totality itself what the different contributions were. One might, in this respect, compare the concept of necessity to the concept of communal belief, i.e. to the concept of what is believed by some member of a given community. It would clearly be absurd to attempt to recover what a given individual believes from what his community believes. But if I am right, there is a similar absurdity involved in attempting to recover the essential properties of things from the class of necessary truths.

Indeed, it seems to me that far from viewing essence as a special case of metaphysical necessity, we should view metaphysical necessity as a special case of essence. For each class of objects, be they concepts or individuals or entities of some other kind, will give rise to its own domain of necessary truths, the truths which flow from the nature of the objects in question. The metaphysically necessary truths can then be identified with the propositions which are true in virtue of the nature of all objects whatever.[1]

Other familiar concepts of necessity (though not all of them) can be understood in a similar manner. The conceptual necessities can be taken to be the propositions which are true in virtue of the nature of all concepts; the logical necessities can be taken to be the propositions which are true in virtue of the nature of all logical concepts; and, more generally, the necessities of a given discipline, such as mathematics or physics, can be taken to be those propositions which are true in virtue of the characteristic concepts and objects of the discipline.

I turn now to the connection between essence and definition. One of the ways the connection reveals itself is through a systematic analogy between necessity and analyticity, on the one hand, and essence and meaning, on the other; as essence is to necessity, so is meaning to analyticity.

An analytic truth is commonly taken to be a sentence which is true in virtue of the meaning of terms. But if there is an intelligible notion of a sentence being true in virtue of the meaning of all terms, it is natural to suppose that there is an intelligible notion of a sentence being true in virtue of certain terms as opposed to others. Consider the familiar example 'all bachelors are unmarried men'. It is plausible that this sentence is true in virtue of the meaning of the term 'bachelor' but not in virtue of the meanings of the terms 'unmarried' and 'man'.

The possibility of relativizing analyticity becomes even more apparent under the traditional explication of the notion. For under this explication,

the meaning of a term is identified with a set of defining sentences and the relation between the meanings of the terms, as so understood, and the given sentence is taken be logical consequence. The analytic sentences are thus the logical consequences of the totality of definitions.

But in that case, the sentences true in virtue of the meanings of certain selected terms may be taken to be the logical consequences of the definitions of those terms. The sentence 'all bachelors are unmarried men', for example, will be analytic in 'bachelor' since it follows from the definition of 'bachelor' as 'unmarried man', while the sentence will not be analytic in 'unmarried' and 'man', since there are no legitimate definitions of these terms from which it follows.

We therefore have a direct analogy with the relativized form of necessity. Just as a necessary truth may be true in virtue of the identity of certain objects as opposed to others, so an analytic truth may be true in virtue of the meanings of certain terms as opposed to others.

One might, of course, be sceptical of the intuitions upon which such a distinction rests. One might think that the sentence 'all bachelors are unmarried men' is no more true in virtue of the meaning of the term 'bachelor' than of the terms 'unmarried' and 'man', or that if it is legitimate to define 'bachelor' as 'unmarried man' then it is equally legitimate to define 'unmarried' as 'bachelor or spinster' or 'man' as 'bachelor or husband'. One might even be some sort of semantical holist and think that the meaning of one term cannot properly be separated from the meaning of any other term. I do not myself find these views plausible; it seems quite clear to me, for example, that the concept of marital status is not at all involved in the concept of being a man. However, just as in the essentialist case, the important issue concerns intelligibility rather than truth. We want to know if there could be a genuine difference of opinion as to whether 'man' is correctly definable as 'bachelor or husband' or as to whether some form of holism is correct; and when the point is put in this way, it seems hard to see how it could be denied.

Granted the intelligibility of the relativized form of analyticity, the question arises as to whether it can be explained in other terms; and we find that, just as there have been those who have attempted to explain the concept of essence in terms of necessity, so there have been those who have attempted to explain the concept of meaning in terms of analyticity. They have thought, for example, that synonymy between expressions might be defined as an appropriate form of analytic equivalence and that the meaning of a term might then be identified with the class of its synonyms.

But the attempt to reduce meaning to analyticity is as futile as the attempt to reduce essence to necessity. For an adequate account of meaning must at least explain when a sentence is true in virtue of the meanings of certain terms as opposed to others; it must provide us with a satisfactory account of relativized analyticity. But how is this to be done? Consider the case of the term 'bachelor'. We want the sentence 'something is a bachelor iff it is an unmarried man' to be true in virtue of the meaning of 'bachelor'. But what for our reductionist can render it true in virtue of the meaning of the term beyond the fact that it is analytic? It would appear that he can only appeal at this point to the further fact that the sentence has the form of an explicit definition. Thus he must maintain that any analytic sentence of the form 'something is a P iff ...' will be true in virtue of the meaning of the predicate P.

But such a view leads to absurdity. For it would follow that the sentence 'something is a bachelor iff it as an unmarried man and all triangles are three sided' is true in virtue of the meaning of 'bachelor'. Yet surely it is no part of our understanding of 'bachelor' that something should be a bachelor only when all triangles have three sides.

Indeed, under the proposed view the distinction between the different relativizations virtually disappears. For let P be a one-place predicate (similar considerations apply to the other cases); and let A be an arbitrary analytic truth. Then 'for all x, Px iff (Px iff A)' is analytic and hence true in virtue of the meaning of P. But A is a logical consequence of this sentence and hence presumably also true in virtue of the meaning of P. Thus we reach the ridiculous conclusion that someone who knows the meaning of one term (in so far as it can be given by an explicit definition) thereby knows the meaning of all terms.

Nor does any other definition of the relative in terms of the absolute notion appear to be available. For just as it appeared to be possible to agree on the modal facts and yet disagree on the essentialist facts, so it appears to be possible to agree on the facts of analyticity and yet disagree on the facts of meaning. A plausible case can perhaps be constructed around the claim, familiar from discussions of personal identity, that a person can only remember his own experiences. Some philosophers have thought that the sentence expressing this claim is true in virtue of the meaning of 'remember'; to remember an experience, if one is a person, is to "quasi-remember" an experience which is yours. Others have thought that the sentence is true in virtue of the meaning of 'person'; to be a person is, at least in part, to be a being which only remembers its own experiences. It is not clear that these philosophers need differ over what they take to be analytic; and if this is so, we would then have a case of the desired sort.

These considerations are relevant to our understanding of semantics or "conceptual analysis". For they suggest that even when all questions of analyticity have been resolved, real issues as to their source will still remain. The study of semantics is no more exhausted by the claims of analyticity than is the metaphysics of identity exhausted by the claims of necessity.

The previous considerations are also relevant to the question of how one should understand the traditional account of analyticity. Under this account, it will be recalled, the notion of analytic truth was understood in terms of the notion of definitional truth; the analytic truths were taken to be the logical consequences of the definitional truths. But how are we to understand the notion of a definitional truth? Let us suppose, for simplicity, that all of the definitional truths are explicit in form; one thing is defined as another. Then how should we understand the relationship between the definiendum and the definiens?

The only answer available to the reductionist was that the two should be synonyms; the corresponding biconditional, or what have you, should be analytic. But if this is the case, then it is hard to see what the traditional account achieves. It is, for one thing, unnecessarily complicated. Quine himself has pointed out, in section 5 of *Two Dogmas of Empiricism*, that, once equipped with the notion of synonymy, we can define an analytic truth as one that is synonymous with a logical truth. But we can do better than that. For fixing on any particular analytic truth S_0, we can define an analytic truth to be any sentence synonymous with S_0. (Alternatively, we can define an analytic truth T to be one synonymous with 'if T then T'). Thus there is not even any need to appeal to the notion of logical truth.

But, more significantly, we must give up the traditional idea that the logical derivation of an analytic statement from the definitions of its terms constitutes an analysis of that statement, one which may enable us to see that it is true. For there is nothing in the underlying conception of definitional truth which will force the resulting derivations to be analyses in any meaningful sense of the term. Indeed, as far as this conception goes, one might as well extract any predicate P from the given analytic statement and use the artificial "definition" above to provide it with a trivial pseudo-analysis.

These difficulties are avoided if we require the definitional truths which figure in the account of analyticity to be true in virtue of the meanings of their defined terms. For the account is then as about as direct as it could be; and real content is given to the idea of analysis. The given analytic statement is derived from definitions which in a significant sense provide one with the meanings of the individual terms.

We have seen that there exists a certain analogy between defining a term and giving the essence of an object; for the one results in a sentence which is true in virtue of the meaning of the term, while the other results in a proposition which is true in virtue of the identity of the object. However, I am inclined to think that the two cases are not merely parallel but are, at bottom, the same.

For what is involved in giving a definition? What makes it correct, for example, to define 'bachelor' as 'unmarried man'? On one common view it is an empirical fact about linguistic usage that 'bachelor' means what it does and hence is correctly definable as unmarried man. But this is to accept a particular conception of a word as a mere sequence of letters. On a thicker and perhaps more natural conception, a word would be constituted in part by its meaning. There would thus be two words 'bank' in English, one meaning river bank and the other meaning money bank.

Under this alternative conception, what would be an empirical fact is that the word, or a token of it, existed. But given the word, it would be essential that it meant what it did. A definition, on this view, would therefore state an essential property of the word.

But there is a deeper connection between definition and the formulation of essence which can still be made out, even when we drop the thicker conception of what a word is. For in attempting to define a term, such as 'bachelor', we are attempting to specify its meaning. But not every specification of the meaning is appropriate. We cannot properly say that the meaning of 'bachelor' is the one most often referred to in the recent philosophical literature on analyticity. We should not even say that the meaning of 'bachelor' is the same as the meaning of the phrase 'unmarried man' (which is the form of locution preferred by Quine); for, strictly speaking, it is irrelevant to the meaning of 'bachelor' that the phrase 'unmarried man' means what it does.

So what is an appropriate specification of the meaning? The only satisfactory answer appears to be that the specification should make clear what the meaning (essentially) is; it should provide us, that is to say, with some account of the meaning's essence. Thus we find again that in giving a definition we are giving an essence – though not now of the word itself, but of its meaning.

Of course, even if this is correct, the essentialist engagement is only with meanings. But there are many philosophers who would be happy with the idea that one can say what a meaning or concept is, at least in the sense of providing it with an analysis, but who would balk at the thought that one can in a comparable sense say what an *object* is. On their view, it is only concepts or meanings which can be defined, not objects.

The difficulty with this position is to see what is so special about concepts. It is granted that the concept bachelor may be defined as unmarried man; this definition states, in the significant essentialist sense, what the concept *is*. But then why is it not equally meaningful to define a particular set in terms of its members or to define a particular molecule of water in terms of its atomic constituents? Why is the one any more a definition or account of what the object is than the others?

Indeed, I believe that what is properly regarded as a definition of an object is sometimes treated as a definition of a concept or of a word, presumably because of some prejudice against real definition. A case in point is the definition of the numerals as they are found in natural language. It is supposed that the numeral '1' should be defined as 'the successor of 0', the numeral '2' as 'the successor of 1', and so on. But why is this view taken to be so plausible? Why could one not, with equal or greater plausibility, understand the numeral '1' independently of the numeral '0', or define '12' as 'the sum of 10 and 2'? I suspect that what these philosophers really have in mind is that the number 1 is to be defined as the successor of 0 and that this thought is then transferred, without regard for the linguistic evidence, from the number to the numeral. We therefore have a reversal of what is usually regarded as the traditional mistake in this area; the definition is illegitimately transferred, not from the word to the object, but from the object to the word.

If I am right, there is more to the idea of real definition than is commonly conceded. For the activities of specifying the meaning of a word and of stating what an object is are essentially the same; and hence each of them has an equal right to be regarded as a form of definition.[2]

Notes

1   This account of necessity has been anticipated by Husserl. In the third of the *Logical Investigations*, section 7, he describes the necessity relevant to his discussion as an "a priori necessity rooted in the essences of things". I do not follow him in treating the necessity in question as a priori or in taking the essences of things to be universal; and he does not follow me in treating the account as a definition of one notion in terms of another. But still, the underlying idea is the same.

2   This paper was presented as the second *Philosophical Perspectives* Lecture at California State University, Northridge in the Fall of 1992. I am grateful to James Tomberlin and his colleagues for the occasion. Other versions have been given elsewhere; and I should like to thank the members of the different philosophical audiences for their valuable comments. The ideas behind the paper go back to two unpublished sets of notes on identity and on necessity, respectively.

Some points of contact with the recent literature should be noted, Wiggins, in his paper *The De Re*

Must ... and elsewhere, argues against what I have called the modal account of essentialist claims. But the point of his arguments is quite different from my own. He wishes to claim that the de re modal statement does not give the correct logical form of an essentialist attribution. But he would be perfectly prepared to concede, given a suitable understanding of necessity, that the two were extensionally, and perhaps even analytically, equivalent. My concern, however, is to argue against the equivalence of the two.

Almog's *The What and the How* is closer in theme to the present paper. He introduces the notion of a primal truth, i.e. of a "truth in actuality solely in virtue of what the subject is" (p. 226); and this notion seems to be like my notion of a proposition's being true in virtue of the identity of certain objects. But the following major disparities between the two notions and between our treatments of them should be noted. (1) The qualification "in actuality" seems to bear some force which makes the two intuitive notions different. For whereas it is a primal truth that Socrates exists, this is not something true in virtue of the identity of Socrates; and nor is existence, at least according to the traditional conception of essence, any part of the essence of Socrates. (2) Almog takes primality to be a property of truths. Given any truth, he extracts the subject (and presumably the subjects, if there is more than one) and asks whether the truth is true solely in virtue of what the subject (or subjects) are. On the other hand, my notion is a relativized property. Given any proposition and any objects (which may or may not he subjects of the proposition), I ask whether it is true in virtue of the identity of those objects. The relativized notion gives us much greater flexibility in saying what we want to say. We may distinguish, for example, between the proposition that Socrates is a member of singleton Socrates being true in virtue of the singleton but not true in virtue of Socrates. It is not clear on Almog's approach how such distinctions are to be expressed; and I doubt that the kinds of notion we are both trying to get at should be regarded as yet another property of truths, alongside necessity, apriolicity and the like. (3) We both argue against our notions being modal; but the arguments are quite different. Mine depend critically upon there being two or more "subjects". His do not; and it is not clear to me, for this reason, that they are as compelling. (4) We understand the connection between our notions and necessity differently. I take a metaphysical necessity to be a proposition true in virtue of the identity of all objects. However, he supposes that some primal truths are not metaphysically necessary and views the two as somehow operating in different conceptual spheres. (5) Almog gives an analogue of the modal account of essence; for he takes P to be a primal trait of x iff "it has to be actually true that, if x exists, x is P" (p. 230). Now I assume that the operator 'it has to be actually true that' is subject-indifferent, at least to the extent of conforming to certain weak modal principles. But then my objections against the modal account of essence will also apply to this account of primal trait. I might also add that there is a difficulty in knowing how this elucidation is to be understood. For either it has to be actually true that Socrates exists or this is not the case. (It is not completely clear to me from the paper what Almog would want to say on this question). If it is the case, then the antecedent expression 'if x exists' is redundant and the elucidation does no work. If it is not the case, then the operator would appear to express a more fundamental concept and the elucidation would actually constitute an analysis of primal truth in terms of this more fundamental concept.

References

Almog, J., The What and the How, *Journal of Philosophy* 91: 225–44.

Aristotle, *Metaphysics* and *Topics*.

Husserl, E. *Logische Untersuchungen*, 1st ed., Halle: Niemeyer, 1900–1, translated as *Logical Investigations* by J. N. Findlay, London: Routledge, 1970.

Locke, J. *An Essay Concerning Human Understanding*.

Moore, G. E. *External and Internal Relations*, Proceedings of the Aristotelian Society, 1917–18, reprinted in *Philosophical Studies*, London: Routledge and Kegan, (1922).

Mill, J. S. *A System of Logic*.

Quine, W. V., Two Dogmas of Empiricism, *Philosophical Review* 60: 20–43, reprinted in *From a Logical Point of View*, Cambridge, Mass.: Harvard University Press (1953).

Wiggins, D., *The De Re 'Must': A Note on the Logical Form of Essentialist Claims*, in *Truth and Meaning*, ed. G. Evans and J. McDowell, Oxford: Clarendon Press (1976).

PART IV
Properties

Introduction

Some things are red: this patch of paint here, that apple over there, and so on. But, in addition to these particular red objects, is there also redness, something had in common by all and only red things? Put more generally, in addition to the particular things that are F, is there also such a thing as F-ness, a property shared by all and only F things? If there are such entities as properties, what sort of thing are they? Is there a property corresponding to every meaningful predicative expression ('red', 'not red', 'red or large', 'located ten miles due north of Providence', 'being sought by Ponce de León')? Can properties exist independently of us or independently of their instances? If one property has all the same instances as another, are they the same property? Or do properties have more demanding identity conditions and, if so, what are they? Are some properties privileged with respect to others, by virtue of being more "natural" or "basic"? These are some of the central questions about properties.

Many philosophers are fairly liberal about which properties they take there to be. They are willing to countenance such properties as the property of being non-black and even the property of being either green and having been observed before the year 2000 or else blue and not having been observed before 2000 (aka the property of being grue). But for certain purposes, it is crucial to recognize a privileged group of properties which (unlike being grue and being non-black) underwrite a genuine similarity among the things that have them. W. V. Quine calls these properties "kinds". In "Natural Kinds" (chapter 20), Quine calls attention to the centrality of the notion of kinds to our conceptual scheme. He shows that kinds play a crucial role in inductive reasoning (and in solving various puzzles of induction) and that the notion of kinds is deeply connected to our notions of dispositions and causation. He also observes some of the difficulties involved in analyzing the notions of similarity and kinds. Quine expresses skepticism about the value and objectivity of our judgments about similarity, but allows that these judgments can be refined as science progresses.

In "Causality and Properties" (chapter 21), Sydney Shoemaker examines the individuation conditions of properties: if P is a property and Q is property, under what conditions is P is same property as Q? Shoemaker defends the *causal structuralist* view that the identity of a property is determined by the causal powers that it bestows upon its bearers. He argues that knowledge of properties and reference to properties is possible only on a causal structuralist account of property identity, and he shows how this account may be put to use in distinguishing genuine properties from so-called "Cambridge" properties

Metaphysics: An Anthology, Second Edition. Edited by Jaegwon Kim, Daniel Z. Korman and Ernest Sosa.
Editorial material and organization © 2012 Blackwell Publishing Ltd. Published 2012 by Blackwell Publishing Ltd.

(e.g., relational properties, like the property of being located ten miles due north of Providence). In the final sections of the paper, Shoemaker observes that this account of property identity implies that the laws of nature are logically necessary, and he addresses the complaint that the laws must be contingent because we can so easily conceive of things being governed by different laws of nature.

In "The Metaphysic of Abstract Particulars" (chapter 22), Keith Campbell defends a view of properties on which properties are abstract particulars, or "tropes." Tropes are abstract insofar as we conceive of them by means of a mental act of abstraction. Tropes are particular insofar as they do not have multiple instances: the whiteness of the wall and the whiteness of the chalk are distinct entities – not a single entity as proponents of multiply instantiable "universals" would have it (see, e.g., chapter 24). Campbell defends trope theory by showing how well it explains various phenomena having to do with causation, perception, the ontological structure of concrete particulars, and general relativity.

In "New Work for a Theory of Universals" (chapter 23), David Lewis presents a number of reasons for allowing universals into one's ontology. (Lewis uses 'universals' to pick out those "elite" properties that Quine calls 'kinds'. Others use 'universals' more liberally, to cover all properties and relations.) Lewis begins with a discussion of one traditional reason for countenancing universals – namely, that they are required for an account of similarity and for an analysis of predication – and he contends that such arguments are unsuccessful. But, according to Lewis, there is still work for universals to do. By accepting a theory of universals, one can elucidate various philosophically important notions, including duplication, supervenience, materialism, and laws of nature. Lewis also argues that universals can play a role in solving various puzzles having to do with the content of our thoughts and utterances – specifically, Putnam's paradox and the "Kripkenstein" paradox.

In "Universals as Attributes" (chapter 24), D. M. Armstrong argues for a particular conception of which universals there are and of the relationship between universals and particulars. He rejects the Platonic conception of universals (as "transcendent" and instance-independent) in favor of the *in rebus* conception of universals, on which universals exist only if something instantiates them at some point in time, and on which universals are ("immanent") constituents of spatiotemporal particulars. He denies that there are universals answering to just any general term in the language and, in particular, argues that there are no disjunctive or negative universals. He then defends an ontology which includes not only individuals and the universals that they instantiate, but also states of affairs involving those individuals and universals. For instance, in addition to a given electron and its charge, there is a further entity: the state of affairs of that electron's having that charge. Armstrong concludes by addressing the objection that the *in rebus* conception of universals commits one to the view that a single thing can have multiple locations.

Further Reading

Bealer, G. (1982). *Quality and Concept*. Oxford: Oxford University Press.

Bealer, G. (1993). "Universals," *The Journal of Philosophy* 90: 5–32.

Devitt, M. (1980). "'Ostrich Nominalism' or 'Mirage Realism'?," *Pacific Philosophical Quarterly*, 61: 433–9.

Hirsch, E. (1993). *Dividing Reality*. New York: Oxford University Press.

MacBride, F. (2005). "The Particular–Universal Distinction: A Dogma of Metaphysics?," *Mind* 114: 565–614.

Mellor, D. H. (1974). "In Defense of Dispositions," *Philosophical Review* 83: 157–81.

Mellor, D. H., and Oliver, A. (eds.) (1997). *Properties*. Oxford: Oxford University Press.

Oliver, A. (1996). "The Metaphysics of Properties," *Mind* 105: 1–80.

Putnam, H. (1969). "On Properties," in N. Rescher et al. (eds.), *Essays in Honor of Carl G. Hempel*. Dordrecht: Reidel.

Van Cleve, J. (1985). "Three Versions of Bundle Theory," *Philosophical Studies* 47: 95–107.

Williams, D. C. (1953). "On the Elements of Being: I," *The Review of Metaphysics* 7: 3–18.

20

Natural Kinds

W. V. Quine

What tends to confirm an induction? This question has been aggravated on the one hand by Hempel's puzzle of the non-black non-ravens,[1] and exacerbated on the other by Goodman's puzzle of the grue emeralds.[2] I shall begin my remarks by relating the one puzzle to the other, and the other to an innate flair that we have for natural kinds. Then I shall devote the rest of the paper to reflections on the nature of this notion of natural kinds and its relation to science.

Hempel's puzzle is that just as each black raven tends to confirm the law that all ravens are black, so each green leaf, being a non-black non-raven, should tend to confirm the law that all non-black things are non-ravens, that is, again, that all ravens are black. What is paradoxical is that a green leaf should count toward the law that all ravens are black.

Goodman propounds his puzzle by requiring us to imagine that emeralds, having been identified by some criterion other than color, are now being examined one after another, and all up to now are found to be green. Then he proposes to call anything *grue* that is examined today or earlier and found to be green or is not examined before tomorrow and is blue. Should we expect the first one examined tomorrow to be green, because all examined up to now were green? But all examined up to now were also grue; so why not expect the first one tomorrow to be grue, and therefore blue?

The predicate "green," Goodman says,[3] is *projectible*; "grue" is not. He says this by way of putting a name to the problem. His step toward solution is his doctrine of what he calls entrenchment,[4] which I shall touch on later. Meanwhile the terminological point is simply that projectible predicates are predicates ζ and η whose shared instances all do count, for whatever reason, toward confirmation of ⌜All ζ are η⌝.

Now I propose assimilating Hempel's puzzle to Goodman's by inferring from Hempel's that the complement of a projectible predicate need not be projectible. "Raven" and "black" are projectible; a black raven does count toward "All ravens are black." Hence a black raven counts also, indirectly, toward "All non-black things are non-ravens," since this says the same thing. But a green leaf does not count toward "All non-black things are non-ravens," nor, therefore, toward "All ravens are black"; "non-black" and "non-raven" are not projectible. "Green" and "leaf" are projectible, and the green leaf counts toward "All leaves are

Metaphysics: An Anthology, Second Edition. Edited by Jaegwon Kim, Daniel Z. Korman and Ernest Sosa.
Editorial material and organization © 2012 Blackwell Publishing Ltd. Published 2012 by Blackwell Publishing Ltd.

green" and "All green things are leaves"; but only a black raven can confirm "All ravens are black," the complements not being projectible.

If we see the matter in this way, we must guard against saying that a statement ⌈All ζ are η⌉ is lawlike only if ζ and η are projectible. "All non-black things are non-ravens" is a law despite its non-projectible terms, since it is equivalent to "All ravens are black." Any statement is lawlike that is logically *equivalent* to ⌈All ζ are η⌉ for some projectible ζ and η.[5]

Having concluded that the complement of a projectible predicate need not be projectible, we may ask further whether there is *any* projectible predicate whose complement is projectible. I can conceive that there is not, when complements are taken strictly. We must not be misled by limited or relative complementation; "male human" and "non-male human" are indeed both projectible.

To get back now to the emeralds, why do we expect the next one to be green rather than grue? The intuitive answer lies in similarity, however subjective. Two green emeralds are more similar than two grue ones would be if only one of the grue ones were green. Green things, or at least green emeralds, are a kind.[6] A projectible predicate is one that is true of all and only the things of a kind. What makes Goodman's example a puzzle, however, is the dubious scientific standing of a general notion of similarity, or of kind.

The dubiousness of this notion is itself a remarkable fact. For surely there is nothing more basic to thought and language than our sense of similarity; our sorting of things into kinds. The usual general term, whether a common noun or a verb or an adjective, owes its generality to some resemblance among the things referred to. Indeed, learning to use a word depends on a double resemblance: first, a resemblance between the present circumstances and past circumstances in which the word was used, and second, a phonetic resemblance between the present utterance of the word and past utterances of it. And every reasonable expectation depends on resemblance of circumstances, together with our tendency to expect similar causes to have similar effects.

The notion of a kind and the notion of similarity or resemblance seem to be variants or adaptations of a single notion. Similarity is immediately definable in terms of kind; for things are similar when they are two of a kind. The very words for "kind" and "similar" tend to run in etymologically cognate pairs. Cognate with "kind" we have "akin" and "kindred." Cognate with "like" we have "ilk." Cognate with "similar" and "same" and "resemble" there are "*sammeln*" and "assemble," suggesting a gathering into kinds.

We cannot easily imagine a more familiar or fundamental notion than this, or a notion more ubiquitous in its applications. On this score it is like the notions of logic like identity, negation, alternation, and the rest. And yet, strangely, there is something logically repugnant about it. For we are baffled when we try to relate the general notion of similarity significantly to logical terms. One's first hasty suggestion might be to say that things are similar when they have all or most or many properties in common. Or, trying to be less vague, one might try defining comparative similarity – "*a* is more similar to *b* than to *c*" – as meaning that *a* shares more properties with *b* than with *c*. But any such course only reduces our problem to the unpromising task of settling what to count as a property.

The nature of the problem of what to count as a property can be seen by turning for a moment to set theory. Things are viewed as going together into sets in any and every combination, describable and indescribable. Any two things are joint members of any number of sets. Certainly then, we cannot define "*a* is more similar to *b* than to *c*" to mean that *a* and *b* belong jointly to more sets than *a* and *c* do. If properties are to support this line of definition where sets do not, it must be because properties do not, like sets, take things in every random combination. It must be that properties are shared only by things that are significantly similar. But properties in such a sense are no clearer than kinds. To start with such a notion of property, and define similarity on that basis, is no better than accepting similarity as undefined.

The contrast between properties and sets which I suggested just now must not be confused with the more basic and familiar contrast between properties, as intensional, and sets as extensional. Properties are intensional in that they may be counted as distinct properties even though wholly coinciding in respect of the things that have them. There is no call to reckon kinds as intensional. Kinds can be seen as sets, determined by their members. It is just that not all sets are kinds.

If similarity is taken simple-mindedly as a yes-or-no affair, with no degrees, then there is no containing of kinds within broader kinds. For, as remarked, similarity now simply means belonging to some one same kind. If all colored things comprise a kind, then all colored things count as similar, and the set of all red things is too narrow to count as a kind. If on the other hand the set of all red things counts as a kind, then colored things do not all count as similar, and the set of all colored things is too broad to count as a kind. We cannot have it both ways. Kinds can, however, overlap; the red things can comprise one kind, the round another.

When we move up from the simple dyadic relation of similarity to the more serious and useful triadic relation of comparative similarity, a correlative change takes place in the notion of kind. Kinds come to admit now not only of overlapping but also of containment one in another. The set of all red things and the set of all colored things can now both count as kinds; for all colored things can now be counted as resembling one another more than some things do, even though less, on the whole, than red ones do.

At this point, of course, our trivial definition of similarity as sameness of kind breaks down; for almost any two things could count now as common members of some broad kind or other, and anyway we now want to define comparative or triadic similarity. A definition that suggests itself is this: *a* is more similar to *b* than to *c* when *a* and *b* belong jointly to more kinds than *a* and *c* do. But even this works only for finite systems of kinds.

The notion of kind and the notion of similarity seemed to be substantially one notion. We observed further that they resist reduction to less dubious notions, as of logic or set theory. That they at any rate be definable each in terms of the other seems little enough to ask. We just saw a somewhat limping definition of comparative similarity in terms of kinds. What now of the converse project, definition of kind in terms of similarity?

One may be tempted to picture a kind, suitable to a comparative similarity relation, as any set which is "qualitatively spherical" in this sense: it takes in exactly the things that differ less than so-and-so much from some central norm. If without serious loss of accuracy we can assume that there are one or more actual things (*paradigm cases*) that nicely exemplify the desired norm, and one or more actual things (*foils*) that deviate just barely too much to be counted into the desired kind at all, then our definition is easy: *the kind with paradigm a and foil b is the set of all the things to which a is more similar than a is to b.* More generally, then, a set may be said to be a *kind* if and only if there are *a* and *b*, known or unknown, such that the set is the kind with paradigm *a* and foil *b*.

If we consider examples, however, we see that this definition does not give us what we want as kinds. Thus take red. Let us grant that a central shade of red can be picked as norm. The trouble is that the paradigm cases, objects in just that shade of red, can come in all sorts of shapes, weights, sizes, and smells. Mere degree of overall similarity to any one such paradigm case will afford little evidence of degree of redness, since it will depend also on shape, weight, and the rest. If our assumed relation of comparative similarity were just comparative chromatic similarity, then our paradigm-and-foil definition of kind would indeed accommodate red-kind. What the definition will not do is distill purely chromatic kinds from mixed similarity.

A different attempt, adapted from Carnap, is this: a set is a kind if all its members are more similar to one another than they all are to any one thing outside the set. In other words, each non-member differs more from some member than that member differs from any member. However, as Goodman showed in a criticism of Carnap,[7] this construction succumbs to what Goodman calls the difficulty of imperfect community. Thus consider the set of all red round things, red wooden things, and round wooden things. Each member of this set resembles each other member somehow: at least in being red, or in being round, or in being wooden, and perhaps in two or all three of these respects or others. Conceivably, moreover, there is no one thing outside the set that resembles every member of the set to even the least of these degrees. The set then meets the proposed definition of kind. Yet surely it is not what anyone means by a kind. It admits yellow croquet balls and red rubber balls while excluding yellow rubber balls.

The relation between similarity and kind, then, is less clear and neat than could be wished.

Definition of similarity in terms of kind is halting, and definition of kind in terms of similarity is unknown. Still the two notions are in an important sense correlative. They vary together. If we reassess something *a* as less similar to *b* than to *c*, where it had counted as more similar to *b* than to *c*, surely we will correspondingly permute *a*, *b*, and *c* in respect of their assignment to kinds; and conversely.

I have stressed how fundamental the notion of similarity or of kind is to our thinking, and how alien to logic and set theory. I want to go on now to say more about how fundamental these notions are to our thinking, and something also about their non-logical roots. Afterward I want to bring out how the notion of similarity or of kind changes as science progresses. I shall suggest that it is a mark of maturity of a branch of science that the notion of similarity or kind finally dissolves, so far as it is relevant to that branch of science. That is, it ultimately submits to analysis in the special terms of that branch of science and logic.

For deeper appreciation of how fundamental similarity is, let us observe more closely how it figures in the learning of language. One learns by *ostension* what presentations to call yellow; that is, one learns by hearing the word applied to samples. All he has to go on, of course, is the similarity of further cases to the samples. Similarity being a matter of degree, one has to learn by trial and error how reddish or brownish or greenish a thing can be and still be counted yellow. When he finds he has applied the word too far out, he can use the false cases as samples to the contrary; and then he can proceed to guess whether further cases are yellow or not by considering whether they are more similar to the in-group or the out-group. What one thus uses, even at this primitive stage of learning, is a fully functioning sense of similarity, and relative similarity at that: *a* is more similar to *b* than to *c*.

All these delicate comparisons and shrewd inferences about what to call yellow are, in Sherlock Holmes's terminology, elementary. Mostly the process is unconscious. It is the same process by which an animal learns to respond in distinctive ways to his master's commands or other discriminated stimulations.

The primitive sense of similarity that underlies such learning has, we saw, a certain complexity of structure: *a* is more similar to *b* than to *c*. Some people have thought that it has to be much more complex still: that it depends irreducibly on *respects*, thus similarity in color, similarity in shape, and so on. According to this view, our learning of yellow by ostension would have depended on our first having been told or somehow apprised that it was going to be a question of color. Now hints of this kind are a great help, and in our learning we often do depend on them. Still one would like to be able to show that a single general standard of similarity, but of course comparative similarity, is all we need, and that respects can be abstracted afterward. For instance, suppose the child has learned of a yellow ball and block that they count as yellow, and of a red ball and block that they do not, and now he has to decide about a yellow cloth. Presumably he will find the cloth more similar to the yellow ball and to the yellow block than to the red ball or red block; and he will not have needed any prior schooling in colors and respects. Carnap undertook to show long ago how some respects, such as color, could by an ingenious construction be derived from a general similarity notion;[8] however, this development is challenged, again, by Goodman's difficulty of imperfect community.

 A standard of similarity is in some sense innate. This point is not against empiricism; it is a commonplace of behavioral psychology. A response to a red circle, if it is rewarded, will be elicited again by a pink ellipse more readily than by a blue triangle; the red circle resembles the pink ellipse more than the blue triangle. Without some such prior spacing of qualities, we could never acquire a habit; all stimuli would be equally alike and equally different. These spacings of qualities, on the part of men and other animals, can be explored and mapped in the laboratory by experiments in conditioning and extinction.[9] Needed as they are for all learning, these distinctive spacings cannot themselves all be learned; some must be innate.

If then I say that there is an innate standard of similarity, I am making a condensed statement that can be interpreted, and truly interpreted, in behavioral terms. Moreover, in this behavioral sense it can be said equally of other animals that they have an innate standard of similarity too. It is part of our animal birthright. And, interestingly enough, it is characteristically animal in its lack of intellectual status. At any rate we noticed earlier how alien the notion is to mathematics and logic.

This innate qualitative spacing of stimulations was seen to have one of its human uses in the ostensive learning of words like "yellow." I should add as a cautionary remark that this is not the only way of learning words, nor the commonest; it is merely the most rudimentary way. It works when the question of the reference of a word is a simple question of spread: how much of our surroundings counts as yellow, how much counts as water, and so on. Learning a word like "apple" or "square" is more complicated, because here we have to learn also where to say that one apple or square leaves off and another begins. The complication is that apples do not add up to an apple, nor squares, generally, to a square. "Yellow" and "water" are mass terms, concerned only with spread; "apple" and "square" are terms of divided reference, concerned with both spread and individuation. Ostension figures in the learning of terms of this latter kind too, but the process is more complex.[10] And then there are all the other sorts of words, all those abstract and neutral connectives and adverbs and all the recondite terms of scientific theory; and there are also the grammatical constructions themselves to be mastered. The learning of these things is less direct and more complex still. There are deep problems in this domain, but they lie aside from the present topic.

Our way of learning "yellow," then, gives less than a full picture of how we learn langue. Yet more emphatically, it gives less than a full picture of the human use of an innate standard of similarity, or innate spacing of qualities. For, as remarked, every reasonable expectation depends on similarity. Again on this score, other animals are like man. Their expectations, if we choose so to conceptualize their avoidance movements and salivation and pressing of levers and the like, are clearly dependent on their appreciation of similarity. Or, to put matters in their methodological order, these avoidance movements and salivation and pressing of levers and the like are typical of what we have to go on in mapping the animals' appreciation of similarity, their spacing of qualities.

Induction itself is essentially only more of the same: animal expectation or habit formation. And the ostensive learning of words is an implicit case of induction. Implicitly the learner of "yellow" is working inductively toward a general law of English verbal behavior, though a law that he will never try to state; he is working up to where he can in general judge when an English speaker would assent to "yellow" and when not.

Not only is ostensive learning a case of induction; it is a curiously comfortable case of induction, a game of chance with loaded dice. At any rate this is so if, as seems plausible, each man's spacing of qualities is enough like his neighbor's. For the learner is generalizing on his yellow samples by similarity considerations, and his neighbors have themselves acquired the use of the word "yellow," in their day, by the same similarity considerations. The learner of "yellow" is thus making his induction in a friendly world. Always, induction expresses our hope that similar causes will have similar effects; but when the induction is the ostensive learning of a word, that pious hope blossoms into a foregone conclusion. The uniformity of people's quality spaces virtually assures that similar presentations will elicit similar verdicts.

It makes one wonder the more about other inductions, where what is sought is a generalization not about our neighbor's verbal behavior but about the harsh impersonal world. It is reasonable that our quality space should match our neighbor's, we being birds of a feather; and so the general trustworthiness of induction in the ostensive learning of words was a put-up job. To trust induction as a way of access to the truths of nature, on the other hand, is to suppose, more nearly, that our quality space matches that of the cosmos. The brute irrationality of our sense of similarity, its irrelevance to anything in logic and mathematics, offers little reason to expect that this sense is somehow in tune with the world – a world which, unlike language, we never made. Why induction should be trusted, apart from special cases such as the ostensive learning of words, is the perennial philosophical problem of induction.

One part of the problem of induction, the part that asks why there should be regularities in nature at all, can, I think, be dismissed. *That* there are or have been regularities, for whatever reason, is an established fact of science; and we cannot ask better than that. *Why* there have been regularities is an obscure question, for it is hard to see what would count as an answer. What does make clear sense is this other part of the problem of induction: why does our innate subjective spacing of qualities accord so well with the functionally relevant groupings in nature as to make our inductions tend to come out right? Why should our subjective spacing of qualities have a special purchase on nature and a lien on the future?

There is some encouragement in Darwin. If people's innate spacing of qualities is a gene-linked trait, then the spacing that has made for the most successful inductions will have tended to predominate through natural selection.[11] Creatures inveterately wrong in their inductions have a pathetic but praiseworthy tendency to die before reproducing their kind.

At this point let me say that I shall not be impressed by protests that I am using inductive generalizations, Darwin's and others, to justify induction, and thus reasoning in a circle. The reason I shall not be impressed by this is that my position is a naturalistic one; I see philosophy not as an a priori propaedeutic or groundwork for science, but as continuous with science. I see philosophy and science as in the same boat – a boat which, to revert to Neurath's figure as I so often do, we can rebuild only at sea while staying afloat in it. There is no external vantage point, no first philosophy. All scientific findings, all scientific conjectures that are at present plausible, are therefore in my view as welcome for use in philosophy as elsewhere. For me, then, the problem of induction is a problem about the world: a problem of how we, as we now are (by our present scientific lights), in a world we never made, should stand better than random or coin-tossing chances of coming out right when we predict by inductions which are based on our innate, scientifically unjustified similarity standard. Darwin's natural selection is a plausible partial explanation.

It may, in view of a consideration to which I next turn, be almost explanation enough. This consideration is that induction, after all, has its conspicuous failures. Thus take color. Nothing in experience, surely, is more vivid and conspicuous than color and its contrasts. And the remarkable fact, which has impressed scientists and philosophers as far back at least as Galileo and Descartes, is that the distinctions that matter for basic physical theory are mostly independent of color contrasts. Color impresses man; raven black

impresses Hempel; emerald green impresses Goodman. But color is cosmically secondary. Even slight differences in sensory mechanisms from species to species, Smart remarks,[12] can make overwhelming differences in the grouping of things by color. Color is king in our innate quality space, but undistinguished in cosmic circles. Cosmically, colors would not qualify as kinds.

Color is helpful at the food-gathering level. Here it behaves well under induction, and here, no doubt, has been the survival value of our color-slanted quality space. It is just that contrasts that are crucial for such activities can be insignificant for broader and more theoretical science. If man were to live by basic science alone, natural selection would shift its support to the color-blind mutation.

Living as he does by bread and basic science both, man is torn. Things about his innate similarity sense that are helpful in the one sphere can be a hindrance in the other. Credit is due to man's inveterate ingenuity, or human sapience, for having worked around the blinding dazzle of color vision and found the more significant regularities elsewhere. Evidently natural selection has dealt with the conflict by endowing man doubly: with both a color-slanted quality space and the ingenuity to rise above it.

He has risen above it by developing modified systems of kinds, hence modified similarity standards for scientific purposes. By the trial-and-error process of theorizing he has regrouped things into new kinds which prove to lend themselves to many inductions better than the old.

A crude example is the modification of the notion of fish by excluding whales and porpoises. Another taxonomic example is the grouping of kangaroos, opossums, and marsupial mice in a single kind, marsupials, while excluding ordinary mice. By primitive standards the marsupial mouse is more similar to the ordinary mouse than to the kangaroo; by theoretical standards the reverse is true.

A theoretical kind need not be a modification of an intuitive one. It may issue from theory full-blown, without antecedents; for instance the kind which comprises positively charged particles.

We revise our standards of similarity or of natural kinds on the strength, as Goodman remarks,[13] of second-order inductions. New groupings, hypothetically adopted at the suggestion of a growing theory, prove favorable to inductions and so become "entrenched." We newly establish the projectibility of some predicate, to our satisfaction, by successfully trying to project it. In induction nothing succeeds like success.

Between an innate similarity notion or spacing of qualities and a scientifically sophisticated one, there are all gradations. Sciences, after all, differ from common sense only in degree of methodological sophistication. Our experiences from earliest infancy are bound to have overlaid our innate spacing of qualities by modifying and supplementing our grouping habits little by little, inclining us more and more to an appreciation of theoretical kinds and similarities, long before we reach the point of studying science systematically as such. Moreover, the later phases do not wholly supersede the earlier; we retain different similarity standards, different systems of kinds, for use in different contexts. We all still say that a marsupial mouse is more like an ordinary mouse than a kangaroo, except when we are concerned with genetic matters. Something like our innate quality space continues to function alongside the more sophisticated regroupings that have been found by scientific experience to facilitate induction.

We have seen that a sense of similarity or of kinds is fundamental to learning in the widest sense – to language learning, to induction, to expectation. Toward a further appreciation of how utterly this notion permeates our thought, I want now to point out a number of other very familiar and central notions which seem to depend squarely on this one. They are notions that are definable in terms of similarity, or kinds, and further irreducible.

A notable domain of examples is the domain of dispositions, such as Carnap's example of solubility in water. To say of some individual object that it is soluble in water is not to say merely that it always dissolves when in water, because this would be true by default of any object, however insoluble, if it merely happened to be destined never to get into water. It is to say rather that it *would* dissolve if it were in water; but this account brings small comfort, since the device of a subjunctive conditional involves all the perplexities of disposition terms and more. Thus far I simply repeat Carnap.[14] But now I want to point out what could be done in this connection with the notion of kind. Intuitively, what qualifies a thing as soluble though it never gets

into water is that it is of the same kind as the things that actually did or will dissolve; it is similar to them. Strictly we can't simply say "*the* same kind," nor simply "similar," when we have wider and narrower kinds, less and more similarity. Let us then mend our definition by saying that the soluble things are the common members of *all* such kinds. A thing is soluble if *each* kind that is broad enough to embrace all actual victims of solution embraces it too.

Graphically the idea is this: we make a set of all the sometime victims, all the things that actually did or will dissolve in water, and then we add just enough other things to round the set out into a kind. This is the water-soluble kind.

If this definition covers just the desired things, the things that are really soluble in water, it owes its success to a circumstance that could be otherwise. The needed circumstance is that a sufficient variety of things actually get dissolved in water to assure their not all falling under any one kind narrower than the desired water-soluble kind itself. But it is a plausible circumstance, and I am not sure that its accidental character is a drawback. If the trend of events had been otherwise, perhaps the solubility concept would not have been wanted.

However, if I seem to be defending this definition, I must now hasten to add that of course it has much the same fault as the definition which used the subjunctive conditional. This definition uses the unreduced notion of kind, which is certainly not a notion we want to rest with either; neither theoretical kind nor intuitive kind. My purpose in giving the definition is only to show the link between the problem of dispositions and the problem of kinds.

As between theoretical and intuitive kinds, certainly the theoretical ones are the ones wanted for purposes of defining solubility and other dispositions of scientific concern. Perhaps "amiable" and "reprehensible" are disposition terms whose definitions should draw rather on intuitive kinds.[15]

Another dim notion, which has intimate connections with dispositions and subjunctive conditionals, is the notion of cause; and we shall see that it too turns on the notion of kinds. Hume explained cause as invariable succession, and this makes sense as long as the cause and effect are referred to by general terms. We can say that fire causes heat, and we can mean thereby, as Hume would have it, that each event classifiable under the head of fire is followed by an event classifiable under the head of heat, or heating up. But this account, whatever its virtues for these general causal statements, leaves singular causal statements unexplained.

What does it mean to say that the kicking over of a lamp in Mrs Leary's barn caused the Chicago fire? It cannot mean merely that the event at Mrs Leary's belongs to a set, and the Chicago fire belongs to a set, such that there is invariable succession between the two sets: every member of the one set is followed by a member of the other. This paraphrase is trivially true and too weak. Always, if one event happens to be followed by another, the two belong to *certain* sets between which there is invariable succession. We can rig the sets arbitrarily. Just put any arbitrary events in the first set, including the first of the two events we are interested in; and then in the other set put the second of those two events, together with other events that happen to have occurred just after the other members of the first set.

Because of this way of trivialization, a singular causal statement says no more than that the one event was followed by the other. That is, it says no more if we use the definition just now contemplated; which, therefore, we must not. The trouble with that definition is clear enough: it is the familiar old trouble of the promiscuity of sets. Here, as usual, kinds, being more discriminate, enable us to draw distinctions where sets do not. To say that one event caused another is to say that the two events are of *kinds* between which there is invariable succession. If this correction does not yet take care of Mrs Leary's cow, the fault is only with invariable succession itself, as affording too simple a definition of general causal statements; we need to hedge it around with provisions for partial or contributing causes and a good deal else. That aspect of the causality problem is not my concern. What I wanted to bring out is just the relevance of the notion of kinds, as the needed link between singular and general causal statements.

We have noticed that the notion of kind, or similarity, is crucially relevant to the notion of disposition, to the subjunctive conditional, and to singular causal statements. From a scientific point of view these are a pretty disreputable lot.

The notion of kind, or similarity, is equally disreputable. Yet some such notion, some similarity sense, was seen to be crucial to all learning, and central in particular to the processes of inductive generalization and prediction which are the very life of science. It appears that science is rotten to the core.

Yet there may be claimed for this rot a certain undeniable fecundity. Science reveals hidden mysteries, predicts successfully, and works technological wonders. If this is the way of rot, then rot is rather to be prized and praised than patronized.

Rot, actually, is not the best model here. A better model is human progress. A sense of comparative similarity, I remarked earlier, is one of man's animal endowments. Insofar as it fits in with regularities of nature, so as to afford us reasonable success in our primitive inductions and expectations, it is presumably an evolutionary product of natural selection. Secondly, as remarked, one's sense of similarity or one's system of kinds develops and changes and even turns multiple as one matures, making perhaps for increasingly dependable prediction. And at length standards of similarity set in which are geared to theoretical science. This development is a development away from the immediate, subjective, animal sense of similarity to the remoter objectivity of a similarity determined by scientific hypotheses and posits and constructs. Things are similar in the later or theoretical sense to the degree that they are interchangeable parts of the cosmic machine revealed by science.

This progress of similarity standards, in the course of each individual's maturing years, is a sort of recapitulation in the individual of the race's progress from muddy savagery. But the similarity notion even in its theoretical phase is itself a muddy notion still. We have offered no definition of it in satisfactory scientific terms. We of course have a behavioral definition of what counts, for a given individual, as similar to what, or as more similar to what than to what; we have this for similarity old and new, human and animal. But it is no definition of what it means really for *a* to be more similar to *b* than to *c*; really, and quite apart from this or that psychological subject.

Did I already suggest a definition to this purpose, metaphorically, when I said that things are similar to the extent that they are interchangeable parts of the cosmic machine? More literally, could things be said to be similar in proportion to how much of scientific theory would remain true on interchanging those things as objects of reference in the theory? This only hints a direction; consider for instance the dimness of "how much theory." Anyway the direction itself is not a good one; for it would make similarity depend in the wrong way on theory. A man's judgments of similarity do and should depend on his theory, on his beliefs; but similarity itself, what the man's judgments purport to be judgments of, purports to be an objective relation in the world. It belongs in the subject matter not of our theory of theorizing about the world, but of our theory of the world itself. Such would be the acceptable and reputable sort of similarity concept, if it could be defined.

It does get defined in bits: bits suited to special branches of science. In this way, on many limited fronts, man continues his rise from savagery, sloughing off the muddy old notion of kind or similarity piecemeal, a vestige here and a vestige there. Chemistry, the home science of water-solubility itself, is one branch that has reached this stage. Comparative similarity of the sort that matters for chemistry can be stated outright in chemical terms, that is, in terms of chemical composition. Molecules will be said to *match* if they contain atoms of the same elements in the same topological combinations. Then, in principle, we might get at the comparative similarity of objects *a* and *b* by considering how many pairs of matching molecules there are, one molecule from *a* and one from *b* each time, and how many unmatching pairs. The ratio gives even a theoretical measure of relative similarity, and thus abundantly explains what it is for *a* to be more similar to *b* than to *c*. Or we might prefer to complicate our definition by allowing also for degrees in the matching of molecules; molecules having almost equally many atoms, or having atoms whose atomic numbers or atomic weights are almost equal, could be reckoned as matching better than others. At any rate a lusty chemical similarity concept is assured.

From it, moreover, an equally acceptable concept of kinds is derivable, by the paradigm-and-foil definition noted early in this paper. For it is a question now only of distilling purely chemical kinds from purely chemical similarity; no admixture of other respects of similarity

interferes. We thus exonerate water-solubility, which, the last time around, we had reduced no further than to an unexplained notion of kind. Therewith also the associated subjunctive conditional, "If this were in water, it would dissolve," gets its bill of health.

The same scientific advances that have thus provided a solid underpinning for the definition of solubility in terms of kinds, have also, ironically enough, made that line of definition pointless by providing a full understanding of the mechanism of solution. One can redefine water-solubility by simply describing the structural conditions of that mechanism. This embarrassment of riches is, I suspect, a characteristic outcome. That is, once we can legitimize a disposition term by defining the relevant similarity standard, we are apt to know the mechanism of the disposition, and so bypass the similarity. Not but that the similarity standard is worth clarifying too, for its own sake or for other purposes.

Philosophical or broadly scientific motives can impel us to seek still a basic and absolute concept of similarity, along with such fragmentary similarity concepts as suit special branches of science. This drive for a cosmic similarity concept is perhaps identifiable with the age-old drive to reduce things to their elements. It epitomizes the scientific spirit, though dating back to the pre-Socratics: to Empedocles with his theory of four elements, and above all to Democritus with his atoms. The modern physics of elementary particles, or of hills in space-time, is a more notable effort in this direction.

This idea of rationalizing a single notion of relative similarity, throughout its cosmic sweep, has its metaphysical attractions. But there would remain still need also to rationalize the similarity notion more locally and superficially, so as to capture only such similarity as is relevant to some special science. Our chemistry example is already a case of this, since it stops short of full analysis into neutrons, electrons, and the other elementary particles.

A more striking example of superficiality, in this good sense, is afforded by taxonomy, say in zoology. Since learning about the evolution of species, we are in a position to define comparative similarity suitably for this science by consideration of family trees. For a theoretical measure of the degree of similarity of two individual animals we can devise some suitable function that depends on proximity and frequency of their common ancestors. Or a more significant concept of degree of similarity might be devised in terms of genes. When kind is construed in terms of any such similarity concept, fishes in the corrected, whale-free sense of the word qualify as a kind, while fishes in the more inclusive sense do not.

Different similarity measures, or relative similarity notions, best suit different branches of science; for there are wasteful complications in providing for finer gradations of relative similarity than matter for the phenomena with which the particular science is concerned. Perhaps the branches of science could be revealingly classified by looking to the relative similarity notion that is appropriate to each. Such a plan is reminiscent of Felix Klein's so-called *Erlangerprogramm* in geometry, which involved characterizing the various branches of geometry by what transformations were irrelevant to each. But a branch of science would only qualify for recognition and classification under such a plan when it had matured to the point of clearing up its similarity notion. Such branches of science would qualify further as unified, or integrated into our inclusive systematization of nature, only insofar as their several similarity concepts were *compatible*; capable of meshing, that is, and differing only in the fineness of their discriminations.

Disposition terms and subjunctive conditionals in these areas, where suitable senses of similarity and kind are forthcoming, suddenly turn respectable; respectable and, in principle, superfluous. In other domains they remain disreputable and practically indispensable. They may be seen perhaps as unredeemed notes; the theory that would clear up the unanalyzed underlying similarity notion in such cases is still to come. An example is the disposition called intelligence – the ability, vaguely speaking, to learn quickly and to solve problems. Sometime, whether in terms of proteins or colloids or nerve nets or overt behavior, the relevant branch of science may reach the stage where a similarity notion can be constructed capable of making even the notion of intelligence respectable. And superfluous.

In general we can take it as a very special mark of the maturity of a branch of science that it no longer needs an irreducible notion of similarity and kind. It is that final stage where the animal vestige is wholly absorbed into the theory. In this career of the similarity notion, starting in its innate phase, developing over the years in the light of accumulated experience, passing then from the intuitive phase into theoretical similarity, and finally disappearing altogether, we have a paradigm of the evolution of unreason into science.

Notes

1   C. G. Hempel, *Aspects of Scientific Explanation and Other Essays* (New York: Free Press, 1965), p. 15.
2   Nelson Goodman, *Fact, Fiction, and Forecast* (1st edn, Cambridge, Mass.: Harvard University Press, Indianapolis: 1955; 2nd edn, Bobbs-Merrill, 1965), p. 74. I am indebted to Goodman and to Burton Dreben for helpful criticisms of earlier drafts of the present paper.
3   Goodman, *Fact*, pp. 82f.
4   Ibid., pp. 95ff.
5   I mean this only as a sufficient condition of lawlikeness. See Donald Davidson, "Emeroses by other names," *Journal of Philosophy* 63 (1966), pp. 778–80.
6   This relevance of kind is noted by Goodman, *Fact*, 1st edn, pp. 119f; 2nd edn, pp. 121f.
7   Nelson Goodman, *The Structure of Appearance*, 2nd edn (Indianapolis: Bobbs-Merrill, 1966), pp. 163f.
8   Rudolf Carnap, *The Logical Structure of the World* (Berkeley: University of California Press, 1967), pp. 141–7 (German edn, 1928).
9   See my *Word and Object* (Cambridge, Mass.: MIT Press, 1960), pp. 83f, for further discussion and references.
10 See ibid., pp. 90–5.
11 This was noted by S. Watanabe on the second page of his paper "Une explication mathématique du classement d'objets," in S. Dockx and P. Bernays (eds), *Information and Prediction in Science* (New York: Academy Press, 1965).
12 J. J. C. Smart, *Philosophy and Scientific Realism* (New York: Humanities Press, 1963), pp. 68–72.
13 Goodman, *Fact*, pp. 95ff.
14 Rudolf Carnap, "Testability and meaning," *Philosophy of Science* 3 (1936), pp. 419–71; 4 (1937), pp. 1–40.
15 Here there followed, in previous printings, 26 lines which I have deleted. They were concerned with explaining certain subjunctive conditionals on the basis of the notion of kind. Paul Berent pointed out to me that the formulation was wrong, for it would have equated those conditionals to their converses.

21

Causality and Properties

Sydney Shoemaker

I

It is events, rather than objects or properties, that are usually taken by philosophers to be the terms of the causal relationship. But an event typically consists of a change in the properties or relationships of one or more objects, the latter being what Jaegwon Kim has called the "constituent objects" of the event.[1] And when one event causes another, this will be in part because of the properties possessed by their constituent objects. Suppose, for example, that a man takes a pill and, as a result, breaks out into a rash. Here the cause and effect are, respectively, the taking of the pill and the breaking out into a rash. Why did the first event cause the second? Well, the pill was pencillin, and the man was allergic to penicillin. No doubt one could want to know more – for example, about the biochemistry of allergies in general and this one in particular. But there is a good sense in which what has been said already explains why the one event caused the other. Here the pill and the man are the constituent objects of the cause event, and the man is the constituent object of the effect event. Following Kim we can also speak of events as having "constituent properties" and "constituent times." In this case the constituent property of the cause event is the relation expressed by the verb "takes", while the constituent property of the effect event is expressed by the predicate "breaks out into a rash". The constituent times of the events are their times of occurrence. Specifying the constituent objects and properties of the cause and effect will tell us what these events consisted in, and together with a specification of their constituent times will serve to identify them; but it will not, typically, explain why the one brought about the other. We explain this by mentioning certain properties of their constituent objects. Given that the pill was penicillin, and that the man was allergic to penicillin, the taking of the pill by the man was certain, or at any rate very likely, to result in an allergic response like a rash. To take another example, suppose a branch is blown against a window and breaks it. Here the constituent objects include the branch and the window, and the causal relationship holds because of, among other things, the massiveness of the one and the fragility of the other.

It would appear from this that any account of causality as a relation between events should involve, in a central way, reference to the properties

Sydney Shoemaker, "Causality and Properties," in Peter van Inwagen (ed.), *Time and Cause* (Dordrecht: Reidel, 1980). Reproduced by kind permission of Springer Science + Business Media B.V.

of the constituent objects of the events. But this should not encourage us to suppose that the notion of causality is to be analyzed away, in Humean fashion, in terms of some relationship between properties – for example, in terms of regularities in their instantiation. For as I shall try to show, the relevant notion of a property is itself to be explained in terms of the notion of causality in a way that has some strikingly non-Humean consequences.

II

Philosophers sometimes use the term "property" in such a way that for every predicate F true of a thing there is a property of the thing which is designated by the corresponding expression of the form "being F". If "property" is used in this broad way, every object will have innumerable properties that are unlikely to be mentioned in any causal explanation involving an event of which the object is a constituent. For example, my typewriter has the property of being over one hundred miles from the current heavyweight boxing champion of the world. It is not easy to think of a way in which its having this property could help to explain why an event involving it has a certain effect, and it seems artificial, at best, to speak of my typewriter's acquisition of this property as one of the causal effects of the movements of the heavyweight champion.

It is natural, however to feel that such properties are not "real" or "genuine" properties. Our intuitions as to what are, and what are not, genuine properties are closely related to our intuitions as to what are, and what are not, genuine changes. A property is genuine if and only if its acquisition or loss by a thing constitutes a genuine change in that thing. One criterion for a thing's having changed is what Peter Geach calls the "Cambridge criterion." He formulates this as follows: "The thing called 'x' has changed if we have '$F(x)$ at time t' true and '$F(x)$ at time t'' false, for some interpretations of 'F,' 't,' and 't'.'"[2] But, as Geach points out, this gives the result that Socrates undergoes a change when he comes to be shorter than Theaetetus in virtue of the latter's growth, and even that he undergoes a change every time a fresh schoolboy comes to admire him. Such "changes", those that intuitively are not

genuine changes, Geach calls "mere 'Cambridge' changes." For Geach, real changes are Cambridge changes, since they satisfy the Cambridge criterion, but some Cambridge changes, namely those that are *mere* Cambridge changes, fail to be real changes. Since it is mere Cambridge changes, rather than Cambridge changes in general, that are to be contrasted with real or genuine changes, I shall introduce the hyphenated expression "mere-Cambridge" to characterize these. And I shall apply the terms "Cambridge" and "mere-Cambridge" to properties as well as to changes. Mere-Cambridge properties will include such properties as being "grue" (in Nelson Goodman's sense), historical properties like being over twenty years old and having been slept in by George Washington, relational properties like being fifty miles south of a burning barn,[3] and such properties as being such that Jimmy Carter is President of the United States.

It is worth mentioning that in addition to distinguishing between real and mere-Cambridge properties and changes, we must also distinguish between real and mere-Cambridge resemblance or similarity, and between real and mere-Cambridge differences. Cambridge similarities hold in virtue of the sharing of Cambridge properties. And mere-Cambridge similarities hold in virtue of the sharing of mere-Cambridge properties: there is such a similarity between all grue things; there is one between all things fifty miles south of a burning barn; there is one between all beds slept in by George Washington; and there is one between all things such that Jimmy Carter is President of the United States. It will be recalled that the notion of similarity, or resemblance, plays a prominent role in Hume's account of causality. His first definition of *cause* in the *Treatise* is "an object precedent and contiguous to another, and where all the objects resembling the former are plac'd in a like relation of priority and contiguity to those objects, that resemble the latter."[4] Hume clearly regarded the notion of resemblance as quite unproblematical and in no need of elucidation.[5] Yet it is plain that he needs a narrower notion of resemblance than that of Cambridge resemblance if his definition of causality is to have the desired content. Cambridge resemblances are too easily come by; any two objects share infinitely many Cambridge properties, and so "resemble" one another in infinitely many ways. There are also infinitely many Cambridge differences between any two objects. What Hume needs is a notion of resemblance and difference which is such that some things resemble a given thing more than others do, and such that some things may resemble a thing exactly (without being numerically identical to it) while others resemble it hardly at all. Only "real" or "genuine" resemblance will serve his purposes. If it turns out, as I think it does, that in order to give a satisfactory account of the distinction between real and mere-Cambridge properties, changes, similarities, and differences, we must make use of the notion of causality, the Humean project of defining causality in terms of regularity or "constant conjunction", notions that plainly involve the notion of resemblance, is seriously undermined.

I have no wish to legislate concerning the correct use of the terms "property", "changes", "similar", and so forth. It would be rash to claim that the accepted use of the term "property" is such that what I have classified as mere-Cambridge properties are not properties. But I do think that we have *a* notion of what it is to be a property which is such that this is so – in other words, which is such that not every phrase of the form "being so and so" stands for a property which something has just in case the corresponding predicate of the form "is so and so" is true of it, and is such that sometimes a predicate is true of a thing, not because (or only because) of any properties *it* has, but because something else, perhaps something related to it in certain ways, has certain properties. It is this narrow conception of what it is to be a property, and the correlative notions of change and similarity, that I am concerned to elucidate in this essay. (I should mention that I am concerned here only with the sorts of properties with respect to which change is possible; my account is not intended to apply to such properties of numbers as being even and being prime.)

III

John Locke held that "*Powers make a great part of our complex* Ideas *of substances.*"[6] And there is one passage in which Locke seems to suggest that all qualities of substances are powers; he says, in explanation of his usage of the term 'quality', that "the Power to produce any *Idea* in our mind, I call *quality* of the Subject wherein that power is."[7] This suggests a theory of properties, namely that properties are causal powers, which is akin to the theory I shall be defending. As it happens, this is not Locke's view. If one ascribed it to him on the basis of the passage just quoted, one would have to ascribe to him the view that all qualities are what he called 'secondary qualities' – powers to produce certain mental effects ('ideas') in us. But Locke recognized the existence of powers that are not secondary qualities, namely powers (for example, the power in the sun to melt wax) to produce effects in material objects. These have been called 'tertiary qualities'. And he distinguished both of these sorts of powers from the 'primary qualities' on which they 'depend'. Nevertheless, the view which Locke's words unintentionally suggest is worth considering.

What would seem to be the same view is sometimes put by saying that all properties are dispositional properties. But as thus formulated, this view seems plainly mistaken. Surely we make a distinction between dispositional and nondispositional properties, and can mention paradigms of both sorts. Moreover, it seems plain that what dispositional properties something has, what powers it has, depends on what nondispositional properties it has – just as Locke thought that the powers of things depend on their primary qualities and those of their parts.

In fact, I believe, there are two different distinctions to be made here, and these are often conflated. One is not a distinction between kinds of *properties* at all, but rather a distinction between kinds of *predicates*. Sometimes it belongs to the meaning, or sense, of a predicate that if it is true of a thing, then under certain circumstances the thing will undergo certain changes or will produce certain changes in other things. This is true of what are standardly counted as dispositional predicates, for example, 'flexible', 'soluble', 'malleable', 'magnetized', and 'poisonous'. Plainly not all predicates are of this sort. Whether color predicates are is a matter of controversy. But whatever we say about this, it seems plain that predicates like 'square', 'round' and 'made of copper' are not dispositional in this sense. There are causal powers associated with being made of copper – for example, being an electrical conductor.

But presumably this association is not incorporated into the meaning of the term 'copper'.

The first distinction, then, is between different sorts of predicates, and I think that the term 'dispositional' is best employed as a predicate of predicates, not of properties. A different distinction is between powers, in a sense I am about to explain, and the properties in virtue of which things have the powers they have.[8] For something to have a power, in this sense, is for it to be such that its presence in circumstances of a particular sort will have certain effects.[9] One can think of such a power as a function from circumstances to effects. Thus if something is poisonous, its presence in someone's body will produce death or illness; in virtue of this, being poisonous is a power. Here it is possible for things to have the same power in virtue of having very different properties. Suppose that one poisonous substance kills by affecting the heart, while another kills by directly affecting the nervous system and brain. They produce these different effects in virtue of having very different chemical compositions. They will of course differ in their powers as well as in their properties, for one will have the power to produce certain physiological effects in the nervous system, while the other will have the power to produce quite different physiological effects in the heart. But there is one power they will share, in virtue of having these different powers, namely that of producing death if ingested by a human being. Properties here play the role, vis-à-vis powers, that primary qualities play in Locke; it is in virtue of a thing's properties that the thing has the powers (Locke's secondary and tertiary qualities) that it has.

There is a rough correspondence between this distinction between powers and properties and the earlier distinction between dispositional and non-dispositional predicates. By and large, dispositional predicates ascribe powers, while nondispositional monadic predicates ascribe properties that are not powers in the same sense.

IV

On the view of properties I want to propose, while properties are typically not powers of the sort ascribed by dispositional predicates, they are related to such powers in much the way that such powers are related to the causal effects which they are powers to produce. Just as powers can be thought of as functions from circumstances to causal effects, so the properties on which powers depend can be thought of as functions from properties to powers (or, better, as functions from sets of properties to sets of powers). One might even say that properties are second-order powers; they are powers to produce first-order powers (powers to produce certain sorts of events) if combined with certain other properties. But the formulation I shall mainly employ is this: what makes a property the property it is, what determines its identity, is its potential for contributing to the causal powers of the things that have it. This means, among other things, that if under all possible circumstances properties X and Y make the same contribution to the causal powers of the things that have them, X and Y are the same property.

To illustrate this, let us take as our example of a property the property of being 'knife-shaped' – I shall take this to be a highly determinate property which belongs to a certain knife in my kitchen and to anything else of exactly the same shape. Now if all that I know about a thing is that it has this property, I know nothing about what will result from its presence in any circumstances. What has the property of being knife-shaped could be a knife, made of steel, but it could instead be a piece of balsa wood, a piece of butter, or even an oddly shaped cloud of some invisible gas. There is no power which necessarily belongs to all and only the things having this property. But if this property is combined with the property of being knife-sized and the property of being made of steel, the object having these properties will necessarily have a number of powers. It will have the power of cutting butter, cheese, and wood, if applied to these substances with suitable pressure, and also the power of producing various sorts of sense-impressions in human beings under appropriate observational conditions, and also the power of leaving an impression of a certain shape if applied to soft wax and then withdrawn, and so on. The combination of the property of being knife-shaped with the property of being made of glass will result in a somewhat different set of powers, which will overlap with the set which results from its combination with the property of being made of steel. Likewise with its combination with the property of being made of wood, the property of being made of butter, and so on.

Let us say that an object has power P conditionally upon the possession of the properties in set Q if it has some property r such that having the properties in Q together with r is causally sufficient for having P, while having the properties in Q is not by itself causally sufficient for having P. Thus, for example, a knife-shaped object has the power of cutting wood conditionally upon being knife-sized and made of steel; for it is true of knife-shaped things, but not of things in general, that if they are knife-sized and made of steel, they will have the power to cut wood. When a thing has a power conditionally upon the possession of certain properties, let us say that this amounts to its having a *conditional power*. Our knife-shaped object has the conditional power of being able to cut wood if knife-sized and made of steel. The identity condition for conditional powers is as follows: if A is the conditional power of having power P conditionally upon having the properties in set Q and B is the conditional power of having P' conditionally upon having the properties in set Q', then A is identical to B just in case P is identical to P' and Q is identical to Q'. Having introduced this notion of a conditional power, we can express my view by saying that properties are clusters of conditional powers. (I shall count powers *simpliciter* as a special case of conditional powers.) I have said that the identity of a property is determined by its causal potentialities, the contributions it is capable of making to the causal powers of things that have it. And the causal potentialities that are essential to a property correspond to the conditional powers that make up the cluster with which the property can be identified; for a property to have a causal potentiality is for it to be such that whatever has it has a certain conditional power.

This account is intended to capture what is correct in the view that properties just are powers, or that all properties are dispositional, while acknowledging the truth of a standard objection to that view, namely that a thing's powers or dispositions are distinct from, because 'grounded in', its intrinsic properties.[10]

Before I give my reasons for holding this view, I should mention one prima facie objection to it.

Presumably the property of being triangular and the property of being trilateral do not differ in the contributions they make to the causal powers of the things that have them, yet it is natural to say that these, although necessarily coextensive, are different properties. It seems to me, however, that what we have good reason for regarding as distinct are not these properties, as such, but rather the concepts of triangularity and trilaterality, and the meanings of the expressions 'triangular' and 'trilateral'. If we abandon, as I think we should, the idea that properties are the meanings of predicate expressions, and if we are careful to distinguish concepts from what they are concepts of, I see no insuperable obstacle to regarding the properties themselves as identical.

V

My reasons for holding this theory of properties are, broadly speaking, epistemological. Only if some causal theory of properties is true, I believe, can it be explained how properties are capable of engaging our knowledge, and our language, in the way they do.

We know and recognize properties by their effects, or, more precisely, by the effects of the events which are the activations of the causal powers which things have in virtue of having the properties. This happens in a variety of ways. Observing something is being causally influenced by it in certain ways. If the causal potentialities involved in the possession of a property are such that there is a fairly direct causal connection between the possession of it by an object and the sensory states of an observer related to that object in certain ways, e.g., looking at it in good light, we say that the property itself is observable. If the relationship is less direct, e.g., if the property can affect the sensory states of the observer only by affecting the properties of something else which the observer observes, a scientific instrument, say, we speak of inferring that the thing has the property from what we take to be the effects of its possession. In other cases we conclude that something has a property because we know that it has other properties which we know from other cases to be correlated with the one in question. But the latter way of knowing about the properties of things is parasitic on the earlier ways; for unless the instantiation of the property had, under some circumstances, effects from which its existence could be concluded, we could never discover laws or correlations that would enable us to infer its existence from things other than its effects.

Suppose that the identity of properties consisted of something logically independent of their causal potentialities. Then it ought to be possible for there to be properties that have no potential whatever for contributing to causal powers, i.e., are such that under no conceivable circumstances will their possession by a thing make any difference to the way the presence of that thing affects other things or to the way other things affect it. Further, it ought to be possible that there be two or more different properties that make, under all possible circumstances, exactly the same contribution to the causal powers of the things that have them. Further, it ought to be possible that the potential of a property for contributing to the production of causal powers might change over time, so that, for example, the potential possessed by property A at one time is the same as that possessed by property B at a later time, and that possessed by property B at the earlier time is the same as that possessed by property A at the later time. Thus a thing might undergo radical change with respect to its properties without undergoing any change in its causal powers, and a thing might undergo radical change in its causal powers without undergoing any change in the properties that underlie these powers.

The supposition that these possibilities are genuine implies, not merely (what might seem harmless) that various things might be the case without its being in any way possible for us to know that they are, but also that it is impossible for us to know various things which we take ourselves to know. If there can be properties that have no potential for contributing to the causal powers of the things that have them, then nothing could be good evidence that the overall resemblance between two things is greater than the overall resemblance between two other things; for even if A and B have closely resembling effects on our senses and our instruments while C and D do not, it might be (for all we know) that C and D share vastly more properties of the causally impotent kind than do A and B. Worse, if two properties can have exactly the same potential for

contributing to causal powers, then it is impossible for us even to know (or have any reason for believing) that two things resemble one another by sharing a single property. Moreover, if the properties and causal potentialities of a thing can vary independently of one another, then it is impossible for us to know (or have any good reason for believing) that something has retained a property over time, or that something has undergone a change with respect to the properties that underlie its causal powers. On these suppositions, there would be no way in which a particular property could be picked out so as to have a name attached to it; and even if, *per impossibile*, a name did get attached to a property, it would be impossible for anyone to have any justification for applying the name on particular occasions.

It may be doubted whether the view under attack has these disastrous epistemological consequences. Surely, it may be said, one can hold that it is a contingent matter that particular properties have the causal potentialities they have, and nevertheless hold, compatibly with this, that there are good theoretical reasons for thinking that as a matter of fact different properties differ in their causal potentialities, and that any given property retains the same potentialities over time. For while it is logically possible that the latter should not be so, according to the contingency view, the simplest hypothesis is that it is so; and it is reasonable to accept the simplest hypothesis compatible with the data.

Whatever may be true in general of appeals to theoretical simplicity, this one seems to me extremely questionable. For here we are not really dealing with an explanatory hypothesis at all. If the identity of properties is made independent of their causal potentialities, then in what sense do we explain sameness or difference of causal potentialities by positing sameness or difference of properties? There are of course cases in which we explain a constancy in something by positing certain underlying constancies in its properties. It is genuinely explanatory to say that something retained the same causal power over time because certain of its properties remained the same. And this provides, *ceteris paribus*, a simpler, or at any rate more plausible, explanation of the constancy than one that says that the thing first had one set of underlying properties and then a different set, and that both sets were sufficient to give it that particular power. For example, if the water supply was poisonous all day long, it is more plausible to suppose that this was due to the presence in it of one poisonous substance all day rather than due to its containing cyanide from morning till noon and strychnine from noon till night. But in such cases we presuppose that the underlying property constancies carry with them constancies in causal potentialities, and it is only on this presupposition that positing the underlying constancies provides the simplest explanation of the constancy to be explained. Plainly this presupposition cannot be operative if what the 'inference to the best explanation' purports to explain is, precisely, that sameness of property goes with sameness of causal potentialities. It is not as if a property had the causal potentialities in question as a result of having yet *other* causal potentialities, the constancy of the latter explaining the constancy of the former. This disassociation of property identity from identity of causal potentiality is really an invitation to eliminate reference to properties from our explanatory hypotheses altogether; if it were correct, then we could, to use Wittgenstein's metaphor, 'divide through' by the properties and leave the explanatory power of what we say about things untouched.

It might be objected that even if my arguments establish that the causal potentialities of a genuine property cannot change over time, they do not establish that these causal potentialities are essential to that property, in the sense of belonging to it in all possible worlds. The immutability of properties with respect to their causal potentialities, it might be said, is simply a consequence of the immutability of laws – of the fact that it makes no sense to speak of a genuine law holding at one time and not at another. And from the fact that the laws governing a property cannot change over time, it does not follow, it may be said, that the property cannot be governed by different laws in different possible worlds.

Let me observe first of all that in conceding that the immutability of the causal potentialities of genuine properties is a consequence of the immutability of laws, the objection concedes a large part of what I want to maintain. It is not true in general of mere-Cambridge properties that their causal potentialities cannot change over time; for example, this is not true of *grueness* on

the Barker–Achinstein definition of *grue*, where something is grue just in case it is green and the time is before T (say AD 2000) or it is blue and the time is T or afterwards.[11] That genuine properties are marked off from mere-Cambridge properties by their relation to causal laws (and that it is nonsense to speak of a world in which it is the mere-Cambridge properties rather than the genuine ones that are law-governed in a way that makes their causal potentialities immutable) is a central part of my view.

There is, moreover, a prima facie case for saying that the immutability of the causal potentialities of a property does imply their essentiality; or in other words, that if they cannot vary across time, they also cannot vary across possible worlds. Most of us do suppose that *particulars* can (or do) have different properties in different possible worlds. We suppose, for example, that in some possible worlds I am a plumber rather than a philosopher, and that in some possible worlds my house is painted yellow rather than white. But it goes with this that particulars can change their properties over time. It is possible that I, the very person who is writing this essay, might have been a plumber, because there is a possible history in which I start with the properties (in this case relational as well as intrinsic) which I had at some time in my actual history, and undergo a series of changes which result in my eventually being a plumber. If I and the world were never such that it was then possible for me to *become* a plumber, it would not be true that I might have been a plumber, or (in other words) that there is a possible world in which I am one. There is, in short, a close linkage between identity across time and identity across possible worlds; the ways in which a given thing can be different in different possible worlds depend on the ways in which such a thing can be different at different times in the actual world. But now let us move from the case of particulars to that of properties. There is no such thing as tracing a property through a series of changes in its causal potentialities – not if it is a genuine property, i.e., one of the sort that figures in causal laws. And so there is no such thing as a possible history in which a property starts with the set of causal potentialities it has in the actual world and ends with a different set. To say the least, this calls into question the intelligibility of the suggestion that the very properties we designate with words like 'green', 'square', 'hard', and so on, might have had different causal potentialities than they in fact have.

However, this last argument is not conclusive. My earlier arguments, if sound, establish that there is an intimate connection between the identity of a property and its causal potentialities. But it has not yet been decisively established that *all* of the causal potentialities of a property are essential to it. The disastrous epistemological consequences of the contingency view would be avoided if for each property we could identify a proper subset of its causal potentialities that are essential to it and constitutive of it, and this would permit some of a property's causal potentialities, those outside the essential cluster, to belong to it contingently, and so not belong to it in some other possible worlds. There would, in this case, be an important difference between the trans-world identity of properties and that of particulars – and it is a difference which there is in my own view as well. If, as I believe, the assertion that a certain particular might have had different properties than it does in the actual world (that in some other possible world it does have those properties) implies that there is a possible history 'branching off' from the history of the actual world in which it acquires those properties, this is because there is, putting aside historical properties and 'identity properties' (like being identical to Jimmy Carter), no subset of the properties of such a thing which constitutes an individual essence of it, i.e., is such that, in any possible world, having the properties in that subset is necessary *and sufficient* for being that particular thing. To put this otherwise, the reason why the possible history in which the thing has different properties must be a branching-off from the history of the actual world is that the individual essence of a particular thing must include historical properties. Now I am not in a position to object to the suggestion that properties differ from particulars in having individual essences which do not include historical properties and which are sufficient for their identification across possible worlds; for I hold that the totality of a property's causal potentialities constitutes such an individual essence. So a possible alternative to my view is one which holds that for each property there is a proper subset of its causal potentialities that constitutes its individual essence. Such a view

has its attractions, and is compatible with much of what I say in this essay; in particular, it is compatible with the claim that within any possible world properties are identical just in case they have the same causal potentialities. But I shall argue in section IX that this view is unworkable, and that there is no acceptable alternative to the view that all of the causal potentialities of a property are essential to it.

VI

As was intended, my account of properties does not apply to what I have called mere-Cambridge properties. When my table acquired the property of being such that Gerald Ford is President of the United States, which it did at the time Nixon resigned from the presidency, this presumably had no effect on its causal powers. Beds that were slept in by George Washington may command a higher price than those that lack this historical property, but presumably this is a result, not of any causal potentialities in the beds themselves, but of the historical beliefs and interests of those who buy and sell them. And grueness, as defined by Goodman, is not associated in the way greenness and blueness are with causal potentialities. (In this sense, which differs from that invoked in section V, something is grue at a time just in case it is green at that time and is first examined before T, say, AD 2000, or is blue at that time and is not first examined before T.) It can happen that the only difference between something that is grue and something that is not is that one of them has and the other lacks the historical property of being (or having been) first examined before the time T mentioned in Goodman's definition of *grue*; and presumably this does not in itself make for any difference in causal potentialities. It can also happen that two things share the property of being grue in virtue of having properties that have different potentialities – that is, in virtue of one of them being green (and examined before T) and the other being blue (and not so examined).

There is an epistemological way of distinguishing genuine and mere-Cambridge properties that is prima facie plausible. If I wish to determine whether an emerald is green at t, the thing to do, if I can manage it, is to examine the emerald at t. But examination of a table will not tell me it is such that Gerald Ford is President of the United States, or whether it is fifty miles south of a burning barn. And if I am ignorant of the date, or if t is after T (the date in Goodman's definition), examination of an emerald will not tell me whether it is grue. Likewise, while scrutiny of a bed may reveal a plaque claiming that it was slept in by George Washington, it will not tell me whether this claim is true. Roughly, if a question about whether a thing has a property at a place and time concerns a genuine nonrelational property, the question is most directly settled by observations and tests in the vicinity of that place and time, while if it concerns a mere-Cambridge property it may be most directly settled by observations and tests remote from that place and time, and observations and tests made at that place and time will either be irrelevant (as in the case of the property of being such that Jimmy Carter is President) or insufficient to settle the question (as in the case of grue).

It would be difficult to make this into a precise and adequate criterion of genuineness of property, and I do not know whether this could be done. But I think that to the extent that it is adequate, its adequacy is explained by my account of properties in terms of causal powers. Properties reveal their presence in actualizations of their causal potentialities, a special case of this being the perception of a property. And the most immediate and revealing effects of an object's having a property at a particular place and time are effects that occur in the immediate vicinity of that place and time. To be sure, we cannot rule out on purely philosophical grounds the possibility of action at a spatial and/or temporal distance. And the more prevalent such action is, the less adequate the proposed epistemological criterion will be. But there do seem to be conceptual limitations on the extent to which causal action can be at a spatial or temporal distance. It is doubtful, to say the least, whether there could be something whose causal powers are *all* such that whenever any of them is activated the effects of its activation are spatially remote from the location of the thing at that time, or occur at times remote from the time of activation.

Causation and causal powers are as much involved in the verification of ascriptions of mere-Cambridge properties as in the verification of ascriptions of genuine ones. But in the case of

mere-Cambridge properties some of the operative causal powers will either belong to something other than the object to which the property is ascribed, or will belong to that object at a time other than that at which it has that property. Thus if I verify that a man has the property of being fifty miles south of a burning barn, it will be primarily the causal powers of the barn, and of the intervening stretch of land (which, we will suppose, I measure), rather than the causal powers of the man, that will be responsible for my verifying observations.

VII

It will not have escaped notice that the account of properties and property identity I have offered makes free use of the notion of a property and the notion of property identity. It says, in brief, that properties are identical, whether in the same possible world or in different ones, just in case their coinstantiation with the same properties gives rise to the same powers. This is, if anything, even more circular than it looks. For it crucially involves the notion of sameness of powers, and this will have to be explained in terms of sameness of circumstances and sameness of effects, the notions of which both involve the notion of sameness of property. And of course there was essential use of the notion of a property in my explanation of the notion of a conditional power.

It is worth observing that there is a distinction between kinds of powers that corresponds to the distinction, mentioned earlier, between genuine and mere-Cambridge properties.[12] Robert Boyle's famous example of the key can be used to illustrate this.[13] A particular key on my key chain has the power of opening locks of a certain design. It also has the power of opening my front door. It could lose the former power only by undergoing what we would regard as real change, for example, a change in its shape. But it could lose the latter without undergoing such a change; it could so do in virtue of the lock on my door being replaced by one of a different design. Let us say that the former is an intrinsic power and the latter a mere-Cambridge power. It is clear that in my account of properties the word 'power' must refer only to intrinsic powers. For if it refers to mere-Cambridge powers as well, then what seems clearly to be a mere-Cambridge property of my key, namely being such that my door has a lock of a certain design, will make a determinate contribution to its having the powers it has, and so will count as a genuine property of it. But it seems unlikely that we could explain the distinction between intrinsic and mere-Cambridge powers without making use of the notion of a genuine change and that of a genuine property. And so again my account of the notion of a property in terms of the notion of a power can be seen to be circular.

How much do these circularities matter? Since they are, I think, unavoidable, they preclude a reductive analysis of the notion of a property in terms of the notion of causality. But they by no means render my account empty. The claim that the causal potentialities of a property are essential to it, and that properties having the same causal potentialities are identical, is certainly not made vacuous by the fact that the explanation of the notion of a causal potentiality, or a conditional power, must invoke the notion of a property. As I see it, the notion of a property and the notion of a causal power belong to a system of internally related concepts, no one of which can be explicated without the use of the others. Other members of the system are the concept of an event, the concept of similarity, and the concept of a persisting substance. It can be worthwhile, as a philosophical exercise, to see how far we can go in an attempt to reduce one of these concepts to others – for both the extent of our success and the nature of our failures can be revealing about the nature of the connections between the concepts. But ultimately such attempts must fail. The goal of philosophical analysis, in dealing with such concepts, should not be reductive analysis but rather the charting of internal relationships. And it is perfectly possible for a "circular" analysis to illuminate a network of internal relationships and have philosophically interesting consequences.

VIII

According to the theory of properties I am proposing, all of the causal potentialities possessed by a property at any time in the actual world are essential to it and so belong to it at all times and in all possible worlds. This has a very strong consequence, namely that causal necessity is just a species of logical necessity. If the introduction into circumstances of a thing having certain properties causally necessitates the occurrence of certain effects, then it is impossible, logically impossible, that such an introduction could fail to have such an effect, and so logically necessary that it has it. To the extent that causal laws can be viewed as propositions describing the causal potentialities of properties, it is impossible that the same properties should be governed by different causal laws in different possible worlds, for such propositions will be necessarily true when true at all.

It is not part of this theory, however, that causal laws are analytic or knowable a priori. I suppose that it is analytic that flexible things bend under suitable pressure, that poisonous things cause injury to those for whom they are poisonous, and so on. But I do not think that it is analytic that copper is an electrical conductor, or that knife-shaped things, if knife-sized and made of steel, are capable of cutting butter. Nor does it follow from the claim that such truths are necessary that they are analytic. Kripke has made a compelling case for the view that there are propositions that are necessary a posteriori, that is, true in all possible worlds but such that they can only be known empirically.[14] And such, according to my theory, is the status of most propositions describing the causal potentialities of properties. The theory can allow that our knowledge of these potentialities is empirical, and that it is bound to be only partial. But in order to show how, in the theory, such empirical knowledge is possible, I must now bring out an additional way in which the notion of causality is involved in the notion of a property.

One of the formulations of my theory says that every property is a cluster of conditional powers. But the converse does not seem to me to hold; not every cluster of conditional powers is a property. If something is both knife-shaped and made of wax, then it will have, among others, the following conditional powers: the power of being able to cut wood conditionally upon being knife-sized and made of steel (this it has in virtue of being knife-shaped), and the power of being malleable conditionally upon being at a temperature of 100°F (this it has in virtue of being made of wax). Intuitively, these are not common components of any single property. By contrast, the various conditional powers a thing has in virtue of being knife-shaped – for example, the power of being able to cut wood conditionally upon being knife-sized and made of steel, the power of being able to cut butter conditionally upon being knife-sized and made of wood, the power of having a certain visual appearance conditionally upon being green, the power of having a certain other visual appearance conditionally upon being red, and so on – are all constituents of a single property, namely the property of being knife-shaped. The difference, I think, is that in the one case the set of conditional powers has, while in the other it lacks, a certain kind of causal unity. I shall now try to spell out the nature of this unity.

Some subsets of the conditional powers which make up a genuine property will be such that it is a consequence of causal laws that whatever has any member of the subset necessarily has all of its members. Thus, for example, something has the power of leaving a six-inch-long knife-shaped impression in soft wax conditionally upon being six inches long if and only if it has the power of leaving an eight-inch-long knife-shaped impression in soft wax conditionally upon being eight inches long. Now some conditional powers will belong to more than one property cluster; thus, for example, there are many different shape properties that give something the power of being able to cut wood conditionally upon being made of steel. But where a conditional power can be shared by different properties in this way, it will belong to a particular property cluster only if there is another member of that cluster which is such that it is a consequence of causal laws that whatever has that other member has the conditional power in question. And at the core of each cluster there will be one or more conditional powers which are such that as a consequence of causal laws whatever has any of them has all of the conditional powers in the cluster. For example, if something has, conditionally upon being made of steel, the power of leaving a knife-shaped impression in soft wax, then it cannot fail to be knife-shaped, and so cannot fail to have all of the other conditional powers involved in being knife-shaped. I suggest, then, that conditional powers X and Y belong to the same property if and only if it is a consequence of causal laws that either (1) whatever has either of them has the other, or (2) there is some third conditional power such that whatever has it has both X and Y.

Returning now to the conditional power of being able to cut wood conditionally upon being made of steel and the conditional power of being malleable conditionally upon being at a temperature of 100°F, it seems to me that these do not qualify under the proposed criterion as belonging to a common property. It is obviously not true that whatever has one of them must have the other. And it does not appear that there is any third conditional power which is such that whatever has it must have the two conditional powers in question.

If I am right in thinking that the conditional powers constituting a property must be causally unified in the way indicated, it is not difficult to see how knowledge of the causal potentialities of properties can develop empirically. The behavior of objects, that is, the displays of their powers, will reveal that they have certain conditional powers. Once it is discovered that certain conditional powers are connected in a lawlike way, we can use these to 'fix the reference' of a property term to the cluster containing those conditional powers and whatever other conditional powers are related to them in the appropriate lawlike relationships.[15] And we can then set about to determine empirically what the other conditional powers in the cluster are.

IX

As I observed earlier, my theory appears to have the consequence that causal laws are logically necessary, and that causal necessity is just a species of logical necessity. While to some this may be an attractive consequence, to many it will seem counterintuitive. It does seem to most of us that we can conceive of possible worlds which resemble the actual world in the kinds of properties that are instantiated in them, but differ from it in the causal laws that obtain. My theory must maintain either that we cannot really conceive of this or that conceivability is not proof of logical possibility.

Anyone who finds both of these alternatives unacceptable, but is persuaded by the arguments in section V that the identity of properties is determined by their causal potentialities, will look for ways of reconciling that conclusion with the view that there can be worlds in which some of the causal laws are different from, and incompatible with, those that obtain in the actual world. I want now to consider two ways in which one might attempt to achieve such a reconciliation. First, it might be held that while propositions describing the causal potentialities of properties are necessarily true if true at all, there are other lawlike propositions, namely those asserting lawlike connections between conditional powers, which are contingent and so true in some possible worlds and false in others. According to this view, when we seem to be conceiving of worlds in which the same properties are governed by different laws, what we are really conceiving of are worlds in which the same conditional powers stand to one another in different lawlike connections than they do in the actual world, and so are differently clustered into properties. Second, it might be held that my condition for the identity of properties across possible worlds is too strict. The theory I have advanced might be called the 'total cluster theory'; it identifies a property with a cluster containing all of the conditional powers which anything has in virtue of having that property, and maintains that in any possible world anything that has that property must have all of the members of that cluster. One might attempt to replace this with a 'core cluster theory', which identifies the property with some proper subset of the conditional powers something has in virtue of having that property. On this theory, it is only some of the causal potentialities possessed by a property in the actual world, namely those constituted by the conditional powers in its core cluster, that are essential to it – so it is possible for the same property to have somewhat different causal potentialities in different possible worlds, because of different laws relating the conditional powers in its core cluster with other conditional powers.

I do not believe, however, that either of these attempted reconciliations is successful. The first involves the suggestion that it is at least sometimes a contingent matter whether two conditional powers belong to the same property, and hence that there could be a world in which some of the same conditional powers are instantiated as in this world, but in which, owing to the holding of different laws, these are differently clustered into properties. The difficulty with this is that the specification of a conditional power always involves, in two different ways, reference to properties that are instantiated in our world and which, *ex hypothesi*, would not be instantiated in the alternative world in question. It involves reference to the properties on which the power is conditional, and also to the properties in the instantiation of which the exercise of the power would result. For example, one of the conditional powers in the property of being knife-shaped is the power, conditionally upon being made of steel, of leaving a knife-shaped impression if pressed into soft wax and then withdrawn. This conditional power, although not by itself identical to the property of being knife-shaped, could not be exercised without that property being instantiated. Neither could it be exercised without the property of being made of steel being instantiated. And a conditional power could not be instantiated in a world in which the causal laws would not allow an exercise of it. So in general, a conditional power could not be instantiated in a world in which the causal laws did not permit the instantiation of the properties whose instantiation would be involved in its instantiation or in its exercise.

Nothing I have said precludes the possibility of there being worlds in which the causal laws are different from those that prevail in this world. But it seems to follow from my account of property identity that, if the laws are different, then the properties will have to be different as well. And it does not appear that we have the resources for describing a world in which the properties that can be instantiated differ from what I shall call the 'actual world properties', that is, those that can be instantiated in the actual world. We have just seen that we cannot do this by imagining the conditional powers that exist in this world to be governed by different laws, and so to be differently grouped into properties.

It might seem that we can at least imagine a world in which *some* of the properties that can be instantiated are actual world properties while others are not. But a specification of the causal potentialities of one property will involve mention of other properties, a specification of the causal potentialities of those other properties will involve mention of still other properties, and so on. If there could be a world in which some but not all of the actual world properties can be instantiated, this could only be because those properties were causally insulated, as it were, from the rest – that is, were such that their causal potentialities could be fully specified without reference to the rest and vice versa. It seems unlikely that any proper subset of the actual world properties is causally insulated in this way – and any that are insulated from all properties we know about are thereby insulated from our knowledge and our language. But could there be a world in which the properties that can be instantiated include all of the actual world properties plus some others? This would be possible only if the two sets of properties, the actual world properties and the properties that cannot be instantiated in the actual world, were causally insulated from one another. And because of this, it would be impossible for us to say anything about the properties that cannot be instaniated in the actual world; for what we can describe is limited to what can be specified in terms of properties that can be so instantiated. What we could describe of such a world would have to be compatible with the laws that specify the causal potentialities of the actual world properties and, what we have found to be inseparable from these, the laws describing the lawlike connections between the conditional powers that constitute these properties.

Now let us consider the second attempt to reconcile the claim that the identity of a property is determined by its causal potentialities with the apparent conceivability of worlds in which the causal laws that obtain are different from, and incompatible with, those that obtain in the actual world. This involves the proposal that we adopt a 'core cluster theory' in place of the 'total cluster theory', and make the identity of a property depend on a proper subset, rather than on the totality, of the causal potentialities it has in the actual world. Like the first attempted reconciliation, this involves the idea that at least some of the lawlike connections between conditional powers hold only contingently; it is this that is supposed to make it possible for the composition of the total cluster associated with a property to differ from one possible world to another, owing to different conditional powers being causally linked with the conditional powers in the property's essential core cluster. But it would seem that the lawlike connections between those conditional powers included in the essential core cluster will have to hold of logical necessity, i.e., in all possible worlds. For if they held only contingently, then in some possible worlds they would not hold. In such a world, the individual conditional powers which in the actual world constitute the essential core of the property could be instantiated, but the property itself could not be instantiated. Even if these conditional powers could be instantiated together in such a world, their coinstantiation would not count as the instantiation of a property, and so of that property, since the requisite causal unity would be lacking. But I have already argued, in discussing the first attempted reconciliation, that it is not possible that there should be a world in which conditional powers that are instantiated in the actual world can be instantiated while actual world properties cannot be instantiated.

But if, as I have just argued, the lawlike connections between conditional powers within the essential core cluster will have to hold of logical necessity, then we are faced with a problem. Some lawlike connections between conditional powers will hold contingently (according to the core cluster theory), while others will hold as a matter of logical necessity. How are we to tell which are which? It does not appear that we can distinguish these lawlike connections epistemologically, i.e., by the way in which they are known. For if, as I am assuming, there are truths that are necessary a posteriori, the fact that a connection is discovered empirically is no guarantee that it does not hold necessarily. Nor can it be said that we identify the necessary connections by the fact that they hold between conditional powers belonging to some property's essential core cluster; for this presupposes that we have some way of identifying essential core clusters, and how are we to do this if we do not already know which connections between conditional powers are necessary and which are contingent?

It might be suggested that what constitutes a set of conditional powers as constituting an essential core cluster is just its being a lawlike truth that whatever has any of its members has all of them, and that it is by discovering such lawlike truths that we identify essential core clusters. Given that the lawlike connections between members of essential core clusters hold of logical necessity, this would amount to the claim that if two conditional powers are so related that the possession of either of them is both causally necessary and causally sufficient for the possession of the other, then the lawlike connection between them holds as a matter of logical necessity, while if the possession of one is causally sufficient but not causally necessary for the possession of the other, then the lawlike connection may be contingent. I have no knock-down argument against this view, but it seems to me implausible. If it is possible for it to be a contingent fact that the possession of one conditional power is causally sufficient for the possession of another, then it seems to me that it ought to be possible for it to be a contingent fact that the possession of one conditional power is both causally necessary and causally sufficient for the possession of another; that is, it ought to be possible for it to be contingently true of two conditional powers that the possession of either of them is causally sufficient for the possession of the other. So if we deny that the latter is a possibility, we should also deny that the former is.

It may be suggested that it is our linguistic conventions that make certain causal potentialities essential to a property, and so determine the makeup of a property's essential core cluster. But this cannot be so. It may in some cases belong to the conventionally determined sense of a property word that the property it designates has certain causal potentialities; while I think there is no need for property words to have such Fregean senses, and think that such words often function much as Kripke thinks natural kind terms do, I have no wish to deny that a property word can have a conventionally determined sense. But there is only so much that linguistic conventions can do; and one thing they cannot do is to dictate to reality, creating lawlike connections and *de re* necessities. Having discovered that certain conditional powers necessarily go together, and so are appropriately related for being part of an essential core cluster, we can lay down the convention that a certain word applies, in any possible world, to those and only those things having those conditional powers. But this leaves open the question of how we know that the conditional powers in question are appropriately related – that they must go together in any world in which either can be instantiated. And here appeal to convention cannot help us.

It begins to appear that if we hold that some lawlike connections are contingent, there is no way in which we could discover which of the lawlike connections between conditional powers are logically necessary and which are logically contingent, and so no way in which we could identify the essential core clusters of properties. This means that when we conceive, or seem to be conceiving, of a possible world in which the actual world properties are governed by somewhat different laws, there is no way in which we can discover whether we are conceiving of a genuine possibility. All that any of our empirical investigations can tell us is what lawlike connections obtain in the actual world; and without some way of telling which of these connections are contingent and which necessary, this gives us no information about what can be the case in other possible worlds. This makes all talk about what logically might be and might have been completely idle, except where questions of logical possibility can be settled a priori. If the core cluster theory makes the modal status of causal connections, their being necessary or contingent, epistemologically indeterminate in this way, it does not really save the intuitions which lead us to resist the total cluster theory, according to which all such connections are necessary. Unless we are prepared to abandon altogether the idea that there is a 'fact of the matter' as to whether there are logically possible circumstances in which a given property would make a certain contribution to the causal powers of its subject, I think we must accept the total cluster theory and its initially startling consequence that all of the causal potentialities of a property are essential to it.

X

If, as my theory implies, there are no situations that are logically but not causally possible, how is it that we are apparently able to conceive or imagine such situations? Saul Kripke has suggested one answer to a very similar question.[16] He holds that it is a necessary truth that heat is molecular motion, but recognizes that it seems as if we can imagine heat turning out to be something other than this. According to Kripke, this appearance of conceivability is something to be explained away, and he explains it away by claiming that the seeming conceivability of heat turning out not to be molecular motion consists in the actual conceivability of something else: namely, of sensations of a certain sort, those that we in fact get from heat, turning out to be caused by something other than molecular motion. The latter really is conceivable, he holds, and for understandable reasons we mistake its conceivability for the conceivability of something that is in fact not conceivable.

But if conceivability is taken to imply possibility, this account commits one to the possibility that the sensations we get from heat might standardly be caused by something other than molecular motion (and so something other than heat); more than that, it commits one to the possibility that this might be so and that these sensations might be related to other sensations and sense experiences in all the ways they are (or have been to date) in the actual world. And since the property of having such sensations is one that is actualized in this world, this would commit one, in my view, to the claim that it is compatible with the laws of nature that prevail in the actual world that these sensations should be so caused and so related to other experiences. Now this claim may be true – if 'may be' is used epistemically. But it is hard to see how we are entitled to be confident that it is. For might there not be laws, unknown to us, that make it impossible that the standard cause of these sensations should be anything other than it is, given the way they are related to the rest of our experience? If the seeming conceivability of heat turning out to be something other than molecular motion does not prove the actual possibility of this, why should the seeming conceivability of certain sensations being caused by something other than molecular motion prove the actual, and so causal, possibility of that? And if seeming conceivability no more proves possibility in the latter case than in the former, there seems little point in distinguishing between conceivability and seeming conceivability; we may as well allow that it is conceivable (and not just seemingly conceivable) that heat should turn out not to be molecular motion, and then acknowledge that conceivability is not conclusive proof of possibility. We could use the term 'conceivable' in such a way that it is conceivable that P just in case not-P is not provable a priori. Or we could use it in such a way that it is conceivable that P just in case it is epistemically possible

that it is possible that P should be the case – that is, just in case P's being possible is compatible, for all we know, with what we know. These uses of 'conceivable' are not equivalent, but on both of them it is possible to conceive of what is not possible.

XI

Although many of the implications of the account I have advanced are radically at odds with Humean views about causality, it does enable us to salvage one of the central tenets of the Humean view: namely, the claim that singular causal statements are 'implicitly general'. As I see it, the generality of causal propositions stems from the generality of properties, that is, from the fact that properties are universals, together with the fact which I began this essay by pointing out: namely, that causal relations hold between particular events in virtue of the properties possessed by the constituent objects of those events, and the fact, which I have tried to establish in the essay, that the identity of a property is completely determined by its potential for contributing to the causal powers of the things that have it. If I assert that one event caused another, I imply that the constituent objects of the cause event had properties which always contribute in certain ways to the causal powers of the things that have them, and that the particular episode of causation at hand was an actualization of some of these potentialities. I may of course not know what the relevant properties of the cause event were; and if I do know this, I may know little about their causal potentialities. This is closely related to the now familiar point that in claiming to know the truth of a singular causal statement one is not committed to knowing the laws in virtue of which it holds.[17] Moreover, a singular causal statement does not commit one to the claim that the instantiation of the relevant properties in relevant similar circumstances always produces the effect that it did in the case at hand, for the laws governing these properties may be statistical; the powers to which the properties contribute may, accordingly, be statistical tendencies or propensities, and the causation may be nonnecessitating. Also, the claim that singular causal statements are implicitly general does not, as here interpreted, imply anything about how such statements are known – in particular, it does not imply the Humean view that causal relationships can only be discovered via the discovery of regularities or 'constant conjunctions'. But where the present theory differs most radically from theories in the Humean tradition is in what it claims about the modality of the general propositions, the laws, that explain the truth of singular causal propositions; for whereas on the Humean view the truth of these propositions is contingent, on my view it is logically necessary. I thus find myself, in what I once would have regarded as reactionary company, defending the very sort of 'necessary connection' account of causality which Hume is widely applauded for having refuted.

Postscript[18]

Richard Boyd has offered the following as a counterexample to the account of properties proposed in this essay. Imagine a world in which the basic physical elements include substances A, B, C, and D. Suppose that X is a compound of A and B, and Y is a compound of C and D. We can suppose that it follows from the laws of nature governing the elements that these two compounds, although composed of different elements, behave exactly alike under all possible circumstances – so that the property of being made of X and the property of being made of Y share all of their causal potentialities. (This means, among other things, that it follows from the laws that once a portion of X or Y is formed, it cannot be decomposed into its constituent elements.) It would follow from my account of properties that being made of X and being made of Y are the same property. And this seems counterintuitive. If, as appears, X and Y would be different substances, the property of being composed of the one should be different from the property of being composed of the other.

I think that this example does show that my account needs to be revised. I propose the following as a revised account which is still clearly a causal account of properties: for properties F and G to be identical, it is necessary *both* that F and G have the same causal potentialities *and* (this is the new requirement) that whatever

set of circumstances is sufficient to cause the instantiation of F is sufficient to cause the instantiation of G, and vice versa. This amounts to saying that properties are individuated by their possible causes as well as by their possible effects. No doubt Boyd's example shows that other things I say in the essay need to be amended.

Notes

1 See Jaegwon Kim, "Causation, nomic subsumption, and the concept of event," *Journal of Philosophy* 70 (1973), pp. 27–36. I should mention that it was reflection on this excellent paper that first led me to the views developed in the present one.

2 Peter Geach, *God and the Soul* (London: Routledge and Kegan Paul, 1969), p. 71. See also Jaegwon Kim, "Non-causal connections", *Noûs* 8 (1974), pp. 41–52, and *idem*, "Events as property exemplifications," in M. Brand and D. Walton (eds), *Action Theory* (Dordrecht: Reidel, 1976), pp. 159–77.

3 I take this example from Kim, "Causation, nomic subsumption, and the concept of event."

4 David Hume, *A Treatise of Human Nature*, ed. L. A. Selby-Bigge (Oxford: Clarendon Press, 1888), p. 170 (bk 1, pt iii, sect. 14).

5 "When any objects *resemble* each other, the resemblance will at first strike the eye, or rather the mind, and seldom requires a second examination" (ibid., p. 70 (bk I, pt iii, sect. 1)).

6 John Locke, *Essay Concerning Human Understanding*, ed. Peter H. Nidditch (Oxford: Clarendon Press, 1975), p. 300 (bk II, ch. 23, sect. 8).

7 Ibid., p. 134 (bk II, ch. 8, sect. 8).

8 What does 'in virtue of' mean here? For the moment we can say that a thing has a power in virtue of having certain properties if it is a lawlike truth that whatever has those properties has that power. On the theory I shall be defending, it turns out that this is a matter of the possession of the properties entailing the possession of the power (i.e., its being true in all possible worlds that whatever has the properties has the power).

9 In speaking of "circumstances" I have in mind the relations of the object to other objects; instead of speaking of "presence in circumstances of a particular sort" I could instead speak of "possession of particular relational properties." Being in such and such circumstances is a mere-Cambridge property of an object, not a genuine (intrinsic) property of it.

10 After this was written, I found that Peter Achinstein has advanced a causal account of

property identity which, despite a different approach, is in some ways similar to the account proposed here. See his "The identity of properties," *American Philosophical Quarterly* 11 (1974), pp. 257–76. There are also similarities, along with important differences, between my views and those presented by D. H. Mellor in "In defense of dispositions," *Philosophical Review* 83 (1974), pp. 157–81, and those presented by R. Harré and E. H. Madden in *Causal Powers: A Theory of Natural Necessity* (Oxford: Clarendon Press, 1975).

11 See S. F. Barker and P. Achinstein, "On the new riddle of induction," *Philosophical Review* 69 (1960), pp. 511–22. The definition given there is not equivalent to that originally given by Goodman, in *Fact, Fiction and Forecast*, 3rd edn (Indianapolis: Bobbs-Merrill, 1975), p. 74, and it is the latter which is employed elsewhere in the present essay.

12 This was called to my attention by Nicholas Sturgeon.

13 See Boyle, "The origins and forms of qualities," in *The Works of the Honourable Robert Boyle* (5 vols, London, 1744), vol. 2, pp. 461 ff.

14 See Saul Kripke, "Naming and necessity," in D. Davidson and G. Harman (eds), *Semantics of Natural Language* (Dordrecht: Reidel, 1972), pp. 253–355.

15 For the notion of 'reference fixing', see ibid., pp. 269–75.

16 Ibid., pp. 331–42.

17 See, e.g., Donald Davidson, "Causal relations," this volume, ch. 27.

18 This was appended to the original publication of this essay as a "Note added in proof."

22

The Metaphysic of Abstract Particulars

Keith Campbell

[handwritten note: This gives us a method by which to view art, wherein we do not pull apart & abstract from the piece some preconceived notions, but rather invest our time contemplating its totality]

1 The Conception of Properties as Particular

A classic tradition in first philosophy, descending from Plato and Aristotle, and recently reaffirmed by D. M. Armstrong,[1] proposes two equally essential, yet mutually exclusive, categories of reality: Substances (or Particulars), which are particular and concrete, and Properties (and Relations), which are universal and abstract. Material bodies are the most familiar examples of Concrete Particulars, and their characteristics, conceived of as repeatable entities common to many different objects, are paradigms of Abstract Universals.

Particular being's distinguishing mark is that it is exhausted in the one embodiment, or occasion, or example. For the realm of space, this restricts particulars to a single location at any one time. Particulars thus seem to enjoy a relatively unproblematic mode of being.

Universals, by contrast, are unrestricted in the plurality of different locations in space-time at which they may be wholly present. Altering the number of instances of a universal (*being a bee*, for example), increasing or decreasing it by millions, in no way either augments or diminishes the universal itself. In my opinion, the difficulty in comprehending how any item could enjoy this sort of reality has been the scandal which has motivated much implausible Nominalism in which, with varying degrees of candor, the existence of properties and relations is denied.

The scandal would disappear if properties were not really universal after all. In modern times, it was G. F. Stout who first explicitly made the proposal that properties and relations are as particular as the substances that they qualify.[2] Others have given the notion some countenance,[3] but its most wholehearted advocate, perhaps, has been D. C. Williams.[4] What are its merits?

In the first place, that a property should, in some sense, enjoy particular being, is not a contradiction in terms. The opposite of *Particular* is *Universal*, whereas the opposite of *Concrete* is *Abstract*. In this context, an item is abstract if it is got before the mind by an act of abstraction, that is, by concentrating attention on some, but not all, of what is presented. A complete material body, a shoe, ship, or lump of sealing wax, is concrete; all of what is where the shoe is belongs to

Keith Campbell, "The Metaphysic of Abstract Particulars," *Midwest Studies in Philosophy*, 6 (1981): 477–88.

Metaphysics: An Anthology, Second Edition. Edited by Jaegwon Kim, Daniel Z. Korman and Ernest Sosa.

the shoe – its color, texture, chemical composition, temperature, elasticity, and so on are all aspects or elements included in the being of the shoe. But these features or characteristics considered individually, e.g., the shoe's color or texture, are by comparison abstract.

The distinction between abstract and concrete is different from that between universal and particular, and logically independent of it. That some particulars as well as universals should be abstract, and that, specifically, cases or instances of properties should be particulars, is at least a formal possibility.

In the second place, it is plain that one way or another, properties must take on or meet particularity in their instances. Consider two pieces of red cloth. There are two pieces of cloth, *ex hypothesi*. Each is red. So there are two occurrences of redness. Let them be two occurrences of the very same shade of redness, so that difference in quality between them does not cloud the issue. We can show that there really are two pieces of cloth (and not, for example, that one is just a reflection of the other) by selective destruction – burn one, leaving the other unaffected. We can show that there really are two cases of redness in the same sort of way: dye one blue, leaving the other unaffected. In this case there remain two pieces of cloth. But there do *not* remain two cases of redness. So the cases of redness here are not to be identified with the pieces of cloth. They are a pair of somethings, distinct from the pair of pieces of cloth. A pair of what? The fact that there are two of them, each with its bounded location, shows that they are particulars, The fact that they are a pair of rednesses shows them to be qualitative in nature. The simplest thesis about them is that they are not the compound or intersection of two distinct categories, but are as they seem to reflection to be, items both abstract and particular. Williams dubs abstract particulars *tropes*.

The argument above is to the effect that tropes are required in any proper understanding of the nature of concrete particulars (in this case specimen material bodies, pieces of cloth) and that this becomes evident in the analysis of local qualitative change.

A third ground for admitting tropes in our ontology is to be found in the problem of universals itself. The problem of universals is the problem of determining the minimum ontological schedule adequate to account for the similarities between different things, or the recurrence of like qualities in different objects. Take a certain shade of red as an example. Many different items are the same color, this certain shade of red. There is a multiple occurrence involved. But what, exactly, is multiple? The *universal* quality, the shade of red, is common to all the cases but is not plural. On the other hand, the red *objects* are plural enough, but they are heterogeneous. Some are pieces of cloth, others bits of the skin of berries, others exotic leaves, dollops of paint, bits of the backs of dangerous spiders, and so on. There is no common recurrent substance.

What does recur, the only element that does recur, is the color. But it must be the color as a particular that is involved in the recurrence, for only particulars can be many in the way required for recurrence.

It is the existence of resembling tropes which poses the problem of universals. The accurate expression of that problem is: What, if anything, is common to a set of resembling tropes?

2 Tropes as Independent Existences

Williams claims more for tropes than just a place in our ontology; he claims a fundamental place. Tropes constitute, for him, "the very alphabet of being," the independent, primitive elements which in combination constitute the variegated and somewhat intelligible world in which we find ourselves.

To take this line, we must overcome a long-standing and deeply ingrained prejudice to the effect that *concrete* particulars, atoms or molecules or larger swarms, are the minimal beings logically capable of independent existence.

We are used to the idea that the redness of our piece of cloth, or Julius Caesar's baldness, if they are beings at all, are essentially dependent ones. Without Julius Caesar to support it, so the familiar idea runs, his baldness would be utterly forlorn. Without the cloth, no redness of the cloth. On this view, concrete particulars are the basic particulars. Tropes are at best parasitic.

Being used to an idea, of course, is not a sufficient recommendation for it. When it is conceded that, as a matter of fact, tropes tend to come in clusters and that a substantial collection of them, clinging together in a clump, is the normal minimum which we do in fact encounter, we have conceded all that this traditional point of view has a right to claim. The question at issue, however, is not what is in fact the ordinary minimum in what is "apt for being," but what that minimum is of metaphysical necessity. The least which could exist on its own may well be less than a whole man or a whole piece of cloth. It may be just a single trope or even a minimal part of a single trope.

And some aspects of experience encourage the view that abstract particulars are capable of independent existence. Consider the sky; it is, to appearance at least, an instance of color quite lacking the complexity of a concrete particular. The color bands in a rainbow seem to be tropes dissociated from any concrete particular.

All Williams requires here, of course, is that dissociated tropes be possible (capable of independent existence), not that they be actual. So the possibility of a Cheshire Cat face, as areas of color, or a massless, inert, impenetrable zone as a solidity trope, or free-floating sounds and smells, are sufficient to carry the point.

The way concrete particularity dissolves in the subatomic world, and in the case of black holes, suggests that dissociated tropes are not just possibilities but are actually to be encountered in this world.

On the view that tropes are the basic particulars, concrete particulars, the whole man and the whole piece of cloth, count as dependent realities. They are collections of co-located tropes, depending on these tropes as a fleet does upon its component ships.

3   The Analysis of Causation

D. Davidson has provided powerful reasons why some singular causal statements, like

The short circuit caused the fire,

are best interpreted as making reference to events.[5] Davidson's example is a specimen of an *event-event* singular causal claim.

But by no means all singular causal statements are of this type. Many involve *conditions* as terms in causal connections. For example:

Condition-event:	The weakness of the cable caused the collapse of the bridge.
Event-condition:	The firing of the auxiliary rocket produced the eccentricity in the satellite's orbit.
Condition-condition:	The high temperature of the frying pan arises from its contact with the stove.

Now the conditions referred to in these examples, the cable's weakness, the orbit's eccentricity, the frying pan's temperature, are properties, but the particular cases of properties involved in particular causal transactions. It is the weakness of this particular cable, not weakness in general or the weakness of anything else, which is involved in the collapse of this bridge on this occasion. And it is not the cable's steeliness, rustiness, mass, magnetism, or temperature which is at all involved. To hold that the whole cable, as concrete particular, is the cause of the collapse is to introduce a mass of irrelevant characteristics.

The cause of the collapse is the weakness of this cable (and not any other), the whole weakness, and nothing but the weakness. It is a particular, a specific condition at a place and time: so it is an abstract particular. It is, in short, a trope.

Events, the other protagonists in singular causal transactions, are widely acknowledged to be particulars. They are plainly not ordinary concrete particulars.[6] They are, in my opinion, best viewed as trope-sequences, in which one condition gives way to others, Events, on this view, are changes in which tropes replace one another. This is a promising schema for many sorts of change.

Attempts to avert reference to tropes by use of *qua*-clauses do not succeed. If we affirm that

The cable *qua* weak caused the collapse

yet deny that

The cable *qua* steely caused the collapse,

then we are committed to the view that

The cable *qua* weak ≠ the cable *qua* steely.

So at least one of these terms refers to something other than the cable. What could it be referring to? – only the weakness (or steeliness) of the cable, that is, only to the trope.

The philosophy of cause calls for tropes. That on its own is virtually sufficient recommendation for a place in the ontological sun.

4 Perception and Evaluation

The introduction of tropes into our ontology gives us an extremely serviceable machinery for analyzing any situation in which specific *respects* of concrete particulars are involved.

In the philosophy of perception, tropes appear not only as terms of the causal relations involved but also, epistemically, as the immediate objects of perception. The difficulties involved in Direct Realism with material objects disappear. Notoriously, we do not see an entire cat, all there is to a cat, for a cat has a back not now perceived and an interior never perceived. The immediate object of vision cannot even be part of the front surface of the cat, for that front surface has a texture and temperature which are not visible, and a microscopic structure not perceptible by any means. So that when you look at a cat what you most directly see is neither a cat nor part of its front surface. This conclusion has, to say the least, encouraged Idealist claims that the immediate object of perception is of a mental nature, a percept or representation standing in some special relation to the cat.

In the trope philosophy, a Direct Realist theory of perception would hold that not cats, but tropes of cats, are what is seen, touched, and so on. The cat's shape and color, but not its temperature or the number of molecules it contains, are objects of vision. Some of the tropes belonging to the cat are perceptible, some not. On any one occasion, some of the perceptible ones are perceived, others are hidden. That is the way in which the senses are selectively sensitive: that is why there is no need for embarrassment in admitting that the senses can give us knowledge only of certain aspects of concrete particulars.

Evaluation is another field in which the admission of tropes does away with awkwardness. Concrete particulars can be simultaneously subject to conflicting evaluations – in different respects, of course. A wine's flavor can be admirable and its clarity execrable, a pole vaulter's strength be splendid and his manners ill. On a trope analysis, the immediate object of evaluation *is* the trope, so that strictly speaking, different objects are being evaluated when we consider the flavor and the clarity of the wine, and thus the incompatible evaluations give rise to no problem at all.

5 The Problem of Concrete Individuals

The problem of concrete individuals is the problem of how it is possible for many different qualities to belong to one and the same thing. To answer it is to give the constitution of a single individual. For convenience's sake, we tend to discuss the issue in terms of items of medium scale, such as books, chairs, or tables, although we know such objects are not really single units but assemblies of parts which are themselves also individuals. The question of the constitution of a single individual is, of course, quite distinct from the relationship between complex wholes and their simpler parts. To avoid confusion we might do better to use as an example some more plausible specimen of a single concrete individual, such as one corpuscle in classical Atomism. Our question is: what is it, in the reality of one corpuscle, in virtue of which it is one, single, complete, distinct individual?

In an ontology that recognizes properties and relations only as *universals*, no satisfactory solution to this question can be found. There are two ways of tackling it:

(i) A complete individual is the union of universal properties with some additional, particularizing reality.

For Aristotelians, this will be the Prime Matter that qualities inform, for Lockeans the substratum in which qualities inhere. The common ground of objection to solutions of this type lies in their introduction of a some-what which, because it lies beyond qualities, lies by its very nature beyond our explorations, describings, and imaginings, all of which are of necessity restricted to the qualities things have. We do well to postpone as long as possible the admission into our ontology of elements essentially elusive and opaque to the understanding.

To avoid such elements, we must deny that in the ontic structure of an individual is to be found any non-qualitative element. Which is precisely the course followed in the other main tradition:

(ii) A complete individual is no more than a Bundle of qualities, viz., all and only the qualities that, as we would ordinarily say, the thing has.

In banishing "metaphysical" particularizers, such views are appealing to Empiricists, for as long as they can forget their Nominalism, which is, of course, incompatible with any Bundle theory.

Where the bundle is a bundle of universals, the very same repeatable item crops up in many different bundles (the same property occurs in many different instances). And herein lies the theory's downfall. For it is a necessary truth that each individual is distinct from each other individual. So each bundle must be different from every other bundle. Since the bundles contain nothing but qualities, there must be at least one qualitative difference between any two bundles. In short, this theory requires that the Identity of Indiscernibles be a necessary truth.

Unfortunately, the Identity of Indiscernibles is not a necessary truth. There are possible worlds in which it fails, ranging from very simple worlds with two uniform spheres in a non-absolute space to very complex ones, without temporal beginning or end, in which the same sequence of events is cyclically repeated, with non-identical indiscernibles occurring in the different cycles.

Bundle theories with elements that are universal qualities thus come to grief over the status of the Identity of Indiscernibles. But where the elements in the bundle are not repeatable universals but particular cases of qualities, not smoothness-in-general but the particular smoothness here, in this place, qualifying this particular tile, the situation is quite different. Now the elements in the bundles are tropes, and no matter how similar they are to one another, the smoothness trope in one tile is quite distinct from the smoothness trope in every other tile. So the bundles can never have any common elements, let alone coincide completely. The question of the Identity of Indiscernibles becomes the question whether all the elements in one bundle match perfectly with all the elements in any other, which is, as it should be, an *a posteriori* question of contingent fact.

Tropes of different sorts can be *compresent* (present at the same place). In being compresent

they, in common speech, "belong to the same thing." Taken together, the maximal sum of compresent tropes constitutes a complete being, a fully concrete particular. Each fully concrete individual is, of necessity, distinct from every other.

There is no need for any non-qualitative particularizer, nor any problem over the Identity of Indiscernibles. In the trope philosophy, the Problem of Individuals has an elegant solution.

A. Quinton recently proposed that an individual is the union of a group of qualities and a position, and D. M. Armstrong has endorsed a similar view.[7] If we take this as a version of the Lockean *substratum* strategy, it invites the criticism that it involves an *a priori* commitment to absolute space or space-time, anterior to the placing of qualities. To avoid such objectionable *a priori* cosmology, we must hold not that place and the quality present at that place are distinct beings, one the particularizer and the other a universal, but that quality-at-a-place is itself a single, particular, reality. And this second view is just the trope doctrine re-expressed.

6   The Problem of Universals

Tropes can be compresent; this makes possible a solution to the problem of individuals. Tropes can also resemble one another, more or less closely. Williams holds that this facilitates a solution to the problem of universals. I regret to report that I cannot fully share his optimism.

The Problem of Universals is the problem of how the same property can occur in any number of different instances. "The Problem of Universals" is not really a good name, since the principal issue is whether there *are* any universals; the problem is: what ontological structure, what array of real entities, is necessary and sufficient to account for the likenesses among different objects which ground the use on different occasions of the same general term, 'round', 'square', 'blue', 'black', or whatever. "The Problem of Resemblance" would thus be a better name; proposed solutions consist in theories of the nature of properties.

As with the problem of individuals, philosophical tradition exhibits an ominous unstable oscillation between unsatisfactory alternatives. Realism claims the existence of a new category of entities, not particular, not having any restricted location, literally completely present, the very

Differing 'kinds' of tropes?
This smacks of a 'universal trope'

same item, in each and every different circular object, or square one, or blue one, or whatever. Nominalism holds that roundness and squareness are no more than shadows cast by the human activity of classifying together, and applying the same description to, sundry distinct particular objects. The classic objection to Realism is Locke's *dictum* that all things that exist are only particulars. This amounts to the difficulty of believing in universal beings. The objection to Nominalism is its consequence that if there were no human race (or other living things), nothing would be like anything else.

Can a philosophy of abstract particulars be of any assistance? Williams claims that a property, such as smoothness, is a set of resembling tropes. Members of this set are instances of the property. Tile A's smoothness, tile B's smoothness, tile C's smoothness, insofar as they resemble one another, all belong to a set S. There are no *a priori* limits on how many members S should have, or how they should be distributed through space and time. So in this respect S behaves as a universal must. Moreover, since the members of S are particular smoothnesses, each of them is fully smooth, not merely partly smooth. This is again a condition which anything proposed as a universal must meet.

The closeness of resemblance between the tropes in a set can vary. These variations correspond to the different degrees to which different properties are specific. According to this view, Resemblance is taken as an unanalyzable primitive, and there are no non-particular realities beyond the sets of resembling tropes. So this view holds that there is *no* entity literally common to the resembling tropes; it is a version of Particularism.

Can we take Resemblance as a primitive? Resemblance between tropes, rather than between concrete particulars, avoids two classic objections to this line.

Objection 1. The companionship difficulty[8]

Attempts to construct a property as a Resemblance-Class of the items that "have the property" face this objection: there could be two *different* properties (say, *having a heart* and *having a kidney*) which, as a matter of fact, happen to be present in the very same objects. But if each property is no more than the Resemblance-Class containing all

and only those objects, since these two different properties determine the same Resemblance-Class it will turn out that the 'two' properties are not different after all. The theory falsely identifies *having a heart* with *having a kidney*, and indeed any pair of co-extensive properties.

This problem cannot arise where the members of the Resemblance-Class are *tropes* rather than whole concrete particulars. Although the *animals* that have hearts coincide with the animals with kidneys, the instances of having a heart, as abstract particulars, are quite different items from the instances of having a kidney. The Resemblance-Classes for the two properties have no members in common, and there is no basis for the objectionable identification.

Objection 2. The difficulty of imperfect community[9]

In constructing a Resemblance-Class, we cannot just select some object O and take all the objects that resemble O in some way or other. That would yield an utterly heterogeneous collection, with 'nothing in common', as we would intuitively put it.

To avoid saying that the members of the Resemblance-Class must all resemble O in the same respect, which introduces *respects* as Realistically conceived universals, we have to require that all the members of the Resemblance-Class must not only resemble O but must also resemble one another.

But although necessary, this restriction is not sufficient. For consider the case where

O_1 has features P Q R
O_2 has features Q R S
O_3 has features R S T
O_4 has features S T P

Each of these objects does resemble all the others. But they share no common property. This is the phenomenon of *imperfect community*. Family resemblance classes are examples. Not all resemblance classes pick out a genuine universal property. More precisely, this is the case where the members of the resemblance classes are objects with many different features.

The problem of imperfect community cannot arise where our resemblance sets are sets of tropes. For tropes, by their very nature and mode of differentiation, *can* only resemble in one respect. An instance of solidity, unlike a complete material object, does not resemble a host of different objects in a host of heterogeneous ways. The difficulty of imperfect community springs from the complexity of concrete particulars. The simplicity of tropes puts a stop to it.

Although the prospects for a resolution of the problem of universals through appeal to resemblances between tropes are better than those for resemblance between concrete particulars, it is by no means plain that this line succeeds.

The difficulty is that we have an answer to the question: What do two smooth tiles have in common, in virtue of which they are both smooth? They both contain a trope of smoothness; *matching* tropes occur in their makeup. But then we at once invite the question: What do two smooth tropes have in common, in virtue of which they match? And now we have no answer, or only answers that restate the situation: These tropes resemble, or are alike, in virtue of their nature, in virtue of what they are. This leaves us with no answer to the question: Why isn't the way a rough trope is, a ground for matching a smooth trope? We cannot say it is the wrong *sort* of thing. We must just say: because it isn't.

Now explanations must stop somewhere. But is this a satisfactory place to stop?

7 The Role of Space in a First Philosophy

The metaphysic of abstract particulars gives a central place to Space, or Space-Time, as the frame of the world. It is through *location* that tropes get their particularity. Further, they are identified, and distinguished from one another, by location. Further yet, the continuing identity over time of the tropes that can move is connected with a continuous track in space-time.

Still further, space (and time) are involved in *co-location*, or compresence, which is essential to the theory's account of concrete particulars. So the theory seems to be committed to the thesis that every reality is a spatio-temporal one. This would make a clean sweep of transcendent gods, Thomist angels, Cartesian minds, Kantian noumena, and Berkeley's entire ontology. But that is too swift, too dismissive.

There is, in fact, a less drastic possibility open. That is, that to the extent that there can be non-spatial particulars, to that extent there must be some analogue of the locational order of space.[10] And in that case, there will be an analogue of location to serve as the principle of individuation for non-spatial abstract particulars.

To concede that there can be non-spatial particulars to the extent that they belong in an array analogous to space is generous enough toward such dubious items.

We are, however, not yet at the end of the special status of space. The geometric features of things, their form and volume, have a special role. Form and volume are not tropes like any others. Their presence in any particular sum of tropes is not an optional, contingent, matter. For the color, taste, solidity, salinity, and so on, which any thing has are essentially spread out. They exist, if they exist at all, *all over* a specific area or volume. They cannot be present except by being present in a formed volume. Tropes are, of their essence, regional. And this carries with it the essential presence of shape and size in any trope occurrence. The often-noticed fact that shape and size, like Siamese twins, are never found except together, is part of this special status of the geometrical features.

Color, solidity, strength are never found except as the-color-of-this-region, the-solidity-of-this-region, and so on. So wherever a trope is, there is formed volume. Conversely, shape and size are not genuinely found except in company with other characteristics. A mere region, a region whose boundaries mark no material distinction whatever, is only artificially a single and distinct being.

So the geometric features are doubly special; they are essential to ordinary tropes and in themselves insufficient to count as proper beings. Form and volume are therefore best considered not as tropes in their own right at all. Real tropes are qualities-of-a-formed-volume. The distinctions we can make between color, shape, and size are distinctions in thought to which correspond no distinctions in reality. A change in the size or shape of an occurrence of redness is not the association of the same red trope with different size and shape tropes, but the occurrence of an (at least partly) different trope of redness.

There is no straightforward correlation between distinct *descriptions* and distinct tropes.

That predicates may not go hand-in-hand with tropes is important, for therein lies the possibility of reduction, exhibiting one trope as consisting in tropes which before the discovery of the reduction would have been considered "other" tropes. Reduction is the life and soul of any scientific cosmology. Reductions involving elements in familiar human-scale material bodies provide the best of explanations why tropes ordinarily occur in compresent bundles which cannot be dissociated and whose members resist independent manipulation.

8   The Philosophy of Change and Modern Cosmology

The admission of abstract particulars as the basic ontological category gives us a way into the philosophy of change. We all feel in our bones that there is a quite radical distinction to be made between the sorts of changes involved in becoming bald and the sorts involved in becoming a grandfather. The first sort are closer to home. They are intrinsic, whereas the others are in some way derivative, dependent, or secondary. If we content ourselves with an analysis of change in terms of the applicability of descriptions, however, the two sorts of change seem to be on a par.

We can do justice to the feeling in our bones by distinguishing changes in which different descriptions apply to O in virtue of a new trope situation at O itself, from changes in which the new descriptions apply as a consequence of a new trope situation elsewhere. Trope changes become the metaphysical base from which other sorts of change derive.

We can recognize three basic types of change into which tropes enter:

1. *Motions*, the shifting about of tropes which retain their identity. When a cricket ball moves from the bat to the boundary, it retains its identity, and the tropes that constitute it retain their identity also. Many *instances of relations*, of being so far, in such direction, from such and such, are involved. For all that has been said so far, these are tropes too. Many such enjoy a brief occurrence during any motion. Because there cannot be relations without terms, in a metaphysic that makes first-order tropes the terms of all relations, relational tropes must belong to a second, derivative order.

2. *Substitutions*, in which one, or more, trope passes away and others take its place. Burning is a classic case. The object consumed does not retain its identity. Its constituent tropes are no more. In their place are others which formerly had no existence.

3. *Variations*. An object gets harder or softer, warmer or cooler. With such qualities which admit of degree, I think we should allow that the same trope, determinable in character though determinate at any given point in time, is involved. Call an abstract element in a situation, extending over time, a *thread*. Variations are homogeneous threads; processes, such as burning, are heterogeneous ones.

The concept of a thread is very useful in ordering categories. Stability is represented by the most homogeneous threads of all. Variations in a quantity, as we have seen, involve no deep discontinuity; different parts of the thread are plainly instances of the same type of property. *Events* are of various sorts: a rise in temperature is a quantitative alteration along a homogeneous thread: an explosion terminates many threads and initiates many different ones. Events, processes, stabilities, and continuities are all explicable as variations in the pattern of presence of tropes. All these are categories constructable from the same basis in abstract particulars.

Attempts to relate these three kinds of change are of course a perfectly proper part of cosmology. Classical Atomism, for example, the very apotheosis of concrete particularism, involves the thesis that all three types of change resolve, on finer analysis, into motions, in particular the motions of corpuscles.

But Classical Atomism is false, and any type of atomism looks unpromising at the present time. The cosmology of General Relativity takes a holistic view of space-time. And it seems positively to call for a trope metaphysic and a break with concrete particularism. The distinction between "matter" and "space" is no longer absolute. All regions have, to some degree, those quantities which in sufficient measure constitute the matter of the objects among which we live and move and have our being.

The world is resolved into six quantities, whose values at each point specify the tensor for curved space-time at that point. Material bodies are zones of relatively high curvature.

The familiar concept of a <u>complex, distinct, concrete individual dissolves.</u> In its place we get the concept of quantities with values in regions. Such quantities, at particular locations, are dissociated abstract particulars, or tropes. Considered in their occurrence and variation across all space and all time, they are pandemic homogeneous threads.

The metaphysic of abstract particulars thus finds a vindication in providing the most suitable materials for the expression of contemporary cosmology.

Notes

1   D. M. Armstrong, *Universals and Scientific Realism* (Cambridge, 1978).

2   G. F. Stout, *The Nature of Universals and Propositions* (Oxford [British Academy Lecture], 1921).

3   G. E. L. Owen, "Inherence," *Phronesis* 10 (1965): 97–108; N. Wolterstorff, "Qualities," *Philosophical Review* 69 (1960): 183–200 and *On Universals* (Chicago, 1970). A. Quinton, "Objects and Events," *Mind* 87 (1979): 197–214. J. Levinson. "The Particularisation of Attributes," *Australasian Journal of Philosophy* 58 (1980): 102–15. P. Butchvarov, *Being Qua Being* (Indiana, 1979), pp. 184–206, discusses but rejects the view.

4   D. C. Williams, "The Elements of Being," in *Principles of Empirical Realism* (Springfield, Ill., 1966).

5   D. Davidson, "Causal Relations," *The Journal of Philosophy* 64 (1967): 691–703; "The Logical Form of Action Statements," in *Logic of Decision and Action*, ed. N. Rescher (Pittsburgh, 1966).

6   If Quine is right, they are four-dimensional concrete particulars whose boundaries are determined not by material discontinuities but by discontinuities in other respects, which we pre-theoretically describe as discontinuities in *activity*.

7   A. Quinton, *The Nature of Things*, part 1 (London, 1973): D. M. Armstrong, *Universals*, ch. 11.

8   See N. Goodman, *The Structure of Appearance*, 2nd edn. (Indianapolis, 1966), ch. 5.

9   See *ibid.*, chs. 5 and 6.

10 Cf. P. F. Strawson, *Individuals* (London, 1959), ch. 2.

23

New Work for a Theory of Universals

David Lewis

Introduction

D. M. Armstrong offers a theory of universals as the only adequate answer to a compulsory question for systematic philosophy: the problem of One over Many.[1] I find this line of argument unpersuasive. But I think there is more to be said for Armstrong's theory than he himself has said. For as I bear it in mind considering various topics in philosophy, I notice time and again that it offers solutions to my problems. Whatever we may think of the problem of One over Many, universals can earn their living doing other much-needed work.

I do not say that they are indispensable. The services they render could be matched using resources that are Nominalistic in letter, if perhaps not in spirit.[2] But neither do I hold any presumption against universals, to the effect that they are to be accepted only if we have no alternative. I therefore suspend judgement about universals themselves. I only insist that, one way or another, their work must be done.

I shall investigate the benefits of adding universals to my own usual ontology. That ontology, though Nominalistic, is in other respects generous.

It consists of *possibilia* – particular, individual things, some of which comprise our actual world and others of which are unactualized[3] – together with the iterative hierarchy of classes built up from them. Thus I already have at my disposal a theory of properties as classes of *possibilia*. Properties, so understood, are not much like universals. Nor can they, unaided, take over the work of universals. Nevertheless, they will figure importantly in what follows, since for me they are part of the environment in which universals might operate.

The friend of universals may wonder whether they would be better employed not as an addition to my ontology of *possibilia* and classes, but rather as a replacement for parts of it. A fair question, and an urgent one; nevertheless, not a question considered in this paper.

In the next section, I shall sketch Armstrong's theory of universals, contrasting universals with properties understood as classes of *possibilia*. Then I shall say why I am unconvinced by the One over Many argument. Then I shall turn to my principal topic: how universals could help me in connection with such topics as duplication, supervenience, and divergent worlds; a minimal form of materialism; laws and causation; and the

David Lewis, "New Work for a Theory of Universals," *Australasian Journal of Philosophy*, 61 (Dec. 1983): 343–77.
Reproduced by permission.

Metaphysics: An Anthology, Second Edition. Edited by Jaegwon Kim, Daniel Z. Korman and Ernest Sosa.

content of language and thought. Perhaps the list could be extended.

Universals and Properties

Language offers us several more or less interchangeable words: 'universal'; 'property', 'quality', 'attribute', 'feature', and 'characteristic'; 'type', 'kind', and 'sort'; and perhaps others. And philosophy offers us several conceptions of the entities that such words refer to. My purpose is not to fix on one of these conceptions; but rather to distinguish two (at opposite extremes) and contemplate helping myself to both. Therefore some regimentation of language is called for; I apologize for any inconvenience caused. Let me reserve the word 'universal' for those entities, if such there be, that mostly conform to Armstrong's account. And let me reserve the word 'property' for classes – any classes, but I have foremost in mind classes of things. To have a property is to be a member of the class.[4]

Why call them 'properties' as well as 'classes'? – Just to underline the fact that they need not be classes of *actual* things. The property of being a donkey, for instance, is the class of *all* the donkeys. This property belongs to – this class contains – not only the actual donkeys of this world we live in, but also all the unactualized, otherworldly donkeys.

Likewise I reserve the word 'relation' for arbitrary classes of ordered pairs, triples, … Thus a relation among things is a property of 'tuples of things. Again, there is no restriction to actual things. Corresponding roughly to the division between properties and relations of things, we have the division between 'monadic' and 'polyadic' universals.

Universals and properties differ in two principal ways. The first difference concerns their instantiation. A universal is supposed to be wholly present wherever it is instantiated. It is a constituent part (though not a spatiotemporal part) of each particular that has it. A property, by contrast, is spread around. The property of being a donkey is partly present wherever there is a donkey, in this or any other world. Far from the property being part of the donkey, it is closer to the truth to say that the donkey is part of the property. But the precise truth, rather, is that the donkey is a member of the property.

Thus universals would unify reality[5] in a way that properties do not. Things that share a universal

have not just joined a single class. They literally have something in common. They are not entirely distinct. They overlap.

By occurring repeatedly, universals defy intuitive principles. But that is no damaging objection, since plainly the intuitions were made for particulars. For instance, call two entities *copresent* if both are wholly present at one position in space and time. We might intuit offhand that copresence is transitive. But it is not so, obviously, for universals. Suppose for the sake of argument that there are universals: round, silver, golden. Silver and round are copresent, for here is a silver coin; golden and round are copresent, for there is a gold coin; but silver and golden are not copresent. Likewise, if we add universals to an ontology of *possibilia*, for the relation of being part of the same possible world.[6] I and some otherworldly dragon are not worldmates; but I am a worldmate of the universal golden, and so is the dragon. Presumably I needed a mixed case involving both universals and particulars. For why should any two universals ever fail to be worldmates? Lacking such failures, the worldmate relation among universals alone is trivially transitive.

The second difference between universals and properties concerns their abundance. This is the difference that qualifies them for different work, and thereby gives rise to my interest in having universals and properties both.

A distinctive feature of Armstrong's theory is that universals are sparse. There are the universals that there must be to ground the objective resemblances and the causal powers of things, and there is no reason to believe in any more. All of the following alleged universals would be rejected:

not golden
golden or wooden
metallic
self-identical
owned by Fred
belonging to class *C*
grue
first examined before 2000 AD
being identical
being alike in some respect
being exactly alike
being part of
owning
being paired with by some pair in *R*

(where C and R are utterly miscellaneous classes). The guiding idea, roughly, is that the world's universals should comprise a minimal basis for characterizing the world completely. Universals that do not contribute at all to this end are unwelcome, and so are universals that contribute only redundantly. A satisfactory inventory of universals is a non-linguistic counterpart of a primitive vocabulary for a language capable of describing the world exhaustively.

(That is rough: Armstrong does not dismiss redundant universals out of hand, as the spirit of his theory might seem to demand. Conjunctive universals – as it might be, golden-and-round – are accepted, though redundant; so are analysable structural universals. The reason is that if the world were infinitely complex, there might be no way to cut down to a minimal basis. The only alternative to redundancy might be inadequacy, and if so, we had better tolerate redundancy. But the redundancy is mitigated by the fact that complex universals consist of their simpler – if perhaps not absolutely simple – constituents. They are not distinct entities.[7])

It is quite otherwise with properties. Any class of things, be it ever so gerrymandered and miscellaneous and indescribable in thought and language, and be it ever so superfluous in characterizing the world, is nevertheless a property. So there are properties in immense abundance. (If the number of things, actual and otherwise, is beth-2, an estimate I regard as more likely low than high, then the number of properties of things is beth-3. And that is a big infinity indeed, except to students of the outer reaches of set theory.) There are so many properties that those specifiable in English, or in the brain's language of synaptic interconnections and neural spikes, could be only an infinitesimal minority.

Because properties are so abundant, they are undiscriminating. Any two things share infinitely many properties, and fail to share infinitely many others. That is so whether the two things are perfect duplicates or utterly dissimilar. Thus properties do nothing to capture facts of resemblance. That is work more suited to the sparse universals. Likewise, properties do nothing to capture the causal powers of things. Almost all properties are causally irrelevant, and there is nothing to make the relevant ones stand out from the crowd. Properties carve reality at the joints – and everywhere else as well. If it's distinctions we want, too much structure is no better than none.

It would be otherwise if we had not only the countless throng of all properties, but also an élite minority of special properties. Call these the *natural* properties.[8] If we had properties and universals both, the universals could serve to pick out the natural properties. Afterwards the universals could retire if they liked, and leave their jobs to the natural properties. Natural properties would be the ones whose sharing makes for resemblance, and the ones relevant to causal powers. Most simply, we could call a property *perfectly* natural if its members are all and only those things that share some one universal. But also we would have other less-than-perfectly natural properties, made so by families of suitable related universals.[9] Thus we might have an imperfectly natural property of being metallic, even if we had no such single universal as metallic, in virtue of a close-knit family of genuine universals one or another of which is instantiated by any metallic thing. These imperfectly natural properties would be natural to varying degrees.

Let us say that an *adequate* theory of properties is one that recognizes an objective difference between natural and unnatural properties; preferably, a difference that admits of degree. A combined theory of properties and universals is one sort of adequate theory of properties.

But not the only sort. A Nominalistic theory of properties could achieve adequacy by other means. Instead of employing universals, it could draw primitive distinctions among particulars. Most simply, a Nominalist could take it as a primitive fact that some classes of things are perfectly natural properties; others are less-than-perfectly natural to various degrees; and most are not at all natural. Such a Nominalist takes 'natural' as a primitive predicate, and offers no analysis of what he means in predicating it of classes. His intention is to select the very same classes as natural properties that the user of universals would select. But he regards the universals as idle machinery, fictitiously superimposed on the primitive objective difference between the natural properties and the others.[10]

Alternatively, a Nominalist in pursuit of adequacy might prefer to rest with primitive objective resemblance among things. (He might not think that 'natural' was a very natural primitive, perhaps because it is to be predicated of classes.) Then he could undertake to define natural properties in terms of the mutual resemblance of their members and the failure of resemblance between their members and their non-members. Unfortunately, the project meets with well-known technical difficulties. These can be solved, but at a daunting price in complexity and artificiality of our primitive. We cannot get by with the familiar dyadic 'resembles'. Instead we need a predicate of resemblance that is both contrastive and variably polyadic. Something like

$x_1, x_2,...$ resemble one another and do not likewise resemble any of $y_1, y_2,...$

(where the strings of variables may be infinite, even uncountable) must be taken as understood without further analysis.[11] If adequate Nominalism requires us to choose between this and a primitive predicate of classes, we might well wonder whether the game is worth the candle. I only say we might wonder; I know of no consideration that seems to me decisive.

At this point, you may see very well why it could be a good idea to believe in universals as well as properties; but you may see no point in having properties as well as universals. But properties have work of their own, and universals are ill-suited to do the work of properties.

It is properties that we need, sometimes natural and sometimes not, to provide an adequate supply of semantic values for linguistic expressions. Consider such sentences as these:

(1)   Red resembles orange more than it resembles blue.
(2)   Red is a colour.
(3)   Humility is a virtue.
(4)   Redness is a sign of ripeness.

Prima facie, these sentences contain names that cannot be taken to denote particular, individual things. What is the semantic role of these words? If we are to do compositional semantics in the way that is best developed, we need entities to assign as semantic values to these words, entities that will encode their semantic roles. Perhaps sometimes we might find paraphrases that will absolve us from the need to subject the original sentence to

semantic analysis. That is the case with (1), for instance.[12] But even if such paraphrases sometimes exist – even if they *always* exist, which seems unlikely – they work piecemeal and frustrate any systematic approach to semantics.

Armstrong takes it that such sentences provide a subsidiary argument for universals, independent of his main argument from the One over Many problem.[13] I quite agree that we have here an argument for something. But not for universals as opposed to properties. Properties can serve as the requisite semantic values. Indeed properties are much better suited to the job than universals are. That is plain even from the examples considered. It is unlikely that there are any such genuine universals as the colours (especially determinable colours, like red, rather than determinate shades), or ripeness, or humility. Armstrong agrees[14] that he cannot take (1)–(4) as straightforwardly making reference to universals. He must first subject them to paraphrase. Even if there always is a paraphrase that does refer to, or quantify over, genuine universals, still the need for paraphrase is a threat to systematic semantics. The problem arises exactly because universals are sparse. There is no corresponding objection if we take the requisite semantic values as properties.

Other sentences make my point more dramatically.

(5)   Grueness does not make for resemblance among all its instances.
(6)   What is common to all who suffer pain is being in some or another state that occupies the pain role, presumably not the same state in all cases.

The point is not that these sentences are true – though they are – but that they require semantic analysis. (It is irrelevant that they are not ordinary language.) A universal of grueness would be anathema; as would a universal such that, necessarily, one has it if he is in some state or other that occupies the pain role in his case.[15] But the corresponding properties are no problem.

Indeed, we have a comprehension schema applying to any predicate phrase whatever, however complicated. (Let it even be infinitely long; let it even include imaginary names for entities we haven't really named.) Let x range over things, P over properties (classes) of things. Then:

$$\exists_1 P \square \forall x (x \text{ has } P \equiv \phi x).$$

We could appropriately call this 'the property of ϕ-ing' in those cases where the predicate phrase is short enough to form a gerund, and take this property to be the semantic value of the gerund. Contrast this with the very different relationship of universals and predicates set forth in *Universals*, vol. 2, pp. 7–59.

Consider also those sentences which prima facie involve second-order quantification. From *Universals*, vol. 1, p. 62, and 'Against "ostrich" nominalism' we have these:

(7) He has the same virtues as his father.
(8) The dresses were of the same colour.
(9) There are undiscovered fundamental physical properties.
(10) Acquired characteristics are never inherited.
(11) Some zoological species are cross-fertile.

Prima facie, we are quantifying either over properties or over universals. Again, paraphrases might defeat that presumption, but in a piecemeal way that threatens systematic semantics. In each case, properties could serve as the values of the variables of quantification. Only in case (9) could universals serve equally well. To treat the other cases, not to mention

(12) Some characteristics, such as the colours, are more disjunctive than they seem

as quantifications over universals, we would again have to resort to some preliminary paraphrase.[16] This second semantic argument, like the first, adduces work for which properties are better qualified than universals.

Which is not to deny that a partnership might do better still. Let it be granted that we are dealing with quantifications over properties. Still, these quantifications – like most of our quantifications – may be tacitly or explicitly restricted. In particular, they usually are restricted to natural properties. Not to perfectly natural properties that correspond to single universals, except in special cases like (9), but to properties that are at least somewhat more natural than the great majority of the utterly miscellaneous. That is so for all our

examples, even (12). Then even though we quantify over properties, we still need either universals or the resources of an adequate Nominalism in order to say which of the properties we mostly quantify over.

I also think that it is properties that we need in characterizing the content of our intentional attitudes. I believe, or I desire, that I live in one of the worlds in a certain class, rather than any world outside that class. This class of worlds is a property had by worlds. I believe, or I desire, that my world has that property. (The class of worlds also may be called a *proposition*, in one of the legitimate senses of that word, and my 'propositional attitude' of belief or desire has this proposition as its 'object'.) More generally, subsuming the previous case, I believe or I desire that I myself belong to a certain class of *possibilia*. I ascribe a certain property to myself, or I want to have it. Or I might ascribe a property to something else, or even to myself, under a relation of acquaintance I bear to that thing.[17] Surely the properties that give the content of attitudes in these ways cannot be relied on to be perfectly natural, hence cannot be replaced by universals. It is interesting to ask whether there is any lower limit to their naturalness (see the final section), but surely no very exacting standard is possible. Here again properties are right for the job, universals are not.

One Over Many

Armstrong's main argument for universals is the 'One over Many'. It is because I find this argument unconvincing that I am investigating alternative reasons to accept a theory of universals.

Here is a concise statement of the argument, taken by condensation from 'Against "ostrich" nominalism', pp. 440–1. A very similar statement could have been drawn from the opening pages of *Universals*.

I would wish to start by saying that many different particulars can all have what appears to be the same nature and draw the conclusion that, as a result, there is a *prima facie* case for postulating universals. We are continually talking about different things having the same property or quality, being of the same sort of kind, having the same nature, and so on. Philosophers draw the distinction between sameness of token and sameness of type. But they are only making explicit a distinction which ordinary language (and so, ordinary thought) perfectly recognizes. I suggest that the fact of sameness of type is a Moorean fact: one of the many facts which even philosophers should not deny, whatever philosophical account or analysis they give of such facts. Any comprehensive philosophy must try to give some account of Moorean facts. They constitute the compulsory questions in the philosophical examination paper.

From this point of departure, Armstrong makes his case by criticizing rival attempts to answer the compulsory question, and by rejecting views that decline to answer it at all.

Still more concisely, the One over Many problem is presented as the problem of giving some account of Moorean facts of apparent sameness of type. Thus understood, I agree that the question is compulsory; I agree that Armstrong's postulation of shared universals answers it; but I think that an adequate Nominalism also answers it.

An effort at systematic philosophy must indeed give an account of any purported fact. There are three ways to give an account. (1) 'I deny it' – this earns a failing mark if the fact is really Moorean. (2) 'I analyse it thus' – this is Armstrong's response to the facts of apparent sameness of type. Or (3) 'I accept it as primitive'. Not every *account* is an *analysis*! A system that takes certain Moorean facts as primitive, as unanalysed, cannot be accused of failing to make a place for them. It neither shirks the compulsory question nor answers it by denial. It does give an account.

An adequate Nominalism, of course, is a theory that takes Moorean facts of apparent sameness of type as primitive. It predicates mutual resemblance of the things which are apparently of the same type; or it predicates naturalness of some property that they all share, i.e., that has them all as members; and it declines to analyse these predications any further. That is why the problem of One over Many, rightly understood, does not provide more than a prima facie reason to postulate universals. Universals afford one solution, but there are others.

I fear that the problem does not remain rightly understood. Early in *Universals* it undergoes an unfortunate double transformation. In the course of a few pages[18] the legitimate demand for an

account of Moorean facts of apparent sameness of type turns into a demand for an analysis of predication in general. The analysandum becomes the schema '*a* has the property *F*'. The turning point takes only two sentences:

> How is [the Nominalist] to account for the apparent (if usually partial) identity of numerically different particulars? How can two different things both be white or both be on a table?[19]

And very soon, those who 'refuse to countenance universals but who at the same time see no need for any reductive analyses [of the schema of predication]', those according to whom 'there are no universals but the proposition that *a* is *F* is perfectly all right as it is', stand accused of dodging the compulsory question.[20]

When the demand for an account – for a place in one's system – turned into a demand for an analysis, then I say that the question ceased to be compulsory. And when the analysandum switched, from Moorean facts of apparent sameness of type to predication generally, then I say that the question ceased to be answerable at all. The transformed problem of One over Many deserves our neglect. The ostrich that will not look at it is a wise bird indeed.

Despite his words, I do not think that Armstrong really means to demand, either from Nominalists or from himself, a *fully* general analysis of predication. For none is so ready as he to insist that not just any shared predicate makes for even apparent sameness of type. (That is what gives his theory its distinctive interest and merit.) It would be better to put the transformed problem thus: one way or another, all predication is to be analysed. Some predications are to be analysed away in terms of others. Here we have one-off analyses for specific predicates – as it might be, for 'grue'. But all those predications that remain, after the one-off analyses are finished, are to be analysed wholesale by means of a general analysis of the schema '*a* has property *F*'.

There is to be no unanalysed predication. Time and again, Armstrong wields this requirement against rival theories. One theory after another falls victim to the 'relation regress': in the course of analysing other predications, the theory has resort to a new predicate that cannot, on pain of circularity, be analysed along with the rest. So falls Class Nominalism (including the version with primitive naturalness that I deem adequate): it employs predications of class membership, which predications it cannot without circularity analyse in terms of class membership. So falls Resemblance Nominalism: it fails to analyse predications of resemblance. So fall various other, less deserving Nominalisms. And so fall rival forms of Realism, for instance Transcendent, Platonic Realism: this time, predications of participation evade analysis. Specific theories meet other, specific objections; suffice it to say that I think these inconclusive against the two Nominalisms that I called adequate. But the clincher, the one argument that recurs throughout the many refutations, is the relation regress. And this amounts to the objection that the theory under attack does not achieve its presumed aim of doing away with all unanalysed predication and therefore fails to solve the transformed problem of One over Many.

Doing away with all unanalysed predication is an unattainable aim, and so an unreasonable aim. No theory is to be faulted for failing to achieve it. For how could there be a theory that names entities, or quantifies over them, in the course of its sentences, and yet altogether avoids primitive predication? Artificial tricks aside,[21] the thing cannot be done.

What's true is that a theory may be faulted for its overabundant primitive predications, or for unduly mysterious ones, or for unduly complicated ones. These are not fatal faults, however. They are to be counted against a theory, along with its faults of overly generous ontology or of disagreement with less-than-Moorean commonsensical opinions. Rival philosophical theories have their prices, which we seek to measure. But it's all too clear that for philosophers, at least, there ain't no such thing as a free lunch.

How does Armstrong himself do without primitive predication? – He doesn't. Consider the predicate 'instantiates' (or 'has'), as in 'particular *a* instantiates universal *F*' or 'this electron has unit charge'. No one-off analysis applies to this specific predicate. 'Such identity in nature [as results from the having of one universal in many particulars] is literally inexplicable, in the sense that it cannot be further explained.'[22] Neither do predications of 'instantiates' fall under Armstrong's general analysis of (otherwise unanalysed) predication. His is a *non-relational* Realism: he declines, with good reason, to postulate a dyadic universal of instantiation to bind particulars to their

universals. (And if he did, it would only postpone the need for primitive predication.) So let all who have felt the bite of Armstrong's relation regress rise up and cry 'Tu quoque!' And let us mark well that Armstrong is prepared to give *one* predicate 'what has been said to be the privilege of the harlot: power without responsibility. The predicate is informative, it makes a vital contribution to telling us what is the case, the world is different if it is different, yet ontologically it is supposed not to commit us. Nice work: if you can get it.'[23]

Let us dump the project of getting rid of primitive predication, and return to the sensible – though not compulsory – project of analysing Moorean facts of apparent sameness of type. Now does the relation regress serve Armstrong better? I think not. It does make better sense within the more sensible project, but it still bites Armstrong and his rivals with equal force. Let the Nominalist say 'These donkeys resemble each other, so likewise do those stars, and there analysis ends.' Let the Platonist say 'This statue participates in the Form of beauty, likewise that lecture participates in the Form of truth, and there analysis ends.' Let Armstrong say 'This electron instantiates unit charge, likewise that proton instantiates tripartiteness, and there analysis ends.' It is possible to complain in each case that a fact of sameness of type has gone unanalysed, the types being respectively resemblance, participation, and instantiation. But it is far from evident that the alleged facts are Moorean, and still less evident that the first two are more Moorean than the third. None of them are remotely the equals of the genuine Moorean fact that, in some sense, different lumps of gold are the same in kind.

Michael Devitt has denounced the One over Many problem as a mirage better left unseen.[24] I have found Devitt's discussion instructive, and I agree with much of what he says. But Devitt has joined Armstrong in transforming the One over Many problem. He takes it to be the problem of analysing the schema

a and *b* have the same property (are of the same type), *F*-ness

otherwise than by means of a one-off analysis for some specific *F*. To that problem it is fair to answer as he does that

a is *F*; *b* is *F*

is analysis enough, once we give over the aim of doing without primitive predication. But Devitt has set himself too easy a problem. If we attend to the modest, untransformed One over Many problem, which is no mirage, we will ask about a different analysandum:

a and *b* have some common property (are somehow of the same type)

in which it is not said what *a* and *b* have in common. This less definite analysandum is not covered by what Devitt has said. If we take a clearly Moorean case, he owes us an account: either an analysis or an overt resort to primitive predication of resemblance.

Duplication, Supervenience, and Divergent Worlds

Henceforth I shall speak only of my need for the distinction between natural and unnatural, or more and less natural, properties. It is to be understood that the work I have in store for an adequately discriminatory theory of properties might be new work for a theory of universals, or it might instead be work for the resources of an adequate Nominalism.

I begin with the problem of analysing duplication. We are familiar with cases of approximate duplication, e.g., when we use copying machines. And we understand that if these machines were more perfect than they are, the copies they made would be perfect duplicates of the original. Copy and original would be alike in size and shape and chemical composition of the ink marks and the paper, alike in temperature and magnetic alignment and electrostatic charge, alike even in the exact arrangement of their electrons and quarks. Such duplicates would be exactly alike, we say. They would match perfectly, they would be qualitatively identical, they would be indiscernible.

But they would not have exactly the same properties, in my sense of the word. As in the case of any two things, countless class boundaries would divide them. Intrinsically, leaving out their relations to the rest of the world, they would be just alike. But they would occupy different spatio-temporal positions; and they might have different owners, be first examined in different centuries, and so on.

So if we wish to analyse duplication in terms of shared properties, it seems that we must first distinguish the *intrinsic* (or 'internal') properties from the *extrinsic* (or 'external' or 'relational') properties. Then we may say that two things are duplicates iff they have precisely the same intrinsic properties, however much their extrinsic properties might differ. But our new problem of dividing the properties into intrinsic and extrinsic is no easier than our original problem of analysing duplication. In fact, the two problems are joined in a tight little circle of interdefinability. Duplication is a matter of sharing intrinsic properties; intrinsic properties are just those properties that never differ between duplicates. Property P is intrinsic iff, for any two duplicate things, not necessarily from the same world, either both have P or neither does. P is extrinsic iff there is some such pair of duplicates of which one has P and the other lacks P.[25]

If we relied on our physical theory to be accurate and exhaustive, we might think to define duplication in physical terms. We believe that duplicates must be alike in the arrangement of their electrons and quarks – why not put this forward as a definition? But such a 'definition' is no analysis. It presupposes the physics of our actual world; however physics is contingent and known a posteriori. The definition does not apply to duplication at possible worlds where physics is different, or to duplication between worlds that differ in their physics. Nor does it capture what those ignorant of physics mean when they speak – as they do – of duplication.

The proper course, I suggest, is to analyse duplication in terms of shared properties; but to begin not with the intrinsic properties but rather with natural properties. Two things are qualitative duplicates if they have exactly the same perfectly natural properties.[26]

Physics is relevant because it aspires to give an inventory of natural properties – not a complete inventory, perhaps, but a complete enough inventory to account for duplication among actual things. If physics succeeds in this, then duplication within our world amounts to sameness of physical description. But the natural properties themselves are what matter, not the theory that tells us what they are. If Materialism were false and physics an utter failure, as is the case at some deplorable worlds, there would still be duplication in virtue of shared natural properties.

On my analysis, all perfectly natural properties come out intrinsic. That seems right. The converse is not true. Intrinsic properties may be disjunctive and miscellaneous and unnatural, so long as they never differ between duplicates. The perfectly natural properties comprise a basis for the intrinsic properties; but arbitrary Boolean compounds of them, however unnatural, are still intrinsic. Hence if we adopt the sort of adequate Nominalism that draws a primitive distinction between natural and unnatural properties, that is not the same thing as drawing a primitive distinction between intrinsic and extrinsic properties. The former distinction yields the latter, but not vice versa.

Likewise if we adopt the sort of adequate Nominalism that begins with a suitable relation of partial resemblance, that is not the same thing as taking duplication itself as primitive. Again, the former yields the latter, but not vice versa.

If instead we reject Nominalism, and we take the perfectly natural properties to be those that correspond to universals (in the sense that the members of the property are exactly those things that instantiate the universal), then all the properties that correspond to universals are intrinsic. So are all the Boolean compounds – disjunctions, negations, etc. – of properties that correspond to universals. The universals themselves are intrinsic *ex officio*, so to speak.

But here I must confess that the theory of universals for which I offer new work cannot be exactly Armstrong's theory. For it must reject extrinsic universals; whereas Armstrong admits them, although not as irreducible.[27] I think he would be better off without them, given his own aims. (1) They subvert the desired connection between sharing of universals and Moorean facts of partial or total sameness of nature. Admittedly, there is such a thing as resemblance in extrinsic respects: things can be alike in the roles they play *vis-à-vis* other things, or in the origins they spring from. But such resemblances are not what we mean when we say of two things that they are of the same kind, or have the same nature. (2) They subvert the desired immanence of universals: if something instantiates an extrinsic universal, that is not a fact just about that thing. (3) They are not

needed for Armstrong's theory of laws of nature; any supposed law connecting extrinsic universals of things can be equivalently replaced by a law connecting intrinsic structures of larger systems that have those things as parts.

Thus I am content to say that if there are universals, intrinsic duplicates are things having exactly the same universals. We need not say '… exactly the same *intrinsic* universals,' because we should not believe in any other kind.

Not only is duplication of interest in its own right; it also is needed in dealing with other topics in metaphysics. Hence such topics create a derived need for natural properties. I shall consider two topics where I find need to speak of duplication: supervenience and divergent worlds.

First, supervenience. A supervenience thesis is a denial of independent variation. Given an ontology of *possibilia*, we can formulate such theses in terms of differences between possible individuals or worlds. To say that so-and-so supervenes on such-and-such is to say that there can be no difference in respect of so-and-so without difference in respect of such-and-such. Beauty of statues supervenes on their shape, size, and colour, for instance, if no two statues, in the same or different worlds, ever differ in beauty without also differing in shape or size or colour.[28]

A supervenience thesis is, in a broad sense, reductionist. But it is a stripped-down form of reductionism, unencumbered by dubious denials of existence, claims of ontological priority, or claims of translatability. One might wish to say that in some sense the beauty of statues is nothing over and above the shape and size and colour that beholders appreciate, but without denying that there is such a thing as beauty, without claiming that beauty exists only in some less-than-fundamental way, and without undertaking to paraphrase ascriptions of beauty in terms of shape, etc. A supervenience thesis seems to capture what the cautious reductionist wishes to say.

Even if reductionists ought to be less cautious and aim for translation, still it is a good idea to attend to the question of supervenience. For if supervenience fails, then no scheme of translation can be correct, and we needn't go on Chisholming away in search of one. If supervenience succeeds, on the other hand, then some correct scheme must exist; the remaining question is whether there exists a correct scheme that is less than infinitely complex. If beauty is supervenient on shape, etc., the worst that can happen is that an ascription of beauty is equivalent to an uncountably infinite disjunction of maximally specific descriptions of shape, etc., which descriptions might themselves involve infinite conjunctions.

Interesting supervenience theses usually involve the notion of qualitative duplication that we have just considered. Thus we may ask what does or doesn't supervene on the qualitative character of the entire world, throughout all of history. Suppose that two possible worlds are perfect qualitative duplicates – must they then also have exactly the same distributions of objective probability, the same laws of nature, the same counterfactuals and causal relations? Must their inhabitants have the same *de re* modal properties? If so, it makes sense to pursue such projects as a frequency analysis of probability, a regularity analysis of laws of nature, or a comparative similarity analysis of causal counterfactuals and *de re* modality. If not, such projects are doomed from the start, and we needn't look at the details of the attempts. But we cannot even raise these questions of supervenience unless we can speak of duplicate worlds. And to do that, I have suggested, we need natural properties.

(Note that if possible worlds obey a principle of identity of qualitative indiscernibles, then all these supervenience theses hold automatically. If no two worlds are duplicates, then *a fortiori* no two are duplicates that differ in their probabilities, laws, ... or anything else.)

We might also ask whether qualitative character supervenes on anything less. For instance, we might ask whether global qualitative character supervenes on local qualitative character. Say that two worlds are *local duplicates* iff they are divisible into corresponding small parts in such a way that (1) corresponding parts of the two worlds are duplicates, and (2) the correspondence preserves spatiotemporal relations. (The exact meaning depends, of course, on what we mean by 'small'.) If two worlds are local duplicates, then must they be duplicates *simpliciter*? Or could they differ in ways that do not prevent local duplication – e.g., in external relations, other than the spatiotemporal relations themselves, between separated things? Again, we must make sense of

duplication – this time, both in the large and in the small – even to ask the question.[29]

Next, divergent worlds. I shall say that two possible worlds *diverge* iff they are not duplicates but they do have duplicate initial temporal segments. Thus our world and another might match perfectly up through the year 1945, and go their separate ways thereafter.

Note that we need no identity of times across worlds. Our world through our 1945 duplicates an initial segment of the other world; that otherworldly segment ends with a year that indeed resembles our 1945, but it is part of otherworldly time, not part of our time. Also, we need no separation of time and space that contravenes Relativity – we have initial temporal segments, of this or another world, if we have spatiotemporal regions bounded by spacelike surfaces that cut the world in two.

I distinguish *divergence* of worlds from *branching* of worlds. In branching, instead of duplicate segments, one and the same initial segment is allegedly shared as a common part by two overlapping worlds. Branching is problematic in ways that divergence is not. First, because an inhabitant of the shared segment cannot speak unequivocally of *the* world he lives in. What if he says there will be a sea fight tomorrow, meaning of course to speak of the future of his own world, and one of the two worlds he lives in has a sea fight the next day and the other doesn't? Second, because overlap of worlds interferes with the most salient principle of demarcation for worlds, viz., that two possible individuals are part of the same world iff they are linked by some chain of external relations, e.g., of spatiotemporal relations. (I know of no other example.) Neither of these difficulties seems insuperable, but both are better avoided. That makes it reasonable to prefer a theory of non-overlapping divergent worlds to a theory of branching worlds. Then we need to be able to speak of qualitative duplication of world-segments, which we can do in terms of shared natural properties.

Divergent (or branching) worlds are of use in defining Determinism. The usual definitions are not very satisfactory. If we say that every event has a cause, we overlook probabilistic causation under Indeterminism. If we speak of what could be predicted by a superhuman calculator with unlimited knowledge of history and the laws of nature, we overlook obstacles that might prevent prediction even under Determinism, or else we try to make non-vacuous sense of counterfactuals about what our predictor could do if he had some quite impossible combination of powers and limitations.

A better approach is as follows. First, a system of laws of nature is Deterministic iff no two divergent worlds both conform perfectly to the laws of that system. Second, a world is Deterministic iff its laws comprise a Deterministic system. Third, Determinism is the thesis that our world is Deterministic.[30]

(Alternative versions of Determinism can be defined in similar fashion. For instance, we could strengthen the first step by prohibiting convergence as well as divergence of law-abiding worlds. Or we could even require that no two law-abiding worlds have duplicate momentary slices without being duplicates throughout their histories. Or we could define a weaker sort of Determinism: we could call a world *fortuitously* Deterministic, even if its laws do not comprise a Deterministic system, iff no world both diverges from it and conforms to its laws. The laws and early history of such a world suffice to determine later history, but only because the situations in which the laws fall short of Determinism never arise. We might equivalently define fortuitous Determinism as follows: for any historical fact F and any initial segment S of the world, there are a true proposition H about the history of S and a true proposition L about the laws of nature, such that H and L together strictly imply P.[31] Does this definition bypass our need to speak of duplication of initial segments? Not so, for we must ask what it means to say that H is about the history of S. I take that to mean that H holds at both or neither of any two worlds that both begin with segments that are duplicates of S.)

Divergent worlds are important also in connection with the sort of counterfactual conditional that figures in patterns of causal dependence. Such counterfactuals tend to be temporally asymmetric, and this is what gives rise to the asymmetry of causation itself. Counterfactuals of this sort do not 'backtrack': it is not to be said that if the present were different, a different past would have led up to it, but rather that if the present were different, the same past would have had a different outcome.

Given a hypothesized difference at a certain time, the events of future times normally would be very different indeed, but the events of past times (except perhaps for the very near past) would be no different. Thus actuality and its counterfactual alternatives are divergent worlds, with duplicate initial segments.[32]

Minimal Materialism

There is a difficulty that arises if we attempt to formulate certain reductionist views, for instance Materialism, as supervenience theses. A solution to this difficulty employs natural properties not only by way of duplication but in a more direct way also.

Roughly speaking, Materialism is the thesis that physics – something not too different from present-day physics, though presumably somewhat improved – is a comprehensive theory of the world, complete as well as correct. The world is as physics says it is, and there's no more to say. World history written in physical language is all of world history. That is rough speaking indeed; our goal will be to give a better formulation. But before I try to say more precisely what Materialism is, let me say what it is not. (1) Materialism is not a thesis of finite translatability of all our language into the language of physics. (2) Materialism is not to be identified with any one Materialist theory of mind. It is a thesis that motivates a variety of theories of mind: versions of Behaviourism, Functionalism, the mind-body identity theory, even the theory that mind is all a mistake. (3) Materialism is not just the theory that there are no things except those recognized by physics. To be sure, Materialists don't believe in spirits, or other such non-physical things. But anti-materialists may not believe in spirits either – their complaint needn't be that physics omits some of the things that there are. They may complain instead that physics overlooks some of the ways there are for physical things to differ; for instance, they may think that physical people could differ in what their experience is like. (4) That suggests that Materialism is, at least in part, the thesis that there are no natural properties instantiated at our world except those recognized by physics. That is better, but I think still not right. Couldn't there be a natural property X (in the nature of the case, it is hard to name an example!) which is shared by the physical brains in worlds like ours and the immaterial spirits that inhabit other worlds? Or by this-worldly quarks and certain otherworldly particles that cannot exist under our physics? Physics could quite properly make no mention of a natural property of this sort. It is enough to recognize the special case applicable to our world, X-*cum*-physicality, brainhood or quarkhood as it might be. Then if by physical properties we mean those properties that are mentioned in the language of physics, a Materialist ought not to hold that all natural properties instantiated in our world are physical properties.

At this point, it ought to seem advisable to formulate Materialism as a supervenience thesis: no difference without physical difference. Or, contraposing: physical duplicates are duplicates *simpliciter*. A *fortiori*, no mental difference without physical difference; physical duplicates are mental duplicates. The thesis might best be taken as applying to whole possible worlds, in order to bypass such questions as whether mental life is to some extent extrinsic to the subject. So we have this first of several attempted formulations of Materialism:

M1:   Any two possible worlds that are exactly alike in all respects recognized by physics are qualitative duplicates.

But this will not do. In making Materialism into a thesis about how just any two worlds can and cannot differ, M1 puts Materialism forward as a necessary truth. That is not what Materialists intend. Materialism is meant to be a contingent thesis, a merit of our world that not all other worlds share. Two worlds could indeed differ without differing physically, if at least one of them is a world where Materialism is false. For instance, our Materialistic world differs from a non-materialistic world that is physically just like ours but that also contains physically epiphenomenal spirits.

There is a non-contingent supervenience thesis nearby that might appeal to Materialists:

M2:   There is no difference, *a fortiori* no mental difference, without some non-mental difference. Any two worlds alike in all non-mental respects are duplicates, and

in particular do not differ in respect of the mental lives of their inhabitants.

This seems to capture our thought that the mental is a pattern in a medium, obtaining in virtue of local features of the medium (neuron firings) and perhaps also very global features (laws of nature) that are too small or too big to be mental themselves. But M2 is not Materialism. It is both less and more. Less, obviously, because it never says that the medium is physical. More, because it denies the very possibility of what I shall call *Panpsychistic* Materialism.

It is often noted that psychophysical identity is a two-way street: if all mental properties are physical, then some physical properties are mental. But perhaps not just some but *all* physical properties might be mental as well; and indeed every property of anything might be at once physical and mental. Suppose there are indeed worlds where this is so. If so, presumably there are many such worlds, not all duplicates, differing *inter alia* in the mental lives of their inhabitants. But all differences between such worlds are mental (as well as physical), so none are non-mental. These worlds will be vacuously alike in all non-mental respects, for lack of any non-mental respects to differ in. Then M2 fails. And not just at the trouble-making worlds; M2 is non-contingent, so if it fails at any worlds, it fails at all – even decent Materialistic worlds like ours. Maybe Panpsychistic Materialism is indeed impossible – how do you square it with a broadly functional analysis of mind? – but a thesis that says so is more than just Materialism.

A third try. This much is at least true:

M3:   No two Materialistic worlds differ without differing physically; any two Materialistic worlds that are exactly alike physically are duplicates.

But M3 is not a formulation of Materialism, for the distinction between Materialistic and other worlds appears within M3. All we learn is that the Materialistic worlds comprise a class within which there is no difference without physical difference. But there are many such classes. In fact, any world, however spirit-ridden, belongs to such a class.

A fourth try. Perhaps we should confine our attention to nomologically possible worlds, thus:

M4:   Among worlds that conform to the actual laws of nature no two differ without differing physically; any two such worlds that are exactly alike physically are duplicates.

But again we have something that is both less and more than Materialism: less, because M4 could hold at a world where Materialism is false but where spiritual phenomena are correlated with physical phenomena according to strict laws; more, because M4 fails to hold at a Materialistic, spirit-free world if the laws of that world do not preclude the existence of epiphenomenal spirits. Our world might be such a world, a world where spirits are absent but not outlawed.[33]

So far, a supervenience formulation of Materialism seems elusive. But I think we can succeed if we join the idea of supervenience with the idea that a non-materialistic world would have something extra, something that a Materialistic world lacks. It might have spirits; or it might have physical things that differ in non-physical ways, for instance in what their experience is like. In either case there are extra natural properties, properties instantiated in the non-materialistic world but nowhere to be found in the Materialistic world. Let us say that a property is *alien* to a world iff (1) it is not instantiated by any inhabitant of that world, and (2) it is not analysable as a conjunction of, or as a structural property constructed out of, natural properties all of which are instantiated by inhabitants of that world. (I need the second clause because I am following Armstrong, *mutatis mutandis*, in declining to rule out perfectly natural properties that are conjunctive or structurally complex.[34] It would be wrong to count as alien a complex property analysable in terms of non-alien constituents.) If our world is Materialistic, then it is safe to say that some of the natural properties instantiated in any non-materialistic world are properties alien to our world. Now we can proceed at last to formulate Materialism as a restricted and contingent supervenience thesis:

M5:   Among worlds where no natural properties alien to our world are instantiated, no two differ without differing physically; any two such worlds that are exactly alike physically are duplicates.[35]

We took Materialism to uphold the comprehensiveness of 'something not too different from present-day physics, though presumably somewhat improved'. That was deliberately vague. Materialist metaphysicians want to side with physics, but not to take sides within physics. Within physics, more precise claims of completeness and correctness may be at issue. Physics (ignoring latter-day failures of nerve) is the science that aspires to comprehensiveness, and particular physical theories may be put forward as fulfilling that aspiration. If so, we must again ask what it means to claim comprehensiveness. And again, the answer may be given by a supervenience formulation: no difference without physical difference as conceived by such-and-such grand theory. But again it must be understood as a restricted and contingent supervenience thesis, applying only among worlds devoid of alien natural properties.

Thus the business of physics is not just to discover laws and causal explanations. In putting forward as comprehensive theories that recognize only a limited range of natural properties, physics proposes inventories of the natural properties instantiated in our world. Not complete inventories, perhaps, but complete enough to account for all the duplications and differences that could arise in the absence of alien natural properties. Of course, the discovery of natural properties is inseparable from the discovery of laws. For an excellent reason to think that some hitherto unsuspected natural properties are instantiated – properties deserving of recognition by physics, the quark colours as they might be – is that without them, no satisfactory system of laws can be found.

This is reminiscent of the distinctive a posteriori, scientific character of Armstrong's Realism.[36] But in the setting of an ontology of *possibilia*, the distinction between discovering what universals or natural properties there actually are and discovering which ones are actually instantiated fades away. And the latter question is a posteriori on any theory. What remains, and remains important, is that physics discovers properties. And not just any properties – natural properties. The discovery is, for instance, that neutrinos are not all alike. That is not the discovery that different ones have different properties in my sense, belong to different classes. We knew that much a priori. Rather, it is the surprising discovery that some *natural* property differentiates some neutrinos from others. That discovery has in fact been made; I should like to read an account of it by some philosopher who is not prepared to adopt a discriminatory attitude toward properties and who thinks that all things are equally similar and dissimilar to one another.

Laws and Causation

The observation that physics discovers natural properties in the course of discovering laws may serve to introduce our next topic: the analysis of what it is to be a law of nature. I agree with Armstrong that we need universals, or at least natural properties, in explaining what lawhood is, though I disagree with his account of how this is so.

Armstrong's theory, in its simplest form,[37] holds that what makes certain regularities lawful are second-order states of affairs $N(F, G)$ in which the two ordinary, first-order universals F and G are related by a certain dyadic second-order universal N. It is a contingent matter which universals are thus related by the lawmaker N. But it is necessary – and necessary *simpliciter*, not just nomologically necessary – that if $N(F, G)$ obtains, then F and G are constantly conjoined. There is a necessary connection between the second-order state of affairs $N(F, G)$ and the first-order lawful regularity $\forall x(Fx \supset Gx)$; and likewise between the conjunctive state of affairs $N(F, G)$ & Fa and its necessary consequence Ga.

A parallel theory could be set up with natural properties in place of Armstrong's first- and second-order universals. It would have many of the attractive features that Armstrong claims on behalf of his theory, but at least one merit would be lost. For Armstrong, the lawful necessitation of Ga by Fa is a purely local matter: it involves only a, the universals F and G that are present in a, and the second-order law-making universal that is present in turn in (or between) these two universals. If we replace the universals by properties, however natural, that locality is lost. For properties are classes with their membership spread around the worlds, and are not wholly present in a. But I do not think this a conclusive objection, for our intuitions of locality often seem to lead us astray. The selective regularity theory I shall shortly advocate also sacrifices locality, as does any regularity theory of law.

What leads me (with some regret) to reject Armstrong's theory, whether with universals or with natural properties, is that I find its necessary connections unintelligible. Whatever N may be, I cannot see how it could be absolutely impossible to have $N(F, G)$ and Fa without Ga. (Unless N just *is* constant conjunction, or constant conjunction plus something else, in which case Armstrong's theory turns into a form of the regularity theory he rejects.) The mystery is somewhat hidden by Armstrong's terminology. He uses 'necessitates' as a name for the law-making universal N; and who would be surprised to hear that if F 'necessitates' G and a has F, then a must have G? But I say that N deserves the name of 'necessitation' only if, somehow, it really can enter into the requisite necessary connections. It can't enter into them just by bearing a name, any more than one can have mighty biceps just by being called 'Armstrong'.

I am tempted to complain in Humean fashion of alleged necessary connections between distinct existences, especially when first-order states of affairs in the past supposedly join with second-order states of affairs to necessitate first-order states of affairs in the future. That complaint is not clearly right: the sharing of universals detracts from the distinctness of the necessitating and the necessitated states of affairs. But I am not appeased. I conclude that necessary connections can be unintelligible even when they are supposed to obtain between existences that are not clearly and wholly distinct.[38]

Thus I do not endorse Armstrong's way of building universals, or alternatively natural properties, into the analysis of lawhood. Instead I favour a regularity analysis. But I need natural properties even so.

Certainly not just any regularity is a law of nature. Some are accidental. So an adequate regularity analysis must be selective. Also, an adequate analysis must be collective. It must treat regularities not one at a time, but rather as candidates to enter into integrated systems. For a given regularity might hold either as a law or accidentally, depending on whether other regularities obtain that can fit together with it in a suitable system. (Thus I reject the idea that lawhood consists of 'lawlikeness' plus truth.) Following Mill and Ramsey,[39] I take a suitable system to be one that has the virtues we aspire to in our own theory-building, and that has them to the greatest extent possible given the way the world is. It must be entirely true; it must be closed under strict implication; it must be as simple in axiomatization as it can be without sacrificing too much information content; and it must have as much information content as it can have without sacrificing too much simplicity. A law is any regularity that earns inclusion in the ideal system. (Or, in case of ties, in every ideal system.) The ideal system need not consist entirely of regularities; particular facts may gain entry if they contribute enough to collective simplicity and strength. (For instance, certain particular facts about the Big Bang might be strong candidates.) But only the regularities of the system are to count as laws.

We face an obvious problem. Different ways to express the same content, using different vocabulary, will differ in simplicity. The problem can be put in two ways, depending on whether we take our systems as consisting of propositions (classes of worlds) or as consisting of interpreted sentences. In the first case, the problem is that a single system has different degrees of simplicity relative to different linguistic formulations. In the second case, the problem is that equivalent systems, strictly implying the very same regularities, may differ in their simplicity. In fact, the content of any system whatever may be formulated very simply indeed. Given system S, let F be a predicate that applies to all and only things at worlds where S holds. Take F as primitive, and axiomatize S (or an equivalent thereof) by the single axiom $\forall x Fx$. If utter simplicity is so easily attained, the ideal theory may as well be as strong as possible. Simplicity and strength needn't be traded off. Then the ideal theory will include (its simple axiom will strictly imply) all truths, and *a fortiori* all regularities. Then, after all, every regularity will be a law. That must be wrong.

The remedy, of course, is not to tolerate such a perverse choice of primitive vocabulary. We should ask how candidate systems compare in simplicity when each is formulated in the simplest eligible way; or, if we count different formulations as different systems, we should dismiss the ineligible ones from candidacy. An appropriate standard of eligibility is not far to seek: let the primitive vocabulary that appears in the axioms refer only to perfectly natural properties.

Of course, it remains an unsolved and difficult problem to say what simplicity of a formulation is. But it is no longer the downright insoluble problem that it would be if there were nothing to choose between alternative primitive vocabularies.

(One might think also to replace strict implication by deducibility in some specified calculus. But this second remedy seems unnecessary given the first, and seems incapable of solving our problem by itself.)

If we adopt the remedy proposed, it will have the consequence that laws will tend to be regularities involving natural properties. Fundamental laws, those that the ideal system takes as axiomatic, must concern perfectly natural properties. Derived laws that follow fairly straightforwardly also will tend to concern fairly natural properties. Regularities concerning unnatural properties may indeed be strictly implied, and should count as derived laws if so. But they are apt to escape notice even if we someday possess a good approximation to the ideal system. For they will be hard to express in a language that has words mostly for not-too-unnatural properties, as any language must. (See the next section.) And they will be hard to derive, indeed they may not be finitely derivable at all, in our deductive calculi. Thus my account explains, as Armstrong's does in its very different way, why the scientific investigation of laws and of natural properties is a package deal; why physicists posit natural properties such as the quark colours in order to posit the laws in which those properties figure, so that laws and natural properties get discovered together.

If the analysis of lawhood requires natural properties, then so does the analysis of causation. It is fairly uncontroversial that causation involves laws. That is so according to both of the leading theories of causation: the deductive-nomological analysis, on which the laws are applied to the actual course of events with the cause and effect present; and the counterfactual analysis that I favour, on which the laws are applied to counterfactual situations with the cause hypothesized away. These counterfactual alternatives may need to break actual laws at the point where they diverge from actuality, but the analysis requires that they evolve thereafter in accordance with the actual laws.[40]

According to my counterfactual analysis, causation involves natural properties in a second way too. We need the kind of counterfactuals that avoid backtracking; or else the analysis faces fatal counterexamples involving epiphenomenal side-effects or cases of causal pre-emption. As I have already noted, these counterfactuals are to be characterized in terms of divergent worlds, hence in terms of duplicate initial world-segments, hence in terms of shared natural properties.

Causation involves natural properties in yet another way. (Small wonder that I came to appreciate natural properties after working on the analysis of causation!) Causation holds between events. Unless we distinguish genuine from spurious events, we will be left with too many putative causes. You put a lump of butter in a skillet, and the butter melts. What event causes this? There is one event that we can call a moving of molecules. It occurs in the region where the skillet is, just before the butter melts. This is an event such that, necessarily, it occurs in a spatiotemporal region only if that region contains rapidly moving molecules. Surely this event is a cause of the melting of the butter.

Heat is that phenomenon, whatever it may be, that manifests itself in certain familiar characteristic ways. Let us say: heat is that which occupies the heat-role. (It won't matter whether we take the definite description plain, as I prefer, or rigidified.) In fact, but contingently, it is molecular motion that occupies the heat-role. It might have been molecular non-motion, or caloric fluid, or what you will. Now consider an alleged second event, one that we may call a having-the-occupant-of-the-heat-role. This second event occurs just when and where the first does, in the region where the hot skillet is. It occurs there in virtue of the two facts (1) that the skillet's molecules are moving rapidly, and (2) that the region in question is part of a world where molecular motion is what occupies the heat-role. But this second event differs from the first. The necessary conditions for its occurrence are different. Necessarily, it occurs in a region only if that region contains whatever phenomenon occupies the heat-role in the world of which that region is part. So in those worlds where caloric fluid occupies the heat-role and molecular motion does not, the first event occurs only in regions with molecular motion whereas the second occurs only in regions with caloric fluid.

Certainly the first event causes the melting of the butter, but shall we say that the second event does so as well? No; that seems to multiply causes beyond belief by playing a verbal trick. But if there really are two events here, I cannot see why the second has less of a claim than the first to be a cause of the melting of the butter. It is out of the question to say that the first and the second events are one and the same – then this one event would have different conditions of occurrence from itself. The best solution is to deny that the alleged second event is a genuine event at all. If it isn't, of course it can't do any causing.

Why is the first event genuine and the second spurious? Compare the properties involved: containing rapidly moving molecules versus containing whatever phenomenon occupies the heat-role. (I mean these as properties of the spatiotemporal region; other treatments of events would take instead the corresponding properties of the skillet, but my point would still apply.) The first is a fairly natural, intrinsic property. The second is highly disjunctive and extrinsic. For all sorts of different phenomena could occupy the heat-role; and whether the phenomenon going on in a region occupies the role depends not only on what goes on in the region but also on what goes on elsewhere in the same world. Thus the distinction between more and less natural properties gives me the distinction between genuine and spurious events that I need in order to disown an overabundance of causes. If a property is too unnatural, it is inefficacious in the sense that it cannot figure in the conditions of occurrence of the events that cause things.[41]

The Content of Language and Thought

Hilary Putnam has given an argument which he regards as a refutation of a 'radically non-epistemic' view of truth, but which I regard rather as a *reductio* against Putnam's premises.[42] In particular, it refutes his assumption that '*we* interpret our languages or nothing does,'[43] so that any constraint on reference must be established by our own stipulation in language or thought. Gary Merrill has suggested that Putnam may be answered by appeal to a constraint that depends on an objective structure of properties and relations in the world.[44]

I agree, and find here another point at which we need natural properties.

Putnam's argument, as I understand it, is as follows. First, suppose that the only constraint on interpretation of our language (or perhaps our language of thought) is given by a description theory of reference of a global and futuristic sort. An 'intended interpretation' is any interpretation that satisfies a certain body of theory: viz., the idealized descendant of our current total theory that would emerge at the end of inquiry, an ideal theory refined to perfection under the guidance of all needed observation and our best theoretical reasoning. If so, intended interpretations are surprisingly abundant. For *any* world can satisfy *any* theory (ideal or not), and can do so in countless very different ways, provided only that the world is not too small and the theory is consistent. Beyond that, it doesn't matter what the world is like or what the theory says. Hence we have radical indeterminacy of reference. And we have the coincidence that Putnam welcomes between satisfaction under all intended intrepretations and 'epistemic truth'. For the ideal theory is the whole of 'epistemic truth', the intended interpretations are just those interpretations of our language that satisfy the ideal theory, and (unless the world is too small or ideal theory is inconsistent) there are some such interpretations.

I take this to refute the supposition that there are no further constraints on reference. But Putnam asks: how *could* there be a further constraint? How could we ever establish it? By stipulation, by saying or thinking something. But whatever we say or think will be in language (or language of thought) that suffers from radical indeterminacy of interpretation. For the saving constraint will not be there until we succeed in establishing it. So the attempted stipulation must fail. The most we can do is to contribute a new chapter to current and ideal theory, a chapter consisting of whatever we said or thought in our stipulation. And this new theory goes the way of all theory. So we cannot establish a further constraint; and 'we interpret our language or nothing does'; so there cannot be any further constraint. We cannot lift ourselves by our bootstraps, so we must still be on the ground.

Indeed we cannot lift ourselves by our bootstraps, but we are off the ground, so there must be another way to fly. Our language

does have a fairly determinate interpretation (a Moorean fact!) so there must be some constraint not created *ex nihilo* by our stipulation.

What can it be? Many philosophers would suggest that it is some sort of causal constraint. If so, my case is made, given my arguments in the previous section: we need natural properties to explain determinacy of interpretation. But I doubt that it really is a causal constraint, for I am inclined to think that the causal aspect of reference *is* established by what we say and think. Thus: I think of a thing as that which I am causally acquainted with in such-and-such way, perhaps perceptually or perhaps through a channel of acquaintance that involves the naming of the thing and my picking up of the name. I refer to that thing in my thought, and derivatively in language, because it is the thing that fits this causal and egocentric description extracted from my theory of the world and of my place in the world.[45]

I would instead propose that the saving constraint concerns the referent – not the referrer, and not the causal channels between the two. It takes two to make a reference, and we will not find the constraint if we look for it always on the wrong side of the relationship. Reference consists in part of what we do in language or thought when we refer, but in part it consists in eligibility of the referent. And this eligibility to be referred to is a matter of natural properties.

That is the suggestion Merrill offers. (He offers it not as his own view, but as what opponents of Putnam ought to say; and I gratefully accept the offer.) In the simplest case, suppose that the interpretation of the logical vocabulary somehow takes care of itself, to reveal a standard first-order language whose non-logical vocabulary consists entirely of predicates. The parts of the world comprise a domain; and sets, sets of pairs, ..., from this domain are potential extensions for the predicates. Now suppose we have an all-or-nothing division of properties into natural and unnatural. Say that a set from the domain is *eligible* to be the extension of a one-place predicate iff its members are just those things in the domain that share some natural property; and likewise for many-place predicates and natural relations. An *eligible interpretation* is one that assigns none but eligible extensions to the predicates. A so-called 'intended' interpretation is an eligible interpretation that satisfies the ideal theory. (But the name is misleading: it is not to be said that our intentions establish the constraint requiring eligibility. That way lies the futile bootstrap-tugging that we must avoid.) Then if the natural properties are sparse, there is no reason to expect any overabundance of intended interpretations. There may even be none. Even ideal theory runs the risk of being unsatisfiable, save in 'unintended' ways. Because satisfaction is not guaranteed, we accomplish something if we manage to achieve it by making a good fit between theory and the world. All this is as it should be.

The proposal calls for refinement. First, we need to provide for richer forms of language. In this we can be guided by familiar translations, for instance between modal language with higher-order quantification and first-order language that explicitly mentions *possibilia* and classes built up from them. Second, it will not do to take naturalness of properties as all-or-nothing. Here, above all, we need to make naturalness – and hence eligibility – a comparative matter, or a matter of degree. There are salient sharp lines, but not in the right places. There is the line between the perfectly natural properties and all the rest, but surely we have predicates for much-less-than-perfectly natural properties. There is the line between properties that are and that are not finitely analysable in terms of perfectly natural properties, but that lets in enough highly unnatural properties that it threatens not to solve our problem. We need gradations; and we need some give and take between the eligibility of referents and the other factors that make for 'intendedness', notably satisfaction of appropriate bits of theory. (Ideal theory, if we keep as much of Putnam's story as we can.) Grueness is not an absolutely ineligible referent (as witness my reference to it just now), but an interpretation that assigns it is to that extent inferior to one that assigns blueness instead. *Ceteris paribus*, the latter is the 'intended' one, just because it does better on eligibility.

Naturalness of properties makes for differences of eligibility not only among the properties themselves, but also among things. Compare Bruce with the cat-shaped chunk of miscellaneous and ever-changing matter that follows him around, always a few steps behind. The former is a highly eligible referent, the latter is not. (I haven't succeeded in referring to it, for I didn't say just which such chunk 'it' was to be.) That is because

Bruce, unlike the cat-shaped chunk, has a boundary well demarcated by differences in highly natural properties. Where Bruce ends, there the density of matter, the relative abundance of the chemical elements, …abruptly change. Not so for the chunk. Bruce is also much more of a locus of causal chains than is the chunk; this too traces back to natural properties, by the considerations of the previous section. Thus naturalness of properties sets up distinctions among things. The reverse happens also. Once we are away from the perfectly natural properties, one thing that makes for naturalness of a property is that it is a property belonging exclusively to well-demarcated things.

You might well protest that Putnam's problem is misconceived, wherefore no need has been demonstrated for resources to solve it. Putnam seems to conceive of language entirely as a repository of theory, and not at all as a practice of social interaction. We have the language of the encyclopedia, but where is the language of the pub? Where are the communicative intentions and the mutual expectations that seem to have so much to do with what we mean? In fact, where is thought? It seems to enter the picture, if at all, only as the special case where the language to be interpreted is hard-wired, unspoken, hidden, and all too conjectural.

I think the point is well taken, but I think it doesn't matter. If the problem of intentionality is rightly posed, there will still be a threat of radical indeterminacy, there will still be a need for saving constraints, there will still be a remedy analogous to Merrill's suggested answer to Putnam, and there will still be a need for natural properties.

Set language aside and consider instead the interpretation of thought. (Afterward we can hope to interpret the subject's language in terms of his beliefs and desires regarding verbal communication with others.) The subject is in various states, and could be in various others, that are causally related to each other, to the subject's behaviour, and to the nearby environment that stimulates his senses. These states fit into a functional organization, they occupy certain causal roles. (Most likely they are states of the brain. Maybe they involve something that is language-like but hard-wired, maybe not. But the nature of the states is beside the point.) The states have their functional roles in the subject as he now is, and in the subject as he is at other times and as he might have been under other circumstances, and even in other creatures of the same kind as the subject. Given the functional roles of the states, the problem is to assign them content. Propositional content, some would say; but I would agree only if the propositions can be taken as egocentric ones, and I think an 'egocentric proposition' is simply a property. States indexed by content can be identified as a belief that this, a desire for that, a perceptual experience of seeming to confront so-and-so, an intention to do such-and-such. (But not all ordinary ascriptions of attitudes merely specify the content of the subject's states. Fred and Ted might be alike in the functional roles of their states, and hence have states with the same content in the narrowly psychological sense that is my present concern, and hence believe alike, e.g., by each believing himself to have heard of a pretty town named 'Castlemaine'. Yet they might be acquainted via that name with different towns, at opposite ends of the earth, so that Fred and not Ted believes that Castlemaine, Victoria, is pretty.) The problem of assigning content to functionally characterized states is to be solved by means of constraining principles. Foremost among these are principles of fit. If a state is to be interpreted as an intention to raise one's hand, it had better typically cause the hand to go up. If a state (or complex of states) is to be interpreted as a system of beliefs and desires – or better, degrees of belief and desire – according to which raising one's hand would be a good means to one's ends, and if another state is to be interpreted as an intention to raise one's hand, then the former had better typically cause the latter. Likewise on the input side. A state typically caused by round things before the eyes is a good candidate for interpretation as the visual experience of confronting something round; and its typical impact on the states interpreted as systems of belief ought to be interpreted as the exogenous addition of a belief that one is confronting something round, with whatever adjustment that addition calls for.

So far, so good. But it seems clear that preposterous and perverse misinterpretations could nevertheless cohere, could manage to fit the functional roles of the states because misassignment of content at one point compensates for misassignment at another. Let us see just how this could

happen, at least under an oversimplified picture of interpretation as follows. An interpretation is given by a pair of functions C and V. C is a probability distribution over the worlds, regarded as encapsulating the subject's dispositions to form beliefs under the impact of sensory evidence: if a stream of evidence specified by proposition E would put the subject into a total state S – for short, if E yields S – we interpret S to consist in part of the belief system given by the probability distribution $C(-/E)$ that comes from C by conditionalizing on E. V is a function from worlds to numerical desirability scores, regarded as encapsulating the subject's basic values: if E yields S, we interpret S to consist in part of the system of desires given by the $C(-/E)$-expectations of V. Say that C and V *rationalize* behaviour B after evidence E iff the system of desires given by the $C(-/E)$-expectations of V ranks B at least as high as any alternative behaviour. Say that C and V *fit* iff, for any evidence-specifying E, E yields a state that would cause behaviour rationalized by C and V after E. That is our only constraining principle of fit. (Where did the others go? – We built them into the definitions whereby C and V encapsulate an assignment of content to various states.) Then any two interpretations that always rationalize the same behaviour after the same evidence must fit equally well. Call two worlds *equivalent* iff they are alike in respect of the subject's evidence and behaviour, and note that any decent world is equivalent *inter alia* to horrendously counterinductive worlds and to worlds where everything unobserved by the subject is horrendously nasty. Fit depends on the total of C for each equivalence class, and on the C-expectation of V within each class, but that is all. Within a class, it makes no difference which world gets which pair of values of C and V. We can interchange equivalent worlds *ad lib* and preserve fit. So, given any fitting and reasonable interpretation, we can transform it into an equally fitting perverse interpretation by swapping equivalent worlds around so as to enhance the probabilities of counterinductive worlds, or the desirabilities of nasty worlds, or both. *Quod erat demonstrandum.*

(My simplifications were dire: I left out the egocentricity of belief and desire and evidence, the causal aspect of rationalized behaviour, the role of intentions, change of basic values, limitations of logical competence, ... But I doubt that these omissions matter to my conclusion.

I conjecture that if they were remedied, we could still transform reasonable interpretations into perverse ones in a way that preserves fit.)

If we rely on principles of fit to do the whole job, we can expect radical indeterminacy of interpretation. We need further constraints, of the sort called principles of (sophisticated) charity, or of 'humanity'.[46] Such principles call for interpretations according to which the subject has attitudes that we would deem reasonable for one who has lived the life that he has lived. (Unlike principles of crude charity, they call for imputations of error if he has lived under deceptive conditions.) These principles select among conflicting interpretations that equally well conform to the principles of fit. They impose a priori – albeit defeasible – presumptions about what sorts of things are apt to be believed and desired; or rather, about what dispositions to develop beliefs and desires, what inductive biases and basic values, someone may rightly be interpreted to have.

It is here that we need natural properties. The principles of charity will impute a bias toward believing that things are green rather than grue, toward having a basic desire for long life rather than for long-life-unless-one-was-born-on-Monday-and-in-that-case-life-for-an-even-number-of-weeks. In short, they will impute eligible content, where ineligibility consists in severe unnaturalness of the properties the subject supposedly believes or desires or intends himself to have. They will impute other things as well, but it is the imputed eligibility that matters to us at present.

Thus the threat of radical indeterminacy in the assignment of content to thought is fended off. The saving constraint concerns the content – not the thinker, and not any channels between the two. It takes two to index states with content, and we will not find the constraint if we look for it always on the wrong side of the relationship. Believing this or desiring that consists in part in the functional roles of the states whereby we believe or desire, but in part it consists in the eligibility of the content. And this eligibility to be thought is a matter, in part, of natural properties.

Consider the puzzle whereby Kripke illustrates Wittgenstein's paradox that 'no course of action could be determined by a rule, because every course of action can be made out to accord with the rule'.[47] A well-educated person working

arithmetic problems intends to perform addition when he sees the '+' sign. He does not intend to perform quaddition, which is just like addition for small numbers but which yields the answer 5 if any of the numbers to be quadded exceeds a certain bound. Wherefore does he intend to add and not to quadd? Whatever he says and whatever is written in his brain can be perversely (mis)interpreted as instructing him to quadd. And it is not enough to say that his brain state is the causal basis of a disposition to add. Perhaps it isn't. Perhaps if a test case arose, he would abandon his intention, he would neither add nor quadd but instead would put his homework aside and complain that the problems are too hard.

The naïve solution is that adding means going on in the same way as before when the numbers get big, whereas quadding means doing something different; there is nothing present in the subject that constitutes an intention to do different things in different cases; therefore he intends addition, not quaddition. We should not scoff at this naïve response. It is the correct solution to the puzzle. But we must pay to regain our naïveté. Our theory of properties must have adequate resources to somehow ratify the judgement that instances of adding are all alike in a way that instances of quadding are not. The property of adding is not perfectly natural, of course, not on a par with unit charge or sphericality. And the property of quadding is not perfectly unnatural. But quadding is worse by a disjunction. So quaddition is to that extent less of a way to go on doing the same, and therefore it is to that extent less of an eligible thing to intend to do.

It's not that you couldn't possibly intend to quadd. You could. Suppose that today there is as much basis as there ever is to interpret you as intending to add and as meaning addition by your word 'addition' and quaddition by 'quaddition'; and tomorrow you say to yourself in so many words that it would be fun to tease the philosophers by taking up quaddition henceforth, and you make up your mind to do it. But you have to go out of your way. Adding and quadding aren't on a par. To intend to add, you need only have states that would fit either interpretation and leave it to charity to decree that you have the more eligible intention. To intend to quadd, you must say or think something that creates difficulties of fit for the more eligible intention and thereby defeats the presumption in its favour. You must do something that, taking principles of fit and presumptions of eligibility and other principles of charity together, tilts the balance in favour of an interpretation on which you intend to quadd. How ironic that we were worried to find nothing positive to settle the matter in favour of addition! For the lack of anything positive that points either way just *is* what it takes to favour addition. Quaddition, being less natural and eligible, needs something positive in its favour. Addition can win by default.

What is the status of the principles that constrain interpretation, in particular the charitable presumption in favour of eligible content? We must shun several misunderstandings. It is not to be said (1) that as a contingent psychological fact, the contents of our states turn out to be fairly eligible, we mostly believe and desire ourselves to have not-too-unnatural properties. Still less should it be said (2) that we should daringly presuppose this in our interpreting of one another, even if we haven't a shred of evidence for it. Nor should it be said (3) that as a contingent psychological fact we turn out to have states whose content involves some properties rather than others, and that is what makes it so that the former properties are more natural. (This would be a psychologistic theory of naturalness.) The error is the same in all three cases. It is supposed, wrongly as I think, that the problem of interpretation can be solved without bringing to it the distinction between natural and unnatural properties; so that the natural properties might or might not turn out to be the ones featured in the content of thought according to the correct solution, or so that they can afterward be defined as the ones that are so featured. I think this is over-optimistic. We have no notion how to solve the problem of interpretation while regarding all properties as equally eligible to feature in content. For that would be to solve it without enough constraints. Only if we have an independent, objective distinction among properties, and we impose the presumption in favour of eligible content a priori as a constitutive constraint, does the problem of interpretation have any solution at all. If so, then any correct solution must automatically respect the presumption. There's no contingent fact of psychology here to be believed, either on evidence or daringly.

Compare our selective and collective theory of lawhood: lawhood of a regularity just consists in its fitting into an ideally high-scoring system, so it's inevitable that laws turn out to have what it takes to make for high scores. Likewise, I have suggested, contenthood just consists in getting assigned by a high-scoring interpretation, so it's inevitable that contents tend to have what it takes to make for high scores. And in both cases, I've suggested that part of what it takes is naturalness of the properties involved. The reason natural properties feature in the contents of our attitudes is that naturalness is part of what it is to feature therein. It's not that we're built to take a special interest in natural properties, or that we confer naturalness on properties when we happen to take an interest in them.

Notes

I am indebted to comments by Gilbert Harman, Lloyd Humberstone, Frank Jackson, Mark Johnston, Donald Morrison, Kim Sterelny, and others; and especially to discussion and correspondence with D. M. Armstrong over several years, without which I might well have believed to this day that set theory applied to *possibilia* is all the theory of properties that anyone could ever need.

1 D. M. Armstrong, *Universals and Scientific Realism* (Cambridge: Cambridge University Press, 1978), henceforth cited as *Universals*; see also his 'Against "ostrich" nominalism: a reply to Michael Devitt.' *Pacific Philosophical Quarterly* 61 (1980), pp. 440–9.

2 Here I follow Armstrong's traditional terminology: 'universals' are repeatable entities, wholly present wherever a particular instantiates them; 'Nominalism' is the rejection of such entities. In the conflicting modern terminology of Harvard, classes count as 'universals' and 'Nominalism' is predominantly the rejection of classes. Confusion of the terminologies can result in grave misunderstanding; see W. V. Quine, 'Soft impeachment disowned', *Pacific Philosophical Quarterly* 61 (1980), pp. 450–1.

3 Among 'things' I mean to include all the gerrymandered wholes and undemarcated parts admitted by the most permissive sort of mereology. Further, I include such physical objects as spatiotemporal regions and force fields, unless an eliminative reduction of them should prove desirable. Further, I include such non-physical objects as gods and

spooks, though not – I hope – as parts of the same world as us. Worlds themselves need no special treatment. They are things – big ones, for the most part.

4   My conception of properties resembles the doctrine of Class Nominalism considered in *Universals*, vol. 1, pp. 28–43. But, strictly speaking, a Class Nominalist would be someone who claims to solve the One over Many problem simply by means of properties taken as classes, and that is far from my intention.

5   *Universals*, vol. 1, p. 109.

6   If universals are to do the new work I have in store for them, they must be capable of repeated occurrence not only within a world but also across worlds. They would then be an exception to my usual principle – meant for particulars, of course – that nothing is wholly present as part of two different worlds. But I see no harm in that. If two worlds are said to overlap by having a coin in common, and if this coin is supposed to be wholly round in one world and wholly octagonal in the other, I stubbornly ask what shape it is, and insist that shape is not a relation to worlds. (See my 'Individuation by acquaintance and by stipulation', *Philosophical Review* 92 (1983), pp. 3–32.) I do not see any parallel objection if worlds are said to overlap by sharing a universal. What contingent, non-relational property of the universal could we put in place of shape of the coin in raising the problem? I cannot think of any.

7   See *Universals*, vol. 2, pp. 30–42 and 67–71.

8   See ibid., vol. 1, pp. 38–41; Anthony Quinton, 'Properties and classes', *Proceedings of the Aristotelian Society* 48 (1957), pp. 33–58; and W. V. Quine, 'Natural kinds', this volume, ch. 20. See also George Bealer, *Quality and Concept* (Oxford: Oxford University Press, 1982), esp. pp. 9–10 and 177–87. Like me, Bealer favours an inegalitarian twofold conception of properties: there are abundant 'concepts' and sparse 'qualities', and the latter are the ones that 'determine the logical, causal, and phenomenal order of reality' (p. 10). Despite this point of agreement, however, Bealer's views and mine differ in many ways.

9   Here I assume that some solution to the problem of resemblance of universals is possible, perhaps along the lines suggested by Armstrong in *Universals*, vol. 2, pp. 48–52 and 101–31; and that such a solution could be carried over into a theory of resemblance of perfectly natural properties, even if we take naturalness of properties as primitive.

10 This is the Moderate Class Nominalism considered in ibid., vol. 1, pp. 38–41. It is akin to the view of Quinton, 'Properties and classes'; but plus the unactualized members of the natural classes, and minus any hint that 'natural' could receive a psychologistic analysis.

11 Such a theory is a form of Resemblance Nominalism, in Armstrong's classification, but it is unlike the form that he principally considers. See *Universals*, vol. 1, pp. 44–63. For discussions of the problem of defining natural classes in terms of resemblance, and of the trickery that proves useful in solving this problem, see Nelson Goodman, *The Structure of Appearance* (Cambridge, Mass.: Harvard University Press, 1951), chs 4–6; Quine, this vol., ch. 18; and Adam Morton, 'Complex individuals and multigrade relations', *Noûs* 9 (1975), pp. 309–18.

To get from primitive resemblance to perfectly natural properties, I have in mind a definition as follows. We begin with R as our contrastive and variably polyadic primitive. We want it to turn out that $x_1, x_2, \ldots Ry_1, y_2, \ldots$ iff some perfectly natural property is shared by all of $x_1, x_2, \ldots$ but by none of $y_1, y_2, \ldots$. We want to define N, another variably polyadic predicate, so that it will turn out that $Nx_1, x_2, \ldots$ iff $x_1, x_2, \ldots$ are all and only the members of some perfectly natural property. Again we must allow for, and expect, the case where there are infinitely many x's. We define $Nx_1, x_2, \ldots$ as:

$$\exists y_1, y_2, \ldots \forall z(z, x_1, x_2, \ldots Ry_1, y_2, \ldots \equiv$$
$$z = x_1 \vee z = x_2 \vee \ldots).$$

Then we finish the job by defining a perfectly natural property as a class such that, if $x_1, x_2, \ldots$ are all and only its members, then $Nx_1, x_2, \ldots$.

We might have taken N as primitive instead of R. But would that have been significantly different, given the interdefinability of the two? On the other hand, taking N as primitive also seems not significantly different from taking perfect naturalness of classes as primitive. It is only a difference between speaking in the plural of individuals and speaking in the singular of their classes, and that seems no real difference. Is plural talk a disguised form of class talk? Or vice versa? (See the discussion in *Universals*, vol. 1, pp. 32–4; also Max Black, 'The elusiveness of sets', *Review of Metaphysics* 24 (1971), pp. 614–36; Eric Stenius, 'Sets', *Synthese* 27 (1974), pp. 161–88; and Kurt Gödel, 'Russell's mathematical logic', in P. A. Schilpp (ed.), *The Philosophy of Bertrand Russell* (Cambridge: Cambridge University Press, 1944).) At any rate, it is not at all clear to me that Moderate Class Nominalism and Resemblance Nominalism in its present form are two different theories, as opposed to a single theory presented in different styles.

12 In virtue of the close resemblance of red and orange, it is possible for a red thing to resemble an orange one very closely; it is not possible for a red thing to resemble a blue one quite so closely. Given our ontology of *possibilia*, all possibilities are realized. So we could paraphase (1) by

(1′) Some red thing resembles some orange thing more than any red thing resembles any blue thing.

so long as it is understood that the things in question needn't be part of our world, or of any one world. Or if we did not wish to speak of unactualized things, but we were willing to take ordinary-language modal idioms as primitive, we could instead give the paraphrase:

(1″) A red thing can resemble an orange thing more closely than a red thing can resemble a blue thing.

It is necessary to use the ordinary-language idioms, or some adequate formalization of them, rather than standard modal logic. You cannot express (1″) in modal logic (excluding an enriched modal logic that would defeat the point of the paraphrase by quantifying over degrees of resemblance or whatnot) because you cannot express cross-world relations, and in particular cannot express the needed cross-world comparison of similarity.

13 *Universals*, vol. 1, pp. 58–63; also his 'Against "ostrich" nominalism'. He derives the argument, and a second semantic argument to be considered shortly, from Arthur Pap, 'Nominalism, empiricism, and universals: I, *Philosophical Quarterly* 9 (1959), pp. 330–40, and F. C. Jackson, 'Statements about universals', *Mind* 86 (1977), pp. 427–9.

14 *Universals*, vol. 1, p. 61.

15 Or better, in the case of creatures of his kind. See my 'Mad pain and Martian pain', in Ned Block (ed.), *Readings in Philosophy of Psychology*, vol. 1 (Cambridge, Mass.: Harvard University Press, 1980).

16 Armstrong again agrees: *Universals*, vol. 1, p. 63.

17 See my 'Attitudes *de dicto* and *de se*', *Philosophical Review* 88 (1979), pp. 513–43; and 'Individuation by acquaintance and by stipulation'.

18 *Universals*, vol. 1, pp. 11–16.

19 Ibid., p. 12.

20 Ibid., pp. 16–17.

21 Let S be the syntactic category of sentences, let N be the category of names, and for any categories x and y, let x/y be the category of expressions that attach to y-expressions to make x-expressions. Predicates, then, are category S/N. (Or $(S/N)/N$ for two-place predicates, and so on.) To embed names (or variables in the category of names) into sentences without primitive predication, take any category Q which is neither S nor N, nor S/N, and let there be primitives of categories Q/N and S/Q. Or take Q_1 and Q_2, different from S and N and S/N and each other, and let the primitives be of categories Q_1/N, Q_2/Q_1, and S/Q_2. Or .... I cannot see how this trickery could be a genuine alternative to, rather than a disguise for, primitive predication.

22 *Universals*, vol. 1, p. 109.

23 Compare Armstrong on Quine's treatment of predication, 'Against "ostrich" nominalism', p. 443.

24 Michael Devitt, '"Ostrich nominalism" or "mirage realism"?', *Pacific Philosophical Quarterly* 61 (1980), pp. 433–9. Devitt speaks on behalf of Quine as well as himself; Quine indicates agreement with Devitt in 'Soft impeachment disowned'.

25 Given duplication, we can also subdivide the extrinsic properties, distinguishing pure cases from various mixtures of extrinsic and intrinsic. Partition the things, of this and other worlds, into equivalence classes under the relation of duplication. A property may divide an equivalence class, may include it, or may exclude it. A property P is extrinsic, as we said, if it divides at least some of the classes. We have four subcases. (1) P divides every class; then we may call P *purely extrinsic*. (2) P divides some classes, includes some, and excludes none; then P is the disjunction of an intrinsic property and a purely extrinsic property. (3) P divides some, excludes some, and includes none; then P is the conjunction of an intrinsic property and a purely extrinsic property. (4) P divides some, includes some, and excludes some; then P is the conjunction of an intrinsic property and an impurely extrinsic property of the sort considered in the second case, or equivalently is the disjunction of an intrinsic property and an impurely extrinsic property of the sort considered in the third case.

We can also classify relations as intrinsic or extrinsic, but in two different ways. Take a dyadic relation, i.e. a class of ordered pairs. Call the relation *intrinsic to its relata* iff, whenever a and a' are duplicates (or identical) and b and b' are duplicates (or identical), then both or neither of the pairs $<a, b>$ and $<a', b'>$ stand in the relation. Call the relation *intrinsic to its pairs* iff, whenever the pairs $<a, b>$ and $<a', b'>$ themselves are duplicates, then both or neither of them stand in the relation. In the second case, a stronger requirement is imposed on the pairs. For instance they might fail to he duplicate pairs because the distance between *a* and *b* differs from the distance between *a′* and *b′*, even though *a* and *a′* are duplicates and *b* and *b′* are duplicates. In traditional terminology, 'internal relations' are intrinsic to their *relata*; 'external relations' are intrinsic to their pairs but not to their *relata*; and relations extrinsic even to their pairs, such as the relation of belonging to the same owner, get left out of the classification altogether.

Our definition of intrinsic properties in terms of duplication closely resembles the definition of 'differential properties' given by Michael Slote in 'Some thoughts on Goodman's riddle', *Analysis* 27 (1967), pp. 128–32, and in *Reason and Scepticism* (London: George Allen & Unwin, 1970). But where I quantify over *possibilia*, Slote applies modality to ordinary, presumably actualist, quantifiers. That makes a difference. An extrinsic property might differ between duplicates, but only when the duplicates inhabit different worlds; then Slote would count the property as differential. An example is the property of being a sphere that inhabits a world where there are pigs or a cube that inhabits a world without pigs.

See my 'Extrinsic properties', *Philosophical Studies* 44 (1983), pp. 197–200 for further discussion of the circle from duplication to intrinsicness and back.

26 Likewise <*a*, *b*> and <*a′*, *b′*> are duplicate pairs iff *a* and *a′* have exactly the same perfectly natural properties, and so do *b* and *b′*, and also the perfectly natural relations between *a* and *b* are exactly the same as those between *a′* and *b′*.

27 See *Universals*, vol. 2, pp. 78–9.

28 For a general discussion of supervenience, see Jaegwon Kim, 'Supervenience and nomological incommensurables', *American Philosophical Quarterly* 15 (1978), pp. 149–56.

29 Such a thesis of supervenience of the global on the local resembles the 'holographic hypothesis' considered and rejected by Saul Kripke in 'Identity through Time', presented at the 1979 conference of the American Philosophical Association, Eastern Division, and elsewhere.

30 This approach is due, in essence, to Richard Montague, 'Deterministic theories', in *Decisions, Values and Groups*, vol. 2 (Oxford: Pergamon Press, 1962), and in his *Formal Philosophy* (New Haven: Yale University Press, 1974). But Montague did not speak as I have done of duplication of initial segments of worlds in virtue of the sharing of certain élite properties. Instead, he used sameness of description in a certain vocabulary, which vocabulary was left as an unspecified parameter of his analysis. For he wrote as a logician obliged to remain neutral on questions of metaphysics.

31 A closely related definition appears in Peter van Inwagen, 'The incompatibility of free will and determinism', *Philosophical Studies* 27 (1975), pp. 185–99.

32 See my 'Counterfactual dependence and time's arrow', *Noûs* 13 (1979), pp. 455–76; Jonathan Bennett's review of my *Counterfactuals*, *Canadian Journal of Philosophy* 4 (1974), pp. 381–402; P. B. Downing, 'Subjunctive conditionals, time order, and causation', *Proceedings of the Aristotelian Society* 59 (1959), pp. 125–40; Allan Gibbard and William Harper, 'Counterfactuals and two kinds of expected utility', in C. A. Hooker, J. T. Leach, and E. F. McClennen (eds), *Foundations and Applications of Decision Theory* (Dordrecht: Reidel, 1978), and in W. L. Harper, R. Stalnaker, and G. Pearce (eds), *Ifs* (Dordrecht: Reidel, 1981); and Frank Jackson, 'A causal theory of counterfactuals', *Australasian Journal of Philosophy* 55 (1977), pp. 3–21.

33 This objection against M4 as a formulation of 'the ontological primacy of the microphysical' appears in Terence Horgan, 'Supervenience and microphysics', *Pacific Philosophical Quarterly* 63 (1982), pp. 29–43.

34 See *Universals*, vol. 2, pp. 30–42 and 67–71.

35 This formulation resembles one proposed by Horgan, 'Supervenience and microphysics'. The principal difference is as follows. Horgan would count as alien (my term, not his) any property cited in the fundamental laws of otherworldly microphysics that is not also explicitly cited in the fundamental laws of this-worldly microphysics. Whether the property is instantiated in either world doesn't enter into it. But must an alien property figure in laws of otherworldly *physics*? Must it figure in any otherworldly laws at all? It seems that a Materialistic world might differ without differing physically from a world where there are properties alien in my sense but not in Horgan's – perhaps a world where laws are in short supply.

36 *Universals*, vol. 1, pp. 8–9 and *passim*.

37 Ibid., vol. 2, pp. 148–57. A more developed form of the theory appears in D. M. Armstrong, *What Is a Law of Nature?* (Cambridge: Cambridge University Press, 1983). Similar theories have been proposed in Fred I. Dretske, 'Laws of nature', *Philosophy of Science* 44 (1977), pp. 248–68, and in Michael Tooley, 'The nature of laws', *Canadian Journal of Philosophy* 4 (1977), pp. 667–98.

38 Armstrong's more developed theory in *What Is a Law of Nature?* complicates the picture in two ways. First, the second-order state of affairs $N(F, G)$ is itself taken to be a universal, and its presence

in its instances detracts yet further from the distinctness of the necessitating and the necessitated states of affairs. Second, all laws are defeasible. It is possible after all to have $N(F, G)$ and Fa without Ga, namely if we also have $N(E \mathrel{\&} F, H)$ and Ea, where H and G are incompatible. (The law that F's are G's might be *contingently* indefeasible, if no such defeating state of affairs $N(E \mathrel{\&} F, H)$ obtains; but no law has its indefeasibility built in essentially.) It remains true that there are alleged necessary connections that I find unintelligible, but they are more complicated than before. To necessitate a state of affairs, we need not only the first- and second-order states of affairs originally considered, but also a negative existential to the effect that there are no further states of affairs of the sort that could act as defeaters.

39 John Stuart Mill, *A System of Logic* (London: Parker, 1843), bk III, ch. 4, sect. 1; F. P. Ramsey, 'Universals of law and of fact', in his *Foundations* (London: Routledge & Kegan Paul, 1978). Ramsey regarded this theory of law as superseded by the different theory in his 'General propositions and causality', also in *Foundations*, but I prefer his first thoughts to his second. I present a theory of lawhood along the lines of Ramsey's earlier theory in my *Counterfactuals* (Oxford: Blackwell, 1973), pp. 73–5. A revision to that discussion is needed in the probabilistic case, which I here ignore.

40 See my 'Causation', this volume, ch. 29.

41 See the discussion of impotence of dispositions in Elizabeth W. Prior, Robert Pargetter, and Frank Jackson, 'Three theses about dispositions', *American Philosophical Quarterly* 19 (1982), pp. 251–7. If a disposition is not identified with its actual basis, there is a threat of multiplication of putative causes similar to that in my example. We would not wish to say that the breaking of a struck glass is caused both by its fragility and by the frozen-in stresses that are the basis thereof; and if forced to choose, we should choose the latter. I suggest that the fragility is inefficacious because it is too unnatural a property, too disjunctive and extrinsic, to figure in the conditions of occurence of any event.

42 Hilary Putnam, 'Realism and reason', in his *Meaning and the Moral Sciences* (London: Routledge & Kegan Paul, 1978), and 'Models and reality', *Journal of Symbolic Logic* 45 (1980), pp. 464–82. The reader is warned that the argument as I present it may not be quite as Putnam intended it to be. For I have made free in reading between the lines and in restating the argument in my own way.

43 Putnam, 'Models and reality', p. 482.

44 G. H. Merrill, 'The model-theoretic argument against realism', *Philosophy of Science* 47 (1980), pp. 69–81.

45 See Stephen Schiffer, 'The basis of reference', *Erkenntnis* 13 (1978), pp. 171–206.

46 See my 'Radical interpretation', *Synthese* 23 (1974), pp. 331–44; and Richard E. Grandy, 'Reference, meaning and belief', *Journal of Philosophy* 70 (1973), pp. 439–52.

47 See Saul A. Kripke, 'Wittgenstein on rules and private language: an elementary exposition', in Irving Block (ed.), *Perspectives on Wittgenstein* (Oxford: Blackwell, 1981).

24

Universals as Attributes

D. M. Armstrong

1 Uninstantiated Universals?

If we abandon the idea that particulars are nothing but bundles of universals but still want to recognize universals, then we must return to the traditional view that particulars, tokens, *instantiate* universals: having properties and standing to each other in relations. If we do this, then there are a number of controversial questions that have to be settled. One key question is this. Should we, or should we not, accept a Principle of Instantiation for universals? That is, should we, or should we not, demand that every universal be instantiated? That is, for each property universal must it be the case that it is a property of some particular? For each relation universal must it be the case that there are particulars between which the relation holds?

We certainly should not demand that every universal should be instantiated *now*. It would be enough if a particular universal was not instantiated now, but was instantiated in the past, or would be instantiated in the future. The Principle of Instantiation should be interpreted as ranging over all time: past, present, and future. But should we uphold the principle even in this relatively liberal form?

This is a big parting of the ways. We can call the view that there are uninstantiated universals the Platonist view. It appears to have been the view held by Plato, who was also, apparently, the first philosopher to introduce universals. (He spoke of Forms or Ideas – but there was nothing psychological about the Ideas.)

Once you have uninstantiated universals, you need somewhere special to put them, a "Platonic heaven," as philosophers often say. They are not to be found in the ordinary world of space and time. And since it seems that any instantiated universal might have been uninstantiated – for example, there might have been nothing past, present, or future that had that property – then if uninstantiated universals are in a Platonic heaven, it will be natural to place all universals in that heaven. The result is that we get two realms: the realm of universals and the realm of particulars, the latter being ordinary things in space and time. Such universals are often spoken of as *transcendent*. (A view of this sort was explicitly held by Russell in his earlier days before he adopted a bundle-of-universals view.[1]) Instantiation then becomes a very big deal: a relation between universals and particulars that crosses realms. The Latin tag used by the Scholastics for a theory of this sort is

D. M. Armstrong, "Universals as Attributes," originally published in D. M. Armstrong, *Universals: An Opinionated Introduction* (1989), ch. 5. Copyright by Westview Press. Reprinted by permission of the publisher.

Metaphysics: An Anthology, Second Edition. Edited by Jaegwon Kim, Daniel Z. Korman and Ernest Sosa.
Editorial material and organization © 2012 Blackwell Publishing Ltd. Published 2012 by Blackwell Publishing Ltd.

universalia ante res, "universals before things." Such a view is unacceptable to Naturalists, that is, to those who think that the space-time world is all the world that there is. This helps to explain why Empiricists, who tend to be sympathetic to Naturalism, often reject universals.

It is interesting to notice that a separate-realm theory of universals permits of a blob as opposed to a layer-cake view of particulars. For on this view, what is it for a thing to have a property? It is not the thing's having some internal feature, but rather its having a relationship, the instantiation relationship, to certain universals or Forms in another realm. The thing itself could be bloblike. It is true that the thing could also be given a property structure. But then the properties that make up this structure cannot be universals but must be particulars. They would have to be tropes. The particular involves property tropes, but these property tropes are put into natural classes by their instantiating a certain universal in the realm of the universals. At any rate, without bringing in tropes in addition, it seems that Platonic theories of universals have to treat particulars as bloblike rather than layer-caked. I think that this is an argument against Platonic theories.

If, however, we reject uninstantiated universals, then we are at least in a position, if we want to do it, to bring the universals down to earth. We can adopt the view whose Latin tag is *universalia in rebus*, "universals in things." We can think of a thing's properties as constituents of the thing and think of the properties as universals. This may have been the position of Aristotle. (The scholars differ. Some make him a Nominalist. Some think he believed in this-worldly universals. Certainly, he criticized Plato's otherworldly universals.) *Universalia in rebus* is, of course, a layer-cake view, with properties as universals as part of the internal structure of things. (Relations will be *universalia inter res*, "universals between things."[2])

There are difficulties in this position, of course, objections that can be brought, as with every other solution to the Problem of Universals. One thing that has worried many philosophers, including perhaps Plato, is that on this view we appear to have multiple location of the same thing. Suppose *a* is F and *b* is also F, with F a property universal. The very same entity has to be part of the structure of two things at two places.

How can the universal be in two places at once? I will come back to this question later.

Just to round things off, I will mention the third Scholastic tag: *universalia post res*, "universals after things." This was applied to Nominalist theories. It fits best with Predicate or Concept Nominalism, where properties, etc. are as it were created by the classifying mind: shadows cast on things by our predicates or concepts.

But our present task is to decide whether or not we ought to countenance uninstantiated universals. The first point to be made is that the onus of proof seems to be firmly on the side of the Platonists. It can hardly be doubted that there is a world of space and time. But a separate realm of universals is a mere hypothesis, or postulation. If a postulation has great explanatory value, then it may be a good postulation. But it has to prove itself. Why should we postulate uninstantiated universals?

One thing that has moved many philosophers is what we may call the argument from the meaning of general terms. Plato, in his *Republic*, had Socrates say, "shall we proceed as usual and begin by assuming the existence of a single essential nature or Form for every set of things which we call by the same name?"[3] Socrates may have been thinking along the following lines. Ordinary names, that is, proper names, have a bearer of the name. If we turn to general terms – words like 'horse' and 'triangular' that apply to many different things – then we need something that stands to the word in the same general sort of relation that the bearer of the proper name stands to the proper name. There has to be an object that constitutes or corresponds to the meaning of the general word. So there has to be something called horseness and triangularity. But now consider a general word that applies to nothing particular at all, a word like 'unicorn' for instance. It is perfectly meaningful. And if it is meaningful, must there not be something in the world that constitutes or corresponds to the word? So there must be uninstantiated universals.

This "argument from meaning" is a very bad argument. (In fairness to Socrates, it is not clear whether he was using it. Other philosophers have, though, often at a rather unselfconscious level.) The argument depends on the assumption that in every case where a general word has meaning, there is something in the world that constitutes or

Russell's theory of meanings

corresponds to that meaning. Gilbert Ryle spoke of this as the 'Fido'–Fido fallacy. Fido corresponds to the word 'Fido', but there does not have to be some single thing corresponding to a general word.

To go along with the argument from meaning is to be led into a very promiscuous theory of universals. If it is correct, then we know a priori that for each general word with a certain meaning, there exists a universal. This lines up predicates and properties in a nice neat way, but it is a way that we ought to be very suspicious of. Is it that easy to discover what universals there are?

Plato had another line of thought that led him toward uninstantiated universals. This is the apparent failure of things in the ordinary world to come up to exact standards. It seems that nothing in the world is perfectly straight or circular, yet in geometry we discuss the properties of perfectly straight lines or perfect circles. Again, no thing is perfectly changeless. Yet again, it may well be that no act is perfectly just. Certainly no person is perfectly virtuous, and no state is perfectly just. Yet in ethical and political discussion (e.g., in the *Republic*) we can discuss the nature of virtue and justice. In general, we perceive the world as falling short of certain standards. This can be explained if, whether we know it or not, we are comparing ordinary things to Forms, which the ordinary things can never fully instantiate. (This can lead one, and perhaps led Plato, to the difficult notion of degrees of instantiation, with the highest degree never realized.)

It is interesting to notice that this argument did not quite lead Plato where he wanted to go in every case. Consider geometry. In geometry one might wish to consider the properties of, say, two intersecting circles. These circles will be perfectly circular. But also, of course, there is only *one* Form of the circle. So what are these two perfect circles? Plato, apparently, had to introduce what he called the Mathematicals. Like the mathematical Forms they were perfect and thus were unlike ordinary things. But unlike the Forms, there could be many tokens of the same type, and in this they were like ordinary things. They were particulars, although perfect particulars. But if this is so, though perhaps the falling away from standards gave Plato an argument for the Mathematicals, it is not clear that it is any argument for the Forms.

But in any case, cannot ideal standards simply be things that we merely think of? We can quite knowingly form thoughts of that which does not exist. In the case of ideal standards nothing comes up to the standard, but by extrapolating from ordinary things that approximate to the standard in different degrees, we can form the thought of something that does come up to the standard. It turns out to be useful to do so. Why attribute metaphysical reality to such standards? They could be useful fictions. As a matter of fact, in the geometrical case it appears that such notions as that of a perfectly straight line or a perfectly circular object may be acquired directly in experience. For cannot something look perfectly straight or perfectly circular, even if it is not in fact so?

One should note that one thing that seems to keep a theory of uninstantiated universals going is the widespread idea that it is sufficient for a universal to exist if it is merely possible that it should be instantiated. I have found in discussion that this idea has particular appeal if it is empirically possible (that is, compatible with the laws of nature) that the alleged universal should have actual instances. Suppose, for instance, that somebody describes a very complex pattern of wallpaper but does not ever sketch the pattern or manufacture the wallpaper. Suppose nobody else does either in the whole history of the universe. It is clear that there was nothing in the laws of nature that prevented the pattern's ever having an instance, from ever having a token of the type. But is not that pattern a monadic universal, a complex and structural universal to be sure, but a universal nonetheless?

In this way, apparently, it is natural for philosophers to argue. But for myself I do not see the force of the argument. Philosophers do not reason that way about particulars. They do not argue that it is empirically possible that present-day France should be a monarchy and therefore that the present king of France exists, although, unfortunately for French royalists, he is not instantiated. Why argue in the same way about universals? Is it that philosophers think that universals are so special that they can exist whether or not particular things, which are contingent only, exist? If so, I think that this is no better than a prejudice, perhaps inherited from Plato.

There is one subtle variation of the argument to uninstantiated universals from their empirical possibility that I think has more weight. It has been developed by Michael Tooley.[4] However, it depends upon deep considerations about the nature of the laws of nature, which cannot be discussed here. And in any case, the argument depends upon the laws' being found to have a very special structure, which it is unlikely that they actually have. As a result, it seems that the best that the argument shows is that uninstantiated universals are possible rather than actual. And even this conclusion may be avoidable.[5]

It may also be thought that considerations from mathematics, and the properties and relations postulated by mathematicians, push toward the recognition of uninstantiated universals. However, the whole project of bringing together the theory of universals with the disciplines of mathematics, although very important, cannot be undertaken here. I have sketched out, rather broadly, the way that I think it ought to go in a book on the nature of possibility.[6]

From this point on, therefore, I am going to assume the truth of the Principle of Instantiation. As already noted, this does not compel one to abandon a two-realm doctrine. It does not compel one to bring the universals down among ordinary things. But it does *permit* one to do this, and to do so seems the natural way to develop the theory once one rejects uninstantiated universals.

2 Disjunctive, Negative, and Conjunctive Universals

For simplicity, in this section I will consider property universals only. But the points to be made appear to apply to relations also. We have already rejected uninstantiated universals. But it seems that the potential class of universals needs to be cut down a great deal further if we are to get a plausible theory. I will begin by giving reasons for rejecting disjunctive property universals. By a *disjunctive property* I mean a disjunction of (property) universals. Let us assume that particular electric charges and particular masses are universals. Then having charge C or having mass M (with C and M dummies for determinate, that is, definite values) would be an example of a disjunctive property. Why is it not a universal? Consider two objects. One has charge C but lacks mass M. The other lacks charge C but has mass

M. So they have the disjunctive property having-charge-C-or-having-mass-M. But surely that does not show that, in any serious sense, they thereby have something identical? The whole point of a universal, however, is that it should be identical in its different instances.

There is another reason to deny that a disjunction of universals is a universal. There is some very close link between universals and causality. The link is of this nature. If a thing instantiates a certain universal, then, in virtue of that, it has the power to act in a certain way. For instance, if a thing has a certain mass, then it has the power to act upon the scalepan of a balance, or upon scales, in a certain way. Furthermore, different universals bestow different powers. Charge and mass, for instance, manifest themselves in different ways. I doubt if the link between universals and powers is a necessary one, but it seems real. Moreover, if, as seems abstractly possible, two different universals bestowed the very same powers, how could one ever know that they were two different universals? If they affect all apparatus, including our brains, in exactly the same way, will we not judge that we are dealing with one universal only?

Now suppose that a thing has charge C but lacks mass M. In virtue of charge C, it has certain powers to act. For instance, it repels things with like charge. Possession of the disjunctive property (C or M) adds nothing to its power. This suggests that while (C) may be a genuine universal (C or M) is not.

So I think that we should reject disjunctive universals. A similar case seems to hold against negative universals: the lack or absence of a property is not a property. If having charge C is the instantiation of a universal, then not having C is not the instantiating of a universal.

First, we may appeal to identity again. Is there really something in common, something identical, in everything that lacks charge C? Of course, there might be some universal property that just happened to be coextensive with lacking charge C. But the lack itself does not seem to be a factor found in each thing that lacks charge C.

Second, causal considerations seem to point in the same direction. It is a strange idea that lacks or absences do any causing. It is natural to say that a thing acts in virtue of positive factors alone. This also suggests that absences of universals are not universals.

It is true that there is some linguistic evidence that might be thought to point the other way. We do say things like "lack of water caused his death." At the surface, the statement says that a lack of water caused an absence of life. But how seriously should we take such ways of expressing ourselves? Michael Tooley has pointed out that we are unhappy to say "lack of poison causes us to remain alive." Yet if the surface way of understanding the first statement is correct, then the second statement should be understood in the same way and thought to be true. Certain counterfactual statements are true in both cases: If he had had water, then he would (could) have still been alive; if we had taken poison, we would have been dead now. These are causal truths. But they tell us very little about the actual causal factors operative in the two cases. We believe, I think, that these actual causal factors could be spelled out in purely positive terms.

It is interesting to notice that conjunctions of universals (having both charge C and mass M) escape the two criticisms leveled against disjunctive and negative universals. With conjunctions we do have identity. The very same conjunction of factors is present in each instance. There is no problem about causality. If a thing instantiates the conjunction, then it will have certain powers as a consequence. These powers will be different from those that the thing would have had if it had had just one of the conjuncts. It may even be that the conjunction can do more than the sum of what each property would do if each was instantiated alone. (As scientists say: There could be synergism. The effect could be more than the sum of each cause acting by itself.)

But there is one condition that ought to be put on conjunctive universals. Some thing (past, present, future) must actually have both properties and at the same time. This, of course, is simply the Principle of Instantiation applied to conjunctive universals.

3 Predicates and Universals

What has been said about uninstantiated universals, and also about disjunctions and negations of universals, has brought out a most important point. It is that there is no automatic passage from predicates (linguistic entities) to universals. For instance, the expression "either having charge C or having mass M" is a perfectly good predicate. It could apply to, or be true of, innumerable objects. But as we have seen, this does not mean that there is a universal corresponding to this predicate.

Wittgenstein made a famous contribution to the Problem of Universals with his discussion of *family resemblances*. Wittgenstein was an anti-metaphysician, and his object was to dissolve rather than to solve the Problem of Universals. He seems to have thought that what he said about family resemblances was (among other things) a step toward getting rid of the problem. But I think that the real moral of what he said is only that predicates and universals do not line up in any simple way.

In his *Philosophical Investigations* he considered the notion of a *game*. He had this to say about it:[7]

66. Consider for example the proceedings that we call "games." I mean board-games, card-games, ball-games, Olympic games, and so on. What is common to them all? – Don't say: "There *must* be something common, or they would not be called 'games'" – but *look and see* whether there is anything common to all – For if you look at them you will not see something that is common to *all*, but similarities, relationships, and a whole series of them at that. To repeat: don't think, but look! – Look for example at board-games, with their multifarious relationships. Now pass to card-games; here you find many correspondences with the first group, but many common features drop out, and others appear. When we pass next to ball-games, much that is common is retained, but much is lost. – Are they all "amusing"? Compare chess with noughts and crosses. Or is there always winning and losing, or competition between players? Think of patience. In ball games there is winning and losing; but when a child throws his ball at the wall and catches it again, this feature has disappeared. Look at the parts played by skill and luck; and at the difference between skill in chess and skill in tennis. Think now of games like ring-a-ring-a-roses; here is the element of amusement, but how many other characteristic features have disappeared! And we can go through the many, many other groups of games in the same way; we can see how similarities crop up and disappear.

And the result of this examination is: we see a complicated network of similarities overlapping and criss-crossing: sometimes overall similarities, sometimes similarities of detail.

67. I can think of no better expression to characterize these similarities than "family resemblances"; for the various resemblances between members of a family: build, features, colour of eyes, gait, temperament, etc. etc. overlap and criss-cross in the same way. – And I shall say: "games" form a family.

This has been a very influential passage. Wittgenstein and his followers applied the point to all sorts of notions besides those of a game, including many of the central notions discussed by philosophers. But what should a believer in universals think that Wittgenstein has shown about universals?

Let us agree, as we probably should, that there is no universal of gamehood. But now what of this "complicated network of similarities overlapping and criss-crossing" of which Wittgenstein speaks? All the Realist has to do is to analyze each of these similarities in terms of common properties. That analysis of similarity is not a difficult or unfamiliar idea, though it is an analysis that would be contested by a Nominalist. But there will not be any property that runs through the whole class and makes them all games. To give a crude and oversimplified sketch, the situation might be like this:

Particulars: *a*   *b*   *c*   *d*   *e*
Their properties: FGHJ GHJK HJKL JKLM KLMN(F)

Here F to M are supposed to be genuine property universals, and it is supposed that the predicate "game" applies in virtue of these properties. But the class of particulars {*a* ... *e*}, which is the class of all tokens of games, is a family in Wittgenstein's sense. Here, though, I have sketched an account of such families that is completely compatible with Realism about universals.

However, Wittgenstein's remarks do raise a big question. How does one decide whether one is or is not in the presence of a genuine property or relation? Wittgenstein says of games, "don't think, but look!" As a general recipe, at least, that seems far too simple.

I do not think that there is any infallible way of deciding what are the true universals. It seems clear that we must not look to semantic considerations. As I said in section 1, those who argue to particular universals from semantic data, from predicates to a universal corresponding to that predicate, argue in a very optimistic and unempirical manner. I call them *a priori realists*. Better, I think, is *a posteriori realism*. The best guide that we have to just what universals there are is total science.

For myself, I believe that this puts physics in a special position. There seem to be reasons (scientific, empirical, a posteriori reasons) to think that physics is *the* fundamental science. If that is correct, then such properties as mass, charge, extension, duration, space-time interval, and other properties envisaged by physics may be the true monadic universals. (They are mostly ranges of quantities. Quantities raise problems that will need some later discussion.) Spatiotemporal and causal relations will perhaps be the true polyadic universals.

If this is correct, then the ordinary types – the type red, the type horse, in general, the types of the manifest image of the world – will emerge as preliminary, rough-and-ready classifications of reality. For the most part they are not false, but they are rough-and-ready. Many of them will be family affairs, as games appear to be. To the one type will correspond a whole family of universals and not always a very close family. And even where the ordinary types do carve the beast of reality along its true joints, they may still not expose those joints for the things that they are. But let it be emphasized that any identification of universals remains rather speculative. In what I have just been saying I have been trying to combine a philosophy of universals with Physicalism. Others may have other ideas.

4   States of Affairs

In the Universals theory that we are examining, particulars instantiate properties, pairs of particulars instantiate (dyadic) relations, triples of particulars instantiate (triadic) relations, and so on as far as is needed. Suppose that *a* is F, with F a universal, or that *a* has R to *b*, with R a universal. It appears that we are required to recognize *a*'s being F and *a*'s having R to *b* as items in our ontology. I will speak of these items as *states of affairs.* Others have called them facts.[8]

Why do we need to recognize states of affairs? Why not recognize simply particulars, universals (divided into properties and relations), and, perhaps, instantiation? The answer appears by considering the following point. If *a* is F, then it is entailed that *a* exists and that the universal F exists. However, *a* could exist, and F could exist, and yet it fail to be the case that *a* is F (F is instantiated, but instantiated elsewhere only). *a*'s being F involves something more than *a* and F. It is no good simply adding the fundamental tie or nexus of instantiation to the sum of *a* and F. The existence of *a*, of instantiation, and of F does not amount to *a*'s being F. The something more must be *a*'s being F – and this is a state of affairs.

This argument rests upon a general principle, which, following C. B. Martin, I call the truth-maker principle. According to this principle, for every contingent truth at least (and perhaps for all truths contingent or necessary) there must be something in the world that makes it true. "Something" here may be taken as widely as may be wished. The "making" is not causality, of course: Rather, it is that in the world in virtue of which the truth is true. Gustav Bergmann and his followers have spoken of the "ontological ground" of truths, and I think that this is my "something in the world" that makes truths true. An important point to notice is that different truths may all have the same truth-maker, or ontological ground. For instance, that this thing is colored, is red, and is scarlet are all made true by the thing's having a particular shade of color.

The truth-maker principle seems to me to be fairly obvious once attention is drawn to it, but I do not know how to argue for it further. It is to be noted, however, that some of those who take perfectly seriously the sort of metaphysical investigation that we are here engaged upon nevertheless reject the principle.[9]

Accepting the truth-maker principle will lead one to reject Quine's view[10] that *predicates* do not have to be taken seriously in considering the ontological implications of statements one takes to be true. Consider the difference between asserting that a certain surface is red and asserting that it is green. An upholder of the truth-maker principle will think that there has to be an ontological ground, a difference in the world, to account for the difference between the predicate 'red' applying to the surface and the predicate 'green' so applying. Of course, what that ontological ground is, is a further matter. There is no high road from the principle to universals and states of affairs.

Returning now to states of affairs, it may be pointed out that there are some reasons for accepting states of affairs even if the truth-maker principle is rejected. First, we can apparently refer to states of affairs, preparatory to saying something further about them. But it is generally, if not universally, conceded by philosophers that what can be referred to exists. Second, states of affairs are plausible candidates for the terms of causal relations. The state of affairs of *a*'s being F may be the cause of *b*'s being G. Third, as we shall see in section 8, states of affairs can help to solve a fairly pressing problem in the theory of universals: how to understand the multiple location of property universals and the nonlocation of relation universals.

It is interesting to see that states of affairs seem not to be required by a Class Nominalist or a Resemblance Nominalist, and of course that is an important economy for their respective theories. The Class Nominalist analyzes *a*'s being F as *a*'s being a member of a class (or natural class) containing {*a*, *b*, *c*, ...}. But here we have simply *a* and the class. The class-membership relation is internal, dictated by the nature of the terms. So we need not recognize it as something additional to the terms. The terms by themselves are sufficient truth-makers. Hence we do not need states of affairs.

The Resemblance Nominalist analyzes *a*'s being F as a matter of resemblance relations holding between *a* and, say, suitable paradigm Fs. But that relation is also internal, dictated by what I called the particularized nature of *a* and the paradigm objects. Once again, states of affairs are not needed.

(But it seems that a Predicate Nominalist *will* require states of affairs. *a*'s being F is analyzed as *a*'s falling under the predicate F. But how can the falling under be dictated simply by *a* and the linguistic object F? Falling under is an external relation.)

Now for something very important. States of affairs have some rather surprising characteristics. Let us call *a*, *b*, F, R, etc., the constituents of states of affairs. It turns out that it is possible for there to be two different states of affairs that nevertheless have *exactly the same constituents*.

Here is a simple example. Let R be a non-symmetrical relation (for instance, loves). Let it be the case, contingently, that *a* has R to *b* and *b* has R to *a*. Two distinct states of affairs exist: *a*'s having R to *b*, and *b*'s having R to *a* (*a*'s loving *b* and *b*'s loving *a*). Indeed, these states of affairs are *wholly* distinct, in the sense that it is possible for either state of affairs to fail to obtain while the other exists. Yet the two states of affairs have exactly the same constituents.

You can get the same phenomenon with properties as well as relations.[11] Assume, as I think it is correct to assume, that a conjunction of states of affairs is itself a state of affairs. Then consider (1) *a*'s being F and *b*'s being G; and (2) *a*'s being G and *b*'s being F. Two wholly distinct states of affairs, it may be, but the very same constituents.

At this point, it is worth realizing that states of affairs may be required not simply by those who recognize universals but also by any philosophy that recognizes properties and relations, whether as universals or as particulars. [...]

Suppose that *a* has R_1 to *b*, with R_1 a particular, but a nonsymmetrical, relation. If *b* has 'the same' relation to *a*, then, on a philosophy of tropes, we have *b*'s having R_2 to *a*: two states of affairs with different (though overlapping) constituents. For the loving that holds between *a* and *b* is a different object from the loving that holds between *b* and *a*. Nevertheless, *a*'s having R_1 to *b* entails the existence of constituents *a*, R_1, and *b*, but the existence of these constituents does not entail that *a* has R_1 to *b*. So states of affairs still seem to be something more than their constituents.

With tropes, you never get different states of affairs constructed out of exactly the same constituents. But given just one set of constituents, more than one state of affairs having just these constituents is *possible*. From *a*, trope R_1, and *b*, for instance, we could get *a*'s having R_1 to *b* or *b*'s having R_1 to *a*. There is a way for a philosophy of tropes to avoid having to postulate states of affairs. But let us leave that aside for now.

I have spoken of the constituents of states of affairs. Could we also think and speak of them as *parts* of states of affairs? I think that it would be very unwise to think and speak of them in this way. Logicians have paid some attention to the notions of whole and part. They have worked out a formal calculus for manipulating these notions, which is sometimes called the calculus of individuals or, better, *mereology* (in Greek *meros* means a part). One philosopher who helped to work this out was Nelson Goodman, and in his book *The Structure of Appearance* an account of mereology is given.[12] There is one mereological principle that is very important for us here: If there are a number of things, and if they have a sum, that is, a whole of which they are parts, then they have just one sum.

I say *if* they have a sum, because it is controversial whether a number of things *always* have a sum. Do the square root of 2 and the Sydney Opera House have a sum? Philosophers differ on how permissive a mereology should be, that is, on whether there are limits to what you can sum, and if there are limits, where the limits fall. I myself would accept total permissiveness in summing. But all that is needed here is something that is agreed by all: where things can be summed, for each collection of things there is just one sum. We have just seen, however, that the complete constituents of a state of affairs are capable of being, and may actually even be, the complete constituents of a different state of affairs. Hence constituents do not stand to states of affairs as parts to whole.

It is worth noticing that complex universals have constituents rather than parts. At any rate this is so if we accept the Principle of Instantiation. Consider, for instance, conjunctive universals. If being P and Q is a conjunctive universal, then there must exist some particular, *x*, such that *x* is both P and Q. But to say that is to say that there exists at least one state of affairs of the form *x* is P and *x* is Q. For the conjunctive universal to exist is for there to be a state of affairs of a certain sort. As a result, it is misleading to say that P and Q are *parts* of the conjunctive universal, a thing that I myself did say in the past.[13]

A very important type of complex universal is a *structural* property. A structural property involves a thing instantiating a certain pattern, such as a flag. Different parts (mereological parts) of the thing that instantiates the structural property will have certain properties. If the structural property involves relations, as a flag does, some or all of these parts will be related in various ways. It is easy to see that states of affairs must be appealed to. If *a* has P, and *b* has Q, and *a* has R to *b*, then and only then the object [*a* + *b*] has the structural property that may be presented in a shorthand way as P-R-Q.

A final point before leaving this particularly important section. The fact that states of affairs, if they exist, have a nonmereological mode of composition may have consequences for the view that particulars are no more than bundles of universals. (I understand that this point comes from Mark Johnston.) We have seen that different states of affairs can have exactly the same constituents (*a*'s loving *b*, and *b*'s loving *a*). We have previously argued [in chapter 4 of the volume, not reproduced in the present selection] against the Bundle theory that two bundles containing exactly the same universals are impossible. They would be the very same bundle. Yet, considering the matter independently of the Bundle theory, why should not two different particulars be exactly alike? But now suppose that, as is plausible, we treat a bundling of universals as a state of affairs. Why should not exactly the same universals be bundled up in different ways?

In reply, I think it must be admitted that this is conceivable. But it would depend upon the Bundle theorist's working out a scheme that allowed for different bundling of the very same things. This is not provided for in the actual Bundle theories that have been developed. So if they want to take this path, then the onus is on Bundle theorists to try to develop their theory in a new way.

5   A World of States of Affairs?

In the previous section it was argued that a philosophy that admits both particulars and universals ought to admit states of affairs (facts), which have particulars and universals as constituents (not as parts). As a matter of fact, we saw that to introduce properties and relations at all, even as particulars, would apparently involve states of affairs. But our present concern is with universals.

The suggestion to be put forward now is that we should think of the world as a world of states of affairs, with particulars and universals only having existence within states of affairs. We have already argued for a Principle of Instantiation for universals. If this is a true principle, then the way is open to regard a universal as an identical element present in certain states of affairs. A particular that existed outside states of affairs would not be clothed in any properties or relations. It may be called a *bare* particular. If the world is to be a world of states of affairs, we must add to the Principle of Instantiation a Principle of the Rejection of Bare Particulars.

This second principle looks plausible enough. In a Universals theory, it is universals that give a thing its nature, kind, or sort. A bare particular would not instantiate any universals, and thus would have no nature, be of no kind or sort. What could we make of such an entity? Perhaps a particular need not have any relations to any other particular – perhaps it could be quite isolated. But it must instantiate at least one property.

6   The Thin and the Thick Particular

Here is a problem that has been raised by John Quilter.[14] He calls it the "Antinomy of Bare Particulars." Suppose that particular *a* instantiates property F. *a* is F. This "is" is obviously not the "is" of identity, as in *a* is *a* or F is F. *a* and F are different entities, one being a particular, the other a universal. The "is" we are dealing with is the "is" of instantiation – of a fundamental tie between particular and property. But if the "is" is not the "is" of identity, then it appears that *a* considered in itself is really a bare particular lacking any properties. But in that case *a* has not got the property F. The property F remains outside *a* – just as transcendent forms remain outside the particular in Plato's theory.

I believe that we can at least begin to meet this difficulty by drawing the important distinction between the *thin* and the *thick* particular.[15] The thin particular is *a*, taken apart from its properties (substratum). It is linked to its properties by instantiation, but it is not identical with them. It is not bare, because to be bare it would have to be not instantiating any properties. But though clothed, it is thin.

However, this is not the only way that a particular can be thought of. It can also be thought of as involving its properties. Indeed, that seems to be the normal way that we think of particulars. This is the thick particular. But the thick particular, because it enfolds both thin particulars and properties, held together by instantiation, can be nothing but a state of affairs.

Suppose that *a* instantiates F, G, H,…. They comprise the totality of *a*'s (nonrelational) properties. Now form the conjunctive property F & G & H…. Call this property N, where N is meant to be short for *a*'s nature. *a* is N is true, and *a*'s being N is a (rather complex) state of affairs. It is also the thick particular. *The thick particular is a state of affairs.* The properties of a thing are "contained within it" because they are constituents of this state of affairs. (Notice that states of affairs, such as *a*'s being N, are not repeatable. So, along with thin particulars, they can be called particulars also.)

Therefore, in one sense a particular is propertyless. That is the thin particular. In another sense it enfolds properties within itself. In the latter case it is the thick particular and is a state of affairs. I think that this answers the difficulty raised by the Antinomy of Bare Particulars.

Two points before leaving this section: First, the distinction between thin and thick particulars does not depend upon a doctrine of properties as universals. It does presuppose a substance-attribute account of a particular, rather than a bundle view. But we have already seen [in chapter 4 of the volume, not reproduced in the present selection] that it is possible to take a substance-attribute view with the attributes as particulars, that is, as tropes. The thin particular remains the particular with its attributes abstracted away. The thick particular is again a state of affairs: the thin particular's having the (particular) attributes that it has.

Second, the thin and the thick particular are really the two ends of a scale. In between is the particular clothed with some, but only some, of its properties. They may be properties that are, for one reason or another, particularly important. This intermediate particular will, of course, be a state of affairs, but a less comprehensive one than the state of affairs that is the thick particular.

7 Universals as Ways

The discussion in the previous section is not entirely satisfactory as it stands. It still leaves us with a picture of the thin particular and its properties as distinct metaphysical nodules that are linked together in states of affairs to form the thick particular. This makes the Principles of Instantiation and of the Rejection of Bare Particulars seem a bit arbitrary. Why must the nodules occur together? Could they not come apart? But would they then not be those unwanted creatures: uninstantiated universals and bare particulars?

Here I turn to a suggestion that has often been in the air, but had not, I think, been expounded systematically before David Seargent's book on Stout's theory of universals.[16] Unlike Stout, Seargent accepts universals, and in chapter 4 he argues that we should think of them as *ways*. Properties are ways things are. The mass or charge of an electron is a way the electron is (in this case, a way that any electron is). Relations are ways things stand to each other.

If a property is a way that a thing is, then this brings the property into very intimate connection with the thing, but without destroying the distinction between them. One can see the point of thinking of instantiation as a fundamental connection, a tie or nexus closer than mere relation. Nor will one be much tempted by the idea of an uninstantiated property. A way that things are could hardly exist on its own.

Again, one will not be tempted by the idea that the way a thing stands to other things, a relation, could exist on its own, independent of the things. (Not that the idea was ever very tempting! It is easier to substantialize properties than relations.)

It may be objected that the phrases "ways things are" and "ways things stand to each other" beg the question against uninstantiated universals. Should I not have spoken of ways things could be and ways things could stand to each other, thus canceling the implication that the ways must be the ways of actual things?

However, my argument is not attempting to take advantage of this semantic point. My contention is that once properties and relations are thought of not as things, but as ways, it is profoundly unnatural to think of these ways as floating free from things. Ways, I am saying, are naturally construed only as ways actual things are or ways actual things stand to each other. The idea that properties and relations can exist uninstantiated is nourished by the idea that they are not ways but things.

Before concluding this section, I should like to note that the conception of properties and relations as ways does not depend upon taking them as universals. We can still think of a's property as a way that a is, even if the property is particular, a trope. It will just be the case that no other thing besides a can be that way. Similarly, a relation holding between a and b can still be a way a and b stand to each other, even if this way is non-repeatable.

It is very important to realize that the notions of states of affairs and their constituents, the distinction between the thin and the thick particular, and the conception of properties and relations as ways things are and ways things stand to other things are available, if desired, to a philosophy of tropes as much as to a philosophy of universals.

8   Multiple Location

To bring universals from a Platonic realm down to earth, down to space-time, seems to involve saying something rather strange. It seems to follow that universals are, or may be, multiply located. For are they not to be found wherever the particulars that instantiate them are found? If two different electrons each have charge e, then e, one thing, a universal, is to be found in two different places, the places where the two electrons are, yet entirely and completely in each place. This has seemed wildly paradoxical to many philosophers.

Plato appears to be raising this difficulty in the *Philebus*, 15b–c. There he asked about a Form: "Can it be as a whole outside itself, and thus come to be one and identical in one thing and in several at once – a view which might be thought to be the most impossible of all?"[17] A theory that kept universals in a separate realm from particulars would at least avoid this difficulty!

You might try just accepting the multiple location of universals. Some philosophers have. But then a difficulty can be raised: What about relations? Perhaps one can give *properties* a multiple location. But just where will you locate the "multiply located" relations? In the related things? That does not sound right. If a precedes b, is the relation in both a and b? Or in the thing $[a + b]$? Neither answer sounds right. But if it is not in the things, where is it?

I am inclined to meet the difficulty by saying that talk of the location of universals, while better than placing them in another realm, is also not quite appropriate. What should be said first, I think, is that the world is a world of states of affairs. These states of affairs involve particulars having properties and standing in relations to each other. The properties and relations are universals, which means both that different particulars can have the very same property and that different pairs, triples, ..., of particulars can stand in the very same relation to each other. I do not think that all that is too startling a claim.

But if Naturalism is true, then the world is a single spatiotemporal manifold. What does this come to in terms of the states of affairs theory? That is, how do we reconcile Naturalism with the view sketched in the previous paragraph? It would be an enormous undertaking, presumably involving both fundamental science and philosophy, to give an answer involving even the sketchiest detail. All that can be said here is that the space-time world would have to be an enormous plurality or conjunction of states of affairs, with all the particulars that feature in the states of affairs linked up together (in states of affairs) by spatiotemporal relations.

To talk of locating universals in space-time then emerges as a crude way of speaking. Space-time is not a box into which universals are put. Universals are constituents of states of affairs. Space-time is a conjunction of states of affairs. In that sense universals are "in" space-time. But they are in it as helping to constitute it. I think that this is a reasonable understanding of *universalia in rebus*, and I hope that it meets Plato's objection.[18]

Notes

It is suggested that ch. 11 of D. M. Armstrong's *Nominalism and Realism* (Cambridge: Cambridge University Press, 1978) and chs 13–17 of his *A Theory of Universals* (Cambridge: Cambridge University Press, 1978) be used as companion readings to this chapter.

1   See his introductory book *The Problems of Philosophy* (London: Williams and Norgate, 1912), chs 9 and 10.

2   F. E. Abbott, *Scientific Theism* (London: Macmillan, 1886).

3 Plato, *Republic*, trans. F. M. Cornford (New York: Oxford University Press, 1947), p. 595.

4 Michael Tooley, *Causation* (Oxford: Clarendon Press, 1987), sects 3.1.4 and 3.2.

5 See D. M. Armstrong, *What is a Law of Nature?* (Cambridge: Cambridge University Press, 1983), ch. 8.

6 D. M. Armstrong, *A Combinatorial Theory of Possibility* (Cambridge: Cambridge University Press, 1989), ch. 10.

7 L. Wittgenstein, *Philosophical Investigations* (Oxford: Blackwell, 1953), sects 66 and 67.

8 E.g., L. Wittgenstein, *Tractatus Logico-Philosophicus* (Oxford: Blackwell, 1961); B. Skyrms, "Tractarian nominalism," *Philosophical Studies* 40 (1981).

9 See in particular David Lewis, "New work for a theory of universals," this volume, ch. 23.

10 W. V. Quine, "On what there is," this volume, ch. 1.

11 As pointed out by David Lewis, "Comment on Forrest and Armstrong," *Australasian Journal of Philosophy* 64 (1986).

12 Nelson Goodman, *The Structure of Appearance* (Cambridge, Mass.: Harvard University Press, 1966).

13 Armstrong, *Theory of Universals*, ch. 15, sect. 2.

14 John Quilter, "What has properties?," *Proceedings of the Russellian Society* (Sydney University, Philosophy Dept., 1985), p. 10.

15 This distinction is discussed in greater detail in D. M. Armstrong's *Universals: An Opinionated Introduction* (Boulder, Colo.: Westview Press, 1989), from which the present selection is taken.

16 D. A. J. Seargent, *Plurality and Continuity, an Essay on G. F. Stout's Theory of Universals* (Martinus Nijhoff, 1985).

17 Plato, *Philebus*, trans. A. E. Taylor.

18 For more on this topic see my "Can a naturalist believe in universals?", in E. Ullmann-Margalit (ed.), *Science in Reflection*, (Kluwer Academic Publishers, 1988); together with critical comment in the same volume by Gilead Bar-Elli.

PART V

Causation

Introduction

David Hume set the stage for contemporary discussions of causation with the following remark about its nature: "We may define cause to be an object followed by another, and where all the objects, similar to the first, are followed by objects similar to the second. Or, in other words, where, if the first object had not been, the second never had existed." As David Lewis observes (in chapter 29), Hume actually seems to have articulated two importantly different accounts of causation. In the first sentence of the quote, Hume articulates a regularity approach to defining causation, on which causation is understood in terms of the "constant conjunction" of similar sorts of events. In the second, he articulates a counterfactual account of causation: one event causes another just in case, if (contrary to the facts) the former had not occurred, the latter would not have occurred either.

In "On the Notion of Cause" (chapter 25), Bertrand Russell contends that our ordinary conception of causation is, in an important sense, defective. His complaint focuses on a tension between two aspects of our notion of cause. First, a cause is meant to ensure, or necessitate, the occurrence of its effects. Second, events of the same type as the cause and the effect must appear in constant conjunction. But now we face a dilemma. If we build too little information into the specification of the cause – for instance, if we say that striking the match caused it to light – the cause won't ensure the effect. A struck match can fail to light due to a strong gust of wind passing through right as the match is struck. Suppose, then, that we build a great deal of information into the specification of the cause, enough to entail the absence of every possible kind of interfering event. In that case, we end up with an event so specific that there almost certainly has never been, and will never be, another event of exactly that sort. But, in that case, that sort of event is not in constant conjunction with anything! So it would seem to be impossible for any event to satisfy both of these central features of our notion of cause. Russell takes these defects in our notion of causation to be reasons for eliminating it from philosophical discourse altogether. Indeed, he maintains that scientists have already dispensed with the notion of cause: "the reason why physics has ceased to look for causes is that, in fact, there are no such things."

Philosophers have, however, continued to search for a more viable notion of cause. In "Causes and Conditions" (chapter 26), J. L. Mackie offers an analysis of causation as an "INUS condition." This is a

Metaphysics: An Anthology, Second Edition. Edited by Jaegwon Kim, Daniel Z. Korman and Ernest Sosa.
Editorial material and organization © 2012 Blackwell Publishing Ltd. Published 2012 by Blackwell Publishing Ltd.

form of the regularity approach to causation (an exact interpretation of Mackie on this point depends on how one understands his conception of sufficiency and necessity). On this approach, a singular causal relation – that is, a causal relation between two individual events – must be covered by a lawful regularity between kinds of events under which the cause and effect fall. According to Mackie, a cause is a condition that, though *insufficient* in itself for its effect, is a *necessary* part of a condition that is *unnecessary* for the effect (since there often are alternative possible causes) but *sufficient* for the effect. If this sounds complicated, you will see that Mackie provides perspicuous examples and explanations.

Donald Davidson's aim in his "Causal Relations" (chapter 27) is not to offer an analysis of causation (although a regularity approach lurks in the background), but to clarify some important issues that are prior to such an analysis. One such issue concerns the *relata* of causal relations: what sort of entities are linked by causal relations? For Davidson, causation is an extensional binary relation between concrete individual events. He maintains that causation is importantly different from explanation, insofar as the truth of explanation claims (unlike causal claims) is sensitive to how the events in questions are described. Davidson also emphasizes how insensitivity to the distinction between a partial description of an event and a description of a part of an event has led to much confusion.

Russell, as we saw, followed Hume in supposing that in order for an event to count as the cause of another event, the event must necessitate its effect, and the causal relation must be underwritten by some exceptionless generalization linking events of the same type as the cause with events of the same type as the effect. In "Causality and Determination" (chapter 28), G. E. M. Anscombe challenges this widespread supposition. Contra Hume, she contends that we acquire our concept of causation by directly observing causal relations (e.g., scraping and pushing), not by observing that certain sorts of events appear in constant conjunction. She suggests that causes are more properly understood as *sources* of effects (or as that from which effects *derive*), not as necessitating their effects. She goes on to examine the view that effects are *determined* by their causes, whether this view is presupposed in contemporary physics, and whether it is undermined by quantum theory.

In "Causation" (chapter 29), David Lewis presents an account of causation in terms of counterfactual dependence. It is a development of the familiar idea that a cause is a *sine qua non* condition for its effect – a condition without which the effect would not have occurred. He argues that his approach resolves many of the difficulties that beset the nomic regularity approach. (Lewis develops his approach further, and discusses many new points, in his several substantial postscripts to this paper; see his *Philosophical Papers*, volume II [Oxford University Press].)

Wesley C. Salmon, in "Causal Connections" (chapter 30), rejects the nomic regularity account of causation in favor of an account of causation in terms of the *production* of effects. According to Salmon, processes, rather than events, must be taken as fundamental in understanding causation, and the basic problem of causation, or "Hume's challenge," is to provide a principled distinction between genuine causal processes and pseudo-processes. Pseudo-processes are processes that, although they exhibit regular, even lawlike, connections between their elements (like the successive shadows cast by a moving car), are not real causal processes. The main question for Salmon then is this: what distinguishes causal processes from pseudo-processes? As an answer to this question, he develops the idea that causal processes are those that are able to "transmit a mark."

In "Causation: Reductionism Versus Realism" (chapter 31), Michael Tooley argues that all reductive accounts of causation, as well as reductive accounts of laws of nature, are bound to fail. A reductive account of causal relations is one in which the facts about causal processes are entirely fixed by the causal laws together with the noncausal properties of events and the noncausal relations that hold among them. Tooley presents a series of counterexamples aimed to show that the laws together with the noncausal features of a world underdetermine which causal relations obtain in that world. Tooley concludes that we should embrace a *realist* theory on which the facts about causal relations are primitive, that is, not analyzable in terms of such noncausal features.

In "Two Concepts of Causation" (chapter 32), Ned Hall argues that we have two, fundamentally distinct, notions of causation. He defends this claim by examining a special sort of causal interaction (which he calls "double prevention"). Hall argues that these sorts of cases pose a prima facie problem for any theory of causation – including counterfactual theories like Lewis's and production theories like Salmon's – that requires either that causal relations be intrinsic, or that they be transitive, or that causes be connected to their effects by spatiotemporally continuous sequences of intermediates. This sort of case is meant to be problematic even if one allows omissions and absences to serve as causal intermediates. Hall concludes that our intuitions that effects counterfactually depend on their causes and our intuitions that effects are produced by their causes are tracking different causal relations.

Further Reading

Beebee, H. (2004). "Causing and Nothingness," in L. A. Paul, E. J. Hall, and J. Collins (eds.), *Causation and Counterfactuals*. Cambridge, MA: MIT Press, pp. 291–308.

Dowe, P. (2007). *Physical Causation*. Cambridge: Cambridge University Press.

Cartwright, N. (1979). "Causal Laws and Effective Strategies," *Noûs* 13: 419–37.

Ehring, D. (1997). *Causation and Persistence*. New York: Oxford University Press.

Lewis, D. (2000). "Causation as Influence," *The Journal of Philosophy* 97: 182–97.

Mackie, J. L. (1974). *The Cement of the Universe*. Oxford: Clarendon Press.

Paul, L. A. (2000). "Aspect Causation," *The Journal of Philosophy* 97: 235–56.

Schaffer, J. (2000a). "Trumping Preemption," *The Journal of Philosophy* 97: 165–81.

Schaffer, J. (2000b). "Causation by Disconnection," *Philosophy of Science* 67: 285–300.

Sosa, E., and Tooley M. (1993). *Causation*. Oxford: Oxford University Press.

Tooley, M. (1987). *Causation: A Realist Approach*. Oxford: Clarendon Press.

Woodward, J. (2005). *Making Things Happen: A Theory of Causal Explanation*. Oxford: Oxford University Press.

25

On the Notion of Cause

Bertrand Russell

In the following paper I wish, first, to maintain that the word "cause" is so inextricably bound up with misleading associations as to make its complete extrusion from the philosophical vocabulary desirable; secondly, to inquire what principle, if any, is employed in science in place of the supposed "law of causality" which philosophers imagine to be employed; thirdly, to exhibit certain confusions, especially in regard to teleology and determinism, which appear to me to be connected with erroneous notions as to causality.

All philosophers, of every school, imagine that causation is one of the fundamental axioms or postulates of science, yet, oddly enough, in advanced sciences such as gravitational astronomy, the word "cause" never occurs. Dr. James Ward, in his *Naturalism and Agnosticism*, makes this a ground of complaint against physics: the business of science, he apparently thinks, should be the discovery of causes, yet physics never even seeks them. To me it seems that philosophy ought not to assume such legislative functions, and that the reason why physics has ceased to look for causes is that, in fact, there are no such things. The law of causality, I believe, like much that passes muster among philosophers, is a relic of a bygone age, surviving, like the monarchy, only because it is erroneously supposed to do no harm.

In order to find out what philosophers commonly understand by "cause," I consulted Baldwin's *Dictionary*, and was rewarded beyond my expectations, for I found the following three mutually incompatible definitions:–

"CAUSALITY. (1) The necessary connection of events in the time-series....

"CAUSE (notion of). Whatever may be included in the thought or perception of a process as taking place in consequence of another process....

"CAUSE AND EFFECT. (1) Cause and effect.... are correlative terms denoting any two distinguishable things, phases, or aspects of reality, which are so related to each other, that whenever the first ceases to exist, the second comes into existence immediately after, and whenever the second comes into existence, the first has ceased to exist immediately before."

Let us consider these three definitions in turn. The first, obviously, is unintelligible without a

Bertrand Russell, "On the Notion of Cause," *Proceedings of the Aristotelian Society*, NS 13 (1912–13): 1–26. Reprinted by permission of John Wiley & Sons, Inc.

Metaphysics: An Anthology, Second Edition. Edited by Jaegwon Kim, Daniel Z. Korman and Ernest Sosa.
Editorial material and organization © 2012 Blackwell Publishing Ltd. Published 2012 by Blackwell Publishing Ltd.

definition of "necessary." Under this head, Baldwin's *Dictionary* gives the following:–

"NECESSARY. That is necessary which not only is true, but would be true under all circumstances. Something more than brute compulsion is, therefore, involved in the conception; there is a general law under which the thing takes place."

The notion of cause is so intimately connected with that of necessity that it will be no digression to linger over the above definition, with a view to discovering, if possible, *some* meaning of which it is capable; for, as it stands, it is very far from having any definite signification.

The first point to notice is that, if any meaning is to be given to the phrase "would be true under all circumstances," the subject of it must be a propositional function, not a proposition.[1] A proposition is simply true or false, and that ends the matter: there can be no question of "circumstances." "Charles I's head was cut off" is just as true in summer as in winter, on Sundays as on Mondays. Thus when it is worth saying that something "would be true under all circumstances," the something in question must be a propositional function, *i.e.* an expression containing a variable, and becoming a proposition when a value is assigned to the variable; the varying "circumstances" alluded to are then the different values of which the variable is capable. Thus if "necessary" means "what is true under all circumstances," then "if x is a man, x is mortal" is necessary, because it is true for any possible value of x. Thus we should be led to the following definition:–

"NECESSARY is a predicate of a propositional function, meaning that it is true for all possible values of its argument or arguments."

Unfortunately, however, the definition in Baldwin's *Dictionary* says that what is necessary is not only "true under all circumstances" but is also "true." Now these two are incompatible. Only propositions can be "true," and only propositional functions can be "true under all circumstances." Hence the definition as it stands is nonsense. What is meant seems to be this: "A proposition is necessary when it is a value of a propositional function which is true under all circumstances, *i.e.* for all values of its argument or arguments." But if we adopt this definition, the same proposition will be necessary or contingent according as we choose one or other of its terms as the argument to our propositional function. For example, "if Socrates is a man, Socrates is mortal," is necessary if Socrates is chosen as argument, but not if *man* or *mortal* is chosen. Again, "if Socrates is a man, Plato is mortal," will be necessary if either Socrates or *man* is chosen as argument, but not if Plato or *mortal* is chosen. However, this difficulty can be overcome by specifying the constituent which is to be regarded as argument, and we thus arrive at the following definition:

"A proposition is *necessary* with respect to a given constituent if it remains true when that constituent is altered in any way compatible with the proposition remaining significant."

We may now apply this definition to the definition of causality quoted above. It is obvious that the argument must be the time at which the earlier event occurs. Thus an instance of causality will be such as: "If the event e_1 occurs at the time t_1, it will be followed by the event e_2." This proposition is intended to be necessary with respect to t_1, *i.e.* to remain true however t_1 may be varied. Causality, as a universal law, will then be the following: "Given any event e_1 there is an event e_2 such that, whenever e_1 occurs, e_2 occurs later." But before this can be considered precise, we must specify how much later e_2 is to occur. Thus the principle becomes:

"Given any event e_1, there is an event e_2 and a time-interval τ such that, whenever e_1 occurs, e_2 follows after an interval τ."

I am not concerned as yet to consider whether this law is true or false. For the present, I am merely concerned to discover what the law of causality is supposed to be. I pass, therefore, to the other definitions quoted above.

The second definition need not detain us long, for two reasons. First, because it is psychological: not the "thought or perception" of a process, but the process itself, must be what concerns us in considering causality. Secondly, because it is circular: in speaking of a process as "taking place in consequence of" another process, it introduces the very notion of cause which was to be defined.

The third definition is by far the most precise; indeed as regards clearness it leaves nothing to be desired. But a great difficulty is caused by the temporal contiguity of cause and affect which the definition asserts. No two instants are contiguous, since the time-series is compact; hence either the cause or the effect or both must, if the definition is correct, endure for a finite time; indeed, by the wording of the definition it is plain that both are assumed to endure for a finite time. But then we are faced with a dilemma: if the cause is a process involving change within itself, we shall require (if causality is universal) causal relations between its earlier and later parts; moreover, it would seem that only the later parts can be relevant to the effect, since the earlier parts are not contiguous to the effect, and therefore (by the definition) cannot influence the effect. Thus we shall be led to diminish the duration of the cause without limit, and however much we may diminish it, there will still remain an earlier part which might be altered without altering the effect, so that the true cause, as defined, will not have been reached, for it will be observed that the definition excludes plurality of causes. If, on the other hand, the cause is purely static, involving no change within itself, then, in the first place, no such cause is to be found in nature, and in the second place, it seems strange – too strange to be accepted, in spite of bare logical possibility – that the cause, after existing placidly for some time, should suddenly explode into the effect, when it might just as well have done so at any earlier time, or have gone on unchanged without producing its effect. This dilemma, therefore, is fatal to the view that cause and effect can be contiguous in time; if there are causes and effects, they must be separated by a finite time-interval τ, as was assumed in the above interpretation of the first definition.

What is essentially the same statement of the law of causality as the one elicited above from the first of Baldwin's definitions is given by other philosophers. Thus John Stuart Mill says: –

"The Law of Causation, the recognition of which is the main pillar of inductive science, is but the familiar truth, that invariability of succession is found by observation to obtain between every fact in nature and some other fact which has preceded it."[2]

And Bergson, who has rightly perceived that the law as stated by philosophers is worthless, nevertheless continues to suppose that it is used in science. Thus he says: –

"Now, it is argued, this law [the law of causality] means that every phenomenon is determined by its conditions, or, in other words, that the same causes produce the same effects."[3]

And again : –

"We perceive physical phenomena, and these phenomena obey laws. This means: (1) That phenomena a, b, c, d, previously perceived, can occur again in the same shape; (2) that a certain phenomenon P, which appeared after the conditions a, b, c, d, and after these conditions only, will not fail to recur as soon as the same conditions are again present."[4]

A great part of Bergson's attack on science rests on the assumption that it employs this principle. In fact, it employs no such principle, but philosophers – even Bergson – are too apt to take their views on science from each other, not from science. As to what the principle is, there is a fair consensus among philosophers of different schools. There are, however, a number of difficulties which at once arise. I omit the question of plurality of causes for the present, since other graver questions have to be considered. Two of these, which are forced on our attention by the above statement of the law, are the following : –

(1) What is meant by an "event"?
(2) How long may the time-interval be between cause and effect?

(1) An "event," in the statement of the law, is obviously intended to be something that is likely to recur, since otherwise the law becomes trivial. It follows that an "event" is not a particular, but some universal of which there may be many instances. It follows also that an "event" must be something short of the whole state of the universe, since it is highly improbable that this will recur. What is meant by an "event" is something like striking a match, or dropping a penny into the slot of an automatic machine. If such an event is to recur, it must not be defined too narrowly: we must not state with what degree of force the match is to be struck, nor what is to be the temperature of the penny. For if such considerations were relevant, our "event" would occur at most once, and the law would cease to give information. An "event," then, is a universal defined sufficiently widely to admit of many particular occurrences in time being instances of it.

(2) The next question concerns the time-interval. Philosophers, no doubt, think of cause and effect as contiguous in time, but this, for reasons already given, is impossible. Hence, since there are no infinitesimal time-intervals, there must be some finite lapse of time τ between cause and effect. This, however, at once raises insuperable difficulties. However short we make the interval τ, something may happen during this interval which prevents the expected result. I put my penny in the slot but before I can draw out my ticket there is an earthquake which upsets the machine and my calculations. In order to be sure of the expected effect, we must know that there is nothing in the environment to interfere with it. But this means that the supposed cause is not, by itself, adequate to insure the effect. And as soon as we include the environment, the probability of repetition is diminished, until at last, when the whole environment is included, the probability of repetition becomes almost *nil*.

In spite of these difficulties, it must, of course, be admitted that many fairly dependable regularities of sequence occur in daily life. It is these regularities that have suggested the supposed law of causality; where they are found to fail, it is thought that a better formulation could have been found which would have never failed. I am far from denying that there may be such sequences which in fact never do fail. It may be that there will never be an exception to the rule that when a stone of more than a certain mass, moving with more than a certain velocity, comes in contact with a pane of glass of less than a certain thickness, the glass breaks. I also do not deny that the observation of such regularities, even when they are not without exceptions, is useful in the infancy of a science: the observation that unsupported bodies in air usually fall was a stage on the way to the law of gravitation. What I deny is that science assumes the existence of invariable uniformities of sequence of this kind, or that it aims at discovering them. All such uniformities, as we saw, depend upon a certain vagueness in the definition of the "events." That bodies fall is a vague qualitative statement; science wishes to know how fast they fall. This depends upon the shape of the bodies and the density of the air. It is true that there is more nearly uniformity when they fall in a vacuum; so far as Galileo could observe, the uniformity is then complete. But later it appeared that even there the latitude made a difference, and the altitude. Theoretically, the position of the sun and moon must make a difference. In short, every advance in a science takes us farther away from the crude uniformities which are first observed, into greater differentiation of antecedent and consequent, and into a continually wider circle of antecedents recognized as relevant.

The principle "same cause, same effect," which philosophers imagine to be vital to science, is therefore utterly otiose. As soon as the antecedents have been given sufficiently fully to enable the consequent to be calculated with some exactitude, the antecedents have become so complicated that it is very unlikely they will ever recur. Hence, if this were the principle involved, science would remain utterly sterile.

The importance of these considerations lies partly in the fact that they lead to a more correct account of scientific procedure, partly in the fact that they remove the analogy with human volition which makes the conception of cause such a fruitful source of fallacies. The latter point will become clearer by the help of some illustrations. For this purpose I shall consider a few maxims which have played a great part in the history of philosophy.

(1) "Cause and effect must more or less resemble each other." This principle was prominent in the philosophy of occasionalism, and is still by no means extinct. It is still often thought, for example, that mind could not have grown up in a universe which previously contained nothing mental, and one ground for this belief is that matter is too dissimilar from mind to have been able to cause it. Or, more particularly, what are termed the nobler parts of our nature are supposed to be inexplicable, unless the universe always contained something at least equally noble which could cause them. All such views seem to depend upon assuming some unduly simplified law of causality; for, in any legitimate sense of "cause" and "effect," science seems to show that they are usually very widely dissimilar, the "cause" being, in fact, two states of the whole universe, and the "effect" some particular event.

(2) "Cause is analogous to volition, since there must be an intelligible *nexus* between cause and effect." This maxim is, I think, often unconsciously in the imaginations of philosophers who would reject it when explicitly stated. It is probably operative in the view we have just been

considering, that mind could not have resulted from a purely material world. I do not profess to know what is meant by "intelligible"; it seems to mean "familiar to imagination." Nothing is less "intelligible," in any other sense, than the connection between an act of will and its fulfilment. But obviously the sort of nexus desired between cause and effect is such as could only hold between the "events" which the supposed law of causality contemplates; the laws which replace causality in such a science as physics leave no room for any two events between which a nexus could be sought.

(3) "The cause *compels* the effect in some sense in which the effect does not compel the cause." This belief seems largely operative in the dislike of determinism; but, as a matter of fact, it is connected with our second maxim, and falls as soon as that is abandoned. We may define "compulsion" as follows: – "Any set of circumstances is said to compel A when A desires to do something which the circumstances prevent, or to abstain from something which the circumstances cause." This presupposes that some meaning has been found for the word "cause" – a point to which I shall return later. What I want to make clear at present is that compulsion is a very complex notion, involving thwarted desire. So long as a person does what he wishes to do, there is no compulsion, however much his wishes may be calculable by the help of earlier events. And where desire does not come in, there can be no question of compulsion. Hence it is, in general, misleading to regard the cause as compelling the effect.

A vaguer form of the same maxim substitutes the word "determine" for the word "compel": we are told that the cause *determines* the effect in a sense in which the effect does not *determine* the cause. It is not quite clear what is meant by "determining"; the only precise sense, so far as I know, is that of a function or one-many relation. If we admit plurality of causes, but not of effects, that is, if we suppose that, given the cause, the effect must be such and such, but, given the effect, the cause may have been one of many alternatives, then we may say that the cause determines the effect, but not the effect the cause. Plurality of causes, however, results only from conceiving the effect vaguely and narrowly and the cause precisely and widely. Many antecedents may "cause" a man's death, because his death is vague and narrow. But if we adopt the opposite course,

taking as the "cause" the drinking of a dose of arsenic, and as the "effect" the whole state of the world five minutes later, we shall have plurality of effects instead of plurality of causes. Thus the supposed lack of symmetry between "cause" and "effect" is illusory.

(4) "A cause cannot operate when it has ceased to exist, because what has ceased to exist is nothing." This is a common maxim, and a still more common unexpressed prejudice. It has, I fancy, a good deal to do with the attractiveness of Bergson's "*durée*": since the past has effects now, it must still exist in some sense. The mistake in this maxim consists in the supposition that causes "operate" at all. A volition "operates" when what it wills takes place; but nothing can operate except a volition. The belief that causes "operate" results from assimilating them, consciously or unconsciously, to volitions. We have already seen that, if there are causes at all, they must be separated by a finite interval of time from their effects, and thus cause their effects after they have ceased to exist.

It may be objected to the above definition of a volition "operating" that it only operates when it "causes" what it wills, not when it merely happens to be followed by what it wills. This certainly represents the usual view of what is meant by a volition "operating," but as it involves the very view of causation which we are engaged in combating, it is not open to us as a definition. We may say that a volition "operates" when there is some law in virtue of which a similar volition in rather similar circumstances will usually be followed by what it wills. But this is a vague conception, and introduces ideas which we have not yet considered. What is chiefly important to notice is that the usual notion of "operating" is not open to us if we reject, as I contend that we should, the usual notion of causation.

(5) "A cause cannot operate except where it is." This maxim is very widespread; it was urged against Newton, and has remained a source of prejudice against "action at a distance." In philosophy it has led to a denial of transeunt action, and thence to monism or Leibnizian monadism. Like the analogous maxim concerning temporal contiguity, it rests upon the assumption that causes "operate," *i.e.*, that they are in some obscure way analogous to volitions. And, as in the case of temporal contiguity, the inferences drawn from this maxim are wholly groundless.

I return now to the question, What law or laws can be found to take the place of the supposed law of causality?

First, without passing beyond such uniformities of sequence as are contemplated by the traditional law, we may admit that, if any such sequence has been observed in a great many cases, and has never been found to fail, there is an inductive probability that it will be found to hold in future cases. If stones have hitherto been found to break windows, it is probable that they will continue to do so. This, of course, assumes the inductive principle, of which the truth may reasonably be questioned; but as this principle is not our present concern, I shall in this discussion treat it as indubitable. We may then say, in the case of any such frequently-observed sequence, that the earlier event is the *cause* and the later event the *effect*.

Several considerations, however, make such special sequences very different from the traditional relation of cause and effect. In the first place, the sequence, in any hitherto unobserved instance, is no more than probable, whereas the relation of cause and effect was supposed to be necessary. I do not mean by this merely that we are not sure of having discovered a true case of cause and effect; I mean that, even when we have a case of cause and effect in our present sense, all that is meant is that, on grounds of observation, it is probable that when one occurs the other will also occur. Thus in our present sense, A may be the cause of B even if there actually are cases where B does not follow A. Striking a match will be the cause of its igniting, in spite of the fact that some matches are damp and fail to ignite.

In the second place, it will not be assumed that *every* event has some antecedent which is its cause in this sense; we shall only believe in causal sequences where we find them, without any presumption that they always are to be found.

In the third place, *any* case of sufficiently frequent sequence will be causal in our present sense; for example, we shall not refuse to say that night is the cause of day. Our repugnance to saying this arises from the ease with which we can imagine the sequence to fail, but owing to the fact that cause and effect must be separated by a finite interval of time, *any* such sequence *might* fail through the interposition of other circumstances in the interval. Mill, discussing this instance of night and day, says: –

"It is necessary to our using the word cause, that we should believe not only that the antecedent always *has* been followed by the consequent, but that as long as the present constitution of things endures, it always *will* be so."[5]

In this sense, we shall have to give up the hope of finding causal laws such as Mill contemplated; any causal sequence which we have observed may at any moment be falsified without a falsification of any laws of the kind that the more advanced sciences aim at establishing.

In the fourth place, such laws of probable sequence, though useful in daily life and in the infancy of a science, tend to be displaced by quite different laws as soon as a science is successful. The law of gravitation will illustrate what occurs in any advanced science. In the motions of mutually gravitating bodies, there is nothing that can be called a cause, and nothing that can be called an effect; there is merely a formula. Certain differential equations can be found, which hold at every instant for every particle of the system, and which, given the configuration and velocities at one instant, or the configurations at two instants, render the configuration at any other earlier or later instant theoretically calculable. That is to say, the configuration at any instant is a function of that instant and the configurations at two given instants. This statement holds throughout physics, and not only in the special case of gravitation. But there is nothing that could be properly called "cause" and nothing that could be properly called "effect" in such a system.

No doubt the reason why the old "law of causality" has so long continued to pervade the books of philosophers is simply that the idea of a function is unfamiliar to most of them, and therefore they seek an unduly simplified statement. There is no question of repetitions, of the "same" cause producing the "same" effect; it is not in any sameness of causes and effects that the constancy of scientific laws consists, but in sameness of relations. And even "sameness of relations" is too simple a phrase; "sameness of differential equations" is the only correct phrase. It is impossible to state this accurately in non-mathematical language; the nearest approach would be as follows:—"There is a constant relation between the state of the universe at any instant and the rate of change in the rate at which any part of the universe is changing at that instant, and this relation is many-one, *i.e.* such that the rate of change in the rate of change is determinate when the state of the universe is given." If the "law of causality" is to be something actually discoverable in the practice of science, the above proposition has a better right to the name than any "law of causality" to be found in the books of philosophers.

In regard to the above principle, several observations must be made –

(1) No one can pretend that the above principle is *a priori* or self-evident or a "necessity of thought." Nor is it, in any sense, a premiss of science: it is an empirical generalization from a number of laws which are themselves empirical generalizations.

(2) The law makes no difference between past and future: the future "determines" the past in exactly the same sense in which the past "determines" the future. The word "determine," here, has a purely logical significance: a certain number of variables "determine" another variable if that other variable is a function of them.

(3) The law will not be empirically verifiable unless the course of events within some sufficiently small volume will be approximately the same in any two states of the universe which only differ in regard to what is at a considerable distance from the small volume in question. For example, motions of planets in the solar system must be approximately the same however the fixed stars may be distributed, provided that all the fixed stars are very much farther from the sun than the planets are. If gravitation varied directly as the distance, so that the most remote stars made the most difference to the motions of the planets, the world might be just as regular and just as much subject to mathematical laws as it is at present, but we could never discover the fact.

(4) Although the old "law of causality" is not assumed by science, something which we may call the "uniformity of nature" is assumed, or rather is accepted on inductive grounds. The uniformity of nature does not assert the trivial principle "same cause, same effect," but the principle of the permanence of laws. That is to say, when a law exhibiting, *e.g.*, an acceleration as a function of the configuration has been found to hold throughout the observable past, it is expected that it will continue to hold in the future, or that, if it does not itself hold, there is some other law, agreeing with the supposed law as regards the past, which will hold for the future. The ground of this principle is simply the inductive ground that it has been found to be true in very many instances; hence the principle cannot be considered certain, but only probable to a degree which cannot be accurately estimated.

The uniformity of nature, in the above sense, although it is assumed in the practice of science, must not, in its generality, be regarded as a kind of major premiss, without which all scientific reasoning would be in error. The assumption that *all* laws of nature are permanent has, of course, less probability than the assumption that this or that particular law is permanent; and the assumption that a particular law is permanent for all time has less probability than the assumption that it will be valid up to such and such a date. Science, in any given case, will assume what the case requires, but no more. In constructing the *Nautical Almanac* for 1915 it will assume that the law of gravitation will remain true up to the end of that year; but it will make no assumption as to 1916 until it comes to the next volume of the almanac. This procedure is, of course, dictated by the fact that the uniformity of nature is not known *a priori*, but is an empirical generalization, like "all men are mortal." In all such cases, it is better to argue immediately from the given particular instances to the new instance, than to argue by way of a major premiss; the conclusion is only probable in either case, but acquires a higher probability by the former method than by the latter.

In all science we have to distinguish two sorts of laws: first, those that are empirically verifiable but probably only approximate; secondly, those that are not verifiable, but may be exact. The law of gravitation, for example, in its applications to the solar system, is only empirically verifiable when it is assumed that matter outside the solar system may be ignored for such purposes; we believe this to be only approximately true, but we cannot empirically verify the law of universal gravitation which we believe to be exact. This point is very important in connection with what we may call "relatively isolated systems." These may be defined as follows: –

A system relatively isolated during a given period is one which, within some assignable margin of error, will behave in the same way throughout that period, however the rest of the universe may be constituted.

A system may be called "practically isolated" during a given period if, although there *might* be states of the rest of the universe which would produce more than the assigned margin of error, there is reason to believe that such states do not in fact occur.

Strictly speaking, we ought to specify the respect in which the system is relatively isolated. For example, the earth is relatively isolated as regards falling bodies, but not as regards tides; it is *practically* isolated as regards economic phenomena, although, if Jevons' sun-spot theory of commercial crises had been true, it would not have been even practically isolated in this respect.

It will be observed that we cannot prove in advance that a system is isolated. This will be inferred from the observed fact that approximate uniformities can be stated for this system alone. If the complete laws for the whole universe were known, the isolation of a system could be deduced from them; assuming, for example, the law of universal gravitation, the practical isolation of the solar system in this respect can be deduced by the help of the fact that there is very little matter in its neighbourhood. But it should be observed that isolated systems are only important as providing a possibility of *discovering* scientific laws; they have no theoretical importance in the finished structure of a science.

The case where one event A is said to "cause" another event B, which philosophers take as fundamental, is really only the most simplified instance of a practically isolated system. It may happen that, as a result of general scientific laws, whenever A occurs throughout a certain period, it is followed by B; in that case, A and B form a system which is practically isolated throughout that period. It is, however, to be regarded as a piece of good fortune if this occurs; it will always be due to special circumstances, and would not have been true if the rest of the universe had been different though subject to the same laws.

The essential function which causality has been supposed to perform is the possibility of inferring the future from the past, or, more generally, events at any time from events at certain assigned times. Any system in which such inference is possible may be called a "deterministic" system. We may define a deterministic system as follows: –

A system is said to be "deterministic" when, given certain data, $e_1, e_2, \ldots, e_n$, at times $t_1, t_2, \ldots, t_n$ respectively, concerning this system, if E_t is the state of the system at any time t, there is a functional relation of the form

$$\mathbf{E}_t = f(e_1, t_1, e_2, t_2, \ldots, e_n, t_n, t).$$

The system will be "deterministic throughout a given period" if t, in the above formula, may be any time within that period, though outside that period the formula may be no longer true. If the universe, as a whole, is such a system, determinism is true of the universe; if not, not. A system which is part of a deterministic system I shall call "determined"; one which is not part of any such system I shall call "capricious."

The events $e_1, e_2, \ldots, e_n$ I shall call "determinants" of the system. It is to be observed that a system which has one set of determinants will in general have many. In the case of the motions of the planets, for example, the configurations of the solar system at any two given times will be determinants.

We may take another illustration from the hypothesis of psycho-physical parallelism. Let us assume, for the purposes of this illustration, that to a given state of brain a given state of mind always corresponds, and *vice versa, i.e.,* that there is a one-one relation between them, so that each is a function of the other. We may also assume, what is practically certain, that to a given state of a certain brain a given state of the whole material universe corresponds, since it is highly improbable that a given brain is ever twice in exactly the same state. Hence there will be a one-one relation between the state of a given person's mind and the state of the whole material universe. It follows that, if n states of the material universe are determinants of the material universe, then n states of a given man's mind are determinants of the whole material and mental universe – assuming, that is to say, that psycho-physical parallelism is true.

The above illustration is important in connection with a certain confusion which seems to have beset those who have philosophized on the relation of mind and matter. It is often thought that, if the state of the mind is determinate when the state of the brain is given, and if the material world forms a deterministic system, then mind is "subject" to matter in some sense in which matter is not "subject" to mind. But if the state of the brain is also determinate when the state of the mind is given, it must be exactly as true to regard matter as subject to mind as it would be to regard mind as subject to matter. We could, theoretically, work out the history of mind without ever mentioning matter, and then, at the end, deduce that matter must meanwhile have gone through the corresponding history. It is true that if the relation of brain to mind were many-one, not one-one, there would be a one-sided dependence of mind on brain, while conversely, if the relation were one-many, as Bergson supposes, there would be a one-sided dependence of brain on mind. But the dependence involved is, in any case, only logical; it does not mean that we shall be compelled to do things we desire not to do, which is what people instinctively imagine it to mean.

As another illustration we may take the case of mechanism and teleology. A system may be defined as "mechanical" when it has a set of determinants that are purely material, such as the positions of certain pieces of matter at certain times. It is an open question whether the world of mind and matter, as we know it, is a mechanical system or not; let us suppose, for the sake of argument, that it is a mechanical system. This supposition – so I contend – throws no light whatever on the question whether the universe is or is not a "teleological" system. It is difficult to define accurately what is meant by a "teleological" system, but the argument is not much affected by the particular definition we adopt. Broadly, a teleological system is one in which purposes are realized, *i.e.*, in which certain desires – those that are deeper or nobler or more fundamental or more universal or what not – are followed by their realization. Now the fact – if it be a fact – that the universe is mechanical has no bearing whatever on the question whether it is teleological in the above sense. There might be a mechanical system in which all wishes were realized, and there might be one in which all wishes were thwarted. The question whether, or how far, our actual world is teleological, cannot, therefore, be settled by proving that it is mechanical, and the desire that it should be teleological is no ground for wishing it to be not mechanical.

There is, in all these questions, a very great difficulty in avoiding confusion between what we can infer and what is in fact determined. Let us consider, for a moment, the various senses in which the future may be "determined." There is one sense – and a very important one – in which it is determined quite independently of scientific laws, namely, the sense that it will be what it will be. We all regard the past as determined simply by the fact that it has happened; but for the accident that

memory works backward and not forward, we should regard the future as equally determined by the fact that it will happen. "But," we are told, "you cannot alter the past, while you can to some extent alter the future." This view seems to me to rest upon just those errors in regard to causation which it has been my object to remove. You cannot make the past other than it was – true, but this is a mere application of the law of contradiction. If you already know what the past was, obviously it is useless to wish it different. But also you cannot make the future other than it will be; this again is an application of the law of contradiction. And if you happen to know the future – *e.g.*, in the case of a forthcoming eclipse – it is just as useless to wish it different as to wish the past different. "But," it will be rejoined, "our wishes can *cause* the future, sometimes, to be different from what it would be if they did not exist, and they can have no such effect upon the past." This, again, is a mere tautology. An effect being *defined* as something subsequent to its cause, obviously we can have no *effect* upon the past. But that does not mean that the past would not have been different if our present wishes had been different. Obviously, our present wishes are conditioned by the past, and therefore could not have been different unless the past had been different; therefore, if our present wishes were different, the past would be different. Of course, the past cannot be different from what it was, but no more can our present wishes be different from what they are; this again is merely the law of contradiction. The facts seem to be merely (1) that wishing generally depends upon ignorance, and is therefore commoner in regard to the future than in regard to the past, (2) that where a wish concerns the future, it and its realization very often form a "practically independent system," *i.e.*, many wishes regarding the future are realized. But there seems no doubt that the main difference in our feelings arises from the fact that the past but not the future can be known by memory.

Although the sense of "determined" in which the future is determined by the mere fact that it will be what it will be is sufficient (at least so it seems to me) to refute some opponents of determinism, notably M. Bergson and the pragmatists, yet it is not what most people have in mind when they speak of the future as determined. What they have in mind is a formula by means of which the future can be exhibited, and at least theoretically calculated, as a function of the past. But at this point we meet with a great difficulty, which besets what has been said above about deterministic systems, as well as what is said by others.

If formulæ of any degree of complexity, however great, are admitted, it would seem that any system, whose state at a given moment is a function of certain measurable quantities, *must* be a deterministic system. Let us consider, in illustration, a single material particle, whose co-ordinates at time t are x_t, y_t, z_t. Then, however, the particle moves, there must be, theoretically, functions f_1, f_2, f_3, such that

$$x_t = f_1(t), \qquad y_t = f_2(t), \qquad z_t = f_3(t).$$

It follows that, theoretically, the whole state of the material universe at time t must be capable of being exhibited as a function of t. Hence our universe will be deterministic in the sense defined above. But if this be true, no information is conveyed about the universe in stating that it is deterministic. It is true that the formulæ involved may be of strictly infinite complexity, and therefore not practically capable of being written down or apprehended. But except from the point of view of our knowledge, this might seem to be a detail: in itself, if the above considerations are sound, the material universe *must* be deterministic, *must* be subject to laws.

This, however, is plainly not what was intended. The difference between this view and the view intended may be seen as follows. Given some formula which fits the facts hitherto – say the law of gravitation – there will be an infinite number of other formulæ, not empirically distinguishable from it in the past, but diverging from it more and more in the future. Hence, even assuming that there are persistent laws, we shall have no reason for assuming that the law of the inverse square will hold in future; it may be some other hitherto indistinguishable law that will hold. We cannot say that *every* law which has held hitherto must hold in the future, because past facts which obey one law will also obey others, hitherto indistinguishable but diverging in future. Hence there must, at every moment, be laws hitherto unbroken which are now broken for the first time. What science does, in fact, is to select the *simplest* formula that will fit the facts. But this, quite obviously, is merely a methodological precept, not a law of Nature. If the simplest formula ceases, after a time, to be applicable, the simplest formula that remains applicable is selected, and science has no sense that an axiom

has been falsified. We are thus left with the brute fact that, in many departments of science, quite simple laws have hitherto been found to hold. This fact cannot be regarded as having any *a priori* ground, nor can it be used to support inductively the opinion that the same laws will continue; for at every moment laws hitherto true are being falsified, though in the advanced sciences these laws are less simple than those that have remained true. Moreover it would be fallacious to argue inductively from the state of the advanced sciences to the future state of the others, for it may well be that the advanced sciences are advanced simply because, hitherto, their subject-matter has obeyed simple and easily-ascertainable laws, while the subject-matter of other sciences has not done so.

The difficulty we have been considering seems to be met partly, if not wholly, by the principle that the *time* must not enter explicitly into our formulæ. All mechanical laws exhibit acceleration as a function of configuration, not of configuration and time jointly; and this principle of the irrelevance of the time may be extended to all scientific laws. In fact we might interpret the "uniformity of nature" as meaning just this, that no scientific law involves the time as an argument, unless, of course, it is given in an integrated form, in which case *lapse* of time, though not absolute time, may appear in our formulæ. Whether this consideration suffices to overcome our difficulty completely, I do not know; but in any case it does much to diminish it.

It will serve to illustrate what has been said if we apply it to the question of free will.

(1) Determinism in regard to the will is the doctrine that our volitions belong to some deterministic system, *i.e.*, are "determined" in the sense defined above. Whether this doctrine is true or false, is a mere question of fact; no *a priori* considerations (if our previous discussions have been correct) can exist on either side. On the one hand, there is no *a priori* category of causality, but merely certain observed uniformities. As a matter of fact, there are observed uniformities in regard to volitions; thus there is some empirical evidence that volitions are determined. But it would be very rash to maintain that the evidence is overwhelming, and it is quite possible that some volitions, as well as some other things, are not determined, except in the sense in which we found that everything must be determined.

(2) But, on the other hand, the subjective sense of freedom, sometimes alleged against determinism, has no bearing on the question whatever. The view that it has a bearing rests upon the belief that causes compel their effects, or that nature enforces obedience to its laws as governments do. These are mere anthropomorphic superstitions, due to assimilation of causes with volitions and of natural laws with human edicts. We feel that our will is not compelled, but that only means that it is not other than we choose it to be. It is one of the demerits of the traditional theory of causality that it has created an artificial opposition between determinism and the freedom of which we are introspectively conscious.

(3) Besides the general question whether volitions are determined, there is the further question whether they are *mechanically* determined, *i.e.*, whether they are part of what was above defined as a mechanical system. This is the question whether they form part of a system with purely material determinants, *i.e.*, whether there are laws which, given certain material data, make all volitions functions of those data. Here again, there is empirical evidence up to a point, but it is not conclusive in regard to all volitions. It is important to observe, however, that even if volitions are part of a mechanical system, this by no means implies any supremacy of matter over mind. It may well be that the same system which is susceptible of material determinants is also susceptible of mental determinants; thus a mechanical system may be determined by sets of volitions, as well as by sets of material facts. It would seem, therefore, that the reasons which make people dislike the view that volitions are mechanically determined are fallacious.

(4) The notion of *necessity*, which is often associated with determinism, is a confused notion not legitimately deducible from determinism. Three meanings are commonly confounded when necessity is spoken of: –

(α) An *action* is necessary when it will be performed however much the agent may wish to do otherwise. Determinism does not imply that actions are necessary in this sense.

(β) A *propositional function* is necessary when all its values are true. This sense is not relevant to our present discussion.

(γ) A *proposition* is necessary with respect to a given constituent when it is the value, with that constituent as argument, of a necessary propositional function, in other words, when it remains true however that constituent may be varied. In this sense, in a deterministic system, the connection of a volition with its determinants is necessary, if the time at which the determinants occur be taken as the constituent to be varied, the time-interval between the determinants and the volition being kept constant. But this sense of necessity is purely logical, and has no emotional importance.

We may now sum up our discussion of causality. We found first that the law of causality, as usually stated by philosophers, is false, and is not employed in science. We then considered the nature of scientific laws, and found that, instead of stating that one event A is always followed by another event B, they stated functional relations between certain events at certain times, which we called determinants, and other events at earlier or later times or at the same time. We were unable to find any *a priori* category involved: the existence of scientific laws appeared as a purely empirical fact, not necessarily universal, except in a trivial and scientifically useless form. We found that a system with one set of determinants may very likely have other sets of a quite different kind, that, for example, a mechanically determined system may also be teleologically or volitionally determined. Finally we considered the problem of free will: here we found that the reasons for supposing volitions to be determined are strong but not conclusive, and we decided that even if volitions are mechanically determined, that is no reason for denying freedom in the sense revealed by introspection, or for supposing that mechanical events are not determined by volitions. The problem of free will *versus* determinism is therefore, if we were right, mainly illusory, but in part not yet capable of being decisively solved.

Notes

1   A propositional function is an expression containing a variable, or undetermined constituent, and becoming a proposition as soon as a definite value is assigned to the variable. Examples are: "A is A," "*x* is a number." The variable is called the *argument* of the function.

2   *Logic*, Bk. III, Chap. V, § 2.

3   *Time and Free Will*, p. 199.

4   *Ibid.*, p. 202.

5   *Loc. cit.*, § 6.

26

Causes and Conditions

J. L. Mackie

Asked what a cause is, we may be tempted to say that it is an event which precedes the event of which it is the cause, and is both necessary and sufficient for the latter's occurrence; briefly, that a cause is a necessary and sufficient preceding condition. There are, however, many difficulties in this account. I shall try to show that what we often speak of as a cause is a condition not of this sort, but of a sort related to this. That is to say, this account needs modification, and can be modified, and when it is modified, we can explain much more satisfactorily how we can arrive at much of what we ordinarily take to be causal knowledge; the claims implicit within our causal assertions can be related to the forms of the evidence on which we are often relying when we assert a causal connection.

1 Singular Causal Statements

Suppose that a fire has broken out in a certain house, but has been extinguished before the house has been completely destroyed. Experts investigate the cause of the fire, and they conclude that it was caused by an electrical short circuit at a certain place. What is the exact force of their statement that this short circuit caused this fire? Clearly the experts are not saying that the short circuit was a necessary condition for this house's catching fire at this time; they know perfectly well that a short circuit somewhere else, or the overturning of a lighted oil stove, or any one of a number of other things might, if it had occurred, have set the house on fire. Equally, they are not saying that the short circuit was a sufficient condition for this house's catching fire; for if the short circuit had occurred, but there had been no inflammable material nearby, the fire would not have broken out, and even given both the short circuit and the inflammable material, the fire would not have occurred if, say, there had been an efficient automatic sprinkler at just the right spot. Far from being a condition both necessary and sufficient for the fire, the short circuit was, and is known to the experts to have been, neither necessary nor sufficient for it. In what sense, then, is it said to have caused the fire?

At least part of the answer is that there is a set of conditions (of which some are positive and some are negative), including the presence of inflammable material, the absence of a suitably placed sprinkler, and no doubt quite a number of others, which combined with the short circuit constituted a complex condition that was

J. L. Mackie, "Causes and Conditions," *American Philosophical Quarterly*, 2 (1965): 245–64. Reproduced by permission.

Metaphysics: An Anthology, Second Edition. Edited by Jaegwon Kim, Daniel Z. Korman and Ernest Sosa.

sufficient for the house's catching fire – sufficient, but not necessary, for the fire could have started in other ways. Also, of *this* complex condition, the short circuit was an indispensable part: the other parts of this condition, conjoined with one another in the absence of the short circuit, would not have produced the fire. The short circuit which is said to have caused the fire is thus an indispensable part of a complex sufficient (but not necessary) condition of the fire. In this case, then, the so-called cause is, and is known to be, an *insufficient* but *necessary* part of a condition which is itself *unnecessary* but *sufficient* for the result. The experts are saying, in effect, that the short circuit is a condition of this sort, that it occurred, that the other conditions which conjoined with it form a sufficient condition were also present, and that no other sufficient condition of the house's catching fire was present on this occasion. I suggest that when we speak of the cause of some particular event, it is often a condition of this sort that we have in mind. In view of the importance of conditions of this sort in our knowledge of and talk about causation, it will be convenient to have a short name for them: let us call such a condition (from the initial letters of the words italicized above), an INUS condition.[1]

This account of the force of the experts' statement about the cause of the fire may be confirmed by reflecting on the way in which they will have reached this conclusion, and the way in which anyone who disagreed with it would have to challenge it. An important part of the investigation will have consisted in tracing the actual course of the fire; the experts will have ascertained that no other condition sufficient for a fire's breaking out and taking this course was present, but that the short circuit did occur, and that conditions were present which in conjunction with it were sufficient for the fire's breaking out and taking the course that it did. Provided that there is some necessary and sufficient condition of the fire – and this is an assumption that we commonly make in such contexts – anyone who wanted to deny the experts' conclusion would have to challenge one or another of these points.

We can give a more formal analysis of the statement that something is an INUS condition. Let 'A' stand for the INUS condition – in our example, the occurrence of a short circuit at that place – and let 'B' and 'C̄' (that is, 'not-C', or the absence

of C) stand for the other conditions, positive and negative, which were needed along with A to form a sufficient condition of the fire – in our example, B might be the presence of inflammable material, C̄ the absence of a suitably placed sprinkler. Then the conjunction 'ABC̄' represents a sufficient condition of the fire, and one that contains no redundant factors; that is, ABC̄ is a minimal sufficient condition for the fire.[2] Similarly let DĒF, GH̄I, etc., be all the other minimal sufficient conditions of this result. Now provided that there is some necessary and sufficient condition for this result, the disjunction of all the minimal sufficient conditions for it constitutes a necessary and sufficient condition.[3] That is, the formula "ABC̄ or DĒF or GH̄I or ..." represents a necessary and sufficient condition for the fire; each of its disjuncts, such as 'ABC̄', represents a minimal sufficient condition; and each conjunct in each minimal sufficient condition, such as 'A', represents an INUS condition. To simplify and generalize this, we can replace the conjunction of terms conjoined with 'A' (here 'BC̄') by the single term 'X', and the formula representing the disjunction of all the other minimal sufficient conditions – here 'DĒF or GH̄I or ...' – by the single term 'Y'. Then an INUS condition is defined as follows:

> A is an INUS condition of a result P if and only if, for some X and for some Y, (AX or Y) is a necessary and sufficient condition of P, but A is not a sufficient condition of P, and X is not a sufficient condition of P.

We can indicate this type of relation more briefly if we take the provisos for granted and replace the existentially quantified variables 'X' and 'Y' by dots. That is, we can say that A is an INUS condition of P when (A ... or ...) is a necessary and sufficient condition of P.

(To forestall possible misunderstandings, I would fill out this definition as follows.[4] First, there could be a set of minimal sufficient conditions of P, but no necessary conditions, not even a complex one; in such a case, A might be what Marc-Wogau calls a moment in a minimal sufficient condition, but I shall not call it an INUS condition. I shall speak of an INUS condition only where the disjunction of all the minimal sufficient conditions is also a necessary condition. Secondly, the definition leaves it open that the INUS condition A might be a conjunct in each of the minimal sufficient conditions. If so, A would be itself a necessary condition of the result. I shall still call A an INUS condition in these circumstances: it is not part of the definition of an INUS condition that it should *not* be necessary, although in the standard cases, such as that sketched above, it is not in fact necessary.[5] Thirdly, the requirement that X by itself should not be sufficient for P insures that A is a nonredundant part of the sufficient condition AX; but there is a sense in which it may not be strictly necessary or indispensable even as a part of *this* condition, for it may be replaceable: for example KX might be another minimal sufficient condition of P.[6] Fourthly, it *is* part of the definition that the minimal sufficient condition, AX, of which A is a nonredundant part, is not also a necessary condition, that there is another sufficient condition Y (which may itself be a disjunction of sufficient conditions). Fifthly, and similarly, it *is* part of the definition that A is not by itself sufficient for P. The fourth and fifth of these points amount to this: I shall call A an INUS condition only if there are terms which actually occupy the places occupied by 'X' and 'Y' in the formula for the necessary and sufficient condition. However, there may be cases where there is only one minimal sufficient condition, say AX. Again, there may be cases where A is itself a minimal sufficient condition, the disjunction of all minimal sufficient conditions being (A or Y); again, there may be cases where A itself is the only minimal sufficient condition, and is itself both necessary and sufficient for P. In any of these cases, as well as in cases where A is an INUS condition, I shall say that A is *at least an* INUS *condition*. As we shall see, we often have evidence which supports the conclusion that something is *at least* an INUS condition; we may or may not have other evidence which shows that it is *no more than* an INUS condition.)

I suggest that a statement which asserts a singular causal sequence, of such a form as "A caused P", often makes, implicitly, the following claims:

(i) A is at least an INUS condition of P – that is, there is a necessary and sufficient condition of P which has one of these forms: (AX or Y), (A or Y), AX, A.

(ii) A was present on the occasion in question.

(iii) The factors represented by the 'X', if any, in the formula for the necessary and sufficient condition were present on the occasion in question.

(iv) Every disjunct in 'Y' which does not contain 'A' as a conjunct was absent on the occasion in question. (As a rule, this means that whatever 'Y' represents was absent on this occasion. If 'Y' represents a single conjunction of factors, then it was absent if at least one of its conjuncts was absent; if it represents a disjunction, then it was absent if each of its disjuncts was absent. But we do not wish to exclude the possibility that 'Y' should be, or contain as a disjunct, a conjunction one of whose conjuncts is A, or to require that *this* conjunction should have been absent.[7])

I do not suggest that this is the whole of what is meant by "A caused P" on any occasion, or even that it is a part of what is meant on every occasion: some additional and alternative parts of the meaning of such statements are indicated below.[8] But I am suggesting that this is an important part of the concept of causation; the proof of this suggestion would be that in many cases the falsifying of any one of the above-mentioned claims would rebut the assertion that A caused P.

This account is in fairly close agreement, in substance if not in terminology, with at least two accounts recently offered of the cause of a single event.

Konrad Marc-Wogau sums up his account thus:

when historians in singular causal statements speak of a cause or the cause of a certain individual event β, then what they are referring to is another individual event α which is a moment in a minimal sufficient and at the same time necessary condition *post factum* β.[9]

He explained his phrase "necessary condition *post factum*" by saying that he will call an event a_1 a necessary condition *post factum* for x if the disjunction "a_1 or a_2 or a_3 ... or a_n" represents a necessary condition for x, and of these disjuncts only a_1 was present on the particular occasion when x occurred.

Similarly Michael Scriven has said:

Causes are *not* necessary, even contingently so, they are not sufficient – but they are, to talk that language, *contingently sufficient....* They are part of *a* set of conditions that does guarantee the outcome, and they are non-redundant in that the rest of *this* set (which does not include all the other conditions present) is not alone sufficient for the outcome. It is not even true that they are relatively necessary, i.e., necessary with regard to that set of conditions rather than the total circumstances of their occurrence, for there may be several possible replacements for them which happen not to be present. There remains a ghost of necessity; a cause is a factor from a set of possible factors the presence of one of which (*any* one) is necessary in order that a set of conditions actually present be sufficient for the effect.[10]

There are only slight differences between these two accounts, or between each of them and that offered above. Scriven seems to speak too strongly when he says that causes are not necessary: it is, indeed, not part of the definition of a cause of this sort that it should be necessary, but, as noted above, a cause, or an INUS condition, may be necessary, either because there is only one minimal sufficient condition or because the cause is a moment in each of the minimal sufficient conditions. On the other hand, Marc-Wogau's account of a minimal sufficient condition seems too strong. He says that a minimal sufficient condition contains "only those moments relevant to the effect" and that a moment is relevant to an effect if "it is a necessary condition for β : β would not have occurred if this moment had not been present". This is less accurate than Scriven's statement that the cause only needs to be non-redundant.[11] Also, Marc-Wogau's requirement, in his account of a necessary condition *post factum*, that only one minimal sufficient condition (the one containing α) should be present on the particular occasion, seems a little too strong. If two or more minimal sufficient conditions (say a_1 and a_2) were present, but α was a moment in each of them, then though neither a_1 nor a_2 was necessary *post factum*, α would be so. I shall use this phrase "necessary *post factum*" to include cases of this sort: that is, α is a necessary condition *post factum* if it is a moment in every minimal sufficient condition that was present. For example, in a cricket team the wicket-keeper is also a good batsman. He is injured during a match, and does not bat in the second innings,

and the substitute wicket-keeper drops a vital catch that the original wicket-keeper would have taken. The team loses the match, but it would have won if the wicket-keeper had *both* batted *and* taken that catch. His injury was a moment in two minimal sufficient conditions for the loss of the match; either his not batting, or the catch's not being taken, would on its own have insured the loss of the match. But we can certainly say that his injury caused the loss of the match, and that it was a necessary condition *post factum*.

This account may be summed up, briefly and approximately, by saying that the statement "*A* caused *P*" often claims that *A* was necessary and sufficient for *P* in the circumstances. This description applies in the standard cases, but we have already noted that a cause is nonredundant rather than necessary even in the circumstances, and we shall see that there are special cases in which it may be neither necessary nor nonredundant.

2 Difficulties and Refinements[12]

Both Scriven and Marc-Wogau are concerned not only with this basic account, but with certain difficulties and with the refinements and complications that are needed to overcome them. Before dealing with these, I shall introduce, as a refinement of my own account, the notion of a causal field.[13]

This notion is most easily explained if we leave, for a time, singular causal statements and consider general ones. The question "What causes influenza?" is incomplete and partially indeterminate. It may mean "What causes influenza in human beings in general?" If so, the (full) cause that is being sought is a difference that will mark off cases in which human beings contract influenza from cases in which they do not; the causal field is then the region that is to be thus divided, *human beings in general.* But the question may mean, "Given that influenza viruses are present, what makes some people contract the disease whereas others do not?" Here the causal field is *human beings in conditions where influenza viruses are present.* In all such cases, the cause is required to differentiate, within a wider region in which the effect sometimes occurs and sometimes does not, the sub-region in which it occurs: this wider region is the causal field. This notion can now be applied to singular causal questions and statements. "What caused this man's skin cancer?"[14] may mean "Why did this man develop skin cancer now when he did not develop it before?" Here the causal field is the career of this man: it is within this that we are seeking a difference between the time when skin cancer developed and times when it did not. But the same question may mean "Why did this man develop skin cancer, whereas other men who were also exposed to radiation did not?" Here the causal field is the class of men thus exposed to radiation. And what is the cause in relation to one field may not be the cause in relation to another. Exposure to a certain dose of radiation may be the cause in relation to the former field: it cannot be the cause in relation to the latter field, since it is part of the description of that field, and being present throughout that field it cannot differentiate one sub-region of it from another. In relation to the latter field, the cause may be, in Scriven's terms, "Some as-yet-unidentified constitutional factor".

In our first example of the house which caught fire, the history of this house is the field in relation to which the experts were looking for the cause of the fire: their question was "Why did this house catch fire on this occasion, and not on others?" However, there may still be some indeterminacy in this choice of a causal field. Does this house, considered as the causal field, include all its features, or all its relatively permanent features, or only some of these? If we take all its features, or even all of its relatively permanent ones, as constituting the field, then some of the things that we have treated as conditions – for example, the presence of inflammable material near the place where the short circuit occurred – would have to be regarded as parts of the field, and we could not then take them also as conditions which in relation to this field, as additions to it or intrusions into it, are necessary or sufficient for something else. We must therefore take the house, in so far as it constitutes the causal field, as determined only in a fairly general way, by only some of its relatively permanent features, and we shall then be free to treat its other features as conditions which do not constitute the field, and are not parts of it, but which may occur within it or be added to it. It is in general an arbitrary matter whether a particular feature is regarded as a condition (that is, as a possible causal factor) or as part of the field, but it cannot be treated in both ways at once. If we are to say that something happened to this house because of, or partly because of, a certain feature, we are implying that it would still have been *this* house, the house in relation to which we are seeking the cause of this happening, even if it had not had this particular feature.

I now propose to modify the account given above of the claims often made by singular causal statements. A statement of such a form as "A caused P" is usually elliptical, and is to be expanded into "A caused P in relation to the field F." And then in place of the claim stated in (i) above, we require this:

(i a)   A is at least an INUS condition of P in the field F – that is, there is a condition which, given the presence of whatever features characterize F throughout, is necessary and sufficient for P, and which is of one of these forms: $(AX$ or $Y)$, $(A$ or $Y)$, AX, A.

In analysing our ordinary causal statements, we must admit that the field is often taken for granted or only roughly indicated, rather than specified precisely. Nevertheless, the field in relation to which we are looking for a cause of this effect, or saying that such-and-such is a cause, may be definite enough for us to be able to say that certain facts or possibilities are irrelevant to the particular causal problem under consideration, because they would constitute a shift from the intended field to a different one. Thus if we are looking for the cause, or causes, of influenza, meaning its cause(s) in relation to the field *human beings*, we may dismiss, as not directly relevant, evidence which shows that some proposed cause fails to produce influenza in rats. If we are looking for the cause of the fire in *this house*, we may similarly dismiss as irrelevant the fact that a proposed cause would not have produced a fire if the house had been radically different, or had been set in a radically different environment.

This modification enables us to deal with the well-known difficulty that it is impossible, without including in the cause the whole environment, the whole prior state of the universe (and so excluding any likelihood of repetition), to find a genuinely sufficient condition, one which is "by itself, adequate to secure the effect".[15] It may be hard to find even a complex condition which was absolutely sufficient for this fire because we should have to include, as one of the negative conjuncts, such an item as the earth's not being destroyed by a nuclear explosion just after the occurrence of the suggested INUS condition; but it is easy and reasonable to say simply that such an explosion would, in more senses than one, take us outside the field in which we are considering this effect. That is to say, it may be not so difficult to find a condition which is sufficient in relation to the intended field. No doubt this means that causal statements may be vague, in so far as the specification of the field is vague, but this is not a serious obstacle to establishing or using them, either in science or in everyday contexts.[16]

It is a vital feature of the account I am suggesting that we can say that A caused P, in the sense described, without being able to specify exactly the terms represented by 'X' and 'Y' in our formula. In saying that A is at least an INUS condition for P in F, one is *not* saying what other factors, along with A, were both present and nonredundant, and one is *not* saying what other minimal sufficient conditions there may be for P in F. One is not even claiming to be able to say what they are. This is in no way a difficulty: it is a readily recognizable fact about our ordinary causal statements, and one which this account explicitly and correctly reflects.[17] It will be shown (in section 5) that this elliptical or indeterminate character of our causal statements is closely connected with some of our characteristic ways of discovering and confirming causal relationships: it is precisely for statements that are thus "gappy" or indeterminate that we can obtain fairly direct evidence from quite modest ranges of observation. On this analysis, causal statements implicitly contain existential quantifications; one can assert an existentially quantified statement without asserting any instantiation of it, and one can also have good reason for asserting an existentially quantified statement without having the information needed to support any precise instantiation of it. I can know that there is someone at the door even if the question. "Who is he?" would floor me.

Marc-Wogau is concerned especially with cases where "there are two events, each of which independently of the other is a sufficient condition for another event". There are, that is to say, two minimal sufficient conditions, both of which actually occurred. For example, lightning strikes a barn in which straw is stored, and a tramp throws a burning cigarette butt into the straw at the same place and at the same time. Likewise for a historical event there may be more than one "cause", and each of them may, on its own, be sufficient.[18] Similarly Scriven considers a case where

> ... conditions (perhaps unusual excitement plus constitutional inadequacies) [are] present at 4.0 P.M. that guarantee a stroke at 4.55 P.M. and consequent death at 5.0 P.M.; but an entirely unrelated heart attack at 4.50 P.M. is still correctly called the cause of death, which, as it happens, does occur at 5.0. P.M..[19]

Before we try to resolve these difficulties, let us consider another of Marc-Wogau's problems: Smith and Jones commit a crime, but if they had not done so, the head of the criminal organization would have sent other members to perform it in their stead, and so it would have been committed anyway.[20] Now in this case, if 'A' stands for the actions of Smith and Jones, what we have is that AX is one minimal sufficient condition of the result (the crime), but $\bar{A}Z$ is another, and both X and Z are present. A combines with one set of the standing conditions to produce the result by one route: but the absence of A would have combined with another set of the standing conditions to produce the same result by another route. In this case we *can* say that A was a necessary condition *post factum*. This sample satisfies the requirements of Marc-Wogau's analysis, and of mine, of the statement that A caused this result; and this agrees with what we would ordinarily say in such a case. (We might indeed add that there was *also* a deeper cause – the existence of the criminal organization, perhaps – but this does not matter: our formal analyses do not insure that a particular result will have a unique cause, nor does our ordinary causal talk require this.) It is true that in this case we cannot say what will usually serve as an informal substitute for the formal account, that the cause, here A, was necesary (as well as sufficient) in the circumstances; for $\bar{A}$ would have done just as well. We cannot even say that A was nonredundant. But this shows merely that a formal analysis may be superior to its less formal counterparts.

Now in Scriven's example, we might take it that the heart attack prevented the stroke from occurring. If so, then the heart attack *is* a necessary condition *post factum*: it is a moment in the only minimal sufficient condition that was present in full, for the heart attack itself removed some factor that was a necessary part of the minimal sufficient condition which has the excitement as one of its moments. This is strictly parallel to the Smith and Jones case. Again it is odd to say that the heart attack was in any way necessary, since the absence of the heart attack would have done just as well: this absence would have been a moment in that other minimal sufficient condition, one of whose other moments was the excitement. Nevertheless, the heart attack was necessary *post factum*, and the excitement was not. Scriven draws the distinction, quite correctly, in terms of continuity and discontinuity of causal chains: "the heart attack was, and the excitement was not the cause of death because the 'causal chain' between the latter and death was interrupted, while the former's 'went to completion.'" But it is worth nothing that a break in the causal chain corresponds to a failure to satisfy the logical requirements of a moment in a minimal sufficient condition that is also necessary *post factum*.

Alternatively, if the heart attack did not prevent the stroke, then we have a case parallel to that of the straw in the barn, or of the man who is shot by a firing squad, and two bullets go through his heart simultaneously. In such cases the requirements of my analysis, or of Marc-Wogau's, or of Scriven's, are not met: each proposed cause *is* redundant and not even necessary *post factum*, though the disjunction of them is necessary *post factum* and nonredundant. But this agrees very well with the fact that we *would* ordinarily hesitate to say, of either bullet, that it caused the man's death, or of either the lightning or the cigarette butt that it caused the fire, or of either the excitement or the heart attack that it was the cause of death. As Marc-Wogau says, "in such a situation as this we are unsure also how to use the word 'cause.'" Our ordinary concept of cause does not deal clearly with cases of this sort, and we are free to decide whether or not to add to our ordinary use, and to the various more or less formal descriptions of it, rules which allow us to say that where more than one at-least-INUS-

condition, and its conjunct conditions, are present, each of them caused the result.[21]

The account thus far developed of singular causal statements has been expressed in terms of statements about necessity and sufficiency; it is therefore incomplete until we have added an account of necessity and sufficiency themselves. This question is considered in section 4 below. But the present account is independent of any particular analysis of necessity and sufficiency. Whatever analysis of these we finally adopt, we shall use it to complete the account of what it is to be an INUS condition, or to be at least an INUS condition. But in whatever way this account is completed, we can retain the general principle that at least part of what is often done by a singular causal statement is to pick out, as the cause, something that is claimed to be at least an INUS condition.

3   General Causal Statements

Many general causal statements are to be understood in a corresponding way. Suppose, for example, that an economist says that the restriction of credit causes (or produces) unemployment. Again, he will no doubt be speaking with reference to some causal field; this is now not an individual object, but a class, presumably economics of a certain general kind; perhaps their specification will include the feature that each economy of the kind in question contains a large private enterprise sector with free wage-earning employees. The result, unemployment, is something which sometimes occurs and sometimes does not occur within this field, and the same is true of the alleged cause, the restriction of credit. But the economist is not saying that (even in relation to this field) credit restriction is either necessary or sufficient for unemployment, let alone both necessary and sufficient. There may well be other circumstances which must be present along with credit restriction, in an economy of the kind referred to, if unemployment is to result; these other circumstances will no doubt include various negative ones, the absence of various counteracting causal factors which, if they were present, would prevent this result. Also, the economist will probably be quite prepared to admit that in an economy of this kind, unemployment could be brought about by other combinations of circumstances in which the restriction of credit plays no part. So once again the claim that he is making is merely that the restriction of credit is, in economics of this kind, a nonredundant part of one sufficient condition for unemployment: that is, an INUS condition. The economist is probably assuming that there is some condition, no doubt a complex one, which is both necessary and sufficient for unemployment in this field. This being assumed, what he is asserting is that, for some X and for some Y, (AX or Y) is a necessary and sufficient condition for P in F, but neither A nor X is sufficient on its own, where 'A' stands for the restriction of credit, 'P' for unemployment, and 'F' for the field, economies of such-and-such a sort. In a developed economic theory the field F may be specified quite exactly, and so may the relevant combinations of factors represented here by 'X' and 'Y'. (Indeed, the theory may go beyond statements in terms of necessity and sufficiency to ones of functional dependence, but this is a complication which I am leaving aside for the present.) In a preliminary or popular statement, on the other hand, the combinations of factors may either be only roughly indicated or be left quite undetermined. At one extreme we have the statement that (AX or Y) is a necessary and sufficient condition, where 'X' and 'Y' are given definite meanings; at the other extreme we have the merely existentially quantified statement that this holds for *some* pair X and Y. Our knowledge in such cases ordinarily falls somewhere between these two extremes. We can use the same convention as before, deliberately allowing it to be ambignous between these different inter-pretations, and say that in any of these cases, where A is an INUS condition of P in F, (A... or ...) is a necessary and sufficient condition of P in F.

A great deal of our ordinary causal knowledge is of this form. We know that the eating of sweets causes dental decay. Here the field is human beings who have some of their own teeth. We do not know, indeed it is not true, that the eating of sweets by any such person is a sufficient condition for dental decay: some people have peculiarly resistant teeth, and there are probably measures which, if taken along with the eating of sweets, would protect the eater's teeth from decay. All we know is that sweet-eating combined with a set of positive and negative factors which we can specify,

if at all, only roughly and incompletely, constitutes a minimal sufficient condition for dental decay – but not a necessary one, for there are other combinations of factors, which do not include sweet-eating, which would also make teeth decay, but which we can specify, if at all, only roughly and incompletely. That is, if 'A' now represents sweet-eating, 'P' dental decay, and 'F' the class of human beings with some of their own teeth, we can say that, for some X and Y, (AX or Y) is necessary and sufficient for P in F, and we *may* be able to go beyond this merely existentially quantified statement to at least a partial specification of the X and Y in question. That is, we can say that (A ... or ...) is a necessary and sufficient condition, but that A itself is only an INUS condition. And the same holds for many general causal statements of the form "A causes (or produces) P". It is in this sense that the application of a potential difference to the ends of a copper wire produces an electric current in the wire; that a rise in the temperature of a piece of metal makes it expand; that moisture rusts steel; that exposure to various kinds of radiation causes cancer, and so on.

However, it is true that not all ordinary general causal statements are of this sort. Some of them are implicit statements of functional dependence. Functional dependence is a more complicated relationship of which necessity and sufficiency can be regarded as special cases. Here too what we commonly single out as causing some result is only one of a number of factors which jointly affect the result. Again, some causal statements pick out something that is not only an INUS condition, but also a necessary condition. Thus we may say that the yellow fever virus is the cause of yellow fever. (This statement is not, as it might appear to be, tautologous, for the yellow fever virus and the disease itself can be independently specified.) In the field in question – human beings – the injection of this virus is not by itself a sufficient condition for this disease, for persons who have once recovered from yellow fever are thereafter immune to it, and other persons can be immunized against it. The injection of the virus, combined with the absence of immunity (natural or artificial), and perhaps combined with some other factors, constitutes a sufficient condition for the disease. Beside this, the injection of the virus is a necessary condition of the disease. If there is more than one complex sufficient condition for yellow fever, the injection of the virus into the patient's bloodstream (either by a mosquito or in some other way) is a factor included in every such sufficient condition. If '*A*' stands for this factor, the necessary and sufficient condition has the form (*A* ... or *A* ... etc.), where *A* occurs in every disjunct. We sometimes note the difference between this and the standard case by using the phrase "the cause". We may say not merely that this virus *causes* yellow fever, but that it is *the cause* of yellow fever; but we would say only that sweet-eating *causes* dental decay, not that it is *the cause* of dental decay. But about an individual case we could say that sweet-eating was *the cause* of the decay of this person's teeth, meaning (as in section 1 above) that the only sufficient condition present here was the one of which sweet-eating is a nonredundant part. Nevertheless, there will not in general be any one item which has a unique claim to be regarded as *the cause* even of an individual event, and even after the causal field has been determined. Each of the moments in the minimal sufficient condition, or in each minimal sufficient condition, that was present can equally be regarded as the cause. They may be distinguished as predisposing causes, triggering causes, and so on, but it is quite arbitrary to pick out as "main" and "secondary", different moments which are equally non-redundant items in a minimal sufficient condition, or which are moments in two minimal sufficient conditions each of which makes the other redundant.[22]

4   Necessity and Sufficiency

One possible account of general statements of the forms "*S* is a necessary condition of *T*" and "*S* is a sufficient condition of *T*" – where '*S*' and '*T*' are general terms – is that they are equivalent to simple universal propositions. That is, the former is equivalent to "All *T* are *S*" and the latter to "All *S* are *T*". Similarly, "*S* is necessary for *T* in the field *F*" would be equivalent to "All *FT* are *S*", and "*S* is sufficient for *T* in the field *F*" to "All *FS* are *T*". Whether an account of this sort is adequate is, of course, a matter of dispute; but it is not disputed that these statements about necessary and sufficient conditions at least *entail* the

corresponding universals. I shall work on the assumption that this account is adequate, that general statements of necessity and sufficiency are equivalent to universals: it will be worthwhile to see how far this account will take us, how far we are able, in terms of it, to understand how we use, support, and criticize these statements of necessity and sufficiency.

A directly analogous account of the corresponding singular statements is not satisfactory. Thus it will not do to say that "A short circuit here was a necessary condition of a fire in this house" is equivalent to "All cases of this house's catching fire are cases of a short circuit occurring here", because the latter is automatically true if this house has caught fire only once and a short circuit has occurred on that occasion, but this is not enough to establish the statement that the short circuit was a necessary condition of the fire; and there would be an exactly parallel objection to a similar statement about a sufficient condition.

It is much more plausible to relate singular statements about necessity and sufficiency to certain kinds of non-material conditionals. Thus "A short circuit here was a necessary condition of a fire in this house" is closely related to the counterfactual conditional "If a short circuit had not occurred here this house would not have caught fire", and "A short circuit here was a sufficient condition of a fire in this house" is closely related to what Goodman has called the factual conditional, "Since a short circuit occurred here, this house caught fire".

However, a further account would still have to be given of these non-material conditionals themselves. I have argued elsewhere[23] that they are best considered as condensed or telescoped *arguments*, but that the statements used as premises in these arguments are no more than simple factual universals. To use the above-quoted counterfactual conditional is, in effect, to run through an incomplete argument: "Suppose that a short circuit did not occur here, then the house did not catch fire." To use the factual conditional is, in effect, to run through a similar incomplete argument: "A short circuit occurred here; therefore the house caught fire." In each case the argument might in principle be completed by the insertion of other premises which, together with the stated premise, would entail the stated conclusion. Such additional premises may be said to *sustain* the nonmaterial conditional. It is an important point that someone can use a non-material conditional without completing or being able to complete the argument, without being prepared explicitly to assert premisses that would sustain it, and similarly that we can understand such a conditional without knowing exactly how the argument would or could be completed. But to say that a short circuit here was a necessary condition of a fire in this house is to say that there is some set of true propositions which would sustain the above-stated counterfactual, and to say that it was a sufficient condition is to say that there is some set of true propositions which would sustain the above-stated factual conditional. If this is conceded, then the relating of singular statements about necessity and sufficiency to non-material conditionals leads back to the view that they refer indirectly to certain simple universal propositions. Thus if we said that a short circuit here was a necessary condition for a fire in this house, we should be saying that there are true universal propositions from which, together with true statements about the characteristics of this house, and together with the supposition that a short circuit did not occur here, it would follow that the house did not catch fire. From this we could infer the universal proposition which is the more obvious, but unsatisfactory, candidate for the analysis of this statement of necessity, "All cases of this house's catching fire are cases of a short circuit occurring here", or, in our symbols, "All FP are A". We can use this to represent approximately the statement of necessity, on the understanding that it is to be a consequence of some set of wider universal propositions, and is not to be automatically true merely because there is only this one case of an FP, of this house's catching fire.[24] A statement that A was a sufficient condition may be similarly represented by "All FA are P". Correspondingly, if all that we want to say is that $(A \ldots$ or $\ldots)$ was necessary and sufficient for P in F, this will be represented approximately by the pair of universals "All FP are $(A \ldots$ or $\ldots)$ and all $F(A \ldots$ or $\ldots)$ are P", and more accurately by the statement that there is some set of wider universal propositions from which, together with true statements about the features of F, this pair of universals follows. This, therefore, is the fuller analysis of the claim that in a particular case A is an INUS condition of P in F, and hence of the singular statement that A caused P. (The statement that A is *at least* an INUS condition includes other alternatives, corresponding to cases where the necessary and sufficient condition is $(A$ or $\ldots)$, $A \ldots$, or A.)

Let us go back now to general statements of necessity and sufficiency and take F as a class, not as an individual. On the view that I am adopting, at least provisionally, the statement that Z is a necessary and sufficient condition for P in F is equivalent to "All FP are Z and all FZ are P". Similarly, if we cannot completely specify a necessary and sufficient condition for P in F, but can only say that the formula "$(A \ldots$ or $\ldots)$" represents such a condition, this is equivalent to the pair of incomplete universals, "All FP are $(A \ldots$ or $\ldots)$ and all $F(A \ldots$ or $\ldots)$ are P". In saying that our general causal statements often do no more than specify an INUS condition, I am therefore saying that much of our ordinary causal knowledge is knowledge of such pairs of incomplete universals, of what we may call elliptical or *gappy* causal laws.

[Sections 5–7 omitted]

8 The Direction of Causation

This account of causation is still incomplete, in that nothing has yet been said about the direction of causation, about what distinguishes A causing P from P causing A. This is a difficult question, and it is linked with the equally difficult question of the direction of time. I cannot hope to resolve it completely here, but I shall state some of the relevant considerations.[25]

First, it seems that there is a relation which may be called *causal priority*, and that part of what is meant by "A caused P" is that this relation holds in one direction between A and P, not the other. Secondly, this relation is not identical with temporal priority; it is conceivable that there should be evidence for a case of backward causation, for A being causally prior to P whereas P was temporally prior to A. Most of us believe, and I think with good reason, that backward causation does not occur, so that we can and do normally use temporal order to limit the possibilities about causal order; but the connection between the two is synthetic. Thirdly, it could be objected to the analysis of "necessary" and "sufficient" offered in section 4 above that it omits any reference to causal order, whereas our most common use of "necessary" and "sufficient" in causal contexts includes such a reference. Thus "*A* is (causally) sufficient for *B*" says "If *A*, then *B*, and *A* is causally prior to *B*", but "*B* is (causally) necessary for *A*" is not equivalent to this: it says "If *A*, then *B*, and *B* is causally prior to *A*". However, it is simpler to use "necessary" and "sufficient" in senses which exclude this causal priority, and to introduce the assertion of priority separately into our accounts of "*A* caused *P*" and "*A* causes *P*." Fourthly, although "*A* is (at least) an INUS condition of *P*" is not synonymous with "*P* is (at least) an INUS condition of *A*", this difference of meaning cannot exhaust the relation of causal priority. If it did exhaust it, the direction of causation would be a trivial matter, for, given that there is some necessary and sufficient condition of *A* in the field, it can be proved that if *A* is (at least) an INUS condition of *P*, then *P* is also (at least) an INUS condition of *A*: we can construct a minimal sufficient condition of *A* in which *P* is a moment.[26]

Fifthly, it is often suggested that the direction of causation is linked with controllability. If there is a causal relation between *A* and *B*, and we can control *A* without making use of *B* to do so, and the relation between *A* and *B* still holds, then we decide that *B* is not causally prior to *A* and, in general, that *A* is causally prior to *B*. But this means only that if one case of causal priority is known, we can use it to determine others: our rejection of the possibility that *B* is causally prior to *A* rests on our knowledge that our action is causally prior to *A*, and the question how we know the latter, and even the question of what causal priority is, have still to be answered. Similarly, if one of the causally related kinds of event, say *A*, can be randomized, so that occurrences of *A* are either not caused at all, or are caused by something which enters this causal field *only* in this way, by causing *A*, we can reject both the possibility that *B* is causally prior to *A* and the possibility that some common cause is prior both to *A* and separately to *B*, and we can again conclude that *A* is causally prior to *B*. But this still means only that we can infer causal priority in one place if we first know that it is absent from another place. It is true that our knowledge of the direction of causation in ordinary cases is

thus based on what we find to be controllable, and on what we either find to be random or find that we can randomize; but this cannot without circularity be taken as providing a full account either of what we mean by causal priority or of how we know about it.

A suggestion put forward by Popper about the direction of time seems to be relevant here.[27] If a stone is dropped into a pool, the entry of the stone will explain the expanding circular waves. But the reverse process, with contracting circular waves, "would demand a vast number of distant coherent generators of waves the coherence of which, to be explicable, would have to be shown … as originating from one centre". That is, if *B* is an occurrence which involves a certain sort of "coherence" between a large number of separated items, whereas *A* is a single event, and *A* and *B* are causally connected, *A* will explain *B* in a way in which *B* will not explain *A* unless some other single event, say *C*, first explains the coherence in *B*. Such examples give us a *direction of explanation*, and it may be that this is the basis, or part of the basis, of the relation I have called causal priority.

9 Conclusions

Even if Mill was wrong in thinking that science consists mainly of causal knowledge, it can hardly be denied that such knowledge is an indispensable element in science, and that it is worthwhile to investigate the meaning of causal statements and the ways in which we can arrive at causal knowledge. General causal relationships are among the items which a more advanced kind of scientific theory explains, and is confirmed by its success in explaining. Singular causal assertions are involved in almost every report of an experiment: doing such and such *produced* such and such an effect. Materials are commonly identified by their causal properties: to recognize something as a piece of a certain material, therefore, we must establish singular causal assertions about it, that this object affected that other one, or was affected by it, in such and such a way. Causal assertions are embedded in both the results and the procedures of scientific investigation.

The account that I have offered of the force of various kinds of causal statements agrees both with our informal understanding of them and with accounts put forward by other writers: at the same time it is formal enough to show how such statements can be supported by observations and experiments, and thus to throw a new light on philosophical questions about the nature of causation and causal explanation and the status of causal knowledge.

One important point is that, leaving aside the question of the direction of causation, the analysis has been given entirely within the limits of what can still be called a regularity theory of causation, in that the causal laws involved in it are no more than straightforward universal propositions, although their terms may be complex and perhaps incompletely specified. Despite this limitation, I have been able to give an account of the meaning of statements about singular causal sequences, regardless of whether such a sequence is or is not of a kind that frequently recurs: repetition is not essential for causal relation, and regularity does not here disappear into the mere fact that this single sequence has occurred. It has, indeed, often been recognized that the regularity theory could cope with single sequences if, say, a unique sequence could be explained as the resultant of a number of laws each of which was exemplified in many other sequences; but my account shows how a singular causal statement can be interpreted, and how the corresponding sequence can be shown to be causal, even if the corresponding complete laws are not known. It shows how even a unique sequence can be directly recognized as causal.

One consequence of this is that it now becomes possible to reconcile what have appeared to be conflicting views about the nature of historical explanation. We are accustomed to contrast the "covering-law" theory adopted by Hempel, Popper, and others with the views of such critics as Dray and Scriven who have argued that explanations and causal statements in history cannot be thus assimilated to the patterns accepted in the physical sciences.[28] But while my basic analysis of singular causal statements in sections 1 and 2 agrees closely with Scriven's, I have argued in section 4 that this analysis can be developed in terms of complex and elliptical universal propositions, and this means that wherever we have a singular causal statement we shall still have a covering law, albeit a complex and perhaps elliptical one. Also, I have shown in

section 5, and indicated briefly, for the functional dependence variants, in section 7 [omitted from this selection], that the evidence which supports singular causal statements also supports general causal statements or covering laws, though again only complex and elliptical ones. Hempel recognized long ago that historical accounts can be interpreted as giving incomplete "explanation sketches", rather than what he would regard as full explanations, which would require fully stated covering laws, and that such sketches are also common outside history. But in these terms what I am saying is that explanation sketches and the related elliptical laws are often all that we can discover, that they play a part in all sciences, that they can be supported and even established without being completed, and do not serve merely as preliminaries to or summaries of complete deductive explanations. If we modify the notion of a covering law to admit laws which not only are complex but also are known only in an elliptical form, the covering-law theory can accommodate many of the points that have been made in criticism of it, while preserving the structural similarity of explanation in history and in the physical sciences. In this controversy, one point at issue has been the symmetry of explanation and prediction, and my account may help to resolve this dispute. It shows, in agreement with what Scriven has argued, how the actual occurrence of an event in the observed circumstances may be a vital part of the evidence which supports an explanation of that event, which shows that it was A that caused P on this occasion. A prediction on the other hand cannot rest on observation of the event predicted. Also, the gappy law which is sufficient for an explanation will not suffice for a prediction (or for a retrodiction): a statement of initial conditions together with a gappy law will not entail the assertion that a specific result will occur, though of course such a law may be, and often is, used to make tentative predictions the failure of which will not necessarily tell against the law. But the recognition of these differences between prediction and explanation does not affect the covering-law theory as modified by the recognition of elliptical laws.

Although what I have given is primarily an account of physical causation, it may be indirectly relevant to the understanding of human action and mental causation. It is sometimes suggested that our ability to recognize a single occurrence as an instance of mental causation is a feature which distinguishes mental causation from physical or "Humean" causation.[29] But this suggestion arises from the use of too simple a regularity account of physical causation. If we first see clearly what we mean by singular causal statements in general, and how we can support such a statement by observation of the single sequence itself, even in a physical case, we shall be better able to contrast with this our awareness of mental causes, and to see whether the latter has any really distinctive features.

This account also throws light on both the form and the status of the "causal principle", the deterministic assumption which is used in any application of the methods of eliminative induction. These methods need not presuppose determinism in general, but only that each specific phenomenon investigated by such a method is deterministic. Moreover, they require not only that the phenomenon should have some cause, but that there should be some restriction of the range of possibly relevant factors (at least to spatio-temporally neighbouring ones). Now the general causal principle, that every event has some cause, is so general that it is peculiarly difficult either to confirm or to disconfirm, and we might be tempted either to claim for it some a priori status, to turn it into a metaphysical absolute presupposition, or to dismiss it as vacuous. But the specific assumption that this phenomenon has some cause based somehow on factors drawn from this range, or even that this phenomenon has some neighboring cause, is much more open to empirical confirmation and disconfirmation: indeed, the former can be conclusively falsified by the observation of a positive instance of P, and a negative case in which P does not occur, but where each of the factors in the given range is either present in both or absent from both. This account, then, encourages us to regard the assumption as something to be empirically confirmed or disconfirmed. At the same time it shows that there must be some principle of the confirmation of hypotheses other than the eliminative methods themselves, since each such method rests on an empirical assumption.

Notes

1 This term was suggested by D. C. Stove, who has also given me a great deal of help criticizing earlier versions of this article.

2 The phrase "minimal sufficient condition" is borrowed from Konrad Marc-Wogau, "On historical explanation," *Theoria* 28 (1962), pp. 213–33. This article gives an analysis of singular causal statements, with special reference to their use by historians, which is substantially equivalent to the account I am suggesting. Many further references are made to this article, especially in n. 9 below.

3 Cf. p. 227, n. 8, where it is pointed out that in order to infer that the disjunction of all the minimal sufficient conditions will be a necessary condition, "it is necessary to presuppose that an arbitrary event C, if it occurs, must have sufficient reason to occur." This presupposition is equivalent to the presupposition that there is some (possibly complex) condition that is both necessary and sufficient for C.

It is of some interest that some common turns of speech embody this presupposition. To say "Nothing but X will do," or "Either X or Y will do, but nothing else will," is a natural way of saying that X, or the disjunction (X or Y), is a *necessary* condition for whatever result we have in mind. But taken literally, these remarks say only that there is no sufficient condition for this result other than X, or other than (X or Y). That is, we use to mean "a necessary condition" phrases whose literal meanings would be "the only sufficient condition," or "the disjunction of all sufficient conditions." Similarly, to say that Z is "all that's needed" is a natural way of saying that Z is a sufficient condition, but taken literally, this remark says that Z is the only necessary condition. But, once again, that the only necessary condition will also be a sufficient one follows only if we presuppose that some condition is both necessary and sufficient.

4 I am indebted to the referees appointed by *American Philosophical Quarterly*, in which this material was first published, for the suggestion that these points should be clarified.

5 Special cases where an INUS condition is also a necessary one are mentioned at the end of sect. 3.

6 This point, and the term "nonredundant", are taken from Michael Scriven's review of Nagel's *The Structure of Science*, in *Review of Metaphysics* (1964). See esp. the passage on p. 408 quoted below.

7 See example of the wicket-keeper discussed below.

8 See sects 7, 8 [not included in this selection].

9 See Marc-Wogau, "On historical explanation", pp. 226–7. Marc-Wogau's full formulation is as follows:

"Let 'msc' stand for minimal sufficient condition and 'nc' for necessary condition. Then suppose we have a class K of individual events $a_1, a_2, \ldots a_n$. (It seems reasonable to assume that K is finite; however, even if K were infinite, the reasoning below would not be affected.) My analysis of the singular causal statement: α is the cause of β, where α and β stand for individual events, can be summarily expressed in the following statements:

(1) $(EK) (K = \{a_1, a_2, \ldots, a_n\})$;

(2) $(x) (x \in K \equiv x \text{ msc } \beta)$;

(3) $(a_1 \vee a_2 \vee \ldots a_n) \text{ nc } \beta$;

(4) $(x) ((x \in Kx \neq a_1) \supset x \text{ is not fulfilled when } \alpha$ occurs$)$;

(5) α is a moment in a_1.

(3) and (4) say that a_1 is a necessary condition *post factum* for β. If a_1 is a necessary condition *post factum* for β, then every moment in a_1 is a necessary condition *post factum* for β, and therefore also α. As has been mentioned before (n. 6) there is assumed to be a temporal sequence between α and β; β is not itself an element in K."

10 Scriven, review, p. 408.

11 However, Marc-Wogau "On historical explanation," pp. 222–3, n. 7, draws attention to the difficulty of giving an accurate definition of "a moment in a sufficient condition". Further complications are involved in the account given in sect. 5 [not included in this selection] of "clusters" of factors and the progressive localization of a cause. A condition which is minimally sufficient in relation to one degree of analysis of factors may not be so in relation to another degree of analysis.

12 This section is something of an aside: the main argument is resumed in sect. 3.

13 This notion of a causal field was introduced by John Anderson. He used it, e.g., in "The problem of causality," first published in the *Australasian Journal of Psychology and Philosophy* 16 (1938), and repr. in *Studies in Empirical Philosophy* (Sydney: Angus and Robertson, 1962), pp. 126–36, to overcome certain difficulties and paradoxes in Mill's account of causation. I have also used this notion to deal with problems of legal and moral responsibility, in "Responsibility and language," *Australasian Journal of Philosophy* 33 (1955), pp. 143–59.

14 These examples are borrowed from Scriven, review, pp. 409–10. Scriven discusses them with reference to what he calls a "contrast class", the class of cases where the effect did not occur with which the case where it did occur is being contrasted. What I call the causal field is the logical sum of the case (or cases) in which [...] being said to be caused with what [...] the contrast class.

15 Cf. Bertrand Russell, "On the notion of cause," in *Mysticism and Logic* (London: Allen & Unwin, 1917), p. 187 [ch. 25 in the present volume]. Cf. also Scriven's first difficulty (op. cit., p. 409): "First, there are virtually no known sufficient conditions, literally speaking, since human or accidental interference is almost inexhaustibly possible, and hard to exclude by specific qualification without tautology." The introduction of the causal field also automatically covers Scriven's third difficulty and third refinement, that of the contrast class and the relativity of causal statements to contexts.

16 J. R. Lucas, "Causation", R. J. Butler (ed.), *Analytical Philosophy* (Oxford: Blackwell, 1962), pp. 57–9, resolves this kind of difficulty by an informal appeal to what amounts to this notion of a causal field: "… these circumstances [cosmic cataclysms, etc.] … destroy the whole causal situation in which we had been looking for Z to appear … predictions are not expected to come true when quite unforeseen emergencies arise."

17 This is related to Scriven's second difficulty (op. cit., p. 409): "there still remains the problem of saying what the other factors are which, with the cause, make up the sufficient condition. If they can be stated, causal explanation is then simply a special case of subsumption under a law. If they cannot, the analysis is surely mythological." Scriven correctly replies that "a combination of the thesis of macro-determinism … and observation-plus-theory frequently gives us the very best of reasons for saying that a certain factor combines with an unknown sub-set of the conditions present into a sufficient condition for a particular effect." He gives a statistical example of such evidence, but the whole of my account of typical sorts of evidence for causal relationships in sects 5 and 7 [not included in this selection] is an expanded defence of a reply of this sort.

18 Marc-Wogau, "On historical explanation", pp. 228–33.

19 Scriven, op. cit., pp. 410–11: this is Scriven's fourth difficulty and refinement.

20 Marc-Wogau, "On historical explanation", p. 232: the example is taken from P. Gardiner, *The Nature of Historical Explanation* (Oxford: Oxford University Press, 1952), p. 101.

21 Scriven's fifth difficulty and refinement are concerned with the direction of causation. This is considered briefly in sect. 8 below.

22 Cf. Marc-Wogau's concluding remarks, "On historical explanation", pp. 232–3.

23 J. L. Mackie, "Counterfactuals and causal laws",
R. J. Butler (ed.) *Analytical Philosophy* (Oxford:
Blackwell, 1962), pp. 56–80.

24 This restriction may be compared with one which
Nagel imposes on laws of nature: "the vacuous
truth of an unrestricted universal is not sufficient
for counting it a law; it counts as a law only if there
is a set of other assumed laws from which the
universal is logically derivable" (Ernest Nagel, *The
Structure of Science* (New York: Harcourt, Brace
and World, 1961), p. 60). It might have been better
if he had added "or if there is some other way in
which it is supported (ultimately) by empirical
evidence". Cf. my remarks in "Counterfactuals and
causal laws" pp. 72–4, 78–80.

25 As was mentioned in n. 21, Scriven's fifth difficulty
and refinement are concerned with this point (op.
cit., pp. 411–12), but his answer seems to me inadequate. Lucas touches on it ('Causation', pp. 51–3).
The problem of temporal asymmetry is discussed,
e.g., by J. J. C. Smart, *Philosophy and Scientific
Realism* (London: Routledge and Kegan Paul,
1963), pp. 142–8, and by A. Grünbaum in the article cited in n. 28 below.

26 I am indebted to one of the referees of *American
Philosophical Quarterly* for correcting an inaccurate statement on this point in an earlier version.

27 Karl Popper, "The arrow of time", *Nature* 177
(1956), p. 538; also vol. 178, p. 382 and vol. 179,
p. 1297.

28 See e.g., C. G. Hempel, "The function of general
laws in history", *Journal of Philosophy*, 39 (1942),
repr. in H. Feigl and W. Sellars (eds), *Readings
in Philosophical Analysis* (New York, Appleton-
Century-Crofts, 1949), pp. 459–71; C. G. Hempel
and P. Oppenheim, "Studies in the logic of
explanation", *Philosophy of Science* 15 (1948), repr.
in H. Feigl and M. Brodbeck (eds), *Readings in
the Philosophy of Science* (New York: Appleton-
Century-Crofts, 1953), pp. 319–52; K. R. Popper,
Logik der Forschung (Vienna: J. Springer, 1934),
trans. as *The Logic of Scientific Discovery* (New
York: Harper & Row, 1959), pp. 59–60, also *The
Open Society* (London: Routledge and Kegan Paul,
1952), vol. 2, p. 262; W. Dray, *Laws and Explanation
in History* (Oxford: Oxford University Press, 1957);
N. Rescher, 'On prediction and explanation', *British
Journal for the Philosophy of Science* 9, (1958),
pp. 281–90; various papers in H. Feigl and
G. Maxwell (eds), *Minnesota Studies in the Philosophy
of Science*, vol. 3 (Minneapolis: University of
Minnesota Press, 1962); A. Grünbaum, "Temporally-
asymmetric principles, parity between explanation
and prediction, and mechanism versus teleology",
Philosophy of Science, 29 (1962), pp. 146–70.

Dray's criticisms of the covering-law theory
include the following: we cannot state the law used
in a historical explanation without making it so
vague as to be vacuous (*Laws*, esp. pp. 24–37) or so
complex that it covers only a single case and is
trivial on that account (p. 39); the historian does
not come to the task of explaining an event with a
sufficient stock of laws already formulated and
empirically validated (pp. 42–3); historians do not
need to replace judgement about particular cases
with deduction from empirically validated laws
(pp. 51–2). It will be clear that my account resolves
each of these difficulties. Grünbaum draws an
important distinction between (1) an asymmetry
between explanation and prediction with regard
to the grounds on which we claim to know that
the explanaudum is true, and (2) an asymmetry
with respect to the logical relation between the
explanans and the explanandum; he thinks that
only the former sort of asymmetry obtains. I suggest that my account of the use of gappy laws will
clarify both the sense in which Grünbaum is right
(since an explanation and a tentative prediction
can use similarly gappy laws which are similarly
related to the known initial conditions and the
result) and the sense in which, in such a case, we
may contrast an entirely satisfactory explanation
with a merely tentative prediction. Scriven (in his
most recent statement, the review cited in n. 6
above) says that "we often pin down a factor as a
cause by excluding other possible causes. Simple –
but disastrous for the covering-law theory of
explanation, because we can eliminate causes only
for something *we know has occurred*. And if the
grounds for our explanation of an event *have* to
include knowledge of that event's occurrence, they
cannot be used (without circularity) to predict
the occurrence of that event" (p. 414). That is, the
observation of this event in these circumstances
may be a vital part of the evidence that justifies the
particular causal explanation that we give of
this event: it may itself go a long way toward
establishing the elliptical law in relation to which
we explain it (as I have shown in sect. 5 [not
included here]), whereas a law used for prediction
cannot thus rest on the observation of the event
predicted. But as my account also shows, this does
not introduce an asymmetry of Grünbaum's second sort, and is therefore not disastrous for the
covering-law theory.

29 See, e.g., G. E. M. Anscombe, *Intention* (Oxford:
Blackwell, 1957), esp. p. 16; J. Teichmann, "Mental
cause and effect", *Mind*, 70 (1961), pp. 36–52.
Teichmann speaks (p. 36) of "the difference between
them and ordinary (or 'Humean') sequences of

cause and effect", and says (p. 37) "it is sometimes in order for the person who blinks to say absolutely dogmatically that the cause is such-and-such, and to say this independently of his knowledge of any previously established correlations," and again, "if the noise is a cause it seems to be one which is known to be such in a special way. It seems that while it is necessary for an observer to have knowledge of a previously established correlation between noises and Smith's jumpings, before he can assert that one causes the other, it is not necessary for Smith himself to have such knowledge."

27

Causal Relations

Donald Davidson

What is the logical form of singular causal statements like: 'The flood caused the famine', 'The stabbing caused Caesar's death', 'The burning of the house caused the roasting of the pig'? This question is more modest than the question how we know such statements are true, and the question whether they can be analyzed in terms of, say, constant conjunction. The request for the logical form is modest because it is answered when we have identified the logical or grammatical roles of the words (or other significant stretches) in the sentences under scrutiny. It goes beyond this to define, analyze, or set down axioms governing, particular words or expressions.

I

According to Hume, "we may define a cause to be an object, followed by another, and where all the objects similar to the first are followed by objects similar to the second." This definition pretty clearly suggests that causes and effects are entities that can be named or described by singular terms; probably events, since one can follow another. But in the *Treatise*, under "rules by which to judge of causes and effects," Hume says that "where several different objects produce the same effect, it must be by means of some quality, which we discover to be common amongst them. For as like effects imply like causes, we must always ascribe the causation to the circumstances, wherein we discover the resemblance." Here it seems to be the "quality" or "circumstances" of an event that is the cause rather than the event itself, for the event itself is the same as others in some respects and different in other respects. The suspicion that it is not events, but something more closely tied to the descriptions of events, that Hume holds to be causes, is fortified by Hume's claim that causal statements are never necessary. For if events were causes, then a true description of some event would be 'the cause of b', and, given that such an event exists, it follows logically that the cause of b caused b.

Mill said that the cause "is the sum total of the conditions positive and negative taken together ... which being realized, the consequent invariably follows." Many discussions of causality have concentrated on the question whether Mill was right in insisting that the "real Cause" must

Donald Davidson, "Causal Relations," *Journal of Philosophy*, 64/21 (Nov. 1967): 692–703.
Copyright by Donald Davidson. Reprinted by permission of the author's estate and Columbia University.

Metaphysics: An Anthology, Second Edition. Edited by Jaegwon Kim, Daniel Z. Korman and Ernest Sosa.
Editorial material and organization © 2012 Blackwell Publishing Ltd. Published 2012 by Blackwell Publishing Ltd.

include all the antecedent conditions that jointly were sufficient for the effect, and much ingenuity has been spent on discovering factors, pragmatic or otherwise, that guide and justify our choice of some "part" of the conditions as the cause. There has been general agreement that the notion of cause may be at least partly characterized in terms of sufficient and (or) necessary conditions.[1] Yet it seems to me we do not understand how such characterizations are to be applied to particular causes.

Take one of Mill's examples: some man, say Smith, dies, and the cause of his death is said to be that his foot slipped in climbing a ladder. Mill would say we have not given the whole cause, since having a foot slip in climbing a ladder is not always followed by death. What we were after, however, was not the cause of death in general but the cause of Smith's death: does it make sense to ask under what conditions Smith's death invariably follows? Mill suggests that part of the cause of Smith's death is "the circumstance of his weight," perhaps because if Smith had been light as a feather, his slip might not have injured him. Mill's explanation of why we don't bother to mention this circumstance is that it is too obvious to bear mention, but it seems to me that if it was Smith's fall that killed him, and Smith weighed twelve stone, then Smith's fall was the fall of a man who weighed twelve stone, whether or not we know it or mention it. How could Smith's actual fall, with Smith weighing, as he did, twelve stone, be any more efficacious in killing him than Smith's actual fall?

The difficulty has nothing to do with Mill's sweeping view of the cause, but attends any attempt of this kind to treat particular causes as necessary or sufficient conditions. Thus Mackie asks, "What is the exact force of [the statement of some experts] that this short circuit caused this fire?" And he answers, "Clearly the experts are not saying that the short circuit was a necessary condition for this house's catching fire at this time; they know perfectly well that a short circuit somewhere else, or the overturning of a lighted oil stove ... might, if it had occurred, have set the house on fire."[2] Suppose the experts know what they are said to; how does this bear on the question whether the short circuit was a necessary condition of this particular fire? For a short circuit elsewhere could not have caused *this* fire, nor could the overturning of a lighted oil stove.

To talk of particular events as conditions is bewildering, but perhaps causes aren't events (like the short circuit, or Smith's fall from the ladder), but correspond rather to sentences (perhaps like the fact that this short circuit occurred, or the fact that Smith fell from the ladder). Sentences can express conditions of truth for others – hence the word 'conditional'.

If causes correspond to sentences rather than singular terms, the logical form of a sentence like:

(1)   The short circuit caused the fire

would be given more accurately by:

(2)   *The fact that* there was a short circuit *caused it to be the case that* there was a fire.

In (2) the italicized words constitute a sentential connective like 'and' or 'if...then...'. This approach no doubt receives support from the idea that causal laws are universal conditionals, and singular causal statements ought to be instances of them. Yet the idea is not easily implemented. Suppose, first, that a causal law is (as it is usually said Hume taught) nothing but a universally quantified material conditional. If (2) is an instance of such, the italicized words have just the meaning of the material conditional, 'If there was a short circuit, then there was a fire'. No doubt (2) entails this, but not conversely, since (2) entails something stronger: namely, the conjunction 'There was a short circuit *and* there was a fire'. We might try treating (2) as the conjunction of the appropriate law and 'There was a short circuit and there was a fire' – indeed, this seems a possible interpretation of Hume's definition of cause quoted above – but then (2) would no longer be an instance of the law. And aside from the inherent implausibility of this suggestion as giving the logical form of (2) (in contrast, say, to giving the grounds on which it might be asserted), there is also the oddity that an inference from the fact that there was a short circuit and there was a fire, and the law, to (2) would turn out to be no more than a conjoining of the premises.

Suppose, then, that there is a non-truth-functional causal connective, as has been proposed by many.[3] In line with the concept of a cause as a condition, the causal connective is conceived as a conditional, though stronger than the truth-functional conditional. Thus Arthur Pap writes, "The distinctive property of causal implication as compared with material implication is just that the falsity of the antecedent is no ground for inferring the truth of the causal implication."[4] If the connective Pap had in mind were that of (2), this remark would be strange, for it is a property of the connective in (2) that the falsity of either the "antecedent" or the "consequent" is a ground for inferring the falsity of (2). That treating the causal connective as a kind of conditional unsuits it for the work of (1) or (2) is perhaps even more evident from Burks's remark that "p is causally sufficient for q is logically equivalent to $\sim q$ is causally sufficient for $\sim p$."[5] Indeed, this shows not only that Burks's connective is not that of (2), but also that it is not the subjunctive causal connective 'would cause'. My tickling Jones would cause him to laugh, but his not laughing would not cause it to be the case that I didn't tickle him.

These considerations show that the connective of (2), and hence by hypothesis of (1), cannot, as is often assumed, be a conditional of any sort, but they do not show that (2) does not give the logical form of singular causal statements. To show this needs a stronger argument, and I think there is one, as follows.

It is obvious that the connective in (2) is not truth-functional, since (2) may change from true to false if the contained sentences are switched. Nevertheless, substitution of singular terms for others with the same extension in sentences like (1) and (2) does not touch their truth-value. If Smith's death was caused by the fall from the ladder and Smith was the first man to land on the moon, then the fall from the ladder was the cause of the death of the first man to land on the moon. And if the fact that there was a fire in Jones's house caused it to be the case that the pig was roasted, and Jones's house is the oldest building on Elm Street, then the fact that there was a fire in the oldest building on Elm Street caused it to be the case that the pig was roasted. We must accept the principle of extensional substitution, then. Surely also we cannot change the truth-value of the likes of (2) by substituting logically equivalent sentences for sentences in it. Thus (2) retains its truth if for 'there was a fire' we substitute the logically equivalent '$\hat{x}(x = x$ & there

was a fire) $= \hat{x}(x = x)$'; retains it still if for the left side of this identity we write the coextensive singular term '$\hat{x}(x = x$ & Nero fiddled)'; and still retains it if we replace '$\hat{x}(x = x$ & Nero fiddled) $= \hat{x}(x = x)$' by the logically equivalent 'Nero fiddled' Since the only aspect of 'there was a fire' and 'Nero fiddled' that matters to this chain of reasoning is the fact of their material equivalence, it appears that our assumed principles have led to the conclusion that the main connective of (2) is contrary to what we supposed, truth-functional.[6]

Having already seen that the connective of (2) cannot be truth-functional, it is tempting to try to escape the dilemma by tampering with the principles of substitution that led to it. But there is another, and, I think, wholly preferable way out: we may reject the hypothesis that (2) gives the logical form of (1), and with it the ideas that the 'caused' of (1) is a more or less concealed sentential connective, and that causes are fully expressed only by sentences.

II

Consider these six sentences:

(3) *It is a fact that* Jack fell down.
(4) Jack fell down *and* Jack broke his crown.
(5) Jack fell down *before* Jack broke his crown.
(6) Jack fell down, *which caused it to be the case that* Jack broke his crown.
(7) *Jones forgot the fact that* Jack fell down.
(8) *That* Jack fell down *explains the fact that* Jack broke his crown.

Substitution of equivalent sentences for, or substitution of coextensive singular terms or predicates in, the contained sentences, will not alter the truth-value of (3) or (4): here extensionality reigns. In (7) and (8), intensionality reigns, in that similar substitution in or for the contained sentences is not guaranteed to save truth. (5) and (6) seem to fall in between; for in them substitution of coextensive singular terms preserves truth, whereas substitution of equivalent sentences does not. However this last is, as we just saw with respect to (2), and hence also (6), untenable middle ground.

Our recent argument would apply equally against taking the 'before' of (5) as the sentential connective it appears to be. And of course we don't interpret 'before' as a sentential connective, but rather as an ordinary two-place relation true of ordered pairs of times; this is made to work by introducing an extra place into the predicates ('x fell down' becoming 'x fell down at t') and an ontology of times to suit. The logical form of (5) is made perspicuous, then, by:

(5')   There exist times t and t' such that Jack fell down at t, Jack broke his crown at t' and t preceded t'.

This standard way of dealing with (5) seems to me essentially correct, and I propose to apply the same strategy to (6), which then comes out:

(6')   There exist events e and e' such that e is a falling down of Jack, e' is a breaking of his crown by Jack, and e caused e'.

Once events are on hand, an obvious economy suggests itself: (5) may as well be construed as about events rather than times. With this, the canonical version of (5) becomes just (6'), with 'preceded' replacing 'caused'. Indeed, it would be difficult to make sense of the claim that causes precede, or at least do not follow, their effects if (5) and (6) did not thus have parallel structures. We will still want to be able to say when an event occurred, but with events this requires an ontology of pure numbers only. So 'Jack fell down at 3 p.m.' says that there is an event e that is a falling down of Jack, and the time of e, measured in hours after noon, is three; more briefly, $(\exists e)$ $(F \text{ (Jack, } e) \ \& \ t(e) = 3)$.

On the present plan, (6) means some fall of Jack's caused some breaking of Jack's crown; so (6) is not false if Jack fell more than once, broke his crown more than once, or had a crown-breaking fall more than once. Nor, if such repetitions turned out to be the case, would we have grounds for saying that (6) referred to one rather than another of the fracturings. The same does not go for 'The short circuit caused the fire' or 'The flood caused the famine' or 'Jack's fall caused the breaking of Jack's crown'; here singularity is imputed. ('Jack's fall', like 'the day after tomorrow', is no less a singular term because it may refer to different entities on different occasions.) To do justice to 'Jack's fall caused the breaking of Jack's crown' what we need is something like. 'The one and only falling down of Jack caused the one and only breaking of

his crown by Jack'; in some symbols of the trade, '(ιe) F(Jack, e) caused (ιe) B (Jack's crown, e)'.

Evidently (1) and (2) do not have the same logical form. If we think in terms of standard notations for first-order languages, it is (1) that more or less wears its form on its face; (2), like many existentially quantified sentences, does not (witness 'Somebody loves somebody'). The relation between (1) and (2) remains obvious and close: (1) entails (2), but not conversely.[7]

III

The salient point that emerges so far is that we must distinguish firmly between causes and the features we hit on for describing them, and hence between the question whether a statement says truly that one event caused another and the further question whether the events are characterized in such a way that we can deduce, or otherwise infer, from laws or other causal lore, that the relation was causal. "The cause of this match's lighting is that it was struck. – Yes, but that was only *part* of the cause; it had to be a dry match, there had to be adequate oxygen in the atmosphere, it had to be struck hard enough, etc." We ought now to appreciate that the "Yes, but" comment does not have the force we thought. It cannot be that the striking of this match was only part of the cause, for this match was in fact dry, in adequate oxygen, and the striking was hard enough. What is partial in the sentence "The cause of this match's lighting is that it was struck" is the *description* of the cause; as we add to the description of the cause, we may approach the point where we can deduce, from this description and laws, that an effect of the kind described would follow.

If Flora dried herself with a coarse towel, she dried herself with a towel. This is an inference we know how to articulate, and the articulation depends in an obvious way on reflecting in language an ontology that includes such things as towels: if there is a towel that is coarse and was used by Flora in her drying, there is a towel that was used by Flora in her drying. The usual way of doing things does not, however, give similar expression to the similar inference from 'Flora dried herself with a towel on the beach at noon' to 'Flora dried herself with a towel', or for that matter, from the last to 'Flora dried herself'. But if, as I suggest, we render 'Flora dried herself' as about an event, as well as about Flora, these inferences turn out to be quite parallel to the more familiar ones. Thus if there was an event that was a drying by Flora of herself and that was done with a towel, on the beach, at noon, then clearly there was an event that was a drying by Flora of herself – and so on.

The mode of inference carries over directly to causal statements. If it was a drying she gave herself with a coarse towel on the beach at noon that caused those awful splotches to appear on Flora's skin, then it was a drying she gave herself that did it; we may also conclude that it was something that happened on the beach, something that took place at noon, and something that was done with a towel, that caused the tragedy. These little pieces of reasoning seem all to be endorsed by intuition, and it speaks well for the analysis of causal statements in terms of events that on that analysis the arguments are transparently valid.

Mill, we are now in better position to see, was wrong in thinking we have not specified the whole cause of an event when we have not wholly specified it. And there is not, as Mill and others have maintained, anything elliptical in the claim that a certain man's death was caused by his eating a particular dish, even though death resulted only because the man had a particular bodily constitution, a particular state of present health, and so on. On the other hand Mill was, I think, quite right in saying that "there certainly is, among the circumstances that took place, some combination or other on which death is invariably consequent … the whole of which circumstances perhaps constituted in this particular case the conditions of the phenomenon …".[8] Mill's critics are no doubt justified in contending that we may correctly give the cause without saying enough about it to demonstrate that it was sufficient; but they share Mill's confusion if they think every deletion from the description of an event represents something deleted from the event described.

The relation between a singular causal statement like 'The short circuit caused the fire' and necessary and sufficient conditions seems, in brief, to be this. The fuller we make the description of the cause, the better our chances of demonstrating that it was sufficient (as described) to produce the effect, and the worse our chances

of demonstrating that it was necessary; the fuller we make the description of the effect, the better our chances of demonstrating that the cause (as described) was necessary, and the worse our chances of demonstrating that it was sufficient. The symmetry of these remarks strongly suggests that in whatever sense causes are correctly said to be (described as) sufficient, they are as correctly said to be necessary. Here is an example. We may suppose there is some predicate '$P(x, y, e)$' true of Brutus, Caesar, and Brutus's stabbing of Caesar and such that any stab (by anyone of anyone) that is P is followed by the death of the stabbed. And let us suppose further that this law meets Mill's requirements of being *unconditional* – it supports counterfactuals of the form 'If Cleopatra had received a stab that was P, she would have died'. Now we can prove (assuming a man dies only once) that Brutus's stab was sufficient for Caesar death. Yet it was not the cause of Caesar's death, for Caesar's death was the death of a man with more wounds than Brutus inflicted, and such a death could not have been caused by an event that was P ('P' was chosen to apply only to stabbings administered by a single hand). The trouble here is not that the description of the cause is partial, but that the event described was literally (spatiotemporally) only part of the cause.

Can we then analyze 'a caused b' as meaning that a and b may be described in such a way that the existence of each could be demonstrated, in the light of causal laws, to be a necessary and sufficient condition of the existence of the other? One objection, foreshadowed in previous discussion, is that the *analysandum* does, but the *analysans* does not, entail the existence of a and b. Suppose we add, in remedy, the condition that either a or b, as described, exists. Then on the proposed analysis one can show that the causal relation holds between any two events. To apply the point in the direction of sufficiency, imagine some description '$(\iota x)Fx$' under which the existence of an event a may be shown sufficient for the existence of b. Then the existence of an arbitrary event c may equally be shown sufficient for the existence of b: just take as the description of c the following: '$(\iota y)(y = c \; \& \; (\exists!x)Fx)$'.[9] It seems unlikely that any simple and natural restrictions on the form of allowable descriptions would meet this difficulty, but since I have abjured the analysis of the causal relation, I shall not pursue the matter here.

There remains a legitimate question concerning the relation between causal laws and singular causal statements that may be raised independently. Setting aside the abbreviations successful analysis might authorize, what form are causal laws apt to have if from them, and a premise to the effect that an event of a certain (acceptable) description exists, we are to infer a singular causal statement saying that the event caused, or was caused by, another? A possibility I find attractive is that a full-fledged causal law has the form of a conjunction:

$$(L)\begin{cases} (S) & (e)(n)((Fe \& t(e) = n) \to \\ & (\exists! f)(Gf \& t(f) = n + \varepsilon \& \\ & C(e, f))) \text{ and} \\ (N) & (e)(n)((Ge \& t(e) = n + \varepsilon) \to \\ & (\exists! f)(Ff \& t(f) = n \& C(f, e))) \end{cases}$$

Here the variables 'e' and 'f' range over events, 'n' ranges over numbers, F and G are properties of events, '$C(e, f)$' is read 'e causes f', and 't' is a function that assigns a number to an event to mark the time the event occurs. Now, given the premise:

(P) $(\exists! e)(Fe \& t(e) = 3)$
(C) $(\iota e)(Fe \& t(e) = 3)$ caused
$(\iota e)(Ge \& t(e) = 3 + \varepsilon)$

It is worth remarking that part (N) of (L) is as necessary to the proof of (C) from (P) as it is to the proof of (C) from the premise '$(\exists! e)(Ge \& t(e) = 3 + \varepsilon)$'. This is perhaps more reason for holding that causes are, in the sense discussed above, necessary as well as sufficient conditions.

Explaining "why an event occurred," on this account of laws, may take an instructively large number of forms, even if we limit explanation to the resources of deduction. Suppose, for example, we want to explain the fact that there was a fire in the house at 3:01 p.m. Armed with appropriate premises in the form of (P) and (L), we may deduce: that there was a fire in the house at 3:01 p.m.; that it was caused by a short circuit at 3:00 p.m.; that there was only one fire in the house at 3:01 p.m.; that this fire was caused by the one and only short circuit that occurred at 3:00 p.m. Some of these explanations fall short of using all that is given by the premises; and this is lucky, since we often know less. Given only (S) and (P), for example, we cannot prove there was only one fire in the house at 3:01 p.m., though we can prove

there was exactly one fire in the house at 3:01 p.m. that was caused by the short circuit. An interesting case is where we know a law in the form of (N), but not the corresponding (S). Then we may show that, given that an event of a particular sort occurred, there must have been a cause answering to a certain description, but, given the same description of the cause, we could not have predicted the effect. An example might be where the effect is getting pregnant.

If we explain why it is that a particular event occurred by deducting a statement that there is such an event (under a particular description) from a premise known to be true, then a simple way of explaining an event, for example the fire in the house at 3:01 p.m., consists in producing a statement of the form of (C); and this explanation makes no use of laws. The explanation will be greatly enhanced by whatever we can say in favor of the truth of (C); needless to say, producing the likes of (L) and (P), if they are known true, clinches the matter. In most cases, however, the request for explanation will describe the event in terms that fall under no full-fledged law. The device to which we will then resort, if we can, is apt to be redescription of the event. For we can explain the occurrence of any event a if we know (L), (P), and the further fact that $a = (\iota e)(Ge \& t(e) = 3 + \varepsilon)$. Analogous remarks apply to the redescription of the cause, and to cases where all we want, or can, explain is the fact that there was *an* event of a certain sort.

The great majority of singular causal statements are not backed, we may be sure, by laws in the way (C) is backed by (L). The relation in general is rather this: if 'a caused b' is true, then there are descriptions of a and b such that the result of substituting them for 'a' and 'b' in 'a caused b' is entailed by true premises of the form of (L) and (P); and the converse holds if suitable restrictions are put on the descriptions.[10] If this is correct, it does not follow that we must be able to dredge up a law if we know a singular causal statement to be true; all that follows is that we know there must be a covering law. And very often, I think, our justification for accepting a singular causal statement is that we have reason to believe an appropriate causal law exists, though we do not know what it is. Generalizations like 'If you strike a well-made match hard enough against a properly prepared surface, then, other conditions being favorable, it will light' owe their importance not to the fact that we can hope eventually to render them untendentious and exceptionless, but rather to the fact that they summarize much of our evidence for believing that full-fledged causal laws exist covering events we wish to explain.[11]

If the story I have told is true, it is possible to reconcile, within limits, two accounts thought by their champions to be opposed. One account agrees with Hume and Mill to this extent: it says that a singular causal statement 'a caused b' entails that there is a law to the effect that "all the objects similar to a are followed by objects similar to b" and that we have reason to believe the singular statement only in so far as we have reason to believe there is such a law. The second account (persuasively argued by C. J. Ducasse[12]) maintains that singular causal statements entail no law and that we can know them to be true without knowing any relevant law. Both of these accounts are entailed, I think, by the account I have given, and they are consistent (I therefore hope) with each other. The reconciliation depends, of course, on the distinction between knowing there is a law "covering" two events and knowing what the law is: in my view, Ducasse is right that singular causal statements entail no law; Hume is right that they entail there is a law.

IV

Much of what philosophers have said of causes and causal relations is intelligible only on the assumption (often enough explicit) that causes are individual events, and causal relations hold between events. Yet, through failure to connect this basic aperçu with the grammar of singular causal judgments, these same philosophers have found themselves pressed, especially when trying to put causal statements into quantificational form, into trying to express the relation of cause to effect by a sentential connective. Hence the popularity of the utterly misleading question: can causal relations be expressed by the purely extensional material conditional, or is some stronger (non-Humean) connection involved? The question is misleading because it confuses two separate matters: the logical form of causal statements and the analysis of causality. So far as form is concerned, the issue of nonextensionality does not arise, since the relation of causality between events can be expressed (no matter how "strong" or "weak" it is) by an ordinary two-place predicate in an ordinary, extensional first-order language. These plain resources will perhaps be outrun by an adequate account of the form of causal laws, subjunctives, and counterfactual conditionals, to which most attempts to analyze the causal relation turn. But this is, I have urged, another question.

This is not to say there are no causal idioms that directly raise the issue of apparently non-truth-functional connectives. On the contrary, a host of statement forms, many of them strikingly similar, at least at first view, to those we have considered, challenge the account just given. Here are samples: 'The failure of the sprinkling system caused the fire', 'The slowness with which controls were applied caused the rapidity with which the inflation developed', 'The collapse was caused, not by the fact that the bolt gave way, but by the fact that it gave way so suddenly and unexpectedly', 'The fact that the dam did not hold caused the flood'. Some of these sentences may yield to the methods I have prescribed, especially if failures are counted among events, but others remain recalcitrant. What we must say in such cases is that in addition to, or in place of, giving what Mill calls the "producing cause," such sentences tell, or suggest, a causal story. They are, in other words, rudimentary causal explanations. Explanations typically relate statements, not events. I suggest therefore that the 'caused' of the sample sentences in this paragraph is not the 'caused' of straightforward singular causal statements, but is best expressed by the words 'causally explains'.[13]

A final remark. It is often said that events can be explained and predicted only in so far as they have repeatable characteristics, but not in so far as they are particulars. No doubt there is a clear and trivial sense in which this is true, but we ought not to lose sight of the less obvious point that there is an important difference between explaining the fact that there was an explosion in the broom closet and explaining the occurrence of the explosion in the broom closet. Explanation of the second sort touches the particular event as closely as language can ever touch any particular. Of course this claim is persuasive only if there are such things as events to which singular terms, especially definite descriptions, may refer. But the assumption, ontological and metaphysical, that there are events, is one without which we cannot make sense of much of our most common talk;

or so, at any rate, I have been arguing. I do not know any better, or further, way of showing what there is.

Notes

I am indebted to Harry Lewis and David Nivison, as well as to other members of seminars at Stanford University to whom I presented the ideas in this paper during 1966/67, for many helpful comments. I have profited greatly from discussion with John Wallace of the questions raised here; he may or may not agree with my answers. My research was supported in part by the National Science Foundation.

1 For a recent example, with reference to many others, see J. L. Mackie, "Causes and conditions," this volume, ch. 26.

2 Ibid. p. 362.

3 For example by: Mackie, ibid. p. 370; Arthur Burks, "The logic of causal propositions," *Mind*, 60/239 (July 1951), pp. 363–82; and Arthur Pap, "Disposition concepts and extensional logic," in H. Feigl, M. Scriven, and G. Maxwell (eds), *Minnesota Studies in the Philosophy of Science*, vol. 2, (Minneapolis: University of Minnesota Press, 1958), pp. 196–224.

4 Pap, "Disposition concepts," p. 212.

5 Burks, "Logic of causal propositions," p. 369.

6 This argument is closely related to one spelled out by Dagfinn Føllesdal, in "Quantification into causal contexts" in R. S. Cohen and M. W. Wartofsky (eds), *Boston Studies in the Philosophy of Science*, vol. 2 (New York: Humanities Press, 1966), pp. 263–74, to show that unrestricted quantification into causal contexts leads to difficulties. His argument is in turn a direct adaptation of Quine's *Word and Object* (Cambridge, Mass.: MIT Press, 1960), pp. 197–8) to show that (logical) modal distinctions collapse under certain natural assumptions. My argument derives directly from Frege.

7 A familiar device I use for resting hypotheses about logical grammar is translation into standard quantificational form; since the semantics of such languages is transparent, translation into them is a way of providing a semantic theory (a theory of the logical form) for what is translated. In this employment, canonical notation is not to be conceived as an improvement on the vernacular, but as a comment on it.

For elaboration and defense of the view of events sketched in this section, see my "The logical form of action sentences," in Nicholas Rescher (ed.), *The Logic of Action and Preference*, (Pittsburgh: Pittsburgh University Press, 1967).

8 J. S. Mill, *A System of Logic* (orig. pub. 1843; London: Routledge & Sons, 1872), bk III, ch. 5, sect. 3.

9 Here I am indebted to Professor Carl Hempel, and in the next sentence to John Wallace.

10 Clearly this account cannot be taken as a definition of the causal relation. Not only is there the inherently vague quantification over expressions (of what language?), but there is also the problem of spelling out the "suitable restrictions."

11 The thought in these paragraphs, like much more that appears here, was first adumbrated in my "Actions, reasons, and causes," *Journal of Philosophy* 60/23 (7 Nov. 1963), pp. 685–700, esp. pp. 696–9; repr. in Bernard Berofsky (ed.), *Free Will and Determinism*, (New York: Harper & Row, 1966). This conception of causality was subsequently discussed and, with various modifications, employed by Samuel Gorovitz, "Causal judgments and causal explanations," *Journal of Philosophy* 62/23 (2 Dec. 1965), pp. 695–711, and by Bernard Berofsky, "Causality and general laws," *Journal of Philosophy*, 63/6 (17 Mar. 1966), pp. 148–57.

12 See C. J. Ducasse, "Critique of Hume's conception of causality," *Journal of Philosophy* 63/6 (17 Mar. 1966); pp. 141–8; *idem*, *Causation and the Types of Necessity* (Seattle: University of Washington Press, 1924); *idem*, *Nature, Mind, and Death* (La Salle, Ill.: Open Court, 1951), pt 2. I have omitted from my "second account" much that Ducasse says that is not consistent with Hume.

13 Zeno Vendler has ingeniously marshalled the linguistic evidence for a deep distinction, in our use of 'cause', 'effect', and related words, between occurrences of verb-nominalizations that are fact-like or propositional, and occurrences that are event-like. (See Zeno Vendler, "Effects, results and consequences," in R. J. Butler (ed.), *Analytic Philosophy* (New York: Barnes & Noble, 1962), pp. 1–15.) Vendler concludes that the 'caused' of 'John's action caused the disturbance' is always flanked by expressions used in the propositional or fact-like sense, whereas 'was an effect of' or 'was due to' in 'The shaking of the earth was an effect of (was due to) the explosion' is flanked by expressions in the event-like sense. My distinction between essentially sentential expressions and the expressions that refer to events is much the same as Vendler's and owes much to him, though I have used more traditional semantic tools and have interpreted the evidence differently.

My suggestion that 'caused' is sometimes a relation, sometimes a connective, with corresponding changes in the interpretation of the expressions flanking it, has much in common with the thesis of J. M. Shorter's "Causality, and a method of analysis," in *Analytic Philosophy*, II, 1965, pp. 145–57.

28

Causality and Determination

G. E. M. Anscombe

1

It is often declared or evidently assumed that causality is some kind of necessary connection, or alternatively, that being caused is – non-trivially – instancing some exceptionless generalization saying that such an event always follows such antecedents. Or the two conceptions are combined.

Obviously there can be, and are, a lot of divergent views covered by this account. Any view that it covers nevertheless manifests one particular doctrine or assumption. Namely:

> If an effect occurs in one case and a similar effect does not occur in an apparently similar case, there must be a relevant further difference.

Any radically different account of causation, then, by contrast with which all those diverse views will be as one, will deny this assumption. Such a radically opposing view can grant that often – though it is difficult to say generally when – the assumption of relevant difference is a sound principle of investigation. It may grant that there are necessitating causes, but will refuse to identify causation as such with necessitation. It can grant that there are situations in which, given the initial conditions and no interference, only one result will accord with the laws of nature; but it will not see general reason, in advance of discovery, to suppose that any given course of things has been so determined. So it may grant that in many cases difference of issue can rightly convince us of a relevant difference of circumstances; but it will deny that, quite generally, this *must* be so.

The first view is common to many philosophers of the past. It is also, usually but not always in a neo-Humean form, the prevailing received opinion throughout the currently busy and productive philosophical schools of the English-speaking world, and also in some of the European and Latin American schools where philosophy is pursued in at all the same sort of way; nor is it confined to these schools. So firmly rooted is it that for many even outside pure philosophy, it routinely determines the meaning of 'cause', when consciously used as a theoretical term: witness the terminology of the contrast between "causal" and "statistical" laws, which is drawn by writers on physics – writers, note, who would not conceive themselves to be addicts of any philosophic school when they use this language to express that contrast.

G. E. M. Anscombe, "Causality and Determination: An Inaugural Lecture," © Cambridge University Press 1971. Reproduced with permission.

Metaphysics: An Anthology, Second Edition. Edited by Jaegwon Kim, Daniel Z. Korman and Ernest Sosa.
Editorial material and organization © 2012 Blackwell Publishing Ltd. Published 2012 by Blackwell Publishing Ltd.

The truth of this conception is hardly debated. It is, indeed, a bit of *Weltanschauung*: it helps to form a cast of mind which is characteristic of our whole culture.

The association between causation and necessity is old; it occurs for example in Aristotle's *Metaphysics*: 'When the agent and patient meet suitably to their powers, the one acts and the other is acted on OF NECESSITY.' Only with "rational powers" an extra feature is needed to determine the result: 'What has a rational power [e.g. medical knowledge, which can kill *or* cure] OF NECESSITY does what it has the power to do and as it has the power, when it has the desire.'[1]

Overleaping the centuries, we find it an axiom in Spinoza, 'Given a determinate cause, the effect follows OF NECESSITY, and without its cause, no effect follows.'[2] And in the English philosopher Hobbes: 'A cause simply, or an entire cause, is the aggregate of all the accidents both of the agents how many soever they be, and of the patients, put together; which when they are supposed to be present, IT CANNOT BE UNDERSTOOD BUT THAT THE EFFECT IS PRODUCED at the same instant; and if any of them be wanting, IT CANNOT BE UNDERSTOOD BUT THAT THE EFFECT IS NOT PRODUCED.'[3]

It was this last view, where the connection between cause and effect is evidently seen as *logical* connection of some sort, that was overthrown by Hume, the most influential of all philosophers on this subject in the English-speaking and allied schools. For he made us see that, given any particular cause – or "total causal situation" for that matter – and its effect, there is not in general any contradiction in supposing the one to occur and the other not to occur. That is to say, we'd know what was being described – what it would be like for it to be true – if it were reported, for example, that a kettle of water was put, and kept, directly on a hot fire, but the water did not heat up.

Were it not for the preceding philosophers who had made causality out as some species of logical connection, one would wonder at this being called a discovery on Hume's part: for vulgar humanity has always been over-willing to believe in miracles and marvels and *lusus naturae*. Mankind at large saw no contradiction, where Hume worked so hard to show the philosophic world – the Republic of Letters – that there was none.

The discovery was thought to be great. But as touching the equation of causality with necessitation, Hume's thinking did nothing against this but curiously reinforced it. For he himself assumed that NECESSARY CONNECTION is an essential part of the idea of the relation of cause and effect,[4] and he sought for its nature. He thought this could not be found in the situations, objects, or events called 'causes' and 'effects', but was to be found in the human mind's being determined, by experience of CONSTANT CONJUNCTION, to pass from the sensible impression or memory of one term of the relation to the convinced idea of the other. Thus to say that an event was caused was to say that its occurrence was an instance of some exceptionless generalization connecting such an event with such antecedents as it occurred in. The twist that Hume gave to the topic thus suggested a connection of the notion of causality with that of deterministic laws – i.e. laws such that always, given initial conditions and the laws, a unique result is determined.

The well-known philosophers who have lived after Hume may have aimed at following him and developing at least some of his ideas, or they may have put up a resistance; but in no case, so far as I know,[5] has the resistance called in question the equation of causality with necessitation.

Kant, roused by learning of Hume's discovery, laboured to establish causality as an a priori conception and argued that the objective time order consists 'in that order of the manifold of appearance according to which, IN CONFORMITY WITH A RULE, the apprehension of that which happens follows upon the apprehension of that which precedes ... In conformity with such a rule there must be in that which precedes an event the condition of a rule according to which this event INVARIABLY and NECESSARILY follows.'[6] Thus Kant tried to give back to causality the character of a *justified* concept which Hume's considerations had taken away from it. Once again the connection between causation and necessity was reinforced. And this has been the general characteristic of those who have sought to oppose Hume's conception of causality. They have always tried to establish the necessitation that they saw in causality: either a priori, or somehow out of experience.

Since Mill it has been fairly common to explain causation one way or another in terms of 'necessary' and 'sufficient' conditions. Now 'sufficient condition' is a term of art whose users may therefore lay down its meaning as they please. So they are in their rights to rule out the query: 'May not the sufficient conditions of an event be present, and the event yet not take place?' For 'sufficient condition' is so used that if the sufficient conditions for X are there, X occurs. But at the same time, the phrase cozens the understanding into not noticing an assumption. For 'sufficient condition' sounds like: 'enough'. And one certainly *can* ask: 'May there not be *enough* to have made something happen – and yet it not have happened?'

Russell wrote of the notion of cause, or at any rate of the "law of causation" (and he seemed to feel the same way about "cause" itself), that, like the British monarchy, it had been allowed to survive because it had been erroneously thought to do no harm. In a destructive essay of great brilliance he cast doubt on the notion of necessity involved, unless it is explained in terms of universality, and he argued that upon examination the concepts of determination and of invariable succession of like objects upon like turn out to be empty: they do not differentiate between any conceivable course of things and any other. Thus Russell too assumes that necessity or universality is what is in question, and it never occurs to him that there may be any other conception of causality.[7]

Now it's not difficult to show it prima facie wrong to associate the notion of cause with necessity or universality in this way. For, it being much easier to trace effects back to causes with certainty than to predict effects from causes, we often know a cause without knowing whether there is an exceptionless generalization of the kind envisaged, or whether there is a necessity.

For example, we have found certain diseases to be contagious. If, then, I have had one and only one contact with someone suffering from such a disease, and I get it myself, we suppose I got it from him. But what if, having had the contact, I ask a doctor whether I will get the disease? He will usually only be able to say, 'I don't know – maybe you will, maybe not.'

But, it is said, knowledge of causes here is partial; doctors seldom even know any of the conditions under which one invariably gets a disease, let alone all the sets of conditions. This comment betrays the assumption that there is

such a thing to know. Suppose there is: still, the question whether there is does not have to be settled before we can know what we mean by speaking of the contact as cause of my getting the disease.

All the same, might it not be like this: knowledge of causes is possible without any satisfactory grasp of what is involved in causation? Compare the possibility of wanting clarification of "valency" or "long-run frequency", which yet have been handled by chemists and statisticians without such clarification; and valencies and long-run frequencies, whatever the right way of explaining them, have been known. Thus one of the familiar philosophic analyses of causality, or a new one in the same line, may be correct, though knowledge of it is not necessary for knowledge of causes.

There is something to observe here, that lies under our noses. It is little attended to, and yet still so obvious as to seem trite. It is this: causality consists in the derivativeness of an effect from its causes. This is the core, the common feature, of causality in its various kinds. Effects derive from, arise out of, come of, their causes. For example, everyone will grant that physical parenthood is a causal relation. Here the derivation is material, by fission. Now analysis in terms of necessity or universality does not tell us of this derivedness of the effect; rather it forgets about that. For the necessity will be that of laws of nature; through it *we* shall be able to derive knowledge of the effect from knowledge of the cause, or vice versa, but that does not show us the cause as source of the effect. Causation, then, is not to be identified with necessitation.

If A comes from B, this does not imply that every A-like thing comes from some B-like thing or set-up or that every B-like thing or set-up has an A-like thing coming from it; or that given B, A had to come from it, or that given A, there had to be B for it to come from. Any of these may be true, but if any is, that will be an additional fact, not comprised in A's coming from B. If we take 'coming from' in the sense of travel, this is perfectly evident.

'But that's because we can observe travel!' The influential Humean argument at this point is that we can't similarly observe causality in the individual case.[8] So the reason why we connect what we call the cause and what we call the effect as we do must lie elsewhere. It must lie in the fact that the succession of the latter upon the former is of a kind regularly observed.

There are two things for me to say about this. *First*, as to the statement that we can never observe causality in the individual case. Someone who says this is just not going to count anything as "observation of causality". This often happens in philosophy; it is argued that "all we find" is such-and-such, and it turns out that the arguer has excluded from his idea of "finding" the sort of thing he says we don't "find". And when we consider what we are allowed to say we do "find", we have the right to turn the tables on Hume, and say that neither do we perceive bodies, such as billiard balls, approaching one another. When we "consider the matter with the utmost attention", we find only an impression of travel made by the successive positions of a round white patch in our visual fields ... etc. Now a "Humean" account of causality has to be given in terms of constant conjunction of physical things, events, etc., not of experiences of them. If, then, it must be allowed that we "find" bodies in motion, for example, then what theory of perception can justly disallow the perception of a lot of causality? The truthful – though unhelpful – answer to the question: "How did we come by our primary knowledge of causality?" is that in learning to speak we learned the linguistic representation and application of a host of causal concepts. Very many of them were represented by transitive and other verbs of action used in reporting what is observed. Others – a good example is 'infect' – form, not observation statements, but rather expressions of causal hypotheses. The word 'cause' itself is highly general. How does someone show that he has the concept *cause*? We may wish to say: only by having such a word in his vocabulary. If so, then the manifest possession of the concept presupposes the mastery of much else in language. I mean: the word 'cause' can be *added* to a language in which are already represented many causal concepts. A small selection: *scrape, push, wet, carry, eat, burn, knock over, keep off, squash, make* (e.g. noises, paper boats), *hurt*. But if we care to imagine languages in which no special causal concepts are represented, then no description of the use of a word in such languages will be able to present it as meaning *cause*. Nor will it even contain words for natural kinds of stuff, nor yet words equivalent to 'body', 'wind', or 'fire'. For learning to use special causal verbs is part and parcel of learning to apply the concepts answering to these, and many other, substantives. As surely as we learned to call people by name or to report from seeing it that the cat was on the table, we also learned to report from having observed it that someone drank up the milk or that the dog made a funny noise or that things were cut or broken by whatever we saw cut or break them.

(I will mention, only to set on one side, one of the roots of Hume's argument, the implicit appeal to Cartesian scepticism. He confidently challenges us to 'produce some instance, wherein the efficacy is plainly discoverable to the mind, and its operations obvious to our consciousness or sensation'.[9] Nothing easier: is cutting, is drinking, is purring not "efficacy"? But it is true that the apparent perception of such things may be only apparent: we may be deceived by false appearances. Hume presumably wants us to "produce an instance" in which *efficacy* is related to sensation as *red* is. It is true that we can't do that; it is not *so* related to sensation. He is also helped, in making his argument that we don't perceive "efficacy", by his curious belief that 'efficacy' means much the same thing as 'necessary connection'! But as to the Cartesian-sceptical root of the argument, I will not delay upon it, as my present topic is not the philosophy of perception.)

Second, as to that instancing of a universal generalization, which was supposed to supply what could not be observed in the individual case, the causal relation, the needed examples are none too common. 'Motion in one body in all past instances that have fallen under our observation, is follow'd upon impulse by motion in another':[10] so Hume. But, as is always a danger in making large generalizations, he was thinking only of the cases where we do observe this – billiard balls against free-standing billiard balls in an ordinary situation: not billiard balls against stone walls. Neo-Humeans are more cautious. They realize that if you take a case of cause and effect, and relevantly describe the cause A and the effect B, and then construct a universal proposition, 'Always, given an A, a B follows', you usually won't get anything true. You have got to describe the absence of circumstances in which an A would not cause a B. But the task of excluding all such circumstances can't be carried out. There is, I suppose, a vague association in people's minds between the universal propositions which would be examples of the required type of generalizations, and scientific laws. But there is no similarity.

Suppose we were to call propositions giving the properties of substances "laws of nature". Then there will be a law of nature running 'The flash-point of such a substance is ...', and this will be important in explaining why striking matches usually causes them to light. This law of nature has not the form of generalization running 'Always, if a sample of such a substance is raised to such a temperature, it ignites'; nor is it equivalent to such a generalization, but rather to: 'If a sample of such a substance is raised to such a temperature and doesn't ignite, there must be a cause of its not doing so.' Leaving aside questions connected with the idea of a pure sample, the point here is that "normal conditions" is quite properly a vague notion. That fact makes generalizations running 'Always ...' merely fraudulent in such cases; it will always be necessary for them to be hedged about with clauses referring to normal conditions; and we may not know in advance whether conditions are normal or not, or what to count as an abnormal condition. In exemplar analytical practice, I suspect, it will simply be a relevant condition in which the generalization, 'Always, if such and such, such and such happens ...', supplemented with a few obvious conditions that have occurred to the author, turns out to be untrue. Thus the conditional 'If it doesn't ignite then there must be some cause' is the better gloss upon the original proposition, for it does not pretend to say specifically, or even disjunctively specifically, what *always* happens. It is probably these facts which make one hesitate to call propositions about the action of substances "laws of nature". The law of inertia, for example, would hardly be glossed: 'If a body accelerates without any force acting on it, there must be some cause of its doing so.' (Though I wonder what the author of *Principia* himself would have thought of that.) On the other hand just such "laws" as that about a substance's flash-point are connected with the match's igniting because struck.

Returning to the medical example, medicine is of course not interested in the hopeless task of constructing lists of all the sets of conditions under each of which people always get a certain disease. It is interested in finding what that is special, if anything, is always the case when people get a particular disease; and, given such a cause or condition (or in any case), in finding circumstances in which people don't get the disease, or tend not to. This is connected with medicine's concern first, and last, with things as they happen in the messy and mixed up conditions of life: only between its first and its last concern can it look for what happens unaffected by uncontrolled and inconstant conditions.

2

Yet my argument lies always open to the charge of appealing to ignorance. I must therefore take a different sort of example.

Here is a ball lying on top of some others in a transparent vertical pipe. I know how it got there: it was forcibly ejected with many others out of a certain aperture into the enclosed space above a row of adjacent pipes. The point of the whole construction is to show how a totality of balls so ejected always build up in rough conformity to the same curve. But I am interested in this one ball. Between its ejection and its getting into this pipe, it kept hitting sides, edges, other balls. If I made a film of it I could run it off in slow motion and tell the impact which produced each stage of the journey. Now was the result necessary? We would probably all have said it was in the time when Newton's mechanics was undisputed for truth. It was the impression made on Hume and later philosophers by that mechanics, that gave them so strong a conviction of the iron necessity with which everything happens, the 'absolute fate' by which 'Every object is determin'd to a certain degree and direction of its motion'.[11]

Yet no one could have deduced the resting place of the ball – because of the indeterminateness that you get even in the Newtonian mechanics, arising from the finite accuracy of measurements. From exact figures for positions, velocities, directions, spins, and masses you might be able to calculate the result as accurately as you chose. But the minutest inexactitudes will multiply up factor by factor, so that in a short time your information is gone. Assuming a given margin of error in your initial figure, you could assign an associated probability to that ball's falling into each of the pipes. If you want the highest probability you assign to be really high, so that you can take it as practical certainty, it will be a problem to reckon how tiny the permitted margins of inaccuracy must be – analogous to the problem: how small a fraction of a grain of millet must I demand is put on the first square of the chess board, if after doubling up at every square I end up having to pay out only a pound of millet? It would be a figure of such smallness as to have no meaning as a figure for a margin of error.

However, so long as you believed the classical mechanics you might also think there could be no such thing as a figure for a difference that had no meaning. Then you would think that though it was not feasible for us to find the necessary path of the ball because our margins of error are too great, yet there *was* a necessary path, which could be assigned a sufficient probability for firm acceptance of it, by anyone (not one of us) capable of reducing his limits of accuracy in measurement to a sufficiently small compass. Admittedly, so small a compass that he'd be down among the submicroscopic particles and no longer concerned with the measurements, say, of the ball. And now we can say: with certain degrees of smallness we get to a region where Newton's mechanics is no longer believed.

If the classical mechanics can be used to calculate a certain real result, we may give a sense to, and grant, the "necessity" of the result, given the antecedents. Here, however, you can't use the mechanics to calculate the result, but at most to give yourself a belief in its necessity. For this to be reasonable the system has got to be acknowledged as true. Not, indeed, that would be enough; but if so much were secured, then it would be worthwhile to discuss the metaphysics of absolute measures of continuous quantities.

The point needs some labouring precisely because "the system does apply to such bodies" – that is, to moderately massive balls. After all, it's Newton we use to calculate Sputniks! 'The system applies to these bodies' is true only in the sense and to the extent that it yields sufficient results of calculations about these bodies. It does not mean: in respect of these bodies the system is the truth, so that it just doesn't matter that we can't use it to calculate such a result in such a case. I am not

saying that a deterministic system involves individual predictability: it evidently does not. But in default of predictability the determinedness declared by the deterministic system has got to be believed because the system itself is believed.

I conclude that we have no ground for calling the path of the ball determined – at least, until it has taken its path – but, it may be objected, is not each state of its path determined, even though we cannot determine it? My argument has partly relied on loss of information through multiplicity of impacts. But from one impact to the next the path is surely determined, and so the whole path is so after all.

It sounds plausible to say: each stage is determined and so the whole is. But what does 'determined' mean? The word is a curious one (with a curious history); in this sort of context it is often used as if it *meant* 'caused'. Or perhaps 'caused' is used as if it meant 'determined'. But there is at any rate one important difference – a thing hasn't been caused until it has happened; but it may be determined before it happens.

(It is important here to distinguish between being *determined* and being *determinate*. In indeterministic physics there is an apparent failure of both. I am concerned only with the former.)

When we call a result determined we are implicitly relating it to an antecedent range of possibilities and saying that all but one of these is disallowed. What disallows them is not the result itself but something antecedent to the result. The antecedences may be logical or temporal or in the order of knowledge. Of the many – antecedent – possibilities, *now* only one is – antecedently – possible.

Mathematical formulae and human decisions are limiting cases; the former because of the obscurity of the notion of antecedent possibilities, and the latter because decisions can be retrieved.

In a chess-game, the antecedent possibilities are, say, the powers of the pieces. By the rules, a certain position excludes all but one of the various moves that were in that sense antecedently possible. This is logical antecedence. The next move is determined.

In the zygote, sex and eye-colour are already determined. Here the antecedent possibilities are the possibilities for sex and eye-colour for a child; or more narrowly: for a child of these parents. *Now,* given the combination of this ovum and this spermatozoon, all but one of these antecedent possibilities is excluded.

It might be said that anything was determined once it had happened. There is now no possibility open: it *has* taken place! It was in this sense that Aristotle said that past and present were necessary. But this does not concern us: what interests us is *pre*-determination.

Then 'each stage of the ball's path is determined' must mean 'Upon any impact, there is only one path possible for the ball up to the next impact (and assuming no air currents, etc.).' (But what ground could one have for believing this, if one does not believe in some system of which it is a consequence?) Consider a steel ball dropping between two pins on a Galton board to hit the pin centred under the gap between them. That it should balance on this pin is not to be expected. It has two possibilities; to go to the right or to the left. If you have a system which forces this on you, you can say: 'There has to be a determining factor; otherwise, like Buridan's ass, the ball must balance.' But if you have not, then you should say that the ball may be undetermined until it does move to the right or the left. Here the ball had only two significant possibilities and was perhaps unpredetermined between them. This was because it cannot be called determined – no reasonable account can be given of insisting that it is so – within a small range of possibility, actualization within which will lead on to its falling either to the right or to the left. With our flying ball there will also be such a small range of possibility. The further consequences of the path it may take are not tied down to just two significant possibilities, as with one step down the Galton board: the range of further possibility gets wider as we consider the paths it may take. Otherwise, the two cases are similar.

We see that to give content to the idea of something's being determined, we have to have a set of possibilities, which something narrows down to one – before the event.

This accords well with our understanding of part of the dissatisfaction of some physicists with the quantum theory. They did not like the undeterminedness of individual quantum phenomena. Such a physicist might express himself by saying 'I believe in causality!' He meant: I believe that the real physical laws and the initial conditions must entail uniqueness of result. Of course, within a range of co-ordinate and mutually exclusive identifiable possible results, only one happens: he means that the result that happens ought to be understood as the only one that was possible before it happened.

Must such a physicist be a "determinist"? That is, must he believe that the whole universe is a system such that, if its total states at t and t' are thus and so, the laws of nature are such as then to allow only one possibility for its total state at any other time? No. He may not think that the idea of a total state of the universe at a time is one he can do anything with. He may even have no views on the uniqueness of possible results for whatever may be going on in any arbitrary volume of space. For 'Our theory should be such that only the actual result was possible for that experiment' doesn't mean 'Our theory should have excluded the experiment's being muffed or someone's throwing a boot, so that we didn't get the result', but rather: 'Our theory should be such that only this result was possible as *the result of the experiment*.' He hates a theory, even if he has to put up with it for the time being, that essentially assigns only probability to a result, essentially allows of a range of possible results, never narrowed down to one until the event itself.

It must be admitted that such dissatisfied physicists very often have been determinists. Witness Schrödinger's account of the "principle of causality": 'The exact physical situation at *any* point P at a given moment t is unambiguously determined by the exact physical situation within a certain surrounding of P at any previous time, say $t - \tau$. If τ is large, that is if that previous time lies far back, it may be necessary to know the previous situation for a wide domain around P.'[12] Or Einstein's more modest version of a notorious earlier claim: if you knew all about the contents of a sphere of radius 186,000 miles, and knew the laws, you would be able to know for sure what would happen at the centre for the next second. Schrödinger says: *any* point P; and *a* means *any* sphere of that radius. So their view of causality was not that of my hypothetical physicist, who I said may not have views on the uniqueness of possible results for whatever may be going on in any arbitrary volume of space. My physicist restricts his demand for uniqueness of result to situations in which he has got certain processes going in isolation from inconstant external influences, or where they do not matter, as the weather on a planet does not matter for predicting its course round the sun.

The high success of Newton's astronomy was in one way an intellectual disaster: it produced an illusion from which we tend still to suffer. This illusion was created by the circumstance that Newton's mechanics *had a good model in the solar system*. For this gave the impression that we had here an ideal of scientific explanation; whereas the truth was, it was mere obligingness on the part of the solar system, by having had so peaceful a history in recorded time, to provide such a model. For suppose that some planet had at some time erupted with such violence that its shell was propelled rocket-like out of the solar system. Such an event would not have violated Newton's laws; on the contrary, it would have illustrated them. But also it would not have been calculable as the past and future motions of the planets are presently calculated on the assumption that they can be treated as the simple "bodies" of his mechanics, with no relevant properties but mass, position, and velocity and no forces mattering except gravity.

Let us pretend that Newton's laws were still to be accepted without qualification: no reserve in applying them in electrodynamics; no restriction to bodies travelling a good deal slower than light; and no quantum phenomena. Newton's mechanics is a deterministic system: but this does not mean that believing them commits us to determinism. We could say: of course nothing violates those axioms or the laws of the force of gravity. But animals, for example, run about the world in all sorts of paths and no path is dictated for them by those laws, as it is for planets. Thus in relation to the solar system (apart from questions like whether in the past some planet has blown up), the laws are like the rules of an infantile card game: once the cards are dealt we turn them up in turn, and make two piles each, one red, one black; the winner has the biggest pile of red ones. So once the cards are dealt the game is determined, and from any position in it you can derive all others back to the deal and forward to win or draw. But in relation to what happens on and inside a planet the laws are, rather, like the rules of chess; the play is seldom determined, though nobody breaks the rules.[13]

Why this difference? A natural answer is: the mechanics does not give the special laws of all the forces. Not, for example, for thermal, nuclear, electrical, chemical, muscular forces. And now the Newtonian model suggests the picture: given the laws of all the forces, then there is total coverage of what happens and then the whole game of motion is determined; for, by the first law, any acceleration implies a force of some kind, and must not forces have laws? My hypothetical physicist at least would think so; and would demand that they be deterministic. Nevertheless he still does not have to be a "determinist"; for many forces, unlike gravity, can be switched on and off, are generated, and also shields can be put up against them. It is one thing to hold that in a clear-cut situation – an astronomical or a well-contrived experimental one designed to discover laws – "the result" should be determined: and quite another to say that in the hurly-burly of many crossing contingencies whatever happens next must be determined; or to say that the generation of forces (by human experimental procedures, among other things) is always determined in advance of the generating procedure; or to say that there is always a law of composition, of such a kind that the combined effect of a set of forces is determined in every situation.

Someone who is inclined to say those things, or implicitly to assume them, has almost certainly been affected by the impressive relation between Newton's mechanics and the solar system.

> We remember how it was in mechanics. By knowing the position and velocity of a particle at one single instant, by knowing the acting forces, the whole future path of the particle could be foreseen. In Maxwell's theory, if we know the field at one instant only, we can deduce from the equations of the theory how the whole field will change in space and time. Maxwell's equations enable us to follow the history of the field, just as the mechanical equations enabled us to follow the history of material particles ... With the help of Newton's laws we can deduce the motion of the earth from the force acting between the sun and the earth.[14]

'By knowing the acting forces' – that must of course include the *future* acting forces, not merely the present ones. And similarly for the equations which enable us to follow the history of the field; a change may be produced by an external influence. In reading both Newton and later writers one is often led to ponder that word 'external'. Of course, to be given "the acting forces" is to be given the external forces too and any new forces that may later be introduced into the situation. Thus those first sentences are true, if true, without the special favour of fate, being general truths of mechanics and physics, but the last one is true by favour, by the brute fact that only the force acting between earth and sun matters for the desired deductions.

The concept of necessity, as it is connected with causation, can be explained as follows: a cause C is a necessitating cause of an effect E when (I mean: on the occasions when) if C occurs it is certain to cause E unless something prevents it. C and E are to be understood as general expressions, not singular terms. If "certainty" should seem too epistemological a notion: a necessitating cause C of a given kind of effect E is such that it *is* not possible (on the occasion) that C should occur and should not cause an E, nor should there be anything that prevents an E from occurring. A non-necessitating cause is then one that can fail of its effect without the intervention of anything to frustrate it. We may discover *types* of necessitating and non-necessitating cause; e.g. rabies is a necessitating cause of death, because it is not possible for one who has rabies to survive without treatment. We don't have to tie it to the occasion. An example of a non-necessitating cause is mentioned by Feynman: a bomb is connected with a Geiger counter, so that it will go off if the Geiger counter registers a certain reading; whether it will or not is not determined, for it is so placed near some radioactive material that it may or may not register that reading.

There would be no doubt of the cause of the reading or of the explosion if the bomb did go off. Max Born is one of the people who has been willing to dissociate causality from determinism: he explicates cause and effect in terms of dependence of the effect on the cause. It is not quite clear what "dependence" is supposed to be, but at least it seems to imply that you would not get the effect without the cause. The trouble about this is that you might – from some other cause. That this effect was produced by this cause does not at all show that it could not, or would

not, have been produced by something else in the absence of this cause.

Indeterminism is not a possibility unconsidered by philosophers. C. D. Broad, in his inaugural lecture, given in 1934, described it as a possibility; but added that whatever happened without being determined was accidental. He did not explain what he meant by being accidental; he must have meant more than not being necessary. He may have meant being uncaused: but, if I am right, not being determined does not imply not being caused. Indeed, I should explain indeterminism as the thesis that not all physical effects are necessitated by their causes. But if we think of Feynman's bomb, we get some idea of what is meant by "accidental". It was random: it "merely happened" that the radioactive material emitted particles in such a way as to activate the Geiger counter enough to set off the bomb. Certainly the motion of the Geiger counter's needle is caused; and the actual emission is caused too; it occurs because there is this mass of radioactive material here. (I have already indicated that, contrary to the opinion of Hume, there are many different sorts of causality.) But all the same the *causation* itself is, one could say, *mere hap*. It is difficult to explain this idea any further.

Broad used the idea to argue that indeterminism, if applied to human action, meant that human actions are "accidental". Now he had a picture of choices as being determining causes, analogous to determining physical causes, and of choices in their turn being either determined or accidental. To regard a choice as such – i.e. any case of choice – as a predetermining causal event now appears as a naïve mistake in the philosophy of mind, though that is a story I cannot tell here.

It was natural that when physics went indeterministic, some thinkers should have seized on this indeterminism as being just what was wanted for defending the freedom of the will. They received severe criticism on two counts: one, that this "mere hap" is the very last thing to be invoked as the physical correlate of "man's ethical behaviour"; the other, that quantum laws predict statistics of events when situations are repeated; interference with these, by the *will's* determining individual events which the laws of nature leave undetermined, would be as much a violation of natural law as would have been interference which falsified a deterministic mechanical law.

Ever since Kant it has been a familiar claim among philosophers that one can believe in both physical determinism and "ethical" freedom. The reconciliations have always seemed to me to be either so much gobbledegook, or to make the alleged freedom of action quite unreal. My actions are mostly physical movements; if these physical movements are physically predetermined by processes which I do not control, then my freedom is perfectly illusory. The truth of physical indeterminism is thus indispensable if we are to make anything of the claim to freedom. But certainly it is insufficient. The physically undetermined is not thereby "free". For freedom at least involves the power of acting according to an idea, and no such thing is ascribed to whatever is the subject (what would be the relevant subject?) of unpredetermination in indeterministic physics. Nevertheless, there is nothing unacceptable about the idea that that "physical haphazard" should be the only physical correlate of human freedom of action; and perhaps also of the voluntariness and intentionalness in the conduct of other animals which we do not call "free". The freedom, intentionalness, and voluntariness are not to be analysed as the same thing as, or as produced by, the physical haphazard. Different sorts of pattern altogether are being spoken of when we mention them, from those involved in describing elementary processes of physical causality.

The other objection is, I think, more to the point. Certainly if we have a statistical law, but undetermined individual events, and then enough of these are supposed to be pushed by will in one direction to falsify the statistical law, we have again a supposition that puts will into conflict with natural laws. But it is not at all clear that the same train of minute physical events should have to be the regular correlate of the same action; in fact, that suggestion looks immensely implausible. It is, however, required by the objection.

Let me construct an analogy to illustrate this point. Suppose that we have a large glass box full of millions of extremely minute coloured particles, and the box is constantly shaken. Study of the box and particles leads to statistical laws, including laws for the random generation of small unit patches of uniform colour. Now the box is remarkable for also presenting the following phenomenon: the word 'Coca-Cola', formed like a mosaic, can always be read when one looks at one of the sides. It is not always the same shape in the formation of its letters, not always the same size or in the same position, it varies in its colours; but there it always is. It is not at all clear that those statistical laws concerning the random motion of the particles and their formation of small unit patches of colour would have to be supposed violated by the operation of a cause for this phenomenon which did not derive it from the statistical laws.

It has taken the inventions of indeterministic physics to shake the rather common dogmatic conviction that determinism is a presupposition, or perhaps a conclusion, of scientific knowledge. Not that that conviction has been very much shaken even so. Of course, the belief that the laws of nature are deterministic has been shaken. But I believe it has often been supposed that this makes little difference to the assumption of macroscopic determinism: as if undeterminedness were always encapsulated in systems whose internal workings could be described only by statistical laws, but where the total upshot, and in particular the outward effect, was as near as makes no difference always the same. What difference does it make, after all, that the scintillations, whereby my watch dial is luminous, follow only a statistical law – so long as the gross manifest effect is sufficiently guaranteed by the statistical law? Feynman's example of the bomb and Geiger counter smashes this conception; but as far as I can judge it takes time for the lesson to be learned. I find deterministic assumptions more common now among people at large, and among philosophers, than when I was an undergraduate.

The lesson is welcome, but indeterministic physics (if it succeeds in giving the lesson) is only culturally, not logically, required to make the deterministic picture doubtful. For it was always a mere extravagant fancy, encouraged in the "age of science" by the happy relation of Newtonian mechanics to the solar system. It ought not to have mattered whether the laws of nature were or were not deterministic. For them to be deterministic is for them, together with the description of the situation, to entail unique results in situations defined by certain relevant objects and measures, and where no part is played by inconstant factors external to such definition. If that is right, the laws' being deterministic does not tell as whether "determinism" is true. It is the total coverage of every motion that happens that is a fanciful claim. But I do not mean that any motions lie outside the scope of physical laws, or that one cannot say, in any given context, that certain motions would be violations of physical law. Remember the contrast between chess and the infantile card game.

Meanwhile in non-experimental philosophy it is clear enough what are the dogmatic slumbers of the day. It is over and over again assumed that any singular causal proposition implies a universal statement running 'Always when this, then that'; often assumed that true singular causal statements are derived from such "inductively believed" universalities. Examples indeed are recalcitrant, but that does not seem to disturb. Even a philosopher acute enough to be conscious of this, such as Davidson, will say, without offering any reason at all for saying it, that a singular causal statement implies *that there is* such a true universal proposition[15] – though perhaps we can never have knowledge of it. Such a thesis needs some reason for believing it! "Regularities in nature": that is not a reason. The most neglected of the key topics in this subject are: interference and prevention.

Notes

1 *Metaphysics*, bk. ix. ch. 5.

2 *Ethics*. i. 3.

3 *Elements of Philosophy Concerning Body*. ch. 9.

4 *Treatise of Human Nature*, i. 3. sects. 2 and 6.

5 My colleague Ian Hacking has pointed out C. S. Peirce to me as an exception to this generalization.

6 *Critique of Pure Reason*, bk. ii. ch. 2. sect. 3. Second Analogy.

7 'The Notion of Cause', in *Mysticism and Logic*. [Reproduced as chapter 25 of the present volume.]

8 *Treatise of Human Nature*, i. 3. sect. 2.

9 Ibid. i. 3. sect. 14.

10 Ibid. ii. 3. sect. 1.

11 Ibid. ii. 3. sect. 1.

12 Erwin Schrödinger, *Science and Humanism* (Cambridge, 1951).

13 I should have made acknowledgements to Gilbert Ryle (*The Concept of Mind* (London, 1949), 77) for this comparison. But his use of the openness of chess is somewhat ambiguous and is not the same as mine. For the contrast with a closed card game I was indebted to A. J. P. Kenny.

14 Albert Einstein and Leopold Infeld. *The Evolution of Physics* (New York, 1938; paperback edn. 1967). 146.

15 Donald Davidson, 'Causal Relations', *Journal of Philosophy*, 64 (Nov. 1967) [ch. 27 in the present volume].

29

Causation

David Lewis

Hume defined causation twice over. He wrote: "we may define a cause to be *an object followed by another, and where all the objects, similar to the first, are followed by objects similar to the second. Or, in other words, where, if the first object had not been, the second never had existed.*"[1]

Descendants of Hume's first definition still dominate the philosophy of causation: a causal succession is supposed to be a succession that instantiates a regularity. To be sure, there have been improvements. Nowadays we try to distinguish the regularities that count – the "causal laws" – from mere accidental regularities of succession. We subsume causes and effects under regularities by means of descriptions they satisfy, not by overall similarity. And we allow a cause to be only one indispensable part, not the whole, of the total situation that is followed by the effect in accordance with a law. In present-day regularity analyses, a cause is defined (roughly) as any member of any minimal set of actual conditions that are jointly sufficient, given the laws, for the existence of the effect.

More precisely, let C be the proposition that c exists (or occurs), and let E be the proposition that e exists. Then c causes e, according to a typical regularity analysis,[2] iff (1) C and E are true; and (2) for some nonempty set L of true law-propositions and some set F of true propositions of particular fact, L and F jointly imply $C \supset E$, although L and F jointly do not imply E, and F alone does not imply $C \supset E$.[3]

Much needs doing, and much has been done, to turn definitions like this one into defensible analyses. Many problems have been overcome. Others remain: in particular, regularity analyses tend to confuse causation itself with various other causal relations. If c belongs to a minimal set of conditions jointly sufficient for e, given the laws, then c may well be a genuine cause of e. But c might rather be an effect of e: one which could not, given the laws and some of the actual circumstances, have occurred otherwise than by being caused by e. Or c might be an epiphenomenon of the causal history of e: a more or less inefficacious effect of some genuine cause of e. Or c might be a preempted potential cause of e: something that did not cause e, but that would have done so in the absence of whatever really did cause e.

It remains to be seen whether any regularity analysis can succeed in distinguishing genuine causes from effects, epiphenomena, and preempted

David Lewis, "Causation," *Journal of Philosophy*, 70/17 (10 Oct. 1973): 556–67. Reproduced by permission.

potential causes – and whether it can succeed without falling victim to worse problems, without piling on the epicycles, and without departing from the fundamental idea that causation is instantiation of regularities. I have no proof that regularity analyses are beyond repair, nor any space to review the repairs that have been tried. Suffice it to say that the prospects look dark. I think it is time to give up and try something else.

A promising alternative is not far to seek. Hume's "other words" – that if the cause had not been, the effect never had existed – are no mere restatement of his first definition. They propose something altogether different: a counterfactual analysis of causation.

The proposal has not been well received. True, we do know that causation has something or other to do with counterfactuals. We think of a cause as something that makes a difference, and the difference it makes must be a difference from what would have happened without it. Had it been absent, its effects – some of them, at least, and usually all – would have been absent as well. Yet it is one thing to mention these platitudes now and again, and another thing to rest an analysis on them. That has not seemed worthwhile.[4] We have learned all too well that counterfactuals are ill understood, wherefore it did not seem that much understanding could be gained by using them to analyze causation or anything else. Pending a better understanding of counterfactuals, moreover, we had no way to fight seeming counterexamples to a counterfactual analysis.

But counterfactuals need not remain ill understood, I claim, unless we cling to false preconceptions about what it would be like to understand them. Must an adequate understanding make no reference to unactualized possibilities? Must it assign sharply determinate truth-conditions? Must it connect counterfactuals rigidly to covering laws? Then none will be forthcoming. So much the worse for those standards of adequacy. Why not take counterfactuals at face value: as statements about possible alternatives to the actual situation, somewhat vaguely specified, in which the actual laws may or may not remain intact? There are now several such treatments of counterfactuals, differing only in details.[5] If they are right, then sound foundations have been laid for analyses that use counterfactuals.

In this paper, I shall state a counterfactual analysis, not very different from Hume's second definition, of some sorts of causation. Then I shall try to show how this analysis works to distinguish genuine causes from effects, epiphenomena, and preempted potential causes.

My discussion will be incomplete in at least four ways. Explicit preliminary settings-aside may prevent confusion.

(1) I shall confine myself to causation among *events*, in the everyday sense of the word: flashes, battles, conversations, impacts, strolls, deaths, touchdowns, falls, kisses, and the like. Not that events are the only things that can cause or be caused; but I have no full list of the others, and no good umbrella-term to cover them all.

(2) My analysis is meant to apply to causation in particular cases. It is not an analysis of causal generalizations. Presumably those are quantified statements involving causation among particular events (or non-events), but it turns out not to be easy to match up the causal generalizations of natural language with the available quantified forms. A sentence of the form "C-events cause E-events," for instance, can mean any of

(a)   For some c in C and some e in E, c causes e.
(b)   For every e in E, there is some c in C such that c causes e.
(c)   For every c in C, there is some e in E such that c causes e.

not to mention further ambiguities. Worse still, "Only C-events cause E-events" ought to mean

(d)   For every c, if there is some e in E such that c causes e, then c is in C.

if "only" has its usual meaning. But no; it unambiguously means (b) instead! These problems are not about causation, but about our idioms of quantification.

(3) We sometimes single out one among all the causes of some event and call it "the" cause, as if there were no others. Or we single out a few as the "causes," calling the rest mere "causal factors" or "causal conditions." Or we speak of the "decisive" or "real" or "principal" cause. We may select the abnormal or extraordinary causes, or those under human control, or those we deem good or bad, or

just those we want to talk about. I have nothing to say about these principles of invidious discrimination.[6] I am concerned with the prior question of what it is to be one of the causes (unselectively speaking). My analysis is meant to capture a broad and nondiscriminatory concept of causation.

(4) I shall be content, for now, if I can give an analysis of causation that works properly under determinism. By determinism I do not mean any thesis of universal causation, or universal predictability-in-principle, but rather this: the prevailing laws of nature are such that there do not exist any two possible worlds which are exactly alike up to some time, which differ thereafter, and in which those laws are never violated. Perhaps by ignoring indeterminism I squander the most striking advantage of a counterfactual analysis over a regularity analysis: that it allows undetermined events to be caused.[7] I fear, however, that my present analysis cannot yet cope with all varieties of causation under indeterminism. The needed repair would take us too far into disputed questions about the foundations of probability.

Comparative Similarity

To begin, I take as primitive a relation of *comparative overall similarity* among possible worlds. We may say that one world is *closer to actuality* than another if the first resembles our actual world more than the second does taking account of all the respects of similarity and difference and balancing them off one against another.

(More generally, an arbitrary world w can play the role of our actual world. In speaking of our actual world without knowing just which world is ours, I am in effect generalizing over all worlds. We really need a three-place relation: world w_1 is closer to world w than world w_2 is. I shall henceforth leave this generality tacit.)

I have not said just how to balance the respects of comparison against each other, so I have not said just what our relation of comparative similarity is to be. Not for nothing did I call it primitive. But I have said what *sort* of relation it is, and we are familiar with relations of that sort. We do make judgments of comparative overall similarity – of people, for instance – by balancing off many respects of similarity and

difference. Often our mutual expectations about the weighting factors are definite and accurate enough to permit communication. I shall have more to say later about the way the balance must go in particular cases to make my analysis work. But the vagueness of overall similarity will not be entirely resolved. Nor should it be. The vagueness of similarity does infect causation, and no correct analysis can deny it.

The respects of similarity and difference that enter into the overall similarity of worlds are many and varied. In particular, similarities in matters of particular fact trade off against similarities of law. The prevailing laws of nature are important to the character of a world; so similarities of law are weighty. Weighty, but not sacred. We should not take it for granted that a world that conforms perfectly to our actual laws is *ipso facto* closer to actuality than any world where those laws are violated in any way at all. It depends on the nature and extent of the violation, on the place of the violated laws in the total system of laws of nature, and on the countervailing similarities and differences in other respects. Likewise, similarities or differences of particular fact may be more or less weighty, depending on their nature and extent. Comprehensive and exact similarities of particular fact throughout large spatiotemporal regions seem to have special weight. It may be worth a small miracle to prolong or expand a region of perfect match.

Our relation of comparative similarity should meet two formal constraints. (1) It should be a weak ordering of the worlds: an ordering in which ties are permitted, but any two worlds are comparable. (2) Our actual world should be closest to actuality, resembling itself more than any other world resembles it. We do *not* impose the further constraint that for any set A of worlds there is a unique closest A-world, or even a set of A-worlds tied for closest. Why not an infinite sequence of closer and closer A-worlds, but no closest?

Counterfactuals and Counterfactual Dependence

Given any two propositions A and C, we have their *counterfactual* $A \;\square\!\!\rightarrow C$: the proposition that if A were true, then C would also be true. The operation $\square\!\!\rightarrow$ is defined by a rule of truth, as follows. $A \square\!\!\rightarrow C$ is true (at a world w) iff either (1) there are no possible A-worlds (in which case $A \square\!\!\rightarrow C$ is *vacuous*), or (2) some A-world where C holds is closer (to w) than is any A-world where C does not hold. In other words, a counterfactual is nonvacuously true iff it takes less of a departure from actuality to make the consequent true along with the antecedent than it does to make the antecedent true without the consequent.

We did not assume that there must always be one or more closest A-worlds. But if there are, we can simplify: $A \square\!\!\rightarrow C$ is nonvacuously true iff C holds at all the closest A-worlds.

We have not presupposed that A is false. If A is true, then our actual world is the closest A-world, so $A \square\!\!\rightarrow C$ is true iff C is. Hence $A \square\!\!\rightarrow C$ implies the material conditional $A \supset C$; and A and C jointly imply $A \square\!\!\rightarrow C$.

Let $A_1, A_2, \ldots$ be a family of possible propositions, no two of which are compossible; let $C_1, C_2, \ldots$ be another such family (of equal size). Then if all the counterfactuals $A_1 \square\!\!\rightarrow C_1, A_2 \square\!\!\rightarrow C_2, \ldots$ between corresponding propositions in the two families are true, we shall say that the C's *depend counterfactually* on the A's. We can say it like this in ordinary language: whether C_1 or C_2 or $\ldots$ depends (counterfactually) on whether A_1 or A_2 or....

Counterfactual dependence between large families of alternatives is characteristic of processes of measurement, perception, or control. Let $R_1, R_2, \ldots$ be propositions specifying the alternative readings of a certain barometer at a certain time. Let $P_1, P_2, \ldots$ specify the corresponding pressures of the surrounding air. Then, if the barometer is working properly to measure the pressure, the R's must depend counterfactually on the P's. As we say it: the reading depends on the pressure. Likewise, if I am seeing at a certain time, then my visual impressions must depend counterfactually, over a wide range of alternative possibilities, on the scene before my eyes. And if I am in control over what happens in some respect, then there must be a double counterfactual dependence, again over some fairly wide range of alternatives. The outcome depends on what I do, and that in turn depends on which outcome I want.[8]

Causal Dependence among Events

If a family $C_1, C_2, \ldots$ depends counterfactually on a family $A_1, A_2, \ldots$ in the sense just explained, we will ordinarily be willing to speak also of causal dependence. We say, for instance, that the barometer reading depends causally on the pressure, that my visual impressions depend causally on the scene before my eyes, or that the outcome of something under my control depends causally on what I do. But there are exceptions. Let $G_1, G_2, \ldots$ be alternative possible laws of gravitation, differing in the value of some numerical constant. Let $M_1 M_2, \ldots$ be suitable alternative laws of planetary motion. Then the M's may depend counterfactually on the G's, but we would not call this dependence causal. Such exceptions as this, however, do not involve any sort of dependence among distinct particular events. The hope remains that causal dependence among events, at least, may be analyzed simply as counterfactual dependence.

We have spoken thus far of counterfactual dependence among propositions, not among events. Whatever particular events may be, presumably they are not propositions. But that is no problem, since they can at least be paired with propositions. To any possible event e, there corresponds the proposition $O(e)$ that holds at all and only those worlds where e occurs. This $O(e)$ is the proposition that e occurs.[9] (If no two events occur at exactly the same worlds – if, that is, there are no absolutely necessary connections between distinct events – we may add that this correspondence of events and propositions is one to one.) Counterfactual dependence among events is simply counterfactual dependence among the corresponding propositions.

Let $c_1, c_2, \ldots$ and $e_1, e_2, \ldots$ be distinct possible events such that no two of the c's and no two of the e's are compossible. Then I say that the family $e_1, e_2, \ldots$ of events *depends causally* on the family $c_1, c_2, \ldots$ iff the family $O(e_1), O(e_2), \ldots$ of propositions depends counterfactually on the family $O(c_1), O(c_2), \ldots$. As we say it: whether e_1 or e_2 or $\ldots$ occurs depends on whether c_1 or c_2 or $\ldots$ occurs.

We can also define a relation of dependence among single events rather than families. Let c and e be two distinct possible particular events. Then e *depends causally* on c iff the family

$O(e)$, $\sim O(e)$ depends counterfactually on the family $O(c)$, $\sim O(c)$. As we say it: whether e occurs or not depends on whether c occurs or not. The dependence consists in the truth of two counterfactuals: $O(c) \;\square\!\!\rightarrow\; O(e)$ and $\sim O(c) \;\square\!\!\rightarrow\; \sim O(e)$. There are two cases. If c and e do not actually occur, then the second counterfactual is automatically true because its antecedent and consequent are true: so e depends causally on c iff the first counterfactual holds. That is, iff e would have occurred if c had occurred. But if c and e are actual events, then it is the first counterfactual that is automatically true. Then e depends causally on c iff, if c had not been, e never had existed. I take Hume's second definition as my definition not of causation itself, but of causal dependence among actual events.

Causation

Causal dependence among actual events implies causation. If c and e are two actual events such that e would not have occurred without c, then c is a cause of e. But I reject the converse. Causation must always be transitive; causal dependence may not be; so there can be causation without causal dependence. Let c, d, and e be three actual events such that d would not have occurred without c, and e would not have occurred without d. Then c is a cause of e even if e would still have occurred (otherwise caused) without c.

We extend causal dependence to a transitive relation in the usual way. Let c, d, e, ... be a finite sequence of actual particular events such that d depends causally on c, e on d, and so on throughout. Then this sequence is a *causal chain*. Finally, one event is a *cause* of another iff there exists a causal chain leading from the first to the second. This completes my counterfactual analysis of causation.

Counterfactual versus Nomic Dependence

It is essential to distinguish counterfactual and causal dependence from what I shall call *nomic dependence*. The family C_1, C_2, ... of propositions depends nomically on the family A_1, A_2, ... iff there are a nonempty set L of true law-propositions and a set F of true propositions of particular fact such that L and F jointly imply (but F alone does not imply) all the material conditionals $A_1 \supset C_1$, $A_2 \supset C_2$, ... between the corresponding propositions in the two families. (Recall that these same material conditionals are implied by the counterfactuals that would comprise a counterfactual dependence.) We shall say also that the nomic dependence holds *in virtue of* the premise sets L and F.

Nomic and counterfactual dependence are related as follows. Say that a proposition B is *counterfactually independent* of the family A_1, A_2, ... of alternatives iff B would hold no matter which of the A's were true – that is, iff the counterfactuals $A_1 \;\square\!\!\rightarrow\; B$, $A_2 \;\square\!\!\rightarrow\; B$, ... all hold. If the C's depend nomically on the A's in virtue of the premise sets L and F, and if in addition (all members of) L and F are counterfactually independent of the A's, then it follows that the C's depend counterfactually on the A's. In that case, we may regard the nomic dependence in virtue of L and F as explaining the counterfactual dependence. Often, perhaps always, counterfactual dependences may be thus explained. But the requirement of counterfactual independence is indispensable. Unless L and F meet that requirement, nomic dependence in virtue of L and F does not imply counterfactual dependence, and, if there is counterfactual dependence anyway, does not explain it.

Nomic dependence is reversible, in the following sense. If the family C_1, C_2, ... depends nomically on the family A_1, A_2, ... in virtue of L and F, then also A_1, A_2, ... depends nomically on the family AC_1, AC_2, ..., in virtue of L and F, where A is the disjunction $A_1 \vee A_2 \vee$.... Is counterfactual dependence likewise reversible? That does not follow. For, even if L and F are independent of A_1, A_2, ... and hence establish the counterfactual dependence of the C's on the A's, still they may fail to be independent of AC_1, AC_2, ..., and hence may fail to establish the reverse counterfactual dependence of the A's on the AC's. Irreversible counterfactual dependence is shown in figure 29.1: @ is our actual world, the dots are the other worlds, and distance on the page represents similarity "distance."

The counterfactuals $A_1 \;\square\!\!\rightarrow\; C_1$, $A_2 \;\square\!\!\rightarrow\; C_2$, and $A_3 \;\square\!\!\rightarrow\; C_3$ hold at the actual world; wherefore the C's depend on the A's. But we do not have the

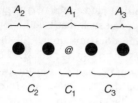

Figure 29.1

reverse dependence of the A's on the AC's, since instead of the needed $AC_2 \, \square\!\!\rightarrow A_2$ and $AC_3 \, \square\!\!\rightarrow A_3$ we have $AC_2 \, \square\!\!\rightarrow A_1$ and $AC_3 \, \square\!\!\rightarrow A_1$.

Just such irreversibility is commonplace. The barometer reading depends counterfactually on the pressure – that is as clear-cut as counterfactuals ever get – but does the pressure depend counterfactually on the reading? If the reading had been higher, would the pressure have been higher? Or would the barometer have been malfunctioning? The second sounds better: a higher reading would have been an incorrect reading. To be sure, there are actual laws and circumstances that imply and explain the actual accuracy of the barometer, but these are no more sacred than the actual laws and circumstances that imply and explain the actual pressure. Less sacred, in fact. When something must give way to permit a higher reading, we find it less of a departure from actuality to hold the pressure fixed and sacrifice the accuracy, rather than vice versa. It is not hard to see why. The barometer, being more localized and more delicate than the weather, is more vulnerable to slight departures from actuality.[10]

We can now explain why regularity analyses of causation (among events, under determinism) work as well as they do. Suppose that event c causes event e according to the sample regularity analysis that I gave at the beginning of this paper, in virtue of premise sets L and F. It follows that L, F, and $\sim O(c)$ jointly do not imply $O(e)$. Strengthen this: suppose further that they do imply $\sim O(e)$. If so, the family $O(e)$, $\sim O(e)$ depends nomically on the family $O(c)$, $\sim O(c)$ in virtue of L and F. Add one more supposition: that L and F are counterfactually independent of $O(c)$, $\sim O(c)$. Then it follows according to my counterfactual analysis that e depends counterfactually and causally on c, and hence that c causes e. If I am right, the regularity analysis gives conditions that are almost but not quite sufficient for explicable causal dependence. That is not quite the same

thing as causation; but causation without causal dependence is scarce, and if there is inexplicable causal dependence we are (understandably!) unaware of it.[11]

Effects and Epiphenomena

I return now to the problems I raised against regularity analyses, hoping to show that my counterfactual analysis can overcome them.

The *problem of effects*, as it confronts a counterfactual analysis, is as follows. Suppose that c causes a subsequent event e, and that e does not also cause c. (I do not rule out closed causal loops a priori, but this case is not to be one.) Suppose further that, given the laws and some of the actual circumstances, c could not have failed to cause e. It seems to follow that if the effect e had not occurred, then its cause c would not have occurred. We have a spurious reverse causal dependence of c on e, contradicting our supposition that e did not cause c.

The *problem of epiphenomena*, for a counterfactual analysis, is similar. Suppose that e is an epiphenomenal effect of a genuine cause c of an effect f. That is, c causes first e and then f, but e does not cause f. Suppose further that, given the laws and some of the actual circumstances, c could not have failed to cause e; and that, given the laws and others of the circumstances, f could not have been caused otherwise than by c. It seems to follow that if the epiphenomenon e had not occurred, then its cause c would not have occurred and the further effect f of that same cause would not have occurred either. We have a spurious causal dependence of f on e, contradicting our supposition that e did not cause f.

One might be tempted to solve the problem of effects by brute force: insert into the analysis a stipulation that a cause must always precede its effect (and perhaps a parallel stipulation for causal dependence). I reject this solution. (1) It is worthless against the closely related problem of epiphenomena, since the epiphenomenon e does precede its spurious effect f. (2) It rejects a priori certain legitimate physical hypotheses that posit backward or simultaneous causation. (3) It trivializes any theory that seeks to define the forward direction of time as the predominant direction of causation.

The proper solution to both problems, I think, is flatly to deny the counterfactuals that cause the trouble. If e had been absent, it is not that c would have been absent (and with it f, in the second case). Rather, c would have occurred just as it did but would have failed to cause e. It is less of a departure from actuality to get rid of e by holding c fixed and giving up some or other of the laws and circumstances in virtue of which c could not have failed to cause e, rather than to hold those laws and circumstances fixed and get rid of e by going back and abolishing its cause c. (In the second case, it would of course be pointless not to hold f fixed along with c.) The causal dependence of e on c is the same sort of irreversible counterfactual dependence that we have considered already.

To get rid of an actual event e with the least overall departure from actuality, it will normally be best not to diverge at all from the actual course of events until just before the time of e. The longer we wait, the more we prolong the spatiotemporal region of perfect match between our actual world and the selected alternative. Why diverge sooner rather than later? Not to avoid violations of laws of nature. Under determinism *any* divergence, soon or late, requires some violation of the actual laws. If the laws were held sacred, there would be no way to get rid of e without changing all of the past; and nothing guarantees that the change could be kept negligible except in the recent past. That would mean that if the present were ever so slightly different, then all of the past would have been different – which is absurd. So the laws are not sacred. Violation of laws is a matter of degree. Until we get up to the time immediately before e is to occur, there is no general reason why a later divergence to avert e should need a more severe violation than an earlier one. Perhaps there are special reasons in special cases – but then these may be cases of backward causal dependence.

Preemption

Suppose that c_1 occurs and causes e; and that c_2 also occurs and does not cause e, but would have caused e, if c_1 had been absent. Thus c_2 is a potential alternate cause of e, but is preempted by the actual cause c_1. We may say that c_1 and c_2 overdetermine e, but they do so asymmetrically.[12] In virtue of what difference does c_1 but not c_2 cause e?

As far as causal dependence goes, there is no difference: e depends neither on c_1 nor on c_2. If either one had not occurred, the other would have sufficed to cause e. So the difference must be that, thanks to c_1, there is nor causal chain from c_2 to e; whereas there is a causal chain of two or more steps from c_1 to e. Assume for simplicity that two steps are enough. Then e depends causally on some intermediate event d, and d in turn depends on c_1. Causal dependence is here intransitive: c_1 causes e via d even though e would still have occurred without c_1.

So far, so good. It remains only to deal with the objection that e does *not* depend causally on d, because if d had been absent, then c_1 would have been absent, and c_2, no longer preempted, would have caused e. We may reply by denying the claim that if d had been absent, then c_1 would have been absent. That is the very same sort of spurious reverse dependence of cause on effect that we have just rejected in simpler cases. I rather claim that if d had been absent, c_1 would somehow have failed to cause d. But c_1 would still have been there to interfere with c_2, so e would not have occurred.

Notes

I thank the American Council of Learned Societies, Princeton University, and the National Science Foundation for research support.

1 David Hume, *An Enquiry Concerning Human Understanding*, sec. 7.
2 Not one that has been proposed by any actual author in just this form, so far as I know.
3 I identify a *proposition*, as is becoming usual, with the set of possible worlds where it is true. It is not a linguistic entity. Truth-functional operations on propositions are the appropriate Boolean operations on sets of worlds; logical relations among propositions are relations of inclusion, overlap, etc. among sets. A sentence of a language *expresses* a proposition iff the sentence and the proposition are true at exactly the same worlds. No ordinary language will provide sentences to express all propositions; there will not be enough sentences to go around.

4   One exception: Ardon Lyon, "Causality," *British Journal for the Philosophy of Science*, 18/1 (May 1967), pp. 1–20.

5   See, for instance, Robert Stalnaker, "A theory of conditionals," in Nicholas Rescher (ed.), *Studies in Logical Theory* (Oxford: Blackwell, 1968); and my *Counterfactuals* (Oxford: Blackwell, 1973).

6   Except that Morton G. White's discussion of causal selection, in *Foundations of Historical Knowledge* (New York: Harper & Row, 1965), pp. 105–81, would meet my needs, despite the fact that it is based on a regularity analysis.

7   That this ought to be allowed is argued in G. E. M. Anscombe, *Causality and Determination: An Inaugural Lecture* (Cambridge: Cambridge University Press, 1971) [see ch. 28 in this volume]; and in Fred Dretske and Aaron Snyder, "Causal irregularity," *Philosophy of Science*, 39/1 (Mar. 1972), pp. 69–71.

8   Analyses in terms of counterfactual dependence are found in two papers of Alvin I. Goldman: "Toward a theory of social power," *Philosophical Studies* 23 (1972), pp. 221–68; and "Discrimination and perceptual knowledge," presented at the 1972 Chapel Hill Colloquium.

9   Beware: if we refer to a particular event *e* by means of some description that *e* satisfies, then we must take care not to confuse $O(e)$, the proposition that *e* itself occurs, with the different proposition that some event or other occurs which satisfies the description. It is a contingent matter, in general, what events satisfy what descriptions. Let *e* be the death of Socrates – the death he actually died, to be distinguished from all the different deaths he might have died instead. Suppose that Socrates had fled, only to be eaten by a lion. Then *e* would not have occurred, and $O(e)$ would have been false; but a different event would have satisfied the description "the death of Socrates" that I used to refer to *e*. Or suppose that Socrates had lived and died just as he actually did, and afterwards was resurrected and killed again and resurrected again, and finally became immortal. Then no event would have satisfied the description. (Even if the temporary deaths are real deaths, neither of the two can be *the* death.) But *e* would have occurred, and $O(e)$ would have been true. Call a description of an event *e* rigid iff (1) nothing but *e* could possibly satisfy it, and (2) *e* could not possibly occur without satisfying it. I have claimed that even such commonplace descriptions as "the death of Socrates" are nonrigid, and in fact I think that rigid descriptions of events are hard to find. That would be a problem for anyone who needed to associate with every possible event *e* a sentence $\Phi(e)$ true at all and only those worlds where *e* occurs. But we need no such sentences – only propositions, which may or may not have expressions in our language.

10 Granted, there are contexts or changes of wording that would incline us the other way. For some reason, "If the reading had been higher, that would have been because the pressure was higher" invites my assent more than "If the reading had been higher, the pressure would have been higher." The counterfactuals from readings to pressures are much less clear-cut than those from pressures to readings. But it is enough that some legitimate resolutions of vagueness give an irreversible dependence of readings on pressures. Those are the resolutions we want at present, even if they are not favored in all contexts.

11 I am not here proposing a repaired regularity analysis. The repaired analysis would gratuitously rule out inexplicable causal dependence, which seems bad. Nor would it be squarely in the tradition of regularity analyses any more. Too much else would have been added.

12 I shall not discuss symmetrical cases of overdetermination, in which two overdetermining factors have equal claim to count as causes. For me these are useless as test cases because I lack firm naïve opinions about them.

30

Causal Connections

Wesley C. Salmon

Basic Problems

As a point of departure for the discussion of causality, it is appropriate for us to take a look at the reasons that have led philosophers to develop theories of explanation that do not require causal components. To Aristotle and Laplace it must have seemed evident that scientific explanations are inevitably causal in character. Laplacian determinism is causal determinism, and I know of no reason to suppose that Laplace made any distinction between causal and noncausal laws.

It might be initially tempting to suppose that all laws of nature are causal laws, and that explanation in terms of laws is *ipso facto* causal explanation. It is, however, quite easy to find law-statements that do not express causal relations. Many regularities in nature are not direct cause-effect relations. Night follows day, and day follows night; nevertheless, day does not cause night, and night does not cause day. Kepler's laws of planetary motion describe the orbits of the planets, but they offer no causal account of these motions.[1] Similarly, the ideal gas law

$$PV = nRT$$

relates pressure (P), volume (V), and temperature (T) for a given sample of gas, and it tells how these quantities vary as functions of one another, but it says nothing whatever about causal relations among them. An increase in pressure might be brought about by moving a piston so as to decrease the volume, or it might be caused by an increase in temperature. The law itself is entirely noncommittal concerning such causal considerations. Each of these regularities – the alternation of night with day; the regular motions of the planets; and the functional relationship among temperature, pressure, and volume of an ideal gas – can be *explained* causally, but they do not *express* causal relations. Moreover, they do not afford causal explanations of the events subsumed under them. For this reason, it seems to me, their value in providing scientific explanations of particular events is, at best, severely limited. These are regularities that need to be explained, but that do not, by themselves, do much in the way of explaining other phenomena.

To untutored common sense, and to many scientists uncorrupted by philosophical training, it is evident that causality plays a central role in

Wesley C. Salmon, "Causal Connections," in *Scientific Explanation and the Causal Structure of the World* (Princeton, NJ: Princeton University Press, 1984). © 1984 Princeton University Press. Reprinted by permission of Princeton University Press.

Metaphysics: An Anthology, Second Edition. Edited by Jaegwon Kim, Daniel Z. Korman and Ernest Sosa.
Editorial material and organization © 2012 Blackwell Publishing Ltd. Published 2012 by Blackwell Publishing Ltd.

scientific explanation. An appropriate answer to an explanation-seeking why-question normally begins with the word "because," and the causal involvements of the answer are usually not hard to find.[2] The concept of causality has, however, been philosophically suspect ever since David Hume's devastating critique, first published in 1739 in his *Treatise of Human Nature*. In the "Abstract" of that work, Hume wrote:

> Here is a billiard ball lying on the table, and another ball moving toward it with rapidity. They strike; the ball which was formerly at rest now acquires a motion. This is as perfect an instance of the relations of cause and effect as any which we know either by sensation or reflection. Let us therefore examine it. It is evident that the two balls touched one another before the motion was communicated, and that there was no interval betwixt the shock and the motion. *Contiguity* in time and place is therefore a requisite circumstance to the operation of all causes. It is evident, likewise, that the motion which was the cause is prior to the motion which was the effect. *Priority* in time is, therefore, another requisite circumstance in every cause. But this is not all. Let us try any other balls of the same kind in a like situation, and we shall always find that the impulse of the one produces motion in the other. Here, therefore, is a *third* circumstance, viz., that of *constant conjunction* betwixt the cause and the effect. Every object like the cause produces always some object like the effect. Beyond these three circumstances of contiguity, priority, and constant conjunction I can discover nothing in this cause.[3]

This discussion is, of course, more notable for factors Hume was unable to find than for those he enumerated. In particular, he could not discover any 'necessary connections' relating causes to effects, or any 'hidden powers' by which the cause 'brings about' the effect. This classic account of causation is rightly regarded as a landmark in philosophy.

In an oft-quoted remark that stands at the beginning of a famous 1913 essay, Bertrand Russell warns philosophers about the appeal to causality:

> All philosophers, of every school, imagine that causation is one of the fundamental axioms or postulates of science, yet, oddly enough, in

advanced sciences such as gravitational astronomy, the word "cause" never occurs.... To me it seems that ... the reason why physics has ceased to look for causes is that, in fact, there are no such things. The law of causality, I believe, like much that passes muster among philosophers, is a relic of a bygone age, surviving, like the monarchy, only because it is erroneously supposed to do no harm.[4]

It is hardly surprising that, in the light of Hume's critique and Russell's resounding condemnation, philosophers with an empiricist bent have been rather wary of the use of causal concepts. By 1927, however, when he wrote *The Analysis of Matter*,[5] Russell recognized that causality plays a fundamental role in physics; in *Human Knowledge*, four of the five postulates he advanced as a basis for all scientific knowledge make explicit reference to causal relations.[6] It should be noted, however, that the causal concepts he invokes are *not* the same as the traditional philosophical ones he had rejected earlier.[7] In contemporary physics, causality is a pervasive ingredient.[8]

Two Basic Concepts

A standard picture of causality has been around at least since the time of Hume. The general idea is that we have two (or more) distinct events that bear some sort of cause–effect relations to one another. There has, of course, been considerable controversy regarding the nature of both the relation and the relata. It has sometimes been maintained, for instance, that facts or propositions (rather than events) are the sorts of entities that can constitute relata. It has long been disputed whether causal relations can be said to obtain among individual events, or whether statements about cause–effect relations implicitly involve assertions about classes of events. The relation itself has sometimes been taken to be that of sufficient condition, sometimes necessary condition, or perhaps a combination of the two.[9] Some authors have even proposed that certain sorts of statistical relations constitute causal relations.

The foregoing characterization obviously fits J. L. Mackie's sophisticated account in terms of INUS conditions – that is, *insufficient* but *nonredundant* parts of *unnecessary* but *sufficient* conditions.[10] The idea is this. There are several different causes that might account for the burning down of a house: careless smoking in bed, an electrical short circuit, arson, being struck by lightning. With certain obvious qualifications, each of these may be taken as a sufficient condition for the fire, but none of them can be considered necessary. Moreover, each of the sufficient conditions cited involves a fairly complex combination of conditions, each of which constitutes a nonredundant part of the particular sufficient condition under consideration. The careless smoker, for example, must fall asleep with his cigarette, and it must fall upon something flammable. It must not awaken the smoker by burning him before it falls from his hand. When the smoker does become aware of the fire, it must have progressed beyond the stage at which he can extinguish it. Any one of these necessary components of some complex sufficient condition can, under certain circumstances, qualify as a cause. According to this standard approach, events enjoy the status of fundamental entities, and these entities are 'connected' to one another by cause–effect relations.

It is my conviction that this standard view, in all of its well-known variations, is profoundly mistaken, and that a radically different notion should be developed. I shall not, at this juncture, attempt to mount arguments against the standard conception. Instead, I shall present a rather different approach for purposes of comparison. I hope that the alternative will stand on its own merits.

There are, I believe, two fundamental causal concepts that need to be explicated, and if that can be achieved, we will be in a position to deal with the problems of causality in general. The two basic concepts are *propagation* and *production*, and both are familiar to common sense. When we say that the blow of a hammer drives a nail, we mean that the impact produces penetration of the nail into the wood. When we say that a horse pulls a cart, we mean that the force exerted by the horse produces the motion of the cart. When we say that lightning ignites a forest, we mean that the electrical discharge produces a fire. When we say that a person's embarrassment was due to a thoughtless remark, we mean that an inappropriate comment produced psychological discomfort. Such examples of causal production occur frequently in everyday contexts.

Causal propagation (or transmission) is equally familiar. Experiences that we had earlier in our lives affect our current behavior. By means of memory, the influence of these past events is transmitted to the present.[11] A sonic boom makes us aware of the passage of a jet airplane overhead; a disturbance in the air is propagated from the upper atmosphere to our location on the ground. Signals transmitted from a broadcasting station are received by the radio in our home. News or music reaches us because electromagnetic waves are propagated from the transmitter to the receiver. In 1775, some Massachusetts farmers – in initiating the American Revolutionary War – "fired the shot heard 'round the world."[12] As all of these examples show, what happens at one place and time can have significant influence upon what happens at other places and times. This is possible because causal influence can be propagated through time and space. Although causal production and causal propagation are intimately related to one another, we should, I believe, resist any temptation to try to reduce one to the other.

Processes

One of the fundamental changes that I propose in approaching causality is to take processes rather than events as basic entities. I shall not attempt any rigorous definition of processes; rather, I shall cite examples and make some very informal remarks. The main difference between events and processes is that events are relatively localized in space and time, while processes have much greater temporal duration, and in many cases, much greater spatial extent. In space-time diagrams, events are represented by points, while processes are represented by lines. A baseball colliding with a window would count as an event; the baseball, traveling from the bat to the window, would constitute a process. The activation of a photocell by a pulse of light would be an event; the pulse of light, traveling, perhaps from a distant star, would be a process. A sneeze is an event. The shadow of a cloud moving across the landscape is a process. Although I shall deny that all processes qualify as causal processes, what I mean by a process is similar to what Russell characterized as a causal line:

A causal line may always be regarded as the persistence of something – a person, a table, a photon, or what not. Throughout a given causal line, there may be constancy of quality, constancy of structure, or a gradual change of either, but not sudden changes of any considerable magnitude.[13]

Among the physically important processes are waves and material objects that persist through time. As I shall use these terms, even a material object at rest will qualify as a process.

Before attempting to develop a theory of causality in which processes, rather than events, are taken as fundamental, I should consider briefly the scientific legitimacy of this approach. In Newtonian mechanics, both spatial extent and temporal duration were absolute quantities. The length of a rigid rod did not depend upon a choice of frame of reference, nor did the duration of a process (such as the length of time between the creation and destruction of a material object). Given two events, in Newtonian mechanics, both the spatial distance and the temporal separation between them were absolute magnitudes. A 'physical thing ontology' was thus appropriate to classical physics. As everyone knows, Einstein's special theory of relativity changed all that. Both the spatial distance and the temporal separation were relativized to frames of reference. The length of a rigid rod and the duration of a temporal process varied from one frame of reference to another. However, as Minkowski showed, there is an invariant quantity – the space-time interval between two events. This quantity is independent of the frame of reference; for any two events, it has the same value in each and every inertial frame of reference. Since there are good reasons for according a fundamental physical status to invariants, it was a natural consequence of the special theory of relativity to regard the world as a collection of events that bear space-time relations to one another. These considerations offer support for what is sometimes called an 'event ontology'.

There is, however, another way (originally developed by A. A. Robb) of approaching the special theory of relativity; it is done entirely with paths of light pulses. At any point in space-time, we can construct the Minkowski light cone – a two-sheeted cone whose surface is generated by the paths of all possible light pulses that converge upon the point (past light cone) and the paths of all possible light pulses that could be emitted from the point (future light cone). When all of the light cones are given, the entire space-time structure of the world is determined.[14] But light pulses, traveling through space and time, are processes. We can, therefore, base special relativity upon a 'process ontology'. Moreover, this approach can be extended in a natural way to general relativity by taking into account the paths of freely falling material particles; these moving gravitational test particles are also processes.[15] It is, consequently, entirely legitimate to approach the space-time structure of the physical world by regarding physical processes as the basic types of physical entities. The theory of relativity does not mandate an 'event ontology'.

Whether one adopts the event-based approach or the process-based approach, causal relations must be accorded a fundamental place in the special theory of relativity. As we have seen, any given event E_0 occurring at a particular space-time point P_0, has an associated double-sheeted light cone. All events that could have a causal influence upon E_0 are located in the interior or on the surface of the past light cone, and all events upon which E_0 could have any causal influence are located in the interior or on the surface of the future light cone. All such events are *causally connectable* with E_0. Those events that lie on the surface of either sheet of the light cone are said to have a *lightlike separation* from E_0, those that lie within either part of the cone are said to have a *timelike separation* from E_0, and those that are outside of the cone are said to have a *spacelike separation* from E_0. The Minkowski light cone can, with complete propriety, be called "the cone of causal relevance," and the entire space-time structure of special relatively can be developed on the basis of causal concepts.[16]

Special relativity demands that we make a distinction between *causal processes* and *pseudo-processes*. It is a fundamental principle of that theory that light is a *first signal* – that is, no signal can be transmitted at a velocity greater than the velocity of light in a vacuum. There are, however, certain processes that can transpire at arbitrarily high velocities – at velocities vastly exceeding that of light. This fact does not violate the basic relativistic principle, however, for these 'processes' are incapable of serving as signals or of transmitting information. Causal processes are those that are capable of transmitting signals; pseudo-processes are incapable of doing so.

Consider a simple example. Suppose that we have a very large circular building – a sort of super-Astrodome, if you will – with a spotlight mounted at its center. When the light is turned on in the otherwise darkened building, it casts a spot of light upon the wall. If we turn the light on for a brief moment, and then off again, a light pulse travels from the light to the wall. This pulse of light, traveling from the spotlight to the wall, is a paradigm of what we mean by a causal process. Suppose, further, that the spotlight is mounted on a mechanism that makes it rotate. If the light is turned on and set into rotation, the spot of light that it casts upon the wall will move around the outer wall in a highly regular fashion. This 'process' – the moving spot of light – seems to fulfill the conditions Russell used to characterize causal lines, but it is not a causal process. It is a paradigm of what we mean by a pseudo-process.

The basic method for distinguishing causal processes from pseudo-processes is the criterion of mark transmission. A causal process is capable of transmitting a mark; a pseudo-process is not. Consider, first, a pulse of light that travels from the spotlight to the wall. If we place a piece of red glass in its path at any point between the spotlight and the wall, the light pulse, which was white, becomes and remains red until it reaches the wall. A single intervention at one point in the process transforms it in a way that persists from that point on. If we had not intervened, the light pulse would have remained white during its entire journey from the spotlight to the wall. If we do intervene locally at a single place, we can produce a change that is transmitted from the point of intervention onward. We shall say, therefore, that the light pulse constitutes a causal process whether it is modified or not, since in either case it is capable of transmitting a mark. Clearly, light pulses can serve as signals and can transmit messages; remember Paul Revere, "One if by land and two if by sea."

Now, let us consider the spot of light that moves around the wall as the spotlight rotates. There are a number of ways in which we can intervene to change the spot at some point; for example, we can place a red filter at the wall with the result that the spot of light becomes red at that point. But if we make such a modification in the traveling spot, it will not be transmitted

beyond the point of interaction. As soon as the light spot moves beyond the point at which the red filter was placed, it will become white again. The mark can be made, but it will not be transmitted. We have a 'process', which, in the absence of any intervention, consists of a white spot moving regularly along the wall of the building. If we intervene at some point, the 'process' will be modified *at that point*, but it will continue on beyond that point just as if no intervention had occurred. We can, of course, make the spot red at other places if we wish. We can install a red lens in the spotlight, but that does not constitute a *local* intervention at an isolated point in the process itself. We can put red filters at many places along the wall, but that would involve *many* interventions rather than a single one. We could get someone to run around the wall holding a red filter in front of the spot continuously, but that would not constitute an intervention *at a single point* in the 'process'.

This last suggestion brings us back to the subject of velocity. If the spot of light is moving rapidly, no runner could keep up with it, but perhaps a mechanical device could be set up. If, however, the spot moves too rapidly, it would be physically impossible to make the filter travel fast enough to keep pace. No material object, such as the filter, can travel at a velocity greater than that of light, but no such limitation is placed upon the spot on the wall. This can easily be seen as follows. If the spotlight rotates at a fixed rate, then it takes the spot of light a fixed amount of time to make one entire circuit around the wall. If the spotlight rotates once per second, the spot of light will travel around the wall in one second. This fact is independent of the size of the building. We can imagine that without making any change in the spotlight or its rate of rotation, the outer walls are expanded indefinitely. At a certain point, when the radius of the building is a little less than 50,000 kilometers, the spot will be traveling at the speed of light (300,000 km/sec). As the walls are moved still farther out, the velocity of the spot exceeds the speed of light.

To make this point more vivid, consider an actual example that is quite analogous to the rotating spotlight. There is a pulsar in the Crab nebula that is about 6,500 light-years away. This pulsar is thought to be a rapidly rotating neutron star that sends out a beam of radiation. When the beam is directed toward us, it sends out radiation that we detect later as a pulse. The pulses arrive at the rate of 30 per second; that is the rate at which the neutron star rotates. Now, imagine a circle drawn with the pulsar at its center, and with a radius equal to the distance from the pulsar to the earth. The electromagnetic radiation from the pulsar (which travels at the speed of light) takes 6,500 years to traverse the radius of this circle, but the 'spot' of radiation sweeps around the circumference of this circle in 1/30th of a second; at that rate, it is traveling at about 4×10^{13} times the speed of light. There is no upper limit on the speed of pseudo-processes.[17]

Another example may help to clarify this distinction. Consider a car traveling along a road on a sunny day. As the car moves at 100 km/hr, its shadow moves along the shoulder at the same speed. The moving car, like any material object, constitutes a causal process; the shadow is a pseudo-process. If the car collides with a stone wall, it will carry the marks of that collision – the dents and scratches – along with it long after the collision has taken place. If, however, only the shadow of the car collides with the stone wall, it will be deformed momentarily, but it will resume its normal shape just as soon as it has passed beyond the wall. Indeed, if the car passes a tall building that cuts it off from the sunlight, the shadow will be obliterated, but it will pop right back into existence as soon as the car has returned to the direct sunlight. If, however, the car is totally obliterated – say, by an atomic bomb blast – it will not pop back into existence as soon as the blast has subsided.

A given process, whether it be causal or pseudo, has a certain degree of uniformity – we may say, somewhat loosely, that it exhibits a certain structure. The difference between a causal process and a pseudo-process, I am suggesting, is that the causal process transmits its own structure, while the pseudo-process does not. The distinction between processes that do and those that do not transmit their own structures is revealed by the mark criterion. If a process – a causal process – is transmitting its own structure, then it will be capable of transmitting certain modifications in that structure.

In *Human Knowledge*, Russell placed great emphasis upon what he called "causal lines," which he characterized in the following terms:

A "causal line," as I wish to define the term, is a temporal series of events so related that, given some of them, something can be inferred about the others whatever may be happening elsewhere. A causal line may always be regarded as the persistence of something – a person, table, a photon, or what not. Throughout a given causal line, there may be constancy of quality, constancy of structure, or gradual change in either, but not sudden change of any considerable magnitude.[18]

He then goes on to comment upon the significance of causal lines:

That there are such more or less self-determined causal processes is in no degree logically necessary, but is, I think, one of the fundamental postulates of science. It is in virtue of the truth of this postulate – if it is true – that we are able to acquire partial knowledge in spite of our enormous ignorance.[19]

Although Russell seems clearly to intend his causal lines to be what we have called causal processes, his characterization may appear to allow pseudo-processes to qualify as well. Pseudo-processes, such as the spot of light traveling around the wall of our Astrodome, sometimes exhibit great uniformity, and their regular behavior can serve as a basis for inferring the nature of certain parts of the pseudo-process on the basis of observation of other parts. But pseudo-processes are not self-determined; the spot of light is determined by the behavior of the beacon and the beam it sends out. Moreover, the inference from one part of the pseudo-process to another is *not* reliable *regardless of what may be happening elsewhere*, for if the spotlight is switched off or covered with an opaque hood, the inference will go wrong. We may say, therefore, that our observations of the various phenomena going on in the world around us reveal processes that exhibit considerable regularity, but some of these are genuine causal processes and others are pseudo-processes. The causal processes are, as Russell says, self-determined; they transmit their own uniformities of qualitative and structural features. The regularities exhibited by the pseudo-processes, in contrast, are parasitic upon causal regularities exterior to the 'process' itself – in the case of the Astrodome, the behavior of the beacon; in the case of the shadow traveling along the roadside, the behavior of the car and the sun. The ability to transmit a mark is the criterion that distinguishes causal processes from pseudo-processes, for if the modification represented by the mark is propagated, the process is transmitting its own characteristics. Otherwise, the 'process' is not self-determined, and is not independent of what goes on elsewhere.

Although Russell's characterization of causal lines is heuristically useful, it cannot serve as a fundamental criterion for their identification for two reasons. First, it is formulated in terms of our ability to infer the nature of some portions from a knowledge of other portions. We need a criterion that does not rest upon such epistemic notions as knowledge and inference, for the existence of the vast majority of causal processes in the history of the universe is quite independent of human knowers. This aspect of the characterization could, perhaps, be restated nonanthropocentrically in terms of the persistence of objective regularities in the process. The second reason is more serious. To suggest that processes have regularities that persist "whatever may be happening elsewhere" is surely an overstatement. If an extremely massive object should happen to be located in the neighborhood of a light pulse, its path will be significantly altered. If a nuclear blast should occur in the vicinity of a mail truck, the letters that it carries will be totally destroyed. If sunspot activity reaches a high level, radio communication is affected. Notice that, in each of these cases, the factor cited does not occur or exist on the world line of the process in question. In each instance, of course, the disrupting factor initiates processes that intersect with the process in question, but that does not undermine the objection to the claim that causal processes transpire in their self-determined fashion regardless of what is happening elsewhere. A more acceptable statement might be that a causal process would persist even if it were isolated from external causal influences. This formulation, unfortunately, seems at the very least to flirt with circularity, for external causal influences must be transmitted to the locus of the process in question by means of other processes. We shall certainly want to keep clearly in mind the notion that causal processes are not parasitic upon other processes, but it does not seem likely that this rough idea could be transformed into a useful basic criterion.

It has often been suggested that the principal characteristic of causal processes is that they transmit energy. While I believe it is true that all and only causal processes transmit energy, there is, I think, a fundamental problem involved in employing this fact as a basic criterion – namely, we must have some basis for distinguishing situations in which energy is transmitted from those in which it merely appears in some regular fashion. The difficulty is easily seen in the 'Astrodome' example. As a light pulse travels from the central spotlight to the wall, it carries radiant energy; this energy is present in the various stages of the process as the pulse travels from the lamp to the wall. As the spot of light travels around the wall, energy appears at the places occupied by the spot, but we do not want to say that this energy is transmitted. The problem is to distinguish the cases in which a given bundle of energy is transmitted through a process from those in which different bundles of energy are appearing in some regular fashion. The key to this distinction is, I believe, the mark method. Just as the detective makes his mark on the murder weapon for purposes of later identification, so also do we make marks in processes so that the energy present at one space-time locale can be identified when it appears at other times and places.

A causal process is one that is self-determined and not parasitic upon other causal influences. A causal process is one that transmits energy, as well as information and causal influence. The fundamental criterion for distinguishing self-determined energy-transmitting processes from pseudo-processes is the capability of such processes of transmitting marks. In the next section, we shall deal with the concept of transmission in greater detail.

Our main concern with causal processes is their role in the propagation of causal influences; radio broadcasting presents a clear example. The transmitting station sends a carrier wave that has a certain structure – characterized by amplitude and frequency, among other things – and modifications of this wave, in the form of modulations of amplitude (AM) or frequency (FM), are imposed for the purpose of broadcasting. Processes that transmit their own structures are capable of transmitting marks, signals, information, energy, and causal influence. Such processes are the means by which causal influence is propagated in our world.

Causal influences, transmitted by radio, may set your foot to tapping, or induce someone to purchase a different brand of soap, or point a television camera aboard a spacecraft toward the rings of Saturn. A causal influence transmitted by a flying arrow can pierce an apple on the head of William Tell's son. A causal influence transmitted by sound waves can make your dog come running. A causal influence transmitted by ink marks on a piece of paper can gladden one's day or break someone's heart.

It is evident, I think, that the propagation or transmission of causal influence from one place and time to another must play a fundamental role in the causal structure of the world. As I shall argue next, causal processes constitute precisely the causal connections that Hume sought, but was unable to find.

The 'At-At' Theory of Causal Propagation

In the preceding section, I invoked Reichenbach's mark criterion to make the crucial distinction between causal processes and pseudo-processes. Causal processes are distinguished from pseudo-processes in terms of their ability to transmit marks. In order to qualify as causal, a process need not actually be transmitting a mark; the requirement is that it be capable of doing so.

When we characterize causal processes partly in terms of their ability to transmit marks, we must deal explicitly with the question of whether we have violated the kinds of strictures Hume so emphatically expounded. He warned against the uncritical use of such concepts as 'power' and 'necessary connection'. Is not the *ability to transmit* a mark an example of just such a mysterious power? Kenneth Sayre expressed his misgivings on this score when, after acknowledging the distinction between causal interactions and causal processes, he wrote:

> The causal process, continuous though it may be, is made up of individual events related to others in a causal nexus…. it is by virtue of the relations among the members of causal series that we are enabled to make the inferences by which causal processes are characterized…. if we do not have an adequate conception of the relatedness between individual members in a causal series,

there is a sense in which our conception of the causal process itself remains deficient.[20]

The 'at-at' theory of causal transmission is an attempt to remedy this deficiency.

Does this remedy illicitly invoke the sort of concept Hume proscribed? I think not. Ability to transmit a mark can be viewed as a particularly important species of constant conjunction – the sort of thing Hume recognized as observable and admissible. It is a matter of performing certain kinds of experiments. If we place a red filter in a light beam near its source, we can observe that the mark – redness – appears at all places to which the beam is subsequently propagated. This fact can be verified by experiments as often as we wish to perform them. If, contrariwise (returning to our Astrodome example of the preceding section), we make the spot on the wall red by placing a filter in the beam at one point just before the light strikes the wall (or by any other means we may devise), we will see that the mark – redness – is not present at all other places in which the moving spot subsequently appears on the wall. This, too, can be verified by repeated experimentation. Such facts are straightforwardly observable.

The question can still be reformulated. What do we mean when we speak of *transmission*? How does the process *make* the mark appear elsewhere within it? There is, I believe, an astonishingly simple answer. The transmission of a mark from point A in a causal process to point B in the same process *is* the fact that it appears at each point between A and B *without further interactions*. If A is the point at which the red filter is inserted into the beam going from the spotlight to the wall, and B is the point at which the beam strikes the wall, then only the interaction at A is required. If we place a white card in the beam at any point between A and B, we will find the beam red at that point.

The basic thesis about mark transmission can now be stated (in a principle I shall designate MT for "mark transmission") as follows:

MT: *Let P be a process that, in the absence of interactions with other processes, would remain uniform with respect to a characteristic Q, which it would manifest consistently over an interval that includes both of the space-time points A and B $(A \neq B)$.*

Then, a mark (consisting of a modification of Q into Q'), which has been introduced into process P by means of a single local interaction at point A, is transmitted to point B if P manifests the modification Q' at B and at all stages of the process between A and B without additional interventions.

This principle is clearly counterfactual, for it states explicitly that the process P would have continued to manifest the characteristic Q if the specific marking interaction had not occurred. This subjunctive formulation is required, I believe, to overcome an objection posed by Nancy Cartwright (in conversation) to previous formulations. The problem is this. Suppose our rotating beacon is casting a white spot that moves around the wall, and that we mark the spot by interposing a red filter at the wall. Suppose further, however, that a red lens has been installed in the beacon just a tiny fraction of a second earlier, so that the spot on the wall becomes red at the moment we mark it with our red filter, but it remains red from that point on because of the red lens. Under these circumstances, were it not for the counterfactual condition, it would appear that we had satisfied the requirement formulated in MT, for we have marked the spot by a single interaction at point A, and the spot remains red from that point on to any other point B we care to designate, without any additional interactions. As we have just mentioned, the installation of the red lens on the spotlight does not constitute a marking of the spot on the wall. The counterfactual stipulation given in the first sentence of MT blocks situations, of the sort mentioned by Cartwright, in which we would most certainly want to deny that any mark transmission occurred via the spot moving around the wall. In this case, the moving spot would have turned red because of the lens even if no marking interaction had occurred locally at the wall.

A serious misgiving arises from the use of counterfactual formulations to characterize the distinction between causal processes and pseudo-processes; it concerns the question of objectivity. The distinction is fully objective. It is a matter of fact that a light pulse constitutes a causal process, while a shadow is a pseudo-process. Philosophers have often maintained, however, that counterfactual conditionals involve unavoidably pragmatic aspects. Consider the famous example about Verdi and Bizet. One person might say, "If Verdi had been a compatriot of Bizet, then Verdi would have been French," whereas another might maintain, "If Bizet had been a compatriot of Verdi, then Bizet would have been Italian." These two statements seem incompatible with one another. Their antecedents are logically equivalent; if, however, we accept both conditionals, we wind up with the conclusion that Verdi would be French, that Bizet would be Italian, and they would still not be compatriots. Yet both statements can be true. The first person could be making an unstated presupposition that the nationality of Bizet is fixed in this context, while the second presupposes that the nationality of Verdi is fixed. What remains fixed and what is subject to change – which are established by pragmatic features of the context in which the counterfactual is uttered – determine whether a counterfactual is true or false. It is concluded that counterfactual conditional statements do not express objective facts of nature; indeed, van Fraassen[21] goes so far as to assert that science contains no counterfactuals. If that sweeping claim were true (which I seriously doubt),[22] the foregoing criterion MT would be in serious trouble.

Although MT involves an explicit counterfactual, I do not believe that the foregoing difficulty is insurmountable. Science has a direct way of dealing with the kinds of counterfactual assertions we require: namely, the experimental approach. In a well-designed controlled experiment, the experimenter determines which conditions are to be fixed for purposes of the experiment and which allowed to vary. The result of the experiment establishes some counterfactual statements as true and others as false under well-specified conditions. Consider the kinds of cases that concern us; such counterfactuals can readily be tested experimentally. Suppose we want to see whether the beam traveling from the spotlight to the wall is capable of transmitting the red mark. We set up the following experiment. The light will be turned on and off one hundred times. At a point midway between the spotlight and the wall, we station an experimenter with a random number generator. Without communicating with the experimenter who turns the light on and off, this second experimenter uses his device to make a random selection of fifty trials in which he will make a mark and fifty in which he will not. If all and only the fifty instances in which the marking interaction occurs are those in which the spot on the wall is red, as well as all the intervening stages in the process, then we may conclude with reasonable certainty that the fifty cases in which the beam was red subsequent to the marking interaction are cases in which the beam would not have been red if the marking interaction had not occurred. On any satisfactory analysis of counterfactuals, it seems to me, we would be justified in drawing such a conclusion. It should be carefully noted that I am *not* offering the foregoing experimental procedure as an analysis of counterfactuals; it is, indeed, a result that we should expect any analysis to yield.

A similar experimental approach could obviously be taken with respect to the spot traversing the wall. We design an experiment in which the beacon will rotate one hundred times, and each traversal will be taken as a separate process. We station an experimenter with a random number generator at the wall. Without communicating with the experimenter operating the beacon, the one at the wall makes a random selection of fifty trials in which to make the mark and fifty in which to refrain. If it turns out that some or all of the trials in which no interaction occurs are, nevertheless, cases in which the spot on the wall turns red as it passes the second experimenter, then we know that we are *not* dealing with cases in which the process will not turn from white to red if no interaction occurs. Hence, if in some cases the spot turns red and remains red after the mark is imposed, we know we are not entitled to conclude that the mark has actually been transmitted.

The account of mark transmission embodied in principle MT – which is the proposed foundation for the concept of propagation of causal influence – may seem too trivial to be taken seriously. I believe such a judgment would be mistaken. My reason lies in the close parallel that can be drawn between the foregoing solution to the problem of mark transmission and the solution of an ancient philosophical puzzle.

About 2,500 years ago, Zeno of Elea enunciated some famous paradoxes of motion, including the well-known paradox of the flying arrow. This paradox was not adequately resolved until the early part of the twentieth century. To establish an intimate connection between this problem and our problem of causal transmission, two observations are in order. First, a physical object (such as the arrow) moving from one place to another constitutes a causal process, as can be demonstrated easily by application of the mark method – for example, initials carved on the shaft of the arrow before it is shot are present on the shaft after it hits its target. And there can be no doubt that the arrow propagates causal influence. The hunter kills his prey by releasing the appropriately aimed arrow; the flying arrow constitutes the causal connection between the cause (release of the arrow from the bow under tension) and the effect (death of a deer). Second, Zeno's paradoxes were designed to prove the absurdity not only of motion, but also of every kind of process or change. Henri Bergson expressed this point eloquently in his discussion of what he called "the cinematographic view of becoming." He invites us to consider any process, such as the motion of a regiment of soldiers passing in review. We can take many snapshots – static views – of different stages of the process, but, he argues, we cannot really capture the movement in this way, for,

> every attempt to reconstitute change out of states implies the absurd proposition, that movement is made out of immobilities.
>
> Philosophy perceived this as soon as it opened its eyes. The arguments of Zeno of Elea, although formulated with a very different intention, have no other meaning.
>
> Take the flying arrow.[23]

Let us have a look at this paradox. At any given instant, Zeno seems to have argued, the arrow is where it is, occupying a portion of space equal to itself. During the instant it cannot move, for that would require the instant to have parts, and an instant is *by definition* a minimal and indivisible element of time. If the arrow did move during the instant, it would have to be in one place at one part of the instant and in a different place at another part of the instant. Moreover, for the arrow to move during the instant would require that during that instant it must occupy a space larger than itself, for otherwise it has no room to move. As Russell said:

> It is never moving, but in some miraculous way the change of position has to occur *between* the instants, that is to say, not at any time whatever.

This is what M. Bergson calls the cinematographic representation of reality. The more the difficulty is meditated, the more real it becomes.[24]

There is a strong temptation to respond to this paradox by pointing out that the differential calculus provides us with a perfectly meaningful definition of instantaneous velocity, and that this quantity *can* assume values other than zero. Velocity is change of position with respect to time, and the derivative dx/dt furnishes an expression that can be evaluated for particular values of t. Thus an arrow can be at rest at a given moment – that is, dx/dt may equal 0 for that particular value of t. Or it can be in motion at a given moment – that is, dx/dt might be 100 km/hr for another particular value of t. Once we recognize this elementary result of the infinitesimal calculus, it is often suggested, the paradox of the flying arrow vanishes.

This appealing attempt to resolve the paradox is, however, unsatisfactory, as Russell clearly realized. The problem lies in the definition of the derivative; dx/dt is defined as the limit as Δt approaches 0 of $\Delta x/\Delta t$, where Δt represents a nonzero interval of time and Δx may be a nonzero spatial distance. In other words, instantaneous velocity is defined as the limit, as we take decreasing time intervals, of the noninstantaneous average velocity with which the object traverses what is – in the case of nonzero values – a nonzero stretch of space. Thus in the definition of instantaneous velocity, we employ the concept of noninstantaneous velocity, which is precisely the problematic concept from which the paradox arises. To put the same point in a different way, the concept of instantaneous velocity does not genuinely characterize the motion of an object at an isolated instant all by itself, for the very definition of instantaneous velocity makes reference to neighboring instants of time and neighboring points of space. To find an adequate resolution of the flying arrow paradox, we must go deeper.

To describe the motion of a body, we express the relation between its position and the moments of time with which we are concerned by means of a mathematical function; for example, the equation of motion of a freely falling particle near the surface of the earth is

(1) $x = f(t) = 1/2gt^2$

where $g = 9.8$ m/sec^2. We can therefore say that this equation furnishes a function $f(t)$ that relates the position x to the time t. But what is a mathematical function? It is a set of pairs of numbers; for each admissible value of t, there is an associated value of x. To say that an object moves in accordance with equation (1) is simply to say that *at any given moment* t it is *at point* x, where the correspondence between the values of t and of x is given by the set of pairs of numbers that constitute the function represented by equation (1). To move from point A to point B is simply to be *at* the appropriate point of space *at* the appropriate moment of time – no more, no less. The resulting theory is therefore known as "the 'at-at' theory of motion." To the best of my knowledge, it was first clearly formulated and applied to the arrow paradox by Russell.

According to the 'at-at' theory, to move from A to B is simply to occupy the intervening points at the intervening instants. It consists in being *at* particular points of space *at* corresponding moments. There is no *additional* question as to how the arrow *gets from* point A *to* point B; the answer has already been given – by being at the intervening points at the intervening moments. The answer is emphatically *not* that it gets from A to B by zipping through the intermediate points at high speed. Moreover, there is no additional question about how the arrow gets from one intervening point to another – the answer is the same, namely, by being at the points between them at the corresponding moments. And clearly, there can be no question about how the arrow gets from one point to the next, for in a continuum there is no next point. I am convinced that Zeno's arrow paradox is a profound problem concerning the nature of change and motion, and that its resolution by Russell in terms of the 'at-at' theory of motion represents a distinctly nontrivial achievement.[25] The fact that this solution can – if I am right – be extended in a direct fashion to provide a resolution of the problem of mark transmission is an additional laurel.

The 'at-at' theory of mark transmission provides, I believe, an acceptable basis for the mark method, which can in turn serve as the means to distinguish causal processes from pseudo-processes. The world contains a great many types of causal processes – transmission of light waves, motion of material objects, transmissions of sound waves, persistence of crystalline structure, and so forth. Processes of any of these types may occur without having any mark imposed. In such instances, the processes still qualify as causal. *Ability* to transmit a mark is the criterion of causal processes; processes that are *actually* unmarked may be causal. Unmarked processes exhibit some sort of persistent structure, as Russell pointed out in his characterization of causal lines; in such cases, we say that the structure is transmitted within the causal process. Pseudo-processes may also exhibit persistent structure; in these cases, we maintain that the structure is *not transmitted* by means of the 'process' itself, but by some other external agency.

The basis for saying that the regularity in the causal process is transmitted via the process itself lies in the ability of the causal process to transmit a modification in its structure – a mark – resulting from an interaction. Consider a brief pulse of white light; it consists of a collection of photons of various frequencies, and if it is not polarized, the waves will have various spatial orientations. If we place a red filter in the path of this pulse, it will absorb all photons with frequencies falling outside of the red range, allowing only those within that range to pass. The resulting pulse has its structure modified in a rather precisely specifiable way, and the fact that this modification persists is precisely what we mean by claiming that the mark is transmitted. The counterfactual clause in our principle MT is designed to rule out structural changes brought about by anything other than the marking interaction. The light pulse could, alternatively, have been passed through a polarizer. The resulting pulse would consist of photons having a specified spatial orientation instead of the miscellaneous assortment of orientations it contained before encountering the polarizer. The principle of structure transmission (ST) may be formulated as follows:

ST: *If a process is capable of transmitting changes in structure due to marking interactions, then that process can be said to transmit its own structure.*

The fact that a process does not transmit a particular type of mark, however, does not mean that it is not a causal process. A ball of putty constitutes a causal process, and one kind of mark it will transmit is a change in shape imposed by indenting it with the thumb. However, a hard rubber ball is equally a causal process, but it will not transmit the same sort of mark, because of its elastic properties. The fact that a particular sort of structural modification does not persist, because of some inherent tendency of the process to resume its earlier structure, does not mean it is not transmitting its own structure; it means only that we have not found the appropriate sort of mark for that kind of process. A hard rubber ball can be marked by painting a spot on it, and that mark will persist for a while.

Marking methods are sometimes used in practice for the identification of causal processes. As fans of Perry Mason are aware, Lieutenant Tragg always placed 'his mark' upon the murder weapon found at the scene of the crime in order to be able to identify it later at the trial of the suspect. Radioactive traces are used in the investigation of physiological processes – for example, to determine the course taken by a particular substance ingested by a subject. Malodorous substances are added to natural gas used for heating and cooking in order to ascertain the presence of leaks; in fact, one large chemical manufacturer published full-page color advertisements in scientific magazines for its product "La Stink."

One of the main reasons for devoting our attention to causal processes is to show how they can transmit causal influence. In the case of causal processes used to transmit signals, the point is obvious. Paul Revere was caused to start out on his famous night ride by a light signal sent from the tower of the Old North Church. A drug, placed surreptitiously in a drink, can cause a person to lose consciousness because it retains its chemical structure as it is ingested, absorbed, and circulated through the body of the victim. A loud sound can produce a painful sensation in the ears because the disturbance of the air is transmitted from the origin to the hearer. Radio signals sent to orbiting satellites can activate devices aboard because the wave retains its form as it travels from earth through space. The principle of propagation of causal influence (PCI) may be formulated as follows:

PCI: *A process that transmits its own structure is capable of propagating a causal influence from one space-time locale to another.*

The propagation of causal influence by means of causal processes *constitutes*, I believe, the mysterious connection between cause and effect which Hume sought.

In offering the 'at-at' theory of mark transmission as a basis for distinguishing causal processes from pseudo-processes, we have furnished an account of the transmission of information and propagation of causal influence without appealing to any of the 'secret powers' which Hume's account of causation soundly proscribed. With this account we see that the mysterious connection between causes and effects is not very mysterious after all.

Our task is by no means finished, however, for this account of transmission of marks and propagation of causal influence has used the unanalyzed notion of a causal interaction that produces a mark. Unless a satisfactory account of causal interaction and mark production can be provided, our theory of causality will contain a severe lacuna.[26] Nevertheless, we have made significant progress in explicating the fundamental concept, introduced at the beginning of the chapter, of *causal propagation* (or *transmission*).

This chapter is entitled "Causal Connections," but little has actually been said about the way in which causal processes provide the connection between cause and effect. Nevertheless, in many common-sense situations, we talk about causal relations between pairs of spatiotemporally separated events. We might say, for instance, that turning the key causes the car to start. In this context we assume, of course, that the electrical circuitry is intact, that the various parts are in good working order, that there is gasoline in the tank, and so forth, but I think we can make sense of a cause–effect relation only if we can provide a *causal connection* between the cause and the effect. This involves tracing out the causal processes that lead from the turning of the key and the closing of an electrical circuit to various occurrences that eventuate in the turning over of the engine and the ignition of fuel in the cylinders. We say, for another example, that a tap on the knee causes the foot to jerk. Again, we believe that there are neutral impulses traveling from the place at which the tap occurred to the muscles that control the movement of the foot, and processes in those muscles that lead to movement of the foot itself. The genetic relationship between parents and offspring provides a further example. In this case, the molecular biologist refers to the actual process of information transmission via the DNA molecule employing the 'genetic code'.

In each of these situations, we analyze the cause–effect relations in terms of three components – an event that constitutes the cause, another event that constitutes the effect, and a causal process that connects the two events. In some cases, such as the starting of the car, there are many intermediate events, but in such cases, the successive intermediate events are connected to one another by spatiotemporally continuous causal processes. A splendid example of multiple causal connections was provided by David Kaplan. Several years ago, he paid a visit to Tucson, just after completing a boat trip through the Grand Canyon with his family. The best time to take such a trip, he remarked, is when it is very hot in Phoenix. What is the causal connection to the weather in Phoenix, which is about 200 miles away? At such times, the air-conditioners in Phoenix are used more heavily, which places a greater load on the generators at the Glen Canyon Dam (above the Grand Canyon). Under these circumstances, more water is allowed to pass through the turbines to meet the increased demand for power, which produces a greater flow of water down the Colorado River. This results in a more exciting ride through the rapids in the Canyon.

In the next chapter,[27] we shall consider events – especially causal interactions – more explicitly. It will then be easier to see how causal processes constitute precisely the physical connections between causes and effects that Hume sought – what he called "the cement of the universe." These causal connections will play a vital role in our account of scientific explanation.

It is tempting, of course, to try to reduce causal processes to chains of events; indeed, people frequently speak of causal chains. Such talk can be seriously misleading if it is taken to mean that causal processes are composed of discrete events that are serially ordered so that any given event has an immediate successor. If, however, the continuous character of causal processes is kept clearly in mind, I would not argue that it is philosophically incorrect to regard processes as collections of events. At the same time, it does seem heuristically disadvantageous to do so, for this practice seems almost inevitably to lead to the puzzle (articulated by Sayre in the quotation given previously) of how these events, which make up a given process, are causally related to one another. The point of the 'at-at' theory, it seems to me, is to show that no such question about the causal relations among the constituents of the process need arise – for the same reason that, aside from occupying interme- diate positions at the appropriate times, there is no further question about how the flying arrow gets from one place to another. With the aid of the 'at- at' theory, we have a complete answer to Hume's penetrating question about the nature of causal connections. For this heuristic reason, then, I con- sider it advisable to resist the temptation always to return to formulations in terms of events.

Notes

1   It might be objected that the alternation of night with day, and perhaps Kepler's "laws," do not consti- tute genuine lawful regularities. This consideration does not really affect the present argument, for there are plenty of regularities, lawful and nonlaw- ful, that do not have explanatory force, but that stand in need of causal explanation.

2   Indeed, in Italian, there is one word, *perche*, which means both "why" and "because." In interrogative sentences it means "why," and in indicative sentences it means "because." No confusion is engendered as a result of the fact that Italian lacks two distinct words.

3   David Hume, *An Enquiry Concerning Human Understanding* (Indianapolis: Bobbs-Merrill, 1955), which also contains "An abstract of *A Treatise of Human Nature*," pp. 186–7.

4   Bertrand Russell, *Mysticism and Logic* (New York: W. W. Norton, 1929) p. 180 [see p. 350 in this volume].

5   Bertrand Russell, *The Analysis of Matter* (London: George Allen and Unwin, 1927).

6   Bertrand Russell, *Human Knowledge, Its Scope and Limits* (New York: Simon and Schuster, 1948), pp. 487–96.

7   In the same place, regrettably, Russell felt com- pelled to relinquish empiricism. I shall attempt to avoid such extreme measures.

8   Patrick Suppes, *A Probabilistic Theory of Causality* (Amsterdam: North-Holland, 1970), pp. 5–6.

9   See J. L. Mackie, *The Cement of the Universe* (Oxford: Clarendon Press, 1974), for an excellent historical and systematic survey of the various approaches.

10 Ibid., p. 62.

11 Deborah A. Rosen, "An argument for the logical notion of a memory trace," *Philosophy of Science* 42 (1975), pp. 1–10.

12 Ralph Waldo Emersom, "Hymn sung at the completion of the battle monument, Concord."

13 Russell, *Human Knowledge*, p. 459.

14 See John Winnie, "The causal theory of space- time," in John Earman, Clark Glymour, and John Stachel (eds), *Minnesota Studies in the Philosophy of Science*, vol. 8 (Minneapolis: University of Minnesota Press, 1977), pp. 134–205.

15 See Adolf Grünbaum, *Philosophical Problems of Space and Time*, 2nd edn (Dordrecht: D. Reidel, 1973), pp. 735–50.

16 Winnie, "Causal theory."

17 Milton A. Rothman, "Things that go faster than light," *Scientific American* 203/1 (July 1960), pp. 142–52, contains a lively discussion of pseudo-processes.

18 Russell, *Human Knowledge*, p. 459.

19 Ibid.

20 Kenneth M. Sayre, "Statistical models of causal relations," *Philosophy of Science* 44 (1977), pp. 203–14, at p. 206.

21 Bas C. van Fraassen, *The Scientific Image* (Oxford: Clarendon Press, 1980), p. 118.

22 For example, our discussion of the Minkowski light cone made reference to paths of possible light rays; such a path is one that would be taken by a light pulse if it were emitted from a given space-time point in a given direction. Special relativity seems to be permeated with reference to possible light rays and possible causal connections, and these involve counterfactuals quite directly. See Wesley C. Salmon, "Foreword," in Hans Reichenbach, *Laws, Modalities, and Counterfactuals* (Berkeley/ Los Angeles/London: University of California Press, 1976), pp. vii–xlii, for further elaboration of this issue, not only with respect to special relativity but also in relation to other domains of physics. A strong case can be made, I believe, for the thesis that counterfactuals are scientifically indispensable.

23 Bergson, *Creative Evolution* (New York: Holt, Reinhart and Winston, 1911), p. 308.

24 Russell, *Mysticism and Logic*, p. 187.

25 Zeno's arrow paradox and its resolution by means of the 'at-at' theory of motion are discussed in Wesley C. Salmon, *Space, Time, and Motion* (Encino, Calif.: Dickenson, 1975; 2nd edn, Minneapolis: University of Minnesota Press, 1980), ch. 2. Relevant writings by Bergson and Russell are reprinted in *idem*, *Zeno's Paradoxes* (Indianapolis: Bobbs- Merrill, 1970); the introduction to this anthology also contains a discussion of the arrow paradox.

26 Salmon offers an account of these notions in his *Scientific Explanation and the Causal Structure of the World* (Princeton: Princeton University Press, 1984), ch. 6.

27 Ibid.

31

Causation: Reductionism Versus Realism

Michael Tooley

Any adequate approach to causation must provide accounts of causal laws, and of causal relations between states of affairs, or events, and, in each case, one is confronted with the choice between reductionism and realism. With respect to causal laws, the relevant issue concerns the relation between causal laws and the totality of events. According to reductionism, causal laws are supervenient upon the total history of the world. According to realism, they are not. With respect to causal relations, the central issue is whether causal relations between events are reducible to other states of affairs, including the non-causal properties of, and relations between, events. The reductionist holds that they are; the realist that they are not.

These choices between reductionist and non-reductionist approaches to causal laws and causal relations are surely among the most fundamental in the philosophy of causation. But in spite of that fact, they have received very little discussion. For, although there have been exceptions, the history of the philosophy of causation since the time of Hume has been largely the history of attempts to offer reductionist accounts of causal laws and of causal relations, and most

philosophers have been content simply to assume that a reductionist approach to causation must be correct.

In this paper, I shall argue that reductionist accounts of causation are exposed to decisive objections, and that the time has come to explore realist alternatives.

1 Reductionist and Realist Alternatives

1.1 Causation and logical supervenience

Some recent discussions of causation have been concerned with the question of what causation is *in this world*, and it has been proposed, for example, that causation in this world can be identified with the transference of energy and/or momentum.[1] Such contingent identity theses concerning the nature of causation clearly constitute one sort of reductionism. It is not, however, the sort that I shall be concerned with here. For I shall be focusing, instead, upon questions such as whether causal laws are reducible, as a matter of *logical* necessity, to facts about the total history of the world, and, similarly, whether facts about causal relations

Michael Tooley, "Causation: Reductionism versus Realism," *Philosophy and Phenomenological Research*, 50, supplement (Autumn 1990): 215–36. Reproduced by permission of John Wiley & Sons, Inc.

Metaphysics: An Anthology, Second Edition. Edited by Jaegwon Kim, Daniel Z. Korman and Ernest Sosa.
Editorial material and organization © 2012 Blackwell Publishing Ltd. Published 2012 by Blackwell Publishing Ltd.

between events are reducible, as a matter of *logical necessity*, to facts about other states of affairs.

A traditional way of putting these questions is in terms of the *analysability*, in certain ways, of causal concepts. Perhaps a slightly preferable way of formulating the matter, however, is in terms of the concept of *logical supervenience*. Let us say that two worlds, W and W^*, agree with respect to all of the properties and relations in some set, S, if and only if there is some one-to-one mapping, f, such that (1) for any individual x in world W, and any property P in set S, x has property P if and only if the corresponding individual, x^*, in W^*, also has property P, and vice versa, and (2) for any n-tuple of individuals, $x_1, x_2, \ldots x_n$ in W, and any relation R in set S, $x_1, x_2, \ldots x_n$ stand in relation R if and only if the corresponding individuals, x_1^*, $x_2^*, \ldots x_n^*$, in W^*, also stand in relation R, and vice versa. Then to say that the properties and relations in set T are logically supervenient upon the properties and relations in set S is to say that, for any two worlds W and W^*, if W and W^* agree with respect to the properties and relations in set S, they must also agree with respect to the properties and relations in set T.

Given these concepts, the reductionist theses that I shall be considering may now be characterized as follows. First, reductionism with respect to causal relations. This comes in two forms, depending upon what the reduction base is claimed to be:

Strong Reductionism with Respect to Causal Relations
Any two worlds that agree with respect to all of the non-causal properties of, and relations between, particular events or states of affairs, must also agree with respect to all of the causal relations between states of affairs. Causal relations are, in short, logically supervenient upon non-causal properties and relations.

Weak Reductionism with Respect to Causal Relations
Any two worlds that agree both with respect to all of the non-causal properties of, and relations between, particular events or states of affairs, and with respect to all causal laws, must also agree with respect to all of the causal relations between states of affairs.

Secondly, reductionism with respect to causal laws. The central contention here is that what

causal laws there are is fixed by the total history of the world. That contention can also take, however, a stronger form and a weaker form:

Strong Reductionism with Respect to Causal Laws
Any two worlds that agree with respect to all of the *non-causal* properties of, and relations between, particular events, must also agree with respect to causal laws.

Weak Reductionism with Respect to Causal Laws
Any two worlds that agree with respect to all of the *causal and non-causal* properties of, and relations between, particular events, must also agree with respect to causal laws.

There are some obvious interrelations here. Strong reductionism for causal relations, when combined with weak reductionism for causal laws, entails strong reductionism for causal laws. Similarly, strong reductionism for causal laws, combined with weak reductionism for causal relations, entails strong reductionism for causal relations.

Strong reductionism on either issue cannot, accordingly, be combined with only weak reductionism on the other. But what about being merely a weak reductionist with regard to both causal laws and causal relations? This combination also seems impossible. For, on the one hand, if causal laws are logically supervenient upon the non-causal properties of, and relations between, particular events, together with the causal relations between events, then causal laws would seem to be ontologically less basic than causal relations, while if causal relations are logically supervenient upon causal laws plus the non-causal properties of, and relations between, particular events, then causal laws are ontologically more basic than causal relations. It would seem impossible, therefore, to formulate a coherent ontology if one attempts to embrace only weak reductionism both with respect to causal laws and with respect to causal relations.

Accordingly, if one is going to be a reductionist with respect to both causal laws and causal relations, it is the strong reductionist views that one must embrace, and it is precisely this combination of positions that has been the dominant one since the time of Hume. Not all philosophers who are thoroughgoing reductionists with respect to causation fall, however, within the Humean tradition. For in the case of philosophers who approach causation in a broadly Humean way, what is fundamental is the acceptance of strong reductionism with respect to causal laws and weak reductionism with respect to causal relations: strong reductionism with respect to causal relations is a further conclusion that is drawn from those more fundamental commitments. It is possible, however, to start instead from weak reductionism with respect to causal laws, together with strong reductionism with respect to causal relations, and then to accept strong reductionism with respect to causal laws as a further consequence.

C. J. Ducasse is a good example of a philosopher who rejected a Humean approach to causation, but who was a strong reductionist nonetheless. For consider, first, the following passage:

The supposition of recurrence is thus wholly irrelevant to the meaning of cause; that supposition is relevant only to the meaning of law. And recurrence becomes related at all to causation only when a law is considered which happens to be a generalization of facts themselves individually causal to begin with. A general proposition concerning such facts is, indeed, a causal law, but it is not causal because general. It is general, i.e., a law, only because it is about a class of resembling facts; and it is causal only because each of them already happens to be a causal fact individually and in its own right (instead of, as Hume would have it, by right of its co-membership with others in a class of pairs of successive events).[2]

As this passage makes clear, weak reductionism with respect to causal relations is not a starting point for Ducasse, since he rejects the idea that causal relations presuppose causal laws. His fundamental commitment with respect to causal relations is, instead, to a strong reductionist view, for he holds that causation can be analysed in terms of relations which Hume granted are observable in the individual instance – the relations, namely, of spatial and temporal contiguity, and of temporal priority.[3] On the other hand, weak reductionism with respect to causal laws is a starting point for Ducasse, for he believes that causal laws are simply uniformities involving causal relations between particular events. So Ducasse is led to a thoroughgoing reductionism, but by a non-Humean route.

What alternatives are open if one rejects strong reductionism with respect to either causal laws, or causal relations, or both? Essentially there are four. First, realism with respect to causal laws can be combined with weak reductionism with respect to causal relations. The result is what might be characterized as a Humean view of causation plus a non-Humean view of laws.

Secondly, realism with respect to causal laws can also be combined with strong reductionism with respect to causal relations. This is the sort of position that results when a singularist reductionist approach to causation – such as Ducasse's – is combined with a realist approach to laws.

Thirdly, one can opt instead for a realist approach to causal relations, while accepting a reductionist a view of causal laws. In that case, however, one would need to adopt a weak reductionist view. For according to a strong reductionist view of causal laws, the latter are logically supervenient upon the non-causal properties of, and relations between, events, and it is hard to see how this could be the case if causal relations were not supervenient upon the same ontological base.

Finally, one can abandon all forms of reductionism with respect to causation, and embrace realism with respect to both causal laws and causal relations. This is, I shall argue, the preferred alternative.

2 Reductionism with Respect to Causal Laws

The distinction between strong and weak reductionism with respect to causal laws is important for understanding what options are open when one is setting out an account of the nature of causation. It is not, however, important with respect to the choice between reductionist and realist approaches to laws, since strong and weak reductionist views are exposed to precisely the same objections.

Since a number of philosophers have recently argued, and in a detailed way, that reductionist accounts of the nature of laws are exposed to very strong objections,[4] my discussion here will be brief. I shall simply mention some of the more important objections that have been raised to reductionist accounts of the nature of laws.

First, then, there is the familiar problem of distinguishing between laws and accidental regularities. For example, there may well be some number N such that, at no time or place in the total history of the universe will there ever be a sphere of radius N centimeters that contains only electrons. But if there is such a number, does that mean that it is a *law* that no sphere of radius N centimeters can contain only electrons? Might it not, instead, be merely an accident that no such sphere exists? But if so, what serves to differentiate laws from mere cosmic regularities?[5]

A second objection concerns the possibility of basic, uninstantiated laws, and may be put as follows. For sake of illustration, let us suppose that our world involves psychophysical laws connecting different sorts of stimulation with emergent properties of experiences, so that it is a causal law, for example, that when a normal human looks at something that is a specific shade of purple, under standard conditions, that gives rise to an experience with some specific emergent property. Let us suppose, further, that at least some of these psychophysical laws are basic laws – that is, incapable of being derived from any other laws, psychophysical or otherwise. Finally, let us assume that, for at least some of those basic psychophysical laws, the only instances of them at any time in the history of the universe involve sentient beings on our earth. Given these assumptions, consider what would have been the case if our world had been different in certain respects. Suppose, for example, that the earth had been destroyed by an explosion of the sun just before the point when, for the first time in history, a sentient being would have observed a purple flower, and so would have had an experience with the corresponding emergent property. What counterfactuals are true in the alternative possible world just described? In particular, what would have been the case if the sun had not gone supernova when it did? Would it not have been the case that a sentient being would have looked at a purple flower, and therefore have been stimulated in such a way as to have had an experience with the relevant emergent property?

It seems to me very plausible to hold that the counterfactual in question is true in that possible world. But that counterfactual cannot be true unless the appropriate psychophysical law obtains in that world. But in the world where the sun explodes before any sentient being has looked at a purple flower, the law in question will not have any instances. So if the counterfactual is true in that world, it follows that there can be basic causal laws that lack all instances. But if that is so, then causal laws cannot be logically supervenient upon the total history of the universe.[6]

A third objection concerns a problem posed by probabilistic laws. Consider a world where it is a law that the probability that an event with property P has property Q is equal to one half. It does not follow that precisely one half of the events with property P will have property Q. Indeed, the proportion that have property Q need not be anywhere near one half: it can be absolutely any value whatever.

The existence of the law in question does have, of course, *probabilistic* implications with respect to the proportion that will have property Q. In particular, as the number of events with property P becomes larger and larger, the *probability* that the proportion of events with property P which also have property Q will be within any specified interval around the value one half approaches indefinitely close to one. But this fact is, of course, perfectly compatible with the fact that the existence of the law in question does not *entail* any restrictions upon the proportion of events with property P that have property Q.

More generally, any probabilistic law is compatible with *any* distribution of properties over events. In this respect, there is a sharp difference between probabilistic laws and non-probabilistic laws. Any non-probabilistic law imposes a constraint upon the total history of any world containing that law – namely, the corresponding regularity must obtain. But a probabilistic law, in contrast, imposes no constraint upon the total history of the world. Accordingly, unless one is prepared to supplement one's ontology in a very unHumean way, by postulating something like objective, *single-case* chances, there would not seem to be even a potential reduction base in the case of probabilistic laws.[7]

The fourth and final objection that I shall mention concerns an epistemological problem that arises if one attempts to identify laws either with cosmic regularities in general, or with regularities that satisfy certain additional constraints. On the one hand, the evidence for any law consists of a finite number of observations. On the other, any law has a potentially infinite number of instances. Can such a finite body of evidence possibly justify one in believing that some law obtains, if laws are essentially just regularities? For if laws are merely certain kinds of regularities, with no further ontological backing, isn't it in fact likely that the regularities that have held with respect to the cases that have been observed so far will break down at some point?

This objection can be formulated in a more rigorous way by appealing to some general, quantitative account of confirmation, according to which any generalization of the sort that expresses a possible law has probability zero relative to any finite body of evidence. Carnap's system of confirmation, for example, has that property.[8] It is possible to argue, of course, that any system with this property is necessarily defective. But then the challenge is to construct a system that assigns non-zero probability to generalizations expressing possible laws, upon finite observational evidence, in an infinite universe, and while there have certainly been attempts to meet this challenge,[9] I think it can be argued that they are *ad hoc*, and fail to appeal to independently plausible principles.

But how is the realist any better placed with respect to this epistemological problem? The answer is that a realist can view the existence of a causal law as constituted by a single, atomic state of affairs, rather than as a potentially infinite conjunction of states of affairs. On the view that I favor, for example, laws are to be identified with certain second order, atomic states of affairs involving irreducible relations between universals, and I have tried to show elsewhere, in a detailed way, that the adoption of this sort of realist account enables one to prove that quite a limited body of evidence may make it very probable that a given law obtains.[10]

To sum up. Reductionist accounts of causal laws face at least four serious objections. First, they appear unable to draw a satisfactory distinction between laws and accidental uniformities. Secondly, they cannot allow for the possibility of basic, uninstantiated laws. Thirdly, probabilistic laws seem to pose an intractable problem. And finally, it is difficult to see how one can ever be justified in believing that there are laws, if one adopts a reductionist account. A realist approach,

in contrast, can provide satisfactory answers to all of these problems.

3 Reductionism with Respect to Causal Relations

Philosophers have gradually become more aware of the seriousness of the problems confronting a reductionist approach to laws. Much less well known, however, is the fact that reductionist approaches to causal relations are also exposed to very strong objections.

The latter fall into two groups. First, there are objections that center upon the problem of giving an account of the direction of causal processes, and which claim that there are possible causal worlds where reductionist accounts of the direction of causation either do not apply at all, or else do apply, but give the wrong answers.

Secondly, there are objections involving what may be referred to as problems of underdetermination. For what these objections attempt to establish is that there can be worlds that agree with respect to, first, all of the non-causal properties of, and relations between, events, secondly, all causal laws, and thirdly, the direction of causation, but which disagree with respect to the causal relations between corresponding events.

3.1 Direction of causation objections

I shall consider two objections which focus upon the direction of causation. The thrust of the first is that there are possible causal worlds to which reductionist accounts of the direction of causation do not apply, while that of the second is that there are other possible causal worlds for which reductionist accounts yield wrong answers with respect to the direction of causal processes.

3.1.1 Simple worlds

Our world is a complex one, with a number of features that might be invoked as the basis of a reductionist account of the direction of causation. First of all, it is a world where the direction of increase in entropy is the same in the vast majority of isolated or quasi-isolated systems. Secondly, the temporal direction in which order is propagated – such as by the circular waves that result when a stone strikes a pond, or by the spherical wavefronts associated with a point source of light – is invariably the same. Thirdly, consider the causal forks that are involved when two events have either a common cause, or a common effect. A fork may be described as open if it does not involve both a common cause and a common effect. Then it is a fact about our world that all, or virtually all, open forks are open in the same direction – namely, towards the future.[11]

Can such features provide a satisfactory account of the direction of causation? One objection arises out of possible causal worlds that are much simpler than our own. In particular, consider a world that contains only two uncharged particles, of the same type, that rotate endlessly about one another, on circular trajectories, in accordance with the laws of Newtonian physics. Each particle will undergo acceleration of a constant magnitude, due to the force of gravity exerted on it by the other particle. So the world is certainly a causal one. But it is also a world that is utterly devoid of changes of entropy, of propagation of order, and of open forks. So there is no hope of basing an account of the direction of causation upon any of those features.

What account can a reductionist give, then, of the direction of causation? The answer is that there is only one possibility. For, given that the simple world just described is completely symmetrical in time, events themselves do not exhibit any structure that serves to distinguish between the direction from cause to effect and the inverse one from effect to cause. So if the direction of causation is to be reduced to anything else, it can only be to the direction of time. But, then, in turn, one will have to be a realist with respect to the latter. There will be no possibility of reducing the direction of time to any structure present in the arrangement of events in time.

3.1.2 Inverted worlds

It is the year 4004 BC. A Laplacean-style deity is about to create a world rather similar to ours, but one where Newtonian physics is true. Having selected the year 2000 AD as a good time for Armageddon, the deity works out what the world will be like at that point, down to the last detail. He then creates two spatially unrelated worlds: the one just mentioned, together with another whose initial state is a flipped over version of the state of the first world immediately prior to

Armageddon – i.e., the two states agree exactly, except that the velocities of the particles in the one state are exactly opposite to those in the other.

Consider, now, any two complete temporal slices of the first world, A and B, where A is earlier than B. Since the worlds are Newtonian ones, and since the laws of Newtonian physics are invariant with respect to time reversal, the world that starts off from the reversed, 2000 AD type state will go through corresponding states, B^* and A^*, where these are flipped over versions of B and A respectively, and where B^* is earlier than A^*. So while the one world goes from a 4004 BC, Garden of Eden state to a 2000 AD, pre-Armageddon state, the other world will move from a reversed, pre-Armageddon type state to a reversed, Garden of Eden type state.

In the first world, the direction of causation will coincide with such things as the direction of increase in entropy, the direction of the propagation of order in non-entropically irreversible processes, and the direction defined by most open forks. But in the second world, whereas the direction of causation runs from the initial state created by the deity – that is, the flipped over 2000 AD type state – through to the flipped over 4004 BC type state, the direction in which entropy increases, the direction in which order is propagated, and the direction defined by open forks will all be the opposite one. So if any of the latter were used to define the direction of causation, it would generate the wrong result in the case of the second world.

As with the 'simple universes' argument, it is open to a reductionist to respond by holding that the direction of causation is to be defined in terms of the direction of time. But here, as before, this response is only available if one is prepared to adopt a realist view of the direction of time. For any reductionist account of the latter in terms of the structure exhibited by events in time cannot possibly generate the right results in both cases for two worlds that are 'inverted twins' – such as the two worlds just described.

3.2 Underdetermination objections

A reductionist approach to causal relations is exposed to at least four other objections, which I shall now describe. The thrust of all four is that fixing all of the non-causal properties of, and relations between, events, all of the laws, both causal and non-causal, and, finally, the direction of causation for all possible causal relations that might obtain, does not always suffice to fix what causal relations there are between events.

The first three arguments are, in effect, variations on a single theme – all of them focusing upon problems that arise concerning causal relations in indeterministic worlds. They do differ slightly, however, in their assumptions. The first argument assumes only that indeterministic causal laws are logically possible. The second argument, on the other hand, incorporates the further assumption that there is nothing incoherent in the idea of an uncaused event, while the third argument also involves that assumption, together with the additional assumption that probabilistic laws are logically possible.

The final argument, in contrast, does not appeal to the possibility of indeterministic worlds. Its thrust is that, even in a fully deterministic world, causal relations between events need not be logically supervenient upon the direction of causation, the totality of laws, both causal and non-causal, and the non-causal properties of, and relations between, events.

3.2.1   The argument from the possibility of indeterministic laws

A world with at least some basic probabilistic laws is necessarily an indeterministic world, so this first argument might equally well start from the assumption that probabilistic laws are logically possible. But there can be indeterministic laws that are not probabilistic. For example, it might be a law that an instance of property P will give rise *either* to an instance of property Q *or* to an instance of property R, without its being the case that there is any number k such that it is a law that an instance of property P will give rise, with probability k, to an instance of property Q. Accordingly, since indeterministic laws need not be probabilistic, and since the concept of a probabilistic law has been thought by some to be more problematic than that of a non-probabilistic law, it seems preferable to start from the slightly more modest assumption.

Given that probabilistic laws are indeterministic, and that quantum physics seems to lend strong support to the idea that the basic laws of nature may well be probabilistic, the assumption that indeterministic causal laws are logically

possible is surely very plausible – though by no means indubitable. Let us consider, then, a world with only the following two basic causal laws – both of which, though not probabilistic, are indeterministic:

> For any object x, x's having property P for a temporal interval of length Δt either causes x to acquire property Q, or else causes x to acquire property R, but does not do both;

> For any object x, x's having property S for a temporal interval of length Δt either causes x to acquire property Q, or else causes x to acquire property R, but does not do both.

Suppose now that a is an object in such a world, that a has property P, but not property S, throughout some interval of length Δt, and then acquires property Q, but not property R. In view of the first of the above laws, it must be the case that a's acquisition of property Q was caused by its possession of property P. Similarly, if a had property S, but not property P, throughout some interval of length Δt, and then acquired property Q, but not property R, it would have to be the case, given the second law, that a's acquisition of property Q was caused by its possession of property S. But what if a had acquired properties P and S at the same time, and had retained both throughout an interval of length Δt? If a then acquired only property Q, there would be no problem: it would simply be a case of causal overdetermination. Similarly, if it acquired only property R. But what if the situation were as follows:

Time t through time $t + \Delta t$	Time $t + \Delta t$
Pa and Sa	Qa and Ra

Here, a has acquired *both* property Q *and* property R, and, as a result, there are two possibilities concerning the relevant causal relations:

Possibility 1	Possibility 2
Pa causes Qa, and Sa causes Ra	Pa causes Ra, and Sa causes Qa

One is therefore confronted with the question of what the relevant causal relations are. Was it the possession of property P, for the appropriate interval, that caused the acquisition of property Q, and the possession of S that caused the acquisition of R? Or was it, instead, the other way around? Given a reductionist view, however, no answer is possible. For the causal laws in question, together with the non-causal properties of the object, and its non-causal relations to other objects, plus facts about the direction of causation in all potential causal processes, do not entail that it was one way rather than the other.

How might a reductionist respond to this argument? One try would be to say that where an object acquires property P and property S at the same time, and then, after the relevant interval, acquires both property Q and property R, there are *no* causal relations at all involved. But given that, for example, the first of the above laws can only obtain if the possession of property P *always* causes an event that is of one of two sorts, this response would seem to entail that indeterministic laws of the above sort are not really logically possible – a claim that surely needs to be supported by some independent argument. Moreover, given that the present argument can easily be formulated in terms of probabilistic laws, the latter would also have to be rejected as incoherent.

Another response would be to argue that, although there are causal relations in the situation, they are not quite as determinate as one might initially assume. The idea here would be that, in the crucial situation where the object has both P and S, and then acquires both Q and R, it is not the case either that the possession of P for the relevant interval causes the acquisition of Q, or that it causes the acquisition of R. What is true, rather, is simply that the possession of property P for the relevant interval causes the state of affairs which involves either the acquisition of property Q, or the acquisition of property R.

But this response is also very dubious, since it appears to involve a confusion between, on the one hand, certain non-linguistic, non-conceptual entities which are the relata of causal relations – namely, states of affairs – and, on the other, certain linguistic expressions that may be used to designate states of affairs. Thus, in referring to states of affairs, one may certainly use disjunctive expressions to pick them out – such as the expression "the state of affairs that involves either *a*'s acquisition of property Q, or *a*'s acquisition of property R." But while states of affairs can be referred to in what way, it makes no sense to speak of states of affairs as themselves disjunctive in nature. The only states of affairs that can be picked out by the disjunctive expression in question are the state of affairs that consists of *a*'s acquiring property Q, and the state of affairs that consists of *a*'s acquiring property R. Accordingly, if the situation described above is to involve causal relations falling under the relevant laws, it must be the case either that the possession of property P for the relevant interval caused the acquisition of property Q, or that it caused the acquisition of property R, and similarly for property S.

3.2.2   The argument from the possibility of uncaused events

The second argument is, in a sense, a simpler version of the previous one. It does involve, however, one additional assumption – namely, that there is nothing incoherent in the idea of an uncaused event.

Given that further assumption, one can consider a world where objects sometimes acquire property Q without there being any cause of their doing so, and similarly for property R, and where, in addition, the following two statements are true:

(1)   It is a law that, for any object x, x's having property P for a temporal interval of length Δt either causes x to acquire property Q, or else causes x to acquire property R.

(2)   It can *never* be the case, for any object x, that x's having property P for a temporal interval of length Δt causes x to acquire *both* property Q *and* property R.

Suppose, finally, that an object a in such a world, having had property P for the appropriate interval, acquires both Q and R. In view of the law described in statement (1), either the acquisition of Q was caused by the possession of P for the relevant interval, or else the acquisition of R was so caused. But, given statement (2), it cannot be the case that the possession of P for the relevant interval caused *both* the acquisition of Q *and* the acquisition of R. So once again, it must be the case that one of two causal states of affairs obtains, but the totality of facts concerning, first, the non-causal properties of, and relations between, events, secondly, what laws there are, and thirdly, the direction of causation in all potential causal processes, does not suffice to fix which causal state of affairs obtains.

A possible reductionist response is that if it is a law that objects always acquire either property Q or property R, after having had property P for a relevant interval, and if, in addition, they sometimes acquire both property Q and property R in such circumstances, then the following must be the case:

(3) It is a law that, for any object x, x's having property P for a temporal interval of length Δt either causes x to acquire property Q, or causes x to acquire property R, or, finally, causes x to acquire both property Q and property R.

But if the latter is the case, then statement (2) cannot be true.

This response, however, does not seem satisfactory. For in the first place, the claim that, in the situation described, statement (3) must be true, surely calls for support What sort of argument might be offered? The only possibility, I think, is to appeal to a reductionist view of causal laws, according to which they are to be identified with certain sorts of regularities.

In the second place, even if the contention in question is granted, for the sake of discussion, the underlying difficulty is only shifted. For now when an object acquires both Q and R, after having had P for the appropriate interval, we can say that it *may* have been the case that the latter state of affairs caused both the acquisition of Q and the acquisition of R. But, equally, it may instead have been the case that, say, only the acquisition of Q was so caused, and that the acquisition of R was an uncaused event. Or perhaps it was the other way around. There are, in short, three distinct possibilities with respect to the causal relations involved, and which of these obtains in any given case is not fixed by the facts in the proposed reductionist base.

3.2.3 The argument from the possibility of uncaused events plus probabilistic, causal laws
The argument just set out can be reinforced, moreover, if one replaces the assumption that there can be indeterministic causal laws with the slightly stronger assumption that it is logically possible for there to be basic, probabilistic, causal laws. Given that assumption, the argument runs as follows. Imagine a world where objects sometimes acquire property Q without there being any cause of that occurrence. Suppose, further, that the following is a law:

For any object x, x's having property P for a time interval Δt causally brings it about, with probability 0.75, that x has property Q.

If objects sometimes acquire property Q without there being any cause of their doing so, why shouldn't this also take place in cases where an object happens to have had property P for the relevant time interval, Δt? Indeed, might there not be excellent reason for thinking that there were such cases? For suppose that objects that have property P for the relevant interval go on to acquire property Q 76 percent of the time, rather than 75 percent of the time, and that this occurs even over the long term. Other things being equal, this would be grounds for doubting whether the above law obtained, and for thinking that the relevant law was rather that:

For any object x, x's having property P for a time interval Δt causally brings it about, with probability 0.76, that x has property Q.

But other things might not be equal. In particular, it might be the case that the first of the above possible laws was derivable from a very powerful, simple, and well-confirmed theory, whereas competing possibilities were not.

If that were the case, one would have reason for believing that, over the long term, of the 76 cases out of a 100 where an object that has had property P for the relevant interval acquires property Q, 75 of those will be ones where the acquisition of property Q is caused by the possession of property P, while the other case will be one where property Q is spontaneously acquired.

There can, in short, be situations where there would be good reason for believing that not all cases where an object has property P for an interval Δt, and then acquires Q, are causally the same. There is, however, no hope of making sense of this, given a reductionist approach to causal relations. For the cases do not differ with respect to relevant non-causal properties and relations, nor with respect to causal laws, nor with respect to the direction of causation in any potential causal relations.

3.2.4 The argument from the possibility of exact replicas of causal situations

The three arguments just set out all appeal to the possibility of indeterministic worlds. The thrust of this final argument, in contrast, is that a reductionist approach to causation is exposed to counterexamples even in the case of deterministic worlds.

Suppose that event P causes event M. In general, there will certainly be nothing impossible about there also being an event, M^*, which has precisely the same properties[12] as M, both intrinsic and relational, but which is not caused by P. But what about relations? Is it logically possible for it also to be the case that either (1) the only relation between P and M is that of causation, or else (2) any other relation that holds between P and M also holds between P and M^*?

If either situation obtained, one would have a counterexample to a reductionist approach to causal relations. For on a reductionist view, P's causing M is logically supervenient upon the non-causal properties of, and the non-causal relations between, P and M, together with the causal laws. So if M^* has precisely the same non-causal properties as M, and also stands to P in the same non-causal relations as M does, then it follows, on a reductionist view, that P must also cause M^*, contrary to hypothesis.

But are such situations possible? In support of the claim that they are, I want to mention two considerations.[13] The first appeals to the logical possibility of there being immaterial minds that are not located in space. If that possibility is granted, the argument runs as follows. First, though the contrary view has been defended, it is hard to see why there could not be two immaterial minds, existing simultaneously, whose mental contents were the same at every instant – either by a grand accident, or because of identical initial conditions in a world with deterministic laws governing mental events. Secondly, a plausible case can be made out, I believe, for the view that identity over time must be analysed in terms of causal relations between different events in the history of the enduring entity in question. But if

this is right, then consider any two qualitatively indistinguishable immaterial minds, A and A^*. Let P and M be any two temporal slices of mind A, and P^* and M^* be the corresponding temporal slices of A^*. Then P will be causally related to M but not to M^*, even though M does not differ from M^*, either with respect to its properties, or with respect to the non-causal relations in which it stands to P.

A similar sort of case, which also turns upon the idea that it is causal relations between the temporal parts of an object that unite those parts into a single, enduring entity, can be constructed for physical objects, given a world that satisfies two conditions. First, it must be a world where the only *basic* external relations between different temporal slices of the world, or between parts of different temporal slices, are temporal relations and causal relations. Secondly, it must possess an appropriate sort of symmetry – specifically, rotational symmetry, such as characterized the simple Newtonian world, described earlier, which consisted of only two uncharged particles, of the same type, rotating endlessly about one another on circular trajectories.

Consider, then, that very simple Newtonian world, and assume, further, that the only basic, external relations obtaining between things existing at different times are temporal relations and causal relations. Let P be the extended temporal part of one particle, which consists of all temporal parts of that particle which exist at times prior to some time t, and let M be the extended temporal part that consists of all the temporal parts of it existing at t or later. Similarly, let P^* and M^* be the corresponding parts of the other particle. Then, in view of the above assumption about identity over time, P is causally related to M in a way that it is not to M^*.

Can a reductionist approach to causal relations cope with this sort of case? Since M and M^* do not differ with respect to their non-causal properties, a reductionist needs to point to some non-causal relation in which one of them stands to P, while the other does not. What might that relation be? A natural suggestion is the relation of spatiotemporal continuity, given that M is spatiotemporally continuous with P, whereas M^* is not. But this suggestion assumes, of course, that causal relations do not enter into spatiotemporal continuity.

One way of attempting to support the latter assumption is by offering an analysis of spatiotemporal continuity in terms of a generalized betweenness relation that, rather than being restricted to locations at a given time, can hold between spacetime points belonging to different temporal slices, and then maintaining, as some philosophers do, that such a generalized betweenness relation can properly be treated as primitive.[14] My own view is that the latter contention is unsound, and that, on the contrary, a generalized betweenness relation, rather than being analytically basic, stands in need of analysis. But even if that were to turn out not to be so, the strategy just sketched would still not provide the reductionist with any reply to the present argument, since spatiotemporal betweenness is not a basic relation *in the possible world in question*. For there the only basic external relations between things existing at different times are temporal relations and causal relations.

Moreover, it is not only an account of spatiotemporal continuity in terms of generalized spatiotemporal betweenness that is precluded for the world in question: no account that does not involve causal relations will do. For there is a simple, general argument, which runs as follows, and which shows that *any* external relation which obtains between P and M, but not between P and M^*, must involve causation. Consider any such relation. In view of the fact that the world is one where the only basic external relations holding between things existing at different times are temporal relations and causal relations, a relation that did not involve causation could hold between P and M, while not holding between P and M^*, only if there were some temporal relation that obtained between P and M, but not between P and M^*, or vice versa. But the latter is impossible, given that M and M^* are simultaneous. Accordingly, there cannot be any non-causal relation that holds between P and M, but not between P and M^*, or vice versa.

This in turn means that a reductionist account cannot be given for the causal relations in question. For, by hypothesis, M and M^* do not differ with respect to their properties, and we have just seen that there cannot be any non-causal relation that obtains between P and M, but not between P and M^*, or vice versa. Nevertheless, P causes M, but not M^*. So we have another counterexample to any reductionist approach to causation.

4 Causal Relations, Singularism, and Singularist Reductionism

One issue that needs to be addressed, at least very briefly, is that of the relation between the case against reductionism and the case for a singularist conception of causation. For while the two arguments concerned with the problem of the direction of causation have no bearing upon the question of whether there can be causal relations that do not fall under causal laws, the four arguments set out in section 3.2, on the other hand, are variants of arguments that I have used elsewhere in support of a singularist conception of causation.[15]

Essentially, there are two points that need to be made. The first is that the arguments set out in section 3.2 are basically arguments against reductionism. They need to be supplemented, before they will lend any support to a singularist conception of causation. In particular, one needs to appeal to considerations of simplicity, if one is to move on from an anti-reductionist conclusion to the view that there can be causal relations that do not fall under causal laws.

The second point is that, although those arguments can be supplemented in order to generate support for a singularist conception of causation, the singularist conception in question must be a realist one. For the underdetermination arguments in section 3.2, no less than the direction of causation arguments in section 3.1, are arguments against any form of reductionism with respect to causal relations, including singularist reductionism.[16]

5 Realism with Regard to Causal Relations

If reductionism must be abandoned, what form should a realist approach to causation take? The basic choice here is between two views. First, the view that causal relations are observable, not only in the everyday sense of that term, but in a much stronger sense which entails that concepts of causal relations are analytically basic. Secondly, the view that causal concepts are theoretical concepts, so that causal relations can only be characterized, indirectly, as those relations that satisfy some appropriate theory.

A number of philosophers have favored the former view, but their arguments in support of it have sometimes been very weak. Elizabeth Anscombe appeals, for example, to the fact that one often acquires observational knowledge of causal states of affairs: one sees the stone break the window, or the knife cut through the butter.[17] But observational knowledge, in this broad, everyday sense, would not seem to provide adequate grounds for concluding that the relevant concepts are analytically basic. One can, for example, quite properly speak of physicists as seeing electrons when they look into cloud chambers, even though the concept of an electron is certainly capable of being analysed in terms of simpler concepts.

More sophisticated arguments have, however, been offered. David Armstrong, for example, distinguishes very carefully between perceptual knowledge in a broad sense, which may involve inference, and perceptual knowledge in a narrow sense, which is completely free of all inference, and he contends that we do have non-inferential knowledge of causal states of affairs, such as the fact that something is pressing against one's body.[18] More recently, Evan Fales has offered a very detailed and careful defense of the view that one can have non-inferential knowledge of causal facts.[19]

This issue is not, I believe, easily resolved, for it seems to me that whether one can have non-inferential knowledge of causal relations between events depends upon what the correct account of non-inferential knowledge is. If, as Armstrong holds, direct realism is correct, then I think it can be plausibly held that one has non-inferential knowledge of causal states of affairs. My own view, on the other hand, is that a satisfactory account of non-inferential knowledge requires a strong notion of direct acquaintance, according to which what properties one is directly acquainted with is logically supervenient upon the phenomenological content of one's experience, and I think it can be shown that such an account of non-inferential knowledge entails the conclusion that causal relations cannot be immediately perceived. Essentially, the argument would turn upon the idea that there could be worlds – call them Berkeleyan worlds – where the contents of one's experiences would be as they are now, but where the events that one observed did not stand in causal relations to one another. I shall not, however, attempt to develop that argument at this point.

If this is right, and there is no epistemologically neutral way of showing either that one can, or that one cannot, have non-inferential knowledge of causal relations between events, are there any other grounds that can be offered for preferring one form of realism to the other? I believe that there are. In the first place, causal relations would seem to have certain formal properties. For even if it is true, as some have argued, that there could be causal loops, it is surely impossible for any event to be the *immediate* cause of itself. I have argued elsewhere, however, that a satisfactory explanation of the formal properties of causation can be given if causal relations are treated as theoretical relations.[20] A realist view that holds, on the other hand, that the intrinsic nature of causal relations (or of some causal relations) is given in immediate perception is forced, in contrast, to treat the relevant formal properties as brute facts, incapable of any explanation.

In the second place, although the direction of causation is not, I have argued, to be reduced to features such as the direction of increase in entropy, or the direction of the transmission of order in non-entropic, irreversible processes, or the direction of open forks, it is surely true that these and other facts often provide evidence concerning how events are causally connected. Again, if causal relations are treated as theoretical relations, then it is possible to show that the features in question do provide evidence for causal connections[21] – something which cannot, I believe, be done, if one assumes that causal relations are basic and unanalysable.

6   Summing Up

I have argued that reductionist accounts, both of causal laws and of causal relations, are open to very serious objections. In the case of laws, I mentioned the problems posed by cosmic, but accidental uniformities, by uninstantiated basic laws, and by probabilistic laws, together with the difficulty of showing that one is justified in believing that laws obtain, if one holds that laws are, basically, cosmic uniformities. In the case of causal relations, I advanced two sorts of objections. First, there were the objections that focused upon the problem of explaining the direction of causation. I argued that a reductionist approach is unable to provide a satisfactory account of the direction of causation either for certain very simple universes, or for inverted universes, unless one is prepared both to define the direction of causation in terms of the direction of time, and to adopt a realist view of the latter. Secondly, there were the underdetermination objections, the thrust of which was that causal relations between events are not logically supervenient even upon the totality of all non-causal facts, together with all laws, both causal and non-causal, plus the direction of causation in all potential causal processes.

For a long time, reductionist approaches to laws and to causal relations were the only ones on offer. This is not, of course, surprising, for it is only comparatively recently that satisfactory realist accounts of the semantics of theoretical terms have been available. What is rather curious, however, is that while the emergence of such accounts has resulted in realism being quite widely espoused in philosophy of science, the philosophy of causation has remained largely untouched by that development. But if the arguments set out above are sound, the time has come to abandon reductionist approaches to causal relations and causal laws, and to explore realist alternatives, for only the latter offer any hope of success.

Notes

I am indebted to David Armstrong for detailed and very helpful comments on an earlier draft.

1 See, for example David Fair, "Causation and the Flow of Energy," *Erkenntnis* 14 (1979): 219–50.
2 C. J. Ducasse, "The Nature and the Observability of the Causal Relation," *Journal of Philosophy* 23 (1926): 57–67, and reprinted in Ernest Sosa (ed.), *Causation and Conditionals* (Oxford: Oxford University Press, 1975), pp. 144–25. See p. 118.
3 Ibid., p. 116.
4 Fred I. Dretske, "Law of Nature" *Philosophy of Science* 44 (1977): 248–68; David M. Armstrong, *What is a Law of Nature?* (Cambridge: Cambridge University Press 1983), esp. chs. 1–5; and my own discussions in "The Nature of Laws," *Canadian Journal of Philosophy* 7 (1977): 667–98, and in *Causation – A Realist Approach* (Oxford: Oxford University Press, 1988), section 2.1.1.
5 For a much fuller discussion of the problem of distinguishing between laws and accidental uniformities, see Armstrong, op. cit., ch. 2.

6 I have discussed the question of the possibility of uninstantiated basic laws in more detail in *Causation*, pp. 47–51.
7 A fuller account of the problem posed by probabilistic laws can be found in *Causation*, pp. 142–47.
8 For a discussion of this, see Rudolf Carnap, *Logical Foundations of Probability*, 2nd edition (Chicago: University of Chicago Press, 1962), pp. 570–75.
9 See, for example, Jaakko Hintikka, "A Two-Dimensional Continuum of Inductive Methods," in Jaakko Hintikka and Patrick Suppes (eds.), *Aspects of Inductive Logic* (Amsterdam: North Holland, 1966), pp. 113–32.
10 *Causation*, pp. 129–37.
11 For the first, see Hans Reichenbach, *The Direction of Time* (Berkeley: University of California Press, 1156), pp. 117–43, and Adolf Grünbaum, *Philosophical Problems of Space and Time*, 2nd edition (Dordrecht: D. Reidel, 1973), pp. 254–64. For the second, see Karl Popper "The Arrow of Time," *Nature* 177 (1956): 538. For the third, see Reichenbach, op. cit., pp. 161–3, and Wesley Salmon, "Why Ask 'Why?'?," *Proceedings and Addresses of the American Philosophical Association* 51 (1978): 696.
12 The only restriction upon properties here is that they must not involve particulars – so that, for example, being five miles from the Grand Canyon does not count as a property.
13 I have offered additional support for this claim in "Laws and Causal Relations," in P. A. French, T. E. Uehling, and H. K. Wettstein (eds.), *Midwest Studies in Philosophy* 9 (Minneapolis: University of Minnesota Press, 1985), pp. 93–112. See pp. 99–107.
14 Compare Hartry Field's formulation of the theory of Newtonian spacetime in his *Science Without Numbers* (Princeton: Princeton University Press, 1980), pp. 52–3.
15 Most recently is "The Nature of Causation: A Singularist Account," in David Copp (ed.), *Canadian Philosophers: Celebrating Twenty Years of the CJP* (Calgary: University of Calgary Press, 1990).
16 Singularist reductionism is also exposed to other objections, including a very strong Humean-style argument. See, for example, section 2 of "The Nature of Causation: A Singularist Account."
17 G. E. M. Anscombe, "Causality and Determination," in E. Sosa (ed.), *Causation and Conditionals*, pp. 63–81 [ch. 28 in the this volume].
18 David M. Armstrong, *A Materialist Theory of the Mind* (New York: Humanities Press, 1968), p. 97.
19 Evan Fales, *Causation and Universals*, Routledge, 2002.
20 *Causation*, pp. 274–87.
21 Ibid., pp. 299–302.

32

Two Concepts of Causation

Ned Hall

1 Introduction

Causation, understood as a relation between events, comes in at least two basic and fundamentally different varieties. One of these, which I call "dependence," is simply that: counterfactual dependence between wholly distinct events. In this sense, event c is a cause of (distinct) event e just in case e depends on c; that is, just in case, had c not occurred, e would not have occurred. The second variety is rather more difficult to characterize, but we evoke it when we say of an event c that it helps to *generate* or *bring about* or *produce* another event e, and for that reason I call it "production." Here I will articulate, defend, and begin to explore the consequences of this distinction between dependence and production. A synopsis:

After taking care of some preliminaries (sec. 2), I will argue for the distinction in a slightly devious manner, by starting with a broad-strokes critique of counterfactual analyses of causation (sec. 3). The reason for this approach is plain: Since I end up endorsing the simplest kind of counterfactual analysis – albeit only as an analysis of *one* kind of event-causation – it makes sense to pay some attention to the prospects for this and kindred analyses, and to examine why there is no hope of turning them into analyses of a *univocal* concept of event-causation. Specifically, my critique will aim to show that the best attempts to shore up counterfactual analyses in the face of well-known and stubborn counterexamples (involving certain kinds of overdetermination) rely on three general theses about causation:

Transitivity: If event c is a cause of d, and d is a cause of e, then c is a cause of e.

Locality: Causes are connected to their effects via spatiotemporally continuous sequences of causal intermediates.

Intrinsicness: The causal structure of a process is determined by its intrinsic, non-causal character (together with the laws).

These theses – particularly the second and third – will require more discussion and elaboration, which will come in due time. For now, contrast them with the thesis that lies at the heart of all counterfactual analyses of causation:

Ned Hall, "Two Concepts of Causation," in John Collins, Ned Hall, and L. A. Paul (eds.), *Causation and Counterfactuals* (Cambridge, MA: MIT Press, 2004), pp. 225–276, © 2004 Massachusetts Institute of Technology, by permission of the MIT Press.

Metaphysics: An Anthology, Second Edition. Edited by Jaegwon Kim, Daniel Z. Korman and Ernest Sosa.
Editorial material and organization © 2012 Blackwell Publishing Ltd. Published 2012 by Blackwell Publishing Ltd.

Dependence: Counterfactual dependence between wholly distinct events is
sufficient for causation.

The simplest counterfactual analysis adds that
dependence is *necessary* for causation. As a *general*
analysis of causation, it fails for well-known reasons,
which we will review shortly. Consequently, very
few counterfactual analysts endorse this necessary
condition (but see Coady 2004). But to my
knowledge, all endorse the sufficient condition
codified in the thesis of *Dependence*. Indeed, it is
probably safe to say that *Dependence* is the
cornerstone of every counterfactual analysis.

What is the trouble? Simply this: A hitherto
ignored class of examples involving what I call
"double-prevention" reveals deep and intractable
tensions between the theses of *Transitivity,
Locality,* and *Intrinsicness,* on the one hand, and
Dependence, on the other (sec. 4).

In section 5, I'll add to my case by arguing that
exactly parallel tensions divide the first three
theses from the thesis of

Omissions: Omissions – failures of events to
occur – can both cause and be
caused.

This thesis will also need further elaboration and
discussion.

One immediate result is that counterfactual
analyses are doomed to failure (unless, as I think,
they are understood to be targeted narrowly at
just one *kind* of event-causation): for they *need*
the first three theses if they are to cope with the
well-known counterexamples involving overdetermination, but they *cannot abide* these theses
if they are to cope with the counterexamples
involving double-prevention (or, for that matter,
if they admit omissions as causes and effects).

Although important, this result is eclipsed by a
more significant lesson that I will develop in
section 6. For the five theses I have mentioned are,
I claim, all *true*. Given the deep and intractable
tensions between them, that can only be because
they characterize *distinct concepts of causation*.
Events can stand in one kind of causal relation –
dependence – for the explication of which the
counterfactual analysis is perfectly suited (and for
which omissions can be perfectly suitable relata).
And they can stand in an entirely different kind of

causal relation – production – which requires an
entirely different kind of analysis (and for which
omissions are *not* suitable relata). *Dependence*
and *Omissions* are true of the first of these causal
relations; *Transitivity, Locality,* and *Intrinsicness*
are true of the second. I'll close section 6 by
defending this claim against some of the most
obvious objections.

How are production and dependence to be
analyzed? Dependence, I think, is easy; it is counterfactual dependence, nothing more nor less
(with, perhaps, me proviso that counterfactual
dependence itself can come in different varieties;
see sec. 7 for brief discussion). Production is
trickier, and in section 7 I'll offer a speculative
proposal about its analysis, confined to the special
case of deterministic laws that permit no action at
a temporal distance or backward causation. But
I'll say at once that I am much more confident of
the propriety of the distinction than I am of this
particular gloss on the "production" half of it.

I'll close, in section 8, by suggesting some ways
in which the distinction between production and
dependence might be put to work, and by
highlighting what I think are the most important
bits of unfinished business. [Sections 7 and 8 are
not included in this selection.]

2   Preliminaries, and a Brief Methodological Sermon

There are, in the literature, more than a dozen
versions of a counterfactual analysis of causation
that I am aware of. To attack them all, in detail,
would require (to borrow an apt term from Tim
Maudlin) a kind of philosophical "trench warfare" that only deeply committed partisans could
find engaging. I'll confess to a taste for trench
warfare, but I won't indulge it here. Instead, I will
follow a different strategy, focusing my critique
on the simplest counterfactual analysis, according
to which causation is counterfactual dependence
between wholly distinct events. It will be far more
illuminating to explore the most basic problems
for this analysis – along with the clearest and
most plausible strategies for confronting them –
than it would be to wind through the convolutions
built into the multitude of more sophisticated
variants.

In order to develop this critique as constructively as possible, we must avoid various methodological pitfalls. For that reason, it will be important to characterize, if only in a rough way, the causal relation that is the target of the counterfactual analysis. I take the analysis to concern the concept of causation as a transitive, egalitarian relation between localized, datable events. Let's look at the parts of this characterization in turn.

Begin with the relata. In understanding them to be *events*, I am taking sides on an issue that has seen much recent controversy.[1] I grant that there may be senses in which nonevents – facts, properties, maybe even things – can cause and be caused; certainly we speak of event *types* as doing so, as when we say that lightning causes fires. All the same, I assume that there is a clear and central sense of "cause" – the one at issue here – in which causes and effects are always events. (In sec. 6, I'll qualify this assumption slightly, suggesting that dependence, at least, can admit more kinds of relata.)

I will, furthermore, follow common practice by stretching ordinary usage of the term "event" to cover such things as, for example, the presence, at the appropriate time, of the oxygen and dry timber that combine with the lightning bolt to produce the forest fire. I will also take it for granted that we can adequately discern when two events fail to be *wholly distinct* – that is, when they stand in some sort of logical or mereological relationship that renders them unsuited to stand in *causal* relationships – and that we can tell when a description is too disjunctive or extrinsic to succeed in picking out an event. Without such assumptions, it is far too easy to make a hash of the simple analysis, and the analyses that build on it, by way of alleged counterexamples to the claim that counterfactual dependence is sufficient for causation.[2]

Of course, I do not at all mean to suggest that it is an easy matter to provide an adequate philosophical account of events that meets these criteria. I certainly won't try to provide any such account here. What I *will* do is avoid choosing examples where any of the controversies surrounding the nature of events makes a difference.[3]

Turn next to the characterization of the relation. Transitivity is straightforward enough: If event *a* is a cause of event *b*, and *b* a cause of *c*, then *a* is thereby a cause of *c*. What I mean by "egalitarian" can best be made clear by contrast

with our usual practice. When delineating the causes of some given event, we typically make what are, from the present perspective, invidious distinctions, ignoring perfectly good causes because they are not sufficiently salient. We say that the *lightning bolt* caused the forest fire, failing to mention the contribution of the oxygen in the air, or the presence of a sufficient quantity of flammable material. But in the egalitarian sense of "cause," a complete inventory of the fire's causes must include the presence of oxygen and of dry wood. (Note that transitivity helps make for an egalitarian relation: Events causally remote from a given event will typically not be *salient* – but will still be among its causes, for all that.)

Now for a brief methodological sermon: If you want to make trouble for an analysis of causation – but want to do so on the cheap – then it's convenient to ignore the egalitarian character of the *analysandum*. Get your audience to do the same, and you can proceed to elicit judgments that will appear to undermine the analysis, but which are in fact irrelevant to it. Suppose that my favorite analysis counts the big bang as among the causes of today's snowfall (a likely result, given transitivity). How easy it is to refute me, by observing that if asked what *caused* the snowfall (better still: what was *the* cause of it), we would never cite the big bang! Of course, the right response to this "refutation" is obvious: It conflates the transitive, egalitarian sense of "cause" with a much more restrictive sense (no doubt greatly infected with pragmatics) that places heavy weight on salience.

A simple mistake, it would seem. But the same sort of mistake shows up, in more subtle forms, in examples drawn from the literature. It will be helpful to work through a few illustrative cases – ones that show, incidentally, how even first-rate authors can sometimes go astray.

First, Bennett (1987, pp. 222–3; italics in the original), who is here concerned with Lombard's thesis that an event's time is essential to it:

> Take a case where this is true:
>
> There was heavy rain in April and electrical storms in the following two months; and in June the lightning took hold and started a forest fire. *If it hadn't been for the heavy rain in April, the forest would have caught fire in May.*
>
> Add Lombard's thesis to that, and you get

If the April rain hadn't occurred the forest fire wouldn't have occurred.

Interpret that in terms of the counterfactual analysis and you get

The April rains caused the forest fire.

That is unacceptable. A good enough theory of events and of causation might give us reason to accept some things that seem intuitively to be false, but no theory should persuade us that delaying a forest's burning for a month (or indeed for a minute) is causing a forest fire.

Lombard agrees that Bennett's result "is unacceptable. It is a bit of good common sense that heavy rains can put out fires, they don't start them; it *is* false to say that the rains caused the fire" (Lombard 1990, p. 197; italics in the original).

Lombard discusses a second example that shows that the essentiality of an event's time is not at issue (ibid., pp. 197–8):

> Suppose that Jones lives in a very dangerous neighborhood, and that one evening Smith attempts to stab him to death. Jones is saved because of the action of Brown who frightens Smith off. However, a year later, Jones is shot to death by the persistent Smith. So, if Brown's action had not occurred, Jones's death due to the shooting would not have occurred, since he would have died of stab wounds a year earlier. But, I find it intuitively quite unacceptable to suppose that Brown's action was a cause of Jones's dying as a result of gunshot a year later.

Finally, Lewis discusses a similar example (Lewis 1986d, p. 250):

> It is one thing to postpone an event, another to cancel it. A cause without which it would have occurred later, or sooner, is not a cause without which it would not have occurred at all. Who would dare be a doctor, if the hypothesis under consideration [that an event's time is essential to it] were right? You might manage to keep your patient alive until 4:12, when otherwise he would have died at 4:08. You would then have caused his death. For his death was, in fact, his death at 4:12. If that time is essential, his death is an event that would not have occurred had he died at 4:08, as he would have done without your action. That will not do.

If these examples are meant to provide rock-solid "data" on which the counterfactual analysis (and perhaps others) founders, then they uniformly fail – for in each case, we can find *independently plausible* premises that entail the allegedly unacceptable consequences. Of course that doesn't show that the consequences are *true*. But it *does* show that we make a serious methodological mistake if we treat those of our intuitions that run counter to them as nonnegotiable "data."

First we must disentangle irrelevant but confusing issues. It is probably right that an event's time is not in every case essential to it; but (*pace* Lewis) that doesn't help in any of the three cases. This is more or less obvious in the first two cases (the June fire is not the same as the fire that would have happened in May; the death by shooting is not the same as the death by stabbing that would have happened a year earlier). So consider Lewis's case. Supposedly, it "will not do" to assert that the doctor's action is among the causes of the patient's death. But what does this have to do with the proximity of the actual time of death to the time at which the patient would have died? Suppose you manage to keep your patient alive until June of 2004, when otherwise he would have died in June of 2003. Would you then have caused his death, since without your action the death he in fact died would not have occurred? It is no less (and no more) unacceptable to say "yes" in this case than it is to say "yes" in Lewis's case. But if, following Lewis, we conclude that the actual death is the same as the death that would have occurred a year earlier, then we are taking the denial of the essentiality of times to a ridiculous extreme. Such a denial, however warranted, does not give the counterfactual analyst the means to respond effectively even to Lewis's problem.

The analyst can, however, draw on our brief methodological sermon to point to two sorts of judgments about causation that the three examples implicitly trade on – but illegitimately, since these judgments concern types of causation that are not at issue. We can all agree that "heavy rains can put out fires, they don't start them," just as we can agree that smoking causes lung cancer, but regular exercise doesn't. So what? The intuitions called on here do not concern the concept of causation as a transitive, egalitarian relation between events, but rather some other concept of causation as an inegalitarian relation between *event-types.* (Never mind that *starting* a fire is not the only way to be one of its causes!) Similarly, we can all agree that it is the *lightning* that causes the forest fire, and nothing else – including the heavy rains. Again, so what? Here we seem to have in mind a restricted, inegalitarian concept of event-causation according to which events that are to count as causes must be particularly salient in some respect; but judgments involving *this* concept matter not at all to the counterfactual analysis, since it concerns the weaker and more inclusive transitive, egalitarian concept.

Unfortunately, Bennett, Lombard, and Lewis have all muddied the question of whether the counterfactual analysis is adequate by choosing examples where intuitions of the two types just discussed are particularly strong and *seemingly* salient: It's not the *rainfall* that causes the June fire, but rather the lightning; moreover, it's just "good common sense" that heavy rains don't cause fires![4] Of course, while recognizing these points you might still judge these cases to have some intuitive force as counterexamples. Fair enough; they do. But a more careful examination shows how hasty it would be to take any such intuitions as decisive. I'll make the case against Bennett, after which it will be clear enough how to proceed against Lombard and Lewis that we can leave those cases aside.

The idea is to find an event intermediate between the cause and its alleged effect that is *clearly* a cause of the second, and at least plausibly an effect of the first. So observe that among the causes of the June fire is not just the lightning but also the very presence of the forest, filled with flammable material. The presence of the forest in the hours before the lightning strikes is itself an event, or perhaps a collection of events. This event is a cause of the June fire (albeit not a salient cause). What are *its* causes? A typical counterfactual analysis will claim that one of its causes is the April rainfall, since without the rainfall the forest would have been destroyed in May. But we can argue for the plausibility of this claim independently, by noting that the following judgments seem, intuitively, to be correct: It is in part *because of* the April rains that the forest is present in June; any complete *causal explanation* of the forest's presence must cite the role of the April rains in preventing its destruction; the April rains are at least in part *responsible for* the presence of the forest in June.[5]

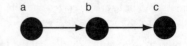

Figure 32.1

One could deny the truth of these judgments, or deny that they show that the April rainfall is a cause of the forest's presence in June, or deny that causation is transitive in the way that is needed to complete the inference to the claim that the April rainfall is among the causes of the June forest fire. But unless one can find some grounds for supporting such denials – grounds independent of the more intuitive implausibility of the claim in question – then this implausibility will fail to provide a particularly compelling reason for giving up the counterfactual analysis. (Exactly parallel points apply to the other two examples.) Happily, I think the conclusions drawn in section 6 clear up what is going on in the rainfall case (and the other cases), precisely by showing that counterfactual analyses utterly fail to capture one important sense of "cause" – production – and that in this sense the April rains are *not* among the causes of the June fire. But it will take some work to get there, and along the way we must not be distracted by the temptations of such bogus "refutations" as those we have just examined. Intuitions about cases must be heeded, to be sure. But not blindly.

Onward. It will help to have a means of representing simple causal structures; accordingly, I will adopt the "neuron" diagrams used by Lewis (1986b).

The diagram in figure 32.1 depicts a pattern of neuron firings. Dark circles represent firing neurons, while arrows represent stimulatory connections between neurons. The order of events is left to right: In figure 32.1 neuron *a* fires, sending a stimulatory signal to neuron *b*, causing it to fire; *b*'s firing in turn sends a stimulatory signal to neuron *c*, causing it to fire. We will also need a way to represent *prevention* of one event by another. So let us add inhibitory connections to the neuron diagrams, represented by a line ending in a solid dot, as shown in figure 32.2. In the left-hand diagram, neurons *a* and *c* fire simultaneously; *c*'s firing causes *d* to fire, which in turn causes *e* to fire. However, thanks to the inhibitory signal from *c*, *a*'s firing does *not* cause *b* to fire; *b*'s failure to fire is represented by leaving its circle unshaded.

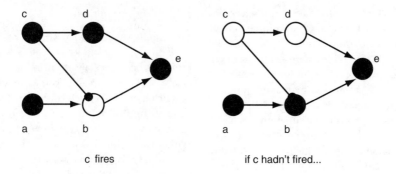

c fires   if c hadn't fired...

Figure 32.2

The right-hand diagram shows what would have happened if *c* had not fired.

Calling these diagrams "neuron diagrams" is merely picturesque; what is important about them is that they can provide, in a readily digestible form, partial representations of many causal structures.

3   The Simple Counterfactual Analysis, and Two Kinds of Overdetermination

3.1   The simple analysis

Both for simplicity and to avoid needless controversies, I will focus only on the counterfactual analysis as it applies to worlds with *deterministic* laws that permit neither backwards causation nor action at a temporal distance (although the lessons of the paper apply much more generally, as far as I can see). I will also leave aside cases, if such there be, where a cause is simultaneous with one of its effects.

Here and throughout I will denote events by lower-case italicized letters "*a*," "*b*," "*c*," and so forth; the proposition that an event *e* occurs by "*Oe*"; and the counterfactual or subjunctive conditional by "□→" (read: "were it the case that … then it would be the case that …").[6] The simple analysis is as follows:

Event *c* is a cause of event *e* iff

(i)   *c* and *e* are wholly distinct events;
(ii) Oc, Oe, and $\neg Oc \,\square\!\!\rightarrow \neg Oe$ are all true.

An immediate problem arises, whose solution requires the counterfactual conditional to be understood in a rather specific way. In figure 32.1, it is certainly correct to say that if *a* hadn't fired, *c* wouldn't have; but it may also be correct to say that if *c* hadn't fired, *a* wouldn't have. (If you don't like the sound of that, try the happier locution: If *c* hadn't fired, it would have to have been that *a* didn't fire.) If so, the analysis wrongly says that *c* is a cause of *a*. (Note the harmless but convenient ambiguity: Letters sometimes refer to events, sometimes to neurons.)

Two responses seem possible. We could augment the analysis by adding some third condition to guarantee the asymmetry of causation (for example: causes must precede their effects). Or we could deny the truth of the offending counterfactual, appealing to an account of the conditional that secured the falsehood of all such "backtrackers" (to use Lewis's apt term: see his 1979). Swain (1978), for example, opts for the first alternative, Lewis (1979 and 1986a) (and most other counterfactual analysts) for the second.[7]

The first response doesn't work, partly for reasons that have been well explored and that I won't rehearse in detail here (e.g., merely adding the requirement that causes precede their effects won't help if, say, *c* and *e* are joint effects of some event *a*, with *c* occurring before *e*; for we could still reason that if *c* hadn't happened, it would have to have been that *a* didn't happen, and therefore that *e* didn't happen). A different, often unnoticed reason for rejecting the first response deserves some discussion, however: The problem is that this response implicitly supposes that backtrackers threaten only the *sufficiency* of the above analysis. If that were true, it would make sense to add further conditions, so as to make the analysis less liberal. But backtrackers also undermine its *necessity*, as figure 32.2 shows.

In figure 32.2, d is, clearly, a cause of e. But if, in evaluating counterfactuals with the antecedent "d does not occur," we proceed by making minimal alterations to the past events that led to d, then we will reach a counterfactual situation in which c does not occur, but a still does – that is, a counterfactual situation in which e occurs. That is, if we allow as true the backtracker $\neg Od \;\square\!\!\rightarrow\; \neg Oc$, then the right-hand diagram *also* describes what would have happened if d hadn't fired, and so the conditional $\neg Od \;\square\!\!\rightarrow\; \neg Oe$ is false. Then how can it be that d turns out to be a cause of e? Adding *extra* conditions to (i) and (ii) provides no answer.[8] (Nor will it help to liberalize the analysis in the standard way, by taking causation to be the *ancestral* of counterfactual dependence. For the problem that threatens the connection between e and d will equally threaten the connection between e and any event that mediates between d and e.)

In short, reading the counterfactual in a backtracking manner destroys the dependence of e on d. That's not only trouble for the simple analysis: It's just wrong, since it manifestly *is* the case that if d hadn't fired, e wouldn't have. Or, more cautiously, there manifestly *is* an acceptable reading of the counterfactual conditional according to which this is true. I will henceforth take it for granted that both the simple analysis and its more elaborate kin employ such a "nonbacktracking" reading of the conditional.

It is not obvious how to provide a general semantics for the counterfactual that will secure this reading. Fortunately, for the purposes of this paper we need only come up with a rule for evaluating counterfactuals of the form $\neg Oc \;\square\!\!\rightarrow\; \neg Oe$, where c and e both occur, and c precedes e. Following Maudlin (2007), I suggest the following: Letting t be the time of occurrence of the given event c, we evaluate the conditional $\neg Oc \;\square\!\!\rightarrow\; \neg Oe$ by altering the state of the world at t just enough to make the antecedent true, evolving that state forward in time in accordance with the (actual) laws, and seeing whether the consequent comes out true.[9] So, in figure 32.2, if d hadn't fired, circumstances contemporaneous with its firing such as the nonfiring of b would have been unchanged, and so e would not have fired.

3.2 Early preemption

The simple analysis may appear quite able to stave off challenges to its *sufficiency*. But obvious problems beset its claim to necessity. Consider a case of ordinary preemption, as in figure 32.2. The firing of e is overdetermined by the simultaneous firings of a and c. But not in a way that leaves us at all uncertain as to what causes what: Without question, c (and not a) is a cause of e, even though if c hadn't occurred, e would have occurred anyway, thanks to an alternative process, beginning with a, that c preempts.

There is an obvious strategy for handling this kind of case. First, we liberalize our analysis, by taking causation to be the *ancestral* of counterfactual dependence: c is a cause of e iff there are events $d_1, ..., d_n$ such that d_1 counterfactually depends on c, d_2 depends on d_1, ..., and e depends on d_n. Next, we look for an event d (or sequence of events) intermediate between the preventing cause c and the effect e, such that e depends on d and likewise d on c. The strategy works handily in the case before us (provided, once again, that we are careful *not* to interpret the counterfactual in a "backtracking" sense, according to which, had d not fired, it would have to have been the case that c didn't fire, and so b would have fired, and so e would still have fired).

Observe how natural this embellishment to the simple analysis is – and observe that it gives a central role to the *Transitivity* thesis.

3.3 Late preemption

Other, quite ordinary cases of overdetermination require a different treatment. Consider a case of so-called late preemption, as in figure 32.3. Neurons a and c fire simultaneously, so that e fires at the same time as b; the inhibitory signal from e therefore prevents d from firing. If c hadn't fired, e still would have; for in that case d would not have been prevented from firing and so would have stimulated e to fire. Likewise for *every* event in the causal chain leading from c to e: If that event had not occurred, e would nevertheless have fired. So the strategy of finding suitable intermediates breaks down; for it to succeed, e would have to depend on at least *one* event in the chain leading back to c, and it does not.

Here is another example, with a slightly different structure; it illustrates how absolutely

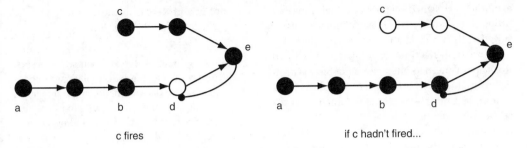

Figure 32.3

mundane these cases are. Suzy and Billy, expert rock-throwers, are engaged in a competition to see who can shatter a target bottle first. They both pick up rocks and throw them at the bottle, but Suzy throws hers a split second before Billy. Consequently Suzy's rock gets there first, shattering the bottle. Since both throws are perfectly accurate, Billy's would have shattered the bottle if Suzy's had not occurred, so the shattering is overdetermined.

Suzy's throw is a cause of the shattering, but Billy's is not. Indeed, every one of the events that constitute the trajectory of Suzy's rock on its way to the bottle is a cause of the shattering. But the shattering depends on none of these events, since had any of them not occurred the bottle would have shattered anyway, thanks to Billy's expert throw. So the transitivity strategy fails.

Three alternative strategies for dealing with this kind of case suggest themselves. The first rests on the observation that Suzy's throw makes a difference to the time and manner of the shattering, whereas Billy's does not. The second rests on the observation that Suzy's throw is connected to the shattering by a spatiotemporally continuous chain of causal intermediates, whereas Billy's is not. And the third rests on the observation that there is a sequence of events connecting Suzy's throw to the shattering that has the right sort of *intrinsic* character to count as a causal sequence, whereas no such sequence connects Billy's throw to the shattering. Let us consider these strategies in turn.

There are various ways to implement the first strategy. For example, we could deny that the effect that does the preventing is numerically the same as the effect that would have occurred via the alternative process. (e.g., in figure 32.3, the

firing of e that *would have* occurred, had c not fired, is not the same event as the firing that *actually* occurs.) If so, then our two examples *do* exhibit the needed pattern of counterfactual dependence, since the effect that actually occurred would not have occurred without its cause (although a very similar event would have occurred in its place). Alternatively, we could remain silent about the individuation of events, and simply employ a slightly different counterfactual in the analysis – say, by counting c a cause of e if and only if, had c not occurred, e would not have occurred at the time it *actually* did (Paul 1998). Lewis (2000) argues that we should count c a cause of e if there is a suitable pattern of counterfactual dependence between various different ways c or something like it might have occurred and correspondingly different ways in which e or something like it might have occurred. (Lewis proposes taking causation itself to be the ancestral of this relation.)

These approaches are uniformly nonstarters. Never mind the well-known problems (e.g., that noncauses can easily make a difference to the time and manner of an event's occurrence – a gust of wind that alters the course of Suzy's rock ever so slightly, for example). What seems to have gone unnoticed is that it is not at all essential to examples of late preemption that the genuine cause make *any* difference to the time or manner of the effect. As Steve Yablo pointed out to me, it's easy enough to construct cases in which c is clearly a cause of e, but in which neither c nor any event causally intermediate between it and e makes the slightest difference to the way e occurs. Yablo observes that we can simply alter the story of Billy and Suzy. This time, Billy throws a Smart Rock, equipped with an onboard computer, exquisitely designed sensors, a lightning-fast propulsion system – and instructions to make sure that the bottle shatters in exactly the way it does, at exactly the time it does. In fact, the Smart Rock doesn't need to intervene, since Suzy's throw is just right. But had it been any different – indeed, had her rock's trajectory differed in the slightest, at any point – the Smart Rock would have swooped in to make sure the job was done properly. Sure, the example is bizarre. But not in a way that matters in the slightest to the evaluation of the causal status of Suzy's throw: Smart Rock notwithstanding, her throw is *still* a cause of the shattering – even though neither it nor any event that mediates between it and the shattering makes a difference to the time or manner of that shattering.

I won't consider these approaches further. It will be far more instructive for us to focus on the two alternative strategies.

Suzy's throw is spatiotemporally connected to the shattering in the right way, but Billy's is not. So perhaps we should add the *Locality* thesis as a constraint on the analysis: Causes have to be connected to their effects via spatiotemporally continuous sequences of causal intermediates. Now, on the face of it this is a step in entirely the *wrong* direction, since it makes the *analysans* more stringent. But if we simultaneously liberalize the analysis in other respects, this strategy might work. For example, we might say that *c* is a cause of *e* just in case there is a spatiotemporally continuous sequence of events connecting *c* with *e* and a (possibly empty) set *S* of events contemporaneous with *c* such that each later event in the sequence (including *e*) depends on each earlier event – or at least *would have*, had the events in *S* not occurred. That will distinguish Suzy's throw as a cause, and Billy's as a noncause.

Of course, since action at a distance is surely *possible*, and so *Locality* at best a highly interesting contingent truth, this amended counterfactual analysis lacks generality. But it is patently general enough to be of value. At any rate, it is not so important for our purposes whether this strategy, or some variant, can handle all cases of late preemption. What is important is that it is a plausible and natural strategy to pursue – and it gives a central role to the *Locality* thesis.

Lewis has proposed a third, different strategy. He begins with the intuition that the causal structure of a process is intrinsic to it (given the laws). As he puts it (1986b, p. 205):

> Suppose we have processes – courses of events, which may or may not be causally connected – going on in two distinct spatiotemporal regions, regions of the same or of different possible worlds. Disregarding the surroundings of the two regions, and disregarding any irrelevant events that may be occurring in either region without being part of the process in question, what goes on in the two regions is exactly alike. Suppose further that the laws of nature that govern the two regions are exactly the same. Then can it be that we have a causal process in one of the regions but not the other? It seems not. Intuitively, whether the process going on in a region is causal depends only on the intrinsic character of the process itself, and on the relevant laws. The surroundings, and even other events in the region, are irrelevant.

In cases of late preemption, the process connecting cause to effect does not exhibit the right pattern of dependence – but only because of accidental features of its surroundings. The process that begins with Suzy's throw and ends with a shattered bottle does not exhibit the right pattern of dependence (thanks to Billy's throw), but it is intrinsically just like other possible processes that do (namely, processes taking place in surroundings that lack Billy, or a counterpart of him). Lewis suggests, in effect, that *for that reason* Suzy's throw should count as a cause.

Clearly, Lewis is trying to parlay something like the *Intrinsicness* thesis into an amended counterfactual analysis, one adequate to handle cases of late preemption. Now, I think there are serious problems with the details of Lewis's own approach (spelled out in the passage following that just quoted), but since that way lies trench warfare, I won't go into them. I do, however, want to take issue with his statement of the *Intrinsicness* thesis, which is too vague to be of real use. What, after all, is a "process" or "course of events"? If it is just any old sequence of events, then what he says is obviously false: We might have a sequence consisting of the lighting of a fuse, and an explosion – but whether the one is a cause of the other is not determined by the intrinsic character of this two-event "process," since it obviously matters whether *this* fuse was connected to *that* exploding bomb.

I will simply give what I think is the right statement of the *Intrinsicness* thesis, one that eschews undefined talk of "processes."[10] Suppose an event *e* occurs at some time *t′*. Then consider the structure of events that consists of *e*, together with all of its causes back to some arbitrary earlier time *t*. That structure has a certain intrinsic character, determined by the way the constituent events happen, together with their spatiotemporal relations to one another. It also has a certain causal character: In particular, each of the constituent events is a cause of *e* (except *e* itself, of course). Then the *Intrinsicness* thesis states that any possible structure of events that exists in a world with the same laws, and that has the same intrinsic character as our given structure, *also* duplicates this aspect of its causal character – that is, each duplicate of one of *e*'s causes is itself a cause of the *e*-duplicate.[11]

Three observations: First, "same intrinsic character" can be read in a very strict sense, according to which the two structures of events must be *perfect* duplicates. Read this way, I think the *Intrinsicness* thesis is close to incontrovertible. But it can also be read in a less strict sense, according to which the two structures must be, in some sense, sufficiently *similar* in their intrinsic characters. Read this way, the thesis is stronger but still highly plausible. Consider again the case of Billy and Suzy, and compare the situation in which Billy throws his rock with the situation in which he doesn't. Clearly, there is a strong intuition that the causal features of the sequence of events beginning with Suzy's throw and ending in the shattering should be the *same* in each case, precisely *because* Billy's throw is extrinsic to this sequence. But it is too much to hope for that the corresponding sequences, in each situation, be *perfect* duplicates; after all, the gravitational effects of Billy's rock, in the situation where he throws, will make minute differences to the exact trajectory of Suzy's rock, and so on. So if it is the *Intrinsicness* thesis that gives voice to our conviction that, from the standpoint of Suzy's throw, the two situations must be treated alike, then we should read the "same intrinsic character" clause in that thesis in the less stringent way.

Doing so quite obviously leaves us with the burden of explaining what near-but-not-quite-perfect duplication of intrinsic character consists in. I won't try to unload that burden here. It will emerge that for my *main* purposes, that doesn't matter, since in order to use the *Intrinsicness* thesis to argue that dependence and production are two distinct kinds of causation, I can read "same intrinsic character" in the more stringent sense. (Alas, we will also see [in sec. 7, not in this selection] that my own preferred *analysis* of production will require the less stringent reading. For extensive discussion of these and other issues involving *Intrinsicness*, see Hall 2002.)

The second observation to make about the *Intrinsicness* thesis is that it is somewhat limited in scope: it does not apply, in general, to situations in which there is causation at a temporal distance, or to situations in which there is backward causation. Roughly, the problem is that the relevant structure of events must be *complete* in a certain respect, consisting in a complete set of joint causes of the given effect *e*, together with all those events that mediate between these causes and *e*. I won't go into the reasons why it must exhibit this kind of completeness (but see Hall 2002). But consider a case where the effect takes place at one o'clock, and we have collected together all of its causes that occur at noon, as well as those that occur between noon and one. If there is action at a temporal distance, then some of the other causes with which the noon causes combine to bring about the effect might have occurred *before* noon, in which case our structure won't be sufficiently complete. If there is backward causation, then some of the events that mediate between the noon causes and the effect might occur *outside* the given interval, in which case our structure won't be sufficiently complete. Either way, there is trouble. It is partly in order to finesse this trouble that I have limited my focus by ignoring both backward causation and causation at a temporal distance.

The third observation to make about the *Intrinsicness* thesis is that we must assume – on pain of rendering the thesis trivially false – that the structure of events against which we compare a given structure includes no *omissions*. Let the structure *S* consist of *e*, together with all of its causes back to some arbitrary earlier time *t*. And let the structure *S′* simply consist of *S*, together with some arbitrary omission that "occurs" at some point in the relevant interval. Plausibly, this omission will contribute nothing to the intrinsic character of S' – for it simply consists in the *failure* of some type of genuine event to occur. So S' will perfectly match S. If we apply the *Intrinsicness* thesis uncritically, we immediately get the absurd result that the added omission – whatever it is – counts as a cause of e. Now, it was already fairly clear that whatever the guiding intuition is behind the *Intrinsicness* thesis, it does not concern omissions. This result confirms the suspicion. So the final clause of the *Intrinsicness* thesis should read: "… any possible structure of *genuine* events (not including any omissions) that exists in a world with the same laws, and that has the same intrinsic character as our given structure, *also* duplicates.…" (It doesn't follow that S – the structure picked out as consisting of e, together with all of its causes back to some earlier time t – must include no omissions. We'll take up the question of whether it can in sec. 5, below.)

Perhaps the counterfactual analyst can use the *Intrinsicness* thesis to handle the problem of Billy and Suzy. After all, in the alternative circumstances in which Billy's throw is absent, it seems correct to say that the causal history of the shattering (back to the time of Suzy's throw) consists exactly of those events on which it depends. What's more, this structure matches a structure that takes place in the actual circumstances, where Billy's throw confounds the counterfactual relations; Suzy's throw, being a part of this structure, will therefore count as a cause of the shattering, thanks to the *Intrinsicness* thesis. To be sure, this is no more than a suggestion of a revised analysis. But again, what is important is that it is a plausible and natural suggestion to pursue – and it gives a central role to the *Intrinsicness* thesis.

4   Double Prevention

And now for something completely different: a kind of example that spells trouble for the *sufficiency* of the simple analysis, by showing that the cornerstone thesis of *Dependence* runs headlong into conflict with each of *Transitivity*, *Locality*, and *Intrinsicness*.

4.1   Example

Suzy and Billy have grown up, just in time to get involved in World War III. Suzy is piloting a bomber on a mission to blow up an enemy target, and Billy is piloting a fighter as her lone escort. Along comes an enemy fighter plane, piloted by Enemy. Sharp-eyed Billy spots Enemy, zooms in, pulls the trigger, and Enemy's plane goes down in flames. Suzy's mission is undisturbed, and the bombing takes place as planned. If Billy hadn't pulled the trigger, Enemy would have eluded him and shot down Suzy, and the bombing would not have happened.

This is a case of what I call "double prevention": one event (Billy's pulling the trigger) prevents another (Enemy's shooting down Suzy), which had it occurred would have prevented yet another (the bombing). The salient causal structure is depicted in figure 32.4. Neurons a, b, and c all fire simultaneously. The firing of c prevents e from firing; if e had fired, it would have caused f to fire, which in turn would have prevented g from firing. Thus, if c had not fired, g would not have. So c is a cause of g: Billy's pulling the trigger is a cause of the bombing.

This consequence of the counterfactual analysis might seem natural enough. After all, wouldn't we give Billy part of the credit for the success of the mission? Isn't Billy's action part of the explanation for that success? And so on. On the other hand, it might seem quite unnatural – for the scuffle between Billy and Enemy takes place, let us suppose, hundreds of miles away from Suzy, in such a way that not only is she completely oblivious to it, but it has absolutely no effect on her whatsoever. Here she is, in one region, flying her plane on the way to her bombing mission. Here Billy and Enemy are, in an entirely separate region, acting out their fateful drama. Intuitively, it seems entirely unexceptionable to claim that the events in the second region have no causal connection to the events in the first – for isn't it plain that no *physical* connection unites them?

So far, it might seem that we have a stalemate: two contrary intuitions about the case, with no way to decide between them. (Indeed, my informal polling suggests that intuitive judgments vary quite a lot.) Not so: Both the judgment that we have a case of causation here, and the thesis of *Dependence* that endorses this judgment, run into trouble with each of the theses of *Locality*, *Intrinsicness*, and *Transitivity*.

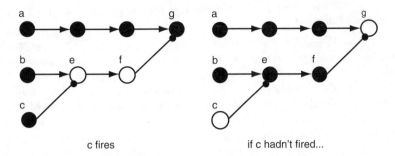

c fires   if c hadn't fired...

Figure 32.4

4.2 Problems with Locality

We all know what action at a distance is: We have a case of it if we have a cause, at least one of whose effects is not connected to it via any spatiotemporally continuous causal chain.[12] I take it that action at a distance is possible, but that its manifestation in a world is nevertheless a highly nontrivial fact about that world. Yet if Billy's action counts as a cause of the bombing, then the quite ordinary and mundane relationship it bears to the bombing also counts as a case of action at a distance. Worse: It counts as a case of action at a *temporal* distance – something that one might reasonably argue is *not* possible, and at any rate something for which one will search the history of physics in vain for precedent. Is *this* all it takes to achieve such non-locality? (And to think that philosophers have been fussing over Bell's inequalities!) If so, we would be hard pressed to describe laws that *didn't* permit action at a (temporal) distance. For example, even the classical laws that describe perfectly elastic collisions would have to be judged nonlocal, since they permit situations in which one collision prevents a second, which, had it happened, would have prevented a third – so that we have dependence of the third collision on the first, but no connecting sequence of causal intermediates. In short, it appears that while *Dependence* doesn't *quite* contradict *Locality*, it renders it satisfiable only by the most trivial laws (e.g., laws that say that nothing ever changes). That's wrong: The distinction between laws that do and laws that don't permit action at a distance is interesting; to assimilate it to the all-but-vacuous distinction between laws that do and laws that don't permit double prevention is a mistake.

A remarkably frequent but entirely unsatisfactory response is the following: Billy's action *is* connected to the bombing via a spatiotemporally continuous causal chain – it's just that this chain consists, in part, of *omissions* (namely, the various failures of Enemy to do what he would have done, had Billy not fired). Now, it's not just that such reliance on causation by omission is desperate on its face. It's that even if we grant that these omissions exist and are located where the events omitted would have occurred (a nontrivial supposition: right now I am at home, and hence fail to be in my office; is this omission located there or here?), it doesn't help. For there is no reason to believe that the region of spacetime these omissions occupy intersects the region of spacetime that Suzy and her bomber *actually* occupy; to hold otherwise is just to mistake *this* region with the region she *would have* occupied, had Billy not fired. We can agree that had Billy not fired, then the Enemy-region would have intersected the Suzy-region; but if, say, Suzy would have swerved under those circumstances, then it's just false to suppose that this counterfactual Enemy-region (= the *actual* omission-of-Enemy-region) intersects the *actual* Suzy-region.

Of course, the debate can take various twists and turns from here: There are further stratagems one might resort to in an effort to interpolate a sequence of omissions between Billy and the bombing; alternatively, one might deny that causation without a connecting sequence of causal intermediates really *is* sufficient for action at a distance. It won't profit us to pursue these twists and turns (but see Hall 2000); suffice it to say that the stratagems fail, and the prospects for a replacement for the sufficient condition seem hopeless.

4.3   Problems with Intrinsicness

Let's first recall what the *Intrinsicness* thesis says, in its careful formulation: Suppose an event *e* occurs at some time *t'*. Consider the structure of events *S* that consists of *e*, together with all of its causes back to some arbitrary earlier time *t*. Then any possible structure of events that exists in a world with the same laws, and that has the same intrinsic character as *S*, *also* has the same causal character, at least with respect to the causal generation of *e*.

For the purposes of this section, we can read "has the same intrinsic character as" as "perfectly duplicates" – we won't need to compare structures of events that exhibit near-but-not-quite-perfect match of intrinsic character.

Now for some more detail. When Billy shot him down, Enemy was waiting for his home base – hundreds of miles away – to radio him instructions. At that moment, Enemy had no particular intention of going after Suzy; he was just minding his own business. Still, if Billy hadn't pulled the trigger, then Enemy would have eluded him, and moments later would have received instructions to shoot down the nearest suitable target (Suzy, as it happens). He would then have done so. But Billy does shoot him down, so he never receives the instructions. In fact, the home base doesn't even bother to send them, since it has been monitoring Enemy's transmissions and knows that he has been shot down.

Focus on the causal history of the bombing, back to the time of Billy's action. There is, of course, the process consisting of Suzy flying her plane, and so on (and, less conspicuously, the process consisting in the persistence of the target). If *Dependence* is true, then the causal history must also include Billy's action and its immediate effects: the bullets flying out of his gun, their impact with Enemy's fuselage, the subsequent explosion. (Perhaps we should also throw in some omissions: the failure of Enemy to do what he would have done, had he somehow eluded Billy. It makes no difference, since their contribution to the *intrinsic character* of the resulting causal history is nil.) Let this structure of events be *S*.

Two problems now emerge. In the first place, the intrinsic character of *S* fails to determine, together with the laws, that there are no *other* factors that would (i) stop Enemy, if Billy somehow failed to; (ii) do so in a way that would reverse the intuitive verdict (such as it is) that Billy's action is a cause of the bombing. Suppose, for instance, that we change the example by adding a bomb under Enemy's seat, which would have gone off seconds after the time at which Billy fired. And suppose that within this changed example, we can find a duplicate of *S* – in which case the specification of the intrinsic character of *S* must leave out the presence of the bomb. That shows (what was, perhaps, apparent already) that the dependence of the bombing on Billy's action is a fact *extrinsic* to *S*. If we decide that in this changed example, Billy's action is *not* a cause of the bombing (since, thanks to the bomb under Enemy's seat, he in fact poses no threat to Suzy), then we must either give up the *Intrinsicness* thesis, or grant that the causal history of the bombing (back to the time of Billy's action) wasn't described completely by *S*. Neither option is attractive. Let us call this the problem of the *extrinsic absence of disabling factors* (disabling in the sense that if they were present, there would be no dependence of the bombing on Billy's action).

Much more serious is the problem of the extrinsic *presence* of *enabling* factors (enabling in the sense that if they were absent, there would be no dependence of the bombing on Billy's action). For consider a third case, exactly like the first except in the following critical respect: The home base has no intentions of sending Enemy orders to shoot anyone down. In fact, if Billy hadn't pulled the trigger, then the instructions from the home base would have been for Enemy to return immediately. So Enemy poses no threat whatsoever to Suzy. Hence Billy's action is *not* a cause of the bombing. Yet the structure of events *S* is duplicated *exactly* in this scenario. So if the *Intrinsicness* thesis is right, then that causal history *S* must not in fact have been *complete*; we must have mistakenly excluded some events for which the third scenario contains no duplicates. Presumably, these events will be the ones that constitute the monitoring of Enemy by his home base, together with the intentions of his superiors to order him to shoot down the nearest appropriate target.

But now we are forced to say that these events count as *causes* of the bombing. That is ridiculous. It is not that they have *no* connection to the bombing, it's just that their connection is much

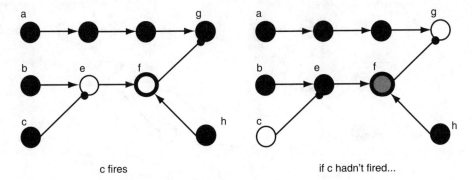

c fires   if c hadn't fired...

Figure 32.5

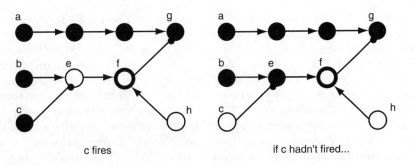

c fires   if c hadn't fired...

Figure 32.6

more oblique: All we can say is that if they hadn't happened, then the bombing would not have depended on Billy's action. And notice, finally, that it is exactly the inclusion of Billy's action as part of the causal history *S* that is the culprit: Once we include it, we must also include (on pain of denying *Intrinsicness*) all those events whose occurrence is required to secure the counterfactual dependence of the bombing on this action.

To see this problem more vividly, compare the events depicted in figures 32.5 and 32.6. Here, *f* is a stubborn neuron, needing two stimulatory signals in order to fire. Neuron *h*, in figure 32.5, fires shortly after the time at which neurons *a*, *b*, and *c* all fire (so I have abused the usual left-to-right conventions slightly). In the left-hand diagram of figure 32.5, *g* depends on *c*, but in figure 32.6 it does not; indeed, it would be quite ridiculous to claim, about the left-hand diagram of figure 32.6, that *c* was in *any* sense a cause of *g*.

But now consider the causal history of *g*, in the left-hand diagram of figure 32.5, and suppose that – in keeping with *Dependence* – we count *c* as

part of this causal history. Then it would seem that this causal history is duplicated *exactly* in the left-hand diagram of figure 32.6 – in which case either *Intrinsicness* is false, or *c* in figure 32.6 is, after all, a cause of *g*. The only way out of this dilemma is to deny *Dependence* – or else to insist, against all good sense, that the causal history of *g*, in figure 32.5, *also* includes the firing of *h* (which is not duplicated in figure 32.6). But of course it does not: In figure 32.5, the firing of *h* is necessary, in order for *g* to depend on *c*; but that does not make it one of *g*'s causes.

4.4   Problems with Transitivity

A more striking problem appears when we focus on the transitivity of causation. I begin by adding yet more detail to the example.

Early in the morning on the day of the bombing, Enemy's alarm clock goes off. A good thing, too: if it hadn't he never would have woken up in time to go on his patrolling mission. Indeed, if has alarm clock hadn't gone off, Enemy would

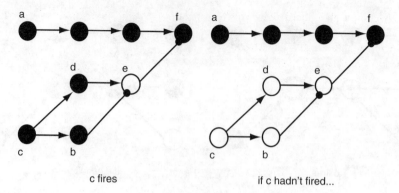

Figure 32.7

have been nowhere near the scene at which he was shot down. It follows that if Enemy's alarm clock hadn't gone off, then Billy would not have pulled the trigger. But it is also true that if Billy hadn't pulled the trigger, then the bombing would never have taken place. By transitivity, this ringing is one of the causes of the bombing.

Figure 32.7 helps to reinforce the absurdity of this conclusion. Neuron *e* can never fire. If *c* does not fire, then *e* won't get stimulated by *d*, whereas if *c* *does* fire, then the stimulation from *d* will be blocked by the inhibitory signal from *b*. So *e* poses no threat whatsoever to the firing of *f*. The little four-neuron network that culminates in *e* is, from the standpoint of *f*, totally inert.

Clearly, *c*'s firing cannot be a cause of *f*'s firing. At most, we might characterize *c*'s firing as something which *threatens to prevent f*'s firing, by way of the *c-d-e* connection – with the threat blocked by the *c-b-e* connection. Yet if both *Dependence* and *Transitivity* are correct, then *c*'s firing *is* a cause of *f*'s firing. For if *c* hadn't fired, then *b* would not have fired. Likewise, if *b* had not fired, then *f* would not have fired (recall here that backtracking is forbidden: We cannot say that if *b* had not fired, then it would have been that *c* didn't fire, and so *f* would have fired all the same). Since *f* depends on *b*, and *b* depends on *c*, it follows from *Dependence* and *Transitivity* that *c*'s firing is a cause of *f*'s firing. That consequence is unacceptable.

Certain examples with this structure border on the comic. Billy spies Suzy about to throw a rock at a window. He rushes to stop her, knowing that as usual he's going to take the blame for her act of vandalism. Unfortunately for him, he trips over a

tree-root, and Suzy, quite oblivious to his presence, goes ahead and breaks the window. If he hadn't tripped, he would have stopped her – so the breaking depends on the tripping. But if he hadn't *set out* to stop her, he wouldn't have tripped – so, by the combination of *Transitivity* and *Dependence*, he has helped cause the breaking after all, merely by setting out to stop it! That conclusion is, of course, just silly.[13]

Conclusion: If the thesis of *Dependence* is true, then each of *Locality*, *Intrinsicness*, and *Transitivity* is false. More precisely, if *Dependence* is true at a world, and the events in that world exhibit a causal structure rich enough to provide even one case of double prevention like each of the ones we have been examining, then each of *Locality*, *Intrinsicness*, and *Transitivity* is false at that world. In the next section, we'll see that an exactly parallel conclusion can be drawn with respect to the thesis that omissions can be causes and effects.

5 Omissions

The thesis of *Omissions* brings in its wake a number of difficult questions of ontology: Does it imply a commitment to a peculiar kind of "event" whose occurrence conditions essentially involve the *failure* of some ordinary type of event to occur? Does it make sense to speak of "the failure of *c* to occur," where "*c*" is supposed to refer to some ordinary event? (For perhaps such singular reference to nonactual events is impossible; alternatively, perhaps it is possible, but the circumstances in which we want to cite some omission as a cause or effect typically underdetermine which ordinary event is "omitted.") Do omissions have locations in space and time? If so, what determines these locations? (Recall the remarks in sec. 4.2: Right now I am at home and hence fail to be in my office; is this omission located there or here?) And so on. I am simply going to gloss over all of these issues and assume that a counterfactual supposition of the form "omission o does not occur" is equivalent to the supposition that some ordinary event of a given type C *does* occur (at, perhaps, a specific place and time) – where the type in question will be fixed, somehow, by the specification of o (or perhaps by context, or perhaps by both). At any rate, however justified complaints about the ontological status of omissions might be, they are emphatically not what is at issue, as we're about to see.

In what follows, I'll make the case that examples of causation *by* omission routinely violate each of *Locality* and *Intrinsicness*. The techniques I employ can be adapted so straightforwardly to make the same points about prevention (i.e., causation *of* omission) that we can safely leave those cases aside. Displaying the conflict between *Omissions* and *Transitivity* will require a case in which we treat an omission as an effect of one event and as a cause of another.

Finally, I am also going to gloss over the remarkably tricky question of when, exactly, we *have* a case of causation by or of omission – a question to which the thesis of *Omissions* only gives the vague answer, "sometimes." For example, is it enough to have causation of e by the failure of an event of type C to occur for e to counterfactually depend on this omission? Or must further constraints be satisfied? If not – if dependence is all that is required – we get such unwelcome results as that my act of typing has among its causes a quite astonishing multitude of omissions: the failure of a meteorite to strike our house moments ago, the failure of the President to walk in and interrupt me, and so on. If, on the other hand, we insist that mere dependence is not enough for causation by omission, then we face the unenviable task of trying to characterize the further constraints. I'm going to sidestep these issues by picking cases that are uncontroversial examples of causation by omission – uncontroversial, that is, on the assumption that there are *any* such cases.

5.1   Problems with Locality

We can draw on the story of Suzy, Billy, and Enemy to show that, even if we waive worries about whether omissions have determinate locations, *Locality* fails for typical cases of causation by omission. Focus on a time t at which Enemy would have been approaching Suzy to shoot her down, had he not been shot down himself. Had Enemy not been absent, Suzy's mission would have failed; so the bombing depends on, as we might put it, the omission of Enemy's attack. More than this: The omission of Enemy's attack is among the *causes* of the bombing – at least, if there is to be causation by omission *at all,* this case should certainly be an example. But once again, it appears that the connection between this omission and the bombing must also qualify as a case of action at a distance, for no spatiotemporally continuous sequence of causal intermediates connects the two events. As before, the problem is not with finding a suitable location for the omission; it is rather that nothing guarantees that the sequence of omissions that proceeds from it (Enemy's failure to approach, pull the trigger, etc.) will intersect Suzy's *actual* flight. We can grant that the region of spacetime in which these omissions "take place" intersects the region she *would have* occupied, had Enemy not been absent. But to suppose that this region is the same as the region she *actually* occupies is to commit the same mistake as before.

5.2   Problems with Intrinsicness

Whatever omissions are, they are notably lacking in intrinsic character. We already saw that, for this reason, the *Intrinsicness* thesis needed to be phrased rather carefully: When we have picked out an event e and a structure of events S comprising e and all causes of e back to some earlier time, it is to be understood that any structure against which we compare S is composed solely of *genuine* events, not omissions. (On the other hand, no harm comes of letting S include omissions, at least on the assumption that they contribute nothing to its intrinsic character.) Still, it is for all that consistent to hold that *Intrinsicness* applies to causation by omission, as follows: Suppose that e occurs at time t', and that S consists of e and all causes of e back to some earlier time t. Suppose

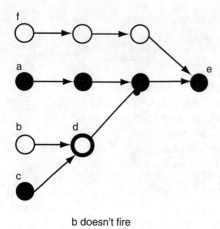

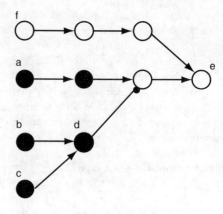

Figure 32.8

further that we count the omission o as one of e's causes, and that o "occurs" (in whatever sense is appropriate for omissions) in the interval between t and t'. Then if structure S' intrinsically matches S, there must be some omission o' "corresponding" to o that causes the event e' in S' that corresponds to e in S (never mind that o' is not *part* of S'). In short, we might think that causation of an event by omission supervenes on the intrinsic character of that event's "positive" causal history.

This conjecture is false. To show why, I'll argue that both of the problems we saw in section 4.3 – the problem of the extrinsic lack of disabling factors and the problem of the extrinsic presence of enabling factors – recur in this context. A simple neuron diagram will serve to illustrate each. In figure 32.8, d is a dull neuron that needs two stimulatory signals in order to fire. Thus, d fails to fire even though stimulated by c; still, since c fires, e's firing depends on the *failure* of b to fire (at, say, time t, which we will take to be the time of a's firing). Note finally that if b had fired and f had as well (at t), then e would have fired all the same.

Let us suppose, in keeping with the *Omissions* thesis, that the failure of b to fire at t is among the causes of e's firing. Let S consist of e, together with all of its (positive) causes back to time t. Then if *Intrinsicness* applies to causation by omission in the way we have suggested, any nomologically possible structure that duplicates S will exhibit the same causal relationships: In particular, there will be an omission that "duplicates" b's failure to

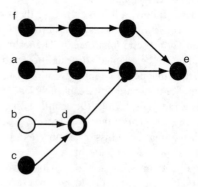

Figure 32.9

fire and that will be a cause of the event that duplicates e's firing. Shown in figure 32.9 is one such possible structure, embedded in slightly different surroundings. And another is shown in figure 32.10, again in different surroundings.

The problem is that in each case, b's failure to fire is no longer a cause of e's firing, *contra* the requirements of our conjecture about how *Intrinsicness* covers causation by omission. In figure 32.9, the firing of f renders b's failure to fire quite irrelevant to whether e fires, showing that when b's failure to fire *is* a cause of e's firing, this is owing in part to the extrinsic absence of disabling factors. Likewise, in figure 32.10, c's failure to fire renders the behavior of b irrelevant, showing that when b's failure to fire is a cause of e's firing, this is owing in part to the extrinsic presence of enabling factors. So the leading idea

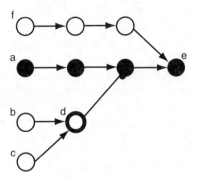

Figure 32.10

behind the *Intrinsicness* thesis – that it is the intrinsic character of some event's causal history that (together with the laws) makes it the case that this *is* its causal history – comes directly into conflict with the *Omissions* thesis.

5.3 Problems with Transitivity

As before, more striking problems emerge when we combine the theses of *Omissions* and *Transitivity*. To see how easy it is to concoct an absurdity from these two ingredients, consider the following variant on our story: This time, Enemy's superiors on the ground had no intention of going after Suzy – until, that is, Billy shoots Enemy down. Outraged by this unprovoked act of aggression, they send out an all-points-bulletin, instructing any available fighter to go after Suzy (a much more valuable target than Billy). Alas, Enemy was the only fighter in the area. Had he somehow been present at the time of the broadcast, he would have received it and promptly targeted and shot down Suzy; his *absence* is thereby a cause of the bombing. But, of course, his absence is itself caused by Billy's action. So by *Transitivity*, we get the result that Billy's action is a cause of the bombing. Lest the details of the case be distracting, let's be clear: *All Billy does is to provoke a threat to the bombing;* luckily for him, the very action that provokes the threat also manages to counteract it. Note the similarity to our earlier "counterexample" to *Transitivity*: Enemy's action (taking off in the morning) both causes a threat to the bombing (by putting Enemy within striking range of Suzy) and counteracts that threat (by likewise putting Enemy within Billy's striking range).

Conclusion: If the thesis of *Omissions* is true, then each of *Locality, Intrinsicness,* and *Transitivity* is false. More precisely, if *Omissions* is true at a world, and the events in that world exhibit a causal structure rich enough to provide cases of the kinds we have just considered, then each of *Locality, Intrinsicness,* and *Transitivity* is false at that world.

6 Diagnosis: Two Concepts of Causation

Here are two opposed reactions one might have to the discussion so far:

Counterfactual dependence is *not* causation. In the first place, it's not (as everyone recognizes) necessary for causation. In the second place, the best attempts to tart it up in such a way as to yield a full-blown analysis of causation rely on the three theses of *Locality, Intrinsicness,* and *Transitivity* – and the lesson of double prevention (a lesson also supported by considering the causal status of omissions) is that these theses *contradict* the claim that dependence is sufficient for causation. The theses are too important; this latter claim must be given up. But give up *Dependency* and you've torn the heart out of counterfactual analyses of causation.

Nonsense; counterfactual dependence *is too* causation. Here we have two wholly distinct events; moreover, if the first had not happened, then the second would not have happened. So we can say – notice how smoothly the words glide off the tongue – that it is in part *because* the first happened that the second happened, that the first event is partly *responsible for* the second event, that the occurrence of the first event helps to *explain why* the second event happened, and so on. Nor do we reverse these verdicts when we discover that the dependence arises by way of double prevention; that seems quite irrelevant. All of these locutions are *causal* locutions, and their appropriateness can, quite clearly, be justified by the claim that the second event depends counterfactually on the first event. So how could this relation fail to be causal? To be sure, it's another question whether we can use it to construct a full-blown analysis of causation, but at the very least we have the result that counterfactual dependence (between wholly distinct events) is *sufficient* for causation – which is just to say that *Dependence* is true.

The claims of both of the foregoing paragraphs are correct, but not by making a contradiction true: Rather, what is meant by "causation" in each case is *different*. Counterfactual dependence is causation in one sense: But in *that* sense of "cause," *Transitivity, Locality*, and *Intrinsicness* are all false. Still, they are not false *simpliciter*; for there is a *different* concept of causation – the one I call "production" – that renders them true. Thus, what we have in the standard cases of over-determination we reviewed in section 3 are not merely counterexamples to some hopeless attempt at an analysis of causation, but cases that reveal one way the concepts of dependence and production can come apart: These cases uniformly exhibit production without dependence. What we have in the cases of double prevention and causation by omission we examined in sections 4 and 5 are not merely more nails in the coffin of the counterfactual analysis, but cases that reveal the other way the two causal concepts can come apart: These cases uniformly exhibit dependence without production. Similarly, we can now diagnose the intuitions Bennett is pumping in his April rains/June forest fire case. For while there is a sense in which the rains *do* cause the fire – the fire clearly depends on the rains – there is an equally good sense in which they don't – the rains do not help to produce the fire. That is because (surprise!) we have here a case of double prevention: The rains prevent an event (fire in May) that, had it occurred, would have prevented the June fires (by destroying the flammable material).

The principal virtues of my claim are thus clear: It allows us to maintain each of the five theses. It provides us with a natural and compelling diagnosis of the most important problem cases for analyses of causation. And it should come as no surprise that the distinction between production and dependence has gone unnoticed, for *typically* the two relations coincide (more exactly, I think production typically coincides with the ancestral of dependence).

An additional virtue of the position, perhaps less obvious than the foregoing ones, concerns the ontological status of omissions. Those who endorse the *Omissions* thesis might worry that they are thereby committed to the existence of a special sort of event – as if the truth of "the failure of an event of type *C* to occur caused *e* to occur" required the existence of something that answered to the description, "failure of an event of type *C* to occur." But if the only sense in which omissions can cause and be caused is that they can enter into relations of counterfactual dependence, then this worry is quite misplaced. For talk of causation by and of omissions turns out to be nothing more than a way of talking about claims of the form, "if an event of type *C* had occurred, then …" and "if …, then an event of type *C* would have occurred." Manifestly, neither locution carries an ontological commitment to a strange sort of "negative" event. So, if I am right, anxieties about whether we can find a place for omissions in the causal order rest on a basic confusion about what it means to attribute causal status to omissions.

This observation connects to a broader point, which is that dependence, understood as a relation *between events*, is unduly restrictive. Quite generally there can be counterfactual dependence between *facts* (true propositions), where these can be "positive," "negative," "disjunctive," or whatever – and where only rarely can we shoehorn the facts so related into the form, "such-and-such an event occurred." When we can – when we can say that the fact that *e* occurred depends on the fact that *c* occurred – then we can go ahead and call this a kind of event-causation. But to see it as anything but a special case of a causal relation with a much broader domain would be, I think, a mistake.[14]

We can bring my thesis into still sharper focus by considering some of the more obvious objections to it. It seems wise to begin by directly confronting what many will see as the most damning objection – which is simply that it posits *two* concepts of event-causation. This might strike some as an extravagantly high price to pay: After all, when possible we should be conservative, and conservatism argues for taking our concept of event-causation to be univocal. At the very least, shouldn't we view the bifurcation of our concept of event-causation as a serious cost of my proposal?

No, we should not – and not because we shouldn't be conservative. It's rather that this objection mistakes a perfectly sensible *methodological maxim* with a *reason to believe*. The methodological maxim goes: When trying to come up with an analysis of a concept, start out by operating under the assumption that the concept is univocal. I think that's sound. But it doesn't at all follow that it is somehow *antecedently more probable* that the concept in question is univocal – let alone *so* probable that any analysis that says otherwise pays a "high price." In the face of the right sorts of reasons to prefer a nonunivocal analysis, we should give up our operative assumption – and we shouldn't expect those reasons to have to carry an extra-heavy burden of proof because of the "intrinsic plausibility" of the hypothesis of univocality.

To think otherwise manifests a basic confusion. It's rather as if I had lost my keys somewhere in this room; I have no idea where. They might be over there, where it's dark and a lot of debris obscures things; or they might be over here, where it's sunny and uncluttered. It makes exceedingly good sense for me to start by looking in the sunny and uncluttered part of the room – to *act as if* I believed my keys were there. But that is not because I *do* believe they are there, or even because I consider it more likely than the alternative (as if the hypothesis that life is easy has some intrinsic plausibility to it!). It's rather that if my keys *are* in the uncluttered area, then I will soon find them – and if they are not, I will quickly find that out as well.

In the same way, when we go to analyze some concept of philosophical interest, it makes exceedingly good sense to start by looking for a univocal analysis. For even if we are wrong, and some hidden ambiguity lurks in our ordinary applications of the concept, the very problems we will encounter in trying to come up with a univocal analysis will (if we are careful and attentive) be diagnostic of this ambiguity. (The critique of the counterfactual analysis carried out in secs. 3–5 was partly designed to be a case in point.) But it is foolishness to mistake this advice for a reason to *believe* that the concept is univocal. Indeed, if I consider the hypothesis that our concept of event-causation is univocal, I see no reason whatsoever to judge it to be highly probable, antecedently to any investigation. And *after* sufficient investigation – in particular, after basic principles governing our application of "cause" have been shown to come into conflict – I think its plausibility is just about nil.

A more subtle objection is the following: What I have really shown is not that there are two *concepts* of causation, but rather that there are two *kinds* of causation, two different ways in which

one event can be a cause of another. That may well be right; certainly, I was happy to begin this paper by announcing that event-causation comes in two "varieties." I do not know how to judge the matter, because I am not sufficiently clear on what underlies this distinction between concepts and kinds. Compare a nice example borrowed from Tim Maudlin: There are at least three different ways of being a mother. We might call them "DNA-mother," "womb-mother," and "nurturing mother." Does that mean we have three different concepts of mother – an ambiguity largely unnoticed only because those we call "mothers" are typically all three? I don't know. At any rate, in the case at hand it doesn't matter in the slightest. I am quite content to agree that I have (merely) shown that there are two kinds of causation – as long as those who insist on this rendering of my thesis agree that the two kinds answer to very different criteria and consequently require very different analyses. That claim alone is enough to show how unwise it would be, when attempting to provide a philosophical account of event-causation, merely to forge blindly ahead, trying to come up with an analysis that can successfully run the gauntlet of known problem cases. If I am right, any such *single* analysis is doomed to failure.

A third, more congenial objection begins by granting the distinction between production and dependence, but denying that dependence deserves to be counted a kind of causation at all. Now, I think there is *something* right about this objection, in that production does seem, in some sense, to be the more "central" causal notion. As evidence, consider that when presented with a paradigm case of production without dependence – as in, say, the story of Suzy, Billy, and the broken bottle – we unhesitatingly classify the producer as a cause; whereas when, presented with a paradigm case of dependence without production – as in, say, the story of Suzy, Billy, and Enemy – our intuitions (well, those of some of us, anyway) about whether a genuine causal relation is manifested are shakier. Fair enough. But I think it goes too far to deny that counterfactual dependence between wholly distinct events is not a kind of *causal* relation. Partly this is because dependence plays the appropriate sort of roles in, for example, explanation and decision. (See sec. 8 [omitted here], below, for more discussion of this point.) And partly it is because I do not see how to accommodate causation of and by omissions (as we should) as a species of production; counterfactual dependence seems the only appropriate causal relation for such "negative events" to stand in.

This last point brings up a fourth possible objection, which is that in claiming that there are two kinds of causation, each characterized by a different subset of the five theses, I have overstepped my bounds. After all, even if the arguments of sections 4 and 5 succeed, all they establish is, roughly, (i) that *Dependence* contradicts each of *Locality, Intrinsicness,* and *Transitivity;* and (ii) that *Omissions* likewise contradicts each of *Locality, Intrinsicness,* and *Transitivity,* It obviously doesn't follow that *Dependence* and *Omissions* should be bundled together and taken to characterize one kind of causation, nor that *Locality, Intrinsicness,* and *Transitivity* should be bundled together and taken to characterize another. Perhaps the ambiguity in our ordinary causal talk is more multifarious and messy than this claim allows.

Dead right. And even though I think that further investigation could unearth more positive reasons for dividing the five theses into the two groups I have chosen, I do not have such reasons to offer here. For what it's worth, I do have a strong hunch that, as noted above, there couldn't *be* anything more to causation of and by omissions than counterfactual dependence; hence the pairing of *Omissions* with *Dependence.* And in the next section [omitted here] I'll propose an analysis of production that gives central roles to both *Intrinsicness* and *Transitivity,* as well as to a slightly weakened version of *Locality.* But that's hardly enough to warrant conviction. Rather, what's wanted are more probing arguments as to why our ordinary notion of event-causation should fracture cleanly along the lines I have drawn. Lacking such arguments, I will fall back on the methodological maxim discussed above: Given that we can no longer take it as a working hypothesis that the concept of causation is univocal, let us nevertheless adopt the most conservative working hypothesis available to us. Since we have yet to find any reason to think that *Dependence* conflicts with *Omissions,* or that conceptual tensions threaten the happy union of *Locality, Intrinsicness,* and *Transitivity,* let us assume – again, as a working hypothesis – that the first two theses characterize one causal notion, the last three another.

[...]

Notes

1 See for example Mellor (1997) and Bennett (1988).
2 See Kim (1973) and Lewis (2000).
3 For excellent discussions of the issues involved in providing a full-blown philosophical account of events, see Lewis (1986c) and Bennett (1988).
4 Notice also that Bennett and Lewis both use the locution "*A* causes *B*" rather than the weaker "*A* is *a* cause of *B*" – thus illegitimately suggesting that a particularly *salient* causal connection is being asserted. That won't do; after all, doesn't it also sound wrong to say, e.g., that the forest's presence caused the fire? But it doesn't sound so bad to say that it was *a* cause of, or *among* the causes of, the fire.
5 Notice that the distracting intuitions evoked by Bennett's example are silent here: There is no "good bit of common sense" analogous to Lombard's observation that "heavy rains … don't start [fires]"; furthermore, no event stands out as a particularly salient cause of the forest's presence (although in the right context, the April rains just might).
6 For standard treatments of the counterfactual, see, e.g., Stalnaker (1968), Lewis (1973a), and Lewis (1973b). Whether these standard treatments are adequate to the needs of the counterfactual analysis is a question we will take up shortly.
7 Note that Lewis's account of the counterfactual conditional does not rule out backtrackers in principle, but only when the world exhibits an appropriate sort of (contingent) global asymmetry; in this way he hopes to leave room for the possibility of backward causation.
8 Swain (1978, see especially pp. 13–14) has overlooked this point. He considers a case with exactly the structure of that described by figure 32.2, yet fails to notice that his views on counterfactuals deny him the resources needed to secure the link between *c* and *e*.
9 The usual caveats apply: There might be more than one such minimal alteration to the state at *t*, or there might be an infinite sequence of minimal alterations, each more minimal than its predecessor. Either way, the proper fix is to take the conditional to be true just in case there is some alteration *A* such that the consequent comes out true for every choice of alteration *A′* that is at least as minimal as *A*. Note also that we would need to amend this rule, if we wanted our analysis to accommodate backward causation and action at a temporal distance.
10 But see Hall (2002) for detailed argument and discussion.

11 The word "structure" is intentionally ambiguous: We could take the structure to be the mereological fusion of all the events, or we could take it to be a set-theoretic construction out of them (most simply, just the set of them). It doesn't matter, as long as we're clear on what duplication of event-structures amounts to.

12 For various reasons not worth the long digression their spelling out would require, I do not think we can add an "only if" to the "if" to get "iff." See Hall (2002) for discussion.

13 There are, in the literature, various other apparent counterexamples to *Transitivity* that cannot be handled merely by denying *Dependence* (see, e.g., McDermott 1995). But on my view they are only apparent; see Hall 2000 for detailed discussion.

14 I do not think that *whenever* we have counterfactual dependence between two facts, the statement asserting this dependence should be construed as causal. It depends on why the dependence holds. For example, "If it hadn't been that *P*, it wouldn't have been that *Q*" could be true because *Q* entails *P*, in which case we shouldn't view this sentence as expressing a *causal* truth. Alas, I don't think we can hope to circumscribe the *causal* dependence claims merely by demanding that the facts in question be logically independent; for what of counternomics, such as "If gravity had obeyed an inverse-cube law, then the motion of the planets would not have obeyed Kapler's law"? While it seems intuitively clear when we have a relation of dependence that holds for the right sorts of reasons to count as causal and when we don't, I will leave the project of elucidating these reasons for another occasion.

References

Bennett, Jonathan. 1987. "Event Causation: the Counterfactual Analysis." *Philosophical Perspectives* 1: 367–86. Reprinted in Sosa and Tooley (1993): 217–33.

Bennett, Jonathan. 1988. *Events and Their Names*. Indianapolis, Ind.: Hackett.

Coady, David. 2004. "Preempting Preemption." In John Collins, Ned Hall, and L. A. Paul (eds.), *Causation and Counterfactuals*, 325–39. Cambridge: MIT Press.

Collins, John, Ned Hall, and L. A. Paul. 2004. "Counterfactuals and Causation: History, Problems, and Prospects." In John Collins, Ned Hall, and L. A. Paul (eds.), *Causation and Counterfactuals*, 1–57. Cambridge: MIT Press.

Hall, Ned. 2000. "Causation and the Price of Transitivity." *Journal of Philosophy* 97: 198–222.

Hall, Ned. 2002. "The Intrinsic Character of Causation." In Dean Zimmerman (ed.), *Oxford Studies in Metaphysics*, volume 1. Oxford: Oxford University Press, 2002.

Hall, Ned. 2004. "Causation and the Price of Transitivity." In John Collins, Ned Hall, and L. A. Paul (eds.), *Causation and Counterfactuals*, 181–203. Cambridge: MIT Press.

Kim, Jaegwon. 1973. "Causes and Counterfactuals." *Journal of Philosophy* 70: 570–2.

Lewis, David. 1973a. "Causation." *Journal of Philosophy* 70: 556–67. Reprinted in Lewis (1986a): 159–72 [ch. 29 in this volume].

Lewis, David. 1973b. *Counterfactuals*. Cambridge: Harvard University Press.

Lewis, David. 1979. "Counterfactual Dependence and Time's Arrow." *Noûs* 13: 455–76. Reprinted with postscripts in Lewis (1986a): 32–66.

Lewis, David. 1986a. *Philosophical Papers*, volume II. Oxford: Oxford University Press.

Lewis, David. 1986b. "Postscripts to 'Causation.'" In Lewis (1986a): 172–123.

Lewis, David. 1986c. "Causal Explanation." In Lewis (1986a): 214–40.

Lewis, David. 1986d. "Events." In Lewis (1986a): 241–69.

Lewis, David. 2000. "Causation as Influence." *Journal of Philosophy* 97: 182–97.

Lombard, Lawrence. 1990. "Causes, Enablers, and the Counterfactual Analysis." *Philosophical Studies* 59: 195–211.

Maudlin, Tim. 2007. "A Modest Proposal Concerning Laws, Counterfactuals, and Explanation." In *The Metaphysics within Physics*. Oxford: Oxford University Press.

McDermott, Michael. 1995. "Redundant Causation." *British Journal for the Philosophy of Science* 46: 523–44.

Mellor, D. H. 1997. "Properties and Predicates." In Mellor and Oliver (1997): 255–67.

Mellor, D. H. 2004. "For Facts as Causes and Effects." In John Collins, Ned Hall, and L. A. Paul (eds.), *Causation and Counterfactuals*, 309–23. Cambridge: MIT Press.

Mellor, D. H., and A. Oliver (eds.). 1997. *Properties*. Oxford: Oxford University Press.

Paul, L. A. 1998. "Keeping Track of the Time: Emending the Counterfactual Analysis of Causation." *Analysis* 58: 191–8.

Sosa, Ernest, and Michael Tooley (eds.). 1993. *Causation*. Oxford: Oxford University Press.

Stalnaker, Robert. 1968. "A Theory of Conditionals." In Nicholas Rescher (ed.), *Studies in Logical Theory*. Oxford: Blackwell.

Swain, Marshall. 1978. "A Counterfactual Analysis of Event Causation." *Philosophical Studies* 34: 1–19.

PART VI

Persistence

Introduction

Things change over time. Rivers flow, trees grow, and mountains erode. To say that something has changed evidently means that it had a certain property at an earlier time that it does not now have. This seems to imply that the thing that had that property at the earlier time is the very thing that now lacks it. But there are numerous puzzles associated with persistence through change. One such puzzle is that of the Ship of Theseus: a ship at sea very gradually undergoes a complete change in parts. Someone then collects the discarded original parts and constructs a ship that is indistinguishable from the original ship. The end result is two ships, each of which has a strong claim to being the original ship. But obviously they cannot *both* be the one ship that we started with. So which is the original ship: the ship at sea or the reconstructed ship?

In "Identity Through Time" (chapter 33), Roderick M. Chisholm defends a "mereological essentialist" solution to the Ship of Theseus puzzle. Strictly speaking, no object can persist through a change in parts. Once a part is removed from a ship and is replaced with a new part, that ship ceases to exist and is replaced by a new ship. Chisholm goes on to explain that there is a loose way of talking about identity, on which it is acceptable to say that the original ship is the same ship as the ship with new parts, but that speaking "strictly and philosophically" they are distinct. Chisholm gives a detailed account of the truth conditions for loose statements about identity and addresses potential problems having to do with claims about the number of ships and the past and future properties of a given ship.

Those who maintain that material objects can survive a change in parts and properties owe us some account of *what it is* for an object to persist through a change. In "Identity, Ostension, and Hypostasis" (chapter 34), W. V. Quine articulates and defends what has come to be called the *four-dimensionalist*, or *perdurantist*, theory of persistence. On this account, ordinary objects are composed of different temporal parts (or "stages") at different times, and they exist at different times by virtue of having temporal parts that exist at just those times – just as things occupy different regions of space at a single time by having spatial parts that fully occupy those regions. According to Quine, Heraclitus was wrong when he famously said that one cannot bathe in the same river twice. What one cannot do is bathe in the same river *stage* twice, where a river stage is a particular aggregate of water molecules. But one can

Metaphysics: An Anthology, Second Edition. Edited by Jaegwon Kim, Daniel Z. Korman and Ernest Sosa.
Editorial material and organization © 2012 Blackwell Publishing Ltd. Published 2012 by Blackwell Publishing Ltd.

bathe in the same river twice by bathing in two river stages that are stages of one and the same river. Quine introduces this theory of persistence in the course of giving an account of ostensive reference, that is, an account of how we manage to refer to a particular entity by pointing in its direction and uttering a name or demonstrative (e.g., 'that'). He considers not only reference to persisting material objects, but also apparent reference to attributes (like triangularity) which, he argues, cannot be identified with concrete entities (for instance, the fusion of all triangular objects).

In "Parthood and Identity Across Time" (chapter 35), Judith Jarvis Thomson criticizes the metaphysic of temporal parts, favoring a *three-dimensionalist* view on which ordinary material objects do not have temporal parts but, rather, are "wholly present" at each moment of their existence. She begins by supplying a perspicuous statement of the theory of temporal parts (on her opponents' behalf) and showing how puzzles of material constitution motivate the temporal parts view. (We describe one such puzzle in the introduction to Part II, in connection with Allan Gibbard's "Contingent Identity.") Thomson argues that this is a "crazy metaphysic" by calling attention to a number of counterintuitive implications of the view. For instance, the view looks to imply that when I seem to be holding an unchanging bit of chalk in my hand, in fact there is new chalk coming into existence every moment, right there in my hand! Thomson rejects the temporal parts view, develops a theory of parthood on which parthood is a three-place relation that holds between a part, a whole, and a time, and offers an alternative solution to the puzzles of material constitution, which involves conceding that ordinary objects are not identical to the stuff of which they are made.

In "Temporal Parts of Four-Dimensional Objects" (chapter 36), Mark Heller supplies a careful exposition and defense of the four-dimensionalist approach. He argues that four-dimensionalism yields the best solution to the puzzles of material constitution, and in particular, it allows one to avoid commitment to distinct but exactly colocated entities. Heller also responds to Thomson's "crazy metaphysic" objection, maintaining that the appearance of craziness fades (at least to some extent) once one appreciates that ordinary objects are temporally extended "space-time worms", not three-dimensional "wholly present" objects.

The fact that objects can persist through changes in their properties leads to a puzzle that is sometimes known as "the puzzle of change" or "the problem of temporary intrinsics." Here is the problem. Objects can undergo alterations: a candle can be straight and then later be bent. But straightness and bentness are incompatible properties; nothing can have both. So how can it be that a single thing – the candle – can have both of these properties? The answer may seem straightforward: surely there's no inconsistency in the candle *now* being bent and the candle *earlier* being straight. But, on closer inspection, there turn out to be a variety of ways of fleshing out this sort of response, none of which seems entirely satisfactory.

In "The Problem of Temporary Intrinsics" (chapter 37) – an excerpt from his *On the Plurality of Worlds* – David Lewis introduces the problem and maintains that three-dimensionalists (or "endurantists") cannot give an adequate response to the problem. He argues that three-dimensionalists must either maintain that properties like *being bent* are in fact nonintrinsic relational properties (relating a subject to a time) or else embrace a theory of time on which there are no times other than the present. Lewis maintains that the problem is best handled by a four-dimensionalist account of persistence on which the bearers of the relevant intrinsic properties are distinct temporal parts of familiar objects.

In "Endurance and Temporary Intrinsics" (chapter 38), Sally Haslanger defends an endurantist response to the problem of temporary intrinsics. She begins by observing that Lewis's own response does not respect the intuition that drives the problem of temporary intrinsics. On Lewis's account, it is the temporal parts of the candle, not the candle itself, that have the intrinsic properties of bentness and straightness. But intuitively, ordinary objects like candles *themselves* have different intrinsic properties at different times. Haslanger contends that persistence through change consists in a given state of affairs – the state of affairs of the relevant object's having a certain intrinsic property – obtaining relative to one time and not obtaining relative to another time. She thereby avoids having to say either that change requires objects to have temporal parts or that the properties in question are relational (nonintrinsic) properties of persisting objects (e.g., *being straight on Monday* and *being bent on Tuesday*).

In "All The World's a Stage" (chapter 39), Theodore Sider develops an alternative version of four-dimensionalism. Like Quine, Lewis, and Heller, Sider takes there to be temporally extended "space-time worms" that are composed of temporal stages. But unlike Quine and Heller, Sider holds that familiar objects like persons and coins are the instantaneous stages of the worms, not the worms themselves. Sider argues that this version of four-dimensionalism provides a superior account of certain puzzles of personal identity (discussed in chapters 42 and 43) and the aforementioned puzzles of material constitution. But if you are an instantaneous stage, doesn't that mean that *you yourself* were never a child and that you will not exist one moment from now? Sider defends his stage theory against such objections by supplying a ("counterpart-theoretic") analysis of these sorts of temporal claims, which renders them consistent with the view that you are identical to a momentary stage.

Further Reading

Fine, K. (2006). "In Defense of Three-Dimensionalism," *The Journal of Philosophy* 103: 699–714.

Haslanger, S. (2003). "Persistence Through Time," in M. J. Loux and D. W. Zimmerman (eds.), *The Oxford Handbook of Metaphysics*. Oxford: Oxford University Press, pp. 315–54.

Haslanger S., and Kurtz, R. M. (2006). *Persistence: Contemporary Readings*. Cambridge, MA: MIT Press.

Hawley, K. (2001). *How Things Persist*. Oxford: Oxford University Press.

Hinchliff, M. (1996). "The Puzzle of Change," *Philosophical Perspectives* 10: 119–36.

Hirsch, E. (1982). *The Concept of Identity*. New York: Oxford University Press.

Johnston, M. (1987). "Is There a Problem about Persistence?," *Proceedings of the Aristotelian Society* suppl. vol. 61: 107–35.

Merricks, T. (1995). "On the Incompatibility of Enduring and Perduring Entities," *Mind* 104: 523–31.

Rea, M. (1998). "Temporal Parts Unmotivated," *The Philosophical Review* 107: 225–60.

Sider, T. (2001). *Four-Dimensionalism*. Oxford: Clarendon Press.

Van Cleve, J. (1986). "Mereological Essentialism, Mereological Conjunctivism, and Identity through Time," *Midwest Studies in Philosophy* 11: 141–56.

Zimmerman, D. W. (1998). "Temporal Parts and Supervenient Causation," *Australasian Journal of Philosophy*, 76(2): 265–88.

33

Identity through Time

Roderick M. Chisholm

The identity of a person is a perfect identity; wherever it is real, it admits of no degrees; and it is impossible that a person should be in part the same, and in part different…For this cause, I have first considered personal identity, as that which is perfect in its kind, and the natural measure of that which is imperfect.

Thomas Reid[1]

1 The Ship of Theseus

To understand the philosophical problems involved in persistence, in the fact that one and the same thing may endure through a period of time, we will begin with what Reid would have called the 'imperfect' cases and remind ourselves of some ancient philosophical puzzles. One such puzzle is suggested by the familiar dictum of Heraclitus: 'You could not step twice in the same river; for other and yet other waters are ever flowing on.'[2] Another is the problem of the Ship of Theseus.[3]

Updating the latter problem somewhat, let us imagine a ship – the Ship of Theseus – that was made entirely of wood when it came into being. One day a wooden plank is cast off and replaced by an aluminum one. Since the change is only slight, there is no question as to the survival of the Ship of Theseus. We still have the ship we had before; that is to say, the ship that we have now is identical with the ship we had before. On another day, another wooden plank is cast off and also replaced by an aluminum one. Still the same ship, since, as before, the change is only slight. The changes continue, in a similar way, and finally the Ship of Theseus is made entirely of aluminum. The aluminum ship, one may well argue, *is* the wooden ship we started with, for the ship we started with survived each particular change, and identity, after all, is transitive.

But what happened to the discarded wooden planks? Consider this possibility, suggested by Thomas Hobbes: 'If some man had kept the old planks as they were taken out, and by putting them afterwards together in the same order, had again made a ship of them, this, without doubt, had also been the same numerical ship with that

Metaphysics: An Anthology, Second Edition. Edited by Jaegwon Kim, Daniel Z. Korman and Ernest Sosa.
Editorial material and organization © 2012 Blackwell Publishing Ltd. Published 2012 by Blackwell Publishing Ltd.

which was at the beginning; and so there would have been two ships numerically the same, which is absurd.'[4] Assuming, as perhaps one has no right to do, that each of the wooden planks survived intact throughout these changes, one might well argue that the reassembled wooden ship *is* the ship we started with. 'After all, it is made up of the very same parts, standing in the very same relations, whereas that ugly aluminum object doesn't have a single part in common with our original ship.'

To compound the problem still further, let us suppose that the captain of the original ship had solemnly taken the vow that, if his ship were ever to go down, he would go down with it. What, now, if the two ships collide at sea and he sees them start to sink together? Where does his duty lie – with the aluminum ship or with the reassembled wooden ship?

'The carriage' is another ancient version of the problem. Socrates and Plato change the parts of their carriages piece by piece until, finally, Socrates' original carriage is made up of all the parts of Plato's carriage and Plato's carriage is made up of all the parts of Socrates' original carriage. Have they exchanged their carriages or not, and if so, at what point?

Perhaps the essence of the problem is suggested by an even simpler situation. Consider a child playing with his blocks. He builds a house with ten blocks, uses it as a garrison for his toy soldiers, disassembles it, builds many other things, then builds a house again, with each of the ten blocks occupying the position it had occupied before, and he uses it again as a garrison for his soldiers. Was the house that was destroyed the same as the one that subsequently came into being?

These puzzles about the persistence of objects through periods of time have their analogues for the extension of objects through places in space. Consider the river that is known in New Orleans as 'the Mississippi.' Most of us would say that the source of the river is in northern Minnesota. But what if one were to argue instead that the source is in Montana, where it is known as 'the Missouri'? Or that its source is in Pittsburgh, where it is known as 'the Ohio', or that its source is farther back where it is called 'the Allegheny', or in still another place where it is called 'the Monongahela'?[5]

The accompanying diagram (Fig. 33.1) provides us with a schematic illustration.

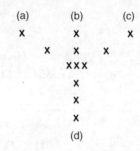

Figure 33.1

Of the river that has its central point at (d), one might wonder whether it flows south-easterly from (a), or due south from (b), or south-westerly from (c). (For simplicity, we ignore the Allegheny and the Monongahela.) If we are puzzled about the beginning of the Mississippi, we should be equally puzzled about the end of the Rhine. Reading our diagram from bottom to top (and again oversimplifying), we could say that if the Rhine begins at (d), then it ends either with the Maas at (a), or with the Waal at (b), or with the Lek at (c).[6]

Perhaps we can imagine three philosophers looking down at the river(s) that end(s) at (d). One insists that the river flows between (a) and (d), another that it flows between (b) and (d) and the third that it flows between (c) and (d); and each insists that, since the arms (or tributaries) to which the other two philosophers refer are distinct not only from each other but from the river itself, neither of the other two can be right. Their dispute, clearly, would be analogous in significant respects to the problem of the Ship of Theseus.

What are we to say of such puzzles? We might follow the extreme course that Carneades took and simply deny the principle of the transitivity of identity.[7] In other words, we might say that things identical with the same thing need not be identical with each other. But if we thus abandon reason and logic at the very outset, we will have no way of deciding at the end what is the most reasonable thing to say about ourselves and *our* persistence through time.

We might be tempted to deny the possibility of alteration. Thus one could say: 'Strictly speaking, nothing alters – nothing is such that at one time it has one set of properties and at another time it has another set of properties. What happens is, rather, that at one time there is a thing having the one set of properties and at the other time there is another thing having the other set of properties.' But this supposition, if we apply it to ourselves, is inconsistent with the data with which we have begun. Each of us knows with respect to himself that he now has properties he didn't have in the past and that formerly he had properties he doesn't have now. ('But a thing x isn't identical with a thing y unless they have all their properties in common. And if the present you has one set of properties and the past you another, how can they be the same thing?') The answer is, of course, that there aren't two you's, a present one having one set of properties and a past one having another. It is rather that you *are* now such that you have these properties and lack those, whereas formerly you *were* such that you had those properties and lacked these. The 'former you' *has* the same properties that the 'present you' now has, and the 'present you' *had* the same properties that the 'former you' then had.[8]

Bishop Butler suggested that it is only in 'a loose and popular sense' that we may speak of the persistence of such familiar things as ships, plants and houses. And he contrasted this 'loose and popular sense' with 'the strict and philosophical sense' in which we may speak of the persistence of *persons*.[9] Let us consider these suggestions.

2 Playing Loose with the 'Is' of Identity

We will not pause to ask what Butler meant in fact. Let us ask what he could have meant. He suggested that there is a kind of looseness involved when we say that such things as the Ship of Theseus persist through time. What kind of looseness is this?

It could hardly be that the Ship of Theseus, in contrast with other things, is only loosely identical with itself. Surely one cannot say that, while some things are only loosely identical with themselves, other things are tightly identical with themselves.[10] The statement 'This thing is more loosely identical with itself than that thing', if it says anything at all, tells us only that the first thing is more susceptible than the second to loss of identity, and this means only that the first is more readily perishable than the second.

We should construe Butler's remark as saying, not that there is a loose kind of identity, but

rather that there is a loose sense of 'identity' – a loose (and popular) use of the 'is' of identity.

What would be a *loose* sense of 'A is B' or 'A is identical with B' – a sense of 'A is B' which is consistent with a denial of the *strict* sense of 'A is B'? I suggest this: we use the locution 'A is B', or 'A is identical with B' in a *loose* sense, if we use it in such a way that it is consistent with saying 'A has a certain property that B does not have' or 'Some things are true of A that aren't true of B'.

Do we ever use the locution 'A is B' in this loose way? It would seem, unfortunately, that we do.

I will single out five different types of such misuse.

(1)   One may say: 'Route 6 is Point Street in Providence and is Fall River Avenue in Seekonk.' Here we would seem to have the 'is' of identity, since it is followed in each occurrence by a term ('Point Street' and 'Fall River Avenue') and not by a predicate expression. But since Point Street and Fall River Avenue have different properties (one is in Providence and not in Seekonk, and the other is in Seekonk and not in Providence), the statement may be said to play loose with 'is'.

As our brief discussion of the rivers may make clear, this use of 'is' is readily avoided. We have only to replace 'is' by 'is part of' and then switch around the terms, as in: 'Point Street in Providence is part of Route 6 and Fall River Avenue in Seekonk is part of Route 6.' Or we could also say, of course: 'Point Street is part of Route 6 in Providence and Fall River Avenue is part of Route 6 in Seekonk.'[11]

(2)   One may say 'This train will be two trains after Minneapolis', or, traveling in the other direction, 'Those two trains will be one train after Minneapolis'. In the first case ('fission'), we are not saying that there is one thing which will subsequently be identical with two things. We are saying, rather, that there is one thing which will be divided into two things, neither of them being identical with the original thing, but each of them being a part of the original thing. And in the second case ('fusion'), we are not saying that there are two things which are subsequently to become identical with each other, or with a third thing. We are saying rather that there are two things which will both become parts of a third thing. (Why not cite an

amoeba as an instance of 'fission'? There is the offchance that amoebas are persons, or at least may be thought to be persons, and in such a case, as we shall see [in ss. 5-6 of the original, omitted here], our treatment would have to be somewhat different.)

(3)　One may say: 'The President of the United States was Eisenhower in 1955, Johnson in 1965, and Ford in 1975.'[12] Here one may seem to be saying that there is, or was, something – namely, the President of the United States – which was identical with Eisenhower in 1955, with Johnson in 1965, and with Ford in 1975. And so, given that Eisenhower, Johnson and Ford were three different people, one may seem to be saying that there is one thing which has been identical with three different things. But this talk, too, is readily avoided. We have only to reformulate the original sentence in such a way that the temporal expression ('in 1955', 'in 1965' and 'in 1975') may be seen to modify, not the verb 'was', but the term 'the President of the United States'. Thus we could say: 'The President of the United States in 1955 (the person who officially presided over the United States in 1955) was Eisenhower; the President of the United States in 1965 was Johnson; and the President of the United States in 1975 was Ford.'[13]

(4)　Pointing to a musical instrument, one man may say to another: 'What you have there is the same instrument that I play, but the one that I play isn't as old as that one.' The first 'is' might be taken to be the 'is' of identity, for it would seem to be followed by a term ('the same instrument that I play'), but the man is saying, of the thing designated by the first term ('what you have there'), that it is older than the thing designated by the second. But of course he didn't need to talk that way. He could have said: 'What you have there is an instrument of the same sort as the one that I play.'

We note a second example of this way of playing loose with 'is' – not because the example introduces any new considerations (for it doesn't), but because it has attracted the attention of philosophers.

Consider the following list:

Socrates is mortal.
Socrates is mortal.

How many sentences have been listed? We could say either 'exactly one' or 'exactly two'. That these incompatible answers are both possible indicates that the question is ambiguous. And so it has been suggested that, to avoid the ambiguity, we introduce the terms 'sentence-token' and 'sentence-type' and then say 'There are two sentence-tokens on the list and one sentence-type'. But if we say this, then we can say: 'The first item on the list is the same sentence-type as the second (for they are syntactically just alike and say the same thing), but the two are different sentence-tokens (for they are two, one being in one place and the other in another).' Here, once again, we are playing loose with 'is'.[14] We *needn't* speak this way in order to deal with the ambiguity of 'How many sentences are there?' We could say there *are* two sentence-tokens and they are tokens *of* the same (sentence-)type. The example does not differ in principle, then, from 'The instrument Jones plays is the same as the one Smith plays but is somewhat older'.

It is sometimes said that we should distinguish the two locutions 'A is identical with B and A is a so-and-so' and 'A is the same so-and-so as B'. It has even been suggested that, for purposes of philosophy, the first of these two locutions should be abandoned in favour of the second.[15] According to this suggestion, we should never' say, simply and absolutely, 'A is identical with B'; we should 'relativize the ascription of identity to a sortal', and say something of the form 'A is the same so-and-so as B', where the expression replacing 'so-and-so' is a count-term, or sortal, such as 'man', 'dog', 'horse'. But this suggestion has point only if we can find instances of the following:

A is the same so-and-so as B, and A is a such-and-such but is not the same such-and-such as B.

Are there really any such A's and B's?

What would be an instance of the above formula? In other words, what would be an instance of an A which is 'the same so-and-so' as something B, but which is not 'the same such-and-such' as B? The only instances which have ever been cited, in defending this doctrine of 'relativized identity', would seem to be instances of one or the other of the four ways of playing loose with 'is' that we have just distinguished.

For example: 'Different official personages may be one and the same man' or 'This is the same word as that'. What the suggestion comes to, then, is that we abandon the strict use of 'is' and replace it by one or more of the loose uses just discussed. There may be advantages to this type of permissiveness, but it will not help us with our philosophical problems.[16]

Do these ways of playing loose with 'is' suggest a true interpretation of the thesis we have attributed to Bishop Butler – the thesis according to which it is only in 'a loose and popular sense' that we may speak of the persistence through time of such familiar physical things as ships, plants and houses? Is it only by playing loose with 'is' that we may say, of the Ship of Theseus, that it is one and the same thing from one period of time to another?

We *can*, of course, play loose with 'is' in one or another of these ways when we talk about the Ship of Theseus. Knowing that it is going to be broken up into two ships, we might say: 'It's going to be two ships.' Or knowing that it was made by joining two other ships, we might say: 'Once it had been two ships.' Or knowing that it makes the same ferry run as does the Ship of Callicles, we might say: 'The Ship of Theseus and the Ship of Callicles are the same ferry.' But the Ship of Theseus doesn't have to be talked about in these loose and popular ways any more than anything else does.

(5)   It may be that the Ship of Theseus and the carriage and other familiar things involve still another way of playing loose with 'is'. Thus Hume said that it is convenient to 'feign identity' when we speak about things which, though they 'are supposed to continue the same, are such only as consist of succession of parts, connected together by resemblance, contiguity, or causation'.[17] What Hume here has in mind by 'feigning' may have been put more clearly by Thomas Reid. (Though Reid and Hume were far apart with respect to most of the matters that concern us here, they seem to be together with respect to this one.) Reid wrote:

All bodies, as they consist of innumerable parts that may be disjoined from them by a great variety of causes, are subject to continual changes of their substance, increasing, diminishing, changing insensibly. When such alterations are gradual, because language could not afford a different name for every different state of such a changeable being, it retains the same name, and is considered as the same thing. Thus we say of an old regiment that it did such a thing a century ago, though there now is not a man alive who then belonged to it. We say a tree is the same in the seed-bed and in the forest. A ship of war, which has successively changed her anchors, her tackle, her sails, her masts, her planks, and her timbers, while she keeps the same name is the same.[18]

I believe that Reid is here saying two things. The first is that, whenever there is a change of parts, however insignificant the parts may be, then some old thing ceases to be, and some new thing comes into being. This presupposes that, strictly speaking, the parts of a thing are essential to it, and therefore when, as we commonly say, something loses a part, then that thing strictly and philosophically ceases to be.[19]

The second thing I take Reid to be saying is this. If, from the point of view of our practical concerns, the new thing that comes into being upon the addition of parts is sufficiently similar to the old one, then it is much more convenient for us to treat them as if they were one than it is for us to take account of the fact that they are diverse. This point could also be put by saying that such things as the Ship of Theseus and indeed most familiar physical things are really 'fictions', or as we would say today, 'logical constructions'. They are logical constructions upon things which *cannot* survive the loss of their parts.

If Reid is right, then, 'The Ship of Theseus was in Athens last week and will be in Kerkyra Melaina next week' need not be construed as telling us that there *is* in fact a certain ship that was in Athens last week and will be in Kerkyra Melaina next week. It does not imply that any ship that was in the one place is identical with any ship that will be in the other place. And so if this is true, and if all the same we say 'A ship that was in Athens last week is identical with a ship that will be in Kerkyra Melaina next week', then, once again, we are playing loose with the 'is' of identity.

3   An Interpretation of Bishop Butler's Theses

We have found a way, then, of interpreting Bishop Butler's two theses.

According to the first, familiar physical things such as trees, ships, bodies and houses persist 'only in a loose and popular sense'. This thesis may be construed as presupposing that these things are 'fictions', logical constructions or *entia per alio*. And it tells us that, from the fact that any such physical thing may be said to exists at a certain place P at a certain time *t* and also at a certain place Q at a certain other time *t'*, we may *not* infer that what exists at P at *t* is identical with what exists at Q at *t'*.

According to the second thesis, persons persist 'in a strict and philosophical sense'. This may be construed as telling us that persons are not thus 'fictions', logical constructions or *entia per alio*. And so it implies that, if a person may be said to exist at a certain place P at a certain time *t* and also at a certain place Q at a certain other time *t'*, then we *may* infer that something existing at P at *t* is identical with something existing at Q at *t'*.

We now consider the two theses in turn.

4   Feigning Identity

Could we think of familiar physical things, such as ships and trees and houses, as being logical constructions? Let us consider just one type of physical thing, for what we say about it may be applied, *mutatis mutandis,* to the others (see Fig. 33.2).

Consider the history of a very simple table. On Monday it came into being when a certain thing A was joined with a certain other thing B. On Tuesday A was detached from B and C was joined to B, these things occurring in such a way that a table was to be found during every moment of the process. And on Wednesday B was detached from C and D was joined with C, these things, too, occurring in such a way that a table was to be found during every moment of the process. Let us suppose that no other separating or joining occurred.

I suggest that in this situation there are the following three wholes among others: AB, that is, the thing made up of A and B; BC, the thing made up of B and C; and CD, the thing made up of C and D. I will say that AB 'constituted' our table on Monday, that BC 'constituted' our table on Tuesday, and that CD 'constituted' our table on Wednesday. Although AB, BC and CD are three different things, they all constitute the same table.

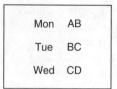

Figure 33.2

We thus have an illustration of what Hume called 'a succession of objects'.[20]

One might also say, of each of the three wholes, AB, BC and CD, that it 'stands in for' or 'does duty for' our table on one of the three successive days. Thus if we consider the spatial location of the three wholes, we see that the place of the table was occupied by AB on Monday, by BC on Tuesday, and by CD on Wednesday. Again, the table was red on Monday if and only if AB was red on Monday, and it weighed 10 pounds on Monday if and only if AB weighed 10 pounds on Monday. And analogously for BC on Tuesday and for CD on Wednesday.

The situation may seem to involve two somewhat different types of individual thing. On the one hand, there is what might be called the *ens successivum* – the 'successive table' that is made up of different things at different times.[21] And on the other hand, there are the things that do duty on the different days for the successive table: namely, AB, BC and CD. But any *ens successivum* may be viewed as a logical construction upon the various things that may be said to do duty for it.

Considering, then, just the simple situation I have described, can we express the information we have about the *ens successivum* in statements that refer only to the particular things that stand in or do duty for it? It should be clear that we can, but let us consider the situation in some detail.

Looking back to our diagram, we can see that Monday's table evolved into Tuesday's table, and that Tuesday's table evolved into Wednesday's table. We began with AB; then A was separated from B and replaced by C, but in such a way that there was a table to be found at every moment during the process; then, in a similar way, B was separated from C and replaced by D. We could say, then, that BC was a 'direct table successor' of AB and that CD was a 'direct table successor' of BC.

Making use of the undefined concept of *part*, or *proper part*, we may define the concept of 'table successor' in the following way:

D. III. 1 x is at t a direct table successor of y at $t' = {}_{Df}$ (i) t does not begin before t'; (ii) x is a table at t and y is a table at t'; and (iii) there is a z, such that z is a part of x at t and a part of y at t', and at every moment between t' and t inclusive z is itself a table.

Thus z is a table which is a proper part of a table. (If we cut off a small part of a table, we may still have a table left. But if the thing that is left is a table, then, since it was there before, it was then a table that was a proper part of a table.) The concept *part*, as it is understood here, is discussed in detail in Appendix B ('Mereological essentialism').[22]

We may also say, more generally, that the CD of Wednesday is a 'table successor' of the AB of Monday, even though CD is not a *direct* table successor of AB. The more general concept is this:

D. III. 2 x is at t a table successor of y at $t' = {}_{Df}$ (i) t does not begin before t'; (ii) x is a table at t, and y is a table at t'; and (iii) x has at t every property P such that (a) y has P at t' and (b) all direct table successors of anything having P have P.

The definition assures us that a direct table successor of a direct table successor is a table successor; so, too, for a direct table successor of a direct table successor … of a direct table successor.[23]

We may now say that things that are thus related by table succession 'constitute the same successive table'.

D. III. 3 x constitutes at t the same successive table that y constitutes at $t' = {}_{Df}$ either (a) x and only x is at t a table successor of y at t', or (b) y and only y is at t' a table successor of x at t.

Each such thing may be said to 'constitute a successive table'.

D. III. 4 x constitutes at t a successive table $= {}_{Df}$ There are a y and a t' such that y is other than x, and x constitutes at t the same table that y constitutes at t'.

We are on the way, then, to reducing our successive table to those things that are said to constitute it.

Certain propositions, ostensibly about the successive table, may be reduced in a straightforward way to propositions about the things that are said to constitute it. For example:

D. III. 5   There is exactly one successive table at place P at time $t = {}_{Df}$ There is exactly one thing at place P at time t that constitutes a successive table at t.

Our definition of 'constituting the same successive table' (D. III. 3) assures us that nothing will constitute more than one successive table at any given time.

Some of the properties that the table has at any given time are thus such that the table borrows them from the thing that constitutes it at that time; but others are not. An example of a property of the first sort may be that of *being red*; an example of a property of the second sort may be that of *having once been blue*. How are we to mark off the former set of properties?

Some properties may be said to be 'rooted outside the times at which they are had'. Examples are the property of *being a widow* and the property of *being a future President*. If we know of anything that it has the former property at any given time, then we can deduce that the thing existed prior to that time. And if we know of anything that it has the latter property at any given time, then we can deduce that the thing continues to exist after that time. Let us say:

D. III. 6   G is rooted outside times at which it is had $= {}_{Df}$ Necessarily, for any x and for any period of time t, x has the property G throughout t only if x exists at some time before or after t.

Some properties may – but need not – be rooted outside the times at which they are had. An example is the property of *being such that it is or was red*. Our successive table may derive this from its present constituent – if its present constituent is red. But it may derive it from a former constituent – if its present constituent is not red. The definition of this type of property is straightforward:

D. III. 7   G may be rooted outside times at which it is had = $_{Df}$ G is equivalent to a disjunction of two properties one of which is, and the other of which is not, rooted outside times at which it is had.

Some properties, finally, are *not* such that they may be rooted outside the times at which they are had.[24] An example is *being red*.

Of the properties that our successive table has at any given time, which are the ones that it borrows from the thing that happens to constitute it at that time? The answer is: those of its properties which are *not* essential to it, and those of its properties which are *not* such that they may be rooted outside the times at which they are had. But the essential properties of the successive table – e.g., that it *is* a successive table – and those of its properties which may be rooted outside the times at which they are had – e.g., that it was blue or that it was or will be blue – are not such that, for any time, they are borrowed from the thing that constitutes the successive table at that time.

We may say, more generally, of the *ens successivum* and the thing that constitutes it at any given time, that they are exactly alike at that time with respect to all those properties which are such that they are not essential to either and they may not be rooted outside the times at which they are had.

Consider now the following definitional schema:

D. III. 8   The successive table that is at place P at time *t* is F at *t* = $_{Df}$ There is exactly one thing at place P at *t* that constitutes a successive table at *t*, and that thing is F at *t*.

This definition is applicable only if the predicates that replace the schematic letter 'F' are properly restricted. For the properties designated by such predicates should be those which are not essential to either and are not such that they may be rooted outside the times at which they are had. Hence acceptable replacements for 'F' would be: 'red', '10 feet square', and 'such that it weighs 10 pounds'.

But not all the properties of the successive table are derivable in this straightforward way from the properties of things that constitute it. For example, if AB ceased to be after Monday, we could say of the successive table on Monday, but not of AB, that it was going to persist through Wednesday. Or if CD came into being on Wednesday, we could say of the successive table on Wednesday, but not of CD, that it is at least two days old. Moreover, on Monday, the successive table, but not AB, was such that it would be constituted by CD on Wednesday; while on Wednesday, the successive table, but not CD, was such that it was constituted by AB on Monday.

Nevertheless all such truths about the successive table may be reduced to truths about AB, BC and CD. That this is so should be apparent from these definitions.

D. III. 9   The successive table that is at place P at time *t* has existed for at least three days = $_{Df}$ There is exactly one *x* such that *x* is at place P at time *t* and *x* constitutes a successive table at *t*; there are a *y* and a time *t'* such that *x* is at *t* a table-successor of *y* at *t'*; and *t* and *t'* are separated by a period of three days.

This definition tells us, then, what it is for a successive table to persist through time. And the following definition suggests the way in which, at any time, the successive table may borrow its properties from things that constitute it at *other* times:

D. III. 10 The successive table that is at place P at time *t* is constituted by *x* at *t'* = $_{Df}$ There is a *y* such that *y* is at place P at time *t*; *y* constitutes a successive table at *t*; and either *x* is identical with *y*, and *t* is identical with *t'*, or *y* constitutes at *t* the same successive table that *x* constitutes at *t'*.

It should now be obvious how to say such things as 'the successive table is red on Monday and green on Wednesday'.

One may object, 'You are committed to saying that AB, BC, CD, and our table are four different things. It may well be, however, that each of the three things AB, BC, CD satisfies the conditions of any acceptable definition of the term "table". Indeed your definitions presuppose that each of them *is* a table. Hence you are committed to saying that, in the situation described, there are *four* tables. But this is absurd; for actually you have described only *one* table. '

We will find a reply to this objection, if we distinguish the strict and philosophical sense of such expressions as 'There are four tables' from their ordinary, or loose and popular, sense. To say that there are four tables, in the strict and philosophical sense, is to say that there are four different things, each of them a table. But from the fact that there are four tables, in this strict and philosophical sense, it will not follow that there are four tables in the ordinary, or loose and popular, sense. If there are to be four tables in the ordinary, or loose and popular, sense, it must be the case that there are four things, not only such that each constitutes a table, but also such that no two of them constitute the same table. In other words, there must be four *entia successiva*, each of them a table.

We may, therefore, explicate the ordinary, or loose and popular, sense of 'There are *n* so-and-so's at *t*' (or 'The number of so-and-so's at *t* is *n*') in the following way:

D. III. 11   There are, in the loose and popular sense, *n* so-and-so's at *t* = $_{Df}$ There are *n* things each of which constitutes a so-and-so at *t*, and no two of which constitute the same so-and-so at *t*.

The term 'so-and-so' in this schematic definition may be replaced by any more specific count-term, e.g., 'table' or 'ship'. And the *definiendum* could be replaced by 'The number of successive so-and-so's at *t* is *n*'.

Hence the answer to the above objection is this: in saying that there are exactly *three* tables in the situation described, one is speaking in the strict and philosophical sense and not in the loose and popular sense. In saying that there is exactly *one* table, one is speaking in the loose and popular sense and not in the strict and philosophical sense. But the statement that there are *four* tables – AB, BC, CD and the successive table – is simply the result of confusion. One is trying to speak both ways at once.[25] The sense in which we may say that there *is* the successive table is not the sense in which we may say that there *is* the individual thing AB, or BC, or CD.[26]

The foregoing sketch, then, makes clear one way in which we may feign identity when what we are dealing with is in fact only a 'succession of related objects'. The ways in which we do thus feign identity are considerably more subtle and complex. Playing loose with 'is' and 'same', we may even speak of the sameness of a table when we are dealing with successions of objects which are related, not by what I have called table succession, but in much more tenuous ways. Nevertheless, it should be clear that if we are saying something we really know, when we thus speak of the sameness of a table, what we are saying could be re-expressed in such a way that we refer only to the related objects and not to the ostensible entities we think of them as making up. And so, too, for other familiar things – ships and trees and houses – that involve successions of related objects that stand in or do duty for them at different times.

We could say, then, that such things are *entia per alio*. They are ontological parasites that derive all their properties from other things – from the various things that do duty for them. An *ens per alio* never is or has anything on its own. It is what it is in virtue of the nature of something other than itself. At every moment of its history an *ens per alio* has something other than itself as its stand-in.

But if there are *ensia per alio*, then there are also *entia per se*.

[ss. 5 and 6 omitted here]

Notes

1   Thomas Reid, *Essays on the Intellectual Powers of Man,* essay III, ch. 14 in Sir William Hamilton (ed.), *The Works of Thomas Reid. D. D.* (Edinburgh: Maclachlan & Stewart, 1854), p. 345.

2   Fragment 41–2, as translated in Milton C. Nahm, *Selections from Early Greek Philosophy* (New York: F. S. Crofts, 1934), p. 91.

3   See Plato, *Phaedo,* 58A, and Xenophon, *Memorabilia,* 4. 8. 2. Leibniz speaks of the Ship of Theseus in *New Essays Concerning Human Understanding,* II, ch. 27, sect. 4, noting that any ordinary physical body may be said to be 'like a river which always changes its water, or like the ship of Theseus which the Athenians were always repairing' (Open Court edn), p. 240.

4   Thomas Hobbes, *Concerning Body,* ch. 11 ('Of identity and difference'), sect. 7.

5 Cf. W. V. Quine: 'Thus take the question of the biggest fresh lake. Is Michigan-Huron admissible, or is it a pair of lakes? ... Then take the question of the longest river. Is the Mississippi-Missouri admissible, or is it a river and a half?' (*Word and Object* (New York: John Wiley, 1960), p. 128).

6 Using terms not commonly applied to rivers, we may note for future reference that when our diagram is read from top to bottom it illustrates *fusion* and when it is read from bottom to top it illustrates *fission*.

7 See note c of the article 'Carneades' in Pierre Bayle's *A General Dictionary: Historical and Critical,* trans. Rev. J. P. Bernard, Rev. Thomas Birch, John Lockeman et al. (10 vols, London: James Bettenham, 1734–41): 'He found uncertainty in the most evident notions. All logicians know that the foundation of the syllogism, and consequently the faculty of reasoning, is built on this maxim: Those things which are identical with a third are the same with each other (*Quae sunt idem uno tertio sunt idem inter se*). It is certain that Carneades opposed it strongly and displayed all his subtleties against it.'

8 Further aspects of this kind of problem are discussed in Roderick M. Chisholm, *Person and Object* (La Salle, Ill.: Open Court, 1976), Appendix A ('The Doctrine of Temporal Parts').

9 Dissertation 1, in *The Whole Works of Joseph Butler, LL.D.* (London: Thomas Tegg, 1839), pp. 263–70. But compare Locke's third letter to the Bishop of Worcester. 'For it being his body both before and after the resurrection, everyone ordinarily speaks of his body as the same, though, in a strict and philosophical sense, as your lordship speaks, it be not the very same.'

10 I have heard it suggested, however, that (a) whereas the evening star is strictly identical with the evening star, nevertheless (b) the evening star is identical but not strictly identical with the morning star. The facts of the matter would seem to be only these: the evening star (i.e., the morning star) is necessarily self-identical; it is not necessarily such that it is visible in the evening or in the morning; it would be contradictory to say that the evening star exists and is not identical with the evening star, or that the morning star exists and is not identical with the morning star; but it would not be contradictory to say that the morning star exists and the evening star exists and the morning star is not identical with the evening star; and whatever is identical with the evening star (i.e., with the morning star) has all the properties that it does.

11 This example of the roads, like that of the rivers above ('the Mississippi-Missouri'), may suggest that the key to our puzzles about identity through time may be found in the doctrine of 'temporal parts'. According to this doctrine, every individual thing x is such that, for every period of time through which x exists, there is a set of parts which are such that x is made up of them at that time and they do not exist at any other time. (Compare: every individual thing x is such that, for every portion of space that x occupies at any time, there is at that time a set of parts of x which then occupy that place and no other place.) I consider this doctrine in detail in *Person and Object*, Appendix A. I there conclude that it will not help us with our problems about identity through time and that there is no sufficient reason for accepting it.

12 Contrast P. T. Geach, *Reference and Generality* (Ithaca, NY: Cornell University Press, 1962), p. 157: '... different official personages may be one and the same man.' Possibly an illustration would be: 'The fire-chief isn't the same personage as the Sunday-school superintendent (for one is charged with putting out fires and the other with religious instruction); yet Jones is both.' But here one seems to be playing loose with 'isn't', for what one has in mind, presumably, is something of this sort: 'Being the fire-chief commits one to different things than does being the Sunday-school superintendent, and Jones is both.'

13 There may be temptations in thus playing loose with 'is'. Suppose there were a monarchy wherein the subjects found it distasteful ever to affirm that the monarch vacated his throne. Instead of saying that there have been so many dozen kings and queens in the history of their country, they will say that the monarch has now exited for many hundreds of years and has had so many dozen different names. At certain times it has been appropriate that these names be masculine, like 'George' and 'Henry', and at other times it has been appropriate that they be feminine, like 'Victoria' and 'Elizabeth'. What, then, if we knew about these people and were to hear such talk as this: 'There has existed for many hundreds of years an x such that x is our monarch; x is now feminine, though fifty years ago x was masculine, and fifty years before that x was feminine'? We should not conclude that there was in that land a monarch who is vastly different from any of the people in ours. We should conclude rather that the speakers were either deluded or pretending.

14 Other examples are suggested by: 'He has a copy of *The Republic* on his desk and another on the table, and he doesn't have any other books. How many books does he have?' 'He played the *Appassionata* once in the afternoon and once again in the evening, but nothing further. How many sonatas did he play?'

15 Compare P. T. Geach in *Logic Matters* (Berkeley and Los Angeles: University of California Press, 1972), pp. 238–49; and *Reference and Generality*, pp. 149ff. The suggestion is criticized in detail by David Wiggins, in *Identity and Spatio-Temporal Continuity* (Oxford: Blackwell, 1967), pp. 1–26. Compare W. V. Quine in a review of *Reference and Generality* in *Philosophical Review*, 73 (1964), pp. 100–4, and Fred Feldman, 'Geach and relativized identity', *Review of Metaphysics* 22 (1968), pp. 547–55.

16 Compare P. T. Geach: 'Even if the man Peter Geach is the same person as the man Julius Caesar, they are certainly different men; they were for example born at different times to a different pair of parents' (*God and the Soul* (London: Routledge & Kegan Paul, 1969), p. 6). John Locke says very similar things; see the Fraser edn of the *Essay Concerning Human Understanding*, pp. 445, 450ff.

17 David Hume, *A Treatise of Human Nature*, bk I, sect. 6; L. A. Selby-Bigge edn. (Oxford: Clarendon Press, 1896), p. 255.

18 Reid, *Essays on the Intellectual Powers of Man*, p. 346.

19 This thesis is discussed and defended in my *Person and Object*, Appendix B ('Mereological essentialism').

20 Sea Hume, *Treatise of Humam Nature*, bk I, pt iv, sect. 6 (Selby-Bigge edn, p. 255): 'all objects, to which we ascribe identity, without observing their invariableness and uninterruptedness, are such as consist of a succession of related objects.' In this same section. Hume affirms a version of the principle of mereolgical essentialism.

21 We could define an *ens successivum* by saying, with St Augustine, that it is 'a single thing ... composed of many, all of which exist not together'; see *Confessions*, bk IV, ch. 11. St Thomas says in effect that a *successivum* is a thing such that some of its parts do not coexist with others of its parts ('una pars non est cum alia parte'); see the *Commentary on the Sentences*, bk I, dist. VIII, Q. 2, Art 1, ad 4. The term *ens successivum* has traditionally been applied to such things as periods of time (e.g., days, weeks, months) and events; compare Aristotle's *Physics*, bk III, ch. 6, 206a.

22 See Chisholm, *Person and Object*.

23 Definition D. III. 2 thus makes use of the general device by means of which Frege defined the ancestral relation; see G. Frege, *The Foundations of Arithmetic* (Oxford: Blackwell, 1950), sect. 79. A more intuitive reading of clause (iii) might be: '(iii) x belongs at t to every class c which is such that (a) y belongs to c at t' and (b) all direct table successors of anything belonging to c belong to c.'

24 The distinction among these several types of property are used in my *Person and Object*, ch. 4, to mark off those states of affairs that are *events*. (We had noted in the previous chapter that, although 'John is walking' refers to an event, 'John will walk' and 'John is such that either he is walking or he will walk' do not refer to events.)

25 Compare Hume: 'Tho' we commonly be able to distinguish pretty exactly betwixt numerical and specific identity, yet it sometimes happens that we confound them, and in our thinking and reasoning employ the one for the other.' (*Treatise of Human Nature*, bk I, pt iv, sect 6 ('Of Personal Identity'), Selby-Bigge edn, pp. 257–8.

26 It may be noted that we have defined the loose and popular sense of the expression 'There are n so-and-so's at t' and not the more general 'The number of so-and-so's that there ever will have been is n'. For the loose and popular sense of this latter expression is not sufficiently fixed to be explicated in any strict and philosophical sense. The following example may make this clear. In the infantry of the United States Army during World War II each private carried materials for half a tent – something like one piece of canvas, a pole and ropes. Two privates could then assemble their materials and create a tent which would be disassembled in the morning. On another night the two privates might find different tent companions. Occasionally when the company was in camp, the various tent parts were collected, stored away, and then reissued, but with no attempt to assign particular parts to their former holders. Supposing, to simplify the matter considerably, that all the tents that there ever will have been were those that were created by the members of a certain infantry company, how, making use of our ordinary criteria, would we go about answering the question 'Just how many tents *have* there been?' Would an accounting of the history of the joinings of the various tent parts be sufficient to give us the answer?

34

Identity, Ostension,
and Hypostasis

W. V. Quine

I

Identity is a popular source of philosophical perplexity. Undergoing change as I do, how can I be said to continue to be myself? Considering that a complete replacement of my material substance takes place every few years, how can I be said to continue to be I for more than such a period at best?

It would be agreeable to be driven, by these or other considerations, to belief in a changeless and therefore immortal soul as the vehicle of my persisting self-identity. But we should be less eager to embrace a parallel solution of Heracleitus's parallel problem regarding a river: 'You cannot bathe in the same river twice, for new waters are ever flowing in upon you.'

The solution of Heracleitus's problem, though familiar, will afford a convenient approach to some less familiar matters. The truth is that you *can* bathe in the same *river* twice, but not in the same river stage. You can bathe in two river stages which are stages of the same river, and this is what constitutes bathing in the same river twice. A river is a process through time, and the river stages are its momentary parts. Identification of the river bathed in once with the river bathed in

again is just what determines our subject matter to be a river process as opposed to a river stage.

Let me speak of any multiplicity of water molecules as a *water*. Now a river stage is at the same time a water stage, but two stages of the same river are not in general stages of the same water. River stages are water stages, but rivers are not waters. You may bathe in the same river twice without bathing in the same water twice, and you may, in these days of fast transportation, bathe in the same water twice while bathing in two different rivers.

We begin, let us imagine, with momentary things and their interrelations. One of these momentary things, called *a*, is a momentary stage of the river Caÿster, in Lydia, around 400 BC. Another, called *b*, is a momentary stage of the Caÿster two days later. A third, *c*, is a momentary stage, at this same latter date, of the same multiplicity of water molecules which were in the river at the time of *a*. Half of *c* is in the lower Caÿster valley, and the other half is to be found at diffuse points in the Aegean Sea. Thus *a*, *b*, and *c* are three objects, variously related. We may say that *a* and *b* stand in the relation of river kinship, and that *a* and *c* stand in the relation of water kinship.

W. V. Quine, "Identity, Ostension, and Hypostasis," *Journal of Philosophy*, 47/22 (26 Oct. 1950): 621–33. Reprinted by permission of the Journal of Philosophy and Dr. Douglas B. Quine, literary executor.

Metaphysics: An Anthology, Second Edition. Edited by Jaegwon Kim, Daniel Z. Korman and Ernest Sosa.
Editorial material and organization © 2012 Blackwell Publishing Ltd. Published 2012 by Blackwell Publishing Ltd.

Now the introduction of rivers as single entities, namely, processes or time-consuming objects, consists substantially in reading identity in place of river kinship. It would be wrong, indeed, to say that a and b are identical; they are merely river-kindred. But if we were to point to a, and then wait the required two days and point to b, and affirm identity of the objects pointed to, we should thereby show that our pointing was intended not as a pointing to two kindred river stages but as a pointing to a single river which included them both. The imputation of identity is essential, here, to fixing the reference of the ostension.

These reflections are reminiscent of Hume's account of our idea of external objects. Hume's theory was that the idea of external objects arises from an error of identification. Various similar impressions separated in time are mistakenly treated as identical; and then, as a means of resolving this contradiction of identifying momentary events which are separated in time, we invent a new non-momentary object to serve as subject matter of our statement of identity. Hume's charge of erroneous identification here is interesting as a psychological conjecture on origins, but there is no need for us to share that conjecture. The important point to observe is merely the direct connection between identity and the positing of processes, or time-extended objects. To impute identity rather than river kinship is to talk of the river Caÿster rather than of a and b.

Pointing is of itself ambiguous as to the temporal spread of the indicated object. Even given that the indicated object is to be a process with considerable temporal spread, and hence a summation of momentary objects, still pointing does not tell us *which* summation of momentary objects is intended, beyond the fact that the momentary object at hand is to be in the desired summation. Pointing to a, if construed as referring to a time-extended process and not merely to the momentary object a, could be interpreted either as referring to the river Caÿster of which a and b are stages, or as referring to the water of which a and c are stages, or as referring to any one of an unlimited number of further less natural summations to which a also belongs.

Such ambiguity is commonly resolved by accompanying the pointing with such words as 'this river', thus appealing to a prior concept of a river as one distinctive type of time-consuming process, one distinctive form of summation of momentary objects. Pointing to a and saying 'this river' – or ὅδε ὁ ποταμός, since we are in 400 BC – leaves no ambiguity as to the object of reference if the word 'river' itself is already intelligible. 'This river' means 'the riverish summation of momentary objects which contains this momentary object'.

But here we have moved beyond pure ostension and have assumed conceptualization. Now suppose instead that the general term 'river' is not yet understood, so that we cannot specify the Caÿster by pointing and saying 'This river is the Caÿster'. Suppose also that we are deprived of other descriptive devices. What we may do then is point to a and two days later to b and say each time, 'This is the Caÿster'. The word 'this' so used must have referred not to a nor to b, but beyond to something more inclusive, identical in the two cases. Our specification of the Caÿster is not yet unique, however, for we might still mean any of a vast variety of other collections of momentary objects, related in other modes than that of river kinship; all we know is that a and b are among its constituents. By pointing to more and more stages additional to a and b, however, we eliminate more and more alternatives, until our listener, aided by his own tendency to favor the most natural groupings, has grasped the idea of the Caÿster. His learning of this idea is an induction: from our grouping the sample momentary objects a, b, d, g, and others under the head of Caÿster, he projects a correct general hypothesis as to what further momentary objects we would also be content to include.

Actually there is in the case of the Caÿster the question of its extent in space as well as in time. Our sample pointings need to be made not only on a variety of dates, but at various points up and down stream, if our listener is to have a representative basis for his inductive generalization as to the intended spatiotemporal spread of the four-dimensional object Caÿster.

In ostension, spatial spread is not wholly separable from temporal spread, for the successive ostensions which provide samples over the spatial spread are bound to consume time. The inseparability of space and time characteristic of relativity theory is foreshadowed, if only superficially, in this simple situation of ostension.

The concept of identity, then, is seen to perform a central function in the specifying of spatiotemporally broad objects by ostension. Without identity, n acts of ostension merely specify up to n objects, each of indeterminate spatiotemporal spread. But when we affirm identity of object from ostension to ostension, we cause our n ostensions to refer to the same large object, and so afford our listener an inductive ground from which to guess the intended reach of that object. Pure ostension plus identification conveys, with the help of some induction, spatiotemporal spread.

II

Now between what we have thus far observed and the ostensive explanation of *general* terms, such as 'red' or 'river', there is an evident similarity. When I point in a direction where red is visible and say 'This is red', and repeat the performance at various places over a period of time, I provide an inductive basis for gauging the intended spread of the attribute of redness. The difference would seem to be merely that the spread concerned here is a conceptual spread, generality, rather than spatiotemporal spread.

And is this really a difference? Let us try shifting our point of view so far as to think of the word 'red' in full analogy to 'Caÿster'. By pointing and saying 'This is Caÿster' at various times and places, we progressively improve our listener's understanding as to what portions of space-time we intend our word 'Caÿster' to cover; and by pointing and saying 'This is red' at various times and places, we progressively improve our listener's understanding as to what portions of space-time we intend our word 'red' to cover. The regions to which 'red' applies are indeed not continuous with one another as those are to which 'Caÿster' applies, but this surely is an irrelevant detail; 'red' surely is not to be opposed to 'Caÿster', as abstract to concrete, merely because of discontinuity in geometrical shape. The territory of the United States including Alaska is discontinuous, but it is nonetheless a single concrete object; and so is a bedroom suite, or a scattered deck of cards. Indeed, every physical object that is not subatomic is, according to physics, made up of spatially separated parts. So why not view 'red' quite on a par with 'Caÿster', as naming a single concrete object extended in space and time? From this point of view, to say that a certain drop is red is to affirm a simple spatiotemporal relation between two concrete objects; the one object, the drop, is a spatiotemporal part of the other, red, just as a certain waterfall is a spatiotemporal part of Caÿster.

Before proceeding to consider how it is that a general equating of universals to particulars breaks down, I want to go back and examine more closely the ground we have already been over. We have seen how identity and ostension are combined in conceptualizing extended objects, but we have not asked why. What is the survival value of this practice? Identity is more convenient than river kinship or other relations, because the objects related do not have to be kept apart as a multiplicity. As long as what we may propose to say about the river Caÿster does not in itself involve distinctions between momentary stages a, b, etc., we gain formal simplicity of subject matter by representing our subject matter as a single object, Caÿster, instead of a multiplicity of objects a, b, etc., in river kinship. The expedient is an application, in a local or relative way, of Occam's razor: the entities concerned in a particular discourse are reduced from many, a, b, etc., to one, the Caÿster. Note, however, that from an overall or absolute point of view the expedient is quite opposite to Occam's razor, for the multiple entities a, b, etc., have not been dropped from the universe; the Caÿster has simply been added. There are contexts in which we shall still need to speak differentially of a, b, and others rather than speaking indiscriminately of the Caÿster. Still the Caÿster remains a convenient addition to our ontology because of the contexts in which it does effect economy.

Consider, somewhat more generally, a discourse about momentary objects all of which happen still to be river stages, but not entirely river kindred. If it happens in this particular discourse that whatever is affirmed of any momentary object is affirmed also of every other which is river kindred to it, so that no distinctions between stages of the same river are relevant, then clearly we can gain simplicity by representing our subject matter as comprising a few rivers rather than the many river stages. Diversities remain among our new objects, the rivers, but no diversities remain beyond the needs of the discourse with which we are occupied.

I have been speaking just now of integration of momentary objects into time-consuming wholes, but it is clear that similar remarks apply to integration of individually indicable localities into spatially extensive wholes. Where what we want to say about certain broad surfaces does not concern distinctions between their parts, we simplify our discourse by making its objects as few and large as we can – taking the various broad surfaces as single objects.

Analogous remarks hold, and very conspicuously, for conceptual integration – the integrating of particulars into a universal. Suppose a discourse about person stages, and suppose that whatever is said about any person stage, in this particular discourse, applies equally to all person stages which make the same amount of money. Our discourse is simplified, then, by shifting its subject matter from person stages to income groups. Distinctions immaterial to the discourse at hand are thus extruded from the subject matter.

In general we might propound this maxim of the *identification of indiscernibles*: Objects indistinguishable from one another within the terms of a given discourse should be construed as identical for that discourse. More accurately: the references to the original objects should be reconstrued for purposes of the discourse as referring to other and fewer objects, in such a way that indistinguishable originals give way each to the same new object.

For a striking example of the application of this maxim, consider the familiar so-called propositional calculus. To begin with, let us follow the lead of some modern literature by thinking of the 'p', 'q', etc. of this calculus as referring to propositional concepts, whatever they may be. But we know that propositional concepts alike in truth value are indistinguishable within the terms of this calculus, interchangeable so far as anything expressible in this calculus is concerned. Then the canon of identification of indiscernibles directs us to reconstrue 'p', 'q', etc. as referring merely to truth values – which, by the way, was Frege's interpretation of this calculus.

For my own part, I prefer to think of 'p', 'q', etc. as schematic letters standing in place of statements but not referring at all. But if they are to be treated as referring, the maxim is in order.

Our maxim of identification of indiscernibles is relative to a discourse, and hence vague insofar as the cleavage between discourses is vague. It applies best when the discourse is neatly closed, like the propositional calculus; but discourse generally departmentalizes itself to some degree, and this degree will tend to determine where and to what degree it may prove convenient to invoke the maxim of identification of indiscernibles.

III

Now let us return to our reflections on the nature of universals. Earlier we represented this category by the example 'red', and found this example to admit of treatment as an ordinary spatiotemporally extended particular on a par with the Caÿster. Red was the largest red thing in the universe – the scattered total thing whose parts are all the red things. Similarly, in the recent example of income groups, each income group can be thought of simply as the scattered total spatiotemporal thing which is made up of the appropriate person stages, various stages of various persons. An income group is just as concrete as a river or a person, and, like a person, it is a summation of person stages. It differs from a person merely in that the person stages which go together to make up an income group are another assortment than those which go together to make up a person. Income groups are related to persons much as waters are related to rivers; for it will be recalled that the momentary object a was part in a temporal way both of a river and of a water, while b was a part of the same river but not of the same water, and c was a part of the same water but not of the same river. Up to now, therefore, the distinction between spatiotemporal integration and conceptual integration appears idle; all is spatiotemporal integration.

Now let me switch to a more artificial example. Suppose our subject matter consists of the visibly outlined convex regions, small and large, in figure 34.1. There are 33 such regions. Suppose

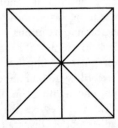

Figure 34.1

further that we undertake a discourse relatively to which any geometrically similar regions are interchangeable. Then our maxim of identification of indiscernibles directs us for purposes of this discourse to speak not of similarity but of identity; to say not that x and y are similar but that $x = y$, thus reconstruing the objects x and y as no longer regions but shapes. The subject matter then shrinks in multiplicity from 33 to 5: the isosceles right triangle, the square, the two-to-one rectangle, and two forms of trapezoid.

Each of these five is a universal. Now just as we have reconstrued the color red as the total spatiotemporal thing made up of all the red things, so suppose we construe the shape square as the total region made up by pooling all the five square regions. Suppose also we construe the shape isosceles right triangle as the total region made up by pooling all the 16 triangular regions. Similarly suppose we construe the shape two-to-one rectangle as the total region made up by pooling the four two-to-one rectangular regions; and similarly for the two trapezoidal shapes. Clearly this leads to trouble, for our five shapes then all reduce to one, the total region. Pooling all the triangular regions gives simply the total square region; pooling all the square regions gives the same; and similarly for the other three shapes. We should end up, intolerably, by concluding identity among the five shapes.

So the theory of universals as concrete, which happened to work for red, breaks down in general.[1] We can imagine that universals in general, as entities, insinuated themselves into our ontology in the following way. First we formed the habit of introducing spatiotemporally extended concrete things, according to the pattern considered earlier. Red entered with Caÿster and the others as a concrete thing. Finally triangle, square, and other universals were swept in on a faulty analogy with red and its ilk.

Purely as philosophical sport, without supposing there to be any serious psychological or anthropological import in our reflections, let us now go back to Hume's theory of external objects and carry it a step further. Momentary impressions, according to Hume, are wrongly identified with one another on the basis of resemblance. Then, to resolve the paradox of identity among temporally disparate entities, we invent time-consuming objects as objects of the

identity. Spatial spread, beyond what is given momentarly in an impression, may be supposed introduced in similar fashion. The entity red, call it a universal or a widespread particular as you please, may be viewed as entering by the same process (though we are now beyond Hume). Momentary localized red impressions are identified one with another, and then a single entity red is appealed to as vehicle of these otherwise untenable identities. Similarly for the entity square, and the entity triangle. Square impressions are identified with one another, and then the single entity square is imported as vehicle for the identity; and correspondingly for triangle.

So far, no difference is noted between the introduction of particulars and universals. But in retrospect we have to recognize a difference. If square and triangle were related to the original square and triangular particulars in the way in which concrete objects are related to their momentary stages and spatial fragments, then square and triangle would turn out to be identical with each other – as lately observed in terms of our artificial little universe of regions.

Therefore we come to recognize two different types of association: that of concrete parts in a concrete whole, and that of concrete instances in an abstract universal. We come to recognize a divergence between two senses of 'is': 'This is the Caÿster' versus 'This is square'.

IV

Interrupting this speculative psychology, let us return to our analysis of ostension of spatiotemporally extended objects, and see how it differs from what may be called the ostension of irreducible universals such as square and triangle. In ostensively explaining the Caÿster, we point to a, b, and other stages, and say each time 'This is the Caÿster', identity of indicated object being understood from each occasion to the next. In ostensively explaining 'square', on the other hand, we point to various particulars and say each time 'This is square' *without* imputing identity of indicated object from one occasion to the next. These various latter pointings give our listener the basis for a reasonable induction as to what we might in general be willing to point out as square, just as our various former pointings gave him the basis for a reasonable induction as to what we might willingly point to as the Caÿster. The difference in the two cases is merely that in the one case an identical indicated object is supposed, and in the other case not. In the second case what is supposed to be identical from pointing to pointing is not the indicated object, but, at best, an attribute squareness which is *shared by* the indicated objects.

Actually there is no need, up to this point, to suppose such entities as attributes at all in our ostensive clarification of 'square'. We are clarifying, by our various pointings, our use of the words 'is square'; but neither is an object squareness supposed as object pointed to, nor need it be supposed available as reference of the word 'square'. No more need be demanded, in explication of 'is square' or any other phrase, than that our listener learn when to expect us to apply it to an object and when not; there is no need for the phrase itself to be a name in turn of a separate object of any kind.

These contrasts, then, have emerged between general terms and singular terms. First, the ostensions which introduce a general term differ from those which introduce a singular term in that the former do not impute identity of indicated object between occasions of pointing. Second, the general term does not, or need not, purport to be a name in turn of a separate entity of any sort, whereas the singular term does.

These two observations are not independent of each other. The accessibility of a term to identity contexts was urged by Frege as the standard by which to judge whether that term is being used as a name.[2] Whether or not a term is being used as naming an entity is to be decided, in any given context, by whether or not the term is viewed as subject in that context to the algorithm of identity: the law of putting equals for equals.

It is not to be supposed that this doctrine of Frege's is connected with a repudiation of abstract entities. On the contrary, we remain free to admit names of abstract entities; and, according to Frege's criterion, such admission will consist precisely in admitting abstract terms to identity contexts subject to the regular laws of identity. Frege himself, incidentally, was rather a Platonist in his own philosophy.

It is clearest, I think, to view this step of hypostasis of abstract entities as an additional step which follows after the introduction of the corresponding general terms. First we may suppose the idiom 'This is square', or 'x is square', introduced – perhaps by ostension as previously considered, or perhaps by other channels, such as the usual geometrical definition in terms of prior general terms. Then as a separate step we derive the attribute *squareness*, or, what comes to much the same thing, *the class of squares*. A new fundamental operator 'class of', or '-ness', is appealed to in this step.

I attach much importance to the traditional distinction between general terms and abstract singular terms, 'square' versus 'squareness', because of the ontological point: use of the general term does not of itself commit us to the admission of a corresponding abstract entity into our ontology; on the other hand, the use of an abstract singular term, subject to the standard behavior of singular terms such as the law of putting equals for equals, flatly commits us to an abstract entity named by the term.

It is readily conceivable that it was precisely because of failure to observe this distinction that abstract entities gained their hold upon our imaginations in the first place. Ostensive explanation of general terms such as 'square' is, we have seen, much like that of concrete singular terms such as 'Caÿster', and indeed there are cases such as 'red' where no difference need be made at all. Hence the natural tendency not only to introduce general terms along with singular ones, but to treat them on a par as names each of a single entity. This tendency is no doubt encouraged by the fact that it is often convenient for purely syntactical reasons, reasons, for example, of word order or cross-reference, to handle a general term like a proper name.

V

The conceptual scheme in which we grew up is an eclectic heritage, and the forces which conditioned its evolution from the days of Java man onward are a matter of conjecture.[3] Expressions for physical objects must have occupied a focal position from the earliest linguistic periods, because such objects provided relatively fixed points of reference for language as a social development. General terms also must have appeared at an early stage, because similar stimuli tend psychologically to induce similar responses; similar objects tend to be called by the same word. We have seen, indeed, that the ostensive acquisition of a concrete general term proceeds in much the same way as that of a concrete singular term. The adoption of abstract singular terms, carrying with it the positing of abstract entities, is a further step and a philosophically revolutionary one; yet we have seen how this step in turn could have been made without conscious invention.

There is every reason to rejoice that general terms are with us, whatever the cause. Clearly language would be impossible without them, and thought would come to very little. On the admission of abstract entities, however, as named by abstract singular terms, there is room for divergent value judgements. For clarity it is important in any case to recognize in their introduction an additional operator, 'class of' or '-ness'. Perhaps, as just now suggested, it was failure to appreciate the intrusion of such an additional unexplained operator that engendered belief in abstract entities. But this genetic point is independent of the question whether abstract entities, once with us, are not a good thing from the point of view of conceptual convenience after all – happy accident though their adoption may have been.

Anyway, once abstract entities are admitted, our conceptual mechanism goes on and generates an unending hierarchy of further abstractions as a matter of course. For, it must be noted to begin with that the ostensive processes which we have been studying are not the only way of introducing terms, singular or general. Most of us will agree that such introduction is fundamental; but once a fund of ostensively acquired terms is at hand, there is no difficulty in explaining additional terms discursively, through paraphrase into complexes of the terms already at hand. Now discursive explanation, unlike ostension, is just as available for defining new general terms applicable to abstract entities, for example, 'shape' or 'zoological species', as for defining general terms applicable to concrete entities. Applying then the operator '-ness' or 'class of' to such abstract general terms, we get second-level abstract singular terms, purporting to name such entities as the attribute of being a shape or zoological species, or the class of all shapes or

zoological species. The same procedure can be repeated for the next level, and so on, theoretically without end. It is in these higher levels that mathematical entities such as numbers, functions of numbers, etc., find their place, according to the analyses of the foundations of mathematics which have been usual from Frege onward through Whitehead and Russell.

The fundamental-seeming philosophical question, How much of our science is merely contributed by language and how much is a genuine reflection of reality? is perhaps a spurious question which itself arises wholly from a certain particular type of language. Certainly we are in a predicament if we try to answer the question; for to answer the question, we must talk about the world as well as about language, and to talk about the world we must already impose upon the world some conceptual scheme peculiar to our own special language.

Yet we must not leap to the fatalistic conclusion that we are stuck with the conceptual scheme that we grew up in. We can change it bit by bit, plank by plank, though meanwhile there is nothing to carry us along but the evolving conceptual scheme itself. The philosopher's task was well compared by Neurath to that of a mariner who must rebuild his ship on the open sea.

We can improve our conceptual scheme, our philosophy, bit by bit while continuing to depend on it for support; but we cannot detach ourselves from it and compare it objectively with an unconceptualized reality. Hence it is meaningless, I suggest, to inquire into the absolute correctness of a conceptual scheme as a mirror of reality. Our standard for appraising basic changes of conceptual scheme must be, not a realistic standard of correspondence to reality, but a pragmatic standard.[4] Concepts are language, and the purpose of concepts and of language is efficacy in communication and in prediction. Such is the ultimate duty of language, science, and philosophy, and it is in relation to that duty that a conceptual scheme has finally to be appraised.

Elegance, conceptual economy, also enters as an objective. But this virtue, engaging though it is, is secondary – sometimes in one way and sometimes in another. Elegance can make the difference between a psychologically manageable conceptual scheme and one that is too unwieldy for our poor minds to cope with effectively. Where this happens, elegance is simply a means to the end of a pragmatically acceptable conceptual scheme. But elegance also enters as an end in itself – and quite properly so as long as it remains secondary in another respect; namely, as long as it is appealed to only in choices where the pragmatic standard prescribes no contrary decision. Where elegance doesn't matter, we may and shall, as poets, pursue elegance for elegance's sake.

Notes

1 Nelson Goodman, *The Structure of Appearance* (Cambridge, Mass.: Harvard University Press, 1951), pp. 46–51.

2 Gottlob Frege, 'On sense and nominatum', in H. Feigl and W. Sellars (eds), *Readings in Philosophical Analysis* (New York: Appleton-Century-Crofts, 1949).

3 The unrefined and sluggish mind
    Of *Homo javanensis*
  Could only treat of things concrete
    And present to the senses.

4 On this theme see Pierre Duhem, *La Théorie physique: son objet et sa structure* (Paris, 1906), pp. 34, 280, 347; or Armand Lowinger, *The Methodology of Pierre Duhem* (New York: Columbia University Press, 1941), pp. 41, 121, 145.

35

Parthood and Identity Across Time

Judith Jarvis Thomson

Temporal parts have come in handy in a number of areas in philosophy.[1] Let us take a close look at one use to which some may be inclined to want to put them.

I

Suppose I own some Tinkertoys. I make a house out of them, finishing the task at 1:00. I put the house, which I shall call "H," on an otherwise empty shelf. Since H is the only Tinkertoy house now on the shelf, and since also the time now is 1:15, we may truly say

(1) H = the Tinkertoy house on the shelf at 1:15.

A Tinkertoy house is made of Tinkertoys. And surely a Tinkertoy house is made only of Tinkertoys: surely it has no additional ingredients, over and above the Tinkertoys it is made of. (Perhaps there is such an entity as "house-shape." Even if there is, it certainly is not literally part of any Tinkertoy house.)

It is an attractive idea that the logic of parthood is the Leonard–Goodman Calculus of Individuals,[2] which takes "x D y" (read: x is

discrete from y) as primitive, defines "$x < y$" (read: x is part of y) and "x O y" (read: x overlaps y) as follows:

$$x < y =_{df} (z)(z \, D \, y \supset z \, D \, x)$$
$$x \, O \, y =_{df} (\exists z)(z < x \, \& \, z < y)$$

and contains the following distinctive axioms:

(CI$_1$) $(x = y) \equiv (x < y \, \& \, y < x)$ identity axiom

(CI$_2$) $(x \, O \, y) \equiv \sim(x \, D \, y)$ overlap axiom

(CI$_3$) $(\exists x)(x \in S) \supset (\exists y)(y \, \text{Fu} \, S)$ fusion axiom

where "x Fu S" (read: x fuses S, or the Ss, or the members of S) is defined as follows:

$$x \, \text{Fu} \, S =_{df} (y)[y \, D \, x \equiv (z)(z \in S \supset y \, D \, z)]$$

(Another way in which we might have defined "x Fu S" is this: x fuses S just in case a thing y is part of x if and only if every part of y overlaps a member of S.)

It is worth stressing that the fusion axiom says only that if anything is a member of S, then there is a thing that fuses the Ss. What I shall call *the fusion principle*[3] says that if anything is a member of S, then there is a unique thing that fuses the Ss.

Judith Jarvis Thomson, "Parthood and Identity Across Time," *Journal of Philosophy*, 80 (1983): 201–20. Reproduced by permission.

$(\exists x)(x \in S) \supset (\exists! y)(y \text{ Fu } S)$ fusion principle

Or, as we may put it: if anything is a member of S, then there is such a thing as *the fusion of* the Ss. The fusion principle is provable in the Calculus of Individuals.

I said it is an attractive idea that the logic of parthood is the Leonard–Goodman Calculus of Individuals. If the axioms are true under their intended interpretation, then so is the fusion principle. There are Tinkertoys on the shelf at 1:15; so the fusion principle tells us that there is such a thing as the fusion of the Tinkertoys on the shelf at 1:15. I shall call it "W"; so we can say

(2) W = the fusion of the Tinkertoys on the shelf at 1:15.

Surely a Tinkertoy house is made only of Tinkertoys. The Tinkertoys H is made of are the Tinkertoys on the shelf at 1:15. So it very naturally suggests itself that we should say

(3) $H = W$.

So far so good; no problem yet.

II

But we should take note of the fact that that fusion axiom makes some people feel nervous. Few, I think, feel nervous about the definitions or about the identity and overlap axioms, but many object to the idea that there is something that fuses (as it might be) the set whose members are all giraffes and all apples. They think the fusion axiom grossly overstrong.

But why? The fusion axiom does commit us to the existence of some pretty odd things, but, so far as I can see, their oddity is no objection to them.

Never mind: the problem I want to set before you arises even if we reject the fusion axiom.

For suppose you have some bits of wood in your hand now; doesn't it follow that there is such a thing as *the wood* in your hand now?

There are some Tinkertoys on the shelf at 1:15, and, since Tinkertoys are bits of wood, it seems right to say there therefore is such a thing as the wood on the shelf at 1:15. Let us call it "W'"; so we can say

(2′) W' = the wood on the shelf at 1:15.

Surely a Tinkertoy house is made only of Tinkertoys. The Tinkertoys H is made of are the Tinkertoys on the shelf at 1:15. The Tinkertoys on the shelf at 1:15 are themselves bits of wood. So it very naturally suggests itself that we should say

(3′) $H = W'$.

If the fusion principle is true, then there is such a thing as the fusion of the Tinkertoys on the shelf at 1:15. I gave that thing the name "W". If there is such a thing as W, it seems plausible to suppose that W' is identical with it; i.e., it seems plausible to suppose that the wood on the shelf at 1:15 is the fusion of the Tinkertoys on the shelf at 1:15.

Even if the fusion principle is not true – in that the fusion axiom is overstrong – it seems plausible to suppose that there is such a thing as W, and that W' is identical with it; i.e., even if the fusion principle is not (in general) true, it seems plausible to suppose that there is such a thing as the fusion of the Tinkertoys on the shelf at 1:15, and that the wood on the shelf at 1:15 is identical with it.

But whether or not there is such a thing as W, it really does seem plausible to suppose that there is such a thing as W', the wood on the shelf at 1:15. *And* that the Tinkertoy house H is identical with it. That will suffice for generating the problem I want to set before you.

III

For let us give the name "alpha" to one of the sticks that help attach the roof of the house to its front wall. At 1:30, I remove alpha; I then replace alpha with a new stick, beta, and I throw alpha on the floor. Shortly thereafter, the time is 1:45. Is H still on the shelf at 1:45? That is, can we truly say

(4) H is on the shelf at 1:45?

Most of us are, I think, inclined to think we can: most of us are inclined to think that H survives replacement of alpha by beta and is still on the shelf at 1:45.

Now there is trouble. For the conjunction of (3′) and (4) entails

(5′)   W′ is on the shelf at 1:45,

which is not true, for W′ is only partly on the shelf at 1:45 – the wood on the shelf at 1:15 is partly on the floor at 1:45, since alpha is on the floor at 1:45.

So also of course the conjunction of (3) and (4) entails

(5)   W is on the shelf at 1:45,

which is also not true, even if there is such a thing as W. For W is only partly on the shelf at 1:45 – the fusion of the Tinkertoys on the shelf at 1:15 is partly on the floor at 1:45, since alpha is on the floor at 1:45.

What to do? Something has to give.

Well, we really must retain (4). Surely that is H on the shelf at 1:45. (This is the typewriter I bought five years ago, though I've had a key replaced.)

So it is the identity sentences (3) and (3′) which have to go. But it seemed intuitively right to say that a Tinkertoy house is made only of Tinkertoys. It was that intuition which led us to identify H first with W and then, anyway, with W′. There has got to be something right in that intuition; but what is the something right in it, if (3) and (3′) are not true? How is H related to W′ – and to W, if there is such a thing as W?

David Wiggins,[4] I think, would say that W, or anyway W′, constitutes H at 1:15, and that that is the most that can be retained of the intuition that a Tinkertoy house is made only of Tinkertoys. He may be right. But we cannot tell until we are made clearer than Wiggins makes us about just what it is for a thing x to constitute a thing y at a time t.

Richard Cartwright[5] draws attention to a solution that appeals to temporal parts. By hypothesis, H came into existence at 1:00, and alpha was removed from H at 1:30. H was in existence throughout that time; and suppose we allow ourselves to say that H therefore had a temporal part that came into existence at 1:00 and went out of existence at 1:30. If you like the fusion principle, you will think there is such a thing as W. It too was in existence throughout that time; and suppose we allow ourselves to conclude that it too had a temporal part that came into existence at 1:00 and went out of existence at 1:30. Let us call these entities, respectively, "H-from-1:00-to-1:30"

and "W-from-1:00-to-1:30." Friends of temporal parts take it that the temporal parts of a thing are, literally, parts of it; so we should say

H-from-1:00-to-1:30 is part of H

and

W-from-1:00-to-1:30 is part of W.

A Tinkertoy house is made only of Tinkertoys. Throughout 1:00 to 1:30, H was made of the Tinkertoys that W fuses; so shouldn't we say

H-from-1:00-to-1:30 = W-from-1:00-to-1:30,

and thus that H and W share a part – that they literally overlap? Tinkertoy houses may be made of different Tinkertoys at different times, however, so don't we preserve as much as anyone could want of the spirit of "A Tinkertoy house is made only of Tinkertoys" if we say, quite generally, that, for every temporal part x of a Tinkertoy house, there is a Tinkertoy fusion y such that x is identical with, or at least overlaps, some temporal part of y?

Of course you may not think there is any such thing as W. Then you are cordially invited to rewrite the preceding paragraph, replacing "W" by "W′", and making the necessary changes elsewhere in it.

But what exactly are these putative entities H-from-1:00-to-1:30 and W-from-1:00-to-1:30? Friends of "temporal parts" do seem to be just a bit casual about the manner in which they explain their use of that term; and a number of people have, rightly, complained that we are owed something more careful in the way of an account of them than we are commonly given.

IV

There are a number of different ways of defining the expression "temporal part". I shall try to define it in such a way as to lend the greatest possible plausibility to the metaphysical theses commonly asserted by use of it.

What we are interested in here is physical objects and their parts. Could I have said, more briefly, that what we are interested in here is physical objects? That is, is *not* every part of a physical object itself a physical object? I should think so. But let us not assume this. (I shall come back to it below.) Let us take the variables "x", "y", etc. to range over physical objects and their parts. Then the first of the metaphysical theses that must be accommodated is this:

(M$_1$) If x is a temporal part of y, then x is part of y.

As I said, friends of temporal parts take it that the temporal parts of a thing are *literally* part of it.

Or at least I think they do. For all I know, there may be those who think that the temporal parts of a thing are not parts of it, but only parts of something else, perhaps of the thing's history. I shall ignore that idea. (In any case, it is not clear exactly how appeal to temporal parts is to help anyone see how H is related to W and W' if their temporal parts are not among their parts.)

I should think that M$_1$ rules out taking the temporal parts of a physical object to be sets. Thus the temporal parts of my chair, for example, cannot be identified (as it might be) with the sets whose members are the chair and a time-point or time-stretch at or through which the chair exists, for I should think that no set is literally part of my chair.

What I suggest we do is attend to places as well as times. We have the idea that no two things can occupy the same place at the same time. Well, I hope that on reflection we shall conclude that that idea is false. But if two things occupy the same place at the same time then don't they at least overlap? Don't they literally share a part? That at any rate is the root idea that generates the definitions I shall give.

It will be simplest if we can make a certain assumption: viz., that every physical object, and every part of every physical object, exactly occupies exactly one place at every time-point at which it exists. I mean to include among "places," of course, discontinuous places, since there are physical objects that occupy such places now – for example, my suit now occupies a discontinuous place, the jacket being on one hanger and the skirt on another.

On one way of construing "places," that is a strong, and presumably false, assumption. Suppose we take places to have "sharp boundaries."

(Because they are sets of space-points? Because they are fusions of sets of space-points? No matter.) Common or garden physical objects presumably do not have sharp spatial boundaries. (What *exactly* are the spatial boundaries of my chair now?) But let us simply ignore the questions raised here. Let us take places to have sharp boundaries, and ignore the fact that making the assumption therefore involves spatial idealizing.

We are letting "x", "y", etc. range over physical objects and their parts. Let "P" range over places. Let t range over time-points, and "T" over times. I include time-stretches among the times. I also include time-points among the times, since many (most? all?) friends of temporal parts take it that physical objects have temporal parts that exist only at a time-point – i.e., that physical objects have temporal "slices" as well as temporal "chunks." (So the range of "t" is included in the range of "T".)

We go in two steps. Let us say, first,

x is a cross-sectional temporal part of y = $_{df}$ $(\exists T)[y$ and x exist through T & no part of x exists outside T & $(t)(t$ is in $T \supset (P)(y$ exactly occupies P at $t \supset x$ exactly occupies P at $t))]$.

Consider again the Tinkertoy house H. It existed through the time-stretch 1:00 to 1:30. If there is an x such that x exists through that time-stretch and such that no part of x exists through that time-stretch and such that, for all time-points in that time-stretch, if H exactly occupies a place, then x exactly occupies it too – if there is such an x, then this definition tells us that x is a cross-sectional temporal part of H. The definition does not tell us that there is such an x. The friends of temporal parts, of course, think there is; but telling us there is is the job, not of any definition, but of a second metaphysical thesis: viz.,

(M$_2$)$(T)[y$ exists through $T \supset (\exists x)(x$ exists through T & no part of x exists outside T & (t) $(t$ is in $T \supset (P)(y$ exactly occupies P at $t \supset x$ exactly occupies P at $t))]$.

Consider again alpha, the stick that was in H until I removed it at 1:30. M$_2$ tells us that alpha had a cross-sectional temporal part that existed only from 1:00 to 1:30. Shouldn't all cross-sectional temporal parts of alpha which existed only during that time be temporal parts not merely of alpha, but also of *H* itself? Presumably they should; so let us say

> *x* is a temporal part of *y* = $_{df}$
> $(\exists T)[y$ and *x* exist through *T* & no part of *x* exists outside *T* & $(t)(t$ is in $T \supset (P)$ $(y$ exactly occupies *P* at $t \supset x$ exactly occupies *P*, or a place in *P*, at $t))]$.

This definition tells us that cross-sectional temporal parts of alpha which exist only during 1:00 to 1:30 are temporal parts of alpha – and of *H*.

Nothing so far said ensures uniqueness. For example, nothing so far said ensures that, if *H* exists through 1:00 to 1:30, then there is *exactly one x* such that *x* exists through that time-stretch and such that no part of *x* exists outside that time-stretch and such that, for all time-points in that time-stretch, if *H* exactly occupies a place, then *x* exactly occupies it too. But shouldn't uniqueness be ensured? I think that friends of temporal parts would like it ensured; indeed, I think they accept a third metaphysical thesis: viz.,

> (M$_3$) If *x* is part of *y* and *y* is part of *x*, then *x* is identical with *y*.[6]

Between them, M$_1$ and M$_3$ ensure the desired uniqueness. For suppose, for example, that *x* and *x'* both have that rather complicated relation to *H* which I just drew attention to. Then *x* and *x'* have it to each other. Then *x* and *x'* are cross-sectional temporal parts of each other and, hence, temporal parts of each other and, hence, by M$_1$, parts of each other. It follows, by M$_3$, that *x* is identical with *x'*.

M$_3$ is obviously a consequence of the identity axiom

$$(x = y) \equiv (x < y) \;\&\; (y < x)$$

of the Calculus of Individuals under its intended interpretation. Friends of temporal parts need not assent to all the axioms of that Calculus: for all I know, some of them reject the fusion axiom as too strong. (So far as I can see, there is nothing in the metaphysic of temporal parts which commits its adherents to the existence of a thing that fuses the set whose members are all giraffes and all apples.) But I think they are all of them happy to assent to the identity axiom.

M$_2$ tells us that there is an *x* that is a cross-sectional temporal part of alpha lasting only from 1:00 to 1:05 and that there is a *y* that is a cross-sectional temporal part of *H* lasting only from 1:10 to 1:15; and the definition of "temporal part" tells us that both *x* and *y* are temporal parts of *H*. Does it follow that there is an entity that fuses *x* and *y*? I think that even those friends of temporal parts who think that the fusion axiom is not (in general) true would assent to

> If *x* is a temporal part of *z* and *y* is a temporal part of *z*, then there is a *z'* that fuses the set whose members are *x* and *y*.

If this is true, then (in light of what precedes) they can say that there is exactly one such *z'* and that it is, itself, a temporal part of *z*. But I do not give this further metaphysical thesis a name, since I suppose it is just barely possible that some friend of temporal parts thinks that even *this* "fusion thesis" is too strong.

I have obviously been so using the expression "is part of" to stand for a reflexive relation: I have been throughout using it in such a way as to make it true to say that everything is part of itself. I think all friends of temporal parts use the expression "is a temporal part of" in that way too – i.e., in such a way as to make their fourth and final metaphysical thesis

> (M$_4$)   *x* is a temporal part of *x*

true.

That looks at first glance like an uninteresting metaphysical thesis; so it pays us to take note of the fact that it is very strong indeed.

In the first place, with M$_4$ in hand we can now easily deduce that every physical object, and every part of every physical object, is the fusion of its temporal parts. But after all, that consequence is presumably just as it should be – the friends of temporal parts would welcome it.

In the second place, we should ask: do "times" have "sharp boundaries"? If so, something that is presumably false now follows. Consider a common or garden physical object – my chair, for example. M$_4$ tells us it is a temporal part of itself. The definition of "temporal part" tell us that this means there is a time *T* such that my chair exists through *T* and such that no part of my chair exists outside T, and so, in particular, such that my chair itself does not exist outside T. But is there? Is there a time-point t such that my chair was in existence at t and at no time before t? Or a time-point t such that my chair was not in existence at or before t, but was in existence at times as close after t as you like? I should think not: I should think there is no such thing as the *exact* temporal boundary of a chair.

Well, temporal idealizing is presumably no worse than spatial idealizing, and those who are still reading are already engaging in the latter activity – see p. 483 above.

The third consequence is far more serious. M_4 tells us that my chair is a temporal part of itself, and this means there is a time T such that my chair exists through T and such that no part of my chair exists outside T, and so, in particular, such that my chair exists through and only through T and no part of it exists before T. Now my chair was made out of wood: four wooden legs, a wooden seat, and a wooden back were screwed together to make that chair. So the legs, seat, and back existed before the chair existed; so neither the legs, seat, nor back of the chair are parts of the chair. What an absurd result to have arrived at!

"No doubt it sounds odd," says the friend of temporal parts with a sigh. "But it can be lived with. For keep this in mind: if the legs, seat, and back of the chair are not themselves parts of the chair, they do at all events overlap the chair – since they have temporal parts that are temporal parts of the chair."

And perhaps the friend of temporal parts doesn't even sigh. A Tinkertoy house is made only of Tinkertoys; and isn't a chair made only of bits of wood, metal, cloth, etc.? And how is this intuition to be more tidily accommodated than by saying that every temporal part of a chair overlaps a temporal part of one or other of the bits of wood, metal, cloth, etc. of which it is made – and that the chair itself just is the fusion of its temporal parts?

More precisely: by saying that every temporal part of a chair overlaps a temporal part of one or other of the bits of wood, etc., of which the chair is at some time or other made. A Tinkertoy house is made only of Tinkertoys, but it may be made of different Tinkertoys at different times – remember the replacement of beta for alpha in H. Similarly, a chair may be made of different bits of wood, etc.,

at different times. How better to capture what goes on when a chair or house is made or when a bit of stuff is replaced in a chair or house, than by adoption of the metaphysic of temporal parts?

V

It seems to me a crazy metaphysic – obviously false. But it seems to me also that there is no such thing as a *proof* that it is false.[7]

Some people have the idea that it follows from this metaphysic that the world is static, that nothing changes, and that, that being false, the metaphysic must be false. But why should we think that this does follow? A thing changes if and only if it has a feature at an earlier time which it lacks at a later time. And a friend of temporal parts says that changes take place all the time, but that a thing does have a feature at an earlier time which it lacks at a later time if and only if earlier cross-sectional temporal parts of the thing have it and later cross-sectional temporal parts of the thing lack it.

Again, some people object to the fact that this metaphysic yields that more than one thing can occupy a given place at a given time – e.g., the cross-sectional temporal part of H which exists only from 1:00 to 1:30 occupies the very same place at 1:15 as H itself occupies at 1:15. But should we take this seriously? On reflection, it does not appear to be a conclusive objection. For after all, the metaphysic also yields that those two things, though not identical, are not discrete – it yields that the former is part of the latter.

I have deliberately refrained from including among the metaphysical theses anything that says that the temporal parts of a thing are ontologically or epistemologically "prior" to it. These are dark notions; but I think we have *some* grip on what they are, enough perhaps to be able to construct a (more or less messy) argument to the effect that the temporal parts of a physical object are not ontologically or epistemologically prior to it. No matter. What concerns me now is not their priority, but their very existence.

Why should we accept this metaphysic? I am inclined to think that the friends of temporal parts are largely motivated by two things: one, the fact that so many problems in philosophy having to do with identity across time can be so tidily solved by appeal to them, and, two, what might be called "the spatial analogy." I shall come back to the first later; let us attend now to the second.

Suppose I have a piece of chalk in my hands now, one end in my right hand, the other in my left. It is a plausible idea that there is such a thing as the "right-hand half" of the bit of chalk. (No part of it is in my left hand.) If there is such a thing, we might as well call it "Alfred."

Friends of temporal parts say that, analogously, there is such a thing as the "later half" of the bit of chalk. (No part of it existed when the chalk first came into existence.) If there is such a thing, we might as well call it "Bert."

I think it is not merely plausible to think that there is such a thing as Alfred, but that we are under considerable pressure to say that there is. For I can break the bit of chalk in half. (Actually, it isn't easy to break a bit of chalk *exactly* in half, but I might be lucky.) If I do, I will have something in my right hand which is white, roughly cylindrical in shape, dusty, etc.; and it could hardly be said that that thing will come into existence at breaking-time – surely the thing does exist before I break it (note that "it") off. And surely the thing does exist now, even if I never break it off.

There is no analogous pressure to say that there is such a thing as Bert. (Homework: try breaking a bit of chalk into its two temporal halves.)

Friends of temporal parts are quite unmoved by this difference. They say: No doubt there are differences, but why shouldn't we take lasting through time to be analogous with extending through space? Why shouldn't we say that, just as there is Alfred, so also there is Bert?

Let us look at the consequences for Bert of the idea that Bert is to be Alfred's temporal analogue.

Is Alfred a physical object? It would presumably be wrong to say that Alfred is a bit or piece or chunk of chalk. If I break Alfred off, Alfred will become a bit of chalk; but I have not in fact broken Alfred off. It is an interesting and not easily answerable question why Alfred is not now a bit of chalk. The point isn't that Alfred isn't independently movable, for you can glue two bits of wood together, which are then two bits of wood that are not independently movable. (Of course you could break off one of the bits of wood; but so could you break Alfred off.) And I think the point isn't that Alfred is continuous with more chalk; for if Alfred had been broken off and were now being held

carefully in place again, it is arguable that Alfred would have been a bit of chalk continuous with another bit of chalk. No matter: as things stand, Alfred is not a bit or piece or chunk of chalk.

Something similar should presumably be said of Bert, viz., that it too is not a bit or piece or chunk of chalk. (For temporal parts come and go during a time in which I have only one bit of chalk in my hand.)

Now perhaps it may be thought that a thing is not a physical object unless it is a bit or piece or chunk of stuff of some kind. It would be no surprise if one who took this view thought that neither Alfred nor Bert is a physical object. It was to allow for the possibility that someone might take this view that I said we should take "x", "y" etc. to range not merely over physical objects, but also over anything that is part of a physical object.

What are Alfred and Bert then? Well, perhaps it will be said that they are quantities[8] of chalk. Or portions[9] of chalk. Which leaves it open for them to be perfectly respectable entities, with any number of ordinary physical properties. Thus Alfred presumably is white, roughly cylindrical in shape, and dusty; if the bit of chalk now weighs three ounces, then Alfred presumably now weighs an ounce and a half; and so on. And shouldn't we say, analogously, that Bert is white, roughly cylindrical in shape, and dusty? Perhaps by the time Bert comes into existence, the bit of chalk will weigh less than three ounces; but surely Bert will have some weight or other at every time at which it exists – just as Alfred does. If Alfred and Bert are not bits of chalk, and therefore not physical objects, they are anyway, both of them, surely *chalk*.

If Bert has not got these properties, then it is very obscure what Bert is, and hard to see why drawing our attention to Alfred should incline us to think there is such a thing as Bert.

I said this seems to me a crazy metaphysic. It seems to me that its full craziness comes out only when we take the spatial analogy seriously. The metaphysic yields that if I have had exactly one bit of chalk in my hand for the last hour, then there is something in my hand which is white, roughly cylindrical in shape, and dusty, something which also has a weight, something which is chalk, which was not in my hand three minutes ago, and indeed, such that no part of it was in my hand three minutes ago. As I hold the bit of chalk in my hand, new stuff, new chalk keeps constantly coming into existence *ex nihilo*. That strikes me as obviously false.

At a minimum, we ought to see whether there isn't some less extravagant way of solving the problem with which we began.

VI

What exactly is the problem? Whether or not there is such a thing as W (the fusion of the Tinkertoys on the shelf at 1:15), there is such a thing as W' (the wood on the shelf at 1:15). A Tinkertoy house is made only of Tinkertoys; that is an intuition we should like to preserve. Tinkertoys are bits of wood. So it seems right to say that the Tinkertoy house H is identical with W'. But at 1:30, I remove alpha from H, and then replace it with beta. H is on the shelf at 1:45, but W' is not then on the shelf, for alpha is on the floor at 1:45. So how is H related to W'?

I spoke earlier of alpha's having been "in H" until 1:30, when I removed it from H and replaced it with beta. I have been trying throughout (not without difficulty) to avoid speaking as common sense speaks. Common sense says: alpha was part of H, and then ceased to be; beta was not part of H, but became part of H.

It really is the most obvious common sense that a physical object can acquire and lose parts. Parthood surely is a three-place relation, among a pair of objects and a time. If you want to construe parthood as a two-place relation, you really will have to indulge in temporal parts to accommodate what common sense calls acquisition and loss of parts. But why should anyone want to?

If parthood is a three-place relation, then it is not possible to read the expression "$x < y$" of the Calculus of Individuals as: x is part of y. And it cannot be said that the logic of parthood is the Calculus of Individuals.

But we can easily construct a Cross-temporal Calculus of Individuals, by emending the Leonard–Goodman definitions and axioms. I think it pays us to do so.

Let us take as primitive "x D y @ t", and read it as: x is discrete from y at t.[10]

But we cannot move on just yet. For the intended interpretation of "x D y @ t" to be fixed, it has to be fixed for all threesomes of a pair of objects and a time-point which make "x D y @ t" true and which make it false. There is no difficulty if both objects exist at the time-point: your nose is now discrete from my nose, your nose is not now discrete from your face, and so on. But what if one or more of the objects does not exist at the time-point? Is Caesar's nose now discrete from your nose?

Looking ahead, we know that the intended interpretation of "x D y @ t" is to be such as to link it with parthood-at-a-time. For example, the threesome containing A, B, and 9 p.m. should make "x D y @ t" true if and only if A and B have no part in common at 9 p.m. More precisely: if and only if there is no z such that z is part of A at 9 p.m. and z is part of B at 9 p.m. Well, is there a z such that z is *now* part of Caesar's nose? After all, Caesar's nose does not exist now. I think it will seem right to say: if x does not exist at t, then there is no z such that z is part of x at t. (If my car goes out of existence at midnight tonight, nothing will be part of it tomorrow.) If we do adopt this view, we are committed to saying that there is no z that is now part of Caesar's nose and, therefore, no z that is now part of both Caesar's nose and your nose and, thus, that Caesar's nose is now discrete from your nose. More generally, adopting this view is adopting an existence principle expressible as follows:

$$x \text{ does not exist at } t \supset (y)(x \text{ D } y @ t)$$
$$\text{first existence principle}$$

I think it really does seem right to say these things – until it strikes us that it follows that not even Caesar's nose is now part of Caesar's nose and that Caesar's nose is now discrete even from itself. There is no entirely happy alternative in the offing here. We might weaken the first existence principle; e.g., we might choose to say, instead,

$$x \text{ does not exist at } t \supset (y)(x \text{ D } y @ t \equiv y \neq x).$$

But this has its own unhappy consequence, viz., that a thing is atomic at all times at which it does not exist; and choosing it would impose complications elsewhere. So I suggest we accept the unhappy consequences of what I called the "first existence principle," and take it to control the intended interpretation of "x D y @ t".

We should surely say also that, if everything is now discrete from a thing, then that thing does not now exist – more generally, that

$$(y)(x \,D\, y @ t) \supset x \text{ does not exist at t}$$
second existence principle

The conjunction of the first and second existence principles is

$$x \text{ does not exist at } t \equiv (y)(x \,D\, y @ t)$$

or, alternatively,

$$x \text{ exists at } t \equiv \sim(y)(x \,D\, y @ t).$$

So we may introduce "$x \,E@\, t$" (read: x exists at t) by definition as follows:

$$x \,E@\, t =_{df} \sim(y)(x \,D\, y @ t)$$

"$x < y @ t$" (read: x is part of y at t) and "$x \,O\, y @ t$" read: x overlaps y at t) are now definable as follows:

$$x < y @ t =_{df} x \,E@\, t \,\&\, y \,E@\, t \,\&$$
$$(z)(z \,D\, y @ t \supset z \,D\, x @ t)$$
$$x \,O\, y @ t =_{df} (\exists z)(z < x @ t \,\&\, z < y @ t)$$

The old overlap axiom is easy enough to emend: what we want is

$$(CCI_2) \quad (x \,O\, y @ t) \equiv \sim(x \,D\, y @ t)$$

new overlap axiom

The old identity axiom is not so easily emended, however. That is, we obviously cannot replace it with

$$(x = y) \equiv (x < y @ t \,\&\, y < x @ t),$$

for this tells us that, whatever time you choose, x is identical with y only if x is part of y at that time and y is part of x at that time and, thus (by the definition of "$x < y @ t$"), only if x and y exist at that time. That is far too restrictive. Caesar's nose is surely identical with Caesar's nose, even if it does not exist now.

What we want is instead this: x is identical with y if and only if for all times t such that one or the other of them exists at t, x is part of y at t, and y is part of x at t – i.e.,

$$(CCI_1) \quad (x = y) \equiv (t)[(x \,E@\, t \vee y \,E@\, t) \supset$$
$$(x < y @ t \,\&\, y < x @ t)]$$
new identity axiom

A great many analogues of theorems of the Calculus of Individuals are now provable in the Cross-temporal Calculus of Individuals. It is perhaps just worth drawing attention to the fact that, although "$x < x$" is provable in the Calculus of Individuals, "$x < x @ t$" is not provable in the Cross-temporal Calculus of Individuals. But it plainly ought not be; for what it tells us is that, whatever time you choose, x is part of itself at that time and thus (by the definition of "$x < y @ t$") that everything exists all the time. What is provable in the Cross-temporal Calculus of Individuals is, instead, this:

$$x \,E@\, t \equiv x < x @ t,$$

which says only that, whatever time you choose, x is part of itself at that time if and only if it exists at that time.

The old fusion axiom presents a different kind of problem. If things can have different parts at different times, then a thing can fuse one set at one time and a different set at a different time. Indeed, fusing has to be regarded as relativized to times, and I suggest we redefine it as follows:

$$x \,Fu\, S @ t =_{df} x \,E@\, t \,\&\, (y)$$
$$[y \,D\, x @ t \equiv (z)[(z \in S \,\&\, z \,E@\, t) \supset t \,D\, z @ t]]$$

One possible analogue of the old fusion axiom is, then, this:

$$(CCI_3) \quad (\exists x)(x \in S \,\&\, x \,E@\, t) \supset (\exists y)$$
$$(y \,Fu\, S @ t).$$

But that is only one of the possibilities. It is, after all, rather weak. It allows us to say, for example, that there is something that fuses Caesar's nose in 44 BC and that there is something that fuses Nixon's nose in 1979; but it does not allow us to conclude that there is something that both fuses Caesar's nose in 44 BC and fuses Nixon's nose in 1979. Admirers of the Calculus of Individuals will surely want that there be such a thing and will, therefore, regard the axiom I set out as too weak to be regarded as the appropriate analogue of the old fusion axiom.

There are a number of available middle grounds, but I suspect that the truly devoted friends of fusions will want to go the whole distance. The simplest way of expressing their view is to take them to say that there is not one fusion axiom in the Cross-temporal Calculus of Individuals, but indefinitely many, the procedure for generating them being this. Take any set of n sets $S_1 \ldots S_n$. For $n = 1$, write what I earlier called (CCI_3). For $n = 2$, write

$$[t_1 \neq t_2 \ \& \ (\exists x)(x \in S_1 \ \& \ x \ E@ \ t_1) \ \& \\ (\exists y) \ (y \in S_2 \ \& \ y \ E@ \ t_2)] \supset (\exists z)(z \ Fu \ S_1 @ \ t_1 \\ \& \ z \ Fu \ S_2 @ \ t_2)$$

and so on. For my own part, I have no objection – it seems to me that one has only to live with fusions for a while to come to love them. But I shall not argue for all or even any of these fusion axioms. I do not know what an argument for them would look like. By the same token, however, I do not know what an argument against them would look like, "What an odd entity!" not seeming to me to count as an argument. So I shall leave it open which fusion axiom or axioms should be regarded as replacing the old fusion axiom.

More precisely, I shall leave it open which fusion axiom or axioms should be regarded as replacing the old fusion axiom, so long as the axiom or axioms chosen do not guarantee the uniqueness of fusions. For we do not want an analogue of what I earlier called "the fusion principle" to be provable in the Cross-temporal Calculus of Individuals. The fusion principle, it will be remembered, says that, if anything is a member of S, then there is a unique thing that fuses the Ss. We do not want to have it provable that if anything is a member of S and exists at t, then there is a unique entity that fuses the Ss at t: we want, precisely, to leave open that there may be more than one. My reason for saying that issues from the use to which I would like to be able to put these notions. Consider again the Tinkertoy house H. A Tinkertoy house is made only of Tinkertoys; and H is, at 1:15, made only of the Tinkertoys on the shelf at 1:15. I would like, therefore, to be able to say that H fuses, at 1:15, the Tinkertoys on the shelf at 1:15. And what about W', the wood on the shelf at 1:15? I would like to be able to say that that too fuses the

Tinkertoys on the shelf at 1:15. But nothing can be true if it licenses our concluding from this that H is identical with W'.

With fusions now relativized to times, we cannot single out a thing to call "W" as I did in section I above:

(2) W = the fusion of the Tinkertoys on the shelf at 1:15

now lacks a sense, for there now is no fusing *simpliciter*, there is only fusing-at-a-time. And, without an analogue of the fusion principle, we cannot even single out a thing to call "W" by drawing attention to the fact that there is something that fuses, at 1:15, the Tinkertoys on the shelf at 1:15: i.e., we cannot replace (2) with

    W = the unique thing that fuses, at 1:15, the Tinkertoys on the shelf at 1:15,

for there may be more than one thing that does this. Indeed, I suggest we agree that there are at least two things which do this, viz., H and W'.

Perhaps you have no taste for fusions, and regard the new fusion axioms (like the old one) as grossly overstrong. All the same, the difficulty we began with can be eliminated, and without appeal to temporal parts, if we say that parthood is a three-place relation[11] and that the new identity axiom (interpreted as I indicated) is true. How is H related to W'? We can say, quite simply, that

$$H < W' @ t \ \& \ W' < H @ t$$

is true for all times t between 1:00 and 1:30 (which was when alpha was removed from H); but that it is not true for any other times t. Since H and W' exist at times at which it is not true, H is not identical with W'.[12]

More generally, a Tinkertoy house is made only of Tinkertoys, and Tinkertoys are bits of wood; so, at every time throughout its life, a Tinkertoy house is part of, and contains as part, the wood it is made of at that time.

VII

There is a difficulty analogous to the one we began with, which I suggest we look at briefly.

Let us supply the Tinkertoy house H with a different history. Suppose H came into existence on a shelf at 1:00 and that all the Tinkertoys it was then made of, indeed, all the bits of wood, indeed, all of the stuff it was then made of, came into existence at 1:00 along with H. Suppose that the whole thing rested quietly on the shelf until 5:00, and then everything – house, bits of wood, stuff – all went out of existence together. Let W' be, as before, the wood on the shelf at 1:15. Now we can say more than that W' is part of H from 1:00 to 1:30, and H part of W' from 1:00 to 1:30: we can say that, for all times t such that either of them exists at t, W' and H are parts of each other at t. It follows, by the new identity axiom, that H is identical with W'.

Is that an acceptable conclusion? I am sure that there are those who will say it is not. For isn't it true of W', and false of H, that W' could have failed to have the form of a house? Can't wood come into existence in ship-shape as well as in house-shape? But houses can't.

But is that a possible history? Normally, a house that *is* made of Tinkertoys *was* made of Tinkertoys; i.e., normally, the Tinkertoys existed before the house did, and the house was then built out of them. Could a house, and the Tinkertoys it is made of, come into existence together?

Again, could some wood have come into existence *ex nihilo*? (Compare the temporal parts of the bit of chalk.)

Well, I was being unfair to those who think there is a problem in the offing here. Let us suppose I make a house, not out of Tinkertoys, but out of ice. I do so, not by fitting bits of ice together, but by pouring water into a house-shaped ice-tray, and freezing it. Four hours later, I melt the whole thing down, and throw out the water. Worries about temporal idealizing apart, we can say that the house and the ice it was made of came into existence (and went out of existence) together. And the ice didn't come into existence *ex nihilo* – it came into existence *ex aqua*. But surely (it will be said) the house is not identical with the ice. For the ice, but not the house, could have failed to have the form of a house. I could have poured that very same water into a ship-shaped ice-tray instead.

I don't myself find it obvious that a piece of house-shaped ice could have been a piece of ship-shaped ice; but my informants tell me it could have been. If they are right, we must give up the Cross-temporal Calculus of Individuals, because we must give up the new identity axiom[13].

Suppose they are right. Then we must take the logic of parthood to be a modal logic, which might be called the Modal Cross-temporal Calculus of Individuals.

I shall not construct such a logic, since I think it does not pay to rehearse the alternative possible replacements for the fusion axiom or axioms. What matters for present purposes, in any case, is really only what should be said about identity. It seems to me, however, that that is plain enough: we should replace CCI_1 with:

$$(MCCI_1)\ (x=y) \equiv \Box(t)[(x\ E@\ t \lor y\ E@\ t) \supset \\ (x<y\ @\ t\ \&\ y<x\ @\ t)]$$

That eliminates the difficulty. Let "House" be the name of the house, and "Ice" be the name of the ice it is made of. Then (if my informants are right) there is a world, and a time t in that world, such that

Ice E@ t

is true, and (since House does not exist in that world)

Ice < House @ t & House < Ice @ t

is false. That being so, $MCCI_1$ tells us that House is not identical with Ice.

But this is of interest only if my informants are right about this case, or would be right about a better case.

Notes

I am grateful to George Boolos, Paul Horwich, Fred Katz, and Sydney Shoemaker for comments on an earlier draft.

1   It is familiar enough that they have been used by those interested in the metaphysics of matter. But so also have they been used by those interested in philosophy of mind (cf., e.g., David Lewis, "Survival and identity," repr. in A. O. Rorty (ed.), *The Identities of Persons* (Berkeley: University of

California Press, 1976) [ch. 43 in this volume]),
and even by moral philosophers (cf., e.g., Allan
Gibbard, "Natural property rights," *Nous* 10/1
(Mar. 1976), pp. 77–88, and the views of Jonathan
Edwards on moral responsibility, described by
Roderick Chisholm in Appendix A of his *Person
and Object* (London: Allen & Unwin, 1976)).

2   Henry S. Leonard and Nelson Goodman, "The
calculus of individuals and its uses," *Journal of
Symbolic Logic* 5/2 (June 1940), pp. 45–55. For
perspicuousness in the discussion to come, I have
strengthened their identity axiom.

3   Following Richard Cartwright, in "Scattered
objects," in Keith Lehrer (ed.), *Analysis and
Metaphysics* (Buston: Reidel, 1975).

4   David Wiggins, *Sameness and Substance* (Cambridge,
Mass.: Harvard University Press, 1980), pp. 30ff.

5   Cartwright, "Scattered objects."

6   But see section VII, n. 13 in particular.

7   But see section VII, n. 13 in particular.

8   In the sense singled out by Helen Morris
Cartwright, in "Quantities," *Philosophical Review*,
79/1 (Jan. 1970), pp. 25–42.

9   Following Allan Gibbard, in "Contingent Identity,"
this volume, ch. 11.

10 The variables of the Calculus of Individuals range
only over existing entities. In the same spirit, the
variables "x", "y", etc. of the Cross-temporal
Calculus of Individuals are to range only over
entities that exist at some time or other.

11 Unlike physical objects, events really do have
temporal parts (though the term must be defined
differently for events); hence there is no need to
use tenses in ascribing parthood relations to
events. We can take events to be a model of the
Cross-temporal Calculus of Individuals (reading
x E@ t as: x is occurring at t). But the event-
identities so obtained would be the same as those
I obtained (in *Acts and Other Events* (Ithaca,
NY: Cornell University Press, 1977)) by taking
events to be a model of the simpler Calculus of
Individuals.

12 David Wiggins would say that W' constitutes H at
1:15 – see p. 482 above. I said: fine, but what is it
for a thing x to constitute a thing y at a time t? I
have no great confidence in the likelihood of his
accepting the gift, but I offer him the following:

$$x \text{ constitutes } y \text{ at } t =_{df} x < y @ t \text{ \& } y < x @ t.$$

On this account of the matter, H constitutes W' at
1:15 if W' constitutes H at 1:15; but that strikes me
as harmless.

13 If my informants are right, then the friends of
temporal parts must give up metaphysical thesis
M_3 and, therefore, the old identity axiom and,
therefore, the Calculus of Individuals. They can
still construe parthood as a two-place relation; but
they must take identity to be governed, instead, by

$$(x = y) \equiv \Box[(x < y) \text{ \& } (y < x)]$$

36

Temporal Parts of Four-Dimensional Objects

Mark Heller

1 The General Camp

The ontology of physical objects I will defend in this work is that of four-dimensional hunks of matter. Some of these hunks are temporal parts of others. Thus, I place myself in the same general camp as Willard Van Orman Quine, John Perry, and David Lewis.[1] Lewis mentions a common objection to such an ontology, and begins to answer it:

> Some would protest that they do not know what I mean by 'more or less momentary person-stages, or time-slices of continuant persons, or persons-at-times.' ... [This] objection is easy to answer, especially in the case where the stages are less momentary rather than more. Let me consider that case only, though I think that instantaneous stages also are unproblematic; I do not really need them. A person-stage is a physical object, just as a person is. (If persons had a ghostly part as well, so would person-stages.) It does many of the same things that a person does: it talks and walks and thinks, it has beliefs and desires, it has a size and shape and location. It even has a temporal duration. But

only a brief one, for it does not last long. (We can pass over the question how long it can last before it is a segment rather than a stage, for that question raises no objection of principle.) It begins to exist abruptly, and it abruptly ceases to exist soon after. Hence a stage cannot do everything that a person can do, for it cannot do those things that a person does over a longish interval.[2]

In spite of its insightfulness, this brief response may not be completely satisfactory to those who do not already understand the notion of a person-stage. The primary goal of this chapter is to develop a clear account of the nature of temporal parts. (Notice that temporal parts, unlike Lewis's stages, are not vague.) Once this account is developed, I will attempt to answer some criticisms of an ontology that includes temporal parts.

The confusion over the nature of temporal parts is increased by the fact that such phrases as 'temporal part', 'temporal phase', and 'temporal slice' have been used in ways that suggest such varied purported objects as processes, events, ways things are, sets, and portions of careers or histories. Judith Jarvis Thomson, not herself a friend of temporal parts, makes a reasonable

Mark Heller, "Temporal Parts of Four-Dimensional Objects," in *The Ontology of Physical Objects* (Cambridge: Cambridge University Press, 1990), ch. 1 (pp. 1–29). © Cambridge University Press 1990. Reproduced by permission.

Metaphysics: An Anthology, Second Edition. Edited by Jaegwon Kim, Daniel Z. Korman and Ernest Sosa.
Editorial material and organization © 2012 Blackwell Publishing Ltd. Published 2012 by Blackwell Publishing Ltd.

attempt to get clear about the notion.[3] (In the following read '$\leq$' as 'is earlier than or simultaneous with', and read '$\geq$' as 'is later than or simultaneous with'.) Consider an object O which exists from time t_0 to t_3. On Thomson's account, a temporal part of O, call it P, is an object that comes into existence at some time $t_1 \geq t_0$ and goes out of existence at some time $t_2 \leq t_3$ and takes up some portion of the space that O takes up for all the time that P exists. (This might better have been called a spatiotemporal part.)

2 Unpleasant Alternatives

As she begins to explain the inner writings of her notion of a temporal part, the existence of such objects begins to look implausible. The basic problem with Thomson's account is that it seems to be developed against the background of an unhelpful presupposition about the nature of physical objects. She seems to think of physical objects as being three-dimensional and enduring through time. I am prepared to admit from the outset that this is our normal philosophical way of thinking of physical objects.[4] But it is this way of thinking that makes temporal parts seem implausible. I see nothing in favor of it other than the fact that it is our standard view, and I put very little weight on this advantage.

Furthermore, the three-dimensional view of objects in general leads to having to choose between what I take to be unpleasant alternatives. The alternatives are:

(a) there is no such physical object as my body,
(b) there is no physical object in the space that we would typically say is now exactly occupied by all of me other than my left hand,
(c) no physical object can undergo a loss of parts,
(d) there can be distinct physical objects exactly occupying the same space at the same time,
(e) identity is not transitive.

To deny each of these alternatives and to accept three-dimensional enduring objects would lead to a contradiction. To show this I present a slightly altered version of an argument of Peter van Inwagen's.[5] If we deny alternative (a), then there is such an object as my body. Call it 'Body'.

If we deny alternative (b), then there is an object that is all of me other than my left hand. Call that object 'Body-minus'. Now consider some time t at which my left hand is cut off. This does not affect Body-minus, so:

(1) the thing that, before t, is Body-minus = the thing that, after t, is Body-minus.

If we also deny alternative (c), then my losing my hand does not end my body's existence, so:

(2) the thing that, after t, is Body = the thing that, before t, is Body.

Further, if we deny (d), it *seems* to follow that:

(3) the thing that, after t, is Body-minus = the thing that, after t, is Body.

If we then deny (e), by transitivity of identity it follows that:

(4) the thing that, before t, is Body-minus = the thing that, before t, is Body.

But since Body was bigger before t than Body-minus was before t:

(5) the thing that, before t, is Body-minus $\neq$ the thing that, before t, is Body,

and (5) contradicts (4).

In the end, Thomson's preferred way of avoiding that contradiction is to accept (d).[6] In contrast, van Inwagen avoids the contradiction by accepting (b).[7] Roderick Chisholm instead accepts (c).[8] And Peter Geach seems to accept (e), or at least something that will have the same effect for this argument as accepting (e).[9] My way of avoiding the contradiction is to claim that (3) does not follow from the denial of (d) unless we accept the additional thesis that physical objects are three-dimensional and endure through time. I will deny this additional thesis. Doing so will allow me to claim that Body and Body-minus are distinct objects that, even after t, do not occupy the same space at the same time. It is incumbent upon me, then, to offer a reasonable alternative to the three-dimensional view of physical objects.

[handwritten notes at top of page: "These particles are belonging more strongly connected to each other from our perspective" and "Naming doesn't make an object metaphysically exist but for Naming ... convin..."]

3　Four-Dimensional Objects

I propose that a physical object is not an enduring spatial hunk of matter, but is, rather, a spatiotemporal hunk of matter. Instead of thinking of matter as filling up regions of space, we should think of matter as filling up regions of space-time. A physical object is the material content of a region of space-time.

Just as such an object has spatial extent, it also has temporal extent – it extends along four dimensions, not just three. To see the contrast clearly, consider an object that is created at noon and destroyed at one. If we think of the object as three-dimensional and enduring through time, it would be appropriate to say that the object exists at different times; the same object exists at noon and at one. Such an object has boundaries along only three dimensions. The whole object is that hunk of matter that entirely fills up those boundaries. The whole object, therefore, exists at noon and still exists at one.

A four-dimensional object, on the other hand, has boundaries along an additional dimension. The whole object must fill up all of its boundaries and, therefore, does not exist at a single moment. If we accept that physical objects are four-dimensional, the appropriate thing to say about the object under consideration is that it takes up more than an instantaneous region of time. It does not exist *at* noon and *at* one; rather, it exists *from* noon *until* one. Thinking of it as an enduring three-dimensional object, we might still say that it exists from noon until one, but only because we would say that it exists *at* every time between noon and one. Instead of thinking of an object as existing at various times, we should, adopting the four-dimensional stance, think of it as existing within regions of time.

Insofar as time is just one more dimension, roughly alike in kind to the three spatial dimensions, we should expect that our claims about an object's spatial characteristics have analogues with respect to its temporal characteristics. For instance, just as we might talk about the distance between two points along a line in space, we can also talk about the distance between two points in time. This allows us to understand the notion of temporal boundaries as analogous to that of spatial boundaries. Furthermore, there is an analogy with respect to the part/whole relationship. Just as a spatial part fills up a subregion of the space occupied by the whole, a temporal part fills up a subregion of the time occupied by the whole.

Another important analogy is that, for both spatial and temporal parts, we can point at or perceive or name a whole by pointing at, perceiving, or indicating a part. When naming a person at birth, I might place my finger on that person's chest and say, "Let us call this Kaitlin" or "This is Kaitlin." In doing so, I did not name the piece of skin directly beneath my finger, nor did I name the chest, nor the surface of the baby. I named the whole person. It is an interesting question as to how this is done, but it is not one that must be taken up here. The point is that on the four-dimensional view there is an analogy. 'Kaitlin' does not name a temporally tiny four-dimensional object that exists for just the amount of time that I am pointing or for just as long as it takes for me to utter my naming sentence. I named the whole person. *The*

It should be noted that an object's temporal characteristics are not completely analogous to its spatial characteristics. This is because time is not completely alike in kind to the three spatial dimensions. Time, for instance, seems to have a direction to it. Also, our perception along the temporal dimension is only one-directional (memory) and is discontinuous (I can remember things that happened on my third and fourth birthdays without remembering anything that happened between them). Furthermore, temporal units of measurement are not of the same kind as spatial units of measurement. These disanalogies will not have any significance for the present work.

One question about four-dimensional objects is whether it is possible to have zero extent along the temporal dimension – Can there be instantaneous objects? I do not have a strong opinion about this one way or the other. What should be noted is that this is no more an issue with respect to the temporal dimension than with any of the spatial dimensions – again we have an analogy. Could there be a physical object such as the surface of a cube? Thinking according to our standard three-dimensional picture, such an object would have zero extent along one of the spatial dimensions. It could, therefore, be called a two-dimensional object. According to our new four-dimensional picture, such an object would still have zero extent along one of the spatial dimensions. It could, therefore, be called a three-dimensional object, one of the three being the temporal dimension. I emphasize that, because a thing's parts are no more ontologically fundamental than the thing itself, existence of four-dimensional objects in no way depends upon their being built up out of instantaneous objects.

4 Refinements

I do not pretend to be in a position to evaluate scientific theses. The ontology I present should end up being consistent with any plausible story that the scientist might tell us about the inner workings of the world. If it turns out that matter just is space-time (perhaps any bit of space-time is matter, or perhaps only bits with a certain shape), then physical objects just are pieces of space-time. (I am prepared to set aside the question of how much the scientific proclamation is really based upon controversial philosophy.) Along these same lines, though for simplicity's sake I assume that all nonrelational properties of an object are a function of the configuration of that object's parts, I am prepared to revise my claims if scientists should determine that there really are irreducible properties (for instance, the flavor of a quark may be such a property).

In saying that a physical object is the material content of a region of space-time, I do not mean to suppose that there are any empty regions. Nor do I mean to suppose the opposite. My point is simply that if there are any regions that do not contain matter, then they do not contain any physical objects. What of a region that is empty in parts and full in other parts? Such a region can be divided into two subregions (perhaps they are scattered subregions), the one that is full and the one that is empty. If the full one is the right shape (perhaps every shape is right, perhaps not), then it contains an object, and, therefore, so does the original region that is partly full. The empty subregion does not contain an object nor any part of an object. So, for instance, if there really is empty space between the parts of an atom, then atoms are really scattered objects, since the region of space that an atom exactly fills at any given time is not connected. Similarly, those everyday objects around us that are composed of atoms are also, on the present hypothesis, scattered objects; the region that a given object exactly fills (the region that contains that object, no other matter, and no empty space) is really a lot smaller than we had thought.

It is not part of my account of the nature of four-dimensional objects to suppose that such an object must stand out from its surroundings in some significant way. Nor is it part of my account to suppose the opposite. The notion of four-dimensional objects can be understood without answering the question of which filled regions of space-time contain such objects. In particular, we do not have to answer such questions as whether a statue can exist inside a boulder, just waiting to be carved out. I would in fact argue that for *every* filled region there is one object that exactly fills it.[10] But this should not be built into the very concept of a four-dimensional object.

The claim that every filled region of space-time is exactly filled by a physical object presupposes a clear distinction between those regions that are full and those that are not. However, contemporary physics raises a problem for that supposition. Quantum mechanics seems to tell us that when we get down to a small enough level, there just is no fact of the matter as to where a given particle is, and therefore, it would seem, no fact of the matter as to whether a certain region is full. (Again, I am prepared to set aside the question of how much of this scientific proclamation is really based upon controversial philosophy.) I am prepared to accept this little bit of imprecision into my ontology. I accept this imprecision, not because it is so small, but because it is the right thing to do. If there is real indeterminacy in the world, if there really is no fact of the matter as to whether a given region of space-time is full, then the world is really imprecise, and that must be reflected in the true ontology. This is a very different sort of imprecision from that which is involved in the vagueness of our everyday objects (as I will argue later); the imprecision here arises from the structure of the world, not just from our way of conceptualizing the world.

But there are other ways to raise doubts about my assumption that for every region there is a determinate fact as to whether that region is exactly filled, If matter is just space-time of a certain shape, so that not all space-time counts as matter, then 'filled' is, in effect, a shape predicate.

As such, it may very well be vague. There may be no precise line between those shapes that count as a region's being full and those that count as the region's not being full. It could be that certain regions are shaped in such a way that they neither count as full nor count as not full.

This proposal has the presupposition that matter is space-time. Thus, given what I have said above, the physical objects proposed by my theory are themselves regions of space-time. If it should turn out that 'filled' is a vague shape predicate, then I should revise my ontology by allowing every region of space-time to be a physical object, not just the filled regions. Perhaps I could not continue to call these objects *physical*, since some of the space-time regions included are clearly empty (they are not among the borderline cases of being empty), and it seems inappropriate to say that an empty region of space-time contains a physical object. (For a region of space-time to contain a physical object, on the present proposal, is just for it to be a physical object.) Instead I would be offering an ontology of spatiotemporal objects, to be distinguished, perhaps, from such purported nonspatiotemporal objects as mental entities and abstract entities.

But suppose that it turns out that 'filled' is a vague predicate even without equating matter with space-time. That is, suppose that it turns out that matter is distinct from the spatiotemporal regions that it fills, that it does not fill all regions, and that there are some regions for which, for reasons having nothing to do with quantum mechanics, there is no fact of the matter as to whether those regions are full or not. In this case expanding my ontology to include objects that are in clearly empty regions would seem very odd. Even an empty region would contain an object, and here "contains" is not just another word for "be". I could avoid the apparent oddness by simply stipulating that "contains" is another word for "be" in this context, stipulating that matter is space-time. But that is not the sort of thing that should be built into an ontology by stipulation. That is the sort of thing we should wait for science to rule upon.

I do not think I need to be forced into such a strange-sounding position. For a spatiotemporal region to be full, in the sense in which I am using that term, is just for it to contain no empty subregions. Because what it is for one spatiotemporal

region to contain another is not in any way vague, 'full' is only as vague as 'empty'. And 'empty' seems to be a paradigm non-vague term. If a region can possibly contain less than it does in fact contain, then it is not empty. Thus the only way for 'empty' to be vague is for there to be cases in which it is indeterminate whether a given region can possibly contain less than it does. And it seems unlikely that there will be any way for this to be indeterminate other than the two that I have already discussed, or relatives of those two: the first being real physical indeterminacy as posited by quantum mechanics and the second being an indeterminacy due to the fact that the supposed filler (i.e., matter) is just space-time of a certain sort.

It should be noted that while I talk of matter as the ultimate filler, I would be prepared to accept that matter is itself composed of particles. The question of which is more basic (in the sense of which is composed of which), stuff or things, is one to be answered by scientists, not philosophers. Perhaps matter is composed of particles that are themselves composed of matter that is itself composed of smaller particles, and on and on. Regardless of which proves to be the basic one, and even if the series continues *ad infinitum*, there should still be a determinate fact for any specified region whether that region could have less in it than it does (barring the two options for letting in indeterminacy that I discuss above).

It could turn out that every particle is itself composed of particles that are spread out in space-time. If this is this case, then any continuous region that is extended along all four dimensions will contain some empty space-time, and hence, there will be no full extended regions. The terms 'empty' and 'full' do not seem to be applicable to nonextended regions, but the supposition that all particles are composed of separated particles does seem to require a distinction between two kinds of points, a distinction that is analogous to that between 'full' and 'empty'. Using the terms in an expanded sense, then, we could say that some points are full, and, further, that some discontinuous regions of space-time are full. In the kind of world now being considered, four-dimensional physical objects turn out to be scattered in the extreme. The region exactly containing a physical object will be a collection of discrete points.

It is crucial for my overall project that the objects of my ontology have precise boundaries;

for any of the objects in my proposed ontology there is a unique and determinate region that that object exactly fills. Given my characterization of a four-dimensional object as the material content of a filled region of space-time, and given that there is a determinate fact as to which regions are full and which are not, four-dimensional objects can have the precision that I require. I do not deny, however, that there could be other ways of characterizing four-dimensional objects that do not imply their having precise boundaries. In principle, precise boundaries need be no more a part of the concept of a four-dimensional object than it is part of the concept of a three-dimensional object. However, I will build this precision into my concept of a four-dimensional object.[11]

Given the precision of four-dimensional objects and the apparent imprecision of the objects of our standard ontology, there are serious questions about the relationship between the two kinds of objects. For the remainder of this essay I will set aside any further discussion of imprecision and will pretend that either the boundaries of our standard objects are as precise as those of my four-dimensional objects or the boundaries of the four-dimensional objects are as imprecise as those of our standard objects.

5 Parts

A four-dimensional object is the material content of a filled region of space-time. A spatiotemporal part of such an object is the material content of a subregion of the space-time occupied by the whole. For instance, consider a particular object O and the region R of space-time that O fills. A spatiotemporal part of O is the material content of a subregion of R. A spatiotemporal part, as long as it has greater than zero extent along every dimension, is itself a four-dimensional physical object. A spatiotemporal part is not a set or a process or a way something is at a place and time. It, like the object it is part of, is a hunk of matter.

If Heller is a physical object, then so is Heller's-left-hand-from-(1:00 p.m. 3 January, 1990)-to-(1:01 p.m. 3 January, 1990). This spatiotemporal part of me could have, between 1:00 p.m. and 1:01 p.m. on 3 January, 1990, been felt, seen, heard, smelled, and, if need be, tasted. It had weight and volume. Thinking of spatiotemporal

parts as physical objects corresponds to the way we ordinarily think of parts on our old three-dimensional picture. When not being swayed by specific philosophical arguments, we have no doubt that my hand is a physical object. Accepting the account of four-dimensional objects presented here, we may continue to hold the general principle that a part of a physical object is itself a physical object.

The fact that any part of O is the material content of a subregion of R does not entail that every filled subregion of R contains a part of O. This point directly parallels the fact that it is not part of the concept of a four-dimensional object that every filled region contains such an object. One could consistently accept all three of the following:

(i) there are four-dimensional objects and spatiotemporal parts of such objects,

(ii) not every filled region of space-time contains a physical object,

(iii) even for a region of space-time that does contain a physical object, not every subregion contains a spatiotemporal part of that object.

I take it that typically someone who accepts all three of these would be accepting (iii) for the same reasons that he accepts (ii). Someone might accept (ii) if he thought that there is good reason to reject scattered objects. Or (ii) might be accepted if independent grounds could be found for some claim like 'every object must contain its principle of unity within itself' (whatever that might mean). My immediate goal is not to supply a means for answering every question of the form 'Is there a spatiotemporal part here?', but rather to make clear the concept of spatiotemporal parthood.

It is now easy to understand the notion of a temporal part. Any proper part of a four-dimensional object is smaller than the whole object along at least one dimension. A proper temporal part is smaller along just one dimension, the temporal dimension. A temporal part of O is a spatiotemporal part that is the same spatial size as O for as long as that part exists, though it may be a smaller temporal size. Let us suppose that object O exactly fills the temporal region from t_0 to t_3. That is, the region of space-time filled by O, namely region R, has the temporal boundaries t_0 and t_3. Now consider a certain subregion of R the temporal boundaries of which are $t_1 \geq t_0$ and $t_2 \leq t_3$ and the spatial boundaries of which are just the spatial boundaries of R from t_1 to t_2. Call this subregion S. If the material content of S is an object, then it is a temporal part of O. In general, using the single letters as variables rather than names, a temporal part of O is the material content of a temporal subregion of R. 'Temporal subregion of R' means spatiotemporal subregion that shares all of R's spatial boundaries within that subregion's temporal boundaries. A temporal part of me which exists from my fifth birthday to my sixth is the same spatial size that I am from age five to age six.

6 Strictly Speaking

One matter of detail that is particularly important for temporal parts specifically and four-dimensional objects in general is how to understand such phrases as ' ___ exists in region ___ ' or ' ___ exists at time ___ '. Physical objects are four-dimensional hunks of matter. They therefore have precise spatiotemporal boundaries. Consider a particular physical object, this piece of paper (assuming that this piece of paper does have precise boundaries). Call this object 'Whitey'. Whitey has certain spatiotemporal boundaries – there is a region that it exactly occupies. But we also think it is true to say that Whitey now exists. This way of talking may be misleading. If Whitey exists now and existed a minute ago, then it is the same object that exists at both times. But this suggests the old three-dimensional picture that we have been denying.

This confusion is easily avoided. When we say that Whitey exists now, this should be taken as a loose way of saying that part of Whitey exists now. If we meant strictly that Whitey exists now, we would be saying something false. Whitey names the whole piece of paper, and that object does not exist now. Strictly speaking, Whitey is temporally too large to exist now.[12] Here, then, is the major difference between the three-dimensional and four-dimensional viewpoints. On the three-dimensional picture, if we said that Whitey exists now and really meant it, we would be saying something true. It is Whitey that exists at different times. On the other hand, on the four-dimensional picture Whitey does not, strictly speaking, exist at different times. Whitey's parts exist at different times (different parts at different times), and in virtue of this fact, we say, in our loose way of speaking, that Whitey exists at those times.

This can be made clearer by considering a spatial analogy. Put Whitey mostly in a drawer, but leave a small corner sticking out. Now if asked where Whitey is, you will answer that it is in the drawer. Strictly speaking, however, your answer would be false. Even on the three-dimensional picture, part of Whitey is not in the drawer. But 'Whitey' names the whole piece of paper, so if it is not the whole piece in the drawer, then it is not Whitey in the drawer. We say that Whitey is in the drawer because a part of Whitey is in there. Notice also that with some rewording it can be seen that how large a portion of the paper is in the drawer is not crucial. If only a corner of the paper were inside, we would be less likely to say that Whitey is in the drawer when asked where Whitey is. But if asked 'Does Whitey exist inside that drawer?' I think that we would all say 'yes'.

Recognizing that we have this loose way of speaking even when using our three-dimensional picture, it is not surprising that we also have this loose way of speaking when using the four-dimensional picture. Recognizing that such a phrase as 'Whitey exists now' is just loose speaking, we see that, strictly speaking, Whitey only exists within the spatiotemporal region that it exactly fills and regions of which that one is a subregion. To loosely say that Whitey exists now is to strictly say that the present time is within Whitey's temporal boundaries. If there are instantaneous temporal parts, then this is equivalent to saying that Whitey has a temporal part that exists now.

7 Coincidence

One nice consequence of these considerations is that an object and a proper temporal part of that object do not, strictly speaking, exist in the same space at the same time. An object should not be coincident with any of its proper parts. Intuitively, the problem with coincident entities is that of overcrowding. There just is not enough room for them. On the account provided above, an object and a proper spatiotemporal part of that object do not compete for room. There is a certain spatiotemporal region exactly occupied by the part; the whole object is not in that region. There is only as much of the object there as will fit – namely, the part. This intuitive understanding of the relationship between part and whole is what I intended to capture with my discussion of our loose way of speaking. When we say that Whitey is in the drawer, that is just a loose way of saying that part of Whitey is there. When we say that Whitey exists now, we are only saying that a part of Whitey exists now. Keeping this in mind allows us to avoid being committed to coincident entities.

Let us consider a spatial case. Even adopting a three-dimensional picture, we are not tempted to say that Heller and Heller's left hand are coincident entities. These are not two distinct entities in one place at one time. Strictly speaking, there is only one object in that hand-shaped region of space – my hand. Whatever truth there is in saying that I am in that region can be wholly captured by saying that a part of me is there. The relation between my hand and me is not that of coincidence, but, rather, that of part to whole. Similar points are relevant to cases of spatial overlap. My living room and my dining room share a common wall. But this does not entail that there is a wall-shaped region of space occupied by both my living room and my dining room. That region is occupied by the wall, and that wall happens to be part of both rooms.

If we adopt the four-dimensional view of physical objects, then similar remarks can be made about the relation between an object and its temporal parts. Heller is not coincident with Heller-during-1983. The only truth there is in saying that I occupy that year-long region of time is that I have a part that occupies that region. Strictly speaking, there is only one entity in the relevant spatiotemporal region – my 1983 part. Also, analogous to the case of spatial overlap, there may be cases of temporal overlap. If I were to undergo fission next year, that should not tempt us to say that prior to 1984 there were two objects in the same space at the same time.[13] Rather, we should say that two four-dimensional objects overlapped prior to 1984 – they shared a common temporal part.

Perhaps a less controversial case would be a hunk of gold that is shaped into a ring. The ring then undergoes a gradual replacement of matter until it is entirely composed of silver. Many would be tempted to say that the ring and the hunk of gold were, for a period of time, coincident entities. However, adopting the four-dimensional view, we can say that the gold and the ring temporally overlap. The gold has a ring-shaped temporal part, the ring has a golden temporal part, and the gold's part is identical with the ring's part. The relationship between the part of the one and the part of the other is identity, not coincidence. The relationship between the gold and the ring is that they share a common part; they overlap.[14] Similar considerations would allow an ontology of four-dimensional objects to avoid an attack based on the Ship of Theseus paradox.[15]

In contrast, trying to make sense of temporal parts without shifting to a four-dimensional picture would require a commitment to objectionable coincident entities. On Thomson's account, Heller and Heller-now are, in the strictest and most problematic sense, two distinct entities occupying the same space at the same time.[16] Heller is, at any given time between his birth and his death, complete. My existing now is not merely my having a part that exists now. Right now I exactly fill all of my three-dimensional boundaries. But that supposed temporal part of me, Heller-now, also exactly fills those same boundaries. Yet the two entities are distinct because I have a much longer career than Heller-now. Thomson cannot claim that strictly speaking I am temporally too big to be coincident with my instantaneous temporal part, because she avails herself of only three dimensions along which to measure. Along those dimensions I am now exactly the same size as Heller-now.

8 A Crazy Metaphysic

In fact, Thomson's problem of coincident entities is a symptom of a much deeper problem with trying to explain temporal parts without rejecting the old three-dimensional picture. Let us return to Whitey, the piece of paper. Even given my meaning hypothesis (according to which it is strictly false that Whitey is in the drawer), the old picture has the consequence that it is strictly true that Whitey exists now (because Whitey now fills the relevant boundaries along all three of the available dimensions). Since 'Whitey' names the whole piece of paper, we get the consequence that it is strictly true that the whole piece of paper exists now. If all of Whitey exists now, then Whitey has no parts that do not exist now. Even though Whitey will continue to exist for the next several hours, 'Whitey-from-(now + one hour)-to-(now + two hours)' does not designate a part of Whitey unless that part exists now. But if there were such a temporal part, it would not yet have come into existence. So Whitey has no temporal parts other than the one that exists now. Indeed, it does not even have that temporal part, since Whitey – all of it – existed an hour ago, and the temporal part that supposedly exists now did not exist then. If one holds the three-dimensional view of physical objects, it is perfectly reasonable to think of an ontology including temporal parts as a 'crazy metaphysic.'[17]

Of course, this is not Thomson's reason for calling it a crazy metaphysic. She does not draw attention to the three-dimensional/four-dimensional distinction at all. Thomson writes:

> I said this seems to me a crazy metaphysic. It seems to me that its full craziness only comes out when we take the spatial analogy seriously. The metaphysic yields that if I have had exactly one bit of chalk in my hand for the last hour, then there is something in my hand which is white, roughly cylindrical in shape, and dusty, something which also has a weight, something which is chalk, which was not in my hand three minutes ago, and indeed, such that no part of it was in my hand three minutes ago. As I hold the bit of chalk in my hand, new stuff, new chalk keeps constantly coming into existence *ex nihilo*. That strikes me as obviously false.[18]

I suggest that this attack on temporal parts depends on accepting the thesis that physical objects are three-dimensional.

Why does Thomson think that temporal parts would come into existence *ex nihilo*? It is obviously not because nothing exists before the temporal part. It is not even because everything that exists before the temporal part continues to exist, for there are prior temporal parts that go out of existence at just the moment that the part in question comes into existence. It may simply be that none of the temporal part's parts exist before the temporal part does, but if that is all, then there is still the question of why this should be objectionable. I suggest that Thomson's objection is founded on

the belief that there is no significant material change occurring at the time that the temporal part is supposed to be coming into existence. The piece of chalk does not undergo any alteration. No molecules need be altering their internal structure or their relationship to other molecules. No matter from outside the chalk is added, nor is any matter that was part of chalk released into the surrounding atmosphere. In short, nothing has occurred that would be enough to bring an object into existence. The temporal part just seems to pop into existence without any sufficient cause.

But this argument reflects an unwarranted prejudice in favor of the three-dimensional picture over the four-dimensional picture. If we accept a four-dimensional view of physical objects, then all it is for an object to come into existence at t_0 is for it to have t_0 as its lower temporal boundary. The question of what caused it to come into existence at t_0 is just the question of what causes it to have the lower temporal boundary that it does, and this question is no more or less answerable than the question of what causes a certain object to have the spatial boundaries it does. There seem to be only two reasonable interpretations of such a question: 'What causes those particular boundaries to be the boundaries of an object?' and 'What causes those boundaries to be filled?' Each of these questions is as answerable for temporal parts as for spatial parts.

Recall that it is not built into the concept of a temporal part that every region should contain such a part. Hence, there may be some explanation for why a given part comes into existence at the particular time that it does, an explanation for what causes those particular boundaries to be the boundaries of an object. For instance, we might think of a person as being one object from birth to death. Still there seems a natural division between the person's prepubescent part and postpubescent part. We can explain why the change from prepubescence to postpubescence should mark the beginning of a new object, because that change will have significant ramifications. The boundaries around the person's postpubescent part seem hardly less significant than the boundaries around the person's heart. Accepting the existence of these temporal parts does not commit us to the existence of a part for every subregion of the region the person exactly fills. A separate argument is required in order to get this rather more cluttered view of what parts there are. Such an argument would also provide an explanation for why the boundaries of each of the objects should be the boundaries of an object.

I suspect that much of the initial impression that temporal parts would have to come into existence *ex nihilo* is based on a picture of these physical objects popping into existence merely because of the passage of time. The phrase '*ex nihilo*' suggests a complete independence from previous events. The objects that I am defending do not just pop into existence. It is not as if there is empty space and then, poof, the space is filled. It is the causal mechanisms together with the material configuration of matter at any given time that affect which parts will exist at the next moment. (Whether this is a deterministic relationship is an independent question.) So, for any particular temporal part there is an answer to the question 'What causes its boundaries to be filled?', or at least as much of an answer as there is for spatial parts. The structure of the world at one moment does affect the structure of the world at the next moment.

9   In Favor of Temporal Parts

To support temporal parts and the four-dimensional view of physical objects, recall that earlier in this chapter I argued that thinking of objects as three-dimensional and enduring would commit us to one of the following five unpleasant alternatives:

(a)   there is no such physical object as my body,
(b)   there is no physical object in the space that we would typically say is now exactly occupied by all of me other than my left hand,
(c)   no physical object can undergo a loss of parts,
(d)   there can be distinct physical objects exactly occupying the same space at the same time,
(e)   identity is not transitive.

We are now in a position to see how viewing objects as four-dimensional allows us to avoid all of these alternatives. Once we adopt the four-dimensional picture, we can deny all five alternatives without having to be committed to:

(3)   the thing that, after *t*, is Body-minus = the thing that, after *t*, is Body.

The objects claimed to be identical in (3) are distinct and do not, except in a loose sense, occupy the same space at the same time.

Body and Body-minus are distinct four-dimensional objects, since they have different spatial shapes before *t*. But then, it might be objected, they seem to be distinct but coincident entities – co-occupying a single spatiotemporal region *R* that begins at *t*. The response is that, strictly speaking, neither of them is in *R*. They are both temporally too big. They each take up a spatiotemporal region that is temporally larger than *R*, because their regions begin before *t*. Of course, each has a temporal part that is in *R*, but that does not entail that either Body or Body-minus is in that region. They overlap in *R*, but neither one exactly fills *R*.[19]

Perhaps there may be another way of generating the coincident entity problem. Instead of comparing Body with Body-minus, let us compare that part of Body which does exactly fill *R* with that part of Body-minus which also exactly fills *R*. It might be claimed that here we have an example of two distinct objects in the same space at the same time. But this again would be a mistake. These temporal parts are not two distinct objects, but, rather, one object under two descriptions. Body and Body-minus have a common temporal part, just as my living room and my dining room have a common spatial part.[20]

The thesis that there are temporal parts allows us to avoid an otherwise troublesome metaphysical puzzle. Moreover, the existence of such objects seems entirely plausible once we are prepared to think of objects as four-dimensional rather than three-dimensional and enduring. However, not everyone agrees about the plausibility of these entities. Their existence becomes especially dubious to some philosophers when considering the case of people. No matter what other objects are like, it might be claimed, we can at least be sure that people do not have temporal parts.

[...]

14   Modal Properties

Peter van Inwagen presents an argument against the thesis that people have temporal parts.[20] [...] The key premise to van Inwagen's argument is that a person could have existed for less time than he does in fact exist. Insofar as such a premise could be generalized to objects other than people, the thesis that those objects have temporal parts would be equally vulnerable to arguments of this type. Actually, van Inwagen's is an argument against the thesis that people have *arbitrary* temporal parts. Van Inwagen suggests that if there are any nonarbitrary temporal parts, they are momentary slices. Personally, I am more certain of the existence of temporally extended temporal parts than I am of momentary ones. The objects that van Inwagen is arguing against are precisely the ones that I include in my ontology. His argument is fairly simple once we grant him his key premise about an individual's modal properties.

Van Inwagen argues by indirect proof. Assume that Descartes has temporal parts. Then there is some thing that begins to exist when Descartes begins to exist and ceases existing exactly one year before Descartes ceases to exist and is exactly the same spatial size that Descartes is for as long as that part exists. Call that object 'Descartes-minus'. Given the premise that Descartes could have lived for a year less than he did, Descartes could have been the same size that Descartes-minus in fact is. If we also accept that Descartes-minus would have been the same size that it is even if Descartes had not existed beyond the time that Descartes-minus in fact exists, then it follows that Descartes and Descartes-minus could have occupied exactly the same spatiotemporal region. But no distinct objects can occupy exactly the same region. So we must deny our assumption that there is such a thing as Descartes-minus.

This argument depends upon the following premises. First, that Descartes could have lived for a year less than he in fact did. Second, that Descartes-minus would have been the same spatiotemporal shape that it in fact is even if Descartes had lived for a year less than he in fact did. And third, that coincident entities are impossible. I accept the last two of these premises. In fact, I would argue for both of them. But I reject the first of his premises. I grant that most of us believe that it is true, but I deny that we are right in our belief or that we even have any very good reason for it. I might reject this premise on the following grounds: It, together with other premises that I accept, has the consequence that there are no temporal parts; but I am more convinced of the existence of temporal parts than I am of the truth of the premise in question; therefore, I conclude that the premise in question is false. I might reject the premise on these grounds, but I do not. I hope that I can present more persuasive grounds.[21]

Notes

1 For instance: Quine, "Identity, ostension, and hypostasis," this volume, ch. 34; John Perry, "Can the self divide?" *Journal of Philosophy* 69 (Sept. 1972), pp. 463–88; David Lewis, "Survival and identity," in *Philosophical Papers*, vol. 1 (New York: Oxford University Press, 1983) [reproduced without postscript in ch. 43 of this volume].

2 Lewis, "Survival and identity," p. 76.

3 Judith Jarvis Thomson, "Parthood and identity across time," this volume, ch. 35.

4 In conversation Jim Hudson and Michael Tye have each expressed doubts about whether they even understand the three-dimensional view, and they claim that the four-dimensional view is in fact the standard view. I am not much concerned about what the standard view really is, but I do think that our standard use of language does reflect at least a tendency to treat time as importantly disanalogous with the three spatial dimensions. Quine puts the point this way: "Our ordinary language shows a tiresome bias in its treatment of time" (*Word and Object* (Cambridge, Mass.: MIT Press, 1960), p. 170). Also, I suspect that many philosophical difficulties would never have arisen if it were not for some tendency toward a three-dimensional view.

5 Peter van Inwagen, "The doctrine of arbitrary undetached parts," *Pacific Philosophical Quarterly* 62 (Apr. 1981), pp. 123–37.

6 Thomson, "Parthood and identity across time."

7 Van Inwagen, "Doctrine of arbitrary undetached parts."

8 Roderick Chisholm, "Parts as essential to their wholes," *Review of Metaphysics* 26 (1973), pp. 581–603.

9 Peter Geach, "Identity," *Review of Metaphysics* 21 (1967–8), pp. 3–12.

10 See Mark Heller, *The Ontology of Physical Objects* (Cambridge: Cambridge University Press, 1990), ch. 2, sect. 9.

11 See Heller, *Ontology of Physical Objects*, chs 2 and 3.

12 Notice that my claims do not presuppose a description theory of names. I am not merely supposing that 'Whitey' *means* the whole piece of paper. On a causal theory of names 'Whitey' refers to the whole piece of paper if and only if it was the whole piece

that was originally indicated when the reference of 'Whitey' was fixed.

13 Compare this to David Lewis's discussion, "Survival and identity."

14 Compare this to John Perry's discussion in "The same *F*," *The Philosophical Review* 79/2 (Apr. 1970), pp. 198–9.

15 See my "The best candidate approach to diachronic identity," *Australasian Journal of Philosophy* 65 (Dec. 1987), pp. 434–51. On my "strictly speaking" ploy many of our ordinary utterances end up being false unless they are treated as loose speaking. It is strictly false that Whitey is in the drawer and that Whitey exists now. What is strictly true is that part of Whitey is in the drawer and part of Whitey exists now. One might prefer to hold that it is strictly true that Whitey is in the drawer, but that this just means that part of Whitey is in the drawer. Similarly, it is strictly true that Whitey exists now, and this just means that part of Whitey exists now. (Actually, if now is supposed to be an instant, and if there are no instantaneous objects, then the strict truth is that now is within Whitey's temporal boundaries.) This suggestion agrees with my earlier claims concerning the nonlinguistic facts, but disagrees about the strict/loose distinction. Perhaps the claim that part of Whitey is in the drawer is in fact the strictest interpretation of 'Whitey is in the drawer'. Someone who adopts the present suggestion will be forced to say that my hand and I do occupy the same space at the same

time, but he can still accept that we do not have to compete for the space, since my occupying that space just is my having a part (my hand) that occupies it. The sort of coincidence just described is not an objectionable sort of coincidence. It is not the sort of coincidence discussed in the next paragraph of the text.

16 Thomson, "Parthood and identity across time," p. 485.

17 Thomson calls it "a crazy metaphysic" on pp. 485 and 486.

18 Ibid., pp. 486–7.

19 Jan Cover has suggested to me that on the four-dimensional view both halves of the identity claim in (3) are nonreferring: There is no thing that, after *t*, is Body-minus. But this is to forget that we can refer to a whole object without having the whole object present. Body-minus (the whole four-dimensional object that begins to exist long before *t*) is Body-minus at all times during its existence, including the after-*t* times.

20 It may appear that in order to get this benefit from temporal parts we will have to accept that every moment within Body's existence is the beginning of a new temporal part (since *t* was arbitrarily selected). I do in fact accept this, but all we really need in the present case is that Body and Body-minus be too big to fit in region *R*. We do not need to claim that there is anything that does exactly fill *R*.

21 For the author's argument see Heller, *Ontology of Physical Objects*, ch. 2.

37

The Problem of Temporary Intrinsics

David Lewis

Let us say that something *persists* iff, somehow or other, it exists at various times; this is the neutral word.[1] Something *perdures* iff it persists by having different temporal parts, or stages, at different times, though no one part of it is wholly present at more than one time; whereas it *endures* iff it persists by being wholly present at more than one time. Perdurance corresponds to the way a road persists through space; part of it is here and part of it is there, and no part is wholly present at two different places. Endurance corresponds to the way a universal, if there are such things, would be wholly present wherever and whenever it is instantiated. Endurance involves overlap: the content of two different times has the enduring thing as a common part. Perdurance does not.

(There might be mixed cases: entities that persist by having an enduring part and a perduring part. An example might be a person who consisted of an enduring entelechy ruling a perduring body; or an electron that had a universal of unit negative charge as a permanent part, but did not consist entirely of universals. But here I ignore the mixed cases. And when I speak of ordinary things as perduring, I shall ignore their enduring universals, if such there be.)

Discussions of endurance versus perdurance tend to be endarkened by people who say such things as this: 'Of course you are wholly present at every moment of your life, except in case of amputation. For at every moment all your parts are there: your legs, your lips, your liver....' These endarkeners may think themselves partisans of endurance, but they are not. They are perforce neutral, because they lack the conceptual resources to understand what is at issue. Their speech betrays – and they may acknowledge it willingly – that they have no concept of a temporal part. (Or at any rate none that applies to a person, say, as opposed to a process or a stretch of time.) Therefore they are on neither side of a dispute about whether or not persisting things are divisible into temporal parts. They understand neither the affirmation nor the denial. They are like the people – fictional, I hope – who say that the whole of the long road is in their little village, for not one single lane of it is missing. Meaning less than others do by 'part', since they omit parts cut crosswise, they also mean less than others do by 'whole'. They say the 'whole' road is in the village; by which they mean that every 'part' is; but by that, they only mean that every part cut lengthwise is.

David Lewis, from chapter 4 of *On the Plurality of Worlds* (Oxford: Blackwell, 1986). Reprinted by permission of John Wiley & Sons, Inc.

Metaphysics: An Anthology, Second Edition. Edited by Jaegwon Kim, Daniel Z. Korman and Ernest Sosa.
Editorial material and organization © 2012 Blackwell Publishing Ltd. Published 2012 by Blackwell Publishing Ltd.

Divide the road into its least lengthwise parts; they cannot even raise the question whether those are in the village wholly or only partly. For that is a question about crosswise parts, and the concept of a crosswise part is what they lack. Perhaps 'crosswise part' really does sound to them like a blatant contradiction. Or perhaps it seems to them that they understand it, but the village philosophers have persuaded them that really they couldn't, so their impression to the contrary must be an illusion. At any rate, *I* have the concept of a temporal part; and for some while I shall be addressing only those of you who share it.[2]

Endurance through time is analogous to the alleged trans-world identity of common parts of overlapping worlds; perdurance through time is analogous to the 'trans-world identity', if we may call it that, of a trans-world individual composed of distinct parts in non-overlapping worlds. Perdurance, which I favour for the temporal case, is closer to the counterpart theory which I favour for the modal case; the difference is that counterpart theory concentrates on the parts and ignores the transworld individual composed of them.

The principal and decisive objection against endurance, as an account of the persistence of ordinary things such as people or puddles, is the problem of temporary intrinsics. Persisting things change their intrinsic properties. For instance, shape: when I sit, I have a bent shape; when I stand, I have a straightened shape. Both shapes are temporary intrinsic properties; I have them only some of the time. How is such change possible? I know of only three solutions.

(It is *not* a solution just to say how very commonplace and indubitable it is that we have different shapes at different times. To say that is only to insist – rightly – that it must be possible somehow. Still less is it a solution to say it in jargon – as it might be, that bent-on-Monday and straight-on-Tuesday are compatible because they are 'time-indexed properties' – if that just means that, somehow, you can be bent on Monday and straight on Tuesday.)

First solution: contrary to what we might think, shapes are not genuine intrinsic properties. They are disguised relations, which an enduring thing may bear to times. One and the same enduring thing may bear the bent-shape relation to some times, and the straight-shape relation to others. In itself, considered apart from its relations to other things, it has no shape at all. And likewise for all other seeming temporary intrinsics; all of them must be reinterpreted as relations that something with an absolutely unchanging intrinsic nature bears to different times. The solution to the problem of temporary intrinsics is that there aren't any temporary intrinsics. This is simply incredible, if we are speaking of the persistence of ordinary things. (It might do for the endurance of entelechies or universals.) If we know what shape is, we know that it is a property, not a relation.

Second solution: the only intrinsic properties of a thing are those it has at the present moment. Other times are like false stories; they are abstract representations, composed out of the materials of the present, which represent or misrepresent the way things are. When something has different intrinsic properties according to one of these ersatz other times, that does not mean that it, or any part of it, or anything else, just *has* them – no more so than when a man is crooked according to the *Times*, or honest according to the *News*. This is a solution that rejects endurance, because it rejects persistence altogether. And it is even less credible than the first solution. In saying that there are no other times, as opposed to false representations thereof, it goes against what we all believe. No man, unless it be at the moment of his execution, believes that he has no future; still less does anyone believe that he has no past.

Third solution: the different shapes, and the different temporary intrinsics generally, belong to different things. Endurance is to be rejected in favour of perdurance. We perdure; we are made up of temporal parts, and our temporary intrinsics are properties of these parts, wherein they differ one from another. There is no problem at all about how different things can differ in their intrinsic properties.

[...]

Notes

1 My discussion of this parallel problem is much indebted to D. M. Armstrong, 'Identity through time', in Peter van Inwagen (ed.), *Time and Cause: Essays Presented to Richard Taylor* (Dordrecht: Reidel, 1980), and to Mark Johnston, *Particulars and Persistence* (Ph.D. dissertation, Princeton University, 1983). I follow Johnston in terminology.

2 I attempt to explain it to others in *Philosophical Papers* (Oxford: Oxford University Press, 1983), vol. 1, pp. 76–7. But I have no great hopes, since any competent philosopher who does not understand something will take care not to understand anything else whereby it might be explained.

38

Endurance and Temporary Intrinsics

Sally Haslanger

In a number of places David Lewis has argued that the problem of temporary intrinsics rules out the possibility that objects endure through change.[1] Lewis maintains that to account for temporary intrinsics we should say that objects do not endure through change, but rather perdure.[2] I disagree; Lewis's arguments do not demonstrate that an endurance theory cannot accommodate temporary intrinsics.

The problem of temporary intrinsics is this: ordinary objects persist through changes in their intrinsic properties, i.e. those properties which an object has in virtue of the way *it* is, independently of anything else. To use Lewis's example, 'when I sit I'm bent, when I stand. I'm straight'. But an object cannot have incompatible properties. So how is intrinsic change possible?

Lewis initially outlines three solutions to this problem, of which he favours the third. The first is the view that properties are really relations to times; the second is the view that only the present exists; the third is the doctrine of temporal parts. It is important to note that Lewis's solution, like the others he mentions, requires a trade off in our intuitions about intrinsic change. Although on his

view it is true that there are persisting objects (the perdurers), and it is also true that properties such as shape are genuinely intrinsic (to the stages), there is nothing such that it persists through a change in *its* intrinsic properties. The intrinsic properties of the stages are not properties of the perdurer. The perdurer itself is not simply bent and then straight; if it were we'd be left with the original problem. The perdurer has properties which are significantly correlated with these, e.g. the property of having a part which is bent (and one which is straight), but these properties involve a relation between the perdurer and one of its momentary parts. Even if one were to hold that a perdurer's relations to its distinct parts are intrinsic (which is not obviously correct), at any rate such properties of the perdurer are not temporary. So what persists is not what has the relevant temporary intrinsic. Like the other 'solutions', Lewis must say that it is not possible for an object to persist through a change in *its* intrinsic properties. So why are we forced to make Lewis's compromise?

I have argued elsewhere for the importance of maintaining endurance in an account of change to accommodate the idea that the past (causally)

Sally Haslanger, "Endurance and Temporary Intrinsics," *Analysis*, 49/3 (June 1989): 119–25. Reproduced by permission.

Metaphysics: An Anthology, Second Edition. Edited by Jaegwon Kim, Daniel Z. Korman and Ernest Sosa.
Editorial material and organization © 2012 Blackwell Publishing Ltd. Published 2012 by Blackwell Publishing Ltd.

constrains the present (see [1]). If one is concerned to preserve endurance, there are at least two options which hold some appeal. The first is to bite the bullet and deny that there are temporary *intrinsics*, i.e. treat all temporary properties as relational. I will not discuss this option here. The second is to develop what Lewis calls the 'adverbial' variant of the first alternative in such a way that it avoids the problems he indicates (see [4] p. 65, fn. 1). I prefer this second option, and will sketch some ways to carry it out.

The intuitive idea behind the so-called 'adverbial' option is that objects have properties at times, and that time should modify this 'having', rather than the subject or the property. Lewis interprets this in terms of a commitment to a three-place instantiation relation which takes objects, properties, and times as arguments. He rightly points out that this interpretation of the view still treats intrinsic properties as relational; and raises the further question, 'what does standing in some relation to straightness have to do with just plain being straight?' (in [4] p. 66, fn. 1).

I think the right response here is to deny that the intuitions underlying the 'adverbial' account need commit one to the three-place instantiation relation. Along these lines, E. J. Lowe, in his response to Lewis, suggests that we should take the account to claim that '*a*'s having a bent shape *obtains at t* while *a*'s having a straight shape *obtains at t*' ([5] p. 75). He also remarks that, 'a thing's *being shaped* itself stands in relation to times, not that a thing's being shaped is partly a matter of *that thing's* standing in relations to times' ([5] p. 75).

In developing the idea that objects have properties at times, we may note that there are a variety of semantical options one might take in spelling out the role of temporal elements in propositions.[3] Reviewing a number of these semantical options facilitates a discussion of the ontological options suggested by the semantics. For the purposes of responding to Lewis, the endurance theorist may remain agnostic about which of the options is semantically superior; and at this point, the endurance theorist may even remain agnostic about the details of the ontology. The goal is simply to show that there are some ways of developing the idea that objects have properties at times without falling prey to Lewis's objections.

Lowe's comments suggest two ways to incorporate temporal elements into one's semantics: the first is to leave temporal elements out of propositions and instead to evaluate propositions with respect to times (just as one evaluates propositions with respect to worlds); the second is to include temporal elements in the proposition without incorporating them into the semantical value of the predicate (or the subject). Treating time as part of the circumstances of evaluation (as in the first suggestion) offers a temporalist view of propositions such that propositions can change truth-value from time to time; treating time as an additional constituent of the proposition (perhaps not explicit in the sentence expressing the proposition but determined via the context of utterance) offers eternalist propositions. On neither view is the property of the object construed as a relation to a time (though, of course, there may be some propositions which do concern a relation between a property and a time); and on neither view have we reified a distinct instantiation relation.[4]

One might complain, however, that none of the options I have indicated avoids commitment to a three-place instantiation relation which holds between an object, a property, and a time; so we have not been given a model which demonstrates how we might construe temporary predications without relying on such a relation. For example, consider the option of accepting temporal propositions which are evaluated with respect to times. On this view, the temporal proposition that Lewis is bent is true at some times and not others. We may note that given that at some time *t*, the proposition that Lewis is bent is true, there is a three-place relation between Lewis, bentness, and a time *t*, such that the proposition that Lewis is bent holds at *t*. In spite of the fact that this temporalist account does not employ a *primitive* three-place instantiation relation, nevertheless, we may define an analogous three-place relation within the temporalist framework. Therefore, the commitment to such a relation remains.[5]

But does the recognition of this defined three-place instantiation relation demonstrate that we must construe the relation between an object and its properties as problematically relational? I think not. The danger of a three-place instantiation relation is that it invites us to treat objects as related to their properties as individuals are related to other individuals; this would be undesirable. But note that the three-place relation indicated above, viz., the relation between an object a, property F, and time t, such that the proposition that a is F holds at t, is a relation defined partly in terms of a more basic notion of a's being F, i.e., of an object instantiating its properties. Even if we grant that the three-place relation is an instantiation relation, the primary instantiation of the property F by the object a need not be construed relationally. Lewis is bent by instantiating bentness, and this instantiation holds at some times and not others. The fact that we can further define a three-place relation between the object, the property, and the time, need not commit us to treating the basic notion of an object's instantiating its properties as relational. Thus, at least one of the options offers a genuine alternative that Lewis has not addressed. This response suggests a strategy which we might also employ in defending other options.

The question remains, however, whether any of these options make metaphysical sense. Lewis thinks that they don't; his worry is that a temporary predication (of whatever sort) does not adequately capture the connection between an object and its intrinsic properties. We can find the basis for his concern about the adverbial variants by considering his argument against the original proposal that properties are 'really' relations to times. He writes,

> Imagine trying to draw a picture of two different times: t_1 when I sit, and t_2 when I stand. You draw two circles, overlapping because I exist at both times so you want to draw me in the intersection. But then you have to draw me bent and also straight, which you can't do; and if *per impossibile* you could, you still wouldn't have done anything to connect the bentness to t_1 and the straightness to t_2 instead of vice versa. What to do? The first solution says to draw the circles overlapping, draw me in the intersection as a mere dot or shapeless blob, draw a line labelled 'bent-at' from me to the t_1 circle and a line labelled 'straight-at' to the t_2 circle. A queer way to draw a shape! ([4] p. 67)

Presumably, to capture the adverbial variant, Lewis would draw two circles overlapping; himself a dot or shapeless blob in the intersection. But this time, bentness and straightness

would be abstract entities outside the circles, and the picture would include two branched lines labelled 'instantiates at', one linking himself, bentness, and the t_1 circle, and the other linking himself, straightness, and the t_2 circle. Like the original picture, this is a 'queer way to draw a shape'.

The argument seems to be this: if the enduring thing has a particular shape, e.g. bent, then to say that *it* (the enduring thing) is straight results in contradiction. Instead, we must say that the shapeless thing has shape by being related to bentness or straightness (at times) – or alternatively is related to times by a 'bent-at' or 'straight at' relation. Given this model, we find ourselves committed to a modified substratum (modified because it may have some permanent intrinsics, and so needn't be a bare substratum), combined with a relational conception of temporary intrinsic predication. Such a relational conception of predication fails to treat the properties in question as genuinely intrinsic; e.g. standing in some relation to shape is not the same as being shaped.

There are three crucial premises in this argument. The first is that the enduring thing has no shape intrinsically; the second is that if the enduring thing has no shape intrinsically, then it has shapes by standing in some relation to them; the third is that a relational conception of having shape is unacceptable. I will focus on the first premise.

On Lewis's view, there is some way that a temporal part can be shaped, e.g. bent, that is not available to an enduring thing. But why not? Why can't the endurance theorist simply insist that the enduring thing is bent in just the same way that the temporal part is bent, except that the enduring thing is not bent in this way throughout its existence? In other words, why must we represent the enduring object as 'a shapeless blob'?

Lewis suggests that if the enduring thing is bent at one time and straight at another, then it must have these shapes extrinsically and not intrinsically.[6] It is because shape is only extrinsic to the enduring thing that it is properly represented as 'shapeless'. But why must we say that temporary properties are extrinsic? Admittedly, if we say that the enduring thing is intrinsically both bent and straight, this results in contradiction. However, there is no contradiction in saying that it is intrinsically bent at one time and intrinsically straight at another. Moreover, if we take seriously the proposals mentioned above, we are fully entitled to make this claim; as we saw, one need not construe an object's having a property at a time either in terms of its standing in relation to a time, or in terms of its standing in a temporarily relativized instantiation relation to the property in question. To assume that an enduring object's temporary properties must be extrinsic is to assume what is at stake in the debate with the ('adverbial') endurance theorist.

Let me put this in more positive terms. Consider the idea of an intrinsic property. Lewis suggests that a property is intrinsic iff the object has the property in virtue of the way *it* is independently of anything else. An endurance theorist will demand a temporally sensitive construal of this condition, e.g. that a property is (at a time) intrinsic iff the object has (at that time) the property in virtue of the way *it* is (at that time), independently of anything else. On this revised condition Lewis is intrinsically bent (at one time) and intrinsically straight (at another).[7] One might deny this interpretation of the condition and insist on a temporally insensitive construal of intrinsic properties, yet in doing so one fails to address the endurance theorist's position.

Lewis might complain, however, that the ontology of the endurance picture remains mysterious. Suppose we want to describe the enduring subject of predication in a way which captures how it is throughout its existence. The endurance theorist is likely to claim that such a description will involve a characterization of it as having different properties at different times. But there is still a question about how it is, abstracted from its changing history, i.e. abstracted from its variation from time to time. We cannot describe the enduring object in these terms as simply bent or straight; so it could only be shapeless. But how can this shapeless thing be the subject of the relevant shape predications?

The endurance theorist's response is to point out that although a description of the enduring object which abstracts from its changing history does not include a particular shape as part of that description (though it may include 'being shaped' since this description applies throughout its changes), such a description is incomplete; most importantly, it doesn't include all of the intrinsic properties of the object because some of the intrinsic properties of the object are had at some times and not at others. Returning to Lewis's diagram, we might say that it is not surprising that the 'shapeless blob' in the intersection of the circles seems incomplete, for to take the exercise as adequately characterizing the enduring object is to assume that we can draw how the enduring thing intrinsically is, once and for all. But if some of its properties, e.g. shape, are temporary intrinsics, this is not possible. The endurance theorist denies that the description which characterizes the object 'timelessly' is the description which captures all of the intrinsic properties of the object. The enduring object is bent and then straight; it is not a shapeless blob.

There is a sense in which these responses to Lewis's concerns are simply a stubborn resistance to his intuitions about what it is to predicate an intrinsic property of an object. Admittedly, predication is a murky issue, and more work needs to be done in working out a theory of endurance through change. However, the temporal parts theory does not offer a sufficiently compelling account of predication to rule out an account which is consistent with a commitment to endurance. Although Lewis's concerns are rightly placed on the issue of predication, his argument rests on assumptions which the endurance theorist need not grant. Although the endurance theorist's resistance does not demonstrate that endurance is preferable to perdurance overall, it does offer a response to the charge that the endurantist position is metaphysically untenable. That the position is tenable is significant, for it is the endurance theory which allows us to preserve the intuition that there are some objects which persist through a change in their intrinsic properties.

Notes

I am grateful to John Broome, Mark Johnston, David Lewis, George Myro, Scott Soames, and Stephen Yablo, for helpful discussions on the issues addressed in this paper.

1 Most recently Lewis argues this in [4]; and in [3], pp. 203–5 [ch. 37, p. 505, in the present volume].
2 I follow Lewis's terminology here, see [3], p. 202 [p. 505 in the present volume].
3 For simplicity, I am considering only simple propositions which contain no explicit temporal operators. The problems become much more complex

when we consider sentences embedded within temporal (and other) operators and the function of temporal indexicals. See, e.g., D. Kaplan [2], and M. Richard [6].

4   There are other options. See, e.g., Nathan Salmon's treatment of time as a component of the 'information value' of the predicate in an eternalist proposition in [7] Ch. 2.

5   I owe this objection to David Lewis.

6   This pattern of inference has a venerable history. Some find it in Aristotle's comments about prime matter (e.g., see *Metaphysics* VII:3), and it is clearly linked to the arguments which some have used to argue for bare substrata.

7   Further, on the endurance theory, a duplicate of an enduring object will also be an enduring object. If the original undergoes change, its duplicate undergoes changes as well. Thus, if an enduring object undergoes a change from being bent to being straight, its duplicate will undergo a change from being bent to being straight, though the change may occur at a different time.

References

[1] Sally Haslanger, 'Persistence, Change, and Explanation', *Philosophical Studies* 56/1 (1989), pp. 1–28.

[2] David Kaplan, 'Demonstratives', in Joseph Almog, John Perry, and Howard Wettstein, eds., *Themes from Kaplan* (New York: Oxford University Press, 1989), pp. 481–563.

[3] David Lewis, *On the Plurality of Worlds* (Oxford: Basil Blackwell, 1986) [see ch. 37 in the present volume].

[4] David Lewis, 'Rearrangement of Particles: A Reply to Lowe', *Analysis* 48 (March 1988) 65–72.

[5] E. J. Lowe, 'The Problem of Intrinsic Change: Rejoinder to Lewis', *Analysis* 48 (March 1988) 72–7.

[6] Mark Richard, 'Tenses, Propositions, and Meanings', *Philosophical Studies* 41 (1982) 337–51.

[7] Nathan Salmon, *Frege's Puzzle* (Cambridge, MA: MIT Press, 1986).

39

All the World's a Stage

Theodore Sider

Some philosophers believe that everyday objects are four-dimensional space-time worms, that a person (for example) persists through time by having temporal parts, or stages, at each moment of her existence. None of these stages is identical to the person herself; rather, she is the aggregate of all her temporal parts.[1] Others accept 'three-dimensionalism', rejecting stages in favour of the notion that persons 'endure', or are 'wholly present' throughout their lives.[2] I aim to defend an apparently radical third view: not only do I accept person stages; I claim that we *are* stages.[3] Likewise for other objects of our everyday ontology: statues are statue-stages, coins are coin-stages, etc.

At one level, I accept the ontology of the worm view. I believe in space-time worms, since I believe in temporal parts and aggregates of things I believe in. I simply don't think space-time worms are what we typically call persons, name with proper names, quantify over, etc.[4] The metaphysical view shared by this 'stage view' and the worm view may be called 'four-dimensionalism', and may be stated roughly as the doctrine that temporally extended things divide into temporal parts.

In this paper I aim to provide what might be called 'a philosopher's reasons' to believe the stage view, by arguing that it resolves various puzzles about identity over time better than its rivals. After replying to objections, I conclude that a strong case exists for accepting the stage view. At the very least, I aim to show that the stage view deserves more careful consideration that it usually is given.

I   The Worm Theory and Parfit's Puzzle

I begin with Derek Parfit's famous argument that two plausible views about self-interested concern, or 'what matters', cannot both be correct.[5] According to the view that 'identity is what matters', a future person matters to me iff he *is* me,[6] according to the view that 'psychological continuity is what matters', a future person matters to me iff he is psychologically continuous with me.[7] Both ideas initially seem correct (to some of us anyway), but consider the much discussed case of the 'division' of a person.[8] If I divide into two persons, Fred and Ed, who are exactly similar to me in all psychological respects, the doctrine that psychological continuity is what matters implies that both Fred and Ed matter to me; but this

Theodore Sider, "All the World's a Stage," *Australasian Journal of Philosophy*, 74/3 (Sept. 1996): 433–53. Reproduced by permission.

contradicts the idea that identity is what matters since I cannot be identical both to Fred and to Ed.

Parfit's solution to his puzzle is to reject the idea that identity is what matters: I do not exist after fission, but nevertheless what matters to me is preserved.[9] This seems counter-intuitive. I could have moral concern for others, but how could such concern be like the everyday a concern I have for myself? I believe, though I won't argue for it here, that rejecting the idea that psychological continuity is what matters also earns low marks; a way to preserve both ideas would be the ideal solution. And even if some relation other than psychological continuity is what matters (e.g., bodily continuity), if it can take a branching form then a problem formally analogous to the present one will arise, and there still will be a need to resolve the apparent conflict between two ideas about what matters.

In his 'Survival and Identity', David Lewis has attempted to provide just such a resolution. On his version of the worm view, the relation of psychological continuity is identical to the 'I-relation', or 'the unity relation for persons' – that relation which holds between person stages iff they are parts of some one continuing person.[10] By identifying these relations Lewis can claim that each is what matters, and hence claim to have resolved the conflict between our two ideas about what matters. In the case of fission, this identification commits Lewis to holding that two distinct persons can share a common person stage, for in that case, a stage in the present is psychologically continuous with future stages of two distinct people. Figure 39.1 illustrates this in the case where I divide into Fred and Ed:

According to Lewis, in such a case we have a total of two people: Ed, who is made up of stages T_1, T_2, T_3, E_4, E_5, and E_6, and Fred, who is made up of T_1, T_2, T_3, F_4, F_5, and F_6. Before division, Fred and Ed overlapped; before division, the name 'Ted' was ambiguous between Ed and Fred.

So, Lewis resolves Parfit's puzzle by claiming that since the I-relation and the relation of psychological continuity are one and the same relation, both can be what matters. But the original puzzle involved *identity*, not the I-relation. I follow Derek Parfit in questioning whether Lewis' claim that the I-relation is what matters adequately captures the spirit of the 'commonsense platitude' (as Lewis calls it) that identity is what matters.[11] How exactly does Lewis understand that commonsense platitude? One possibility would be the following:

(I.1)   A person stage matters to my present stage if and only if it bears the I-relation to my present stage.

The problem is that (I.1) concerns what matters to person stages. When in everyday life we speak of 'what matters', surely the topic is what matters to persons, so if Lewis is to vindicate the *commonsense* platitude that identity is what matters, his version of that platitude must concern what matters to persons. Unless persons *are* person stages, which they are not for Lewis, (I.1) does not address the present topic.

Let us then consider a mattering relation that applies to persons. Where P is a person, and what

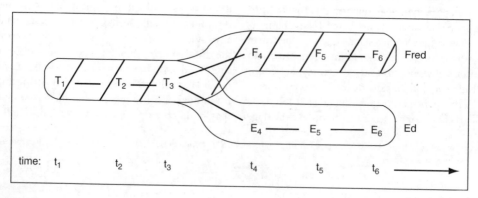

Figure 39.1

happens to future person P* matters to P in the special way at issue here, let us write 'M(P*, P)'. (Actually, the relation is four place since it involves two times. 'M(P*, t*, P, t)' means that what happens to P* at t* matters to P at t. I will mostly leave the times implicit.) The doctrine that psychological continuity is what matters would seem to be the following:

(PC)   For any person P and any person P* existing at some time in the future, M(P*, P) iff P's current stage is psychologically continuous with P*'s stage at that time.

As for the doctrine that identity is what matters, the only two possibilities seem to be:

(I.2)   For any person P and for any person P* existing at some time in the future, M(P*, P) iff P = P*; and

(I.3)   For any person P and for any person P* existing at some time in the future, M(P*, P) iff P's current stage bears the I-relation to P*'s stage at that time.

(I.2) clearly does express the 'platitude of common sense' that what matters to me now is what will happen to me later. But, as Parfit notes, combined with (PC) it rules out the possibility of a stage of one person being psychologically continuous with a stage of another person, and is thus inconsistent with Lewis' approach to fission. (I.3) avoids this problem, but at the cost of failing to capture the spirit of the commonsense platitude that what matters is *identity*. Suppose that, after division, Fred is tortured while Ed lies in the sun in Hawaii. Since according to Lewis T_3 bears the I-relation to F_4, (I.3) implies that M(Fred, Ed). So if (I.3) were true, Ed ought to fear something that will never happen to him!

In the postscript to [14, p. 74], Lewis makes some remarks that suggest an objection to this argument against (I.3). According to Lewis, at t_3, it is simply impossible for Ed to desire anything uniquely on his own behalf:

The shared stage [T_3] does the thinking for both of the continuants to which it belongs. Any thought it has must be shared. It cannot desire

one thing on behalf of [Ed] and another thing on behalf of [Fred].

I complained that (I.3) implies that what happens to Fred matters to Ed. Lewis' reply, apparently, is that to think otherwise would be to assume that Ed can have desires about what happens to Ed *as opposed to* happens to Fred.

I believe this objection can be answered. We can, I think, ask what *matters* to a person (in the relevant sense) independently of asking what that person is capable of desiring. Suppose I am comatose, but will recover in a year. Though I am currently incapable of having desires, it seems that what will happen to me in a year matters to me now, in the relevant sense. The fact that I will be tortured in the future is *bad for me now*, even though I cannot appreciate this fact. So, regardless of what Ed can desire, if we wish to stay faithful to the spirit behind the commonsense platitude that identity is what matters, we must reject the idea that Fred can matter to Ed. I conclude, then, that Lewis' attempt to preserve the view that both psychological continuity and identity matter in survival cannot succeed.

A three-dimensionalist could follow Lewis' solution to the puzzle up to a point, by claiming that before fission, there are two co-located wholly present persons.[12] Though the possibility of two persons in the same place at the same time seems implausible to me, three-dimensionalists have made similar claims (which I discuss below) in other cases, for example, in the case of a statue and the lump of matter from which it is constituted. The problem for such a three-dimensionalist, however, is the same as the problem for Lewis: since Ed is psychologically continuous with Fred, the doctrine that psychological continuity is what matters contradicts the commonsense platitude's requirement that what happens to Fred cannot matter to Ed. As noted above, two main responses are available to Lewis: speaking of what matters to stages, and the quoted reply that Ed is incapable of desiring things uniquely on behalf of himself. But the first response is unavailable to the three-dimensionalist (since she rejects stages), and the second response, as I argued above, is unsuccessful. I know of no other possibilities for reconciling both ideas about what matters that are based either on three-dimensionalism or the worm view. But there is such a possibility if we accept the stage view.

II The Stage View and Parfit's Puzzle

First, I will need to present the stage view in more detail. In particular, I need to address a problem that initially seems devastating. I once was a boy; this fact seems inconsistent with the stage view, for the stage view claims that I am an instantaneous stage that did not exist before today, and will not exist after today.

Properly construed, the stage view has no untoward consequences in this area. If we accept the stage view, we should analyze a tensed claim such as 'Ted was once a boy' as meaning roughly that there is some past person stage, x, such that x is a boy, and x bears the I-relation to Ted. (I spell out this analysis more carefully in section VII.) Since there is such a stage, the claim is true. Despite being a stage, Ted *was* a boy. The 'I-relation' I invoke here is the same relation used by the worm theorist. (It should be noted that the stage view is independent of particular theories of the nature of the I-relation; a stage theorist could analyze the I-relation in terms of memory, bodily continuity, take it as 'brute', etc.)

There is a close analogy here with Lewis' counterpart theory of *de re* modality.[13] According to counterpart theory, an object, x, has the property *possibly being F* iff there is some object in some possible world that has F, and bears the counterpart relation to x. The I-relation plays the role for the stage view that the counterpart relation plays in counterpart theory. The temporal operator 'was', and also other temporal operators like 'will be', 'will be at t', etc., are analogous to the modal operator 'possibly'. (The analogy is only partial, for there are no modal analogues of metrical tense operators like 'will be in 10 seconds'.) This analogy between the stage view and counterpart theory will be important in what follows.

I'll consider several objections to the stage view in section VI below, but one should be considered right away. It can be phrased as follows: 'According to the stage view, statements that look like they are about what once happened to me are *really* about what once happened to someone else. That's absurd.'

The stage view does *not* have this consequence. According to the stage view, 'Ted was once a boy' attributes a certain temporal property, the property of *once being a boy*, to me, not to anyone else.

Of course, the stage view does analyze my having this property as involving the boyhood of another object, but I am the one with the temporal property, which is the important thing. My answer to this objection parallels Lewis' answer to a famous objection to counterpart theory that was given by Saul Kripke:[14]

> [According to counterpart theory,] ... if we say 'Humphrey might have won the election (if only he had done such-and-such)', we are not talking about something that might have happened to *Humphrey* but to someone else, a 'counterpart'. Probably, however, Humphrey could not care less whether someone *else*, no matter how much resembling him, would have been victorious in another possible world.

Lewis replied that the objection is mistaken: Humphrey himself has the modal property of *possibly winning*. Granted,

> Counterpart theory does say ... that someone else - the victorious counterpart - enters into the story of ... how it is that Humphrey might have won.

But what is important is that Humphrey have the modal property:[15]

> Thanks to the victorious counterpart, Humphrey himself has requisite modal property: we can truly say that *he* might have won.

(I will discuss this objection further in section VI.)

Given the stage view's 'counterpart-theory of temporal properties', we can accept both that psychological continuity is what matters (in the sense of (PC)), and the following version of the doctrine that identity is what matters:

(I.4) For any person P and any person P* existing at some time in the future, M(P*, P) iff P *will be* identical to P* then.

What happens to a person in the future matters to me if and only if I will be that person. We cannot say that the person must, timelessly, *be* me, for I am not identical to persons at other times. But I *will* be identical to persons at other times, for

I bear the I-relation to future stages that are identical to such persons. (I.4) adequately captures the spirit of the commonsense platitude that identity is what matters, for it says that what matters to me is what will happen to me.

Back to the case of fission. Since both Fred and Ed – stages, according to the stage view – are psychologically continuous with me, each matters to me, according to (PC). (I.4) then implies that I will be Fred, and that I will be Ed. This does *not* imply that I will be both Fred and Ed, nor does it imply that Fred is identical to Ed. The following sentences must be distinguished:

(1a)   I will be Fred, and I will be Ed

(1b)   I will be both Fred and Ed.

(1a) is a conjunction of two predications; it may be thought of as having the form:

(a)   futurely-being-F(me) & futurely-being-G(me).

In contrast, (1b) is a predication of a single conjunctive temporal property; its form is:

(b)   futurely-being-F&G(me).

(1b) implies the absurd conclusion that Fred = Ed, since it says that I am I-related to some stage in the future that is identical to both Fred and Ed.[16] Fortunately, all the stage view implies is (1a), which follows from the facts of the case, (PC), and (I.4). It merely says that I am I-related to some future stage that is identical to Fred, and also that I'm I-related to some *possibly different* future stage that is identical to Ed.[17]

III   Counting Worms

I have another objection to Lewis' multiple occupancy approach, which also applies to the three-dimensionalist version of Lewis' approach that I mentioned at the end of section I. Quite simply, the idea that in fission cases there would be two persons in a single place at one time is preposterous.[18] Before division, imagine I am in my room alone. According to Lewis, there were two persons in the room. Was one of them hiding

under the bed? Since each weighs 150 pounds, why don't the two of them together weigh 300 pounds? These are traditional rhetorical questions asked of those who defend the possibility of two things being in one place at a time. I think they have force.

These questions are by no means unanswerable since Lewis can always reply that there is only a single stage present. The two persons don't weigh 300 pounds together because they aren't wholly distinct now – they overlap. The point is simply to draw attention to the immense prima facie implausibility of such cohabitation. The conclusion that two distinct persons could overlap and coexist at one place at some time is one that should be avoided if at all possible. Since I accept that for any class of person stages there is an aggregate of that class, I accept the existence of space-time worms that overlap in a single person stage at a given time. But since I say that no two persons can ever share spatial location at a time, I take this to show that these worms aren't persons.

Lewis' response to this problem is to defend an unorthodox view of counting.[19] If roads A and B coincide over a stretch that a person (Jane, let us call her) must cross, when she asks how many roads she must cross to reach her destination, it would be appropriate to tell her 'one'. According to Lewis, in counting here, we go through the things to be counted (roads) and count off positive integers, as usual. But we do not use a new number for each road – rather, we use a new number only when the road fails to bear a certain relation to the other roads we have already counted. In this case, the relation is that of *identity along Jane's path*, which is borne by one road to another iff they both cross Jane's path and share sections wherever they do. Let us say that persons are identical-at-t iff they have stages at t that are identical. (A three-dimensionalist might say instead that objects are identical-at-t iff they have the same part at t.) Counting by the relation *identity-at-t*, there is but one person in the room. In this way, Lewis tries to explain our intuition that there is only one person in the room. But is this *counting*? I think not. It seems clear to me that it is part of the meaning of 'counting' that counting is by identity. When we count a group of objects, we are interested in how many numerically distinct objects there are. Suppose I am alone in a room, and someone tells me on the

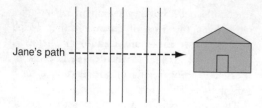

Figure 39.2

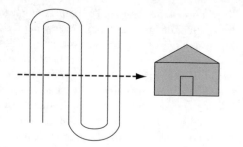

Figure 39.3

telephone that there are actually two persons in the room. Then imagine she clarifies this remark: 'well, actually, there is only one person, counting by identity-at-the-present-time'. I would suspect double talk. I would rephrase my question: 'how many numerically distinct persons are in the room?'. The literal answer then would be two. And it seems to me that I just rephrased my original question, in such a way as to be sure that I was getting a literal answer. Lewis may introduce a procedure of associating natural numbers with groups of persons or objects, but it is misleading to call this 'counting'.

Lewis' example of counting one road while giving directions, however, is designed to show that we *do* sometimes count by relations other than identity. I grant that we would indeed say that Jane needs to cross one road, but Lewis' interpretation of this is not the only one possible. I would prefer to say that we have counted *road segments* by identity. What matters to Jane is how many road segments she crosses, and we have told her: one.[20] Granted, the question was about roads. But I think that it is quite plausible to claim that the predicate 'road' does not always apply to 'continuant' roads – it sometimes applies to road segments. Whether a given speaker means road segments or continuant roads by 'road' depends

on his or her interests (and may sometimes be indeterminate).

I support this view with an additional example. Suppose Jane is walking to the farm. As far as we know, her path is as shown in Figure 39.2. If she asks: 'how many roads must I cross to get to the barn?', we will answer 'three'. But suppose that, unknown to us, because of their paths miles away, the 'three' roads are connected, as in Figure 39.3. In a sense, she only crosses one road (albeit three times). If we count continuant roads, we count one road that she crosses, whether we count by identity or by identity-across-Jane's-path. But I believe we gave the correct answer, when we said 'three'. We told her what she wanted to know: the number of road segments she needed to cross. If someone came to me later and asked me for directions, my short answer would still be 'three'. I might add 'actually, you cross one road three times'. This might indicate that her question was ambiguous: does she want to know the number of roads or the number of road segments? But the first answer was satisfactory, for it is likely that she is more interested in road segments.[21]

This way of understanding the case of directions is, I believe, more attractive than counting by relations other than identity. Lewis cites the roads case as a precedent for the practice of counting by relations other than identity. Since this case can be controverted, there is no precedent. Counting is by identity.

IV The Stage View and Counting

The advantage of the stage view over the worm view when it comes to counting is clear.[22] Before division, when I am alone in my room there is but one stage, and therefore one person, if persons are stages. In trying to weigh the importance of this advantage of the stage view over the worm view, it may be instructive to return to the analogy with counterpart theory. Accroding to counterpart theory, I exist only in the actual world; my otherworldly selves are distinct objects related to me merely by the counterpart relation. But this version of Lewis' modal realism is not inevitable; Lewis could have taken me to be the sum of all my counterparts, an object that spans worlds just as a space-time worm spans times. Why not take objects to be transworld sums? In part, Lewis' reason is this. Even if I don't actually divide, I might have; thus, at some worlds I have two counterparts; thus, there are two transworld persons that overlap in the actual world; thus, even though I don't actually divide, there are in the actual world two persons at the same place at the same time! The solution of counting by relations other than identity would be required in the *actual* case, as well as in the bizarre case of fission. Comparing the case of temporal fission with modal fission, Lewis writes:[23]

> We will have to say something counter-intuitive, but we get a choice of evils. We could say that there are two people;… or that there is one, and we're counting people, but we're not counting them by identity … It really isn't nice to have to say any of these things – but after all, we're talking about something that doesn't really ever happen to people except in science fiction stories and philosophy examples, so is it really so very bad that peculiar cases have to get described in peculiar ways? We get by because ordinary cases are not pathological. But modality is different: pathology is everywhere.

But I don't see why the frequency of the puzzle cases, or the question of whether they are actual, is relevant. Consider the following two claims:

(i) In fact, there is just one person (counting by identity) in the room;

(ii) If I were about to divide tomorrow, there would *now* be one person (counting by identity) in the room.

Since I am currently alone in my apartment, I find (i) compelling. But I find (ii) compelling as well; I find the possibility of two persons sharing a single body, a single mind, etc., nearly as implausible as its actuality. Granted, bizarre cases require bizarre descriptions, but not bizarre descriptions in just any respect. The stage view accounts correctly for the case's strangeness: it is a case in which a person has two futures – for every action that either Fred or Ed commits after t_4, Ted will do it. Bizarre though this is, it doesn't seem to warrant us saying that two persons are present before division.

If Lewis' method of counting by relations other than identity works, then it works no matter how frequently we must apply it – why would frequency matter? On the other hand, if it *doesn't* work for everyday cases, then I don't think it works in the rare or counterfactual cases either. So, I say, we should give a unified treatment of the two cases of overpopulation due to non-actual fission and overpopulation due to actual fission. The best thing to say, in each case, is that there is only one person. Only the stage view is consistent with this claim.

V Spatially Coincident Objects

A related virtue of the stage view is that it can be extended to handle other metaphysical problems involving two objects being at one place at a time. Suppose a certain coin is melted down on Tuesday. It seems that the coin, but not the lump of copper from which it is made, ceases to exist; but then it seems that the lump and the coin are distinct, because they differ with respect to the property *existing after Tuesday*. But how can this be? Today, the coin and the lump share spatial location, angular momentum, mass, etc.

David Wiggins would allow the coincidence because the objects are of different kinds,[24] but I think the counter intuition is strong. Surely, we don't *say* 'here are two coin-shaped objects in the same place'. This talk is clearly intended to be literal (as opposed to talk of 'the average family'), and is accompanied by robust intuitions ('shouldn't two coin-like things weigh twice as much as one?'). While not decisive, these intuitions create an at least prima facie reason to look for a theory that respects them. One might appeal to counting by relations other than identity, but I have already argued against that response. And aside from the question of the proper way to interpret counting in everyday English, surely we can count by identity 'in the philosophy room', and even in the philosophy room I don't find it plausible to count two coin-shaped objects. To me, this 'reeks of double-counting', to use a phrase of Lewis'.[25] I don't think that we should distinguish the coin from the lump today, just because 'they' will differ tomorrow. The more plausible view is that of temporary identity – the coin and the lump are identical today, although they won't be tomorrow. But of course I don't reject Leibniz's Law. I account for the truth of:

(2)   The lump of copper is such that it will
        exist after Tuesday; and

(3)   The coin is not such that it will exist after
        Tuesday,

while denying that this implies that the coin and
the lump of copper have different properties, by
making a natural adjustment to the stage view. On
the resulting version of the stage view, the expression
'will exist after Tuesday' is ambiguous, so there is no
one property that (2) predicates of the lump of
copper, but (3) withholds from the coin.

The ambiguity involves I-relations. An I-relation
specifies what sort of 'continuity' a thing must
exhibit over time in order to continue to exist.
Memory theorists like Lewis say the I-relation for
persons is one of psychological continuity. Things
are different for non-sentient things like coins.
When a coin gets melted, a certain kind of continuity is destroyed, for the item has not retained a
coin-like shape. Let us say that the *coin I-relation*
does not hold between the coin and the lump that
is present afterwards. But there is another kind of
continuity that is not destroyed when the coin is
melted: the copper atoms present after the process
are the same as those that were present before.
We can speak of the *lump-of-matter I-relation*,
which does hold between the coin and the lump
afterwards.[26]

The ambiguity in tensed expressions I invoke is
ambiguity about which I-relation is involved. In
complete sentences uttered in context, the ambiguity is typically resolved. (2) is true because it
means:

(2*)   The lump of copper is lump I-related to
        something that exists after Tuesday;

whereas (3) means:

(3*)   The coin is not coin I-related to any-
        thing that exists after Tuesday.

Clearly, the property attributed to the lump by
(2*) is different from that withheld from the coin
by (3*). The use of the lump I-relation in
interpreting (2) is triggered by the term 'lump of
copper', as was the use of the coin I-relation in
(3) by the presence of the word 'coin'. All this is

consistent with the coin and the lump being one
and the same thing. Here I have again exploited
the analogy between the stage view and counterpart theory. Just as I can account for temporary
identity using multiple unity relations, Lewis has
accounted for contingent identity in a parallel
way using multiple counterpart relations.[27]

In certain contexts the ambiguity in temporal
constructions may be inadequately resolved.
Uttered out of the blue, a query 'how long has *that*
existed?', even accompanied by a gesture towards
the coin, may have no determinate answer. But
this is to be expected, given that we are admitting
that both (2) and (3) are true. Moreover, this consequence is not particular to the stage view – a
worm theorist who accepts overlapping worms
will admit the same indeterminacy, but locate it
in the referential indeterminacy of the demonstrative 'that', rather than in the tense operator as
I do. As Quine has pointed out, a term whose
reference is spatially fixed at some time may still
be indeterminate, because it may be unclear what
the temporal extent of the referent is.[28] Likewise
for a three-dimensionalist like Wiggins who
accepts distinct but coincident objects.

On the stage view, then, people, statues, coins,
quarks, etc. never coincide. I do grant the existence of aggregates of stages, and such aggregates
do sometimes coincide; but I deny that these
aggregates are people, statues, coins, quarks, etc.
Moreover, I deny that these objects are (typically)
in the range of our quantifiers.[29] Thus, the stage
theorist can deny that any of the material objects
over which we typically quantify ever coincide.
Neither three-dimensionalists nor worm theorists can match the stage view's resources here.
(2) and (3) seem to commit us to the view that
'the coin' does not denote the same thing as 'the
lump of copper'. As I have argued, a stage theorist
can avoid this consequence by appeal to ambiguity in temporal constructions, but no such
manoeuvre seems available to worm theorists or
three-dimensionalists. So to avoid being committed to spatial coincidence, a three-dimensionalist
or worm theorist would have to reject either
(2) or (3). (3) seems the likely candidate here: the
claim would be that the coin does not go out of
existence upon melting; it merely ceases to be
coin-like. I find this approach implausible. We
surely think of artifacts like coins, statues, tables
and chairs as being destroyed in certain cases,

rather than conceiving of these as being merely cases of radical alteration. Moreover, this approach requires a distinguished 'stopping place'. Here I have a thing which is currently a coin; what is the permanent 'kind' of the object? Is the object a coin? A lump of copper? There are other possibilities; we might take it to be a *chunk of quarks*, for consider separating the copper atoms into their constituent particles; to disallow coincidence between a lump of copper and a chunk of quarks we might say that the former persists through this procedure, while ceasing to be lump-of-copper-like. To avoid arbitrariness the final extreme looks most plausible, but it requires us to deny so many of our everyday intuitions about when objects are destroyed that the stage view looks preferable.

Another way to reject (2) or (3) would be to deny the existence of one of the involved entities. By denying the existence of lumps of matter, for example, one could reject (2). A more radical but probably more theoretically satisfying approach would be to follow Peter van Inwagen in rejecting the existence of both lumps of matter and coins, and composite material objects generally! (van Inwagen makes an exception for living things.[30]) The latter view would eliminate the need to find a principled reason why coins are countenanced, for example, but not lumps of matter. I find both of these suggestions implausible, and I suspect many others would as well; I would rather accept the stage view than deny the existence of either lumps of matter or coins. (I argue elsewhere that there are other reasons to reject van Inwagen's radical view.[31])

The importance of employing multiple unity relations extends beyond cases of temporary identity between artifacts and the quantities of matter that constitute them. First, we can use multiple unity relations to answer an objection to the stage view. I claim that I am identical to an *instantaneous* stage, and also that I will exist for more than an instant – how can I have it both ways? The answer is that when I say that a stage is instantaneous and so will not exist tomorrow, I am denying that it is *stage* I-related to any stage in the future. The stage I-relation is that of identity – since stages do not persist through time, their I-relation never relates stages at different times (nor, of course, distinct stages at a given time). But I am (and so my current stage, with which I am identical, is) *person*

I-related to stages tomorrow; this is what I assert when I say that I will exist tomorrow.

Secondly, multiple unity relations can help with other puzzles of spatial coincidence that have been discussed in the literature. Consider, for example, Peter Geach's paradox of Tibbles, a cat, and Tib, a certain large proper part of Tibbles which consists of all of Tibbles except for the tail.[32] If Tibbles loses her tail at some time, t, it seems that both Tibbles and Tib survive: Tibbles, because a cat can survive the loss of a tail, and Tib, because all that has happened to it is that a certain external object (the tail) has become detached from it. After t, Tibbles and Tib share spatial location. But it seems that they're not identical – after all, Tib, but not Tibbles, seems to have the property *being a proper part of a cat before t*. If we accept the stage view we can identify Tibbles and Tib, using multiple unity relations to explain away their apparently differing temporal properties.

Finally, I'd like very briefly to mention some other puzzle cases that are handled nicely by the stage view: cases of degrees of personal identity and of a person gradually turning into another (Lewis), and cases of vague identity sentences where the terms involved have no 'spatial vagueness' (Robert Stalnaker).[33] In each case, for worm theorists and three-dimensionalists alike there is pressure to admit coincident entities in order to avoid contradicting formal properties of the identity relation in the first place, or admitting 'genuine vagueness-in-the-world' in the second. But a stage theorist can avoid these pitfalls more adroitly, by appealing to unity relations that come in degrees in the first case, and, in the second case, by locating the vagueness in which of various unity relations are used in the interpretation of temporal constructions.

The examples I have discussed in this section provide, I think, the strongest support for the stage view. Though the contrary view has perhaps become familiar to metaphysicians, there really is a strong pre-theoretical motivation to reject spatial coincidence between distinct material objects. Moreover, unlike the case of fission, the cases of the present section are neither bizarre nor counterfactual, and so provide a response to a possible objection to my presentation through to section IV: that the motivation for the stage view is merely from a bizarre, counterfactual case.[34] (Though, as

I said above, I think we have strong intuitions even about the bizarre case of fission.)

VI   Objections to the Stage View

My argument for the stage view has been that it solves puzzles better than either three-dimensionalism on the worm view. It remains to show that the stage view has no outweighing defects. The first objection I want to consider involves the fact that certain identity statements that we might have thought were true turn out on the stage view to be false. When I look back on my childhood, and say 'I am that irritating young boy', the stage view pronounces my utterance false. I accept this consequence. Assuming the account of temporal predication I sketched in section II, the stage view does allow me to say truly, that 'I *was* that irritating young boy"; why can't we accept that the former is false when we know that we can say the latter? It seems to me that the latter is what we mean, anyway. A related objection is that on the stage view, nothing persists through time. If by 'Ted persists through time' we mean 'Ted exists at more than one time', then the stage view does indeed have this consequence. But in another sense of 'persists through time', the stage view does not rule out persistence through time, for in virtue of its account of temporal predication, the stage view allows that I both exist now and *previously* existed in the past. Given that the stage view allows the latter kind of persistence, I think that the denial of the former sort is no great cost.

Next I would like to consider in more detail the objection I addressed in section II: the analogue of Kripke's Humphrey objection to counterpart theory. This objection, which we might call the semantic objection, has been given by John Perry against the stage view:[35]

> ... [on the stage view] the little boy stealing apples is *strictly speaking* not identical with the general before me ... [The stage view] denies what is clearly true: that when I say of someone that he will do such and such, I mean that he will do it. The events in my future are events that will happen to me, and not merely events that will happen to someone else of the same name.

I believe that it is the semantic objection that is the source of the common attitude of metaphysicians that the stage view is obviously false. But, on its face, it seems to be a mistake. Perry says that the stage view denies that when I say 'You will do it', I mean that you will do it. But as I argued above (following the lead of Lewis in the modal case), the stage view is perfectly consistent with stages having temporal properties; it is just that these properties are analyzed in terms of the I-relation and other stages.

Perry and I both agree that the events in my future will happen to me, that I was once a child, and that (hopefully) I will be an old man one day; what Perry must be finding objectionable is the stage view's analysis of these facts. I can think of two kinds of worry one might have about the analysis. While I don't think either constitutes a knockdown argument, I grant that each is a legitimate cause for concern. To those with these concerns, I acknowledge that the stage view has costs, but claim that they are outweighed by its benefits. The first concern is this: the fact that I was once a child and will one day be an old man is, according to the stage view, really a fact about two different objects, a stage that is a child and a stage that is an old man. Notice that this feature is not unique to the stage view: the worm theorist also analyzes change as difference between temporal stages. This makes it clear that the concern here is simply the familiar objection that the four-dimensionalist conception of change is not genuine change at all.[36] Only if three-dimensionalism is true can we avoid the need to analyze change in terms of stages, by invoking a single 'wholly present' changing thing. I think that there are independent reasons to prefer four-dimensionalism to three-dimensionalism (see my [29]). And even those who remain unconvinced by direct arguments for four-dimensionalism should weigh their certainty that change cannot be analyzed in terms of stages against the other attractive consequences of the stage view.

The second concern is simply that the stage view's analysis of temporal properties is flat-out implausible: the property *being I-related to some stage in the past that is F* is just not the same property as the property *previously being F*. The conception of persistence over time that the stage view can offer, the objection runs, is simply not common sense persistence at all. But I just don't agree. All that can be counted part of common sense is that objects typically have temporal properties (like *existing ten minutes ago)*, and the stage view is consistent with this part of common sense. Further claims about the analysis of such properties are theoretical, not part of common sense, and so a theory that looks best from the perspective of a global cost-benefit analysis is free to employ a non-standard analysis of temporal predication.[37] I do not say that intuitions about theoretical analyses carry no weight at all, only that they are negotiable. Indeed, I partially based my rejection of Lewis' account of counting on such intuitions. I grant that my analysis of tensed predication is unexpected, to say the least; my claim is that this is not a decisive consideration.

A final objection is difficult to answer. If we take the 'timeless perspective' and ask how many people there ever will be, or how many people have been (say) sitting in my office during the last hour, the stage view seems not to have an easy answer.[38] Persons on this view are identified with stages and there are infinitely many stages between any two times, assuming that time is continuous and that there is a stage for each moment of time.

In response I propose a partial retreat. The stage view should be restricted to the claim that *typical* references to persons are to person stages. But, in certain circumstances, such as when we take the timeless perspective, reference is to worms rather than stages.[39] When discussing the cases of counting roads above, I suggested that we sometimes use 'road' to refer to extended roads and sometimes to road segments, depending on our interests. In typical cases of discussing persons, our interests are in stages, for example when I ask how many coin-shaped things are in my pocket, whether identity is what matters, etc. But in extreme cases, such as that of timeless counting, these interests shift.

This admission might be thought to undermine my arguments for the stage view.[40] Those arguments depended on the claim that the ordinary material objects over which we quantify never coincide, but now I admit that in some contexts we quantify over space-time worms, which do sometimes coincide. However, I don't need the premise that there is *no* sense in which material objects coincide; it is enough that there is some legitimate sense in which, e.g., the coin is numerically identical to the lump of copper, for I can claim that our anti-coincidence intuitions are based on this sense. Indeed, in making claims about coincidence in section V, I intended to use terms like 'coin', 'lump of copper', etc., in the ordinary sense, in which they apply to stages rather than worms.

Trouble for this response comes from mixed sentences such as:

(M)   There is some set, S, such that S has finitely many members, S contains every coin or lump of copper that ever exists, and no two members of S ever exist at the same place at the same time,

since on neither sense of 'coin' and 'lump of copper' is sentence (M) true. The best a stage theorist can do here is to claim that intuition is well enough served by pointing out that each of the following sentences has a reading on which it is true:

(Ml)   There is some set, S, such that S has finitely many members and S contains every coin or lump of copper that ever exists;

(M2)   No two coins or lumps of copper ever exist at the same place at the same time.

The 'special exception' to the main claim of the stage view that I have granted in this section admittedly detracts from the stage view's appeal, but not fatally so. On balance, I believe the case for the stage view remains strong. In the next section I attempt to fill out the stage view by discussing certain semantic issues that confront a stage theorist.

VII   Amplifications

A good place to start is the stage theorist's treatment of proper names. In a formal development of the stage view, with each (disambiguated) name we would associate a certain property of person stages. The referent of that name, relative to any time (in any possible world) would be the one and only stage that has the property.[41] This

but, because this stage shares the I-relation with other stages, practically speaking, we name all stages property may be thought of as being something like an individual concept. Given a name, such as 'Ted', I'll speak of stages with the associated individual concept as being 'Ted-stages'. It must be emphasized that talk of these individual concepts doesn't require a descriptivist view of reference. A stage theorist can, if she wishes, adopt a theory of reference in harmony with the picture Kripke sketches in *Naming and Necessity*.[42] A name is introduced by an initial baptism, where it is affixed to some stage. At least in normal cases where there is no fission or the like, that baptism completely determines what the referent of the name will be at any later time: it will refer to the stage existing at that later time (if there is one) that bears the I-relation to the originally baptized stage. Likewise for stages at other possible worlds: whether or not they have one of these individual concepts is determined by factors that the user of a given name need not know about. I myself would prefer to say that at another world the referent of a name is determined in some way by the holding of a counterpart relation between actual stages to which the name refers and other-worldly stages, but this view is not inevitable for a stage theorist. At any rate, the point is that a stage theorist can agree that a user of a name need not have in her possession descriptive information that uniquely identifies its referent; she need only be at the end of an appropriate causal chain extending back to an initial baptism. Thus, there is no assumption that these individual concepts are 'qualitative' or 'purely descriptive'.

The meaning of an n-place predicate should be taken to be an n-place relation over stages, rather than over worms. It should not be assumed, however, that these relations are temporally local or intrinsic to stages. Critics of temporal parts have often expressed skepticism about the possibility of reducing predicates like 'believes' to temporally local features of stages, but these doubts do not apply here since I am not proposing any such reduction. If I have a relational property, such as the property *being surrounded,* this is so in virtue of my relations to other things, but I myself have the property just the same, for I am the one that is surrounded. Analogously, a stage can have the property of *believing that snow is white* even if its having this property depends on properties of other stages (to which it is I-related). It is quite consistent with the stage view that it would be

impossible for a momentary stage that existed in isolation from all other stages to have any beliefs.[43]

Let us now consider the analysis of various types of sentence. The simplest case is a present tense assertion about a presently existing object, for example, 'Clinton is president'. One could take this sentence to express a so-called 'singular proposition' about Clinton's present stage. Likewise for what I will call '*de re* temporal predications', which occur when we single out a presently existing stage and assert something about what *will* happen, or what *has* happened, to it. If I say 'Clinton was once governor of Arkansas', we may take this as having subject-predicate form (the predicate is complex and involves a temporal operator); it expresses a singular proposition about Clinton, to the effect that he has the temporal property *previously being governor of Arkansas.* Ignoring the further complication that 'Arkansas' might be taken to denote a stage, this property is that had by a stage, x, iff x is I-related to some stage that (i) exists before x in time, and (ii) is governor of Arkansas.

Things are different with other temporal predications.[44] The sentence 'Socrates was wise' cannot be a *de re* temporal claim about the present Socrates-stage since there is no such present stage Nor can we take it as being about one of Socrates' past stages, for lack of a distinguished stage that the sentence concerns. What we must do is interpret the sentence as a *de dicto* temporal claim. Syntactically, the sentence should be taken as the result of applying a sentential operator 'WAS' to the sentence 'Socrates is wise'; the resulting sentence means that at some point in the past, there is a Socrates-stage that is wise. This is somewhat like, and somewhat unlike, the claim that 'once there were dinosaurs that roamed the earth'. The latter is not about any particular dinosaurs, but is rather about the past generally. The former is like this in not being about any particular Socrates-stage, but unlike it in not being a purely 'qualitative' claim about the past, since the notion of a Socrates-stage may not be qualitative or descriptive. Various modal and counterfactual claims will also require *de dicto* readings. The sentence 'If Socrates hadn't existed, then Plato wouldn't have been a good philosopher' cant be *de re* with respect to 'Socrates' (or 'Plato') for lack of present stages or distinguished past stages. Thus, assuming the Stalnaker-Lewis semantics for counterfactuals, it must be a *de dicto* claim to the effect that in the nearest world containing no Socrates-stages, the Plato-stages aren't good philosophers.[45]

The distinction I am appealing to here is a bit like one required by a 'presentist' such as A.N. Prior. Prior rejects past objects and so can't interpret 'Socrates is wise' as being about Socrates, but rather must interpret it as being about the past generally. (This is in contrast to temporal predications of current objects, which the presentist can take as being *de re*.[46]) Notice, however, the differences between the presentist and the stage theorist. For one thing, the stage theorist requires *de dicto* temporal claims not because of a lack of past objects, but because of a lack of a *distinguished* past object. Also, there is some pressure for a presentist to interpret *de dicto* claims about the past in purely descriptive terms, on the grounds that if past objects don't exist at all, then neither will their non-qualitative identity properties.[47] The stage theorist (one who isn't a presentist, at any rate) need have no such qualms about admitting non-qualitative individual concepts of merely past entities.

It is important that the stage view has the means to express both *de re* and *de dicto* temporal claims. We clearly need the *de dicto* analysis for sentences concerning past individuals. The *de re* reading seems required for, e.g., the case where I look you in the eye, grab your shoulder, and say that *you* will be famous in the year 2000. Another reason we need the means to express *de re* temporal claims comes from the fission case. I want to say, before fission, that Ted will exist at t_4. But the *de dicto* claim 'It will be true at t_4 that: Ted exists' will be false, since it is plausible to say that 'Ted' lacks denotation at t_4. What is true is that at times before division, Ted has the temporal property *futurely existing at t_4*.[48]

VIII   Conclusion

Despite its shock value and a bit of unsteadiness in connection with timeless counting, the stage view on balance seems to stand up well to scrutiny. I submit that it gives a more satisfying resolution of the various puzzle cases of identity over time than its competitors, the worm theory and three-dimensionalism. Stage theorists can accept that:

Both identity and psychological continuity matter in survival;
There is only one person in the room before I divide;
The lump of copper is identical to the coin, Tibbles is identical to Tib, etc.

I think the benefits outweigh the costs. These are, as promised, my reasons as a philosopher for accepting the stage view.

Notes

I would like to thank David Braun, Phillip Bricker, Earl Conee, David Cowles, Fergus Duniho, Fred Feldman, Rich Feldman, Ed Gettier, David Lewis, Ned Markosian, Cranston Paull, Sydney Shoemaker, and anonymous referees for helpful comments and criticism.

1   By the 'worm view', I primarily have in mind Lewis' version of this view (see Lewis [14, pp. 58–60]), as opposed to the view defended in Perry [22]; see further n. 22 below. See also Heller [7, 8 and 9], Lewis [13, pp. 202–4, and 14, postscript B, pp. 76–7], and Quine [24, pp. 859–60] on four-dimensionalism.

2   Elsewhere [29], I argue against three-dimensionalism and take up the important task of precisely stating three and four-dimensionalism. For criticisms of four-dimensional, and defences and/or assertions of three-dimensionalism, see Mellor [17, p. 104], Simons [30, p. 175 ff.], Thomson [33], and van Inwagen [36].

3   Contemporary philosophers seem to dismiss the stage view as obviously false, almost as if it were being used as an example of a bad theory. See Peter van Inwagen's discussion of 'Theory 1' in [36, p. 248]; John Perry [22, pp. 479–80]; David Kaplan [10, pp. 503–4]; and Nathan Salmon [27, pp. 97–9]. An exception seem to be Forbes [4, p. 252, 258 n. 27], although his remarks are terse. Some philosophers in the middle part of this century may have accepted something like the stage view. J. J. C. Smart, for example, says

> When … I say that the successful general is the same person as the small boy who stole the apples I meant only that the successful general I see before me is a time slice of the same four-dimensional object of which the small boy stealing apples is an earlier time slice. [31, p. 143].

One also sometimes heard the assertion that 'identity over time is not true identity, but rather genidentity'. To my knowledge, these early stage theorists did not hold the account of temporal predication I defend below, nor do they defend the stage view by appealing to its ability to solve the puzzles of identity over time that I discuss.

4 I say 'typically' because of a problem of timeless counting that I consider in section VI.

5 I follow Lewis [14] in exposition. The gloss of mattering as 'self-interested concern' is misleading, for it is crucial that we not rule out Parfit's view of the matter by definition. The idea is that we have a general notion of concern, which in *normal* cases is only for what happens to oneself.

6 Actually, a case can be made (see Feldman [3, ch. 6] that people typically continue to exist after death: as dead people (corpses). If this view is correct, then the idea that identity is what matters should be taken to be the idea that continued existence is a necessary condition for the preservation of what matter. (The sufficiency claim would be false, since existence as a corpse presumably does not preserve what matters.)

7 This relation of psychological continuity is the relation claimed to be the unity relation for persons by those who hold descendants of Locke's memory identity. There are various versions of this theory, between which I will not distinguish in this paper. (For example, some include a causal component to the psychological theory.) See Perry [21] for excerpts from Locke, his contemporary defenders, and their critics. See Lewis [14, p. 58] and Parfit [18, section 78] for discussions of psychological continuity.

8 See Parfit [20, p. 200 ff] for a representative example of the division case.

9 See Parfit [18, pp. 254–66], and Parfit [20, p. 200 ff]. I have simplified Parfit's views slightly. He claims that the question of whether or not I survive division is an empty question. But, he says, some empty questions should be given an answer by us. The case of fission is such a case, and there is a best answer: I do not survive fission at all.

10 See Lewis [14, pp. 59–60], and Perry's introduction to [21, esp. pp. 7–12].

11 Parfit [19, pp. 92–5].

12 Denis Robinson [26] takes such a line in the case of the division of an amoeba.

13 See Lewis [16].

14 Kripke [11, p. 45].

15 See Lewis [13, p. 196]. See also Hazen [6].

16 More care is required with this example than I take in the text, since I do not formulate the stage view with much precision before section VII. In the terminology of that section, (1b) should be understood as being *de re* with respect to 'I', but *de dicto* with respect to 'Ed' and 'Fred' – it says roughly that

I now have the property of being I-related to a stage in the future that is identical both to the referent of 'Ed' then and to the referent of 'Fred' then. But this implies that the referent of 'Fred' at t and the referent of 'Ed' at t are identical – that is, it implies the *de dicto* claim that at some time in the future, Fred will be identical to Ed. Since this is false, (1b) is false.

17 Perry [22, p. 479] makes similar remarks regarding distinguishing 'It will be not-P' from 'Not-it will be P'.

18 Perry [22, pp. 472, 480] agrees.

19 See Lewis [14, p. 64].

20 Objection: there are infinitely many segments that Jane crosses – they have varying spatial extents. For example, there is the segment that is just wide enough to encompass her footsteps, another a little bit wider, etc. How then can I say that she crosses but one segment? Clearly, however, we do say that she crosses but one segment. I take it that we have here a case of the so called 'problem of the many' (see, for example, Lewis [12] and Unger [34]); its solution is independent of the issues I discuss here.

21 Another way to think about these cases is that, in Lewis' road example, the correct answer is really 'two', and that the correct answer in my case is 'one', but when we give directions we sometimes speak falsely to avoid being misleading. I have no strong view about whether this is so; what I do claim is that if we must make our speech literally true in Lewis' road case, we should count segments by identity, not extended roads by some other relation.

22 There is a version of the worm view that may appear to avoid my counting objections: John Perry's account of persons in 'Can the Self Divide?'. In fact I think this appearance is deceiving; see Lewis [14, pp. 71–2]. Anyway, Perry's version of the worm view is of no special help in the cases of coincidence I consider in section V.

23 Lewis [13, pp. 218–19].

24 See Wiggins [38].

25 Lewis [13, p. 252]. In this passage Lewis is discussing actual overpopulation due to possible fission, but I think the 'double-counting' intuition is equally strong in the case of the lump and the coin.

26 I ignore the complicating fact that the lump I-relation is surely vague (as probably are most I-relations).

27 See Lewis [15].

28 See Quine [25, pp. 67–8].

29 Caveat: I grant at the end of section VI that in certain special contexts involving timeless counting, we quantify over worms. My claim in the text should be understood as being made in an ordinary

context where we aren't taking the timeless perspective.

30 See van Inwagen [35, esp. chs. 9 and 12].

31 See my [28].

32 Wiggins introduces the example in Wiggins [38], attributing it to Geach. For other discussions of this puzzle, see van Inwagen [37] and Cartwright [2, pp. 164–6].

33 See Lewis [14] and Stalnaker [32].

34 Lewis made this objection in a helpful conversation about an earlier draft of this paper.

35 Perry [22, pp. 479, 480]. Nathan Salmon also appears to be giving an objection of this sort to a theory like the stage view in Salmon [27, pp. 97–9].

36 See Heller [7] for a discussion of this issue.

37 Allen Hazen makes similar points in the case of the Kripke objection to counterpart theory in Hazen [6, pp.320–4].

38 Compare Lewis [14, p. 72].

39 Or perhaps, in certain cases, to proper segments of such sums: if I ask how many persons exist during 1994, I will not want to count twice a person who will divide in 1995. I thank Fergus Duniho for this point.

40 Here I thank an anonymous referee for helpful comments.

41 Compare Perry [22, p. 477].

42 See Kripke [11, pp. 91–7].

43 I thank David Braun and Sydney Shoemaker for bringing this matter to my attention. Compare John Perry's distinction between basic and non-basic properties in [22, pp. 470–1].

44 I thank Sydney Shoemaker for raising a helpful objection here.

45 I thank an anonymous referee for drawing my attention to this example. I gloss over the question of whether at the world in question, it must be that all, or some, or most, etc. Plato-stages aren't good philosophers; as I see it, the original sentence is ambiguous.

46 See Prior [23].

47 See Adams [1].

48 Compare Perry's distinction between primary and secondary referents in his [22, pp. 482–3].

References

[1] Adams, Robert M., 'Time and Thisness' in P. French, T. Uehling and H. Wettstein (eds.), *Midwest Studies is Philosophy* XI (Minneapolis: University of Minnesota Press, 1986) pp. 315–29.

[2] Cartwright, Richard, 'Scattered Objects' in Keith Lehrer (ed.), *Analysis and Metaphysics* (Dordrecht: Reidel, 1975).

[3] Feldman, Fred, *Confrontations with the Reaper* (New York Oxford University Press, 1992).

[4] Forbes, Graham, 'Thisness and Vagueness', *Synthese* 19 (1983) pp. 235–59.

[5] Gibbard, Allan, 'Contingent Identity', *Journal of Philosophical Logic* 4 (1975) pp. 187–221 [ch. 11 in this volume].

[6] Hazen, Allen, 'Counterpart-Theoretic Semantics for Modal Logic', *The Journal of Philosophy* 76 (1979) pp. 319–38.

[7] Heller, Mark, 'Things Change', *Philosophy and Phenomenological Research* 52 (1992) pp. 695–704.

[8] Heller, Mark, *The Ontology of Physical Objects: Four Dimensional Hunks of Matter* (Cambridge: Cambridge University Press, 1990) [partly reproduced in ch. 36 of this volume].

[9] Heller, Mark, 'Temporal Parts of Four Dimensional Objects', *Philosophical Studies* 46 (1984) pp. 323–34.

[10] Kaplan, David, 'Bob and Carol and Ted and Alice' in J. Hintikka et al. (eds.), *Approaches to Natural Language* (Dordrecht: Reidel, 1973) pp. 490–518.

[11] Kripke, Saul, *Naming and Necessity* (Cambridge, MA: Harvard University Press, 1972).

[12] Lewis, David, 'Many, but Almost One' in Keith Campbell, John Bacon, and Lloyd Reinhardt (eds.), *Ontology, Causality and Mind: Essays on the Philosophy of D. M. Armstrong* (Cambridge: Cambridge University Press, 1993) pp. 23–38 [ch. 48 in this volume].

[13] Lewis, David, *On the Plurality of Worlds* (Oxford: Blackwell, 1986) [partly reproduced in chs 16 and 37 of this volume].

[14] Lewis, David, 'Survival and Identity' in his *Philosophical Papers, Vol. I* (New York: Oxford University Press, 1983) pp. 55–77 [reproduced without postscript in ch. 43 of this volume].

[15] Lewis, David, 'Counterparts of Persons and Their Bodies', *The Journal of Philosophy* 68 (1971) pp. 203–11.

[16] Lewis, David, 'Counterpart Theory and Quantified Modal Logic' *The Journal of Philosophy* 65 (1968) pp. 113–26.

[17] Mellor, D. H., *Real Time* (Cambridge: Cambridge University Press, 1981).

[18] Parfit, Derek, *Reasons and Persons* (Oxford: Clarendon Press, 1984).

[19] Parfit, Derek, 'Lewis, Perry, and What Matters' in Amelie O. Rorty (ed.), *The Identities of Persons* (Berkeley: University of California Press, 1976) pp. 91–107.

[20] Parfit, Derek, 'Personal Identity' in [21] [ch. 42 in this volume].

[21] Perry, John (ed.), *Personal Identity* (Berkeley: University of California Press, 1975).

[22] Perry, John, 'Can the Self Divide?', *The Journal of Philosophy* 69 (1972) pp. 463–88.

[23] Prior, A.N., 'Changes in Events and Changes in Things' in his *Papers on Time and Tense* (Oxford: Clarendon Press, 1968) chapter 1.

[24] Quine, W. V. O., 'Worlds Away', *The Journal of Philosophy* 73 (1976) pp. 859–63.

[25] Quine, W. V. O., 'Identity, Ostension, and Hypostasis' in his *From a Logical Point of View* (New York: Harper and Row, 1963) pp. 65–79 [ch. 34 in this volume].

[26] Robinson, Denis, 'Can Amoebae Divide Without Multiplying?', *Australasian Journal of Philosophy* 63 (1985) pp. 299–319.

[27] Salmon, Nathan, 'Modal Paradox: Parts and Counterparts, Points and Counterpoints' in P. French, T. Uehling and H. Wettstein (eds.), *Midwest Studies in Philosophy, XI* (Minneapolis: University of Minnesota Press, 1986) pp. 75–120.

[28] Sider, Theodore, 'van Inwagen and the Possibility of Gunk', *Analysis* 53 (1993) pp. 285–9.

[29] Sider, Theodore, 'Four Dimensionalism' *Philosophical Review* 106 (1997) pp. 197–231.

[30] Simons, Peter, *Parts: A Study in Ontology* (Oxford: Oxford University Press, 1987).

[31] Smart, J. J. C., 'Sensations and Brain Processes'. *The Philosophical Review* 68 (1959) pp. 141–56.

[32] Stalnaker, Robert, 'Vague Identity' in D. F. Austin (ed.), *Philosophical Analysis* (Dordrecht: Kluwer, 1938) pp. 349–60 [ch. 13 in this volume].

[33] Thomson, Judith Jarvis, 'Parthood and Identity Across Time', *The Journal of Philosophy* 80 (1983) pp. 201–20 [ch. 35 in this volume].

[34] Unger, Peter, 'The Problem of the Many' in P. French, T. Uehling, and H. Wettstein (eds.), *Midwest Studies in Philosophy,* V (Minneapolis: University of Minnesota Press, 1980) pp. 411–67.

[35] van Inwagen, Peter, (1990a) *Material Beings* (Ithaca, NY: Cornell University Press).

[36] van Inwagen, Peter, (1990b) 'Four-Dimensional Objects', *Noûs* 24 pp. 245–55.

[37] van Inwagen, Peter, 'The Doctrine of Arbitrary Undetached Parts', *Pacific Philosophical Quarterly* 62 (1981) pp. 123–37.

[38] Wiggins, David, 'On Being in the Same Place at the Same Time', *The Philosophical Review* 77 (1968) pp. 90–5.

PART VII
Persons

Introduction

You currently occupy a certain region of space. Exactly located in that region of space – right where you are – is a person, an organism, a human animal, and your body. Perhaps this description makes that region sound more crowded than it in fact is. Plausibly, there is just one thing occupying that region (you!), and 'person', 'organism', 'human animal', and 'body' are just different ways of describing that one thing.

Or perhaps not. Suppose that your brain is taken from your body and is successfully transplanted into a new body, at which point the original body is destroyed. Not surprisingly, the resultant person knows all sorts of things about your past and insists that it is you. And plausibly it *is* you. Although this is only an imaginary scenario, it nevertheless stands to tell us quite a bit about personal identity. You can survive such a procedure; but the animal, organism, and body that are located where you are cannot. So, you cannot be identical to any of those things (see the discussion of the Indiscernibility of Identicals in the Introduction to Part II). The scenario also seems to show that the persistence of your body (or the human animal) is not necessary for your persistence. Our intuitions about this scenario suggest that it is psychological continuity, rather than bodily continuity, that accounts for personal identity.

For these sorts of reasons, a great many metaphysicians endorse a psychological criterion of personal identity. There is a tradition, going back at least as far as John Locke, of giving pride of place to memory. On one (rather flat-footed) way of developing the memory criterion, one might suggest that a person at one time is identical to a person at a later time just in case the latter can remember some experience that the former had. But there are numerous problems for this version of the memory criterion. First, you probably cannot now remember any of the experiences you were having on this date exactly fifteen years ago. So, this criterion would seem to entail that you did not exist exactly fifteen years ago. Second, saying that one person remembers an experience that an earlier person was having already seems to *presuppose* that it is the same person, in which case this cannot be an informative criterion of personal identity. Third, one can conceive of cases in which a person "divides in two," so to speak, resulting in two separate people who remember your experiences. In these cases, the simple-minded memory criterion articulated above would imply that they are both identical to the original person, which is impossible. In "Persons and their Pasts" (chapter 40), Sydney Shoemaker supplies a more sophisticated version of the memory criterion which is designed to avoid these problems (see, especially, sections 4–7).

In "The Self and the Future" (chapter 41), Bernard Williams defends a bodily criterion of identity, on which a person at one time is the same person as a person at a later time just in case they have the same body. He does so by casting doubt upon the sorts of body-switching cases that are meant to motivate psychological accounts of personal identity. For instance, imagine a case in which your personality and memories are somehow transferred to another brain, and someone else's personality and memories are transferred into your brain. Many feel a strong temptation to say that you thereby get a new body (not that you get a new personality and new memories), which suggests that it is mental continuity that accounts for the persistence of persons, not bodily continuity. Williams shows that, by simply redescribing the case, he can elicit exactly the opposite intuition: that this is a case in which you retain the same body and (in more than one sense) lose your mind. It hardly matters to your own survival and well-being whether someone else loses her mind as well and starts thinking that she is you. Williams addresses various responses to his treatment of the case, including the objection that which of the resultant people is you is determined by our conventions.

In "Personal Identity" (chapter 42), Derek Parfit examines a number of puzzle cases which put a tremendous strain on our concept of personal identity, for instance, cases of fission in which the left and right hemispheres of a person's brain are successfully transplanted into two separate bodies. Which of the two resultant people is identical to the original person? No answer seems acceptable. We cannot say that she is both of them since the resultant people are distinct (and identity is transitive). We cannot say that she is neither of them since (as Parfit says) this is a "double success," not a failure. And it would simply be arbitrary to identify her with one rather than the other. Parfit maintains that, in such cases, there simply is no fact of the matter whether either of the resultant people is the original person. This may seem deeply unsatisfying: whether any later person is *you* matters too much for there not to be a fact of the matter. Parfit addresses this objection by maintaining that it is not identity, but rather the psychological connectedness of earlier and later selves, that truly matters to us.

In "Survival and Identity" (chapter 43), David Lewis attempts to resist Parfit's conclusion by supplying an account of persons and personal identity on which identity and psychological continuity are not in competition. Lewis maintains that, in cases of fission, the two people who exist post-fission both existed, and were entirely colocated, prior to the fission. He goes on to argue that, despite appearances, his account is compatible with our judgment that there was only one person pre-fission, not two. He also shows how his account can handle other objections that Parfit raises, having to do with individuals with extraordinarily long lives and the observation that psychological continuity can come in degrees.

These first four entries in this section are primarily concerned with the question of the *persistence* of persons. The remaining chapters concern the *ontology* of persons: what sort of thing is a person? One historically popular view is that persons are (or are partly constituted by) "souls." Your soul, on one understanding, is intimately related to, but not identical to, your body, or any other material being. In "Lonely Souls: Causality and Substance Dualism" (chapter 44), Jaegwon Kim offers a new argument, "the pairing problem," in defense of the traditional objection to the dualist view of persons, namely, that one who takes persons to be immaterial cannot account for how persons cause things to happen in a physical world. Kim argues that this leads to the problem of explaining why a given soul is paired (or united) with one particular body rather than some other body.

In "The Ontological Status of Persons" (chapter 45), Lynne Rudder Baker defends a view on which persons are not identical to their bodies but are nevertheless material beings. On her view, persons are *constituted* by their bodies. Baker begins with a general discussion of the relation of constitution in which she explains what accounts for the nonidentity of items standing in the constitution relation, and why such entities share so many of their properties if (as she thinks) they are not identical. Baker then argues that personhood has "ontological significance," which is to say that when the property of being a person comes to have new instances, new things come into existence. (By contrast, the property of being a student lacks ontological significance. When it comes to have new instances, nothing new comes into existence. Rather, something that already existed simply comes to have a new property.) Baker goes on to argue that Animalism – the thesis that persons are most fundamentally animals – is incompatible with the view that personhood is ontologically significant.

In "An Argument for Animalism" (chapter 46), Eric T. Olson defends the view that each of us is identical to a human animal. (He calls this view 'Animalism', but notice that his use of the label is slightly different from Baker's.) This should seem fairly commonsensical: there is a human animal located exactly where you are, and it is you! But, as we have seen, the view is widely rejected, as a result of reflection of the sorts of hypothetical cases that purport to show that you can exist in the absence of that particular animal and vice versa. Olson presents and defends a powerful argument for identifying persons with animals, which runs as follows: there is a human animal where you are; if so, it is thinking; yet there is only one thing thinking where you are; so you are a human animal. In order to resist this argument, it seems that one must either deny that the animal where you are thinks (despite having a fully functional brain!) or insist – quite counterintuitively – that there is more than one thing in your exact location that is thinking.

Further Reading

Chisholm, R. (1976). *Person and Object*. London, George Allen & Unwin.

Chisholm, R. (1991). "On the Simplicity of the Soul," *Philosophical Perspectives* 5: 167–81.

Hudson, H. (2001). *A Materialist Metaphysics of the Human Person*. Ithaca, NY: Cornell University Press.

Johnston, M. (1987). "Human Beings," *The Journal of Philosophy* 84: 59–83.

Martin, R., and Barresi, J. (2003). *Personal Identity*. Oxford: Blackwell.

Parfit, D. (1984). *Reasons and Persons*. Oxford: Clarendon Press.

Perry, J. (1975). *Personal Identity*. Berkeley: University of California Press.

Rorty, A. O. (1976). *Identities of Persons*. Berkeley: University of California Press.

Shoemaker, S., and Swinburne, R. (1984). *Personal Identity*. Oxford: Blackwell.

Unger, P. (1979). "I Do Not Exist," in G. F. MacDonald (ed.), *Perception and Identity*. London: Macmillan.

Van Inwagen, P., and Zimmerman, D. (2007). *Persons: Human and Divine*. Oxford: Oxford University Press.

40

Persons and their Pasts

Sydney Shoemaker

Persons have, in memory, a special access to facts about their own past histories and their own identities, a kind of access they do not have to the histories and identities of other persons and other things. John Locke thought this special access important enough to warrant a special mention in his definition of "person," viz., "a thinking, intelligent Being, that has reason and reflection, *and can consider it self as it self, the same thinking thing, in different times and places…*"[1] In this essay I shall attempt to explain the nature and status of this special access and to defend Locke's view of its conceptual importance. I shall also attempt to correct what now seem to me to be errors and oversights in my own previous writings on this topic.

I

As a first approximation, the claim that persons have in memory a special access to their own past histories can be expressed in two related claims, both of which will be considerably qualified in the course of this essay. The first is that it is a necessary condition of its being true that a person remembers a given past event that he, that same person, should have observed or experienced the event, or known of it in some other direct way, at the time of its occurrence. I shall refer to this as the "previous awareness condition" for remembering.[2]

The second claim is that an important class of first-person memory claims are in a certain respect immune to what I shall call "error through misidentification." Consider a case in which I say, on the basis of my memory of a past incident, "I shouted that Johnson should be impeached," and compare this with a case in which I say, again on the basis of my memory of a past incident, "John shouted that Johnson should be impeached." In the latter case it could turn out that I do remember someone who looked and sounded just like John shouting that Johnson should be impeached, but that the man who shouted this was nevertheless not John – it may be that I misidentified the person as John at the time I observed the incident, and that I have preserved this misidentification in memory, or it may be that I subsequently misidentified him as John on the basis of what I (correctly) remembered about him. Here my statement would be false, but its falsity would not be due to a mistake or fault of my memory; my memory could be as accurate and complete as any

Sydney Shoemaker, "Persons and their Pasts," *American Philosophical Quarterly*, 7 (1970). Reproduced by permission.

memory could be without precluding this sort of error. But this sort of misidentification is not possible in the former case. My memory report could of course be mistaken, for one can misremember such incidents, but it could not be the case that I have a full and accurate memory of the past incident but am mistaken in thinking that the person I remember shouting was myself. I shall speak of such memory judgments as being immune to error through misidentification with respect to the first-person pronouns, or other "self-referring" expressions, contained in them.[3]

I do not contend that all memory claims are immune to error through misidentification with respect to the first-person pronouns contained in them. If I say "I blushed when Jones made that remark" because I remember seeing in a mirror someone, whom I took (or now take) to be myself, blushing, it could turn out that my statement is false, not because my memory is in any way incomplete or inaccurate, but because the person I saw in the mirror was my identical twin or double.[4] In general, if at some past time I could have known of someone that he was ϕ, and could at the same time have been mistaken in taking that person to be myself, then the subsequent memory claims I make about the past occasion will be subject to error through mis-identification with respect to the first-person pronouns. But if, as is frequently the case, I could not have been mistaken in this way in the past in asserting what I then knew by saying "I am ϕ," then my subsequent memory claim "I was ϕ" will be immune to error through misidentification relative to "I"; that is, it is impossible in such cases that I should accurately remember someone being ϕ but mistakenly take that person to be myself. We might express this by saying that where the present-tense version of a judgment is immune to error through misidentification relative to the first-person pronouns contained in it, this immunity is *preserved* in memory.[5] Thus if I claim on the strength of memory that I saw John yesterday, and have a full and accurate memory of the incident, it cannot be the case that I remember someone seeing John but have misidentified that person as myself; my memory claim "I saw John" is subject to error through misidentification with respect to the term "John" (for it could have been John's twin or double that I saw), but not with respect to "I."

II

In his early paper, "Personal Identity," H. P. Grice held that the proposition "One can only remember one's own past experiences" is analytic but pointed out that this would be analytic in only a trivial way "if 'memory' were to be defined in terms of 'having knowledge of one's own past experiences.'" He says that "even if we were to define 'memory' in this sort of way, we should still be left with a question about the proposition, 'one can only have knowledge of one's own past experiences,' which seems to me a necessary proposition."[6] Now I doubt very much if Grice, or any other philosopher, would now want to hold that it is necessarily true, or that it is true at all, that one's own past experiences are the only past experiences of which one can have knowledge. But one does not have to hold this to hold, with Grice, that it is not just a trivial analytic truth that one's own experiences are the only ones that one can remember, i.e., that it is not the case that the necessity of this truth derives merely from the fact that we refuse to *call* someone's having knowledge of a past experience a case of his remembering it unless the past experience belonged to the rememberer himself.

Grice's remarks are explicitly about memory of past experiences, but they raise an important question about all sorts of "event memory." Supposing it to be a necessary truth that the previous witnessing condition must be satisfied in any genuine case of remembering, is this necessarily true because we would refuse to *count* knowing about a past event as remembering it if the previous awareness condition were not satisfied, or is it necessary for some deeper reason? I think that many philosophers would hold that if this is a necessary truth at all, it is so only in the former way, i.e., in such a way as to make its necessity trivial and uninteresting. Thus G. C. Nerlich, in a footnote to his paper "On Evidence for Identity," says that it is true only of *our* world, not of all possible worlds, that only by being identical with a witness to past events can one have the sort of knowledge of them one has in memory.[7] On this view it is logically possible that we should have knowledge of past events which we did not ourselves witness, of experiences we did not ourselves have, and of actions we did not ourselves perform, that is in all important respects like the knowledge we have of past events, experiences, and actions in remembering them. If one takes this view, it will seem a matter of small importance, if indeed it is true, that the having of such knowledge could not be called "remembering."

It is of course not absolutely clear just what it means to speak of knowledge as being "in all important respects like" memory knowledge, if this is not intended to imply that the knowledge *is* memory knowledge. Presumably, knowledge of past events that is "just like" memory knowledge must not be inferred from present data (diaries, photographs, rock strata, etc.) on the basis of empirical laws and generalizations. But while this is necessary, it is not sufficient. When a person remembers a past event, there is a correspondence between his present cognitive state and some past cognitive and sensory state of his that existed at the time of the remembered event and consisted in his experiencing the event or otherwise being aware of its occurrence. I shall say that remembering a past event involves there being a correspondence between the rememberer's present cognitive state and a past cognitive and sensory state that was "of" the event. In actual memory this past cognitive and sensory state is always a past state of the rememberer himself. What we need to consider is whether there could be a kind of knowledge of past events such that someone's having this sort of knowledge of an event does involve there being a correspondence between his present cognitive state and a past cognitive and sensory state that was of the event, but such that this correspondence, although otherwise just like that which exists in memory, does not necessarily involve that past state's having been a state of the very same person who subsequently has the knowledge. Let us speak of such knowledge, supposing for the moment that it is possible, as "quasi-memory knowledge," and let us say that a person who has this sort of knowledge of a past event "quasi-remembers" that past event. Quasi-remembering, as I shall use the term, includes remembering as a special case. One way of characterizing the difference between quasi-remembering and remembering is by saying that the former is subject to a weaker previous awareness condition than the latter. Whereas someone's claim to remember a past event implies that he himself was aware of the event at the time of its occurrence, the claim to quasi-remember a past event implies only that someone or other was

aware of it. Except when I indicate otherwise, I shall use the expression "previous awareness condition" to refer to the stronger of these conditions.

Our faculty of memory constitutes our most direct access to the past, and this means, given the previous awareness condition, that our most direct access to the past is in the first instance an access to *our own* past histories. One of the main questions I shall be considering in this essay is whether it is conceivable that our most direct access to the past should be a faculty of quasi-remembering which is not a faculty of remembering. Is it conceivable that we should have, as a matter of course, knowledge that is related to past experiences and actions other than our own in just the way in which, as things are, our memory knowledge is related to our own past experiences and actions? In our world all quasi-remembering is remembering; what we must consider is whether the world could be such that most quasi-remembering is not remembering.

Before going on to consider this question, I should mention two reasons why I think it important. The first is its obvious bearing on the question of the relationship between the concepts of memory and personal identity. If there can be quasi-remembering that is not remembering, and if remembering can be defined as quasi-remembering that is of events the quasi-rememberer was aware of at the time of their occurrence (thus making it a trivial analytic truth that one can remember an event only if one was previously aware of it), then it would seem that any attempt to define or analyze the notion of personal identity in terms of the notion of remembering will be viciously circular. I shall have more to say about this in section V. But this question also has an important bearing on the question of how a person's memory claims concerning his own past are grounded. In previous writings I have claimed, and made a great deal of the claim, that our memory knowledge of our own past histories, unlike our knowledge of the past histories of other things, is not grounded on criteria of identity.[10] Strawson makes a similar claim in *The Bounds of Sense*, saying that "When a man (a subject of experience) ascribes a current or directly remembered state of consciousness to himself, no use whatever of any criteria of personal identity is required to justify his use of the pronoun 'I' to refer to the subject of that experience." He remarks that "it is because Kant recognized this truth that his treatment of the subject is so greatly superior to Hume's."[11] Now it can easily seem that this claim follows immediately from the fact that remembering necessarily involves the satisfaction of the previous awareness condition. If one remembers a past experience, then it has to have been one's own, and from this it may seem to follow that it makes no sense to inquire concerning a remembered experience whether it was one's own and then to try to answer this question on the basis of empirical criteria of identity. But suppose that it were only a trivial analytic truth that remembering involves the satisfaction of the previous awareness condition, and suppose that it were possible to quasi-remember experiences other than one's own. If this were so, one might remember a past experience but not know whether one was remembering it or only quasi-remembering it Here, it seems, it would be perfectly appropriate to employ a criterion of identity to determine whether the quasi-remembered experience was one's own, i.e., whether one remembered it as opposed to merely quasi-remembering it. Thus the question of whether the knowledge of our own identities provided us by memory is essentially non-critical turns on the question of whether it is possible to quasi-remember past actions and experiences without remembering them.

III

There is an important respect in which my characterization of quasi-remembering leaves that notion inadequately specified. Until now I have been ignoring the fact that a claim to remember a past event implies, not merely that the rememberer experienced such an event, but that his present memory is in some way *due to*, that it came about *because of*, a cognitive and sensory state the rememberer had at the time he experienced the event. I am going to assume, although this is controversial, that it is part of the previous awareness condition for memory that a veridical memory must not only correspond to, but *must also stand in* an appropriate *causal relationship* to, a past cognitive and sensory state of the rememberer.[12] It may seem that if quasi-memory is to be as much like memory as

possible, we should build a similar requirement into the previous awareness condition for quasi-memory, i.e., that we should require that a veridical quasi-memory must not only correspond to, but must also stand in an appropriate causal relationship to, a past cognitive and sensory state of someone or other. On the other hand, it is not immediately obvious that building such a requirement into the previous awareness condition for quasi-memory would not make it equivalent to the previous awareness condition for memory, and thus destroy the intended difference between memory and quasi-memory. But there is no need for us to choose between a previous awareness condition that includes the causal requirement and one that does not, for it is possible and useful to consider both. In the present section I shall assume that the previous awareness condition for quasi-memory does not include the causal requirement, and that it includes nothing more than the requirement that a quasi-memory must, to be a veridical quasi-memory of a given event, correspond in content to a past cognitive and sensory state that was of that event. In the sections that follow I shall consider the consequences of strengthening this condition to include the causal requirement.

The first thing we must consider is what becomes of the immunity of first-person memory claims to error through misidentification if we imagine the faculty of memory replaced by a faculty of quasi-memory. As things are now, there is a difference between, on the one hand, remembering an action of someone else's – this might consist, for example, in having a memory of seeing someone do the action – and, on the other hand, remembering *doing* an action, which can be equated with remembering *oneself* doing the action. In the case of quasi-remembering, the distinction corresponding to this is that between, on the one hand, the sort of quasi-memory of a past action whose corresponding past cognitive and sensory state belonged to someone who was watching someone else do the action and, on the other hand, the sort of quasi-memory of a past action whose corresponding past cognitive and sensory state belonged to the very person who did the action. Let us call these, respectively, quasi-memories of an action "from the outside" and quasi-memories of an action "from the inside." Now whereas I can remember an action from the inside only if it was my action, a world in which there is quasi-remembering that is not remembering will be one in which it is not true that any action one quasi-remembers from the inside is thereby an action he himself did. So – assuming that ours may be such a world – if I quasi-remember an action from the inside, and say on this basis that I did the action, my statement will be subject to error through misidentification; it may be that my quasi-memory of the action is as accurate and complete as it could be, but that I am mistaken in thinking that I am the person who did it. There is another way in which a first-person quasi-memory claim could be mistaken through misidentification. If there can be quasi-remembering that is not remembering, it will be possible for a person to quasi-remember an action of his own from the outside. That is, one might quasi-remember an action of one's own as it appeared to someone else who observed it; one might, as it were, quasi-remember it through the eyes of another person. But of course, if I were to quasi-remember someone who looks like me doing a certain action, and were to say on that basis that I did the action, I might be mistaken through no fault of my quasi-memory; it might be that the person who did the action was my identical twin or someone disguised to look like me.

What I have just said about the quasi-remembering of past actions also applies to the quasi-remembering of past experiences and of other mental phenomena. If I remember a past pain from the inside – i.e., remember the pain itself, or remember having the pain, as opposed to remembering seeing someone manifest pain behavior – then the pain must have been mine. But the fact that I *quasi*-remember a pain from the inside will be no guarantee that the pain was mine. Any quasi-memory claim to have been in pain on some past occasion, or to have had a certain thought, or to have made a certain decision, will be subject to error through misidentification.

What is shown by the foregoing is that the immunity of first-person memory claims to error through misidentification exists only because remembering requires the satisfaction of the previous awareness condition, and that this feature disappears once we imagine this requirement dropped. Quasi-memory, unlike memory, does not preserve immunity to error through misidentification relative to the first-person

pronouns. To consider the further consequences of replacing memory with quasi-memory, I must first say something more about memory.

To refer to an event of a certain sort as one that one remembers does not always uniquely identify it, since one may remember more than one event of a given sort, but it does go some way toward identifying it. In referring to an event in this way, one to a certain extent locates it in space and time, even if the description of the event contains no place-names, no names of objects by reference to which places can be identified, and no dates or other temporal indicators. For in saying that one remembers the event, one locates it within a spatiotemporal region which is defined by one's own personal history. The spatiotemporal region which is "rememberable" by a given person can be charted by specifying the intervals of past time during which the person was conscious and by specifying the person's spatial location, and indicating what portions of his environment he was in a position to witness, at each moment during these intervals. If someone reports that he remembers an event of a certain kind, we know that unless his memory is mistaken, an event of that kind occurred within the spatiotemporal region rememberable by him, and in principle we can chart this region by tracing his history back to its beginning.

Ordinarily, of course, we have far more knowledge than this of the spatiotemporal location of a remembered event, for usually a memory report will fix this position by means of dates, place-names, and other spatial and temporal indicators. But it must be noted that memory claims are subject to error through misidentification with respect to spatial indicators. If a man says "I remember an explosion occurring right in front of that building," it is possible for this to be false even if the memory it expresses is accurate and detailed; the remembered explosion may have occurred, not in front of the building indicated, but in front of another building exactly like it. This remains true no matter how elaborate and detailed we imagine the memory claim to be. For any set of objects that has actually existed in the world, even if this be as extensive as the set of buildings, streets, parks, bridges, etc. that presently make up New York City, it is logically possible that there should somewhere exist, or that there should somewhere and at some time have existed, a numerically different but exactly similar set of objects arranged in exactly the same way. So memory claims are, in principle, subject to error through misidentification even with respect to such place names as "New York City." Here I am appealing to what Strawson has referred to as the possibility of 'massive reduplication.'[13]

When a memory report attempts to fix the location of a remembered event by reference to some landmark, we are ordinarily justified in not regarding it as a real possibility that the claim involves error through misidentification owing to the reduplication of that landmark. Certainly we are so justified if the landmark is New York City. But it is important to see why this is so. It is not that we have established that nowhere and at no time has there existed another city exactly like New York; as a self-consistent, unrestricted, negative existential claim, this is something that it would be impossible in principle for us to establish.[14] What we can and do know is that New York is not reduplicated within any spatiotemporal region of which anyone with whom we converse can have had experience. Whether or not New York is reduplicated in some remote galaxy or at some remote time in the past, we know that the man who claims to remember doing or experiencing something in a New York-like city cannot have been in any such duplicate. And from this we can conclude that if he does remember doing or experiencing something in a New York-like city, then it was indeed in New York, and not in any duplicate of it, that the remembered action or event occurred. But we can conclude this only because remembering involves the satisfaction of the previous awareness condition.

Even when a landmark referred to in someone's memory claim is reduplicated within the spatiotemporal region rememberable by that person, we can often be confident that the claim does not involve error through misidentification. Suppose that someone locates a remembered event, say an explosion, by saying that it occurred in front of his house, and we know that there are many houses, some of which he has seen, that are exactly like his. If he reported that he had simply found himself in front of his house, with no recollection of how he had gotten there, and that after seeing the explosion he had passed out and awakened later in a hospital, we would think it quite possible that he had misidentified the place

at which the remembered explosion occurred. But suppose instead that he reports that he remembers walking home from work, seeing the explosion in front of his house, and then going inside and being greeted by his family. Here a misidentification of the place of the explosion would require the reduplication, not merely of his house, but also of his family, his place of work, and the route he follows in walking home from work. We could know that no such reduplication exists within the spatiotemporal region of which he has had experience, and could conclude that his report did not involve an error through misidentification. But again, what would enable us to conclude this is the fact remembering involves the satisfaction of the previous awareness condition.

Presumably, what justifies any of us in using such expressions as "New York" and "my house" in his own memory reports are considerations of the same kind as those that justify others in ruling out the possibility that claims containing such expressions involve error through misidentification. What justifies one is the knowledge that certain sorts of reduplication do not in fact occur within the spatiotemporal regions of which any of us have had experience. Normally no such justification is needed for the use of "I" in memory reports; this is what is involved in saying that memory claims are normally immune to error through misidentification relative to the first-person pronouns. But what makes such a justification possible in the case of "New York" is the same as what makes it unnecessary in the case of "I": namely, the fact that remembering involves the satisfaction of the previous awareness condition. So it is because of this fact that remembering can provide us, not merely with the information that an event of a certain sort has occurred somewhere or other in the vicinity of persons and things satisfying certain general descriptions, but with the information that such an event occurred in a certain specified place, in a certain specifiable spatial relationship to events presently observed, and in the vicinity of certain specified persons or things. But this is also to say that it is this fact about remembering that makes is possible for us to know that an object or person to which one remembers something happening is, or is not, identical with an object or person presently observed. And it will emerge later that it is also this fact about remembering that makes it possible to know that different memories are, or are not, of events in the history of a single object or person.

But now let us consider the consequences of replacing the faculty of memory by a faculty of quasi-memory. Quasi-remembering does not necessarily involve the satisfaction of the previous awareness condition, and first-person quasi-memory claims are, as we have seen, subject to error through misidentification. It is a consequence of this that even if we are given that someone's faculty of quasi-memory is highly reliable, in the sense that when he seems to quasi-remember an event of a certain sort he almost always does quasi-remember such an event, nevertheless, his quasi-memory will provide neither him nor us with any positive information concerning the spatial location of the events he quasi-remembers, or with any information concerning the identity, or concerning the history, of any object or person to which he quasi-remembers something happening. The fact that he quasi-remembers an event of a certain sort will not provide us with the information that such an event has occurred within the spatiotemporal region of which he has had experience. But in consequence of this, if he attempts to locate the quasi-remembered event by reference to some object or place known to us, e.g., New York or Mt. Everest, it is impossible for us to rule out on empirical grounds the possibility that his claim involves error through misidentification owing to the reduplication of that object or place. To rule this out, we would have to have adequate grounds for asserting, not merely that there is no duplicate of New York (say) in the spatiotemporal region of which he has had experience, but that at no place and time has there been a duplicate of New York. And this we could not have.[15] But this means that in expressing his quasi-memories he could not be justified in using such expressions as "New York" and "Mt. Everest," or such expressions as "I" "this," and "here," to refer to the places, persons, and things in or to which he quasi-remembers certain things happening. The most he could be entitled to assert on the basis of his quasi-memories would be a set of general propositions of the form "An event of type ϕ at some time occurred in the history of an object of type A while it stood in relations $R_1, R_2, R_3 \ldots$ to objects of types $B, C, D \ldots$" And given only a set of

propositions of this sort, no matter how extensive, one could not even begin to reconstruct any part of the history of the world; one could not even have grounds for asserting that an object mentioned in one proposition in the set was one and the same as an object mentioned in another proposition of the set.

So far I have been ignoring the fact that the events and actions we remember generally have temporal duration, and the fact that we sometimes remember connected sequences of events and actions lasting considerable lengths of time. What will correspond to this if remembering is replaced with quasi-remembering? If someone says "I remember doing X and then doing Y," it would make no sense to say to him, "Granted that your memory is accurate, and that such a sequence of actions did occur, are you sure that it was one and the same person who did both X and Y?" But now suppose that someone says "I quasi-remember doing X and then doing Y," and that the world is such that there is quasi-remembering that is not remembering. Here it is compatible with the accuracy of the man's quasi-memory that he should be mistaken in thinking that he himself did X and Y. And as I shall now try to show, it must also be compatible with the accuracy of this man's quasi-memories that he should be mistaken in thinking even that one and the same person did both X and Y.

Suppose that at time t_1 a person, call him A, does action Y and has while doing it a quasi-memory from the inside of the immediately previous occurrence of the doing of action X. A's having this quasi-memory of the doing of X is of course compatible with X's having been done by someone other than himself. At t_1, A's cognitive state includes this quasi-memory from the inside of the doing of X together with knowledge from the inside of the doing of Y; we might say that it includes knowledge from the inside of the action sequence X-followed-by-Y. But now suppose that at a later time t_2 someone, call him B, has a quasi-memory corresponding to the cognitive state of A at t_1. It would seem that B's quasi-memory will be a quasi-memory from the inside of the action sequence X-followed-by-Y. This quasi-memory will be veridical in the sense that it corresponds to a past cognitive state that was itself a state of knowledge, yet its being veridical in this way is compatible with X and Y having been done by different persons. If A were mistakenly to assert at t_1 that X and Y were done by the same person, his mistake would not be due to a faulty quasi-memory. And if B's cognitive state at t_2 corresponds to A's cognitive state at t_1, then if B were mistaken at t_2 in thinking that X and Y were done by the same person, this mistake would not be due to a faulty quasi-memory.

If, as I have been arguing, someone's quasi-remembering from the inside the *action* sequence X-followed-by-Y provides no guarantee that X and Y were done by the same person, then by the same reasoning someone's quasi-remembering the *event* sequence X-followed-by-Y provides no guarantee that X and Y were witnessed by the same person, and therefore no guarantee that they occurred in spatial proximity to one another. But any temporally extended event can be thought of as a succession of temporally and spatially contiguous events; e.g., a stone's rolling down a hill can be thought of as consisting in its rolling half of the way down followed by its rolling the other half of the way. Suppose, then, that someone has a quasi-memory of the following event sequence: stone rolling from top of hill to middle followed by stone rolling from middle of hill to bottom. If we knew this to be a memory, and not just a quasi-memory, we would know that if it is veridical, then one and the same person observed both of these events, one immediately after the other, and this together with the contents of the memory could guarantee that one and the same hill and one and the same stone were involved in both, and that a single stone had indeed rolled all the way down a hill. But the veridicality of this quasi-memory *qua* quasi-memory would be compatible with these events having been observed by different persons, and with their involving different stones and different hills; it would be compatible with no stone's having rolled all of the way down any hill. And since any temporally extended event can be thought of as a succession of temporally and spatially contiguous events, it follows that someone's quasi-remembering what is ostensibly a temporally extended event of a certain kind is always compatible with there actually being no such event that he quasi-remembers, for it is compatible with his quasi-memory being, as it were, compounded out of quasi-memories of a number of different events that were causally

unrelated and spatiotemporally remote from one another. The knowledge of the past provided by such a faculty of quasi-memory would be minimal indeed.[16]

IV

But now we must consider the consequences of strengthening the previous awareness condition for quasi-remembering to include the requirement that a veridical quasi-memory must not only correspond to, but must also stand in an appropriate causal relationship to, a past cognitive and sensory state of someone or other. Clearly, much of what I have said about quasi-remembering ceases to hold once its previous awareness condition is strengthened in this way. If, as is commonly supposed, causal chains must be spatiotemporally continuous, then if quasi-memory claims implied the satisfaction of this strengthened previous awareness condition, they would, when true, provide some information concerning the location of the quasi-remembered events and actions. We would know at a minimum that the spatiotemporal relationship between the quasi-remembered event and the making of the quasi-memory claim is such that it is possible for them to be linked by a spatiotemporally continuous causal chain, and if we could trace the causal ancestry of the quasi-memory, we could determine precisely when and where the quasi-remembered event occurred. Thus if we construe the previous awareness condition of quasi-memory as including this causal requirement, it seems that a faculty of quasi-remembering could enable us to identify past events and to reidentify persons and things, and it seems at first glance (though not, I think, on closer examination) that it would enable us to do this without giving us a special access to our own past histories.

It must be stressed that this strengthened previous awareness condition is an improvement on the weaker one *only* on the assumption that causal chains (or at any rate the causal chains that link cognitive and sensory states with subsequent quasi-memories) must be spatiotemporally continuous, or at least must satisfy a condition similar to spatiotemporal continuity. If the sort of causality operating here allowed for action at a spatial or temporal distance, and if there were no limit on the size of the spatial or temporal gaps that could exist in a causal chain linking a cognitive and sensory state with a subsequent quasi-memory, then the claim that a quasi-memory originated in a corresponding cognitive and sensory state would be as unfalsifiable, and as uninformative, as the claim that it corresponds to a past cognitive and sensory state of someone or other.

To consider the consequences of strengthening the previous awareness condition for quasi-memory in the way just suggested, I shall have to introduce a few technical expressions. First, I shall use the expressions "quasi$_c$-remember" and "quasi$_c$-memory" when speaking of the sort of "quasi-remembering whose previous awareness condition includes the causal requirement. Second, I shall use the term "M-type causal chain" to refer to the sort of causal chain that must link a quasi$_c$-memory with a corresponding past cognitive and sensory state if they are to be "of" the same event, or if the former is to be "of" the latter. Since quasi$_c$-remembering is to be as much like remembering as is compatible with the failure of the strong previous awareness condition, M-type causal chains should resemble as much as possible the causal chains that are responsible for actual remembering, i.e., should resemble them as much as is compatible with their sometimes linking mental states belonging to different persons. At any given time a person can be said to have a total mental state which includes his memories or quasi$_c$-memories and whatever other mental states the person has at that time. Let us say that two total mental states, existing at different times, are directly M-connected if the later of them contains a quasi$_c$-memory which is linked by an M-type causal chain to a corresponding cognitive and sensory state contained in the earlier. And let us say, by way of giving a recursive definition, that two total mental states are M-connected If either (1) they are directly M-connected, or (2) there is some third total mental state to which each of them is M-connected.[17]

Now there are two cases we must consider. Either the world will be such, or it will not, that a total mental state existing at a particular time can be M-connected with at most one total mental state existing at each other moment in time. Or, what comes to the same thing, either the world will be such, or it will not, that no two total mental states existing at the same time can be M-connected. Let us begin by considering the case in which the former of these alternatives holds. This is the case that will exist if there is no "branching" of M-type causal chains, i.e., if it never happens that an M-type causal chain branches into two such chains which then produce quasi$_c$-memories belonging to different and simultaneously existing total mental states, and if it never happens that different M-type causal chains coalesce and produce in a single total mental state quasi$_c$-memories whose corresponding past cognitive and sensory states belonged to different and simultaneously existing total mental states. This is presumably the situation that exists in the actual world. And I think that in any world in which this situation exists, M-connected total mental states will be, to use a term of Bertrand Russell's, "copersonal," i.e., states of one and the same person, and quasi$_c$-remembering will reduce to remembering. There seems to me to be at least this much truth in the claim that memory is constitutive of personal identity.[18] (But more about this in section V.)

Now let us consider the case in which M-type causal chains do sometimes branch, and in which, as a result, it can happen that two or more simultaneously existing total mental states are M-connected. Here we cannot claim that if two total mental states are M-connected, they are thereby copersonal without committing ourselves to the unattractive conclusion that a person can be in two different places, and can have two different total mental states, at one and the same time. But it is still open to us to say that if a total mental state existing at time t_1 and a total mental state existing at time t_2 are M-connected, then they are copersonal *unless* the M-type causal chain connecting them branched at some time during the interval $t_1 - t_2$. If we can say this, as I think we can, then even in a world in which there is branching of M-type causal chains, the fact that a person quasi$_c$-remembers a past event or action would create a presumption that he, that same person, experienced the event or did the action, and therefore a presumption that the quasi$_c$-memory was actually a memory. This presumption would stand as long as there was no evidence that the M-type causal chain linking the past action or experience with the subsequent quasi$_c$-memory had branched during the interval between them.

Worlds of the sort we are now considering, i.e., worlds in which M-type causal chains sometimes branch, could be of several kinds. Consider first a world in which people ocasionally undergo fission or fusion; i.e., people sometimes split, like amoebas, both offshoots having quasi$_c$-memories of the actions done prior to the fission by the person who underwent it, and two people sometimes coalesce into a single person who then has quasi$_c$-memories of both of their past histories. Here we cannot say that a person did whatever actions he quasi$_c$-remembers from the inside without running afoul of Leibniz' Law and the principle of the transitivity of identity. But we can say something close to this. Suppose that someone, call him Jones, splits into two persons, one of whom is me and the other is someone I shall call Jones II. Both Jones II and I have quasi$_c$-memories from the inside of Jones's past actions, and no one else does. If anyone now alive is identical with Jones, it is either myself or Jones II, and any objection to saying that I am Jones is equally an objection to saying that Jones II is Jones. I think that we can say here that I am identical with Jones if anyone now alive is identical with him. Or suppose that two people, call them Brown and Smith, coalesce, resulting in me. I have quasi$_c$-memories from the inside of Brown's actions and also of Smith's actions. There are serious objections to identifying me with either Brown or Smith, but it seems clear here that if anyone now alive is identical with either Brown or Smith, I am. So in such a world the following principle holds: if at time t a person A quasi$_c$-remembers a past action X from the inside, then A is identical with the person who did X if anyone alive at t is identical with him.[19]

But I think that we can imagine a world in which this principle would not hold. In the case in which two persons coalesce, the M-type causal chains involved might be represented by a river having two "forks" of equal width. Suppose that instead of this we have an M-type causal chain, or a connected set of such causal chains, that could be represented by a river having several small tributaries. For example, suppose, very fancifully, that memories were stored, by some sort of chemical coding, in the blood rather than in the brain cells, and that as a result of being given a blood transfusion, one sometimes acquired quasi$_c$-memories "from the inside" of a few of the actions of the blood donor. Here the blood transfusion would be a "tributary" into what apart from its tributaries would be the sort of M-type causal chain that occurs in the history of a single person. Now I do not think that we would deny that A, existing at time t_2, was the same person as B, who existed at an earlier time t_1, merely because A quasi$_c$-remembers from the inside, as the result of a blood transfusion, an action at t_1 that was not done by B. Nor would we deny that another person C, the blood donor, is the person who did that past action merely because there is someone other than himself, namely A, who quasi$_c$-remembers it from the inside. So here it would not be true that if at time t a person quasi$_c$-remembers a past action from the inside, then he is identical with the person who did it if anyone existing at t is identical with the person who did it.

Yet even in such a world it seems essential that in any total mental state the memories, i.e., the quasi$_c$-memories produced by the past history of the person whose total mental state it is, should outnumber the quasi$_c$-memories produced by any given tributary. If the quasi$_c$-memories produced by a given tributary outnumbered the memories, then surely the tributary would not be a tributary at all, but would instead be the main stream. But this implies that if a person quasi$_c$-remembers an action from the inside, then, in the absence of evidence to the contrary, he is entitled to regard it as more likely that the action was done by him than that it was done by any other given person. And this, taken together with my earlier point that if someone quasi$_c$-remembers an action from the inside, there is a presumption that he is the person who did it, gives us a sense in which quasi$_c$-memory can be said to provide the quasi$_c$-rememberer with "special access" to his own past history. This is of course a much weaker sense of "special access" than that explained in section I – but in this sense it will be true in *any* possible world, and not merely in ours, that people have a special access to their own past histories.

V

In the preceding sections it was assumed that remembering, as opposed to (mere) quasi$_c$-remembering, necessarily involves the satisfaction of the strong previous awareness condition; that is, it was assumed that in any genuine case of event memory the memory must correspond to a past cognitive and sensory state of the rememberer himself. And this is commonly supposed in discussions of memory and personal identity. But it is not really clear that this assumption is correct. For consider again the hypothetical case in which a man's body "splits" like an amoeba into two physiologically identical bodies, and in which both offshoots produce memory claims corresponding to the past life of the original person. Or, to take a case that lies closer to the realm of real possibility, consider the hypothetical case in which a human brain is split, its two hemispheres are transplanted into the newly vacated skulls of different bodies, and both transplant recipients survive, regain consciousness, and begin to make memory claims that correspond to the past history of the brain "donor."[20] In neither case can we identify both of the physiological offshoots of a person with the original person, unless we are willing to take the drastic step of giving up Leibniz' Law and the transitivity of identity. But is it clear that it would be wrong to say that each of the offshoots remembers the actions, experiences, etc. of the original person? There is, to be sure, awkwardness about saying that each offshoot remembers *doing* an action done by the original person, for this seems to imply that an action done by one and only one person was done by each of the two nonidentical offshoots. But perhaps we can say that each of the offshoots does remember the action "from the inside." In our world, where such bizarre cases do not occur, the only actions anyone remembers from the inside are those that he himself performed, so it is not surprising that the only idiomatic way of reporting that one remembers an action from the inside is by saying that one remembers doing the action. But this need not prevent us from describing my hypothetical cases by saying that both offshoots do remember the actions of the original person, and it does not seem to me unnatural to describe them in this way. If this is a correct way of describing them, then perhaps my second sort of quasi-remembering, i.e., quasi$_c$-remembering, turns out to be just remembering, and the previous awareness condition for remembering turns out to be the causal requirement discussed in the preceding section rather than the stronger condition I have been assuming it to be.

If the suggestion just made about the conditions for remembering is correct, the logical connection between remembering and personal identity is looser than I have been supposing it to be. Yet adopting this suggestion does not prevent one from defending the claim that remembering is constitutive of and criterial for personal identity; on the contrary, this makes it possible to defend the letter of this claim, and not just its spirit, against the very common objection that any attempt to analyze personal identity in terms of memory will turn out to be circular.

Bishop Butter objected against Locke's account of personal identify that "one should really think it self-evident, that consciousness of personal identity presupposes, and therefore cannot constitute, personal identity, any more than knowledge, in any other case, can constitute truth, which it presupposes."[21] More recently several writers have argued that while "S remembers doing A" entails "S did A" (and so entails "S is identical with the person who did A"), this is only because "S remembers doing A" is elliptical for "S remembers himself doing A"[22] To offer as a partial analysis of the notion of personal identity, and as a criterion of personal identity, the formula "If S remembers (himself) doing action A, S is the same as the person who did A" would be like offering as a partial definition of the word "red," and as a criterion of redness, the formula "If S knows that X is red, then X is red." In both cases the concept allegedly being defined is illicitly employed in the formulation of the defining condition. Likewise, it has been argued that while someone's remembering a past event is a sufficient condition of his being identical with a witness to the event, we cannot use the former as a criterion for the latter, since in order to establish that a person really does remember a given past event, we have to establish that he, that very person, was a witness to the event. And if this is so, the formula "If S remembers E, S is identical with someone who witnessed E" will be circular if offered as a partial analysis of the concept of personal identity.[23]

Such objections assume that renumbering involves the satisfaction of the strong previous awareness condition, and they can be avoided on the assumption that the previous awareness condition is weaker than this, e.g., is that given for quasi$_c$-remembering in section IV. Or, better, they can be avoided if we explicitly use "remember" in a "weak" sense ("remember$_w$") rather than in a "strong" sense ("remember$_s$"), the strength of the sense depending on the strength of the associated previous awareness condition. Although there are perhaps other possibilities, let us take "remember$_w$" to be synonymous with "quasi$_c$-remember." Clearly, to establish that S remembers$_w$ event E (or remembers$_w$ action A from the inside) it is not necessary to establish that S himself witnessed E (or did A), for it will be enough if S is the offshoot of someone who witnessed E (did A). And while we cannot claim that statements about what events or actions a man remembers$_w$ logically entail statements about his identity and past history, this does not prevent the truth of the former from being criterial evidence for, and from being partially constitutive of, the truth of the latter. For we can still assert as a logical truth that if S remembers$_w$ event E (or remembers$_w$ action A from the inside), *and* if there has been no branching of M-type causal chains during the relevant stretch of S's history, then S is one of the witnesses of E (is the person who did A). Here we avoid the circularity that Butler and others have thought to be involved in any attempt to give an account of personal identity, and of the criteria of personal identity, in terms of memory.

In the actual world, people remember$_w$ whatever they remember$_w$ and this makes it difficult to settle the question of whether it is the weak or the strong sense of "remember" that is employed in ordinary discourse. It is possible that this question has no answer; since branching of M-type causal chains does not in fact occur, and is seldom envisaged, people have had no practical motive for distinguishing between the strong and the weak senses of "remember." But I do not think that this question is especially important. We can defend the spirit of the claim that memory is a criterion of personal identity without settling this question, although in order to defend the letter of that claim, we must maintain that in its ordinary use "remember" means "remember$_w$."

At this point I should say something about why it is important to insist on the claim that there is a causal element in the notion of memory. For this claim has recently come under attack.[24] It has been argued that the notion of memory should be analyzed in terms of the *retention*, rather than the causation, of knowledge, and that the notion of retention is not itself a causal notion. Now I

have no objection to saying that remembering, consists in the retention of knowledge. But I believe that unless we understand the notion of retention, as well as that of memory, as involving a causal component, we cannot account for the role played by the notion of memory, or even the concept of similarity, in judgements of personal identity.

Here it will be useful to consider a hypothetical case I have discussed at some length elsewhere.[25] Let us suppose that the brain from the body of one man, Brown, is transplanted into the body of another man, Robinson, and that the resulting creature – I call him "Brownson" – survives and upon regaining consciousness begins making memory claims corresponding to the past history of Brown rather than that of Robinson. We can also suppose that Brownson manifests personality traits strikingly like those previously manifested by Brown and quite unlike those manifested by Robinson. Although Brownson has Robinson's (former) body, I doubt if anyone would want to say that Brownson is Robinson, and I think that most people would want to say that Brownson is (is the same person as) Brown.

But what can we offer as evidence that Brownson is Brown? Clearly the mere correspondence of Brownson's ostensible memories to Brown's past history, and the similarity of Brownson's personality to Brown's, is far from being sufficient evidence. And it is equally clear that the notion of the *retention* of knowledge and traits is of no use here. To be sure, once we take ourselves to have established that Brownson is Brown, we can say that Brownson retains knowledge, and also personality traits, acquired by Brownson in the past. But the latter assertion presupposes the identity of Brownson and Brown, and cannot without circularity be offered as evidence for it. Indeed, the circularity is the same as what would be involved in offering as evidence of this identity the fact that Brownson remembers$_s$ Brown's past experiences and actions.

We do not, however, beg the question about identity if we take Brownson's possession of what used to be Brown's brain, together with the empirical facts about the role played by the brain in memory, as establishing that Brown's ostensible memories are directly M-connected with Brown's past actions and experiences, i.e., are causally related to them in essentially the same ways as people's memories are generally connected with their own past experiences and actions. This in turn establishes that Brownson quasi$_c$-remembers, and so remembers$_w$, Brown's past experiences and actions. And from this in turn, and from the fact that we have good reason to suppose that no other person's memories are M-connected with Brown's past history in this way, i.e., that there has been no 'branching' of M-type causal chains, we can conclude that Brownson is Brown.[26]

We can reason in this way only if we can assert that there is a causal connection between Brownson's past history and Brownson's ostensible memories. And this, it seems to me, we are clearly entitled to do. Given that Brownson has Brown's former brain, there is every reason to think that had Brown's history been different in certain ways, there would (ceteris paribus) be corresponding differences in what Brownson ostensibly remembers. I can see no reason for doubting that such counterfactuals assert causal connections. Similar remarks can be made about the similarity between Brownson's and Brown's personality traits. Given that Brownson has Brown's former brain, we have reason to think that had Brown developed a different set of personality traits, Brownson would (ceteris paribus) have those personality traits rather than the ones he has. And while we cannot naturally speak of Brown's having a certain trait at one time as causing Brownson to have the same trait at a subsequent time, we can speak of the former as being an important part of a causally sufficient condition for the latter. It is only where we suppose that the traits of things at different times are causally related in this way that we are entitled to take the similarity of something at one time and something at another time as evidence of identity.

VI

We are now in a position to reassess the view, mentioned in section II, that the knowledge of our own pasts and our own identities provided us by memory is essentially "noncriterial." If I remember$_s$ an action or experience from the inside, and know that I do, it makes no sense for me to inquire whether that action or experience was my own. But it seems logically possible that one should remember$_w$ an action or experience from the inside (i.e., quasi$_c$-remember$_w$ it) without remembering$_s$ it. So if one remembers$_w$ an action or experience from the inside, it can make sense to inquire whether it was one's own (whether one remember$_s$ it), and it would seem offhand that there is no reason why one should not attempt to answer this question on the basis of criteria of personal identity.

But while an action I remember$_w$ from the inside can fail to be mine, there is only one way in which this can happen: namely, through there having been branching in the M-type causal chain linking it with my present memory. So in asking whether the action was mine, the only question I can significantly be asking is whether there was such branching. If I go on to verify that there was no branching, I thereby establish that a sufficient criterion of personal identity is satisfied. If instead I conclude on inductive grounds that there was no branching, relying on my general knowledge that M-type causal chains seldom or never branch (or that it is physiologically impossible for them to do so), I thereby conclude that a sufficient criterion of personal identity is satisfied. But an important part of what the satisfaction of this criterion consists in, namely my remembering$_w$ the past action from the inside, is not something I establish, and not something I necessarily presuppose in inquiring concerning my relation to the remembered$_w$ action. In cases where one remembers$_w$ a past action from the inside, and knows of it only on that basis, one cannot significantly inquire concerning it whether one does remember$_w$ it – for as I tried to bring out in my discussion of quasi-remembering, there is no way of knowing the past that stands to remembering$_w$ as remembering$_w$ stands to remembering$_s$, i.e., is such that one can know of a past event this way and regard it as an open question whether in so knowing of it one is remembering$_w$ it. So in such cases the satisfaction of this part of the memory criterion for personal identity is a precondition of one's being able to raise the question of identity, and cannot be something one establishes in attempting to answer that question.

That one remembers$_w$ a past action is not (and could not be) one of the things one remembers$_w$ about it, and neither is the fact that there is no branching in the M-type causal chain linking it with one's memory of it. And normally there is no set of remembered$_w$ features of an action one remembers$_w$ from the inside, or of the person who did the action, by which one identifies the action as one's own and the agent as oneself. If one has not identified a remembered person as oneself on the basis of his remembered$_w$ features, then of course it cannot be the case that one has *mis*identified him on this basis. This is not to say that there is no basis on which one might misidentify a remembered$_w$ person as oneself. If there can, logically, be remembering$_w$ that is not remembering$_s$, then where one remembers$_w$ an action from the inside, one's judgment that one did the action will not be logically immune to error through misidentification in the sense defined in section II – though given the contingent fact that all remembering$_w$ is remembering$_s$, such judgments can be said to have a *de facto* immunity to error through misidentification. But the sort of error through misidentification to which a statement like "I saw a canary" is liable, if based on a memory$_w$ from the inside, is utterly different from that to which a statement like "John saw a canary" is liable when based on a memory$_w$ of the incident reported. If the making of the latter statement involves an error through misidentification, this will be because either (1) the speaker misidentified someone as John at the time the reported incident occurred, and retained this misidentification in memory, or (2) at some subsequent time, perhaps at the time of speaking, the speaker misidentified a remembered$_w$ person as John on the basis of his remembered$_w$ features. But if I remember$_w$ from the inside someone seeing a canary, and am mistaken in thinking that person to have been myself, it is absurd to suppose that this mistake originated at the time at which the remembered$_w$ seeing occurred. Nor, as I have said, will this be a misidentification based on the remenbered$_w$ features of the person who saw the canary. What could be the basis for a misidentification in this case is the mistaken belief that there is no branching in the M-type causal chain linking one's memory with the past incident. But a misidentification on this basis, while logically possible, would be radically unlike the misidentifications that actually occur in the making of third-person reports.

VII

Because I have taken seriously the possibility of worlds in which M-type causal chains sometimes branch, and thus the possibility of quasi$_c$-remembering (remembering$_w$) that is not remembering$_s$, I have had to qualify and weaken my initial claims about the "special access" people have to their own past histories. But if our concern is with the elucidation of our present concept of personal identity, and with personal identity as something that has a special sort of importance for us, then it is not clear that the possibility of such worlds, and the qualifications this requires, should be taken as seriously as I have taken them. For there is reason to think (1) that some of our concepts, perhaps including the concept of a person, would necessarily undergo significant modification in their application to such worlds, and (2) that in such worlds personal identity would not *matter* to people in quite the way it does in the actual world.

There are important connections between the concept of personal identity and the concepts of various "backward-looking" and "forward-looking" mental states. Thus the appropriate objects of remorse, and of a central sort of pride, are past actions done by the very person who is remorseful or proud, and the appropriate objects of fear and dread, and of delighted anticipation, are events which the subject of these emotions envisages as happening to himself. And intentions have as their "intentional objects" actions to be done by the very person who has the intention. It is difficult to see how the notion of a person could be applied, *with these conceptual connections remaining intact*, to a world in which M-type causal chains frequently branch, e.g., one in which persons frequently undergo fission. If I remember$_w$ from the inside a cruel or deceitful action, am I to be relieved of all tendency to feel remorse if I discover that because of fission someone else remembers$_w$ it too? May I not feel proud of an action I remember$_w$ from the inside even though I know that I am only one of several offshoots of the person who did it, and so cannot claim to be identical with him? Am I not to be afraid of horrible things I expect to happen to my future offshoots, and not to view with pleasant anticipation the delights that are in prospect for them? And is it to be impossible, or logically inappropriate, for me knowingly to form intentions, and make decisions and plans, which because of the prospect of immanent fission will have to be carried out by my offshoots rather than by me? To the extent that I can imagine such a world I find it incredible to suppose that these questions must be answered in the affirmative. The prospect of immanent fission might not be appealing, but it seems highly implausible to suppose that the only rational attitude toward it would be that appropriate to the prospect of immanent death (for fission, unlike death, would be something "lived through"). It seems equally implausible to suppose that a person's concern for the well-being of his offshoots should be construed as altruism; surely this concern would, or at any rate could, be just like the self-interested concern each of us has for his own future well-being. Yet a negative answer to my rhetorical questions would suggest that either the concept of a person or such concepts as those of pride, remorse, fear, etc., would undergo significant modification in being applied to such a world.[27]

A person's past history is the most important source of his knowledge of the world, but it is also an important source of his knowledge, and his conception, of himself; a person's "self-image," his conception of his own character, values, and potentialities, is determined in a considerable degree by the way in which he views his own past actions. And a person's future history is the primary focus of his desires, hopes, and fears.[28] If these remarks do not express truths about the concept of personal identity, they at least express truths about the *importance* of this concept in our conceptual scheme, or in our "form of life." It seems plausible to suppose that in a world in which fission was common, personal identity would not have this sort of importance. Roughly speaking, the portion of past history that would matter to a person in this special way would be that which it is possible for him to remember$_w$, and not merely that which it is possible for him to remember$_s$. And the focus of people's "self-interested" attitudes and emotions would be the future histories of their offshoots, and of their offshoots' offshoots, and so on, as well as their own future histories. In the actual world it is true both that (1) remembering$_w$ is always remembering$_s$ (and thus that there is special access in the strong sense characterized in section I), and that

(2) the primary focus of a person's "self-interested" attitudes and emotions is his own past and future history. It is surely no accident that (1) and (2) go together.

Notes

1 John Locke, *Essay Concerning Human Understanding*, ed. Peter H. Nidditch (Oxford: Clarendon Press, 1975), p. 335 (bk 11, ch. 27, sect. 9); italics added.

2 In their paper "Remembering," (*Philosophical Review* 75 (1966)), C. B. Martin and Max Deutscher express what I call the previous awareness condition by saying that "a person can be said to remember something happening or, in general, remember something directly, only if he has observed or experienced it." Their notion of direct remembering seems to be much the same as Norman Malcolm's notion of "personal memory" (see his "Three forms of memory," in *Knowledge and Certainty* (Englewood Cliffs, NJ: Prentice-Hall, 1963), pp. 203–21). To remember that Caesar invaded Britain, I need not have had any experience of the invasion, but no one who lacked such experience could directly or personally remember that Caesar invaded Britain. In this essay I am primarily concerned with memories that are of events, i.e., of something happening, and do not explicitly consider what Malcolm calls "factual memory," i.e., memories that such and such was (or is, or will be) the case; but what I say can be extended to cover all cases of direct or personal memory. Martin and Deutscher hold, and I agree, that remembering something happening is always direct remembering.

There are apparent counterexamples to the previous witnessing condition as I have formulated it. I can be said to remember Kennedy's assassination, which is presumably an event, yet I did not witness or observe it, and the knowledge I had of it at the time was indirect. But while I can be said to remember the assassination, I could hardly be said to remember Kennedy being shot (what I do remember is hearing about it, and the impact this made on me and those around me). Perhaps I can be said to remember the assassination because we sometimes mean by "the assassination" not only the events in Dallas but their immediate effects throughout the nation and world. In any case, when I speak of memories of events in this essay, I mean what Martin and Deutscher speak of as memories of something happening.

3 Although self-reference is typically done with first-person pronouns, it can be done with names, and even with definite descriptions – as when de Gaulle says "De Gaulle intends…" and the chairman of a meeting says "The Chair recognizes…." In such cases these expressions are "self-referring," not merely because their reference is in fact to the speaker, but also because the speaker intends using them to refer to himself.

4 There is a subtle distinction between this sort of case and cases like the following, which I would not count as a case of error through misidentification. Suppose that Jones says "You are a fool," and I mistakenly think that he is speaking to me. Subsequently I say "I remember Jones calling me a fool," and my statement is false through no fault of my memory. While this is a case of knowing *that* Jones called someone (someone or other) a fool and mistakenly thinking that he was calling me a fool, it is not a case of knowing *of* some particular person that Jones called him a fool but mistakenly identifying that person as oneself. Whereas in the other case we can say, not merely that I know that someone or other blushed, and mistakenly think that it was I, but that I know *of* some particular person (namely the man I saw in the mirror) that he blushed and have mistakenly identified him as myself.

5 I have discussed the immunity to error through misidentification of first-person present-tense statements in Sydney Shoemaker, *Identity, Cause and Mind* (Cambridge: Cambridge University Press, 1984), Essay I. There I made the mistake of associating this feature with the peculiarities of the first-person pronouns. But in fact present tense statements having the appropriate sorts of predicates are immune to error through misidentification with respect to any expressions that are "self-referring" in the sense of n. 3, above, including names and definite descriptions. If someone says "De Gaulle intends to remove France from NATO," and is using "de Gaulle" to refer to himself, his statement is in the relevant sense immune to error through misidentification, regardless of whether he is right in thinking that his name is "de Gaulle" and that he is the President of France.

6 H. P. Grice, "Personal identity," *Mind* 50 (1941), pp. 330–50, at p. 344.

7 G. C. Nerlich, "On evidence for identity," *Australasian Journal of Philosophy*, 37 (1959), pp. 201–14, at p. 208.

8 I am not here endorsing the view, which I in fact reject, that remembering consists in the having of an image, or some other sort of mental "representation," in which the memory content is in some way encoded. It is sufficient for the existence at *t* of the "cognitive state" of remembering such and such that it be true of the person at *t* that he remembers such and such; I am not here committing myself to any account of what, if anything, someone's remembering such and such "consists in."

9 I should make it clear that I am not saying that what we remember is always, or even normally, a past cognitive and sensory state. I am not propounding the view, which is sometimes held but which is clearly false, that "strictly speaking" one can remember only one's own past experiences. I am saying only that if a person remembers an event that occurred at time *t*, then at *t* there must have been a corresponding cognitive and sensory state – which the person may or may not remember – that was of that event. It would not be easy to specify just what sort of correspondence is required here, and I shall not attempt to do so. But I take it as obvious that the claim to remember firing a gun requires, for its truth, a different sort of past cognitive and sensory state than the claim to remember hearing someone else fire a gun, and that the latter, in turn, requires a different sort of past cognitive and sensory state than the claim to remember seeing someone fire a gun. Sometimes one remembers a past event but no longer remembers just how one knew of it at the time of its occurrence; in such a case one's memory, because of vagueness and incompleteness, corresponds to a wider range of possible cognitive and sensory states than (say) a memory of seeing the event or a memory of being told about it.

10 See my book *Self-Knowledge and Self-Identity* (Ithaca, NY: Cornell University Press, 1953), esp. ch. 4, and my paper "Personal identity and memory," *Journal of Philosophy* 56 (1959), pp. 868–82.

11 P. F. Strawson, *The Bounds of Sense* (London: Methuen, 1966), p. 165.

12 I owe to Norman Malcolm the point that to be memory knowledge, one's knowledge must be in some way due to, must exist because of, a past cognitive and sensory state of oneself – see his "Three forms of Memory." Malcolm holds that "due to" does not here express a causal relationship, but I have been persuaded otherwise by Martin's and Deutscher's "Remembering." See also my paper "On knowing who one is" (*Common Factor* 4 (1966)), and David Wiggins's *Identity and Spatio-Temporal Continuity* (Oxford: Blackwell, 1967), esp. pp. 50ff. The view that there is a causal element in the concept of memory is attacked by Roger Squires in his recent paper "Memory unchained," *Philosophical Review* 78 (1969), pp. 178–96; I make a very limited reply to this in section V of this essay.

13 P. F. Strawson, *Individuals* (London: Methuen, 1959), p. 20.

14 It will perhaps be objected that the dictum that unrestricted negative existential claims are unverifiable in principle is brought into question by the possibility that we might discover – what some cosmologists hold there is good reason for believing – that space and past time are finite. If we discovered this, why shouldn't we be able, at least in principle, to establish that at no place does there exist, and at no time in the past has there existed, a duplicate of New York?

One way of countering this objection would be to introduce the possibility, which has been argued by Anthony Quinton in his paper "Spaces and times," *Philosophy 57* (1962), pp. 130–41, of there being a multiplicity of different and spatially unrelated spaces. Establishing that there is no duplicate of New York in our space would not establish that there is no space in which there is such a duplicate, and if it is possible for there to be multiplicity of spaces, there would seem to be no way in which the latter could be established.

But we needn't have recourse to such recondite possibilities in order to counter this objection, if it is viewed as an objection to my claim that it is the fact that remembering involves the satisfaction of the previous awareness condition that makes it possible for us to rule out the possibility that memory claims are false through misidentification owing to the reduplication of landmarks. For to discover that space or past time is finite, and that massive reduplication does not occur, one would have to have a vast amount of empirical information about the world, including information about the histories of particular things. But, as I think the remainder of my discussion should make clear, one could not be provided with such information by memory (or by quasi-memory) unless one were *already* entitled in a large number of cases to refer to particular places and things in one's memory reports without having to regard it as possible that one's references were mistaken owing to massive reduplication. So this entitlement would have to precede the discovery that space and past time are finite, and could not depend on it.

15 The point made in the preceding note can now be expressed by saying that even if we, who have the faculty of memory, could establish that at no place and time has there been a duplicate of New York, this could not be established by someone whose faculty of knowing the past was a faculty of quasi-memory.

16 It may be objected that I have overlooked one way in which a quasi-rememberer might begin to reconstruct his own past history, and the histories of other things, from the information provided him by his quasi-memories. The quasi-rememberer's difficulties would be solved if he had a way of sorting out those of his quasi-memories that are of his own past, i.e., are memories, from those that are not. But it may seem that the quasi-rememberer could easily tell which of his quasi-memories of the very recent past are of his own past, namely by noting which of them have contents very similar to the contents of his *present* experiences; e.g., if he quasi-remembers from the inside the very recent seeing of a scene that resembles very closely the scene he presently sees, it may seem that he can justifiably conclude that the quasi-remembered seeing was his own. And it may seem that by starting in this way he could trace back his own history by finding among his quasi-memories a subset of situations that form a spatiotemporally continuous series of situations, that series terminating in the situation he presently perceives.

This objection assumes that the quasi-rememberer can know the degree of recentness of the situations of which he has quasi-memories, but I shall not here question this assumption. What I shall question is the assumption that if the quasi-rememberer knows that a quasi-remembered scene occurred only a moment or so ago, and that it closely resembles the scene he presently sees, he is entitled to believe that it is numerically the same scene as the one he presently sees and that in all probability it was he who saw it. For of course it could be the case that there is somewhere else a duplicate of the scene he sees, and that his quasi-memory is of that duplicate. It will perhaps be objected that while this is logically possible (given the possibility of quasi-remembering that is not remembering), it is highly improbable. But while it may be intrinsically improbable that a highly complicated situation should be reduplicated within some limited spatiotemporal area, it does not seem intrinsically improbable that such a situation should be reduplicated somewhere or other in the universe – unless the universe is finite, which is something the quasi-rememberer could have no reason for believing (see nn. 14 and 15 above). Moreover, one could not be in a position to know how rare or frequent such reduplication is in fact, and therefore how likely or unlikely it is that a given situation is reduplicated, unless one already had a way of reidentifying places and things. So the quasi-rememberer could not be in a position to know this, for he could have a way of reidentifying places and things only if he were already in a position to rule out reduplication as improbable.

17 It is worth mentioning that if quasi$_c$-remembering is to be as much like remembering as possible, then not just any causal chain linking a past cognitive and sensory state with a subsequent

quasi$_c$-memory can be allowed to count as an M-type causal chain. For as Martin and Deutscher ("Remembering") point out, there are various sorts of cases in which a man's knowledge of a past event is causally due to his previous experience of it, but in which the causal connection is obviously not of the right kind to permit us to say that he remembers the event. E.g., I have completely forgotten the event, but know of it now because you told me about it, and you came to know about it through my telling you about it prior to my forgetting it. It is easier to decide in particular cases whether the causal connection is "of the right kind" than it is to give a general account of what it is for the causal connection to be of the right kind, i.e., what it is for there to be an M-type causal chain. I shall not attempt to do the latter here. The notion of an M-type causal chain would of course be completely useless if it were impossible to determine in any particular case whether the causal connection is "of the right kind" without already having determined that the case is one of remembering – but I shall argue in section V that is not impossible.

18 In his paper "Bodily continuity and personal identity: a reply," *Analysis* 21 (1960), pp. 42–8), B. A. O. Williams says that "identity is a one–one relation, and… no principle can be a criterion of identity for things of type *T* if it relies on what is logically a one–many or many–many relation between things of type *T*," and remarks that the relation "being disposed to make sincere memory claims which exactly fit the life of" is a many–one relation and "hence cannot possibly be adequate in logic to constitute a criterion of identity" (pp. 44–5). Now it may seem that my version of the view that memory is a criterion of personal identity is open to the same objection, for if M-type causal chains can branch and coalesce, then the relation "has a quasi-memory which is linked by an M-type causal chain with a cognitive and sensory state of" is not logically a one–one relation. But while this relationship i s not logically one–one, the relationship "has a quasi-memory which is linked by a *non-branching* M-type causal chain with a cognitive and sensory state of" is logically one–one, and it is the holding of the latter relationship that I would hold to be a criterion, in the sense of being a sufficient condition, for personal identity.

19 A. N. Prior has defended the view that in cases of fission *both* offshoots can be identified with the original person, although not with each other. This of course involves modifying the usual account of the logical features of identity. See his "'Opposite number'" *Review of Metaphysics* 2

(1957), pp. 196–201 and his "Time, existence and identity," *Proceedings of the Aristotelian Society* (1965–6), pp. 183–92. Roderick Chisholm takes a very different view. Considering the supposition that "you knew that your body, like that of an amoeba, would one day undergo fission and that you would go off, so to speak, in two different directions," he says "it seems to me, first, that there is no possibility whatever that *you* would be *both* the person on the right and the person on the left. It seems to me, secondly that there *is* a possibility that you would be one or the other of those two persons" ("The loose and popular and the strict and philosophical senses of identity," in Norman S. Care and Robert H. Grimm (eds) *Perception and Personal Identity* (Cleveland: Press of Case Western Reserve University, 1969), p. 106). It is not clear to me whether Chisholm would hold that one (but not both) of the offshoots might be me if the memories of each stood in the same causal relationships to my actions and experiences as the memories of the other, and if each resembled me, in personality, appearance, etc. as much as the other. If so, I would disagree.

20 See Wiggins, *Identity and Spatio-Temporal Continuity*, p. 53, where such a case is discussed.

21 Joseph Butler, "Of personal identity," First Dissertation to the *Analogy of Religion*, repr. in J. Perry (ed.), *Personal Identity* (Berkeley and Los Angeles: University of California Press, 1975).

22 See A. J. Ayer, *The Problem of Knowledge* (Harmondsworth Penguin, 1956), p. 196, and B. A. O. Williams, "Personal identity and individuation," in *Problem of the Self* (Cambridge: Cambridge University Press, 1973), pp. 3–4.

23 See Williams, "Personal identity and individuation," pp. 4–5, and my "Personal identity and memory," pp. 869–70 and 877. In the latter, and in *Self-Knowledge and Self-Identity*, I attempted to reduce the force of this objection by arguing that it is a "conceptual truth" that memory claims are generally true, and that we can therefore be entitled to say that a person remembers a past event without already having established, or having inductive evidence, that some other criterion of personal identity (one not involving memory) is satisfied. This way of handling the objection no longer seems to me satisfactory.

24 See Squires's "Memory unchained."

25 Shoemaker, *Self-Knowledge and Self-Identity*, pp. 23–5 and 245–7.

26 In *Self-Knowledge and Self-Identity* I held that saying that Brownson is Brown would involve making a "decision" about the relative weights to be assigned to different criteria of personal identity, and that in the absence of such a decision

there is no right answer to the question whether Brownson is Brown. I have come to believe that there is a right answer to this question, namely that Brownson is Brown, and that my former view overlooked the importance of the causal component in the notion of memory (see my treatment of this example to "On knowing who one is").

27 On this and related questions, see my exchange with Chisholm in Care and Grimm (eds), *Perception and Personal Identity*, pp. 107–27.

28 This is not to deny the possibility or occurrence of unselfish attitudes and emotions. Even the most unselfish man, who is willing to suffer that others may prosper, does not and cannot regard the pleasures and pains that are in prospect for him in the same light as he regards those that are in prospect for others. He may submit to torture, but he would hardly be human if he could regularly view his own future sufferings with the same detachment (which is not indifference) as he views the future suffering of others.

41

The Self and the Future

Bernard Williams

[handwritten annotation: Because we attend to state the conditions for preserving personhood w/o defining personhood itself]

Suppose that there were some process to which two persons, *A* and *B*, could be subjected as a result of which they might be said — question-beggingly — to have *exchanged bodies*. That is to say – less question-beggingly – there is a certain human body which is such that when previously we were confronted with it, we were confronted with person *A*, certain utterances coming from it were expressive of memories of the past experiences of *A*, certain movements of it partly constituted the actions of *A* and were taken as expressive of the character of *A*, and so forth; but now, after the process is completed, utterances coming from this body are expressive of what seem to be just those memories which previously we identified as memories of the past experiences of *B*, its movements partly constitute actions expressive of the character of *B*, and so forth; and conversely with the other body.

There are certain important philosophical limitations on how such imaginary cases are to be constructed, and how they are to be taken when constructed in various ways. I shall mention two principal limitations, not in order to pursue them further here, but precisely in order to get them out of the way.

There are certain limitations, particularly with regard to character and mannerisms, to our ability to imagine such cases even in the most restricted sense of our being disposed to take the later performances of that body which was previously *A*'s as expressive of *B*'s character; if the previous *A* and *B* were extremely unlike one another both physically and psychologically, and if, say, in addition, they were of different sex, there might be grave difficulties in reading *B*'s dispositions in any possible performances of *A*'s body. Let us forget this, and for the present purpose just take *A* and *B* as being sufficiently alike (however alike that has to be) for the difficulty not to arise; after the experiment, persons familiar with *A* and *B* are just *overwhelmingly struck* by the *B*-ish character of the doings associated with what was previously *A*'s body, and conversely. Thus the feat of imagining an exchange of bodies is supposed possible in the most restricted sense. But now there is a further limitation which has to be overcome if the feat is to be not merely possible in the most restricted sense, but also is to have an outcome which, on serious reflection, we are prepared to describe as *A* and *B* having changed bodies – that is, an outcome where, confronted with what was previously *A*'s body, we are prepared seriously to say that we are now confronted with *B*.

Metaphysics: An Anthology, Second Edition. Edited by Jaegwon Kim, Daniel Z. Korman and Ernest Sosa.
Editorial material and organization © 2012 Blackwell Publishing Ltd. Published 2012 by Blackwell Publishing Ltd.

A-Body-Person = having B's mind

It would seem a necessary condition of so doing that the utterances coming from that body be taken as genuinely expressive of memories of B's past. But memory is a causal notion; and as we actually use it, it seems a necessary condition of x's present knowledge of x's earlier experiences constituting memory of those experiences that the causal chain linking the experiences and the knowledge should not run outside x's body. Hence if utterances coming from a given body are to be taken as expressive of memories of the experiences of B, there should be some suitable causal link between the appropriate state of the body and the original happening of those experiences to B. One radical way of securing that condition in the imagined exchange case is to suppose, with Shoemaker,[1] that the brains of A and of B are transposed. We may not need so radical a condition. Thus suppose it were possible to extract information from a man's brain and store it in a device while his brain was repaired, or even renewed, the information then being replaced: it would seem exaggerated to insist that the resultant man could not possibly have the memories he had before the operation. With regard to our knowledge of our own past, we draw distinctions between merely recalling, being reminded, and learning again, and those distinctions correspond (roughly) to distinctions between no new input, partial new input, and total new input with regard to the information in question; and it seems clear that the information-parking case just imagined would not count as new input in the sense necessary and sufficient for 'learning again'. Hence we can imagine the case we are concerned with in terms of information extracted into such devices from A's and B's brains and replaced in the other brain; this is the sort of model which, I think not unfairly for the present argument, I shall have in mind.

We imagine the following. The process considered above exists; two persons can enter some machine, let us say, and emerge changed in the appropriate ways. If A and B are the persons who enter, let us call the persons who emerge the A-body-person and the B-body-person: the A-body-person is that person (whoever it is) with whom I am confronted with, after the experiment, I am confronted with that body which previously was A's body – that is to say, that person who would naturally be taken for A by someone who just saw this person, was familiar with A's appearance before the experiment, and did not know about the happening of the experiment. A non-question-begging description of the experiment will leave it open which (if either) of the persons A and B the A-body-person is; the description of the experiment as 'persons changing bodies' of course implies that the A-body-person is actually B.

We take two persons A and B who are going to have the process carried out on them. (We can suppose, rather hazily, that they are willing for this to happen; to investigate at all closely at this stage why they might be willing or unwilling, what they would fear, and so forth, would anticipate some later issues.) We further announce that one of the two resultant persons, the A-body-person and the B-body-person, is going after the experiment to be given $100,000, while the other is going to be tortured. We then ask each of A and B to choose which treatment should be dealt out to which of the persons who will emerge from the experiment, the choice to be made (if it can be) on selfish grounds.

Suppose that A chooses that the B-body-person should get the pleasant treatment and the A-body-person the unpleasant treatment; and B chooses conversely (this might indicate that they thought that 'changing bodies' was indeed a good description of the outcome). The experimenter cannot act in accordance with both these sets of preferences, those expressed by A and those expressed by B. Hence there is one clear sense in which A and B cannot both get what they want: namely, that if the experimenter, before the experiment, announces to A and B that he intends to carry out the alternative (for example), of treating the B-body-person unpleasantly and the A-body-person pleasantly – then A can say rightly, 'That's not the outcome I chose to happen', and B can say rightly, 'That's just the outcome I chose to happen'. So, evidently, A and B before the experiment can each come to know either that the outcome he chose will be that which will happen, or that the one he chose will not happen, and in that sense they can get or fail to get what they wanted. But is it also true that when the experimenter proceeds after the experiment to act in accordance with one of the preferences and not the other, then one of A and B will have got what he wanted, and the other not?

"download" info from A + B, then upload A into B + vice versa

There seems very good ground for saying so. For suppose the experimenter, having elicited A's and B's preference, says nothing to A and B about what he will do; conducts the experiment; and then, for example, gives the unpleasant treatment to the B-body-person and the pleasant treatment to the A-body-person. Then the B-body-person will not only complain of the unpleasant treatment as such, but will complain (since he has A's memories) that that was not the outcome he chose, since he chose that the B-body-person should be well treated; and since A made his choice in selfish spirit, he may add that he precisely chose in that way because he did not want the unpleasant things to happen to *him*. The A-body-person meanwhile will express satisfaction both at the receipt of the $100,000, and also at the fact that the experimenter has chosen to act in the way that he, B, so wisely chose. These facts make a strong case for saying that the experimenter has brought it about that B did in the outcome get what he wanted and A did not. It is therefore a strong case for saying that the B-body-person really is A, and the A-body-person really is B; and therefore for saying that the process of the experiment really is that of changing bodies. For the same reasons it would seem that A and B in our example really did choose wisely, and that it was A's bad luck that the choice he correctly made was not carried out, B's good luck that the choice he correctly made was carried out. This seems to show that to care about what happens to me in the future is not necessarily to care about what happens to *this* body (the one I now have); and this in turn might be taken to show that in some sense of Descartes's obscure phrase, I and my body are 'really distinct' (though, of course, nothing in these considerations could support the idea that I could exist without a body at all).

These suggestions seem to be reinforced if we consider the cases where A and B make other choices with regard to the experiment. Suppose that A chooses that the A-body-person should get the money, and the B-body-person get the pain, and B chooses conversely. Here again there can be no outcome which matches the expressed preferences of both of them: they cannot both get what they want. The experimenter announces, before the experiment, that the A-body-person will in fact get the money, and the B-body-person will get the pain. So A at this stage gets what he wants (the announced outcome matches his expressed preference). After the experiment, the distribution is carried out as announced. Both the A-body-person and the B-body-person will have to agree that what is happening is in accordance with the preference that A originally expressed. The B-body-person will naturally express this acknowledgement (since he has A's memories) by saying that this is the distribution he chose; he will recall, among other things, the experimenter announcing this outcome, his approving it as what he chose, and so forth. However, he (the B-body-person) certainly does not like what is now happening to him, and would much prefer to be receiving what the A-body-person is receiving – namely, $100,000. The A-body-person will on the other hand recall choosing an outcome other than this one, but will reckon it good luck that the experimenter did not do what he recalls choosing. It looks, then, as though the A-body-person has got what he wanted, but not what he chose, while the B-body-person has got what he chose, but not what he wanted. So once more it looks as though they are, respectively, B and A; and that in this case the original choices of both A and B were unwise.

Suppose, lastly, that in the original choice A takes the line of the first case and B of the second: that is, A chooses that the B-body-person should get the money and the A-body-person the pain, and B chooses exactly the same thing. In this case, the experimenter would seem to be in the happy situation of giving both persons what they want – or at least, like God, what they have chosen. In this case, the B-body-person likes what he is receiving, recalls choosing it, and congratulates himself on the wisdom of (as he puts it) his choice; while the A-body-person does not like what he is receiving, recalls choosing it, and is forced to acknowledge that (as he puts it) his choice was unwise. So once more we seem to get results to support the suggestions drawn from the first case.

Let us now consider the question, not of A and B choosing certain outcomes to take place after the experiment, but of their willingness to engage in the experiment at all. If they were initially inclined to accept the description of the experiment as 'changing bodies', then one thing that would interest them would be the character of the other person's body. In this respect also, what would happen after the experiment would seem to suggest that 'changing bodies' was a good description of the experiment. If A and B agreed to the experiment, being each not displeased with the appearance, physique, and so forth of the other person's body; after the experiment the B-body-person might well be found saying such things as: 'When I agreed to this experiment, I thought that B's face was quite attractive, but now I look at it in the mirror, I am not so sure'; or the A-body-person might say, 'When I agreed to this experiment, I did not know that A had a wooden leg; but now, after it is over, I find that I have this wooden leg, and I want the experiment reversed.' It is possible that he might say further that he finds the leg very uncomfortable, and that the B-body-person should say, for instance, that he recalls that he found it very uncomfortable at first, but one gets used to it: but perhaps one would need to know more than at least I do about the physiology of habituation to artificial limbs to know whether the A-body-person would find the leg uncomfortable: that body, after all, has had the leg on it for some time. But apart from this sort of detail, the general line of the outcome regarded from this point of view seems to confirm our previous conclusions about the experiment.

Now let us suppose that when the experiment is proposed (in non-question-begging terms) A and B think rather of their psychological advantages and disadvantages. A's thoughts turn primarily to certain sorts of anxiety to which he is very prone, while B is concerned with the frightful memories he has of past experiences which still distress him. They each hope that the experiment will in some way result in their being able to get away from these things. They may even have been impressed by philosophical arguments to the effect that bodily continuity is at least a necessary condition of personal identity: A, for example, reasons that, granted the experiment comes off, then the person who is bodily continuous with him will not have this anxiety, and while the other person will no doubt have some anxiety – perhaps in some sense his anxiety – at least that person will not be he. The experiment is performed, and the experimenter (to whom A and B previously revealed privately their several difficulties and hopes) asks the A-body-person whether he has got rid of his anxiety. This person presumably replies that he does not know what the man is talking about; he never had such anxiety, but he did have some very disagreeable memories, and recalls engaging in the experiment to get rid of them, and is disappointed to discover that he still has them. The B-body-person will react in a similar way to questions about his painful memories, pointing out that he still has his anxiety. These results seem to confirm still further the description of the experiment as 'changing bodies'. And all the results suggest that the only rational thing to do, confronted with such an experiment, would be to identify oneself with one's memories, and so forth, and not with one's body. The philosophical arguments designed to show that bodily continuity was at least a necessary condition of personal identity would seem to be just mistaken.

Let us now consider something apparently different. Someone in whose power I am tells me that I am going to be tortured tomorrow. I am frightened, and look forward to tomorrow in great apprehension. He adds that when the time comes, I shall not remember being told that this was going to happen to me, since shortly before the torture something else will be done to me which will make me forget the announcement. This certainly will not cheer me up, since I know perfectly well that I can forget things, and that there is such a thing as indeed being tortured unexpectedly because I had forgotten or been made to forget a prediction of the torture: that will still be a torture which, so long as I do know about the prediction, I look forward to in fear. He then adds that my forgetting the announcement will be only part of a larger process: when the moment of torture comes, I shall not remember any of the things I am now in a position to remember. This does not cheer me up, either, since I can readily conceive of being involved in an accident, for instance, as a result of which I wake up in a completely amnesiac state and also in great pain; that could certainly happen to me, I should not like it to happen to me, nor to know that it was going to happen to me. He now further adds that at the moment of torture I shall not only not remember the things I am now in a position to remember, but will have a different set of impressions of my past, quite different from the memories I now have. I do not think that this would cheer me up, either. For I can at least conceive the possibility, if not the concrete reality,

The intuition is that, because the prospect of future bodily harm to a body continuous w/ ours, shows a link between personal identity + our bodies

of going completely mad, and thinking perhaps that I am George IV or somebody; and being told that something like that was going to happen to me would have no tendency to reduce the terror of being told authoritatively that I was going to be tortured, but would merely compound the horror. Nor do I see why I should be put into any better frame of mind by the person in charge adding lastly that the impressions of my past with which I shall be equipped on the eve of torture will exactly fit the past of another person now living, and that indeed I shall acquire these impressions by (for instance) information now in his brain being copied into mine. Fear, surely, would still be the proper reaction: and not because one did not know what was going to happen, but because in one vital respect at least one did know what was going to happen – torture, which one can indeed expect to happen to oneself, and to be preceded by certain mental derangements as well.

If this is right, the whole question seems now to be totally mysterious. For what we have just been through is of course merely one side, differently represented, of the transaction which we considered before; and it represents it as a perfectly hateful prospect, while the previous considerations represented it as something one should rationally, perhaps even cheerfully, choose out of the options there presented. It is differently presented, of course, and in two notable respects; but when we look at these two differences of presentation, can we really convince ourselves that the second presentation is wrong or misleading, thus leaving the road open to the first version which at the time seemed so convincing? Surely not.

The first difference is that in the second version the torture is throughout represented as going to happen to *me*: 'you', the man in charge persistently says. Thus he is not very neutral. But should he have been neutral? Or, to put it another way, does his use of the second person have a merely emotional and rhetorical effect on me, making me afraid when further reflection would have shown that I had no reason to be? It is certainly not obviously so. The problem just is that through every step of his predictions I seem to be able to follow him successfully. And if I reflect on whether what he has said gives me grounds for fearing that I shall be tortured, I could consider that behind my fears lies some principle such as this: that my undergoing physical pain in the future is not

excluded by any psychological state I may be in at the time, with the platitudinous exception of those psychological states which in themselves exclude experiencing pain, notably (if it is a psychological state) unconsciousness. In particular, what impressions I have about the past will not have any effect on whether I undergo the pain or not. This principle seems sound enough.

It is an important fact that not everything I would, as things are, regard as an evil would be something that I should rationally fear as an evil if it were predicted that it would happen to me in the future and also predicted that I should undergo significant psychological changes in the meantime. For the fact that I regard that happening, things being as they are, as an evil can be dependent on factors of belief or character which might themselves be modified by the psychological changes in question. Thus if I am appallingly subject to acrophobia, and am told that I shall find myself on top of a steep mountain in the near future, I shall to that extent be afraid; but if I am told that I shall be psychologically changed in the meantime in such a way as to rid me of my acrophobia (and as with the other prediction, I believe it), then I have no reason to be afraid of the predicted happening, or at least not the same reason. Again, I might look forward to meeting a certain person again with either alarm or excitement because of my memories of our past relations. In some part, these memories operate in connection with my emotion, not only on the present time, but projectively forward: for it is to a meeting itself affected by the presence of those memories that I look forward. If I am convinced that when the time comes I shall not have those memories, then I shall not have just the same reasons as before for looking forward to that meeting with the one emotion or the other. (Spiritualism, incidentally, appears to involve the belief that I have just the same reasons for a given attitude toward encountering people again after I am dead, as I did before: with the one modification that I can be sure it will all be very nice.)

Physical pain, however, the example which for simplicity (and not for any obsessional reason) I have taken, is absolutely minimally dependent on character or belief. No amount of change in my character or my beliefs would seem to affect substantially the nastiness of tortures applied to me; correspondingly, no degree of predicted change in my character and beliefs can unseat the fear of torture which, together with those changes, is predicted for me.

I am not at all suggesting that the *only* basis, or indeed the only rational basis, for fear in the face of these various predictions is how things will be relative to my psychological state in the eventual outcome. I am merely pointing out that this is one component; it is not the only one. For certainly one will fear and otherwise reject the changes themselves, or in very many cases one would. Thus one of the old paradoxes of hedonistic utilitarianism; if one had assurances that undergoing certain operations and being attached to a machine would provide one for the rest of one's existence with an unending sequence of delicious and varied experiences, one might very well reject the option, and react with fear if someone proposed to apply it compulsorily; and that fear and horror would seem appropriate reactions in the second case may help to discredit the interpretation (if anyone has the nerve to propose it) that one's reason for rejecting the option voluntarily would be a consciousness of duties to others which one in one's hedonic state would leave undone. The prospect of contented madness or vegetableness is found by many (not perhaps by all) appalling in ways which are obviously not a function of how things would then be for them, for things would then be for them not appalling. In the case we are at present discussing, these sorts of considerations seem merely to make it clearer that the predictions of the man in charge provide a double ground of horror: at the prospect of torture, and at the prospect of the change in character and in impressions of the past that will precede it. And certainly, to repeat what has already been said, the prospect of the second certainly seems to provide no ground for rejecting or not fearing the prospect of the first.

I said that there were two notable differences between the second presentation of our situation and the first. The first difference, which we have just said something about, was that the man predicted the torture for *me*, a psychologically very changed 'me'. We have yet to find a reason for saying that he should not have done this, or that I really should be unable to follow him if he does; I seem to be able to follow him only too well. The second difference is that in this presentation he does not mention the other man, except in the somewhat incidental role of being the provenance of the impressions of the past I end up with. He does not mention him at all as someone who will end up with impressions of the past derived from me (and, incidentally, with $100,000 as well – a consideration which, in the frame of mind appropriate to this version, will merely make me jealous).

But why *should* he mention this man and what is going to happen to him? My selfish concern is to be told what is going to happen to me, and now I know: torture, preceded by changes of character, brain operations, changes in impressions of the past. The knowledge that one other person, or none, or many will be similarly mistreated may affect me in other ways, of sympathy, greater horror at the power of this tyrant, and so forth; but surely it cannot affect my expectations of torture? But – someone will say – this is to leave out exactly the feature which, as the first presentation of the case showed, makes all the difference: for it is to leave out the person who, as the first presentation showed, will be you. It is to leave out not merely a feature which should fundamentally affect your fears, it is to leave out the very person for whom you are fearful. So of course, the objector will say, this makes all the difference.

But can it? Consider the following series of cases. In each case we are to suppose that after what is described, A is, as before, to be tortured; we are also to suppose the person A is informed beforehand that just these things followed by the torture will happen to him:

(i)   A is subjected to an operation which produces total amnesia;

(ii) amnesia is produced in A, and other interference leads to certain changes in his character;

(iii) changes in his character are produced, and at the same time certain illusory 'memory' beliefs are induced in him: these are of a quite fictitious kind and do not fit the life of any actual person;

(iv) the same as (iii), except that both the character traits and the 'memory' impressions are designed to be appropriate to another actual person, B;

(v)   the same as (iv), except that the result is produced by putting the information into

A from the brain of *B*, by a method which leaves *B* the same as he was before;

(vi) the same happens to *A* as in (v), but *B* is not left the same, since a similar operation is conducted in the reverse direction.

I take it that no one is going to dispute that *A* has reasons, and fairly straightforward reasons, for fear of pain when the prospect is that of situation (i); there seems no conceivable reason why this should not extend to situation (ii), and the situation (iii) can surely introduce no difference of principle – it just seems a situation which for more than one reason we should have grounds for fearing, as suggested above. Situation (iv) at least introduces the person *B*, who was the focus of the objection we are now discussing. But it does not seem to introduce him in any way which makes a material difference; if I can expect pain through a transformation which involves new 'memory'-impressions, it would seem a purely external fact, relative to that, that the 'memory'-impressions had a model. Nor, in (iv), do we satisfy a causal condition which I mentioned at the beginning for the 'memories' actually being memories; though notice that if the job were done thoroughly, I might well be able to elicit from the *A*-body-person the kinds of remarks about his previous expectations of the experiment – remarks appropriate to the original *B* – which so impressed us in the first version of the story. I shall have a similar assurance of this being so in situation (v), where, moreover, a plausible application of the causal condition is available.

But two things are to be noticed about this situation. First, if we concentrate on *A* and the *A*-body-person, we do not seem to have added anything which from the point of view of his fears makes any material difference; just as, in the move from (iii) to (iv), it made no relevant difference that the new 'memory'-impressions which precede the pain had, as it happened, a model, so in the move from (iv) to (v) all we have added is that they have a model which is also their cause: and it is still difficult to see why that, to him looking forward, could possibly make the difference between expecting pain and not expecting pain. To illustrate that point from the case of character: if *A* is capable of expecting pain, he is capable of expecting pain preceded by a change in his dispositions – and to that expectation it can

make no difference, whether that change in his dispositions is modelled on, or indeed indirectly caused by, the dispositions of some other person. If his fears can, as it were, reach through the change, it seems a mere trimming how the change is in fact induced. The second point about situation (v) is that if the crucial question for *A*'s fears with regard to what befalls the *A*-body-person is whether the *A*-body-person is or is not the person *B*,[2] then that condition has not yet been satisfied in situation (v): for there we have an undisputed *B* in addition to the *A*-body-person, and certainly those two are not the same person.

But in situation (vi), we seemed to think, that is finally what he is. But if *A*'s original fears could reach through the expected changes in (v), as they did in (iv) and (iii), then certainly they can reach through in (vi). Indeed, from the point of view of *A*'s expectations and fears, there is less difference between (vi) and (v) than there is between (v) and (iv) or between (iv) and (iii). In those transitions, there were at least differences – though we could not see that they were really relevant differences – in the content or cause of what happened to him; in the present case there is absolutely no difference at all in what happens to him, the only difference being in what happens to someone else. If he can fear pain when (v) is predicted, why should he cease to when (vi) is?

I can see only one way of relevantly laying great weight on the transition from (v) to (vi); and this involves a considerable difficulty. This is to deny that, as I put it, the transition from (v) to (vi) involves merely the addition of something happening to *somebody else*; what rather it does, it will be said, is to involve the reintroduction of *A* himself, as the *B*-body-person; since he has reappeared in this form, it is for this person, and not for the unfortunate *A*-body-person, that *A* will have his expectations. This is to reassert, in effect, the viewpoint emphasized in our first presentation of the experiment. But this surely has the consequence that *A* should not have fears for the *A*-body-person who appeared in situation (v). For by the present argument, the *A*-body-person in (vi) is not *A*; the *B*-body-person is. But the *A*-body-person in (v) is, in character, history, everything, exactly the same as the *A*-body-person in (vi); so if the latter is not *A*, then neither is the former. (It is this point, no doubt, that encourages one to speak of the difference that goes with (vi) as being, on the present view, the *reintroduction* of *A*.) But no one else in (v) has any better claim to be *A*. So in (v), it seems, *A* just does not exist. This would certainly explain why A should have no fears for the state of things in (v) – though he might well have fears for the path to it. But it rather looked earlier as though he could well have fears for the state of things in (v). Let us grant, however, that that was an illusion, and that A really does not exist in (v); then does he exist in (iv), (iii), (ii), or (i)? It seems very difficult to deny it for (i) and (ii); are we perhaps to draw the line between (iii) and (iv)?

Here someone will say: you must not insist on drawing a line – borderline cases are borderline cases, and you must not push our concepts beyond their limits. But this well-known piece of advice, sensible as it is in many cases, seems in the present case to involve an extraordinary difficulty. It may intellectually comfort observers of *A*'s situation; but what is *A* supposed to make of it? To be told that a future situation is a borderline one for its being myself that is hurt, that it is conceptually undecidable whether it will be me or not, is something which, it seems, I can do nothing with; because, in particular, it seems to have no comprehensible representation in my expectations and the emotions that go with them.

If I expect that a certain situation, *S*, will come about in the future, there is of course a wide range of emotions and concerns, directed on *S*, which I may experience now in relation to my expectation. Unless I am exceptionally egoistic, it is not a condition on my being concerned in relation to this expectation, that I myself will be involved in *S* – where my being 'involved' in *S* means that I figure in *S* as someone doing something at that time or having something done to me, or, again, that *S* will have consequences affecting me at that or some subsequent time. There are some emotions, however, which I will feel only if I will be involved in *S*, and fear is an obvious example.

Now the description of *S* under which it figures in my expectations will necessarily be, in various ways, indeterminate; and one way in which it may be indeterminate is that it leaves open whether I shall be involved in *S* or not. Thus I may have good reason to expect that one of us five is going to get hurt, but no reason to expect it to be me rather than one of the others. My present emotions will be correspondingly affected by this indeterminacy. Thus, sticking to the egoistic concern involved in

fear, I shall presumably be somewhat more cheerful than if I knew it was going to be me, somewhat less cheerful than if I had been left out altogether. Fear will be mixed with, and qualified by, apprehension; and so forth. These emotions revolve around the thought of the eventual determination of the indeterminacy; moments of straight fear focus on its really turning out to be me, of hope on its turning out not to be me. All the emotions are related to the coming about of what I expect: and what I expect in such a case just cannot come about save by coming about in one of the ways or another.

There are other ways in which indeterminate expectations can be related to fear. Thus I may expect (perhaps neurotically) that something nasty is going to happen to me, indeed expect that when it happens, it will take some determinate form, but have no range, or no closed range, of candidates for the determinate form to rehearse in my present thought. Different from this would be the fear of something radically indeterminate – the fear (one might say) of a nameless horror. If somebody had such a fear, one could even say that he had, in a sense, a perfectly determinate expectation: if what he expects indeed comes about, there will be nothing more determinate to be said about it after the event than was said in the expectation. Both these cases of course are cases of *fear* because one thing that is fixed amid the indeterminacy is the belief that it is me to whom the things will happen.

Central to the expectation of *S* is the thought of what it will be like when it happens – thought which may be indeterminate, range over alternatives, and so forth. When *S* involves me, there can be the possibility of a special form of such thought: the thought of how it will be for me, the imaginative projection of myself as participant in *S*.[3] I do not have to think about *S* in this way, when it involves me; but I may be able to. (It might be suggested that this possibility was even mirrored in the language, in the distinction between 'expecting to be hurt' and 'expecting that I shall be hurt'; but I am very doubtful about this point, which is in any case of no importance.)

Suppose now that there is an *S* with regard to which it is for conceptual reasons undecidable whether it involves me or not, as is proposed for the experimental situation by the line we are discussing. It is important that the expectation of *S* is not *indeterminate* in any of the ways we have just been considering. It is not like the nameless horror, since the fixed point of that case was that it was going to happen to the subject, and that made his state unequivocally fear. Nor is it like the expectation of the man who expects one of the five to be hurt; his fear was indeed equivocal, but its focus, and that of the expectation, was that when S came about, it would certainly come about in one way or the other. In the present case, fear (of the torture, that is to say, not of the initial experiment) seems neither appropriate, nor inappropriate, nor appropriately equivocal. Relatedly, the subject has an incurable difficulty about how he may think about S. If he engages in projective imaginative thinking (about how it will be for him), he implicitly answers the necessarily unanswerable question; if he thinks that he cannot engage in such thinking, it looks very much as if he also answers it, though in the opposite direction. Perhaps he must just refrain from such thinking; but is he just refraining from it, if it is incurably undecidable whether he can or cannot engage in it?

It may be said that all that these considerations can show is that fear, at any rate, does not get its proper footing in this case; but that there could be some other, more ambivalent, form of concern which would indeed be appropriate to this particular expectation, the expectation of the conceptually undecidable situation. There are, perhaps, analogous feelings that actually occur in actual situations. Thus material objects do occasionally undergo puzzling transformations which leave a conceptual shadow over their identity. Suppose I were sentimentally attached to an object to which this sort of thing then happened; it might be that I could neither feel about it quite as I did originally, nor be totally indifferent to it, but would have some other and rather ambivalent feeling towards it. Similarly, it may be said, toward the prospective sufferer of pain, my identity relations with whom are conceptually shadowed, I can feel neither as I would if he were certainly me, nor as I would if he were certainly not, but rather some such ambivalent concern.

But this analogy does little to remove the most baffling aspect of the present case – an aspect which has already turned up in what was said about the subject's difficulty in thinking either projectively or non-projectively about the situation. For to regard the prospective pain-sufferer *just* like the transmogrified object of sentiment, and to conceive of my ambivalent distress about his future pain as just like ambivalent distress about some future damage to such an object, is of course to leave him and me clearly distinct from one another, and thus to displace the conceptual shadow from its proper place. I have to get nearer to him than that. But is there any nearer that I can get to him without expecting his pain? If there is, the analogy has not shown us it. We can certainly not get nearer by expecting, as it were, *ambivalent* pain; there is no place at all for that. There seems to be an obstinate bafflement to mirroring in my expectations a situation in which it is conceptually undecidable whether I occur.

The bafflement seems, moreover, to turn to plain absurdity if we move from conceptual undecidability to its close friend and neighbour, conventionalist decision. This comes out if we consider another description, overtly conventionalist, of the series of cases which occasioned the present discussion. This description would reject a point I relied on in an earlier argument – namely, that if we deny that the A-body-person in (vi) is A (because the B-body-person is), then we must deny that the A-body-person in (v) is A, since they are exactly similar. 'No', it may be said, 'this is just to assume that we say the same in different sorts of situation. No doubt when we have the very good candidate for being A – namely, the B-body-person – we call him A; but this does not mean that we should not call the A-body-person A in that other situation when we have no better candidate around. Different situations call for different descriptions.' This line of talk is the sort of thing indeed appropriate to lawyers deciding the ownership of some property which has undergone some bewildering set of transformations; they just have to decide, and in each situation, let us suppose, it has got to go to somebody, on as reasonable grounds as the facts and the law admit. But as a line to deal with a person's fears or expectations about his own future, it seems to have no sense at all. If A's fears can extend to what will happen to the A-body-person in (v), I do not see how they can be rationally diverted from the fate of the exactly similar person in (vi) by his being told that someone would have a reason in the latter situation which he would not have in the former for deciding to call another person A.

Thus, to sum up, it looks as though there are two presentations of the imagined experiment and the choice associated with it, each of which carries conviction, and which lead to contrary conclusions. The idea, moreover, that the situation after the experiment is conceptually undecidable in the relevant respect seems not to assist, but rather to increase, the puzzlement; while the idea (so often appealed to in these matters) that it is conventionally decidable is even worse. Following from all that, I am not in the least clear which option it would be wise to take if one were presented with them before the experiment. I find that rather disturbing.

Whatever the puzzlement, there is one feature of the arguments which have led to it which is worth picking out, since it runs counter to something which is, I think, often rather vaguely supposed. It is often recognized that there are 'first-personal' and 'third-personal' aspects of questions about persons, and that there are difficulties about the relations between them. It is also recognized that 'mentalistic' considerations (as we may vaguely call them) and considerations of bodily continuity are involved in questions of personal identity (which is not to say that there are mentalistic and bodily criteria of personal identity). It is tempting to think that the two distinctions run in parallel: roughly, that a first-person approach concentrates attention on mentalistic considerations, while a third-personal approach emphasizes considerations of bodily continuity. The present discussion is an illustration of exactly the opposite. The first argument, which led to the 'mentalistic' conclusion that A and B would change bodies and that each person should identify himself with the destination of his memories and character, was an an argument entirely conducted in third-personal terms. The second argument, which suggested the bodily continuity identification, concerned itself with the first-personal issue of what A could expect. That this is so seems to me (though I will not discuss it further here) of some significance.

I will end by suggesting one rather shaky way in which one might approach a resolution of the problem, using only the limited materials already available.

The apparently decisive arguments of the first presentation, which suggested that A should identify himself with the B-body-person, turned on the extreme neatness of the situation in satisfying, if any could, the description of 'changing bodies'. But this neatness is basically artificial; it is the product of the will of the experimenter to produce a situation which would naturally elicit, with minimum hesitation, that description. By the sorts of methods he employed, he could easily have left off earlier or gone on further. He could have stopped at situation (v), leaving B as he was; or he could have gone on and produced two persons each with A-like character and memories, as well as one or two with B-like characteristics. If he had done either of those, we should have been in yet greater difficulty about what to say; he just chose to make it as easy as possible for us to find something to say. Now if we had some model of ghostly persons in bodies, which were in some sense actually moved around by certain procedures, we could regard the neat experiment just as the *effective* experiment: the one method that really did result in the ghostly persons' changing places without being destroyed, dispersed, or whatever. But we cannot seriously use such a model. The experimenter has not in the sense of that model *induced* a change of bodies; he has rather produced the one situation out of a range of equally possible situations which we should be most disposed to call a change of bodies. As against this, the principle that one's fears can extend to future pain whatever psychological changes precede it seems positively straightforward. Perhaps, indeed, it is not; but we need to be shown what is wrong with it. Until we are shown what is wrong with it, we should perhaps decide that if we were the person A then, if we were to decide selfishly, we should pass the pain to the B-body-person. It would be risky: that there is room for the notion of a *risk* here is itself a major feature of the problem.

Notes

1 Sydney Shoemaker, *Self-Knowledge and Self-Identity* (Ithaca, NY: Cornell University Press, 1963), pp. 23ff.

2 This of course does not have to be the crucial question, but it seems one fair way of taking up the present objection.

3 For a more detailed treatment of issues related to this, see 'Imagination and the self', in Bernard Williams, *Problems of the Self* (Cambridge: Cambridge University Press, 1973), pp. 38ff.

42

Personal Identity

Derek Parfit

We can, I think, describe cases in which, though we know the answer to every other question, we have no idea how to answer a question about personal identity. These cases are not covered by the criteria of personal identity that we actually use.

Do they present a problem?

It might be thought that they do not, because they could never occur. I suspect that some of them could. (Some, for instance, might become scientifically possible.) But I shall claim that even if they did, they would present no problem.

My targets are two beliefs: one about the nature of personal identity, the other about its importance.

The first is that in these cases the question about identity must have an answer.

No one thinks this about, say, nations or machines. Our criteria for the identity of these do not cover certain cases. No one thinks that in these cases the questions "Is it the same nation?" or "Is it the same machine?" must have answers.

Some people believe that in this respect they are different. They agree that our criteria of personal identity do not cover certain cases, but they believe that the nature of their own identity through time is, somehow, such as to guarantee that in these cases questions about their identity must have answers. This belief might be expressed as follows: "Whatever happens between now and any future time, either I shall still exist, or I shall not. Any future experience will either be *my* experience, or it will not."

This first belief – in the special nature of personal identity – has, I think, certain effects. It makes people assume that the principle of self-interest is more rationally compelling than any moral principle. And it makes them more depressed by the thought of aging and of death.

I cannot see how to disprove this first belief. I shall describe a problem case. But this can only make it seem implausible.

Another approach might be this. We might suggest that one cause of the belief is the projection of our emotions. When we imagine ourselves in a problem case, we do feel that the question "Would it be me?" must have an answer. But what we take to be a bafflement about a further fact may be only the bafflement of our concern.

I shall not pursue this suggestion here. But one cause of our concern is the belief which is my second target. This is that unless the question about identity has an answer, we cannot answer

Derek Parfit, "Personal Identity." In the public domain. Currently published by Duke University Press.

Metaphysics: An Anthology, Second Edition. Edited by Jaegwon Kim, Daniel Z. Korman and Ernest Sosa.
Editorial material and organization © 2012 Blackwell Publishing Ltd. Published 2012 by Blackwell Publishing Ltd.

certain important questions (questions about such matters as survival, memory and responsibility).

Against this second belief my claim will be this. Certain important questions do presuppose a question about personal identity. But they can be freed of this presupposition. And when they are, the question about identity has no importance.

I

We can start by considering the much discussed case of the man who, like an amoeba, divides.[1]

Wiggins has recently dramatized this case.[2] He first referred to the operation imagined by Shoemaker.[3] We suppose that my brain is transplanted into someone else's (brainless) body, and that the resulting person has my character and apparent memories of my life. Most of us would agree, after thought, that the resulting person is me. I shall here assume such agreement.[4]

Wiggins then imagined his own operation. My brain is divided, and each half is housed in a new body. Both resulting people have my character and apparent memories of my life.

What happens to me? There seem only three possibilities: (1) I do not survive; (2) I survive as one of the two people; (3) I survive as both.

The trouble with (1) is this. We agreed that I could survive if my brain were successfully transplanted. And people have in fact survived with half their brains destroyed. It seems to follow that I could survive if half my brain were successfully transplanted and the other half were destroyed. But if this is so, how could I *not* survive if the other half were also successfully transplanted? How could a double success be a failure?

We can move to the second description. Perhaps one success is the maximum score. Perhaps I shall be one of the resulting people.

The trouble here is that in Wiggins's case each half of my brain is exactly similar, and so, to start with, is each resulting person. So how can I survive as only one of the two people? What can make me one of them rather than the other?

It seems clear that both of these descriptions – that I do not survive, and that I survive as one of the people – are highly implausible. Those who have accepted them must have assumed that they were the only possible descriptions.

What about our third description: that I survive as both people?

It might be said, "If 'survive' implies identity, this description makes no sense – you cannot be two people. If it does not, the description is irrelevant to a problem about identity."

I shall later deny the second of these remarks. But there are ways of denying the first. We might say, "What we have called 'the two resulting people' are not two people. They are one person. I do survive Wiggins's operation. Its effect is to give me two bodies and a divided mind."

It would shorten my argument if this were absurd. But I do not think it is. It is worth showing why.

We can, I suggest, imagine a divided mind. We can imagine a man having two simultaneous experiences, in having each of which he is unaware of having the other.

We may not even need to imagine this. Certain actual cases, to which Wiggins referred, seem to be best described in these terms. These involve the cutting of the bridge between the hemispheres of the brain. The aim was to cure epilepsy. But the result appears to be, in the surgeon's words, the creation of "two separate spheres of consciousness,"[5] each of which controls one half of the patient's body. What is experienced in each is, presumably, experienced by the patient.

There are certain complications in these actual cases. So let us imagine a simpler case.

Suppose that the bridge between my hemispheres is brought under my voluntary control. This would enable me to disconnect my hemispheres as easily as if I were blinking. By doing this, I would divide my mind. And we can suppose that when my mind is divided, I can, in each half, bring about reunion.

This ability would have obvious uses. To give an example: I am near the end of a maths exam, and see two ways of tackling the last problem. I decide to divide my mind, to work, with each half, at one of two calculations, and then to reunite my mind and write a fair copy of the best result.

What shall I experience?

When I disconnect my hemispheres, my consciousness divides into two streams. But this division is not something that I experience. Each of my two streams of consciousness seems to have been straightforwardly continuous with my one stream of consciousness up to the moment of division. The only changes in each stream are the disappearance of half my visual field and the loss of sensation in, and control over, half my body.

Consider my experiences in what we can call my "right-handed" stream. I remember that I assigned my right hand to the longer calculation. This I now begin. In working at this calculation I can see, from the movements of my left hand, that I am also working at the other. But I am not aware of working at the other. So I might, in my right-handed stream, wonder how, in my left-handed stream, I am getting on.

My work is now over. I am about to reunite my mind. What should I, in each stream, expect? Simply that I shall suddenly seem to remember just having thought out two calculations, in thinking out each of which I was not aware of thinking out the other. This, I submit, we can imagine. And if my mind was divided, these memories are correct.

In describing this episode, I assumed that there were two series of thoughts, and that they were both mine. If my two hands visibly wrote out two calculations, and if I claimed to remember two corresponding series of thoughts, this is surely what we should want to say.

If it is, then a person's mental history need not be like a canal, with only one channel. It could be like a river, with islands, and with separate streams.

To apply this to Wiggins's operation: we mentioned the view that it gives me two bodies and a divided mind. We cannot now call this absurd. But it is, I think, unsatisfactory.

There were two features of the case of the exam that made us want to say that only one person was involved. The mind was soon reunited, and there was only one body. If a mind was permanently divided and its halves developed in different ways, the point of speaking of one person would start to disappear. Wiggins's case, where there are also two bodies, seems to be over the borderline. After I have had his operation, the two "products" each have all the attributes of a person. They could live at opposite ends of the earth. (If they later met, they might even fail to recognize each other.) It would become intolerable to deny that they were different people.

Suppose we admit that they are different people. Could we still claim that I survived as both, using "survive" to imply identity?

We could. For we might suggest that two people could compose a third. We might say, "I do survive Wiggins's operation as two people. They can be different people, and yet be me, in just the way in which the Pope's three crowns are one crown."[6]

This is a possible way of giving sense to the claim that I survive as two different people, using "survive" to imply identity. But it keeps the language of identity only by changing the concept of a person. And there are obvious objections to this change.[7]

The alternative, for which I shall argue, is to give up the language of identity. We can suggest that I survive as two different people without implying that I am these people.

When I first mentioned this alternative, I mentioned this objection: "If your new way of talking does not imply identity, it cannot solve our problem. For that is about identity. The problem is that all the possible answers to the question about identity are highly implausible."

We can now answer this objection.

We can start by reminding ourselves that this is an objection only if we have one or both of the beliefs which I mentioned at the start of this paper.

The first was the belief that to any question about personal identity, in any describable case, there must be a true answer. For those with this belief, Wiggins's case is doubly perplexing. If all the possible answers are implausible, it is hard to decide which of them is true, and hard even to keep the belief that one of them must be true. If we give up this belief, as I think we should, these problems disappear. We shall then regard the case as like many others in which, for quite unpuzzling reasons, there *is* no answer to a question about identity. (Consider "Was England the same nation after 1066?")

Wiggins's case makes the first belief implausible. It also makes it trivial. For it undermines the second belief. This was the belief that important questions turn upon the question about identity. (It is worth pointing out that those who have only this second belief do not think that there must *be* an answer to this question, but rather that we must decide upon an answer.)

Against this second belief my claim is this. Certain questions do presuppose a question about personal identity. And because these questions *are* important, Wiggins's case does present a problem.

But we cannot solve this problem by answering the question about identity. We can solve this problem only by taking these important questions and prizing them apart from the question about identity. After we have done this, the question about identity (though we might for the sake of neatness decide it) has no further interest.

Because there are several questions which presuppose identity, this claim will take some time to fill out.

We can first return to the question of survival. This is a special case, for survival does not so much presuppose the retaining of identity as seem equivalent to it. It is thus the general relation which we need to prize apart from identity. We can then consider particular relations, such as those involved in memory and intention.

"Will I survive?" seems, I said, equivalent to "Will there be some person alive who is the same person as me?"

If we treat these questions as equivalent, then the least unsatisfactory description of Wiggins's case is, I think, that I survive with two bodies and a divided mind.

Several writers have chosen to say that I am neither of the resulting people. Given our equivalence, this implies that I do not survive, and hence, presumably, that even if Wiggins's operation is not literally death, I ought, since I will not survive it, to regard it as death. But this seemed absurd.

It is worth repeating why. An emotion or attitude can be criticized for resting on a false belief, or for being inconsistent. A man who regarded Wiggins's operation as death must, I suggest, be open to one of these criticisms.

He might believe that his relation to each of the resulting people fails to contain some element which is contained in survival. But how can this be true? We agreed that he would survive if he stood in this very same relation to only one of the resulting people. So it cannot be the nature of this relation which makes it fail, in Wiggins's case, to be survival. It can only be its duplication.

Suppose that our man accepts this, but still regards division as death. His reaction would now seem wildly inconsistent. He would be like a man who, when told of a drug that could double his years of life, regarded the taking of this drug as death. The only difference in the case of division is that the extra years are to run concurrently.

This is an interesting difference. But mean that there are no years to run.

I have argued this for those who think that there must, in Wiggins's case, be a true answer to the question about identity. For them, we might add, "Perhaps the original person does lose his identity. But there may be other ways to do this than to die. One other way might be to multiply. To regard these as the same is to confuse nought with two."

For those who think that the question of identity is up for decision, it would be clearly absurd to regard Wiggins's operation as death. These people would have to think, "We could have chosen to say that I should be one of the resulting people. If we had, I should not have regarded it as death. But since we have chosen to say that I am neither person, I do." This is hard even to understand.[8]

My first conclusion, then, is this. The relation of the original person to each of the resulting people contains all that interests us – all that matters – in any ordinary case of survival. This is why we need a sense in which one person can survive as two.[9]

One of my aims in the rest of this paper will be to suggest such a sense. But we can first make some general remarks.

II

Identity is a one–one relation. Wiggins's case serves to show that what matters in survival need not be one–one.

Wiggins's case is of course, unlikely to occur. The relations which matter are, in fact, one–one. It is because they are that we can imply the holding of these relations by using the language of identity.

This use of language is convenient. But it can lead us astray. We may assume that what matters is identity and, hence, has the properties of identity.

In the case of the property of being one–one, this mistake is not serious. For what matters is in fact one–one. But in the case of another property, the mistake is serious. Identity is all-or-nothing. Most of the relations which matter in survival are, in fact, relations of degree. If we ignore this, we shall be led into quite ill-grounded attitudes and beliefs.

How would Parfit feel about I-relation seems to be that I am me, now, at this stage

The claim that I have just made – that most of what matters are relations of degree – I have yet to support. Wiggins's case shows only that these relations need not be one–one. The merit of the case is not that it shows this in particular, but that it makes the first break between what matters and identity. The belief that identity *is* what matters is hard to overcome. This is shown in most discussions of the problem cases which actually occur: cases, say, of amnesia or of brain damage. Once Wiggins's case has made one breach in this belief, the rest should be easier to remove.[10]

To turn to a recent debate: most of the relations which matter can be provisionally referred to under the heading "psychological continuity" (which includes causal continuity). My claim is thus that we use the language of personal identity in order to imply such continuity. This is close to the view that psychological continuity provides a criterion of identity.

Williams has attacked this view with the following argument. Identity is a one–one relation. So any criterion of identity must appeal to a relation which is logically one–one. Psychological continuity is not logically one–one. So it cannot provide a criterion.[11]

Some writers have replied that it is enough if the relation appealed to is always in fact one–one.[12]

I suggest a slightly different reply. Psychological continuity is a ground for speaking of identity when it is one–one.

If psychological continuity took a one–many or branching form, we should need, I have argued, to abandon the language of identity. So this possibility would not count against this view.

We can make a stronger claim. This possibility would count in its favor.

The view might be defended as follows. Judgments of personal identity have great importance. What gives them their importance is the fact that they imply psychological continuity. This is why, whenever there is such continuity, we ought, if we can, to imply it by making a judgment of identity.

If psychological continuity took a branching form, no coherent set of judgments of identity could correspond to, and thus be used to imply, the branching form of this relation. But what we ought to do, in such a case, is take the importance which would attach to a judgment of identity and attach this importance directly to each limb of the branching relation. So this case helps to show that judgments of personal identity do derive their importance from the fact that they imply psychological continuity. It helps to show that when we can, usefully, speak of identity, this relation is our ground.

This argument appeals to a principle which Williams put forward.[13] The principle is that an important judgment should be asserted and denied only on importantly different grounds.

Williams applied this principle to a case in which one man is psychologically continuous with the dead Guy Fawkes, and a case in which two men are. His argument was this. If we treat psychological continuity as a sufficient ground for speaking of identity, we shall say that the one man is Guy Fawkes. But we could not say that the two men are, although we should have the same ground. This disobeys the principle. The remedy is to deny that the one man is Guy Fawkes, to insist that sameness of the body is necessary for identity.

Williams's principle can yield a different answer. Suppose we regard psychological continuity as more important than sameness of the body.[14] And suppose that the one man really is psychologically (and causally) continuous with Guy Fawkes. If he is, it would disobey the principle to deny that he is Guy Fawkes, for we have the same important ground as in a normal case of identity. In the case of the two men, we again have the same important ground. So we ought to take the importance from the judgment of identity and attach it directly to this ground. We ought to say, as in Wiggins's case, that each limb of the branching relation is as good as survival. This obeys the principle.

To sum up these remarks: even if psychological continuity is neither logically, nor always in fact, one–one, it can provide a criterion of identity. For this can appeal to the relation of *non-branching* psychological continuity, which is logically one–one.[15]

The criterion might be sketched as follows. "*X* and *Y* are the same person if they are psychologically continuous and there is no person who is contemporary with either and psychologically continuous with the other." We should need to explain what we mean by "psychologically continuous" and say how much continuity the criterion requires. We should then, I think, have described a sufficient condition for speaking of identity.[16]

non-branching psychological continuity is logically
1 – 1 an can be a criterion for personal identity

We need to say something more. If we admit that psychological continuity might not be one–one, we need to say what we ought to do if it were not one–one. Otherwise our account would be open to the objections that it is incomplete and arbitrary.[17]

I have suggested that if psychological continuity took a branching form, we ought to speak in a new way, regarding what we describe as having the same significance as identity. This answers these objections.[18]

We can now return to our discussion. We have three remaining aims. One is to suggest a sense of "survive" which does not imply identity. Another is to show that most of what matters in survival are relations of degree. A third is to show that none of these relations needs to be described in a way that presupposes identity.

We can take these aims in the reverse order.

III

The most important particular relation is that involved in memory. This is because it is so easy to believe that its description must refer to identity.[19] This belief about memory is an important cause of the view that personal identity has a special nature. But it has been well discussed by Shoemaker[20] and by Wiggins.[21] So we can be brief.

It may be a logical truth that we can only remember our own experiences. But we can frame a new concept for which this is not a logical truth. Let us call this "q-memory".

To sketch a definition[22] I am q-remembering an experience if (1) I have a belief about a past experience which seems in itself like a memory belief, (2) someone did have such an experience, and (3) my belief is dependent upon this experience in the same way (whatever that is) in which a memory of an experience is dependent upon it.

According to (1), q-memories seem like memories. So I q-remember having experiences.

This may seem to make q-memory presuppose identity. One might say, "My apparent memory of having an experience is an apparent memory of my having an experience. So how could I q-remember my having other people's experiences?"

This objection rests on a mistake. When I seem to remember an experience, I do indeed seem to remember having it.[23] But it cannot be a part of

what I seem to remember about this experience that I, the person who now seems to remember it, am the person who had this experience.[24] That I am is something that I automatically assume. (My apparent memories sometimes come to me simply as the belief that I had a certain experience.) But it is something that I am justified in assuming only because I do not in fact have q-memories of other people's experiences.

Suppose that I did start to have such q-memories. If I did, I should cease to assume that my apparent memories must be about my own experiences. I should come to assess an apparent memory by asking two questions: (1) Does it tell me about a past experience? (2) If so, whose?

Moreover (and this is a crucial point) my apparent memories would now come to me as q-memories. Consider those of my apparent memories which do come to me simply as beliefs about my past: for example, "I did that." If I knew that I could q-remember other people's experiences, these beliefs would come to me in a more guarded form: for example, "Someone – probably I – did that." I might have to work out who it was.

I have suggested that the concept of q-memory is coherent. Wiggins's case provides an illustration. The resulting people, in his case, both have apparent memories of living the life of the original person. If they agree that they are not this person, they will have to regard these as only q-memories. And when they are asked a question like "Have you heard this music before?", they might have to answer "I am sure that I q-remember hearing it. But I am not sure whether I remember hearing it. I am not sure whether it was I who heard it, or the original person."

We can next point out that on our definition every memory is also a q-memory. Memories are, simply, q-memories of one's own experiences. Since this is so, we could afford now to drop the concept of memory and use in its place the wider concept q-memory. If we did, we should describe the relation between an experience and what we now call a "memory" of this experience in a way which does not presuppose that they are had by the same person.[25]

This way of describing this relation has certain merits. It vindicates the "memory criterion" of personal identity against the charge of circularity.[26] And it might, I think, help with the problem of other minds.

But we must move on. We can next take the relation between an intention and a later action. It may be a logical truth that we can intend to perform only our own actions. But intentions can be redescribed as q-intentions. And one person could q-intend to perform another person's actions.

Wiggins's case again provides the illustration. We are supposing that neither of the resulting people is the original person. If so, we shall have to agree that the original person can, before the operation, q-intend to perform their actions. He might, for example, q-intend, as one of them, to continue his present career, and, as the other, to try something new.[27] (I say "q-intend as one of them" because the phrase "q-intend that one of them" would not convey the directness of the relation which is involved. If I intend that someone else should do something, I cannot get him to do it simply by forming this intention. But if I am the original person, and he is one of the resulting people, I can.)

The phrase "q-intend as one of them" reminds us that we need a sense in which one person can survive as two. But we can first point out that the concepts of q-memory and q-intention give us our model for the others that we need: thus, a man who can q-remember could q-recognize, and be a q-witness of, what he has never seen; and a man who can q-intend could have q-ambitions, make q-promises, and be q-responsible for.

To put this claim in general terms: many different relations are included within, or are a consequence of, psychological continuity. We describe these relations in ways which presuppose the continued existence of one person. But we could describe them in new ways which do not.

This suggests a bolder claim. It might be possible to think of experiences in a wholly "impersonal" way. I shall not develop this claim here. What I shall try to describe is a way of thinking of our own identity through time which is more flexible, and less misleading, than the way in which we now think.

This way of thinking will allow for a sense in which one person can survive as two. A more important feature is that it treats survival as a matter of degree.

IV

We must first show the need for this second feature. I shall use two imaginary examples.

The first is the converse of Wiggins's case: fusion. Just as division serves to show that what matters in survival need not be one–one, so fusion serves to show that it can be a question of degree.

Physically, fusion is easy to describe. Two people come together. While they are unconscious, their two bodies grow into one. One person then wakes up.

The psychology of fusion is more complex. One detail we have already dealt with in the case of the exam. When my mind was reunited, I remembered just having thought out two calculations. The one person who results from a fusion can, similarly, q-remember living the lives of the two original people. None of their q-memories need be lost.

But some things must be lost. For any two people who fuse together will have different characteristics, different desires, and different intentions. How can these be combined?

We might suggest the following. Some of these will be compatible. These can coexist in the one resulting person. Some will be incompatible. These, if of equal strength, can cancel out, and if of different strengths, the stronger can be made weaker. And all these effects might be predictable.

To give examples – first, of compatibility: I like Palladio and intend to visit Venice. I am about to fuse with a person who likes Giotto and intends to visit Padua. I can know that the one person we shall become will have both tastes and both intentions. Second, of incompatibility: I hate red hair, and always vote Labour. The other person loves red hair, and always votes Conservative. I can know that the one person we shall become will be indifferent to red hair, and a floating voter.

If we were about to undergo a fusion of this kind, would we regard it as death?

Some of us might. This is less absurd than regarding division as death. For after my division the two resulting people will be in every way like me, while after my fusion the one resulting person will not be wholly similar. This makes it easier to say, when faced with fusion, "I shall not survive", thus continuing to regard survival as a matter of all-or-nothing.

This reaction is less absurd. But here are two analogies which tell against it.

First, fusion would involve the changing of some of our characteristics and some of our

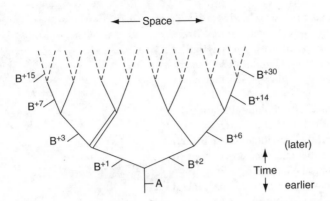

Figure 42.1

desires. But only the very self-satisfied would think of this as death. Many people welcome treatments with these effects.

Second, someone who is about to fuse can have, beforehand, just as much "intentional control" over the actions of the resulting individual as someone who is about to marry can have, beforehand, over the actions of the resulting couple. And the choice of a partner for fusion can be just as well considered as the choice of a marriage partner. The two original people can make sure (perhaps by "trial fusion") that they do have compatible characters, desires and intentions.

I have suggested that fusion, while not clearly survival, is not clearly failure to survive, and hence that what matters in survival can have degrees.

To reinforce this claim, we can now turn to a second example. This is provided by certain imaginary beings. These beings are just like ourselves except that they reproduce by a process of natural division.

We can illustrate the histories of these imagined beings with the aid of a diagram (Fig. 42.1). The lines on the diagram represent the spatiotemporal paths which would be traced out by the bodies of these beings. We can call each single line (like the double line) a "branch"; and we can call the whole structure a "tree". And let us suppose that each "branch" corresponds to what is thought of as the life of one individual. These individuals are referred to as "A", "B + 1", and so forth.

Now, each single division is an instance of Wiggins's case. So A's relation to both B + 1 and B + 2 is just as good as survival. But what of A's relation to B + 30?

I said earlier that what matters in survival could be provisionally referred to as "psychological continuity". I must now distinguish this relation from another, which I shall call "psychological connectedness".

Let us say that the relation between a q-memory and the experience q-remembered is a "direct" relation. Another "direct" relation is that which holds between a q-intention and the q-intended action. A third is that which holds between different expressions of some lasting q-characteristic.

"Psychological connectedness", as I define it, requires the holding of these direct psychological relations. "Connectedness" is not transitive, since these relations are not transitive. Thus, if X q-remembers most of Y's life, and Y q-remembers most of Z's life, it does not follow that X q-remembers most of Z's life. And if X carries out the q-intentions of Y, and Y carries out the q-intentions of Z, it does not follow that X carries out the q-intentions of Z.

"Psychological continuity", in contrast, only requires overlapping chains of direct psychological relations. So "continuity" is transitive.

To return to our diagram. A is psychologically continuous with B + 30. There are between the two continuous chains of overlapping relations. Thus, A has q-intentional control over B + 2, B + 2 has q-intentional control over B + 6, and so on up to B + 30. Or B + 30 can q-remember the life of B + 14, B + 14 can q-remember the life of B + 6, and so on back to A.[28]

A, however, need *not* be psychologically connected to B + 30. Connectedness requires direct relations. And if these beings are like us, A cannot stand in such relations to every individual in his indefinitely long "tree". Q-memories will weaken with the passage of time, and then fade away. Q-ambitions, once fulfilled, will be replaced by others. Q-characteristics will gradually change. In general, A stands in fewer and fewer direct psychological relations to an individual in his "tree" the more remote that individual is. And if the individual is (like B + 30) sufficiently remote, there may be between the two *no* direct psychological relations.

Now that we have distinguished the general relations of psychological continuity and psychological connectedness, I suggest that connectedness is a more important element in survival. As a claim about our own survival, this would need more arguments than I have space to give. But it seems clearly true for my imagined beings. A is as close psychologically to B + 1 as I today am to myself tomorrow. A is as distant from B + 30 as I am from my great-great-grandson.

Even if connectedness is not more important than continuity, the fact that one of these is a relation of degree is enough to show that what matters in survival can have degrees. And in any case the two relations are quite different. So our imagined beings would need a way of thinking in which this difference is recognized.

V

What I propose is this.

First, A can think of any individual, anywhere in his "tree", as "a descendant self". This phrase implies psychological continuity. Similarly, any later individual can think of any earlier individual on the single path[29] which connects him to A as "an ancestral self".

Since psychological continuity is transitive, "being an ancestral self of" and "being a descendant self of" are also transitive.

To imply psychological connectedness, I suggest the phrases "one of my future selves" and "one of my past selves".

These are the phrases with which we can describe Wiggins's case. For having past and future selves is, what we needed, a way of continuing to exist which does not imply identity through time. The original person does, in this sense, survive Wiggins's operation: the two resulting people are his

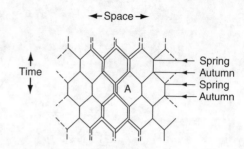

Figure 42.2

later selves. And they can each refer to him as "my past self". (They can share a past self without being the same self as each other.)

Since psychological connectedness is not transitive, and is a matter of degree, the relations "being a past self of" and "being a future self of" should themselves be treated as relations of degree. We allow for this series of descriptions: "my most recent self", "one of my earlier selves", "one of my distant selves", "hardly one of *my* past selves (I can only q-remember a few of his experiences)," and, finally, "not in any way one of *my* past selves – just an ancestral self."

This way of thinking would clearly suit our first imagined beings. But let us now turn to a second kind of being. These reproduce by fusion as well as by division.[30] And let us suppose that they fuse every autumn and divide every spring. This yields Figure 42.2.

If A is the individual whose life is represented by the three-lined "branch," the two-lined "tree" represents those lives which are psychologically continuous with A's life. (It can be seen that each individual has his own "tree," which overlaps with many others.)

For the imagined beings in this second world, the phrases "an ancestral self" and "a descendant self" would cover too much to be of much use. (There may well be pairs of dates such that every individual who ever lived before the first date was an ancestral self of every individual who ever will live after the second date.) Conversely, since the lives of each individual last for only half a year, the word "I" would cover too little to do all of the work which it does for us. So part of this work would have to be done, for these second beings, by talk about past and future selves.

We can now point out a theoretical flaw in our proposed way of thinking. The phrase "a past self of"

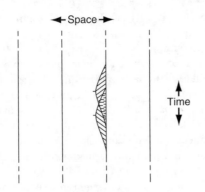

Figure 42.3

implies psychological connectedness. Being a past self of is treated as a relation of degree, so that this phrase can be used to imply the varying degrees of psychological connectedness. But this phrase can imply only the degrees of connectedness between different lives. It cannot be used within a single life. And our way of delimiting successive lives does not refer to the degrees of psychological connectedness. Hence there is no guarantee that this phrase, "a past self of," could be used whenever it was needed. There is no guarantee that psychological connectedness will not vary in degree within a single life.

This flaw would not concern our imagined beings. For they divide and unite so frequently, and their lives are in consequence so short, that within a single life psychological connectedness would always stand at a maximum.

But let us look, finally, at a third kind of being.

In this world there is neither division nor union. There are a number of everlasting bodies, which gradually change in appearance. And direct psychological relations, as before, hold only over limited periods of time. This can be illustrated with a third diagram (Figure 42.3). In this diagram the two shadings represent the degrees of psychological connectedness to their two central points.

These beings could not use the way of thinking that we have proposed. Since there is no branching of psychological continuity, they would have to regard themselves as immortal. It might be said that this is what they are. But there is, I suggest, a better description.

Our beings would have one reason for thinking of themselves as immortal. The parts of each "line"

are all psychologically continuous. But the parts of each "line" are not all psychologically connected. Direct psychological relations hold only between those parts which are close to each other in time. This gives our beings a reason for *not* thinking of each "line" as corresponding to one single life. For if they did, they would have no way of implying these direct relations. When a speaker says, for example, "I spent a period doing such and such," his hearers would not be entitled to assume that the speaker has any memories of this period, that his character then and now are in any way similar, that he is now carrying out any of the plans or intentions which he then had, and so forth. Because the word "I" would carry none of these implications, it would not have for these "immortal" beings the usefulness which it has for us.[31]

To gain a better way of thinking, we must revise the way of thinking that we proposed above. The revision is this. The distinction between successive selves can be made by reference, not to the branching of psychological continuity, but to the degrees of psychological connectedness. Since this connectedness is a matter of degree, the drawing of these distinctions can be left to the choice of the speaker and be allowed to vary from context to context.

On this way of thinking, the word "I" can be used to imply the greatest degree of psychological connectedness. When the connections are reduced, when there has been any marked change of character or style of life, or any marked loss of memory, our imagined beings would say, "It was not I who did that, but an earlier self." They could then describe in what ways, and to what degree, they are related to this earlier self.

This revised way of thinking would suit not only our "immortal" beings. It is also the way in which we ourselves could think about our lives. And it is, I suggest, surprisingly natural.

One of its features, the distinction between successive selves, has already been used by several writers. To give an example, from Proust: "we are incapable, while we are in love, of acting as fit predecessors of the next persons who, when we are in love no longer, we shall presently have become…"[32]

Although Proust distinguished between successive selves, he still thought of one person as being these different selves. This we would not do on the way of thinking that I propose. If I say,

"It will not be me, but one of my future selves," I do not imply that I will be that future self. He is one of my later selves, and I am one of his earlier selves. There is no underlying person who we both are.

To point out another feature of this way of thinking. When I say, "There is no person who we both are," I am only giving my decision. Another person could say, "It will be you," thus deciding differently. There is no question of either of these decisions being a mistake. Whether to say "I," or "one of my future selves," or "a descendant self" is entirely a matter of choice. The matter of fact, which must be agreed, is only whether the disjunction applies. (The question "Are X and Y the same person?" thus becomes "Is X *at least* an ancestral (or descendant) self of Y?")

VI

I have tried to show that what matters in the continued existence of a person are, for the most part, relations of degree. And I have proposed a way of thinking in which this would be recognized.

I shall end by suggesting two consequences and asking one question.

It is sometimes thought to be especially rational to act in our own best interests. But I suggest that the principle of self-interest has no force. There are only two genuine competitors in this particular field. One is the principle of biased rationality: do what will best achieve what you actually want. The other is the principle of impartiality: do what is in the best interests of everyone concerned.

The apparent force of the principle of self-interest derives, I think, from these two other principles.

The principle of self-interest is normally supported by the principle of biased rationality. This is because most people care about their own future interests.

Suppose that this prop is lacking. Suppose that a man does not care what happens to him in, say, the more distant future. To such a man, the principle of self-interest can only be propped up by an appeal to the principle of impartiality. We must say, "Even if you don't care, you ought to take what happens to you then equally into account." But for this, as a special claim, there seem to me no good arguments. It can only be supported as part of the general claim, "You ought to take what happens to everyone equally into account."[33]

The special claim tells a man to grant an *equal* weight to all the parts of his future. The argument for this can only be that all the parts of his future are *equally* parts of *his* future. This is true. But it is a truth too superficial to bear the weight of the argument. (To give an analogy: The unity of a nation is, in its nature, a matter of degree. It is therefore only a superficial truth that all of a man's compatriots are *equally* his compatriots. This truth cannot support a good argument for nationalism.)[34]

I have suggested that the principle of self-interest has no strength of its own. If this is so, there is no special problem in the fact that what we ought to do can be against our interests. There is only the general problem that it may not be what we want to do.

The second consequence which I shall mention is implied in the first. Egoism, the fear not of near but of distant death, the regret that so much of one's *only* life should have gone by – these are not, I think, wholly natural or instinctive. They are all strengthened by the beliefs about personal identity which I have been attacking. If we give up these beliefs, they should be weakened.

My final question is this. These emotions are bad, and if we weaken them, we gain. But can we achieve this gain without, say, also weakening loyalty to, or love of, other particular selves? As Hume warned, the "refined reflections which philosophy suggests ... cannot diminish ... our vicious passions ... without diminishing ... such as are virtuous. They are ... applicable to all our affections. In vain do we hope to direct their influence only to one side."[35]

That hope *is* vain. But Hume had another: that more of what is bad depends upon false belief. This is also my hope.

Notes

I have been helped in writing this by D. Wiggins, D. F. Pears, P. F. Strawson, A. J. Ayer, M. Woods, N. Newman, and (through his publications) S. Shoemaker.

1   Implicit in John Locke, *Essay Concerning Human Understanding*, ed. John W. Yolton, (London:

J. M. Dent and New York: E. P. Dutton, 1961) vol. 2, ch. 27, sect. 18 and discussed by (among others) A. N. Prior in "Opposite number," *Review of Metaphysics* 11 (1957–8), and *idem*, "Time, existence and identity," *Proceedings of the Aristotelian Society* 57 (1965–6); J. Bennett in "The simplicity of the soul," *Journal of Philosophy* 64 (1967); and R. Chisholm and S. Shoemaker in "The loose and popular and the strict and the philosophical senses of identity," in Norman Care and Robert H. Grimm, *Perception and Personal Identity: Proceeding of the 1967 Oberlin Colloquium in Philosophy*, (eds), (Cleveland: Press of Case Western Reserve University, 1967).

2 David Wiggins, *Identity and Spatio-Temporal Continuity* (Oxford: Blackwell, 1967), p. 50.

3 S. Shoemaker, *Self-Knowledge and Self-Identity* (Ithaca, NY: Cornell University Press, 1963), p. 22.

4 Those who would disagree are not making a mistake. For them my argument would need a different case. There must be some multiple transplant, faced with which these people would both find it hard to believe that there must be an answer to the question about personal identity, and be able to be shown that nothing of importance turns upon this question.

5 R. W. Sperry, *Brain and Conscious Experience*, ed. J. C. Eccles (New York: Springer Verlag, 1966), p. 299.

6 Cf. Wiggins, *Identity*, p. 40.

7 Suppose the resulting people fight a duel. Are there three people fighting, one on each side, and one on both? And suppose one of the bullets kills. Are there two acts, one murder and one suicide? How many people are left alive? One? Two? (We could hardly say, "One and a half".) We could talk in this way. But instead of saying that the resulting people are the original person – so that the pair is a trio – it would be far simpler to treat them as a pair, and describe their relation to the original person in some new way. (I owe this suggested way of talking, and the objections to it, to Michael Woods.)

8 Cf. Sydney Shoemaker, in *Perception and Personal Identity*, p. 54.

9 Cf. Wiggins *Identity*.

10 Bernard Williams's "The self and the future," this volume, ch. 41, is relevant here. He asks the question "Shall I survive?" in a range of problem cases, and he shows how natural it is to believe (1) that this question must have an answer, (2) that the answer must be all-or-nothing, and (3) that there is a "risk" of our reaching the wrong answer. Because these beliefs are so natural, we should need in undermining them to discuss their causes. These, I think, can be found in the ways in which we misinterpret what it is to remember (cf. sect. III) and to anticipate (cf. Williams's "Imagination and the self," *Proceedings of the British Academy* 52 (1966), pp. 105–24); and also in the way in which certain features of our egoistic concern – e.g., that it is simple, and applies to all imaginable cases – are "projected" onto its object. (For another relevant discussion, see Terence Penelhum's *Survival and Disembodied Existence* (New York: Humanities Press, 1970, final chapters.)

11 Bernard Williams, "Personal identity and Individuation," *Proceedings of the Aristotelian Society* 57 (1956–7), pp. 229–53; also his "Bodily continuity and personal identity: a reply," *Analysis* 21 (1960–61), 43–8.

12 J. M. Shorter, "More about bodily continuity and personal identity," *Analysis* 22 (1961–2), pp. 79–85; and J. M. R. Jack (unpublished), who requires that this truth be embedded in a causal theory.

13 Williams, "Bodily Continuity," p. 44.

14 For the reasons given by A. M. Quinton in "The soul," *Journal of Philosophy* 59 (1962), pp. 393–409.

15 Cf. S. Shoemaker, "Persons and their pasts," this volume, ch. 40, and *idem*, "Wiggins on identity," *Philosophical Review* 79 (1970), p. 542.

16 But not a necessary condition, for in the absence of psychological continuity, bodily identity might be sufficient.

17 Cf. Williams, "Personal identity and individuation," pp. 240–1, and *idem*, "Bodily continuity," p. 44; and also Wiggins, *Identity*, p. 38: "if coincidence under [the concept] *f* is to be *genuinely* sufficient we must not withhold identity … simply because transitivity is threatened."

18 Williams produced another objection to the "psychological criterion," that it makes it hard to explain the difference between the concepts of identity and exact similarity ("Bodily continuity," p. 48). But if we include the requirement of causal continuity, we avoid this objection (and one of those produced by Wiggins in his n. 47).

19 Those philosophers who have held this belief, from Butler onward, are too numerous to cite.

20 Shoemaker, this volume, ch. 40.

21 In a paper on Butler's objection to Locke (not yet published).

22 I here follow Shoemaker's "quasi-memory." Cf. also Penelhum's "retrocognition," in his article on "Personal identity," in Paul Edwards (ed.), *Encyclopedia of Philosophy*.

23 As Shoemaker put it, I seem to remember the experience "from the inside" (this volume, ch. 40).

24 This is what so many writers have overlooked. Cf. Thomas Reid: "My memory testifies not only that this was done, but that it was done by me who

now remember it" ("Of identity," in *Essays on the Intellectual Powers of Man*, ed. A. D. Woozley (London: Macmillan, 1941), p. 203). This mistake is discussed by A. B. Palma in "Memory and personal identity," *Australasian Journal of Philosophy* 42 (1964), p. 57.

25 It is not logically necessary that we only *q*-remember our own experiences. But it might be necessary on other grounds. This possibility is intriguingly explored by Shoemaker in his "Persons and their pasts," this volume, ch. 40. He shows that *q*-memories can provide a knowledge of the world only if the observations which are *q*-remembered trace out fairly continuous spatiotemporal paths. If the observations which are *q*-remembered traced out a network of frequently interlocking paths, they could not, I think, be usefully ascribed to persisting observers, but would have to be referred to in some more complex way. But in fact the observations which are *q*-remembered trace out single and separate paths; so we can ascribe them to ourselves. In other words, it is epistemologically necessary that the observations which are *q*-remembered should satisfy a certain general condition, one particular form of which allows them to be usefully self-ascribed.

26 Cf. Wiggins's paper on Butler's objection to Locke.

27 There are complications here. He could form *divergent* *q*-intentions only if he could distinguish, in advance, between the resulting people (e.g., as "the left-hander" and "the right-hander"). And he could be confident that such divergent *q*-intentions would be carried out only if he had reason to believe that neither of the resulting people would change their (inherited) mind.

Suppose he was torn between duty and desire. He could not solve this dilemma by *q*-intending, as one of the resulting people, to do his duty, and, as the other, to do what he desires. For the one he *q*-intended to do his duty would face the same dilemma.

28 The chain of continuity must run in one direction of time. B + 2 is not, in the sense I intend, psychologically continuous with B + 1.

29 Cf. Wiggins, *Identity*.

30 Cf. Shoemaker in "Persons and their pasts," this volume, ch. 40.

31 Cf. Austin Duncan Jones, "Man's mortality," *Analysis* 28 (1967–8), pp. 65–70.

32 Proust, *Within a Budding Grove* (New York: Modern Library, 1949), vol. 1, p. 226 (my own translation).

33 Cf. Thomas Nagel's *The Possibility of Altruism* (Oxford: Clarendon Press, 1970), in which the special claim is in effect defended as part of the general claim.

34 The unity of a nation we seldom take for more than what it is. This is partly because we often think of nations, not as units, but in a more complex way. If we thought of ourselves in the way that I proposed, we might be less likely to take our own identity for more than what it is. We are, for example, sometimes told, "It is irrational to act against your own interests. After all, it will be you who will regret it." To this we could reply, "No, not me. Not even one of my future selves. Just a descendant self."

35 Hume, "The Sceptic," in "Essays Moral, Political and Literary," *Hume's Moral and Political Philosophy* (New York, 1959), p. 349.

43

Survival and Identity

David Lewis

What is it that matters in survival? Suppose I wonder whether I will survive the coming battle, brainwashing, brain transplant, journey by matter-transmitter, purported reincarnation or resurrection, fission into twins, fusion with someone else, or what not. What do I really care about? If it can happen that some features of ordinary, everyday survival are present but others are missing, then what would it take to make the difference between something practically as good as commonplace survival and something practically as bad as commonplace death?

I answer, along with many others: *what matters in survival is mental continuity and connectedness.* When I consider various cases in between commonplace survival and commonplace death, I find that what I mostly want in wanting survival is that my mental life should flow on. My present experiences, thoughts, beliefs, desires, and traits of character should have appropriate future successors. My total present mental state should be but one momentary stage in a continuing succession of mental states. These successive states should be interconnected in two ways. First, by bonds of similarity. Change should be gradual rather than sudden, and (at least in some respects) there

should not be too much change overall. Second by bonds of lawful causal dependence. Such change as there is should conform, for the most part, to lawful regularities concerning the succession of mental states – regularities, moreover, that are exemplified in everyday cases of survival. And this should be so not by accident (and also not, for instance, because some demon has set out to create a succession of mental states patterned to counterfeit our ordinary mental life) but rather because each succeeding mental state causally depends for its character on the states immediately before it.

I refrain from settling certain questions of detail. Perhaps my emphasis should be on *connectedness*: direct relations of similarity and causal dependence between my present mental state and each of its successors; or perhaps I should rather emphasize *continuity*: the existence of step-by-step paths from here to there, with extremely strong local connectedness from each step to the next. Perhaps a special place should be given to the special kind of continuity and connectedness that constitute memory; or perhaps not. Perhaps the "mental" should be construed narrowly, perhaps broadly. Perhaps

David K. Lewis, "Survival and Identity," from David Lewis, *Philosophical Papers*, vol. 1 (Oxford: Oxford University Press), pp. 55–77.

Metaphysics: An Anthology, Second Edition. Edited by Jaegwon Kim, Daniel Z. Korman and Ernest Sosa.

nonmental continuity and connectedness – in my appearance and voice, for instance – also should have at least some weight. It does not matter, for the present, just which version I would prefer of the thesis that what matters is mental continuity and connectedness. I am sure that I would endorse some version, and in this paper I want to deal with a seeming problem for any version.

The problem begins with a well-deserved complaint that all this about mental connectedness and continuity is too clever by half. I have forgotten to say what should have been said first of all. What matters in survival is survival. If I wonder whether I will survive, what I mostly care about is quite simple. When it's all over, will I myself – the very same person now thinking these thoughts and writing these words – still exist? Will any one of those who do exist afterward be me? In other words, *what matters in survival is identity* – identity between the I who exists now and the surviving I who will, I hope, still exist then.

One question, two answers! An interesting answer, plausible to me on reflection but far from obvious:[1] that what matters is mental connectedness and continuity between my present mental state and other mental states that will succeed it in the future. And a compelling commonsense answer an unhelpful platitude that cannot credibly be denied: what matters is identity between myself, existing now, and myself, still existing in the future.

If the two answers disagreed and we had to choose one, I suppose we would have to prefer the platitude of common sense to the interesting philosophical thesis. Else it would be difficult to believe one's own philosophy! The only hope for the first answer, then, is to show that we need not choose: the answers are compatible, and both are right. That is the claim I wish to defend. I say that it cannot happen that what matters in survival according to one answer is present while what matters in survival according to the other answer is lacking.

I Parfit's Argument

Derek Parfit has argued that the two answers cannot both be right, and we must therefore choose.[2] (He chooses the first). His argument is as follows:

(a) Identity is a relation with a certain formal character. It is one-one and it does not admit of degree.

(b) A relation of mental continuity and connectedness need not have that formal character. We can imagine problem cases in which any such relation is one-many or many-one, or in which it is present to a degree so slight that survival is questionable.

Therefore, since Parfit believes as I do that what matters in survival is some sort of mental continuity or connectedness,

(c) What matters in survival is not identity. At most, what matters is a relation that coincides with identity to the extent that the problem cases do not actually arise.

Parfit thinks that if the problem cases did arise, or if we wished to solve them hypothetically, questions of personal identity would have no compelling answers. They would have to be answered arbitrarily, and in view of the discrepancy stated in (a) and (b), there is no answer that could make personal identity coincide perfectly with the relation of mental continuity and connectedness that matters in survival.

Someone else could just as well run the argument in reverse. Of course what matters in survival is personal identity. Therefore what matters cannot be mental continuity or connectedness, in view of the discrepancy stated in premises (a) and (b). It must be some better-behaved relation.

My task is to disarm both directions of the argument and show that the opposition between what matters and identity is false. We can agree with Parfit (and I think we should) that what matters in questions of personal identity is mental continuity or connectedness, and that this might be one-many or many-one, and admits of degree. At the same time we can consistently agree with common sense (and I think we should) that what matters in questions of personal identity – even in the problem cases – is identity.

I do not attack premises (a) and (b). We could, of course, say "identity" and just mean mental continuity and connectedness. Then we would deny that "identity" must have the formal character stated in (a). But this verbal maneuver would not meet the needs of those who think, as I do, that what matters in survival is literally *identity*: that relation that everything bears to itself and to no other thing. As for (b), the problem cases clearly are possible under Parfit's conception of the sort of mental continuity or connectedness that matters in survival: or under any conception I might wish to adopt. The questions about continuity and connectedness which I left open are not relevant, since no way of settling them will produce a relation with the formal character of identity. So we do indeed have a discrepancy of formal character between identity and any suitable relation of mental continuity and connectedness.

But what does that show? Only that the two relations are different. And we should have known that from the start, since they have different relata. He who says that what matters in survival is a relation of mental continuity and connectedness is speaking of a relation among more or less momentary person-stages, or time-slices of continuant persons, or persons-at-times. He who says that what matters is survival is identity, on the other hand, must be speaking of identity among temporally extended continuant persons with stages at various times. What matters is that one and the same continuant person should have stages both now and later. Identity among stages has nothing to do with it, since stages are momentary. Even if you survive, your present stage is not identical to any future stage.[3] You know that your present stage will not survive the battle – that is not disconcerting – but will *you* survive?

II   The R-Relation and the I-Relation

Pretend that the open questions have been settled, so that we have some definite relation of mental continuity and connectedness among person-stages in mind as the relation that matters in survival. Call it the *R-relation*, for short. If you wonder whether you will survive the coming battle or what-not, you are wondering whether any of the stages that will exist afterward is R-related to you-now, the stage that is doing the wondering. Similarly for other "questions of personal identity." If you wonder whether this is your long-lost son, you mostly wonder whether the stage before you now is R-related to certain past stages. If you also wonder whether he is a reincarnation of Nero, you

wonder whether this stage is R-related to other stages farther in the past. If you wonder whether it is in your self-interest to save for your old age, you wonder whether the stages of that tiresome old gaffer you will become are R-related to you-now to a significantly greater degree than are all the other person-stages at this time or other times. If you wonder as you step into the duplicator whether you will leave by the left door, the right door, both, or neither, you are again wondering which future stages, if any, are R-related to you-now.

Or so say I. Common sense says something that sounds different: in wondering whether you will survive the battle, you wonder whether you – a continuant person consisting of your present stage along with many other stages – will continue beyond the battle. Will you be identical with anyone alive then? Likewise for other questions of personal identity.

Put this way, the two answers seem incomparable. It is pointless to compare the formal character of identity itself with the formal character of the relation R that matters in survival. Of course the R-relation among stages is not the same as identity either among stages or among continuants. But identity among continuant persons induces a relation among stages: the relation that holds between the several stages of a single continuant person. Call this the *I-relation*. It is the I-relation, not identity itself, that we must compare with the R-relation. In wondering whether you will survive the battle, we said, you wonder whether the continuant person that includes your present stage is identical with any of the continuant persons that continue beyond the battle. In other words: whether it is identical with any of the continuant persons that include stages after the battle. In other words: you wonder whether any of the stages that will exist afterward is I-related to – belongs to the same person as – your present stage. If questions of survival, or personal identity generally, are questions of identity among continuant persons, then they are also questions of I-relatedness among person-stages; and conversely. More precisely: *if common sense is right that what matters in survival is identity among continuant persons, then you have what matters in survival if and only if your present stage is I-related to future stages.* I shall not distinguish henceforth between the thesis that what matters in survival is identity and the thesis that what matters in survival is the I-relation. Either way, it is a compelling platitude of common sense.

If ever a stage is R-related to some future stage but I-related to none, or if ever a stage is I-related to some future stage but R-related to none, then the platitude that what matters is the I-relation will disagree with the interesting thesis that what matters is the R-relation. But no such thing can happen, I claim; so there can be no such disagreement. In fact, I claim that *any stage is I-related and R-related to exactly the same stages.* And I claim this not only for the cases that arise in real life, but for all possible problem cases as well. Let us individuate relations, as is usual, by necessary coextensiveness. Then I claim that *the I-relation is the R-relation.*

A continuant person is an aggregate[4] of person-stages, each one I-related to all the rest (and to itself). For short: a person is an I-*inter*related aggregate. Moreover, a person is not part of any larger I-interrelated aggregate; for if we left out any stages that were I-related to one another and to all the stages we included, then what we would have would not be a whole continuant person but only part of one. For short: a person is a maximal I-interrelated aggregate. And conversely, any maximal I-interrelated aggregate of person-stages is a continuant person. At least, I cannot think of any that clearly is not.[5] So far we have only a small circle, from personhood to I-interrelatedness and back again. That is unhelpful; but if the I-relation is the R-relation, we have something more interesting: a noncircular definition of person-hood. I claim that *someting is a continuant person if and only if it is a maximal R-interrelated aggregate of person-stages.* That is: if and only if it is an aggregate of person-stages, each of which is R-related to all the rest (and to itself), and it is a proper part of no other such aggregate.

I cannot tolerate any discrepancy in formal character between the I-relation and the R-relation, for I have claimed that these relations are one and the same. Now although the admitted discrepancy between identity and the R-relation is harmless in itself, and although the I-relation is not identity, still it may seem that the I-relation inherits enough of the formal character of identity to lead to trouble. For suppose that $S_1, S_2, \ldots$ are person-stages; and suppose that C_1 is the continuant person of whom S_1 is a stage, C_2 is the continuant person of whom S_2 is a stage, and so

on. Then any two of these stages S_i and S_j are I-related if and only if the corresponding continuant persons C_i and C_j are identical. The I-relations among the stages mirror the structure of the identity relations among the continuants.

I reply that the foregoing argument wrongly takes it for granted that every person-stage is a stage of one and only one continuant person. That is so ordinarily; and when that is so, the I-relation does inherit much of the formal character of identity. But ordinarily the R-relation also is well behaved. In the problem cases, however, it may happen that a single stage S is a stage of two or more different continuant persons. Worse, some or all of these may be persons to a diminished degree, so that it is questionable which of them should count as persons at all. If so, there would not be any such thing (in any straightforward way) as *the* person of whom S is a stage. So the supposition of the argument would not apply. It has not been shown that the I-relation inherits the formal character of identity in the problem cases. Rather it might be just as ill behaved as the R-relation. We shall examine the problem cases and see how that can happen.[6]

It would be wrong to read my definition of the I-relation as saying that person-stages S_1 and S_2 are I-related if and only if the continuant person of whom S_1 is a stage and the continuant person of whom S_2 is a stage are identical. The definite articles require the presupposition that I have just questioned. We should substitute the indefinite article: S_1 and S_2 are I-related if and only if a continuant person of whom S_1 is a stage and a continuant person of whom S_2 is a stage are identical. More simply: if and only if there is some one continuant person of whom both S_1 and S_2 are stages.

One seeming discrepancy between the I-relation and the R-relation need not disturb us. The I-relation must be symmetrical, whereas the R-relation has a direction. If a stage S_2 is mentally connected to a previous stage S_1, S_1 is available in memory to S_2 and S_2 is under the intentional control of S_1 to some extent – not the other way around.[7] We can say that S_1 is R-related *forward* to S_2, whereas S_2 is R-related *backward* to S_1. The forward and backward R-relations are converses of one another. Both are (normally) anti-symmetrical. But although we can distinguish the forward and backward R-relations, we can also merge them into a symmetrical relation. That is the R-relation I have in mind: S_1 and S_2 are R-related simpliciter if and only if S_1 is R-related either forward or backward to S_2.

While we are at it, let us also stipulate that every stage is R-related – forward, backward, and simpliciter – to itself. The R-relation, like the I-relation, is reflexive.

Parfit mentions two ways for a discrepancy to arise in the problem cases. First, the R-relation might be one-many or many-one. Second, the R-relation admits in principle of degree, and might be present to a degree that is markedly subnormal and yet not negligible. Both possibilities arise in connection with fission and fusion of continuant persons, and also in connection with immortality or longevity.

III Fission and Fusion

Identity is one-one, in the sense that nothing is ever identical to two different things. Obviously neither the I-relation nor the R-relation is one-one in that sense. You-now are a stage of the same continuant as many other stages, and are R-related to them all. Many other stages are stages of the same continuant as you-now, and are R-related to you-now. But when Parfit says that the R-relation might be one-many or many-one, he does not just mean that. Rather, he means that one stage might be R-related to many stages that are not R-related to one another, and that many stages that are not R-related to one another might all be R-related to one single stage. (These possibilities do not differ once we specify that the R-relation is to be taken as symmetrical.) In short, the R-relation might fail to be transitive.

In a case of fission, for instance, we have a prefission stage that is R-related forward to two different, simultaneous postfission stages that are not R-related either forward or backward to each other. The forward R-relation is one-many, the backward R-relation is many-one, and the R-relation simpliciter is intransitive.

In a case of fusion we have two prefusion stages, not R-related either forward or backward to each other, that are R-related forward to a single postfusion stage. The forward R-relation is many-one, the backward R-relation is one-many, and the R-relation simpliciter is again intransitive.

Identity must be transitive, but the I-relation is not identity. The I-relation will fail to be transitive if and only if there is partial overlap among continuant persons. More precisely: if and only if two continuant persons C_1 and C_2 have at least one common stage, but each one also has stages that are not included in the other. If S is a stage of both, S_1 is a stage of C_1 but not C_2, and S_2 is a stage of C_2 but not C_1, then transitivity of the I-relation fails. Although S_1 is I-related to S which in turn is I-related to S_2, yet S_1 is not I-related to S_2. In order to argue that the I-relation, unlike the R-relation, must be transitive, it is not enough to appeal to the uncontroversial transitivity of identity. The further premise is needed that partial overlap of continuant persons is impossible.

Figure 43.1 shows how to represent fission and fusion as cases of partial overlap. The continuant persons involved, C_1 and C_2, are the two maximal R-interrelated aggregates of stages marked by the two sorts of cross-hatching. In the case of fission, the prefission stages are shared by both continuants. In the case of fusion, the postfusion stages are likewise shared. In each case, we have a shared stage S that is I-related to two stages S_1 and S_2 that are not I-related to each other. Also S is R-related to S_1 and S_2 (forward in the case of fission, backward in the case of fusion) but S_1 and S_2 are not R-related to each other. More generally, the I-relation and the R-relation coincide for all stages involved in the affair.

There is, however, a strong reason for denying that continuant persons can overlap in this way. From this denial it would indeed follow (as it does not follow from the transitivity of identity alone) that the I-relation cannot share the possible intransitivities of the R-relation.

The trouble with overlap is that it leads to overpopulation. To count the population at a given time, we can count the continuant persons who have stages at that time; or we can count the stages. If there is overlap, there will be more continuants than stages. (I disregard the possibility that one of the continuants is a time traveler with distinct simultaneous stages.) The count of stages is the count we accept; yet we think we are counting persons, and we think of persons as continuants rather than stages. How, then, can we tolerate overlap?

For instance, we say that in a case of fission *one* person becomes *two*. By describing fission as initial

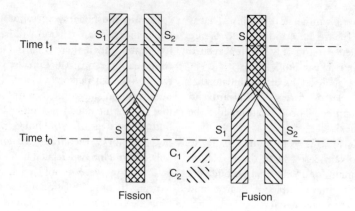

Figure 43.1

stage-sharing we provide for the two, but not for the one. There are two all along. It is all very well to say from an eternal or postfission standpoint that two persons (with a common initial segment) are involved, but we also demand to say that on the day before the fission only *one* person entered the duplication center; that his mother did not bear twins; that until he fissions he should only have one vote; and so on. Counting at a time, we insist on counting a person who will fission as one. We insist on a method of counting persons that agrees with the result of counting stages, though we do not think that counting persons just *is* counting (simultaneous) stages.

It is not so clear that we insist on counting a product of fusion as one (or a time traveler meeting himself as two). We are not sure what to say. But suppose we were fully devoted to the doctrine that the number of different persons in existence at a time is the number of different person-stages at that time. Even so, we would not be forced to deny that continuant persons could overlap. We would therefore not be driven to conclude that the I-relation cannot share the possible intransitivities of the R-relation.

The way out is to deny that we must invariably count two nonidentical continuants as two. We might count not by identity but by a weaker relation. Let us say that continuants C_1 and C_2 are *identical-at-time-t* if and only if they both exist at t and their stages at t are identical. (More precisely: C_1 and C_2 both have stages at t, and all and only stages of C_1 at t are stages of C_2 at t.) I shall speak of such relations of identity-at-a-time as relations of *tensed identity*. Tensed identity is not a kind of identity. It is not identity among stages, but rather a derivative relation among continuants which is induced by identity among stages. It is not identity among continuants, but rather a relation that is weaker than identity whenever different continuants have stages in common. If we count continuants by tensed identity rather than by identity, we will get the right answer – the answer that agrees with the answer we get by counting stages – even if there is overlap. How many persons entered the duplication center yesterday? We may reply: C_1 entered and C_2 entered, and no one else; although C_1 and C_2 are not identical today, and are not identical simpliciter, they were identical yesterday. So counting by identity-yesterday, there was only one. Counting by identity-today, there were two; but it is inappropriate to count by identity-today when we are talking solely about the events of yesterday. Counting by identity simpliciter there were two; but in talking about the events of yesterday it is as unnatural to count by identity as it is to count by identity-today. There is a way of counting on which there are two all along; but there is another way on which there are first one and then two. The latter has obvious practical advantages. It should be no surprise if it is the way we prefer.

It may seem far-fetched to claim that we ever count persons otherwise than by identity simpliciter. But we sometimes *do* count otherwise. If an infirm man wishes to know how many roads he must cross to reach his destination, I will count by identity along-his-path rather than by identity. By crossing the Chester A. Arthur Parkway and Route 137 at the brief stretch where they have merged, he can cross both by crossing only one road. Yet these two roads are certainly not identical.

You may feel certain that you count persons by identity, not by tensed identity. But how can you be sure? Normal cases provide no evidence. When no stages are shared, both ways of counting agree. They differ only in the problem cases: fission, fusion, and another that we shall soon consider. The problem cases provide no very solid evidence either. They are problem cases just because we cannot consistently say quite all the things we feel inclined to. We must strike the best compromise among our conflicting initial opinions. Something must give way; and why not the opinion that of course we count by identity, if that is what can be sacrificed with least total damage?

A relation to count by does not have to be identity, as the example of the roads shows. But perhaps it should share the key properties of identity. It should at least be an *equivalence* relation: reflexive, symmetrical, and transitive. Relations of tensed identity are equivalence relations. Further, it should be an *indiscernibility* relation; not for all properties whatever, as identity is, but at least for some significant class of properties. That is, it ought to be that two related things have exactly the same properties in that class. Identity-at-time-t is an indiscernibility relation for a significant class of properties of continuant persons: those properties of a person which are logically determined by the properties of his stage at t. The class includes the properties of walking, being tall, being in a certain room, being thirsty, and believing in God at time t; but not the properties of being forty-three years old, gaining weight, being an ex-Communist, or remembering one's childhood at t. The class is sizable enough, at any rate, to make clear that a relation of tensed identity is more of an indiscernibility relation than is identity-along-a-path among roads.

If we are prepared to count a product of fusion as two, while still demanding to count a person who will fission as one, we can count at t by the relation of identity-at-all-times-up-to-t. This is the relation that holds between continuants C_1 and C_2 if and only if (1) they both exist at

some time no later than t, (2) at any time no later than t, either both exist or neither does, and (3) at any time no later than t when both exist, they have exactly the same stages. Again, this is a relation among continuants that is weaker than identity to the extent that continuants share stages. Although derived from identity (among stages) it is of course not itself identity. It is even more of an indiscernibility relation than identity-at-t, since it confers indiscernibility with respect to such properties as being forty-three years old, gaining weight (in one sense), being an ex-Communist, and remembering one's childhood at t; though still not with respect to such properties as being, at t, the next winner of the State Lottery.

It may be disconcerting that we can have a single name for one person (counting by tensed identity) who is really two nonidentical persons because he will later fission. Isn't the name ambiguous? Yes; but so long as its two bearers are indiscernible in the respects we want to talk about, the ambiguity is harmless. If C_1 and C_2 are identical-at-all-times-up-to-now and share the name "Ned" it is idle to disambiguate such remarks as "Ned is tall," "Ned is waiting to be duplicated," "Ned is frightened," "Ned only decided yesterday to do it," and the like. These will be true on both disambiguations of "Ned," or false on both. Before the fission, only predictions need disambiguating. After the fission, on the other hand, the ambiguity of "Ned" will be much more bother. It can be expected that the ambiguous name "Ned" will then fall into disuse, except when we wish to speak of the shared life of C_1 and C_2 before the fission.

But what if we don't know whether Ned will fission? In that case, we don't know whether the one person Ned (counting by identity-now) is one person, or two, or many (counting by identity). Then we don't know whether "Ned" is ambiguous or not. But if the ambiguity is not a practical nuisance, we don't need to know. We can wait and see whether or not we have been living with a harmless ambiguity.

This completes my discussion of fission and fusion. To summarize: if the R-relation is the I-relation, and in particular if continuant persons are maximal R-interrelated aggregates of person-stages, then cases of fission and fusion must be treated as cases of stage-sharing between different, partially overlapping continuant persons. If so, the R-relation and the I-relation are alike intransitive, so there is no discrepancy on that score. If it is granted that we may count continuant persons by tensed identity, then this treatment does not conflict with our opinion that in fission one person becomes two; nor with our opinion (if it really is our opinion) that in fusion two persons become one.

IV Longevity

I turn now to a different problem case. Parfit has noted that mental connectedness will fade away eventually. If the R-relation is a matter of direct connectedness as well as continuity, then intransitivities of the R-relation will appear in the case of a person (if it is a person!) who lives too long.

Consider Methuselah. At the age of 100 he still remembers his childhood. But new memories crowd out the old. At the age of 150 he has hardly any memories that go back before his twentieth year. At the age of 200 he has hardly any memories that go back before his seventieth year; and so on. When he dies at the age of 969, he has hardly any memories that go beyond his 839th year. As he grows older he grows wiser; his callow opinions and character at age 90 have vanished almost without a trace by age 220, but his opinions and character at age 220 also have vanished almost without a trace by age 350. He soon learns that it is futile to set goals for himself too far ahead. At age 120, he is still somewhat interested in fulfilling the ambitions he held at age 40; but at age 170 he cares nothing for those ambitions, and it is beginning to take an effort of will to summon up an interest in fulfilling his aspirations at age 80. And so it goes.

We sometimes say in later life I will be a different person. For us short-lived creatures, such remarks are an extravagance. A philosophical study of personal identity can ignore them. For Methuselah, however, the fading-out of personal identity looms large as a fact of life. It is incumbent on us to make it literally true that he will be a different person after one and one-half centuries or so.

I should imagine that this is so just in virtue of normal aging over 969 years. If you disagree,

imagine that Methuselah lives much longer than a bare millennium (Parfit imagines the case of immortals who change mentally at the same rate as we do). Or imagine that his life is punctuated by frequent amnesias, brain-washings, psycho-analyses, conversions, and what not, each one of which is almost (but not quite) enough to turn him into a different person.

Suppose, for simplicity, that any two stages of Methuselah that are separated by no more than 137 years are R-related; and any two of his stages that are separated by more than 137 years are not R-related. (For the time being, we may pretend that R-relatedness is all-or-nothing, with a sharp cutoff.)

If the R-relation and the I-relation are the same, this means that two of Methuselah's stages belong to a single continuant person if and only if they are no more than 137 years apart. (Therefore the whole of Methuselah is not a single person.) That is the case, in particular, if continuant persons are maximal R-interrelated aggregates. For if so, then segments of Methuselah are R-interrelated if and only if they are no more than 137 years long; whence it follows that all and only the segments that are exactly 137 years long are maximal R-interrelated aggregates; so all and only the 137-year segments are continuant persons.

If so, we have intransitivity both of the R-relation and of the I-relation. Let S_1 be a stage of Methuselah at the age of 400; let S_2 be a stage of Methuselah at the age of 500; let S_3 be a stage of Methuselah at the age of 600. By hypothesis S_1 is R-related to S_2 and S_2 is R-related to S_3, but S_1 and S_3 are not R-related. Being separated by 200 years, they have no direct mental connections. Since S_1 and S_2 are linked by a 137-year segment (in fact, by infinitely many) they are I-related; likewise S_2 and S_3 are I-related. But S_1 and S_3 are not linked by any 137-year segment, so they are not I-related. The R-relation and the I-relation are alike intransitive.

The problem of overpopulation is infinitely worse in the case of Methuselah than in the cases of fission or fusion considered hitherto. Methuselah spends his 300th birthday alone in his room. How many persons are in that room? There are infinitely many different 137-year segments that include all of Methuselah's stages on his 300th birthday. One begins at the end of Methuselah's 163rd birthday and ends at the end of his 300th birthday; another begins at the beginning of his 300th and ends at the beginning of his 437th. Between these two are a continuum of other 137-year segments. No two of them are identical. Every one of them puts in an appearance (has a stage) in Methuselah's room on Methuselah's 300th birthday. Every one of them is a continuant person, given our supposition that Methuselah's stages are R-related if and only if they are not more than 137 years apart, and given that continuant persons are all and only maximal R-interrelated aggregates of person-stages. It begins to seem crowded in Methuselah's room!

Tensed identity to the rescue once more. True, there are continuum many nonidentical continuant persons in the room. But, counting by the appropriate relation of tensed identity, there is only one. All the continuum many nonidentical continuant persons are identical-at-the-time-in-question, since they all share the single stage at that time. Granted that we may count by tensed identity, there is no overcrowding.

V   Degree

We turn now to the question of degree. Identity certainly cannot be a matter of degree. But the I-relation is not defined in terms of identity alone. It derives also from personhood: the property of being a continuant person. Thus personal identity may be a matter of degree because personhood is a matter of degree, even though identity is not. Suppose two person-stages S_1 and S_2 are stages of some one continuant that is a person to a low, but not negligible, degree. Suppose further that they are not stages of anything else that is a person to any higher degree. Then they are I-related to a low degree. So if personhood admits of degree, we have no discrepancy in formal character between the I-relation and the R-relation.

Parfit suggests, for instance, that if you fuse with someone very different, yielding a fusion product mentally halfway between you and your partner, then it is questionable whether you have survived. Not that there is a definite, unknown answer. Rather, what matters in survival – the R-relation – is present in reduced degree. There is less of it than in clear cases of survival, more than in clear cases of nonsurvival.[8] If we want the I-relation and the R-relation to coincide, we may take it that C_1 and C_2 (see Fig. 43.1 for cases of

fusion) are persons to reduced degree because they are broken by abrupt mental discontinuities. If persons are maximal R-interrelated aggregates, as I claim, that is what we should expect; the R-relations across the fusion point are reduced in degree, hence the R-interrelatedness of C_1 and C_2 is reduced in degree, and hence the personhood of C_1 and C_2 is reduced in degree. C_1 and C_2 have less personhood than clear cases of persons, more personhood than continuant aggregates of stages that are clearly not persons. Then S and S_1, or S and S_2, are I-related to reduced degree just as they are R-related to reduced degree.

Personal identity to reduced degrees is found also in the case of Methuselah. We supposed before that stages no more than 137 years apart are R-related while states more than 137 years apart were not. But if the R-relation fades away at all – if it is a relation partly of connectedness as well as continuity – it would be more realistic to suppose that it fades away gradually. We can suppose that stages within 100 years of each other are R-related to a high enough degree so that survival is not in doubt; and that stages 200 or more years apart are R-related to such a low degree that what matters in survival is clearly absent. There is no significant connectedness over long spans of time, only continuity. Then if we want the R-relation and the I-relation to coincide, we could say roughly this: 100-year segments of Methuselah are persons to a high degree, whereas 200-year segments are persons only to a low degree. Then two stages that are strongly R-related also are strongly I-related, whereas stages that are weakly R-related are also weakly I-related. Likewise for all the intermediate degrees of R-relatedness of stages, of personhood of segments of Methuselah, and hence of I-relatedness of stages.

It is a familiar idea that personhood might admit of degrees. Most of the usual examples, however, are not quite what I have in mind. They concern continuants that are said to be persons to a reduced degree because their stages are thought to be person-stages to a reduced degree. If anyone thinks that the wolf-child, the "dehumanized" proletarian, or the human vegetable is not fully a person, that is more because he regards the stages themselves as deficient than because the stages are not strongly enough R-interrelated. If anyone thinks that personhood is partly a matter of species membership, so that a creature of sorcery or a freak offspring of hippopotami could not be fully a person no matter how much he resembled the rest of us, that also would be a case in which the stages themselves are thought to be deficient. In this case the stages are thought to be deficient not in their intrinsic character but in their causal ancestry; there is, however, nothing wrong with their R-interrelatedness. A severe case of split personality, on the other hand, does consist of perfectly good person-stages that are not very well R-related. If he is said not to be fully a person, that *is* an example of the kind of reduced personhood that permits us to claim that the R-relation and the I-relation alike admit of degrees.

Let us ignore the complications introduced by deficient person-stages. Let us assume that all the stages under consideration are person-stages to more or less the highest possible degree. (More generally, we could perhaps say that the degree of I-relatedness of two stages depends not on the absolute degree of personhood of the continuant, if any, that links them; but rather on the relative degree of personhood of that continuant compared to the greatest degree of personhood that the degree of person-stage-hood of the stages could permit. If two wolf-child-stages are person-stages only to degree 0.8, but they are stages of a continuant that is a person to degree 0.8, we can say that the stages are thereby I-related to degree 1.)

If we say that a continuant person is an aggregate of R-interrelated person-stages, it is clear that personhood admits of degree to the extent that the R-relation does. We can say something like this: the degree of R-interrelatedness of an aggregate is the minimum degree of R-relatedness between any two stages in the aggregate. (Better: the greatest lower bound on the degrees of R-relatedness between any two stages.) But when we recall that a person should be a maximal such aggregate, confusion sets in. Suppose we have an aggregate that is R-interrelated to degree 0.9, and it is not included in any larger aggregate that is R-interrelated to degree 0.9 or greater. Suppose, however, that it *is* included in a much larger aggregate that is R-interrelated to degree 0.88. We know the degree to which it qualifies as an R-interrelated aggregate, but to what degree does it qualify as a maximal one? That is, to what degree does it qualify as a person, if persons are maximal R-interrelated aggregates? I am inclined

to say: it passes the R-interrelatedness test for personhood to degree 0.9, but at the same time it flunks the maximality test to degree 0.88. Therefore it is a person only to degree 0.02!

This conclusion leads to trouble. Take the case of Methuselah. Assuming that R-relatedness fades out gradually, every segment that passes the R-interrelatedness rest to a significant degree also flunks the maximality test to almost the same degree. (If the fadeout is continuous, delete "almost.") So *no* segment of Methuselah passes both tests for personhood to any significant degree. No two stages, no matter how close, are stages of some *one* continuant that is a person to high degree. Rather, nearby stages are strongly I-related by being common to many continuants, each one of which is strongly R-interrelated, is almost as strongly nonmaximal, and therefore is a person only to a low degree.

We might sum the degrees of personhood of all the continuants that link two stages, taking the sum to be the degree of I-relatedness of the stages.

But there is a better way. Assume that R-relatedness can come in all degrees ranging from 0 to 1 on some scale. Then every number in the interval from 0 to 1 is a possible location for an arbitrary boundary between pairs of stages that are R-related and pairs that are not. Call every such number a *delineation* of this boundary. Every delineation yields a decision as to which stages are R-related. It thereby yields a decision as to which continuants are R-interrelated; a decision as to which continuants are included in larger R-interrelated aggregates; a decision as to which continuants are persons, given that persons are maximal R-interrelated aggregates; and thence a decision as to which stages are I-related. We can say that a certain continuant is a person, or that a certain pair of stages are I-related, *relative* to a given delineation. We can also say whether something is the case relative to a set of delineations, provided that all the delineations in the set agree on whether it is the case. Then we can take the degree to which it is the case as the size (more precisely: Lebesgue measure) of that set. Suppose, for instance, that two stages count as I-related when we set the cut-off for R-relatedness anywhere from 0 to 0.9, but not when we set the cut-off more stringently between 0.9 and 1. Then those two stages are I-related relative to delineations from 0 to 0.9, but not relative to delineations from 0.9 to 1. They are I-related to degree 0.9 – the size of the delineation interval on which they are I-related. Yet there may not be any continuant linking those stages that is a person to degree more than 0. It may be that any continuant that links those stages is both R-interrelated and maximal only at a single delineation. At any more stringent delineation, it is no longer R-interrelated; while at any less stringent delineation it is still R-interrelated but not maximal.

The strategy followed here combines two ideas. (1) When something is a matter of degree, we can introduce a cut-off point. However, the choice of this cut-off point is more or less arbitrary. (2) When confronted with an arbitrary choice, the thing to do is not to make the choice. Rather, we should see what is common to all or most ways (or all or most reasonable ways) of making the choice, caring little what happens on any particular way of making it. The second idea is van Fraassen's method of supervaluations.[9]

On this proposal the I-relation admits of degree; and further, we get perfect agreement between degrees of I-relatedness and degrees of R-relatedness, regardless of the degrees of personhood of continuants. For at any one delineation, two stages are R-related if and only if they belong to some one maximal R-interrelated aggregate; hence if and only if they belong to some one continuant person; hence if and only if they are I-related. Any two stages are R-related and I-related relative to exactly the same set of delineations. Now if two stages are R-related to a degree x, it follows (given our choice of scale and measure) that they are R-related at all and only the delineations in a certain set of size x. Therefore they are I-related at all and only the delineations in a certain set of size x; which means that they are I-related to degree x. The degree of I-relatedness equals the degree of R-relatedness. In this way personal identity can be just as much a matter of degree as the mental continuity or connectedness that matters in survival.

VI Perry's Treatment of Fission

It is instructive to contrast my way and John Perry's way[10] of overcoming the seeming discrepancies in character between personal identity and mental continuity or connectedness. Perry and I have the same goals, but our priorities differ. Perry does not need to resort to tensed identity to rescue the common opinion that in fission there is only one person beforehand. However, Perry's way does not permit identification of the R-relation and the I-relation themselves, but only of certain time-dependent subrelations thereof. Further, he must introduce an unintuitive discrimination among the persons who exist at (have stages at) any given time. Some of them (all, except in the problem cases) are classified as *determinable* at that time. These are the ones who count. There may be others, not determinable at that time, who are left out of consideration for certain purposes.

Say that Stage S_1 is *R-related at time* t – for short, R_t-*related* – to stage S_2 if and only if stages S_1 and S_2 are R-related simpliciter, and also S_2 is located at time t. The R_t-relation, then, is the R-relation between stages at t and stages at other times (or at t).

Say that stage S_1 is *I-related at time* t – for short, I_t-*related* – to stage S_2 if and only if both S_1 and S_2 are stages of some one continuant person who is determinable at time t, and S_2 is located at time t. The I_t-relation, then, is the I-relation between stages at t and stages at other times (or at t), if we leave out any continuant persons who are not determinable at t.

Perry proposes that something C is a continuant person determinable at t if and only if, for some person-stage S located at t, C is the aggregate comprising all and only the stages R_t-related to S. A continuant person, in general, is a continuant person determinable at some time. (No one is doomed to permanent indeterminability.) If something is a continuant person according to this proposal, Perry calls it a *lifetime*. If something is a continuant person according to my proposal – that is, if it is a maximal R-interrelated aggregate of person-stages – Perry calls it a *branch*. In normal cases, all and only lifetimes are branches.

In a case of fission, however, some lifetimes are not branches (see Fig. 43.1 for cases of fission). Branch C_1 is a lifetime determinable at t_1, since it comprises all and only the stages R_{t1}-related to S_1. Likewise branch C_2 is a lifetime determinable at t_1. But C – the whole thing – though not a branch, is a lifetime determinable at t_0, since it comprises all and only the stages R_{t0}-related to S. Note that C_1 and C_2 are not yet determinable at t_0, whereas C is no longer determinable at t_1.

On Perry's proposal, the R-relation is not the same as the I-relation in this case. Since C is a lifetime, and hence according to Perry a continuant person, S_1 and S_2 are I-related. However, they are not R-related.

What does follow from Perry's proposal is that, for any time t, the R_t-relation is the same as the I_t-relation. Perhaps that is good enough. Any particular question of survival, or of personal identity in general, arises at some definite time. If the question arises at time t, it is the R_t-relation and the I_t-relation that are relevant. We want them to give the same answer. The rest of the R-relation and the I-relation are not involved. In particular, it is harmless that S_1 and S_2 are I-related, since they are neither I_{t0}-related nor I_{t1}-related, nor indeed I_t-related for any time t whatever.

On Perry's proposal, any person-stage existing at any time must belong to exactly one continuant person who is determinable at that time. Persons can share stages, to be sure. More so on Perry's proposal than on mine, in fact: stage S in the fission case belongs to three lifetimes (C, C_1, and C_2) but only two branches (C_1 and C_2). Stage S_1 belongs to two lifetimes (C and C_1) but only one branch (C_1). But Perry's persons share stages only when all but one of the sharers is not determinable. Therefore we can count by identity, counting only the persons determinable at the time, and we will get the right answer. One determinable person (counting by identity) exists before the fission, but two exist afterward. There are three all along, counting by identity but including the nondeterminables; but at the fission one loses determinability and the other two gain it.

I grant that counting by tensed identity is somewhat counterintuitive; but isn't excluding the nondeterminable persons just as bad? They *are* (timelessly speaking) persons; they *do* exist at (have stages at) the time; they are *not* identical to persons we are counting. If we want to count the persons at the time, is it not gratuitous to exclude them? Perry can say: Yes, but we just do. Or: we do it for excellent practical reasons. I will say the same about counting by tensed identity without any exclusions. Both are counterintuitive; neither is unbeatably so; either is better than not having any way to count that gives the correct answer; either is better than permitting the possibility of fission to create a discrepancy between personal identity and what matters in survival.

Perry considers only fission and fusion, but his proposal can apply also to the case of Methuselah. I do not know whether Perry would wish so to apply it. He might prefer to let mental continuity predominate over connectedness in the R-relation, so that the whole of Methuselah is both a branch and a lifetime, and thus an unproblematic person.

Suppose as before, however, that the R-relation fades out with an (arbitrary) cut-off at 137 years. For me, the 137-year segments (the branches) are the continuant persons; for Perry, the 274-year segments (the lifetimes) are the continuant persons. For instance, a segment that begins on Methuselah's 420th birthday and ends at the same time on his 694th comprises all and only the stages R_t-related to a certain stage S on his 557th, t being the time of that stage. The lifetimes are not branches and the branches are not lifetimes. (With a trivial exception: the initial and final 137-year segments are both branches and lifetimes. More generally: the initial and final lifetimes are shorter than the others, being cut off by birth or death.) Any stage at any time belongs to exactly one person determinable at that time, and to infinitely many nondeterminable persons. Counting by identity gives the right answer, provided the nondeterminable hordes are left out. The R_t-relation and the I_t-relation are the same for any time t, but the R-relation and the I-relation disagree for any two stages separated by more than 137 years but no more than 274.

Perry says nothing about degrees of personal identity. However, there is nothing to prevent him from taking over all I have said. If the R-relation admits of degree, then so does personhood, no matter whether continuant persons are branches or lifetimes. Then the I_t-relations also admit of degree, and there is no obstacle here to identifying them with the corresponding R_t-relations.

I have one serious misgiving about Perry's treatment of the problem. Perry has concentrated on making things come out as they should from the standpoint of any particular time, provided that persons not then determinable are not counted among the persons existing at that time. But what shall we do when we wish to generalize over persons existing at various times? Exclusion of the nondeterminables requires a definite point of reference, which is lacking. Overpopulation sets in again. Of course my cure for overpopulation – counting by tensed identity – also requires a definite point of reference. But let us count by identity, if we count from the standpoint of no definite time. How many persons were involved in an episode of fission long ago? I say two. Perry says: three. Or else he says: none now determinable. Isn't two the correct answer?

Notes

1 Better, *quasi-memory*: that process which is memory when it occurs within one single person, but might not be properly so-called if it occurred in a succession of mental states that did not all belong to a single person.

2 Derek Parfit, "Personal Identity," *Philosophical Review* 80 (1971): 3–27 [ch. 42 in this volume].

3 Unless time is circular, so that it is in its own future in the same way that places are to the west of themselves. But that possibility also has nothing to do with survival.

4 It does not matter what sort of "aggregate." I prefer a mereological sum, so that the stages are literally parts of the continuant. But a class of stages would do as well, or a sequence or ordering of stages, or a suitable function from moments or stretches of time to stages.

5 The least clear-cut cases are those in wh stages cannot be given any "personal time" ordering with respect to which they vary in the way that the stages of an ordinary person vary with respect to time. But it is so indeterminate what we want to say about such bizarre cases that they cannot serve as counterexamples to any of my claims.

6 The argument also takes it for granted that every person-stage is a stage of at least one person. I do not object to that. If there is no way to unite a stage in a continuant with other stages, let it be a very short-lived continuant person all by itself.

7 As before, it would be better to speak here of quasi-memory; and likewise of quasi-intentional control.

8 No similar problem arises in cases of fission. We imagine the immediate postfission stages to be pretty much alike, wherefore they can all be strongly R-related to the immediate prefission stages.

9 See Bas van Fraassen, "Singular Terms, Truth-Value Gaps, and Free Logic," *Journal of Philosophy* 63 (1966): 481–95. See also the discussion of vagueness in my "General Semantics," *Synthese* 22 (1970): 18–67.

10 John Perry, "Can the Self Divide?," *Journal of Philosophy* 69 (1972): 463–88.

44

Lonely Souls: Causality and Substance Dualism

Jaegwon Kim

I   The Problem

We commonly think that we, as persons, have both a mental and a bodily dimension – or, if you prefer, mental aspects and material aspects. Something like this dualism of personhood, I believe, is common lore shared across most cultures and religious traditions, although such beliefs are not always articulated in the form of an explicit set of dogmas as in some established religions. It is often part of this "folk dualism" that we are able to survive bodily deaths, as "pure spirits," and retain all or most of the spiritual aspects of ourselves after our bodies are gone.

Spirits and souls as conceived in popular lore seem to have physical properties as well, if only vestigially physical ones, and are not what Descartes and other philosophical dualists would call souls or minds – wholly immaterial and non-physical substances outside physical space with no physical properties whatever. For example, souls are commonly said to *leave* the body when a person dies and *rise upward* toward heaven, indicating that they are thought to have, and are able to change, locations in physical space. And they

can be heard and seen, we are told, by people endowed with special virtues and in especially propitious mental states. Souls are sometimes pictured as balls of bright light, causing the air to stir barely perceptibly as they move and even emitting some unearthly sounds. Perhaps, they are composed of pure immaterial Cartesian souls and some rare and strange matter unknown to science. As is well known, Descartes thought of persons in a similar way – the difference is that for Descartes a person is a combination, or "union" as he called it, of an immaterial soul and a human body composed of ordinary matter, not some weird and ethereal stuff.

But does this conception of a person, as something made up of two radically diverse components, a body and an immaterial soul, make sense, whether the body is made up of ordinary matter or some mysterious ethereal stuff? One contention of this paper is that there is reason to think that such a conception of a person is ultimately unintelligible. My arguments will be principally based on considerations on causation – specifically, I will try to undermine the idea that immaterial souls can causally interact with

Jaegwon Kim, "Lonely Souls: Causality and Substance Dualism," in Kevin Corcoran (ed.),
Soul, Body, and Survival: The Metaphysics of the Human Person (Ithaca, NY: Cornell University Press, 2001).
Copyright © 2001 by Cornell University. Reproduced by permission of the publisher.

Metaphysics: An Anthology, Second Edition. Edited by Jaegwon Kim, Daniel Z. Korman and Ernest Sosa.
Editorial material and organization © 2012 Blackwell Publishing Ltd. Published 2012 by Blackwell Publishing Ltd.

material bodies, thereby forming a "union" with them. If I am right, it is an idea that we cannot make intelligible. In fact, it will be seen that much of the interest of my discussion, such as it is, concerns issues about mental causation and, more generally, causation itself, and, if the general drift of my arguments is correct, it will cast serious doubts on the usefulness and viability of the very notion of immaterial substance. My claim about the Cartesian "two-component" conception of persons will fall out as a corollary of what I have to say about mind-body causation under substance dualism.

II   Descartes and Mental Causation

Conventional wisdom has it that the downfall of Cartesian mind-body dualism was due to its inability to account for mental causation. In particular, as has often been noted, his radical dualism of mental and material substances was thought to be inconsistent with the possibility of causal transactions between them. Princess Elisabeth of Bohemia famously asked Descartes to explain "how man's soul, being only a thinking substance, can determine animal spirits so as to cause voluntary action."[1] According to one commentator, Richard A. Watson, the perceived inconsistency between the radical duality of minds and bodies and their causal interaction was not only a major theoretical flaw in Cartesianism but also the historical cause of its demise.[2]

The reason standardly offered for the supposed incoherence of Cartesian interactionist dualism is that it is difficult to conceive how two substances with such radically diverse natures, one in space-time with mass, inertia, and the like and the other lacking wholly in material properties and not even located in physical space, could stand in causal relations to each other. Apparently, various principles about causation, such as that cause and effect must show a certain degree of mutual affinity or "essential likeness," or that there can be no "greater reality" in an effect than there is in its cause, seem to have played a role. Anthony Kenny, for example, writes: "On Descartes' principles it is difficult to see how an unextended thinking substance can cause motion in an extended unthinking substance and how the extended unthinking substance can cause sensations in the unextended

thinking substance. The properties of the two kinds of substance seem to place them in such diverse categories that it is impossible for them to interact."[3] That is pretty much all that Kenny has to say about Descartes's troubles with mind-body causation – and, as far as I know, that is pretty much all we get from Descartes's critics and commentators. But as an argument this is incomplete and unsatisfying. As it stands, it is not much of an argument – it hardly gets started; rather, it only expresses a vague dissatisfaction of the sort that ought to prompt us to look for a real argument. Why is it incoherent to think that there can be causal relations between "diverse substances"? Why is it "impossible," as Kenny puts it, for things with diverse natures to enter into causal relations with one another? Just what sorts of diverseness make trouble and why?

It has not been an easy matter to pin down exactly what is wrong with positing causal relations between substances with diverse natures and explain in concrete terms what it is about the natures of mental and material substance that make them unfit to enter into causal relations with each other. And there have been commentators who have defended Descartes against the Kenny-style charge of incoherence. Louis Loeb is one of them.[4] Loeb's defense rests on his claim that Descartes was a proto-Humean about causation – namely that, for Descartes, causality amounted to nothing more than brute regularity, or "constant conjunction," and there can be no a priori metaphysical constraint, such as resemblance or mutual affinity, on what events can be causally joined with what other events. Loeb quotes from Descartes:

> There is no reason to be surprised that certain motions of the heart should be naturally connected in this way with certain thoughts, which they in no way resemble. The soul's natural capacity for union with a body brings with it the possibility of an association between thoughts and bodily motions or conditions so that when the same conditions recur in the body they impel the soul to the same thought; and conversely when the same thought recurs, it disposes the body to return to the same conditions.[5]

On Loeb's view, then, the fact that soul and body are of such diverse natures was, for Descartes, no barrier at all for their entering into the most intimate of causal relations, to form a "union" that is a person. Taking Loeb's word for it that Descartes was indeed a proto-Humean on the nature of causation, his point seems to me sufficient as a response to the kind of vaguely worded and inchoate objection of the sort that Kenny and many others have advanced. But does the constant conjunction view of causation really help save Descartes? I don't think it does, and the reason, I think, is simple to see and also instructive.

Suppose that two persons, Smith and Jones, are "psychophysically synchronized," as it were, in such a way that each time Smith's mind wills to raise his hand so does Jones's, and vice versa, and every time they will to raise their hands, their hands rise. There is a constant conjunction between Smith's mind's willing to raise a hand and Smith's hand's rising, and, similarly, between Jones's mind's willing to raise a hand and Jones's hand's going up. If you are a pure constant conjunctivist about causation, this would suffice for saying that a given instance of Smith's willing to raise a hand is a cause of the subsequent rising of his hand, and similarly in the case of Jones. But there is a problem here. For we see that instances of Smith's mind's willing to raise a hand are constantly conjoined not only with his hand's rising but *also with Jones's hand's rising*, and, similarly, instances of Jones's mind's willing to raise a hand are constantly conjoined with Smith's hand's rising. So why is it not the case that Smith's volition causes Jones's hand to go up, and that Jones's volition causes Smith's hand to go up?

If, however, you believe in the idea of "causal necessity" and think that constant conjunction, if it is to support a causal relation, must hold with necessity in some form, you have a prima facie answer: the constant and regular conjunction between Smith's mind's willing to raise a hand and Jones's hand's going up is only coincidental, carrying no force of necessity. And this is perhaps manifest in the fact that there are no counterfactual dependencies between these events: for example, it is not true that if Smith had not willed that a hand should rise, Jones's hand would not have gone up.

But it won't do to say that after all Smith wills *his* hand to rise and that's why his willing causes his hand, not Jones's hand, to rise. It isn't clear what this reply can accomplish, but it begs the question on hand. The reason is that, according to the standard interpretation of Descartes, what makes Smith's hand Smith's, not Jones's – that is, what makes Smith's body the body with which Smith's mind is "united" – is the fact that there is specially intimate and direct causal commerce between the two. To say that this is the body with which this mind is united is to say that this body is the only material thing that this mind can *directly* affect – that is, without other bodies serving as causal intermediaries – and that all changes this mind can cause in other bodies are caused by changes in this body. This is *my* body, and this is *my* arm, because it is something that I can move without moving any other body. I can raise *your* arm only by grabbing it with my hand and pulling it up.[6] And something similar must obtain in the direction of body-to-mind causation as well. The "union" of a mind and a body that Descartes speaks of, therefore, presupposes mental causation. Whether or not this interpretation of Descartes is historically correct, a causal account of "ownership" seems the most natural option for substance dualists, and I do not know of noncausal alternatives that make any real sense.

I have heard some people say that we could simply take the concept of the mind's "union" with a body as a primitive, and that it is simply a primitive fact, perhaps divinely ordained, that this mind and this body are integrated into a proper union that is a person. But I find such an approach unintelligible. For it seems to concede that the notion of "union" of minds and bodies, and hence the notion of a person, are unintelligible. If God chose to unite my body with my mind, just what is it that he did? I am not asking *why* he chose to unite this particular mind with this particular body, or *why* he decided to engage in such activities as uniting minds and bodies at all, or *whether* he, or anyone else, could have powers to do things like that. If God united my mind and my body there must be a relationship R such that a mind stands in relation R to a body if and only if that mind and that body constitute a unitary person. In uniting my mind and my body, God related the two with R. Unless we know what R is, we do not know what God did. Again, we are not asking *how* God managed to establish R between a mind and a body – as far as we are concerned, that can remain a mystery forever. We only want to know *what* God did.

III   Causation and the "Pairing" Problem

The difficulty we have seen with Loeb's interpretation of Descartes as a Humean in matters of causation, I believe, points to a more fundamental difficulty in the idea that mental substances, outside physical space, can enter into causal relations with objects in physical space, a difficulty that is not resolved when, as above, some sort of "necessary connection" is invoked as a constituent of causal relations. What is perhaps more surprising, the very same difficulty besets the idea that such nonspatial mental substances can enter into any sort of causal relations, whether with material things or with other mental substances.

Let us begin with a simple example of physical causation: two rifles, A and B, are simultaneously fired, and this results in the simultaneous death of two persons, Andy and Buddy. What makes it the case that the firing of rifle A caused Andy's death and the firing of rifle B caused Buddy's death, and not the other way around? What are the principles that underlie the correct and incorrect *pairings* of cause and effect in a situation like this? We can call this "the causal pairing problem," or "the pairing problem" for short.[7]

Two possible ways for handling this problem come to mind.

1.   We can trace a continuous causal chain from the firing of rifle A to Andy's death, and another such chain from the firing of B to Buddy's death. (Indeed, we can, with a high-speed camera, trace the bullet's path from rifle A to Andy, etc.) No causal chain exists from the firing of A to Buddy's death, or from the firing of B to Andy's death.

2.   We look for a "pairing relation," R, that holds between A's firing and Andy's death and between B's firing and Buddy's death, but not between A's firing and Buddy's death or B's firing and Andy's death. In this particular case, when the two rifles were fired, rifle A, not rifle B, was located at a certain distance from Andy and pointed in his direction, and similarly with rifle B and Buddy. It is these *spatial relations* (distance, orientation, etc.) that help pair the firing of A with Andy's death and the firing of B with Buddy's

death. Spatial relations seem to serve as the "pairing relations" in this case, and perhaps for all cases of physical causation involving distinct objects.

The two methods may be related, but let us set aside this question for now.

Let us now turn to a situation involving non-physical Cartesian souls as causal agents. There are two souls, A and B, and they perform a certain mental action, as a result of which a change occurs in material substance M. We may suppose that mental actions of the kind involved generally cause physical changes of the sort that happened in M, and, moreover, that in the present case it is soul A's action, not soul B's, that caused the change in M. Surely, such a possibility must exist. But ask: What relation might perform the job of pairing soul A's action with the change in M, a relation that is absent in the case of soul B's action and the change in M? Evidently, no spatial relations can be invoked to answer this question, for souls are not in space and are not able to bear spatial relations to material things. Soul A cannot be any "nearer" to material object M, or more appropriately "oriented" with respect to it, than soul B is. Is there anything that can do for souls what space, or the network of spatial relations, does for material things?

Let us now consider the possibility of causality within a purely mental world – a world inhabited only by Cartesian souls. Soul A acts in a certain way at time *t* and so does soul B at the same time. This is followed by certain changes in two other souls, A* and B*. Suppose that actions of A and B are causes of the changes in A* and B*. But which cause caused which effect? If we want a solution that is analogous to case 2 above for rifle firings and dyings, what we need is a pairing relation R such that R holds, say, for A and A*, and for B and B*, but not for A and B*, or for B and A*. Since the entities are immaterial souls outside physical space, R cannot be a spatial, or any other kind of physical, relation. The radical non-spatiality of mental substances rules out the possibility of invoking any spatial relationship for the cause-effect pairing.

Evidently, then, the pairing relation R must be some kind of psychological relation. But what could that be? Could R be some kind of intentional relation, such as thinking of, picking out,

and referring? Perhaps, soul A gazes at soul A*
and B*, and then pick outs A*, and causes a
change in it. But how do we understand these
relations like gazing at and picking out? What is it
for A to pick out A* rather than B*? To pick out
something outside us, we must be in a certain
episternic relationship with it; we must perceive it
somehow and be able to distinguish it from other
things around it – that is, perceptually identify it.
Take perception: What is it for me to perceive this
tree, not another tree which is hidden behind it
and which is qualitatively indistinguishable from
it? The only credible answer is that the tree I perceive is the one that is causing my perceptual
experience as of a tree, and that I do not see the
hidden tree because it bears no causal relation to
my perceptual experience.[8] Ultimately, these
intentional relations must be explained on the
basis of causal relations (this is not to say that
they are entirely reducible to causality), and I do
not believe we can explain what it is for soul A to
pick out soul A* rather than B* except by positing
some kind of causal relation that holds for A and
A* but not for A and B*. If this is right, invoking
intentional relations to do causal pairings begs
the question: we need causal relations to understand intentional relations. Even if intentional
relations were free of causal involvements, that
would not in itself show that they would suffice as
pairing relations. In addition, they must satisfy
certain structural requirements; this will become
clear below.

We are not necessarily supposing that one single R will suffice for all causal relations between
two mental substances. But if the physical case is
any guide, we seem to be in need of a certain kind
of "space," not physical space of course, but some
kind of a nonphysical coordinate system that gives
every mental substance and every event involving
a mental substance a *unique location* (at a time),
and which yields for each pair of mental entities a
determinate relationship defined by their locations. Such a system of "mental space" could provide us with a basis for a solution to the pairing
problem, and enable us to make sense of causal
relations between nonspatial mental entities. But I
don't think that we have the foggiest idea what
such a framework might look like – what psychological relations might generate such a structure.

What about using the notion of causal chain
to connect the souls in the right cause-effect

relationships? Can there be a causal chain between
soul A's action and the change in soul A*, and
between soul B's action and the change in soul
B*? But do we have an understanding of such
purely mental causal chains? What could such
chains be like outside physical space? Hume
required that a cause-effect pair of events that are
spatiotemporally separated be connected by a
causal chain of *spatially contiguous* events. It is
difficult to imagine what kind of causal chain
might be inserted between events involving two
mental substances. Presumably we have to place a
third soul, C, between soul A and soul A*, such
that A's action causes a change in C which in turn
causes the change in A*. But what could "between"
mean here? What is it for an immaterial and
nonspatial thing to be "between" two other immaterial and nonspatial things? In the physical case it
is physical space that gives a sense to betweenness.
In the mental case, what would serve the role that
space serves in the physical case?

One might say: For C to be "between" A and A*
in a sense relevant to present purposes is for A's
action to cause a change in C and for this change
to cause a change in A*. That is, betweenness is to
be taken simply as causal betweenness. This of
course is the idea of a causal chain, but it is clear
that this idea does not give us an independent
handle on the pairing problem. The reason is
simple: it begs the question. Our original question was: How do we pair soul A's action with a
change in soul A*? Now we have two pairing
problems instead of one: First, we need to pair
soul A's action with a change in a third soul, C,
and then pair this change in C with the change in
A*. This means that methods 1 and 2 above are
not really independent. The very idea of a causal
chain makes sense only if an appropriate notion
of causation is already on hand, and this requires
a prior solution to the pairing problem. This
means that method 2 is the only thing we have.

We are, therefore, back with 2 – that is,
with the question what psychological relations
might serve the role that spatial relations serve
in the case of physical causation. The problem
here is independent of the Humean constant
conjunction view of causation, and therefore
independent of the difficulty we raised for Loeb's
defense of Descartes. For suppose that there is a
"necessary," counterfactual sustaining, regularity
connecting properties F and G of immaterial mental

substances. A mental substance, A has F at t, and at t^*, and an instant later, two mental substances, B and C, acquire property G. I think we would like the following to be a possible situation: A's having F at t causes B to have G at t^*, but it does not cause C to have G at t^*. If so, there must be an intelligible account of why A acts on B but not on C, and such an account must be grounded in a certain relation, a "pairing relation," holding for A and B but not for A and C. What conceivable psychological or intentional relation, or system of such relations, could serve this purpose? I don't have a clue.

If these reflections are not entirely wrongheaded, our idea of causation requires that the causally connected items be situated in a spacelike framework. It has been widely believed, as we noted, that Cartesian dualism of two substances runs into insurmountable difficulties in explaining the possibility of causal relations across the two domains, mental-to-physical and physical-to-mental – especially the former. But what our considerations show is that there is an even deeper difficulty – substantival dualism is faced with difficulties even in explaining how mental-to-mental causation is possible, how two distinct Cartesian souls could be in causal commerce with each other. Perhaps Leibniz was wise to renounce all causal relations between individual substances, or monads – although I have no idea as to his actual reasons for this view. A purely Cartesian world seems like a pretty lonely place, inhabited by immaterial souls each of which is an island unto itself, totally isolated from all other souls. Even the actual world, if we are immaterial souls, would be a lonely place for us; each of us, as an immaterial entity, would be entirely cut off from anything else, whether physical or nonphysical, in our surroundings. Can you imagine any existence that is lonelier than an immaterial self?

IV   Causation and Space

The fact, assuming this to be a fact, that the causal pairing problem for physical causation is solved only by invoking spatial relations tells us, I believe, something important about physical causation and the physical domain. By locating each and every physical item – object and event – in an all-encompassing coordinate system, this framework imposes a determinate relation on every pair of items in the physical domain. Causal structure of the physical domain, or our ability to impose a causal structure on it, presupposes this space-time framework. Causal relations must be selective and discriminating, in the sense that there can be two objects with identical intrinsic properties such that a third object causally acts on one of them but not the other (this can be stated for events as well), and, similarly, that there can be two intrinsically indiscernible objects such that one of them, but not the other, causally acts on a third object. If so, there must be a principled way of distinguishing the two intrinsically indiscernible objects in such causal situations, and it seems that spatial relations provide us with the principal means for doing this. Although this isn't the place to enter into detailed discussion, spatial relations have the right sorts of properties; for example, causal influences generally diminish as distance in space increases, and various sorts of barriers can be set up in the right places in space to prevent or impede propagation of causal influences (though perhaps not gravity!). In general, causal relations between physical objects or events depend crucially on their spatiotemporal relations to each other; just think of the point of establishing alibis – "I wasn't there," if true, is sufficient for "I didn't do it." And the temporal order alone will not be sufficient to provide us with such a basis. We need a full space-time framework for this purpose. It wasn't for nothing, after all, that Hume included "contiguity" in space and time, as well as constant conjunction, among his conditions for causal relations. From our present perspective, Hume's contiguity condition can be seen as a response to the pairing problem.

If this is right, it gives us one plausible way of vindicating the critics of Descartes who, as we saw, argued that the radically diverse natures of mental and material substances preclude causal relations between them. It is of the essence of material substances that they have determinate positions in the space-time framework and that there is a determinate spatiotemporal relationship between each pair of them. Descartes of course talked of extendedness in space as the essence of matter, but we can broadly construe this to include other spatial properties and relations for material substances. Now consider the mental side: as I take it, the Cartesian doctrine has it that it is part of the souls' essential nature that they are outside the spatial order and lack all spatial properties, though they do belong to the temporal order. And it is this essential nonspatiality that makes trouble for their participation in causal structures. What is interesting is that it isn't just mind-to-body causation but also mind-to-mind causation that is put in jeopardy.

We have already seen how difficulties arise for mind-to-body and mind-to-mind causation. Unsurprisingly, body-to-mind causation fares no better. Let's quickly run through this: Consider a physical object causally acting on a mental sub-stance, causing it to have property F at time t. Suppose that there is another mental substance that begins to have F at t, but not as a causal result of the physical object's action. How might the pair-ing problem be solved in this case? To solve it, we need to identify a relation R that holds between the physical object and the mental substance it causally affects but which does not hold between the physi-cal object and the second mental substance. The only relation that can do this for physical objects is the spatial relation, but the very essence of a mental substance excludes it from any and all spatial rela-tions. Moreover, given the fact that we could not devise a system of pairing relations for the domain of mental substances, it seems out of the question that we could generate a system that would work across the divide between the mental and material realms. If this is true, not even epiphenomenalism is an option for the substance dualist.

I am not claiming that these considerations are what motivated the anti-Cartesian argument that mind-body causal interaction is incoherent given the radically diverse natures of minds and bodies, or the absence of similarity or affinity between them. I am only suggesting that this may be one way to flesh out the critics' worries and show that there is a real and concrete basis for these worries. Causal interaction is precluded between mental and material substances because of their diverse essential natures – more specifically, because of the essential spatiality of bodies and the essential nonspatiality of minds. Causality requires a pair-ing relation, and this diversity between minds and bodies does not permit such relations connecting minds and bodies. What the critics perhaps didn't see was the possibility that essentially the same difficulty bedevils causal relations *within* the realm of the minds as well.

V   Can We Locate Souls in Space?

These reflections might lead one to wonder whether it would help the cause of substance dualism if mental substances were at least given spatial locations, not as extended substances like material bodies but as extensionless geometric points. After all, Descartes spoke of the pineal gland as "the seat" of the soul, and it is easy to find passages in his writings that seem to give souls positions in space, although this probably was not part of his official doctrine. And most people who believe in souls, philosophers included, appear to think that our souls are in our bodies at least – my soul in my body, your soul in your body, and so on. But I would hazard that this conviction is closely associated with the idea that my soul is in direct causal contact with my body and your soul with your body. The pineal gland is the seat of the soul for Descartes, as I take it, only because it is where unmediated mind-body causal interaction takes place. If all this is right, this confirms my speculation that mind-body causation generates pressure to somehow bring minds into space, which, for Descartes, is exclusively the realm of the matter.

In any case, putting souls into physical space may create more problems than it solves. For one thing, we need a principled way of locating each soul at a particular point in space. It is difficult to imagine how this can be done (why can't we locate all the souls in the world in one place, say in this empty coffee mug on my desk, like the many angels on the head of a pin?). It would obvi-ously beg the question to locate my soul where my body, or brain, is on the ground that my soul and my body are in direct causal interaction with each other. Second, if locating souls in space is to help with the pairing problem, it must be the case that no more than one soul can occupy an identi-cal spatial point; for otherwise spatial relations would not suffice to uniquely identify each soul in relation to other souls in space. This is analo-gous to the so-called principle of "impenetrabil-ity of matter," a principle whose point can be taken as the claim that space provides us with a criterion of individuation for material things. According to it, material objects occupying exactly the same spatial region are one and the same. What we need is a similar principle for souls, that is, a principle of "impenetrability of souls": Two distinct souls cannot occupy exactly the same point in space. But if souls are subject to spatial exclusion, in addition to the fact that the exercise of their causal powers are constrained by spatial relations, why aren't souls just material objects, albeit of a very special, and strange, kind? Moreover, there is a prior question: Why should we think that a principle of spatial exclusion applies to immaterial souls? To solve the pairing problem for souls by placing them in space requires such a principle, but that's not a reason for thinking that the principle holds; we cannot wish it into being – we need independent reasons and evidence.

Moreover, if a soul, all of it, is at a geometric point, it is puzzling how it could have enough structure to account for all the marvelous causal work it is supposed to perform and explain the differences between souls in regard to their causal powers. You may say: A soul's causal powers arise from its mental structure, and mental structure doesn't take up space. But what is mental structure? What are its parts and how are the parts configured in a structure? If a soul's mental structure is to account for its distinctive causal powers, then, given the pairing problem and the essentiality of spatial relations for causation, it is unclear how wholly nonspatial mental structure could give an explanation of a soul's causal powers. To go on: If souls exclude each other for spatial occupancy, do souls exclude material bodies as well? If not, why not? It may be that one's dualist commitments dictate certain answers to these questions. But that would hardly show they are the "true" answers. We shouldn't do philosophy by first deciding what conclusions we want to prove, or what aims we want to realize, and then posit convenient entities and premises to get us where we want to go. When we think of the myriad problems and puzzles that arise from locating souls in physical space, it is difficult to escape the impression that whatever answers that might be offered would likely look ad hoc and fail to convince.

I have tried to explore considerations that seem to show that the causal relation indeed exerts a strong, perhaps irresistible, pressure toward a degree of homogeneity over its domain, and, moreover, that the kind of homogeneity it requires probably includes, at a minimum, spatiotemporality, which arguably entails physicality.

The more we think about causation, the clearer becomes our realization, I think, that the possibility of causation between distinct objects depends on a shared spacelike coordinate system in which these objects are located, a scheme that individuates objects by their "locations" in the scheme. Are there such schemes other than the scheme of physical space? I don't believe we know of any. This alone makes trouble for serious substance dualisms and dualist conceptions of personhood – unless, like Leibniz, you are prepared to give up causal relations for substances altogether. Malebranche denied causal relations between all finite substances, reserving causal powers exclusively for God, the only genuine causal agent that there is. It is perhaps not surprising that among the dualists of his time, Descartes was the only major philosopher who chose to include minds as an integral part of the causal structure of the world. In defense of Descartes, we can ask: What would be the point of having souls as immaterial substances if they turn out to have no causal powers, not even powers to be affected by things around them? Before we castigate Descartes for his possibly unworkable metaphysics, therefore, we should applaud him for showing a healthy respect for common sense in his defense of mental causation and his insistence on making sense of our intuitive dualistic conception of what it is to be a person.

Notes

Thanks to David Armstrong, Jerry Katz, Noah Latham, Barry Loewer, Eugene Mills, Timothy O'Connor, Alvin Plantinga, and Ernest Sosa for helpful comments and suggestions. This paper is descended from a paper first presented at a conference on mind-body dualism at the University of Notre Dame in March 1998.

1 Margaret Wilson, ed., *The Essential Descartes* (New York: New American Library, 1969), 373.

2 Richard A. Watson, *The Downfall of Cartesianism 1673–1712* (The Hague: Martinus Nijhoff, 1966).

3 Anthony Kenny, *Descartes* (New York: Random House, 1968), 222–3.

4 Louis E. Loeb, *From Descartes to Hume* (Ithaca: Cornell University Press, 1981). See 134–49.

5 Anthony Kenny, trans. and ed., *Descartes' Philosophical Letters* (Oxford: Oxford University Press, 1963), 210. I am rather dubious as to whether

this passage supports Loeb's Humean interpretation of Descartes, for Descartes is using here causal verbs, "impel" and "dispose," to describe the regularities. But Loeb may well be right, and I am not in a position to challenge him on this point.

6 Does this exclude telekinesis? Yes. This probably is the main reason why there is something a priori strange about telekinesis. If telekinesis were a widespread everyday phenomenon, that might very well undermine the idea that each of us has a distinct body.

7 I first discussed this problem in "Causation, Nomic Subsumption, and the Concept of Event," *Journal of Philosophy* 70 (1973): 217–36. I was prompted to reflect on the issues involved here by John Foster's "Psychophysical Causal Relations," *American Philosophical Quarterly* 5 (1968): 64–70.

8 This of course is the causal theory of perception. See H. P. Grice, "The Causal Theory of Perception," *Proceedings of the Aristotelian Society*, supp. vol. 35 (1961).

45

The Ontological Status of Persons

Lynne Rudder Baker

Throughout his illustrious career, Roderick Chisholm was concerned with the nature of persons. On his view, persons are what he called '*entia per se.*' They exist per se, in their own right. I too have developed an account of persons – I call it the 'Constitution View' – an account that is different in important ways from Chisholm's. Here, however, I want to focus on a thesis that Chisholm and I agree on: that persons have ontological significance in virtue of being persons. Although I'll make the notion of ontological significance more precise later, the rough idea is that Fs (persons, or whatever) have ontological significance just in case a new F is a new thing and not just a change in some already-existing thing.

The Constitution View offers a way to place a traditional preoccupation of the great philosophers in the context of the "neo-Darwinian synthesis" in biology.[1] The traditional preoccupation concerns our inwardness – our abilities not just to think, but to think about our thoughts; to see ourselves and each other as subjects; to have rich inner lives. The modern synthesis in biology has made it clear that we are biological beings, continuous with the rest of the animal kingdom.

The Constitution View of human persons recognizes our uniqueness even as it tries to show how we are part of the world of organisms.

On the Constitution View, something is a *person* in virtue of having a first-person perspective (or a narrowly defined capacity for one),[2] and something is a *human* person in virtue of being a person constituted by a human animal (or body).[3] Human persons are material beings, part of the natural order. As I develop the idea of constitution, this view of human persons has the consequence that although I am both a person and an animal, I am most fundamentally a person. Hence, my persistence conditions are the persistence conditions of a person (sameness of first-person perspective), not the persistence conditions of an animal (sameness of biological organism).[4] I could continue to exist without being an animal, but I could not continue to exist without being a person. If parts of my human body were replaced by synthetic parts until the body that constitutes me was no longer a human animal, then, as long as my first-person perspective remained intact, I would continue to exist and I would continue to be a person. But if nothing

Lynne Rudder Baker, "The Ontological Status of Persons," *Philosophy and Phenomenological Research*, 65/2 (Sept. 2002): 370–88. Reproduced by permission.

Metaphysics: An Anthology, Second Edition. Edited by Jaegwon Kim, Daniel Z. Korman and Ernest Sosa.

had my first-person perspective, then there would be no me. To put this controversial thesis in a slogan: Persons are essentially persons.[5]

I'll structure my elucidation and defense of the thesis that persons have ontological significance as follows: First, I'll explain my idea of constitution and its distinctive features. Second, I'll work out an account of ontological significance, on which both Chisholm's view and the Constitution View accord persons ontological significance. Then, I'll turn to Animalism, according to which persons are essentially animals, and show that Animalism in its several forms does not accord persons ontological significance. Finally, I'll urge – against Animalism – that what is distinctive about persons is enough to give them ontological significance.

The Idea of Constitution

The relation of constitution is exemplified all around us: Not only do human bodies constitute persons, but also DNA molecules constitute genes; pieces of plastic constitute drivers' licenses; aggregates of water molecules constitute rivers. So, constitution is a very general relation.

Several features of the idea of constitution will be important here. First, the relation of constitution, which I have discussed in elaborate detail elsewhere,[6] is in some ways like identity. However, constitution is not identity. If you wonder how a relation could be *like* identity, but not *be* identity, think of what philosophers have called "contingent identity." By 'identity,' I mean strict identity: $x = y \rightarrow \Box(x = y)$. The idea of constitution plays the role in my view that the idea of "contingent identity" plays in others' views. (Indeed, one advantage of my views is that I can achieve what other philosophers want when they invoke ersatz "identity," without cheapening the idea of identity.) Identity is necessary; constitution is contingent. Hence, constitution is not identity.

Behind the idea of constitution is an Aristotelian assumption. For any x, we can ask: What most fundamentally is x? The answer will be what I call x's 'primary kind.' Everything that exists is of exactly one primary kind – e.g., a horse or a passport or a cabbage. A thing's primary kind determines its persistence conditions. And since its primary-kind property

determines what a thing most fundamentally is, a thing has its primary-kind property essentially.[7] It could not exist without having its primary-kind property.[8]

Although the idea of primary kinds is inspired by Aristotle, I differ from Aristotle in several ways: First, according to the Constitution View, there are primary kinds of artifacts, as well as of natural objects. Second, according to the Constitution View, a primary kind may be just a kind of thing; it does not have to be a kind of a broader kind (like a kind of furniture). In particular, although on my view, *person* is a primary kind, I need not say that a person is a kind *of* some further kind (such as a kind of animal).[9] Third, as we shall see in the discussion of borrowing properties, something may have a primary-kind property without having that property *as* its primary-kind property. Something may have a primary-kind property contingently when suitably related to something that has it essentially.[10]

Constitution is a relation that things have in virtue of their primary kinds. The basic idea is that when things of certain primary kinds are in certain circumstances, things of new primary kinds, with new kinds of causal powers, come into existence. For example, when a piece of marble is carved by a member of an artworld, a sculptor, to have a certain shape, a new thing of a new kind – a statue – comes into existence. If a piece of marble constitutes a statue, then the primary kind of the marble statue is *statue*. The piece of marble still exists, but the statue now has pre-eminence. What makes the difference between a sculpture and a mere piece of marble is that the existence of the sculpture requires an artworld or an artist's intention or whatever is required by the correct theory of sculptural art.

What makes the difference between a human person and a human animal is that the existence of the person requires a first-person perspective. Your persistence conditions are determined by your having a first-person perspective; your body's persistence conditions are determined by its being a human animal. The organism that constitutes you, the person, retains its persistence conditions even though you-as-constituted-by-that-organism have the persistence conditions of a person.[11]

If constitution is not identity, we need an explanation of the fact that, if x constitutes y at t, then x and y share so many properties at t.

Not only are x and y at the same places at the same times (as long as one constitutes the other), but x and y have many properties in common: weighing 200 lbs., having a toothache, running a 4-minute mile – properties that do not entail the existence of anything at any other time or in any other world.

There is an explanation: Even though constitution is not identity, it is a relation of genuine unity. And because constitution is a relation of genuine unity, if x constitutes y at t, x may borrow properties at t from y and y may borrow properties at t from x. (Chisholm introduced me to the idea of borrowing properties, but I have modified his idea quite a bit for my own purposes. On my view, if x constitutes y at t, then both x and y borrow properties at t from each other.) The intuitive idea of borrowing a property or of having a property derivatively is simple. If x constitutes y at t, then some of x's properties at t have their source (so to speak) in y, and some of y's properties at t have their source in x. I have put this less metaphorically elsewhere by defining 'x has property H at t derivatively,' but here I'll just illustrate the idea. Consider some properties of my drivers' license, which is constituted by a piece of plastic: My drivers' license has the property of being rectangular only because it is constituted by something that could have been rectangular even if it had constituted nothing. And the piece of plastic has the property of impressing the policeman only because it constitutes something that would have impressed the policeman (a valid drivers' license) no matter what constituted it. The drivers' license has the property of being rectangular derivatively, and of impressing the policeman nonderivatively; the piece of plastic that constitutes my drivers' license has the property of being rectangular nonderivatively, and of impressing the policeman derivatively.

The second illustration of having a property derivatively is perhaps more controversial. Person is your primary kind. Human animal is your body's primary kind. You are a person nonderivatively and a human animal derivatively; and your body is a human animal nonderivatively and a person derivatively. Although you are a person and your body is a person, there are not two persons where you are. This is so because constitution is a unity relation. If x constitutes y at t, and x is an F at t derivatively and y is an F at t

nonderivatively – or vice versa – then there are not thereby two Fs.[12] Even though being a person is a primary-kind property that you have nonderivatively, your body has that property derivatively; but it (the property of being a person) is not your body's primary-kind property. Everything has its own primary-kind property essentially; but it can have a second primary-kind property contingently. For example, your body's primary-kind property is the property of being a human animal. Your body has that property essentially; although your body also has the property of being a person contingently, the property of being a person is not your body's primary-kind property. Your body is a person derivatively – solely in virtue of constituting you (who are a person nonderivatively). Your body is not a separate person from you; the fact that your body is a person is just the fact that you are a person (nonderivatively) and your body constitutes you.[13]

Not all properties may be borrowed, or had derivatively.[14] For example, although primary-kind properties – like being a person, or being a human animal – may be had derivatively, other properties – like being a person essentially, or having human animal as one's primary kind – cannot be had derivatively. So, my body has the property of being a person (derivatively), but my body does not have the property of *having being a person as its primary-kind property* at all (not derivatively, not nonderivatively). Rather, my body has the property of being a human organism as its primary-kind property. If being an F and being a G are two primary-kind properties, x may have both – one as its primary-kind property and the other derivatively – but x is not of two primary kinds.[15]

The fact that constitution is a relation of real unity has two implications for the idea of having properties derivatively: On the one hand, if x has a property derivatively, then there are not two separate exemplifications of the property: x has the property solely in virtue of its constitution-relations to something that has the property independently. On the other hand, if x has a property derivatively, x still really has it. I really am a body (derivatively); if my foot itches, then I itch. And my body is really a person (now); when I have a right to be in a certain seat, my body has a right to be in that seat. Constitution is so intimate a relation, so close to identity, that if x constitutes y at t, then – solely in virtue of the fact that x constitutes y – x has properties derivatively at t that x would not have had if x had not constituted y. (And vice versa.) The idea of having properties derivatively accounts for the otherwise strange fact that if x constitutes y at t, x and y share so many properties even though x ≠ y.

Before leaving the topic of constitution, I need to discuss a common criticism of the Constitution View. The criticism is that the Constitution View makes it too easy for new things to come into existence. We certainly do not want to say, for example, that at the founding of the United States a new entity, the President, came into being. But there seems to be nothing in the Constitution View to prevent taking the President to be a new entity, constituted by different people (starting with George Washington) at different times.[16]

The critic has a point. What I need is a theory of primary kinds to distinguish cases of property-acquisition (George Washington merely acquired the property of being President) from cases of constitution (a piece of clay came to constitute a statue). I do have a theory of sorts; at least it is a condition on primary kinds: A kind K is a primary kind just in case (nonderivative) members of K have their persistence conditions in virtue of being members of kind K. Although this seems fine as far as it goes, it may not fully satisfy the critic. For it provides no way to adjudicate disagreements about which properties do determine persistence conditions. For example, I include among primary kinds organisms (e.g., maggots, redwoods, dogs), artifacts (e.g., telephones, submarines, stamps), and artworks (e.g., sculptures, paintings), but not social roles (e.g., President). Others may disagree.

In addition to the condition on primary kinds – that primary-kind properties determine persistence conditions of their nonderivative bearers – I can offer two characteristics that distinguish constitution from property-acquisition. If x constitutes a G, as opposed to just acquiring the property of being a G, then the G has whole classes of causal properties that x would not have had if x had not constituted something. Pieces of paper constitute dollar bills, and dollar bills have a whole range of vastly different kinds of causal properties – e.g., they pay off your debts, bribe the mayor, give you peace of mind, allow you to quench your thirst by inserting them into machines – a whole range of causal properties that the constituting pieces of paper would not have had if they had not constituted anything. A second characteristic of constitution is its relative stability. For example, pieces of metal constitute keys, but if I have a metal dogtag and use it to jimmy a lock, my dogtag does not thereby constitute a key. Rather, it merely acquires the property of being used to jimmy a lock. But both of these characteristics – new causal properties and relative stability – are admittedly vague.

I am satisfied to think of the idea of constitution as offering a form of a theory that needs to be filled out by a theory of primary kinds. For purposes here, however, I only need the claim that *person* is a primary kind, and later, I'll give reasons to consider the person case to be a matter of constitution, and not mere property acquisition.

To conclude the discussion of constitution: The aim of my conception of constitution is to make sense of a relation more intimate than separate existence, but still not identity. I take identity to be necessary or strict identity: If (x = y), then $\Box(x = y)$. Many philosophers think that if x and y are not identical, then they are just two different things, like the sun and the moon. The notion of constitution offers a third position, a position intermediate between identity and separate existence. (Say that x and y have separate existence at t if and only if there is no property F such that x and y are the same F at t.) For any x and y, there are three (not two) possibilities: strict identity, constitution, and separate existence. In *Persons and Bodies*, I give a general definition of 'constitution' that shows that there is "logical space" for such an intermediate position.[17] Thus, any criticism of my view that presupposes that nonidentity entails separate existence begs the question against my view.

Chisholm also uses the term 'constitution,' but for a relation somewhat different from the one I am trying to elucidate. On Chisholm's view, being constituted is a mark of ontological inferiority. On his view, if a table, say, is made up of boards AB on Monday and BC on Tuesday, then the table (which existed on both Monday and Tuesday) is an ontological parasite – a mere *ens successivum* – that does not exist in its own right.[18] Clearly, I am not using 'constitution' in Chisholm's way.[19] On my view, if x constitutes y at t, then x is not just a stand-in at t for y: y exists in its own right. And not only does y borrow properties from x at t, but also x borrows properties from y at t.[20]

Here, then, is a significant contrast between Chisholm's and my conceptions of constitution. Rather than being a relation between a really existing thing and an ontological parasite, constitution on my view is a relation between really existing individuals. A world with assault weapons, fiber-optic cables, and space stations is ontologically richer than a world that contains only the particles produced by the Big Bang. A world with organisms in it is ontologically richer than a world that contains no organisms but contains all the chemicals that make up amino acids and proteins. On Chisholm's view, constitution produces ontological parasites; on my view, constitution provides a vehicle of ontological novelty.

Ontological Significance

Despite these differences between Chisholm's view and mine, Chisholm and I are allies in rejecting views that deny that persons have ontological status.[21] While disagreeing with Chisholm that a person is an *ens per se* – which cannot gain or lose parts nor come into being or pass away gradually – I heartily endorse his larger point that a person is not an ontological parasite. Moreover, Chisholm is right to hold that 'person' is not a phase-sortal like 'child,' nor does it designate a property or an abstract entity, nor does it refer to a logical construction of nonpersonal elements, nor is it just an honorific for human animals. Persons, Chisholm and I agree, are real individuals whose appearance in the world makes an ontological difference. They have ontological significance. Now I want to try to spell out what I mean by saying that persons are ontologically significant.

Intuitively, to say that Fs (tigers, chairs, anything) have ontological significance is to say that the addition of a (nonderivative)[22] F is not just a change in something that already exists, but the coming-into-being of a new thing. The primary bearers of ontological significance are properties; things have ontological significance in virtue of having ontologically significant properties. Every individual thing that exists has

ontological significance in virtue of some property or other. Ontologically significant properties must be essential to their (nonderivative) bearers. For example, being a student is not an ontologically significant property; being a water molecule is: The difference, I think, lies in the idea of persistence conditions.[23] A water molecule has its persistence conditions in virtue of being a water molecule; a student does not have her persistence conditions in virtue of being a student. To generalize:

(OS1)   The property of being an F has ontological significance if and only if, necessarily, if x is an F (nonderivatively), then being an F determines x's persistence conditions.

Here is the rationale for (OS1). Suppose that the property of being an F has ontological significance. Then, the instantiation of that property brings into existence a new thing, an F. Every existing thing has persistence conditions, and has its persistence conditions essentially. Since the F has its persistence conditions essentially, instantiation of the property sufficient for bringing the F into existence must be sufficient for the F's having the persistence conditions that it has. Therefore, if the property of being an F is ontologically significant, then the property of being an F determines the (nonderivative) F's persistence conditions.

On the other hand, if the property of being an F determines the (nonderivative) F's persistence conditions, then the instantiation of the property of being an F entails that there is an F with those persistence conditions. Since things have their persistence conditions essentially, the F could not have existed before the instantiation of the property of being an F (which determines the F's persistence conditions). So, the instantiation of the property of being an F brings into existence a new entity, and the property of being an F has ontological significance. Therefore, if the property of being an F determines the (nonderivative) F's persistence conditions, the property of being an F has ontological significance. Hence, (OS1).

Ontological significance is not only a feature of properties, but also a feature of things that have those properties:

(OS2)   (Nonderivative) Fs have ontological significance in virtue of being Fs if and only if the property of being an F has ontological significance.

I'll use 'Fs have ontological significance' to abbreviate '(nonderivative) Fs have ontological significance in virtue of being Fs'.[24] (OS1) and (OS2) aim to explicate the basic idea of ontological significance: Being an F is an ontologically significant property if and only if the addition of a (nonderivative) F adds to the stock of what there is.[25]

Since 'is a nonderivative F' in the vocabulary of the Constitution View is equivalent to 'is an F' in other vocabularies, the qualification 'nonderivative' in (OS1) and (OS2) is no restriction on the generality of these necessary and sufficient conditions for ontological significance. Outside the context of the Constitution View, the qualification 'nonderivative' may be dropped without loss.

Now it is easy to see that on the Constitution View, persons[26] have ontological significance, given (OS1) and (OS2). Indeed, since every primary-kind property determines the persistence conditions of its (nonderivative) bearers, every primary-kind property has ontological significance – being a person, being a human animal, being a statue, being a piece of marble. So, on the Constitution View, persons and human animals both have ontological significance. Persons have ontological significance in virtue of being persons, even when they are constituted by human animals; human animals have ontological significance in virtue of being human animals, even when they constitute persons.

Likewise, on Chisholm's view, persons are ontologically significant. Indeed, Chisholm begins with the assumption that persons are *entia per se*, and the idea of an *ens per se* is formulated in terms of persistence conditions: *entia per se* cannot gain or lose parts without ceasing to exist, nor can they come into existence or pass away gradually. On one of Chisholm's definitions, a person is "that which is necessarily such that it is physically possible that there is a time at which that thing consciously thinks."[27] And he takes it that anything that instantiates this property is an *ens per se* – a being that has the persistence conditions of persons. So, according to (OS1) and (OS2), persons are ontologically significant both on my view and on Chisholm's.

Animalist Accounts of Persons

Chisholm and I not only agree that persons have ontological significance; we also agree in what we deny. Neither Chisholm nor I thinks that we persons are identical to animals or are essentially animals. With the ascendancy of biology, however, Chisholm and I may be in the minority. Many philosophers today hold that persons are most fundamentally animals. These philosophers – call them 'Animalists'[28] – hold that we persons have the persistence conditions of human organisms.[29]

Suppose that Animalism is correct, and that we have the persistence conditions of human animals, and hence are essentially animals. We are also persons. How may an Animalist understand persons if persons have the persistence conditions of organisms? I'll consider two kinds of possibilities: Being a person, on an Animalist view, either concerns having psychological properties (actually or potentially) or it does not. The only way that I can think of for an Animalist to hold that being a person has nothing to do with having psychological properties, actually or potentially, is to identify the property of being a human person with the property of being a human animal.[30] (To identify the property of being a person with the property of being a human animal would be a nonstarter since it would preclude even the logical possibility of there being nonhuman persons.) Such a 'property-identity' Animalist may claim that persons have ontological significance by means of the following inference:

(1)   Human organisms have ontological significance;

(2)   The property of being a human person = the property of being a human organism;

So, (3)   Human persons have ontological significance.

The inference is valid, but the second premise is untenable for two reasons: First, there are no grounds for holding it; second, it is tantamount to eliminativism about persons.

To see that there are no grounds for the claim of identity between being a human person and being a human organism, consider: Does the assertion have any a priori or a posteriori justification? It has no a posteriori justification. Unlike the assertion of the identity of water and H_2O molecules between 0 and 100 degrees centigrade, there was no empirical discovery that would underwrite an identity of being a human person and being a human animal. Indeed, without some way to characterize the property of being a human person other than in terms of its alleged identity to the property of being a human organism it is logically impossible that there be any *discovery* that underwrites the property-identity claim.

So the justification for the property-identity claim must be a priori, based on the meanings of words. But the meanings of the words give no warrant for asserting identity. The term 'person' was introduced in something like its current meaning to apply to parts of the Christian Trinity – hardly human organisms. It was given wide application by Locke, who explicitly distinguished being a person from being a "man," as he called it. Since historically, 'being a human person' and 'being a human organism' were not taken as denoting the same property, considerations of use or meaning do not do not give a priori justification for the claim of property identity. So, we are left with no justification for the claim of Animalist property-identity.

To see that the thesis of identity between the property of being a human person and the property of being a human organism is tantamount to eliminativism about persons, consider: If being a human organism is identical to being a human person, then by parity of reasoning, being an oyster is identical to being an oyster person. (At any rate, I do not believe that a property-identity Animalist has resources to make a principled objection to the thesis that being an oyster is identical to being an oyster person.) But there is no such property as being an oyster person. If there is no such property as being an oyster person, then by parity of reasoning in the other direction, there is no such property as being a human person. In that case, property-identity Animalism collapses into eliminativism about persons. Eliminativism about persons is hardly compatible with taking persons to have ontological significance. So, premise (2) is false and the argument is unsound.

So, an Animalist who takes having psychological properties to be irrelevant to being a human person does not assign ontological significance

to persons. However, there are several theses available to an Animalist that construe being a person in terms of psychological properties. Consider:

> (1) Necessarily, if x is a human person at t, then x has psychological properties at t.

On Animalism + (1), persons have their persistence conditions not in virtue of being persons but in virtue of being animals; nor would the property of being a person be essential to persons. *Person* would not be a substance-sortal (as it is on the Constitution View), but would be a phase-sortal like *infant* or *puppy*. In this case, being a person would be a contingent property of persons, and persons would have no ontological significance.[31] Now consider:

> (2) Necessarily, if x is a human person at any time, then x has psychological properties at some time or other.

Animalism + (2) has the consequence that whether or not an embryo is a person depends on its subsequent development. If it is miscarried or aborted before it has psychological states, then it is not a person. If it is carried to term and is born normally, then it was a person all along. So, on Animalism + (2), being a person is a contingent property of persons, and persons have no ontological significance. Finally, consider the most plausible notion of personhood available to an Animalist:

> (3) Necessarily, if x is a human person at t, then x has the capacity at t to have psychological properties.

'Capacity' is a notoriously elastic term. For purposes here, I take it that to have a capacity at t to have F is to have an internal structure at t such that it is consistent with the laws of nature that things with that internal structure have F. Now consider a person, Smith, who has suffered irreversible damage to the cerebral cortex, so that it is physically impossible for the brain ever to support psychological properties again. Suppose also that Smith's lower brain that regulates animal life continues to function.[32] Does Smith still exist?

I'll consider two versions of Animalism + (3). On one, suggested by writers on medical ethics, Smith does not still exist. On this construal, when the cerebral cortex is destroyed, so is the human animal. So, although Smith is [identical to] a human animal, destruction of the cerebral cortex is destruction of that human animal and hence destruction of Smith. However, after destruction of the cerebral cortex, an animal still persists, but it is not a human animal (and thus it is not Smith).

I do not believe that this construal is a viable option for Animalists. Here's why. Call the animal with functioning cerebral cortex, H. Call the animal after the cerebral cortex was destroyed, H'. Are H and H' the same animal? If so, then being human is just a contingent property of animals. In that case, being a human animal could not furnish the persistence conditions of human animals – since, assuming that H is the same animal as H', a human animal can lose the property of being human without going out of existence. But if the property of being a human animal does not provide the persistence conditions of human animals, then Animalism is false. So, on the view that holds that a human animal cannot persist after destruction of the cerebral cortex, H and H' must not be the same animal. But if H is not the same animal as H' and both H and H' are animals, then H' must have replaced H.[33] What happened to H? There is no plausible answer. Without anyone's being able to detect that anything was amiss, H just disappeared. I do not believe that the persistence conditions of animals that are countenanced by biologists allow for the undetectable disappearance of one animal and its undetectable replacement by another animal. So, that version of Animalism – that takes destruction of the cerebral cortex to be destruction of the human animal – entails untenable persistence conditions for animals, and I'll not consider it further.

On the other version of Animalism + (3), the persistence conditions of human animals are determined by lower-brain functions like metabolism, digestion, respiration, and circulation.[34] On this version of Animalism, Smith still exists after destruction of his cerebral cortex. If Smith has the persistence conditions of a human animal, then Smith still exists since the lower-brain functions that regulate animal life continue to function. But since there is no longer a capacity for having psychological properties, Smith is no longer a person (according to Animalism + (3)). If Smith can exist without being a person, then being a person is irrelevant to Smith's persistence conditions. In that case, being a person is not an ontologically significant property.

We have considered two versions of Animalism coupled with (3), where (3) is the view of persons that takes personhood to be the capacity to have psychological properties. The two versions of Animalism were, first, the view that takes the destruction of the cerebral cortex to be destruction of the human animal, and, second, the view that takes the persistence conditions of the human animal to be determined by lower-brain functions. On neither of these versions of Animalism + (3) are persons ontologically significant by (OS1) and (OS2).

Notice that Animalism cannot be combined with a Chisholmian construal of a person – as being "that which is necessarily such that it is physically possible that there is a time at which that thing consciously thinks." As Chisholm would agree, human animals do not have this property. First of all, human animals come into and go out of existence gradually, but, as Chisholm argues, no person – no *ens per se* – comes into or goes out of existence gradually.[35] Putting aside that difficulty, however, there is another difficulty with attempting to combine Animalism with Chisholm's definition of a person.

Suppose that H is a human animal that comes into being in the normal way: a fertilized egg undergoes cell division, is implanted in the uterus, and approximately nine months later, a normal baby is born. Now suppose that there is another possible world in which the same egg is fertilized by the same sperm that produced H; but in this other world, the mother-to-be drinks some toxic water which results in impairment, but not destruction, of the fertilized egg just as the new animal comes into existence.[36] Given Animalism, H still comes into being in this other possible world – same egg, same sperm, same time, same uterus – but the impairment is such that there is no physical possibility that H ever consciously think. (The impairment prevents the organism from ever developing a cerebral cortex.) Nevertheless, H, the human animal, still exists in the other possible world. But since it is physically impossible for H in that other world to think, H is not a person in that other world. And, on Chisholm's definition, if H is not a person in every possible world in which H exists, then H is not a person in any possible world in which H exists. So, on Chisholm's view, H – the normal baby born in the actual world – is not and never will be a person in the actual world.

I conclude that nothing with the persistence conditions of an animal can be a person, on Chisholm's view (as Chisholm would be the first to agree). My point is to show that a hybrid position that is part-Animalist and part-Chisholmian is not available to anyone. Given Chisholm's view, it is impossible that H, the normal baby born in the actual world, is or ever will be a person – since there is a possible world in which it is physically impossible that H ever consciously think. Given an Animalist view, it is possible that H, the normal baby born in the actual world, either is or will be a person – since H is just like any other normal baby born in the actual world. It is impossible that both positions be correct.

Therefore, on none of the construals of Animalism that I can think of does Animalism accord persons ontological status. Of course, an Animalist who denies that there is a property of being a person in the first place just concurs with my point that Animalism denies that persons have ontological significance.

To sum up: On Animalism, animals have ontological significance, but persons do not. On Chisholm's view, persons have ontological significance, but animals do not. On the Constitution View, both persons and animals have ontological significance; and we, being essentially persons, have our persistence conditions in virtue of being persons. So, on the Constitution View and on Chisholm's view, persons have ontological significance. On the Animalist view, persons have no ontological significance.

The Upshot

The fact that on the Constitution View persons have ontological significance (in the sense defined) and on the Animalist View they do not have ontological significance has not, I think, been properly appreciated. This fact, however, does not add up to a satisfactory argument for the Constitution View over Animalism, unless persons really do have ontological significance. So, I offer the following argument:

(1) If Animalism is true, then persons do not have ontological significance.

(2) Persons do have ontological significance.

∴ (3) Animalism is not true.

I just established the first premise. Although I cannot embark on a full-scale defense of the second premise in this paper, I shall offer two considerations in favor of it.

The first consideration is this: Persons are self-conscious, and self-consciousness is unique. No other part of the animal kingdom is self-conscious in the way that we are.[37] Self-consciousness is sufficiently different from everything else known to us in the natural world that it is reasonable to say that the difference that self-consciousness makes is an ontological difference. I can almost hear the question: Why not be more Aristotelian and take the "genus and species" approach? An Aristotelian may say that we are animals who differ from other animals in being self-conscious. Then I ask: In virtue of what do I have my persistence conditions? The answer cannot be that I have my persistence conditions in virtue *both* of being a human animal and of being self-conscious. Since the animal that is supposed to be me [nonderivatively, of course] existed before it was self-conscious, I cannot be both essentially an animal and essentially self-conscious. To say that persons are essentially animals, and not essentially self-conscious, is to make properties like *wondering how one should live* irrelevant to what we most fundamentally are, and properties like *having digestion* central to what we fundamentally are. I think that what we most fundamentally are is a matter of what is distinctive about us and not what we share with nonhuman animals.

The second consideration is this: Considered in terms of genetic or morphological properties or biological functioning, there is no discontinuity between chimpanzees and human animals. In fact, human animals are biologically more closely related to certain species of chimpanzees than the chimpanzees are related to gorillas and orangutans.[38] So, biologically speaking, there's no significant difference between us and higher nonhuman animals. But all things considered, there is a huge discontinuity between us and nonhuman animals. And this discontinuity arises from the fact that we, and no other part of the animal kingdom, are self-conscious. (If I thought that chimpanzees or computers really did have first-person perspectives, I would put them in the same category that we are in – namely, persons.)

So, in biological terms, there are no significant differences between us and other higher primates, but there are enormous differences between us and nonhuman animals all things considered. [Only we seek to understand our place in the universe.] Biologists and biologically-oriented philosophers speak with one voice in insisting that the animal kingdom is a seamless whole in which the human animals have no special significance. This suggests that biology does not fully reveal our nature. So, perhaps we should say that biology may well reveal our animal nature, but that our animal nature does not exhaust our nature all things considered. Rather, self-consciousness distinguishes us ontologically from the rest of the animal kingdom. This is to say that self-consciousness – and thus personhood – is an ontologically significant property.

The point here concerns the status of self-consciousness. The issue is not whether or not self-consciousness is a product of evolution, or whether or not it has a neural basis. The Constitutionalist's claim is that when self-consciousness did evolve by natural selection (if it did), it was sufficiently different from every other property in the natural world that it ushered in a new kind of being.[39] Self-consciousness makes an ontological difference whether it is a product of natural selection or not. Since biologists do not recognize any ontological difference between human and nonhuman animals, we should conclude that ontology does not recapitulate biology.

In short, the uniqueness of self-conscious beings – of beings who can think of themselves as themselves, who have inner lives – makes it plausible to hold that to be a person is to be a special kind of thing – a thing that has ontological significance in virtue of being of that kind. Here again I share a Chisholmian intuition: The coming-to-be of a person is not just a change in some already existing – but theretofore nonpersonal – thing.[40] Rather, a new person is a new entity in the world.[41] If this is correct, then persons have ontological significance. And if persons have ontological significance, then Animalism is wrong.

Conclusion

What I have done here is to make precise what I mean by 'the ontological significance of persons,' and then to show that the Constitution View affirms the ontological significance of persons and that the Animalist View denies the ontological significance of persons. Finally, I offered some considerations to show that persons should be regarded as having ontological significance, and hence that the Constitution View is superior to Animalism.

The Constitution View is a materialist view that explains the sense in which we are animals – that is, biological beings, part of the seamless animal kingdom. At the same time, the Constitution View explains the sense in which we are different from other animals in a way that makes us ontologically unique. What makes us ontologically distinctive is the first-person perspective. The property of having an inner life – not just sentience – is so extraordinary, so utterly unlike any other property in the world, that beings with this property are a different kind of thing from beings without it. Only beings with first-person perspectives can write their memoirs or dread old age or discover evolution and intervene in its otherwise blind operations. And in my opinion, what something fundamentally is – its nature – is more a matter of what it can do than of what it is made of.

If the Constitution View is correct, then the property of being a person is not just a contingent property of a fundamentally nonpersonal thing like an organism. Persons have ontological significance. Although my elucidation and defense of this thesis is not very Chisholmian, I am confident that Chisholm would approve of the conclusion.

Notes

I'd like to thank Gary Rosenkrantz, my commentator at the Chisholm Memorial Conference at Brown University, November 10–11, 2000, for helpful comments. Also, thanks are due to Gareth B. Matthews for reading many drafts of this paper and to Katherine A. Sonderegger for searching discussions of these matters.

1 Variations on this term are widely used. For example, see Ernst Mayr, *Toward a New Philosophy of Biology: Observations of an Evolutionist* (Cambridge, MA: The Belknap Press of Harvard University Press, 1988); Philip Kitcher, *Abusing Science: The Case Against Creationism* (Cambridge, MA: The MIT Press, 1982); Daniel C. Dennett, *Darwin's Dangerous Idea: Evolution and the Meanings of Life* (New York: Simon and Schuster, 1995).

2 I explain what I mean by a first-person perspective in "The First-Person Perspective: A Test for Naturalism," *American Philosophical Quarterly* 35 (1998): 327–48, and in *Persons and Bodies: A Constitution View* (Cambridge, MA: Cambridge University Press, 2000): ch. 3.

3 Unlike David Wiggins, who has a different sort of constitution view from mine, I do not distinguish between human animals and human bodies. I use the terms 'human animal' and 'human body' interchangeably.

4 I am aware of the controversies in biology about individuating species. But we do talk about human animals, and human animals do have persistence conditions that are different from the persistence conditions that I take persons to have. That's all I need.

5 A caveat: On my view, this slogan applies only to things that are persons nonderivatively in a sense that I shall explain.

6 See *Persons and Bodies*. For a preliminary discussion of the notion of constitution, see "Unity Without Identity: A New Look at Material Constitution," ed. Peter A. French and Howard K. Wettstein (Boston, MA: Blackwell Publishers, 1999): 144–65.

7 To borrow some paraphrases about essential properties from Chisholm, if x has the property of being a horse essentially, then 'x is such that, if it were not a horse, it would not exist'; or 'God couldn't have created x without making it such that it is a horse'; or 'x is such that in every possible world in which it exists it is a horse.' *Person and Object: A Metaphysical Study* (LaSalle, IL: Open Court Publishing Company, 1976), pp. 25–6. Chisholm gives generalizations of these as paraphrases of the locution 'x is necessarily such that it is F.' But then he goes on to say, rather forlornly, that "if a person doesn't understand 'x is necessarily such that it is F', it is not likely that he will understand the expressions in terms of which we have attempted to clarify it."

8 Since a thing has the same persistence conditions in every possible world and time at which it exists, it has its persistence conditions essentially. Thus, no one who invokes persistence conditions is in a position to object to my view for invoking essential properties.

9 Gareth B. Matthews has made me realize how different my view is from Aristotle's.

10 Many properties (unrelated to this discussion) may be had essentially by some things and nonessentially by other things. A planet has the property of having a closed orbit essentially; a meteor that has a closed orbit has that property nonessentially. (This assumes that planets are planets essentially; otherwise it is only a de dicto necessity that planets have closed orbits.)

11 I have a general definition of 'x constitutes y at t' that I'll not state here. The purpose of the definition is to provide assurance that the idea of constitution-without-identity is coherent; and that constitution-without-identity is not just "spatial co-location" of two otherwise separate things. See *Persons and Bodies*, ch. 2.

12 Being a person essentially and being a person contingently are two ways of having a single property along one dimension; being a person nonderivatively and being a person derivatively are two ways of having a single property along another dimension. But if *being essentially a person* were a distinct property from *being contingently a person*, or if *being nonderivatively a person* were a distinct property from *being derivatively a person*, none of those "properties" could be borrowed. The definition of 'having a property derivatively' would rule out having any of these properties derivatively. See *Persons and Bodies*, ch. 2.

13 For further discussion of this point, see *Persons and Bodies*, ch. 7, and "Materialism With a Human Face," in *Body, Soul, and Survival*, ed. Kevin Corcoran (Ithaca, NY: Cornell University Press, 2001): 159–80.

14 The following kinds of properties cannot be had derivatively: (1) any property expressed in English by 'possibly', 'necessarily', 'essentially', or 'primary-kind property', or variants of these terms – call these 'alethic properties'; (2) any property expressed in English by 'is identical to', 'constitutes', 'derivatively', 'exists' or 'is an object' or variants of these terms – call these 'identity/constitution/existence properties'; (3) any property such that necessarily, x has it at t only if x exists at some time other than t – call these 'properties rooted outside the times that they are had'; (4) any properties that are conjunctions of two or more properties that either entail or are entailed by two or more primary-kind properties (e.g., being a cloth flag, being a human person) – call these 'hybrid properties'. In *Persons and Bodies*, I amend

the definition of 'having a property derivatively' to accommodate having hybrid properties derivatively.

15   There may be conjunctive primary kinds. Assuming that *can-opener* is one primary kind and *corkscrew* is another, then the property of being a can-opener and a corkscrew is a primary-kind property. (I believe that Tom Nagel is responsible for a "can-opener/corkscrew" example.)

16   Dean Zimmerman, among others, has pressed this criticism on me.

17   Constitution offers the fruits of contingent identity, temporal identity, relative identity and so on without tampering with genuine identity.

18   If the boards, AB, constituted the table on Monday and the boards, BC, constituted the table on Tuesday, then what really existed on Chisholm's view were the boards, AB, which "stood in for" the table on Monday, and BC, which "stood in for" the table on Tuesday. To say that the table is an ontological parasite is to imply that all of the intrinsic, present-rooted properties of the table are borrowed (in Chisholm's sense) from the boards that constitute it.

19   I argue for my conception in "Persons in Metaphysical Perspective," in *The Philosophy of Roderick Chisholm* (Library of Living Philosophers, vol. XXV), ed. Lewis Edwin Hahn (Chicago: Open Court Publishing Company, 1997): 433–53.

20   There are further differences between Chisholm and me here. Most important is that, on my view, constitution is a key to understanding human persons. On Chisholm's view, constitution has nothing to do with persons at all; persons exist in their own right; constituted things (on Chisholm's view) are ontological parasites.

21   On Chisholm's view, a person is either an *ens per se* or "just a *façon de parler*." "I am certain, then, that this much is true: if I'm a real thing and not just a *façon de parler*, then neither my coming into being nor my passing away is a gradual process." Roderick Chisholm, *On Metaphysics* (Minneapolis: University of Minnesota Press, 1989): 59. I think that the dichotomy – *ens per se* or "just a façon de parler" – is a false one. See my "Persons in Metaphysical Perspective."

22   A nonderivative F is a thing that is an F nonderivatively. The reason for the qualification 'nonderivative' is that a derivative F may lose the property of being F without thereby going out of existence. E.g., my body is a person derivatively, but if I went out of existence while my body remained, my body would cease to be a person without ceasing to exist altogether. So, the ontological significance of a property is determined only by those things that have the property nonderivatively.

23   In "Why Constitution is Not Identity," *Journal of Philosophy* 94 (1997): 599–621, I argued that everything that can go out of existence altogether has persistence conditions.

24   I.e., 'Fs have ontological significance' is short for: 'For all x, if x is a nonderivative F, then x has ontological significance in virtue of being an F.'

25   Although I avoid the 'qua' locution, the way that I have elucidated 'Fs have ontological significance' suggests that an alternative to that expression might be 'Fs-qua-Fs have ontological significance.'

26   I.e., nonderivative persons. In general, I'll drop the qualification when it seems clear that I am talking about nonderivative Fs.

27   *On Metaphysics*, 59–60. 'Physically possible,' Chisholm tells us, means not contrary to the laws of nature. In *Person and Object*, Chisholm says that a person is "an individual thing which is necessarily such that it is physically possible that there is something which it undertakes to bring about." Chisholm goes on to point out: "Our definition has the consequence that, if an individual thing x is a person, then in every possible world in which x exists, x is a person from the moment it comes into being until the moment it passes away." *Person and Object*, 137.

28   The term 'Animalist' comes from Paul Snowdon, who is an Animalist himself.

29   It may be reasonable to suppose that human organisms are essentially human organisms, but it is a view that Thomas Aquinas would oppose. According to Aquinas (following Aristotle), a zygote formed by a human egg and a human sperm first acquires a vegetative soul, then a sensitive soul. The organism does not become a human organism until it acquires a rational soul (at about 12 weeks). If we take it that there is a single developing organism from zygote on through birth and beyond, then on Aquinas's view, a human organism would not be essentially a human organism – since it exists before acquiring a rational soul and thus before becoming a human organism.

30   Fred Feldman takes the term 'person' to be ambiguous. There are, he says, "four distinguishable concepts of personality." He claims that we have a concept of "biological personality," but he offers no warrant for using the term 'personality' here; indeed, a biological person on his view is nothing other than a human organism from conception to disintegration. There is nothing particularly personal about it. However, on his view, the property of being a biological person (as opposed to the property of being a psychological person) furnishes our persistence conditions. As far as I can tell, Feldman would endorse this property identity for what he calls "biological persons." He seems to

take the property of being a biological person to be the property of being a human animal. See his *Confrontations with the Reaper: A Philosophical Study of the Nature and Value of Death* (New York: Oxford University Press, 1992): 101.

31 What Feldman calls "a psychological person" conforms to Animalism + (1) (or perhaps + (2)). A psychological person on his view is just a "biological person" (a human organism) with psychological properties.

32 Similar thought experiments are used by Eric T. Olson in *The Human Animal: Personal Identity Without Psychology* (New York: Oxford University Press, 1997) to illustrate Animalism. His version is the second one discussed in the text.

33 Speaking from the Constitution View, we should add another conjunct to the antecedent: "…and H and H′ are not related by constitution."

34 See Olson's *The Human Animal*.

35 Roderick M. Chisholm, "Coming into Being and Passing Away: Can the Metaphysician Help?" in *On Metaphysics*, 49–61.

36 Whenever that is. Logically speaking, I do not believe that there could be a new individual until about two weeks after fertilization. Before that time, there is the physical possibility of "twinning." Since it is logically impossible for one thing to be identical to two things, I think that it is a logical error to hold that a new life begins at fertilization.

37 This is not to deny that there are gradations of mentality throughout the animal kingdom. My claim is that there is only one species with a first-person perspective, and that species is obviously different from all the others in what it manages to accomplish and produce.

38 Daniel C. Dennett, *Darwin's Dangerous Idea* (New York: Simon and Schuster, 1995): 336. Dennett is discussing Jared Diamond's *The Third Chimpanzee*.

39 The reason that I do not say that self-consciousness ushered in a new kind of animal is that biologists do not take self-consciousness to distinguish species, and I take the identification of new kinds of animals to be within the purview of biology.

40 Recall the arguments against identifying being a human person with being a human organism.

41 A new nonderivative person, that is. When a body comes to constitute a person, it becomes a person derivatively, but the body is not thereby a new person. The body's being a person is entirely a matter of the body's constitution-relations to a person.

46

An Argument for Animalism

Eric T. Olson

Animal is a part of what ... is to be human

It is a truism that you and I are human beings. It is also a truism that a human being is a kind of animal: roughly a member of the primate species *Homo sapiens*. It would seem to follow that we are animals. Yet that claim is deeply controversial. Plato, Augustine, Descartes, Spinoza, Leibniz, Locke, Berkeley, Hume, Kant, and Hegel all denied it. With the notable exception of Aristotle and his followers, it is hard to find a major figure in the history of Western philosophy who thought that we are animals. The view is no more popular in non-Western traditions. And probably nine out of ten philosophers writing about personal identity today either deny outright that we are animals or say things that are clearly incompatible with it.

This is surprising. Isn't it obvious that we are animals? I will try to show that it isn't obvious, and that Plato and the others have their reasons for thinking otherwise. Before doing that I will explain how I understand the claim that we are animals. My main purpose, though, is to make a case for this unpopular view. I won't rely on the brief argument I began with. My strategy is to ask what it would mean if we weren't animals. Denying that we are animals is harder than you might think.

1 What Animalism Says

When I say that we are animals, I mean that each of us is numerically identical with an animal. There is a certain human organism, and that organism is you. You and it are one and the same. This view has been called "animalism" (not a very nice name, but I haven't got a better one). Simple though it may appear, this is easily misunderstood. Many claims that sound like animalism are in fact different.

First, some say that we are animals and yet reject animalism.[1] How is that possible? How can you be an animal, and yet not be one? The idea is that there is a sense of the verb *to be* in which something can "be" an animal without being identical with any animal. Each of us "is" an animal in the sense of "being constituted by" one. That means roughly that you are in the same place and made of the same matter as an animal. But you and that animal could come apart (more on this later). And since a thing can't come apart from itself, you and the animal are not identical.

I wish people wouldn't say things like this. If you are not identical with a certain animal, that

Eric T. Olson, "An Argument for Animalism," in R. Martin and J. Barresi (eds.), *Personal Identity* (Oxford: Blackwell 2003), pp. 318–24. Reprinted by permission of John Wiley & Sons, Inc.

Metaphysics: An Anthology, Second Edition. Edited by Jaegwon Kim, Daniel Z. Korman and Ernest Sosa.

animal is something other than you. And I doubt whether there is any interesting sense in which you can *be* something other than yourself. Even if there is, expressing a view on which no one is identical with an animal by saying that we *are* animals is badly misleading. It discourages us from asking important questions: what we *are* identical with, if not animals, for instance. Put plainly and honestly, these philosophers are saying that each of us is a non-animal that relates in some intimate way to an animal. They put it by saying that we *are* animals because that sounds more plausible. This is salesman's hype, and we shouldn't be fooled. In any case, the "constitutionalists" do not say that we are animals in the straightforward sense in which I mean it. They are not animalists.

The existence of the "constitution view" shows that animalism is not the same as *materialism*. Materialism is the view that we are material things; and we might be material things but not animals. Animalism implies materialism (animals are material things), but not vice versa. It may seem perverse for a materialist to reject animalism. If we are material things of any sort, surely we are animals? Perverse or not, though, the view that we are material non-organisms is widely held.

Animalism says that we are animals. That is compatible with the existence of non-animal people (or persons, if you prefer). It is often said that to be a person is to have certain mental qualities: to be rational, intelligent, and self-conscious, say. Perhaps a person must also be morally responsible, and have free will. If something like that is right, then gods or angels might be people but not animals.

Nor does our being animals imply that all animals, or even all human animals, are people. Human beings in a persistent vegetative state are biologically alive, but their mental capacities are permanently destroyed. They are certainly human animals. But we might not want to call them people. The same goes for human embryos.

So the view that we are animals does not imply that to be a person is nothing other than to be an animal of a certain sort – that being an animal is part of what it is to be a person. Inconveniently enough, this view has also been called animalism. It isn't the animalism that I want to defend. In fact it looks rather implausible. I don't know whether there could be inorganic people, as for instance

traditional theism asserts. But mere reflection on what it is to be a person doesn't seem to rule it out. Of course, if people are animals by definition, it follows that we are animals, since we are obviously people. But the reverse entailment doesn't hold: we might be animals even if something could be a person without being an animal.

If I don't say that all people are animals, which people do I mean? Is animalism the mere tautology that all animal people are animals? No. I say that you and I and the other people who walk the earth are animals. If you like, all *human* people are animals, where a human person is roughly someone who relates to a human animal in the way that you and I do, whatever way that is. (Even idealists can agree that we are in some sense human, and not, say, feline or angelic.) Many philosophers deny that *any* people are animals. So there is nothing trivial about this claim.

"Animalism" is sometimes stated as the view that we are *essentially or most fundamentally* animals. We are essentially animals if we couldn't possibly exist without being animals. It is less clear what it is for us to be most fundamentally animals, but this is usually taken to imply at least that our identity conditions derive from our being animals, rather than from our being, say, people or philosophers or material objects – even though we *are* people and philosophers and material objects.

Whether our being animals implies that we are essentially or most fundamentally animals depends on whether human animals are essentially or most fundamentally animals. If the animal that you are is essentially an animal, then so are you. If it is only contingently an animal, then you are only contingently an animal. Likewise, you are most fundamentally an animal if and only if the animal that you are is most fundamentally an animal. The claim that each of us is identical with an animal is neutral on these questions. Most philosophers think that every animal is essentially and most fundamentally an animal, and I am inclined to agree. But you could be an animalist in my sense without accepting this.

Is animalism the view that we are identical with our bodies? That depends on what it is for something to be someone's body. If a person's body is by definition a sort of animal, then I suppose being an animal amounts to being one's body. It is often said, though, that someone could have a partly or wholly inorganic body. One's body might include plastic or metal limbs. Someone might even have an entirely robotic body. I take it that no animal could be partly or wholly inorganic. If you cut off an animal's limb and replace it with an inorganic prosthesis, the animal just gets smaller and has something inorganic attached to it. So perhaps after having some or all of your parts replaced by inorganic gadgets of the right sort you would be identical with your body, but would not be an animal. Animalism may imply that you are your body, but you could be your body without being an animal. Some philosophers even say that being an animal rules out being identical with one's body. If you replaced enough of an animal's parts with new ones, they say, it would end up with a different body from the one it began with.

Whether these claims about bodies are true depends on what it is for something to be someone's body. What does it *mean* to say that your body is an animal, or that someone might have a robotic body? I have never seen a good answer to this question (see van Inwagen 1980 and Olson 1997: 144–9). So I will talk about people and animals, and leave bodies out of it.

Finally, does animalism say that we are *merely* animals? That we are nothing more than biological organisms? This is a delicate point. The issue is whether being "more than just" or "not merely" an animal is compatible with being an animal – that is, with being identical with an animal.

If someone complains that the committee is more than just the chairman, she means that it is not the chairman: it has other members too. If we are more than just animals in something like this sense, then we are not animals. We have parts that are not parts of any animal: immaterial souls, perhaps.

On the other hand, we say that Descartes was more than just a philosopher: he was also a mathematician, a Frenchman, a Roman Catholic, and many other things. That is of course compatible with his being a philosopher. We can certainly be more than "mere" animals in this sense, and yet still be animals. An animal can have properties other than being an animal, and which don't follow from its being an animal. Our being animals does not rule out our being mathematicians, Frenchmen, or Roman Catholics – or our being people, socialists, mountaineers, and

many other things. At least there is no evident reason why it should. Animalism does not imply that we have a fixed, "animal" nature, or that we have only biological or naturalistic properties, or that we are no different, in any important way, from other animals. There may be a vast psychological and moral gulf between human animals and organisms of other species. We may be very special animals. But special animals are still animals.

2 Alternatives

One reason why it may seem obvious that we are animals is that it is unclear what else we could be. If we're not animals, what are we? What are the alternatives to animalism? This is a question that philosophers ought to ask more often. Many views about personal identity clearly rule out our being animals, but leave it a mystery what sort of things we might be instead. Locke's account is a notorious example. His detailed account of personal identity doesn't even tell us whether we are material or immaterial.

Well, there is the traditional idea that we are simple immaterial substances, or, alternatively, compound things made up of an immaterial substance and a biological organism.

There is the view, mentioned earlier, that we are material objects constituted by human animals. You and a certain animal are physically indistinguishable. Nonetheless you and it are two different things.

Some say that we are temporal parts of animals. Animals and other persisting objects exist at different times by having different temporal parts or "stages" located at those times. You are made up of those stages of a human animal (or, in science fiction, of several animals) that are "psychologically interconnected" (Lewis 1976). Since your animal's embryonic stages have no mental properties at all, they aren't psychologically connected with anything, and so they aren't parts of you. Hence, you began later than the animal did.

Hume famously proposed that each of us is "a bundle or collection of different perceptions, which succeed each other with an inconceivable rapidity, and are in a perpetual flux and movement" (1888: 252). Strictly speaking you are not made of bones and sinews, or of atoms, or of matter. You are literally composed of thoughts. Whether Hume actually believed this is uncertain; but some do (e.g. Quinton 1962).

Every teacher of philosophy has heard it said that we are something like computer programs. You are a certain complex of information "realized" in your brain. (How else could you survive Star-Trek teletransportation?) That would mean that you are not a concrete object at all. You are a universal. There could literally be more than one of you, just as there is more than one concrete instance of the web browser *Netscape 6.2*.

There is even the paradoxical view that we don't really exist at all. There are many thoughts and experiences, but no beings that *have* those thoughts or experiences. The existence of human people is an illusion – though of course no one is deluded about it. Philosophers who have denied or at least doubted their own existence include Parmenides, Spinoza, Hume, Hegel (as I read them, anyway), Russell (1985: 50), and Unger (1979). We also find the view in Indian Buddhism.

There are other views about what we might be, but I take these to be animalism's main rivals. One of these claims, or another one that I haven't mentioned, must be true. There must be *some* sort of thing that we are. If there is anything sitting in your chair and reading these words, it must have some basic properties or other.

For those who enjoy metaphysics, these are all fascinating proposals. Whatever their merits, though, they certainly are strange. No one but a philosopher could have thought of them. And it would take quite a bit of philosophy to get anyone to believe one of them. Compared with these claims, the idea that we are animals looks downright sensible. That makes its enduring unpopularity all the more surprising.

3 Why Animalism is Unpopular

Why is animalism so unpopular? Historically, the main reason (though by no means the only one) is hostility to materialism. Philosophers have always found it hard to believe that a material object, no matter how physically complex, could produce thought or experience. And an animal is a material object (I assume that vitalism is false). Since it is plain enough that *we* can think, it is easy to conclude that we couldn't be animals.

But why do modern-day materialists reject animalism, or at least say things that rule it out? The main reason, I believe, is that when they think about personal identity they don't ask what sort of things we are. They don't ask whether we are animals, or what we might be if we aren't animals, or how we relate to the human animals that are so intimately connected with us. Or at least they don't ask that first. No one who *began* by asking what we are would hit on the idea that we must be computer programs or bundles of thoughts or non-animals made of the same matter as animals.

The traditional problem of personal identity is not what we are, but what it takes for us to persist. It asks what is necessary, and what is sufficient, for a person existing at one time to be identical with something present at another time: what sorts of adventures we could survive, and what would inevitably bring our existence to an end. Many philosophers seem to think that an answer to this question would tell us all there is to know about the metaphysics of personal identity. This is not so. Claims about what it takes for us to persist do not by themselves tell us what other fundamental properties we have: whether we are material or immaterial, simple or composite, abstract or concrete, and so on. At any rate, the single-minded focus on our identity over time has tended to put other metaphysical questions about ourselves out of philosophers' minds.

What is more, the most popular solution to this traditional problem rules out our being animals. It is that we persist by virtue of some sort of psychological continuity. You are, necessarily, that future being that in some sense inherits its mental features – personality, beliefs, memories, values, and so on – from you. And you are that past being whose mental features you have inherited. Philosophers disagree about what sort of inheritance this has to be: whether those mental features must be continuously physically realized, for instance. But most accept the general idea. The persistence of a human animal, on the other hand, does not consist in mental continuity.

The fact that each human animal starts out as an unthinking embryo and may end up as an unthinking vegetable shows that no sort of mental continuity is necessary for a human animal to persist. No human animal is mentally continuous with an embryo or a vegetable.

To see that no sort of mental continuity is sufficient for a human animal to persist, imagine that your cerebrum is put into another head. The being who gets that organ, and he alone, will be mentally continuous with you on any account of what mental continuity is. So if mental continuity of any sort suffices for you to persist, you would go along with your transplanted cerebrum. You wouldn't stay behind with an empty head.

What would happen to the human animal associated with you? Would *it* go along with its cerebrum? Would the surgeons pare that animal down to a small chunk of yellowish-pink tissue, move it across the room, and then supply it with a new head, trunk, and other parts? Surely not. A detached cerebrum is no more an organism than a detached liver is an organism. The empty-headed thing left behind, by contrast, *is* an animal. It may even remain alive, if the surgeons are careful to leave the lower brain intact. The empty-headed being into which your cerebrum is implanted is also an animal. It looks for all the world like there are two human animals in the story. One of them loses its cerebrum and gets an empty head. The other has its empty head filled with that organ. No animal moves from one head to another. The surgeons merely move an organ from one animal to another. If this is right, then no sort of psychological continuity suffices for the identity of a human animal over time. One human animal could be mentally continuous with another one (supposing that they can have mental properties at all).

If we tell the story in the right way, it is easy enough to get most people, or at any rate most Western-educated philosophy students, to say that *you* would go along with your transplanted cerebrum. After all, the one who got that organ would act like you and think she was you. Why deny that she would be the person she thinks she is? But "your" animal – the one you would be if you were any animal – would stay behind. That means that you and that animal could go your separate ways. And a thing and itself can never go their separate ways.

It follows that you are not that animal, or indeed any other animal. Not only are you not essentially an animal. You are not an animal at all, even contingently. Nothing that is even

contingently an animal would move to a different head if its cerebrum were transplanted. The human animals in the story stay where they are and merely lose or gain organs.[2]

So the thought that leads many contemporary philosophers to reject animalism – or that would lead them to reject it if they accepted the consequences of what they believe – is something like this: You would go along with your transplanted cerebrum; but no human animal would go along with its transplanted cerebrum. More generally, some sort of mental continuity suffices for us to persist, yet no sort of mental continuity suffices for an animal to persist. It follows that we are not animals. If we were animals, we should have the identity conditions of animals. Those conditions have nothing to do with psychological facts. Psychology would be irrelevant to our identity over time. That goes against 300 years of thinking about personal identity.

This also shows that animalism is a substantive metaphysical thesis with important consequences. There is nothing harmless about it.

4 The Thinking-Animal Argument

I turn now to my case for animalism. It seems evident that there *is* a human animal intimately related to you. It is the one located where you are, the one we point to when we point to you, the one sitting in your chair. It seems equally evident that human animals can think. They can act. They can be aware of themselves and the world. Those with mature nervous systems in good working order can, anyway. So there is a thinking, acting human animal sitting where you are now. But you think and act. *You* are the thinking being sitting in your chair.

It follows from these apparently trite observations that you are an animal. In a nutshell, the argument is this: (1) There is a human animal sitting in your chair. (2) The human animal sitting in your chair is thinking. (If you like, every human animal sitting there is thinking.) (3) You are the thinking being sitting in your chair. The one and only thinking being sitting in your chair is none other than you. Hence, you are that animal. That animal is you. And there is nothing special about you: we are all animals. If anyone suspects a trick, here is the argument's logical form:

1 $(\exists x)(x$ is a human animal & x is sitting in your chair)

2 $(x)((x$ is a human animal & x is sitting in your chair$) \supset x$ is thinking)

3 $(x)((x$ is thinking & x is sitting in your chair$) \supset x =$ you)

4 $(\exists x)(x$ is a human animal & $x =$ you)

The reader can verify that it is formally valid. (Compare: A man entered the bank vault. The man who entered the vault – any man who did – stole the money. Snodgrass, and no one else, entered the vault and stole the money. Doesn't it follow that Snodgrass is a man?)

Let us be clear about what the "thinking-animal" argument purports to show. Its conclusion is that we are human animals. That is, one of the things true of you is that you are (identical with) an animal. That of course leaves many metaphysical questions about ourselves unanswered. It doesn't by itself tell us whether we are essentially or most fundamentally animals, for instance, or what our identity conditions are. That depends on the metaphysical nature of human animals: on whether human animals are essentially animals, and what their identity conditions are. These are further questions. I argued in the previous section that no sort of mental continuity is either necessary or sufficient for a human animal to persist. If that is right, then our being animals has important and highly contentious metaphysical implications. But it might be disputed, even by those who agree that we are animals. The claim that we are animals is not the end of the story about personal identity. It is only the beginning. Still, it is important to begin in the right place.

The thinking-animal argument is deceptively simple. I suspect that its very simplicity has prevented many philosophers from seeing its point. But there is nothing sophistical about it. It has no obvious and devastating flaw that we teach our students. It deserves to be better known.[3]

In any case, the argument has three premises, and so there are three ways of resisting it. One could deny that there is any human animal sitting in your chair. One could deny that any such animal thinks. Or one could deny that you are the thinking being sitting there. Anyone who denies that we are animals is committed to

accepting one of these claims. They are not very plausible. But let us consider them.

5 Alternative One: There Are No Human Animals

Why suppose that there is no human animal sitting in your chair? Presumably because there are no human animals anywhere. If there are any human animals at all, there is one sitting there. (I assume that you aren't a Martian foundling.) And if there are no human animals, it is hard to see how there could be any organisms of other sorts. So denying the argument's first premise amounts to denying that there are, strictly speaking, any organisms. There appear to be, of course. But that is at best a well-founded illusion.

There are venerable philosophical views that rule out the existence of organisms. Idealism, for instance, denies that there are any material objects at all (so I should describe it, anyway). And there is the view that nothing can have different parts at different times (Chisholm 1976: 89–113, 145–58). Whenever something appears to lose or gain a part, the truth of the matter is that one object, made of the first set of parts, ceases to exist (or becomes scattered) and is instantly replaced by a numerically different object made of the second set of parts. Organisms, if there were such things, would constantly assimilate new particles and expel others. If nothing can survive a change of any of its parts, organisms are metaphysically impossible. What we think of as an organism is in reality only a succession of different "masses of matter" that each take on organic form for a brief moment – until a single particle is gained or lost – and then pass that form on to a numerically different mass.

But few opponents of animalism deny the existence of animals. They have good reason not to quite apart from the fact that this is more or less incredible. Anything that would rule out the existence of animals would also rule out most of the things we might be if we are not animals. If there are no animals, there are no beings constituted by animals, and no temporal parts of animals. And whatever rules out animals may tell against Humean bundles of perceptions as well. If there are no animals, it is not easy to see what we *could* be.

6 Alternative Two: Human Animals Can't Think

The second alternative is that there is an animal sitting in your chair, but it isn't thinking. (Let any occurrence of a propositional attitude, such as the belief that it's raining or the hope that it won't, count as "thinking".) *You* think, but the animal doesn't. The reason for this can only be that the animal can't think. If it were able to think, it would be thinking now. And if *that* animal can't think – despite its healthy, mature human brain, lengthy education, surrounding community of thinkers, and appropriate evolutionary history – then no human animal can. And if no human animal can think, no animal of any sort could. (We can't very well say that dogs can think but human animals can't.) Finally, if no animal could ever think – not even a normal adult human animal – it is hard to see how any organism could have any mental property whatever. So if your animal isn't thinking, that is apparently because it is impossible for any organism to have mental properties.

The claim, then, is that animals, including human animals, are no more intelligent or sentient than trees. We could of course say that they are "intelligent" in the sense of being the bodies of intelligent people who are not themselves animals. And we could call organisms like dogs "sentient" in the sense of being the bodies of sentient non-animals that stand to those animals as you and I stand to human animals. But that is loose talk. The strict and sober truth would be that only non-organisms could ever think.

This is rather hard to believe. Anyone who denies that animals can think (or that they can think in the way that we think) needs to explain why they can't. What stops a typical human animal from using its brain to think? Isn't that what that organ is *for*?

Traditionally, those who deny that animals can think deny that any material object could do so. That seems natural enough: if *any* material thing could think, it would be an animal. Thinking things must be immaterial, and so must we. Of course, simply denying that any material thing could think does nothing to explain why it couldn't. But again, few contemporary opponents of animalism believe that we are immaterial.

Someone might argue like this: "The human animal sitting in your chair is just your body. It is absurd to suppose that your body reads or thinks about philosophy. The thinking thing there – you – must therefore be something other than the animal. But that doesn't mean that you are immaterial. You might be a material thing other than your body."

It may be false to say that your body is reading. There is certainly *something* wrong with that statement. What is less clear is whether it is wrong because the phrase 'your body' denotes something that you in some sense have – a certain human organism – that is unable to read. Compare the word 'body' with a closely related one: *mind*. It is just as absurd to say that Alice's mind weighs 120 pounds, or indeed any other amount, as it is to say that Alice's body is reading. (If that seems less than obvious, consider the claim that Alice's mind is sunburned.) Must we conclude that Alice has something – a clever thing, for Alice has a clever mind – that weighs nothing? Does this show that thinking beings have no mass? Surely not. I think we should be equally wary of drawing metaphysical conclusions from the fact that the phrase 'Alice's body' cannot always be substituted for the name 'Alice'. In any case, the "body" argument does nothing to explain why a human animal should be unable to think.

Anyone who claims that some material objects can think but animals cannot has his work cut out for him. Shoemaker (1984: 92–7; 1999) has argued that animals cannot think because they have the wrong identity conditions. Mental properties have characteristic causal roles, and these, he argues, imply that psychological continuity must suffice for the bearers of those properties to persist. Since this is not true of any organism, no organism could have mental properties. But material things with the right identity conditions *can* think, and organisms can "constitute" such things. I have discussed this argument in another place (Olson 2002b). It is a long story, though, and I won't try to repeat it here.

7 Alternative Three: You Are Not Alone

Suppose, then, that there is a human animal sitting in your chair. And suppose that it thinks. Is there any way to resist the conclusion that you are that thinking animal? We can hardly say that the animal thinks but you don't. (If anything thinks, you do.) Nor can we deny that you exist, when there is a rational animal thinking your thoughts. How, then, could you fail to be that thinking animal? Only if you are not the only thinker there. If you are not *the* thinking thing sitting there, you must be one of at least two such thinkers. You exist. You think. There is also a thinking human animal there. Presumably it has the same psychological qualities as you have. But it isn't you. There are two thinking beings wherever we thought there was just one. There are two philosophers, you and an animal, sitting there and reading this. You are never truly alone: wherever you go, a watchful human animal goes with you.

This is not an attractive picture. Its adherents may try to comfort us by proposing linguistic hypotheses. Whenever two beings are as intimately related as you and your animal are, they will say, we "count them as one" for ordinary purposes (Lewis 1976). When I write on the copyright form that I am the sole author of this essay, I don't mean that every author of this essay is numerically identical with me. I mean only that every author of this essay bears some relation to me that does not imply identity: that every such author is co-located with me, perhaps. My wife is not a bigamist, even though she is, I suppose, married both to me and to the animal. At any rate it would be seriously misleading to describe our relationship as a *ménage à quatre*.

This is supposed to show that the current proposal needn't contradict anything that we say or believe when engaged in the ordinary business of life. Unless we are doing metaphysics, we don't distinguish strict numerical identity from the intimate relation that each of us bears to a certain human animal. Ordinary people have no opinion about how many numerically different thinking beings there are. Why should they? What matters in real life is not how many thinkers there are strictly speaking, but how many *non-overlapping* thinkers.

Perhaps so. Still, it hardly makes the current proposal easy to believe. Is it not strange to suppose that there are two numerically different thinkers wherever we thought there was just one?

In any event, the troubles go beyond mere overcrowding. If there really are two beings, a person and an animal, now thinking your thoughts and performing your actions, you ought to wonder which one you are. You may think you're the person (the one that isn't an animal). But doesn't the animal think that *it* is a person? It has all the same reasons for thinking so as you have. Yet it is mistaken. If you *were* the animal and not the person, you'd still think you were the person. For all you know, *you're* the one making the mistake. Even if you are a person and not an animal, you could never have any reason to believe that you are.[4]

For that matter, if your animal can think, that ought to make *it* a person. It has the same mental features as you have. (Otherwise we should expect an explanation for the difference, just as we should if the animal can't think at all.) It is, in Locke's words, "a thinking intelligent being, that has reason and reflection, and can consider itself as itself, the same thinking thing, in different times and places" (1975: 335). It satisfies every ordinary definition of 'person'. But it would be mad to suppose that the animal sitting in your chair is a *person* numerically different from you – that each human person shares her location and her thoughts with *another* person. If nothing else, this would contradict the claim that people – all people – have psychological identity conditions, thus sweeping away the main reason for denying that we are animals in the first place.

On the other hand, if rational human animals are not people, familiar accounts of what it is to be a person are all far too permissive. Having the psychological and moral features that you and I have would not be enough to make something a person. There could be rational, intelligent, self-conscious *non*-people. In fact there would be at least one such rational non-person for every genuine person. That would deprive personhood of any psychological or moral significance.

8 Hard Choices

That concludes my argument for animalism. We could put the same point in another way. There are about six billion human animals walking the earth. Those animals are just like ourselves. They sit in our chairs and sleep in our beds. They work, and talk, and take holidays. Some of them do philosophy. They have just the mental and physical attributes that we take ourselves to have.

So it seems, anyway. This makes it hard to deny that *we* are those animals. The apparent existence of rational human animals is an inconvenient fact for the opponents of animalism. We might call it the *problem of the thinking animal*.

But what of the case against animalism? It seems that you would go along with your cerebrum if that organ were transplanted. More generally, some sort of mental continuity appears to suffice for us to persist.[5] And that is not true of any animal. Generations of philosophers have found this argument compelling. How can they have gone so badly wrong?

One reason, as I have said, is that they haven't asked the right questions. They have thought about what it takes for us to persist through time, but not about what we are.

Here is another. If someone is mentally just like you, that is strong evidence for his being you. All the more so if there is continuously physically realized mental continuity between him and you. In fact it is conclusive evidence, given that brain transplants belong to science fiction. Moreover, most of us find mental continuity more interesting and important than brute physical continuity. When we hear a story, we don't much care which person at the end of the tale is the same animal as a given person at the beginning. We care about who is psychologically continuous with that person. If mental and animal continuity often came apart, we might think differently. But they don't.

These facts can easily lead us to suppose that the one who remembers your life in the transplant story is you. Easier still if we don't know how problematic that claim is – if we don't realize that it would rule out our being animals. To those who haven't reflected on the problem of the thinking animal – and that includes most philosophers – it can seem dead obvious that we persist by virtue of mental continuity. But if we are animals, this is a mistake, though an understandable one.

Of course, opponents of animalism can play this game too. They can attempt to explain why it is natural to suppose that there are human animals, or that human animals can think, or that you are the thinking thing sitting in your chair, in a way that does not imply that those claims are true. (That is the point of the linguistic hypotheses I mentioned earlier.) What to do? Well, I invite you to compare the thinking-animal argument with the transplant argument.

Which is more likely? That there are no animals? That no animal could ever think? That you are one of at least two intelligent beings sitting in your chair? Or that you would not, after all, go along with your transplanted cerebrum?

9   What It Would Mean if We Were Animals

What would it mean if we were animals? The literature on personal identity gives the impression that this is a highly counter-intuitive, "tough-minded" idea, radically at odds with our deepest convictions. It is certainly at odds with most of that literature. But I doubt whether it conflicts with anything that we all firmly believe.

If animalism conflicts with any popular beliefs, they will be beliefs about the conditions of our identity over time. As we have seen, the way we react (or imagine ourselves reacting) to certain fantastic stories suggests that we take ourselves to persist by virtue of mental continuity. Our beliefs about *actual* cases, though, suggest no such thing. In every actual case, the number of people we think there are is just the number of human animals. Every actual case in which we take someone to survive or perish is a case where a human animal survives or perishes.

If anything, the way we regard actual cases suggests a conviction that our identity does not consist in mental continuity, or at any rate that mental continuity is unnecessary for us to persist. When someone lapses into a persistent vegetative state, his friends and relatives may conclude that his life no longer has any value. They may even conclude that he has ceased to exist *as a person*. But they don't ordinarily suppose that their loved one no longer exists at all, and that the living organism on the hospital bed is something numerically different from him – even when they come to believe that there is no mental continuity between the vegetable and the person. *That* would be a tough-minded view.

And most of us believe that we were once foetuses. When we see an ultrasound picture of a twelve-week-old foetus, it is easy to believe we are seeing something that will, if all goes well, be born, learn to talk, go to school, and eventually become an adult human person. Yet none of us is in any way mentally continuous with a twelve-week-old foetus.

Animalism may conflict with religious beliefs: in reincarnation or resurrection, for instance (though whether there is any real conflict is less obvious than it may seem: see van Inwagen 1978). But few accounts of personal identity are any more compatible with those beliefs. If resurrection and reincarnation rule out our being animals, they probably rule out our being anything except immaterial substances, or perhaps computer programs. On this score animalism is no worse off than its main rivals.

And don't we have a strong conviction that we are animals? We all think that we are human beings. And until the philosophers got hold of us, we took human beings to be animals. We *seem* to be animals. It is the opponents of animalism who insist that this appearance is deceptive: that the animal you see in the mirror is not really you. That we are animals ought to be the default position. If anything is hard to believe, it's the alternatives.

Notes

I thank Trenton Merricks and Gonzalo Rodriguez-Pereyra for comments on an earlier version of this paper.

1 e.g. Shoemaker 1984: 113f. For what it's worth, my opinion of "constitutionalism" can be found in Olson 2001.

2 For more on this crucial point see Olson 1997: 114–19.

3 The argument is not entirely new. As I see it, it only makes explicit what is implicit in Carter 1989, Ayers 1990: 283f, Snowdon 1990, and Olson 1997: 100–9.

4 Some say that revisionary linguistics can solve this problem too (Noonan 1998). The idea is roughly this. First, not just any rational, self-conscious being is a person, but only those that have psychological identity conditions. Human animals, despite their mental properties, are not people because they lack psychological identity conditions. Second, the word 'I' and other personal pronouns refer only to people. Thus, when the animal associated with you says 'I', it doesn't refer to itself. Rather, it refers to you, the person associated with it. When it says, "I am a person," it does not say falsely that *it* is a person, but truly that *you* are. So the animal is not mistaken about which thing it is, and neither are you. You can infer that you are a person from the linguistic facts that you are whatever you refer to when you say 'I', and that 'I' refers only to people: I discuss this ingenious proposal in Olson 2002a.

5 In fact this is not so. Let the surgeons transplant each of your cerebral hemispheres into a different head. Both offshoots will be mentally continuous with you. But they can't both *be* you, for the simple reason that one thing (you) cannot be identical with two things. We cannot say in general that anyone who is mentally continuous with you must be you. Exceptions are possible. So it ought to come as no great surprise if the original cerebrum transplant is another exception.

References

Ayers, M. 1990. *Locke*, vol. 2. London: Routledge.

Carter, W. R. 1989. How to change your mind. *Canadian Journal of Philosophy* 19: 1–14.

Chisholm, R. 1976. *Person and Object*. La Salle, IL: Open Court [partly reproduced as ch. 33 in this volume].

Hume, D. 1888. *Treatise of Human Nature* (1739), ed. L. A. Selby-Bigge. Oxford: Clarendon Press. Partly repr. in Perry 1975: 159–78.

Lewis, D. 1976. Survival and identity. In A. Rorty, ed., *The Identities of Persons*, Berkeley: University of California Press, pp. 17–40. Repr. in his *Philosophical Papers*, vol. 1, New York: Oxford University Press, 1983, pp. 55–77 [ch. 43 in this volume].

Locke, J. 1975. *An Essay Concerning Human Understanding*, 2nd edn (1694), ed. P. Nidditch. Oxford: Clarendon Press. Partly repr. in Perry 1975: 33–52.

Noonan, Harold. 1998. Animalism versus Lockeanism: a current controversy. *Philosophical Quarterly* 48: 302–18.

Olson, E. 1997. *The Human Animal: Personal Identity without Psychology*. New York: Oxford University Press.

Olson, E. 2001. Material coincidence and the indiscernibility problem. *Philosophical Quarterly* 51: 337–55.

Olson, E. 2002a. Thinking animals and the reference of 'I'. *Philosophical Topics* 30.

Olson, E. 2002b. What does functionalism tell us about personal identity? *Noûs* 36.

Perry, J., ed. 1975. *Personal Identity*. Berkeley: University of California Press.

Quinton, A. 1962. The soul. *Journal of Philosophy* 59: 393–403. Repr. in Perry 1975: 53–72.

Russell, B. 1985. *The Philosophy of Logical Atomism* (1918). La Salle, IL: Open Court.

Shoemaker, S. 1984. Personal identity: a materialist's account. In S. Shoemaker and R. Swinburne, *Personal Identity*, Oxford: Blackwell, pp. 67–132.

Shoemaker, S. 1999. Self, body, and coincidence. *Proceedings of the Aristotelian Society*, supp. vol. 73: 287–306.

Snowdon, Paul. 1990. Persons, animals, and ourselves. In C. Gill, ed., *The Person and the Human Mind*, Oxford: Clarendon Press, pp. 83–107.

Unger, P. 1979. I do not exist. In G. F. MacDonald, ed., *Perception and Identity*, London: Macmillan, pp. 235–51. Repr. in M. Rea, ed., *Material Constitution*, Lanham, MD: Rowman and Littlefield, 1997, pp. 175–90.

van Inwagen, P. 1978. The possibility of resurrection. *International Journal for the Philosophy of Religion* 9: 114–21. Repr. in his *The Possibility of Resurrection and Other Essays in Christian Apologetics*, Boulder, CO: Westview, 1997, pp. 45–51.

van Inwagen, P. 1980. Philosophers and the words 'human body'. In van Inwagen, ed., *Time and Cause*, Dordrecht: Reidel, pp. 283–99.

PART VIII

Objects

Introduction

In recent years, there has been a growing interest among metaphysicians in questions concerning which material objects there are; in particular, what sorts of highly visible, macroscopic things there are. Some have suggested that there are far fewer than we ordinarily take there to be. There are no baseballs, mountains, or bicycles. Some have even gone so far as to deny that they themselves exist! Others have suggested that there are far more things, right before our eyes, than we ordinarily take there to be. For instance, some would say that where there seems to be a single cat on a mat, there are in fact billions of cats. Or that there are billions of non-cats on the mat, each of which is physically indistinguishable from the cat but which differ from the cat by having slightly or wildly different persistence conditions. Or that, in addition to the mat and the cat, there is a single thing composed of the mat and the cat, a "matcat," which is part polyester and part flesh and bone.

In "When are Objects Parts?" (chapter 47), Peter van Inwagen introduces "The Special Composition Question": under what conditions do some objects compose something? Intuitively, sometimes some things do compose something, for instance, a hammer handle and the hammer head to which it is affixed compose something: a hammer. Other things seem not to compose anything, for instance, your nose and the Eiffel Tower do not together compose an object. However it is extraordinarily difficult to give a fully general answer to the Special Composition Question that respects all of our intuitions about when composition occurs. Van Inwagen rejects a number of candidate answers to the question, including "extreme" answers: that any plurality of disjoint objects compose something ("universalism") and that no plurality of objects ever compose something ("nihilism"). He concludes with a discussion of how moderate answers to the Special Composition Question run afoul of the dominant, linguistic account of the nature of vagueness. (In his book *Material Beings*, van Inwagen defends his own preferred response to the question: some things compose something just in case their activities constitute a life. In other words, there are mountain lions but no mountains, apple trees but no apples.)

In "Many, But Almost One" (chapter 48), David Lewis attempts to solve the so-called "Problem of the Many." To see what the problem is, consider a mountain, and call the atoms that compose the mountain "the As." (Never mind that it is vague exactly which atoms those are. As Lewis points out, proper attention to the vagueness of parthood only *amplifies* the problem.) Now consider a particular atom at the very tip of the mountain. Call it "B." Now consider all of the As other than B. They have everything that it takes to compose a mountain. So surely they do compose a mountain. But this can't

Metaphysics: An Anthology, Second Edition. Edited by Jaegwon Kim, Daniel Z. Korman and Ernest Sosa.
Editorial material and organization © 2012 Blackwell Publishing Ltd. Published 2012 by Blackwell Publishing Ltd.

be the same mountain as the mountain mentioned at the outset. After all, that one has B as a part and this other mountain doesn't. So where we thought there was just one mountain, there are at least two. By exactly similar reasoning, we can conclude that there are actually billions of mountains there! Lewis tries to show that there is a perfectly good sense in which there is only one mountain there. Yet he concedes that there is another sense in which there really are many mountains where there looked to be just one, and he maintains that they are nevertheless "almost one" by virtue of their nearly complete overlap.

The Problem of the Many illustrates one way in which philosophical reflection might lead us to postulate far more material objects than we ordinarily take there to be. In "Existential Relativity" (chapter 49), Ernest Sosa notes yet another way in which we might be driven to postulate "extra" entities. We conceive of the world as containing certain kinds of objects with certain kinds of persistence conditions. But we could easily have conceived of the world as containing objects with different kinds of persistence conditions. (Sosa gives the example of *snowdiscalls* which, like snowballs, are constituted by pieces of snow, but which are meant to be different from snowballs in that they can survive being flattened into a disc.) Much of Sosa's paper is devoted to examining the viability of a conceptual relativist view on which objects exist only relative to conceptual schemes. But Sosa ultimately endorses an "absolutist" view, on which both snowballs and snowdiscalls do strictly speaking exist, as do countless other objects answering to alternative ways of carving up the world into objects.

In "The Argument from Vagueness" (chapter 50), Theodore Sider presents and defends an argument for universalism, the thesis that for any (non-overlapping) objects you like, those objects compose something. Here is the main idea behind the argument: If we say that composition only sometimes occurs, then presumably there can be borderline cases of composition – that is, cases where it is vague whether the objects in question compose anything. But there can't be borderline cases of composition. That's because if it were vague whether some things composed something (say, a hammer head that is just beginning to be affixed to a handle) then it would be vague how many things there are (the handle, the head, *and* a hammer, or just the handle and head?). But we can make claims about how many things there are without using any vague language whatsoever. Consequently, those claims can't be vague; they must have determinate truth values. So it can't be vague how many things there are, in which case it can't be vague whether composition occurs. So composition must be unrestricted. So (among other things) there is something composed of your nose and the Eiffel Tower! Sider goes on to argue that composition is unrestricted even across time – in which case there is also something composed of *Socrates'* nose and the Eiffel Tower – and that this supports the four-dimensionalist theory of persistence (see Part VI).

In "Epiphenomenalism and Eliminativism" (chapter 51), Trenton Merricks argues that we should not believe in baseballs and other familiar kinds of macroscopic objects. Merricks observes that everything that a baseball might be thought to cause can already be accounted for by the collective activities of the relevant "atoms arranged baseballwise." But once we see that the activities of these microscopic items can do all of the explanatory work, there would seem to be little reason to suppose that the associated macroscopic objects exist. It is implausible that all of the events that are allegedly caused by baseballs are systematically overdetermined, that is, caused independently by baseballs and by their parts. And we should be unwilling to believe in baseballs if they would have to be mere "epiphenomena," that is, if they would have no causal powers of their own. Merricks also considers and rejects other putative reasons for believing in baseballs and the like (e.g., that we can *see* them).

In "Against Revisionary Ontology" (chapter 52), Eli Hirsch argues that revisionary ontological views about material objects – that is, those that deviate from our pretheoretical conception of which material objects there are or of the persistence conditions of these objects – are fundamentally misguided. He presents an "argument from charity" which purports to show that, unless ordinary speakers are making some massive *empirical* mistake (e.g., we are hallucinating when we seem to see baseballs and other macroscopic objects), the correct interpretation of our language must make the bulk our utterances about the world come out true. These include such utterances as 'There are baseballs', 'There is nothing whose parts are my nose and the Eiffel Tower', and 'This tree once had more branches'. If these sentences are true, then certain revisionary views must be false: eliminativism, universalism, and mereological essentialism. Hirsch also supplies a (hilarious) critique of various attempts to reconcile revisionary views with ordinary discourse about material objects.

In "Strange Kinds, Familiar Kinds, and the Charge of Arbitrariness" (chapter 53), Daniel Z. Korman addresses worries having to do with the apparent arbitrariness of our ordinary judgments about which kinds of things there are and are not. Isn't it arbitrary, for instance, to accept that there are snowballs but deny that there are such things as Sosa's snowdiscalls? Or to deny that there is anything composed of your nose and the Eiffel Tower, while believing in other scattered objects, such as the solar system? Korman examines a variety of cases and attempts to show that our judgments and intuitions in these cases are not as arbitrary as they may at first seem. He also considers whether the mere possibility of communities with radically different conceptual schemes should undermine our confidence about which objects there are.

Further Reading

Baker, L. R. (2008). *The Metaphysics of Everyday Life*. Cambridge: Cambridge University Press.

Cartwright, R. (1975). "Scattered Objects," in K. Lehrer (ed.), *Analysis and Metaphysics*. Boston: Reidel.

Hawley, K. (2002). "Vagueness and Existence," *Proceedings of the Aristotelian Society* 102: 125–40.

Hoffman, J., and Rosenkrantz, G. S. (1997). *Substance: Its Nature and Existence*. New York: Routledge.

Horgan, T., and Potrč, M. (2000). "Blobjectivism and Indirect Correspondence," *Facta Philosophica* 2: 249–70.

Markosian, N. (1998). "Brutal Composition," *Philosophical Studies* 92: 211–49.

Merricks, T. (2001). *Objects and Persons*. New York: Oxford University Press.

Rea, M. C. (1997). *Material Constitution*. Lanham: Rowman & Littlefield.

Simons, P. (1987). *Parts: A Study in Ontology*. New York: Oxford University Press.

Thomasson, A. (2007). *Ordinary Objects*. Oxford: Oxford University Press.

Unger, P. (1979). "There Are No Ordinary Things," *Synthese* 41: 117–54.

Van Inwagen, P. (1990). *Material Beings*. Ithaca, NY: Cornell University Press.

47

When are Objects Parts?

Peter van Inwagen

I

That there are deep and intractable metaphysical problems about material objects is evident from the unresolved antinomies and paradoxes involving material objects. The best known of these are about artifacts, the puzzle of the Ship of Theseus being the best known of all. Others, at least as worthy of remark, involve living organisms. If a cat's tail is cut off, for example, it seems natural to describe this episode in words that appear to imply that the cat becomes identical with a former proper part of itself – a violation of the attractive modal principle that a thing and another thing cannot become a thing and itself. Or, talking of cats, consider a cat that is composed at t of certain atoms arranged in a certain way; it is at least logically possible for those very same atoms to be arranged in exactly the same way at some later time, and then to compose a different cat; but that apparently implies that certain small material objects can compose one large material object at t, and, even though arranged in precisely the same way, compose a distinct material object later. How could that be?

All, or almost all, of the antinomies and paradoxes that the philosophical study of material objects is heir to involve the notion of parthood. I believe, though I shall not argue for this thesis, that most of the great, intractable metaphysical puzzles about material objects could be seen to have quite obvious solutions by one who had a clear understanding of what it was for one material object to be a part of another. In this paper, I shall try to advance our understanding of this notion.

I shall approach the concept of parthood in a somewhat indirect way. There is a mereological concept that I have found it easier to think fruitfully about than I have parthood. (By a mereological concept, I mean one that can be given a trivial definition in terms of parthood.) I call this notion *composition*. I give some examples. Suppose there is a house made entirely of bricks. Then those bricks compose the house. If there are such things as the north and south halves of the house, then those two halves also compose the house, and each of *them* is composed of certain bricks. The eastern third of the house, the western third of the house, and its middle third also compose it. Certain molecules compose the house. Certain atoms compose the house. Certain elementary particles compose the house. These examples should make it intuitively clear what composition is.

Peter van Inwagen, "When are Objects Parts?", in James E. Tomberlin (ed.), *Philosophical Perspectives*, 1: *Metaphysics* (1987). Copyright by Ridgeview Publishing Co., Atascadero, CA. Reprinted by permission of Ridgeview Publishing Company.

Metaphysics: An Anthology, Second Edition. Edited by Jaegwon Kim, Daniel Z. Korman and Ernest Sosa. Editorial material and organization © 2012 Blackwell Publishing Ltd. Published 2012 by Blackwell Publishing Ltd.

I will now formally define composition in terms of parthood. I begin with a bit of formal machinery.

Let us call expressions like 'the *xs*', 'the *ys*', and 'the *zs*' *plural variables*. These expressions stand to the English pronoun 'they' as the familiar singular variables '*x*', '*y*', and '*z*' stand to the English pronoun 'it'. Singular variables combine with *n*-adic predicates to make open sentences like '*x* loves *y*'. Plural variables combine with "variably polyadic" predicates to form open sentences like 'the *xs* are cooperating with the *ys*'. (Or both sorts of variable may occur together: 'the *xs* are conspiring against *y*'.) Plural variables are bound by two plural quantifiers: 'for some *xs*' and 'for any *xs*'. Ordinary open sentences containing *n* free variables express *n*-ary relations: '*x* likes *x* better than *x* likes *y*' expresses a binary relation. Open sentences formed from variably polyadic predicates express relations of a type sometimes called "multigrade": 'the *xs* belong to the same political party' expresses a multigrade relation. (Much of this terminology is confused and confusing; it could easily be greatly improved, but I shall not bother about that here.)

Our definition of composition is in two stages:

(i)   *y* is the sum of the *xs* if and only if the *xs* are parts of *y* and every part of *y* overlaps [shares a part with] at least one of the *xs*;

(ii) the *xs* compose *y* if and only if *y* is the sum of the *xs* and no two of the *xs* overlap.[1]

I believe that this definition of composition is ultimately due to Whitehead. The two stages of the definition could obviously be combined into a single definition of 'compose', but we shall have some use for the notion of "sum" that is introduced in the first stage.

The question that will be our main topic is this: Suppose one had certain non-overlapping material objects, the *xs*, at one's disposal; what would one have to do – what *could* one do – to get the *xs* to compose something? (I have found it to be heuristically useful to put the question in this "practical" way, in a way that invites the inquirer to contemplate various courses of action. But this way of asking the question must not be taken to imply that the *xs* are objects that human beings are able to manipulate. The *xs* may just as well be quarks or stars – or the members of some quite heterogeneous class of material things – as bricks or tinker-toy parts. The inquirer should, therefore, imagine himself to be omnipotent.) An interesting answer to this question must not, of course, involve mereological concepts. It would be no fair to answer it by saying, "To get the *xs* to compose something, cause them to have a sum."

I shall call this question the Special Composition Question. It is important to realize that an answer to the Special Composition Question would not tell us what composition *was*. An answer to the Special Composition Question would merely tell us when, or under what conditions, composition occurred. This point is important enough for a brief digression. Suppose you have an answer to the Special Composition Question; something along these lines:

> To get the *xs* to compose something, you must (and need only) get them to stand in the multigrade relation R.

Then you are in a position to eliminate the sentence '∃*y* the *xs* compose *y*' from your discourse: You can replace it with 'the *xs* stand in R'. But you are not in a position to eliminate just any reference to composition from your discourse. You are not, for example, in a position to eliminate the sentence '∀*y*(F*y* ⊃ ~ the *xs* compose *y*)', for this sentence is not of the form '∃*y* the *xs* compose *y*'. To remove *all* references to composition from your discourse, you would have to have a sentence that you could replace 'the *xs* compose *y*' with – a sentence, of course, in which '*y*' occurred free. An answer to the Special Composition Question will provide us with no such sentence.

Suppose we call the question 'What *is* composition?' the General Composition Question. The General Composition Question is obviously closely related to the question, How can we remove all reference to composition from our discourse? (On one understanding of philosophical analysis, these questions are essentially identical.) To ask how to remove all reference to composition from our discourse is to ask how to remove all sentences of the form 'the *xs* compose *y*'. Therefore, as we have seen, an answer to the Special Composition Question is not an answer to the General Composition Question. This is why the Special Composition Question is not the question: What

what is an improper part?

is composition? This is why it is more like the question: Under what conditions does composition occur? Here is a mathematical analogy. I can tell you when, or under what conditions, a number has a (unique) reciprocal: A number has a reciprocal if that number is not 0. But this piece of information does not tell you what a "reciprocal" is, or what it is for an object to be "the reciprocal of" a given number. Note that, on the basis of the piece of information I have given you, you can eliminate '∃*y* *y* is the reciprocal of *x*' from your discourse: You can replace it with '*x* is not 0'. But this will not enable you to remove all references to reciprocality from your discourse. To be able do that, you would have to have a sentence to replace '*y* is the reciprocal of *x*' with. ('*y* = 1/*x*' is, of course, what is needed.)

I mention the General Composition Question only to distinguish it from the Special Composition Question, and to remark that it is immensely more difficult than the Special Composition Question. The Special Composition Question will be our concern. The Special Composition Question is easier than the General Composition Question,[2] but it is not easy. It is sufficiently difficult that I shall not, in this paper, propose an answer to it; I shall do no more than to reject some unsatisfactory answers.

I said above that I should approach the concept of parthood in a somewhat indirect way. I was alluding to the fact that I shall approach the concept of parthood *via* the concept of composition. I must point out, lest I raise false hopes, that an answer to the Special Composition Question, even if we had it, would not tell us what parthood *was*. This is an obvious corollary of the fact that an answer to the Special Composition Question would not tell us what composition was. Parthood and composition are trivially interdefinable. We have seen how to define composition given parthood. Given composition, we may define parthood as follows:

x is a part of *y* if and only if
there are *z*s such that *x* and the *z*s compose *y*.

Only an answer to the General Composition Question could turn this definition into an explanation of parthood. But an answer to the Special Composition Question will tell us something about parthood: under what conditions it occurs.

That is, if we know, in general, the conditions under which composition occurs, we can easily say under what conditions an object is a proper part of something. (Of course an object is *always* an improper part of something.) An object *x* is a proper part of something if and only if there are *z*s, one of which is not *x*, such that *x* and the *z*s compose something.

I am almost ready to turn to the Special Composition Question. Before doing so, however, I will remark that in the remainder of this paper I am going to be making a controversial assumption about material objects: that material objects are three-dimensional and strictly persist through time. I assume, for example, that a cat is a three-dimensional object (and not a "space-time worm," whatever that is). And I assume that the three-dimensional cat I took to the vet last September is numerically identical with the three-dimensional cat I stroked last week. (I shall be told that the cat I took to the vet and the cat I stroked had different properties and hence cannot have been numerically identical. I reply that *it* had different properties at different times.) I oppose this view to the view that *two* three-dimensional cats – or perhaps I am supposed to call them "cat-slices" – figure in my history, one occupying a point in time last September and the other occupying a point in time last week, these numerically distinct three-dimensional objects having no more intimate connection than that established by their both being slices of one four-dimensional object.

I will mention three facts by way of justifying my making this assumption: (a) I believe it to be true; (b) I find the alternative unintelligible; (c) I can't do everything in one paper. I am willing to defend the "three-dimensionalist" conception of material objects, but to do so is not my project here. Anyone who accepts "four-dimensionalism," or takes this doctrine seriously, may regard this paper as having a conclusion that is conditional in form: '*If* cats and such are three-dimensional and strictly persist through time, *then* composition must have such-and-such features'. Four-dimensionalists may in fact be extremely pleased with my conditional conclusion when they have seen its consequent.

Speaking of controversial assumptions, I am also going to assume that you and I, human beings, men and women, are material objects – the ones you see about you with clothes draped over them, things made of flesh and blood and bone and shaped roughly like statues of human beings. I would justify my making this assumption on grounds similar to those on which I have justified my assumptions about the three-dimensionality of material objects. If you reject this assumption, you may wish to consider the arguments that can be got by replacing all statements about human beings in the sequel with the corresponding statements about human bodies – or cats. *I* find the resulting arguments less persuasive than the arguments I shall give,[3] but you may feel differently.

Let us now examine some answers to the Special Composition Question.

II

Answer (i) Contact

To get the *x*s to compose something, one must, and need only, bring them into contact; if the *x*s are in contact, they compose something and if they are not in contact, they do not compose anything.

I shall assume that we know what it is for *two* objects to be in contact.[4] (It will be technically convenient to treat each object as being in contact with itself, and to stipulate that *two* objects are in contact only if they do not overlap.) For any *x*s, there is a binary relation that holds between *y* and *z* just in the case that *y* and *z* are among the *x*s and are in contact: the contact relation on the *x*s, so to call it. The *x*s are in contact if the <u>ancestral</u> of the contact relation on the *x*s holds between any pair of the *x*s. For example consider six blocks arranged like this and surrounded by empty space:

3	5	7	9		2	4

The six blocks are not in contact. The odd-numbered blocks are in contact. The square, odd-numbered blocks are in contact. (The previous sentence "comes out true" even though there is only one square, odd-numbered block.) The even-numbered blocks are in contact. The square blocks are not in contact. The oblong blocks are not in contact. (The ancestral of *x is in contact with y* holds between any two of the oblong blocks, but the ancestral of *x and y are among the oblong blocks and are in contact* – the contact relation on the oblong blocks – does not: It does not hold between 3 and 7 or between 3 and 9. It is this sort of case that is the source of the complexity of the definition.) Blocks 3, 5, and 7 are in contact.

It is to 'contact' in this sense that the answer to the Special Composition Question called *Contact* refers. If *Contact* is correct, then, in the situation pictured above, there are, in addition to our six blocks, at least seven other objects – seven clumps of blocks, one might call them. "At least seven? Why not exactly seven?" Well, for one thing the blocks may have parts that are not shown. But even if the blocks have no proper parts, *Contact* entails that our picture displays exactly seven composite objects only on the assumption that, for any *x*s, the *x*s compose (at any given moment) at most one thing. (Strictly speaking, if we were not willing to make this assumption, we should have said 'a sum' rather than 'the sum' in our definition of composition. Cf. n. 1.) This assumption could be defended in various ways. For example, it follows from the principle of the identity of indiscernibles, together with the principle that the properties of a composite object are completely determined by the properties of and the relations among its parts. But perhaps these two principles are no more evident than the thesis that follows from them. In the sequel, I shall assume without further discussion that, for any *x*s, the *x*s compose at most one thing at a time.

Contact has a certain intuitive appeal. It seems plausible to say that if one has ten thousand wooden blocks none of which touches any of the others, then there is nothing that those blocks compose. It seems plausible to say that if one proceeds to build a model of Salisbury Cathedral out of them (laying them dry, as it were), then one has brought into existence something that they compose: a model of Salisbury Cathedral. But this answer seems less plausible in simpler cases. If I bring two identical cubes into contact so that a face of one is conterminous with a face of the other, have I thereby brought into existence a new thing, a solid whose volume is twice that of either of the cubes? Or have I merely rearranged the furniture of earth without adding to it? If I cause the cue ball to rebound from the eight ball, do I thereby create a short-lived object shaped like two slightly flattened spheres in contact? One might suspect that there is no answer to these questions laid up in heaven, and that how we answer them – assuming they're worth answering – is going to be simply a matter of convention. But I think that we can see that there are at least some cases in which mere contact is not sufficient for the production of a new object.

Suppose you and I shake hands. Does a new thing at that moment come into existence, a thing shaped like a statue of two people shaking hands, a thing that has you and me as parts and which will perish when we cease to be in contact? Does our handshake generate an object that fits just exactly into the region of space that we jointly occupy? Not in my view. Despite our being in contact, nothing is such that you and I compose it. Or, at least, if you and I compose something, this is not *in virtue of* our being in contact. Some philosophers think that any non-overlapping things compose something, and these philosophers would say that when you and I are shaking hands, there is a thing, the sum of you and me, that occupies the sum of the regions of space that we occupy individually. But, according to the theory these philosophers advocate, the sum of you and me did not come into existence at the moment you and I came into contact; rather, this sum already existed and had existed at every moment at which you and I both existed. (It would, I suppose, be logically possible to hold that you and I had one sum before we were in contact, and another afterwards, this second sum being generated at just the moment we came into contact. But this thesis would have little to recommend it, and I am sure no one in fact holds it.) All that happened to this sum at the moment you and I touched – these philosophers tell us – is that it changed from being a scattered to being a connected object. (A connected object is an object that is "all in one piece": For any *x*s, if the *x*s compose that object, then the *x*s are in contact. A scattered object is a non-connected object.) That is not the theory we are currently considering. We shall examine *that* theory presently. The theory we are considering entails that the thing you and I compose came into existence (or resumed

existence: it might have existed at various earlier times) at the moment we came into contact.

It is a basic conviction of mine that this theory is wrong and that its being wrong is in no sense a matter of convention. I cannot prove this thesis, for I know of no propositions more plausible than itself from which it could be derived. I will content myself for the present by pointing out that if you disagree with me about *Contact*, you face a host of metaphysical problems that I avoid. For example, suppose that I were to touch your knee with my elbow. Would the object that came into existence when this happened be the same one that came into existence when we shook hands or a different one? For that matter, does the same object come into (or resume) existence every time we shake hands? One would like to believe that these questions had answers. (The philosophers I mentioned in the preceding paragraph will of course say that the thing you and I compose when we are shaking hands is the thing that you and I compose when my elbow is touching your knee. But if you believe, as they do not, that the existence at a given time of a thing that is then our sum depends upon our being in contact at that time, then it is far from obvious whether this statement is available to you.) I am happy to have a position that enables me to avoid these difficult questions. Nevertheless, it is not in order to avoid difficulties that I have adopted the position that the coming into contact of two human beings is without metaphysical issue. I have adopted it because it seems to me, on careful consideration, to be true.

We have talked so far only about the case of two human beings coming into contact. Reflection on more complicated cases of human contact (ring-dances, say) convinces me that, however many people we may consider, those people do not begin to compose something at the moment at which they begin to be in contact. Therefore, the relation *the xs come into contact at t* is not (for it is not even coextensive with) the relation *the xs begin at t to compose something*. This is not to say, however, that there may not be some cases in which certain things come to compose something at the moment at which they come into contact. It is to say that the mere fact that they come into contact cannot be a complete explanation of the generation of the new thing that they compose.

Answer (ii) Fastening

To get the xs to compose something, one must, and need only, cause them to be fastened to one another.

To separate two normal, middle-sized material objects that are in contact, one need often do no more than apply to one of them a force that would have sufficed to move it if it had not been in contact with the other. Contact is therefore typically a highly unstable relation, a fact that may lead one who reflects on it to the conclusion that objects that have simply been brought into contact have not really been *joined*. More generally and abstractly, one may be led to the conclusion that if the xs are to compose an object, then the arrangement of the xs should be one of the more stable among the possible arrangements of the xs: If a rather small force could radically change the positions of the xs relative to one another, then one might be inclined to say that the xs did not compose anything; if the direction in which an impulse of a given magnitude was applied to one of the xs were largely immaterial to whether that impulse would radically change the disposition of the xs, then one might be inclined to say that the xs did not compose anything.

Suppose that two objects are in contact and suppose that they are so arranged that, among all the many sequences in which forces of arbitrary direction and magnitude might be applied to either or both of them, *at most only a few* would be capable of separating them without breaking or permanently deforming or otherwise damaging either of them. Then let us say that these two objects are *fastened to each other* or, simply, *fastened*. (If we know what it is for two objects to be fastened to each other, then we can easily give a general explanation of what it is for the xs to be fastened to one another: We need only employ the device that was used to define 'the xs are in contact'. We stipulate, moreover, that each object is fastened to itself and that *two* objects are fastened only if they do not overlap.) For example, if a nut is threaded on to a bolt, then the nut and the bolt are fastened, since most ways of applying force to the nut or to the bolt or to both would not suffice to remove the nut from the bolt: Most ways of applying force would produce no movement of either, or else would cause them to

move as a unit. A structure built of tinker-toy parts, a house, and a watch are examples of things that are, in the main, built up by successively fastening things to one another – at least, assuming that there are such objects as these things and their parts. A watch is unlike a house of blocks in that an arbitrarily applied force will almost certainly not cause the watch to come apart (unless, of course, the force is great enough actually to cause something to break), while a force great enough to move any of the blocks composing a house of blocks "separately" will quite possibly cause the house of blocks to disintegrate. One can toss a watch about, but one cannot toss a house of blocks about.

Now the concept of "fastening" is pretty vague, and my attempts to explain it could probably be improved upon. One source of this vagueness and unsatisfactoriness is the notion of "only a few among all the possible ways of applying forces to a thing." It would not be difficult to devise some set-theoretical constructions to play the parts of "ways of applying forces" to a thing. And if these objects were constructed in any standard or obvious way, the cardinality of, e.g., the set of ways of applying forces to a nut and a bolt that would unthread the nut from the bolt would be just the cardinality of the whole set of ways of applying forces to the nut and the bolt. (Still, there seems to be something to this idea. Consider the ill-named notion of a "child-proof cap." Isn't what differentiates a child-proof cap from a garden-variety cap the fact that comparatively few of the ways of applying force to a child-proof cap will suffice to remove it from its bottle?) But there would be no point in trying to provide a better account of fastening, for it does not seem to be true that if two things become fastened there must at that moment come into existence a new object that has them both as parts, an object that occupies all the space that they individually occupy and which wouldn't have existed if they had merely come into contact. I think we can find perfectly clear cases of two objects becoming fastened, cases that ought to be allowed by any reasonable way of spelling out the concept of fastening, that are simply not cases of anything's coming to be. Suppose again that you and I shake hands. We have already agreed that it would be wrong to suppose that our coming into contact in this way would result in the existence of a new object, one that you and I compose. Now suppose that the fingers of our hands were suddenly to become paralyzed, with the embarrassing consequence that we were unable to let go of each other. Suppose that, in fact, because of the paralysis of our entwined fingers, it had become impossible for anyone to pull us apart by main force, short of doing us damage. On any reasonable account, then, we have suddenly become fastened to each other. But it is certainly not true that an object composed of you and me comes into existence at the instant our fingers become paralyzed. Our paralysis has not added to the furniture of earth; it has merely diminished its capacity to be rearranged. Therefore, composition is not, primarily, a matter of things being fastened to one another. This is not to say that there may not be some cases in which certain things come to compose something at the moment they become fastened to one another; it is to say that the mere fact that they have become fastened is not a complete explanation of the generation of the new thing that they compose.

Answer (iii) Cohesion

….one need only cause them to cohere.

Objects that are merely fastened to one another can often be separated by one who knows how without his breaking anything. It is, of course, possible to join objects so that they can't be pulled apart, or even moved in relation to one another, without breaking some of them. One might, for example, glue two blocks of wood together, using a glue the particles of which attract particles of wood more strongly than particles of wood attract one another. (Perhaps the layer of dried glue is a third object. In that case we have three objects joined in this fashion.) Or one might weld two pieces of metal together. We might say that in such cases one causes objects to *cohere*. If one causes two things to cohere, does one thereby cause a new object to come into being, an object that they compose and which would not have existed if they had merely been in contact or had merely been fastened to each other? It would seem not. Suppose once more that you and I shake hands, this time after I have smeared my hand with one of those glues whose manufacturers warn us that they

"bond skin instantly." No new thing comes to be in the course of our consequent painful adventure.

Answer (iv) Fusion

….one need only cause them to fuse.

Between objects that have been caused merely to cohere, there is a discernible boundary: a welding seam, say, or a layer of dried glue. It is possible to cause objects to be joined more intimately than this, so that they melt into each other in a way that leaves no discoverable boundary. If two very smooth pieces of chemically pure metal are brought together, for example, they become attached to each other in just this intimate way. (Such an event could scarcely occur outside a laboratory: Under normal conditions, each of the pieces of metal would almost immediately acquire a coating of its oxide, and these coatings would be thick and irregular enough to prevent the pieces being brought into effective contact.) Let us say that if two things are caused to "merge" in this way, they become *fused* or that they *fuse*. Is the fusion of two or more objects a sufficient condition for their beginning to compose something? No. Consider Alice and Beatrice, who are identical twins. A mad surgeon cuts off Alice's left hand and Beatrice's right hand and joins their stumps together, so that they look rather as if they were part of a chain of paper dolls. The surgeon thus produces what might be described as a case of artificial Siamese twins. It is at least theoretically possible that the anatomy of Alice's wrist be so nearly an exact match to the anatomy of Beatrice's wrist, and the healing of one to the other be so nearly perfect, that no boundary between Alice and Beatrice be discoverable; it may be that there is a region such that there is simply no answer to the question whether the cells in that region are Alice's cells or Beatrice's cells. And yet, it seems to me, it is quite unreasonable to say that our mad surgeon, like Dr. Frankenstein, created a new being by causing parts of existing beings to fuse. (Perhaps Dr. Frankenstein's success was due to his using only *proper* parts of existing beings.) Despite the fact that they are fused, and separable only by further surgery, there is nothing but Alice and Beatrice (and such undetached parts as they may have) *there*: If R_A is the region of space that Alice fits just exactly into and R_B is the region of space that Beatrice fits just exactly into, there is no one thing that fits just exactly into the region of space that is the sum of R_A and R_B. That is, despite their fusion, nothing is such that Alice and Beatrice compose it. Or, at least, if Alice and Beatrice compose something, this is not *in virtue of* their fusion. It may, of course, be, as we noted in our discussion of *Contact*, that any two non-overlapping objects "automatically" compose something. But if Alice and Beatrice of necessity compose some object at every moment at which they exist, then, surely, they always compose the same object. (While this seems evident enough, it is formally possible to deny it. An analogous possibility was briefly noted in our discussion of *Contact*. We shall discuss this matter more fully later.) And if, necessarily, Alice and Beatrice always compose the same object, then one could not bring the object they compose into existence by surgically fusing them. *Fusion*, therefore, is not the right answer to the Special Composition Question.

We have failed to find an acceptable answer to the Special Composition Question. Perhaps we have been looking in the wrong place for one. Let us divide all possible answers to the Special Composition Question into two classes. One class will comprise those answers that have the following consequence: It is possible for there to be objects that compose something, and it is also possible for there to be objects that do not compose anything. Let us call such answers *Moderate*. If you believe that you and I and the Eiffel Tower exist and have proper parts and yet do not compose anything, then you believe that the right answer to the Special Composition Question is Moderate. Answers that are not Moderate we shall call *Extreme*. While there are many Moderate answers to the Special Composition Question – we have examined four of the simpler ones – there are only two Extreme answers. To these I now turn.

III

Answer (v) Nihilism

It is impossible for one to bring it about that something is such that the *x*s compose it, because, necessarily, (if the *x*s are two or more) nothing is such that the *x*s compose it.[5]

If this answer is correct, then either there is nothing material at all – a possibility I shall not bother to discuss – or else there is nothing material but what I shall call simples: material objects that have no proper parts. In the latter case, the material world consists entirely of simples. These simples might be in constant motion in the void and might affect one another or become fastened to one another (or even cohere with or become fused with one another), but there would never be anything that had two or more simples as its parts. The history of the material universe consists in a continuous rearrangement of simples, but no arrangement out of all the possible arrangements of them could ever give birth to a material object. If Nihilism is the correct answer to the Special Composition Question, then there is at any time one particular number that is the number of material things: It is the number of simples. (Of course, the number of simples might change, for perhaps simples can be annihilated or created out of nothing.)

Nihilism has an interesting and unique logical property. I have said that a correct answer to the Special Composition Question, even if we had it, would not provide us with an answer to the General Composition Question. This is not quite true. Nihilism alone, among all the answers to the Special Composition Question, does entail an answer to the General Composition Question. It entails the answer: The *x*s compose *y* if and only if each of the *x*s is *y*. Suppose, for example, that Cicero is a material simple. Then Nihilism countenances the truth of 'Tully and Cicero compose Cicero', 'The things identical with Tully compose Cicero', and 'The authors of *De Fato* compose Tully'. Unfortunately for the student of the General Composition Question, Nihilism would seem to be false. You and I (and Cicero) are material things and none of us is a simple: There are, if nothing else, elementary particles that compose me and others that compose you. And yet you and I exist.

Answer (vi) Universalism

It is impossible for one to bring it about that something is such that the *x*s compose it, because, necessarily, (if no two of the *x*s overlap) something is such that the *x*s compose it.

According to this answer, one can't bring it about that any non-overlapping material objects, the xs, compose something, because they already do; they do so "automatically." Just as, according to the theory of sets, there has to be associated with the xs a certain uniquely defined object, their set, so, according to Universalism, there has to be associated with the xs a certain uniquely defined object, their sum. Universalism corresponds to a position about sets that almost everyone holds: In every possible world in which, e.g., Tom, Dick, and Harry exist, there also exists a set that contains just them. Nihilism corresponds to nominalism (about sets): In no possible worlds are there any sets. Some philosophers accept Universalism because it is entailed by a certain stronger thesis, which they accept on grounds that are, in theory, independent of their views about material things. This stronger thesis, which we may call Super-universalism, is the thesis that any two objects, whether material or not, have a sum. According to Super-universalism, for example, if there are such things as the color blue and I, then there is an object that has the color blue and me as parts. I do not understand Super-universalism because, though I think that the color blue and I both exist, I am unable to form a sufficiently general conception of parthood to be able to conceive of an object that has me and a color as parts.

Whatever problems Super-universalism may face, however, it is simple Universalism that is our present concern. In my view, Universalism is false: There are non-overlapping material objects that compose nothing whatever. My conviction that Universalism is false rests on three theses that, on reflection, appear to me to be correct. First, Universalism does not seem to force itself upon the mind as true. A theory that denies Universalism is not in *prima facie* trouble, like a theory that denies the reality of time. Secondly, there is no known way to derive Universalism from premises that force themselves upon the mind as true, or even from premises that seem more plausible than not. Thirdly, Universalism is in conflict with certain plausible theses (which I shall presently lay out). Now these three judgments are highly subjective ones. Many philosophers for whom I have the highest respect not only accept Universalism but, apparently, regard it as just obviously true. And many of these phi-

losophers will say that some of the "plausible theses" I shall lay out are obviously, or at least demonstrably, false. Well, I shall have to do the best I can. Here are the theses I regard as plausible and which entail the falsity of Universalism.

(1) I exist now and I existed ten years ago.
(2) I am an organism (in the biological sense) and I have always been an organism.
(3) Every organism is composed of (some) atoms (or other) at every moment of its existence.
(4) Consider any organism that existed ten years ago; all of the atoms that composed it ten years ago still exist.
(5) Consider any organism that exists now and existed ten years ago; none of the atoms that now compose that organism is among those that composed it ten years ago.
(6) If Universalism is true, then the xs cannot ever compose two objects. More formally, if Universalism is true, then it is not possible that $\exists y\, \exists z\, \exists w\, \exists v$(the xs compose y at the moment w, and the xs compose z at the moment v, and y is not identical with z).

Of these propositions, (3), (4), and (5) would appear to express empirical facts.[6] Propositions (1) and (2), however, entail theses that have been denied on various philosophical grounds. At least one philosopher[7] would deny that I ever exist. Many philosophers deny that, in the strict, philosophical sense, objects persists through time, and others find special reasons to doubt that persons – I suppose I am a "person," though what philosophers mean by this word is not always clear – persist through time. And, of course, all manner of philosophers have argued that personal pronouns do not refer to material things and would therefore reject (2).

I should be willing to defend the thesis that such things as you and I exist and strictly persist through time. But to defend a thesis against particular objections is not to prove it, and in any case, my defense would depend on an answer to the Special Composition Question that is inconsistent with Universalism, the refutation of which is our present concern. I have, therefore, nothing to say in defense of (1).

In view of the history of Western philosophy, (2) deserves an extended and careful defense. I have a lot to say that is relevant to the contention that we human beings are organisms – a lot of remarks to make about the ontology of human beings – though I am not sure that what I have to say would add up to a "defense" of premise (2). In any case, most of what I have to say about the ontology of human beings is only very obliquely relevant to our present concerns. But because this topic is a very important one, and because (2) is essential to my argument against Universalism, I will make one remark (more autobiography than argument). Perhaps this remark will explain a certain otherwise puzzling lacuna in my vocabulary.

Many philosophers, I believe, will concede that there is a biological organism, which, though it is not identical with me, stands in a relationship to me that is far more intimate than the relationships in which it stands to anyone else. These philosophers will say that this organism to which I am so intimately related (they will differ among themselves about my intrinsic nature and about my relation to it) is properly referred to as 'my body'. I do not understand them. I believe that 'body', as such philosophers use it, has no clear meaning. It has neither a sense that is supplied by ordinary speech nor a sense that has been supplied by explicit definition. But I have argued for these conclusions elsewhere,[8] and I will not repeat my arguments here. Given that I think this, however, it is not surprising that I do not use the word 'body'. (It should go without saying that I am unwilling to accept the thesis that we "are our bodies." I don't know what that means. I do think, as I have said, that we are material objects, things made of flesh and blood and bone, and that we are shaped roughly like statues of human beings. If this constitutes a belief that we "are our bodies," then I believe that we are our bodies; but I do not know why those words are an expression of my belief.)

Let us turn to (6). All the Universalists I am aware of do accept the consequent of (6). (Generally this acceptance consists simply in treating expressions of the form 'the sum of x and y' as unproblematical proper definite descriptions, ones that no more demand the addition of 'at t' than does 'the set that contains just x and y'.) And I think they are right to. Here is the reason why. The consequent of (6) might reasonably be denied by adherents of certain of the doctrines about parts and wholes that we have considered. Take, for example, those who accept *Contact*. If someone thinks that in building a model of

Salisbury Cathedral out of a set of blocks, I thereby bring a certain object (the model) into existence – that is, that I do not merely transform an already existing scattered object into a connected, cathedral-shaped object – and if he also thinks that in building a model of the Colosseum out of the very same blocks I thereby bring (the object that is) that model of the Colosseum into existence, then perhaps it would be reasonable for him to suppose that the model of the cathedral and the model of the arena are numerically distinct objects, and that, therefore, the same blocks can compose – at different times – numerically distinct objects. But suppose someone thinks (as Universalists do) that the arrangement of the blocks is quite irrelevant to the question whether they compose an object: Suppose he thinks that the blocks must at any moment at which they all exist compose an object, even if at that moment each of them is thousands of miles from the others, and even if they are moving at high velocities relative to one another, and even if they exert no causal influence to speak of on one another. If the arrangement of the blocks is irrelevant to the question whether they compose anything, why should it be supposed to be relevant to the identity of the thing they compose? Consider the object that is said to be composed of the blocks at t, when they are widely scattered and moving rapidly in relation to one another. How long does it last? Only two answers seem possible. (a) It doesn't last at all; it exists only at t. (b) It lasts as long as its constituent blocks do. Any compromise between these two answers would be intolerably arbitrary: If the blocks "automatically" compose an object, then either any rearrangement of the blocks *must* destroy that object, or else no rearrangement *could* destroy it. And the former answer seems intolerably severe: It implies a doctrine beside which mereological essentialism pales: *positional* essentialism, according to which not only the identities of the parts of a whole are essential to that whole, but their relative positions and attitudes as well. It is bad enough to suppose that the replacement of a rusty bolt leaves me with what is, "in the strict, philosophical sense," a new car. It is infinitely worse, and never has the phrase 'infinitely worse' been used more appropriately, to suppose that when I sit in my car and turn the wheel, what I am occupying is, "in the strict, philosophical sense," a compact series of infinitesimally differing cars. Or let us consider a simpler case, easily visualized because it involves only two objects. According to Universalism, this cup and this pen always (when they both exist) compose an object, one that presumably fits exactly into the non-connected region of space they jointly occupy. Assuming we can make sense of this thesis, can we make sense of the thesis that at different times they compose different objects? I think not: If they always compose an object, then they always compose the *same* object. Universalism, therefore, cannot countenance the supposition that at two different times the *xs* compose two different objects. For the Universalist, 'the sum of those blocks' must be a proper definite description – assuming "those blocks" to exist – one that needs no temporal qualification. In this respect it is like 'the product of those numbers' or 'the set containing just exactly those blocks and those numbers'.

It is pretty evident that propositions (1) through (6) entail the denial of Universalism. Here is the argument in outline: Assume the truth of Universalism; consider the atoms that composed me ten years ago; if (6) is true, those atoms compose me now; but those atoms obviously do not compose me now, and Universalism is therefore false. But let us set out the argument in pedantic detail to make sure that nothing has been overlooked.

It follows from (1) and (2) that I existed ten years ago and was then a biological organism. It follows from (3) that ten years ago that organism – I – was composed of certain atoms. Let us use 'T' as an abbreviation for 'the atoms that composed me ten years ago'. By (4), all of T still exist.

Now assume that Universalism is true. Then T now compose something. Call it 'the thing that is at present the sum of T' or '+T'. From Universalism and (6) it follows that T composed +T ten years ago. But, by definition, T composed me ten years ago. Therefore, by (6), I was +T ten years ago. But then I am +T now. If ten years ago a certain object and I were such that there was only one of us, then there is only one of us still: A thing and itself cannot go their separate ways. But I am not now +T. At present, +T, if it exists at all, is (I would suppose) a rarefied spherical shell of atoms, about eight thousand miles in diameter and a few miles thick; in any case, +T is composed

of atoms none of which are now parts of me. Our assumption of Universalism has, therefore, led us to a falsehood and Universalism must be rejected.

We must conclude that Answer (vi) is incorrect: Objects do not necessarily and automatically compose anything. (I would suggest, for example, that T do not now compose anything,[9] though they did once.) Alternatively, it does not follow from the mere existence of certain objects that there is any object that has them all as parts; not every set of objects has a sum.

IV

If the arguments of the previous section are correct, then some Moderate answer to the Special Composition Question is correct: It is at least possible that there are objects that compose something, and it is also at least possible that there are objects that compose nothing. Moreover, the actual world is so rich and complex that it would be hard to believe that these possibilities exist but are unrealized. If, therefore, the arguments of the previous sections are correct, then *there are* objects that compose something, and *there are also* objects that compose nothing. (*I* would say, for example, that the elementary particles that are now parts of me compose something while my two cats and I compose nothing.)

It is not my intention in this paper to endorse an answer to the Special Composition Question. While I do have an opinion about this, I could not possibly defend this opinion adequately in a paper of this length. I have been concerned not to answer the Special Composition Question, but rather to try to make this question "come alive" by showing that the answers to it that come most quickly to mind – the two Extreme answers and several of the more obvious Moderate answers – are unsatisfactory. (And we must not lose sight of the fact that I have been working within the scope of a certain assumption: that one and the same three-dimensional material object can exist at two different times. Many philosophers regard this assumption as incoherent, and will not, therefore, be impressed by arguments that derive incoherencies from positions that incorporate it. A definitive treatment of composition would have to include an examination of the thesis that the only three-dimensional material objects are "slices" of four-dimensional wholes.) In this, the final section of the paper, I wish to explain why I find my position – that the right answer to the Special Composition Question is Moderate – a rather uncomfortable one.

If the correct answer to the Special Composition Question is Moderate, then it seems very likely that the multigrade relation expressed by '∃y the xs compose y' is a causal relation, or is at any rate necessarily coextensive with one. All of the Moderate answers we have examined in this paper have this feature. For example, both 'the xs are in contact' and 'the xs are fastened' express multigrade causal relations.

I will concede that I can think of Moderate answers to the Special Composition Question that are *not* causal. Suppose for example, that the physical universe consists of, and any possible physical universe would have to consist of, exactly two kinds of simples, the as and the bs. And suppose that, loosely speaking, Universalism holds for the as and Nihilism holds for the bs. This supposition amounts to a non-causal but Moderate answer to the Special Composition Question. But it hardly seems plausible, even when stated so abstractly as I have stated it. If just any as compose something, necessarily and automatically, no matter how scattered they may be, how is it that two or more bs never compose anything, however tightly they may be grouped? It seems to me that any plausible Moderate answer to the Special Composition Question will have the following feature: If two or more xs in fact compose something, then it is at least possible that those xs *not* compose anything. Or, to put the matter another way, if there are two or more xs that must, under any circumstances in which they all exist, compose something, this can only be because, for *any* non-overlapping xs, those xs must, in any circumstances in which they all exist, compose something. Or again: If there are two or more xs that *essentially* compose something, this can only be because Universalism is true. I conclude, provisionally, that any plausible Moderate answer to the Special Composition Question will identify the relation expressed by '∃y the xs compose y' with some causal relation.

Why is this an "uncomfortable" position? It is uncomfortable because causal relations – or perhaps I should say 'names for causal relations' – would seem to be inherently vague. Take contact.

Suppose I toss a piece of chalk on the table. You hear a sharp noise and you perhaps suppose that the transition between the chalk's not being in contact with the table and its being in contact with the table was a sharp one. But contact between gross physical objects like tables and pieces of chalk is ultimately a matter of the interaction between continuous electromagnetic fields. I doubt whether the event that was the chalk's coming into contact with the table could be "dated" within a millionth of a second. That is, if you maintained of a certain millionth-second-long interval that the chalk came into contact with the table during *that* interval, and I maintained that this event occurred during the following millionth of a second, it is hard to see how one of us could be right and the other wrong. A dispute between us on this point would be like a dispute about the exact distance in inches between the earth and the sun. Therefore, if *Contact* were the correct answer to the Special Composition Question, there would be a period during which it was not definitely true that the table and the chalk composed something *and* not definitely false that they composed something. (A short period, to be sure, but that is logically irrelevant. And, anyway, we could no doubt produce long-lasting "borderline" cases of contact in a laboratory.) But where is the promised discomfort? Isn't this just a case of vagueness, a philosophical problem we are going to have on our hands no matter what we say about composition? It is a case of vagueness, but it is very unlike the standard philosophical cases of vagueness. To see this, let us examine one of these standard cases.

John is 5'11 1/2" tall. Is he tall? There is (let us suppose, at any rate) no definite answer to this question. What is the source of this indefiniteness? The answer is obvious: its source lies in language, in the adjective 'tall'. For one reason or another, we English-speakers have not bothered to fill in the rules governing the adjective 'tall' in such a way that the speaker who follows these rules will never have cause to hesitate over the question, 'Is that man "tall"?' One is tempted to say of the present case that what we have is a perfectly definite *object*, John, and a fuzzy *adjective*, 'tall'. But it would probably be better not to have to explain what we mean by calling an object "definite." Perhaps we should say that the fuzzy/definite distinction applies only to adjectives and certain other linguistic items, those that have *extensions* in the semantical sense of the word. At any rate, it seems obvious that we should locate the vagueness that infects the question 'Is John tall?' entirely in language. And it is tempting to universalize this obvious thesis: *All* cases of vagueness can be traced in pretty much the same way to the vague extensions of, or to the vague instructions for determining the extensions of, certain linguistic items. Let us call this universal thesis the Linguistic Theory of Vagueness.

A major problem for causal answers to the Special Composition Question is that they seem to generate cases of vagueness that cannot be accounted for by the Linguistic Theory. (I owe this point to David Lewis.) Consider, for example, *Contact*. Suppose *Contact* is right. Suppose that there is nothing material but two one-foot cubes. Suppose that they drift together in such a way that they constitute a borderline case of two material things in contact. Consider the sentence 'There is something larger than a one-foot cube'. Does this sentence express a truth? We can't answer, "Definitely, yes," for that answer would be right only if the two blocks definitely composed something; and that in its turn would be right only if the blocks were definitely in contact – which they are not. A similar argument shows that we cannot answer, "Definitely, no." We appear, therefore, to have a case of vagueness. Can it be explained by the Linguistic Theory of Vagueness? It is hard to see how. The only predicate in this sentence is 'is larger than a one-foot cube'. Is there something in our imaginary universe that is a borderline case of a thing that falls under this predicate? What is it? The obvious answer is: the thing the two cubes compose. But if there is such a thing, it definitely falls under this predicate, and if there is no such thing, then everything is such that it definitely does not fall under this predicate. What seems to be indefinite is this: *whether* there is an object that the two cubes compose. This suggests that the locus of vagueness in our sentence is not in its predicate but in its quantifier. But, really, what could that mean? How could the existential quantifier, as opposed to a predicate it is prefixed to, be vague? I think that there is only one way to make sense of this idea: To suppose, first, that there is a Meinongian realm of non-existent objects, and, secondly, that the function of the existential quantifier is to pick out the items

that do not belong to this Meinongian realm, and, thirdly, that the border between the realm of the existent and the realm of the non-existent is vague. But I am convinced, as are many, that the idea of a non-existent object is a self-contradictory one; therefore, in my view, there can no more be a thing that is a borderline case of a non-existent object than there can be a thing that is a borderline case of a triangular circle. I speculate, moreover, that even convinced Meinongians will be reluctant to say that there are objects of which it is neither definitely true nor definitely false that those objects exist.

What I have said about *Contact* applies, I think, to any interesting Moderate answer to the Special Composition Question. If any interesting Moderate answer – that is, any *causal* answer – to the Special Composition Question is correct, then there will be cases of vagueness that cannot be accounted for by the comfortable and sensible Linguistic Theory of Vagueness. If any causal answer is correct, then the vagueness inherent in multigrade causal relations like *being in contact* and *being fused* will infect notions like existence, number, and identity, that, one would have supposed, cannot, because of their pristine logico-mathematical character, admit of the least tincture of vagueness.

Now the conviction that existence, number, and identity do not in any way involve vagueness can be preserved by one who accepts an Extreme answer to the Special Composition Question. Take, for example, our two-cube universe. If Universalism is true, this universe contains an object that the two cubes compose, and it contains this object whether or not they are in contact. Recall the term 'connected': A connected object is an object such that, for any *xs*, if the *xs* compose that object, then the *xs* are in contact. What we have said about contact entails that the predicate 'is connected' is vague: Sometimes there will be no fact of the matter whether the object our two cubes compose is connected. But *it* will always be there: All the vagueness that we confront when we ask whether it is connected can be traced, *via* the vagueness of the monadic predicate 'is connected', to the vagueness of the variably polyadic predicate 'are in contact'. If Universalism is true, then there is no way for the vagueness involved in contact or in any other causal relation to spill over into the realm of existence, number, and identity, for the extensions of these austere concepts within the class of material objects will be determined by factors quite independent of the causal relations that happen to hold among material objects. If Universalism or Nihilism (or something like our uninteresting Moderate mixture of them) is correct, then the existence and number of composite material objects are determined by the existence and number of material simples, and vagueness in our statements about material objects will be comfortably located in the predicates (such as 'are in contact') that we have devised to talk about them. I have no doubt that many philosophers will regard this result as providing us with a decisive reason for accepting an Extreme answer to the Composition Question, since few philosophers – or so I judge – are prepared to accept any account of vagueness that is at variance with the Linguistic Theory.

I myself find the Linguistic Theory extremely attractive. I can get myself into a frame of mind in which it seems not only attractive but indisputable. Nevertheless, I do not believe we should regard it as sacrosanct. If the problems I have raised in this paper for Universalism – I suppose few people are attracted to Nihilism – prove intractable, then I think we should consider seriously the possibility of trying to work out an account of vagueness that is compatible with a causal answer to the Special Composition Question. Let us remember the fate of the Linguistic Theory of Necessity, the theory that necessary truth is entirely a product of our linguistic conventions. I am just old enough to remember a time when that theory seemed not only attractive but indisputable. The Linguistic Theory of Necessity has had a hard time of it over the last twenty years. It is not beyond all reason to suppose that the Linguistic Theory of Vagueness deserves to be in for a hard time of it.

Notes

The problems raised in this paper are discussed in much greater depth in my book *Material Beings* (Ithaca, NY: Cornell University Press, 1990).

Versions (or ancestors) of this paper have been read at the University of Connecticut, the University of Rochester, Princeton University, the University of Massachusetts at Amherst, Virginia Polytechnic Institute and State University, Memphis State University, the Western Washington Philosophy Colloquium (1985), and the Tenth Annual Symposium in Philosophy at the University of North Carolina at Greensboro (1986). I wish to thank the audiences at these colloquia (and my colleagues at Syracuse University) for their thoughtful criticism. I wish also to thank Joshua Hoffman, who was the only formal commentator on the paper, for his careful and penetrating comments.

Of all the people who have tried to change my mind about composition, I must single out David Lewis as having been especially effective in getting round my deep disinclination to do so. Samuel C. Wheeler III and Peter Unger (whose views are much closer to mine than Lewis's are) have also made me change my mind on various points. I have benefited from conversations with Mark Heller and Mark Johnston.

1 The two *definientia* and the two *definienda* should be understood to be in the present tense: What we have is a definition of 'the xs *now* compose y'. I say this because I wish to leave it an open question whether the xs might compose one object at one time and another object at another time. (Consider the puzzle about cats and atoms touched on in the first paragraph of this paper.) I also wish to leave it an open question whether a given object might be composed of the xs at one time and (exist but) not be composed of the xs at another. Strictly speaking, our *definientia* and *definienda* should include a time-variable: 'y is at t the sum of the xs', and so on.

If I were being really pedantic, I should write not 'the sum of the xs' but 'a sum of the xs', since nothing has been said to justify the assumption that, at any given moment at which the xs all exist, there is at that moment *at most one* object y such that the xs are then parts of y and every part of y then overlaps at least one of the xs. But I doubt whether anyone is likely to reject this assumption, so I shall not be that pedantic. We shall later briefly discuss this assumption. See p. 630.

2 This statement requires some qualification. If one has an answer to the General Composition Question, then one "automatically" has an answer to the Special Composition Question: One has only to prefix an existential quantifier to one's answer to the General Question. But the answer so obtained will not necessarily be the "best" or "deepest" or "most interesting" one. An analogy may indicate the reason for this. Consider two answers to the question, When does a number have a reciprocal?: (a) When there exists something that is the result of dividing 1 by that number; (b) When that number is not 0. Both of these answers, of course, are right. The former is got from the general answer to 'What

is a reciprocal?' by existential quantification. But the latter is the better, the more informative, answer. Something formally similar to this might be true in respect of the Special and General Composition Questions. And it might be that the best or most informative answer to the Special Question is harder to discover than the right answer to the General Question.

3 For one thing, I do not understand the term 'human body' well enough to be comfortable about allowing it to function as what Jonathan Bennett would call a "load-bearing member" in a metaphysical argument. (See my paper, "Philosophers and the Words 'Human Body,'" in *Time and Cause: Essays Presented to Richard Taylor* (Dordrecht: D. Reidel, 1980). While I no longer accept everything I said in that paper, I continue to be puzzled by 'body'.) For another: One of the central arguments of the present paper depends on the premise that human beings – you and I – strictly persist through time. This is a premise that few of us would be willing to reject. But, as regards human *bodies*, even those philosophers who believe that our bodies strictly persist through time would probably be willing to give up this belief if they were presented with a demonstration that it had untoward metaphysical consequences – provided that they could continue to hold that *they themselves* strictly persisted through time. The thesis that each of us is, in the normal course of events, continually "changing bodies" is a rather curious thesis, but one a philosopher might be willing to put up with; the thesis that one exists only at an instant, or only for a few minutes, on the other hand, has the aspect of a moral and metaphysical calamity. I expect most of us would say the same thing about cats: The strict persistence of cats through time is negotiable in a way that the strict persistence of human beings is not. For this reason, an argument whose premise is the strict persistence of human bodies or of cats will be less persuasive than an otherwise similar argument whose premise is the strict persistence of human beings.

4 But we don't really. Not in general. The notion of contact applies only to objects whose dimensions do not differ from ours by more than five or six orders of magnitude. It would make no sense, for example, to speak of protons being (or not being) in contact. And yet protons are proper parts of things if any objects ever are. This consideration alone shows that *Contact* cannot be the right answer to the Special Composition Question. In the text, however, I shall argue that *Contact* can be seen to be wrong independently of such "scientific" considerations. Similar remarks apply to the three proposed answers to the Special Composition Question that we shall examine next after *Contact* (*Fastening, Cohesion,* and *Fusion*).

5 Peter Unger calls himself a nihilist, but he uses the word in a different sense from mine. In my terminology, Unger is a Universalist (*vide infra*, in text) who holds that none of the many objects that exist according to Universalism can correctly be described as a "table" or a "stone" or a "human being" or as falling under any of the other count-nouns that we use in everyday life. See "There Are No Ordinary Things," *Synthese* 41 (1979), pp. 117–154, and "Skepticism and Nihilism," *Noûs* 14 (1980), pp. 517–45.

6 Well, not quite. Organisms have parts that overlap no atom, such as ions, free electrons, and photons. A few of the atoms that composed me ten years ago were unstable (carbon-14 atoms, for example) and no longer exist. The atoms that ten years ago made up the cholesterol molecules in the myelin sheaths around the neurons in my brain are mostly still there, and a few of the atoms expelled from my system ten years ago have no doubt wandered back into it during the last few weeks and are still there. Let us ignore these subtleties.

7 Peter Unger. See "I Do Not Exist," in *Perception and Identity: Essays Presented to A. J. Ayer, with His Replies* (Ithaca: Cornell University Press, 1979). See also Samuel C. Wheeler III. "On That Which Is Not," *Synthese* 41 (1979), pp. 155–73.

8 In "Philosophers and the Words 'Human Body.'" See n. 3.

9 Of course they *might*. It is not impossible for there now to be an object – one that weighs just what I weighed ten years ago – that T compose. It is, however, astronomically improbable.

48

Many, But Almost One

David Lewis

The Problem of the Many

Think of a cloud – just one cloud, and around it clear blue sky. Seen from the ground, the cloud may seem to have a sharp boundary. Not so. The cloud is a swarm of water droplets. At the outskirts of the cloud the density of the droplets falls off. Eventually they are so few and far between that we may hesitate to say that the outlying droplets are still part of the cloud at all; perhaps we might better say only that they are near the cloud. But the transition is gradual. Many surfaces are equally good candidates to be the boundary of the cloud. Therefore many aggregates of droplets, some more inclusive and some less inclusive (and some inclusive in different ways than others), are equally good candidates to be the cloud. Since they have equal claim, how can we say that the cloud is one of these aggregates rather than another? But if all of them count as clouds, then we have many clouds rather than one. And if none of them count, each one being ruled out because of the competition from the others, then we have no cloud. How is it, then, that we have just one cloud? And yet we do.

This is Unger's (1980) 'problem of the many'. Once noticed, we can see that it is everywhere, for all things are swarms of particles. There are always outlying particles, questionably parts of the thing, not definitely included and not definitely not included. So there are always many aggregates, differing by a little bit here and a little bit there, with equal claim to be the thing. We have many things or we have none, but anyway not the one thing we thought we had. That is absurd.

Think of a rusty nail, and the gradual transition from steel, to steel with bits of rust scattered through, to rust adhering to the nail, to rust merely resting on the nail. Or think of a cathode, and its departing electrons. Or think of anything that undergoes evaporation or erosion or abrasion. Or think of yourself, or any organism, with parts that gradually come loose in metabolism or excretion or perspiration or shedding of dead skin. In each case, a thing has questionable parts, and therefore is subject to the problem of the many.

If, as I think, things perdure through time by having temporal parts, then questionable temporal parts add to the problem of the many. If a person comes into existence gradually (whether

David Lewis, "Many, But Almost One," in John Bacon, Keith Campbell, and Lloyd Reinhardt (eds.), *Ontology, Causality, and Mind* (Cambridge: Cambridge University Press, 1993), pp. 23–39.

Metaphysics: An Anthology, Second Edition. Edited by Jaegwon Kim, Daniel Z. Korman and Ernest Sosa.
Editorial material and organization © 2012 Blackwell Publishing Ltd. Published 2012 by Blackwell Publishing Ltd.

over weeks or over years or over nanoseconds doesn't matter for our present purpose) then there are questionable temporal parts at the beginning of every human life. Likewise at the end, even in the most sudden death imaginable. Do you think you are one person? – No, there are many aggregates of temporal parts, differing just a little at the ends, with equal claim to count as persons, and equal claim to count as you. Are all those equally good claims good enough? If so, you are many. If not, you are none. Either way we get the wrong answer. For undeniably you are one.

If, as some think but I do not,[1] ordinary things extend through other possible worlds, then the problem of the many takes on still another dimension. Here in this world we have a ship, the *Enigma*; there in another world is a ship built at about the same time, to plans that are nearly the same but not quite, using many of the same planks and some that are not the same. It is questionable whether the ship in that other world is *Enigma* herself, or just a substitute. If *Enigma* is a thing that extends through worlds, then the question is whether *Enigma* includes as a part what's in that other world. We have two versions of *Enigma*, one that includes this questionable other-worldly part and one that excludes it. They have equal claim to count as ships, and equal claim to count as *Enigma*. We have two ships, coinciding in this world but differing in their full extent. Or else we have none; but anyway not the one ship we thought we had.

The Paradox of 1001 Cats

Cat Tibbles is alone on the mat. Tibbles has hairs $h_1, h_2, \ldots, h_{1000}$. Let c be Tibbles including all these hairs; let c_1 be all of Tibbles except for h_1; and similarly for $c_2, \ldots, c_{1000}$. Each of these c's is a cat. So instead of one cat on the mat, Tibbles, we have at least 1001 cats – which is absurd. This is P. T. Geach's (1980, pp. 215–16) paradox of 1001 cats.

Why should we think that each c_n is a cat? Because, says Geach, 'c_n would clearly be a cat were the hair h_n plucked out, and we cannot reasonably suppose that plucking out a hair *generates* a cat, so c_n must already have been a cat' (p. 215). This need not convince us. We can reply that plucking out h_n turns c_n from a mere proper part of cat Tibbles into the whole of a cat. No new cat is generated,

since the cat that c_n becomes the whole of is none other than Tibbles. Nor do c_n and Tibbles ever become identical *simpliciter* – of course not, since what's true about c_n's past still differs from what's true about Tibbles's past. Rather, c_n becomes the whole of cat Tibbles in the sense that c_n's post-plucking temporal part is identical with Tibbles's post-plucking temporal part. So far, so good; except for those, like Geach, who reject the idea of temporal parts. The rest of us have no paradox yet.

But suppose it is spring, and Tibbles is shedding. When a cat sheds, the hairs do not come popping off; they become gradually looser, until finally they are held in place only by the hairs around them. By the end of this gradual process, the loose hairs are no longer parts of the cat. Sometime before the end, they are questionable parts: not definitely still parts of the cat, not definitely not. Suppose each of $h_1, h_2, \ldots, h_{1000}$ is at this questionable stage. Now indeed all of $c_1, c_2, \ldots, c_{1000}$, and also c which includes all the questionable hairs, have equal claim to be a cat, and equal claim to be Tibbles. So now we have 1001 cats. (Indeed, we have many more than that. For instance there is the cat that includes all but the four hairs h_6, h_{408}, h_{882}, and h_{907}.) The paradox of 1001 cats, insofar as it is a real paradox, is another instance of Unger's problem of the many.

To deny that there are many cats on the mat, we must either deny that the many are cats, or else deny that the cats are many. We may solve the paradox by finding a way to disqualify candidates for cathood: there are the many, sure enough, but the many are not all cats. At most one of them is. Perhaps the true cat is one of the many; or perhaps it is something else altogether, and none of the many are cats. Or else, if we grant that all the candidates are truly cats, we must find a way to say that these cats are not truly different from one another. I think both alternatives lead to successful solutions, but we shall see some unsuccessful solutions as well.

Two Solutions by Disqualification: None of the Many are Cats

We could try saying that not one of the c's is a cat; they are many, sure enough, but not many cats. Tibbles, the only genuine cat on the mat, is something else, different from all of them.

One way to disqualify the many is to invoke the alleged distinction between things and the parcels of matter that constitute them. We could try saying that the c's are not cats. Rather, they are cat-constituting parcels of matter. Tibbles is the cat that each of them constitutes.[2]

This dualism of things and their constituters is unparsimonious and unnecessary. It was invented to solve a certain problem, but a better solution to that problem lies elsewhere, as follows. We know that the matter of a thing may exist before and after the thing does; and we know that a thing may gain and lose matter while it still exists, as a cat does, or a wave or a flame. The dualists conclude that the matter is not the thing; constitution is not identity; there are things, there are the parcels of matter that temporarily constitute those things; these are items of two different categories, related by the special relation of constitution. We must agree, at least, that the temporally extended thing is not the temporally extended parcel of matter that temporarily constitutes that thing. But constitution may be identity, all the same, if it is identity between temporal parts. If some matter constitutes a cat for one minute, then a minute-long temporal segment of the cat is identical to a minute-long temporal segment of the matter. The cat consists entirely of the matter that constitutes it, in this sense: The whole of the cat, throughout the time it lives, consists entirely of temporal segments of various parcels of matter. At any moment, if we disregard everything not located at that moment, the cat and the matter that then constitutes it are identical.[3] So only those who reject the notion of temporal parts have any need for the dualism of things and constituters. But suppose we accept it all the same. At best, this just transforms the paradox of 1001 cats into the paradox of 1001 cat-constituters. Is that an improvement? We all thought there was only one cat on the mat. After distinguishing Tibbles from her constituter, would we not still want to think there was only one cat-constituter on the mat?

Further, even granted that Tibbles has many constituters, I still question whether Tibbles is the only cat present. The constituters are cat-like in size, shape, weight, inner structure, and motion. They vibrate and set the air in motion – in short, they purr (especially when you pat them). Any way a cat can be at a moment, cat-constituters also can be; anything a cat can do at a moment, cat-constituters also can do. They are all too

cat-like not to be cats. Indeed, they may have unfeline pasts and futures, but that doesn't show that they are never cats; it only shows that they do not remain cats for very long. Now we have the paradox of 1002 cats: Tibbles the constituted cat, and also the 1001 all-too-feline cat-constituters. Nothing has been gained.

I conclude that invoking the dualism of cats and cat-constituters to solve the paradox of 1001 cats does not succeed.

A different way to disqualify the many appeals to a doctrine of vagueness in nature. We could try saying that cat Tibbles is a vague object, and that the c's are not cats but rather alternative precisifications of a cat.

In one way, at least, this solution works better than the one before. This time, I cannot complain that at best we only transform the paradox of 1001 cats into the paradox of 1001 cat-precisifications, because that is no paradox. If indeed there are vague objects and precisifications, it is only to be expected that one vague object will have many precisifications.

If the proposal is meant to solve our paradox, it must be meant as serious metaphysics. It cannot just be a way of saying 'in the material mode' that the words 'Tibbles' and 'cat' are vague, and that this vagueness makes it indefinite just which hairs are part of the cat Tibbles. Rather, the idea must be that material objects come in two varieties, vague and precise; cats are vague, the c's are precise, and that is why none of the c's is a cat.

This new dualism of vague objects and their precisifications is, again, unparsimonious and unnecessary. The problem it was made to solve might better be solved another way. It is absurd to think that we have decided to apply the name 'Tibbles' to a certain precisely delimited object; or that we have decided to apply the term 'cat' to each of certain precisely delimited objects. But we needn't conclude that these words must rather apply to certain imprecisely delimited, vague objects. Instead we should conclude that we never quite made up our minds just what these words apply to. We have made up our minds that 'Tibbles' is to name one or another Tibbles-precisification, but we never decided just which one; we decided that 'cat' was to apply to some and only some cat-precisifications, but again we never decided just which ones. (Nor did we ever decide just which things our new-found terms 'Tibbles-precisification' and 'cat-precisification' were to apply to.) It was very sensible of us not to decide. We probably couldn't have done it if we'd tried; and even if we could have, doing it would have been useless folly. Semantic indecision will suffice to explain the phenomenon of vagueness.[4] We need no vague objects.

Further, I doubt that I have any correct conception of a vague object. How, for instance, shall I think of an object that is vague in its spatial extent? The closest I can come is to superimpose three pictures. There is the *multiplicity* picture, in which the vague object gives way to its many precisifications, and the vagueness of the object gives way to differences between precisifications. There is the *ignorance* picture, in which the object has some definite but secret extent. And there is the *fadeaway* picture, in which the presence of the object admits of degree, in much the way that the presence of a spot of illumination admits of degree, and the degree diminishes as a function of the distance from the region where the object is most intensely present. None of the three pictures is right. Each one in its own way replaces the alleged vagueness of the object by precision. But if I cannot think of a vague object except by juggling these mistaken pictures, I have no correct conception.[5]

I can complain as before that we end up with a paradox of 1002 cats: Tibbles the vague cat, and also the 1001 precise cats. Once again, the cat-precisifications are all too cat-like. More so than the cat-constituters, in fact: The precisifications are cat-like not just in what they can do and how they can be at a moment, but also over time. They would make good pets – especially since 1001 of them will not eat you out of house and home!

Don't say that the precisifications cannot be cats because cats cannot be precise objects. Surely there could be cats in a world where nature is so much less gradual that the problem of the many goes away. It could happen that cats have no questionable parts at all, neither spatial nor temporal. (In this world, when cats shed in the spring, the hairs *do* come popping off.) So it is at least possible that cat-like precise objects are genuine cats. If so, how can the presence of one vague cat spoil their cathood?

I conclude that invoking the dualism of vague objects and their precisifications to solve the paradox of 1001 cats does not succeed.

A Better Solution by Disqualification: One of the Many is a Cat

Since all of the many are so cat-like, there is only one credible way to deny that all of them are cats. When is something very cat-like, yet not a cat? – When it is just a little less than a whole cat, almost all of a cat with just one little bit left out. Or when it is just a little more than a cat, a cat plus a little something extra. Or when it is both a little more and a little less.

Suppose we say that one of our many is exactly a cat, no more and no less; and that each of the rest is disqualified because it is a little less than a cat, or a little more, or both more and less. This invokes no unparsimonious and unnecessary dualisms; it disqualifies all but one of the many without denying that they are very cat-like; it leaves us with just one cat. All very satisfactory.

The trouble, so it seems, is that there is no saying which one is a cat. That is left altogether arbitrary. Settling it takes a semantic decision, and that is the decision we never made (and shouldn't have made, and maybe couldn't have made). No secret fact could answer the question, for we never decided how the answer would depend on secret facts. Which one deserves the name 'cat' is up to us. If we decline to settle the question, nothing else will settle it for us.[6]

We cannot deny the arbitrariness. What we can deny, though, is that it is trouble. What shall we do, if semantic indecision is inescapable, and yet we wish to carry on talking? The answer, surely, is to exploit the fact that very often our unmade semantic decisions don't matter. Often, what you want to say will be true under all different ways of making the unmade decision. Then if you say it, even if by choice or by necessity you leave the decision forever unmade, you still speak truthfully. It makes no difference just what you meant, what you say is true regardless. And if it makes no difference just what you meant, likewise it makes no difference that you never made up your mind just what to mean. You say that a famous architect designed Fred's house; it never crossed your mind to think whether by 'house' you meant something that did or that didn't include the attached garage; neither does some established convention or secret fact decide the issue; no matter, you knew that what you said was true either way.

This plan for coping with semantic indecision is van Fraassen's (1966) method of *supervaluations*. Call a sentence *super-true* if and only if it is true under all ways of making the unmade semantic decisions; *super-false* if and only if it is false under all ways of making those decisions; and if it is true under some ways and false under others, then it suffers a super-truth-value gap. Super-truth, with respect to a language interpreted in an imperfectly decisive way, replaces truth *simpliciter* as the goal of a cooperative speaker attempting to impart information. We can put it another way: Whatever it is that we do to determine the 'intended' interpretation of our language determines not one interpretation but a range of interpretations. (The range depends on context, and is itself somewhat indeterminate.) What we try for, in imparting information, is truth of what we say under all the intended interpretations.

Each intended interpretation of our language puts one of the cat-candidates on the mat into the extension of the word 'cat', and excludes all the rest. Likewise each intended interpretation picks out one cat-candidate, the same one, as the referent of 'Tibbles'. Therefore it is super-true that there is just one cat, Tibbles, on the mat. Because it is super-true, you are entitled to affirm it. And so you may say what you want to say: there is one cat. That is how the method of supervaluations solves the paradox of 1001 cats.

Objection. Just one of the candidates is a cat, no more and no less. But don't try to say which one it is. Nothing you might say would be super-true. For it is exactly this semantic decision that remains unmade: it is exactly in this respect that the intended interpretations differ. Although it is super-true that something is a cat on the mat, there is nothing such that it is super-true of it that *it* is a cat on the mat. (It's like the old puzzle: I owe you a horse, but there's no horse such that I owe you that horse.) This is peculiar.

Reply. So it is. But once you know the reason why, you can learn to accept it.

Objection.[7] Supervaluationism works too well: it stops us from ever stating the problem in the first place. The problem supposedly was that all the many candidates had equal claim to cathood. But under the supervaluationist rule, that may not be said. For under any one way of making the

unmade decision, one candidate is picked as a cat. So under any one way of making the decision, the candidates do *not* have equal claim. What's true under all ways of making the decision is super-true. So what's super-true, and what we should have said, is that the candidates do *not* have equal claim. Then what's the problem? And yet the problem was stated. So supervaluationism is mistaken.

Reply. What's mistaken is a fanatical supervaluationism, which automatically applies the supervaluationist rule to any statement whatever, never mind that the statement makes no sense that way. The rule should instead be taken as a defeasible presumption. What defeats it, sometimes, is the cardinal principle of pragmatics: The right way to take what is said, if at all possible, is the way that makes sense of the message. Since the supervaluationist rule would have made hash of our statement of the problem, straightway the rule was suspended. We are good at making these accommodations; we don't even notice when we do it. Under the supervaluationist rule, it's right to say that there's only one cat, and so the candidates have unequal claim. Suspending the rule, it's right to say that the candidates have equal claim, and that all of them alike are not definitely not cats. Suspending the rule, it's even right to say that they are all cats! Is this capitulation to the paradox? – No; it's no harm to admit that in *some* sense there are many cats. What's intolerable is to be without any good and natural sense in which there is only one cat.

Objection.[8] The supervaluationist's notion of indeterminate reference is conceptually derivative from the prior notion of reference *simpliciter*. But if the problem of the many is everywhere, and semantic indecision is inescapable, then reference *simpliciter* never happens. To the extent that we gain concepts by 'fixing the reference' on actual examples, we are in no position to have the concept of reference. Then neither are we in a position to have the derivative concept of indeterminate reference due to semantic indecision.

Reply. We don't need actual examples to have the concept. We have plenty of imaginary examples of reference *simpliciter*, uncomplicated by semantic indecision. These examples are set in sharper worlds than ours: worlds where clouds have no outlying droplets, where cats shed their hairs instantaneously, and so on. When we picked up the concept of reference, in childhood, we probably took for granted that our own world was sharp in just that way. (When not puzzling over the problem of the many, maybe we half-believe it still.) We fixed the reference of 'reference' on these imaginary examples in the sharp world we thought we lived in – and if any theory of reference says that cannot be done, so much the worse for it.

I conclude that the supervaluationist solution to the paradox of 1001 cats, and to the problem of the many generally, is successful. But is it the only successful solution? – I think not. I turn now to the other sort of solution: the kind which concedes that the many are cats, but seeks to deny that the cats are really many.

Relative Identity: The Many are not Different Cats

Geach himself favours one such solution. The paradox of 1001 cats serves as a showcase for his doctrine of relative identity.

> Everything falls into place if we realize that the number of cats on the mat is the number of *different* cats on the mat; and c_{13}, c_{279}, and c are not three different cats, they are one and the same cat. Though none of these 1001 lumps of feline tissue is the same lump of feline tissue as another, each is the same cat as any other: each of them, then, is a cat, but there is only one cat on the mat, and our original story stands…. The price to pay *is* that we must regard '—— is the same cat as ——' as expressing only a certain equivalence relation, not an absolute identity restricted to cats; but this price, I have elsewhere argued, must be paid anyhow, for there is no such absolute identity as logicians have assumed. (1980, p. 216)

'Same cat' is a relation of partial indiscernibility, restricted to respects of comparison somehow associated with the term 'cat', and discernibility by just a few hairs doesn't count. 'Same lump of feline tissue' is a different relation of partial indiscernibility, and a more discerning one.

I agree that sometimes we say 'same', and mean by it not 'absolute identity' but just some relation of partial indiscernibility. I also agree that sometimes we count by relations of partial indiscernibility. As I once wrote:

If an infirm man wishes to know how many roads he must cross to reach his destination, I will count by identity-along-his-path rather than by identity. By crossing the Chester A. Arthur Parkway and Route 137 at the brief stretch where they have merged, he can cross both by crossing only one road. (1976, p. 27 [pp. 580–1 this volume])

I'll happily add that for that brief stretch, the two roads are the same. But though I don't object to this positive part of Geach's view, it doesn't ring true to apply it as he does to the case of the cats.

If you ask me to say whether c_{13}, c_{279}, and c are the same or different, I may indeed be of two minds about how to answer. I might say they're different – after all, I know how they differ! Or I might say they're the same, because the difference is negligible, so I duly ignore it. (Not easy to do while attending to the example as I now am; if I attend to my ignoring of something, *ipso facto* I no longer ignore it.) But if you add the noun phrase, either 'same cat' or 'same lump of feline tissue', it seems to me that I am no less hesitant than before. Just as I was of two minds about 'same', so I am still of two minds about 'same cat' and 'same lump of feline tissue'.

Other cases are different. If you ask me 'same or different?' when you hold Monday's *Melbourne Age* in one hand and Tuesday's *Age* in the other, or when you hold one Monday *Age* in each hand, again I won't know how to answer. But if you ask me 'same or different newspaper?' or 'same or different issue?' or 'same or different copy?' then I'll know just what to say. We can dispute his explanation of what happens, but at least the phenomenon happens exactly as Geach says it does. Not so, I think, for the case of 'same cat' versus 'same lump'.

Something else is lacking in Geach's solution. In other cases where it comes natural to count by a relation other than identity, it seems that identity itself – 'absolute identity' – is not far away. Local identity, as between the Arthur Parkway and Route 137 for the stretch where they have merged, is identity *simpliciter* of spatial parts. Likewise temporary identity, as between a thing and the matter that temporarily constitutes it, is identity *simpliciter* of temporal parts. Qualitative identity is identity *simpliciter* of qualitative character. The newspaper that Monday's *Age* is an issue of and the newspaper that Tuesday's *Age* is an issue of are identical *simpliciter*; likewise my copy and your copy of Monday's *Age* are copies of the identical issue. But Geach never tells us what the 'same cat' relation has to do with identity *simpliciter*.

He wouldn't, of course, because he thinks 'there is no such absolute identity as logicians have assumed'. (Nor would he accept all my examples above; certainly not the one about temporary identity and identity of temporal parts.) But Geach's case against absolute identity is unconvincing. It seems to come down to a challenge: If Geach is determined to construe all that I say in terms of relations of partial indiscernibility, is there any way I can stop him? Can I *force* him to understand? (What's more, can I do it with one hand tied behind my back? Can I do it, for instance, without ever using the second-order quantification that Geach (1967) also challenges?) I suppose not. But I don't see why that should make me doubt that I know the difference between identity and indiscernibility.

We have the concept of identity, *pace* Geach; and if we are to justify denying that the cats are many, we need to show that they are interrelated by a relation closely akin to identity itself. Geach has not shown this, and wouldn't wish to show it. Nevertheless it can be shown, as we shall soon see. But at that point we shall have a solution that bypasses Geach's doctrine of relative identity altogether.

Partial Identity: The Many are Almost One

What is the opposite of identity? *Non*-identity, we'd offhand say. Anything is identical to itself; otherwise we have two 'different' things, two 'distinct' things; that is, two non-identical things. Of course it's true that things are either identical or non-identical, and never both. But the real opposite of identity is distinctness; not distinctness in the sense of non-identity, but rather distinctness in the sense of non-overlap (what is called 'disjointness' in the jargon of those who reserve 'distinct' to mean 'non-identical'). We have a spectrum of cases. At one end we find the complete identity of a thing with itself: it and itself are entirely identical, not at all distinct. At the opposite end we find the case of two things that are entirely distinct: They have no part in common. In between we find all the cases of partial overlap: things with parts

in common and other parts not in common. (Sometimes one of the overlappers is part of the other, sometimes not.) The things are not entirely identical, not entirely distinct, but some of each. They are partially identical, partially distinct. There may be more overlap or less. Some cases are close to the distinctness end of the spectrum: Siamese twins who share only a finger are almost completely distinct, but not quite. Other cases are close to the identity end. For instance, any two of our cat candidates overlap almost completely. They differ by only a few hairs. They are not quite completely identical, but they are almost completely identical and very far from completely distinct.

It's strange how philosophers have fixed their attention on one end of the spectrum and forgotten how we ordinarily think of identity and distinctness. You'd think the philosophers of common sense and ordinary language would have set us right long ago, but in fact it was Armstrong (1978, Vol. 2, pp. 37–8) who did the job. Overshadowed though it is by Armstrong's still more noteworthy accomplishments, this service still deserves our attention and gratitude.

Assume our cat-candidates are genuine cats. (Set aside, for now, the supervaluationist solution.) Then, strictly speaking, the cats are many. No two of them are completely identical. But any two of them are almost completely identical; their differences are negligible, as I said before. We have many cats, each one almost identical to all the rest.

Remember how we translate statements of number into the language of identity and quantification. 'There is one cat on the mat' becomes 'For some x, x is a cat on the mat, and every cat on the mat is identical to x'. That's false, if we take 'identical' to express the complete and strict identity that lies at the end of the spectrum. But the very extensive overlap of the cats does approximate to complete identity. So what's true is that for some x, x is a cat on the mat, and every cat on the mat is almost identical to x. In this way, the statement that there is one cat on the mat is almost true. The cats are many, but almost one. By a blameless approximation, we may say simply that there is one cat on the mat. Is that true? – Sometimes we'll insist on stricter standards, sometimes we'll be ambivalent, but for most contexts it's true enough. Thus the idea of partial and approximate identity affords another solution to the paradox of 1001 cats.

The added noun phrase has nothing to do with it. Because of their extensive overlap, the many are almost the same cat; they are almost the same lump of feline tissue; and so on for any other noun phrase that applies to them all. Further, the relation of almost-identity, closely akin to the complete identity that we call identity *simpliciter*, is not a relation of partial indiscernibility. Of course we can expect almost-identical things to be very similar in a great many ways: size, shape, location, weight, purring, behaviour, not to mention relational properties like location and ownership. But it is hard to think of any very salient respect in which almost-identical things are guaranteed to be entirely indiscernible. Finally, the relation of almost-identity, in other words extensive overlap, is not in general an equivalence relation. Many steps of almost-identity can take us from one thing to another thing that is entirely distinct from the first. We may hope that almost-identity, when restricted to the many cats as they actually are, will be an equivalence relation; but even that is not entirely guaranteed. It depends on the extent to which the cats differ, and on the threshold for almost-identity (and both of these are matters that we will, very sensibly, leave undecided). What this solution has in common with Geach's is just that we count the cats by a relation other than strict, 'absolute' identity. Beyond that, the theories differ greatly.[9]

One Solution Too Many?

We find ourselves with two solutions, and that is one more than we needed. Shall we now choose between the way of supervaluation and the way of partial identity? I think not. We might better combine them. We shall see how each can assist the other.

Here is how to combine them. In the first place, there are two kinds of intended interpretations of our language. Given many almost-identical cat-candidates, some will put every (good enough) candidate into the extension of 'cat'; others will put exactly one. Context will favour one sort of interpretation or the other, though not every context will settle the matter. Sometimes, especially in our offhand and unphilosophical moments,

context will favour the second, one-cat sort of interpretation; and then the supervaluation rule, with nothing to defeat it, will entitle us to say that there is only one cat. But sometimes, for instance when we have been explicitly attending to the many candidates and noting that they are equally cat-like, context will favour the first, many-cat sort of interpretation. (If we start with one-cat interpretations, and we say things that the supervaluation rule would make hash of, not only is the rule suspended but also the many-cat interpretations come into play.) But even then, we still want some good sense in which there is just one cat (though we may want a way to say the opposite as well). That is what almost-identity offers.

This is one way that almost-identity helps a combined solution. It is still there even when we discuss the paradox of 1001 cats, and we explicitly choose to say that the many are all cats, and we thereby make the supervaluation solution go away.

Perhaps it helps in another way too. The supervaluation rule is more natural in some applications than in others. For instance it seems artificial to apply it to a case of unrelated homonyms. 'You said you were going to the bank. Is that true? No worries, you bank at the ANZ, it's right down by the river, so what you said was true either way!' – I don't think such a response is utterly forbidden, but it's peculiar in a way that other applications of the supervaluation rule are not. The two interpretations of 'bank' are so different that presumably you did make up your mind which one you meant. So the means for coping with semantic indecision are out of place. The supervaluation rule comes natural only when the alternative interpretations don't differ too much. If they are one-cat interpretations that differ only by picking almost-identical cats, that's one way for them not to differ much.

How, on the other hand, do supervaluations help the combined solution? Why not let almost-identity do the whole job?

For one thing, not every case of the problem of the many is like the paradox of 1001 cats. The almost-identity solution won't always work well.[10] We've touched on one atypical case already: if not a problem of the many, at least a problem of two. Fred's house taken as including the garage, and taken as not including the garage, have equal claim to be his house. The claim had better be good enough, else he has no house. So Fred has two houses. No! We've already seen how to solve this problem by the method of supervaluations. (If that seemed good to you, it shows that the difference between the interpretations was not yet enough to make the supervaluation rule artificial.) But although the two house-candidates overlap very substantially, having all but the garage in common, they do not overlap nearly as extensively as the cats do. Though they are closer to the identity end of the spectrum than the distinctness end, we cannot really say they're almost identical. So likewise we cannot say that the two houses are almost one.

For another thing, take a statement different from the statements of identity and number that have concerned us so far. Introduce a definite description: 'The cat on the mat includes hair h_{17}'. The obvious response to this statement, I suppose, is that it is gappy. It has no definite truth-value, or no definite super-truth-value, as the case may be. But how can we get that answer if we decide that all the cat-candidates are cats, forsake supervaluations, and ask almost-identity to do the whole job? We might subject the definite description to Russellian translation:

(R1)   There is something that is identical to all and only cats on the mat, and that includes h_{17}.

Or equivalently:

(R2)   Something is identical to all and only cats on the mat, and every cat on the mat includes h_{17}.

Both these translations come out false, because nothing is strictly identical to all and only cats on the mat. That's not the answer we wanted. So we might relax 'identical' to 'almost identical'. When we do, the translations are no longer equivalent: (R1)-relaxed is true, (R2)-relaxed is false. Maybe we're in a state of semantic indecision between (R1)-relaxed and (R2)-relaxed; if so, we could apply the supervaluation rule to get the desired gappiness. Or we might apply the supervaluation rule more directly. Different one-cat interpretations pick out different things as the cat, some that include h_{17} and some that don't. Under any particular one-cat interpretation the Russellian

translations are again equivalent, and different one-cat interpretations give them different truth values; so the translations, and likewise the original sentence, suffer super-truth-value gaps. Or more simply, different one-cat interpretations differ in the referent of 'the cat'; some of these referents satisfy 'includes h_{17}' and some don't, so again we get a super-truth-value gap. Whichever way we go, supervaluations give us the gappiness we want. It's hard to see how else to get it.

Notes

1   See Lewis (1986, pp. 210–20).

2   This is the solution advanced in Lowe (1982).

3   The dualism of things and their constituters is also meant to solve a modal problem: Even at one moment, the thing might have been made of different matter, so what might have been true of it differs from what might have been true of its matter, so constitution cannot be identity. This problem too has a better solution. We should allow that what is true of a given thing at a given world is a vague and inconstant matter. Conflicting answers, equally correct, may be evoked by different ways of referring to the same thing, e.g., as cat or as cat-constituter. My counterpart theory affords this desirable inconstancy; many rival theories do also. See Lewis (1986, pp. 248–63).

4   Provided that there exist the many precisifications for us to be undecided between. If you deny this, you will indeed have need of vague objects. See van Inwagen (1990, pp. 213–83).

5   I grant that the hypothesis of vague objects, for all its faults, can at least be made consistent. If there are vague objects, no doubt they sometimes stand in relations of 'vague identity' to one another. We might think that when a and b are vaguely identical vague objects, the identity statement $a = b$ suffers a truth-value gap; but in fact this conception of vague identity belongs to the theory of vagueness as semantic indecision. As Gareth Evans showed, it doesn't mix with the idea that vague identity is due to vagueness in nature. For if a and b are vaguely identical, they differ in respect of vague identity to a; but nothing, however peculiar it may be, differs in any way from itself; so the identity $a = b$ is definitely false. See Evans (1978). (Evans's too-concise paper invites misunderstanding, but his own testimony confirms my interpretation. See Lewis 1988.) To get a consistent theory of vague objects, different from the bastard theory that is Evans's target, we must disconnect 'vague identity' from truth-value gaps in identity statements. Even if $a = b$ is definitely false,

a and *b* can still be 'vaguely identical' in the sense of sharing some but not all of their precisifications.

6   I do not think reference is entirely up to our choice. Some things are by their nature more eligible than others to be referents or objects of thought, and when we do nothing to settle the contest in favour of the less eligible, then the more eligible wins by default; see Lewis (1984). That's no help here: nature is gradual, no handy joint in nature picks out one of the *c*'s from all the rest.

7   Here I'm indebted to remarks of Saul Kripke many years ago. At his request, I note that what I have written here may not correspond exactly to the whole of what he said on that occasion.

8   Here I'm indebted to Andrew Strauss (personal communication, 1989).

9   There is another way we sometimes count by a relation other than strict identity. You draw two diagonals in a square; you ask me how many triangles; I say there are four; you deride me for ignoring the four large triangles and counting only the small ones. But the joke is on you. For I was within my rights as a speaker of ordinary language, and you couldn't see it because you insisted on counting by strict identity. I meant that, for some w, x, y, z, (1) w, x, y, and z are triangles; (2) w and x are distinct, and … and so are y and z (six clauses); and (3) for any triangle t, either t and w are not distinct, or … or t and z are not distinct (four clauses). And by 'distinct' I meant non-overlap rather than non-identity, so what I said was true.

10 Here I'm indebted to Phillip Bricker (personal communication, 1990).

References

Armstrong, D. M. 1978. *Universals and Scientific Realism*, 2 vols. (Cambridge University Press).

Evans, Gareth. 1978. 'Can There be Vague Objects?', *Analysis* 38: 208. Reprinted in *Collected Papers* (Oxford University Press, 1985) [ch. 12 in this volume].

Geach, P. T. 1967. 'Identity', *Review of Metaphysics* 21: 3–12. Reprinted in *Logic Matters* (Oxford: Blackwell, 1972), pp. 238–47.

Geach, P. T. 1980. *Reference and Generality*, 3rd ed. (Ithaca, NY: Cornell University Press).

Lewis, David. 1976. 'Survival and Identity'. In *The Identities of Persons*, ed. Amélie Rorty (Berkeley: University of California Press), pp. 17–40. Reprinted in Lewis, *Philosophical Papers*, vol. 1 (Oxford University Press, 1983), pp. 55–72 [ch. 43 in this volume].

Lewis, David. 1984. 'Putnam's Paradox', *Australasian Journal of Philosophy* 62: 221–36.

Lewis, David. 1986. *On the Plurality of Worlds* (Oxford: Blackwell).

Lewis, David. 1988. 'Vague Identity: Evans Misunderstood', *Analysis* 48: 128–30.

Lowe, E. J. 1982. 'The Paradox of the 1,001 Cats', *Analysis* 42: 27–30.

Unger, Peter. 1980. 'The Problem of the Many', *Midwest Studies in Philosophy* 5: 411–67.

van Fraassen, Bas C. 1966. 'Singular Terms, Truth-Value Gaps, and Free Logic', *Journal of Philosophy* 63: 481–95.

van Inwagen, Peter. 1990. *Material Beings* (Ithaca, NY: Cornell University Press).

49

Existential Relativity

Ernest Sosa

A Three Ways in Ontology

Artifacts and natural objects are normally composed of stuff or of parts in certain ways. Those that endure are normally composed of stuff or of parts at each instant of their enduring. Moreover, the stuff or parts composing such an object right up to t must be related in certain restricted ways to the stuff or parts that compose it right after t, for any time t within its history.

Thus a snowball exists at a time t and location l only if there is a round quantity of snow at l and t sufficiently separate from other snow, and so forth: and it endures through an interval I only if, for every division of I into a sequence of subintervals $I_1, I_2, \ldots$, there is a corresponding sequence of quantities of snow $Q_1, Q_2, \ldots$, related in certain restricted ways. I mean thus to recall our criteria of existence and perdurance for snowballs.

So much for snowballs. The like is true of chains and constituent links, boxes and constituent sides, and a great variety of artifacts or natural entities such as hills or trees; and the same goes for persons and their constituent bodies. In each case we have criteria of existence and of perdurance, an entity of that sort existing at t (perduring through I) if and only if its criteria of existence are satisfied at t (its criteria of perdurance are satisfied relative to I).

We are supposing a snowball to be constituted by a certain piece of snow as constituent matter and the shape of (approximate) roundness as constituent form. That particular snowball exists at that time because of the roundness of that piece of snow. If at that time that piece of snow were to lose its roundness, then at that time that snowball would go out of existence.

Compare now with our ordinary concept of a snowball the concept of a "snowdiscall," which we may define as an entity constituted by a piece of snow as matter and as form any shape between being round and being disc-shaped. At any given time, therefore, any piece of snow that constitutes a snowball constitutes a snowdiscall, but a piece of snow might at a time constitute a snowdiscall without then constituting a snowball. For every round piece of snow is also in shape between disc-shaped and round (inclusive), but a disc-shaped piece of snow is of course not round.

Any snowball SB must hence be constituted by a piece of snow PS that also then constitutes a snowdiscall SD. Now SB is distinct (a different

Ernest Sosa, "Existential Relativity," *Midwest Studies in Philosophy*, 23 (1999): 132–43. Reprinted by permission of John Wiley & Sons, Inc.

Metaphysics: An Anthology, Second Edition. Edited by Jaegwon Kim, Daniel Z. Korman and Ernest Sosa.

entity from) *PS*, since *PS* would survive squashing and *SB* would not. By similar reasoning, *SD* also is distinct from *PS*. And again by similar reasoning, *SB* must also be distinct from *SD*, since enough partial flattening of *PS* will destroy *SB* but not *SD*. Now, there are infinitely many shapes $S_1, S_2, ...,$ between roundness and flatness of a piece of snow, and, for any shape S_i, having a shape between flatness and S_i would give the form of a distinctive kind of entity to be compared with snowballs and snowdiscalls. Whenever a piece of snow constitutes a snowball, therefore, it constitutes infinitely many entities all sharing its place with it.

Under a broadly Aristotelian conception, therefore, the barest flutter of the smallest leaf creates and destroys infinitely many things, and ordinary reality suffers a sort of "explosion."

This is where we are led by our first option.

We might perhaps resist this "explosion" of our ordinary world by embracing a kind of conceptual relativism. Constituted, supervenient entities do not just objectively supervene on their requisite, constitutive matters and forms, outside all conceptual schemes, with absolute independence from the categories recognized by any person or group. Perhaps snowballs do exist relative to all actual conceptual schemes ever, but not relative to all conceivable conceptual schemes. Just as we do not countenance the existence of snowdiscalls, just so another culture might be unwilling to countenance snowballs. We do not countenance snowdiscalls: our conceptual scheme denies the snowdiscall form (being in shape between round and disc-shaped) the status required for it to be a proper constitutive form of a separate sort of entity – at least not with snow as underlying stuff.

That would block the explosion of reality, but the price is existential relativity. Supervenient, constituted entities do not just exist or not in themselves, free of any dependence on or relativity to conceptual scheme. What thus exists relative to one conceptual scheme may not do so relative to another. In order for such a sort of entity to exist relative to a conceptual scheme, that conceptual scheme must recognize its constituent form as an appropriate way for a distinctive sort of entity to be constituted.

Must we now conceive of the existence even of the conceptual scheme itself and of its framers and users as also relative to that conceptual scheme? And aren't we then caught in a vicious circle? The framers exist only relative to the scheme and this they do in virtue of the scheme's giving their constituent form-cum-matter the required status. But to say that the scheme gives to this form-cum-matter the required status – isn't that just to say that the *framers* of that scheme do so? Yet are not the framers themselves dependent on the scheme for their existence relative to it?

Answer: Existence *relative* to a conceptual scheme is *not* equivalent to existence *in virtue* of that conceptual scheme. Relative to scheme *C* the framers of *C* exist *in virtue* of their constitutive matter and form and how these satisfy certain criteria for existence and perdurance of such subjects (the framers). Their existence is in that way relative to *C* but not in virtue of *C*. There is hence no vicious circularity.

That is our second option.

A third option is a disappearance or elimination theory that refuses to countenance supervenient, constituted objects. But then most if not all of ordinary reality will be lost. Perhaps we shall allow ourselves to continue to use its forms of speech, "but only as a convenience or abbreviation." But in using those forms of speech, in speaking of snowballs, chains, boxes, trees, hills, or even people, we shall *not* believe ourselves to be seriously representing reality and its contents. "As a convenience" ... to *whom* and for what *ends*? "As an abbreviation" ... of *what*?

What follows will first develop and defend our middle, relativist, option; but we shall be led eventually to a compromise position.

Our conceptual scheme encompasses criteria of existence and of perdurance for the sorts of objects that it recognizes. Shall we say now that a sort of object *O* exists (has existed, exists now, or will exist) relative to a scheme *C* at *t* iff, at *t*, *C* recognizes sort *O* by allowing the corresponding criteria? But surely there are sorts of objects that our present conceptual scheme does not recognize, such as artifacts yet uninvented and particles yet undiscovered, to take only two obvious examples. Of course we allow that there might be and probably are many such things. Not that there could be any such entities relative to our *present* conceptual scheme, however, for by hypothesis it does not recognize them. So are there sorts of objects – constituted sorts among them, as are the artifacts at least – such that they exist but not relative to our present scheme C? But then we are back to our problem. What is it for there to be such objects? Is it just the in-itself satisfaction of constitutive forms by constitutive matters? That yields the explosion of reality.

Shall we say then that a constituted, supervenient sort of object O exists relative to our present scheme C if and only if O is recognized by C directly or recognized by it indirectly through being recognized by some predecessor or successor scheme? That, I fear, cannot suffice, since there might be sorts of particles that always go undiscovered by us, and sorts of artifacts in long-disappeared cultures unknown to us, whose conceptual schemes are not predecessors of ours.

Shall we then say that what exists relative to our present scheme O is what it recognizes directly, what it recognizes indirectly through its predecessors or successors, and what it *would* recognize if we had developed appropriately or were to do so now, and had been or were to be appropriately situated? This seems the sort of answer required, but it obviously won't be easy to say what appropriateness amounts to in our formula, in its various guises. Whether it is worth it to specify our formula further so as to assuage the foregoing concerns will depend on whether even our preliminary formulation is defensible against certain natural objections. We next formulate and answer five such objections.

B   Objections and Replies

Objection 1

Take a sort of object O recognized by our scheme C, with various instances; for example, the sort Planet, with various particular planets as instances: Mercury, Venus, etc. The instances, say we, exist, which amounts to saying that they exist relative to our scheme. But if we had not existed there would have been no scheme of ours for anything to exist relative to; nor would there have been our actual scheme C either. For one thing, we may just assume the contingent existence of our actual scheme to depend on people's actually granting a certain status to certain constitutive forms. If we had not existed, therefore, the constitutive form for the sort Planet would not have had, relative to our conceptual scheme, the status that makes it

possible "that there be instances of that sort, particular planets." And from this it apparently follows that if we had not existed there would have been no planets: no Mercury, no Venus, and so on.

Reply. While existing in the actual world x we now have a conceptual scheme C_x relative to which we assert existence, when we assert it at all. Now we suppose a possible world w in which we are not to be found, in which indeed no life of any sort is to be found. Still we may, in x: (a) consider alternative world w and recognize that our absence there would have no effect on the existence or course of a single planet or star, that Mercury, Venus, and the rest would all still make their appointed rounds just as they do in x; while yet (b) this recognition, which after all takes place in x, is still relativized to C_x, so that the existence in w of whatever exists in x relative to C_x need not be affected at all by the absence from w of C_x, and indeed of every conceptual scheme and of every being who could have a conceptual scheme. For when we suppose existence in w, or allow the possibility of existence in w, *we* do so in x, and we do so there still relative to C_x, to our present conceptual scheme, and what it recognizes directly or indirectly, or ideally.

Objection 2

What does it matter whether we "recognize" the snowdiscall form (being in shape between round and disc-shaped, inclusive)? We are anyhow "committed" to there being such a property in any case, to there being the property or condition of being shaped in that inclusive way. If a piece of snow is in shape anywhere between disc-shaped and round then it just is a snowdiscall. So there must be lots of snowdiscalls in existence and that must be nothing new. What is the problem? Could we not even just define a "caog" as anything that is a cat or a dog, and are there not as many caogs in existence as are in the union of the set of cats and the set of dogs? Why should anyone worry about this "explosion"? Why not just admit the obvious: that, yes, there are snowdiscalls, and caogs, even if heretofore they had not been so-called?

Not only is that obvious. If anyone is misguided enough to want to avoid admitting the obvious, it does not really help to introduce some conceptually relative notion of existence according to which the entities that so exist are only those that we are committed to through the properties and kinds that we admit in our ideology and ontology. For if we admit being a dog as an ordinary, harmless enough property, and the kind dog as well, along with being a cat, and so on, then we are implicitly committed to admitting anything that is either a dog or a cat, as being "either a dog or a cat," and that is tantamount to admitting that there are caogs – not under this description, of course, but what does that matter?

Reply. That is all quite true, of course, but not in conflict with existential relativity, which is a thesis about ontological constitution, presupposing as it does that there are levels of individuals, and thus individuals on a higher level, constituted out of individuals on a lower level. How then are the constituted entities constitutable out of the constituting entities? One (partial, Aristotelian) answer: A constituted entity must derive from the satisfaction by the constituting entity (or entities) of a condition (a property or relation, a "form"). *Any* condition? That is absolutism, and leads to the "explosion." Only conditions from a restricted set? *How*, in what way, restricted? Somehow by reference to the conceptual scheme of the speaker or thinker who attributes existence? This is existential relativity (of the sort at issue here).

Returning to the examples of the objection: First, yes, of course there are snowdiscalls if all one means by this is that there are pieces of snow with a shape somewhere between disc-shaped and round. And when something is so shaped and, also, more specifically, round, then it is not only such a snowdiscall but also a round piece of snow, a "snowround," let's say. But one and numerically the same thing is then both the snowdiscall and the snowround. And this is no more puzzling than is the fact that someone can be both a mother and a daughter, or both red and round, or both an apple and a piece of fruit, and so on. When *I* introduced the term "snowdiscall" this is not what I had in mind. In my sense, a "snowdiscall" is not just any piece of snow with a shape between round and disc-shaped. Nor is a snowball just a round piece of snow, a snowround. For a round piece of snow can survive squashing, unlike the snowball that it constitutes, which is destroyed, not just changed, when it is squashed. The question is: what is special

about the form of being round combined with an individual piece of snow, what is special about the ordered pair, let's say, that makes it a suitable matter-form pair for the constitution of a constituted individual, a particular snowball? Would any other shape, between roundness and flatness, also serve as such a form, along with that individual piece of snow? Could they together yield a matter-form pair that might also serve, in its own way, for the formation, the constitution of its own individual: not a snowball, presumably, but its own different kind of individual? It is to *this* question that the absolutist would answer in the affirmative, while the existential relativist might well answer in the negative.

According to existential relativity in ontology, what then is required for a matter-form pair to serve as the form and matter for the constitution of an individual, a constituted individual? Answer: that the sort of matter-form combination in question be countenanced by the relevant conceptual scheme, a conceptual scheme determined by the context of thought or utterance.

Objection 3

If it is granted that things can exist prior to the development of any conceptual scheme whatever, prior to the evolution of any thinkers who could have a conceptual scheme, is that not a concession to absolutism? Is it not being conceded that things exist "out there, in themselves," independently of conceptual schemes altogether, so that things do not exist in virtue of our conceptual choices after all. Rather things exist "in themselves." Reality itself manages somehow to cut the cookies unaided by humans. Isn't this just absolutism after all? What can be left of existential relativity after this has been granted?

Reply. Compare this. If I say, "The Empire State Building is 180 miles away," my utterance is true, but the sentence I utter is true only relative to my present position. If I had uttered that sentence elsewhere then I might well have said something false. So my sentence is true relative to my spatial position, but it is not true or false just on its own, independently of such context. And, in a sense, that the Empire State Building is 180 miles away is true relative to my present position but false relative to many other positions. However, it is not so that the Empire State Building is 180 miles from here *in virtue of* my present position. The Empire State Building would have been 180 miles from here even had I been located elsewhere. Whether I am here or not does not determine the distance of the Empire State Building relative to this place here.

Existential relativity can be viewed as a doctrine rather like the relativity involved in the evaluation of the truth of indexical sentences or thoughts. In effect, "existence claims" can be viewed as implicitly indexical, and that is what my existential relativist is suggesting. So when someone says or thinks that Os exist, this is to be evaluated relative to the position of the speaker or thinker in "ontological space." Relative to the thus distinguished conceptual scheme, it might be that Os do exist, although this is not true relative to many other conceptual schemes.

But what is it about a "conceptual scheme" that determines whether or not it is true to say that "Os exist"? Answer: what determines whether "there are" constituted entities of a certain sort relative to a certain conceptual scheme would be that scheme's criteria of existence (or individuation). And what are these? They are specifications of the appropriate pairings of kinds of individuals with properties or relations. Appropriate for what? For the constitution of constituted entities, *in the dispensation of that conceptual scheme.*

When one says or thinks "Os exist," then, according to existential relativity this is not true or false absolutely. Its truth value must be determined relative to one's conceptual scheme, to one's "conceptual position," including its criteria of existence. However, even if one's claim that "Os exist" must be evaluated relative to one's conceptual position, so that it can be very naturally said that "Os exist" relative to one's conceptual position (in that sense), it does not follow that "Os exist" only *in virtue* of one's conceptual position, in that if one had not existed with some such conceptual scheme, or at least if no one had existed with some such conceptual scheme, then there would have been "no Os in existence." This no more follows than it follows from the relativity of the truth of my statement "The Empire State Building is 180 miles from here" that the Empire State Building is that far from here as a result of *my* being here (even if I am the speaker or thinker). Despite the relativity of the truth of my statement, the Empire State Building *would have*

been exactly where it is, 180 miles from here, even if I had not been here. Similarly, Os might have existed relative to this my (our) conceptual position, even if no one had existed to occupy this position.

Objection 4

It is not easy for me to understand what relative reference in thought would be. Relative reference in *language*, however, seems explicable in terms of conventions to refer *simpliciter* in thought. There is a rule for relative reference (for the first-person pronoun [I]): [I] refers to x relative to y iff $x = y$. But the rule only gives us truth-conditions for propositions attributing relative reference; it doesn't explain it. Correspondingly, I have trouble grasping existential relativity, even when restricted to supervenient entities. If entities in one layer of reality exist and have their properties *simpliciter*, it seems to me that either they determine *simpliciter* the existence and properties of a class of entities or they don't. What would determination relative to a conceptual scheme be? Wouldn't it be more palatable to conclude that there are snowdiscalls as well as snowballs?

Moreover, if we accept existential relativity, can we recognize disagreement between users of "rival" conceptual schemes? One population recognizes snowballs but not snowdiscalls, let us say, while another has the reverse preference. Further, suppose nothing prevents the populations from discussing this difference in what they respectively recognize. Would not each population know both what snowdiscalls would be and what snowballs would be, even if each "recognizes" only one of these? Nevertheless, shouldn't we find in the difference between them some real disagreement? If we say that to recognize Fs is to believe there are Fs, we can of course easily locate such disagreement. But if we say that to recognize Fs is to use a conceptual scheme that recognizes Fs, with no further explanation possible of recognition by schemes, wherein might reside the disagreement?

Reply. Can't one think of it as follows? There is some sort of selection function that for a community or an individual picks out the matter-form pairs that are suitable for object constitution. One's selection function determines one's position in ontological (individuation) space. "The objects that there can be" – this for our relativist view is not an absolutely and objectively denoting description: rather, it denotes relative to a position. So it is in that respect rather like "the objects that are nearby." When you and I occupy sufficiently different spatial positions, we need not disagree if you say "X is nearby" and I say "X is not nearby." Similarly we need not disagree with the alien culture if, speaking of the same place, we say, "There are only snowballs here," and they say, "There are only snowdiscalls here."

Wherein then resides our disagreement? Perhaps just in the fact that we differ in what we include in our respective ontological positions. Well, it resides at least in that. But do we not disagree also in that we believe that there are in fact snowballs and disbelieve that there are snowdiscalls, whereas they believe there are in fact snowdiscalls and disbelieve that there are snowballs? This is the move that seems questionable in the light of our analogy to judgments of what is nearby. Given that what we say is said from relevantly different positions it may just be that we are not disagreeing at all in those respective beliefs.

"There are" and, especially, "there can be" are according to this view covertly indexical. Therefore we cannot report their beliefs by saying that according to their belief there can be no snowballs. They may say, "There can be no snowballs," and they may even say, "There can be no objects composed of a chunk of snow and roundness." But we could not properly describe them as believing that there can be no snowballs or even as believing that there can be no objects so composed. We can no more do that than I (from Providence) can unambiguously describe you as believing that Boston is far away, just because you in Tokyo say sincerely, "Boston is far away."

The lack of agreement ("disagreement" may now well strike one as the wrong word here) would then reside simply in the fact that we are selecting different matter-form categories. Of course there may be reasons why it is better to select one set of categories rather than another, pragmatic reasons at least; rather as there may be reasons why it is better to be at one location rather than another. But this would not show that the actual judgments of "what is nearby" made by those poorly positioned are inferior to the judgments made by those better positioned. Nor would it show that there is any real disagreement

when one says, "X is nearby," and the other says, "X is not nearby." Their only failure of "agreement" is their lack of spatial coincidence. Similarly, to have different positions in ontological space might reveal a lack of coincidence in the selected matter-form object-constituting pairs, but little else by way of real disagreement as to what there can be or what there cannot be. (There might be such disagreement anyway; but it would not derive just from the occupancy of divergent ontological positions. Rather, the disagreement might be over, say, whether there can be things that are cubical and eight-sided, or over similar property combination questions.)

That all seems compatible with its being nontrivial to determine what objects there can be relative to our position in ontological space. Nothing rules out the possibility that the selection function operate beneath the surface, such that it is far from easy to determine our implicit individuation and persistence criteria. Their being relative to the psychology of the individual or the culture of the group would seem compatible with its being a matter of difficult analysis, psychological or cultural, to tease out just what they are.

Objection 5

Surely it will prove difficult to be selective about existential relativity. Could we reasonably say that some things (atoms, perhaps) exist *simpliciter* whereas others (snowballs) exist only relative to our scheme? If we did, wouldn't we be pressed to conclude that snowballs do not *really* exist: they only "exist" courtesy of our scheme? Thus facts about atoms don't determine that there are snowballs, but they might perhaps be said to do so relative to our scheme. If so, doesn't our scheme then commit us to some falsehoods? Our scheme would then seem to attribute existence to snowballs (snowdiscalls), whereas snowballs do not exist (not *really*).

Reply. Evaluable claims as to what is or is not nearby require that the claimant be spatially located. Analogously, sensible judgments as to what objects do or do not exist, or, indeed, might or might not exist, may require a subject located in ontological space. There might still be good reasons to change our ontological position, however, just as there often is good reason to change our spatial location. And if we do move, we might in the new location be able to make true judgments that we were not in any position to make in the earlier location.

Are we precluded from supposing that there might be, or even that there definitely is, or more yet that there must be, some noumenal reality constituted in itself, with no relativity to categories or criteria of individuation and/or persistence contributed by the mind or by the culture? I can't see that we are.

Nevertheless, when we say that there are atoms, the truth of our utterance seems independent of our point of view. Whether there are atoms gives no sign of being relative to our ontological position. Would atoms be like snowballs, so that some alien culture might fail to recognize atoms, might just have some other set of categories? Surely they would just be missing something real if they miss atoms. Well, yes; but perhaps we can do justice to this fact from within existential relativity.

Consider again the analogy to judgments of distance. Boston is nearby. That's a fact I am aware of, and one I probably could not express nonperspectivally. Would someone with a different location, far from here, be unable to grasp that fact? Would they not be missing something real if they missed that fact? Here we would need to consider the coordination of thoughts, starting with simple location-relative thoughts. For example, the fact that Boston is near me now is a fact that someone else far away and in the future might still grasp even though it would be grasped, not by means of that very perspectival proposition, but by some appropriately coordinated one. Someone with a snowdiscall ontology could perhaps grasp a fact that I grasp by saying, "There are snowballs," but only by means of a coordinated proposition such as, perhaps, "There are non-disc-shaped snowdiscalls."

We can always drop down a level if our schemes coincide at the lower level: for example, if we both believe in chunks of snow and we both have a grasp of the properties of roundness and of being disc-shaped, and so on, we can compare notes at that lower level. But if a level recognizes items, be they particles or fields or whatever, and if we think of these items in terms of the matter-form model, with entailed criteria of individuation and persistence, then the same

issues will recur. Nevertheless, every level might allow for agreement or disagreement determined by coordinated, perspectival propositions, such coordination among propositions to be understood in terms of some deeper ontological level, deeper in a sense suggested as follows. When I think, "Boston is near to where I am now," a fact makes that true, one involving two entities and a distance between them. Of course, if one tries to pick out the entity that is oneself, it may not be possible for *us* to do this without doing it perspectivally: either I do it, in which case I use the first-person conceptual mechanism(s), or you do it, in which case you might use some second- or third-person mechanism(s). Actually stating the fact in virtue of which my thought "Boston is nearby" is true may be a problem if one tries to do so nonperspectivally: I actually think it cannot be done, not by humans anyway. But that need not prevent us from supposing that a fact *is* stated and could be stated by any one of a large number of coordinated propositions, which would be used by different, appropriately positioned subjects; a fact, moreover, that is not mind-dependent, in the sense that its being a fact is independent of its being thought of by anyone, in any of the various perspectival ways in which it might be thought of. What is that fact, one might well ask, what could it be? Why not "the fact that Boston is nearby"? The point is that I have no way to state it except perspectivally; and of course the truth of the thought or proposition that I thereby state is not objective or mind-independent. But consider the fact thereby stated, the fact stated in that mind-dependent way, a fact that we humans may be unable to state except in some such mind-dependent way. As far as I can see, it simply does not follow that the fact itself must therefore be mind-dependent. So one single mind-independent fact can be approached from indefinitely many perspectives and can be stated in the corresponding, mutually coordinated perspectival ways. All of these statements, and the thoughts they would express, are of course mind-dependent, at least in the sense that they are not truth-evaluable except relative to the mind that uses them. But from that it does not follow that there is no mind-independent fact that is thereby stated, even if we lack access to that fact except perspectivally, and hence mind-dependently.[1]

C Some Middle Ground?

What then shall we say exists relative to our present scheme C? Assuming the success of our defense against the foregoing objections, may we answer that what so exists is what our scheme C recognizes directly, what it recognizes indirectly through its predecessors or successors, and what it *would* recognize if we had developed appropriately or were to do so now, and had been or were to be appropriately situated? This does seem the sort of answer required by our relativism, but we are still left wondering what "appropriateness" amounts to in our formula, in its various guises. Let us step back and reconsider.

. We are pulled in several directions at once, as is typical of a paradox.

On the one hand, when a certain combination $(w + m)$ of a piece of wood w and a piece of metal m is used both as a doorstop and occasionally as a hammer, it constitutes both that doorstop and that hammer. Are there then three things there: $(w + m)$, the doorstop, and that hammer? Are these distinct entities, occupying the same location? One is drawn here to say that really there is just $(w + m)$, which might be used as a hammer, or used as a doorstop, or both.

On the other hand, why stop with $(w + m)$? Why not say that what really exists in that situation is just w and m severally, which, if properly joined, can be used for hammering, for stopping doors, and the like. But why stop even there? After all, w itself will be a combination of certain molecules, each of which in turn combines certain atoms, and so forth. Where does it all stop? What is the bottom?

How indeed can we know that there *is* a bottom? How do we know that there is a level that does not itself derive from some underlying level of reality in the way the hammer derives from $(w + m)$'s having a certain use, or in the way $(w + m)$ derives from w and m severally, when the two are relevantly joined, or the way w derives from certain molecules being arrayed a certain way? And so on.

Science, so far as I can tell, itself postulates no such bottom. Only philosophers do so. But on what basis? Is this just a metaphysical dogma?

Consider now the eliminativism that rejects the entities at any given level ontologically derivative from an underlying level. To avoid the ontological nihilism for which there is absolutely nothing ever anywhere, such eliminativism must commit itself to the existence of an ontological bottom level. But, again, this seems little better than dogma.

However, if one does therefore admit a layered reality, with ontological levels derived from underlying levels, what governs such derivation? The most general characterization of the way in which ontologically derivative particulars derive from an underlying reality would seem to be our Aristotelian conception according to which a sequence of particulars (matters) at the underlying level exemplifies a property or relation (form), giving rise thereby to a distinctive object at the higher, derived level.

But now our earlier questions recur: One would want to know what restrictions if any there might be on matter-form pairs that constitute derived entities. Why rule out entities of the sort $(w + m)$ or properties of the form: having such and such a function (hammering, stopping doors, etc.)? Why not allow that these can constitute distinctive derived entities? And why not allow not only a piece of snow as matter and approximate roundness as form, but also a piece of snow as matter, and a shape anywhere between roundness and being disc-shaped as form? And if we allow these, then where does it all stop? We seem driven to the explosion.

Compare the claim that a certain irregularly shaped figure f drawn on a surface is "shapeless." Such a claim is interestingly relative to context. On the one hand it might be true iff figure f has no shape whatever, in which case it would of course be false, since f does have some shape or other, surely, however irregular. And yet in another context it might be evaluated as true iff f lacks any of the shapes in some restricted set of shapes: where the context would somehow determine the specific restriction. Thus in one context the religious background may pick out a certain irregular shape as highly significant, in which case items with that shape would not count as "shapeless," whereas in other contexts they would.

On an analogous contextual relativism of *existential* claims, the objects on the derived level relevant to the truth evaluation of an existential claim are those in some restricted set, the context somehow determining the restriction. Compare here: "There is nothing in that box." (What about the air?) Or "there is only a hammer here." (What about the doorstop?) Or even "there is only a snowball here." (What about the snowdiscall?)

So our choices, none pleasant, seem to be these:

- *Eliminativism*: Supposed entities that derive ontologically from underlying entities do not exist, not really. But this carries a commitment to an ontological bottom, one that seems little better than dogma, on pain of nihilism.
- *Absolutism*: Eliminativism is false. Moreover, there are no restrictions on the appropriate matter-form pairs that can constitute objects.[2] *Any* matter-form pair whatever, at any given ontological level, determines a corresponding derived entity at the next higher level, so long as the matter takes that form. This is the "explosion" of reality.
- *Unrestricted absolutism*: Absolutism is true. Moreover, any existential claim is to be assessed for truth or falsity relative to all objects and properties without restriction.
- *Conceptual relativism*: Absolutism is true. Moreover, existential claims are true or false only relative to the context of speech or thought, which restricts the sorts of objects relevant to the assessment. Such restrictions are governed by various pragmatic or theoretical considerations.

Note how moderate this conceptual *relativism* turns out to be. It is even absolutist and objectivist enough to accept the "explosion." Reality is objectively much richer and more bizarre than is perhaps commonly recognized. All sorts of weird entities derive from any given level of particulars and properties. Snowdiscalls are just one straightforwardly simple example. Our objective metaphysics is hence absolutist and latitudinarian, given our inability to find any well-motivated objective restriction on the matter-form pairs that constitute derived entities. Our relativism applies to the truth or falsity of existential and other ontologically committed claims. It is here that a restriction is imposed by the conceptual scheme of the claimant speaker or thinker. But the restriction is as harmless and even trivial as is that involved in a claim that some selected figure *f* is "shapeless" made in full awareness that *f* does have some specific shape, however irregular. Similarly, someone who claims that there are only snowballs at location *L* may be relying on some context-driven restriction of the totality of objects which, in full strictness, one *would* recognize at that location. Speaking loosely and popularly we may hence say that there are only snowballs there, even if strictly and philosophically one would recognize much that is not dreamt of in our ordinary talk.

Have we a robust intuition that snowballs are a different order of entity, somehow less a product of conceptual artifice, than snowdiscalls, or a robust intuition that doorstops are too dependent on the vagaries of human convenience and convention to count as distinctive kinds of entities no matter how artificial? And if doorstops do not count, how or why can cars count? Or is any such intuition displaced under reflection by corresponding intuitions about such natural kinds as animals and elements? But what exactly enables us to distinguish the distinguished classes of entities favored as objectively real, by contrast with the artificial or shadowy snowdiscalls, doorstops, hammers, snowballs, and even cars? I have here raised this question, but any claim of originality would be ludicrous. Here I have tried to frame that question in a context that rejects eliminativism on one side, and questions the "explosion" on the other. But in the end I do express a preference for the latitudinarian "explosion." This preference is motivated by the rejection of eliminativism on one side, and by my failure to find attractive and well-motivated restrictions on allowable matter-form pairs on the other. My preference can only be tentative, however, given the vast history of the issue and the subtle and intricate contemporary discussions of it. I do point to a way in which one might be able to accommodate some of the intuitions that drive the desire for restriction, through a kind of metalinguistic or metaconceptual ascent. And it is through this ascent that our relativism emerges. It remains to be seen, however, whether the accommodation thus made possible will be accommodating enough.

Notes

1 Part A of this paper draws from part C of my "Putnam's Pragmatic Realism," *Journal of Philosophy* 90 (1993): 605–26. My thanks to Matthew McGrath for helpful comments, and also to Reginald Allen and Mitchell Green, for helpful comments at an APA Central session on my earlier paper.
2 Again, the reference should be, more strictly, to "matter(s)-form" pairs, so as to allow plural constitution.

50

The Argument from Vagueness

Theodore Sider

Under what conditions do objects come into and go out of existence? As a believer in temporal parts and unrestricted composition, I say this *always* occurs. Any filled region of spacetime is the total career of some object. Others say that objects come into and go out of existence only under certain conditions. When bits of matter are arranged in certain ways, an object – say, a person – comes into existence; and that thing goes out of existence when the bits cease to be arranged in the appropriate way. But what sorts of arrangements are suitable? If one arrangement is suitable, then a *very* slightly different arrangement would seem to be as well. Iterate this procedure, and we have the conclusion that objects *always* come into and go out of existence, no matter how bits of matter are arranged. But this, it will be seen, is tantamount to admitting that four-dimensionalism is true.[1] The obvious problem with 'slippery slope' arguments of this sort is that they neglect vagueness. But there cannot be vagueness of the sort needed to block the argument. The argument will at this point make some assumptions, most notably that vagueness never results from 'logic' (i.e. from boolean connectives, quantification, or identity). These assumptions could be coherently denied, but they

are very plausible. I also suspect that they are widely held, even among those hostile to temporal parts. There is, therefore, considerable interest in showing that anyone who accepts the assumptions must accept four-dimensionalism.

Those familiar with David Lewis's *On the Plurality of Worlds* (1986) will recognize a parallel here with his argument for the principle of unrestricted mereological composition. In the next section I develop Lewis's argument for unrestricted composition in my own way, and then in the following two sections show how it can be modified to yield an argument for temporal parts.

1 Unrestricted Mereological Composition

Here is Lewis's argument (1986: 212–13):

> We are happy enough with mereological sums of things that contrast with their surroundings more than they do with one another; and that are adjacent, stick together, and act jointly. We are more reluctant to affirm the existence of

Theodore Sider, "The Argument from Vagueness," in *Four Dimensionalism: An Ontology of Persistence and Time* (Oxford: Oxford University Press, 2001), ch. 4, sect. 9 (pp. 120–39).

Metaphysics: An Anthology, Second Edition. Edited by Jaegwon Kim, Daniel Z. Korman and Ernest Sosa.

mereological sums of things that are disparate and scattered and go their separate ways...

The trouble with restricted composition is as follows... To restrict composition in accordance with our intuitions would require a vague restriction. But if composition obeys a vague restriction, then it must sometimes be a vague matter whether composition takes place or not. And that is impossible.

The only intelligible account of vagueness locates it in our thought and language. The reason it's vague where the outback begins is not that there's this thing, the outback, with imprecise borders; rather there are many things, with different borders, and nobody has been fool enough to try to enforce a choice of one of them as the official referent of the word 'outback'. Vagueness is semantic indecision. But not all of language is vague. The truth-functional connectives aren't, for instance. Nor are the words for identity and difference, and for the partial identity of overlap. Nor are the idioms of quantification, so long as they are unrestricted. How could any of these be vague? What would be the alternatives between which we haven't chosen?

The question whether composition takes place in a given case, whether a given class does or does not have a mereological sum, can be stated in a part of language where nothing is vague. Therefore it cannot have a vague answer.... No restriction on composition can be vague. But unless it is vague, it cannot fit the intuitive *desiderata*. So no restriction on composition can serve the intuitions that motivate it. So restriction would be gratuitous. Composition is unrestricted ...

It may be summarized as follows. (I follow Lewis in speaking of parthood atemporally; I consider temporally relativized parthood in the next subsection.) If not every class has a fusion then there must be a restriction on composition. Moreover, the only plausible restrictions on composition would be vague ones. But there can be no vague restrictions on composition, because that would mean that whether composition occurs is sometimes vague. Therefore, every class has a fusion.

There is a weakness in this argument. The first premise of my summary is that if not every class has a fusion then there must exist a 'restriction on composition'. On a natural reading, a 'restriction on composition' is a way of filling in the blank in the following schema:

A class, S, has a fusion if and only if —

such that what goes into the blank is not universally satisfied. That is, a restriction on composition would be an answer to Peter van Inwagen's 'special composition question'.[2] (For example, one answer might be that a class has a fusion iff its members are 'in contact'.) But perhaps the special composition question has no informative answer because whether composition takes place in a given case is a 'brute fact' incapable of informative analysis.[3]

There are two senses in which composition might be brute. Composition is brute in a strong sense if it does not even supervene on causal and qualitative factors. This is extremely implausible; one would need to admit a pair of cases exactly alike in terms of causal integration, qualitative homogeneity, and so on, but which differ over whether objects have a sum. But even if supervenience is admitted, composition might be brute in the weaker sense that there is no natural, finite, humanly statable restriction on composition. Since I do not wish to reject weak brute composition out of hand, I will reformulate Lewis's argument so as not to (directly, anyway) presuppose its falsity.

Let us understand a 'case of composition' ('case', for short) as a possible situation involving a class of objects having certain properties and standing in certain relations. We will ask with respect to various cases whether composition occurs; that is, whether the class in the case would have a fusion. In summary, my version of Lewis's argument runs as follows. If not every class has a fusion, then we can consider two possible cases, one in which composition occurs and another in which it does not, which are connected by a 'continuous series of cases' selected from different possible worlds, each extremely similar to the last. Since composition can never be vague, there must be a sharp cut-off in this series where composition abruptly stops occurring. But that is implausible. So composition always occurs.

More carefully. First, consider any case, C_1, in which composition occurs — the case of a certain class of subatomic particles that are part of my body, for example. Now consider a second case, C_2, which occurs after I die and am cremated, in which my molecules are scattered across the Milky Way. Some would say that in C_2, composition fails to take place: there is nothing that is made up of these scattered, causally unconnected particles. Next, let us further imagine a finite series of cases connecting C_1 and C_2, in which each case in the series is extremely similar to its immediately adjacent cases in all respects that might be relevant to whether composition occurs: qualitative homogeneity, spatial proximity, unity of action, comprehensiveness of causal relations, etc. I call such a series a 'continuous series connecting cases C_1 and C_2.'

My argument's first premise is:

P1: If not every class has a fusion, then there must be a pair of cases connected by a continuous series such that in one, composition occurs, but in the other, composition does not occur.

I can think of only two objections. Given 'nihilism', the view that composition *never* occurs (i.e. that there are no composite objects): since there are no cases of composition at all there cannot exist a continuous series connecting a case of composition to anything.[4] I argue against nihilism in Chapter 5, Section 6 [not reproduced in this selection]. The second objection is that not every pair of cases can be connected by a continuous series. No continuous series connects any case with finitely many objects to a case with infinitely many objects, for example.[5] However, P1 only requires that *some* pair of cases differing over composition be connected by a continuous series, if composition is restricted. No one will want to claim that the jump from finitude to infinity is the thing that makes the difference between composition and its absence. So even if no continuous series connects C_1 with C_2, one can choose another pair of cases C_1' and C_2', like C_1 and C_2 with respect to whether composition occurs, which are connected by a continuous series.

By a 'sharp cut-off' in a continuous series I mean a pair of *adjacent* cases in a continuous series such that in one, composition definitely occurs, but in the other, composition definitely does not occur. Surely there are no such things:

P2: In no continuous series is there a sharp cut-off in whether composition occurs.

Adjacent members in a continuous series are extremely similar in certain respects. By including more and more members in a continuous series, adjacent members can be made as similar as you like. Accepting a sharp cut-off is thus nearly as difficult as rejecting the supervenience of composition on the relevant factors. It would involve saying, for example, that although certain particles definitely compose a larger object, if one of the particles had been 0.0000001 nanometers displaced, those particles would have definitely failed to compose any object at all. Of course, sharp cut-offs in the application of a predicate are not *always* implausible – consider the predicate 'are separated by exactly 3 nanometers'. What I object to is a sharp cut-off in a continuous series of cases of *composition*.

To postulate such a sharp cut-off would be to admit that the realm of the macroscopic is in some sense 'autonomous' of the microscopic. By 'autonomous' I do not mean 'non-supervenient', since accepting a sharp cut-off in a continuous series of cases of composition does not threaten supervenience. Rather, I mean that there would seem to be something 'metaphysically arbitrary' about a sharp cut-off in a continuous series of cases of composition. Why is the cut-off here, rather than there? Granted, everyone must admit *some* metaphysically 'brute' facts, and it is a hard question why one brute fact seems more or less plausible than another. Nevertheless, *this* brute fact seems particularly hard to stomach.[6]

A possible objection to P2 would be based on precisely statable topological restrictions on the regions of space that can possibly be occupied by a composite object, perhaps regions in which any two points are connectable by some continuous path confined to the region. But this would rule out too many objects: galaxies, solar systems, and so on. More importantly, under the classical physics conception of matter, all macroscopic objects are discontinuous. This is less clear on a quantum-mechanical picture, but a classical world should not turn out devoid of macro-objects.[7]

The final premise of the argument is, I think, the most controversial:

P3: In any case of composition, either composition definitely occurs, or composition definitely does not occur.

P1, P2, and P3 imply the desired conclusion. P1 requires that if composition is not unrestricted, we have a case of composition connected by a continuous series to a case of non-composition. By P3, there must be a sharp cut-off in this series where composition abruptly ceases to occur; but this contradicts P2. It must be emphasized that this is not 'just another Sorites'. The correct solution to traditional Sorites paradoxes will surely involve a region in which the relevant predicate ('is a heap', 'is bald', and so on) neither definitely applies nor definitely fails to apply (note: the epistemic theory of vagueness is discussed below). But this is just what P3 prohibits.

I turn now to the defense of P3. Recall that a 'case' was defined as involving a *class* of objects, by which I mean a non-fuzzy class. Thus understood, classes have precisely defined membership, and so must be distinguished from class descriptions, which may well be imprecise. P3 pertains to classes themselves, not their descriptions. Thus, indeterminacy of truth value in the sentence 'The class of molecules in the immediate vicinity of my body has a fusion' would not be inconsistent with P3. In virtue of its vagueness, the subject term of this sentence may well fail to refer uniquely to any one class. Also note that P3 is not concerned with the nature of the resulting fusion, only its existence. It may well be indeterminate whether a given class of molecules has a fusion that counts as a *person*. This is not inconsistent with P3, for the class may definitely have a fusion which is a borderline case of a person.

Lewis's method for establishing P3 appeals to the 'linguistic theory of vagueness'.[8] This view's slogan is that 'vagueness is semantic indecision'. Whenever a sentence is indeterminate in truth value due to vagueness, this is because there is some term in the sentence that is *semantically vague*, in that there are multiple possible meanings for that term, often called 'precisifications', no one of which has been singled out as the term's unique meaning. There is no vagueness 'in the world'; all vagueness is due to semantic indecision. An oversimplified example: 'bald' is vague because no one has ever decided which of its precisifications it is to mean, where the precisifications are properties of the form *having no more than* n *hairs on one's head*, for various integers n in a certain range. (Realistically, baldness depends on more than how many hairs one has on one's head. Distribution, length, and other factors also matter.)

In virtue of the definition of 'fusion' in terms of parthood, we can formulate the assertion that a given class, C, has a fusion as follows:

(F) There is some object, x, such that (1) every member of C is part of x, and (2) every part of x shares a part in common with some member of C.

If (F) has no determinate truth value relative to some assignment to 'C', this must be due to vagueness, for other potential sources of truth value gaps (such as ambiguity or failed presupposition) are not present. Given the linguistic theory of vagueness, one of the terms in (F) would need to have multiple precisifications. But it is difficult to see what the precisifications of logical terms, or the predicates 'is a member of' and 'part of', might be.

The weakest link here is the rejection of precisifications for 'is part of'. Notice that in ruling out 'part of' as a source of vagueness, Lewis is not ruling out all vagueness in *ascriptions* of parthood, for ascriptions of parthood may contain singular terms (e.g. 'the outback') with multiple precisifications. (F), however, apparently contains no vague singular terms. Vague ascriptions of parthood are therefore not a good reason *for* saying that 'part' lacks precisifications. But what is a good reason *against*? Lewis's reason is that it is difficult to see what the precisifications might be. But perhaps this is because they are not easily statable in natural language. *Some* non-logical terms, 'is bald' for example, have prima facie easily statable precisifications (namely, properties expressed by predicates of the form ⌐has a head with less than n hairs⌐, and even then statability is in doubt, given the vagueness of 'head' and 'hair'). But other vague predicates lack easily statable precisifications, for example 'person', 'table', and artifact terms generally. Someone might argue that 'part' has precisifications corresponding to precisifications of answers to van Inwagen's special composition question. I do not say that this response to Lewis can be made to work, but I cannot see how to show that it cannot be made to work.

Fortunately, P3 may be supported without making any assumptions about parthood, for if it were vague whether a certain class had a fusion then it would be vague how many concrete objects exist. Lewis's assumptions about vagueness can then be replaced by weaker assumptions that concern only logical vocabulary.

Let us stipulatively define *concrete* objects as those which do *not* fit into any of the kinds on the following list:

sets and classes
numbers
properties and relations
universals and tropes
possible worlds and situations

If I have missed any 'abstract' entities you believe in, feel free to update the list. Suppose now for *reductio* that P3 is false – that is, that it can be vague whether a given class has a fusion. In such a case, imagine counting all the concrete objects in the world. One would need to include all the objects in the class in question, but it would be indeterminate whether to include another entity: the fusion of the class. Now surely if P3 can be violated, then it could be violated in a 'finite' world, a world with only finitely many concrete objects. That would mean that some *numerical sentence* – a sentence asserting that there are exactly n concrete objects, for some finite n – would be indeterminate. But numerical sentences need contain only logical terms and the predicate 'C' for concreteness (a numerical sentence for $n = 2$ is: $\exists x \exists y \, [Cx \, \& \, Cy \, \& \, x \neq y \, \& \, \forall z \, (Cz \to [x = z \vee y = z])])$. Mereological terms are *not* needed to express numerical sentences, and so need not be assumed to lack precisifications.

To support P3, then, I must argue that numerical sentences can never be indeterminate in truth value. First, note that numerical sentences clearly have no syntactic ambiguity. Secondly, note that the concreteness predicate, 'C', presumably has precise application conditions since it was defined by a list of predicates for fundamental ontological kinds that do not admit of borderline cases. And even if one of the members of the list is ill defined or vague in some way, the vagueness is presumably of a kind not relevant to my argument: any way of eliminating the vagueness would suffice for present purposes. So if any numerical sentence is to be indeterminate in truth value, it must be because one of the logical notions is vague.

Accordingly, the argument's crucial assumption about vagueness is that logical words are never a source of vagueness.[9] Any sentence containing only logical expressions, plus perhaps predicates with determinate application conditions (such as 'is concrete'), must be either definitely true or definitely false. This premise is extremely compelling. Logical concepts are paradigm cases of precision. At the very least, in no case is there evident indeterminacy as with 'bald' and 'heap'.

I am inclined to regard my assumption that logic does not generate vagueness as flowing from two further theses, first, the linguistic theory of vagueness outlined above, and secondly, the assumption that logical terms lack multiple precisifications. The first thesis I simply assume; the second I am about to argue for. But all the argument for four-dimensionalism requires is that the assumption holds, whether or not it is justified by these two theses.

It is overwhelmingly plausible that the boolean operators lack precisifications. That leaves the quantifiers and the identity sign.

Might an unrestricted quantifier have precisifications? It is important to be clear that there is no problem at all with *restricted* quantifiers having precisifications. The restricted quantifier 'all persons' will clearly have precisifications because the restricting predicate 'is a person' has precisifications. But this is irrelevant.

If predicates can have precisifications, why not unrestricted quantifiers? The asymmetry is due to the fact that predicates have subclasses of the universal domain of all things as their extensions, and the universal domain has many subclasses. But there seems to be only one 'everything' for the restricted quantifier to range over.

This can be turned into an argument against the possibility of multiple precisifications for the unrestricted quantifier. Imagine there were two expressions, $\forall_1$ and $\forall_2$, which allegedly expressed precisifications of the unrestricted quantifier. $\forall_1$ and $\forall_2$ will need to differ in extension if they are to make any difference to the kinds of sentences under consideration in this section; merely intensional difference will not do. Thus, there must be some thing, x, that is in the extension of one, but not the other, of $\forall_1$ and $\forall_2$. But in that case, whichever of $\forall_1$ and $\forall_2$ lacks x in its extension will fail to be an acceptable precisification of the unrestricted quantifier. It quite clearly is a restricted quantifier since there is something – x – that fails to be in its extension.

This argument is directed only at those who share my assumption of the linguistic theory of vagueness. Those who believe that objecthood itself is somehow vague might resist the step where I concluded that some object is in the extension of one but not the other of $\forall_1$ and $\forall_2$ from the fact that $\forall_1$ and $\forall_2$ differ extensionally. Suppose, for example, that reality definitely contains objects a and b, but that it is indeterminate whether reality contains a third object, c. Somehow it is indeterminate whether c exists, where this is not due to semantic indeterminacy of any kind. The believer in vague objects might then claim that if $\forall_1$ ranges over a and b, and $\forall_2$ over a, b, and c, then even though $\forall_1$ and $\forall_2$ differ extensionally, it is at least not definitely the case that there is something in $\forall_2$ but not $\forall_1$, for it is not definitely the case that c exists. I mention this position only to set it aside; as I said above, I simply assume that this theory of vagueness is *not* correct.

Someone who shares the linguistic theory of vagueness might still attempt to resist this step of the argument. Its conclusion is that *there is* an object, x, in the extension of one of $\forall_1$ and $\forall_2$. But this 'there is', it might be claimed, must be one or another precisification of the unrestricted quantifier. In particular, it will need to be one that includes x. But then it might be argued that it is illegitimate to conclude that $\forall_2$ is not an acceptable precisification for the unrestricted quantifier just because under one of the *other* precisifications there is an object that is not in $\forall_2$'s extension. There is no Archimedean point from which to quantify, and say that $\forall_2$ is a restricted quantifier. All we have are many precisifications, each of which is complete by its own lights.

It is hard to understand what these precisifications are supposed to be. As mentioned above, precisifications for predicates are unproblematic, and should be acceptable to all since everyone admits the existence of the extensions of those precisifications. But what are these precisifications of 'everything'? It might be claimed that existence and objecthood are somehow relative to 'conceptual scheme', and that the precisifications for the quantifiers correspond to different conceptual schemes, or precisifications of conceptual schemes. This comes in tame and wild variants. The tame claim that different conceptual schemes involve different restrictions on quantifiers, is

surely correct, but is irrelevant, concerning as it does merely restricted quantification. The wild claim is that all quantification, no matter how unrestricted, is relative to conceptual scheme. A claim so wild that I will not consider it is that the world is the way it is because we talk in a certain way. A still wild but nevertheless worthy-of-discussion claim is that the world is in a certain way independent of us, but there is no once-and-for-all correct description of it in terms of quantifiers and variables. Any description using such a 'thing-language' presupposes some division of reality into things, but this division may be done in various ways depending on one's conceptual scheme or linguistic framework. Various ways of doing this division count as precisifications of the concept of an object, and hence correspond to precisifications of the quantifiers. I reject this conception of existence for the reasons explained in the introduction [not reproduced in this selection]. I am pre-supposing that existence of things is univocal, not relative to conceptual schemes or linguistic frameworks.

So I reject the idea that unrestricted quantifiers have precisifications. Might the identity predicate have precisifications? On the face of it, the answer is no: the nature of identity seems conceptually simple and clear. Identity *sentences* can clearly have vague truth conditions when they have singular terms that are indeterminate in reference: 'Michael Jordan is identical to the greatest basketball player of all time', for example. But the only singular terms in numerical sentences are variables relative to assignments, which are not indeterminate in reference. There are those who say that even without indeterminate singular terms, and even without precisifications for the identity predicate, identity ascriptions can be vague in truth value, despite the Evans (1978)/ Salmon (1981) argument to the contrary.[10] I find this doctrine obscure but have nothing to add to the extensive literature on this topic; here I must presuppose it false.

In summary, then, the argument for P3 has been as follows. If it could be vague whether composition occurs, this could happen in a finite world; some numerical sentence would then be indeterminate in truth value. But aside from the predicate 'concrete', which is non-vague, numerical sentences contain only logical vocabulary, and logical vocabulary, I say, can never be a source of vagueness.

A loose end must be tied before proceeding to the parallel argument for temporal parts. Defenders of *epistemicism* claim that vagueness never results in indeterminacy of truth value. Imagine removing the hairs from a man, one at a time. According to the epistemicist there will be a single hair whose removal results in the man becoming bald. Even though no one could ever know where it lies, this sharp cut-off for the predicate 'bald' exists.[11] Since epistemicists are already accustomed to accepting sharp cut-offs for predicates like 'heap' and 'bald', one might think they would also be happy with a sharp cut-off in a continuous series of cases of composition, thus rejecting P2. The epistemic theory seems to me incredible despite its current popularity, but set this aside. I will argue that even an epistemicist should accept P2.

As explained in the introduction [not included in this selection], I assume a 'best-candidate' theory of reference and meaning, according to which meaning is determined jointly by 'use and intrinsic eligibility'. Recall the precisifications for the predicate 'bald': *having no more than* n *hairs on one's head*, for various positive integers n. Most of us think there is no fact of the matter as to which of these candidate properties is meant by 'bald'. The reason, I think, is twofold. First, the candidates appear equally intrinsically eligible. Secondly, it also appears that use does not distinguish between the candidates. Despite this, the epistemicist says that 'bald' means exactly one of them. If the epistemicist accepts the best-candidate theory of meaning (and I think he should), he must therefore say either (1) one candidate is more intrinsically eligible, carves nature at the joints better than the rest, thus granting it *metaphysical* privilege, or (2) one candidate fits use better than the rest, thus granting it *semantic* privilege.

The epistemicist should surely prefer option (2).[12] Somehow, something about our meaning-determining behavior singles out one of the many candidate properties to be the meaning of 'bald'. The epistemicist is therefore committed to the existence of bridge laws from use to meaning that are more fine-grained than one might have expected, but at least he avoids the highly implausible metaphysics of option (1). Epistemicism *per se* should not lead us to revisionary metaphysics.

So the epistemicist's sharp cut-offs would not be 'metaphysical'. Instead of corresponding to unexpected joints in reality, they would represent unanticipated powers of humans to draw metaphysically arbitrary lines. They cannot, therefore, be used to give a plausible objection to premise P2 in my argument. Premise P2 says that there are no sharp cut-offs in a continuous series of cases of composition. A sharp cut-off in whether composition occurs would (in a finite world) result in a sharp cut-off in the number of objects, and thus in the truth value of a sentence stated solely in terms of logical terms and the predicate for concreteness. But, as I have argued, there are no multiple candidates to be meant by these terms. So the epistemicist's explanation of sharp cut-offs due to vagueness – as being the result of use selecting among equally eligible candidate meanings – is unavailable in this case.

If, despite this, the epistemicist were to persist in believing in a sharp cut-off, he would need to revert to the metaphysical explanation. The sharp cut-off would represent a 'logical joint' in reality: on the one and only candidate set of meanings for the logical terms (and 'concrete'), at some point on a continuous series of cases of composition there is an abrupt shift in the truth value of a numerical sentence. This sharp cut-off would be starkly metaphysical. As I have claimed, it is very hard to believe in this sort of cut-off – it feels 'metaphysically arbitrary'. Moreover, at this point epistemicism is no longer playing a role in the objection to P2, for even a non-epistemicist will admit that *if* the *metaphysical* cut-off exists, then there is a sharp shift in the truth value of a numerical sentence. The objection to P2, therefore, is not aided by epistemicism, but rather rests on its own metaphysical credentials, which are unimpressive.

The argument for restricted composition, we have seen, leans most heavily on P3, which in turn rests on the view that logic, and in particular unrestricted quantification and identity, are non-vague. This view is attractive, and I have said some things in its defense, but I doubt I have said enough to convince a determined opponent. My argument for unrestricted composition, therefore, should be taken as showing that anyone who accepts that logic is non-vague must also accept unrestricted composition. In the next two sections I show that everyone who shares this assumption about vagueness must also accept four-dimensionalism.

2   Composition Questions and Temporally Indexed Parthood

The argument of the previous section concerned the question of when a given class has a fusion, where 'fusion' was understood atemporally. To avoid begging any questions against my opponents, the argument for temporal parts will be stated using temporally qualified mereological terms (see Ch. 3, Sect. 3 [not reproduced in this selection]). When the relation *being a fusion of* is indexed to times, various questions of composition must then be distinguished.[13]

The simplest question is that of when a given class has a fusion at a given time. But we are also interested in 'diachronic', or 'cross-time' fusions: things that are fusions of different classes at different times. These are objects that gain and lose parts. One concept of cross-time summation may be introduced as follows. Call an 'assignment' any (possibly partial) function that takes one or more times as arguments and assigns non-empty classes of objects that exist at those times as values; and let us say that an object x is a *diachronic fusion* ('D-fusion', for short) of an assignment f iff for every t in f's domain, x is a fusion-at-t of $f(t)$. For example, consider two times at which I exist, and let f be a function with just those two times in its domain that assigns to each the class of subatomic particles that are part of me then. I am a D-fusion of f, since at each of the two times I am a fusion of the corresponding class of subatomic particles.

A second question of composition, then, is the question of when a given assignment has a D-fusion: given various times and various objects corresponding to each, under what conditions will there be some object that at the various times is composed by the corresponding objects? A third question would be that of the conditions under which there would be such an object that existed *only* at the specified times. This is the question of when a given assignment has a *minimal* D-fusion – a D-fusion of the assignment that exists only at times in the assignment's domain. I am not a minimal D-fusion of the assignment f mentioned above because I exist at times other than the two times in the domain of f. To get an assignment of which I am a minimal D-fusion, extend f to assign to any other time at which I exist the class of subatomic particles that are part of me then.

In an intuitive sense, a minimal D-fusion of some objects at various times consists of those objects at those times and nothing more. Though it required some machinery to state, the question of which assignments have minimal D-fusions is far from being remote and technical. Indeed, we can restate this question in the following woolly yet satisfying fashion: *under what conditions do objects begin and cease to exist?* Suppose we make a model of a park bench from three toy blocks, b_1, b_2, and b_3, by placing one on top of two of the others at time t_1; a few minutes later at t_2 we separate the blocks. Is there something that we brought into existence at the first time and destroyed at the second? This is the question of whether a certain assignment has a minimal D-fusion – namely, the assignment that assigns the class $\{b_1, b_2, b_3\}$ to every time between t_1 and t_2.

3   The Argument from Vagueness for Four-Dimensionalism

Under what conditions does a given assignment have a minimal D-fusion? I say that all assignments have minimal D-fusions; my argument is parallel to the argument for unrestricted composition. Restricting when minimal D-fusions exist would require a cut-off in some continuous series of pairwise similar cases. Just as composition can never be vague, neither can minimal D-fusion. So the cut-off would need to be abrupt, which is implausible:

P1′:   If not every assignment has a minimal D-fusion, then there must be a pair of cases connected by a 'continuous series' such that in one, minimal D-fusion occurs, but in the other, minimal D-fusion does not occur.

P2′:   In no continuous series is there a sharp cut-off in whether minimal D-fusion occurs.

P3′:   In any case of minimal D-fusion, either minimal D-fusion definitely occurs, or minimal D-fusion definitely does not occur.

The notion of a 'case' must be adjusted in the obvious way. A 'continuous series of cases' will now vary in all respects thought to be relevant to whether a given assignment has a minimal D-fusion, including spatial adjacency, qualitative similarity, and causal relations at the various times in the assignment, as well as the beginning and cessation of these factors at various times of the assignment.

The justification of premise P1′ is like that for P1. Like P1, P1′ can be resisted by a nihilist, who rejects the existence of all composites. For the nihilist, only mereological simples exist; there are no composite objects. The only cases of minimal D-fusion concern the entire lifetime of a single particle; such cases cannot be connected continuously with cases in which minimal D-fusion does not take place.[14] Arguments against nihilism must wait until Chapter 5, Section 6 [not reproduced here]. As for P2′, an abrupt cut-off in a continuous series of cases of minimal D-fusion – a pair of cases *extremely* similar in spatial adjacency, causal relations, and so on, but definitely differing in whether minimal D-fusion occurs – seems initially implausible. There is, however, a three-dimensionalist ontology that would secure such a cut-off: a version of mereological essentialism according to which, intuitively, nothing exists but mereological sums, which have their parts permanently, and exist as long as those parts exist. Minimal D-fusions could be restricted non-vaguely: an assignment has a minimal D-fusion, roughly, when and only when it is the temporally longest assignment for a given fixed class of objects. The idea is that mereological fusions of objects 'automatically' come into existence when their parts do, automatically retain those same parts, and automatically go out of existence when any of those parts go out of existence. (Less roughly: where S_1 and S_2 are sets of objects that exist at times t_1 and t_2, respectively, say that pairs $<t_1, S_1>$ and $<t_2, S_2>$ are *equivalent* iff every part-at-t_1 of any member of S_1 overlaps-at-t_2 some member of S_2, and every part-at-t_2 of any member of S_2 overlaps-at-t_1 some member of S_1. The idea is that S_1 and S_2 contain, if not exactly the same members, at least the same stuff, just divided up differently. The non-vague restriction is that an assignment f has a minimal D-fusion iff f is a maximal equivalence-interrelated assignment; that is (construing f as a class of pairs), iff (1) every two pairs in f are equivalent, and (2) if a pair $<t, S>$ is equivalent to some member of f, then some pair $<t, S′>$ (i.e. some pair with the

same time) to which it is equivalent is a member of f.) My argument can therefore be resisted by this sort of mereologist.[15] Other arguments can be given against mereological essentialism; see Chapter 5, Section 7 [not reproduced here].

Just as topological restrictions on regions of space can provide precise restrictions on composition (although I find them unmotivated), topological restrictions on regions of time can provide precise restrictions on minimal D-fusion. Some may favor a restriction to continuous intervals (although cf. Hirsch's 1982: 22 ff. example of a watch that is taken apart for repairs), or to sums of continuous intervals. I regard each as unmotivated, but we need not quarrel. Given either restriction, the argument would still establish a restricted version of four-dimensionalism according to which there exist continuous temporal segments of arbitrarily small duration. For most four-dimensionalists that would be four-dimensionalism enough.

My argument for P3 was that if it is indeterminate whether composition occurs then it will be indeterminate how many objects there are, which is impossible. I use a similar argument to establish P3′. Indeterminacy in minimal D-fusion might be claimed in several situations. But in each case, I will argue, at some possible world there would result 'count indeterminacy' – an indeterminacy in the finite number of concrete objects. This was argued above to be impossible, assuming that logic is not a possible source of vagueness. (Recall the distinction between existence-at and quantification. Count indeterminacy is indeterminacy in how many objects *there are*, not merely in how many objects *exist at* some specified time. It is the former that my assumption about logic prohibits, and hence the former that I must argue would result from indeterminacy in minimal D-fusion.)

I distinguish four situations in which indeterminacy in minimal D-fusion might be claimed:

1 Indeterminacy in whether objects have a fusion at a given time, because (say) they are moderately scattered at that time. This would result in count indeterminacy. For consider a possible world containing some finite number of quarks that are greatly scattered at all times except for a single time, t, at which they are moderately scattered. The quarks would then determinately lack a fusion except

at time t, when it would be indeterminate whether they have a fusion. The result is indeterminacy in how many objects exist: there is one more object depending on whether the quarks have a fusion at t. (Similar remarks would apply if 'scattered' in this paragraph were replaced by various other predicates deemed relevant to the question of whether a class has a fusion at a given time.)

2 Indeterminacy in whether a fusion at t of certain particles is identical to a fusion at some other time, t', of some other particles. This, too, would result in count indeterminacy. Suppose I undergo amnesia in such a way that we feel indeterminacy in whether 'Young Man Ted is identical to Old Man Sider' is true. Presumably we will want to say the same thing about this case if it occurs in a world with only finitely many concrete things. But in this world, if it is really indeterminate whether a certain assignment has a minimal D-fusion (say, one that assigns to times before and after amnesia all my parts at those times), then there will result indeterminacy in the count of the concrete objects there, for if the identity holds there will be one less object than if the identity does not hold.

3 Indeterminacy in when an object begins to exist. Again, this would result in count indeterminacy. Suppose that in some case, C, it is indeterminate when a certain statue comes into existence. Consider next a case much like C, but in which (i) only finitely many concrete things exist, and (ii) the molecules that would make up the statue are all annihilated after the time at which the statue is alleged to indeterminately exist. Then it will be indeterminate whether the statue exists at all, and hence indeterminate how many things there are in the world in question.

4 Indeterminacy in when an object ceases existing. This case is similar to the previous case.

If, then, minimal D-fusion could be indeterminate, it could be indeterminate what the (finite) number of concrete things is. But then there could be a numerical sentence that is neither definitely true nor definitely false. Assuming that no indeterminacy can issue from logic, this is impossible.

So P3′ is true: a given assignment must either definitely have or definitely lack a minimal D-fusion. This is not to say that the phenomena adduced in (1) to (4) are not genuine; they simply must be understood in some way not implying indeterminacy in minimal D-fusion: (1) The indeterminacy is due to indeterminate restrictions on everyday quantification. Typically, we do not quantify over all the objects that there are, only over fusions of objects that are not too scattered. If objects are borderline scattered they still definitely have a fusion, but we have a borderline resistance to admitting that fusion into an everyday domain of quantification. (2) This is a case involving three objects. Object 1 begins around the time of my birth and ends at the amnesia, Object 2 begins at amnesia and lasts until my death, and Object 3 lasts throughout this time interval. The name 'Young Man Ted' is indeterminate in reference between Objects 1 and 3; the name 'Old Man Sider' is indeterminate between Objects 2 and 3; hence the identity sentence is indeterminate in truth value. (3) There are many objects involved differing in when they begin to exist; the term 'the statue' is indeterminate in reference among them; hence the sentence 'The statue begins to exist at t' will be indeterminate in truth value for certain values of 't'. Case (4) is similar to (3).

P1′, P2′, and P3′ jointly imply:

(U) every assignment has a minimal D-fusion.

But (U) is a powerful claim, for it entails four-dimensionalism! The central four-dimensionalist claim is that every object, x, has a temporal part at every moment, t, at which it exists. Let A be the assignment with only t in its domain that assigns $\{x\}$ to t. (U) guarantees the existence of an object, z, that is a minimal D-fusion of A. It may now be shown that z is a temporal part of x at t. I do so by showing that z satisfies clauses (1) to (3) of our earlier definition of a temporal part: x is an instantaneous temporal part of y at instant $t =_{df}$ (1) x exists at, but only at, t; (2) x is part of y at t; and (3) x overlaps at t everything that is part of y at t.[16]

1 z is a fusion of $\{x\}$ at t. It follows from the definition of 'fusion at t' that every part of z at t overlaps x at t; by (PO), z *is part of* x at t.[17]

2 Since z is a *minimal* D-fusion of this assignment, z *exists at but only at* t.

3 Let y be any part of x at t. Since z is a fusion of $\{x\}$ at t, x is part of z at t; thus, y is part of z at t; thus, z overlaps y at t. So: z *overlaps at* t *every part of* x *at* t.

A few people have objected in conversation that the conclusion of the argument, (U), does not entail four-dimensionalism. A thing-event dualist, for example, might say that the objects guaranteed by (U) are temporal parts of events, not of continuants. These events would spatially coincide with continuants, but the continuants would nevertheless endure. This objection is a mistake. Line (1) of the argument shows that z is a *part* of x at t, not merely spatially coincident with x. So x could not be an enduring thing, given (U) – at any moment it (and every other object as well) would have an instantaneous part that overlaps all its parts.

An interesting feature of the argument from vagueness is that it forces one into taking an extreme position in the philosophy of persistence. Take on board the claim that minimal D-fusion can never be vague, and reject as well the existence of a sharp cut-off in a continuous series of cases of composition. What is out at this point are moderate views, such as those of David Wiggins and Michael Burke, who admit minimal D-fusion in cases that match up with ordinary intuition, and even Peter van Inwagen, who admits minimal D-fusion only in the case of living things. The only views left open seem to be nihilism, mereological essentialism, and four-dimensionalism. Each gives a non-vague answer to the question of when minimal D-fusions exist and is thereby unaffected by the argument. I discuss each in the next chapter and argue that four-dimensionalism is the most attractive of the three.

4 On the usual terminology, a mereological atom is the fusion of its unit class; let us understand 'continuous series connecting cases C_1 and C_2' as excluding 'cases' involving only one atom.

5 I thank Earl Conee for this observation.

6 See, however, Markosian (1998).

7 I thank John G. Bennett for helpful observations here. Another precise restriction of fusions, to classes that are sets, seems unmotivated (and of little consequence even if adopted).

8 See e.g. Dummett (1978: 260) (although see Dummett 1981: 440); Fine (1975); Russell (1923).

9 Cf. also Fine (1975: 267, 274–5).

10 See Lewis (1988b); Parsons (1987); Pelletier (1989); Thomason (1982); van Inwagen (1990, ch. 18).

11 See e.g. Sorensen (1988: 217–52), and Williamson (1994).

12 Williamson (1994, sect. 7.5) prefers option (2).

13 See Simons (1987: 183 ff.) and Thomson (1983: 216–17 [pp. 488–9 in the present volume]).

14 More carefully, for the nihilist, an assignment A has a minimal D-fusion iff for some simple, x, A's domain is the set of times at which x exists and A assigns to any such time $\{x\}$.

15 A variant of mereological essentialism would also secure precise cut-offs. According to both mereological essentialism and this variant, if x is ever part of y then whenever x and y both exist, x must be part of y. The mereological essentialist adds that x must exist and be part of y whenever y exists, whereas the variant adds instead that y must exist and contain x as a part whenever x exists. The variant allows a thing to survive the destruction of one of its parts. The criticisms of mereological essentialism in Ch. 5. Sect. 7 [not reproduced] apply to this variant as well.

16 See my *Four-Dimensionalism* (2001; pb edn. Oxford: Oxford University Press, 2003), ch. 3, sect. 2 for further discussion.

17 (PO) is a temporally relativized version of a principle normally called "strong supplementation": If x and y exist at t, but x is not part of y at t, then x has some part at t that does not overlap y at t.

Notes

1 An earlier version of this argument was given in Sider (1997). Compare Quine (1981: 10) and Heller (1990, ch. 2, sect. 9).

2 Actually, the special composition question is slightly different, since it concerns when fusion takes place *at* a given time; see van Inwagen (1990, ch. 2).

3 Thanks to David Cowles and Ned Markosian here. See Markosian (1998).

References

Dummett, Michael. 1981. *The Interpretation of Frege's Philosophy* (London: Duckworth).

Dummett, Michael. 1978. *Truth and Other Enigmas* (London: Duckworth).

Evans, Gareth. 1978. 'Can there be Vague Objects?' *Analysis*, 38: 208 [ch. 12 in the present volume].

Fine, Kit. 1975. 'Vagueness, Truth and Logic', *Synthese*, 30: 265–300.

Heller, Mark. 1990. *The Ontology of Physical Objects: Four Dimensional Hunks of Matter* (Cambridge: Cambridge University Press).

Hirsch, Eli. 1982. *The Concept of Identity* (Oxford: Oxford University Press).

Lewis, David. 1988. 'Vague Identity: Evans Misunderstood', *Analysis*, 48: 128–30.

Lewis, David. 1986. *On the Plurality of Worlds* (Oxford: Basil Blackwell).

Markosian, Ned. 1998. 'Brutal Composition'. *Philosophical Studies*, 92: 211–49.

Parsons, Terence. 1987. 'Entities without Identity', in James Tomberlin, ed., *Philosophical Perspectives*, 1, *Metaphysics* (Atascadero, Calif.: Ridgeview Publishing Company).

Pelletier, Francis Jeffry. 1989. 'Another Argument against Vague Objects', *Journal of Philosophy*, 86: 481–92.

Quine, W. V. O. 1981. *Theories and Things* (Cambridge, Mass.: Harvard University Press).

Russell, Bertrand. 1923. 'Vagueness', *Australasian Journal of Philosophy and Psychology*, 1: 84–92. Repr.

in Rosanna Keefe and Peter Smith, eds., *Vagueness: A Reader* (Cambridge, Mass.: MIT Press, 1996), 61–8.

Salmon, Nathan U. 1981. *Reference and Essence* (Princeton: Princeton University Press).

Sider, Theodore. 1997. 'Four-Dimensionalism', *Philosophical Review*, 106: 197–231.

Simons, Peter. 1987. *Parts: A Study in Ontology* (Oxford: Oxford University Press).

Sorensen, Roy A. 1988. *Blindspots* (Oxford: Clarendon Press).

Thomason, Richard, 1982. 'Identity and Vagueness', *Philosophical Studies*, 42: 329–32.

Thomson, Judith Jarvis. 1983. 'Parthood and Identity Across Time', *Journal of Philosophy*, 80: 201–20 [ch. 35 in the present volume].

van Inwagen, Peter. 1990. *Material Beings* (Ithaca, NY: Cornell University Press).

Williamson, Timothy. 1994. *Vagueness* (London: Routledge).

51

Epiphenomenalism and Eliminativism

Trenton Merricks

Consider the following argument about an alleged baseball causing atoms arranged window-wise to scatter, or, for ease of exposition, causing 'the shattering of a window'.[1]

> (1) The baseball – if it exists – is causally irrelevant to whether its constituent atoms, acting in concert, cause the shattering of the window.
>
> (2) The shattering of the window is caused by those atoms, acting in concert.
>
> (3) The shattering of the window is not overdetermined.
>
> Therefore,
>
> (4) If the baseball exists, it does not cause the shattering of the window.

Overdetermination [handwritten margin note]

The rest of this chapter will, in one way or another, involve this argument, which I shall call 'the Overdetermination Argument'. I shall begin by defending its validity, and then proceed to explicate, and defend the truth of, each of its premisses. I shall conclude by arguing that the moral of the Overdetermination Argument is the truth of eliminativism.[2]

I The Causal Principle

Suppose some individuals, such as the members of an unruly mob, cause the vandalism of a park. Suppose also that the vandalism of the park is not overdetermined. And, finally, suppose that I am 'causally irrelevant' to whether those members cause the vandalism.

This final supposition invites me to explain '*causal irrelevance*'. Causal irrelevance, as I shall understand it, amounts to exactly four things. Those four things, applied to this particular case, are as follows. First, I am not myself one of the members. Second, I am not a 'partial cause' of the vandalism alongside the members; that is, it is not the case that only when combined with my additional causal contribution do the members cause the vandalism. Third, I am not an intermediate in a causal chain between the members and the vandalism; that is, the members do not cause the vandalism by causing me to do something by which I, more proximately, cause the vandalism. And, finally, I do not cause any of the members to cause the vandalism.[3]

It should be clear, given the above suppositions, that I do not cause the park to be vandalized. And

Trenton Merricks, "Epiphenomenalism and Eliminativism," in *Objects and Persons* (Oxford: Oxford University Press, 2001), ch. 3. Reproduced by permission.

Metaphysics: An Anthology, Second Edition. Edited by Jaegwon Kim, Daniel Z. Korman and Ernest Sosa.

that I do not cause the vandalism is the result of the following general (and so implicitly universally quantified) principle:

Causal Principle. Suppose: O is an object. The *x*s are objects. O is causally irrelevant to whether the *x*s, acting in concert, cause a certain effect E (i.e. O is not one of the *x*s, O is not a partial cause of E alongside the *x*s, none of the *x*s cause O to cause E, and O does not cause any of the *x*s to cause E). The *x*s, acting in concert, do cause E. And E is not overdetermined. It follows from all this that O does not cause E.

In this principle, and in the Overdetermination Argument, *overdetermination* is understood in the most literal, straightforward, and natural sense possible. An effect is overdetermined if the following are true: that effect is caused by an object; that object is causally irrelevant to whether some other – i.e. numerically distinct – object or objects cause that effect; and the other object or objects do indeed cause that effect. Given this understanding of overdetermination, the Causal Principle is obviously and demonstrably true.

The Causal Principle is true. As noted above, the Causal Principle implies that I do not cause the park to be vandalized. More interestingly, the Causal Principle implies that the Overdetermination Argument – given how I understand overdetermination in that argument – is valid.

Some will object that I have ignored the fact that, while I stand in *no* salient relations to the mobsters, the baseball is *composed of* the atoms. Because of this fact, they will object, even if a baseball caused an effect also caused by its atoms, it would not overdetermine that effect. Or, better, they will object that although the baseball would 'overdetermine' that effect in the sense of overdetermination I explained above, there is nothing troubling about such 'overdetermination'.

This objection must be addressed. But not here. For any objection along these lines is an objection to neither the Causal Principle nor the validity of the Overdetermination Argument. Such an objection is – as we shall see – an objection to premiss (3) of the Overdetermination Argument. And so I shall delay responding to that objection until I defend that premiss. With this point clarified, there should be no doubt that, as I intend

them to be understood, the Causal Principle is true and the Overdetermination Argument valid.

II   Atomic Causation

(1)   The baseball – if it exists – is causally irrelevant to whether its constituent atoms, acting in concert, cause the shattering of the window.

Suppose that the atoms working in concert only 'partially' caused the window's shattering. Suppose further that the 'full' cause included, alongside and in addition to the work of the atoms, the work of the baseball itself. Then (1) would be false. But the baseball and the atoms are not – according to anyone – relevantly analogous to two rocks jointly shattering the window, either one of which alone could not do so. For while two rocks can do more work than one, a baseball and its constituent atoms cannot do any more than those atoms all by themselves.[4]

Suppose the atoms arranged baseballwise caused the shattering of the window by causing the ball to shatter the window. Then (1) would be false. But there is not a causal chain, starting with the atoms working in concert and ending with the shattering, which includes as an intermediary the work of the baseball. Even if the baseball caused the shattering, its doing so would not be akin to its being the middle domino in a row of three, the domino whose falling allows the first to cause the last to fall.

Or so I say. And I think almost everyone would agree. But suppose that someone claimed that the way the baseball's atoms were at an earlier time caused the baseball, at a later time, to shatter the window. This stays within the pale just so long as he adds that the way the atoms were at the earlier time *also* caused the baseball's atoms to shatter the window at the later time.

Such an argument implies that the baseball, with respect to the shattering of the window, is causally redundant; it merely overdetermines the work of its atoms. And any (even somewhat) plausible way of defending the 'middle domino' objection to (1) requires this sort of systematic overdetermination. As I argue in defence of (3), we should resist just this kind of systematic causal overdetermination. If that argument is sound, then this objection to (1) can be blocked. On the other hand, if what I say in defense of (3) is mistaken and (3) turns out to be false, the Overdetermination Argument is sunk anyway and so this objection doesn't matter. So I shall ignore this objection in what follows.

The final point in defence of (1) is that the baseball does not cause the 'actions' of any of the atoms arranged ballwise. This rejection of 'downward' causation is part of the 'scientific attitude' and 'bottom-up' metaphysics, according to which the final and complete causal stories will involve only the entities over which physics quantifies. Of course, it is controversial whether everything conforms to a bottom-up metaphysics – I'll deny that humans do – but I think few would resist taking the 'scientific attitude' towards, and applying a bottom-up metaphysics to, baseballs (if baseballs exist in the first place).

One might object that while some sorts of 'downward causation' are forbidden by a bottom-up metaphysics of baseballs, not all are. Specifically, one might say, such a metaphysics permits the way a baseball is at one time to cause its atoms to do something at a later time – and so permits downward causation – just as long as those atoms' doing that something at the later time also has a complete causal explanation *wholly in terms of the microphysical*. (Otherwise, as will become clear in the defense of premise (2), the baseball would have 'emergent' causal powers.) Thus – and this is essentially the same sort of move we considered in defence of the 'middle domino' objection – one might claim that bottom-up metaphysics allows downward causation if and only if downward causation *merely overdetermines* microphysical causation, if and only if it is merely redundant.

The only sort of downward causation even arguably consistent with the bottom-up metaphysics of baseballs – and so the only sort that can plausibly generate an objection to premiss (1) – implies systematic causal overdetermination. As noted above, in response to the 'middle domino' objection, I shall argue against systematic overdetermination below. For now, I shall assume that no such over-determination occurs and ignore any objections, including the one just raised, that require it.

Baseballs do not exercise downward causation upon their atoms. Nor is a baseball an inter-mediary in a causal chain, bridging the work of its

atoms to the shattering of the window. Nor is a baseball a partial cause, alongside its atoms, of the window's shattering. These three points above are what it is (given, obviously, that the baseball is not itself one of the atoms) for the baseball to be causally irrelevant to whether its atoms shatter the window. Given my understanding of causal irrelevance, we should be able to see that (1) is true, even uncontroversially so.

(2) The shattering of the window is caused by those atoms acting in concert.

Premise (2) seems obviously correct. After all, each of the window-striking atoms causes *some-thing*. And when you put what one atom causes together with what another causes, and so on for each of the atoms arranged baseballwise, it seems like the cumulative effect must be the shattering of the window.

Suppose someone denied (2) and claimed that our imagined shattering is caused, not by atoms, but by the baseball. He must claim, then, that the baseball causes something that its parts, working in concert, do not. I suppose his idea must be that the baseball causes things in virtue of having some sort of causally efficacious 'emergent' property.[5]

C. D. Broad questioned the assumption of 'Mechanism', the assumption that *every* composite object is causally redundant because it is related to its parts as a clock is to its 'springs, wheels, pendulum, etc.' (1925: 60). But we can oppose the above objection just so long as, were there clocks (or baseballs), they'd be related to some of their parts as a clock is related to its springs, wheels, pendulum, etc. That is, we can oppose the above objection just so long as truly non-redundant causal properties – properties that would allow an object to cause what its parts do not – do not 'emerge' *at the level of artefacts*.[6] And so even opponents of full-blown Mechanism (or full-blown bottom-up metaphysics) should oppose the above objection. For even they should agree that everything a baseball causes is caused by its parts at some level of decomposition.

Any objection to (2) that insists that the baseball – but not its parts – causes the window to shatter is mistaken. For any such objection implies the false claim that baseballs have 'emergent' causal powers. Nevertheless, I'll respond to two more objections of this sort. We

question for lecture on monday

have just seen one reason these objections fail. I'll point out further problems with them below.

The Overdetermination Argument shows that *if* the atoms shattered the window, *then* the baseball did not. So, one might object, since baseballs shatter windows, their constituent atoms do not. In response, no matter what we decide to say about the window's shattering, there will be some things that the atoms seem to cause for which the baseball cannot account. Imagine, for example, the causal effects of the atoms before, or after, they (allegedly) compose the baseball (or, for that matter, when they compose nothing at all). But the converse does not hold. That is, everything that is allegedly caused by a baseball can be accounted for by the work of the atoms that compose it at various times. This asymmetry gives us strong reason, when forced to choose, to favour the causal powers of the atoms over those of the baseball.

Suppose one tried to resist this asymmetry. Suppose one argued that whatever seems to be caused by the parts of the baseball is instead – somehow – caused by the baseball itself. In § IV I'll argue that 'epiphenomenal' material objects ought to be eliminated. Thus rendering the baseball's alleged parts causally inefficacious implies that the baseball is a simple. The claim that atoms arranged baseballwise fail to compose a baseball might be hard to swallow. But it goes down like draught Guinness compared to the claim that baseballs are simples.

Here is a second objection to premiss (2). Just as the baseball is not identical with its constituent atoms, so the shattering of the *window* is not identical with the many scatterings of the *atoms arranged windowwise*. Suppose, then, that the scatterings of the atoms are caused by the atoms arranged ballwise but the shattering of the window is caused by the baseball. This would give us distinct effects with distinct causes, allowing the ball to shatter and the atoms to scatter and neither to overdetermine the work of the other.

There are two important things to note about this objection. First, this objection requires a shift in terminology. Up to this point I have been using 'the shattering of the window' as a plural referring expression, referring to the many scatterings. This objection requires that we now use it as a name of a single, composite event. So let us do so for the remainder of this section.

Second, the 'non-identity' crucial to this objection is *not* between the (single) event of the scattering of the atoms and the (single) event of the shattering of the window. The first event – if it existed – would be identical with the second (cf. Kim 1998: 83–7). For 'the scattering of atoms' would be just another description, a 'micro-description', of the shattering of the window.

There is however, a lack of identity between the shattering of the window and the many events such as this atom's heading thataway and that atom's heading thisaway, and so on, for each of the atoms formerly arranged windowwise. Let us refer to those many events collectively as the 'multiple scatterings', being careful to remember that 'multiple scatterings' refers to many events, not to a single event composed of those many events. Given our rejection of composition as identity, the multiple scatterings cannot be identical with the shattering of the window that they allegedly compose.[7] They are many; it – assuming there is such a composite event – is one.

My response to this second objection to (2) begins by noting that the atoms arranged baseballwise have *multiple* effects, namely the multiple scatterings. And so the most reasonable thing to say is that the atoms' multiple effects include, in addition to the multiple scatterings, the shattering of the window. Moreover, the multiple scatterings *compose* the window's shattering. With this in mind, consider the following:

If some objects cause events $v_1 \ldots v_n$ and $v_1 \ldots v_n$ compose event V, then those objects cause V.

This principle, which I think is correct, implies that if the atoms cause the multiple scatterings, and if there is a composite event of the window's shattering, then the atoms cause that composite event.[8]

This completes my discussion of objections to premiss (2) that require the baseball to cause things its parts do not. But there is a very different sort of objection to premiss (2) – the premiss claiming that the shattering of the window is caused by the atoms arranged baseballwise – worth addressing. This is the objection that only events, not atoms or any other objects, cause things to happen. Now this 'objection' is most plausibly interpreted as merely reminding us that the sense in which events cause things differs from, and is perhaps more basic than, the sense in which objects cause things. But this reminder has no adverse implications for (2). Indeed, a fundamental distinction between event-causation and object-causation strengthens the arguments of this chapter (see §III).

Of course, we could interpret this objection as the claim that there is *no sense* in which objects cause things. This claim implies that (2) is flat-out false. (It also implies that the conclusion of the Overdetermination Argument is flat-out true.) But this claim is mistaken. Consider that however the details may vary, virtually all accounts of perception agree that an object can be perceived only if it causes something.[9] Moreover, recall the familiar charge that, because abstracta would not have causal powers, they simply do not exist. Those who endorse this charge might be inclined to defend Samuel Alexander's principle, called 'Alexander's dictum' by Jaegwon Kim (1993*a*): to be real is to have causal powers.

The point here is not to defend some particular account of perception, Alexander's dictum, or attacks on abstract objects rooted in their alleged causal inertness. The point is that the presence of these views on the philosophical playing field is ample evidence that philosophers generally – and correctly – assume that entities other than events, such as objects, cause things.

Now one might, in light of all the reasons above, accept the truth of (2), yet still be bothered by it. For one might find (2) to be an odd premiss in an argument whose conclusion is that a baseball does not cause a window to shatter. For one might think that, though a baseball is not identical with its atoms, its causing something is nevertheless analyzed as its atoms' (or other parts') causing that same thing. Thus one might object that (2) is simply *another way of saying* that the baseball causes the window to shatter.

This objection does not have the makings of an objection to the truth of (2). Nor, for that matter, will it generate an objection to the truth of (1) or the validity of the Overdetermination Argument. (It doesn't touch the validity of the Over-determination Argument because it doesn't bring into question the Causal Principle.) So in so far as we have here an objection to the soundness of the Overdetermination Argument, it is – perhaps somewhat surprisingly – actually an objection to

premiss (3). And so I shall address this objection in the next section.

III Causal Overdetermination

(3) The shattering of the window is not overdetermined.

Consider a substance dualist (like Mills 1996) who, conceding causal closure of the physical, says that mental events cause physical events only by overdetermining the effects of physical causes. Pre-theoretically, that's an ugly picture. The redundancy is *all by itself* a reason to resist this form of substance dualism. More generally, we always have a reason to resist systematic causal overdetermination, along with any view that implies it.

As I shall explain later, the reasoning behind the Overdetermination Argument quickly generalizes to apply to more than (alleged) baseballs and to more than the shattering of a window. Thus one who responds to the Overdetermination Argument by rejecting (3) must – assuming she wants to save the causal power of more than baseballs – embrace overdetermination in a wide variety of cases. But we should resist widespread and systematic causal overdetermination. And so I think it is most reasonable to endorse (3).

Some will disagree. Some will reply that while *certain kinds* of systematic overdetermination are surely objectionable and to be resisted, over-determination of the sort at issue here – of the sort denied by (3) – is not. For this objection to be principled, our objector must have in mind some principled way to distinguish objectionable overdetermination from the unobjectionable. I'll consider different ways one might draw such a distinction.

To begin to understand the most plausible way of drawing such a distinction, and thus the most serious objection to (3), consider the following claim: an effect is pseudo-overdetermined if it is caused by an object and caused by the event in which that object participates. This claim implies that a window's shattering is pseudo-overdetermined if it is caused by a baseball and caused by the baseball's striking the window. But, I reply, *what it is* for a baseball – if baseballs exist – to shatter a window is for it to participate in a window-shattering event. So, I say, pseudo-overdetermined is *not* overdetermination. Thus, I conclude, any objections one might have to systematic overdetermination should give rise to no objections to systematic pseudo-overdetermination.

Likewise, one might object, *what it is* for the baseball to shatter the window is for its parts – such as its atoms – to shatter the window. (This returns us to the objection raised at the very end of the last section.) So, the objection continues, the sort of 'overdetermination' opposed by premiss (3) is not real overdetermination. It is, instead, like pseudo-overdetermination. As a result, one might conclude, any scruples we have about real systematic overdetermination do not support denying the occurrence of 'overdetermination' denied by (3).

This objection assumes that the overdetermination at issue in (3) is analogous to pseudo-overdetermination. Its central assumption is that a baseball's causing something *just is* its parts causing that same thing. The first step towards seeing that this objection's central assumption is mistaken – and so towards seeing that the objection itself fails – is to consider the following:

Object O's causing an effect E *is analyzed as* O's participating in the appropriate way in an event that causes E.

Nothing turns on the details of this analysis, which is purposefully short on detail. All that matters is that in this analysis – as in *any* analysis of object-causation in terms of event-causation – *causation* appears in both analysandum and analysans. If any such analysis is to have a hope of being correct, it must not be blatantly circular. If it is not circular, then the kind of causation exercised by objects must not be the kind exercised by events. And it is quite plausible that we have different 'kinds' of causation here. To see why, it may be useful to think in terms of metaphysical categories. The causation exercised by events, since events differ categorically from objects, is only *analogically related* to the causation exercised by objects.

The above analysis can survive challenges based on circularity. For object-causation and event-causation are distinct, but interanalysed, phenomena. Again, objects and events do not do the same kind of causal work. On the other hand,

a baseball and its constituent atoms, all being objects, do the same kind of causal work. Thus an analysis of one's causing in terms of the others' causing is bound to be circular. And so any such analysis ought to be abandoned right from the start.

I suppose one might object that the analysis of a composite's causing something in terms of its parts' causing that same thing avoids circularity because 'composite-causation' and 'part-causation' are distinct kinds of causation. This objection is mistaken. As noted above, there is a significant difference between an event's causing something and an object's causing something. But there does not seem to be the same kind or degree of difference between a big object's causing something and a smaller object's causing something, even if the smaller is part of the bigger. Parts of objects and the objects they compose seem to be in the same category – object – and for that reason presumably cause things in the same sense.

And there is another problem with saying that the sense in which composites cause things is distinct from the sense in which their parts cause things. This problem stems from some composites' being themselves parts of other, bigger, composites. For the following sort of claim seems unacceptable: an atom composite-causes an effect and, when part of something else, part-causes that same effect, although these are metaphysically different kinds of causation. I suppose one might try to avoid such claims by insisting that only simples can be parts. But that too seems unacceptable. It is certainly unacceptable to anyone whose ultimate aim is to defend folk ontology, since folk ontology embraces objects with composite parts.

So here is what I conclude thus far. One can plausibly insist that *what it is* for a baseball to shatter a window is for it to participate in a window-shattering event. But one cannot plausibly insist that *what it is* for a baseball to shatter a window is for its constituent atoms to shatter it. Because an object's causing something is not analysed as its parts causing something, the overdetermination denied by premiss (3) is *not* like pseudo-overdetermination. It is real overdetermination.

We can look at essentially the same point in this way. Because an object and an event do not do the same kind of causal work, one cannot redundantly duplicate the work of the other so as to result in overdetermination. But a(n alleged) baseball and its atoms, all being objects, do the same kind of causal work. So if they all caused the same effect – like the shattering of the window – the baseball would thereby redundantly duplicate the work of its atoms. And so the baseball and the atoms would really overdetermine that effect.

I suspect that most who were initially inclined to resist (3) were inclined to do so because the overdetermination (3) opposes seemed to be on a par with the totally innocuous pseudo-overdetermination. But now we know that the overdetermination (3) opposes is not remotely like pseudo-overdetermination. This undermines the primary opposition to (3). Indeed, it provides positive support for (3). For just as the alleged analogy between pseudo-overdetermination and overdetermination by an object and its parts supported denying (3), so the actual disanalogy speaks forcefully in (3)'s favour.

Some might still insist that systematic overdetermination by an object and its parts is not objectionable. Of course, they cannot claim to do so on the grounds that such overdetermination is not genuine. It is genuine. But perhaps they will defend the following argument. The true moral of this chapter thus far is that, like it or not, composition is possible only given overdetermination of the very sort premiss (3) denies. Since, necessarily, to be composite is to be causally redundant, this argument continues, to object to systematic overdetermination by composita is simply to object to *what it is* (in part) to be composite. But composition as such is not objectionable. Therefore, etc.

This argument is unsound. For to be composite is *not*, in its very nature, to be causally redundant, to overdetermine systematically. As I shall argue in the next chapter [not included here], there are composite objects that are not causally redundant. It is a peculiarity of some (alleged) composita, rather than an inevitable result of composition as such, that they are wholly causally redundant. (This gives us another reason to deny that a composite's causing something is *analysed as* its parts' causing that same thing. For, obviously enough, that analysis is inconsistent with a composite's failing to be causally redundant (and thus causing something its parts do not).)

Opponents of (3) might argue in the following way. Genuine and systematic overdetermination

is not objectionable if the overdetermining causes are not 'wholly separate'. The baseball is not wholly separate from its atoms. So we should not resist the claim that the baseball and its atoms overdetermine the shattering.

I think this objection fails. For I reject its claim about what kinds of systematic overdetermination are objectionable. And so do others. Consider a well-known argument in the philosophy of mind. This argument's cornerstone is that mental properties' systematically overdetermining the effects of physical properties would be objectionable (Kim 1989a, b; see also Malcolm 1968). Yet according to this argument, mental properties supervene on the very physical properties whose effects are in question (much as an alleged baseball supervenes on its atoms [...]). The overdetermination this argument targets as objectionable would be the work of entities that are not wholly separate.

I suppose one could deny (3) on the grounds that overdetermination by a baseball and its atoms is not objectionable. This is hardly principled. Nor is there much improvement in the claim – perhaps this is what was behind the 'wholly separate' objection above – that overdetermination by an object and its proper parts is not objectionable. For this claim is tailor-made to resist a premiss like (3). And this claim loses its initial plausibility, I believe, in light of the conclusions noted above. I have in mind here especially the conclusion that an object's causing an effect cannot be analyzed as its parts causing the same effect and the conclusion [...] that some objects cause effects without merely overdetermining what their parts cause.

We always have a reason to resist systematic and genuine overdetermination. Thus, I say, we have a good reason to endorse (3). Some might object that opposition to systematic overdetermination in general does not support (3), since there is something special about the overdetermination (3) opposes. But, I have argued, the various principled ways one might defend this objection fail; these failures rob that objection of its initial plausibility. And so we should conclude that (3) is true.

I want to add one final point in favour of (3). Imagine that someone has been killed by a bullet. Now entertain the possibility that the killing was overdetermined by two bullets arriving simultaneously. But suppose, further, that there is *no reason* to believe that the killing was overdetermined in this way. For, let us suppose, while there is evidence for the existence of one bullet, there is no evidence for the existence of a second. In such a case, I think everyone would agree that we should deny that the killing is overdetermined as a result of a second bullet. For without a reason to think an effect is overdetermined, we should assume it is not.

Obviously enough, one would have a reason for believing that the shattering of the window is overdetermined only if one had a reason for believing that *both* the baseball *and* the atoms arranged baseballwise caused it. And one would have a reason for believing *that* only if one had a reason to believe that the baseball existed. But, I shall argue momentarily, there is no good reason to believe the baseball exists. Without the positive belief that a baseball exists, there is no motivation for believing that the shattering of a window is overdetermined, caused by atoms and a ball. And if there is no such motivation, then we ought to conclude that there is no overdetermination. And thus we have (3) of the Overdetermination Argument.

As just noted, I shall argue that we have no good reason to believe in baseballs. One might then ask why we need the Overdetermination Argument at all. Here is one reply. Even if the defence of (3) to follow fails, the Overdetermination Argument is still sound. For even if that particular defence of (3) fails, we should – for the reasons given above – still accept the truth of (3). There is a second reply. The argument to follow implies only a healthy agnosticism (not a full-blown eliminativism) about baseballs. The Overdetermination Argument shows how that agnosticism leads to the claim that baseballs, if they exist, do not shatter windows. And that, as we shall see (§IV), leads to eliminating baseballs.

Our ordinary reason for believing in baseballs is simply that, so it seems, we can just see them (or feel them or otherwise sense them). Similarly, our ordinary reason for believing in statues is that we can just see them. But we saw earlier that 'just seeing a statue' is not really a good reason to believe that atoms arranged statuewise compose a statue.[10] Likewise, 'just seeing a baseball' is not a good reason to believe that atoms arranged baseballwise compose a baseball. So it turns out that our ordinary reasons for believing in baseballs

aren't good reasons. So unless we have some extraordinary reasons, we have no good reason at all to believe in baseballs. And if we have no good reason to believe in baseballs, then we shouldn't believe in them. (That is, we should either withhold belief or positively disbelieve in them.)

In the course of establishing that 'just seeing a statue' isn't a good reason to believe in a statue, I traded on an analogy. I claimed that whether atoms arranged statuewise compose a statue is analogous to whether atoms arranged my-neighbour's-dogwise and the-top-half-of-the-tree-in-my-backyardwise compose an object. And I said that it would not do to support an affirmative answer to the latter question simply by saying 'I can just see that object'.

This is an important point in what follows. Note that it is *not* controversial. There are many philosophers who believe in arbitrary sums like the 'dog-and-treetop', but none of them – not one – defends the existence of such things on merely perceptual grounds. No one says we should believe that such an object exists simply because we can see it or simply because we can hear it (gnawing on a bone while rustling its leaves).

Part of the reason, presumably, that no one says such things is that one's visual and auditory experiences would be the same whether or not they were caused only by atoms arranged dog-and-treetopwise or were instead overdetermined by those atoms plus the object they compose. But whatever the explanation, it is uncontroversial that philosophical argument is necessary to justify positive belief in the dog-cum-treetop. Likewise, philosophical argument is necessary to justify positive belief in statues and, of course, baseballs.

Anyone who wants to resist this conclusion must insist that the question of whether atoms arranged baseballwise compose a baseball is *not* relevantly analogous to the question of whether atoms arranged dog-and-treetopwise compose something. Now no one should dispute that they are analogous in many ways. Each is a question about whether atoms compose a particular macrophysical object. Each is a question that, if it has an affirmative answer, has an affirmative answer of necessity (and likewise if it has a negative answer). And each of the alleged macrophysical objects, if it exists, *at best* overdetermines our sensory experience of it in *exactly the same way* as does the other.

The only possibly relevant disanalogy between the cases at issue here is that baseballs are, but 'arbitrary sums' like the dog-and-treetop are not, part of our commonsense metaphysics. In light of this, one might object that the objects of folk ontology – unlike arbitrary sums – are presumed innocent until proven guilty.

Let me concede the following. Folk ontology and belief in baseballs is a *justified starting-point* in forming beliefs about the world. Though it is reasonable to start with such beliefs, however, their justification is undermined for those of us familiar with the issues raised in this section of this chapter. For we ought to see that the only difference between arbitrary sums and statues is a matter of conventional wisdom and local custom. *Once this is pointed out*, one is no longer justified in believing that statues exist merely because one can supposedly see them.[11]

Imagine a child reared on an island of philosophers who are enamoured of unrestricted composition. Such a child might take it for granted that arbitrary sums exist. She might even insist that such sums obviously exist because she can 'see them'. I think that child is initially justified in her beliefs. But once she realizes that she could 'see such things' whether or not they were there, seeing no longer justifies believing.

One might reply that belief in folk ontology is not merely *customary*, but somehow epistemically privileged: hard-wired in non-defective cognizers or part of epistemic proper functioning or what have you. But it's hard to see why the folk way of carving up the material world should – barring further argument – be elevated to a loftier status than the unrestricted compositionist way. Note, in particular, that the problem wouldn't be solved simply by folk-ontological beliefs' being *reliably* formed. For even if unrestricted composition were true and 'seeing arbitrary sums' reliable, such seeing would not, on its own, justify believing.

I conclude that whether atoms arranged statuewise compose a statue is in the same epistemic boat as whether atoms arranged treetopwise and neighbour's-dogwise compose an object. In the latter case, one cannot reasonably base one's conclusion simply on what one senses or, more generally, on any of the alleged causal effects of the alleged treetop-plus-dog; likewise, then, in the former. To be justified in believing in baseballs,

we must have philosophical reasons to believe that they exist.

Some will respond that we *do have* philosophical reasons for believing in baseballs. We can better understand their position by considering the possible worlds of David Lewis (1986). Lewis believes that these worlds contain macrophysical objects, like the counterparts of our (alleged) baseball, with which we have no causal–perceptual interaction. This is germane to the present discussion because Lewis thinks he has good (non-perceptual) reasons for believing in these objects, namely, their philosophical utility combined with our modal insights.[12]

Similarly, some think that we have philosophical reasons for believing in this-worldly baseballs. Those reasons, if strong enough, would block my final defence of (3), the defence based on epistemic considerations. But once the locus of the debate moves to philosophical argument and leaves behind what we can 'just see', things look good for eliminativism. In part, this is because once we agree that the way to decide whether baseballs exist is by philosophical argument, various philosophical arguments against the existence of things like baseballs become all the more significant. And, in part, this is because there is very little out there by way of positive, non-question-begging arguments for the existence of baseballs. After all, their existence is generally taken for granted.[13]

But there is something out there that has a right to call itself 'a non-question-begging defence of the existence of baseballs'. I have in mind philosophical defences of unrestricted composition, and specifically defences of unrestricted composition that are also committed to perdurance and the inconstancy of modal predicates.

To see the relevance of perdurance and inconstant modal predicates, consider the following. Unrestricted composition implies that, if there is a baseball B composed of atoms $A_1 \ldots A_n$, then there is some other object composed of all those atoms save A_n. Call that latter object B*. Suppose A_n then ceases to exist. What is the relation between B and B*? One answer implies that B ceases to exist. But then B cannot be a baseball. For the baseballs of folk ontology can survive the loss of a single atom. And we are here concerned with only the unrestricted compositionist who wishes to defend the existence of baseballs.

The unrestricted compositionist who defends the existence of baseballs will probably say that B and B* are co-located after A_n ceases to exist.[14] For the unrestricted compositionist who accepts co-location can easily insist that there are objects persisting in the way that the folk think baseballs do. Each of those objects, then, can be a 'baseball' with the right persistence conditions. Earlier, I argued that co-location leads right to perdurance and inconstant modal predicates.[15] So I'll assume that both are accepted by the unrestricted compositionist who embraces co-location.

The ontology of unrestricted composition and co-location includes the objects of folk ontology. But – with its explosion of macrophysical objects, massive amounts of co-location, and perdurance – it is not the ontology of the folk. So one question is whether this departure from folk ontology is more or less plausible than eliminativism. I think it is less plausible (although many will disagree). The burden of much of this book is showing just how plausible eliminativism really is, thus helping to make the case that it is more plausible than its rivals. [...]

If the usual arguments for eliminativism are only about as persuasive as the philosophical arguments for the existence of baseballs, then the philosophical arguments here end in a draw. But then eliminativism wins. For if the philosophical arguments end in a draw, we have no positive reason to believe in baseballs. And if we have no positive reason to believe in baseballs, we have no positive reason to believe that the overdetermination opposed by (3) occurs. And we should deny overdetermination occurs unless we have a positive reason to believe it does. So we should accept (3): the shattering of the window is not overdetermined.

At the start of this section I considered the objection that what a baseball causes is analysed in terms of what its parts cause. But we saw that this analysis fails. Thus we saw that the alleged overdetermination at issue in (3) is indeed genuine overdetermination. I then countered other objections to (3). And I presented reasons to accept (3). So I concluded that (3) was true, even before developing the point that, because baseballs would be at best causally redundant, none of our ordinary reasons for believing in them are any good.

At that stage of the argument – prior to my developing the 'epistemic point' – I think someone could justifiedly reply that my considerations in support of (3) are outweighed by his certainty that baseballs both exist and cause things. After all, he might add, if baseballs exist and cause things, the Overdetermination Argument is easily transformed into an argument against premiss (3).

But we now know that the belief in baseballs is on a par with the belief in objects like the dog-and-treetop. The belief that baseballs exist (and cause things) is justified, if at all, by philosophical means. And so it merits only the degree of certainty appropriate to that of a speculative philosophical hypothesis. As a result, the denial of (3) is itself likewise speculative and thus relatively vulnerable to defeat. In light of this, I conclude that my earlier considerations in support of (3) are compelling. And so I conclude that (3) is true.

IV   The Moral of the Overdetermination Argument

I have defended the validity of the Overdetermination Argument and the truth of each of its premisses. The Overdetermination Argument is sound. Baseballs do not cause windows to shatter. And there is nothing special about shattering windows as opposed to, say, knocking hapless batters unconscious. Nor is there anything special about whether the shattering or knocking is allegedly caused by a baseball or, for example, a rock. For these reasons, the Overdetermination Argument looks like it will generalize to rob the macrophysical of causal power in a wide range of cases.

We can see how far the Overdetermination Argument generalizes by looking at the following schema of which it is an instance:

(1*)   Object O – if O exists – is causally irrelevant to whether its parts $P_1 \dots P_n$, acting in concert, cause effect E.

(2*) $P_1 \dots P_n$ cause E.

(3*)   E is not overdetermined.

Therefore,

(4*)   If O exists, O does not cause E.

If an alleged effect of an (alleged) object is caused by that object's parts, and if that object is causally irrelevant to whether its parts cause that effect, then that effect is – assuming no overdetermination – not caused by the object in question. Note that, if *every* effect allegedly caused by a composite object is caused by its parts, and if that object is causally irrelevant to whether its parts cause those effects, then – assuming no overdetermination – the object causes *nothing.*

Everything (alleged) baseballs and other non-living macrophysical objects (allegedly) cause is caused by their proper parts at some level of decomposition. Moreover, if baseballs and other non-living macrophysical objects exist, they are causally irrelevant to the causing done by their atoms. At least that's what I say. For these claims are the heart of a 'bottom-up' metaphysics applied to baseballs and other inanimate macroscopica. So here is where the Overdetermination Argument and its opposition to systematic over-determination leads us. If baseballs and other non-living macrophysical objects exist, then – since a 'bottom-up' metaphysics is true of them – they do not cause anything at all.

One is likely to wonder why I restrict this conclusion to non-living macrophysical objects. Developing and defending this restriction will be the central task of the following chapter. But this issue does not need to be settled before establishing this chapter's main thesis up to this point. For that thesis is not that humans or atoms or any other things have causal powers. It is that if non-living macrophysical objects exist, they cause nothing.

If non-living macrophysical objects exist, they cause nothing – they are *epiphenomenal*. This bears directly on eliminativism. For if there were baseballs, they would break windows, they would injure batters, they would cause visual sensations (and so be seen), and they would cause tactile sensations (and so be felt).[16] In general, if there were inanimate macrophysical objects, they would have causal powers. But given the Overdetermination Argument and the schema of which it is an instance, if there were such objects, they would not have causal powers. So there are no such objects.

Arguments linking existence to causal powers are often controversial. Consider such arguments against Platonic Forms or moral properties. But this is no problem. For I do not rely upon the entirely unrestricted thesis that to be is to have causal powers. I claim only that, for *macrophysical objects*, to be is to have causal powers. Macro-physical objects are *exactly* the sort of things about which this kind of causal requirement seems to be true. There should be no controversy on this point. The controversy, instead, is about which other sorts of things are like macrophysical objects in this way.

We can, without too much controversy, extend this 'causal criterion' to events. (At least, we can extend this criterion to a wide range of events. Perhaps the number 7's being prime – even if that event exists – causes nothing.) And, as one might suspect, we can likewise extend the reasoning of the Overdetermination Argument to events. Imagine that my wife and I are lifting a sofa. The sofa's being lifted is a result of two distinct events: my straining at one end of the sofa and my wife's straining at the other. If, in addition to those two events, there is the single composite event of *our* straining, then that composite event would cause the sofa to be lifted only at the price of overdetermination. But that price is too high. So the composite event does not cause the sofa to be lifted. Nor does it cause any-thing else. But then it must not really exist. Thus my ontology of events will end up being sparse for the same reasons, and in much the same way, as my ontology of material objects.[17]

This reasoning also delivers a new reason to reject wholly co-located entities such as a statue and a lump of clay. Suppose, for *reductio*, that a statue and a lump of clay are numerically distinct material objects that are wholly co-located, that is, that share all of their parts at some level of decom-position. Anything the alleged statue is alleged to cause – the breaking of a window, visual sensations – would also be caused by the statue-shaped lump. Anything the alleged lump is alleged to cause would also be caused by the lump-constituted statue. But there is not the sort of systematic causal overdeter-mination that their co-location implies. There-fore, at least one of those objects causes nothing. But every macrophysical object causes something. So either the statue or the lump does not really exist. And so there is not co-location of a statue and a numerically distinct lump after all.

(The general strategy behind the Overdetermination Argument can, we have seen, be adapted to cases where the allegedly overdetermining competitors are an event and its 'parts' and an object and its constituting mass. The application of this sort of reasoning to a property and its supervenience base in the philosophy of mind is already familiar. [...] There may be other areas, not explored in this book, where this strategy can be fruitfully exploited.)

The anti-co-locationist adaptation of the Overdetermination Argument resonates with a common objection to co-location. That objection is that co-location implies – as far as causal explanations are concerned – 'a needless multiplication' of physical objects. It implies this, according to that objection, because everything one co-located object allegedly causes is accounted for by the work of the other. Opponents of co-location who found themselves nodding vigorously as that objection was originally presented should, in consistency, deny that atoms arranged baseballwise compose a baseball. After all, to add the baseball is to needlessly multiply. For everything the baseball allegedly does is accounted for by the work of the atoms. So at least some of what motivates denying co-location also motivates eliminativism.

[...]

Notes

1 I use 'the shattering of a window' as a plural referring expression, shorthand for many scatterings. I am not identifying the many scatterings with some single event, a shattering; that would imply that identity holds one-many. Nor do I claim that 'the shattering of a window' normally means many scatterings.

2 The Overdetermination Argument resembles a familiar overdetermination-based argument in the philosophy of mind, a version of which is advanced by, among others, Jaegwon Kim (e.g. 1989b). [...]

3 One may interpret this last clause as implying that I cannot prevent the members from vandalizing the park. And the first clause – my not being one of the members – can be read as an instance of a more general constraint on causal irrelevance: the xs are causally irrelevant to whether the ys have an effect only if none of the xs are any of the ys. This makes causal irrelevance symmetric.

4 (1) does not imply that the baseball is not a partial cause of the window shattering. (That would presuppose (4).) (1) implies only that the baseball is not a partial cause alongside and augmenting *its constituent atoms*.

5 If we deny (2), we open up the possibility that the baseball, in virtue of its 'emergent' causal properties, causes its atoms to do its bidding. Thus denying (2) might undermine (1). [...]

6 So we need not rule out all non-redundant or emergent causal properties, not even all such purely physical properties. So nothing I defend here is threatened by the apparent evidence Teller (1989) and Maudlin (1994: 210–12) discuss for something like emergent causal properties in physical systems.

7 See *Objects and Persons*, ch. 1, §4.

8 Compare Kim (1998: 42–3): '*To cause a supervenient property to be instantiated, you must cause its base property (or one of its base properties) to be instantiated.* To relieve a headache, you take aspirin: that is, you causally intervene in the brain process on which the headache supervenes.'

9 This is true not only of causal theories of perception of the sort endorsed by Chisholm and Grice, but also of theories like Goldman's that allow non-causal factors a prominent role. (See Alston 1990 for discussion of these views.)

10 *Editors' note*: Merricks presents the argument in ch. 1, §2 of *Objects and Persons*. He reiterates the argument in what follows.

11 We have here something like what Alvin Plantinga (1993: 41) calls an 'undercutting defeater' for one's non-propostional sensory evidence for the existence of a baseball. For more on defeaters, see Lehrer and Paxson (1969), Harman (1973), and Pollock (1974, 1986).

12 Some have objected that, because knowledge of concrete objects requires causal interaction, one could not know of the worlds Lewis posits or the objects in those worlds. Lewis (1986, §2.4) notes, and responds to, objections along these lines found in Richards (1975), Lycan (1979), and Skyrms (1976).

13 It is difficult to find positive arguments for the existence of baseballs. Note, for example, that Ned Markosian (1998) defends baseballs and the like only in the sense – irrelevant to present purposes – that his answer to the special composition question is *consistent with* the existence of such objects. H. Scott Hestevold (1980–1) might get us baseball-sized and -shaped objects, but given Hestevold's avowed mereological essentialism, he does not get us *baseballs*. If sound, Crawford Elder's (1996) arguments might (perhaps) save baseballs, but only by implying that organisms and rocks, among other putative objects beloved of folk ontology, do not exist.

14 These comments about the implications of unrestricted composition reflect the orthodox and standard views. But they are of course controversial. To delve more deeply into these issues, see van Cleve (1986), Rea (1998), and the essays in Rea (1997).

15 *Objects and Persons*, Ch. 2, §3.

16 Epiphenomenalism with regard to non-living macrophysical objects implies that we have no sensory evidence for their existence. This point

differs from the claim suggested during the defence of premiss (3). That claim was that we have no good reason to believe that one's sensory experience caused by atoms arranged baseball-wise is overdetermined by a(n alleged) baseball. The point at hand is that a baseball does not cause one's baseballish sensory experience.

17 A sparse ontology of events supports a view I have defended elsewhere. I believe that objects endure; and this implies, I have argued (1995a), that events endure. That events endure is difficult to reconcile with the claim that, say, the American Civil War existed; for such an event seems never to have been 'wholly present' at any single time. But the endurance of events like my thinking that P is easier to accept.

References

Alston, William P. (1990), 'Externalist Theories of Perception', *Philosophy and Phenomenological Research*, 50: 73–97.

Broad, C. D. (1925), *The Mind and its Place in Nature* (London: Routledge & Kegan Paul).

Elder, Crawford (1996), 'On the Reality of Medium-Sized Objects', *Philosophical Studies*, 83: 191–211.

Harman, Gilbert (1973), *Thought* (Princeton: Princeton University Press).

Hestevold, H. Scott (1980–1), 'Conjoining', *Philosophy and Phenomenological Research*, 41: 371–85.

Kim, Jaegwon (1989a), 'Mechanism, Purpose, and Explanatory Exclusion', in J. Tomberlin (ed.) *Philosophical Perspectives*, 3 (Atascadero, Calif.: Ridgeview); repr. in Kim (1993b).

Kim, Jaegwon (1989b), 'The Myth of Nonreductive Materialism', *Proceedings and Addresses of the American Philosophical Association*, 63: 31–47.

Kim, Jaegwon (1993a), 'The Nonreductivist's Troubles with Mental Causation', in J. Heil and A. Mele (eds.), *Mental Causation* (Oxford: Oxford University Press); repr. in Kim (1993b).

Kim, Jaegwon (1993b), *Supervenience and Mind* (Cambridge: Cambridge University Press).

Kim, Jaegwon (1998) *Mind in a Physical World: An Essay on the Mind–Body Problem and Mental Causation* (Cambridge, Mass.: MIT Press).

Lehrer, Keith and Paxson, Thomas (196 Undefeated Justified True Belie *Philosophy*, 66: 225–37.

Lewis, David (1986), *On the Plurality of V* Blackwell).

Lycan, William (1979), 'The Trouble with Possible Worlds', in Michael Loux (ed.), *The Possible and the Actual* (Ithaca, NY: Cornell University Press).

Malcolm, Norman (1968), 'The Conceivability of Mechanism', *Philosophical Review*, 77: 45–72.

Markosian, Ned (1998), 'Brutal Composition', *Philosophical Studies*, 92: 211–49.

Maudlin, Tim (1994), *Quantum Non-Locality and Relativity: Metaphysical Intimations of Modern Physics* (Oxford: Blackwell).

Merricks, Trenton (1995), 'On the Incompatibility of Enduring and Perduring Entities', *Mind*, 104: 523–31.

Mills, Eugene (1996), 'Interactionism and Over-determination', *American Philosophical Quarterly*, 33: 105–17.

Plantinga, Alvin (1993), *Warrant and Proper Function* (Oxford: Oxford University Press).

Pollock, John (1974), *Knowledge and Justification* (Princeton: Princeton University Press).

Pollock, John (1986), *Contemporary Theories of Knowledge* (Totowa, NJ: Rowman & Littlefield).

Pollock, John (ed.) (1997), *Material Constitution: A Reader* (New York: Rowman & Littlefield).

Rea, Michael C. (1997), *Material Constitution* (Lanham: Rowman & Littlefield).

Rea, Michael C. (1998), 'In Defense of Mereological Universalism', *Philosophy and Phenomenological Research*, 58: 347–60.

Richards, Tom (1975), 'The Worlds of David Lewis', *Australasian Journal of Philosophy*, 53: 105–18.

Skyrms, Brian (1976), 'Possible Worlds, Physics, and Metaphysics', *Philosophical Studies*, 30: 323–32.

Teller, Paul (1989), 'Relativity, Relational Holism, and the Bell Inequalities', in J. Cushing and E. McMullin (eds.), *Philosophical Consequences of Quantum Theory: Reflections on Bell's Theorem* (Notre Dame, Ind.: University of Notre Dame Press).

van Cleve, James (1986), 'Mereological Essentialism, Mereological Conjunctivism, and Identity through Time', in P. French, T. Uehling Jr., and H. Wettstein (eds.), *Midwest Studies in Philosophy*, vol. 11 (Minneapolis: University of Minnesota Press).

52

Against Revisionary Ontology

Eli Hirsch

I

My impression is that the period of the last twenty years or so has been an amazingly bad time for common sense ontology. It seems to me that every third philosopher I talk to has serious doubts about whether tables exist, and of the other two at least one of them thinks that if there are such things as tables then there are also such things as the object composed of the Eiffel Tower and Plato's nose. As I overheard a philosopher saying recently, "Either everything exists or nothing exists." The "everything exists" people are sometimes called "universalists." They hold that for any two things there is a third thing composed of the two. Typically they also hold that if a thing persists through a period of time then there is a second thing, a "temporal part" of the first, which exists only during that period. The world consists, then, of all of the sums of these temporal parts, so that, as Quine often puts it, every materially occupied space-time portion of the world, however discontinuous or gerrymandered, is an object on an equal footing with any other.[1] The "nothing exists" people – perhaps Peter Unger is the most famous recent example (or would be if

he existed) – typically hold that none of the complex entities that people ordinarily seem to be talking about really exist, though they may possibly allow for the existence of metaphysical simples.[2] Even more amazing in a way than the anti-commonsensical stances of the universalists and nihilists is the view of people like Chisholm and van Inwagen who, while agreeing with common sense that the truth lies somewhere between "everything exists" and "nothing exists," claim to have some way of picking and choosing amongst ordinary things, admitting some of them but dismissing others, in a manner I can't help associating with the game played by small children who demand from you an invisible ticket before they'll admit you into their room.[3]

These attacks on common sense amaze me in part because I think they are so badly misguided, but also because when I entered the profession of philosophy during the heyday of the so-called ordinary language movement, I think almost no one would have predicted that before the end of the millennium – even given some predictable end-of-millennium madness – the existence of tables would again be called into question. I think most of us assumed back then that philosophers

Eli Hirsch, "Against Revisionary Ontology," *Philosophical Topics*, 30/1 (Spring 2002): 102–27. Reproduced by permission of the author and the University of Arkansas Press, www.uapress.com.

Metaphysics: An Anthology, Second Edition. Edited by Jaegwon Kim, Daniel Z. Korman and Ernest Sosa.

like Moore, P. F. Strawson, Austin, and Wittgenstein had once and for all established the undeniability of our most basic common sense beliefs – or, if not "once and for all," at least for more than ten years. We were, as it now appears, overly optimistic.

Looking back at those heroes of common sense we can draw a rough distinction, I think, between two general approaches. The first approach, typified by Moore, comes out of basic epistemology. A simple point that Moore made in a number of his papers is that our common sense convictions have more epistemic weight than any fancy philosophical arguments. Suppose you think you have an argument against the existence of tables. Maybe there is some mistake in the argument that you haven't seen. That's possible, isn't it? What is more likely, that there is a mistake in the argument or that there aren't any tables? Moore thought that any sane person who considers that question would soon realize that it is more reasonable to abandon the argument than to abandon tables.[4]

The second approach, which one is likely to associate with the name "ordinary language philosophy," comes out of linguistic rather than epistemological considerations. In arguing against revisionary ontology in the present paper I'm going to develop a version of this second approach. This is not because I think that the more simple Moorean appeal to basic epistemology is insufficient. It ought to suffice, but the trouble is that revisionists tend to be unmoved by it. The revisionary literature often gives the impression that revisionists are people who have heard rumors about the existence of tables at family affairs, and apart from a natural reluctance to offend their non-philosophical relatives, they themselves have no initial intuitive feelings one way or another about whether tables might exist. The simple Moorean appeal to the convictions of sane common sense, therefore, tends to be shrugged off by these philosophers. The argument from language that I'm going to develop will, I hope, be harder for them to ignore.

The basic argument can be summarily put as follows. It is widely acknowledged that a central constraint on interpreting a language is a "principle of charity."[5] Suppose we have two candidate interpretations for a set of sentences that fluent speakers of a language would typically be prepared to assert (or assent to). If one of these interpretations implies that the speakers are correct in asserting these sentences, and the other interpretation implies that they are incorrect, then the principle of charity imposes a presumption in favor of the first interpretation. Revisionists seem to flout this presumption, overriding it for no apparently good reason. Given a set of commonsensical ontological assertions, revisionists seem to perversely insist on interpreting these assertions in a way that makes them incorrect, even though it seems perfectly possible to interpret them in a way that would make them correct.

I'll refer to the above argument as "the argument from charity." This argument is one basis – not the only basis – for explaining why there is always a strong (if defeasible) presumption in favor of common sense. In evaluating this presumption I want to place a great deal of emphasis on a certain distinction. The beliefs expressed by typical speakers of a language may be attacked in two different ways. One way is to claim that these beliefs are *empirically false*. For example, typical speakers of English may at one time have held the empirically false beliefs that the Earth is flat and that whales are fish. The second way is to claim that these beliefs are false on *a priori conceptual* grounds. I take the second way to be characteristic of revisionary or anti-commonsensical ontology. A nihilist like Unger and a mereological essentialist like Chisholm think that it is an a priori mistake to claim that there are tables (i.e., composite tables that persist through mereological changes), and universalists like Lewis think it is an a priori mistake to deny that the Eiffel Tower and Plato's nose compose an object. Quine may not fit into this, if he completely rejects the distinction between the empirical and the a priori. But I assume that distinction in all of my work, as well as in the present paper, and the revisionary ontologists that most concern me assume it too.[6]

The reason why this distinction is important to the argument from charity is that it is generally understood that charity in linguistic interpretation has more to do with *rationality* – with *good reasons* – than with *truth*. People are expected to make empirical mistakes if their sensory data are limited – it may in fact be positively *irrational* for them not to make such mistakes – so that an interpretation of language that ascribes such mistakes to people may be compatible with, or even required by, the principle of interpretive charity. Revisionary ontology, however, as this is understood in the present discussion, has nothing to do with sensory data. If revisionists interpret the ontological assertions of common sense as a priori necessarily false then, assuming there are other available interpretations, this does prima facie violate the principle of charity, since people are not normally thought to have good reason to assert what is a priori necessarily false.

The presumption that typical fluent speakers of a language do not make assertions that are a priori necessarily false is safer – because it demands less – than the more general Moorean presumption that the assertions are true. The central problem for revisionists is that they seem to flout even this presumption. Consider the universalist's claim that any two things, no matter how related (even if not contemporaneous, I'm assuming), make up a thing.[7] When I have presented this position to ordinary people I have sometimes gotten the following response: "These philosophers don't mean by 'a (one) thing' what we ordinarily mean." That response seems to me essentially right. By ignoring the obvious – that is, the charitable – interpretation of what the words "a (one) thing" mean in English, these philosophers are merely "abusing the language." Of course they are entitled to introduce a technical language if they wish, but then they have to say that, and not pretend that they are expressing in plain English a substantive and controversial philosophical discovery.

To be a bit more accurate, it is not the expression "a thing" taken by itself that the universalist misuses, but that expression in such larger contexts as "a thing that is made of flesh at one time and made of metal at a later time." On any reasonably charitable interpretation of the English language that expression doesn't refer to anything, or at least it doesn't refer to anything merely by virtue of a nose existing at one time and a tower existing at a later time. This is because, on any reasonably charitable interpretation, an English expression of the form "the thing that is made up of the F and the G" does not refer to anything unless the things referred to by "the F" and "the G" are connected or united in some relevantly special way. If we compare the universalist's "fusions" or "sums" with sets, the essential contrast, from the point of view of the present discussion, is that typical speakers of English have

no disposition to deny standard assertions about sets. To the extent that the language of set theory is technical, speakers unschooled in this language may be apt to greet an assertion about sets with incomprehension ("What do you mean by 'a set having a member'?"), but certainly there is no tendency to deny the assertion. By contrast, typical speakers of English will regard as sheer lunacy the following assertion: "Something (some physical object) was made of flesh thousands of years ago and it (that same thing) is now made of metal (by virtue of Plato's nose and the Eiffel Tower)." To repeat what I said a moment ago, if universalists intend to introduce a technical language – so that the sentence just mentioned is not to be understood in plain English – then they are not revisionary ontologists in the sense that concerns me, and I have no argument with them (nor, obviously, do they have any argument with common sense).[8]

To spell out a bit further what I mean here by a revisionary ontologist:

> *Revisionary ontology.* Many common sense judgments about the existence or identity of highly visible physical objects are a priori necessarily false.

Perhaps there are common sense judgments about the existence or identity of things other than highly visible physical objects, such as numbers or properties. If so, they are not the topic of this discussion. I am dealing here only with an area of ontology that might be roughly called (in honor of Austin) "the ontology of moderate-sized dry goods."[9] Revisionists, in the present sense, hold that ordinary people make mistakes in their judgments about the existence or identity of the physical objects they claim to perceive in front of them, and not just mistakes, but a priori necessary mistakes. Revisionists hold this because they misinterpret the language, or so the argument from charity says.

A reaction that I have often gotten to this argument is that it is a form of linguistic idealism. "We are doing ontology, not linguistics. We are considering substantive questions about what exists in the world, and if you think that such questions can be settled by an examination of the English language then you must hold the most non-commonsensical view of all, namely, the view that language determines what exists in the world." This objection is off the mark. If we are speaking English then to know the truth-value of the sentence "There are tables" is to know whether there are tables. If we have decided that on the most charitable and reasonable interpretation that sentence is true, then we have decided that: *there are tables*. This has nothing to do with linguistic idealism. It simply follows from the trivial disquotational constraint that (assuming "*p*" is a sentence in the language I am now speaking) "*p*" is true if and only if it is the case that *p*. I say that, on the most charitable and reasonable interpretation of the English sentence "There is something that was made of flesh at one time and made of metal at a later time," the sentence is not made true by the existence of Plato's nose followed by the existence of the Eiffel Tower. In saying this, since I am now speaking (plain, nontechnical) English, I have concluded that there is not (by virtue of Plato's nose and the Eiffel Tower) anything that was made of flesh at one time and made of metal at a later time. My move from the remark about language to the remark about what exists does not commit me to the absurd view that what exists depends upon language. It rather commits me to being responsible to the language that I speak, even – or, I should say, especially – when I am doing philosophy.

"But how," it may still be puzzled, "can an appeal to anything as shallow as ordinary English usage resolve deep issues about what exists in the world?" The answer is that it can't. The issues being debated by revisionists are not deep; they are completely trivial. That's the key to all of this. Revisionists display to the highest degree the philosophical syndrome Wittgenstein called "language gone on holiday."[10] Because they have lost their grip on language they "have a new conception and interpret it as seeing a new object [or the absence of an old object]."[11] Revisionists suffer from the illusion that certain questions are philosophically deep, inviting complicated theoretical debates, when in fact these questions are comically trivial. "Is it possible for a table to exist?," "Is it possible for a car to survive the change of a tire?," "Is it possible for two things not to make up a third thing?" – the only sensible response to such questions is, "Of course, what on Earth are you talking about?" To dismiss the questions in that manner, to treat them as

utterly trivial, is part of what is involved in understanding the words and concepts that enter into them. The argument from charity is a last-ditch effort to bring the revisionists back to their senses, that is, to bring them back to the language that they themselves claim to be using, so that they can recognize utter triviality when it stares them in the face.

II

The argument from charity can be schematically formulated as follows, where "*O*" is some ontological sentence affirmed by ordinary people but denied by some revisionists:

1 Typical fluent speakers of the language assert (or assent to) the sentence "*O*."
2 Therefore, there is the charitable presumption that, on the correct interpretation of "*O*," speakers have good reason to assert "*O*," so that "*O*" is not a priori necessarily false.
3 There is nothing to defeat this presumption.
4 Therefore, "*O*" is not a priori necessarily false.
5 Therefore, it's possible that *O*.
6 Therefore, it's actually the case that *O*.

Let me first comment on line 6. A philosopher might reject 6 on empirical grounds. Such a philosopher, who thinks that *O*'s truth is possible but not actual, would not be a revisionist in the present sense. Revisionists, who think that *O*'s truth is impossible, will typically agree, however, that if they are wrong about that, then common sense is right, and *O* is not merely possibly true but actually true. Van Inwagen, for instance, would probably agree that, if it's possible for a table to exist (as a composite non-living thing), then a table does in fact exist. Why would he want to deny that tables in fact exist once he has accepted their possibility? Again, I'm confident that the universalist Lewis would agree that, if it's possible for there to be things that don't compose anything, then there are in fact many cases of such things. The move from 5 to 6 should actually be carefully examined, but I will not undertake that here. My general assumption – for expository reasons, if nothing else – will be that, if we have refuted the revisionist's claim that common sense ontological judgments are a priori necessarily false, then we have established the truth of those common sense judgments.

In presenting the argument from charity I assume – subject to further discussion – that revisionists who deny commonsensical assertions of some sentence "*O*" will admit that they are able to make intelligible to themselves a prima facie charitable interpretation on which "*O*" is true. By an "interpretation" I simply mean the assignment of truth conditions to "*O*." This need not involve formulating a sentence that is synonymous with "*O*," nor even a sentence that has strictly the same truth conditions as "*O*." All that is required is that one be able to indicate in some – perhaps rough and sketchy – manner what are the possible situations or worlds with respect to which "*O*" (as uttered in some specified kind of context) holds true.

Nihilists and various quasi-nihilists, for instance, deny that there are tables, but agree that there are bits of matter that are table-wise interrelated.[12] It is indeed the latter condition that, according to them, somehow induces ordinary people to make the mistake of thinking that there are tables. The question posed by the argument from charity is why these philosophers don't interpret the English sentence "There are tables" as holding true whenever that condition obtains. Again, universalists will admit that they can make intelligible to themselves a possible use of the sentence "Nothing was first made of flesh and then made of metal" which has as its truth conditions that nothing made of flesh was connected or united in some relevantly special way to something later made of metal. The question posed by the argument from charity is why not interpret that English sentence as having such truth conditions.

Starting now from the beginning of the argument: 1 reports a fact about people's linguistic propensities. 2 comes out of the widely accepted principle of interpretive charity. If 3 is also accepted then it follows that 4 should be accepted: if we assert that there is a presumption in favor of something's being the case, then we should assert that it is the case as soon as we agree that there is nothing to defeat the presumption.[13] The move from the meta-level claim 4 to the object-level claim 5, I have already defended. If there is a hole here I think it is in 3. Revisionists might claim that the presumption is defeated in some way. I'll

presently examine, and criticize, several ways in which this claim might be formulated.

Before turning to this, however, there is a complication that has to be addressed. There are some philosophers who sound like revisionists but who insist that they are not really disagreeing with ordinary people about anything. I will call them, with due respect, *crypto-revisionists*. I think this maneuver never works and only confuses things further. The most familiar form of the maneuver, found in Butler and more recently in Chisholm, is to claim that the assertions standardly made by ordinary folk are perfectly correct in the "loose" sense intended, though philosophers need to realize that these assertions are "strictly" false. Since ordinary people intend the statements only loosely, the philosophers have no disagreement with them.[14]

Now I don't doubt that the distinction between "loose talk" and "strict talk" is potentially of interest to philosophy, and that the distinction may not always be easy to clarify, but the trouble is that Butler and Chisholm seem to make intuitive nonsense of the distinction. The distinction between loose and strict talk must surely be based on the linguistic practices of fluent speakers of the language. Three obvious criteria to determine whether an assertion is strict or loose are: (a) Ask the speakers if they mean the thing strictly or loosely; (b) See if the speakers will make the assertion in a "strict" context, that is, a context calling for careful and thoughtful formulations – such as in a court of law or a formal document; (c) See if the speakers withdraw the assertion when reminded of relevant information. The following is a genuine example of loose talk.[15] *A* and *B* have often bemoaned the fact that since *C* left town she calls very rarely. On this occasion *A* says, "She never calls." Obviously *A* means this only loosely. The proof is that, first, if you asked her whether she means that, strictly speaking, *C* never calls she would say no; second, *A* would not say under oath in court, "*C* never calls"; third, if *B* says to *A*, "Well, she does call once in a while," *A* doesn't say, "That's right, *she never calls*."

Imagine now that a witness for the defense swears that the car involved in the accident was the same one that he later parked in the garage. "Are we getting the strict truth from you? You cannot be claiming that it is the same one – can you, now? – when you yourself have testified that a hubcap fell off on the way to the garage!," triumphantly cries the prosecuting attorney Chisholm. No ordinary person, even under oath, will be induced to reconsider the claim that it was the same car *merely* by being reminded that the hubcap fell off. (It would be question-begging to appeal to what some people might be induced to say by – what I am claiming is – bad philosophy.) The Butler-Chisholm approach seems especially implausible with respect to a statement like, "This tree (is the same one that) had more branches twenty years ago," which mentions the very fact about mereological change that is alleged to make the statement loose. This would be analogous to *A*'s saying, "My friend *C*, who calls on holidays, never calls."

I don't question that there may be hard cases in which it is unclear (or indeterminate) whether we are speaking strictly or loosely, but it seems obvious that, by any sensible criteria, the assertions ordinary people make about the existence and identity of physical objects are typically intended to be true in a perfectly strict sense. This does not imply, of course, that such assertions contain no elements of vagueness. Strictness in the sense of the present discussion must not be confused with precision or non-vagueness. The statement "Rockefeller was wealthy" is normally intended to be strictly true (rather than "loosely true but strictly false"), although "wealthy" is highly vague.

I think many people even in the revisionary camp have come to accept that the "loose"–"strict" distinction is of little help to them.[16] There is, however, another form that crypto-revisionism has recently taken. Lewis has a formulation of the universalist position which says that the ontological assertions of common sense are correct if the quantifiers – such words as "something" and "anything" – are restricted roughly to ordinary or familiar things, but the assertions are false when the quantifiers are interpreted as unrestricted.[17] I think that Lewis himself did not mean to claim that universalists are therefore not in disagreement with common sense, but I have often heard other universalists make that claim. I think it is easy to show that the claim is false. Imagine that I hold up two pieces of wood, one white and one brown, and I ask some ordinary people whether they can see any

wooden thing that is first white and then brown. Of course they say no. Now the universalist – I mean here a "four-dimensionalist" universalist like Lewis, one who believes in temporal parts – believes that any early part of the white piece together with a later part of the brown piece add up to a wooden thing that is first white and then brown. Might this belief be reconciled with what the ordinary folk say by supposing that they only meant – what is surely the case – that there is no ordinary or familiar thing that is first white and then brown? Well, let's ask them: "Now, you're not supposed to restrict yourself to ordinary things, or familiar things, or anything like that. Take into account *anything whatsoever* no matter how peculiar a thing it is. Do you now see some wooden thing that is first white and then brown?" They still answer "no." I assume everyone agrees that that would be the outcome of the experiment. But let's take it one step further, with a final attempt at reconciliation: "Ah, you didn't get the riddle. You see, you kept restricting your attention to just one sort of thing even though you were told not to. The correct answer is that any early part of this one together with any later part of the other one make up a wooden thing that is first white and then brown." Do they say, "Oh yes, how stupid of us! Give us another riddle"? No, they throw you out the window. That there is a stark conflict between common sense beliefs and the universalist's position seems to me undeniable.

I have spoken to philosophers who remain unconvinced. The trouble is, they say, that ordinary people just can't unrestrict the quantifier, no matter what you tell them. Ordinary people don't really disagree with the four-dimensionalist, but in the previous example the quantifier remained restricted to familiar things, or interesting things, or something of that sort.

Does this even make sense? If ordinary people can't unrestrict the quantifier how could the so-called unrestricted quantifier ever have become a part of the English language? If it is part of the English language then fluent speakers must know how to use it. Imagine that someone says, as in one of Lewis's examples, "There's no beer," meaning to restrict the quantifier to beer in his fridge. I say to him. "But of course there is beer in the grocery store." He replies, "No, there is no beer in the grocery store," still restricting the quantifier to beer in his fridge, and saying in effect, "There is no beer in my fridge in the grocery store." I say, "But you'll surely agree that there is beer outside your fridge?" "No," he replies, "there is no beer outside my fridge," still restricting the quantifier to beer in his fridge, and saying in effect, "There is no beer in my fridge outside my fridge." Finally he exclaims, "There is no beer of any sort whatever, anywhere in the world, that can be referred to by anyone!" and he says that because he has never before had occasion to quantify over beer outside his fridge, so he keeps restricting the quantifier to beer in his fridge. That story, it seems to me, makes as much sense as the suggestion that ordinary people are not really disagreeing with the four-dimensionalists, but they just keep restricting the quantifier to familiar and interesting objects even when other objects that they supposedly don't reject are explicitly and emphatically brought to their attention.

III

Let me return to the main thread of the argument. I will henceforth assume that we are dealing, not with crypto-revisionists, but with outright revisionists, philosophers who think it is their job to correct the mistakes ordinary people make about the existence and identity of the moderate-sized dry goods in front of their eyes. I have suggested that the only hope revisionists have to rebut the argument from charity is to claim that there are some considerations that defeat the presumption in favor of an interpretation of the language that makes the ordinary assertions come out true. I will consider these potential defeaters under two headings: *conflicts of charity* and *constraints beyond charity*.

A conflict of charity occurs when typical speakers of the language are disposed to assert conflicting sets of sentences. If we adopt an interpretation that justifies the first set of assertions, this will make it impossible to justify the second set; and if we adopt an interpretation that justifies the second set, this will make it impossible to justify the first set. How do we then decide which interpretation is correct? To which set of assertions do we bestow our interpretive charity?

The standard revisionist literature does not address the argument from charity, but it does often invoke various general principles that are claimed to refute commonsensical assertions about the existence and identity of objects. Insofar as some of these principles are themselves accepted by ordinary people we may have a conflict of charity.

To illustrate this idea let me consider a principle that shows up in a great deal of the revisionary literature, the principle that two things cannot wholly occupy the same place at the same time.[18] It seems that ordinary people are inclined to accept this principle. The principle seems, however, to conflict with various commonsensical assertions about existence and identity. If a sculptor sculpts a statue out of a lump of clay, ordinary people say that the statue but not the lump of clay has just come into existence. It follows (by Leibniz's Law) that the statue and the lump of clay are two things, and they wholly occupy the same place, contrary to the "no-two-things-in-the-same-place" principle. There are numerous examples of this sort, in which the principle seems to conflict with the ordinary person's assertions about existence and identity. Here it seems that we have a conflict of charity. We can interpret the English language in a way that makes the ordinary person's assertion of the principle come out true and numerous ordinary assertions about the existence and identity of objects come out false, or we can interpret the language to the opposite effect.

I think when the options are presented in that way it's immediately clear that the revisionists have no leg to stand on. What possible reason could we have to accept the first interpretation over the second? The most that one can imagine claiming is that there is some degree of indeterminateness here, so that the revisionists' bizarre assertions are after all not determinately false (in plain English). But even that very modest claim – far more modest, obviously, than what revisionists want – cannot, I think, be sustained. the correct interpretation of English is most plausibly the second one, that is, the one that makes ordinary assertions about existence and identity come out true and the "no-two-things-in-the-same-place" principle come out false. Let me try to explain why this is so.

It is a standard assumption in general discussions of the nature of language that the linchpin of language-learning and language-interpretation consists of *examples*, especially perceptual examples.[19] Faced with two candidate interpretations, and a conflict of charity, we must therefore choose the interpretation that does best in sustaining people's assertions about examples, rather than the interpretation that sustains some general principles. General principles are made to be qualified or refined in the face of counter-examples (that's the very idea of a counterexample). This point is a commonplace in philosophy. A famously dramatic instance is the successive qualifications of the principles traditionally defining knowledge in the face of Gettier's counterexamples. In a conflict between accepted principles and accepted examples we normally hold onto the examples and qualify or refine the principles.

So it should be with the "no-two-things-in-the-same-place" principle. Once we become aware of the standard counterexamples to the principle surely the natural move is to qualify the principle in some way so as to accommodate the counter-examples. There are several ways to do this. A famous qualification offered by Locke is to say that the principle applies only to things of the *same sort*, which takes care of at least most of the standard counterexamples.[20] Another possibility is Lewis's plausible suggestion that we sometimes "count by temporary identity."[21] The statue and lump of clay are indeed two things in the Leibnizian sense (i.e., in the sense of "identity" satisfying Leibniz's Law), but the "no-two-things-in-the-same-place" princi-ple remains true in the sense of saying that if what are two things in the Leibnizian sense occupy the same place then they are "temporarily one thing," meaning roughly that they temporarily share all of their properties.

In the next section I will give additional reasons – besides the primacy of examples – for accepting the interpretation that sustains ordinary ontological assertions while qualifying the "no-two-things-in-the same-place" principle. Consider, however, a revisionist who has no wish to contest my ideas about linguistic interpretation but who responds to what I have been saying as follows: "The problem is that to my mind it seems completely clear that two things cannot wholly occupy the same place at the same time. What could make them two things (or, worse, two *sorts* of things) if they share the same (minute) parts? That merely darkens my understanding. In this case, therefore, my concerns about ordinary usage

and correct linguistic interpretation must defer to my deep metaphysical intuitions." This "deep" response, however, misses the essential point of the resolute shallowness of my argument. Perhaps it will help if I formulate the argument in a slightly different way. I am claiming that the correct interpretation of the English language assigns truth conditions to sentences in a way that makes the ontological sentences typically asserted by ordinary people come out true. My assumption at present (subject, as I said, to further discussion) is that the revisionists will admit that they understand well enough the interpretation I have in mind, but they don't think that is the correct interpretation. Let me give the name *Shmenglish* to a hypothetical language for which it is stipulated that this *is* the correct interpretation. Shmenglish sentences are the same (phonetically and syntactically) as English sentences, but it is stipulated that Shmenglish sentences have the truth conditions that I (perhaps mistakenly) take English sentences to have. On my present assump-tion revisionists will admit to understanding well enough how Shmenglish operates. Quasi-nihilists like van Inwagen and Merricks, for instance, will understand that the Shmenglish sentence "A statue was created from a lump of clay" counts as true with respect to any situation in which a continuous succession of (atomic) bits of matter arranged lump-of-clay-wise temporarily coincides with a succession of bits of matter arranged statue-wise – or something roughly to that effect. If the people presently living in North America were speaking Shmenglish then, as even revisionists would admit, their assertions of such sentences as the one just mentioned would be correct.

Consider now the following little argument:

1 In Shmenglish the sentence "Two things can wholly occupy the same place at the same time" is true.
2 On the most reasonably charitable interpre-tation of the dominant language in North America, this language is Shmenglish; that is to say, English is Shmenglish.
3 Therefore (we conclude in English): Two things can wholly occupy the same place at the same time.

I assume that (1) will be accepted by revisionists. For quasi-nihilists, to take them again for illustrative purposes, the Shmenglish sentence "Two things can wholly occupy the same place at the same time" is made true by such facts as the one about lumps-of-clay-wise and statue-wise arrangements of matter that I sketched a moment ago. If there is a flaw in this argument it is evidently not brought out by a philosopher's announcing her deep metaphysical commitment to the "no-two-things-in-the-same-place" principle. Since this philosopher will admit (I am now assuming) that Shmenglish is an intelligible language in which the principle (that is, the sentence expressing the principle) is false, the question that has to be addressed is whether English is Shmenglish. Interpretive charity indicates that it is. And some philosopher's professedly unshakable commitment to the "no-two-things-in-the-same-place" principle seems to have no serious bearing on this question.

Of the various other general principles invoked by revisionists, some seem to be highly contrived philosophical constructions, which have as such no direct relevance to issues of interpretive charity.[22] None have, I think, the intuitive commonsensical appeal of the "no-two-things-in-the-same-place" principle, If any of these principles generate genuine conflicts of charity in interpreting the language they should be dealt with as outlined above. Philosophers who are inclined to assert these principles should first remind themselves that if they were speaking Shmenglish it would be wrong to assert them. Next they should remind themselves that they *are* speaking Shmenglish (if they are speaking English). So they should stop asserting these principles.[23]

That linguistic interpretation leans heavily on examples comes out in one of the most famous passages in the *Philosophical Investigations*.[24] Wittgenstein considers the impulse to think that games must have something in common, or they would not be called "games." "Don't think, but look!" Wittgenstein says. Look at examples of games and you find that they don't satisfy some set of necessary and sufficient conditions. The revisionist might be compared to someone who answers: "I have looked and indeed have found that what common sense calls 'games' do not have anything in common. Since this is absurd I conclude that common sense is *wrong* in its judgments as to which activities are games." We might even imagine this answer giving rise

to counterparts of our three main revisionist positions, universalism, nihilism, and quasi-nihilism: "Every human activity is really a game"; "No human activity is really a game" (two existentialist positions); and, as one tempting counterpart of quasi-nihilism, "The only real game is *dreydl*."

IV

The primacy of (perceptual) examples in resolving conflicts of interpretive charity is evidently only one part of a more complicated story. Certainly there are other considerations that enter into resolving such conflicts, the barest sketch of which must include at least the following. If one interpretation has the effect of sustaining some of the typical speaker's assertions while abandoning others, and a second interpretation has the reverse effect, the correct interpretation is the one that tends as far as possible to favor assertions that are:

A. assigned good reasons (rather than truth)
B. numerous
C. perceptual
D. specific (as in examples)
E. strongly held
F. widely held
G. hard to qualify
H. hard to explain away by a theory of human error

Some of these criteria may be closely related. For instance, assertions that are on the order of general principles (hence, do not satisfy D) tend to be both easily qualified and easily explained away (hence, do not satisfy either G or H). I think that almost all of the criteria favor an interpretation of English that makes ordinary ontological assertions come out true or reasonable and various principles invoked by revisionists come out false or unreasonable.

Criterion H is worth looking at for a moment. If an interpretation abandons some assertions as being false or unreasonable, that interpretation is more credible insofar as we have some plausible way of explaining why people might be expected to make mistakes in those assertions. On my interpretation of English people tend to make mistakes about general principles such as the "no-two-things-in-the-same-place" principle because they generalize too hastily from a few paradigmatic examples that immediately come to their minds. This seems to be a very obvious and plausible explanation. By contrast, revisionists have no plausible way of explaining why people make the mistakes revisionists allege. According to (quasi-) nihilists, for example, people mistakenly judge tables to be in front of them when there are no tables in front of them. Why would people make a mistake like that? The illusion of depth that generates the whole revisionary project also generates the illusion that there is an answer to this question: People make these mistakes because it requires deep philosophical insight to avoid them. But what sense does this make? If there isn't an object of a certain sort in front of people why would they have to be as philosophically acute as Trenton Merricks to avoid the mistake of perceptually judging that such an object is there? Or take this from the (four-dimensionalist) universalist's angle. If when two sticks of different color are held up, as in my earlier example, there are numerous highly visible wooden objects there that change color, why would one have to be as deep as Mark Heller to avoid the mistake of thinking that there are no such objects there? If acknowledging the existence of the sticks requires no great philosophical depth, why would acknowledging the existence of these other stick-sized wooden objects require depth? The fact is, I think, that revisionists standardly delude themselves into thinking that they can plausibly explain why people make the mistakes they allege. It is closer to the truth to say that such mistakes would require some highly selective and seemingly arbitrary forms of genetically or culturally transmitted idiocy.

Criterion A harks back to a point made very early in this paper: the principle of charity pertains primarily to good reasons rather than to truth. This criterion is, I think, the main reason why the correct interpretation of a language can sometimes have the effect that typical speakers make assertions that are empirically (as opposed to a priori) false, even about (perceptual) examples. Suppose that typical speakers are prepared to assert "The Earth is flat." Why not interpret that as being true, as meaning something like "The Earth is locally flat (or looks flat)"? We have

to take into account many other assertions these people will make, such as, "If the Earth is flat, then if you keep moving in as straight a line as possible (over land and sea) on its surface you'll reach a point where you can't go any farther (you fall off)," and "If the Earth is flat it's shaped more like a large pancake than like a large grapefruit." The details are not easy to spell out, but I think it's fairly clear that we are faced with essentially two interpretive choices. On one interpretation "The Earth is flat" turns out to be true, but numerous conditionals asserted by the speakers turn out to be incomprehensibly unreasonable. On the second interpretation the conditionals are correct, and, although "The Earth is flat" is false, people have (tolerably) good reasons for asserting it, given their sensory data. The second interpretation is, therefore, the credible one, by criterion A.

Other examples of attributing empirical falsehoods to typical speakers may involve further complications.[25] The essential point to stress in all of these examples is that they do not involve contravening the principle of charity in the basic sense of criterion A, for we are not denying that, given their sensory experience, the speakers may have good reason to assert what they do. In contrast, revisionists imply that typical speakers of the language make many a priori false ontological judgments for no good reason.

It should be clear that because of criterion A we never seek mere "models" as our interpretations (in the sense of Putnam's "model theoretic" argument against Realism). Suppose that by mapping words of English to certain sets of objects on Alpha Centauri, objects that are causally unrelated to people on Earth, we can make the sentences typically asserted come out true. That mapping would not even qualify as a candidate interpretation, since people on Earth would evidently have no reason to assert sentences that are made true by causally remote objects on Alpha Centauri. A credible interpretation must delineate perceptual sentences that speakers typically assert with good reason when their sensory apparatus is suitably affected by their environment, and then must delineate reasonable connections between these assertions and others typically made. The revisionist's interpretation of English drastically fails to meet these constraints in the most charitable way possible.[26]

As Davidson and others have stressed, interpreting a language is part of the larger project of understanding human behavior. Criteria A through H deal only with assertions, but other forms of linguistic and non-linguistic behavior would ultimately need to be taken into account. I want to especially stress that these criteria are inadequate for interpreting normative language, which is linked essentially to attitudes and non-linguistic behavior. Suppose that typical speakers are prepared to assert, "We're not morally required to make large sacrifices to help starving strangers," and that Peter Singer says he disagrees with this. Here we certainly must not try to appeal to an argument from ordinary language to refute Singer. Questions of value cannot be resolved by appealing to ordinary English usage. On one meta-ethical picture Singer would admit that the "descriptive meaning" he assigns to the words "morally required" is different from that assigned by typical speakers, but the important point is that the "evaluative meaning" of those words is fixed by people's attitudes and behavior. Singer is engaged in a "disagreement of attitude" with ordinary people, and that can't be resolved by straightening out misinterpretations of language. The meta-ethical picture I've just appealed to may be overly crude, but I think the essential point is clear enough.

Questions in the ontology of moderate-sized dry goods, however, typically have no evaluative significance whatever. For instance, my friend van Cleve is a mereological essentialist who claims to believe that when you change a tire on a car you have replaced one car with another one. I would still not hesitate to let him fix my flat: why should I care if he likes to call this "destroying the original car"? It's because questions in the ontology of moderate-sized dry goods have no evaluative significance – and also no empirical significance – that typically the only thing required to answer them correctly is: *Speak plain English.*[27]

V

I turn, finally, to *"constraints beyond charity."* We can introduce this topic by considering a puzzling argument in Richard Cartwright's paper "Scattered Objects," a seminal early universalist formulation.[28] Cartwright begins by giving examples of scattered objects, such as a pipe whose parts are spatially disconnected while it is being cleaned, or a multivolume book whose volumes might be in different places. He then notes that, since some spatially disconnected objects make up an object, it would be "arbitrary" to exclude any disconnected objects from making up an object. He thereby draws the universalist conclusion that any two objects, however disconnected, make up an object.

What kind of argument is this? It seems clear that from the standpoint of common sense an expression of the form "the thing made up of the F and the G" refers to something only if the things referred to by "the F" and "the G" satisfy some suitable kind of unity relation, whether this be spatial, causal, historical, or whatever. Ordinary people would certainly not count Plato's nose and the Eiffel Tower as making up something, since they fail to satisfy any relevant unity relation. What can Cartwright mean by rejecting this ordinary judgment because it is "arbitrary"? Consider that it is *given* that in Shmenglish, as I have defined that language, the sentence "There is something made up of Plato's nose and the Eiffel Tower" is false. I claim that all the linguistic evidence indicates that English is Shmenglish. How can Cartwright rebut this claim by appealing to "arbitrariness"?

Cartwright seems perilously close to carrying on a burlesque battle with the English language. Obviously, if we don't like something about the language – because, perhaps, it strikes us as "arbitrary" – that doesn't entitle us to say that people who are using the language in the conventionally correct way are making mistakes. Of course we can overtly stipulate a *change* in the language, but that's exactly what revisionists like Cartwright say they are not doing.

"Arbitrariness" in philosophical discussions is closely related to "too much complexity" (or "too much complexity of the wrong kind"). Perhaps what is really bothering Cartwright is that the unity relation that seems to enter into the ordinary meaning of the expression "thing made up of the F and the G" is too complex. If it is unclear whether this is the problem that leads Cartwright to universalism it is certainly one of the main problems that leads van Inwagen to his brand of quasi-nihilism.[29] One of van Inwagen's main complaints against common sense is that it seems impossible to give any kind of accurate analysis of what counts as the unity relation for common sense. If ordinary judgments about objects were correct the unity relation would have to turn out to be highly disjunctive and intractably complex. I think it's quite likely that van Inwagen is right about this. He talks primarily about the *composition* relation – that is, the relation that holds between the contemporaneous parts of a unitary thing – but I also have in mind the relation that binds the successive stages of the history of a single thing. An examination of cases suggests, I think, that those successions of (sets of) bits of matter that common sense treats as answering to the history of a persisting object probably do not share some conjunction of conditions that neatly mark them off from sets that are not so treated. In all likelihood, our common sense ontology requires a unity relation that is messily disjunctive and even in some ways grue-like.[30]

But so what? The truth can obviously be told with grue-like expressions: the grass that grew a few years ago was grue, and the grass that grows now is bleen; surely, no one questions that. Van Inwagen, like Cartwright, seems to be battling the language. Let me put the point as before: It's given that in Shmenglish the sentence "There exists a table" is true, and all the linguistic evidence seems to indicate that English is Shmenglish. So how could van Inwagen's complaints about the complexity of the unity relation possibly lead us to his conclusion that "tables don't exist," which implies that English is not Shmenglish?[31]

Perhaps the complexity of the common sense unity relation affects the revisionists in the following way: they simply claim not to understand what this relation is. They don't understand what it is that gets ordinary people to distinguish between "things that make up something" and "things that don't make up something." This is a peculiar impasse. From my point of view such revisionists would merely be pretending not to understand English. Of course, they won't see it that way. They understand English well enough, they would say, but it's my make-believe language Shmenglish that they don't understand. What they don't understand, they say, is the supposedly "most charitable interpretation" of the assertions made by typical North Americans, the interpretation that would make these assertions come out true and that is stipulated to be the correct one

for Shmenglish. "Give us a clear analysis of the unity relation for objects that is supposed to operate in Shmenglish," they demand. And I'm apparently trapped, because I can't give a clear analysis; the most I can do is make some rough sketchy gestures.[32]

Let's consider an analogous case involving an imaginary philosopher named Shmgettier. In this fantasy Gettier never existed. Shmgettier, however, presents a couple of novel examples. One of them concerns someone Smith who has evidence that Jones owns a Ford.... Well, we know the example. It's what we call in the real world a Gettier case. But Shmgettier's approach to this case is very different from that of the real life Gettier case. Shmgettier's point is that our best theory of knowledge, roughly that knowledge is true rational belief, teaches us that this case is a case of knowledge. Of course common sense says otherwise, but, Shmgettier declares, common sense is often wrong, and here is a case where philosophical theory shows us it is wrong.

"But," we object to Shmgettier, "you're merely misusing the English word 'knowledge.' As that word actually functions in the language it obviously doesn't apply to the kind of case you mentioned." "What 'kind of case' is that?" replies Shmgettier. "I simply don't understand how you think the English word 'knowledge' functions, if it doesn't function as I say. Give me a clear analysis of how you think it functions." Of course, that's exactly what we're not able to do.

So does Shmgettier win this argument? No, I think almost everyone will agree he doesn't. The lesson we learn from this case (and numerous others like it) might be put as follows: Charity trumps problems of analysis. When we interpret a language we proceed on the presumption that ordinary speakers are making correct judgments about examples. That presumption is not defeated by the difficulty (or impossibility) of giving a clear analysis of how the language functions.[33]

I think that, in fact, many revisionists ought not even to be tempted by the move I've just been discussing, the move of saying, "We simply don't understand how Shmenglish is supposed to function." The overall story told by revisionists will often provide the resources to say how Shmenglish functions. Four-dimensionalist universalists, for example, will almost always want to distinguish between the broad category of space-time worms that are physical objects and the sub-category of such objects that are talked about outside philosophy. Quine calls this sub-category "bodies."[34] One can then define Shmenglish simply as a language in which the most general word "(some) thing," as this applies within the domain (roughly) of space-occupying perceptible objects, is equivalent to "body." There can therefore be no complaint that the truth conditions of the sentences of Shmenglish have not been made intelligible. We have, then, a kind of *reductio* argument: Since four-dimensionalists distinguish between "bodies" and "other (space-occupying perceptible) objects," they can understand how Shmenglish operates by appealing to the former category. It must be clear to them, therefore, that Shmenglish is the dominant language of North America, i.e., English is Shmenglish. But, then, four-dimensionalists are hoisted with their own petards, for, speaking English, as they claim to be doing, they can no longer distinguish between "bodies" and "other (space-occupying perceptible) objects."

Considerations of complexity may play another kind of role in linguistic interpretation. Lewis has the well-known view that, in interpreting a language, there is the presumption that words express properties that are natural to a relatively high degree.[35] Degrees of naturalness are, for Lewis, the same as degrees of complexity relative to "perfectly" natural properties. This naturalness-presumption, as I will call it, ought to be viewed as a constraint beyond charity. The point is somewhat obscured by the fact that in Lewis's own discussion he seems to treat the naturalness-presumption as a corollary of the principle of charity. I have been talking about charity at the level of assertions: an interpretation is credible to the extent that it makes typical assertions come out reasonable (if not true). Perhaps Lewis thinks that there is another level of charity: the semantic structure of the language itself ought to be made reasonable. If this is the correct explanation of the naturalness-presumption, it would have to be the case that, other things being equal, it is unreasonable for people to have a language whose words express highly unnatural properties. I have devoted a book-length discussion to this question, and,

as far as I can make out, there would in fact be nothing unreasonable about this.[36] This makes me somewhat skeptical about the naturalness-presumption, though I think it would also be possible to take this presumption as irreducible and unrelated to charity at any level. The presumption is, in any case, a constraint beyond charity in my sense, i.e., charity at the level of linguistic behavior.

Perhaps we should back up for a moment and ask what the basis is for the principle of charity itself. The essential answer is given by Davidson: The simplest and most plausible explanation of any human behavior, including linguistic behavior, is, other things being equal, that there is a good reason for the behavior.[37] The principle of interpretive charity is simply an application of this general idea.

If we accept the naturalness-presumption, it might be possible to apply it to the word "unity (of a thing)," with the result that there is a presumption in favor of construing the unity relation as being not too complex. Even so, charity (at the level of assertions) trumps the naturalness-presumption, as Lewis would certainly agree. We see this in countless cases, such as the case of Shmgettier. Shmgettier's interpretation of "knowledge" assigns to this word a much simpler, and therefore more natural property than that assigned by the correct interpretation. Shmgettier is wrong because charity trumps naturalness. Certainly one would have to say the same thing about "unity." The revisionist's interpretation of that word would be wrong for just the same reason that Shmgettier's interpretation of "knowledge" is wrong. Shmgettier's essential folly is to perversely interpret the language in a way that implies that typical speakers make a priori false judgments about examples. That seems to be precisely the revisionist's folly.

The most significant response in the literature (known to me) to the kind of challenge that I am here posing to revisionism is found in some recent work by Theodore Sider.[38] Sider holds that there is, in addition to the principle of charity, and in addition to the naturalness-presumption, a third constraint: language ought to respect the world's "logical joints."[39] The part of the English language that is most closely connected to "logical joints" are such expressions as "(there) exists" and "(some) thing," the so-called quantifiers. Let us say that expressions in a language are *quantifier-like* if they function formally like the English quantifiers (roughly speaking, they satisfy the rules of the predicate calculus). Sider's third constraint implies that the quantifier-like expressions in any possible language must be *genuine quantifiers*, and this means that they must answer to reality's logical joints. There cannot, therefore, be different languages whose quantifier-like expressions have different (referential) meanings. Since quantifier-like expressions play the same formal role in different languages, they might be trivially said to share the same "formal meaning." Sider's position, however, is that such expressions must also share the same meaning in the sense of referring to (ranging over) the same objects.[40]

When it comes to quantifier-like expressions, therefore, charity falls out of the picture. Given that a language contains quantifier-like expressions it is already established that they have the only possible meanings that such expressions can have. Our task as ontologists is to try as best we can to describe *what really exists*, and in doing so we know in advance that we are at the same time describing what is referred to by the quantifier-like expressions of any possible language. Ontology teaches us, therefore, that Shmenglish – the imagined language in which the sentences typically asserted by speakers of English come out true – is a *metaphysically impossible language*. As charitable as we would like to be to ordinary people's ontological assertions, therefore, we cannot avoid the conclusion that many of these assertions are false.

I think that Sider's underlying assumption is that the truth conditions of the sentences of any possible language must be generable by (something approximating to) a Tarski-style referential semantics, with the quantifier-like expressions ranging over everything ("everything" as defined by the true ontology).[41] Of course, if we are operating from *inside* Shmenglish there would be no special problem in generating the imagined truth conditions of its sentences by what looks like a Tarski-style treatment. But that does not suffice, according to Sider, for ontology teaches us in advance that operating from inside Shmenglish is not even a possibility.

It seems to me that Sider's position is the only hope for revisionists, but I find it to be a dim hope. Of course I am bothered (as Sider himself

is) by the heavy metaphysical apparatus of "logical joints," and also by the quite mysterious epistemology that must go with it. But what is more centrally of concern to me is Sider's contention that, as regards quantifier-like expressions, charity doesn't count. Sider's third constraint, therefore, goes far beyond Lewis's naturalness-presumption. It is, in fact, not a presumption, but an absolute and indefeasible requirement. Why should we suppose that there is any such absolute requirement on language? How indeed *can* there be such a requirement? Sider seems willing to say that in an important sense "we can't mean what we want" by the quantifier-like expressions.[42] Worse, in refusing to interpret charitably the English language we actually speak, Sider's position implies that in an important sense we can't possibly mean what we in fact *seem* to mean. Why should anyone accept this? The position seems to me primarily designed to provide revisionists a carte blanche to fly in the face of common sense.

VI

A number of philosophers have reacted to my point of view by cautioning me about the difficulty in determining what ordinary people – typical fluent speakers of the language – really believe about the existence and identity of moderate-sized dry goods. Certainly there are difficulties; I've limited myself here to saying only enough to reveal the basic error of revisionism. Part of the difficulty is to find the proper balance in both acknowledging and not exaggerating the genuine elements of vagueness and indeterminateness in the ordinary language of existence and identity. A familiar experience for a philosophy professor is that some students can easily be induced to accept almost any ontological position. What follows? That all bets are off, that there are no rules of language? No, what follows is that interpreting a language is a delicate matter. First and foremost one has to avoid kicking the language around, pushing it where one wants it to go. Austin called his method "linguistic phenomenology," which I think suggests the idea of allowing the linguistic phenomena to come to light without willful manipulation.[43] The most important linguistic data are not acquired primarily from the conflicting utterances characteristically generated under philosophical pressure, but primarily from the relatively spontaneous and unreflective utterances shared by virtually all speakers, including philosophers.

If our philosophical business is the ontology of moderate-sized dry goods – and that is, obviously, not the only important part of metaphysics – we need to put aside the currently fashionable revisionist's mannerisms: the comical battles with ordinary language, the lawyer's briefs for and against entities, the mock-theoretical debates about what objects exist in front of our eyes. If our business is the ontology of moderate-sized dry goods then our only philosophical task is to explore the currents and undercurrents of our ordinary ways of thinking and talking about the perceptible world around us.

Notes

I owe a debt of gratitude to Ned Markosian. Trenton Merricks, and Ted Sider for many important criticisms of a much earlier draft of this paper, which led to extensive revisions.

1 Universalists who accept temporal parts are often called "four-dimensionalists." Examples are W. V. Quine, *Word and Object* (Cambridge, Mass.: MIT Press, 1960), esp. 171; David Lewis, *On the Plurality of Worlds* (Oxford: Basil Blackwell, 1986), esp. 202–4, 211–13 [and ch. 37 in this volume]; Mark Heller, *The Ontology of Physical Objects: Four-Dimensional Hunks of Matter* (Cambridge: Cambridge University Press, 1990): ch. 1 [ch. 36 in this volume]; Theodore Sider, *Four-Dimensionalism: An Ontology of Persistence and Time* (New York: Oxford University Press, 2001) [partly reproduced as ch. 50 in this volume]. Universalists who reject temporal parts are rare, but include Judith Jarvis Thomson, "Parthood and Identity across Time." *Journal of Philosophy* 80 (1983): 201–20 [ch. 35 in this volume]; and James van Cleve, "Mereological Essentialism, Mereological Conjunctivism, and Identity through Time," *Midwest Studies in Philosophy XI: Studies in Essentialism* (1986). An argument from universalism to temporal parts is given in Richard Cartwright, "Scattered Objects," in *Analysis and Metaphysics*, ed. K. Lehrer (Dordrecht: Reidel, 1975).

2 Peter Unger, "There Are No Ordinary Things," *Synthese* 41 (1980): 117–54, and "I Do Not Exist," in

Perception and Identity: Essays Presented to A. J. Ayer with His Replies to Them, ed. G. F. Macdonald (New York: Macmillan, 1979).

3 Roderick Chisholm is a "mereological essentialist" who holds that the only things that exist are things that have the same parts from moment to moment (and from world to world); see *Person and Object* (LaSalle, Ill.: Open Court, 1976); ch. 3 [ch. 33 in this volume]. This position is defended further in van Cleve, "Mereological Essentialism, Mereological Conjunctivism, and Identity through Time." Peter van Inwagen believes that the only composite things that exist are living things; see *Material Beings* (Ithaca, N.Y.: Cornell University Press, 1990). A variation of this position, defended with different (and clearer) arguments, is given in Trenton Merricks, *Objects and Persons* (Oxford: Oxford University Press, 2001) [partly reproduced in ch. 51 of this volume].

4 G. E. Moore, "A Defense of Common Sense," esp. 41, and "Four Forms of Scepticism," esp. 222, both in *Philosophical Papers* (New York: Collier Books, 1962). A Moorean argument against revisionary ontology is interestingly developed in Ned Markosian, "Brutal Composition," *Philosophical Studies* 92 (1988): 211–49.

5 Quine, *Word and Object*, 59; Donald Davidson, *Inquiries into Truth and Interpretation* (London: Oxford University Press, 1984), esp. "Belief and the Basis of Meaning" and "Thought and Talk"; David Lewis, "Radical Interpretation," in *Philosophical Papers I* (New York: Oxford University Press, 1983), and "New Work for a Theory of Universals," *Australasian Journal of Philosophy* 61 (1983): 343–77, at 370–7 [ch. 23 in this volume].

6 Within the context of this discussion I don't think it's important to worry about distinctions – coming out of Kripke's work – between "a priori necessary," "conceptually necessary," "epistemically necessary," "metaphysically necessary." Although it's the first two that are most crucial to my argument, I think that the typical revisionist is claiming that common sense beliefs are necessarily false in all these ways.

7 Thomson has urged in conversation that ordinary people quite easily accept *portions of matter*, even, for example, the scattered portion of matter that makes up Clinton's nose and the Eiffel Tower. That may be. But I take it for granted that the universalist's "fusions" are not limited to contemporaneous portions of matter.

8 Cf. my papers "Quantifier Variance and Realism," *Philosophical Issues* 12 (2002): 55–6 and "Sosa's Existential Relativism," in John Greco (ed.), *Ernest Sosa and his Critics* (Oxford: Blackwell Publishing), 224–32.

9 J. L. Austin, *Sense and Sensibilia* (London: Oxford University Press, 1962), 8.

10 Ludwig Wittgenstein, *Philosophical Investigations* (Oxford: Blackwell, 1953), 1, 38.

11 Wittgenstein, *Philosophical Investigations*, 1, 401.

12 This is van Inwagen's famous formulation, which has been taken over by many revisionists.

13 This entire paper hovers in the vicinity of, but does not enter into, issues about the ultimate nature of semantic content, especially the issues discussed in Saul A. Kripke, *Wittgenstein on Rules and Private Languages* (Cambridge, Mass.: Harvard University Press, 1982). Do 2 and 3 strictly entail 4 or is the connection in some sense probabilistic? I leave that open. It seems clear, however, that anyone who asserts 2 and 3 should assert 4.

14 Joseph Butler, "Of Personal Identity," in *The Whole Works of Joseph Butler, LLD.* (London: Thomas Tegg, 1836), 263–70; Chisholm, *Person and Object* [partly reproduced as ch. 33 in this volume].

15 The example was offered to me by Donald Baxter to help me to understand what people like Butler and Chisholm are talking about, but I use it to the opposite effect.

16 Closely related to this distinction, and equally obscure, is van Inwagen's attempt to distinguish between what a sentence expresses "in the ordinary business of life" and what it expresses "in the philosophy room." Van Inwagen, *Material Beings*, 98–107, and "Reply to Reviewers," *Philosophy and Phenomenological Research* 53 (1993): 709–19, at 711. For a critique of van Inwagen's crypto-revisionism, see Merricks, *Objects and Persons*, 162–70.

17 Lewis. *On the Plurality of Worlds*, 3 and 212–13.

18 Revisionists from every camp have tried to capitalize on this principle, including Cartwright, van Cleve, van Inwagen, Heller, and Merricks.

19 The role of examples in linguistic interpretation is especially emphasized in Tyler Burge, "Intellectual Norms and Foundations of Mind," *Journal of Philosophy* 83 (1986): 697–720.

20 John Locke, *An Essay concerning Human Understanding* (1690), book 2, ch. 27.

21 David Lewis, "Survival and Identity," in *The Identities of Persons*, ed. A. Rorty (Berkeley: University of California Press, 1976), 26–7 [ch. 43 in this volume].

22 Two examples: first, the principle that a quality cannot be formally treated as a relation between a thing and a time, invoked in behalf of temporal parts in Lewis, *On the Plurality of Worlds*, 202–4; second, the principle that a composite thing cannot be causally redundant in a certain technical sense, invoked in behalf of quasi-nihilism in Merricks, *Objects and Persons*, ch. 3 [ch. 51 in this volume].

23 I suspect that for some philosophers it will be hardest to give up certain principles involving the vagueness of existence and identity which generate problems for common sense. I've tried to directly address these problems in "The Vagueness of Identity," *Philosophical Topics: The Philosophy of Sydney Shoemaker* 26 (1999): 139–58; and "Quantifier Variance and Realism."

24 1, 66.

25 If typical speakers assert "Whales are fish" and we interpret the sentence as being false, this may require an appeal to Lewis's "naturalness-presumption," to be discussed later.

26 Merricks suggests that, although the ontological assertions of ordinary folk are not really supported by any sensory data, and are refutable by a priori philosophical arguments, they are nevertheless a "justified starting-point" because they are "a matter of conventional wisdom and local custom" (*Objects and Persons*, 74–75 [p. 681 in this volume]). Charity, however, requires us to look for an interpretation of these assertions that assigns "good reasons" to them in a more robust sense.

27 Persons, however, may be a specimen of moderate-sized dry goods that have to be treated differently. To the extent that the question "Will that future person be me?" is linked to the normative question "Ought I to have some special concern for that person?", I'm not sure if an appeal to ordinary English usage completely suffices to answer even the first question (let alone, the second). For a slightly different angle on essentially the same point, see Alan Sidelle, "On the Prospects for a Theory of Personal Identity," *Philosophical Topics: The Philosophy of Sydney Shoemaker* 26 (1999): 351–72.

28 The argument I'm referring to is in *Analysis and Metaphysics*, ed. K. Lehrer (Dordrecht: Reidel, 1975).

29 *Material Beings*, esp. 64–71 and 122–3.

30 Markosian, "Brutal Composition," suggests that the unity relation is in principle not amenable to any finitary non-circular analysis. This is, I think, a very interesting possibility, but a lot will turn on what one means by a "non-circular analysis."

31 This question applies even more obviously to those numerous (quasi-) nihilists who repudiate tables by appealing to Ockham's razor: How could that appeal possibly show that English is not Shmenglish?

32 Actually I made 311 pages worth of rough sketchy gestures in *The Concept of Identity* (New York: Oxford University Press, 1982).

33 Note that, unlike Shmgettier's question, classical skeptical issues are typically about our "right to be sure," and this apparently normative component may not be resolvable merely by appealing to ordinary language.

34 W. V. Quine, *The Roots of Reference* (LaSalle, Ill.: Open Court, 1974), 54.

35 David Lewis, "New Work for a Theory of Universals," 370–7 [pp 323–7 in this volume].

36 *Dividing Reality* (New York: Oxford University Press, 1993).

37 *Truth and Interpretation*, esp. 159–60.

38 "Criteria of Personal Identity and the Limits of Conceptual Analysis," in *Philosophical Perspectives* 15 (2001), and the Introduction to *Four Dimensionalism: An Ontology of Persistence and Time*. Sider is, as far us I know, alone amongst current revisionists in recognizing that they face a erious problem with respect to interpretive charity.

39 Sider bases linguistic interpretation on what he calls "use" and "eligibility." The first corresponds roughly to what I call "charity," and the second to what I call "constraints beyond charity." The latter constraints divide up, for Sider, into the naturalness-presumption and the additional constraint about "logical joints."

40 Sider does allow that there could be explicit stipulations that assign different (referential) meanings to quantifier-like expressions, but such different meaning would be by necessity derivative of the primary meaning. He may also allow for the possibility of languages that have no quantifier-like expressions at all. Let me ignore these complications.

41 On possible connections between this formulation and the philosophical positions in Davidson, the *Tractatus*, and the *Philosophical Investigations*, see Kripke, *Wittgenstein on Rules and Private Languages*, 71–2, note 60.

42 A more focused discussion of the specific issue of assigning different meanings to quantifier expressions is given in "Quantifier Variance and Realism" and "Sosa's Existential Relativism."

43 J. L. Austin, "A Plea for Excuses," in *Philosophical Papers* (Oxford: Oxford University Press, 1961), 130.

53

Strange Kinds, Familiar Kinds, and the Charge of Arbitrariness

Daniel Z. Korman

1 Prelude

A snowdiscall is something made of snow that has any shape between being round and being disc-shaped *and* which has the following strange persistence conditions: it can survive taking on all and only shapes in that range. So a round snowdiscall can survive being flattened into a disc but cannot survive being packed into the shape of a brick. Ernest Sosa observes that one can avoid commitment to snowdiscalls, and a plenitude of other strange kinds, by embracing either some form of eliminativism on which there are neither snowballs nor snowdiscalls or else some form of relativism on which material objects do not exist simpliciter but only relative to some conceptual scheme or other.[1] Curiously, the natural view that there are no snowdiscalls, that there are snowballs, and that snowballs exist *simpliciter* is not among the options that Sosa considers.

2 Particularism

Particularism about a given domain of inquiry is the view that our intuitive judgments about cases in the domain are largely correct and that, when intuitive judgments about cases conflict with compelling general principles, the cases should in general be treated as counterexamples to those principles.[2] The distinction between particularists and nonparticularists cuts little ice in most domains. For instance, apart from skeptics, virtually all parties to the debates about empirical knowledge and justification are particularists – reliabilists and evidentialists, foundationalists and coherentists, internalists and externalists, contextualists and invariantists – never straying far from the bulk of our intuitive judgments about cases, even if they cannot accommodate all of them.

The distinction does, however, cut ice in material-object metaphysics, in which many of the dominant views flout wide swaths of our intuitive judgements about cases. Here I especially have in mind views on which there are far more or far fewer things than we intuitively judge there to be: universalist views on which composition is unrestricted at a time or even across time, plenitudinous views on which familiar objects exactly coincide with countless other objects with slightly or wildly different modal profiles, and eliminativist views on which virtually none of the things that we intuitively judge to exist in fact

Daniel Z. Korman, "Strange Kinds, Familiar Kinds, and the Charge of Arbitrariness," *Oxford Studies in Metaphysics*, 5 (2010). Reproduced by permission.

Metaphysics: An Anthology, Second Edition. Edited by Jaegwon Kim, Daniel Z. Korman and Ernest Sosa.

exist.[3] This constitutes a dramatic departure from standard philosophical methodology.

What accounts for this departure? One possible explanation is that metaphysicians have become convinced – for instance, by familiar strategies for reconciling revisionary ontologies with ordinary discourse – that the relevant intuitive judgments are based on intuitions whose contents do not support those judgments and do not entail the falsity of their revisionary ontological theses.[4] But these strategies have little prima facie plausibility, and it is difficult to believe that anyone who was not antecedently convinced that the intuitive judgments were mistaken would be moved by the suggestion that these intuitions are being misreported.[5]

The explanation is rather that they have been convinced by some argument against particularism in material-object metaphysics. These arguments fall into two broad categories: rebutting arguments and undercutting arguments. Rebutting arguments are arguments for conclusions that directly contradict some specific range of intuitive judgments about cases, the most prominent being the argument from vagueness, causal exclusion arguments, and arguments from the impossibility of distinct coincident items. Undercutting arguments are arguments for the conclusion that our intuitive judgments about cases are (probably) unreliable, but that do not purport to demonstrate the falsity of any specific range of intuitive judgments. Although the rebutting arguments are by far the more widely discussed of the two, it is difficult to believe that these arguments are primarily responsible for the widespread aversion to particularism in material-object metaphysics. After all, every philosophical domain has its share of powerful rebutting arguments, yet it is only in material-object metaphysics that such arguments do not typically inspire a Moorean confidence that at least one of the principles that drives the argument must be false.

I suspect that it is rather the undercutting arguments that lie at the root of the aversion to particularism in material-object metaphysics. In what follows, I address one sort of undercutting argument, which turns on the claim that the particularist's differential treatment of strange and familiar kinds is intolerably arbitrary. The literature is now replete with examples of such kinds – apceans, bligers, bonangles, carples,

cdogs, cpeople, cupcups, dwods, gollyswoggles, incars, klables, monewments, shmees, shmrees, trables, trout-turkeys, wakers – and the charge of arbitrariness has been leveled (in one form or another) by numerous authors.[6] But, despite how influential the charge has been, there has been virtually no discussion of how particularists might respond to the charge.

There are at least two other sorts of undercutting arguments worth mentioning (setting aside those that generalize to intuitions in all domains). First, there are a variety of arguments having to do with the subject matter of material-object metaphysics, for instance, that questions in material-object metaphysics concern substantive facts about the world and therefore cannot be settled by (anything like) conceptual analysis.[7] Second, there are a variety of arguments having to do with the apparent impossibility of subsuming our intuitive judgments about cases under interesting general principles.[8]

My ambitions in this paper are modest in one respect, ambitious in another. The modesty lies in its scope. I do not argue for particularism or against revisionary ontologies. I argue only that particularists have the resources to resist the argument from arbitrariness, and I have done my best to disentangle this argument from the others. The ambition lies in the background metaontology. I will show that the argument from arbitrariness can be resisted without retreating to any sort of deflationary view of ontology. Particularists need not embrace any form of relativism about ordinary material objects, nor need they accept the deflationary doctrine of quantifier variance according to which there are counterparts of our quantifiers that are on a par with ours and that range over things that do not exist (but rather, e.g., shmexist).[9] Let us then distinguish between *deflationary particularists*, who couple their particularist ontology with a deflationary metaontology, and *robust particularists*, who opt for a nondeflationary metaontology. I suspect that the argument from arbitrariness owes at least some of its influence to the presumption (implicit in Sosa's trilemma) that robust particularism is a nonstarter and that the only viable alternative to a revisionary ontology is some form of deflationary particularism – or, in the words of John Hawthorne, "a kind of anti-realism that none of us should tolerate."[10]

For ease of exposition, I sometimes refer to "what particularists will say" about a given case. But no less than in other domains, particularism in material-object metaphysics is a matter of degree and can come in endless varieties. Some particularists in epistemology and philosophy of language are willing to bite bullets in at least some cases (fake barn cases, seemingly informative identities, etc.), and particularists in material-object metaphysics may do the same. There also is endless room for disagreement among particularists about which kinds of things there are, about the persistence conditions of various familiar kinds, about whether it is at least possible for various strange kinds to have instances, about what it would take for various strange kinds to have instances, and so forth.

Although particularism possibly deserves the label 'folk ontology' or 'commonsense ontology', I hesitate to use these labels for two reasons. First, particularists can be expected to reject highly intuitive general principles (e.g., about material coincidence) which the folk will assent to and which seem equally deserving of the label 'common sense'. Second, the label may be misleading in the following respect. I wish to understand 'intuitive judgments about cases' not in terms of how the folk respond to philosophical interrogation or surveys, but rather in terms of how things seem to philosophers, who are alert to relevant distinctions and who know the difference between reporting their intuitions and reporting their considered judgments. However important the folk's intuitions may or may not be, they are too likely to misreport or misrepresent their intuitions for their responses to be of much use to philosophers.[11]

3   The Argument from Arbitrariness

The argument from arbitrariness turns on the claim that there is no difference between certain of the familiar kinds that we intuitively judge to exist and certain of the strange kinds that we intuitively judge not to exist that could account for the former's but not the latter's having instances. In short, there is no *ontologically significant difference* between the relevant strange and familiar kinds. Arguments from arbitrariness will have the following form:

(P1)   There is no ontologically significant difference between Ks and K´s.

(P2)   If there is no ontologically significant difference between Ks and K´s, then it is objectionably arbitrary to countenance things of kind K but not things of kind K´.

(C)   So it is objectionably arbitrary to countenance things of kind K but not things of kind K´.

Deflationary particularists will typically deny P2. Countenancing familiar kinds but not strange kinds is objectionably arbitrary only if one thereby privileges the familiar kinds. But deflationary particularists will deny that existent kinds enjoy a privileged status. According to relativists, snowballs exist and snowdiscalls do not exist – relative to our scheme, that is – but, relative to other schemes, snowdiscalls exist and snowballs do not exist.[12] According to quantifier variantists, snowballs exist but do not shmexist, and snowdiscalls shmexist but do not exist. So at bottom there is a uniform treatment of strange and familiar kinds.

This sort of strategy is available only to deflationary particularists and, as indicated above, my goal is to show how robust particularists can resist the charge of arbitrariness. I know of no way for robust particularists to address all instances of the argument *en masse*; we will have to take them case by case. Before turning to the cases, however, let me make three preliminary remarks.

First, in what follows I will identify what seem to be ontologically significant differences between various strange and familiar kinds without taking the further step of attempting to establish that the differences are indeed ontologically significant. I do not consider this a shortcoming of my response to the argument from arbitrariness. An analogy: In explaining why a certain justified true belief counts as knowledge in one case but not in another, one might appeal to some feature F (e.g., having a defeater) that is present in the one case and absent in the other. There is an interesting question – which may or may not have an answer – of why F is epistemically significant, but it would be a mistake to insist that answering this question is a prerequisite to explaining why there is knowledge in one case but not the other. Furthermore, having an account of F's epistemic significance is not required for having a reason to believe that F is epistemically significant: the reason would simply be that the presence of F *seems* to be making a difference both in the case at hand and across a wide range of cases. Analogously, there can be good reason to accept that a certain feature marks an ontologically significant difference between two kinds – that it explains why one kind has instances while another does not – even in the absence of an account of what makes that feature ontologically significant.[13] I will therefore take myself to have defended the particularist against the charge of arbitrariness if I can achieve the more modest goal of identifying differences between strange and familiar kinds that do at least *seem* ontologically significant and that do not simply amount to the former's being unfamiliar, or uninteresting, or intuitively nonexistent, or failing to fall under any of our sortals.

Second, uncovering the metaphysics of familiar kinds is often quite complicated, and I suspect that part of the force of the charge of arbitrariness comes, illegitimately, from the intricacy of these issues and an impatience for long digressions into the metaphysics of snowballs, statues, solar systems, and so forth. If one finds one's intuitions about familiar kinds unmanageable at times, one should bear in mind that this may be because metaphysics is difficult, not because the questions or our intuitions are somehow defective.[14]

Third, although I follow anti-particularists in characterizing these as cases of arbitrariness, this characterization is highly tendentious. Arbitrary judgments are those based on random choice or personal whim. The characterization is apt in other familiar charges of arbitrariness in metaphysics, for instance, that it is arbitrary to identify the number two with $\{\{\emptyset\}\}$ rather than $\{\emptyset, \{\emptyset\}\}$.[15] Here, not only can we find no difference between the two sets that could account for the one but not the other's being the number two, there also is not even prima facie reason to believe that the one but not the other is the number two. By contrast, we do have at least prima facie reason for taking there to be snowballs but no snowdiscalls, for this view has strong intuitive support. Our reasons for the differential treatment of snowballs and snowdiscalls are therefore no different in kind from our reasons for the differential treatment of Gettier cases and paradigm cases of knowledge and are hardly a matter of whim or random choice.[16]

4 Toddlers and Toddlescents

A toddlescent is a material object that comes into existence whenever a child reaches the age of two, ceases to exist when the child reaches the age of fourteen, and is exactly co-located with the child at all times in between. Particularists will deny that there are toddlescents. Yet particularists will accept that there are toddlers. Is this differential treatment of toddlers and toddlescents arbitrary?

Not at all, for there is an important difference between toddlers and toddlescents. Unlike toddlers, toddlescents would have to be things that cease to exist without any of their constitutive matter undergoing any intrinsic change. Toddlers, by contrast, do not cease to exist when they grow up; they merely cease to be toddlers. A separate question is whether there are toddlescent*s, where a toddlescent* is a child between the ages of two and fourteen. Particularists will of course agree that there are toddlescent*s. Some of them are toddlers, others are adolescents – things that we intuitively judge to exist. Toddlescents, however, cannot be either of these things on account of their strange persistence conditions.[17]

One must therefore take care to distinguish between strange phased kinds, like toddlescent*s, and strange individuative kinds, like toddlescents and snowdiscalls, when consulting one's intuitions about strange kinds.[18] Phased kinds are kinds whose instances can cease to belong to that kind without ceasing to exist. Individuative kinds are kinds whose instances cannot cease to belong without ceasing to exist: they are of that kind as a matter of de re necessity. Things belonging to strange phased kinds are often perfectly familiar things with perfectly ordinary persistence conditions; it is the things belonging to strange individuative kinds to which particularists take exception. I have found that those who cannot even see the *pretheoretical* reason for refusing to countenance the strange kinds discussed in the literature are often conflating phased and individuative kinds.

5 Islands and Incars

A full-sized incar is like a car in nearly all respects. The main difference is that, unlike a car, it is metaphysically impossible for an incar to leave a garage. As the incar inches toward the great outdoors, it begins to shrink at the threshold of the garage, at which time an outcar springs into existence and begins growing. What it looks like for an incar to shrink and gradually be replaced by an outcar is exactly the same as what it looks like for a car to leave a garage. But an incar is not a car (or even a part of a car) that is inside a garage, for a (part of a) car that is inside a garage can later be outside the garage.

Hawthorne maintains that "none but the most insular metaphysician should countenance islands while repudiating incars."[19] The suggestion, I take it, is that there is no ontologically significant difference between islands and incars. Hawthorne evidently believes that islands shrink and ultimately cease to exist as their constitutive matter comes to be fully submerged, just as incars shrink and ultimately cease to exist as their constitutive matter leaves the garage.

Particularists should reject this characterization of islands. Suppose that an island is entirely submerged every day at high tide. Intuitively, it is still there at high tide – under the water – and when it re-emerges at low tide, it has not suffered interrupted existence.[20] Incars, by contrast, cease to exist when their constitutive matter leaves the garage, and without any of their constitutive matter undergoing any intrinsic change. This would seem to be an ontologically significant difference between islands and incars.[21]

It may be that those who were initially moved by Hawthorne's objection were confusing incars with incar*s, where an incar* is a car that is inside a garage. There is no ontologically significant difference between islands and incar*s, but particularists will not deny that there are incar*s. Alternatively, it may be that they were confusing the question of whether the island ceases to exist when entirely submerged with the separate (and less pressing) question of whether an island ceases to be *an island* when it is entirely submerged. Some will be inclined to say that nothing that is entirely submerged, even momentarily, is at that time an island; others will say that islands continue to be islands when entirely submerged. I am inclined to say that an island ceases to be an island only when permanently submerged, or else when the waters recede and it comes to be part of a peninsula. Nothing hangs on this question of classification. For however

one answers it, one can agree that all islands have perfectly ordinary persistence conditions and, in particular, that they do not cease to exist when submerged.

6 Pages and Monewments

A monewment is like a monument insofar as it is a material object that has the function of commemorating a certain person or event. But monewments have more permissive persistence conditions than monuments: if the constitutive matter of the monewment is annihilated, and a qualitatively identical material object is erected at the location of the original monewment, that material object is numerically identical to the original monewment. Particularists will deny that there are such things as monewments.

Carl Ginet contends that we already countenance material objects of just this sort, for instance, pages of a typescript:

> Suppose that *this* typescript's 18th page were now constituted of wholly different matter from that which constituted it yesterday, because I spilled coffee over it and had to retype it. The 18th page of this typescript (*this* page, I might say, holding it up) ceased to exist altogether for a while but now it exists again in a new embodiment.[22]

The suggestion is that pages, like monewments, are material objects that can survive undergoing a complete change of matter in a nonpiecemeal fashion. If so, then it may seem that there is no ontologically significant difference between the two.

Particularists should deny that there is a single material object answering to 'the 18th page' that once had coffee spilled on it and is now in Ginet's hand. Obviously, the mere fact that 'the 18th page' once referred to the coffee-stained page and now refers to the page in Ginet's hand does not suffice to show that there is a single material object that was the 18th page at both times, any more than the fact that 'the president' once referred to Clinton and now refers to Obama suffices to show that there is a single individual who was the president at both times. There presumably is a *type* answering to 'the 18th page' which, once the typescript goes to press, will have multiple tokens; and perhaps this is a thing that ceases to exist and comes back into existence in the case that Ginet describes.[23] But this is an abstract object, not a material object. There is a sheet of paper in Ginet's hand, but that sheet never had coffee spilled on it; when the coffee was spilled, that sheet was across the room on top of a stack of other blank sheets. And even those who take the page to be a material object that is distinct from the sheet will insist that the page in Ginet's hand is something that began to exist – not something that came back into existence – when the words were retyped on the new sheet.[24]

So, unlike a monewment, neither the 18th page nor any of its tokens is a material object that can survive a complete and nonpiecemeal replacement of its constitutive matter. This would seem to be an ontologically significant difference between monewments and manuscript pages.

7   Statues and Gollyswoggles

You have absent-mindedly kneaded a piece of clay into an unusual shape. Let us say that anything with exactly that shape is gollyswoggle-shaped. Something is a gollyswoggle just in case it is essentially gollyswoggle-shaped. Particularists will agree that there are statues but deny that there are gollyswoggles: some things are gollyswoggle-shaped, but nothing is essentially gollyswoggle-shaped.

Van Inwagen find this unacceptable: "I should think that if our sculptor brought a statue into existence, then you brought a gollyswoggle into existence."[25] Van Inwagen evidently thinks that there is no ontologically significant difference between statues and gollyswoggles, including the presence of creative intentions in the one case and their absence in the other: "our sculptor intended to produce something statue-shaped while you, presumably, did not intend to produce anything gollyswoggle-shaped. But these facts would seem to be irrelevant to any questions about the existence of the thing produced."[26]

Yet our intuitive judgments about cases suggest that creative intentions are indeed relevant to what kinds of things there are. Suppose that a meteoroid, as a result of random collisions with space junk, temporarily comes to be a qualitative duplicate of some actual statue. Intuitively,

nothing new comes into existence which, unlike the meteoroid, cannot survive further collisions that deprive the meteoroid of its statuesque form.[27] Likewise, unintentionally and momentarily kneading some clay into the shape of a gollyswoggle does not suffice for the creation of something that has that shape essentially. When a piece of clay comes to be, and moments later ceases to be, gollyswoggle-shaped, this does not involve the generation of new objects, any more than a two-year-old's becoming a three-year-old involves the generation of any new object. The particularist should therefore contend that the fact that many have set out to make statues, while no one has ever set out to make a gollyswoggle, is an ontologically significant difference between statues and gollyswoggles, in which case the differential treatment is not arbitrary.[28]

Does this view of artifacts as mind-dependent constitute a departure from the fullblooded ontological realism promised at the outset? Perhaps. But it is important to appreciate just how benign the needed degree of mind-dependence is. The artifacts cannot have begun to exist without us but, once created, they do not depend on us for their continued existence. Moreover, once created, their modal features remain entirely independent of how we later come to use them or conceive of them. This opens the door for community-wide error, for instance, of unearthing ancient cooking utensils and mistaking them for religious relics, or finding the statue-shaped meteoroid and mistakenly taking it to be an artifact and to have its form essentially. This is about as realist as one can get about artifacts.[29]

There are a number of other questions that one might be tempted to ask at this point about the metaphysics of artifacts: Can one bring a new object into existence simply by placing a piece of driftwood in one's living room and using it as a coffee table? Or by signing one's name on a urinal and placing it in a museum? Or by pointing at some stuff, specifying some persistence conditions (however strange), and declaring that that stuff constitutes something with those persistence conditions? Is it possible to *intentionally* make a gollyswoggle (or incar, or snowdiscall)? If not, what are the constraints on our creative powers?

I do not deny that these are difficult questions. There presumably are constraints on the creation of artifacts, and the nature of those constraints has been studied in some detail.[30] But even those particularists who hold that creative powers are radically unconstrained may still insist that there are statues but no gollyswoggles and cite the absence of the relevant creative intentions as an ontologically significant difference between the two. In any event, answering the argument from arbitrariness is one thing, supplying a theory of artifacts is another, and I am here concerned only with the former.

8 Snowballs and Snowdiscalls

Particularists will insist that the presence or absence of the relevant creative intentions is an ontologically significant difference between statues and gollyswoggles. It is open to particularists to account for the difference between snowballs and Sosa's snowdiscalls along similar lines: clumps of snow sometimes constitute snowballs but never snowdiscalls because people have intended to make snowballs but (to my knowledge) no one has ever intended to make a snowdiscall.

For what it is worth, I suspect that (pace Sosa) snowballs are not an individuative kind at all but rather a phased kind. Snowballs are identical to round clumps of snow, and they cease to be snowballs when flattened but do not cease to exist. That snowballs are just clumps of snow, while snowdiscalls are meant to be constituted by (and modally different from) clumps of snow, is itself an ontologically significant difference between snowballs and snowdiscalls. And, as should by now be clear, particularists will have no objection to instances of the associated phased kind, snowdiscall*, where a snowdiscall* is a clump of snow that has any shape between being round and being disc-shaped.

9 Scattered Objects

It is often alleged that there is no ontologically significant difference between the scattered objects that we do countenance and those that we do not.[31] In some cases, there are obvious differences: for instance, the disjoint microscopic parts of the table together exhibit a kind of unity, continuity, and causal covariance that is altogether lacking in the case of the alleged fusion of

my nose and the Eiffel Tower.[32] In other cases, the grounds for differential treatment are less obvious. I will discuss various strategies available to particularists for explaining away the apparent arbitrariness in such cases.

As we have already seen, creative intentions do seem relevant to the existence of artifacts, and scattered artifacts are no exception. Whether a steel ball and steel rod arranged letter-'i'-wise compose something will depend upon whether they came to be so arranged by accident or as a result of someone intending to make a lower-case letter 'i'. Likewise, the ontologically significant difference between a work of art consisting of several disconnected parts and the alleged fusion of my nose and the Eiffel Tower is the presence of relevant creative intentions in the one case and their absence in the other. This account may also be extended to scattered institutional entities, like the Supreme Court, and scattered geopolitical entities, like the state of Michigan.[33] In those cases, something is created without the sort of hands-on labor that is usually involved in bringing an artifact into existence. This is not to say that one can stipulate things into existence willy-nilly; as with ordinary artifacts, there presumably are constraints on the creation of such entities.[34] Some may still feel that if this sort of "spooky action at a distance" is what is needed to vindicate our intuitive judgments about cases, then it is not worth the cost.[35] Such is the difference between them and particularists. The charge of arbitrariness should move only those who already embrace a certain stringent view of what sort of factors are relevant to composition.

Now let us now turn to scattered nonartifacts, taking the solar system as a representative example. Despite being a scattered object, the solar system exhibits a degree of unity altogether lacking in the universalist's strange fusions. The solar system has boundaries demarcated by natural properties: the objects in the solar system are the smallest collection of objects containing the sun, each of whose primary gravitational influences are only the others in the collection. Furthermore, the solar system, not unlike an organism, is self-sustaining: it retains its form by means of forces internal to the system. So there do look to be ontologically significant differences between solar systems and the universalist's strange fusions; though, as indicated in §3, the task of supplying an argument that these differences are ontologically significant lies outside the scope of this paper.[36]

This, however, is not the only response available to particularists. The particularist *could* simply concede that there is no ontologically significant difference between the solar system and the strange fusion and admit that the latter exists. Perhaps the strange fusion is not so strange after all: it too is a system (whose parts exert certain forces on one another) and, when we intuitively judged there to be nothing whose parts are my nose and the Eiffel Tower, it was because we had neglected to consider the system whose parts are my nose and the Eiffel Tower.[37] Particularists who takes this line will still deny that there are such modally strange things as incars, monewments, gollyswoggles, and snowdiscalls. But they evidently must (on pain of arbitrariness) admit that composition is unrestricted, at least when it comes to items that exert some force on one another, thereby comprising a system. This response may seem to be in tension with particularism. But in a way, this would simply be a case of particularism in action: our concrete-case intuitive judgment that there is a system that has them as parts takes precedence over our intuitive judgment about the generalization that there is nothing that has them as parts.

Alternatively, particularists might contend that the ontologically significant difference between the fusion of my nose and the Eiffel Tower and the solar system is that the former, but not the latter, is a single individual.[38] The solar system is not a single individual; it is many individuals. 'The solar system' may be syntactically singular but, on the present account, it is nevertheless semantically plural: it refers, not to a set of heavenly bodies or to a fusion of heavenly bodies, but to some heavenly bodies.[39] One problem with this account is that solar systems do not seem to have the right sort of modal profile to be pluralities. Pluralities presumably have exactly the parts that they do essentially, whereas solar systems can survive gaining and losing parts.[40] However, particularists might take a page from the revisionary ontologist's playbook here and insist that 'solar systems can survive gaining and losing parts' is true only in a loose and misleading sense.[41] Just as no one thing actually becomes longer as the part of this sentence that you have read thus far gets

longer, no one thing needs to get bigger or change parts in order for the solar system to grow or change parts; it is sufficient that one plurality of heavenly bodies is larger than a suitably related, earlier plurality of heavenly bodies. The things that are now (identical to) the solar system may be distinct from the things that had previously been the solar system.[42]

10   Disassembled Objects

Let us turn now to a somewhat different way in which our treatment of cases may appear arbitrary. Thus far, we have been considering pairs of cases that allegedly do not differ in any ontologically significant respects. Now let us consider a single case that seems to admit of multiple permissible, but mutually incompatible descriptions. Suppose that a watch is disassembled and later reassembled. It seems equally permissible to describe the watch as coming back into existence upon reassembly as it is to describe the watch as having been scattered across the workbench prior to reassembly. But these descriptions are incompatible: the watch either did or did not exist after disassembly and prior to reassembly. So if the descriptions are equally permissible, it may seem that (on pain of arbitrarily favoring one over the other) one must either take them to be true of temporarily coincident things – only one of which survived disassembly – or else true only relative to some convention or context.[43]

There is, however, more than one way of being permissible, and being true is only one of them. Another way of being permissible is by conveying something true despite being literally false. The police are looking for Carl, find a heap of bone and meat by the wood chipper, and one says to the other, "I think this is Carl." She certainly does not think that this stuff is (the same thing as) Carl or that Carl still exists. She is speaking loosely. What she meant is that this heap of bone and meat is Carl's remains. She takes herself to have been deliberately misunderstood when her partner replies: "How can this be *Carl*? Carl couldn't have survived *that*!" We react similarly when someone points to the disassembled parts and says, "You really think *this* is a watch? It isn't *shaped* like a watch!" So it is plausible that we are likewise speaking loosely when we refer to the scattered parts as 'a watch'. This could then serve as nonarbitrary grounds for favoring the description of the watch as coming back into existence upon reassembly.[44]

Yet another way of being permissible is by being penumbral. One mark of something's being a borderline case is that either verdict is permissible.[45] It may well be that our ambivalence toward the two descriptions of the watch, and the permissibility of each description, is the result of its being vague whether the watch exists after disassembly. In that case, no more machinery is needed to account for the permissibility of these two descriptions of the watch than is needed to account for the permissibility of describing a borderline bald man as bald or as nonbald.[46]

11 Strange Communities

I have thus far made no mention of strange linguistic communities, though it is common for discussions of strange kinds to be carried out in terms of such communities. So, before concluding, I will make some remarks about communities that employ strange conceptual schemes and their relevance to particularism.

One might think that the mere possibility of communities who make different intuitive judgments about strange and familiar kinds is enough by itself to cause trouble for the particularist. John Hawthorne seems to be suggesting something along these lines when he says:

> Barring a kind of anti-realism that none of us should tolerate, wouldn't it be remarkable if the lines of reality matched the lines that we have words for? The simplest exercises of sociological imagination ought to convince us that the assumption of such a harmony is altogether untoward, since such exercises convince us that it is something of a biological and/or cultural accident that we draw the lines that we do.[47]

Hawthorne seems have in mind an argument along the following lines: we cannot expect intuitive judgments about which kinds of things there are to be correct because (1) we cannot expect intuitive judgments that are largely the result of biocultural accidents to be correct and (2) the intuitive judgments that lead us to draw the lines that we do are largely the result of biocultural accidents. We are meant to be convinced of the second premise by "the simplest exercises of sociological imagination."

Certainly Hawthorne is not suggesting that the mere fact that we are able to imagine strange communities is reason enough to accept (2). After all, just as easily as we can imagine perfectly functional communities who (say) take there to be snowdiscalls but no snowballs, we can imagine perfectly functional communities, no worse off than our own at satisfying their various needs and desires, with different intuitive judgments about the multiple-realizability of mental properties, the moral impermissibility of torturing babies for fun, the supervenience of moral facts on natural facts, the indiscernibility of identicals, the premises of the revisionary ontologists' favorite anti-particularist arguments, and so on for virtually all other intuitive judgments. Whatever reasons there may be for global skepticism about intuitive judgments, the mere imaginability of communities with different intuitive judgments is not one of them.

Perhaps what Hawthorne has in mind is only that, when we imagine such communities, we see that there is no ontologically significant difference between the relevant strange and familiar kinds. But this would render the argument from strange imaginary communities parasitic on P1 of the argument from arbitrariness (§3), and the detour into strange communities superfluous.

Alternatively, perhaps what Hawthorne has in mind is that we can easily imagine the sorts of circumstances that might have led us to draw the lines differently and that, since these circumstances could easily have obtained, we could easily have come to draw the lines differently. To a certain extent, this is right but poses no threat to the particularist. For instance in other (easily imaginable) circumstances, we would have had reason to make different kinds of artifacts and, accordingly, would have taken there to be different kinds of artifacts. To that extent it is indeed a biocultural accident that we countenance the kinds of artifacts that we do. But given the way in which the kinds of artifacts there are depends upon the kinds of artifacts people have intended to make, our ability to judge correctly which kinds of artifacts there are is no more remarkable than our ability to know what kinds of artifacts people have intended to make.

We can likewise easily imagine conditions under which we would have found it convenient to employ strange phased-kind concepts, like *toddlescent** or *incar**. But this would not be a case in which we would have made different intuitive judgments, for (as indicated in §§4–5) we do intuitively judge there to be such things as toddlescent*s and incar*s. So while it is almost certainly a biocultural accident that we employ the phased-kind concepts that we do, this is no indication that it is a biocultural accident that we intuitively judge there to be things answering to the relevant phased kinds.

The real problem cases would be those involving strange nonartifactual individuative kinds, like toddlescents. However, I find it difficult to believe that there could easily have been communities that intuitively judged there to be toddlescents – just as I find it difficult to believe that there could easily have been communities with different intuitive judgments about the indiscernibility of identicals, multiple realizability, moral supervenience, and so forth. Why this could not easily have happened is a difficult question, but one which lies beyond the scope of this paper.[48]

What would be more worrisome is if there turned out to be *actual* communities whose intuitive judgments about which kinds of things there are differed from ours, for one could hardly ask for better evidence that this could easily have happened than that it has happened. Suppose, for instance, that anthropologists or experimental philosophers discover an actual community that apparently takes there to be toddlescents. What then?

Given that this is an actual case, whose details must be discovered (not stipulated), it will be open to debate whether they indeed intuitively judge there to be toddlescents. There will, in such cases, be at least two alternative explanations of whatever linguistic behavior it is that leads one to suspect that they intuitively judge there to be toddlescents. The first and most straightforward is that they have been misinterpreted: they do not take there to be toddlescents but, rather, toddlescent*s. Particularists do not deny that there are toddlescent*s, nor do they deny that there are things answering to countless other strange phased kinds. Consequently, the extensive anthropological literature on strange ways of categorizing has little if any bearing on particularism about material-object metaphysics.

A further possibility is that they do judge there to be toddlescents but do not *intuitively* judge there to be toddlescents. Communities may come to form strange judgments about kinds or persistence conditions for reasons having nothing at all to do with their intuitions. Eli Hirsch discusses a case in which the Rabbis came to the counterintuitive conclusion that a sandal cannot survive the replacement of its straps, more than anything out of a practical need for a manageable criterion of persistence.[49] Even if this judgment came to be shared by the entire religious community, this is not necessarily any indication of a difference in their intuitions about persistence, for they may have come to believe this on authority and *despite* finding it counterintuitive.[50]

Suppose, however, that (for one reason or another) these alternative explanations are untenable. What, according to robust particularists, should we do in that case? The same thing that we would do if we discovered an actual community whose scientists were running the same experiments but consistently obtaining radically different data. We wouldn't throw out our equipment and burn all of our data, nor would be glibly ignore this other community. Rather, we would investigate, looking for possible sources of error on both sides. Likewise, for moral disagreement. Upon encountering communities with different ethical beliefs, we (realists, anyway) do not throw up our hands and conclude that there are no ethical truths or that we are both right relative to our respective standards. Rather we look for potential sources of error or bias. (Perhaps centuries of tyrannical rule have distorted their moral sense; perhaps centuries of overemphasis of the value of autonomy has distorted ours.) I see no reason to think that cross-cultural ontological disagreements need be or should be treated any differently.[51]

12 Conclusion

I have examined numerous strategies for explaining away the apparent arbitrariness of our treatment of various cases: distinguishing between phased and individuative kinds, loose and strict talk, vagueness and arbitrariness, types and tokens, masses and individuals, intentional and unintentional activities, syntactic and semantic singularity, and simply thinking more carefully about the metaphysics of familiar kinds. I have not addressed every sort of case that has been, or might be, claimed to be indicative of arbitrariness (some will think I have gone on long enough already). But our success above is at least some grounds for optimism that there will be a way of handling new problems as they arise.

This has been only a partial defense of robust particularism. Consequently, I do not expect the foregoing to have won many converts. For one, I have not supplied any argument that the apparent ontologically significant differences (in particular, the presence of relevant creative intentions) are indeed ontologically significant. Nor have I shown that, all told, the costs of deeply revisionary ontologies are greater than the costs of robust particularism. This would require (among other things) examining strategies for – and costs associated with – blocking the rebutting arguments and the other undercutting arguments mentioned in §2, as well as assessing various strategies for mitigating the apparent costs of revisionary ontological theories. Nevertheless, I do hope to have emboldened fence-sitters and closet particularists and to have shown that the particularist's treatment of strange and familiar kinds is not as intolerably arbitrary as it is so often taken to be.

Notes

I am grateful to Derek Ball, John Bengson, Reid Blackman, Josh Dever, Kenny Easwaran, Adam Elga, John Hawthorne, Eli Hirsch, Cory Juhl, Shieva Kleinschmidt, Dave Liebesman, Dan López de Sa, Marc Moffett, Bryan Pickel, Raul Saucedo, Peter Simons, Ernest Sosa, Jason Turner, Chris Tillman, Michael Tye, audiences in Laramie and Urbana, and especially to George Bealer, Chad Carmichael, and Trenton Merricks for valuable discussion.

1 See his (1987, 178–9), (1993, 620–2), or (1999, 133–4 [ch. 49, p. 653 in this volume]).

2 By 'intuitive judgments', I mean the judgments that one is inclined to make on the basis of one's intuitions together with either perceived details of actual cases or stipulated details of counterfactual cases when theoretical qualms are set to the side. See Bealer (2004, 14–15) on the primacy of judgments about cases.

3 See, among a great many others, Cartwright 1975, Unger 1979, Lewis 1986, van Cleve 1986, Yablo 1987, Heller 1990, van Inwagen 1990, Rea 1998,

Sosa 1999, Horgan and Potrč 2000, Hudson 2001, Merricks 2001, Sider 2001, Rosen and Dorr 2002, Hawthorne 2006, and Thomasson 2007.

4 Here I have in mind, e.g., the contention that the true content of apparently anti-eliminativist intuitions is only that there are mereological simples arranged thus-and-so (à la van Inwagen 1990) or that the contents of apparently anti-universalist or anti-plenitude intuitions are suitably – and perhaps inscrutably – restricted in such a way as to exclude strange kinds (à la Lewis 1986).

5 See Merricks (2001, 162–70), Hirsch (2002a, 109–12 [ch. 52, pp. 690–2 in this volume]), and my (2008 and 2009) for critical discussion of these reconciliatory strategies.

6 See, e.g., Cartwright (1975, 158), Quine (1981, 13), van Cleve (1986, 145), Yablo (1987, 307), van Inwagen (1990, 126), Hirsch (1993, 690), Hudson (2001, 108–11), Sider (2001, 156–7 and 165), Sidelle (2002, 119–20), Hawthorne (2006, 109), Johnston (2006, 696–8), and Schaffer (2010, §2.1).

7 See Hirsch (2002a, 107 [ch. 52, pp. 688–9 in this volume]) for a statement of one version of this argument, and see Rodriguez-Pereyra (2002, 217) on appeals to intuition in metaphysics generally.

8 See, e.g., van Inwagen (1990, 66–8), Horgan (1993, 695), and Hudson (2001, 109).

9 See Hirsch (2002b).

10 Hawthorne (2006, 109).

11 Cf. Williamson (2007, 191): "Although the philosophically innocent may be free of various forms of theoretical bias, just as the scientifically innocent are, that is not enough to confer special authority on innocent judgment, given its characteristic sloppiness."

12 Then again, relativists may be better understood as denying P1: the difference between snowballs and snowdiscalls that explains why the former but not the latter exist – relative to our scheme, that is – is that the concept *snowball* is part of our conceptual scheme and the concept *snowdiscall* is not.

13 Of course, the mere appearance of ontological significance will not be enough to convince some committed anti-particularists, but in that case their aversion to particularism presumably doesn't rest primarily on the absence of plausible candidates for ontologically significant differences and, therefore, lies beyond the scope of this paper.

14 Moreover, difficulty in specifying a relevant distinction between two cases is not obviously evidence that there is no relevant distinction between them. Cf. Sider: "There are, one must admit, analogies between these cases [of genuine causes and epiphenomena], and it is no trivial philosophical enterprise to say exactly what distinguishes them. But setbacks or even failure

at this task in philosophical analysis should not persuade us that there is no distinction to be made, since failure at philosophical analysis should *never* persuade anyone, on its own anyway, that there is no distinction to be made" (2003, 772). The italics are his.

15 See Benacerraf (1965), as well as Armstrong (1986, 87) on ordered pairs, Bealer (1998, 6–7) on propositions, and Merricks (2003, 532–6) on counterpart theory.

16 Furthermore, we plausibly have reason to treat Gettier cases and paradigm cases of knowledge differently even before we manage to pin down the epistemically significant difference between the cases.

17 Here and elsewhere, I assume that individuals that can survive a given change cannot be identified with individuals that cannot survive that change.

18 Cf. Wiggins (2001, 29–33).

19 Hawthorne (2006, vii).

20 Nor, for that matter, do islands shrink when the water levels rise. Islands are like icebergs: part of the island is above water and the rest of the island is underwater. (Submarines sometimes crash into islands.) And, like icebergs, they shrink by eroding. To the extent that we are ever inclined to say that the island is shrinking when the water levels rise, it seems plausible on reflection that all that is shrinking is the part of the island that is above water, not the island itself. And even this is evidently a *façon de parler*. Nothing really becomes smaller when the part of the island that is above water gets smaller any more than something really becomes longer as the part of this sentence that you have read thus far gets longer.

21 I am grateful to Chad Carmichael here. E. J. Lowe raises similar points about islands in his (2007).

22 Ginet (1985, 220–1).

23 Though, far more plausibly, this abstractum does not cease to exist when the original copy of the 18th page is destroyed, any more than there ceases to be an 18th letter of the alphabet when all of the tokens of that letter are destroyed.

24 This is perhaps easiest to see if one imagines that this page is only one of several back-up copies of the 18th page that were produced after the spill.

25 Van Inwagen (1990, 126).

26 Ibid.

27 Cf. Baker (2008, 211). I leave it open whether this meteoroid is a statue. If so, then it turns out that, while most statues are essentially statues, others are only contingently statues, are identical with pieces of stuff, and share the persistence conditions of the piece of stuff. What matters for our purposes is that nothing with the persistence conditions normally associated with statues (and thus distinct from the meteoroid) comes into existence in the absence of the

relevant creative intentions. Thanks to Reid Blackman and Josh Dever for helpful discussion here.

28 Particularists may hold that gollyswoggles' inability to survive even minimal changes in shape is yet another ontologically significant difference between statues and gollyswoggles.

29 Cf. Thomasson (2003). Some may object even to this minimal degree of mind-dependence and insist that the existence of a certain sort of object is always independent of human intentions and desires. See, e.g., van Cleve (1986, 149), Rea (1998, 353–4), Olson (2001, 347), Sider (2001, 157), and, for a dissenting voice, Baker (2008, 46–7). It is precisely their willingness to reject such intuitive principles in the face of what look to be clear counterexamples that distinguishes particularists from revisionary ontologists.

30 See, e.g., Thomasson (2003, §3) and Baker (2008, 43–66). Some particularists are more liberal than others. Baker (2008, 53) allows that a wine rack can be brought into existence by brushing off a piece of unaltered driftwood and using it as a wine rack, so long as appropriate conventions and practices are in place. I am inclined to agree with Dean Zimmerman (2002, 335) that "changes in our ways of talking about things, even coupled with simple changes in some of our nonverbal reactions to things, could [not] by themselves bring any concrete physical object into existence" and to accept a more conservative view on which at least some alteration is required in order to bring a wine rack into existence (which is not yet to deny that the piece of driftwood is a wine rack; see note 27).

31 See, e.g., Cartwright (1975, 158), Quine (1981, 13), van Cleve (1986, 145), and Hudson (2001, 108–12).

32 There is then the further question of how (and whether) such factors combine to yield necessary and sufficient conditions for composition, a question which lies outside the scope of this paper.

33 The state of Michigan is not identical to the land that it now occupies. The land is a quantity of matter, and particularists need have no objection to arbitrary scattered quantities. There is some land some of which is on one side of Lake Michigan and some of which is on the other. There is even some flesh and metal, some of which is in Paris and some of which is on my face. And what, according to particularists, is the ontologically significant difference between this scattered quantity and the alleged individual whose parts are my nose and the Eiffel Tower? Their ontological category: one is some stuff, the other is an individual.

34 See, e.g., Thomasson, (2003, §2). And even were our creative powers radically unconstrained, the fact that no one has directed such creative intentions at my nose and the Eiffel Tower would

be ontologically significant, from the perspective of particularists, to their not composing anything.

35 See, e.g., van Inwagen (1990, 12–13), Rea (1998, 352), and Hudson (2001, 111).

36 I am grateful here to Kenny Easwaran.

37 It is precisely their immunity to this sort of error – having overlooked nonobvious exceptions – that makes concrete-case intuitions a more secure starting point.

38 Some may insist that strange fusions are mere pluralities and, therefore, "ontologically innocent." If indeed the fusion of my nose and the Eiffel Tower just is my nose and the Eiffel Tower, then universalists and particularists have no disagreement, for they agree that my nose and the Eiffel Tower exist. That said, it is controversial (even among universalists) whether strange fusions are ontologically innocent in this way.

39 See Simons (1987, 142–3) for a related discussion. For what it is worth, the most common dictionary definitions of 'the solar system' are something along the lines of: the sun and the various heavenly bodies that orbit it.

40 Furthermore, the solar system, unlike a mere plurality, would plausibly cease to exist if its parts were scattered across the universe.

41 An alternative would be to contend that some pluralities are mereologically flexible. For instance, Peter Simons (1997, 91–2) maintains that an orchestra is an "empirical collective," which like a mere plurality is many things, not one thing, but unlike a mere plurality can survive gaining and losing parts. Whatever the merits of this view, it cannot (by itself) defuse the charge of arbitrariness, for one would still have to identify an ontologically significant difference between the solar system – understood as an empirical collective – and various strange empirical collectives of my nose and the Eiffel Tower.

42 I am grateful to Derek Ball, John Hawthorne, Dave Liebesman, and Peter Simons for valuable discussions of the points in this section.

43 See Hawthorne and Cortens (1995, 158–60) or Hawthorne (2006, 53–4) for discussion of a related case.

44 Some contend that *all* ordinary talk about nonliving composites (van Inwagen 1990) or mereologically flexible entities (Chisholm 1976) is loose talk about no such things and may go on to insist that there is no principled reason to take apparent reference to some but not other nonliving composites at face value. But there are principled reasons for the differential treatment. For the current appeal to loose talk is plausible and can be (and has just been) independently motivated, whereas these other appeals to loose talk are not plausible and cannot be independently

motivated. Cf. Merricks (2001, 164–7), Hirsch (2002a, 109–11 [ch. 52, pp. 690–1 in this volume]), and my (2009, §3).

45 See Sainsbury (1996, 259), Shapiro (2003, 43–4), and Wright (2003, 92–4).

46 It may well be that more needs to be said in accounting for the *vagueness* in the present case, but that is another matter; we are here concerned with the argument from arbitrariness, and the argument from vagueness will have to wait its turn.

47 Hawthorne (2006, 109). Cf. Hudson (2001, 107), Sider (2001, 156–7), and Rea (2002, chapter 8).

48 Perhaps the case could be made that the correct explanation of why we could not easily have had different intuitive judgments about the indiscernibility of identicals, multiple realizability, moral supervenience (etcetera etcetera) does not carry over to our intuitive judgments about strange and familiar kinds. But I do not see how it would go.

49 Hirsch (1999). Objects that had become impure were not allowed into the temple, so the Rabbis needed principled ways of deciding whether a given object was the same object that at an earlier time had acquired the impurity.

50 Similarly, differences in judgments about unobservables (e.g., "tree spirits") presumably have nothing at all to do with differences in intuitions. See Bealer (2004, 12–13) on the difference between intuition and belief.

51 I am grateful to George Bealer, Adam Elga, Marc Moffett, Bryan Pickel, and Chris Tillman for helpful discussion of points in this section.

References

Armstrong, D. M. (1986), 'In Defence of Structural Universals', *Australasian Journal of Philosophy* 64: 85–8.

Baker, Lynne Rudder (2008), *The Metaphysics of Everyday Life* (Cambridge: Cambridge University Press).

Bealer, George (1998), 'Propositions', *Mind* 107: 1–32.

Bealer, George (2004), 'The Origins of Modal Error', *Dialectica* 58: 11–42.

Benacerraf, Paul (1965), 'What Numbers Could Not Be', *The Philosophical Review* 74: 47–73.

Cartwright, Richard (1975), 'Scattered Objects', in Keith Lehrer (ed.), *Analysis and Metaphysics* (Boston: Reidel).

Chisholm, Roderick M. (1976), *Person and Object* (London, George Allen and Unwin) [partly reproduced as ch. 33 in this volume].

Ginet, Carl (1985), 'Plantinga and the Philosophy of Mind', in James E. Tomberlin and Peter van

Inwagen (eds.), *Alvin Plantinga* (Dordrecht: D. Reidel), pp. 199–223.

Hawthorne, John (2006), *Metaphysical Essays* (Oxford: Oxford University Press).

Hawthorne, John, and Cortens, Andrew (1995), 'Towards Ontological Nihilism', *Philosophical Studies* 79: 143–65.

Heller, Mark (1990), *The Ontology of Physical Objects: Four-Dimensional Hunks of Matter* (New York: Cambridge University Press).

Hirsch, Eli (1993), 'Peter van Inwagen's *Material Beings*', *Philosophy and Phenomenological Research* 53: 687–91.

Hirsch, Eli (1999), 'Identity in the Talmud', *Midwest Studies in Philosophy* 23: 166–80.

Hirsch, Eli (2002a), 'Against Revisionary Ontology', *Philosophical Topics* 30: 103–27 [ch. 52 in this volume].

Hirsch, Eli (2002b), 'Quantifier Variance and Realism', *Philosophical Issues* 12: 51–73.

Horgan, Terence (1993), 'On What There Isn't', *Philosophy and Phenomenological Research* 53: 693–700.

Horgan, Terence, and Potrč, Matjaž (2000), 'Blobjectivism and Indirect Correspondence', *Facta Philosophica* 2: 249–70.

Hudson, Hud (2001), *A Materialist Metaphysics of the Human Person* (Ithaca: Cornell University Press).

Johnston, Mark (2006), 'Hylomorphism', *The Journal of Philosophy* 103: 652–98.

Korman, Daniel Z. (2008), 'Unrestricted Composition and Restricted Quantification', *Philosophical Studies* 140: 319–34.

Korman, Daniel Z. (2009), 'Eliminativism and the Challenge from Folk Belief', *Noûs* 43: 242–64.

Lewis, David (1986), *On the Plurality of Worlds* (Oxford: Blackwell).

Lowe, E. J. (2007), 'Metaphysical Essays', *Notre Dame Philosophical Reviews*. http://ndpr.nd.edu/review.cfm?id=8563

Merricks, Trenton (2001), *Objects and Persons* (New York: Oxford) [partly reproduced as ch. 51 in this volume].

Merricks, Trenton (2003), 'The End of Counterpart Theory', *The Journal of Philosophy* 100: 521–49.

Olson, Eric T. (2001), 'Material Coincidence and the Indiscernibility Problem', *The Philosophical Quarterly* 51: 337–55.

Quine, W. V. O. (1981), *Theories and Things* (Cambridge: Harvard University Press).

Rea, Michael C. (1998), 'In Defense of Mereological Universalism', *Philosophy and Phenomenological Research* 58: 337–55.

Rea, Michael C. (2002), *World Without Design* (Oxford: Oxford University Press).

Rodriguez-Pereyra, Gonzalo (2002), *Resemblance Nominalism: A Solution to the Problem of Universals* (Oxford: Oxford University Press).

Rosen, Gideon, and Dorr, Cian (2002), 'Composition as Fiction', in Richard M. Gale (ed.), *The Blackwell Guide to Metaphysics* (Oxford: Blackwell), pp. 151–74.

Sainsbury, R. M. (1997), 'Concepts Without Boundaries' in R. Keefe and P. Smith (eds.), *Vagueness: A Reader* (Cambridge: MIT Press), pp. 251–64.

Schaffer, Jonathan (2010), 'Monism: The Priority of the Whole', *The Philosophical Review* 119: 31–76.

Shapiro, Stewart (2003), 'Vagueness and Conversation', in J. C. Beall (ed.), *Liars and Heaps: New Essays on Paradox* (Oxford: Oxford University Press), pp. 39–72.

Sidelle, Alan (2002), 'Is There a True Metaphysics of Material Objects?', *Philosophical Issues* 12: 118–45.

Sider, Theodore (2001), *Four-Dimensionalism* (Oxford: Clarendon Press).

Sider, Theodore (2003), 'What's So Bad about Overdetermination?', *Philosophy and Phenomenological Research* 67: 719–26.

Simons, Peter (1987), *Parts: A Study in Ontology* (New York: Oxford University Press).

Simons, Peter (1997), 'Bolzano on Collections', in W. Künne, M. Siebel, and M. Textor (eds.), *Bolzano and Analytic Philosophy* (Amsterdam: Rodopi), pp. 87–108.

Sosa, Ernest (1987), 'Subjects Among Other Things', *Philosophical Perspectives*, 1: 155–87.

Sosa, Ernest (1993), 'Putnam's Pragmatic Realism', *The Journal of Philosophy* 90: 605–26.

Sosa, Ernest (1999), 'Existential Relativity', *Midwest Studies in Philosophy* 23: 132–43.

Thomasson, Amie (2003), 'Realism and Human Kinds', *Philosophy and Phenomenological Research* 57: 580–609.

Thomasson, Amie (2007), *Ordinary Objects* (Oxford: Oxford University Press).

Unger, Peter (1979), 'There Are No Ordinary Things', *Synthese* 41: 117–54.

van Cleve, James (1986), 'Mereological Essentialism, Mereological Conjunctivism, and Identity Through Time', *Midwest Studies in Philosophy* 11: 141–56.

van Inwagen, Peter (1990), *Material Beings* (Ithaca: Cornell University Press).

Wiggins, David (2001), *Sameness and Substance Renewed* (New York: Cambridge University Press).

Williamson, Timothy (2007), *The Philosophy of Philosophy* (Oxford: Blackwell).

Wright, Crispin (2003), 'Vagueness: A Fifth Column Approach', in J. C. Beall (ed.), *Liars and Heaps: New Essays on Paradox* (Oxford: Oxford University Press), pp. 84–105.

Yablo, Stephen (1987), 'Identity, Essence, and Indiscernibility', *The Journal of Philosophy* 84: 293–314.

Zimmerman, Dean W. (2002), 'The Constitution of Persons by Bodies', *Philosophical Topics* 30: 295–338.